CURRENT TRENDS IN LINGUISTICS

Edited by

THOMAS A. SEBEOK

VOLUME 6

Linguistics in South West Asia and North Africa

Associate Editors:

CHARLES A. FERGUSON – CARLETON T. HODGE

HERBERT H. PAPER

Assistant Editors:

JOHN R. KRUEGER – GENE M. SCHRAMM

Assistant to the Editor:

LUCIA HADD ZOERCHER

1970
MOUTON
THE HAGUE · PARIS

The research reported herein was performed pursuant to a contract with the U.S. Department of Health, Education, and Welfare, Office of Education, under the authority of Section 602, Title VI, NDEA.

LIBRARY OF CONGRESS CATALOG CARD NUMBER: 64-3663

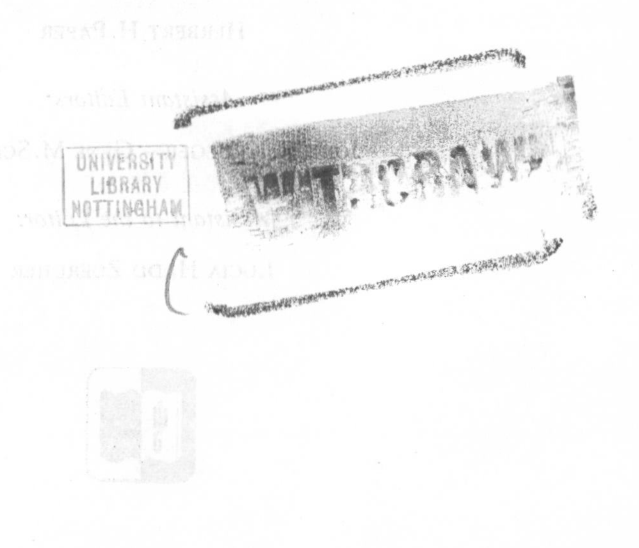

Printed in The Netherlands by Mouton & Co., Printers, The Hague.

CURRENT TRENDS IN LINGUISTICS

VOLUME 6

In memoriam

Joaquim Mattoso Câmara Jr. (1904-1970)

Thomas Welbourne Clark (1904-1969)

EDITOR'S INTRODUCTION

With the publication of *Linguistics in South West Asia and North Africa*, and Vols. 7 and 8 at heel, this series will have passed its halfway mark in the number of volumes — if not necessarily in quantity of sheets printed — envisaged in the plan of *Current Trends in Linguistics*. To recapitulate, these are the six volumes available to date:

Vol. 1, *Soviet and East European Linguistics* (xii + 606 pp.), originally published in 1963, reprinted in 1968. Reviewed, among others, by Olga Akhmanova, *Word* 21.166–181 (1965); J. Bartoš, *Jazykovedný časopis* 17.201–202 (1966); T.V. Bulygina, V.Z. Panfilov, O.N. Trubačev, *et al.*, *Voprosy Jazykoznanija* 1965, No. 3, pp. 147–165; Robert T. Harms, *Slavic Review* 24.354–355 (1965); Karel Horálek, *Linguistics* 9.77–80 (1964) and *Slovo a Slovesnost* 26.76–77 (1965); Henry Kučera, *Language* 41.115–126 (1965); Alfons Nehring, *Deutsche Literaturzeitung für Kritik der internationalen Wissenschaft* 87.109–110 (1966); Dennis Ward, *Journal of Linguistics* 1.207–208 (1965); and L. Zgusta, *Archiv Orientální* 33.113–115 (1965).

Vol. 2, *Linguistics in East Asia and South East Asia* (xix + 979 pp.), published in 1967. Reviewed, among others, by M. A. K. Halliday, *Bulletin of the School of Oriental and African Studies* 32.435–436 (1969), and James A. Matisoff, *Journal of Asian Studies* 28.835–837 (1969).

Vol. 3, *Theoretical Foundations* (xi + 537 pp.), published in 1966. Reviewed, among others, by Robbins Burling, *American Anthropologist* 69.406–408 (1967); James D. McCawley, *Language* 44.556–592 (1968); Wolf Thümmel, *Sprache im technischen Zeitalter* 25.74–85 (1968); and L. Zgusta, *Archiv Orientální* 35.298–301 (1967); also, by sixteen other linguists, preceded by the editor's and authors' precis and followed by the authors' and editor's replies to the reviewers, in *Current Anthropology* 9.125–179 (1968).

Vol. 4, *Ibero-American and Caribbean Linguistics* (xix + 659 pp.), published in 1968.

Vol. 5, *Linguistics in South Asia* (vii + 814 pp.), published in 1969.

The first three volumes were prepared with assistance, under three successive grants, from the National Science Foundation; the following three, under contracts between the U.S. Office of Education and the Indiana University Foundation (the contract for the present volume bore the identification USOE-OEC-3-7-061987-2075). I hereby gratefully acknowledge this indispensable aid. Financing for Vols. 7 through 12 is now also secure and will be acknowledged where due.

In 1970 or early 1971, then, three more volumes will have appeared, and possibly a fourth: this one; Vol. 7, *Linguistics in Sub-Saharan Africa*; Vol. 8, *Linguistics in Oceania*; and Vol. 9, *Linguistics in Western Europe*. Beyond that, there are three further substantial volumes in various stages of preparation:

Vol. 10, *Linguistics in North America*. The contents were planned in collaboration with Associate Editors William Bright (University of California, Los Angeles), Dell Hymes (University of Pennsylvania), John Lotz (Center for Applied Linguistics), Albert H. Marckwardt (Princeton University), and Jean-Paul Vinay (University of Victoria), and are organized into four principal sections. The first of these will deal with the 'major' immigrant languages of North America, that is, English (11 chapters), French (3), and Spanish (1). Other immigrant languages will be covered together in two chapters, one for the U.S. and the other for Canada. The section on the native languages of North America will contain four general chapters, and will then examine in detail areal groupings from the Arctic through California and the Southwest into Mexico (9 chapters); it will also feature a new checklist of the American Indian languages of this continent. The book — which is being prepared for publication in 1972 — will further incorporate up-to-date directories of current U.S. and Canadian activities in linguistics, namely, in university and kindred institutional research, journals and other serial publications, and societies and similar organizations (4 chapters).

Vol. 11, *Diachronic, Areal, and Typological Linguistics*. The contents were planned in collaboration with Associate Editors Henry M. Hoenigswald (University of Pennsylvania) and Robert E. Longacre (Summer Institute of Linguistics). After an introductory chapter on the history of language classification, the book will contain a series of theoretical treatments of selected topics, each matched by one or more illustrative case studies. Thus the chapter dealing with methodological aspects of internal reconstruction will be complemented by a study of internal reconstruction of Finnish; the chapter dealing with general problems in the decipherment and analysis of written records will be exemplified by the unraveling of Linear B; and so forth. Twenty-two chapters have been commissioned for this book, which is also expected to appear in 1972.

Vol. 12, *Linguistics and Adjacent Arts and Sciences*. The contents were planned in collaboration with Associate Editors Arthur S. Abramson (University of Connecticut), Dell Hymes, Herbert Rubenstein (Lehigh University), Edward Stankiewicz (University of Chicago), and Assistant Editor Bernard Spolsky (University of New Mexico). This immense undertaking, which will be finished by the end of 1972, will then appear in three separate tomes. There may be fifteen parts, distributed as follows (with the number of chapters in each part given in parentheses):

Tome 12/1 — Part One, Linguistics and philosophy (5); Two, Semiotics (9); Three, Linguistics and the verbal arts (9); Four, Special languages (3); and Five, Linguistic aspects of translation (1).

Tome 12/2 — Part Six, Linguistics and psychology (8); Seven, Linguistics and sociology (6); Eight, Linguistics and anthropology (3); Nine, Linguistics and economics (1); and Ten, Linguistics and education (7).

Tome 12/3 — Part Eleven, Phonetics (11); Twelve, Bio-medical applications (5); Thirteen, Computer applications (5); and Fourteen, Linguistics as a pilot science (2).

The problem of Vol. 13, *Index to Current Trends in Linguistics, Vols. 1–12*, is at present being intensively explored, and resolves itself into a number of subsidiary questions. The most immediately compelling among these relates to the utility and economy of such secondary information services in general. In other words, we must determine whether the expenditure of time, effort, and money can be justified in terms of the anticipated results: would a particular complex of indexes truly enhance the value of the series for its users? If the answer to this basic question should turn out to be affirmative, then the type and comprehensiveness of indexing, providing maximum ease of access to the information stored in the close to 15,000 pages that will make up Vols. 1–12, must be faced next. At this time, three such lists are under serious consideration: a cumulative index of personal names; a cumulative index of language names, including terms for various subordinate dialects, superordinate families, and the like; and an index of subjects. Each of these implies a host of further questions. For instance, in an index of languages, should an effort be made to tag every entry with an identification code that would provide for its linguistic classification, tell the geographical location of its speakers, and perhaps give, in addition, certain minimal demographic data? Or, as regards an index of subjects, ought one seek to fully or partially conform to existing or developing thesauri, such as those of ERIC or LINCS, or, on the contrary, to specify hierarchic criteria custom-tailored for our particular user-groups, assuming that these can be reasonably well defined?

A different set of questions relates to the extent to which the raw materials preedited for the indexes can be processed by a computer and peripheral equipment. Discussions held so far suggest that it might pay to take advantage of existing technology for the indexes of personal and language names, but hardly for the index of subjects.

Another sort of question is whether it would be preferable to rely on auto-indexing — that is, to request each contributor to index his own article, with the accumulated returns pooled by a skilled editorial staff — or to have the whole job done centrally; each approach seems to have some advantages and some disadvantages, and cost is by no means a negligible factor in choosing between alternatives. In a future Introduction, I hope to return to these and related questions; in the meantime, suggestions of reviewers and other interested readers will be most welcome.

What of the recycling of this series after Vol. 12, or its continuation in perhaps some new format, better suited to the times? It is instructive in connection with this query — which is frequently put to me by colleagues, publishers, and supporting agencies alike — to ponder some of the recommendations contained in the recently published Report of the Committee on Scientific and Technical Communication (SATCOM) of the National Academy of Sciences — National Academy of Engineering (Washington,

D.C.: National Academy of Sciences, Publication 1707, 1969). This important and influential Report emphasizes (p. 40) that '*A singularly pervasive conclusion in regard to scientific and technical communication is that the functions performed by critical reviews and compilations — digesting, consolidating, simplifying, and repackaging for specific categories of users — are essential if information is to be used effectively*' (italics in the original). What every worker needs is 'something that will organize and evaluate what is known about a subject and present it in a language that he can understand at the level of detail that he wants'; moreover, the preparation of such consolidations of information — state-of-the-art surveys or review articles — 'often requires great intellectual creativity' (*Synopsis*, p.24).

Should this type of service remain in the hands of for-profit organizations or should technical societies take collective responsibility in linguistics, as scientific organizations have done in some other fields? If the former, consumers cannot fairly complain, as Burling has done, about the 'ghastly price' of compilations such as this. If, on the other hand, economically reasonable terms are demanded, private enterprise must yield to cooperative arrangements; as the authors of the SATCOM Report put it, '*Scientific and technical societies must develop, propose, and assist in implementing new and better ways to identify needs for critical reviews and data compilations and to further efficient preparation of them*...' (p.41; italics in the original). If there are any linguistic organizations willing and able to systematically commission, finance, and distribute critical and evaluative articles of the 'Annual Review of...' or 'Advances in...' type, which aim to relate and clarify findings with their disciplinary and cross-disciplinary implications, I don't know about them.

Current Trends should certainly not be continued in its present format, because this is both too slow and too expensive. This cycle will have taken just about a decade to complete, with the cost per page mounting distressingly from volume to volume (the tangible costs of Vol. 12 alone will exceed one hundred thousand dollars). Alternative proposals that have been put forward to date are not very convincing and are unlikely, in my opinion, to succeed. I intend to return to them on another occasion, with some counterproposals of my own.

As in all previous volumes, the contents envisaged by the Editorial Board don't precisely match what is included in this book. As usual, the original design was richer than what could be realized, because of the involuntary withdrawal of some collaborators, felled by illness, or the dereliction of others, perhaps overwhelmed by their commitments. (I particularly regret the omission of the chapter on the Northwest Semitic languages.)

Editorial policy requires that all manuscripts submitted in a foreign language be translated, and that the English version be approved by the author as well as the pertinent members of the Editorial Board. Many of the articles in this book were translated from either French or German. Whether this time-consuming, tiresome, and very expensive procedure yields results commensurate with our exertions, each reader must judge for himself. We shall continue to present all contributions in English, with the sole exception of those articles written in French for Vol. 10 that deal with Canadian French subjects.

Authors are instructed to prepare their mss. essentially in accordance with the LSA Style Sheet, adopted for publications of the Linguistic Society of America, as announced in the Society's annual *Bulletin*. In 1966, this Style Sheet was altered; new rules were established particularly in regard to bibliographical reference (cf. *Bulletin* No. 39, et seq.). This change is also reflected in the *Current Trends* series, beginning with Vol. 6.

The Editorial Board for this volume agreed at the outset that each member would assume prime responsibility for one of its sections: Herbert H. Paper (University of Michigan), Indo-European languages; John R. Krueger (Indiana University), Altaic languages; Carleton T. Hodge (Indiana University), Afroasiatic languages, save Semitic, which were allocated to Gene M. Schramm (University of Michigan); and Charles A. Ferguson (Stanford University), regional language issues and studies in Afghanistan, the Arab countries, Iran, Israel, and Turkey. The Master List of Abbreviations, Index of Languages, and Index of Names were compiled by Lucia Hadd Zoercher, who also prepared all articles for press and coordinated the two successive proofreading cycles with our far-flung authors, editors, and production department. To the six friends mentioned in this paragraph, the twenty-two contributors to this book, and the staff of Mouton & Co., go my thanks for their cooperation.

Bloomington, November 15, 1969 THOMAS A. SEBEOK

CONTENTS

A: *Semitic*

B: *Other Languages*

PART FOUR: REGIONAL LANGUAGE ISSUES AND STUDIES

MASTER LIST OF ABBREVIATIONS

AAntH	*Acta Antiqua Academiae Scientiarum Hungaricae* (Budapest).
AAWL	*Abhandlungen der Akademie der Wissenschaften und der Literatur in Mainz, Geistes- und sozialwissenschaftliche Klasse* (Wiesbaden).
ABAW	*Abhandlungen der Bayerischen Akademie der Wissenschaften. Philosophisch-historische Klasse* (Munich).
ACISE	*Atti del convegno internazionale di studi etiopici (Roma, 2–4 aprile, 1959).* Accademia Nazionale dei Lincei 357 (1960).
ACLS	American Council of Learned Societies (New York).
Acme	*Acme.* Facoltà di filosofia e lettere (Università, Milan).
AcOr	*Acta Orientalia, ediderunt Societates Orientales Danica Norvegica Svecica (Le Monde Oriental)* (Leiden and Copenhagen).
ADAW	*Abhandlungen der Deutschen Akademie der Wissenschaften zu Berlin, Klasse für Sprachen, Literatur und Kunst* (Berlin).
AE	*Annales d'Ethiopie* (Paris).
Aegyptus	*Aegyptus.* Revista Italiana di Egittologia e di Papirologia (Milan).
AESJ	*Afrikanskij ètnografičeskij sbornik*, III, *Jazykoznanie.*
Aevum	*Aevum.* Rassegna di Scienze, Filologiche, Linguistiche e Storiche (Milan).
AfO	*Archiv für Orientforschung.* Internationale Zeitschrift für die Wissenschaft vom Vorderen Orient (Graz).
Africa	*Africa.* Journal of the International African Institute (London).
Afr. Ital.	*Africa italiana* (Naples).
AfrLS	*African Language Studies* (London).
AGI	*Archivio Glottologico Italiano* (Florence).
AHw	*Akkadisches Handwörterbuch. Unter Benützung des lexikalischen Nachlasses von Bruno Meissner (1868–1947)* bearbeitet von Wolfram von Soden (Wiesbaden, Harrassowitz, 1959–).
AION-L	*Annali, Istituto Universitario Orientale, Sezione Linguistica* (Naples).
AION-O	*Annali, Istituto Universitario Orientale di Napoli, Sezionale Orientale* (Naples).
AIP	*Annuaire de l'Institut de philologie et d'histoire orientales et slaves* (Brussels).
AIUO	*Annali dell'Istituto Universitario Orientale di Napoli, Nuova serie* (Naples).
AJSL	*American Journal of Semitic Languages and Literatures* (Chicago).
AL-AN	*Al-Andalus.* Revista de las Escuelas de estudios árabes de Madrid y Granada (Madrid and Granada).
ALH	*Acta Linguistica Academiae Scientiarum Hungaricae* (Budapest).
ALZ	*Allgemeine Literatur-Zeitung* (Jena and Leipzig).
AM	*Asia Major.* New Series (London).
AmA	*American Anthropologist* (Menasha, Wisconsin).
AnL	*Anthropological Linguistics* (Bloomington, Indiana).
AnnIEO	*Annales de l'Institut d'Études orientales de la Faculté des Lettres de l'Université* (Algiers).
AnnLat	*Annali del Pontificio Museo Missionario Etnologico già Lateranensi* (Vatican City).
Anthropos	*Anthropos.* Revue internationale d'ethnologie et de linguistique/Internationale Zeitschrift für Volker- und Sprachenkunde (Fribourg, Switzerland).

AO *Archiv Orientální* (Prague).

AOH *Acta Orientalia Academiae Scientiarum Hungaricae* (Budapest).

APAW *Abhandlungen der Preussischen Akademie der Wissenschaften* (Berlin).

Arabica *Arabica.* Revue d'études arabes (Leiden).

ArchL *Archivum Linguisticum.* A Review of Comparative Philology and General Linguistics (Glasgow).

Archs. Berb. *Les Archives berbères.* Publication du Comité d'études berbères de Rabat (Paris).

Ariel *Ariel.* A Quarterly of the Arts and Sciences in Israel (Jerusalem).

ASGIM *Atti del Sodalizio Glottologico Milanese* (Milan).

ASLU *Acta Societas Linguisticae Upsaliensis*, Nova Series (Uppsala). (Continuation of SprSUF).

ASP *Actes de la Société Philologique* (Paris).

AÜ Ankara Üniversitesi.

AUC-Ph *Acta Universitatis Carolinae Philologica* (Prague).

AÜDTCFD *Ankara Üniversitesi Dil ve Tarih-Coğrafya Fakültesi Dergisi* (Ankara).

AÜDTCFY *Ankara Üniversitesi Dil Tarih-Coğrafya Fakültesi Yayınları* (Ankara).

AWAW *Anzeiger der Kaiserlichen Akademie der Wissenschaften in Wien.*

BA *Beiträge zur Assyriologie und vergleichenden semitischen Sprachwissenschaft* (Leipzig).

BALM *Bollettino dell'Atlante Linguistico Mediterraneo* (Venice and Rome).

Bar-Ilan *Bar-Ilan.* Annual of the Bar-Ilan University (Ramat Gan, Israel).

Basha'ar *Basha'ar.* A Journal for Problems of Society and Culture (Merhavia, Israel).

BASOR *Bulletin of the American Schools of Oriental Research* (New Haven, Conn.).

BEO *Bulletin d'Études Orientales* (Damascus).

Biblica *Biblica.* Commentarii editi cura Pontificii Instituti Biblici (Rome).

BIFAN *Bulletin de l'Institut Français d'Afrique Noire.* Série B (Dakar).

BIFAO *Bulletin de l'Institut Français d'Archéologie Orientale* (Cairo).

BiOr *Bibliotheca Orientalis* (Leiden).

BL *Bibliographie linguistique/Linguistic Bibliography.* Comité Internationale Permanent des Linguistes (Utrecht and Antwerp).

BNF *Beiträge zur Namenforschung* (Heidelberg).

BSAC *Bulletin de la Société d'Archéologie Copte* (Cairo).

BSGI *Bollettino della Società Geografica Italiana* (Rome).

BSL *Bulletin de la Société de Linguistique de Paris* (Paris).

BSOAS *Bulletin of The School of Oriental and African Studies, University of London* (London).

BSOS *Bulletin of The School of Oriental Studies* (London) (= BSOAS).

BTNK Bongah-e Tarjomeh va Nashr-e Ketab/The Royal Institute for Translation and Publication (Tehran).

Bull. corr. afr. *Bulletin de correspondance africaine.* Publications de la Faculté des Lettres de l'Université (Algiers).

CAD *The Assyrian Dictionary of the Oriental Institute of The University of Chicago* (Chicago and Glückstadt, J.J. Augustin Inc., 1950–).

CAJ *Central Asiatic Journal* (The Hague and Wiesbaden).

CdÉ *Chronique d'Égypte.* Bulletin périodique de la Fondation Egyptologique Reine Élisabeth (Brussels).

CFS *Cahiers Ferdinand de Saussure* (Geneva).

CR *The Classical Review.* New Series (London).

Crum Studies *Coptic Studies in Honor of W.E. Crum* (Boston, 1950).

CSCO *Corpus Scriptorum Christianorum Orientalium* (Louvain).

CT *Cultura Turcica* (Ankara).

DANTadž *Doklady Akademii Nauk Tadžikskoj SSR* (Stalinabad [Dušanbe]).

EArmS *Erevanskij armjanskij gosudarstvennyj pedagogičeskij institut im. Chačatur Abovjana.* Sbornik naučnych trudov. Serija russkogo jazyka (Erevan).

EḤ *Enṣiqlōpediyya Ḥinnūxīt. Mōsad Bialik* (Jerusalem, 1959–69).

EI *Encyclopedia of Islam.* Second Edition (Leiden, E.J. Brill).

ĖIRJa *Ėtimologičeskie issledovanija po russkomu jazyku* (Moscow).

EO *Ethiopia Observer* (Addis Ababa and London).

Ereṣ Yisra'el	*Ereṣ Yisra'el*. Annual of the Israel Exploration Society (Jerusalem).
ĖV	*Ėpigrafika Vostoka* (Moscow and Leningrad).
FIZ	*Farhang-e Irânzamin* (Tehran).
FO	*Folia Orientalia*. Revue des études orientales (Cracow).
GAG	*Grundriss der akkadischen Grammatik*, by Wolfram von Soden. (Analecta Orientalia 33) (Rome, Pontificium Institutum Biblicum, 1952).
Genava	*Genava*. Organe officiel au Musée d'art et d'histoire de Genève, à la Bibliothèque publique et universitaire de Genève et à la Société des amis du Musée (Geneva).
GGA	*Göttingsche Gelehrte Anzeigen* (Göttingen).
GL	*General Linguistics* (University Park, Pennsylvania).
GLECS	*Comptes rendus du Groupe Linguistique d'Études Chamito-Sémitiques* (Paris).
Gnomon	*Gnomon*. Kritische Zeitschrift für die gesamte klassische Altertumswissenschaft (Munich).
GSAI	*Giornale della Società Asiatica Italiana* (Florence).
GUÅ	*Göteborgs Universitets Årsskrift/Acta Universitatis Gotoburgensis* (Göteborg).
HA	*Handēs Amsoreay*. Zeitschrift für armenische Philologie (Vienna).
HandVIFC	*Handelingen van het Vlaamse Filologencongres* (Louvain).
Hesperia	*Hesperia*. Journal of the American School of Classical Studies at Athens (Athens).
Hespéris	*Hespéris*. Bulletin de l'École supérieure de langue arabe et des dialectes berbères de Rabat (= *Archives berbères et bulletin de l'Institut des hautes études marocaines*) (Paris).
HFM	*Historisk-Filosofiske Meddelelser udgivet af Det Kongelige Danske Videnskabernes Selskab* (Copenhagen).
HFSkr	Det Kongelige Danske Videnskabernes Selskab, *Historisk-filosofiske skrifter* 4/3 (Copenhagen).
Ḥī	*ha-Ḥinnūx* (Tel-Aviv).
HKN	*Hogen Kenkyū Nenpo* (Annual Report of Dialectology) (Hiroshima).
HUCA	*Hebrew Union College Annual* (Cincinnati).
Ibla	*Revue de l'Institut des Belles Lettres Arabes* (Tunis).
IEJ	*Israel Exploration Journal* (Jerusalem).
IF	*Indogermanische Forschungen*. Zeitschrift für Indogermanistik und allgemeine Sprachwissenschaft (Berlin).
IFAN	*Mémoires d'Institut Français d'Afrique Noire* (Dakar).
IFŽ	*Patma-banasirakan handes/Istoriko-filologičeskij žurnal*. Akademija Nauk Armjanskoj SSR (Erevan).
IHEM	l'Institut des Hautes Études Marocaines. Bulletin 1922–. Notes et Documents 1948– (Rabat).
IIJ	*Indo-Iranian Journal* (The Hague).
IJAL	*International Journal of American Linguistics* (Baltimore).
IL	*Indian Linguistics*. Journal of the Linguistic Society of India (Poona).
IQ	*The Islamic Quarterly* (London).
IRAL	*International Review of Applied Linguistics in Language Teaching/Internationale Zeitschrift für angewandte Linguistik in der Spracherziehung* (Heidelberg).
Iran	*Iran*. Journal of the British Institute of Persian Studies (Tehran).
IRHT	Institut de Recherche et d'Histoire des Textes, Bulletin (Paris).
Islam	*Der Islam*. Zeitschrift für Geschichte und Kultur des Islamischen Orients (Berlin).
Islamica	*Islamica*. Zeitschrift für die Erforschung der Sprachen und der Kulturen der islamischen Völker (Leipzig).
İÜ	İstanbul Üniversitesi.
İÜEFTDED	*İstanbul Üniversitesi Edebiyat Fakültesi Türk Dili ve Edebiyati Dergisi* (Istanbul).
İÜEFY	*İstanbul Üniversitesi Edebiyat Fakültesi Yayınları* (Istanbul).
IzvAN	*Izvestija Akademii Nauk SSR, Otdelenie literatury i jazyka* (Moscow and Leningrad).
IzvANArm	*Haykakan SSH Gitut'yunneri Akademi*. Lraber hasarakakan gitut'yunneri. Vestnik obščestvennych nauk (Formerly: *Telekagir hasarakakan gitut'yunneri seria*) (Erevan).
IzvANAzerb	*Azärbajğan SSR elmlär akademijasynyn chäbärläri, Iğtimai elmlär serijasy/Izvestija Akademii Nauk Azerbajdžanskoj SSR*. Serija obščestvennych nauk (Baku).

IzvANTadž	*Izvestija Akademii Nauk Tadžikskoj SSR, Otdelenie obščestvennych nauk* (Dušanbe).
IzvANUzb	*Izvestija Akademii Nauk Uzbekskoj SSR* (Taškent).
IzvJOsNII	*Izvestija Jugo-Osetinskogo naučno-issledovetel'skogo instituta* (Cchinval).
IzvSOsNII	*Izvestija Severo-Osetinskogo naučno-issledovatel'skogo instituta. Jazykoznanie* (Ordžonikidze).
JA	*Journal Asiatique* (Paris).
JAF	*Journal of American Folklore* (Philadelphia).
JAfrL	*Journal of African Languages* (London).
JAOS	*Journal of the American Oriental Society* (New Haven, Conn.).
JASB	*Journal of the Asiatic Society of Bengal* (Calcutta).
JBL	*Journal of Biblical Literature* (Philadelphia).
JČ	*Jazykovedný časopis* (Bratislava).
JCS	*Journal of Cuneiform Studies* (New Haven, Conn.).
JEA	*The Journal of Egyptian Archaeology* (London).
JEOL	*Jaarbericht van het Vooraziatisch-Egyptisch Genootschap 'Ex Oriente Lux'/Annuaire de la Société orientale 'Ex Oriente Lux'* (Leiden).
JEthS	*Journal of Ethiopian Studies* (Addis Ababa).
JMS	*Journal of Maltese Studies* (Valetta, Malta).
JNES	*Journal of Near Eastern Studies* (Chicago).
JQR	*Jewish Quarterly Review*. New Series (Philadelphia).
JRAS	*Journal of the Royal Asiatic Society of Great Britain and Ireland* (London).
JRGS	*Journal of the Royal Geographical Society* (London).
JSAfr	*Journal de la Société des Africanistes* (Paris).
JSFOu	*Suomalais-ugrilaisen seuran aikakauskirja/Journal de la Société Finno-ougrienne* (Helsinki).
JSS	*Journal of Semitic Studies* (Manchester).
JWAfrL	*The Journal of West African Languages* (London).
KAWSE	*Kaiserliche Akademie der Wissenschaften. Südarabische Expedition/Akademičeskija izvestija* (Leningrad).
Kratylos	*Kratylos*. Kritisches Berichts- und Rezensionsorgan für indogermanische und allgemeine Sprachwissenschaft (Wiesbaden).
KSINA	*Kratkie Soobščenija Instituta narodov Azii* (Moscow).
KSIV	*Kratkie Soobščenija Instituta vostokovedenija* (now *KSINA*) (Moscow).
KSUzbU	*Kratkie Soobščenija Uzbekskogo gosudarstvennogo universiteta* (Samarkand).
Kush	*Kush*. Journal of the Sudan Antiquities Service (Khartoum).
KZ	*Zeitschrift für Vergleichende Sprachforschung auf dem Gebiete der indogermanischen Sprachen*, begründet von A. Kuhn (Göttingen).
LA	*Al-Lisān al-ʿArabī* (Rabat).
Lěšonénu	*Lěšonénu*. Vaʿad halashon haivrit be-Eretz Yisrael (Tel-Aviv).
Lexis	*Lexis*. Studien zur sprachphilosophie, sprachgeschichte und begriffsforschung (Lahr).
Lg	*Language*. Journal of the Linguistic Society of America (Baltimore).
LGU	*Leningradskij gosudarstvennyj universitet* (Leningrad).
Lingua	*Lingua*. International Review of General Linguistics/Revue internationale de linguistique générale (Amsterdam).
Linguistics	*Linguistics*. An International Review (The Hague).
LL	*Language Learning* (Ann Arbor).
LLA	*Lěšonénu La-ʿam* (Jerusalem).
LPosn	*Lingua Posnaniensis*. Czasopismo poświecone językoznawstwu porównowczemu i ogólnemu (Poznan).
LUÅ	*Lunds Universitets Årsskrift/Acta Universitatis Ludensis* (Lund).
Maʿalot	*Maʿalot*. Monthly of the Secondary School Teachers' Association (Tel-Aviv).
MDAIK	*Mitteilungen des Deutschen Archäologischen Instituts*, Abteilung Kairo.
MEA	*Middle Eastern Affairs* (New York).
MEJ	*The Middle East Journal* (Washington, D.C.).
MGWJ	*Monatsschrift für die Geschichte und Wissenschaft des Judentums* (Berlin).
MH	*Museum Helveticum*. Schweizerische Zeitschrift für klassische Altertumswissenschaft/

	Revue suisse pour l'étude de l'antiquité classique (Basel).
MIFAO	*Mémoires de l'Institut Français d'Archéologie Orientale* (Cairo).
MIO	*Mitteilungen des Instituts für Orientforschung.* Deutsche Akademie der Wissenschaften zu Berlin (Berlin).
MKAI	*Majallat Kulliyat al-Adāb* (Alexandria).
MKNA	*Mededelingen van de Koninklijke Nederlandsche Akademie van Wetenschappen*, afdeling Letterkunde. Nieuwe Reeks (Amsterdam).
MKVA	*Mededelingen van de Koninklijke Vlaamse Academie voor Wetenschappen, Letteren en Schone Kunsten van België.* Klasse der Letteren (Brussels).
MLJ	*Modern Language Journal* (Milwaukee, Wisconsin).
MM	*Mål og Minne.* Norske studier (Oslo).
MMAD	*Majallat al-Majmaʿ al-ʿIlmī al-ʿArabī* (Damascus).
MMII	*Majallat al-Majmaʿ al-ʿIlmī al-ʿIrāqī* (Baghdad).
MMLA	*Majallat Majmaʿ al-Lughah al-ʿArabiyyah* (Cairo).
MMLMP	*Materialy po matematičeskoj lingvistike i mašinnomu perevodu* (Leningrad).
MNy	*Magyar Nyelv* (Budapest).
MO	*Le Monde Oriental.* Revue des Études Orientales/Tidsskrift för Orientalska Studier (Uppsala).
MPhon	*Le Maître Phonétique.* Organe de l'Association Phonétique Internationale (London).
MSFOu	*Mémoires de la Société Finno-ougrienne* (Helsinki).
MSL	*Mémoires de la Société de Linguistique de Paris* (Paris).
MSOS	*Mitteilungen des Seminars für Orientalische Sprachen zu Berlin* (Berlin).
MSS	*Münchener Studien zur Sprachwissenschaft* (Münich).
MT	*Mechanical Translation* (Cambridge, Mass.).
Muséon	*Le Muséon.* Revue d'Études Orientales (Louvain).
MUSJ	*Mélanges de l'Université Saint-Joseph* (Beirut).
MVAG	*Mitteilungen der Vorderasiatischen-aegyptischen Gesellschaft* (Berlin).
NAA	*Narody Azii i Afriki.* Istorija, ékonomika, Kul'tura (Moscow).
NClio	*La Nouvelle Clio* (Brussels).
NS	*Die Neueren Sprachen* (Frankfurt am Main).
NTS	*Norsk Tidsskrift for Sprogvidenskap* (Oslo).
NTTašU	*Naučnye trudy Taškentskogo gosudarstvennogo universiteta im. V. I. Lenina.* Filologičeskie nauki (Tashkent).
Nyr	*Magyar Nyelvőr* (Budapest).
OGand	*Orientalia Gandensia* (Louvain).
OLZ	*Orientalistische Literaturzeitung* (Berlin).
OM	*Oriente Moderno* (Rome).
Or	*Orientalia.* Commentarii periodici Pontificii Instituti Biblici. Nova Series (Rome)
Orbis	*Orbis.* Bulletin international de documentation linguistique (Louvain).
Oriens	*Oriens.* Milletlerarası Şark Tetkikleri Cemiyeti Mecmuası/Journal of the International Society for Oriental Research (Leiden).
OS	*Orientalia Suecana* (Uppsala).
PBA	*Proceedings of the British Academy* (London).
Phonetica	*Phonetica.* Internationale Zeitschrift für Phonetik/International Journal of Phonetics (Basel and New York).
PICL IX	*Proceedings of the 9th International Congress of Linguists, Cambridge, Mass., August 27–31, 1962* (The Hague).
PMLA	*Publications of the Modern Language Association* (Menasha, Wisc.).
PP	*La Parola del Passato.* Revista di studi classici (Naples).
PPS	*Proceedings of the Philological Society* (London).
RA	*Revue Archéologique.* VIe Série (Paris).
RALinc	*Atti della Accademia Nazionale dei Lincei, Rendiconti della Classe di scienze morali, storiche e filologiche.* Serie VIII (Rome).
RAS	Royal Asiatic Society (London).
RAss	*Revue d'Assyriologie et d'Archéologie Orientale* (Paris).
RB	*Revue Biblique* (Paris).

RE	*Revue d'Égyptologie publiée par la Société française d'Égyptologie* (Paris).
REA	*Revue des Études Anciennes* (Bordeaux and Paris).
REArm	*Revue des Études Arméniennes* (Paris).
REIsl	*Revue des Études Islamiques* (Paris).
REJuiv	*Revue des Études Juives* (Paris).
RENLO	*Revue de l'École Nationale des Langues Orientales*. Structures des langues et civilisations du monde contemporain (Paris).
RESm	*Revue des Études Sémitiques* (Paris).
RETP	*Revue d'Ethnographie et des Traditions Populaires* (Paris).
Rev.Afr.	*Revue africaine*. Journal des travaux de la société historique algérienne (Algiers).
RFLIsf	*Našriyye-ye Dâneškade-ye Adabiyyât-e Esfahân/Revue de la Faculté des Lettres d'Isfahan* (Esfahân).
RFLMed	*Majalle-ye Dâneškade-ye Adabiyyât-e Mašhad/Revue de la Faculté des Lettres de Meched* (Mašhad).
RFLTan	*Dânešgâh-e Tehrân, Majalle-ye Dâneškade-ye Adabiyyât va Olum-e Ensâni/Université de Téhéran, Revue de la Faculté des Lettres et Sciences Humaines* (Tehran).
RFLTiz	*Našriyye-ye Dâneškade-ye Adabiyyât-e Tabriz/Université de Tabriz, Revue de la Faculté des Lettres* (Tabriz).
RIL	*Rendiconti dell'Istituto Lombardo di Scienze e Lettere, Classe di lettere e scienze morali e storiche* (Milan).
RIOno	*Revue Internationale d'Onomastique* (Paris).
RL	*Ricerche Linguistiche*. Bollettino dell'Istituto di Glottologia dell'Universitá di Roma (Rome).
RLing	*Revue Roumaine de Linguistique* (Bucarest).
RO	*Rocznik Orientalistyczny* (Warsaw).
RPh	*Revue de Philologie, de Littérature et d'Histoire anciennes*. Troisième série (Paris).
RQ	*Revue de Qumran* (Paris).
RRAL	*Rendiconti della Reale Accademia dei Lincei. Classe di scienze morali, storiche e filologiche* (Rome).
RS	*Revue sémitique d'épigraphie et d'histoire ancienne* (Paris).
RSEt	*Rassegna di Studi Etiopici* (Rome).
RSO	*Rivista degli Studi Orientali* (Rome).
RT	*Recueil de travaux relatifs à la philologie et à l'archéologie égyptiennes et assyriennes* (Paris).
SANGruz	*Soobščenija Akademii Nauk Gruzinskoj SSR* (Tiflis).
SbBAW	*Sitzungsberichte der Bayerischen Akademie der Wissenschaften, Philosophisch-historische Klasse* (Munich).
SbDAW	*Sitzungsberichte der Deutschen Akademie der Wissenschaften zu Berlin, Klasse für Sprachen, Literatur und Kunst* (Berlin).
ScrH	*Scripta Hierosolymitana*. Publications of the Hebrew University (Jerusalem).
SE	*Studi Etruschi* (Florence).
Semit. jaz.	*Semitskie Jazyki*. Akademija Nauk SSSR, Institut Narodov Azii. (Moscow).
SIL	*Studies in Linguistics* (Buffalo, New York).
SIsl	*Studia Islamica* (Paris).
SJA	*Southwestern Journal of Anthropology* (Albuquerque, New Mexico).
SL	*Studia Linguistica*. Revue de linguistique générale et comparée (Lund).
SO	*Studia Orientalia*, edidit Societas Orientalis Fennica (Helsinki).
SovEtn	*Sovetskaja Etnografija* (Moscow and Leningrad).
SPAGI	*Supplementi periodici all'Archivio Glottologico Italiano* (Florence).
SPAW	*Sitzungsberichte der Preussischen Akademie der Wissenschaften* (Berlin).
Sprache	*Die Sprache*. Zeitschrift für Sprachwissenschaft (Vienna).
SprOKrPAN	*Polska Akademia Nauk, Odzial w Krakowie, Sprawozdania z posiedzeń Komisji* (Cracow).
SWAW	*Sitzungsberichte der Wiener Akademie der Wissenschaften*. Philosophisch-historische Klasse (Vienna).
Syria	*Syria*. Revue d'art oriental et d'archéologie (Paris).

TA	*La Traduction automatique* (The Hague and Paris).
TAPS	*Transactions of the American Philosophical Society* (Philadelphia).
Tarbiz	*Tarbiz.* A Quarterly Review of the Humanities. (In Hebrew) (Jerusalem).
TAzU	*Trudy Azerbajdžanskogo gosudarstvennogo universiteta* (Baku).
TBGS	*Transactions of the Bombay Geographical Society* (Bombay).
TD	*Türk Dili* (Ankara).
TDAYB	*Türk Dili Araştırmaları Yıllığı Belleten* (Ankara).
TDB	*Türk Dili Belleten* (Ankara).
TDe	*Türkoloji Dergisi* (Ankara).
TDK	Türk Dil Kurumu (Ankara).
Textus	*Textus.* Annual of the Hebrew University Bible Project (Jerusalem).
TIJa	*Trudy Instituta Jazykoznanija Akademija Nauk SSR* (Moscow).
TIJaGruz	*Trudy Instituta Jazykoznanija Akademii Nauk Gruzinskoj SSR* (Tbilisi).
TK	*Türk Kültürü* (Ankara).
TKA	*Türk Kültürü Araştırmaları* (Ankara).
TKAEY	*Türk Kültürünü Araştırma Enstitüsü Yayınları* (Ankara).
TM	*Türkiyat Mecmuası* (Ankara).
TPhS	*Transactions of the Philological Society* (Oxford).
TSBA	*Transactions of the Society of Biblical Archeology* (London).
TSrAzU	*Trudy Sredne-Aziatskogo gosudarstvennogo universiteta* (Tashkent).
TTadžAN	*Akademii Nauk Tadžikskoj SSR, Institut istorii, arxeologii i étnografii, Trudy* (Stalinabad [Dušanbe]).
TTbilU	*Trudy Tbilisskogo gosud. universiteta.* Serija filologičeskich Nauk/Šromebi. Pilologiur mecnierebate seria (Tiflis).
TTK	Türk Tarih Kurumu.
TVIIJa	*Trudy Voennogo Instituta Inostrannych Jazykov* (Moscow).
UAJb	*Ural-Altaische Jahrbücher* (Wiesbaden).
UAS	*Indiana University Publications,* Uralic and Altaic Series (Bloomington and The Hague).
UUÅ	*Uppsala Universitets Årsskrift* (Uppsala).
UZAzU	*Elmi əsərələr.* Dil və ədəbijat/Učenye zapiski Azerbajdžanskogo gosudarstvennogo universiteta im. S.M. Korova. Jazyk i literatura (Baku).
UZBašU	*Učenye zapiski Baškirskogo gosudarstvennogo universiteta.* Serija filologičeskich nauk (Ufa).
UZIMO	*Učenye zapiski, Institut meždunarodnych otnošenij* (Moscow).
UZIV	*Učenye zapiski instituta vostokovedenija* (Moscow).
UZLU	*Učenye zapiski Leningradskogo ordena Lenina gosudarstvennogo universiteta im. A.A. Ždanova* (Leningrad).
UZMU	*Učenye zapiski Moskovskogo gosudarstvennogo universiteta* (Moscow).
UZStalPI	*Učenye zapiski Stalinabadskogo Pedinstituta* (Stalinabad [Dušanbe]).
UZTadžU	*Učenye zapiski Tadžikskogo gosudarstvennogo universiteta* (Stalinabad [Dušanbe]).
UZVIIJa	*Učenye zapiski voennogo instituta inostrannych jazykov* (Moscow).
VDI	*Vestnik Drevnej Istorii* (Moscow).
VIO	*Veröffentlichungen des Instituts für Orientforschung, Deutsche Akademie der Wissenschaften zu Berlin* (Berlin).
VJa	*Voprosy Jazykoznanija* (Moscow).
VjaStArm	*Voprozy jazyka i stilja/Lezvi ev oči har'er* (Erevan).
VLU	*Vestnik Leningradskogo gosudarstvennogo universiteta* (Leningrad).
VMU	*Vestnik Moskovskogo universiteta.* Serija VII: Filologija (Moscow).
VON	*Vestnik otdelenija obščestvennych nauk, Akademija Nauk Gruzinskoj SSR* (Tiflis).
VT	*Vetus Testamentum.* A Quarterly published by The International Organization of Old Testament Scholars (Leiden).
WI	*Die Welt des Islams* (Leiden).
Word	*Word.* Journal of the Linguistic Circle of New York (New York).
WVM	*Wiener Völkerkundliche Mitteilungen* (Vienna).
WZKM	*Wiener Zeitschrift für die Kunde des Morgenlandes* (Vienna).

WZUB	*Wissenschaftliche Zeitschrift der Humboldt-Universität, Berlin.* Gesellschafts- und sprachwissenschaftliche Reihe (Berlin).
ZA	*Zeitschrift für Assyriologie und verwandte Gebiete.* Neue Folge (Berlin).
ZAPh	*Zeitschrift für Armenische Philologie* (Marburg).
ZÄS	*Zeitschrift für ägyptische Sprache und Altertumskunde* (Berlin).
ZATW	*Zeitschrift für die alttestamentliche Wissenschaft* (Berlin).
ZDMG	*Zeitschrift der Deutschen Morgenländischen Gesellschaft* (Wiesbaden).
ZDPV	*Zeitschrift des Deutschen Palästina-Vereins* (Wiesbaden).
ZES	*Zeitschrift für Eingeborenen-Sprachen* (Berlin).
ZEthn	*Zeitschrift für Ethnologie.* Organ der Deutschen Gesellschaft für Volkerkunde (Braunschweig).
ZFSL	*Zeitschrift für französische Sprache und Literatur* (Wiesbaden).
ZII	*Zeitschrift für Indologie und Iranistik* (Leipzig).
ZKM	*Zeitschrift für die Kunde des Morgenlandes* (Göttingen and Bonn).
ZPhon	*Zeitschrift für Phonetik, Sprachwissenschaft und Kommunikationsforschung* (Berlin).
ZS	*Zeitschrift für Semitistik* (Leipzig).
ZWS	*Zeitschrift für die Wissenschaft der Sprache* (Berlin).

PART ONE

INDO-EUROPEAN LANGUAGES OF THE AREA

INDO-EUROPEAN LANGUAGES

AN OVERVIEW

The Indo-European languages of the Near East are amply covered bibliographically and topically in the several contributions in this volume devoted to Armenian and Iranian. It is abundantly clear that a great deal of scholarly attention is paid to the study of these languages, though the results often appear in languages that are not easily accessible to non-specialists in western Europe and America. Nevertheless, it is equally true that in relation to other branches of Indo-European, the Armenian and Iranian are relatively sparsely populated in scholarly quarters; the former with much fewer specialists than the latter. These remarks will be devoted more specifically to Iranian because of my greater familiarity with that field, though I am sure that much of what I have to say applies equally well to Armenian.

My colleagues Benveniste, Dresden, Lazard, and Redard have presented admirable surveys concerning the state of past accomplishment in the study of various aspects of *Iranistik*. Quite naturally the traditional fields of Old Iranian, Middle Iranian, and especially Modern Persian have received the lion's share of attention from a variety of points of view: comparative-historical linguistics, some dialectology, structural-descriptive studies, textbook grammars, dictionaries, and the usual language plus history, religion, archeology, and other interrelations. Much of what continues to be done on these languages involves elucidation and recovery of intriguing chapters of man's endeavor as expressed in these languages. New discoveries have brought to light hitherto unsuspected Iranian tongues. Khotanese, at the beginning of this century, and Bactrian, within the last decade, represent two enormously important achievements of decipherment and analysis. Yet much of Central Asia and of the Irano-Afghan geographic domain remain to be systematically explored. There is every reason to believe that significant and exciting text discoveries await us in the future. But this aspect primarily concerns recovery of the past.

The present configuration of the Iranian linguistic scene is one that could conceivably attract an army of workers — so varied a laboratory does it provide. Both synchronic and diachronic work beg to be done. If we limit the discussion to the most important literary language, Modern Persian, we find that despite the long interest in the West that has been displayed toward this language and its literature, enormous gaps remain. Concordances (except for Wolff's *Glossar zu Firdosis Schahname*) are non-existent. The whole domain of historical lexicography is virtually untouched. The pioneering work of Lazard in attempting a description of the grammar of the earliest Persian prose is bold, unique, and enormously useful. Similar studies for other periods and even for individual authors need doing. Indeed, it could be argued that more insightful elucidation of literary texts would be the first and most obvious profit to be gained from such purely linguistic studies.

Persian in its current forms has begun to be examined and interesting results have already become manifest. Much more can be accomplished. We know hardly more than the anecdotal about the facts of code-switching in various social settings. Because of the interest that linguists rather than Iranists have devoted in recent years to the modern spoken language, it has become clear that the traditional and widespread identification of 'colloquial' with 'substandard' is a serious error. Furthermore, we are almost totally ignorant of the facts relevant to the current scene with respect to the range of politeness and deferential forms and their usage: pronoun substitutes, verb phrases, etc. That the situation is changing has been attested, again anecdotally, but there is no systematic study available.

When we turn to the dialectology of Modern Persian, it is apparent that despite the abundance of earlier data collected by conscientious and capable field workers, much of it is scattered, unsystematic, and needs redoing either to fill in gaps or to cover areas never before studied and above all to reinterpret in the light of more up-to-date theorizing. Efforts here are few and uncoordinated. The work of the *Atlas Linguistique de l'Iran* needs amplification and publication — here too attention has been primarily devoted to Persian-speaking Afghanistan.

Whatever gaps exist for Modern Persian are of course doubly or triply vacant with respect to the less traditional fields of languages that do not possess the same literary prestige: Kurdish, Pashto, Baluchi, Ossetic — though of course much good work has been done in recent years on these languages. In the Soviet Union, to be sure, especially valuable research continues to be published on these languages and of course on Persian and Tajik. The Western Iranist ignores the Russian materials at his own peril; and it cannot be said that Russian is as familiar to Iranists as are the other scholarly languages, English, French, and German. Our Russian colleagues, with some justice, often complain that their efforts receive scant attention in the West. No doubt there will have to be a continuing effort at translation — in both directions — to make the scholarly literature more accessible. In recent years, there is growing evidence that less nationalistic official fervor has allowed our Russian colleagues to provide their own translations into English and French. This should certainly be applauded. It is clear that there are probably more scholars working full-time on Iranian languages in the USSR than in all the rest of the world.

Ancillary subjects in Iranian linguistics have begun to be opened that bid fair to provide much useful information. Here I am especially thinking of research into Judeo-Persian — a hitherto sadly neglected field (except for the early years of this century), but one where the textual resources promise significant insights into various aspects of Persian linguistic history. Broadly speaking, Judeo-Persian comprehends a millennial tradition of textual attestation — Persian language written in the Hebrew alphabet and in an orthography that differs markedly from that of Islamic Persian. The varied text genres and the independence of orthographic and grammatical tradition combine to provide a fruitful alternative source for elucidating, confirming, and often explicating many features of Persian historical phonology and morphology. For syntax and lexicon there are also important insights to be gained from these texts. The resources are vast; and the workers in this field, few. Furthermore, the various spoken forms of Judeo-Persian that are still actively used throughout the Persian-speaking world as well as outside it await recording and analysis.

The new and exciting realm that is broadly referred to by the term 'sociolinguistics' is virtually untouched in its application to Iranian. The massive bi- and multilingualism of Iran, Afghanistan, and Central Asia ought to be of exciting interest. One aspect that seems especially intriguing is the process whereby the three major forms of Persian — (Iranian) Persian, Dari (Afghan Persian), and Tajik (the Persian spoken in Soviet Tajikistan and neighboring areas) — are growing apart. Here we find a divisiveness stimulated by political, cultural, and geographical factors that is apparently serving to increase the amount of mutual unintelligibility of what are essentially three dialects of one and the same language. The lack of contact across the national borders, the use of Cyrillic script for Tajik, and a studied three-way independence in new vocabulary formation and borrowing — all of these and other factors are, in my opinion, pushing these three forms of Persian farther apart from each other. The process cries out for systematic study.

The Persian-speaking geographical domain could provide an excellent laboratory for investigation of the problem of multilingual societies (with interesting types of diglossia), especially in the matter of learning how to take a language census. The amount of multilingualism that one finds without special effort in Tehran, for example, is staggering. Aside from the use of English and French, learned by Iranians in school both at home and abroad, and depending on familial, ethnic, religious, and other factors, and in addition to the normal kind of formal-to-informal range for Persian, there are many speakers who also control and use with great frequency one or more of the following: a regional Persian dialect (e.g., Rashti), Azeri (Azerbaijani Turkish), Armenian, Russian. Families whose history bears connection with the Caucasus, Azerbaijan, etc. still often carry on the use of one of the pertinent languages in the home or in circles of friends and relatives of similar origin. The linguistic demography and especially the linguistic sociograms of a sufficiently large sample of individuals correlated with their socio-economic classification and family migration history would provide illuminating insights into the structure of Iranian society. Surely the simplistic two-dimensional map that colors Iran a linguistic monolith is much less than a half-truth. The linguistic complexity needs reasonably adequate documentation and description.

The seemingly traditional dialectological view that somehow everything regional is a deviation from 'classical' or 'standard' Persian must be discarded. What is above all needed is systematic collection and analysis of regional dialects on a large scale in which description for its own sake is the paramount motivation. Traditional dialect sampling via a questionnaire that focuses on particular items in the whole range of language structure can still produce excellent and informative results. The burden of all this is simply that the field of Iranian linguistics in its vast complexity of geographic and temporal distribution is virtually wide open for interested students and can cater to every predilection. It is hoped that the Iranian surveys in this volume may stimulate a coming expanded generation of scholars.

HERBERT H. PAPER

A

IRANIAN LANGUAGES

OLD IRANIAN

EMILE BENVENISTE

PREFATORY NOTE

A bibliographic survey of the main publications on Old Iranian from 1904 (the date of Christian Bartholomae's *Altiranisches Wörterbuch*) down to approximately 1960, will be found in J. Duchesne-Guillemin's 'Forschungsbericht: L'étude de l'iranien ancien au vingtième siècle' (*Kratylos* 7.1-44, 1962).

In the following report we have endeavoured to analytically register the books and articles related to this field, published between 1961-62 and 1968. This space of time is too short to allow very definite or new trends to appear. On occasion reference has been made to earlier contributions. The items have been classified, so far as possible, for the reader's convenience, according to the traditional divisions of grammar.

EXTRA-IRANIAN SOURCES

Our knowledge of Old Iranian is furthered by evidence found in other languages which are either geographically close to, or included within, the limits of the Achaemenid Persian Empire.

Several notable publications deal with these areas. We shall present them in the following order: 1. Asia Minor, 2. Aramaic, 3. Elamite, 4. Greek, and 5. Slavic.

1. The documents of El Amarna and Boghaz-Köy have opened up an important subject, that of contacts of Indo-Iranian groups with the Hittites and the Mitanni in Asia Minor, in the middle of the second millennium B.C.

Today one is inclined to consider the proper nouns (names of gods and men) and the few loanwords (in particular the numerals) transcribed in the cuneiform texts, as Indo-Aryan. The Iranist, nevertheless, will benefit greatly from studying these data. He will find this material, collected and analyzed, in the most recent study: Manfred Mayrhofer, *Die Indo-Arier im alten Vorderasien* mit einer analytischen Bibliographie (Wiesbaden, 1966). It is certainly the best work on the subject. It includes two documentary chapters, one linguistic (pp. 18–25), combining the onomastic and lexical data with some comments; the other historical, on the events and conditions which brought the Indo-Aryans into contact with the Mitanni. The largest part of the book (pp. 41–128) is taken up by an analytical bibliography of the subject, from 1884 to 1965, arranged year by year, in which each reference is accompanied by a brief summary of its contents. An index alphabetically rearranges the mass of linguistic material (pp. 129–45), and increases the usefulness of the work.

2. The publication of G. R. Driver, *Aramaic documents of the fifth century B.C.* (Oxford, 1954) has brought to light some valuable official documents written on leather, issued by the Chancery of Aršāma, Persian satrap of Egypt in the fifth century B.C. These Aramaic documents contain a number of still unknown Persian terms and some Iranian proper names. The commentary devoted to the Iranian items, however, has been criticized in responsible quarters. The work is available now in an 'abridged and revised edition' (Oxford, Clarendon Press, 1957), in which the editor has taken into account the remarks made by several Iranists. The commentary has been condensed and widely corrected.

Several Iranian terms for functions, borrowed or transcribed into Aramaic, are studied by F. Rundgren in *OS* 12.89f. (1963), 14–15.75f. (1966).

A fragmentary version of the edicts of Aśoka in Aramaic and Greek has been found in the region of Kandahar (S.E. Afghanistan). It provides completely new facts about the use of these two languages in the frontier provinces of the Maurya Empire. The Aramaic text contains some valuable Iranian lexical elements which have been identified and analyzed by E. Benveniste (*JA* 36f., 1958).

3. The Elamite tablets of Persepolis appear today as an invaluable source of information on Achaemenid onomastics, economy, and society in general. George Cameron published in 1948 a group of tablets from the Treasury, *The Persepolis treasury tablets*, with a valuable commentary; and, in 1965, new tablets from the Persepolis treasury (*JNES* 24.167f.). We are awaiting the forthcoming publication of the so-called Fortification tablets, in the care of Richard T. Hallock. This would be a very rich collection, the importance of which, for Achaemenid studies, cannot be exaggerated. Thanks to the index of personal names provided in manuscript by R. T. Hallock, the very abundant onomastic material (around 1500 names) has already been accessible to E. Benveniste, who has found around 400 Iranian proper names among them, most of them completely unknown. He has studied them in his book, *Titres et noms propres en iranien ancien*, 75–99 (Paris, 1966). See also, by the same author, *JA*, 49f., 1958.

4. Between Achaemenid Persia and Greece there were exchange relations which have left their mark in the Greek vocabulary. These lexical relations have been studied by E. Benveniste in the light of the Persian loanwords in Greek, arranged chronologically. The first of these borrowings go back to a period before historical relations between the two countries. The Persian words quoted by Herodotus, then by

Xenophon, and finally the more recent ones, are reviewed successively, in a chapter of the collective work, *La Persia e il mondo greco-romano*, 479f. (Accademia dei Lincei, Rome, 1966).

A part of this subject, the Median and Persian elements in Herodotus, is also treated by Rüdiger Schmitt in 'Medisches und persisches Sprachgut bei Herodot' (*ZDMG* 117.119f., 1967). But in contrast with the preceding author, he includes all proper names, ethnic and personal, which are very numerous. Each Persian or Median name is considered in the transcription given by Herodotus and, so far as possible, reconstructed in its original form, with full bibliography.

The Greek word *maniakes* 'gold necklace' is shown to be an Iranian loanword by Rüdiger Schmitt (*Sprache* 13.61f., 1967).

Two Iranian proper names in Greek inscriptions from the Pontic region, *Iodesmagos* and *Sandarzios*, are commented on by D. Weber (*Sprache* 12.90f., 1968).

Verse 100 of Aristophane's *Acharnians* is supposed to quote a sentence in Persian, uttered by a messenger of the Great King. This verse has been subjected to many reconstructions and interpretations. The most recent one is that of W. Brandenstein (*Wiener Zeitschrift für die Kunde Süd- und Ostasiens* VIII.43f., 1964). Starting from the text as given by the mss. AC: *iartamanexarxanapissonasatra*, he makes it a greeting formula which would read in Old Persian: *haya (a)rtamanā Ḫšayāršā napaišuv yaunam hšaçam* 'Der frommgesinnte Xerxes (grüsst) das an den Gewässern befindliche griechische Reich!' Neither the construction nor the formulation would seem convincing. The article ends with a useful review of the previous attempts, all of them hypothetical, and always for the same reason: it is impossible to decide whether the sentence is to be taken as Persian or as Persian-like jabber.

5. The question of lexical contacts between Iranian and Slavic can be best mentioned here. E. Benveniste reviews the main facts and shows that it is necessary to set up several levels and varieties in the Irano-Slavic correlations, which have been studied until now in too uniform a manner. Some of them presuppose ancient and long relations between the Iranian and Slavic tribes (*To Honor Roman Jakobson*, I.197f., 1967).

IRANIAN SOURCES

General Works

The main requirement for studies of Old Iranian would be a new edition of Chr. Bartholomae's *Altiranisches Wörterbuch*. This dictionary, published in 1904, is still indispensable. But even with the corrections made by Bartholomae, first in the dictionary's appendix (col. 1880–1900), then in the supplement *Zum Altiranischen Wörterbuch* (Beiheft zum 19. Band der *Indogermanischen Forschungen*, 1906), a complete revision is an urgent need.

It is now possible to look forward to the realization of this new, up-to-date edition in the not too distant future. We are happy to see preliminary work being done on this project: Bernfried Schlerath, *Awesta-Wörterbuch, Vorarbeiten I*: Index locorum zur Secundärliteratur des Awesta (Wiesbaden, O. Harrassowitz, 1968, XXXII + 214 pp.); *Vorarbeiten II*: Konkordanz (1968, XV + 199 pp.). A third volume is planned. The first volume sums up the scientific work devoted to the textual interpretation of the Avesta. After a detailed bibliography (pp. XI–XXXII), an *index locorum*, which takes up the whole volume, gives for each passage of each Avestan text a list of references to all that has been written thereon. One follows thus, line by line, the entire Avesta and can immediately find, for any text or verse, the complete exegetical bibliography. The references are given in abbreviated form, with a system indicating whether the passage is translated entirely or not, merely quoted, or with parallels, etc.

For the scientific references, the author goes back further than Bartholomae, and he covers the material up to 1965. Although the typographic presentation is clear and each paragraph is neatly set forth, with marginal numbering, the work, as a whole, makes at first an overwhelming impression. One could not imagine that the Avesta has given rise to such a massive body of commentaries.

On closer examination, one realizes that this bibliography goes far beyond what was expected, that it even registers the comments of the very first pioneers, Anquetil, Westergaard, Spiegel, or of worthless authors, such as Mills. While it is still useful to collect the opinions of Darmesteter or Geldner, Caland or W. Geiger, it would appear useless to refer today to completely out-of-date works. But it would be unfair to complain of an excess of riches when the scanty bibliographic means available in this field were for so long deplored. The second volume of the *Vorarbeiten* includes a series of concordances numbered A, B, and C. As more than 25 per cent of the Avestan texts consist in entire or partial repetitions of other passages, it is necessary to list all the repeated texts; that is the goal of Concordance A. The initial passage is reproduced *in extenso*, and the repetitions are indexed by reference. As these repetitions sometimes involve a change of the initial text (in case forms, demonstratives, etc.), a second concordance, called Concordance B, lists these variations. There follows a Concordance C, indicating the parallels of expression or of construction between Avestan and Vedic, and occasionally in other ancient languages. Finally, there are indexes by references and by headwords for each of the concordances, which greatly facilitates use.

This short analysis is sufficient to show the value of this bibliographic instrument for the philological or linguistic study of the Avesta, and generally for any research on this text, its composition and its language. It is also worth stressing the importance of the list of agreements between Avestan and Vedic formulas, a subject of great interest to which several articles have recently been devoted (cf. below).

A new instalment of the *Handbuch der Orientalistik*, Iranian Section, deals with the literatures of Iran (*Iranistik*, Zweiter Abschnitt. *Literatur*, Lieferung 1, 1968).

Several chapters are of interest for the study of Old Iranian, particularly that by I. Gershevitch on 'Old Iranian literature' (pp. 1-30, with a bibliography; but note the author's statement that: 'This article was submitted in July, 1955, and slightly revised in July, 1959'). It is a thorough and well-documented survey, with personal views, of the two great literary monuments, the Achaemenid inscriptions on the one hand, and the Avesta on the other, including discussion of their textual nature, literary tradition, and general characteristics of composition and language.

Equally instructive for their frequent references to ancient traditions and texts are the two chapters by Mary Boyce: 'Middle Persian literature' (pp. 32-66) and 'The Manichaean literature in Middle Iranian' (pp. 67–76), very competently bringing together much scattered information. M. J. Dresden offers in the final chapter a 'Survey of the history of Iranian studies' (pp. 168–85) in which Old Persian and Avestan are dealt with (pp. 171–3).

For Old Persian, the *Handbuch des Altpersischen* of Wilhelm Brandenstein and Manfred Mayrhofer (Wiesbaden, 1964) is a very useful work of introduction and reference, rewritten in German from a manual first published in Spanish. To the first author is due a grammatical sketch with the main nominal and verbal inflections conveniently tabulated. The second gives a selection of Old Persian texts together with a lexicon (pp. 100–57), which is the essential part of the work. Under each Persian word there is a detailed bibliography of recent works, which will be profitably consulted.

In the present report, we have not repeated, with rare exception, the Old Persian bibliography already given in this handbook.

A Danish translation of the Old Persian inscriptions has been provided by J. P. Asmussen, *Historiske Tekster fra Achaemenidetiden* (Copenhagen, 1960).

I have not seen Walther Wüst, *Altpersische Studien*, Sprach- und kulturgeschichtliche Beiträge zum Glossar der Achämeniden-Inschriften (München, 1966).

For Avestan, we will note, in Russian, the manual of S. N. Sokolov, *Jazyk avesty* (Leningrad, 1964), which I have not seen.

Two useful general books in Russian are: I. M. Oranskij, *Vvedenie v iranskuju filologiju* (An introduction to Iranian philology) (Moscow, 1960) and *Iranskie jazyki* (Iranian languages, including Old Iranian) (Moscow, 1963), both with detailed bibliography.

New Texts

No new text has been published. A small fragment of a Persian cuneiform inscription from Pasargadae, which was believed to contain part of the name of Cyrus, has been definitely identified by George Cameron as belonging to a duplicate of the inscription of Darius on gold and silver plates unearthed at Persepolis and Hamadan (George G. Cameron, 'An inscription of Darius from Pasargadae', *Iran*, Journal of the British Institute of Persian Studies, 5.7f., 1967).

The whole Avesta has been transcribed in Devanagari script and published by E. M. F. Kanga and N. S. Sontakke (Poona, 1962, in two volumes).

Phonetics

The sound system of Old Iranian is analyzed as a phonemic system by E. Benveniste in *BSL* 62.53f., 1968, who points out the conditions in which the characteristic changes of Iranian occurred, notably the transition from Indo-Iranian *s* to Iranian *h*. In the very complex table of Avestan sounds, the author distinguishes those which have phonemic value and those which are only variants.

Dialectology

The main traits of the Old Iranian dialects are summarized by J. Duchesne-Guillemin, *AGI* 49.105f., 1964.

The dialect variation of the treatment of palatals in Iranian is discussed, in the extreme complexity of detail, by I. Gershevitch in *TPhS* 1f., 1964. In his opinion, the divergent treatments of voiceless *s* and *θ*, and voiced *z* and *d*, cannot be explained by the difference between Persian and Median.

The problem is taken up again by M. Mayrhofer (*Anzeiger der phil. hist. Klasse der Österreichischen Akademie der Wissenschaften*, 1f., 1968) who endeavours to clarify the demonstration of the preceding article and to evaluate its conclusions as to the reconstruction of Median.

Persian Epigraphy

Textual interpretation of Persian texts, or the revision of previously accepted translations, has been the object of several studies.

W. Hinz (*ZDMG* 113.231f., 1963) discusses minutely the three Achaemenid versions and the fragment of translation into Aramaic, of paragraph 14 of the Bisutun inscription. He examines, in particular, the meaning of the terms *gaiθā-*, *abičariš*, *māniya-*, *viθbišča*.

The same author, in *ZDMG* 115.227f., 1965, analyzes and translates again the inscription from Darius' tomb, labelled DNb, in which the meaning of a number of terms is still disputed.

Rüdiger Schmitt (*Or* 32.437f., 1963) discards as a ghostword the alleged OP ordinal '*çita*'. He deals at length with the Vedic and Iranian syntactic function of the enclitic *-ča* in relation to the OP phrase *artăcā brazmaniya*. On this last word, see also W. Hinz, *Or* 33.262, 1964.

M. Mayrhofer (*Or* 33.72f., 1964) discusses various questions concerning the vocalization of the OP script. He also points to an OP proper name, *Ariyāršan-*, that had been misread in a previous publication.

H. Mittelberger (*Sprache* 11.93f., 1965) considers, in numerous instances, the relation between the OP cuneiform script and the phonetic structure of the language. This problem is also treated by J. Kuryłowicz (*ZPhon* 17.563f., 1964).

Jens Juhl Jensen (*KZ* 81.284f., 1967) analyzes the Persian cuneiform system as a regular organization of 36 signs, which can be arranged in a schema of six sign classes. A striking parallel is provided by the Ionian alphabet of the Achaemenid period, which can also be arranged in five similar classes. The author's conclusion is that the Persian cuneiform writing has been formed by imitation of a regular writing system, divided into sign classes, such as could be seen, within the Persian empire, in the Greek alphabet.

The formation of Old Persian fractional numerals, as attested in Elamite transcriptions, is investigated by Karl Hoffmann (*KZ* 79.247f., 1965).

Rüdiger Schmitt, in 'Altpersische Minutien' (*KZ* 81.54f., 1967), revives the former interpretation of *patiyāvanhyaiy* as a 'futurum historicum' (Wackernagel); he proposes to read *ābičarīš* and he understands it to mean 'die von den Knechten/Sklaven bewohnte/bearbeitete Ortlichkeit'; he reads OP *tauviyah* for *tavyah./*; he stresses that OP passive forms always had the full grade of the root.

Under the title 'Old Persian miscellanea', Bo Utas (*OS* 14–15.118f., 1966) examines two passages of the Persian text of Bisutun: 1) *abiš nāviyā āha*, 2) *mātya drauga man(ya)-* and comments at length on their forms or their construction.

We shall merely mention articles such as O. Szemerenyi's 'Iranian Studies I' (*KZ* 76.60f., 1959) and 'Iranica II' (*Sprache* 12.190f., 1966), which touch on a number of etymological questions about Iranian forms, of which several are from Old Persian: in the second article, *Hūža*, *Hvārazmiš*, *arašniš*, *van-*, *anušiya-*, *azdā*, *kamna*, *patiyāvahyaiy*, *duvitāpar(a)nam*, *čašma*, *rādiy*; A. Prosdocimi, 'Note di Persiano antico' (*RSO* 42.27f., 1967); Rüdiger Schmitt, on the mountain-name Paryadres (*Beiträge zur Namenforschung* 15.297, 1964); W. Eilers, on OP *dānaka* as coin-name (*Die Welt des Orients* 2.333, 1959); R. Ghirshman, on the OP script (*JNES* 24.243f., 1965); J. Duchesne-Guillemin, on *baga*, (*Festschrift W. Eilers*, 157, 1967); and O. Klima, on OP *gaiθāmča māniyamča* (*Ibid.*, 202f.). (It has not been possible to make a complete abstract of this Festschrift.)

Accentuation

The main characteristic of accentuation in Old Iranian, that is the fixation of the accent on the penultimate syllable, sometimes on the antepenultimate when the penultimate is short, should be brought into relation with the phonological structure of the word, as J. Kuryłowicz shows (*Indo-Iranica*, Mélanges G. Morgenstierne, 103f., 1964); this placing of the accent was made compulsory in the prehistoric stage of the language by the quantitative syncretism of *ă* and *ā* in final position, thus excluding the last syllable as rhythmic center of the word.

Noun Morphology and Syntax

The problem of the Avestan instrumental case is of great interest for Iranian syntax, since the instrumental is apparently equivalent to the nominative in certain constructions which belong, above all, to the language of the *Gāthās*. The function of this instrumental has been the subject of several studies, in the last few years, one of the most notable being H. Seiler's *Relativsatz, Attribut und Apposition* (143f., 1960).

Another two articles have been devoted to this problem. Ernst Risch analyzes examples of the phrase *Mazdā ašāiča* (vocative coordinated with a dative by *-ča*) and similar constructions. He shows that this phrase would occur when the persons invoked are, grammatically, objects, but that in this case there could also be a comitative instrumental. The use of the instrumental case predominates when the characters are invoked as possessors with the 2nd plural possessive pronoun. There is less coherence when the characters function as subject in the sentence (*MSS* 17.51f., 1964).

In a long article, 'The instrumental in Gāthā' (*FO* 7.119-71, 1966), Tadeusz Pobożniak studies the problem in Old Iranian in general, but he does not seem to know the contributions of all his predecessors (in particular, the above-mentioned article by Risch). He registers the forms and uses of the instrumental, and reviews the various interpretations proposed for the Gāthic passages in which the instrumental alternates with other cases. His conclusions however, are not clear. The article is useful, above all, as a collection of quotations and opinions.

Also dealing with the instrumental is an article by Wolfgang P. Schmid (*IF* 69.213f., 1965), but its object is the construction of the Persian preposition *hačā* with the instrumental, which is presumably secondary to the construction with the ablative.

The Avestan and Old Persian examples of the suffix *-aina-*, forming adjectives of substance, are collected and studied by W. Belardi (*AION* 3.7f., 1961).

The suffix *-vant* in several Avestan examples represents a former *-van-*, developed into *-vant-* as a result of a tendency found also in Indian (E. Benveniste, *Pratidānam: Indian, Iranian and Indo-European studies presented to F. B. J. Kuiper*, 123–7, 1968). The pronominal forms in Old Persian have been studied by K. Strunk in relation to the monosyllabic structure of the word (*KZ* 81.265f., 1967).

On the Nom. Plural ending of the *-a* stems in Avestan, see Rüdiger Schmitt, *Festschrift W. Eilers*, 265f., 1967.

Verb Morphology

Certain phonetically close, yet different, verb roots have forms which are sometimes brought together and associated in new groups.

M. Mayrhofer studies in detail the contamination of the Indo-Iranian roots *takṣ-*, *tvakṣ-* and **tvarṣ-*, especially in Old Persian, *taxš-* 'to be zealous', compared to Av. *θwaχš*; or Av. *θwōrəštar-* 'creator' compared with Ved. *Tvaṣṭar-* (*Indo-Iranica*, Mélanges G. Morgenstierne, 141f., 1964).

Stanley Insler (*IF* 67.55, 1962) explains Av. *daxš-* 'to show, teach' as a doublet from *daēs-*. 'As the doublet *pixšta-/paxšta-* exists as past participles to *paēs-*, so too **di(x)šta-/daxšta-* form a doublet of past parts. to *daēs-* "point out, reveal" and to this *daxšta-* a new present *daxšati* has been formed.'

Several Avestan forms with an *-ō-* vowel written before the inflectional ending are discussed by Insler (*IF* 70.14f., 1965): *aχtōyōi* would represent *aχtō(i)yōi*; the substantive *χᵛāθrōyā-* would be read **χᵛāθrōi *yā*; *akōyā* should be taken as an optative of *ak-* parallel to the optative *isōyā*; similarly, *χšayā* and *zəvīm* would also be optatives. The same author suggests that the Av. form *niγrāire* should be corrected in +*niγnāire* (from *gan-* 'strike') corresponding to Vedic *ni-han-* (*KZ* 81.259f., 1967).

The simple and reduplicated present forms of *dā-*, notably *dāya-*, are studied comparatively in Indo-Iranian by P. Tedesco (*Lg* 44.21, 1968).

Rüdiger Schmitt suggests that the Old Persian verbal theme *rasa-*, *avārasam*, etc., should be read as *rsa-* (= Ved. *ṛccha-*) (*IIJ* 8.275f., 1965).

The Old Persian forms *hagmatā* and *paraitā* are generally considered to be passive participles in *-ta-*, taken in a predicative function: 'they came together', 'they departed'. M. Leumann (*Indo-Iranica*, Mélanges G. Morgenstierne, 124f., 1964) rejects this interpretation. He explains *hagmatā* as a 3rd plural middle form, coming by haplology from *ha(ma)gmatā*, Ved. *sam agmata.* Then this personal form *-gmatā*, having become unrecognizable, was reinterpreted as a participle in *-ta-*, and finally *hagmatā* led to an analogical form *paraitā.*

The reduplication in the Indo-Iranian perfect tense shows important divergences between Indian and Iranian: certain perfect forms have long vowels, others short vowels in the reduplication; there is also a disagreement in the perfect form of *bhū-*, namely Ind. *babhūva* and Av. *bvāva*; finally, certain perfect forms of the Gāthās offer a structure *čāχnaro* (from *kan-*), *čāχrire* from *kar-*), which has no equivalent in Vedic. These pecularities are studied and explained by E. Benveniste in *Symbolae linguisticae Kuryłowicz*, 25f. (Wrocław-Warzsawa-Krakow, 1965).

The third plural perfect form Av. *irīraθar*, *irīriθar*, appears in Bartholomae's Dictionary, under *rāθ-* 'haften'. But the correct reading is *irīriθar* as given in most mss.; the form belongs, with *iriθya- irista-*, etc., to a root *riθ-* 'to mix, to intermingle', which is confirmed by Sogd. *riθ rist* '(se) mêler' (E. Benveniste, *Ibid.*, 30 where it is necessary to read '3rd pl.', line 8 from bottom).

The correlation of the Indian optative-precative in *-eṣ-* with Old Persian *-aiš* (4rd sing. *fraθiyaiš*, 3rd pl. *yadiyaišan*) is underlined by P. Tedesco (*Lg* 44.18, 1968).

vaēdəmna-, middle participle of *vid-*, is examined in its uses by H. P. Schmidt (*IIJ* I.165f., 1957), who links it, not to *vid-* 'to know', but to *vid-* 'to find'.

The relation between the two Iranian roots *nay-* and *vad-* 'lead, conduct' is placed in a comparative, Indo-European setting and in its dialect distribution by E. Benveniste in *Hittite et indo-européen*, 33f. (Paris, 1962).

The Avestan verbal adjective *ainita-* 'unharmed' is revised by F.B.J. Kuiper (*IIJ* 3.137f., 1959) who discards the comparison with the instrumental *inti* as well as the analysis **an-inita-* given by Bartholomae. He takes *ainita-* as *an-īta-* and the abstract *ainiti-* as *an-īti-* in accordance with Ved. *īti-* 'plague, calamity'. The form *inti* merely results from an incorrect manuscript tradition. As for Gāth. *ənaitī*, it should be taken as *an-itī-* opposed in Dvandva to *χᵛīti-* from *hu-itī*.

W. Belardi (*AION* II/1.51f., 1960) attempts to determine the meaning and etymological connections of the Avestan epithet *vāya-spāra* and **spara-* 'shield'.

The verb *stā-* 'to stand' has taken in Sogdian the function of an imperfective auxiliary. The beginning of this development can already be observed in Avestan, in the construction of the present *hišta-* with a predicative participle (E. Benveniste, *AcOr* 30.45f., 1966).

The Avestan present form *uz-vaēdaya-* does not mean 'certiorem facere' (Bartholomae 1317), but 'to menace' (E. Benveniste, *IIJ* 3.132f., 1959).

Syntax

In an article entitled 'An alleged anacoluth in Old Persian' (*JAOS* 85.48f., 1968), Adelaide Hahn studies the syntactic construction which consists in enunciating first the relative proposition, and then renaming the subject by a pronoun in the main proposition ('the man who did..., I punished him'). This Old Persian syntactic use sets forth an Indo-European construction, as attested in other languages.

Phraseology and Poetic Formulas

To the list of stylistic formulas and figures inherited from Indo-Iranian, one should add Bernfried Schlerath's remarks on Av. *χšaθra-* (*Das Königtum im Rig- und Atharvaveda*, 127f., Wiesbaden, 1960): the main Avestan formulaic expressions of 'power' correspond to those of Vedic; notably *kṣatram dhar-*, *vardh-*, *vakṣ-*, *van-*, etc. have parallels in Old Iranian.

Poetic phraseology in Indo-Iranian is the subject of an article by E. Benveniste (*Mélanges Louis Renou*, 73, Paris, 1968), who brings to light a number of parallel poetic phrases or constructions in Vedic and Avestan.

Gerd Gropp, *Wiederholungsformen im Jung-Awesta* (Diss. Hamburg 1967) gives a thorough analysis of the composition of Yasht 13, 1–19, with special reference to the repetitions of formulas and their metrical structure.

Religious Vocabulary

As regards ancient mythology, one should note the article by M. Boyce on the god Mithra in the Zoroastrian and Manichaean pantheon (*A locust's leg*, 44, 1962); the article by W. Lentz on the functions of Mithra in Avesta (*Indo-Iranica*, Mélanges G. Morgenstierne, 108f., 1964); the article by W. B. Henning on the Iranian god *Baga*, corresponding to the Vedic *Bhaga* (*BSOAS* 28.242f., 1965); the article by G. Morgenstierne who, on the basis of a term for 'serpent' in some Pamir dialects, reconstructs an old Indo-Iranian word for 'dragon' as **sušnā*, which he equates with Vedic *Suṣṇa* (*Unvala memorial volume*, 95f., 1964). These studies make use largely of Middle Iranian forms, in order to analyze Old Iranian ones.

Many remarks on Avestan religious terms will be found in recent works on Iranian religions: W. Hinz, *Zarathustra* (Stuttgart, 1961), contains a new translation of the *Gāthās*; M. Molé, *Le problème zorastrien et la tradition mazdéenne* (Paris, 1963); J. Duchesne-Guillemin, *La religion de l'Iran ancien* (Paris, 1962); G. Widengren, *Die Religionen Irans* (Stuttgart, 1965).

Certain notions have been particularly studied: *aša-* by J. Duchesne-Guillemin, *Quaderni della Biblioteca filosofica di Torino* 3.3ff. (1962); A. Radicchi, *Confronti Gathico-Rigvedici, Aša-Rta* (Firenze, 1962); F.B.J. Kuiper, *IIJ* 8.96f. (1964).

-(*χᵛarənah*) *farnah-* by J. Duchesne-Guillemin, *AION* 5.19ff. (1963); G. Gnoli, *Ibid.* 295f. Several religious terms are examined in the appendices of I. Gershevitch's article, 'Zoroaster's own contribution', *JNES* 23.12f. (1964). The Iranian sacrificial terminology has been dealt with by E. Benveniste (*JA*, 45f., 1964), particularly on *zaoθra-* and the varieties of sacrifice, cf. M. Boyce, *JRAS*, 104f., 1966.

In certain enumerations of evil beings in the Avesta the 'demons' (*daēva-*) are associated, strangely enough, with 'men' (*mašya-*). E. Benveniste (*Festschrift W. Eilers*, 144f., 1967) shows that this sequence is inherited from the *Gāthās* where *daēva-* still keeps its former sense of 'god', so that the old god/man opposition is also intended in this case.

dāhi- has been translated 'Schöpfung' by Bartholomae. The corresponding Vedic form *dhāsi-* has been subjected to a detailed study by Klaus Ludwig Janert, *Sinn und Bedeutung des Wortes 'dhāsi'* (Wiesbaden, 1956), who suggests 'Rinnung, Rinnsal, Flüssigkeitsstrahl, Quell'. He extends this meaning to Av. *dāhi-* and translates it as 'source, flow (of water)'; the examples are discussed in two chapters (p. 68ff.).

drav- 'laufen' (Bartholomae), a daēvic verb, actually means 'lead astray', and *draoman-*, 'deception, treachery' (Martin Schwartz, *JRAS*, 119f., 1966).

We may also mention here Av. *haδānaēpatā-*, the name of a tree whose wood is used for ritualistic purposes, left without identification by Bartholomae; it designates the 'pomegranate-tree', which agrees with the Parsee tradition (cf. Tavadia, *Sāyast nē šayast*, p. 133, fn. 5) and with several forms of Pamirian dialects (Morgenstierne, *Indo-Iranian frontier languages* II.190a).

The exact meaning of such terms, so frequent and essential in the *Gāthās*, as 'ox', 'pasture', and 'herdsman', is questioned by George G. Cameron (*IIJ* 10.261f., 1968). These terms, in his opinion, should be understood in the metaphorical sense, and refer to spiritual notions: '... in his preaching Zoroaster would be using metaphors which brought these ideas to expression in concrete terms ...; most of his allusions to cattle would apply not merely to a herd of kine, but to the flock of God; his references to pasturage would pertain not to the open Iranian fields sparse with grain, but to the way of life of believers in God; when he speaks of shepherds he would mean not the herdsmen of the cow and the ox, but those who lead God's fold or who are active in this work; and when he points to nourishment he would be alluding not to the fattening of the draft ox or the milch cow, but that heavenly sustenance — our and his Holy Spirit — which descends on all men of good will' (p. 270).

Lexicography

H. W. Bailey has proposed quite numerous reconstructions of Iranian forms and roots, based on extensive etymological comparisons or on reinterpretations of Persian or Avestan passages. It is physically impossible to survey them here. They can be found, for the most part, in the successive volumes of his *Indo-Scythian studies*, and in particular in the most recent, *Prolexis to the Book of Zambasta* (Khotanese texts, Volume VI, Cambridge University Press, 1967), of which the very learned etymological notes deal with all the Iranian languages.

We may group here several important studies on Iranian plant-names by the late W. B. Henning.

The Old Iranian word for 'mustard' has been set as **siušapa-*, which itself comes from **sinšapa-*, and compares with Skr. **sarṣapa-* and Gr. **sinapi* (Henning, *AION* 6.29f., 1965). The Old Iranian word for 'coriander' has been set as **gṛzna* by W. B. Henning (*AM* 10.195f., 1963).

The Kurdish word for 'elm', *būz*, has always been quoted in the discussions on the Indo-European **bhāgos* 'beech', concerning both its name and geographical distribution. Henning shows that the Kurdish form *būz* points to an ancient **wizu-* or **wizw-* and has nothing to do with the IE *bhāgos* (*AM* 10.68f., 1963).

On the same word, see also a lengthy and erudite contribution by W. Eilers and M. Mayrhofer, 'Kurdisch *bûz* und die indogermanische 'Buchen'-Sippe' (*Mitteilungen der Anthropologischen Gesellschaft in Wien* 92.61f., 1962).

We have thought it useful to survey in alphabetic order the Old Iranian words which, during the last few years, have been especially studied for their meaning or form, and have not been mentioned in the preceding pages. We have not included incidental references to Iranian words in etymological studies dealing with other fields.

avaŋhana- 'Abschluss, Vollendung' (Bartholomae) should mean 'liberation' and correspond to Ved. *ava-sā/si-* 'losbinden', according to H.P. Schmidt (*IIJ* 1.160' 1957).

arzah- designates the 'West'. H.W. Bailey discusses possible etymological connections (*TPhS*, 75f., 1960).

ašasairyas (Sg. nom. of an Avestan proper name) is derived from a stem *ašasaryanč-* 'characterized by a union with Aša' by F.B.J. Kuiper (*IIJ* 8.282, 1965).

āi- (Vd. III 4, 23), of which Bartholomae makes an (otherwise unknown) preverb 'hin/zu-', would be an ancient name for 'earth', neuter in *-i*, corresponding to Greek *aîa* (f.) 'earth', and, in the form **āika*, the prototype of Persian *χāk* 'earth', according to I. Gershevitch (*A locust's leg*, 76f., 1962).

aδu-, which has been translated 'zeal', 'Eifer', means in reality 'grain (of wheat)', in accordance with Sogd. *''δwk* which has this sense. Gāthic *ǝǝādū* (Y. 35.6) is probably the same word (R. E. Emmerick, *TPhS*, 1f., 1966; 204, 1967).

āfant-, which Bartholomae translates 'wasserreich', an adjective derived from *ap-*, is in fact a substantive meaning 'course of time' (E. Benveniste, *Donum natal. H.S. Nyberg*, 17f., 1954; *Etudes sur la langue ossète*, 75, fn. 5, 1959; cf. also I. Gershevitch, *The Avestan hymn to Mithra*, 172, 322, 1959).

azātā- 'free, noble' is discussed in relation to Iranian social structure by A. Perikhanian (*REArm* 5, 1968).

upa.mraodǝšča (Bartholomae 392) is dealt with as to its meaning and etymology by K. Hoffmann (*Festschrift W. Eilers* 177f., 1967).

ušaδā- ('Bezeichnung eines Teils des Rückens (?)' (Bartholomae 415) can now be translated 'neck'; cf. Sogd. *šδ''k* 'neck', Yidgha *šilë* 'id.' (Morgenstierne, *Indo-Iranian frontier languages* II.251b, 1938).

gaodāyu- means properly 'cattle-nourisher' and must be etymologically connected with modern Iranian words for 'grass', such as Persian *giyāh* (I. Gershevitch, *A locust's leg*, 80, 1962).

gaoyaoiti-, i.e. *gau-yauti-*, as well as its corresponding form, Vedic *gav-yūti-*, is usually translated 'pasture'. It is a very significant term, as is seen in the specific epithet of Mithra, *vouru-gaoyaoiti-*. The Avestan and Vedic uses of it are analyzed by E. Benveniste (*JA* 421f., 1960), who stresses the importance of this term for Indo-Iranian social prehistory.

ganza- 'treasure', an Iranian word largely propagated by the Achaemenid administration and borrowed by most neighboring languages, is the Median form of an older **gazna-* preserved in Parthian and in Sogdian, according to W.B. Henning (*AM* 10.196f., 1963).

gav- 'verschaffen' (Bartholomae), found in several compounds and derivatives, means 'to increase'; cf. *gaona-* 'increase, profit', OP *abigāva-* (transcribed *'bg'w* in an Aramaic document of Egypt) 'increase, interest (of money)', etc. (E. Benveniste, *REArm* 1.3, 1964).

čiakazauato, a corrupt Avestan form, left untranslated by Bartholomae 584, should be corrected to *čiąkaδauato*; this is a bad spelling of **čąkaδavato* 'of that which has an elbow or forearm'. It results that the stem is Av. *čąkaδa-* 'elbow, forearm', cf. Pašto *cangal* 'elbow, forearm', etc. (W.B. Henning, *BSOAS* 11.471, fn. 3, 1945).

daγa-, 'Bezeichnung einer schlechten Eigenschaft) des Pferdes' (Bartholomae 675), means 'hairless, bald' (E. Benveniste, *Asiatica*, Festschrift Fr. Weller, 32, 1954).

panti- 'way, road' is considered in its Avestan use in relation to *adwan-* (B. Schlerath, *Unvala memorial volume*, 141, 1965).

pairi-gaēθa-, in the expression *pairigaēθa-vahma-* (Y. 34,2), would mean '(adoration) in which the *gaēθå* (livestock, goods and family, cattle and men) are grouped around the altar as to be dedicated to God and blessed by Him', according to H. Humbach (*Unvala memorial volume*, 271, 1965).

parana- 'former', as stem of the OP adverb *paranam*, is discussed in relation to several Modern Iranian chronological adverbs by I. Gershevitch (*Indo-Iranica*, Mélanges G. Morgenstierne, 83, 1964).

pairiθna- (Vd. 19, 28), left without translation by Bartholomae, is examined by K. Hoffmann (*Unvala memorial volume*, 269f., 1965), who suggests 'fulfillment of lifetime' or 'due lifetime', and analyzes it into *pairi-iθna-*, with **iθna-* derived from *i-* 'to go' and the suffix *-θna-*.

baog- 'to liberate, free' is well known in Avestan and Middle Iranian. But several derivatives, Gath. *buj-*, *buxsa-* in the proper name *Baga-buxša*, Av. *pouru. baoxšna-* cannot admit this meaning. They should be connected with another root *baug-* which would be the Iranian form corresponding to Ved. *bhoj-* 'to enjoy'. The existence of *baug-* 'to enjoy' in Iranian is confirmed by the Armenian verb *əmbošχnem* 'to enjoy', formed from the Iranian loanword *bauχšna-* 'enjoyment', which is attested by Av. *pouru.-baoχšna-* 'endowed with great enjoyment' (to be translated thus, and not 'vielen Rettung, Erlösung bringend' — Bartholomae). Iranian proper names of Greek tradition, like *Mithro-bouzanes*, contain *-baujana-* which also derives from *baug-* 'to feel or give enjoyment' (Benveniste, *Titres et noms propres*, 108f., 1966; *REArm* 3.7f., 1966).

bāzura- must be recognized as an independent word, meaning 'wing'; it appears in the compound *snāvarə.bāzura-* which must be translated 'nerve-winged', describing a sling (E. Benveniste, *Asiatica*, Festschrift Fr. Weller, 33, 1954).

nam- in Old Iranian means 'to bend, to recede', hence 'to move aside, to draw away from'. This sense, as specified by certain preverbs, notably *apa-nam-*, makes it possible to explain certain developments which occur in the Middle Iranian forms of *nam-* (E. Benveniste, *BSOAS* 30.505f., 1967).

nasu-spaya-, usually translated 'interment of the dead', was a practice described as the 'plague' of Arachosia. But this translation is impossible: *spa-* in all its forms means 'to throw, leave on the ground'. It follows that the dead were 'thrown down' and abandoned on the ground, a funerary custom known outside of Iran (E. Benveniste, *A locust's leg*, 39f., 1962).

nāvaya- 'navigable', OP *nāviya-* is also applied to irrigation water. I. Gershevitch (*A locust's leg*, 79f., 1962) infers from this 'that OP *nāu-*, like N Pers. *nāv*, denoted two distinct contrivances: (1) a ship, and (2) a channel presumably consisting, at least originally, of one or more hollowed-out tree-trunk's.

ni-drā- has not been found in Old Iranian, but it can surely be restored, in correspondence with Ved. *ni-drā*, for an Iranian form **ni-drā-* is postulated by the Armenian loan *nirh* 'drowsiness'. Ved. *ni-drā* should be translated 'drowsiness, somnolence' and not 'sleep'; this is also the sense of O.Sl. *drěmľjǫ*, Russian *dremlju* 'to doze' (E. Benveniste, *Beiträge zur Indo-germanistik und Keltologie*, Festschrift J. Pokorny, 11f., Innsbruck, 1967).

manθ- 'to agitate, to shake', and not *mant-* (Bartholomae), is the Old Iranian form postulated by the group of Middle and Modern Iranian dialectal forms, in accordance with Ved. *manth-* which has the same meaning (E. Benveniste, *IIJ* 7.307f., 1963-64).

mazdā is set as an *-ā-* stem and reconstructed in its original inflection by F.B.J. Kuiper (*IIJ* 1.86f., 1957).

marətānō (Y. 30–6) is taken as a nominative plural by H. Humbach (*IIJ* I.306f., 1957).

mərəγa- is the Iranian word for 'bird'. But the corresponding form in Indian, Ved. *mṛga-*, means any animal which can be hunted, primarily the 'gazelle'. This disagreement shows that *mṛga-* is to be taken as a generic term for various animals, each one being specified by a distinctive epithet. Vedic *mṛga-*, associated with *pataru-* 'winged' designates the bird. Iranian has thus limited the sense of *mərəγa-* to the winged species (E. Benveniste, *Festgabe für H. Lommel*, 193f., 1960).

mišti adv., '(in mischung sva.) durcheinander' (Bartholomae 1187), actually means 'always' as is proved by the Armenian loanword *mišt* 'always' and moreover by the Pahlavi tradition; cf. Darmester, *Zend Avesta*, II.394, and Hübschmann, *Armenische Grammatik*, 194.

yat- is an Indian and Iranian root, whose meaning has given rise to very different opinions. The comparison of the ancient uses on the one hand, and of Middle and Modern Iranian forms of *yat-* on the other, makes it possible to settle on the meaning as 'reach one's proper place' (E. Benveniste, *Indo-Iranica*, Mélanges G. Morgenstierne, 21f., 1964).

yāna- 'favour' is derived from *yā-* 'to request, to implore', well attested in Sanskrit, by A.M. Mehendale (*IIJ* 5.63f., 1961), who suggests a feminine stem *yanā-* for the forms *yānå* and *yānāδa*.

vat-, an Indo-Iranian root denoting certain mental capacities 'comprehension, inspiration', etc. is considered in its etymological connections by H.W. Bailey (*TPhS*, 70f., 1960).

varənava- (*varənava-vīša-*), name of a demonic being, could be compared with Ved. *ūrṇa-vābhi-* 'spider'. Therefore *varənava-* can be a compound whose first member *varəna-* would be comparable to Vedic *ūrna-* 'wool' and *va-* with the Ved. root *va-* 'to weave' (A. Debrunner, *Corolla linguistica F. Sommer*, 24, fn. 9, 1955).

vazdah-, with the derivatives *vazdar* etc., which all contain the notion of 'nourishment, fat' is investigated in Indo-Iranian as well as in the modern dialects by H.W. Bailey (*TPhS*, 62f., 1960).

**vasōpuθra-* as the ancient form of the Middle Iranian title *vāspuhr*, with *vāsō* reduced from **vāis* (a vrddhi-form of *vis*) is attested by Babylonian transcriptions as early as the fifth century B.C. (W. Eilers, *A locust's leg*, 55f., 1962).

vi- 'bird', coexists with *mərəγa-*, another term for 'bird'. These are not semantic doublets. They are logically related: *vi-* denotes the bird as genus, and *mərəγa-* the bird as species (E. Benveniste, *Festgabe für H. Lommel*, 193f., 1960).

vībərəθwant- 'by observing the pauses' (i.e. pauses between the three verses of the Ahuna Vairya). This use of Av. *vī-bar-* is connected with the similar use of *vī-har-* 'to separate (with a pause or insertions)' found in the Sanskrit ritual texts (A.M. Mehendale, *IIJ* 5.61, 1961).

**visah-duxtā-* 'daughter of the house', then 'princess', is warranted not only by Middle Iranian *visduxt* 'princess', but also by a survival such as *visite*, *vesita*, 'husband's sister' in the Tākistānī dialect, spoken around Qazvīn (W.B. Henning, *Indo-Iranica*, Mélanges G. Morgenstierne, 95f., 1964).

vispaya irina, a corrupt and meaningless Av. phrase, must simply be written in one word to become a correct and fully intelligible compound, *vispayairina-* 'of all days' cf. Av. *vispo-ayara-* (E. Benveniste, *Unvala memorial volume*, 12, 1964).

rŭ-, *lŭ-*, 'to pluck', an Indo-Iranian root, can be found in a number of Middle and Modern Iranian derivatives which B. Geiger analyzes (*A locust's leg*, 70f., 1962).

snāvar- 'nerve' in Avestan is discussed in relation to corresponding Sanskrit and Middle Indian forms, Ved. *snāvan-*, *snāyu-*, Pali *nhāru*, by P. Tedesco (*Gedenkschrift P. Kretschmer*, II.182f., 1957).

zayan- zyam- 'winter' is studied in its etymological connections with Indo-European words denoting both 'winter' and 'snow', in contrast with Av. *vafra* 'snow' and *snaēža-* 'to snow', by E. Benveniste (*Gedenkschrift P. Kretschmer* I.31f., 1956).

zāviši (Vd. 19, 5–6) is a form generally considered as a Sg. passive aorist from *zav-* 'to call', which raises some difficulties. This form is discussed in length by R.E. Emmerick (*TPhS*, 7f., 1966), who concludes that *zāviši* would be the correct Sg. noun <*zāvišī* 'strength' from a verbal base *zav-* 'to be strong, powerful'; cf. Av. *zəvīštya-* 'swiftest, strongest'.

šənm is a corrupt Avestan form listed without translation by Bartholomae 1708; W.B. Henning shows its source to be the word *šanman* (Yt 10,24); and *šanman* means a part of the lance or the arrow; this is confirmed by Ved. *kṣadman* (*Unvala memorial volume*, 41, 1964).

hapərəsi, an unidentified plant-name (Bartholomae, 1765), is the 'huniper' (Morgenstierne, *NTS* 5.40f.; *TPhS*, 70f., 1948; Henning, *Sogdica*, 41, 1940).

hizū- and *hizvā-*, 'tongue', are examined in their respective morphological structure and compared to the Indian and other forms by E. Benveniste (*Asiatica*, Festschrift Fr. Weller, p. 30, 1954).

hizu.drāǰah- and *zānu.drāǰah-* should mean 'length of the chin, of the tongue' according to Rüdiger Schmitt (*IIJ* 10.183f., 1967).

Addenda (*December* 1969)

Annelies Kammenhuber, *Die Arier im Vorderen Orient* (Heidelberg, 1968), is a critical assessment of the textual evidence.

The collective volume entitled *Pratidānam: Indian, Iranian and Indo-European studies presented to F.B.J. Kuiper*, 1968 (appeared 1969) has not been seen in its entirety and may contain articles on Old Iranian.

MIDDLE IRANIAN

MARK J. DRESDEN

1. INTRODUCTION

1.1 *Delimitation*

Two decisive historical developments stand at the beginning and at the end of the approximate time period during which the Middle Iranian language stage was dominant. At the beginning, the collapse of the Achaemenid administrative structure under the impact of the armies of Alexander the Great and the subsequent emergence of the Parthian dynasty of the Arsacids in 250 B.C.; at the end, the disruption of Sassanian power, caused by the successful invasion of Iran by Muslim Arabic military forces, in the middle of the seventh century A.D. For reasons of convenience and because of the nature of the extant documentation, these crucial events of the fourth and third centuries B.C. and those of the seventh century A.D. are taken to correspond respectively to the end of the Old Iranian (until about 300 B.C.) and the beginning of the New (or Modern) Iranian (700 A.D. and after) linguistic periods. In short, the Middle Iranian language period covers the ten centuries between 300 B.C. and 700 A.D.

1.2 *Earlier Research*

In the history of the study of the Iranian language group as a whole the turn of the twentieth century can be considered a milestone. The publication of the *Grundriss der iranischen Philologie* (1895–1906), under the joint editorship of Wilhelm Geiger and Ernst Kuhn, represents the results of the scholarly research which had been carried out, mainly in the western world, in the fields of Iranian and Persian studies (language, literature, history and geography) since the late eighteenth century, when the publication of Anquetil-Duperron's Avesta translation in 1771 opened new vistas on Zoroaster's religion. At the time, only one Middle Iranian language, Pahlavi, was known. The grammar of this language, in which the religious and secular literature of Sassanian times (226–651 A.D.) is recorded, is the subject of a chapter 'Mittel-persisch' by C. Salemann (*Grundriss*, vol. 1. 249–332; in English, as *A Middle Persian grammar*, 1930, by L. Bogdanov); its literature is described by E. W. West (*Grundriss*, vol. 2. 75–122; a recent survey is J.C.Tavadia, *Die mittelpersische Sprache und Literatur der Zarathustrier*, 1956).

1.3 *Iranian Language Materials from Chinese Turkestan*

Today, several varieties of Middle Iranian are known in addition to Pahlavi. This is due to discoveries made in Chinese Turkestan at the beginning of this century. They were the result of a series of expeditions undertaken by scholars and explorers from England (Mark Aurel Stein in 1900–01 [*Ancient Khotan*, I-II, 1907], 1906–08 [*Serindia*, I-IV, 1921], and 1913–15 [*Innermost Asia*, I-IV, 1928]), France (Paul Pelliot in 1906–08; see, for instance, B.Pauly, 'Fragments sanskrits de Haute Asie', *JA* 253, 1965, 95–105 with bibliography), Germany (A.Grünwedel and A.von Le Coq in 1902–03, 1904–05, 1905–07, and 1913–14; see, for instance, M.Boyce, *A catalogue of the Iranian manuscripts in Manichean script in the German Turfan collection*, 1960, X-XXI, and W.Lentz, 'Fünfzig Jahre Arbeit an den iranischen Handschriften der deutschen Turfan-Sammlung', *ZDMG* 106, 1956, *4*–*22*), Japan (K.Ôtani in 1902, 1908–09, and 1911–14 [*Shin Saiiki ki, New records on Central Asia, being several reports by the Ôtani mission*, I-II, 1937]), Russia (S.Oldenburg in 1909–10 [*Russkaya Turkestanskaya èkspeditsiya, 1909–1910*, 1914]), and other nations. Since this context does not justify comment on the actual events which led to the discovery of the Iranian language materials, reference can be made only to such bibliographical lists as 'Bibliography of the Central Asiatic studies', in *Monumenta Serindica*, II, 1958, 53–87 or M.Paul-David, M.Hallade and V.Hambis, *Toumchouq*, II, 1964, xxx-xxxiii.

1.4 *The Major Middle Iranian Languages*

At present, five major forms of Middle Iranian can be distinguished: (1) Middle Persian, (2) Parthian, (3) Sogdian, (4) Khwarezmian, and (5) Saka dialects of which Khotanese is most abundantly attested. To these can be added: (6) 'Bactrian', and (7) 'Kušān-Hephthalite' materials. A recent detailed review of all of these materials has been given by W.B.Henning ('Mitteliranisch' in *Handbuch der Orientalistik*, Erste Abteilung, Vierter Band, *Iranistik*, Erster Abschnitt, *Linguistik*, 1958, 20–130; reprinted 1967), a contribution of the highest competence without which this article could not have been written. It will be often referred to as *Mitteliranisch*.

On geographical and linguistic grounds Middle Persian and Parthian belong to the western, Sogdian, Khwarezmian, Saka (Khotanese), 'Bactrian', and 'Kušān-Hephthalite" to the eastern group of Iranian languages. The western group shows extensive simplification of the ancient nominal flection and of the verbal conjugation; the eastern group, on the other hand, retains the old endings of nouns and verbs to a large extent (*Mitteliranisch* 89–92). Each of these seven varieties of Middle Iranian will be dicussed in the given order. The available materials will be presented with bibliographical references in section 2. of this survey. Some of the major characteristics of each language will be taken up in section 5.

2. SURVEY OF MIDDLE IRANIAN LANGUAGE MATERIALS

2.1 *Middle Persian and Parthian*

Within the western group, a southwestern and a northwestern group can be distinguished. Among the first, the local language of the old satrapy of (Old Persian) *Pārsa*, now *Fārs*, can be considered as the direct descendant of the Old Persian language of the Achaemenid inscriptions; the Middle Iranian representative of the northwestern group continues or, rather, is closely related to the little known language of the Medes and is generally called Parthian (Old Persian *Pārθawa*). The principal differences between the two subgroups have been determined by P. Tedesco ('Dialektologie der westiranischen Turfantexte', *Le Monde Oriental* 15, 1921, 148–258). For instance, southwestern *zan* 'woman', *dah* 'ten', *čahār* 'four', *dōdīg* 'second', *hil-* 'to let (go)', *kar-* 'to make, do', correspond to northwestern *žan*, *das*, *čafār*, *bidīg*, *hirz-*, and *kun-*.

It should be mentioned at this point that the terms Middle Persian and Parthian are preferable to *Pārsīk* and *Pahlawīk* respectively (*Mitteliranisch* 40 fn. 2 and 43 fn. 3).

2.2 *Middle Persian*

As has already been implied, Middle Persian or *Pahlavi* is the local language of the area of Istakhr-Persepolis, the capital of the province of Persis (*Fārs*). It is documented by (1) coins from local kings of *Fārs*, (2) coins of Sassanian and post-Sassanian times, (3) royal and private Sassanian inscriptions, (4) legends on gems and seals from Sassanian times, (5) Zoroastrian religious and, to a lesser extent, secular literature from late Sassanian times, (6) Manichean texts from Central Asia (Turfan), (7) fragments of a psalter translated from Syriac, (8) materials from Dura-Europos, (9) papyri, ostraca and inscriptions on silver ware, (10) other inscriptional materials.

2.2.1 The issuance of coins by the local rulers of Fārs falls between the middle of the third century B.C. and the beginning of the third century A.D. G. F. Hill (*Catalogue of the Greek coins of Arabia, Mesopotamia and Persia*, 1922) has divided them chronologically in three series. The first series belongs to a ruler who calls himself *prtrkʾ ZY ʾLHYʾ* 'Fratarak the lord'. The oldest specimen of the third series, probably from the end of the second century B.C., reads *dʾryw MLKʾ BRH wtprdt MLKʾ* 'Darius the king, son of Autophradates the king'. The occurrence of *BRH* 'son' elicited the following remark from Henning: 'Das hier reinaramäisch *BR* ersetzende, mit dem späteren mittelpersischen übereinstimmenden *BRH* "Sohn" ist das älteste "aramäische

Ideogram" auf persischen Boden: die Legende beweist, dass der Übergang zur ideographischen Schreibweise jetzt vollzogen ist" (*Mitteliranisch* 25). See 3.3 below.

2.2.2 The early coins from Fārs (2.2.1) are the predecessors of the coinage of the Sassanian rulers. In turn, the Sassanian coin tradition is continued after the dynasty ceased to exist. An up-to-date comprehensive study of Sassanian coins is outstanding. It is the subject of F. D. J. Paruck, *Sassanian coins*, 1924, and of several, more recent publications by R. Göbl ('Stand und Aufgaben der sassanidischen Numismatik', *NClio* 5, 1952, 360–8 and 'Aufbau der Münzprägung' in F. Altheim-R. Stiehl, *Ein asiatischer Staat*, 1954, 51–128). On post-Sassanian coins in the Sassanian tradition, see J. M. Unvala, *Coins of Ṭabaristān and some Sassanian coins from Susa*, 1938; J. Walker, *A catalogue of the Arab-Sassanian coins*, 1941; A. Guillou, *Les monnayages pehlevi-arabes*, 1953.

2.2.3 The royal and private Sassanian inscriptions are a prime source of historical and linguistic information. Among other features common to the Achaemenian and Sassanian inscriptions is the fact that the large majority of the latter is trilingual. The early inscriptions of Ardašīr and Šāpūr I are written in Middle Persian, Parthian and Greek. Later, the Greek version is omitted and in the end only the Middle Persian text remains. Among the more important royal inscriptions are:

(a) inscription on the structure known as *Kaʿbe-yi Zardušt* located at Naqš-i Rustam near Persepolis. It relates the victorious campaigns of Šāpūr I against the Romans and the dedication of fire temples. Bibliography: W. B. Henning, 'The great inscription of Šāpūr I', *BSOS* (now *BSOAS*) 9, 1937–39, 823–49 and 'Notes on the great inscription of Šāpūr I' in *Prof. Jackson Memorial Volume*, 1954, 40–54. — B. Honigmann and A. Maricq, *Recherches sur les Res Gestae Divi Saporis, Académie Royale de Belgique, Classe des lettres et des sciences morales et politiques, Mémoires*, Collection in-8°, Tome XLVII, Fasc. 4, 1953. — A. Maricq, 'Res gestae divi Saporis', *Syria* XXXV, 1958, 296–360. — W. Ensslin, 'Zu den Kriegen des Sassaniden Schapur I.', *SbBAW, Philosophisch-historische Klasse Jahrgang 1947*, Heft 5, 1949.

(b) inscription on the monument of Paikuli in the Zagros mountains on the ancient road from Ctesiphon to Ganzaca. It reports the struggle between king Narseh and Bahrām III and Narseh's coronation. Bibliography: E. Herzfeld, *Paikuli, monument and inscription of the early history of the Sassanian empire* I-II, 1924.

Kartīr (*Kardēr*, written *kltyl*), the founder of the Sassanian Zoroastrian religion, has left several literary documents of his activities. Among them:

(c) inscription on the *Kaʿbe-yi Zardušt*, Bibliography: facsimile in *Corpus Inscriptionum Iranicarum* ... portfolio III, 1963, plates lxxi-lxxix. — Marie-Louise Chaumont, 'L'inscription de Kartir à la "Kaʿbah de Zoroastre"', *JA* 248, 1960, 339–80.

(d) inscription from Naqš-i Rustam. Bibliography: facsimile in *Corpus Inscriptionum Iranicarum* ... portfolio II, 1957, plates xxv-xlviii and portfolio III, 1963, plates xlix-lxx.

(e) inscription of Sar-Mašhad. Bibliography: facsimile in *Corpus Inscriptionum Iranicarum* ... portfolio I, 1955, plates i-xxiv.

(f) inscription of Naqš-i Rajab. Bibliography: facsimile in *Corpus Inscriptionum Iranicarum* ... portfolio III, 1963, plates lxxx-lxxxiv. — R.N. Frye, 'The Middle Persian inscription of Kartīr at Naqš-i Rajab', *IIJ* 8, 1965, 211–25.

Other materials include:

(g) inscription of Fīrūzābād. Bibliography: W.B. Henning, 'The inscription of Firuzabad', *AM*, New Series, 4, 1954, 98–102.

(h) inscription of Hājjīābād. Bibliography: H.S. Nyberg, 'Hājjīābād-Inskriften', *Øst og Vest, Afhandlinger tilegnede Prof. Dr. Phil. Arthur Christensen*, 1945, 62–74.

(i) inscriptions from Persepolis. Bibliography: facsimile in *Corpus Inscriptionum Iranicarum* ... portfolio III, 1963, plates lxxxv-lxxxvii. — R.N. Frye, 'The Middle Persian inscriptions from the time of Shapur II', *Iranian Studies presented to Kaj Barr on his seventieth birthday, June* 26, 1966 (*AcOr* 30. 83–93).

(j) inscription from Šāhpūr. Bibliography: R. Ghirshman, 'Inscription du monument de Châpour Ier à Châpour', *Revue des Arts Asiatiques* X, 1936, 123–9. — O. Hansen, 'Epigraphische Studien 1, Die Inschrift des *Apasāy in Šāhpūr', *ZDMG* 92, 1938, 441–51.

The language of the inscriptions has been described by E. Herzfeld, 'Essay on Pahlavi' in *Paikuli* I, 1924, 52–73. M. Sprengling, *Third century Iran, Sapor and Kartir*, 1953, deals with the inscriptions mentioned under (a), (c), (d), and (f).

2.2.4 Among the earliest publications on carved gems and seals are A. D. Mordtmann, 'Studien über geschittene Steine mit Pehlevi-Inschriften', *ZDMG* 18, 1864, 1–52 and 'Sassanidische Gemmen', *ZDMG* 29, 1875, 199–211. What is needed is a comprehensive and up-to-date study of these materials to replace P. Horn and G. Steindorff, *Sassanidische Siegelsteine*, 1891. The most important official seals have been collected by E. Herzfeld, *Paikuli* I, 1924, 74–82. Some recent publications on individual pieces include: W. B. Henning, 'A misinterpreted Sassanian gem' in F. Altheim, *Literatur und Geschichte im ausgehenden Altertum* II, 1950, 279–80. — J. Harmatta, 'Deux gemmes sassanides à inscriptions', *Bulletin du Musée Hongrois des Beaux-Arts* [Budapest] 10, 1957, 8–20. — S. Eilenberg, 'A Sassanian silver medallion of Varhrān III', *Ars Orientalis* 2, 1957, 487–8.

Another set of similar materials are seal impressions many of which were found in Qaṣr Abū Naṣr near Shiraz; on one such impression see W.B. Henning, *AM*, New Series, 2, 1951–52, 144. For materials found in Susa see J. M. Unvala, "Empreintes de cachets sassanides", *Hazāre-yi Firdausī* [*The millennium of Firdawsi*], 1322/1944, 90–5.

2.2.5 Until the discovery of new Iranian language materials in Central Asia (see 1.3), the language of the Zoroastrian books of late Sassanian times was the main source of documentation for Middle Persian or, more accurately, Zoroastrian Book Pahlavi (Zor.BkPahl.). Before and after the publication of Salemann's grammar (see 1.2), the BkPahl. texts had been the subject of intensive study by western scholars and Parsi savants in India. These efforts have not entirely resulted in producing the needed results, such as reliable editions and translations, a dictionary or a new grammar. Some of the reasons for this, such as incomplete understanding of the nature of the script in its historical development including the ideogrammatic writing system, are inherent to the subject; others such as insufficient strictness in applying the methods of modern editorial techniques or limited familiarity with relevant data from other Middle Iranian as well as Old and New Iranian languages are not due to the intricacies of BkPahl. as such. To what degree comprehensive utilization of all relevant Iranian language materials, not to mention Indic materials, can shed light on BkPahl. problems is shown by H.W. Bailey in his *Zoroastrian problems in the ninth-century books*, 1943. The literature on the subject of Zor.BkPahl. is too large to be listed here; in addition, it is mainly directed towards problems of a philological and historico-religious nature. See the references given above (1.2). As far as the language itself is concerned, little attention has been paid to problems of syntax. Among the exceptions are: M. Boyce, 'The use of relative particles in Western Middle Iranian', *Indo-Iranica, Mélanges présentés à Georg Morgenstierne à l'occasion de son soixante-dixième anniversaire*, 1964, 28–47, and 'Some Middle Persian and Parthian constructions with governed pronouns', *Dr. J. M. Unvala memorial volume*, 1964, 49–56. — D. N. MacKenzie, 'The "indirect affectee" in Pahlavi', *Dr. J. M. Unvala memorial volume*, 1964, 45–8.

2.2.6 Ever since the materials brought to Berlin from the Turfan oasis in Central Asia (Eastern Turkestan) by the first German expedition (see 1.3) began to be studied, it became clear that they were written in several languages. One of them was identified as Middle Persian and it was immediately realized thanks to the penetrating insight of F. W. K. Müller ('Handschriften-Reste in Estrangelo-Schrift aus Turfan, Chinesisch-Turkestan [I]', *SPAW* 1904, 348–52) that this group of texts represented 'Reste der verloren geglaubten manichäischen Literatur'. Soon after it was found by F. C. Andreas that in addition to Middle Persian (more accurately Manichean Middle Persian or Man.MP) another western Iranian language, Parthian (more accurately Manichean Parthian or Man.Pt), thus called by A. Meillet, was present among the Turfan findings. On Parthian see below 2.3, also above 2.1.

Among the major text publications of Man.MP texts are: F. W. K. Müller, 'Handschriften-Reste in Estrangelo-Schrift aus Turfan, Chinesisch-Turkestan II', *APAW*, Anhang, 1904, 1–117; 'Eine Hermas-Stelle in manichäischer Version', *SPAW* 1905, 1077–83; 'Ein Doppelblatt aus einem manichäischen Hymnenbuch (Maḥrnāmag)', *APAW* 1912. — C. Salemann, 'Ein Bruchstück manichaeischen Schrifttums im Asiatischen Museum', *Mémoires de l'Académie Impériale des Sciences de St.-Pétersbourg*, VIIIe série, VI.6, 1904, 1–26; 'Manichaeische Studien I', *Mémoires de l'Académie Impériale des Sciences de St.-Pétersbourg*, VIIIe série, VIII.10, 1908, a revised transliteration in Hebrew characters of Müller's materials; 'Manichaica III-IV', *Bulletin de l'Académie Impériale des Sciences de St.-Pétersbourg*, 1912, 1-50, including Manichean fragments in the St. Petersburg (Leningrad) collection. — E. Waldschmidt and W. Lentz, 'Die Stellung Jesu im Manichäismus', *APAW* 1926, no. 4 and 'Manichäische Dogmatik aus chinesischen und iranischen Texten', *SPAW* 1933, 480–607, including texts in Parthian, Sogdian and Chinese. — F. C. Andreas and W. B. Henning, 'Mitteliranische Manichaica aus Chinesisch Turkestan I', *SPAW* 1932, 175–222; II, *SPAW* 1933, 294–363; III, *SPAW* 1934, 848–912. — W. Henning, 'Ein manichäisches Bet- und Beichtbuch', *SPAW* 1936, X, including Sogdian materials.

As for an analysis of Man.MP, W. B. Henning studied the verb in 'Das Verbum des Mittelpersischen der Turfanfragmente', *Zeitschrift für Indologie und Iranistik* 9, 1933, 158–253, with index by A. Ghilain, 'Index de termes en moyen-iranien', *Muséon* 50, 1937, 367–95. No dictionary or glossary has yet been published.

2.2.7 A fragmentary collection of psalm texts, in Middle Persian, translated from Syriac, was found in Bulayïq, north of Turfan. Although the archaizing form of the script in which these fragments are written seems to point to the sixth century A.D., the actual manuscript was, probably, not written before the seventh or early eighth century (*Mitteliranisch* 47). The psalter was published by F. C. Andreas and K. Barr, 'Bruchstücke einer Pehlevi-Übersetzung der Psalmen', *SPAW* 1933, 91–152.

2.2.8 Excavations at Dura-Europos, on the Euphrates river in present day Syria near the Iraq border, have yielded a number of Middle Iranian, Parthian as well as Middle Persian, documents. In the local synagogue twelve dipinti in Middle Persian and three graffiti in Parthian script were found. The first attempt at interpretation was made by A. Pagliaro ('Le iscrizioni pahlaviche della sinagoga di Dura-Europo', *Atti della Reale Accademia d'Italia, Rendiconti della classe di scienze morali e storiche*, 1941–42, 578–616); a more complete and definitive study was published by B. Geiger (*The synagogue, The Middle Iranian texts*, in *The excavations at Dura-Europos, Final Report* VIII, Part I, C. H. Kraeling ed., 1956, 283–317). The documents originate with the scribes (*dpywr* [*dipiwar*]) of the Persian army which occupied the city in 252–3 A.D. (*Mitteliranisch* 46). Further documents from Dura-Europos include two Middle Persian pieces published by W. B. Henning (*The excavations at Dura-Europos, Final Report* V, Part I, *The parchments and papyri*, 1959, 414–7) and several ostraca, in Middle Persian and Parthian, on which see W. B. Henning, *Gnomon* 26, 1954, 478–9 and J. Harmatta, 'Die parthischen Ostraka aus Dura-Europos', *AAntH* 6, 1958, 87–175. For other Parthian materials from Dura-Europos, see *Mitteliranisch* 41–2.

2.2.9 The major publication on Middle Persian papyri is O. Hansen, 'Die mittelpersischen Papyri der Papyrussammlung der Staatlichen Museum zu Berlin', *ABAW* 1937, Nr. 9. Facsimiles of papyri and ostraca were edited by J. de Menasce (*Ostraca and Papyri, Corpus Inscriptionum Iranicarum*, Portfolio I: Plates I-XXIV, 1957). The majority of the papyri date from a short occupation of Egypt by the Persians in the early seventh century A.D. The strongly cursive character of the script used in the papyri makes decipherment difficult. For a survey of papyrus collections see J. de Menasce, 'Recherches de papyrologie pehlevie', *JA* 241, 1953, 185–96.

The same or a similar kind of cursive writing is also used in inscriptions found on silver objects. Most of these objects are reproduced in I. I. Smirnov, *Vostočnoe serebro*, 1909. Recent articles dealing with individual inscriptions include R. Ghirshman, 'Argenterie d'un seigneur sassanide', *Ars Orientalis* 2, 1957, 177–82 whose readings were corrected by W. B. Henning, 'New Pahlavi inscriptions on silver vessels', *BSOAS* 22, 1959, 132–4. — W. B. Henning, 'A Sassanian silver bowl from Georgia', *BSOAS* 24, 1961, 353–6 and *Mitteliranisch* 49–50.

2.2.10 Other materials in Middle Persian from late Sassanian times are: (a) funeral inscriptions from Fārs, written vertically and dating from the second half of the seventh century (*Mitteliranisch* 47); (b) memorial inscription, found in Bāġ-i Lardī near Seidūn between Istakhr and Sīvand (*Mitteliranisch* 48, and J. de Menasce, 'Inscriptions pehlevies en écriture cursive', *JA* 244, 1956, 423–31 who also deals with a vertical inscription from Maqṣūdābād, south of Persepolis); (c) a series of inscriptions from Derbend on the Caspian some of which are written vertically and dating from the second half of the sixth century (E. A. Paxomov and H. S. Nyberg, *Bulletin de la Société Scientifique d'Azerbaïdjan*, No. 8, V, 1929 and *Izv.Azerbaydžansk.Gos. Naučno-Issled.Inst.* I.2, 1930, 13–6); (d) a fragment of a Pahlavi *frahang*, found in Turfan and dating, perhaps, from the ninth or tenth century (K. Barr, 'Remarks on the Pahlavi ligatures and ', *BSOS* 8, 1935–37, 391–403).

After the fall of the Sassanian empire Middle Persian language and writing continued to exist. Next to inscriptions of the Buyid ruler 'Aḍūd ad-Daulah (from 969–70), of Rādakān in eastern Astārābād, of the tower of Lājim in the Savādkūh (from 1021–22?), materials from southern India originating in the activities of Persian Christians deserve to be mentioned (Quilon copper tablet from the ninth century, crosses from Travancore); see *Mitteliranisch* 50–2.

2.3 *Parthian*

In the preceding paragraph a number of Parthian materials have already been mentioned. The inscriptions of *Ka'be-yi Zardušt*, *Paikuli*, *Hājjīābād* and *Bih-Šāpūr* ('Chapour') are recorded in both Middle Persian and Parthian (2.2.3, a, b, h, j) and some of the Turfan publications (2.2.6) and of the Dura-Europos documents (2.2.8) also contain Parthian materials. To these can be added: (1) documents from Nisā near Ashkhabad, the capital of Turkmenistan, (2) the Awrōmān document, (3) coins, (4) inscriptions, (5) Manichean Parthian texts from Central Asia (Turfan).

2.3.1 Excavations at the site of Nisā, the ancient royal Parthian city, yielded a considerable amount of ostraca in Aramaic script. They belong to the first century B.C.; the type of Aramaic script used points to the wider time span between the second century B.C. and the first century A.D. The ostraca show that at the time of their composition the writing system was in the developmental stage between full Aramaic and ideogrammatic Parthian (see 3.3). The study of these documents was initiated by M. Dyakonov, I. Dyakonov and V. A. Livshic (for instance *VDI* 4, 1953, 114–30); M. Sznycer studied the available materials ('Ostraca d'époque parthe trouvés à Nisa (U.R.S.S.)', *Semitica* 5, 1955, 65–98); Dyakonov and Livshic returned to the subject in a more complete form (*Dokumenty iz Nisy*, 1960). Also: M. Sznycer, 'Nouveaux ostraca de Nisa', *Semitica* 12, 1962, 105–26. — E. J. Bickerman, 'The Parthian ostracon No. 1760 from Nisa', *BiOr* 23, 1966, 15–7.

2.3.2 The document from Awrōmān, in southern Kurdistan, is dated *ŠNT* 300 *YRḤ*' *'rwtt* 'year 300, month (H)arwatāt', taken by W. B. Henning (*Mitteliranisch* 29) to correspond to the period between January 7 and February 5, 53 A.D. The writing of this document (ideograms in the form attested in later Parthian documents: *BRY* 'brother', *YRḤ*' 'month'; Iranian markers appear in such forms as *ZBN-t* 'bought' for Parthian *xrīt*) is similar to that of the Nisā documents (above 2.3.1) and places it in the same stage of development. Bibliography: H. S. Nyberg, 'The Pahlavi documents from Avromān', *Le Monde Oriental* 17, 1923, 182–230. — W. B. Henning, *Mitteliranisch*, 28–30.

2.3.3 Early Arsacid coins are known from about the middle of the first century A.D. First, the legend consists of the abbreviated royal name (*wl*, for *wlgšy*, 'Volagases'); in the second third of the second century A.D. the inscriptions become longer (*wlgšy MLK*' 'Volagases, the king'); the full form (*'ršk wlgšy MLKYN MLK*') appears on copper coins. Bibliography: W. Wroth, *Catalogue of the coins of Parthia*, 1903. — The work of A. Petrowicz, *Arsaciden-Münzen*, 1904, has recently (1967) been reprinted. — Also: R. Ghirshman, 'Trois monnaies parthes inédites', *Centennial publication of the American Numismatic Society* 1958, 279–84.

For Parthian legends on coins from the local kings of Elymais and of the Indo-Parthian king Sanabares (end of the first century A.D.) see *Mitteliranisch* 41.

2.3.4 Besides the materials already mentioned (2.2.3) the following should be listed: (a) inscription of Artabanus V from Susa on a funeral stele and dated in 215 A.D. (*ŠNT iiii c xx xx xx ii YRḤ' spndrmty YWM' mtry* 'year 462, month Spandarmāt, day Mihr' corresponding to September 14, 215). Bibliography: R. Ghirshman's first publication in *Monuments Piot* 44, 1950, 97–107. — W. B. Henning, *AM*, New Series, 2, 1952, 176. — F. Altheim and R. Stiehl, *PP* 8, 1953, 307–9; (b) inscriptions of Kāl-i Jangāl near Birjand in southern Khorasan, probably from the first half of the third century A.D. Bibliography: W. B. Henning, 'A new Parthian inscription', *JRAS* 1953, 132–6.

2.3.5 The Man.MP text publications listed above (2.2.6) often contain both Parthian and Middle Persian texts. The identity of each text is apparent from the indications given by the editors. A collection of Parthian hymns has been published by M. Boyce, *The Manichaean hymn-cycles in Parthian*, 1954. Also, by the same author, 'Sadwēs and Pēsūs', *BSOAS* 13, 1951, 908–15 and 'Some Parthian abecedarian hymns', *BSOAS* 14, 1952, 435–50 and W.B. Henning, 'Geburt und Entsendung des manichäischen Urmenschen', *GGA* 1933, 306–18. The verbal system of Parthian has been studied by A. Ghilain, *Essai sur la langue parthe, son système verbal d'après les textes manichéens du Turkestan oriental*, in *Bibliothèque du Muséon* 9, 1939 (reprint 1966). Vocabularies and lexicographic studies are few in number. Besides the word-lists in *Mitteliranische Manichaica* I-III (above 2.2.6) and other publications, there is W.B. Henning, 'A list of Middle-Persian and Parthian words', *BSOAS* 9, 1937, 79–92.

2.4 *Sogdian*

(a) Early materials in Sogdian consist of coin legends. They are often of uncertain reading and their dates are difficult to establish with accuracy although it seems reasonable to assume that the oldest specimens are from the middle of the second century A.D. Most of the relevant materials are to be found in Allotte de la Fuÿe, 'Monnaies jnsertaines de la Sogdiane et des contrées voisines', *Revue Numismatique* 14, 1910, 6–73 and 281–333; 28, 1925, 26–50 and 143–69; 29, 1926, 29–40 and 141–51. See *Mitteliranisch* 25–6.

(b) The materials from Sogdiana itself are most conveniently classified after the type of Sogdian script used. Three main varieties emerge, the first from Samarkand, the second from Bukhara, and a third, not localized, type (*Mitteliranisch* 52). Documents of different kinds (coins, legends on silver objects, on textile, on leather, ostraca, intaglios) seem to originate from a period which covers the fifth and sixth centuries A.D. For recently discovered Sogdian documents in several archaeological sites in Central Asia, see R.N. Frye, 'The significance of Greek and Kushan archaeology in the history of Central Asia', *Journal of Asian History* 1, 1967, 33–44.

An important collection of over seventy pieces on leather, paper and wood, originating from the Sogdian homeland, was discovered in 1933 as a result of archaeological work conducted at Mt.Mugh in Tadzikistan. They date from the eighth century A.D. After the study of these documents had been initiated by A.A. Freiman (*Sogdijskij Sbornik*, 1934), their decipherment and understanding has been brought to a partly final partly provisional completion by the publication of *Sogdijskie dokumenty s gory Mug, čtenie, perevod, kommentarij* I-III, 1962–63 by A.A. Freiman, V.A. Livshic, M.N. Bogolyubov and O.I. Smirnova. The documents were published in facsimile as part of the *Corpus Inscriptionum Iranicarum* series as *Dokumenty s Gory Mug*, 1963.

(c) The main source of information for Sogdian lies in the discoveries made in the oases of Turfan and Tun-huang in eastern Turkestan where Sogdian refugees had settled after the destruction of Samarkand by Alexander the Great in the second half of the fourth century B.C. The identity of the language as Sogdian was established by F. C. Andreas after the Sogdian calendar terms given by Bērūnī (*Chronologie orientalischer Völker*, ed. E. Sachau, 1878, 46; see F. W. K. Müller, 'Die "persischen" Kalenderausdrücke...', *SPAW* 1907, 465). After the religious sources of inspiration the Sogdian documents can be divided in (1) Buddhist, (2) Manichean, and (3) Christian.

2.4.1 The French scholar R. Gauthiot was among the first to work on the documents brought to Paris by P. Pelliot (see 1.3). His early publications include: 'Une version sogdienne du Vessantara Jātaka', *JA* 1912, 163–93 and 429–510, and 'Le sūtra des religieux Ongles-Longs', *Mémoires de la Société de Linguistique de Paris* 15, 1912, 1–11 (see on the same text F. Weller, 'Bemerkungen zum soghdischen Dīrghanakhasūtra', *AM* [First Series] 10, 1935, 221–8); the same scholar wrote the first volume of a grammar of Buddhist Sogdian (*Essai de grammaire sogdienne* I, *Phonétique*, 1914) which was later completed by E. Benveniste (*Essai de grammaire sogdienne* II, *Morphologie, syntaxe et glossaire*, 1929). These early successful attempts at reading, understanding and analyzing Buddhist Sogdian materials were soon followed: F. Rosenberg, 'Deux fragments sogdien-bouddhiques du Ts'ien-fo-tong de Touen-houang I. Fragment d'un conte', *Bulletin de l'Académie des Sciences de Russie* 1918, 817–42 and II. 'Fragment d'un sūtra', *Bulletin de l'Académie des Sciences de Russie* 1920, 399–420 and 455–74, and 'Un fragment sogdien bouddhique du Musée Asiatique', *IzvAN* 1927, 1375–98. — R. Gauthiot, P. Pelliot and E. Benveniste, *Le sūtra des causes et des effets* I-III, 1920–28. — F. W. K. Müller, 'Reste einer soghdischen Übersetzung des Padmacintāmaṇi-dhāraṇī-sūtra', *SPAW* 1926, 2–8. — H. Reichelt, *Die soghdischen Handschriftenreste des Britischen Museums* I-II, 1928–31; volume I contains Buddhist Sogdian texts (*Vimalakīrtinirdeśa-sūtra*: F. Weller, 'Bemerkungen zum soghdischen Vimalakīrtinirdeśasūtra', *Abhandlungen für die Kunde des Morgenlandes* XXII.6, 1937, 1–87; *Dhyāna* text: F. Weller, 'Bemerkungen zum soghdischen Dhyāna-Texte', *Monumenta Serica* 2, 1936–37, 341–404 and 3, 1938, 78–129, and E. Benveniste, 'Notes sur le fragment sogdien du *Buddhadhyānasamādhisāgarasūtra*', *JA* 223, 1933, 193–248), while volume II provides more Buddhists texts (*Vajracchedikā*: F. Weller, 'Bemerkungen zur soghdischen Vajracchedikā', *AcOr* 14, 1936, 112–46), several documents, and a series of Ancient Letters (W. B. Henning, 'The date of the Sogdian Ancient Letters', *BSOAS* 12, 1948, 601–15). Notes on Reichelt's two volumes were published by E. Benveniste, 'Notes sur les textes sogdiens du British Museum', *JRAS* 1933, 29–68. — The publication by F. W. K. Müller and W. Lentz, *Soghdische Texte* II, *SPAW*, 1934, contains both Christian and Buddhist texts. — All of the Buddhist texts belonging to the Pelliot collection were published by E. Benveniste, *Textes sogdiens, édités, traduits et commentés*, 1940 (see the important review by W. B. Henning, 'The

Sogdian texts of Paris', *BSOAS* 11, 1946, 713–40); the same scholar also edited the Pelliot manuscripts (*Codices Sogdiani*, 1940, *Monumenta Linguarum Asiae Maioris* III) and republished the *Vessantara-jātaka* text (*Vessantara Jātaka, texte sogdien édité, traduit et commenté*, 1946).

2.4.2 While editorial work on the Buddhist texts has been practically completed, the same cannot be said of the Manichean materials. This is partly due to the by and large more fragmentary character of the texts themselves. It is, therefore, particularly fortunate to have a grammar available based on a comprehensive study of the Manichean published as well as unpublished materials (I. Gershevitch, *A grammar of Manichean Sogdian*, 1954). In addition to the Sogdian fragments published by Waldschmidt and Lentz (see 2.2.6 above), the following deserve to be mentioned: W. Henning, 'Ein manichäisches Bet- und Beichtbuch', *APAW*, 1936 which also contains Middle Persian and Parthian texts; *Sogdica*, 1940 (*James G. Forlong Fund* XXI); 'The book of the giants', *BSOAS* 11, 1943, 52–74; 'The murder of the Magi', *JRAS* 1944, 133–44; 'Sogdian tales', *BSOAS* 11, 1945, 465–87; 'The Manichaean feasts', *JRAS* 1945, 146–64; 'Two Manichaean magical texts', *BSOAS* 12, 1947, 39–66; 'A Sogdian fragment of the Manichaean cosmogony', *BSOAS* 12, 1948, 306–18.

2.4.3 Christian Sogdian materials were made known early through F. W. K. Müller, *Soghdische Texte* I, *APAW*, 1912; *Soghdische Texte* II (see 2.4.1 above) included further Christian texts. It took more than another decade for further materials to be published: O. Hansen, *Berliner soghdische Texte* I, *APAW*, 1941 (see I. Gershevitch, 'On the Sogdian St. George Passion', *JRAS* 1946, 179–84 and E. Benveniste, 'Fragments des Actes de saint Georges en version sogdienne', *JA* 234, 1943–45, 91–116) and *Berliner sogdische Texte* II, *AAWL*, 1954 (see E. Benveniste, 'Études sur quelques textes sogdiens chrétiens', *JA* 243, 1955, 297–337 and *JA* 247, 1959, 115–36). A study on Christian Sogdian is S. Telegdi, 'Notes sur la grammaire du sogdien chrétien', *JA* 230, 1938, 205–33.

2.4.4 Besides the religious texts in Sogdian, a number of secular documents some of which have already been mentioned (2.4 above) have survived. They bear witness to the extent of the area in which Sogdian was used. The Ancient Letters, discovered in a watchtower belonging to the Chinese Wall west of Tun-Huang, may well date from the early fourth century A.D. according to W. B. Henning (see 2.4.1 above). Several centuries later are the inscriptions from Ladakh in southwestern Jammu-Kashmir and from Karabalgasun (Qara Balgasun), the ancient capital of the Uigurs on the Orkhon river in Mongolia. The first may date from 841–42 A.D. according to W. B. Henning (*Mitteliranisch* 54); see E. Benveniste, *BSOS* IX, 1937–39, 502–5. The second, dating from the first two decades of the ninth century A.D., is trilingual (Turkish and Chinese besides Sogdian) and has been studied by O. Hansen, 'Zur soghdischen Inschrift auf dem dreisprachigen Denkmal von Karabalgasun', *JSFOu* 44, 1930, 3–39.

2.5 *Khwarezmian*

The earliest stages of the history of the language of Khwārazm, the ancient *Uvārazmiš* of the Old Persian inscriptions, to the south of the Aral Sea between the Oxus and Yaxartes rivers, are difficult to trace. The documents are relatively few, their publication is incomplete and not always satisfactory, and the data they yield are more often than not uncertain. These documents include: coins with Khwarezmian legends of early date (second or third century B.C.), for which see S.P. Tolstov, *VDI* 4 (5), 1938, 120–45 and *Drevnej Xorezm*, 1948, 173-95; inscriptions on wood and leather from Topraq-qal'a, probably from the second half of the second century A.D., see S.P. Tolstov, *Trudy Xorezmskoj Arxeologo-Etnografičeskoj Ėkspedicii* II, 1958, 208–12 and *Po drevnim del'tam Oksa i Yaksarta*, 1962, 217 ff.; inscriptions on ossuaries from Toqqal'a which may be assigned to the seventh century A.D., see S.P. Tolstov and V.A. Livshic, 'Datirovannye nadpisi na xorezmijskix ossyarix s gorodišča Tok-kala', *Sovetskaya Ėtnografia* 2, 1964, 50–69 (in English as 'Decipherment and interpretation of the Khwarezmian inscriptions from Tok Kala', *AAntH* 12, 1964, 231–51); inscriptions on silver vessels with datings between the first half of the sixth and the second half of the seventh centuries A.D.

Of later date and more considerable bulk and substance are the Khwarezmian materials, written in Arabic script, which are to be found in such Arabic writings from the twelfth and thirteenth centuries as Zamakhšarī's *Muqaddimatu'l-Adab* (published in facsimile by Z.V. Togan, *Khorezmian glossary of the Muqaddimat al-Adab*, 1951), Mukhtār az-Zāhidī's *Qunyat'l-Munyah*, the *Yatīmatu'd-dahr fī fatāwī ahli'l-aṣr*, another *fiqh* work like the *Qunyah*. To these the Khwarezmian words quoted by Bērūnī in his *Chronology* (see 2.4 above) should be added.

The first studies on Khwarezmian are those of Z.V. Togan, 'Chwarezmische Sätze in einem arabischen Fiqhwerke', *Islamica* 3, 1927, 190–213, and of Z.V. Togan and W.B. Henning, 'Über die Sprache der alten Chwarezmier' and 'Über die Sprache der Chwarezmier', *ZDMG* 90, 1936, *27–30* and *30–34*. Later publications include: A. A. Freiman, *Xorezmijskij jazyk*, 1951. — W. B. Henning, "The Khwarezmian language', *Zeki Velidi Togan'a Armağan*, 1955, 421–36; 'The structure of the Khwarezmian verb', *AM*, New Series, 5, 1955, 43–9; *Mitteliranisch* 81–4 and 109–20; 'The Choresmian documents', *AM*, New Series, 11, 1965, 166–79. — E. Yarshater, 'Čand nuqte dar bāre-yi zabān-i xwārizmī', *Majalle-yi Dāniškade-yi Adabiyyāt* (Tehran) 1, 1954, 41–8. — N. Rast, 'Zabān-i xwārizmī', *Majalle-yi Dāniškade-yi Adabiyyāt-i Šīrāz* II.4, 1338/1959–60, 11–38. A comprehensive study of the Khwarezmian materials in Zamakhšarī by J. Benzing has been announced for publication under the title *Das chwaresmische Sprachmaterial der 'Muqaddimat al-Adab' von Zamaxšarī*; published 1968.

2.6 *Saka Languages*

Several related types of languages of the Saka peoples, who are known from around

600 B.C. and after to have lived in the large area from the steppes of southern Russia to the Jaxartes river, now Syr Darya, in Kazakhstan, have come to light in the late nineteenth and early twentieth centuries in such places as Tumshuq, near Maralbashi, to the northeast of the city of Kashgar, and Khotan, to the southeast of the same city. The most recent discussion of these Saka languages is by H. W. Bailey ('Languages of the Saka', *Handbuch der Orientalistik*, Erste Abteilung, Vierter Band, *Iranistik*, Erster Abschnitt, *Linguistik*, 1958, 131–54).

2.6.1 The materials from Tumshuq, including one from Murtuq to the east of Turfan, are limited in number. Bibliography: S. Konow, 'Ein neuer Saka-Dialekt', *SPAW*, 1935, 772–823; 'Une nouvelle forme aberrante du khotanais', *JA* 232, 1941–42, 83–104; 'The oldest dialect of Khotanese Saka', *NTS* 14, 1947, 156–90. — H.W. Bailey, 'The Tumshuq Karmavācanā', *BSOAS* 13, 1950, 649–70 and 809–10, and *Languages of the Saka*, 147–54.

From the point of view of orthography the Tumshuq Saka documents fall into two groups both of which seem to represent an older language stage than Khotan Saka.

2.6.2 The amount of texts in Khotanese is very considerable. After the initial work by A. F. Rudolf Hoernle, P. Pelliot, J. N. Reuter, A. von Staël-Holstein and others in in the late nineteenth and early twentieth centuries, the main credit for the development of Khotanese studies goes to E. Leumann, S. Konow and H. W. Bailey. Text editions by Leumann include: *Zur nordarischen Sprache und Literatur*, 1912; *Buddhistische Literatur*, I. *Teil*: *Nebenstücke*, 1920; with M. Leumann, *Das nordarische* (*Sakische*) *Lehrgedicht des Buddhismus*, 1933–36; an extensive collection of notes on vocabulary items in this text was published by H. W. Bailey, *Prolexis to the Book of Zambasta* (*Khotanese Texts* VI), 1967. S. Konow published: *Vajracchedikā* and *Aparimitāyuḥ-sūtra* texts in A. F. R. Hoernle, *Manuscript remains of Buddhist literature found in Eastern Turkestan* I, 1916, 214–356; *Saka Studies*, 1932; 'Zwölf Blätter einer Handschrift des Suvarṇabhāsa-sūtra in Khotan-Sakisch', *SPAW* 1935, 428–86; 'A medical text in Khotanese', *Avhandlinger utgitt av Det Norske Videnskaps-Akademi i Oslo*, II *Hist.-Filos. Klasse*, 1940. Bailey's editorial work is contained in six text volumes (*Khotanese Texts* I, 1945; *Khotanese Buddhist Texts*, 1951; *Indo-Scythian Studies, being Khotanese Texts* II, III, IV and V, 1954, 1956, 1961 and 1963); in addition, several facsimile volumes (*Codices Khotanenses*, *Monumenta Linguarum Asiae Majoris* II, 1938; *Saka Documents*, *Corpus Inscriptionum Iranicarum*, Part II, Vol. V, portfolios I-IV, 1960–67) were edited by the same scholar.

As for comprehensive grammatical studies, the first outline was written by S. Konow, *Khotansakische Grammatik*, 1941 (in English as *Primer of Khotanese Saka*, 1949), followed, more recently, by A. G. Herzenberg, *Xotano-Sakskij jazyk*, 1965; also, R. E. Emmerick, 'Syntax of cases in Khotanese', *BSOAS* 28, 1965, 24–33. Complete glossaries are attached to the English translations of the *Bhadracaryādeśanā* text (J. P. Asmussen, *The Khotanese Bhadracaryādeśanā*, 1961), the *Jātakastava* text (M. J.

Dresden, 'The Jātakastava or "Praise of the Buddha's former births"', *Transactions of the American Philosophical Society*, New Series, 45, Part 5, 1955, 397–508), and Leumann's *Lehrgedicht* new folios of which were published by V.S. Vorob'ev-Desjatovskij and M.I. Vorob'eva-Desjatovskaja (*Skazanie o Bhadre, novye listy sakskoj rukopisi 'E'*, 1954; see R.E. Emmerick, 'Notes on the "Tale of Bhadra"', *BSOAS* 30, 1967, 83–94 and 'The nine new fragments from the book of Zambasta', *AM*, New Series, 12, 1966, 148–78).

The number of articles by H. W. Bailey on specific Khotanese texts or specific problems of historical linguistics or vocabulary is very large. A selected list follows. (a) Texts with commentary and translation: 'Hvatanica III', *BSOS* 9, 1938, 521–43; 'Rāma', *BSOS* 10, 1940, 365–76 and *BSOAS* 10, 1941, 559–98; 'Hvatanica IV', *BSOAS* 10, 1942, 886–924; 'Kanaiṣka', *JRAS* 1942, 14–28; 'The seven princes', *BSOAS* 12, 1948, 616–24; 'Irano-Indica', *BSOAS* 12, 1948, 319–23 and, on the same text, 'A Khotanese text concerning the Turks in Kanṭṣou', *AM*, New Series, 1, 1949, 28–52; 'The Staël-Holstein miscellany', *AM*, New Series, 2, 1951, 1–45; 'Ariaca', *BSOAS* 15, 1953, 530–40; 'Mā'hyara', *S.K. De Felicitation Volume*, 1960, 3–5; 'The profession of prince Tcūṃ-ttehi', *Indological studies in honor of W. Norman Brown*, 1962, 18–22; 'Śrī Viśa Śūra and the Ta-Uang', *AM*, New Series, 11, 1964, 1–26; 'Viśa' Saṃgrāma', *AM*, New Series, 11, 1965, 101–19; 'Vajrayāna texts from Gostana', *Studies of Esoteric Buddhism and Tantrism edited by Koyasan University*, 1965, 27–39; 'A tale of Aśoka', *Bulletin of Tibetology* 3, 1966, 5–11; 'The Sudhana poem of Ṛddhiprabhāva', *BSOAS* 29, 1966, 506–32; 'Altun Khan', *BSOAS* 30, 1967, 95–104. (b) Articles on linguistic and vocabulary problems: 'Iranica', *BSOAS* 11, 1943, 1–5; 'A Turkish-Khotanese vocabulary', *BSOAS* 11, 1943, 290–7; 'Gāndhārī', *BSOAS* 11, 1943, 746–97; 'Indo-Iranica II', *BSOAS* 13, 1949, 121–39; 'Indo-Iranica III', *BSOAS* 13, 1950, 389–409; 'Indo-Iranica IV', *BSOAS* 13, 1951, 920–38; 'Indo-Iranian studies', *TPhS* 1954, 129–56; 'Analecta Indoscythica I', *JRAS* 1953, 95–116; 'Ariana', *Donum Natalicium H.S. Nyberg oblatum*, 1955, 1–16; 'Iranian *miṣṣa*, Indian *bīja*', *BSOAS* 18, 1956, 32–42 and '*Miṣṣa* suppletum', *BSOAS* 21, 1958, 40–7; 'Adversaria Indo-Iranica', *BSOAS* 19, 1957, 49–57; 'Indago ariaca', *R.L. Turner Jubilee Volume* I, 1958, 1–6; 'Ambages Indoiranicae', *AION-L* 1, 1959, 113–46; 'Arya I', *BSOAS* 21, 1958, 522–45; 'Arya II', *BSOAS* 23, 1960, 13–39; 'Vāsta', *AcOr* 30, 1966, 25–43. At some time in the future the data presented in these and other publications will have to be collected in a lexicographical repertory for the use and evaluation of those who want to consult and have access to the Khotanese evidence.

2.7 '*Bactrian*'

The main piece of evidence for this language to which on linguistic and geographical grounds the name Bactrian has been given is an inscription of twenty-five lines in

Greek characters found in 1957 by the Délégation Archéologique Française en Afghanistan during excavations at Surkh-Kotal, the ancient Bagolango, in Afghanistan. The text was first published by A. Maricq, 'La grande inscription de Kaniṣka et l'étéo-tokharien, l'ancienne langue de la Bactriane', *JA* 246, 1958, 345–440. Two other versions of the same inscriptions were published by E. Benveniste, 'Inscriptions de Bactriane', *JA* 249, 1961, 113–52. The discussion of the important linguistic, historical and chronological problems raised by the Surkh-Kotal inscription has found expression in a considerable number of publications. Among them are: W. B. Henning, '"Surkh-Kotal"', *BSOAS* 18, 1956, 366–7; 'The Bactrian inscription', *BSOAS* 23, 1960, 47–55; 'Surkh-Kotal and Kaniṣka', *ZDMG* 115, 1965, 75–87. — A. Maricq, 'Bactrien ou Étéo-Tokharien?', *JA* 248, 1960, 161–6. — R. Göbl, *Die drei Versionen der Kaniška-Inschrift van Surkh Kotal*, 1965 (*Österreichische Akademie der Wissenschaften, Phil.-hist. Klasse, Denkschriften* 88,1). — J. Harmatta, "The great Bactrian inscription', *AAntH* 12, 1964, 373–471; 'Minor Bactrian inscriptions', *AAntH* 13, 1965, 149–205. — M. Mayrhofer, 'Das Bemühen um die Surkh-Kotal-Inschrift', *ZDMG* 112, 1962, 325–44. — H. Humbach, *Baktrische Sprachdenkmäler* I-II, 1966–67. — A. D. H. Bivar, 'The Kaniṣka dating from Surkh-Kotal', *BSOAS* 26, 1963, 498–502. — O. Hansen, 'Zur Sprache der Inschrift von Surḫ-Kotal', *Indo-Iranica, Mélanges présentés à Georg Morgenstierne à l'occasion de son soixante-dixième anniversaire*, 1964, 89–94.

2.8 '*Kušān-Hephthalite*'

Common to the materials classified, rather loosely, as 'Kušān-Hephthalite' are their alphabet, which appears to be derived from the Greek, and the general area of their origin, Afghanistan. Uncertainties connected with the decipherment and interpretation of this 'Greco-Bactrian' alphabet make it often difficult to decide not only on a correct reading but also on the language used. In some cases, the latter appears to be Iranian; in other instances, the language may or may not be Iranian. Among the relevant documentation which is largely of a fragmentary nature are: (1) coins (E. Herzfeld, *Kushano-Sassanian coins, Memoirs of the Archaeological Survey of India* No. 38, 1930. — H. Junker, 'Die hephthalitischen Münzinschriften', *SPAW* 1930, 641–61. — A. D. H. Bivar, 'The Kushano-Sassanian coin series', *Journal of the Numismatic Society of India* 18, 1956, 13–42. — Also: R. B. Whitehead, 'Multan: the House of Gold', *Numismatic Chronicle* 1937, 60–72. — J. Walker, *A catalogue of the Arab-Sassanian coins*, 1941. — R. Ghirshman, *Les Chionites-Hephthalites, Mémoires de la Délégation Archéologique Française en Afghanistan* XIII, 1948. — R. Curiel and D. Schlumberger, *Trésors monétaires d'Afghanistan, Mémoires de la Délégation Archéologique Française en Afghanistan* XIV, 1953); (2) seals (R. B. Whitehead, 'Notes on the Indo-Greeks, Part III', *Numismatic Chronicle* 1950, 231–2. — R. Ghirshman, 'Une intaille hephthalite de la collection de Mrs. Newell', *Numismatic Chronicle*

1953, 123–4. — A.D.H. Bivar, 'Notes on Kushan cursive seal inscriptions', *Numismatic Chronicle* 1955, 203–10); (3) inscriptions (A.D.H. Bivar, 'The inscriptions of Uruzgan', *JRAS* 1954, 112–8. — R. Curiel, 'Inscriptions de Surkh-Kotal', *JA* 243, 1954, 189–205); and (4) book fragments (F.W. Thomas, 'A Tokharī(?) MS.', *JAOS* 64, 1944, 1–3. — O. Hansen, 'Die Berliner Hephthalitenfragmente' in F. Altheim, *Aus Späntike und Christentum*, 1951, 78–103 and 'Ein neues Hephthalitenfragment', *PP* 20, 1951, 361–6. A comprehensive four-volume work has recently been devoted by R. Göbl to these and other Middle Iranian (Pahlavi, Sogdian, Bactrian) materials, from the middle of the fourth to the middle of the eighth century A.D., under the title *Dokumente zur Geschichte der iranischen Hunnen in Baktrien und Indien*, 1967 (I: Katalog, II: Kommentare, III: Fototafeln, IV: Zeichentafeln).

3. ARAMAIC

3.1 *Aramaic and its Importance*

The policy of the Achaemenian rulers by which Aramaic, a Semitic language, was introduced as the common language of administrative communication between the satrapies has had a deep and continuous influence. This is shown by the frequent use of Aramaic ideograms in written Middle Iranian materials and by the adoption of various modified types of Aramaeo-Semitic scripts for purposes of writing in the Middle Iranian period.

3.2

The success of the Achaemenian policy is clear from the extent of the area in which documents in Aramaic have been found. From Egypt come documents sent there by Aršām(a), an Achaemenian prince, from Susa in the fifth century B.C. Other Aramaic materials, from post-Achaemenian times, were recovered in Armenia and Georgia, in the west, and in Taxila, near Rawalpindi in West Pakistan, and Lampāka (Lamghān), on the Kabul river in Afghanistan, in the east. For a discussion of these materials, which falls outside this survey, and bibliographical references, to which now can be added E. Benveniste and A. Dupont-Sommer, 'Une inscription indo-araméenne d'A-soka provenant de Kandahar (Afghanistan)', *JA* 254, 1966, 437–65, see *Mitteliranisch* 22–4, 37–40.

3.3

While these documents were written in Aramaic, there is reason to assume that around 150 A.D. a basic change has taken or is taking place. The coin legend quoted above (2.2.1) presents what seems to be the earliest evidence for a transition from writing in Aramaic to 'ideogrammatic' writing in Iranian, in casu Middle Persian. The technique whereby Middle Persian *pus* 'son' is written Aramaic *BRH*, literally 'his son', for Aramaic *BR* 'son', becomes the accepted one from then on. In the course of the following centuries it shows several modifications and refinements and, in the case of Zoroastrian Book Pahlavi (see 2.2.5), results in such traditional lists, for the use of both educated writers and readers, of (Aramaic) ideograms with their Iranian equivalents as the *Frahang-i Pahlavīg* (see J.C. Tavadia, *Die mittelpersische Sprache und Literatur der Zarathustrier*, 1956, 38).

Refinements of the technique, caused mainly by a need for clarity and specification, are produced by the addition of Iranian flectional and conjugational complements or markers to the Aramaic ideograms. An early verbal example is to be found in the Awrōmān document in which *ZBNt* (line 7) shows Aramaic *ZBN* 'to buy' with *-t* as an indicator of the Parthian past participle [*xrīd*] 'bought' from the present stem *xrīn-* 'to buy' (see 2.3.2 above). The same complementary technique is applied not only in Parthian but in other Middle Iranian languages as well as is shown by forms of the demonstrative pronouns as they occur in Middle Persian, Parthian and Sogdian (*Mitteliranisch* 32–3). The forms in parentheses give the spellings as they occur in non-ideogrammatic writing.

Middle Persian	Parthian	Sogdian
'this' sg. *LZNH* [*im*] (*ʿym*) pl. *LZNHšn* [*imēšān*] (*ʿymyšʾn*)	*ZNH* [*im*] (*ʿym*) *ZNḤn* [*imīn*] (*ʿymyn*)	— —
'that' sg. *ʿLH* [*awē, ōy*] (*ʾwy*) pl. *ʿLHšn* [*awēšān*] (*ʾwyšʾn*)	*LḤw* [*hau, hō*] (*hw*) *LḤwyn* [*hawīn*] (*hwyn*)	masc. *ZK* [*xau, xō*] (*xw*) fem. *ZKh* [*xā*] (*xʾ*) acc. *ZKw* [(*a*)*wu*] (*ʾww*) gen. *ZKy* [(*a*)*wē*] (*ʾwy*) nom. *ZKy* [(*a*)*wē*] gen. *ZKyšnw* [*wēšanu*] (*wyšnw*)
'that also' *ʿLHc* [*awēz, ōyiz*]	*LḤwyš* [*hawiž*]	—

The general concordance in the use of the complementary writing technique with regard to pronouns as well as verbs and nouns in such different geographical localities as Persia, Parthia and Sogdiana is, perhaps, best explained by the close cultural and intellectual contacts and exchanges between these areas.

It should, on the other hand, be kept in mind that the forms of the ideograms underwent considerable changes in the course of history. Sogdian *ḤZYH* 'he sees' (in the *Ancient Letters* from the early fourth century A.D.; see 2.4.1 above) from Aramaic *ḤZH* 'to see' or Parthian *'TYt* '(having) come' (in Sassanian inscriptions) from Aramaic *'TY* 'to come' show the earlier forms if compared with Zor.BkPahl. *ḤZYTWN* [*dīdan*] 'to see' and *Y'TWN* [*āmadan*] 'to come' respectively. In addition, the ideograms show considerable uncertainty in the writing of Aramaic *'ain* and *alef* as is shown by such cases as *'RK'* 'real estate' for Aramaic *'rq'* [*arqā*], *'KBY'* 'heel' for Aramaic *'qb'* [*'iqbā*], or Middle Persian *YK'YMWN* 'to stand', Parthian *ḤQ'YM-* for Aramaic **yq'ym* (from *qwm*). See *Mitteliranisch* 35–6.

Finally, it is clear that no one single interpretation was necessarily attached to the ideograms with or without complements. For instance, in some Middle Persian inscriptional materials final *-t* indicates the 3rd sg.pres.ind. or subj. while past participles are consistently written by means of the plain ideogram; in other cases, the same marker *-t* interchanges with the plain ideogram to indicate the past participle (Kardēr, Ka'be-yi Zardušt, line 4: *'ZLWN* [*šud*] 'he went' and *'BYDWN* [*kard*] 'he did' against *YK'YMWNt* [*ēstād*] 'he stood' and *YḤBWNt* [*dād*] 'he gave').

It goes without saying that these circumstances make for uncertainty in interpretation. Further study and analysis of the ideogrammatic writing system in its long course of practice is an urgent desideratum.

4. ALPHABETS

The common origin of the Middle Iranian writing systems lies in the Aramaic alphabet. Naturally, difficulties arose from the fact that a foreign (Semitic) system was used to record non-Semitic languages. To make matters worse, few or no attempts were made to exhaust the full potential of the available foreign symbols. Generally speaking, Semitic *hē*, *ṭēth*, *ṣādē* and *qāf* remained unused and their use was limited to the writing of ideograms. Diacritics, a device to distinguish by means of additions to individual symbols, were adopted very late after the introduction of the original script; even then, they were rarely used and not written in a consistent way.

What may be called historical, pseudo-historical or inverse spellings are abundant in Middle Iranian. The general principle of procedure is the retention of a fixed, at one time correct, orthography without paying attention to the actual changes of later times. In addition, there is the mechanical adherence to certain once-adopted orthographic rules. Such phenomena are, of course, by no means uncommon in other writing systems. It is the high degree of frequency which is, perhaps, uncommon in the case of Middle Iranian. These and other reasons such as possible failure to recognize and properly evaluate this kind of spelling make it imperative to consider matters of orthography of prime importance. Examples have been collected, discussed and analyzed by Henning (*Mitteliranisch* 63–72). Among them are: Parthian *ptysḥw* 'answer' reflecting **patisahwa(n)* for actual [*passox*], Man.Pt. spelling *pswx*; the retention of final *-y* in Parthian *ʾrtḥštrpry* (proper name) reflecting **artaxšaθra-priya* and its transference to such cases as Parthian *drwzny* 'evil' [*drōžanʸ*], Old Persian *draujana-*; the writing of *-yw-*, in Zor.BkPahl. *gywʾk* 'place' [**giwāk*], for *-y-*, as against Man.MP *gyʾg* [*giyāg*], Man.Pt *wyʾg*, Sogdian *wyʾk*.

5. THE INDIVIDUAL LANGUAGES

5.1 *Middle Persian*

5.1.1 *Scripts*

The alphabets used in the Middle Persian (and Parthian) inscriptions from early Sassanian times show forms which if compared with the simpler shapes of the older coin legends tend towards elegance and monumentality. Handwritten lists of symbols, both Middle Persian and Parthian ideograms, are to be found in H. S. Nyberg, *A manual of Pahlavi* I, 1964, 129; their transliteration is as follows: ʾ, *b*, *g*, *d*, *h* (only final *-H* in Middle Persian and Parthian and occasionally as the indication of the feminine gender), *w*, *z*, *ḥ*, *ṭ* (only in ideograms), *y*, *k*, *l*, *m*, *n*, *s*, ʿ (only in ideograms), *p*, *c* (*Ṣ* only in ideograms), *q* (only in ideograms), *r*, *š*, *t*.

The script in which Zor.BkPahl. is written is the outcome of a centuries' long process. Of the original twenty-two Aramaic symbols only eighteen were retained (ʾ, *b*, *d*, *g*, *w*, *z*, *ḥ*, *y*, *k*, *l*, *m*, *n*, *s*, *p*, *c*, *r*, *š*, and *t*); the remaining four (*hē*, *ṭēth*, *ṣādē* and *qāf*) were limited to their use in writing ideograms. In the course of practice, an embarrassing number of symbols became identical or looked alike: *w*, *r*, *n* (and *ʿain*) became the same, ʾ and *ḥ* looked identical, the distinction between *d*, *g* and *y* was lost, *s* looked like *d* (or *g* or *y*) plus another *d* (or *g* or *y*), *š* sometimes looked like *d* (or *g* or *y*) plus ʾ, final *h* became identical with *m* plus *n*, *c*, if connected to the right, looked like *p*. The result was that only *b*, *z*, *k*, *l*, *š* (to an extent) and *t* remain immediately distinguishable while *m*, *p* and *c* can usually be distinguished. Furthermore, abbreviations (*ZY* looks like *d*, *g* or *y*) and alterations (*-zd-*, *-gd-* or *-yd-* have the appearance of *-ʾ-*) developed and unusual scribal practices (*b* connected to the left, against the normal practice, as in *BYN* [*andar*] 'in') gradually crept in. These developments seem to have resulted in a relatively fixed form in the seventh century A.D. This fixed form of late Sassanian times appears to have served as the example for the newly created Avestan alphabet as it is known from the earliest Avestan manuscript of the early fourteenth century. A table of the Zor.BkPahl. alphabet is to be found, for instance, in H.S. Nyberg, *A manual of Pahlavi* I, 1964, 129; a convenient collection of facsimiles from different Pahlavi manuscripts in O. Hansen, *Mittelpersisches Lesebuch*, 1963.

It goes without saying that the Zor.BkPahl. script is not the only outcome of the Aramaic writing system as used for Middle Persian. Variations occur and can be found in a variety of materials such as coin legends (2.2.2), gem legends (2.2.4), materials from Dura-Europos (2.2.8) and from India (2.2.10), etc. The alphabet used in the Psalter (2.2.7) is an example of the formal type of writing in as much as some of the symbols preserve older shapes. The entire Psalter manuscript material has been published in facsimile in the edition of Andreas and Barr (2.2.7). Next to this more formal type of writing several varieties of cursive writing developed. Such cursive types occur, for instance, on papyri (2.2.9), ostraca (2.2.9) and in inscriptions on silver vessels (2.2.9). A comparative historical study and tabulation of all of these various types from the beginning until early Islamic times is much needed.

Both the Manichean Persian and Parthian manuscripts are written in a variant of the Palmyrenian script with which Mani became familiar in his native Babylonia. He began to apply this script for the recording of his own religious compositions in Middle Persian during the reign of the Sassanian ruler Šāpūr I. The same alphabet was then also used for the notation of Manichean Parthian and Sogdian.

The full retention of the twenty-two original symbols, the apt use of diacritics and the creation of a new symbol if needed, all these in addition to the virtual abandonment of ideogrammatic writing, resulted in an almost ideal instrument which was far superior to the system used for Zor.BkPahl.

In the case of Man.MP the following symbols have been adopted for purposes of transliteration: ʾ, *b*, *g*, *d*, *ẖ* (*hē*), *w*, *z*, *h* (*ḥēth*), *ṯ* (*ṭēth*), *y*, *k*, *x*, *l*, *m*, *n*, *s*, ʿ, *p*, *f* (not consistently distinguished from *p*), *c* (*ṣādē*), *j*, *q*, *r*, *š*, *t* (*tau*). In addition, *ẅ* is used for *ʾwd* [*ud*] 'and' and *š̈* stands for *ʾwš* [*u-š*] 'and he'. A table of the symbols is to be found in F. C. Andreas and W. B. Henning, 'Mitteliranische Manichaica aus Chinesisch Turkestan', *SPAW* 1934, 66. See also Table 1, page 54.

5.1.2 The following text passage is an average specimen of Pahlavi writing. It is presented in transliteration and in transcription with translation after the interpretation of W. B. Henning ('A Pahlavi poem', *BSOAS* 13, 1950, 641–8). The passage shows rhyme and, in general, can be considered to be versified. Analysis of Pahlavi poetry offers many problems. Benveniste approached these problems in terms of isosyllabism in two articles ('Le texte du *Draxt Asūrīk* et la versification pehlevie', *JA* 207, 1930, 193–225 and 'Le Mémorial de Zarēr, poème pehlevi mazdéen', *JA* 220, 1932, 245–93). The unsatisfactory nature of this approach can be seen from the large number of text changes Benveniste was forced to accept in order to fit the traditional text into lines of equal syllables. Better results may be expected and have, in fact, been reached by the assumption that the number of stresses to the line rather than the number of syllables is at the basis of Pahlavi versification. This assumption as proposed by Henning in the article mentioned above seems to be applicable to verse compositions in Manichean Middle Persian, Manichean Parthian and Khotanese.

(a) *dʾlm ʾndlcʾy MN dʾnʾkʾn* *MN gwpt ZY pyšynykʾn*
[*dārom andarz-ē az dānāgān* *az guft-ī pēšēnīgān*]

(b) *ʿL LKWM BRʾ wcʾlm*	*PWN lʾstyḥ BYN gyḥʾn*
[ō šmāh bē wizārom	*pad rāstīh andar gēhān]*
ḤT [ZNH MN L] MQBLWNyt	*YḤWWNyt swt ZY 2 gyḥʾn*
[agar [ēn az man] padīrēd	*bawēd sūd-ī dō gēhān]*
(c) *PWN gytyy wstʾḥw ʿL byt*	*KBD ʾlcwk BYN gyḥʾn*
[pad gētī wistāxw ma bēd	*was-arzōg andar gēhān]*
MH gytyy PWN ʾYŠ Lʾ ŠBQWNt ḤWHd	*Lʾ kwšk W [Lʾ] ḥʾn W mʾn*
[čē gētī pad kas nē hišt hēnd	*nē kušk ud [nē] xān u mān]*
(d) (one line missing?)	
šʾtyḥ ZY PWN LBBMH MH YḤBYBWNyt	*W MH nʾcyt gytyʾn*
[šādīh-ī pad dil čē xandēd	*ud čē nāzēd gētiyān]*
(e) *cnd mtlwmʾn dyt ḤWHm*	*KBD [ʾlcwk] BYN gyḥʾn*
[čand mardomān dīd hom	*was[-arzōg] andar gēhān]*
cnd ḥwtʾyʾn dyt ḤWHm	*mssrdʾlyh QDM mltwmʾn*
[čand xwadāyān dīd hom	*mih-sardārīh abar mardomān]*
(f) *ʿLHšʾn ms wyš mynytʾl*	*BRʾ SGYTWNt ḤWHd BYN gyḥʾn*
[awēšān mih wēš-mēnīdār	*bē raft hēnd andar gēhān]*
ʿLHšʾn ʾp[y]lʾs ʿZLWNt ḤWHd	*LWTH dlt BRʾ SGYTWNt ḤWHd ʾsʾmʾn*
[awēšān abērāh šud hēnd	*abāg dard bē raft hēnd asāmān]*
(g) *KLʾ MNW cygwn ZNH dyt MH lʾy*	*ʾMT wstʾl BYN gyḥʾn*
[harw kē čūn ēn dīd čē rāy	*ka wastār andar gēhān]*
ʾMT Lʾ YḤSNNyt gytyy PWN spnc	*W [Lʾ] tn PWN ʾsʾn*
[ka nē dārēd gētī pad spanǰ	*ud nē tan pad āsān]*

'(a) I have a counsel from the wise, from the saying(s) of the ancient. (b) To you I will explain (it), in truth, in the world; if you accept it from me, (there) will be profit (from it) in both worlds. (c) In world(ly goods) do not put trust, (while) desiring much in the world; for world(ly goods) have not been left to anyone, neither palace, nor house and hearth. (d) Joy in (one's) heart? Why laugh and be proud, (o you) worldlings? (e) How many men have I seen, desiring much in the world! How many princes have I seen — royal power over men! (f) Powerful, excessively proud, they strode in the world; they have gone astray, in pain they went, aimless(ly). (g) Everyone who has witnessed this, what use if he (continues) entrusting (himself) to the world? If he does not consider the world an inn nor the body (something) ephemeral?'

These lines show the utilization of ideogrammatic writing as it is commonly practiced in the Pahlavi books. Markers are added to the verbal ideograms as, for instance, in *YḤSNNyt* (g) [*dārēd*] 'holds, considers' 3 sg.ind.pres., *MQBLWNyt* (b) [*padīrēd*] 'you accept' 2pl. ind.pres., *ḤWHd* [*hēnd*] as auxiliary verb in *ŠBQWNt ḤWHd* (c) [*hišt hēnd*] 'they have left', etc. Among commonly used ideograms for pronouns are:

(a) personal *LKWM* (b) [*šmāh*] 'you' 2 plural; (b) demonstrative *'LHš'n* (f) [*awēšān*] 'those, they'; (c) interrogative *MH* (c) [*čē*] 'what'; (e) indefinite *'YŠ* (c) [*kas*] 'anyone'; (f) the relative *iḍāfe* particle is written *ZY* (d) [*ī*]. Among prepositions are: *'L* (b) [*ō*] 'to', *PWN* (b) [*pad*] 'in, one', *BYN* (b) [*andar*] 'between, in', *LWTH* (f) [*abāg*] 'with, in'.

5.1.3 *Middle Persian phonology*

Middle Persian phonology has not received the attention it deserves. Only recently has an attempt been made to analyze the phonological system on the basis of the Zor.BkPahl., inscriptional, Psalter and Manichean Middle Persian materials by D.N. Mackenzie ('Notes on the transcription of Pahlavi', *BSOAS* 30, 1967, 17–29). His analysis results in:

(a) vocalism	/*ă*/	/*ĭ*/	/*ŭ*/		
	/*ĕ*/	/*ŏ*/			
(b) consonantism	/*p*/	/*t*/	/*č*/	/*k*/	
	/*b*/	/*d*/	/*ǰ*/	/*g*/	
	/*f*/	/*s*/	/*š*/	/*x*/	/*h*/
		/*z*/	(/*ž*/)	/*γ*/	
	/*m*/	/*n*/			
	/*w*/ /*r*/ /*l*/ /*y*/				

The rendering of these phonemes in actual writing can be illustrated by the following examples. Distinction is made between Manichean Middle Persian (M), Zor.BkPahl. (B) and Psalter spellings.

(a) vocalism

/*a*/ : not written M *pd*[*pad*] 'on, in'
/*ā*/ : ' M *d'd* B *d't* [*dād*] 'given'
/*i*/ : *y* M *pyd* B *pyt* [*pid*] 'father'; also not written M *nbyg* [*nibīg*] 'script'
/*ī*/ : *y* M *dyd* B *dyt* [*dīd*] 'seen'
/*u*/ : *w* M *pws*[*pus*] 'son'
/*ū*/ : *w* M *dwr* B *dwl* [*dūr*] 'far'
/*e*/ : *y* M *dyẖ* B *dyh* [*deh*] 'land'; also not written M *bn-* (also *byn-*)[*benn-*] 'bind'
/*ē*/ : *y* M *'yw* Incriptions *'yw* [*ēw*] 'one'
/*o*/ : *w* M *'bryšwm* [*abrēšom*] 'silk'
/*ō*/ : *w* M *rwz* B *lwc* [*rōz*] 'day'

(b) consonantism (in the order of the Manichean alphabet of Table 1, see page 54).

/*b*/ : *b* M *b'd* Psalter *b'tʸ* [*bād*] 'may it be'; in B *p* is also used for /*b*/ M *'b* B *'p* [*āb*] 'water', M *'bgn-* B *'pkn-* [*abgan-*] 'throw'
/*g*/ : *g* M B *g'm* [*gām*] 'step'; /*γ*/ seems to occur in B, written by means of a tailed *k* sign, in *myk* [*mēγ*], Man.Pt *myx* 'nail' and, perhaps, in one or two other words

/d/ : *d* M *dr* B *dl* [*dar*] 'door'; in B *t* is also used for /d/ M *zd* B *zt* [*zad*] 'struck'
/ẖ/ : see /h/
/w/ : *w* M *w'd* B *w't* [*wād*] 'wind'; see under vocalism
/z/ : *z* M *zd* B *zt* [*zad*] 'struck'; in B the *c* sign is regularly used for medial /z/ M *'z'd* B *'c't* [*āzād*] 'free'
/h/ : *h* (or *ẖ*) M *h'm-* B *ḥ'm-* [*hām-*] 'same'; M *-yẖ* B *-yḥ* [*-īh*] abstract suffix
/ṯ/ : see /t/
/y/ : *y* M *yšt* [*yašt*] 'worshipped'; in B *y* is also used for /ǰ/ B *ywdt* M *jwd* [*ǰud*] 'separate'; see under vocalism
/k/ : *k* (or *q*) M *kyrd* (*qyrd*) B *krt* [*kerd*] 'done'; see under /g/
/x/ : *x* (B *ḥ*) M *x'n* B *ḥ'n* [*xān*] 'house'
/l/ : *l* B *llc-* [*larz-*] 'tremble'; in B the first sign is a crossed *l* (*ł*)
/m/: *m* M *m'd* B *m't* [*mād*] 'mother'
/n/ : *n* M *n'z-* B *n'c-* [*nāz-*] 'to be proud'
/s/ : *s* M *swr* B *swl* [*sūr*] 'meal'
/p/ : *p* M *p'd* B *p't* [*pād*] 'protected'; also /f/ M B *n'p* [*nāf*] 'family'; in M the *p* and *f* signs are rarely distinguished
/c/ : *č* M B *cšm* [*čašm*] 'eye'; medial *c* in B represents /z/ see under *z*
/j/ : *ǰ* M *j'r* B *y'wl* [*ǰār*] 'time'; also /ž/ M *ywjdhr* B *ywšd'sl* [*yōždahr*] 'holy'
/q/ : *k* see under *k*
/r/ : *r* M *sr* B *sl* [*sar*] 'head'
/š/ : *š* M B *cšm* [*čašm*] 'eye'
/t/ : *t* (also written *ṯ*) M *tr* B *tl* [*tar*] 'over, across'; in B *t* is also used for /d/ see under *d*

Both the accuracy of the phonemic analysis and the validity of the reconstruction of these forms may be questionable. In fact, the examples rest on one or several assumptions the evidence for which can be tenuous or indecisive as the case may be. Further study both synchronic and diachronic is what is needed before the precise phonemic structure of the Middle Persian language can emerge.

5.1.4 *Further grammatical remarks*

For all practical purposes nominal flection is absent in Middle Persian; only the plural marker *-ān* exists. In inscriptional Middle Persian and in the Psalter a final *-y* is frequently found. It has been the subject of much discussion; it is, perhaps, best considered as a pseudo-historical (see 4.) writing (*Mitteliranisch* 67–9).

The verbal system of (Man.)MP shows: (1) indicative present (1 sg. *-ym* [*-ēm*], 2 sg. *-y(ẖ)* Psalter *-ydy* [*-ē(h)*], 3sg. *-(yy)d* Psalter *-yty* [*-ēd*], 1 pl. *-ym* [*-ēm*] and *-wm* [*-om*], 2 pl. *-y(y)d* [*-ēd*], 3 pl. *-y(y)nd* Psalter *-yndy* [*-ēnd*]); (2) subjunctive present (1 sg. *-'(')n* [*-ān*], 2 sg. *-'y* [*-āy*], 3 sg. *-'(')d* Psalter *'ty* [*-ād*], 1 pl. *-'(')m* [*-ām*], 2 pl. *-'(')d* [*-ād*], 3 pl. *-'nd* Psalter *-'ndy* [*-ānd*]); (3) optative present (3 sg. *-y(y)h* [*-ē(h)*]); (4) imperative present (2 sg. zero Psalter *-y* (*-ē*], 2 pl. *-y(y)d* [*-ēd*]; (5) intransitive preterite expressed by the past participle plus forms of the verb *ah-* 'to be' (*'md hym* [*āmad hēm*] 'I have come') except for the 3 sg. (*'md*[*āmad*] 'he has come') and transitive preterite expressed by a passive construction in which the agent is in the oblique case and the object appears as the (grammatical) subject (*'wm'n ny bwxt hy* [*u-mān nē bōxt hē*] 'and we have not delivered you', lit.: 'and (by) us you have not been delivered') and the less common *kyrd hynd*[*kerd hēnd*] 'they have done' after the intransitive preterite pattern; (6) participle present in *-'n* [*-ān*] (*phryz'n*) [*pahrēzān*] 'protecting'; (7) infinitive in *-tn* [*-tan*] (*bwxtn* [*bōxtan*] 'to deliver'; (8) passive from the present stem with *-yh-* [*-īh-*] (*d'nyh-* [*dānīh-*] 'to be known'), Psalter *-yd-* (*-īh-*] (*'pswsyd-* [*afsōsīh-*] 'to be ridiculed' and the much rarer 3 sg. form of which several examples occur in inscriptions (*'kylydy* [*(a)kerīy*] 'it was made'), see *Mitteliranisch* 101–2; (9) causative from the present stem with *-yn-* [*-ēn-*] (*zywyn-* [*zīwēn-*] 'to make alive'), Psalter *-n-* (*-ēn-*] (*z'ln-* [*zārēn-*] 'to torment').

5.1.5 *Differences between Manichean Middle Persian and Zoroastrian Book Pahlavi*

One of the features which distinghuishes Man.MP from Zor.BkPahl. is the change in the former of *-nd-* to *-nn-* as in *bng* [*ban(n)ag*] 'slave' against *bnd-* in the latter; there are, however, what seem exceptions both ways as Man.MP *'ndrz* [*andarz*] 'counsel' or Zor.BkPahl. *gn'k* [*gannāg*] from *gandāk*. Another such feature is the disappearance of final *-w* in Zor.BkPahl. which results in such pairs as Man.MP *'rd'w* [*ardāw*] and Zor.BkPahl. *'lt'y* [*ardā*] 'true', Man.MP *'yw* [*ēw*] and Zor.BkPahl. *'y* [*ē*] 'one'. Several circumstances interfere with a clear evaluation of the available evidence. Next to differences in the orthographic systems of Man.MP and Zor.BkPahl. and the use of ideograms that cover the actual linguistic forms in Zor.BkPahl., there are the intrusion of later, New Persian, forms into Zor.BkPahl. and the acceptance in both Man.MP and Zor.BkPahl. of dialect forms to be considered as factors which obscure the real situation.

5.2 *Parthian*

5.2.1 *Scripts*

The alphabet used in writing Parthian inscriptions has already been referred to (5.1.1). The symbols used for writing Manichean Parthian are the same as those used for Manichean Middle Persian. In the former case, the following transliteration symbols are in common use: ', *b*, *g*, *d*, *ẖ* (*hē*), *w*, *z*, *ž*, *h* (*ḥēth*), *ṯ* (*ṭēth*), *y*, *k*, *x*, *l*, *m*, *n*, *s*, ', *p*, *f*, *c* (*ṣāde*), *j*, *q*, *r*, *s*, *š*, *t* (*tau*). See also Table 1, page 54.

5.2.2 The phonemic system of Manichean Parthian has not been fully analyzed. By and large, it conforms to that of Manichean Middle Persian (5.1.3). Some of the differences between (Manichean) Parthian and (Manichean) Middle Persian have already been mentioned (2.1). The article by Tedesco remains the fullest treatment of the subject. See also W. Lentz, 'Die nordiranischen Elemente in der neupersischen Literatursprache bei Firdosi', *Zeitschrift für Indologie und Iranistik* 4, 1926, 251–316.

5.2.3 *Further grammatical remarks*

As in Middle Persian, there is no nominal flection in Parthian except for an occasional plural in *-yn* [*-īn*] as in Man.Pt *hwyn* [*hawīn*] 'those, they' or Inscriptions *ḥštrdryn* [*šahrdārīn*] 'rulers'.

The verbal system shows: (1) indicative present (1 sg. *-ʾm* [*-ām*], 2 sg. *-y(y)ẖ -yy* [*-ē(h)*], 3 sg. *-y(y)d -d* [*-ēd*], 1 pl. *-ʾm* [*-ām*], 2 pl. *-y(y)d* [*-ēd*], 3 pl. *-y(y)nd* [*-ēnd*]); (2) subjunctive present (1 sg. *-ʾ(ʾ)n* [*-ān*], 2 sg. *-ʾ(ʾ)ẖ* [*-āh*], 3 sg. *-ʾ(ẖ)* [*-ā(h)*], 1 pl. *-ʾ(ʾ)m* [*-ām*], 2 pl. *-ʾʾd* [*-ād*], 3 pl. *-ʾnd* [*-ānd*]); (3) optative present (2 and 3 sg., 3 pl. *-yndy(y)(ẖ)* [*-ēndē(h)*]; (4) imperative (2 sg. zero, 2 pl. *-y(y)d -d* [*-ēd*]); (5) intransitive preterite expressed by the past participle plus forms of the verb *ah-* 'to be' (*ʾgd ʾyy* [*āgad ē*] 'you have come') except for the 3 sg. (*sd* [*sad*] 'he rose') and transitive preterite expressed by a construction similar to that used in Man.MP (*mn dyšt ʾpdn* [*man dišt ābdan*] 'I built a palace', *ʾwš nmʾd rʾštyft* [*u-š numād rāštīft*] 'he showed the truth', *ʾʾzʾdʾn ʿym sxwn ʿšnwd* [*āzādān im saxwan išnūd*] 'the nobles heard this word'; also by means of a preposition (*ʾw* [*ō*]) *hrwyn ʾfryd ʾw tw* [*harwīn āfrīd ō tō*] 'all honored you'); (6) participle present in *-ynd* (*-ēnd*] (*xndynd* [*xandēnd*] 'laughing'); (7) infinitive in *-tn -dn* [*-tan -dan*] (*bwdn* [*būdan*] 'to be'); (8) causative from the present stem with *-yn-* [*-ēn-*] (*rwcyn-* [*rōžēn-*] 'to illuminate'), with *-ʾn-* [*-ān-*] (*wgrʾn-* [*wigrān-*] 'to awaken') or by lengthening of the stem vowel (*sʾn-* [*sān-*] 'to raise' from *sn-* [*san-*] 'to rise', *frnʾm-* [*franām-*] 'to lead' from *prnm-* [*franam-*] 'to go (toward)').

5.3 *Sogdian*

5.3.1 *Scripts*

The development of scripts in Sogdiana proper has been mentioned above (2.4b). It is the Samarkand type which is represented in a clear form in the Ancient Letters of the beginning of the fourth century A.D. In the majority of the Buddhist texts a special type of script, sometimes called *sūtra* or Sogdian script, appears; it may have reached its final form around 500 A.D. and it continued to exist afterwards in approximately the same form. Another variety, sometimes referred to as Uigur because it was later borrowed and adopted by the Turkish Uigurs, begins to emerge shortly before or in the seventh century A.D.; it is shown fully developed in the documents from Mt.Mugh of the eighth century A.D. In addition, the alphabet of the writers of Manichean Middle Persian and Parthian texts and referred to as Manichean script was also used by the writers of Manichean Sogdian texts.

The following symbols are commonly used for the transliteration of the *sūtra* (Sogdian) script: ʾ, *β*, *γ*, *w*, *z*, *h*, *t*, *y*, *k*, *δ*, *m*, *n*, *s*, *p*, *c*, *r*, *š*, *t*; *hē* and *ʿain* are only used in ideograms and *δ* stands for *L* in ideograms.

The Manichean script is more elaborate: ʾ, *b*, *β*, *g*, *γ*, *d*, *ẖ*, *w*, *z*, *ž*, *h*, *ṯ*, *y*, *k*, *x*, *l*, *δ*, *n*, *s*, ʿ, *p*, *f*, *c*, *j*, *q*, *r*, *š*, *t*. Tabel 1 (page 54) lists the symbols of the *sūtra*, Manichean and Christian scripts with their traditional transliteration.

In the order of the Manichean alphabet the symbols generally express (B Buddhist, M Manichean, C Christian):

ʾ : [*a*] B M *ʾrsk* [*arsk*] 'envy'; *ʾʾ* [*ā*] B M *ʾʾz* [*āz*] 'greed'; see under *w* and *y*

b : [*b*] M *nmb* [*namb*] 'dew'; [*v*] B M *βyr-* C *byr-* [*vīr-*] 'obtain'; alternating with *p* C *ʾb* B M *ʾʾp* [*āb*] [*āp*] 'water', M *kmb-* B *knp-* [*kamb-*] 'lacking, less'

β : [*v*] B M *βγ-* [*vaγ*] 'god' C *bγ-*; [*f*] B *γrβ-* M *γrβ γrf-* C *γrf-* 'many'

g : [*g*] in *-ng-* M *ʾngrnd-* [*angrand-*] B *ʾnkrʾnt-* 'to cut', but M *frkrnd-* B *prkr*(ʾ)*nt-* 'to cut up'

γ : [*γ*] M B *γrʾn* [*γarān*] 'heavy', B *mγδβ-* [*maγδv-*] 'minister', C *nγʾdʾ* [*niγāδa*] 'prayer'; [*x*] B (ʾ)*γw* M C *xw* [*xō*] 'he, the'

d : [*d*] in *-nd-* M *ʾndwxs-* B *ʾntwys-* [*anduxs-*] 'to strive'; [*δ*] C *dsʾ* B M *δsʾ* [*δasa*] 'ten'

h : written or not, at the discretion of the scribe, after final -ʾ or *-y* to fill out a line or surplus space for what seem to be mainly aesthetic reasons

w : [*u*] M *wβyw* [*uvyu*] 'both'; [*o*] M *xwštr* B *γwštr* [*xoštr*] 'camel'; [*ū*] or [*ō*] M C *rwt* [*rūt*] or [*rōt*] 'river'; [*w*] B M C *wyn-* [*wēn-*] 'to see'

z : [*z*] B M C *zyrn* [*zirn*] 'gold'; [*ž*] B *zγʾyr-* M *jγyr-* [*žγēr-*] 'to call'

ž : C *zγyr-* [*žγēr-*] 'to call'; [*ǰ*] only in Sogdian, in what seems to be a Parthian spelling, in *pnž* [*panǰ*], for normal *pnc*, 'five'

h : [*h*] or [*x*] M *hwnx xwnx* [*xōnax*] 'that, he'; [*h*] M *rhnd* ([*a*)*rhand*] 'believer' (Skt. *arhant-*); in B in final position only *ZKh* [*xā*] 'they'

ṯ : same as *t* (see below)

y : [*i*] B M C *wysp-* [*wisp-*] 'all'; [*ī*] or [*ē*] M *mzyyn* [*mazīn*] or [*mazēn*] 'armor'; [*iy*] M *fryʾn* [*friyān*] 'dear ones'; [*ai*] M *ptškwyt* [*ptškwait*] 'he says'; [*y*] M *ywʾr* [*yawār*] 'but'

k : [*k*] B M C *kyrʾn* [*kirān*] 'direction'; [*g*] B *ʾnkrʾnt-* M *ʾngrnd-* [*angrand-*] 'to cut' and in loanwords B M *kwtr* C *qṯwr* [*gotr*(*a*)] 'descendant' Skt. *gotra-*

x : [*x*] M *xwr-* B *wr-* [*xūr*] or [*xōr*] 'sun'; *x* and *γ* alternate in M *ʾwγz- ʾwxz-* [*ōxaz-*] 'to descend'

δ : [*δ*] B M *δyn* C *dyn* [*δēn*] 'religion'; [*θ*] M *myδ*(*δ*) C *myθ* [*mēθ*] 'day', M B *γʾδwk-* [*γāθūk-*] 'throne'; [*l*](?) M *δyw* [*lēw*](?) 'unreliable', M *δwt* [*lūt*](?) 'ewer, pitcher'

m : [*m*] B M C *mʾn* [*mān*] 'mind'

n : [*n*] B M C *nʾm* [*nām*] 'name'; [*m*] B *knp-* M *kmb-* [*kamb-*] 'lacking, less'

s : [*s*] B M C *sr-* [*sar-*] 'head', B M C *δst* [*δast*] 'hand'

ʿ : [*ə*] M *ʿspʾ* [*əspā*] 'army', M *ʿstryc* [*əstrīč*] 'woman'; *ʿy-* [*ī-*] or [*ē-*] M *ʿys-*, also spelled *ʾys-* [*īs-*] or [*ēs-*] 'to come'

p : [*p*] B M C *pr* [*par*] 'in, on'; [*b*] M *ṯmbʾr* B *tnpʾr* [*tambār*] 'body' and in loanwords B *prʾʾmn* [*brāman*] 'Brahmin'; [*f*] B *prmʾy-* M *frmʾy-* [*framāy-*] 'to order'

f : [*f*] M *frmʾy-* [*framāy-*] 'to order', M *ptškʾf* [*ptškāf*] 'to scratch' (infinitive)

c : [*č*] B M C *cšm-* [*čašm-*] 'eye'; [*ǰ*] M *pδδync-* [*paδinǰ-*] 'to pull'; [*tš*] C *pcmʾr* [*pčmār*] B M *ptšmʾr* [*ptšmār*] 'counting'; [*ts*] C *mcʾ* [*matsā*] B M *mrtsʾr* [*martsār*] 'here'; [*dz*] M *pcβwš-* [*pdzvūš-*](?) 'to smell'

j : [ǰ] M *'njmn* [*anǰuman*] 'assembly'; [ž] M *'nwyj-* [*anwēž-*] 'to collect'; see *ž* above
q : same as *k*; M B *kβn-* C *qbn-* [*kavn-*] 'little'
r : [*r*] B M *δwr* [*δūr*] 'far'; [əʳ] B M *mrγ-* [*məʳγ-*] 'bird'; used to represent foreign (Indic) cerebral in B *n'r-*, in *n'rkr'k* 'actor', Skt. *nāṭa-* and foreign *l* in B *krp-* [*kalp-*] Skt. *kalpa-*
š : [*š*] B *š't* [*šāt*] 'happy'
t : [*t*] B *tm-* [*tam-*] 'hell'; [*d*] B *kt'(')m* M *kt'm kδ'm* C *qd'm* [*kadām*] 'which?'; in *-γt-* [*-γd-*] B M *ptmwyt-* [*p(a)tmuγd-*] 'dressed' and *-βt-* [*-vd-*] B *' βt(')* [*avd*] 'seven'
θ : [*θ*] C *xypθ* B *γypδ* M *xypδ* [*xēpaθ*] 'own'

5.3.2 *The rhythmic law*

The preservation or loss of vocalic endings in Sogdian morphology is controlled by what has been termed the 'rhythmic law'. It was first discovered and formulated by P. Tedesco (*Zeitschrift für Indologie und Iranistik* 4, 1926, 102) and, later, rephrased by I. Gershevitch (*A grammar of Manichean Sogdian*, 1954, 72) as follows: 'Given the alterations of OIr. words which the phonetic changes peculiar to Sogdian have brought about, stems with no more than one brief vowel (not counting prothetic or svarabhakti vowels) are light, except when this vowel is *in positione*, viz. followed by *mb*, *xw*, or by a group of consonants beginning with *n* or *r*; all other stems are heavy. Heavy stems lose their vocalic endings, while light stems preserve them'. It was suggested by Gershevitch (*TPhS* 1948, 61–3) that word stress — 'words kept or lost their endings according as the endings were stressed or unstressed' — was responsible for this feature.

By and large, nominal, verbal and pronominal morphology conforms to this rule. Examples are: (a) light nouns B *mγδβy* [*maγδvi*] 'minister' nom.sg. (OIr. ending -**ah*), *mγδβw* [*maγδvu*] acc.sg. (OIr. ending -**am*), *mγδβt'* [*maγδvtā*] nom.-acc.pl. as against heavy nouns B M *wrtn* [*wartan*] 'chariot' nom.-acc.sg., M *wrṯnd* [*wartand*] nom.-acc. pl.; (b) light verbal forms M *sndyy* [*sandi*] 'he rises' 3 sg.pres.ind. (OIr. ending -**ti*), M *stty* [*satti*] 'he rose' 3 sg.intrans.pret. as against heavy verbal forms M *tyst* [*tīst*] 'he enters' 3 sg.pres.ind., B *'np'st* C *'mpsṯ* [*ampast*] 'he fell' 3 sg.intrans.pret.; M *snyy* [*sani*] 'to rise' light infinitive as against M *pyz* [*pēz*] 'to oppress' heavy infinitive.

It has been observed on the other hand that though it is difficult to deny the existence and general validity of the rhythmic law not all cases of loss or retention of short final vowels are covered by it. In other words, there are exceptions either way of light stems without and of heavy stems with vowel endings (*Mitteliranisch* 107–8). Further detailed research is needed before a sure conclusion can be reached.

5.3.3 The Sogdian verbal system shows: (1) indicative present (1 sg. *-'m -m* [*-am*] from OIr. -**ămi*, 2 sg. *-y* [*-ī*] from OIr. *-ahi*, 3 sg. *-ty* [*-ti*] from OIr. -**ati* for light and *-t*[*-t*] for heavy stems, 1 pl. *-ym* [*-īm*] from -**aima* (1 pl. opt. ending) and *-ymn* [*-īman*], 2 pl. *-t'* [*-ta*] *-δ'* [*-θa*] *-δ* [*-θ*], 3 pl. *-'nd* [*-and*] from OIr. -**anti*; (2) subjunctive present (1 sg. *-'(')n* [*-ān*] *-m* [*-ām*] from OIr. -**āni*, and other forms retaining the *-ā-* of the OIr.

	Sūtra (Sogdian)	Manichean	Berliner Soghdische Texte I		Sūtra (Sogdian)	Manichean	Berliner Soghdische Texte I
ʾ				l			
b	–			δ			–
β			–	m			
g	–			n			final medial
γ				s			
d	–			ʿ	–		–
h̲,			–	p			
w				f	–		
z				c			
ž	–			j	–		–
h	–		–	q	–		
t̲	–			r			
y			final medial initial	š			
k				t			–
x	–			ϑ	–	–	

TABLE 1

The symbols used in the table represent only an average selection. It ought to be kept in mind that, regrettably, there is no uniformity in the use of transliteration symbols. This is particularly true with regard to Christian Sogdian. See, for instance, W. B. Henning, *Beichtbuch* (see 2.2.6), 52.

subjunctive); (3) optative present (1 sg. B *-ʾy* [*-ai*] from OIr. -**ai(ya)m* and other forms); (4) imperative present (2 sg. light stems -ʾ [*-a*] from OIr. -**a*, 2 sg. heavy stems zero, 2 pl. light and heavy stems *-δʾ* [*-θa*]); (5) rests of an imperfect active (1 sg. -(ʾ)*w* [*-u*] from OIr. -**am*) and middle; with retention of the augment (**a-*) (M *pʾxwʾy* [*pāxwāy*] 'he cut off' with preverb **apa-*, M *wʾrms* [*wārams*] 'he became quiet' with preverb **awa-*, B *ptʾyγwṯ* [*ptīyōš*] 'he heard' with preverb **pati-*); (6) intransitive preterite expressed by the past participle plus forms of **ah-* and *ʾn-* [*an-*] 'to be' (*ʾʾγtym* [*āγ(a)tīm*] 'I have come') except for the 3 sg. (in *-y* [*-i*] M *stty* [*satti*] 'he rose' for light and zero *zʾt* [*zāt*] 'he is born' for heavy stems; the 3 sg.fem. is retained in C *nyžtʾ* [*niž(i)tā*] 'she went out') and transitive preterite expressed by the past participle in the accusative (*-w* [*-u*] from OIr. **-am*) plus forms of *δʾr-* [*δār-*] 'to have' (*βwγtw δʾr-* [*vuγdu δār-*] 'to deliver' for light and M *wyt δʾr-* [*wīt δār-*] 'to see' and with omission of *-t*, C *wydʾr-* [*wīdār-*] for heavy stems); (7) preterite formed by *-ʾz* [*-āz*] added to the present stem (M *šwʾz skwn* [*šawāz skun*] 'he was going'; see under (8)); (8) durative formations are made by adding B (ʾ)*skwn*, M *skwn*, *sk*, *kn*, *k*, C *sqn* to the indicative present, the imperfect, the optative, etc.; (9) a future tense is formed by adding B M *kʾm*, M *kʾn*, C *qʾn qʾ gʾ* to the present indicative (*βyndmqʾm* [*vindamkām*] 'I shall bind'); the same particles also occur with other tenses such as the subjunctive (*δʾrʾt kʾm* [*δārātkām*] 'he should hold'), the optative, etc.; (10) present participles in M C *-ny -yny*, B *-nʾk ʾynʾk* [*-əne?*] from OIr. **-ānaka-*, in C *-yq* [*-ēk*]; (11) infinitives are based on the present (see above 5.3.2) and on the past stem and end in *-y* [*-i*] for light stems (B *βsty* [*vasti*] 'to bind') and zero for heavy stems (B *snʾʾt* [*snāt*] 'to wash'); (12) rests of a precative, potential and two kinds of irrealis. These and other formations make for a varied and rich verbal system particularly in comparison with western Middle Iranian.

The same richness appears in the nominal flection and in pronominal forms. The former retains traces of grammatical gender. Examples: (a) light stems: singular nom.masc. *-y* [*-i*] from OIr. -**ah* M *βγyy* [*vaγi*] 'god', nom.-acc.neuter *-w* [*-u*] from OIr. -**am* B *δtw* [*δatu*] 'wild animal', nom.fem. -ʾ [*-ă*] from OIr. -**ā* M *wnʾ* [*wană*] 'tree', acc.masc. *-w* [*-u*] from OIr. -**am* M *δsṯww* [*δastu*] 'hand', acc.fem. -ʾ [*-ă*] from OIr. -**ām* M *rwrʾ* B *rwrh* [*rură*] 'plant', gen.-dat.masc. *-y* [*-i*] from OIr. -**ahya* M *cxryy* [*čaxri*] 'wheel', gen.-dat.fem. *-yʾ -yh* [*-ya*] from OIr. -**āyāh* B *wδwyh* [*waδwya*] 'wife', abl.masc. -ʾ [*-a*] from OIr. -**āt* M *δsṯʾ* [*δasta*] 'hand', abl.fem. *-yʾ -yh* [*-ya*] from OIr. -**āyāh* M *wnyʾ* [*wanya*] 'tree', voc.sg. -ʾ [*-a*] from OIr. -**a* *βγʾ* [*vaγa*] 'god'; plural nom.-acc. *-tʾ* [*-tă*] *cšmtʾ* [*čašmtă*] 'eyes', oblique *-tyʾ* [*-tyă*] M *δstyʾẖ* [*δastyă*] 'hands'.

Sogdian is also rich in pronominal forms; they are derived from the pronominal stems *x-* (OP *hauv*), (-)*w-* (OP *ava-*), *y-* (**ayam*), and (-)*m-* (OP *imam*). For instance, the *x-* and (-)*w-* stems show: singular nom.masc. M C *xw* B (ʾ)*γw* [*xō*], nom.fem. M C *xʾ* B *γh* [*xă*], acc.masc. M (ʾ)*ww* [(*a*)*wu*] B *ʾw* [*ō*], acc.fem. M *wʾ* [*wă*], gen.-dat. M *w(y)nyy* [*winē̆*] B *ʾwyn* [*awin*], loc. M *wyʾ* B *ʾwyh* [(*a*)*wyă*]; plural nom. M *xʾ* [*xă*], M acc. *wʾ* [*wă*], obl. M *w(y)nyy* [*winē̆*]. It should be mentioned that analogy causes many crossovers between pronominal forms to take place with the result that many of them appear in more than one syntactical context in apparently different functions.

The pronominal forms are often extended by means of such suffixes as *-n'* [*-na*] (B *w'n' w'n'kh w'n'kw* [*wāna*] acc.sg.fem. 'that'), *-nw* [*-nu*] (B M *'wnw* B *'wn'w 'wn'kw* [*ōnu*] nom.-acc.sg. 'this'), etc. They are equally often prepositioned as in M *cn* B *cnn* M *cwn* M B *c'wn* [*čon*] 'from the(m)' from **hača* and **awana* or M *prywyδ* C *prywyθ* [*pariwiθ*] 'in this' from [*par*] 'in' and [*wiθ*] 'this'. The number of such formations tends to become large; particles and conjunctions are likewise very numerous. These features set Sogdian off against western Middle Iranian.

5.3.4 *Sogdian 'dialects'*

The linguistic differences which can be observed between the Buddhist, Manichean and Christian Sogdian materials have been the subject of a recent discussion by Henning (*Mitteliranisch* 105–8). Among the possible causes for these differences Henning mentions actual phonological and morphological differentiations, the use of different alphabets and the adoption of different orthographic conventions by the scribes of each of the religious communities, differences in social and educational background between these communities, chronological differences and others. Further evaluation of the relevant evidence naturally imposes itself before it can be decided which of a number of possible explanations or which combination of such explanations fits the evidence best.

5.3.5 *Sogdian and other Iranian languages*

As far as the relation of Sogdian with other Iranian languages is concerned two points deserve mention. First is the fact that Sogdian shares certain features with Old Persian: (1) OIr. *θr-* appears as *ç* in OP and as *š* in Sogdian (OP *çitīya-* Man.Sogdian *štyk* 'third', OP **miça-* Man.Sogdian *myš-* 'Miθra'); (2) certain combinations of prepositions and pronouns occur in both OP and Sogdian (OP *hačāma* Sogdian *c'm'* [*čāmă*] 'from me'); (3) lexicographical features such as the existence of OP *gaub-* 'to speak' and Sogdian *γw-* [*γōv-*] 'to praise', etc. Henning tentatively proposes to assume that the Persians in ancient times resided for some time in an area or areas adjacent to ancient Sogdiana. The second point concerns the occurrence of a short *a*, from **ā*, in both Avestan and Sogdian, under certain conditions. For instance: (1) before *y* Av. *zaya-* Man.Sogdian *''jy-* [*ăžay-*] as against New Persian *zāyad*, Skt. *jāyate* 'to be born' or Man.Sogdian *sy'k* B *sy''kh* C *sy'q* [*sayāk*] and Av. *a-saya-* as against New Persian *sāye*, Skt. *chāyā-* 'shadow, canopy'; (b) before *w*(*ă*) Av. *navāza-* Sogdian *nw''z* [*nawāz*] as against Man.Parthian *n'w'z* [*nāwāz*], Skt. *nāvāja-* 'sailor'; see Henning, *TPhS* 1942, 65. These identical developments have been taken as one of the reasons for the assumption that Avestan belongs to the eastern Iranian language group.

5.4 *Khwarezmian*

5.4.1 *Scripts*

Besides the script in which the older Khwarezmian materials were written (see 2.5 above), the Arabic alphabet came to be used, probably in the course of the tenth century A.D., for the writing of Khwarezmian. Diacritics ('points') provided the possibility to render a number of Khwarezmian phonemes for which no existing Arabic symbol was suited. Thus, *p*, *č*, *ž* and *v* were written with three additional points to the existing symbols for *b*, *j*, *z* and *f* (*Mitteliranisch* 81–3). In adopting this method the Khwarezmian scribes followed the pattern set by their Persian colleagues.

5.4.2 *Khwarezmian and other Iranian languages*

The position of Khwarezmian within the eastern Iranian language group is somewhat undecided. Certain objections against H. W. Bailey's suggestion that Khwarezmian is in one group with Ossetic, Sogdian, Saka (Khotanese) and Pashto ('Asica', *TPhS* 1945, 1–38 and 1946, 202–6) have been raised by W. B. Henning ('The Khwarezmian language', *Zeki Velidi Togan'a Armağan* 1955, 421–36). Henning's discussion of the subject is concluded with the statement that Khwarezmian 'takes its place between Sogdian and the southeastern dialects, for instance Pashto and has, in addition, certain features in common with Parthian, others with Ossetic and still others with Avestan' (*Mitteliranisch* 114).

5.4.3 *Grammatical remarks*

The verbal structure of Khwarezmian has been analyzed by W. B. Henning (*AM*, New Series, 5, 1955, 43–9); further materials, on the use of the indicative present and and the injunctive in negative phrases, were provided in *Mitteliranisch* 118–20.

As discovered by Henning, the existence of pause forms is one of the prevailing characteristics of Khwarezmian. This means that generally speaking the vowel before the last consonant of a word is stressed *in pausa* and thereby lengthened or apparently lengthened. In other words, a noun such as *zādik* 'son' appears in two forms as *z'dk* inside the sentence and as *z'dyk* [OIr. **zātaka-*] at the end of the sentence or *in pausa*. Another example is the occurrence of two forms *h'βrd* and *h'βryd* 'he gave' from *hβr-* [*hivr-*] 'to give'; the first [*hāvírda*] is from OIr. **frābárata*, the second (*hāvrída*] from OIr. **frābaráta*. The vowel ending is assured by cases in which a suffix is added as, for instance, in *h'βrd'h* [*hāvirdāhi*] 'he gave him [*-hi*]', *h'βrd'hyn* [*hāvirdāhīna*] 'he gave to them [*-hīna*]' or 'he gave them [*-na*] to him [*-hi*]'. Not only enclitic pronouns but also postpositions (*c*^{i} 'from' OIr. *hačā*, *θa* 'with, to' OIr. **hada*, *b*^{i}*r* 'upon' OIr. **upari*, *da* 'through, beyond, off' OIr. **ati* (?)) can be added in a fixed order to the verbal forms.

Another feature of Khwarezmian sentence structure is that 'if [the verb] precedes the object, the object is expressed a second time by an enclitic pronoun either on the verb itself or on a word before the verb' (Henning, *AM*, New Series, V, 1955, 48). Example: *h'βrnyd y' δwyd'm* [*hāvirnīdi yā δuydāmi*] 'I have given my daughter to you' which can be analyzed as **hāvirnāhīdi* 'I have given [*hāvirna*] her [*hi*] to you (*-di*], my daughter'.

Given the stage in which Khwarezmian studies are, no comprehensive phonological analysis exists. Important historical processes and developments in phonology are the subject of part of Henning's article quoted 5.4.2 and of certain sections in *Mittel-*

iranisch 109–18. The bibliography given above (2.5) provides references which are available at the moment.

5.5 *Khotanese*

5.5.1 *Script*

The Khotanese manuscripts are written in the Indian *Brāhmī* script as it is known, at an older stage, from Kušān inscriptions in India and from Buddhist Sanskrit manuscripts from the Tarim basin in Central Asia. It fully reproduces the vowel system of the language. In fact, Khotanese is an exception in that respect among the Middle Iranian languages. The Tumshuq and Murtuq documents show, by and large, the same writing system but for the addition of a dozen or so new signs which were developed for the notation of Iranian phonemes.

In the Khotanese manuscripts several different forms of script can be observed. There is a gradual development from earlier calligraphic, square type styles to later, more and more cursive, types of writing. In the older periods, the symbols (*akṣara*) are distinct and ligatures clearly show the composing elements modified as they may be; in the later periods there is a gradual increase in the tendency to fuse the components of ligatures.

These scriptural developments are paralleled by the fact that the Khotanese documents, which can be assumed to date from the seventh to the tenth centuries, show successive stages of development of the language itself. This process has been described, somewhat traditionally perhaps, as follows: 'The language ... is attested in two forms in four linguistic stages (1*a*, 1*b* and 2*a*, 2*b*). The earlier form ... may in comparison with Italic and Indo-Aryan languages be placed on a level with Latin or Sanskrit. The intrusion of later phonetic forms (type 1*b*) indicates that for the scribes the language in type 1*a* was already somewhat archaic. The second form (type 2*a*) ... of the eighth to tenth centuries shows regular phonetic system and inflected forms but compared to the first form (1*a* and 1*b*) the final syllable and some internal syllables have lost something of their importance. It is comparable with Italian and Prakrit. The stage 2*b* contemporaneous with 2*a* but displaying less scholastic or clerkly training, approximates to the then rapidly developing spoken language attaining almost to a New Iranian stage. Here the phonetic system has been simplified ... The ending of the genitive plural [OIr. *-*ānām*] can show the four stages: 1*a* -*ānu*, 1*b* -*āni*, 2*a* -*āṃ*, 2*b* -*ā*' (H.W. Bailey, *Khotanese texts* V, 1963, vii–viii).

Not only do the successive forms of handwriting and linguistic system display changes. Spelling conventions also appear to be subject to alterations. For instance, in older Khotanese, *śś*, *ṣṣ* and *s* denote voiceless /*ś*/, /*ṣ*/ and /*s*/ while *ś*, *ṣ* and *ys* indicate voiced /*ź*/, /*ẓ*/ and /*z*/; in later Khotanese *ś*, *ṣ* and *s* are used for the voiceless, *ś*', *ṣ*' (*akṣaras* with additional subscript hook) and *ys* for the voiced sibilants. A summary of other orthographic devices is given by H.W. Bailey: 'The existence of *t*, *d* and *δ* led to the use of *tt* for *t*, *t* for intervocalic *d* in foreign words, and of *d* for *δ* (and *θ* before *r*) and for *d* in *nd*. Older Indian *xr-* was replaced by *gr-*, *fr-* by *br-*, *θr-* by *dr-*. The letters [and ligatures] *tc*, *ts*, *js*, *j*, *ch* represent *ts*, *ts'*, *dz*, *dz'*, *tš'*. The Older Khotanese distinguishes *rr* and *r*, where the Later Khotanese tends to use one for the other. The absence of a recently omitted sound is indicated by a hook below, as for *š* in *pyū̕* from **pati-gauša-* "hear", but *pyūṣḍe* "he hears" from **pati-gaušatai*. The hook was used more often in Later Khotanese, when other sounds still intact in Older Khotanese had been lost, thus in *ba̕ysa-* from *balysa-* ["Buddha"].' (*Languages of the Saka*, 136; see 2.6 above).

5.5.2 *Khotanese phonology*

A full and comprehensive study of Khotanese phonology, either diachronic or synchronic, has not yet been published. The grammar of A. G. Herzenberg (see 2.6.2 above) deals with both (55–71 and 41–54) within the limitations of the amount of data which have been analyzed and can be fully understood. The following passage (H. W. Bailey, *Languages of the Saka*, 139–40; see 2.6 above) lists some of the major historical developments: 'The vowel system was gravely modified in Khotanese by the effect of a following *-i-* and *-y-* ... This *i*-umlaut replaced *ā* by *e*; *a* by *ä*, i and *ī*; *u*, *ū* by *uī*, *vī*; *o au* by *ve*, *e*, as in *bera-* "to be borne" [from **bārya-*], *mästa-*, *mista-* "great" [Av. *masita-*], *bīḍä* "he bears" [from **barati*], *ysīḍaa-* "yellow" [Av. *zarita-*], *paltcīmphāka-* "destroying" [from **pari-sčamf(a)yāka-*], *rräysduīräṇu*, gen. plur., "princesses" [*rräys-dutar-*], *mvīre* "of a precious stone" [*mūrā-*], *hvete* "of power" [*hotā-*, *hautā-*], *heḍä* "he gives" [**frabarati*]. The sequence *-aiva-* was replaced by *-yū-*, as in *dyūva-* "demon", and *byūrru* "10,000", in Old Pers. *daiva-*, Av. *daēva-* and *baēvar-*. Penultimate syllables lost *a*, *i*, *u*, hence *hvarati* "he eats" became *hviḍä* and *frabarati* gave *heḍä* "he gives". From *zarita-* (with *-ka-*) came *ysīḍaa-* "yellow" ... Intervocalic stops became voiced, and voiced stops were lost, thus *kava-* "fish", Sogd. *kp-*, *spāta-* "commander" representing *spāda-pati*, *pitar-* "father" with *-t-* for *-d-*, *pajsāka-* "cooking" from *pač-*; *dai* "fire", loc. *dā̃ña*, from *dāga-*, *rrai* "plain" from *rāga-*, *pā* "foot" from *pāda-*, but *-v-* from *-b-*, as [in] *ākṣuvīndä* "they begin" from **ā-xšaubanti*. The voiced initials *g*, *d*, *b* are found in *ggarä* "mountain", *dār-* "to hold" and *basta-* "bound", but for *b-* before *ŭ* we have *v-* or nothing, thus in *ŭḍa-* "adult" from **bržda-* (IE *bherĝh-*, as in Av. *bərəzant-*, Oss. *bärzond*), and *vūḍa-*, *ŭḍa-* "covered" from **bržda-* (IE *bhelĝh-*, as in Sansk. *upabarhaṇa-* "covering", Oss. *ämbärzän* "covering", *ämbärzun* "to cover"), *väta-* "been" from *būta-*. The old voiceless fricatives *f*, *θ*, *x* became *-h-* between vowels, as in *saha-* "hoof", *raha-* "cart", *khāhā-* "spring of water", Sogd. *γ̕ γ*, and similarly *-xv-* in *paha-* "cooked, digested" like Pašto *pōx*, plur. *pāxə* "cooked, ripe" ... Initially *fr-*, *θr*, *xr-* were written *br-*, *dr-* and *gr-*, as in *briya-*, *brya-* "dear", Av. *frya-* for *friya-*, *draya-* "three" and *gäräta-*, *-grīta-* "brought" in *yusgrī-*, *uysgärya-* ["ransomed"] from *xrīta-*. Medially from *-θr-* and *-xr-* arose *-r-* with lengthened preceding vowel as in *pūra-* "son" from *puθra-*, *tcīrau* "duck" from *čaxravāka-*. The *-fr* left in *-u-* the trace of its *-f-*, as in *baura-* "snow" from *vafra-*. The sound which replaced Old Iranian *č* and *ǰ* from older *k'*, *g'* is the affricate *ts* and *dz*, written in Khotanese *tc* and *js*, as in *tcātaka* "well", *tcäṣ-* "to see", *jsā-* "to go", *jsīnā-* "life" ... Initial *y-* passed to *ǰ-*, written *gy-* and *j-*, as in *gyaysna-*, *jaysna-* "worship", Av. *yasna-* and Old Pers. *yzn*, **yazna-*. Initial *v-* is represented by the three sounds *v-* unchanged, *b-* and *g-*: thus *vala-* "rose" from *vr̥da-*, *birgga-* "wolf", Av. *vəhrka-*, and *ābeiʾsa-* "whirpool", *baiś-* "make to turn", *ggeiʾs* "to turn" from *vart-*, *āci-veʾsāra-* "rolling in flames", *geʾsāra-* "neck", older *ggälsāra-*. While *-rk-* became *-rg-*, and *-rp-* became *-rb-* as in *tcārba-* "fat", *-rg-* lost the sound *-g-*, hence *mura-* "bird", Av. *mərəγa-*. The group *-rt-* was replaced by *-ḍ-* as *käḍa-* "done" from *kr̥ta-*, while *-rd-* passed to *-l-* as in *sala-* "year". Both *xš-* and *fš-* appear as *kṣ* as in *kṣūtä* "pushes", and *kṣāna-*"shoulder", *kṣārma-* "shame", and *kṣundai* "husband", and *xš-* can also appear as *ṣṣ-*, as in *ṣṣavā-* "night", Av. *xšapā-*. But the initial *š-* is confused with *xš-*, as in *kṣū-* "hunger", Av. *šud-*, Oss. *sud*, and *kṣīra-* "place", Av. *šōiθra-*, Armenian loan-word *šēn* "cultivated". The group *-xt-*, *-γd-* has lost the fricative, as in *sīta-*, *sīya-* "learned", from the base *sak-*, pres. *sāj-*, *dīta-*, *dīya-* "burnt" from *dag-*. Similarly *suti-* "shoulder" is from **sufti-*, Av. *supti-*, and *hauda* "seven" from **hafta*, Av. *hapta*. The group *sr* passed to *ṣ(ṣ)*, as in *ṣṣū-* "horn", Av. *sru-*, *ṣṣūkā-* "fame" from *srav-* "be heard of". From *-gn-* the *-g-* is lost, as in *būnaa-* "naked", Oss. *bäγnäg*, and *rrūṇa-* "oil", Av. *raoγna-*. The *-θu̯-* of the word for "four" is replaced by *-h-* in *tcahora*. The groups *-rn-* and *-ršn-* were reduced to *-rr-*, as in *kārra-* "deaf", Av. *karəna-*, *tarra-* "herb" from *tr̥na-*, and *pārra* "heel", Av. *pāšna-*, Sansk. *pārṣṇi-*. From *-rš-* arose *-r-*, as in *hāmura-* "forgetting".'

5.5.3 *Further grammatical remarks*

In older Khotanese, the nominal declension shows singular and plural case endings (nominative, accusative, genitive, instrumental, locative and vocative) of several nominal stems (in *-a-*, *a(k)a-*, *-ā-*, *-a(k)ā-*, *-i-*, *-ī-*, *-u-*, *-r-*, *-nd-*, *-h-*). Each of these endings shows considerable simplification in later Khotanese. For instance, the older paradigm of the *-a-* stem is: singular nom. *balysä*, *balysi* 'Buddha', acc. *balysu*, gen. *balysä*, *balysi*, instr. *dātäna* 'law', loc. *dīśta* (of *dasta-*) 'hand', voc. *gyasta* 'god'; plural nom.-acc. *balysa*, gen. *balysānu*, instr. *balysyau*, *gyastyo*, loc. *gyastuvoʾ*, *gyastuo*, voc. *gyastyau*. In later Khotanese, most final vowels lose their distinctive quality: nom.sg. in *-a*, *-e*, etc., acc.sg. in *-ä*, *-a*, etc., instr.sg. in *-ana*, *-ena*, etc., loc.sg. in *aña-*, gen.pl. in *-āṃ*, *-ā*, *-au*, loc.pl. in *-vā*, etc. Similar changes reducing the number of distinct cases occur in the other nominal stem classes.

The verbal system consists of: (1) indicative present with active and middle endings (active of *puls-* 'to ask' in Older Khotanese: 1 sg. *pulsīmä*, 2 sg. *pulśi*, 3 sg. *pulśtä*, 1 pl. *pulsāmä*, 2 pl. *pulsta*, 3 pl. *pulsīndä*; middle of *häm-* 'to become' in Older Khotanese: 1 sg. *häme*, 2 sg. *häma*, 3 sg. *hämäte*, 1 pl. *hämāmane*, 2 pl. **hämäta*, 3 pl. *hämāre*); (2) subjunctive middle marked by *-ā-* (1 sg. *hämāne*, etc.); (3) optative middle marked by *-ī-* (for instance 3 sg. *yanīya* 'may he do' from *yan-*, 3 pl. *patīro* 'may they fall' from *pat-*) which is often used to express the past; (4) imperative active (2 sg. in *-a* as in *yana* 'do', 2 pl. in *-ta -da* as in *yanda*, 3 sg. in *-tu* as in *pvaʾttu* 'he should fear' from *p(u)vaʾd-*, 3 pl. in *-āndu* as in *saṃbajāndu* 'they should succeed' from *saṃbaj-*);

(5) intransitive preterite expressed by the past participle plus forms of *ah-* 'to be' (*bustämä* 'I have recognized') except for the 3 sg. (*hämätä* 'he became', *hämäta* 'she became') and 3 pl. (*hämäta* 'they became' [masc.], *hämäte* 'they became' [fem.]) and transitive preterite expressed by a formation in *-(*t*)*ānt-*, femenine *-(*t*)*āti-* plus forms of *ah-* 'to be' (1 sg.masc. *dätaimä* 'I have seen' and fem. *dätāmä*, 2 sg.masc. *dätai*, 3 sg.masc. *däte* and fem. *hvatätä* 'she spoke', etc.); (6) present participles in *-and-*, *-anda-*, *-andaa-* (active), *-āna-* (middle), *-ya-*, *-yaa-*, *-āña-* (expressing necessity); (7) past participles in *-ta-* or *-da-* (*hämäta-* 'having become', *purrda-* 'won'), *-āta-* (*huṣṣāta-* 'grown'); (8) infinitives in *-ä* or *-i* added to the present stem (*yanä* 'to do') and *-te* with regressive palatalization (*buśte* 'to recognize').

In general, Khotanese morphology conforms to the eastern Middle Iranian pattern of richness in nominal and verbal forms if compared with the relative poverty of western Middle Iranian.

5.5.4 *Khotanese versification*

Although the manuscripts make it clear by the way they are written whether a given text is prose or poetry, the structure of Khotanese metrics remains difficult to grasp. Similar difficulties are attached to the analysis of other Middle Iranian as well as Old Iranian metrical compositions. See above under 5.1.2. Suggestions as to what the underlying metrical pattern in Khotanese may be are to be found in M. J. Dresden, 'Note on Khotanese poetry', *Indological studies in honor of W. Norman Brown*, 1962, 42–50.

5.6 *Bactrian*

In spite of good progress made in the analysis and understanding of this most recently rediscovered Middle Iranian language, discussions are continuing on many basic problems as well as points of detail. In this case, again, the results of further research have to be awaited before a clear picture of Bactrian phonology and morphology can be obtained.

The designation of the language as Bactrian was preferred by W. B. Henning on the ground that '[it] occupies an intermediary position between Pashto and Yidgha-Munji on the one hand, Sogdian, Khwarezmian, and Parthian on the other: it is thus in its natural and rightful place in Bactria' (*BSOAS* 23, 1960, 47).

6. OUTLOOK

At the conclusion of this survey one is left with mixed feelings. At the one hand, there is a sense of admiration for and satisfaction with the often brilliant pioneering work done since the beginning of Iranian studies and more particularly in the last half century, since the discovery of the Central Asian materials. These efforts opened new and attractive vistas of new fields of study, they filled a rather thinly documented period in Iranian linguistics and they gave unexpected insights into certain aspects and periods of Iranian and Central Asian culture, religion and history. On the other hand, it would be wrong to conceal certain misgivings and almost a sense of disappointment caused by the limitations of the results which have been reached. For reasons which cannot and ought not to be discussed here the Middle Iranian field has remained a closed one and fellow researchers have been slow in joining the initiated few.

This situation in turn has resulted in few if any publications which can claim or for that matter intend to be of an introductory or comprehensive nature. Few would disagree that the lack of such publications can do little else but be disadvantageous to the development of a wider interest. Several of the more noticeable gaps which need to be filled such as a comprehensive historical analysis of the scripts used for recording the Middle Iranian languages, linguistic studies of each of these languages on a historical and descriptive basis, and syntactical as well as comparative studies of various kinds, have already been mentioned or have become apparent. Also on the level of advanced research much remains to be done. A relatively large number of texts is still unpublished, a large number of published texts has not yet been translated, and dictionaries for any one of the languages are nonexistent. In fact, the basic tools for further research have still to be produced. It can only be hoped that the vicious circle which leads from the disinclination to produce such tools among those who work at the advanced level to the need for them among those who want to be informed and back, will soon be broken.

Postcript [February 1969]

1.2 Now also: Mary Boyce, 'Middle Persian literature', in *Iranistik* (*Handbuch der Orientalistik*, Erste Abteilung, Vierter Band), Zweiter Abschnitt, *Literatur*, Lieferung 1, 1968, 31–66.

2.2.2 Also: R. Göbl, *Sasanidische Numismatik*, 1968.

2.2.5 and 2.3.5 See Mary Boyce, 'The Manichean literature in Middle Iranian', in *Iranistik* (*Handbuch der Orientalistik*, Erste Abteilung, Vierter Band), Zweiter Abschnitt, *Literatur*, Lieferung 1, 1968, 67–76.

2.6.2 On the Zambasta text: R.E. Emmerick, 'The ten new folios of Khotanese', *AM*, New Series, 13, 1967, 1–47, and *The Book of Zambasta, a Khotanese poem on Buddhism*, 1968. — Grammar: R.E. Emmerick, *Saka grammatical studies*, 1968, which deals with nominal and verbal morphology.

2.7 On the inscription of Surkh-Kotal: I. Gershevitch, *BSOAS* 26, 1963, 192–6, a review of H. Humbach, *Die Kaniška-Inschrift von Sorkh-Kotal, ein Zeugnis des jüngeren Mithraismus aus Iran*, 1960, and 'The well of Baghlan', *AM*, New Series, 12, 1966, 90–109, a review article of R. Göbl, *Die drei Versionen der Kaniška-Inschrift von Surkh-Kotal*, 1965.

2.8 On the so-called Hephthalite fragments published in H. Humbach, *Baktrische*

Sprachdenkmäler I–II, 1966–67: I. Gershevitch, 'Bactrian inscriptions and manuscripts', *IF* 78, 1967, 25–67.

5.5.3 Khotanese nominal and verbal morphology is analyzed in detail by R.E. Emmerick, *Saka grammatical studies*, 1968.

5.5.4 On metrics also R.E. Emmerick, *The Book of Zambasta*, 1968, 438 ff.

PERSIAN AND TAJIK

GILBERT LAZARD

It is a general rule that, before the birth of linguistic science, grammars and dictionaries were first composed for languages which were not well understood. The Persian language is no exception. It is remarkable that the Iranians, who established classical Arabic grammar and did so much for it, in spite of their attachment to their maternal language, were only very little interested in describing it. This is no surprise. Arabic was both a foreign language and the language of the holy Qoran: it had to be learnt and taught. Persian, as the mother tongue, did not have to be acquired, except in its literary use. For the latter a number of treatises on rhetoric were written. Dictionaries appear as early as the tenth and eleventh centuries A.D., but, as a rule, they are small books giving only rare, local, or obsolete words found in old poetic texts and not easily understandable to later readers. The large 'classical' dictionaries of the Persian language were not compiled until the seventeenth century and after, mostly in India and in Turkey, where a good knowledge of Persian language and literature was an essential part of culture (traditional Persian dictionaries were described and classified by Blochmann 1868, de Lagarde 1884, and Salemann 1888; see also a list and several descriptions by Nafisi et al. 1959).

As for grammar, until a very recent period, there was hardly any work but for a few chapters in books on rhetoric and introductory remarks in dictionaries (on which see Štolbová 1967). Real grammars of the Persian language only began to be written in the East during the nineteenth century (see Homâi 1959). They are generally patterned on Arabic, sometimes influenced by Turkish or French grammar; moreover they are exclusively concerned with the classical literary language and the descriptions (and prescriptions) are based on the written shape of the words in the Arabic script.

In the West, the first Persian grammar was published in 1639 (de Dieu), and the first dictionary in 1684 (Persian-Latin dictionary by Angelicus à S. Joseph). They were followed during the next three centuries by a number of works in Latin, French, English, German, and Russian, mostly written for their colleagues either by drogmans and missionaries in Persia and Turkey or by British officials in India. The dictionaries were based on the indigenous lexicographical tradition with occasional additions, the last and most complete ones being those by Steingass (1892) and Desmaisons (1908–14). Vullers' lexicon (1855–64), of a more philological character, is a corpus of the data given by traditional Persian dictionaries on words of non-Arabic origin; as such it is still indispensable for philologians and linguists. Among grammars (bibliography in Afšâr 1953) it may be useful to mention those by Salemann and Shukovski (1889) — very brief, but accurate, still usable for the classical language; Phillott (1919) — a huge volume full of valuable details, but utterly unsystematic; and Jensen (1931) — interesting for its syntax of classical Persian.

Towards the end of the nineteenth century, the development of historical-comparative linguistics introduced a new dimension in Persian studies. The Iranian group of the Indo-European language family had been established. Darmesteter (1883) defined the position of Persian (New Persian) within the group and showed that it was the modern continuation of Old Persian, the Achaemenian language. Comparative investigations were extensively carried on by neo-grammarian scholars; the results were systematized by Hübschmann (1895) and Horn (1893 and 1895–1901).

In the first part of the twentieth century the discovery of hitherto unknown or little known Middle-Iranian languages — Parthian, Sogdian, Khotanese Saka, Khwarezmian — and a better knowledge of Middle Persian widened the field of comparison and gave the possibility of taking a clearer view of the relations between Persian and other Iranian languages. It appeared that New Persian, although undoubtedly a continuation of Old and Middle Persian, had admitted a considerable proportion of words originating from other Iranian dialects, especially Parthian and Sogdian. Parthian elements were investigated by Lentz (1926) and Sogdian loanwords by Henning (1939). On the other hand many new etymologies were discovered.

Around 1950, there begins a new period in Persian linguistics. On the whole Persian had been hitherto studied and described only for practical uses or for historical-comparative purposes. This language which has a thousand year history, which is attested in literary documents as early as the ninth century A.D., which served for centuries as the main instrument of culture and government in a large part of Asia far beyond the limits of the Iranian plateau, which is now the official language of three different nations, had been generally treated as a monolithic unit — which of course it is not; there are noticeable differences between the language of older and later times, between formal and colloquial styles, and in local usages. Nevertheless that approach is easily understandable. Classical Persian was rather strongly fixed and unified; it enjoyed, and still enjoys, an immense prestige. As the prominent form of the language it almost exclusively attracted the attention of those who wrote about Persian. European drogmans in the Near East and British officials in India were primarily concerned with high style; colloquial Persian was not taught; if needed, it was learnt by practical training among native speakers. On the other hand, for historical-comparative purposes morphology as described in grammars, and words as found in dictionaries, were enough, with special attention paid to old forms, classical and preclassical; neogrammarian scholars were only little interested in contemporary and colloquial aspects of the language; besides, they had scant information about them.

Finally, this state of affairs was felt to be unsatisfactory and the fiction of monolithic unity was abandoned. This change of approach was necessitated both by the new trends in linguistics and by the historical development that had taken place in the Persian-speaking area since the beginning of the twentieth century.

The attention of linguists was now directed much more than before towards description. It appeared that Persian grammar was very far from what might be considered even grossly as more or less adequately described. Since the first condition for a good description is to take as its object a well-defined 'état de langue', some efforts were made in this direction, the contemporary language generally being given preference. Another factor to be taken into account is that a large part of the work was done by Soviet scholars; it benefited by the revival of Soviet linguistics after 1950. There are now more linguists working on Persian (and Tajik) and more publications in the U.S.S.R. in this field than in all the rest of the world (see bibliographies of Soviet works in Rastorgueva and Paxalina 1962, Rastorgueva 1962). Other and more powerful reasons lie in the new cultural, social, and political developments in the countries where Persian is spoken. Modernization, economic growth, increased relations with the West, and social transformations have brought about considerable changes in the cultural life and in the functions and forms of the national language. In Iran, while classical Persian is still studied at school and highly respected, new formal and literary styles, closer to the colloquial, have developed; this modern standard Persian, with its formal and colloquial aspects, is definitely distinct from the classical. In the Soviet republic of Tajikistan, the change has been still more drastic: a new national language (Tajik), written in modified Cyrillic, has been elaborated on the basis of local dialects. In Afghanistan also, where Persian is an official language side by side with Pashto, the traditional high style seems to be losing ground; although it is not clear yet which way the evolution will go and whether the literary language will stick to the Tehran standard or draw nearer the Kabul colloquial, people are conscious of the differences between their Persian, which they now call *dari* (an old and venerated name) and the language of Iran. Everywhere there is a large and ever increasing number of neologisms and loanwords, especially from French, English, and Russian.

These new conditions made the necessity of up-to-date studies on Persian strongly felt. Modern standard forms of the language had to be studied for themselves, in connection with practical needs, and consequently classical Persian appeared as a separate field; modern local dialects also attracted attention. Since World War II, in the Soviet Union, in Europe, in the U.S.A., and, of course, in Persian-speaking countries, a number of books and articles have been devoted to the standard Persian of Iran, to Tajik, to Persian and Tajik dialects, and systematic exploration of old texts was begun. Although on the whole Persian linguistics is still undoubtedly 'underdeveloped', and these achievements, if compared with what has been done for other languages, are not so considerable, they do represent an unprecedented amount of descriptive work, which in its turn is able to shed light on the history and prehistory of the language.

We shall now survey works on the modern formal Persian of Iran, on Persian dialects of Iran and Afghanistan, on standard and dialectal Tajik, on older forms of the language, and on its formation and relation to other languages.

MODERN PERSIAN OF IRAN

During the last fifteen or twenty years, studies on the modern literary language of Iran have been initiated and carried on by a few scholars in western Europe and the U.S.A. and by a greater number in the Soviet Union, where interest in Persian is very much alive. The main features of the structure of the language have been described in a few general works, articles have been published and dissertations written on various points of phonology and grammar. Of course different approaches have been used. Unfortunately, the scholars concerned are too few and too scattered for real and fruitful controversies to take place. Many important problems have hardly been tackled, and those which have did not profit by extensive and active discussion. This being so, a survey of studies can hardly be anything else than a catalogue of questions approached and works published.

All recent Persian grammars published in the West and in the U.S.S.R. are concerned with the contemporary language of Iran: such are, for instance, Lazard (1957a), which considers both the formal and the colloquial language, and Boyle (1966). A descriptive sketch by Nye (1955) is an attempt to apply the techniques of American descriptivists to Persian. Others by Rastorgueva (1953a; English translation by Hill 1964) and Rubinčik (1960) follow the usual, more traditional, method of Russian scholars. Suggestions for description have been made by Lentz (1958).

In phonology, a structural (functional) point of view had been introduced by Krámský (1939). Systematizations of Persian phonemes were presented, in addition to the above-mentioned general works, by Matthews (1956), Hodge (1957), Giunašvili (1965; see also Nalbandjan 1961). Special problems called for particular studies: the phonetic nature of the uvular consonant *q* (Sokolova and collaborators 1952, Giunašvili 1960b), the distribution and interpretation of the glottal stop (Xubua 1947, Ostovar 1958, Scott 1964), the role of voicing in consonants, and, particularly, the ticklish question of vocalic quantity (Shaki 1957, Krámský 1966). The main contributions are those by Soviet specialists in experimental phonetics. Gaprindašvili and Giunašvili published a general experimental study of Persian phonemes (1964). Zav'jalova (1961) investigated the realizations, voiced and unvoiced, of consonants. Sokolova (1951b, et al. 1952) settled the question of vocalic quantity by showing that an opposition of quantity exists, but only in a particular position, namely in open non-final syllables; she constrasts 'unstable' vowels, which are shortened in this position, with 'stable' vowels, which retain their duration in all positions.

Concerning phoneme distribution, we may mention Krámský's inventory of monosyllables (1947). Questions of accent and intonation were approached by several scholars (Bausani 1947, Lucidi 1951, Hamp 1958, Arzumanjan 1966, Atai 1964), above all Ferguson (1957), who gave a clear picture of word stress, and Zav'jalova (1960 and later), who devoted a series of articles to experimental research on stress and pitch in phrases. Fichtner (1965) made an interesting study of the rhythm of Persian prose with statistical data.

In morphology, a general structural sketch was attempted by Milanian (1965). A few studies deal with personal verbal forms, simple or compound (Alizade 1956, 1964; Pejsikov 1958, 1961; Rozenfel'd 1948; Muginov 1960; Lingenfelder 1957), and verbal nouns (Rustamova 1953, 1956, 1958, 1964a and b; Voskanjan 1956; Giunašvili 1957b). If, in Persian, the verb is an easily definable part of speech with specific morphemes, nominal morphology offers much trickier problems, which are still far from being sufficiently investigated, but some of which have been clarified by Hincha's very suggestive study (1961) and Telegdi's penetrating articles (1961, 1962; see also Ovčinnikova 1961). Extensive research on plural morphemes based on a vast corpus has been undertaken by Ovčinnikova (1964). The problem of the 'article' *-i* (studied by Rubinčik [1961; see also Murav'eva and Rubinčik 1959] and Lazard [1966]) bears on both morphology and syntax, because of its connection with the question of relative clauses. Rastorgueva and Paxalina (1962:22–5) mention unpublished Soviet dissertations on other morphological, and also syntactical, points.

In syntax, Arends' book (1941), a pioneer work, written along traditional lines on the basis of a large amount of material drawn from literary and newspaper texts, has remained the only general description, with the exception of the above-mentioned grammars and of Sadeghi's tentative systematic survey of syntactic functions (1967). Pejsikov's important book (1959) is a detailed study of the different types of syntagms and of the 'main members of the clause' (subject and predicate), interesting for its rich data and for its many new observations and suggestive insights, although some aspects of the author's approach call for discussion. One of the most difficult questions of Persian syntax is that of the function of the postposition *râ*, which is a marker of what may be broadly called the object of the verb, but is also used in connection with such categories as concrete/abstract, definite/indefinite, etc.; in spite of the data gathered and suggestions made in some of the above-mentioned works and in articles by Ovčinnikova (1956a) and Xrisanov (1959), it seems that a fruitful method of approaching the problem is still to be found. Other points of the syntax of the simple sentence have been touched on by Mahmudov (1955, 1956, 1964), Šafâi (1953), Arzumanjan (1965), Abdusamatåv (1964), and Rustamova (1964b). As for the syntax of subordination and the compound sentence, several questions have been examined by Kamenskij (1945), Šafâi (1955, 1966, 1967), Šarova (1964), Kuxtin (1961), and especially by Rubinčik in a series of studies.

In word formation, among articles dealing with suffixation and composition (Boyle 1952a; Machalski 1960; Sokolov 1958; Xrisanov 1960; Rzaeva 1953; Giunašvili 1957a, 1958, 1960a; Muxamedova 1962, 1964a and b), Pejsikov's articles on transposition (1964) and on single words derived from phrases (1966), Shaki's studies on nominal compounds (1963a, 1964), and Telegdi's considerations on the so-called compound verbs (1950, 1951), on verbs with preverbs (1955), and on a particular type of ambiguous compound adjectives (1964) are especially notable.

All the above-mentioned works were produced by western scholarship, the greater number in the U.S.S.R., others in central and western Europe and America. In Iran itself, tradition is still almost all-powerful in grammatical writing. Most grammars (for instance those by Qarib and collaborators, a book largely used in teaching and often imitated, Homâyunfarrox, Xayyâmpur, Maškur, Saidiân, Zonnur), follow the old pattern, with no distinction between contemporary Persian and the language of classical texts, where examples are looked for by preference, and with frequent mingling of a formal approach and semantic considerations. In spite of obvious shortcomings, such works are consulted with profit by western linguists. Let us mention, as a particularly detailed and careful study Moin's essays on Persian grammar (1952–62; see Pejsikov 1957). At the present time efforts are being made to renovate the method of grammatical description and teaching (for instance by Xânlari) and to frame a new linguistic terminology in Persian on the western model (Baqâi, Rezâi, Extiâr, Zomorrodiân, Azimâ). There is no linguistic journal in Iran. Many articles published in literary journals concern problems of language. Generally they deal with particular questions along the same lines as the above-mentioned grammars (e.g. Mortazavi 1956, Rahbar 1964). With few exceptions (e.g. Kešâvarz), they are less linguistic than stylistic and normative, and their authors are primarily concerned with the preservation of 'good' Persian and how to reconcile it with the many novelties enforced by western influence and modern life.

The condition and needs of Persian lexicography have been recently stated by Moayyad (1962; see also Rypka 1963). In this field it is difficult and somewhat artificial to separate classical and contemporary Persian; we shall therefore survey here briefly works on the Persian lexicon in general, leaving only historical lexicographical and lexicological studies for later consideration. Extensive dictionaries are in progress. Dehxodâ's *Loqatnâme* is an immense work, fascicles of which have been published for twenty years and which is still far from completion; being of an encyclopaedic as well as lexicographic character, it is an unprecedented collection of words with examples and a valuable tool for the linguist, though somewhat lacking in philological precision. Moin's *Farhang*, a middle-sized dictionary, is, like Dehxodâ's, much more oriented towards the classical language than the modern one. Among bilingual dictionaries (bibliography in Afšâr 1959) the best ones are Hayyim's Persian-English dictionaries, among which the 'one volume' and the 'shorter' one, being later, are richer in neologisms, Miller's Persian-Russian (1953), especially good for modern vocabulary, and Junker and Alavi's Persian-German (1965). A new large Persian-Russian dictionary is now being prepared, with special attention to modern words and phraseology (see Rubinčik 1964a and b).

Apart from dictionaries, lexicological works are few (for Soviet works see Rastorgueva and Paxalina 1962, and Hatəmi 1964). Some special glossaries, published in

Iran or in the U.S.S.R., are collections of technical terms and phrases; most of them are bilingual, either from Persian to a western language or vice versa. Compiled for practical use, they provide data for research on the constitution of modern technical vocabularies. A large number of neologisms have of course been coined in contemporary Persian; Dowlatâbâdi (1954) gives some information on this development.

On general phraseology, an important field since Persian is particularly rich in idioms, we should mention Shaki's works (1958, 1963b; see also Zulfigarova 1963).

DIALECTS OF IRAN AND AFGHANISTAN

Colloquial forms of Persian are rather different from the formal one and from one another; local dialects are not all mutually intelligible. Until recently they were practically ignored by scholars, if we except a few scattered remarks on the 'vulgar' or 'bazari' language of Persia (e.g. Ivanow 1931) and on eastern Persian, that is, Persian of Afghanistan and India and Tajik. Recent studies have shown that Persian dialectology (to be distinguished from Iranian dialectology, which is concerned with Iranian non-Persian dialects) is a rich and promising field.

The socially most important dialect is the colloquial of Tehran, which is rapidly spreading in Iran and becoming the standard colloquial language of the country. It is also making its way in dialogue parts of fictional literature, on which Boyle (1952b) based his observations. Its specific phonological and morphological features were more systematically described by Hodge (1956 and 1957, with a definition of stylistic levels), Pejsikov (1960a), Vahidiân (1964), Hatəmi (1965, with texts and vocabulary; see also Hatəmi 1955), these works being, as it seems, independent of one another. Glossaries of 'vulgar' words were published by Rahmati (1951) and Jamâlzâde (1962), shorter lists of words and phrases by Monteil (1955) and Hinz (1961), and interesting remarks on 'vulgar' vocabulary by Jamâlzâde (1963).

Other dialects of Persian have been but little investigated. A few glossaries have been elaborated in Iran, and several descriptions have been attempted as doctoral dissertations by Iranian students in the West. We can mention for Kerman a dictionary (Sotude 1957) and a descriptive sketch (Baqâi 1961, 1963–67), for Fars a list of words (Behruzi Kâzeruni), for Mašhad a descriptive sketch (Habibollahi 1966) and a list of words (Adib-e Tusi 1962), for Qâen a descriptive sketch (Zomorrodiân 1965, 1966), for Birjand a glossary (Rezâi 1965; see also Ivanow's older notes, 1928), for Sistan linguistic remarks (Grjunberg 1963) and folklore texts (Weryho 1962).

In Afghanistan the main dialect is that of Kabul. In addition to older notes (Morgenstierne 1926:7–9, 1928; Bonelli 1929, 1930, 1936; Bogdanov 1930), it has been dealt with in Farhâdi's book (1955), Paxalina's articles (1963, 1964), and Wilson's manuals (1956, 1960). Influence of colloquial Kabuli is to some extent perceivable in the literary language as used in Afghanistan; these local features of written Afghan Persian have been investigated by Dorofeeva (1959, 1960). Among other dialects, with the exception of Lorimer's phonology of Badakhshan Persian (1922), Grierson's notes on the same dialect and on dēhwārī (1921:452–3 and 527–30), and Farhâdi's remarks on several dialects (1959), only the dialect of the Hazaras of central Afghanistan has been studied (Efimov 1964, 1965; Ligeti 1964). A dictionary of 'vulgar' words was published in Afghanistan (Afghâninawês 1961).

As far as can be seen now, the main division of Persian dialects in general is into a western and an eastern group, the boundary being towards the central deserts of Persia. For different phonological, grammatical and lexical features, dialects of eastern Persia (Khorasan) are, as it seems, better classified together with Afghan Persian and Tajik in the eastern group, which, in spite of important internal differences, may be contrasted with Tehran Persian and other dialects of western Persia. Unfortunately we do not yet possess enough information to make definite statements. It will be the task of future research to collect more extensive data in order to get a more accurate classification. This task is an urgent one, since, at least in Persia, local forms of Persian are progressively yielding ground to the standard language. It is hoped that the Linguistic Atlas of Iran and Afghanistan, which is now being prepared by G. Redard, will provide valuable information on the dialects of the Persian language as well.

STANDARD AND DIALECTAL TAJIK

As said above, until World War I, Tajik (Central Asian Persian) was known only from a few observations. After the founding of the Soviet Republic of Tajikistan, it was raised to the status of a national language. In the twenties and the thirties, linguistic activity in Tajikistan was mainly devoted to the practical work of standardizing the language and its orthography first in Latin, then in Cyrillic script; most publications were practical books, grammars for teaching in school and manuals for non-Tajik, i.e. Russian, speakers. Since that time, the standard (literary) language, being established, has been studied more scientifically and the spoken dialects very actively explored. Naturally, with the exception of a few comparative articles, this work has all taken place in the U.S.S.R.; it has been carried on by Tajik as well as by Russian scholars.

A general description of standard Tajik is available in Rastorgueva's (1954; English translation by Paper 1963) and Nemenova's (1955) sketches, and, more extensively, in the official grammar for higher teaching, a collective work with a large choice of examples (Niyozmuhammadov, Niyozi, and Tojiev 1956, Niyozmuhammadov and Ismatulloyev 1963). These authors as well as the ones mentioned below operate with notions traditional among Russian linguists. In Tajik a whole set of new technical phonological and grammatical terms is used, these neologisms being 'calques' of the corresponding Russian words.

In phonology and phonetics, besides Orfinskaja's article (1945) and Rastorgueva's brief sketch for teaching in colleges (1955), the main work is Sokolova's careful and instructive study of experimental phonetics (1949). The most interesting point is vocalic quantity, which plays the same role as in Persian and most dialects, and contrasts 'unstable' with 'stable' vowels.

A series of sketches on Tajik grammar ('Očerki po grammatike tadžikskogo jazyka') was published in 1953–54 by the Institute of Language and Literature of the Academy of Sciences of Tajikistan, as preliminary studies for an academic grammar; they deal with the morphology and semantics of personal verbal forms (No. 2 and 3: Rastorgueva; No. 4: Rozenfel'd, see also Rozenfel'd 1956c and 1963c), the functions of participles (No. 5: Tadžiev), nominal parts of speech (No. 7: Niyozi), prepositions (No. 6: Nemenova), verbal locutions (No. 1: Rozenfel'd). Rastorgueva (1962) and Niyozmuhammadov and Ismatulloyev (1963) mention a number of other works on different morphological points (e.g. Jalolov 1961a), on the structure of the clause (e.g. Niyozmuhammadov 1956, 1960a; Ismatulloyev 1955), on subordinate clauses (e.g. Huseynov 1960, Niyozmuhammadov 1960b, Kosimova 1962), on word formation. Among more recent publications let us mention Xalilov's book on nominal phrases (1964) and a collective volume edited by Niyozmuhammadov (1964). Although most of these studies are based on a choice of examples, more modern methods with quantitative data are sometimes introduced (e.g. Nikolaev and Normatov 1967 on word order). Certain questions are particularly interesting because they concern specific features of Tajik as contrasted with the language of Persia, such as the construction of nominal determination (Tadžiev 1955, Kerimova 1964), the versatile use of participles (Ėdel'man 1955), compound verbal forms and compound verbs of the type 'participle-gerund + verb' (O.I. Smirnova 1948; Ahmadova 1958, 1960; Rozenfel'd 1953). Rastorgueva and Kerimova's detailed description of the verbal system (1964) is a valuable book.

The lexicon of literary Tajik is registered in Raximi and Uspenskaja's 40,000 word dictionary (1954). Among lexicological works we can mention an interesting extensive article by Tadžiev (1952), Muxammadiev's study of synonyms (1962), Fozilov's book on onomatopoetic and other 'expressive' words (1958) and, by the same author, a phraseological dictionary (1963–64). Some studies on the vocabulary and phraseology of modern writers (e.g. Ma'sumi 1959, Ghaforov 1962) may provide materials for a future larger consideration of the formation of literary Tajik (on this question see Rastorgueva 1964c and Niyozmuhammadov 1964).

Tajik dialects, considering the comparatively small area they occupy, are much differentiated. Twenty years ago little was known about them. Some inquiries had been made, especially by Zarubin, whose materials unfortunately remained unpublished, with the exception of his excellent monograph on the Jewish dialect of Samarkand (1928). Some folklore texts had been published, and Andreev (1930) had recognized the main division between a northwestern and southwestern group of dialects. In the recent period systematic investigations have been undertaken and actively carried on. Monographs published, or still unpublished, are many. Generally they are based on, and accompanied by, abundant and very good samples of not only folklore, but also colloquial texts; and most descriptions, which are made along traditional lines, are detailed and accurate. Today Tajik dialects are by far better known than those spoken in the rest of the Persian area, and few of them remain unexplored. A clear account of the state of studies is given by Rastorgueva (1964b: 3–10).

The most extensive work is Rastorgueva's 'Sketches of Tajik dialectology' (1952–63) in five volumes, the first one of which deals with the dialect of Varzob, north of Dushanbe, in central Tajikistan (see also Rastorgueva 1948), the second, third and fourth with dialects of Ferghana and neighboring regions, in northern Tajikistan and across the political frontier in Uzbekistan, the fifth being a glossary of these dialects. Some of these Ferghana dialects were also treated by Jalolov (1949) and Niyozmuhammadov (1951) and others further north in the upper Chirchik valley in Uzbekistan by Adelung (1959) and Tagirova (1959). All these dialects belong to the northwestern group and so do all those spoken in south Uzbekistan and west Tajikistan: those of Samarkand studied, in addition to Zarubin's above-mentioned work, 1928 — on which Birnbaum's article 1950 is based — by Behbudī 1961), of Foriš, northwest of Samarkand (studied by Kosimov 1966), of Bukhara (described in Kerimova's excellent monograph 1959, and studied by Melex 1964 and also Rajâi, an Iranian professor at Mashad University, 1964), of the Baysun region (studied by Hamroqulov 1958, 1961a and b, 1963), of Shahrtuz and the Kaška-Darya region (studied by Saidova 1962, Niyozmuhammadov 1960c, Ešniyozov 1959, Jūrayev 1967); of Hisar and Karatag (studied by Uspenskaja 1956, 1962, and Saidova 1961), of Penjikent (studied by Ivanova 1956). The dialects of upper Zarafshan in Matcha and Falghar have specific features and form a particular group, as shown by Xromov's (1958b, 1959, 1962, 1963, 1965) and Kerimova's (1963) work. Other data gathered by Kerimova on the Falghar and also the Penjikent dialect are still waiting for publication.

The southwestern dialects have not as yet been as systematically investigated as the northwestern ones. Nevertheless information about them is not scanty. The most northern one, in Karategin, northwest of the Pamir, was explored by Rozenfel'd (1950, 1960). South of this region in the Kulab district there are several different dialects, which were studied by Sokolova (1951a, et al. 1952), Jablonskaja (1954), Bogorad (1956), Jalolov (1961b, 1967), and especially Nemenova (1954a and b, 1956). Information on the Badakhshan dialects was provided by Boldyrev (1948), Bogorad (1963), and Rozenfel'd (1963b), who also published notes on the dialect of the Wanch valley (1952, 1956b, 1962a, 1963a, 1964). The dialect of Darvaz (in the most northern part of the Panj valley and neighboring regions) has very peculiar features and is probably to be classified apart; it was studied by Kisljakov (1936), Vohidov (1954), Rozenfel'd (1956a, 1962b), and Nemenova (1963). Other materials collected by Nemenova on this dialect and by Paxalina on the Badakhshan dialect have not yet been published. A southern dialect spoken by displaced people in Uzbekistan has been studied by Murvatov (1967). Bogoljubov's article (1962) and Rozenfel'd's studies (1966, 1967) deal with grammatical features peculiar to southwestern dialects. Finally we must also mention jargons with Tajik grammar discovered and described by Oranskij (1961, 1964).

The question of the classification of Tajik dialects has been discussed several times (Rozenfel'd 1951, Melex 1960, Rastorgueva 1963a). A detailed classification, based on all the data made available in the last fifteen years, with both structural and historical considerations, is proposed in Rastorgueva's recent book (1964b). An interesting question is that of the contact and interaction of Tajik and Uzbek. Some features of northwestern Tajik manifest a certain convergence with the Turkish linguistic type. The most northern dialects, in regions where bilingualism is massive, are undoubtedly more or less turkicized in their structure. This phenomenon has been discussed by Borovkov (1952, 1953), Livšic (1954), Rastorgueva (1951, and with collaborators 1964), and Doerfer (1967:52–63).

Tajik dialects, at least the northwestern ones, and the literary language, which is founded on moderate forms of northwestern spoken Tajik, possess common characteristic features on the basis of which they can be contrasted with other forms of Persian, including Kabuli. Some of these dialectal differences were studied by Cejpek (1956), Rozenfel'd (1961), and Lorenz (1964). A more comprehensive comparison with the standard Persian of Iran and Kabuli, bearing on phonology, grammar, and vocabulary, was made by Lazard (1957b) and Wei (1962).

CLASSICAL PERSIAN

Linguistic studies on classical Persian are comparatively few. The reason for this may be in part that in this field linguistic work is often dependent upon long preliminary and sometimes difficult philological work. When there are more critical editions of the texts, their linguistic investigation will be easier and lead to more assured results. Classical Persian is generally considered to be a rather rigidly fixed literary language. Actually, careful consideration of well-established texts shows that it is not so uniform as usually assumed and certain lines of evolution can even now be perceived more or less clearly. This fact was especially brought to light and usefully illustrated by Bahâr (1947), an Iranian poet and scholar, by no means a linguist, but a fine connoisseur of his language; his book is a pioneer work for the study of the internal history of Persian. Future study must of course be based on an attentive examination of dated texts. The oldest prose texts, which are especially interesting for their age and for their many particularities, were explored by Lazard (1963), whose book is a large collection of data with discussions on phonetic, morphological, and syntactic points. A few other works register the specific features of individual literary texts (Fozilov 1954; L.P. Smirnova 1959, 1963; Sultanov 1957, 1958; Šafii 1964; Behbudī 1964; Šajii 1966). Moreover most of the good editions of old texts published in Iran comprise more or less copious linguistic remarks which provide useful data.

Another possible approach was to deal with individual grammatical points in one or several texts: verb (Boldyrev 1946, L.P. Smirnova 1957, Kozlov 1959, Jūrayev 1962, Siyoyev 1961, Davlatova 1964); prepositions (L. P. Smirnova 1958b, Garipova 1958, Shariʿat-Razavi 1963); postposition *râ* (Ovčinnikova 1956a and b, Tušišvili 1960, Dabirinegead 1968); and other points (Xubua 1950, Sultanov 1953, Kapranov 1962). As a rule these studies are synchronic and limited to statements of facts. Diachronic considerations are found only in a few articles (Kuryłowicz 1953 on the evolution of the verbal system, Telegdi 1955 on verbal locutions, Lazard 1969 on the change of function of the postposition *râ* from early New Persian to the contemporary language, with quantitative data).

We have already mentioned general Persian dictionaries concerning the classical as well as the modern lexicon, especially Dehxodâ's and Moin's. Another classical dictionary is in preparation in Tajikistan (see Rastorgueva 1963b:62). A dictionary of rare words with examples from classical literature is in progress in Iran (Adib-e Ṭusi 1966). There has been a revival of interest in traditional dictionaries; several of the most important ones have been recently published in Iran. But this is only a preliminary task for a systematic investigation of the lexicon of the classical language. Another and more important one is the lexicological exploration of the texts. Though Wolff's glossary of Ferdowsi's epics (1935) has hitherto remained the only complete concordance of a literary text, several collections of words and phrases used by individual authors have been compiled in Iran. On the other hand, a methodical exploration of selected texts has been initiated in Tehran by the Iranian Culture Foundation for a future historical dictionary, a work which is urgently needed. A different and promising kind of research is the establishment of concordances for linguistic statistics as undertaken by Osmanov (1963).

FORMATION OF THE LANGUAGE; DIALECTAL AND FOREIGN CONTRIBUTIONS

As in the case of any national language, the question of the formation of the Persian language is not a simple one. How did it reach the status of a literary language? How did it impose itself and progressively gain ground against the use of Arabic? What spoken dialects were the basis of this literary language or influenced its development? These problems have still hardly been investigated and some of them have only recently been formulated. Boldyrev (1955, 1956) collected and commented on interesting testimony on the use of literary and scientific Persian and its competition with Arabic in the early centuries. Discussions took place on the meaning of the name *dari*, which undoubtedly denoted literary Persian in the tenth and eleventh centuries, but the exact value of which is not quite clear (Bertel's 1948, 1950; Pejsikov 1960a; Semenov 1960; Kozlov 1964; Frye 1963). Such matters would be to a certain extent clarified by a better knowledge of past Persian dialectal varieties. On this point some clues may be found in old monuments of classical Persian (Lazard 1961a and b) and very interesting data are provided by 'marginal' documents, those not belonging to the main stream of Persian literature. In this respect the most important source is Judeo-Persian literature, written in Hebrew script and exhibiting many peculiar features. It was actively investigated towards the end of the last century and the beginning of the present one, and then these studies came to a standstill. They have been recently resumed. The discovery of new inscriptions contributed to the revival of interest in manuscript documents; publication of texts and linguistic observations are in progress (Sundermann 1966; Asmussen 1965–66; MacKenzie 1966, 1968; Paper 1965–68, 1967a and b), and it is possible to delineate some features of Judeo-Persian dialectology (Lazard 1968). Information on non-standard forms of Persian in the past may also be extracted from transcriptions of Persian texts in Latin script (Bodrogligeti 1961), Zoroastrian writings in Persian (Amouzgar-Yeganeh 1968) and other documents (Navvâbi 1957, Iwamura 1961, Tagirdžanov 1962, MacKenzie 1959). Historical dialectology must of course go hand in hand with the investigation of modern dialects, which is a great help in the interpretation of old data, as shown for instance by Xromov's article (1958a).

On the origins of New Persian and contributions of different Iranian languages to its formation no major work has been done recently, but a number of new etymologies and remarks on historical phonology have been proposed in connection with studies on Old Iranian and Middle Iranian languages. A non-Persian, especially Parthian or Sogdian, origin was pointed out for Persian words (e.g. Benveniste 1963, Livšic 1957, Xromov 1965). Etymologies are scattered in many articles by Iranists on various subjects. A new etymological dictionary of New Persian is now an urgent need. On a quite different line of research we must mention Skalmowski's attempt to apply the methods of communication theory to some aspects of the evolution of the language from Old Persian to New Persian (1961b, 1962, after which Herdan 1964:177–82).

Foreign contribution to the Persian lexicon is an immense question, especially because of the Arabic vocabulary, which in Persian plays very much the same role as Latin vocabulary in English. This problem has been approached from different points of view in a few recent works. Arabic words in Ferdowsi's 'Book of Kings' attracted the attention of scholars (Humbert 1953, Tušišvili 1954) because of their small number, the question being whether this feature is linguistic or stylistic. Koppe (1959–60) made a quantitative and semantic study of Arabic words in the language of a modern writer. Articles by Skalmowski (1961a) and Lazard (1965), on classical and early Persian, respectively, are purely statistical evaluations of the Arabic vocabulary and were used by Herdan (1964:142–3, 1966:329–31). Rubinčik (1965) studied phonetic modifications undergone by Arabic loanwords. For Arabic words in Tajik, see Maḥfūẓ (1964). As for Turkish and Mongolian elements, in addition to older notes (Köprülü 1940–42, Zarinezad 1962), an extensive inventory, with detailed discussions, by Doerfer (1959, 1963–67, also 1967) is in progress.

In modern times a large number of words have been borrowed from western languages (see Dutt 1955–56, Razi 1960, Jazayery 1966), mainly French and also English in Iran, English in Afghanistan, Russian in Tajikistan. This question has been touched on only in a few works (Giese 1956 on French words in Persian of Iran; Kalontarov 1955, Avaliani 1959 on Russian words in Tajik). But it is an important problem and it certainly deserves careful study, though modern borrowing is a difficult and fluid matter, since new loanwords appear practically every day and many are dropped after a short time.

BIBLIOGRAPHY

This bibliography is conceived as large, but not exhaustive. It covers the last twenty years, and includes all important works known to the author, and many minor contributions. As a rule, abstracts of dissertations the contents of which have been published elsewhere, abstracts of communications at conferences, comparatively unimportant articles on minute points of Tajik, articles published in Persia or elsewhere which are more stylistic than linguistic or of a purely factual character, and articles dealing with the etymology or meaning of individual words have been excluded. For Soviet works, an extensive bibliography down to 1961 may be found in Rastorgueva 1962 and Rastorgueva and Paxalina 1962; see also Oranskij 1960, Sverčevskaja 1967:225–32. All items figuring in the following bibliography have been mentioned in the preceding survey.

For the transcription of Persian, the simplified system proposed by the First International Congress of Iranology (Tehran, August-September 1966) has been used. The transcription of Tajik conforms to that of Persian: *j* = [dž] and *y* = [i̯] as in Persian (and unlike Russian, where *j* = [i̯], *y* = [ï]). For Tajik authors whose name has a double form, a Tajik and a Russian one (e.g. Jalolov/Džalalov), all items are mentioned under the Tajik form, with a cross reference, if necessary, under the Russian one. The same principle has been followed for works in Persian with a title page in English or French; a systematic transcription of the author's name and the title in Persian has been preferred to the author or editor's transcription or translation.

ABDUSAMATÅV, M. 1964. Håzirgi zamån fårs tilidagi 'az' komakčisi haqida. NTTašU 229.46–55.

ADELUNG, N.S. 1959. Fonetičeskij stroj bogustanskogo govora tadžikskogo jazyka. IzvANTadž 1 (19) 35–44.

ADIB-E TUSI. 1962. Loqât-e nowqâni (mašhadi). RFLTiz 14.1–41.

——. 1966. Farhang-e loqât-e adabi, Baxš-e noxost. Tabriz.

AFGHÂNINAWÊS, ABDOLLÂH. 1961. Loghât-e âmiâna-ye fârsi-e Afghânestân. Kâbol.

AFŠÂR, IRAJ. 1953. Ketâbšenâsi-e dastur-e zabân-e fârsi. FIZ 2.19–44.

——. 1959. Ketâbšenâsi-e farhanghâ-ye fârsi-orupâi. Loqatnâme, by Dehxodâ, Introduction, 373–78. Tehrân, Dânešgâh.

Ahmadova, Ū. [Axmedova, U.]. 1958. Glagol'nye formy s vspomogatel'nym glagolom *istodan*. IzvANTadž 1.93–102.

——. 1960. Šaklhoi fe'lī bo yoridihandai *istodan* dar asarhoi S. Aynī. IzvANTadž 1/21.131–40.

Əlizadə, Həsən [Alizade, G.A.]. 1953. O prošedšem vremeni glagola v sovremennom literaturnom persidskom jazyke. TAzU, serija vostokovedenija, vyp. 1. [In Azerbaijani].

——. 1956. Vyraženie glagola buduščego vremeni v persidskom jazyke. UZAzU no. 11.

——. 1964. Müasir fars dilinda fe'l sistemi (Xabar formasynyn zamanlary). UZAzU 1.3–25.

Amouzgar-Yeganeh, Jaleh. 1968. Pahlavi et persan. Etudes sur la langue et la littérature mazdéennes en persan. Unpublished Paris dissertation.

Andreev, M.S. 1930. Kratkij obzor nekotoryx osobennostej tadžikskix govorov. Stalinabad-Taškent.

Arends, A.K. 1941. Kratkij sintaksis sovremennogo persidskogo literaturnogo jazyka. Moskva-Leningrad, Izd. AN SSSR.

Arzumanjan, O.A. 1965. O strukturno-semantičeskix tipax voprositel'nyx predloženij v persidskom jazyke. IzvANArm 8.81–92.

——. 1966. Nekotorye itogi eksperimental'nogo issledovanija voprositel'nogo predloženija v persidskom jazyke. Iranskaja filologija, materialy IV vsesojuznoj meživuzovskoj naučnoj konferencii po iranskoj filologii, 60–77. Taškent, Izd. 'FAN' UzSSR.

Asmussen, Jes P. 1965–66. Judaeo-Persica. AcOr 28.245–61; 29.49–60, 247–51; 30. 15–24.

Atai, P. 1964. A contrastive study of English and Persian question signals. University of Michigan dissertation. Ann Arbor, University Microfilms.

Avaliani, Ju.A. 1959. Nekotorye voprosy struktury russkix i internacional'nyx slov v tadžikskom jazyke. KSUzbU, kafedra russkogo jazykoznanija. Samarkand.

Axmedova, U. see Ahmadova, Ū.

Azimâ, Ali-Akbar. Zabânšenâsi-e omumi. Esfahân.

Baghaï, Nasser see Baqâi, Nâser.

Bahâr, Mohammad Taqi. 1947. Sabkšenâsi yâ târix-e tatavvor-e nasr-e fârsi. 3 volumes. Tehrân.

Baqâi, Nâser [Baghaï, Nasser]. 1961. Le persan parlé à Kerman. Unpublished Paris dissertation.

——. 1963–67. Fârsi-e Kermân. RFLTiz 15.15–40, 224–44; 16.46–64, 225–46, 345–60, 507–16; 17.398–402; 18.175–80, 441–58; 19.84–8, 239–46 [still incomplete].

Bausani, Alessandro. 1947. Di una possibile origine dell'accentuazione sull'ultima sillaba in persiano moderno. Oriente moderno 27.123–30.

BEHBUDĪ, N. [BEGBUDI, N. M.]. 1961. Kratkie svedenija o sintaksise samarkandskogo govora tadžikskogo jazyka. Osobennosti postroenija prostogo predloženija, porjadok slov v prostom predloženii. IzvANTadž 3/26.3–20.

——. 1964. Mulohizaho oid ba zaboni osori Rūdakī. Ba'ze mas'alahoi zabonšinosii tojik, ed. by B. N. Niyozmuhammadov, 116–38. Dušanbe, Izd. AN Tadž. SSR.

BEHRUZI KÂZERUNI, A. Loqât-e mahalli-e Fârs. [See Jamâlzâde 1963:64].

BENVENISTE, EMILE. 1963. Le sens du mot persan *shâdurvân*. Mélanges d'orientalisme offerts à Henri Massé, 31–7. Téhéran, Imprimerie de l'Université.

BERTEL'S, E. Ė. 1948. Persidskij-tadžikskij-dari. Izvestija Tadžikskogo filiala Akademii nauk SSSR 12.

——. 1950. Persidskij-dari-tadžikskij. SovEtn 4.55–66.

BIRNBAUM, S. A. 1950. The verb in the Bukharic Language of Samarkand. ArchL 2.60–73, 158–76.

BLOCHMAN, H. 1868. Contributions to Persian lexicography. JASB 37.1–72.

BODROGLIGETI, A. 1961. The Persian translation of the Koran in Latin letters. AOH 13.261–76.

BOGDANOV, L. 1930 [1931]. Stray notes on Kābulī Persian. JASB N.S. 26.1–123.

BOGOLJUBOV, M. N. 1962. Predloženija s arxaičnym pričastiem v govorax tadžikskogo jazyka. UZLU 306.3–5.

BOGORAD, JU. I. 1956. Rogskie govory tadžikskogo jazyka. TIJa 6.133–95.

——. 1963. Goronskij govor tadžikskogo jazyka. Iranskij sbornik k semidesjatipjatiletiju professora I. I. Zarubina, 44–59. Moskva, Izd. vostočnoj literatury.

BOLDYREV, A. N. 1946. Perfekt II v novopersidskom literaturnom jazyke. IzvAN 5.490–6.

——. 1948. Badaxšanskij fol'klor. Sovetskoe vostokovedenie 5.275–94.

——. 1955. Iz istorii razvitija persidskogo literaturnogo jazyka. VJa 5.78–92.

——. 1956. Nekotorye voprosy stanovlenija i razvitija pis'mennyx jazykov v uslovijax feodal'nogo obščestva. VJa 4.31–7.

BONELLI, L. 1929. Appunti fonetici sul volgare persiano di Kābul. Annali, Reale Istituto Orientale di Napoli 1.5–14.

——. 1930. Ancora del volgare persiano di Kābul. Appunti grammaticali. Annali, Reale Istituto Orientale di Napoli 2.24–46, 3.50–62.

——. 1936. Ancora del volgare persiano di Kābul. Appunti lessicali. Annali, Reale Istituto Orientale di Napoli 8.43–53.

BOROVKOV, A. K. 1952. Tadžiksko-uzbekskoe dvujazyčie i vopros o vzaimovlijanii tadžikskogo i uzbekskogo jazykov. UZIV 4.165–200.

——. 1953. Filologičeskie zametki. Sbornik statej ... posvjaščennyj 80-letiju so dnja roždenija A. A. Semenova. Stalinabad.

BOYLE, J. A. 1952a. The changes of meaning undergone by certain Persian nomina agentis in *-tār* (*-dār*). JRAS 13–19.

——. 1952b. Notes on the colloquial language of Persia as recorded in certain recent writings. BSOAS 14.451–62.

Boyle, J. A. 1966. A grammar of modern Persian. (Porta linguarum orientalium, neue Serie, 9). Wiesbaden.

Cejpek, J. 1956. Die verbale Periphrase als ein wichtiges Unterscheidungsmerkmal zwischen Neupersisch und Tağikisch. AO 24.171–82.

Dabirinegead, Badiollah. 1968. Les emplois de la postposition 'râ' dans le 'Golestân' de Sa'di. Unpublished Paris dissertation.

Darmesteter, James. 1883. Etudes iraniennes. 2 volumes. Paris, Vieweg.

Davlatova, M. 1964. Serma'noii fe'lhoi sodda dar 'Zayn-ul-axbor'-i Gardizī. Ba'zi mas'alahoi zabonšinosii tojik, ed. by Niyozmuhammadov, 139–46. Dušanbe, Izd. AN Tadž. SSR.

de Dieu, Ludovicus. 1639. Rudimenta linguae persicae. Lugduni Batavorum, ex officina Elseviriana.

Dehxodâ, Ali-Akbar. 1946–68. Loqatnâme. [French title: Loghat-Nama (Dictionnaire encyclopédique) fondé par Alî Akbar Dehkhodâ]. Publication in progress; 131 fascicles published since 1946. Tehrân, Dânešgâh.

de Lagarde, Paul. 1884. Persische Studien. (Abhandlungen der königlichen Gesellschaft der Wissenschaften zu Göttingen 31). Göttingen, Dieterich.

Desmaisons, Jean-Jacques-Pierre. 1908–14. Dictionnaire persan-fançais. 4 volumes. Rome, Imprimerie polyglotte vaticane.

Doerfer, Gerhard. 1959. Prolegomena zu einer Untersuchung der altaischen Lehnwörter im Neupersischen. CAJ 5.1–26.

——. 1963–67. Türkische und mongolische Elemente im Neupersischen. 3 volumes published. Wiesbaden, Steiner.

——. 1967. Türkische Lehnwörter im Tadzhikischen. (Abhandlungen für die Kunde Morgenlandes, 37.3). Wiesbaden, Steiner.

Dorofeeva, L. N. 1959. O jazyke farsi Afghanistana. KSIV 33.114–27.

——. 1960. Jazyk farsi-kabuli. (Jazyki zarubežnogo vostoka i Afriki). Moskva, Izdatel'stvo vostočnoj literatury.

Dowlatâbâdi, Aziz. 1954. Târix-e tahavvol-e nasr-e fârsi-e moâser. Tabriz.

Dutt, C. 1955–56. Loan-words in Persian. IL 17.114–20.

Džalalov, O. see Jalolov, O.

Džuraev, R. see Jūrayev, R.

Ėdel'man, D. I. 1955. Predikativnye sočetanija s pričastijami na *-gī* i na *-ī* v sovremennom literaturnom tadžikskom jazyke. IzvANTadž 7.67–74.

Efimov, V. A. 1964. Ličnye glagol'nye formy v jakaulangskom dialekte xazara. Indijskaja i iranskaja filologija, 17–39. Moskva, Izd. 'Nauka'.

——. 1965. Jazyk afganskix xazara, jakaulangskij dialekt. (Jazyki zarubežnogo vostoka i Afriki). Moskva, Izd. 'Nauka'.

Ešniyozov, M. 1959. Ba'ze qaydho doir ba leksikai zaboni tojikoni Xardurī. IzvANTadž 1/19.69–79.

Extiâr, Mansur. 1964–65. Šive-ye barresi-e guyešhâ. RFLTan 12.170–215, 13.1–73.

FARHÂDI, ABD-UL-GHAFÛR. 1955. Le persan parlé en Afghanistan. Grammaire du kâboli. Paris, Klincksieck.

——. 1959. Quelques formes démonstratives et interrogatives des parlers persans de l'Afghanistan. Akten des vierundzwanzigsten internationalen Orientalisten-Kongress, 507–09. Wiesbaden, Deutsche morgenländische Gesellschaft.

FAZYLOV, M. F. see Fozilov, M.

FERGUSON C. A. 1957. Word stress in Persian. Lg 33.123–35.

FICHTNER, E. 1965a. Zur statistischen Erfassung des persischen Prosarythmus. WZUB 14.587–92.

——. 1965b. Über sprachliche Form und Rhythmik mittel- und neupersischer Sprüche. MIO 11.55–70.

FOZILOV, M. [FAZYLOV, M. F.]. 1954. Nekotorye osobennosti tadžikskogo literaturnogo jazyka ėpoxi Samanidov (po odnoj starinnoj rukopisi 'Ta'rixi Tabari Bal'ami'). TTadžII 17.173–83.

——. 1958. Izobrazitel'nye slova v tadžikskom jazyke. Stalinabad, Izd. AN Tadž. SSR.

——. 1963–64. Farhangi iborahoi rextai zaboni hozirai tojik (farhangi frazeologī). 2 vols. Dušanbe, Našriyoti davlatii Tojikiston.

FRYE, RICHARD N. 1963. The problem of New Persian and 'Dari'. Indo-Iranica 16.30–2.

GAPRINDAŠVILI, Š. G., and DŽ. Š. GIUNAŠVILI. 1964. Fonetika persidskogo jazyka, I: Zvukovoj sostav. Tbilisi, Izd. 'Mecniereba'.

GARIPOVA, N. D. 1958. Iz istorii razvitija grammatičeskoj kategorii predloga (na materiale iranskix jazykov). UZBašU vyp. 6, serija filologičeskaja, no. 5.

GHAFOROV, R. 1962. Kalimahoi guftugūī-xalqī dar romani Rahim Jalil 'Odamoni jovid'. IzvANTadž 3/30.67–75.

GIESE, W. 1956. Französische Lehnwörter im modernen Persischen. ZFSL 67.69–77.

GIUNAŠVILI, DŽ. Š. 1957a. Slovoobrazovatel'naja funkcija pričastija nastojaščego vremeni na *-ande* v persidskom literaturnom jazyke. TSrAzU 105.39–41.

——. 1957b. Zametki o morfologičeskoj sostave infinitiva v persidskom jazyke. TSrAzU 105.45–9.

——. 1958. Tendencija fonetičeskogo uproščenija i nekotorye voprosy slovoobrazovatel'nogo analiza v persidskom jazyke. Sbornik naučnyx trudov aspirantov Sredne-Aziatskogo gosudarstvennogo universiteta, vyp. 4.299–309. Taškent.

——. 1960a. Glagol'nyj komponent determinativnyx imennyx obrazovanij persidskogo literaturnogo jazyka. TIJaGruz, serija vostočnyx jazykov, 3.225–46.

——. 1960b. K voprosu o proiznošenii *gh*/*q* v sovremennom persidskom jazyke. TTbilU 91.63–76.

——. 1965. Sistema fonem persidskogo jazyka. TTbilU 116.87–141.

GRIERSON, GEORGE A. 1921. Linguistic survey of India. Vol. 10. Calcutta.

GRJUNBERG, A. L. 1963. Seistanskij dialekt v Seraxse. KSINA 67.76–86.

HABIBOLLAHI, MOHAMMAD. 1966. Le persan parlé à Meched. Unpublished Paris dissertation.

HAÏM, S. see Hayyim, Soleymân.

HAMP, E.P. 1958. Stress continuity in Iranian. JAOS 78.115–18.

HAMROQULOV, X. 1958. Pešoyand va pasoyandhoi ševai Darband (az gurūhi ševai Boysun). Očerkho oid ba filologiyai tojik, majmūai ilmii aspirantho, jild 4.136–47. Stalinobod.

——. 1961a. Xususiyathoi fonetiki gurūhi ševahoi Boysun. IzvANTadž 3/26.82–96.

——. 1961b. Xuxusiyathoi morfologii gurūhi ševai Boysun. IzvANTadž 4/27.3–19.

——. 1963. Ševahoi tojikoni rayoni Boysun. Dušanbe.

HATƏMI, N. Z. [XATEMI, N. Z.]. 1955. Nekotorye zametki o fonetike sovremennogo persidskogo jazyka. UZAzU 11. [In Azerbaijani].

——. 1964. Fars dilində çoxmə'naly sözlər. UZAzU 1.27–38.

——. 1965. Fars danyšyg dili. Baky, Azərbajǰan dəvlət tədris-pedagoži ədəbijjaty nəšrijjaty.

HAYYIM, SOLEYMÂN [HAÏM, S.]. 1934–35. New Persian-English dictionary. 2 volumes. Tehran, Beroukhim.

——. 1953. The one-volume Persian-English dictionary. Tehran, Beroukhim.

——. 1963. The shorter Persian-English dictionary. 3rd ed. Tehran, Beroukhim.

HENNING, WALTER B. 1939. Sogdian loan words in New Persian. BSOAS 10.93–106.

HERDAN, GUSTAV. 1964. Quantitative linguistics. London, Butterworths.

——. 1966. Haeckels Biogenetisches Grundgesetz in der Sprachwissenschaft. ZPhon 19.321–38.

HINCHA, G. 1961. Beiträge zu einer Morphemlehre des Neupersischen. Islam 37. 136–201.

HINZ, WALTER. 1961. Beiträge zur Lexicographie der neu-persischen Volks- und Umgangsprache. WZKM 57.118–49.

HODGE, C.T. 1956. Spoken Persian. Washington, Department of State, Foreign Service Institute. [Mimeographed.]

——. 1957. Some aspects of Persian style. Lg 33.355–69.

HOMÂI, JALÂLADDIN. 1959. Dastur-e zabân-e fârsi. Loqatnâme, by Dehxodâ, Introduction, 110–47. Tehrân, Dânešgâh.

HOMÂYUNFARROX, ABDORRAHIM. 1960. Dastur-e jâme'-e zabân-e fârsi. Tehrân, Ali Akbar Elmi.

HORN, PAUL. 1893. Grundriss der neupersischen Etymologie. (Sammlung indogermanischer Wörterbücher, 4.) Strassburg, Trübner.

——. 1895–1901. Neupersische Schriftsprache. Grundriss der iranischen Philologie, ed. by W. Geiger and E. Kuhn, vol. 1, part 2, 1–200. Strassburg, Trübner.

HÜBSCHMANN, H. 1895. Persische Studien. Strassburg, Trübner.

HUMBERT, PAUL. 1953. Observations sur le vocabulaire arabe du Châhnâmeh. (Mémoires de l'Université de Neuchatel, 22.) Neuchatel, Université.

HUSEYNOV, X. 1960. Jumlai murakkabi tobe' bo jumlai payravi zamon dar zaboni adabii tojik. Dušanbe, Našriyyoti Akademiyai fanhoi RSS Tojikiston.

ISMATULLAEV, M. F. 1955. Prjamoe dopolnenie v sovremennom tadžikskom jazyke. Stalinabad.

IVANOVA, S. JU. 1956. Materialy po pendžikentskomu govoru tadžikskogo jazyka. TIJa 6.281–342.

IVANOW, W. 1928 [1929]. Persian as spoken in Birjand. JASB N.S. 24.235–351.

——. 1931. Notes on the phonology of colloquial Persian. Islamica 4.576–95.

IWAMURA, SHINOBU. 1961. The Zirni manuscript: A Persian-Mongolian glossary and grammar. (Results of the Kyoto University expeditions to the Karakoram and the Hindukush, 1955, 6.) Kyoto.

JABLONSKAJA, V. 1954. Osobennosti Daštidžumskogo govora tadžikskogo jazyka. UZStalPI, serija filologičeskaja, t. 4. Stalinabad.

JALOLOV, O. J. [DŽALALOV, O.]. 1949. Otnošenie čustskogo dialekta k tadžikskomu literaturnomu jazyku. (AN SSSR, Tadžikskij filial, Institut istorii, jazyka i literatury, Trudy 25.) Stalinabad.

——. 1961a. Kategoriyai jam' va ba'ze mas'alahoi zaboni hozirai tojik. Stalinobod.

——. 1961b. Ma'lumoti muxtasar dar borai ševahoi rayoni Yovon. IzvANTadž 3/26.75–81.

——. 1967. Gurūhi ševahoi tojikoni rayoni Yovon. Dušanbe, Našriyoti 'Doniš'.

JAMÂLZÂDE, MOHAMMAD ALI. 1962. Farhang-e loqât-e âmiâne. (Entešârât-e Farhang-e Irânzamin, 7.) Tehrân.

——. 1963. Zabân-e avâmâne. FIZ 11.35–69.

JAZAYERY, M. A. 1966. Western influence in contemporary Persian: a general view. BSOAS 29.79–96.

JENSEN, HANS. 1931. Neupersische Grammatik, mit Berücksichtigung der historischen Entwicklung. (Indogermanische Bibliothek, Erste Abt., 1. Reihe, 22. Bd.) Heidelberg, Carl Winter.

JUNKER, HEINRICH, and BOZORG ALAVI. 1965. Persisch-deutsches Wörterbuch. Leipzig, Verlag Enzyklopädie.

JŪRAYEV, R. [DŽURAEV, R.]. 1962. Iz istorii vremen i modal'nyx značenii glagol'nyx form tadžikskogo i persidskogo jazykov (na materiale sočinenija 'Asrār-i tavḥīd'). Dušanbe.

——. 1967. Bandakjonišinho dar lahjahoi arabhoi tojikzabon. IzvANTadž 3/49.54–60.

KALONTAROV, JA. I. 1955. Obogaščenie tadžikskoj leksiki pod vlijaniem russkogo jazyka. IzvANTadž 7.

KAMENSKIJ, N. S. 1945. O propuske podležaščego v pridatočnom predloženii celi v persidskom jazyke. UZVIIJa t. 1, vyp. 2.

——. 1946. O podležaščem-nominativnoj gruppe slov (materialy po sintaksisu sovremennogo persidskogo voennogo jazyka). Trudy Moskovskogo instituta vostokovedenija, vyp. 3.162–68.

KAPRANOV, V. A. 1962. 'Imale' i imalirovannye formy v jazyke tadžikskoj (farsi) klassičeskoj literatury. IzvANTadž 3/30.3–16.

KERIMOVA, A. A. 1959. Govor tadžikov Buxary. Moskva, Izd. vostočnoj literatury.

——. 1963. Osobennosti govora kišlaka Rarza. Iranskij sbornik k semidesjatipjatiletiju professora I. I. Zarubina, 22–44. Moskva, Izd. vostočnoj literatury.

——. 1964. Ob odnoj opredelitel'noj konstrukcii v tadžikskom jazyke. Indijskaja i iranskaja filologija, 279–81. Moskva, Izd. 'Nauka'.

KEŠÂVARZ, KARIM. 1962. Možare' va mâzi-e malmus. Rahnemâ-ye ketâb 5.687–94. Tehrân.

KISLJAKOV, N. A. 1936. Opisanie govora tadžikov Vaxio-Bolo. Trudy Tadžikistanskoj bazy AN SSSR, t. 3, Lingvistika, 29–37.

KOPPE, R. 1959–60. Statistik und Semantik der arabischen Lehnwörter in der Sprache 'Alawi's. WZUB 9.585–619.

KÖPRÜLÜ, M. F. 1940–42. Yeni fârisîde türk unsurları. Türkiyet mecmuası 7–8.1–16.

KOSIMOV, V. 1966. Ba'ze xususiyathoi fonetikii gurūhi ševahoi Foriš. IzvANTadž 1/43.49–75.

KOSIMOVA, M. 1962. Jumlai payravi šartī dar zaboni adabii tojik. Dušanbe.

KOZLOV, G. I. 1959. Glagol'nyj suffiks *-ē* (*ī*) po tekstam 'Istorii Bejhaki'. KSIV 36.61–76.

——. 1964. Iz istorii jazyka dari. KSINA 65 (Sbornik pamjati E. Ė. Bertel'sa) 84–9.

KRÁMSKÝ, J. 1939. A study in the phonology of modern Persian. AO 11.66–83.

——. 1947. A phonological analysis of Persian monosyllables. AO 16.103–34.

——. 1966. Some remarks on the problem of quantity of vowel phonemes in modern Persian. AO 34.215–20.

KURYŁOWICZ, JERZY. 1953. Aspect et temps dans l'histoire du persan. RO 16.531–42.

KUXTIN, V. G. 1961. Vremennye sojuzy v sovremennom persidskom jazyke. KSINA 40.42–63.

LAZARD, GILBERT. 1957a. Grammaire du persan contemporain. Paris, Klincksieck.

——. 1957b. Caractères distinctifs de la langue tadjik. BSL t. 52, fasc. 1.117–86.

——. 1961a. Dialectologie de la langue persane d'après les textes des Xme et XIme siècles ap. J.-C. RFLTiz 13.241–58. [With Persian translation.]

——. 1961b. Obščij jazyk iranskix zemel' i ego dialekty po tekstam X-XI vv. n. ė. NAA 4.176–81. [Russian translation of the preceding article.]

——. 1963. La langue des plus anciens monuments de la prose persane. (Etudes linguistiques, 2.) Paris, Klincksieck.

——. 1965. Les emprunts arabes dans la prose persane du Xe au XIIe siècle: aperçu statistique. RENLO 2.53–67.

——. 1966. L'enclitique nominal *-i* en persan: un ou deux morphèmes? BSL t. 61, fasc. 1.249–64.

LAZARD, GILBERT. 1968. La dialectologie du judéo-persan. Studies in Bibliography and Booklore, 8.77–98. Cincinnati.

——. 1970. Etude quantitative de l'évolution d'un morphème: l'enclitique *râ* en persan. Mélanges Marcel Cohen. La Haye-Paris, Mouton.

LENTZ, WOLFGANG. 1926. Die nordiranischen Elemente in der neupersischen Literatursprache bei Firdosi. ZII 4.251–316.

——. 1958. Das Neupersische. Handbuch der Orientalistik, ed. by B. Spuler, Erste Abt., Vierter Bd., Erster Abschnitt, Linguistik, 179–221. Leiden-Köln, Brill.

LIGETI, L. 1964. Mongol'skie elementy v dialektax xazara v Afganistane. KSINA 83.5–22.

LINGENFELDER, HILTRUDE. 1957. Beiträge zur Erforschung des neupersischen Verbums. Hamburg dissertation.

LIVŠIC, V. A. 1954. O vnutrennyx zakonax razvitija tadžikskogo jazyka. IzvANTadž 5.99–102.

——. 1957. Sogdijskie slova v tadžikskom jazyke. IzvANTadž 12.31–43.

LORENZ, MANFRED. 1964. Die partizipialen Wendungen — ein Unterscheidungsmerkmal des Tağikischen gegenüber dem Persischen. MIO 1.133–9.

LORIMER, D. L. R. 1922. The phonology of the Bakhtiari, Badakhshani and Madaglashti dialects of modern Persian. (Prize publication fund, 6.) London, Royal Asiatic Society.

LUCIDI, M. 1951. L'accento nel persiano moderno. RL 2.108–40.

MACHALSKI, FRANCISZEK. 1960. Sur la productivité des suffixes déverbatifs des adjectifs en persan moderne. FO 2.251–8.

MACKENZIE, D. N. 1959. The language of the Medians. BSOAS 22.354–5.

——. 1966. Ad *Judaeo-Persica II* Hafniensia. JRAS 69.

——. 1968. An early Jewish-Persian argument. BSOAS 31.249–69.

MAḤFŪẒ, H. ʿA. 1964. Āṯār al-lugha al-ʿarabiyya fī al-lugha al-tājīkiyya. MMII 11. 158–81.

MAHMUDOV, H. Š. [MAXMUDOV, G. Š.]. 1955. K postanovke voprosa o glagol'nom upravlenii v sovremennom persidskom literaturnom jazyke. UZAzU 12.87–96.

——. 1956. O klassifikacii glagolov v sovremennom persidskom jazyke po kategorii perexodnosti. UZAzU 2.

——. 1964. Müasir fars dilində ǰumlənin üzvləri. UZAzU 1.67–83.

MAŠKUR, MOHAMMAD JAVÂD. 1966. Dasturnâme dar sarf-o nahv-e zabân-e pârsi. 4th ed. Tehrân, Moassase-ye matbuâti-e Šarq.

MA'SUMI, N. 1959. Očerkho oid ba inkišofi zaboni adabii tojik. Stalinobod.

MATTHEWS, W. K. 1956. The systematization of Persian phonemes. MPhon, ser. 3, ann. 34, 2–6.

MELEX, N. A. 1960. Tadžikskie govory i ix rasprostranenie. VLU 14.149–51.

——. 1964. Fonetičeskie osobennosti gidžuvanskogo govora tadžikskogo jazyka. Iranskaja filologija, Trudy naučnoj konferencii po iranskoj filologii, 27–32 Leningrad, Izd. Leningradskogo universiteta.

MILANIAN, HORMOZ. 1965. Les modalités en persan du point de vue de la linguistique générale. Unpublished Paris dissertation.

MILLER, B. V. 1953. Persidsko-russkij slovar'. 2nd ed. Moskva, Gos.izd. inostrannyx i nacional'nyx slovarej.

MOAYYAD, H. 1962. Zum Problemkreis und Stand der persischen Lexicographie. AION-O 12.1–81.

MOIN, MOHAMMAD. 1952–62. Tarh-e dastur-e zabân-e fârsi. In 5 parts. Tehrân.

——. 1963–66. Farhang-e fârsi. 4 volumes published. Tehrân, Amir-e kabir.

MONTEIL, VINCENT. 1955. Le persan contemporain: Textes et vocabulaires. Paris, Klincksieck.

MORGENSTIERNE, GEORG. 1926. Report on a linguistic mission to Afghanistan. (Instituttet for sammenlignende Kulturforskning, ser. C I, 2.) Oslo, Aschehoug.

——. 1928. Persian texts from Afghanistan. AcOr 6.309–28.

MORTAZAVI, MANUCEHR. 1956. Cand pasvand. Tabriz.

MUGINOV, A. M. 1960. Ob upotreblenii persidskogo glagola *daštän* dlja peredači značenija bližajšego buduščego vremeni. Očerki po istorii russkogo vostokovedenija, sb. 5, pamjati V. A. Žukovskogo, 136–45. Moskva, Izd. AN SSSR.

MURAV'EVA, L. N., and JU. A. RUBINČIK. 1959. Artikl' v sovremennom tadžikskom i persidskom jazykax. KSIV 29.75–87.

MURVATOV, J. 1967. Ismu sifat dar ševahoi tojikoni Andijon. IzvANTadž 3.43–53.

MUXAMEDOVA, N. A. 1962. Xarakteristika sposobov slovoobrazovanija i drugix putej obogaščenija slovarnogo sostava sovremennogo persidskogo jazyka. NTTašU 214.89–114.

——. 1964a. 'Xar' v značenii 'bolšoj' 'velikij' v sostave nekotoryx persidskix slov. NTTašU 229.18–22.

——. 1964b. Prefiksal'nye glagoly v persidskom jazyke. KSINA 72.72–91.

MUXAMMADIEV, M. 1962. Sinonimy v sovremennom tadžikskom literaturnom jazyke, Imennye častej reči. Dušanbe, Tadž.gos.univ.

NADJAMABADI, S. 1966. Der Stand der Neuschöpfung wissenschaftlicher Fachausdrücke im Neupersischen. ZDMG 116.*11*.

NAFISI, SAID, et al. 1959. Farhanghâ-ye fârsi. Loqatnâme, by Dehxodâ, Introduction, 178–379. Tehrân, Dânešgâh.

NALBANDJAN, G. M. 1961. Očerki po fonetike sovremennogo persidskogo jazyka. Erevan, Izd.AN Armjanskoj SSR. [In Armenian.]

NAVVÂBI, MÂHYÂR. 1957. Zabân-e mardom-e Tabriz dar pâyân-e sade-ye dahom va âqâz-e sade-ye yâzdahom-e hejri. RFLTiz 9.221–32, 396–426.

NEMENOVA, R. L. 1954a. Izučenie jugo-vostočnyx tadžikskix govorov. UZTadžU 2, serija guman.nauk, 181–93.

——. 1954b. Nekotorye osobennosti baldžuanskix govorov tadžikskogo jazyka. IzvANTadž 5.137–46.

——. 1954c. Predlogi v tadžikskom jazyke. (Očerki po grammatike tadžikskogo jazyka, 6.) Stalinabad, Izd. AN Tadž. SSR.

NEMENOVA, R. L. 1955. Kratkij očerk grammatika tadžikskogo jazyka. Kratkij tadžiksko-russkij slovar', by Ja. I. Kalontarov, 507–604. Moskva, Gos. izd. inostrannyx i nacional'nyx slovarej.

——. 1956. Kuljabskie govory tadžikskogo jazyka (severnaja gruppa). Stalinabad, Izd. AN Tadž. SSR.

——. 1963. Vokalizm tadžikskix govorov Darvaza. Iranskij sbornik k semidesjatipjatiletiju professora I. I. Zarubina, 60–7. Moskva, Izd. vostočnoj literatury.

NIJAZMUXAMEDOV, B. N. see Niyozmuhammadov, B.

NIKOLAEV, I., and M. NORMATOV. 1967. K voprosu o porjadke slov v prostom predloženii v russkom i tadžikskom jazykax. IzvANTadž 4.46–54.

NIYOZĪ, Š. N. 1954. Ism va sifat dar zaboni tojikī. (Očerki po grammatike tadžikskogo jazyka, 7.) Stalinabad, Izd. AN Tadž. SSR.

NIYOZMUHAMMADOV, B. [NIJAZMUXAMEDOV, B. N.]. 1951. Kanibadamskoe narečie tadžikskogo jazyka. Stalinabad.

——. 1956. Jumlahoi sodda dar zaboni tojikī (ma'lumoti muxtasar). Stalinobod.

——. 1960a. Jumlahoi sodda dar zaboni adabii hozirai tojik. Stalinobod.

——. 1960b. Očerkho oid ba ba'ze mas'alahoi zabonšinosii tojik. Stalinobod, Našriyoti davlatii adabiyoti ta'limī-pedagogii Tojikiston.

——. 1960c. O nekotoryx osobennostjax tadžikskix govorov Šaartuza. IzvANTadž 2.3–9.

——. 1964. O razvitii sovremennogo tadžikskogo literaturnogo jazyka. Voprosy razvitija literaturnyx jazykov narodov SSSR v sovetskuju èpoxu, 261–68. Alma-Ata, Izd. AN Kazax. SSR.

——, ed. 1964. Ba'ze mas'alohoi zabonšinosii tojik. Dušanbe, Izd. AN Tadž. SSR.

NIYOZMUHAMMADOV, B. N., S. N. NIYOZĪ, and Š. N. TOJIEV. 1956. Grammatikai zaboni tojikī, Qismi I: fonetika va morfologiya. Stalinobod, Našriyoti davlatii Tojikiston.

NIYOZMUHAMMADOV, B., and M. ISMATULLOYEV. 1963. Grammatikai zaboni tojikī, Sintaksis. Dušanbe, Našriyoti davlatii Tojikiston.

NYE, GERTRUDE E. 1955. The phonemes and morphemes of modern Persian: a descriptive study. University of Michigan dissertation. Ann Arbor, University microfilms.

ORANSKIJ, I. M. 1960. Vvedenie v iranskuju filologiju. Moskva, Izd. vostočnoj literatury.

——. 1961. Novye svedenija o sekretnyx jazykax (argo) Srednej Azii. KSINA 40. 62–77.

——. 1964. Novye svedenija o sekretnyx jazykax (argo) Srednej Azii, II. Materialy dlja izučenija argo ètnografičeskoj gruppy džugi (gissarskaja dolina). Iranskaja filologija, Trudy naučnoj konferencii po iranskoj filologii, 62–75. Leningrad, Izd. Leningradskogo universiteta.

ORFINSKAJA, V. K. 1945. Materialy k xarakteristike fonetičeskogo sostava tadžikskogo jazyka. Iranskie jazyki I, 87–106. Moskva, Izd. An SSSR.

OSMANOV, N. 1963. On the methods of compiling structure-frequency vocabularies as exemplified by the Rudaki vocabulary. XXVI International Congress of Orientalists, Papers presented by the USSR delegation. Moscow.

OSTOVAR, A. 1958. Voprosy proiznošenija i pravopisanija xamzy v persidskoj jazyke. IzvANUzb 2.77–83.

OVČINNIKOVA, I. K. 1956a. Funkcii posleloga *ra* v sovremennom literaturnom persidskom jazyke. TIJa 6.356–91.

——. 1956b. Ispol'zovanie posleloga *ra* v proizvedenijax tadžikskix-persidskix klassičeskix avtorov (XI-XV vv.). TIJa 6.392–408.

——. 1961. K voprosu o klassifikacii imennyx častej reči v persidskom jazyke. KSINA 30.75–85.

——. 1964. Ob upotrebitel'nosti nepravil'nyx form množestvennogo čisla v sovremennom literaturnom persidskom jazyke (opyt statističeskogo analiza). Indijskaja i iranskaja filologija, 90–103. Moskva, Izd. 'Nauka'.

PAPER, HERBERT H. 1965–68. The Vatican Judaeo-Persian Pentateuch. AcOr 28. 263–340; 29.75–181, 253–310; 31.55–113.

——. 1967a. Judaeo-Persian deverbatives in *-šn* and *-št*. IIJ 10.56–71.

——. 1967b. A note on Judeo-Persian copulas. JAOS 87.227–30.

PAXALINA, T. N. 1963. Vokalizm farsi-kabuli (po dannym eksperimenta). UZAzU 4.21–7.

——. 1964. K xarakteristike kabul'skogo prostorečija. Indijskaja i iranskaja filologija, 44–61. Moskva, Izd. 'Nauka'.

PEJSIKOV, L. S. 1952. K xarakteristike osnovnogo slovarnogo fonda persidskogo jazyka. TVIIJa 1.50–9.

——. 1957. Novye raboty professora M. Moina. VJa 1.132–6.

——. 1958. K tipologii služebnyx glagolov v persidskom jazyke. UZ kafedr inostrannyx jazykov Vostočnogo fakul'teta Instituta meždunarodnyx otnošenij, vyp. 2. Voprosy jazyka i literatury stran Vostoka, 155–74. Moskva, Izd. Instituta meždunarodnyx otnošenij.

——. 1959. Voprosy sintaksisa persidskogo jazyka. Moskva, Izd. Instituta meždunarodnyx otnošenij.

——. 1960a. Tegeranskij dialekt. Moskva, Izd. Instituta meždunarodnyx otnošenij.

——. 1960b. Problema jazyka dari v trudax sovremennyx iranskix učenyx. VJa 2.120–5.

——. 1961. Zametki o persidskix glagolax sostojanija. UZIMO 7, serija filologii, 105–11.

——. 1964. Transpozicija kak sposob slovoobrazovanija v iranskix jazykax. Iranskaja filologija, Trudy naučnoj konferencii po iranskoj filologii, 14–26. Leningrad, Izd. Leningradskogo universiteta.

——. 1966. Složnoproizvodnye slova-sraščenija v persidskom jazyke. Iranskaja filologija, Materialy IV vsesojuznoj meživuzovnoj konferencii po iranskoj filologii, 23–31. Taškent, Izd. 'FAN' UzSSR.

PHILLOTT, D.C. 1919. Higher Persian grammar. Calcutta, University.
QARIB, A., M. T. BAHÂR, B. FORUZÂNFAR, J. HOMÂI, and R. YÂSEMI [n.d.]. Dastur-e zabân-e fârsi. Tehrân, Ali-Akbar Elmi.
RAHBAR, XATIB. 1964. Horuf-e ezâfe. RFLTan 12.150–61.
RAHMATI, YUSEF. 1951. Farhang-e âmiâne. Tehrân.
RAJÂI, AHMAD ALI. 1964. Yâddâšti dar bâre-ye lahje-ye boxârâi. (Entešârât-e Dânešgâh-e Mašhad, 8.) Mašhad, Dânešgâh.
RASTORGUEVA, V. S. 1948. K xarakteristike varzobskogo govora tadžikskogo jazyka. VMU 6.33–9.
——. 1951. Ob ustojčivosti morfologičeskoj sistemy tadžikskogo jazyka. Voprosy teorii i istorii jazyka v svete trudov I. V. Stalina po jazykoznaniju, 225–36. Moskva, Izd. AN SSSR.
——. 1952–63. Očerki po tadžikskoj dialektologii. 5 volumes. Moskva, Izd. AN SSSR.
——. 1953a. Kratkij očerk grammatiki persidskogo jazyka. Persidsko-russkij slovar', by B.V. Miller, 613–68. Moskva, Gos. izd. inostrannyx i nacional'nyx slovarej.
——. 1953b. O formax kon'junktiva (soslagatel'nogo naklonenija) v sovremennom tadžikskom literaturnom jazyke. (Očerki po grammatike tadžikskogo jazyka, 2.) Stalinabad, Izd. AN Tadž. SSR.
——. 1953c. K voprosu o neočevidnyx ili povestvovatel'nyx formax tadžikskogo glagola. (Očerki po grammatike tadžikskogo jazyka, 3.) Stalinabad, Izd. AN Tadž. SSR.
——. 1954. Kratkij očerk grammatiki tadžikskogo jazyka. Tadžiksko-russkij slovar', by M. V. Raximi and L. V. Uspenskaja, 529–70. Moskva, Gos. izd. inostrannyx i nacional'nyx slovarej.
——. 1955. Kratkij očerk fonetiki tadžikskogo jazyka. Stalinabad.
——. 1962. Izučenie tadžikskogo jazyka v SSSR. Očerki po istorii izučenija iranskix jazykov, 33–66. Moskva, Izd. AN SSSR.
——. 1963a. Opyt klassifikacii tadžikskix govorov. Trudy dvadcat' pjatogo meždunarodnogo kongressa vostokovedov, t. II, 296–304. Moskva, Izd. vostočnoj literatury.
——. 1963b. A short sketch of Tajik grammar, transl. by H. H. Paper. (Part II, IJAL, vol. 29, number 4.) Bloomington, Indiana University. [Translation of Rastorgueva 1954.]
——. 1964a. A short sketch of the grammar of Persian, transl. by P. Hill. (Part II, IJAL, vol. 30, number 1.) Bloomington, Indiana University. [Translation of Rastorgueva 1953a.]
——. 1964b. Opyt sravnitel'nogo izučenija tadžikskix govorov. Moskva, Izd. 'Nauka'.
——. 1964c. O razvitii sovremennogo tadžikskogo literaturnogo jazyka. Voprosy razvitija literaturnyx jazykov narodov SSSR v sovetskuju ėpoxu, 253–60. Alma-Ata, Izd. AN Kazax. SSR.

Rastorgueva, V. S., Č. X. Bakaev, M. I. Isaev, A. A. Kerimova, and L. A. Pirejko. 1964. Tipy dvujazyčija u iranskix narodov sovetskogo sojuza. Moskva, Izd. 'Nauka'. [Communication to the VIIth International Congress of Anthropology, Moscow.]

Rastorgueva, V. S., and A. A. Kerimova. 1964. Sistema tadžikskogo glagola. Moskva, Izd. 'Nauka'.

Rastorgueva, V. S., and T. N. Paxalina. 1962. Izučenie persidskogo jazyka v SSSR. Očerki po istorii izučenija iranskix jazykov, 16–32. Moskva, Izd. AN SSSR.

Raximi, M. V., and L. V. Uspenskaja. 1954. Tadžiksko-russkij slovar'. Moskva, Gos. izd. inostrannyx i nacional'nyx slovarej.

Razi, H. 1960. Farhang-e estelâhât-e xâreji dar zabân-e fârsi. Tehrân.

Redard, Georges. 1959. Projet d'un Atlas Linguistique de l'Iran. Akten des vier und zwanzigsten internationalen Orientalisten-Kongresses, 440–4. Wiesbaden, Deutsche morgenländische Gesellschaft.

——. 1963. 'Atlas Linguistique de l'Iran': 1957–60. Trudy dvadcat' pjatogo meždunarodnogo kongressa t. II, 294–6. Moskva, Izd. vostočnoj literatury.

Rezâi, Jamâl. 1965. Guyeš-e Birjand, baxš-e noxost (farhang-e Mollâ Ali Ašraf Sabuhi). Tehrân.

Rozenfel'd, A. Z. 1948. Vspomogatel'naja funkcija glagola *da:štan* v sovremennom persidskom jazyke. Sovetskoe vostokovedenie 5.305–10.

——. 1950. Govory Karategina. Iranskie jazyki II. 145–68. Moskva, Izd. AN SSSR.

——. 1951. Nekotorye voprosy tadžikskoj dialektologii. VLU 6–7.32–40.

——. 1952. Vančskie govory. DANTadž 5.49–53.

——. 1953. Materialy k issledovaniju složno-sostavnyx glagolov v sovremennom tadžikskom literaturnom jazyke. (Očerki po grammatike tadžikskogo jazyka, 1.) Stalinabad, Izd. An Tadž. SSR.

——. 1954. Glagol. (Očerki po grammatike tadžikskogo jazyka, 4.) Stalinabad, Izd. AN Tadž. SSR.

——. 1956a. Darvazskie govory tadžikskogo jazyka. TIJa 6.196–272.

——. 1956b. K voprosu o pamirsko-tadžikskix jazykovyx otnošenijax. TIJa 6.273–80.

——. 1956c. O zalogax tadžikskogo glagola. IzvANTadž 9.105–20.

——. 1960. Govory Karategina. (AN Tadž. SSR, Institut jazyka i literatury, Trudy, 93.) Stalinabad.

——. 1961. Tadžiksko-persidskie jazykovye otnošenija. UZLU 294.12–42.

——. 1962a. Toponimika Vandža. Toponimika Vostoka, 66–72. Moskva.

——. 1962b. Namunahoi folklori Darvoz. Dušanbe.

——. 1963a. Zametki po leksike vančskie govorov tadžikskogo jazyka. Iranskij sbornik k semidesjatipjatiletiju professora I. I. Zarubina, 68–70. Moskva, Izd. vostočnoj literatury.

——. 1963b. Tadžikskie govory sovetskogo Badaxšana i ix mesto sredi drugix jazykov na Pamire. VLU 20.107–12.

——. 1963c. Modal'nye značenija nekotoryx form glagolov *budan* i *šudan* v tadžikskom jazyke. KSINA 67.73–5.
——. 1964. Vandžskie govory tadžikskogo jazyka. Leningrad, Izd. Leningradskogo universiteta.
——. 1966. Sistema glagola v jugo-vostočnyx govorax tadžikskogo jazyka. Avtoreferat dissertacii na soiskanie učenoj stepeni doktora filologičeskix nauk. Leningrad.
——. 1967. Glagol'naja forma perfekta II v jugo-vostočnyx govorax tadžikskogo jazyka. VLU 2, istorija, jazyk, literatura, vyp. 1.133–5.
RUBINČIK, JU. A. 1955. O dvux vidax pridatočnyx opredelitel'nyx predloženij v sovremennom persidskom jazyke. Trudy Voennogo instituta inostrannyx jazykov 7.53–67. Moskva.
——. 1959a. Složnye predloženija s pridatočnymi opredelitel'nymi v sovremennom persidskom jazyke. Moskva, Izd. vostočnoj literatury.
——. 1959b. Priroda i funkcii persidskogo podčinitel'nogo sojuza *ke*. KSIV 36.45–60.
——. 1960. Sovremennyj persidskij jazyk. (Jazyki zarubežnogo Vostoka i Afriki.) Moskva, Izd. vostočnoj literatury.
——. 1961. K xarakteristike imen suščestvitel'nyx *kas* i *čiz* (O xaraktere sočetanija 'imja suščestvitel'noe + artikl''). KSINA 40.31–41.
——. 1963a. Obrazovanie ustojčivyx slovosočetanij na osnove složnyx predloženij s pridatočnymi opredelitel'nymi v sovremennom persidskom jazyke. Iranskij sbornik k semidesjatipjatiletiju professora I. I. Zarubina, 178–85. Moskva, Izd. vostočnoj literatury.
——. 1963b. Strukturno-semantičeskie svojstva složnosočinennyx predloženij v sojuzom *vä* (*o*) v sovremennom persidskom jazyke. Iranskij sbornik k semidesjatipjatiletiju professora I. I. Zarubina, 186–202. Moskva, Izd. vostočnoj literatury.
——. 1964a. Nekotorye principy sostavlenija persidsko-russkogo slovarja. KSINA 72.192–9.
——. 1964b. Struktura i soderžanie slovarnoj stat'i 'Bol'šogo persidsko-russkogo slovarja'. Indijskaja i iranskaja filologija, 80–9. Moskva, Izd. 'Nauka'.
——. 1964c. Osnovnye vidy bessojuznyx složnyx predloženij v persidskom jazyke. Indijskaja i iranskaja filologija, 152–64. Moskva, Izd. 'Nauka'.
——. 1965. O xaraktere fonetičeskix izmenenij arabskix zaimstvovanij v persidskom jazyke. Semitskie jazyki, Materialy pervoj konferencii po semitskim jazykam, vyp. 2, čast' 2.585–97. Moskva, Izd. 'Nauka'.
RÜSTƏMOVA, T. [RUSTAMOVA, T. Z.]. 1953. K postanovke voprosa ob otglagol'nom prilagatel'nom v sovremennom literaturnom persidskom jazyke. TAzU, serija vostokovedenija, vyp. 1. [In Azerbaijani.]
——. 1956. O deepričastii v sovremennom persidskom jazyke. UZAzU 11.
——. 1958. Sposoby vyraženija deepričastij azerbajdžanskogo jazyka v persidskom jazyke. UZAzU 6.

——. 1964a. Fars dilindəki fe'li sifətlərinin morfoloži xüsusijjətləri. UZAzU 1.85–97.

——. 1964b. Fars dilində bitišən əvəzliklər. UZAzU 5.95–102.

RYPKA, JAN. Über eine dringende Aufgabe der neupersischen Lexicographie. Trudy dvadcat' pjatogo meždunarodnogo kongressa vostokovedov t. II, 319–21. Moskva, Izd. vostočnoj literatury.

RZAEVA, A. 1953. Narečie v persidskom jazyke i vidy ego obrazovanija. TAzU, vyp. 1. [In Azerbaijani.]

S. JOSEPH, P. ANGELICUS À. 1684. Gazophylacium lingua Persarum triplici linguarum clavi, italicae, latinae, gallicae, nec non specialibus praeceptis ejusdem linguae referatum. Amstelodami.

SADEGHI, ALI-ACHRAF. 1967. L'indication des fonctions grammaticales en persan. Unpublished Paris dissertation.

ŠAFÂI, A. M. 1953. O xaraktere opredelitel'nyx slovosočetanij sovremennom literaturnom persidskom jazyke. TZAzU, serija vostokovedenija, vyp. 1. [In Azerbaijani.]

——. 1955. K klassifikacii složnopodčinennyx predloženij v persidskom jazyke. UZAzU 11.

——. 1966. Kriterij opredelenija vidov pridatočnyx v sintetičeskix tipax složnopodčinennyx predloženij v sovremennom persidskom jazyke. Iranskaja filologija, materialy IV vsesojuznoj meživuzovskoj naučnoj konferencii po iranskoj filologii, 32–45. Taškent.

——. 1967. Složnopodčinennye predloženija v sovremennom persidskom jazyke. Avtoreferat dissertacii na soiskanie učenoj stepeni doktora filologičeskix nauk. Baku.

ŠAFII, MAHMUD. 1964. Šâhnâme va dastur yâ dastur-e zabân-e fârsi bar pâye-ye Šâhnâme-ye Ferdowsi va sanješ bâ soxan-e guyandegân va nevisandegân-e pišin. Tehrân, Entešârât-e Nil.

SAIDIÂN, ABDOLHOSEYN. 1964. Dastur-e zabân-e fârsi va fonun-e adabi. 2nd ed. Tehrân, Matbuâti-e Moruj.

SAIDOVA, K. 1961. Xususiyathoi fonetikii ševai tojikoni qismi kūhistonii rayoni Hisor. IzvANTadž 3.21–8.

——. 1962. Xususiyathoi fonetikii ševai tojikoni rayoni Šahrtuz. IzvANTadž 3.57–66.

ŠAJII, P. 1966. Bahsi dar bâb-e maâni-e harf-e 'bar'. RFLIsf 2–3.29–35.

SALEMANN, C. 1888. Chronologisches Verzeichnis der Farhange. Mélanges Asiatiques tirés du Bulletin de l'Académie Impériale des Sciences de St.-Pétersbourg 9.505–77.

SALEMANN, C., and V. SHUKOVSKI. 1889. Persische Grammatik. (Porta linguarum orientalium, 12.) Berlin, Reuther.

ŠAROVA, E. N. 1964. Ispol'zovanie form iz'javitel'nogo i soslagatel'nogo naklonenij v toždestvennyx sintaksičeskix uslovijax. Indijskaja i iranskaja filologija, 142–51. Moskva, Izd. 'Nauka'.

Scott, Ch. T. 1964. Syllable structure in Tehran Persian. AnL 6.27–30.

Semenov, A. A. 1960. K voprosu o termine 'darī' kak nazvanii jazyka. Pamjati M. S Andreeva, sbornik statej. Stalinabad.

Shaki, Mansour. 1957. The problem of the vowel phonemes in the Persian language. AO 25.45–55.

——. 1958. A study in the Persian bound phraseology and idioms. AO 26.248–78.

——. 1963a. Nominal compounds in Neo-Persian. AO 31.138–40.

——. 1963b. A Modern Persian phrase-book. Praha, Státní pedagogické nakladatelství.

——. 1964. A study on nominal compounds in Neo-Persian. (Rozpravy Československé Akademie Věd, Ročnik 74, sesit 8.) Praha.

Shari'at-Razavi, Bibifateme. 1963. Les prépositions et les locutions prépositives dans le 'Golestan' de Sa'di. Unpublished Paris dissertation.

Siyoyev, V. 1961. Šaklhoi enklitikii fe'lī dar zaboni 'Ta'rixi Tabarī'-i Bal'amī. IzvANTadž 4/27.20–35.

Skalmowski, W. 1960 [1961]. Statystyczny model komunikacji językowej i kilka parametrów języka nowoperskiego. SprOKrPAN, 278–80.

——. 1961a. Ein Beitrag zur Statistik der arabischen Lehnwörter im Neupersischen. FO 3.171–5.

——. 1961b. Sprachstatistische Untersuchungen zur persischen Sprachentwicklung. WZUB 10.129.

——. 1962. Über einige statistisch erfassbare Züge der persischen Sprachentwicklung. FO 4.47–80.

Smirnova, L. P. 1957. O forme tipa *gūjame* v jazyke klassičeskoj literatury. IzvANTadž 12.67–72.

——. 1958. Sistema predlogov v jazyke 'Ta'rixi Siston'. IzvANTadž 1.65–83.

——. 1959. Jazyk 'Taʿrix-i Sistān' (grammatičeskoe opisanie). (AN Tadž. SSR, Institut jazyka i literatury, Trudy, 110.) Stalinabad.

——. 1963. Osobennosti jazyka 'Fārsnāma'. KSINA 72.102–19.

Smirnova, O. I. 1948. Složnye glagoly s *istodan* i *mondan* v tadžikskom jazyke i ix istoričeskie korni. Sovetskoe vostokovedenie 5.297–304.

Sokolov, S. N. 1958. Oglasovka kauzativnogo suffiksa v zapadnoiranskix jazykax. UZLU 256.147–51.

Sokolova, V. S. 1949. Fonetika tadžikskogo jazyka. Moskva-Leningrad, Izd. AN SSSR.

——. 1951a. Itogi kuljabskoj dialektologičeskoj ekspedicii. Trudy Tadžikskogo filiala AN SSSR, t. 29, Istorija, arxeologija, ètnografija, jazyk i literatura. Stalinabad.

——. 1951b. Ustojčivye i neustojčivye glasnye. Pamjati akad. L. V. Sčerby, 236–44. Leningrad, Izd. Leningradskogo Universiteta.

Sokolova, V. S., R. L. Nemenova, Ju. I. Bogorad, V. A. Livšic, and A. I. Farxadjan. 1952. Novye svedenija po fonetike iranskix jazykov. TIJa 1.154–93.

SOTUDE, MANUCEHR [SOTOODEH, MANOOCHEHR]. 1957. Farhang-e Kermâni. (Entešârât-e Farhang-e Irânzamin, 4.) Tehrân.

STEINGASS, F. 1892. A comprehensive Persian-English dictionary. London, Kegan Paul.

ŠTOLBOVA, E. 1967. Some characteristic features of older Persian linguistic literature. Yádnáme-ye Jan Rypka, Collection of articles on Persian and Tajik literature, 149–54. Prague, Academia.

SULTANOV, R. S. 1953. Sposoby sočetanija imen v persidskom jazyke po dannym 'Golestana' Saadi. TAzU, serija vostokovedenija, 1.28–45.

——. 1957. O nekotoryx grammatičeskix kategorijax persidskogo jazyka po dannym 'Golestana' Saadi (morfologija). Trudy Instituta literatury i jazyka AN Azerb. SSR, t.10, Jazykovedčeskij sbornik. Baku.

——. 1958. O nekotoryx grammatičeskix kategorijax persidkogo jazyka po dannym 'Golestana' Saadi (morfologija). IzvANAzerb 4.77–92.

SUNDERMANN, W. 1966. Zum Judenpersisch der Mas'at Binyāmīn. MIO 11.275–300.

SVERČEVSKAJA, A. K. 1967. Bibliografija Irana, Literatura na russkom jazyke (1917–1965 gg.). Moskva, Izd. 'Nauka'.

TADŽIEV, D. T. 1952. Slovo *ob* 'voda' v sovremennom tadžikskom jazyke (iz materialov po tadžikskoj leksikologii). TIJa 1.120–53.

——. 1954. Pričastija v sovremennom tadžikskom literaturnom jazyke. (Očerki po grammatike tadžikskogo jazyka, 5.) Stalinabad, Izd. AN Tadž. SSR.

——. 1955. Sposoby opredelenija s opredeljaemym v sovremennom tadžikskom jazyke. Stalinabad.

TAGIRDŽANOV, A. 1962. Pamjatnik tadžikskogo razgovornogo jazyka pervoj poloviny XVI v. IzvANTadž, 28–32.

TAGIROVA, K. T. 1959. Tadžikskie govory Bastandykskogo rajona Uzbekskoj SSR. Stalinabad.

TELEGDI, ZS. 1950. Sur les périphrases verbales dites 'verbes composés' en persan. Etudes orientales à la mémoire de P. Hirschler, 32–40. Budapest.

——. 1951. Nature et fonction des périphrases verbales dites verbes composés en persan. AOH 1.315–38.

——. 1955. Beiträge zur historischen Grammatik des Neupersischen, I. Über die Partikelkomposition im Neupersischen. ALH 5.67–183.

——. 1961. Zur Morphologie des Neupersischen. AOH 12.183–99.

——. 1962. Zur Unterscheidung von Substantiv und Adjektiv im Neupersischen. AOH 15.325–36.

——. 1964. Über einen Fall von struktureller Homonymie im Persischen. ALH 14.237–61.

TUŠIŠVILI, L. N. 1954. Arabskie leksičeskie elementy v 'Šax-name' Firdousi. TIJaGruz, t. l, serija vostočnyx jazykov. [In Georgian.]

——. 1960. Funkcii posleloga *ra* v klassičeskom persidskom jazyke. TIJaGruz, serija vostočnyx jazykov, no. 3.

USPENSKAJA, L. V. 1956. Karatagskij govor tadžikskogo jazyka. (AN Tadž. SSR, Institut jazyka i literatury, 46.) Stalinabad, Izd. AN Tadž. SSR.

——. 1962. Govory tadžikov Gissarskogo rajona. Dušanbe.

VAHIDIÂN, TAQI. 1964. Dastur-e zabân-e âmiâne-ye fârsi. Mašhad.

VOHIDOV, Z. 1954. Maqomi *ū* va *u* dar lahjai Darvoz. Sbornik studenčeskix naučnyx rabot Tadžikskogo gos. universiteta, vyp. 1.31–7. Stalinabad.

VOSKANJAN, G. A. 1956. Infinitivnye slovosočetanija, vyražajaščie načalo i dlitel'nost' dejstvija (na materiale persidskogo jazyka). UZIMO vyp. 1.

VULLERS, I. A. 1855–64. Lexicon persico-latinum etymologicum. 2 vol. Bonnae ad Rhenum, impensis Adolphi Marci.

WEI, JACQUELINE. 1962. Dialectal differences between three standard varieties of Persian, Tehran, Kabul and Tajik. Washington, Center for Applied Linguistics. [Mimeographed.]

WERYHO, J. W. 1962. Sīstānī-Persian folklore. IIJ 5.276–307.

WILSON, J. CHRISTY. 1956. An introduction to colloquial Kabul Persian. Monterey, Army Language School. [Mimeographed.]

——. 1960. Kabul Persian. Washington, Department of State, Foreign Service Institute. [Mimeographed.]

WOLFF, FRITZ. 1935. Glossar zu Firdosis Schahname. Berlin, Reichsdrückerei.

XALILOV, A. 1964. Iborahoi izofī dar zaboni adabii tojik. Dušanbe, Našrdavtojik.

XÂNLARI, PARVIZ NÂTEL. 1964a. Zabânšenâsi va zabân-e fârsi. Tehrân.

——. 1964b. Dastur-e zabân-e fârsi barâ-ye sâl-e avval-e dabirestânhâ. Tehrân, Šerkat-e sahâmi-e tab' va našr-e ketâbhâ-ye darsi.

——. [n.d.] Dastur-e zabân-e fârsi barâ-ye sâl-e dovvom-e dabirestânhâ. Tehrân, Šerkat-e sahâmi-e tab' va našr-e ketâbhâ-ye darsi.

XATEMI, N. Z. see Hatəmi, N. Z.

XAYYÂMPUR, A. 1959. Dastur-e zabân-e fârsi. 3rd ed. Tabriz.

——. 1960. Šive-ye enteqâd dar majalle-ye Rahnemâ-ye Ketâb. RFLTiz 12.181–228.

XRISANOV, N. V. 1959. Oformlenie prjamogo dopol'nenija poslelogom *ra*. Sbornik trudov po jazykoznaniju Voennoj akademii Sovetskoj Armii, vyp. 3. Moskva.

——. 1960. Affiksal'nye narečija v sovremennom persidskom jazyke. Sbornik trudov po jazykoznaniju Voennoj akademii Sovetskoj Armii 4.205–34. Moskva.

XROMOV, A. L. 1958a. O nekotoryx slovax jazyka ėpoxi Rudaki, soxranivšixsja v tadžikskix govorax verxov'ev Zeravšana. Rudaki i ego ėpoxa (Sbornik Statej), 222–6. Stalinabad, Tadž. gos. izdat.

——. 1958b. Osobennosti vokalizma matčinskix govorov. IzvANTadž 1.7–20.

——. 1959. Nekotorye grammatičeskie osobennosti govorov Matči. IzvANTadž 1/19.45–68.

——. 1962. Govory tadžikov Matčinskogo rajona. (AN Tadž. SSR, Institut jazyka i literatury, Trudy, 107.) Dušanbe, Izd. AN Tadž. SSR.

——. 1963. K voprosu toponimike Matči. IzvANTadž 1/32.76–82.

——. 1965. Sogdijskie slova v govorax tadžikskogo jazyka. IzvANTadž /341.44–7.

XUBUA, M. 1947. Hamza v persidskoj reči. Soobščenija AN Gruzinskoj SSR 9–10. 677–81.

——. 1950. K obrazovaniju uslovnyx predloženij v persidskom jazyke klassičeskogo perioda. Soobščenija AN Gruzinskoj SSR 6.381–8.

ZARINEZAD, G. 1962. Azerbajdžanskie slova v persidskom jazyke. (Period Sefevidov). Baku, Izd. AN Azerb. SSR.

ZARUBIN, I.I. 1927. Otčet ob ėtnologičeskix rabotax v Srednej Azii letom 1926 g. IzvAN, 351–60.

——. 1928. Očerk razgovornogo jazyka samarkandskix evreev. Iran II.95–180. Leningrad, Izd. AN SSSR.

ZAV'JALOVA, V.N. 1960. K fonetičeskoj xarakteristike sintagmy v persidskom jazyke. VLU 14.125–37.

——. 1961. K xarakteristike persidskix soglasnyx. UZLU 294.43–61.

——. 1962a. Sintagmatičeskoe členenie predloženija v persidskom jazyke. UZLU 305.85–108.

——. 1962b. Intonacija obraščenija v persidskom jazyke. UZLU 306.16–31.

——. 1963. Ob udarenii v persidskom jazyke. Iranskij sbornik k semidesjatipjatiletiju professora I. I. Zarubina, 173–7. Moskva, Izd. vostočnoj literatury.

——. 1964. Dinamičeskaja xarakteristika vokativnoj sintagmy v persidskom jazyke. Iranskaja filologija, trudy naučnoj konferencii po iranskoj filologii, 42–9. Leningrad, Izd. Leningradskogo universiteta.

ZOMORRODIÂN, REZÂ [ZOMORRODIAN, RÉZA]. 1965. Le dialecte de Ghayen, description linguistique. Unpublished Paris dissertation.

——. 1966–67. Barresi-e xosusiyyât-e fonoloži va tatbiq-e ân be lahje-ye Qâyen. RFLMed 1.378–95; 2.40–7, 187–91; 3.68–77. [Still incomplete.]

ZONNUR, R. 1964. Dasturnâme-ye pârsi dar sarf-o nahv va emlâye fârsi. Tehrân, Entešârât-e Kuroš-e Kabir.

ZULFIGAROVA, I.F. 1963. Ob idiomatičeskix vyraženijax v persidskom jazyke. UZAzU 4.52–9.

[manuscript completed March 1968]

OTHER IRANIAN LANGUAGES

GEORGES REDARD

1. SOURCES OF DOCUMENTATION

Apart from the *Bibliographie linguistique* (BL), whose Iranian section has been considerably improved over the last few years, there exists no exhaustive bibliography for the languages under consideration here. The Persian contributions have been meticulously inventoried by I. Afšār, who lists some 6000 articles without, unfortunately, indicating their dates (1961); we also refer the reader to Afšār 1955,[1] to the report by E. R. Oney (1959), and to the references given in that work by E. Yar-Shater, which will surely complete our own.

For Afghanistan one will recall the analytic bibliography of Moh. Akram, whose first volume, the only one as yet to have appeared (Paris, 1947), lists the works published outside of the country (languages and literatures nos. 1698–1897). Also devoted to languages and literatures is the eighth chapter of the bibliography by D. N. Wilber (1956a) who, in the collective work which he edited on Afghanistan (1956b), had entrusted the chapter reserved for languages to Charles A. Ferguson. The most recent publication, the bibliography of T. I. Kuchtina (1965), devotes a rather limited space to linguistics (nos. 5487–5606). A. Bausani has reviewed the studies in Iranology and in Turcology made in Italy since 1941 (1951); G. Morgenstierne gives some useful information for Scandinavia (1941). The Soviet studies are reviewed by M. N. Bogoljubov in his survey of articles published in the UZ vojen. inst. inostr. jazykov (1948), and studies of Iranian linguistics at Leningrad from 1917 to 1957 (1960), while V. I. Abaev has given a brief survey of historical and comparative Iranian linguistics (1959b). A commemorative volume has been dedicated, and with just cause, to V. A. Žukovskij (1858–1918): *Očerki po istorii russkogo vostokovedenija* V, Moskva, Izd. Vost. lit., 1960. Finally, the articles in which A. A. Frejman examines Stalin's language policy and its effects on Iranian linguistics (1951) explain the fate of Iranian languages in the U.S.S.R.

[1] By the same author, cf. *Fehrest-nāme-ye ketạbšenạsīhạ-ye Īrān* (A bibliography of bibliographies on Iranian studies), Tehran 1342/1964. The work by Xān Bābā Mošār (1958) is difficult to consult (titles are classified alphabetically, without a division according to subject); the second volume should be ordered according to authors' names.

We will consider here, in an undeniably arbitrary manner, the contributions since 1940; little mention is made here of the Tājik, Pašto, and Kurdish dialects, which are covered elsewhere in this volume. We have made a selection from among the studies which do not deal explicitly with the dialects, with the intention of publishing separately a complete and descriptive bibliography of Iranian dialectology; in reality, almost all of the articles by H. W. Bailey, E. Benveniste, W. B. Henning, etc., deserve to be cited, for in them there is a consistent appearance of modern forms; similarly, a work such as the *Saka grammatical studies* of R.E. Emmerick (London, 1968) includes a number of Balōčī, Ōrmuṛī, Ossetic, Pamir, etc., words which have not been discussed. There are certainly numerous involuntary omissions too.

For convenience we have adopted, for the languages and dialects (excluding Ossetic), the order followed by G. Morgenstierne (1958a).

2. IRANIAN LANGUAGES IN GENERAL

2.1 *General*

The group of Iranian languages as a whole has been the object of several important studies. There has appeared in Iran itself the useful catalogue by N. Rāst (1953). I. M. Oranskij has contributed two excellent manuals to Iranian studies, which ought to be translated in order to have, in the West, the audience that they deserve; his introduction to Iranian philology (1960:490 pp. and maps) devotes a great deal of space to dialects (p. 304ff. with very good bibliographies); likewise his *Iranskie jazyki* (1963: 127–71). Supplementing these two descriptive reports, V. S. Sokolova and A. Grjunberg have given an historical account of the research done on the Pamir dialects, Yaǧnābī, the Caspian dialects, and Balōčī (1962:118–47). In the *Handbuch der Orientalistik*, G. Morgenstierne (1958a) has presented the modern dialects in an admirable manner: phonetics, morphology (essential characteristic traits), distribution, bibliography.

In addition to the notes by G. Redard (1954), J. Duchesne-Guillemin (1964) and A. M. D'jakov (in a work devoted to the languages and literatures of the peoples of southern Asia, 1963:40), we will mention again, for Afghanistan, the brief report by E. Benveniste (1952) and the list arranged by A. G. R. Farhādī (1967) which corrects the one proposed by the same author in 1956 (Aryana Encyclop. 3, facing p. 791) and in 1957 at the 24th Congress of Orientalists (*Akten*, Wiesbaden, 1959:444–7); in this Farhādī utilizes, for the first time, the term *Iranic*, preferable to *Iranian* which today generally has a political connotation, and he mentions, in addition to Balōčī, the Pahlavānī 'similar to Dari but still distinct, spoken in the village Haji Hamza Khan of Karim Kushta in Chakhansoor province' (1967:84), which calls for serious examination.

2.2 *Special Studies*

2.2.1 D.I. Ėdel'man has attempted to establish a uniform scientific *transcription* of the Iranian languages (1963a, 60 pp.), which ought to serve as the chief topic of discussion at a future congress of Iranology; the question has been debated many times and taken up most recently, for Persian and Pašto, by G.P. Serǰučenko (*Russkaja transkripcija dlja jazykov zarubežnogo vostoka*, 166–42, Moskva, 1967).

2.2.2 The problems posed by the editing of *descriptive grammars* of the Iranian languages — to which we shall return later — have been approached summarily by M.I. Isaev, A.A. Kerimova, L.A. Pirejko, and D.I. Ėdel'man (1964).

2.2.3 *Phonetics* has been the object of important investigations, due principally to V.S. Sokolova; after a preliminary communication dealing with the Balōčī, Tālišī, Tātī, and Kurdish (1950), she took interest in the Persian and Tāǰik dialects of the southeast, with R.L. Nemenova, Ju.I. Bogorad, V.A. Livšic, and A.I. Farchadjan (1952). She then published two studies (1953), the first devoted to Balōčī, to Kurdish of Turkmenistan, to Tālišī and Tātī of Azerbaidjan; the second, to the Ossetic, Yaġnābī, and Pamir languages. For each dialect, V.S. Sokolova gives the system of phonemes whose articulatory characteristics are described with the aid of experimental phonetics. Precise answers are given to some difficult questions, such as, in consonantism, the opposition of voiceless and voiced consonants, and, in vocalism, the oppositions of timbre and quantity.

G. Morgenstierne has collected, in a brief but compact article, the phonetic traits which Iranian has conserved from Indo-European (1956).

2.2.4 In the same perspective, Morgenstierne studies certain aspects of *morphology*: gender, dual, case, verb, pronouns, etc. Considering elsewhere the formation of feminines in *-čī* (1962a), he rejects the explanation of I. Gershevitch (*-ĭkă* > *-ič-* by progressive palatalization) and asserts Sogd. *knč* 'girl' < **kaničī*, cf. Oss. **čîndz/kindza*, Persian *kanīz*, etc., then lists the numerous modern forms where *-č* is characteristic of the feminine (like Šuġnī *rewuxč* 'flown'), which gives evidence of a former **-(a)čī* conserved principally in Eastern Iranian. In the West, the feminine in *-a/e* is preponderant; G. Morgenstierne studies it too (1962b), collecting materials which are sparse, sometimes unpublished (as for the Tākistānī where the feminine was first treated by W.B. Henning 1954:161) or which are as yet unexplained (thus Āštīānī *anazā* compared with Skt. *anyă-jāta* 'begot by another man [than the husband]').

M.N. Bogoljubov has summarized, with excessive brevity, an historical study of the relations of modes and tenses in Iranian (1954). L.S. Pejsikov (1964) has occupied himself, again too briefly, with the type of formation called transposition (the first of five types distinguished by G. Lazard, before suffixation, prefixation, composition, and juxtaposition), which consists in transferring a word or a radical, as the case may be, from one class to another (adjective, substantive, verb); borrowing his examples from Persian, Pašto, Kurdish, and Ossetic, Pejsikov distinguishes between full transpositions (generators of words) and incomplete transpositions, called 'functional'.

2.2.5 The *lexicon* has given rise to numerous monographs. To V.I. Abaev we owe a study of the root *kan-* and the dialectal names for bread in Middle and Modern Iranian (1956d, also the carefully examined contribution of J. Harmatta 1953); in the same article the equivalents of Oss. *wæ jyg*, *-jug* and *fæstinon* are studied. V.I. Abaev has also published a note on the names for steel (1963). From H.W. Bailey we recall notably the four series of *arya* concerning the forms (Iranian, or more precisely Khotanese and Ossetic) *maz-*, *had-*, *kom*, *gad-*, *haik-*, *sor-*, *arva-*, *farva-*, *iza-*, *khoca*, *mala*, *fšar-* (1958), *ahva-*, *āysña-*, *ganīh-*, *barb-*, *kuṃji*, *ysār-*, *hūṣa*, *tau-: tu-*, (dig.) *zurun*, *ttunda-*, *tilläg* (1960), *dru-*, *ara-*, *pandara-* (1961), *gaš-*, *mand-*, *mar-*, *tap-* (1963); then his 'Ambages' (1959a): Bal. *t'ēlaγ* 'eyeball', *-vīya-*, *kalāka-*, Iran. *čirāγ-* 'light, lamp', Iran. *karasta-*, Khot. *haura-*, *bvīysna*; and finally his study published with Alan S.C. Ross on Iran. *pant-* ~ *paθ-* 'path, road', and *paθ-* 'extended' (1961). Studying the expression of 'to be able', E. Benveniste has established that the absence of a personal verb has given rise to the construction with 'to make' and the participle; this innovation, part of Old Persian, is observed in a rather compact group of Middle and Modern dialects, for the most part Eastern (1954). As for the names for 'bird', the same author has noted that the Av. *vi-* has nowhere survived in Iranian, where it has been supplanted by *mrga-* (Oss. *marγ*, etc.) which, being locally specialized — in general into the sense of 'hen' — has been replaced by a new generic term, cf. Persian *parande* literally 'volatile', Sīvandī *bāländä* (*bāl* 'arm, wing'), Baxtīārī *bāndä* (*bāh*(*u*) 'arm'), etc. (1960). Valuable material, notably Balōčī and Baškardī, will be found in the article by I. Gershevitch on adverbial expressions of time (1964b), and an astonishing fan of the names of mushrooms, arranged under semantic headings, made by G. Morgenstierne (1957) to whose article is added that of Ch. M. Kieffer (1965).

3. STUDIES CONCERNING A DIALECT OR A DIALECTAL GROUP

3.1 *Eastern Iranian*

Having established that the group *r* + sibilant evolves in an analogous manner in diverse eastern dialects (Pašto *rs*, *rz* > *x̌t*, *ǵd*, Sanglēčī *rs* > *ṣt*, Šuġnī *rs*, *rz* > *x̌c*, *γj*), G. Morgenstierne shows that this development is best explained by certain characteristics of the phonetic system of Old Eastern Iranian (1948b, additional notes concerning the Pašto 1950). Similarly, Mrs. D.I. Ėdel'man has studied the cerebrals in these dialects (1963d). Pursuing a suggestion made by G. Morgenstierne, according to whom the Persian *tarāšīdan* would be the result of a cross between **tāšīdan* and *xarāšidan*, M. Mayrhofer explains certain eastern forms by the influence of *tarāš-*:

Pašto *tarx̌əj*, Parāčī *tašõ*, Šuġnī *tōrx̌*, Waxī *tarš*, etc., would thus not be native (1964: 47).

3.2 *Kafir (Dardic) Languages*

This denomination covers, as we know, a certain number of languages and dialects spoken in the mountainous northwest angle of the Indo-Aryan linguistic triangle in Afghanistan, Pakistan, and Kashmir. The nomenclature and classification of these languages are still much disputed. For some they share elements of both Indian and Iranian; for others they constitute a group independent of the Indo-Iranian, indeed even (opinion of H. Sköld) of the Indo-European. The bulk of the knowledge which we have of them is due to G. Morgenstierne who, in the period considered here, has produced two monographs (grammar, texts, lexicon) on Prasun, 'the most aberrant of the Kafir languages' (1949), and on Waigalī spoken in southeast Nuristan (1954); the Aṣkūṇ of Wāmā and the dialects of Tregām have been surveyed as well (1951), while certain particular traits have been brought to light: metathesis of liquids (1947b), pronouns of the first and second persons of the plural (1953), etc. — most of these texts, reviewed and augmented by new findings, will appear in a volume now in press, *Irano-dardica* (Wiesbaden, Harrassowitz). We will find in his forthcoming volume notably genealogies completing those already published (1950), and a chapter on the position of the Kafir languages will mark an important achievement. G. Morgenstierne has been studying this difficult problem for a long time. It was forty years ago that he postulated the existence of a third branch of the Indo-Iranian group (*Oostersch Genootschap in Nederland, Verslag van het 5. Congres*, 30–1, Leiden 1927). The position is probed in the important article on IE *k'* in Kāfirī (1945)[2] and, in a less technical manner, in the new Encyclopedia of Islam (1961). The Kāfir group (Katī, Prasun, Aṣkūṇ, Waigalī) is clearly distinguished from the Dardic group in which, except for some traits coming from the former, nothing can be found that could have been derived from the Old Indo-Aryan; the Kāfir dialects, although heavily overlaid with Dardic words and forms, have conserved some decisive non-Indian traits (total loss of aspiration of voiceless and voiced stops, conservation of palatal occlusives and palatalized velars of Indo-European). G. Morgenstierne finds himself thus 'entitled to posit the existence of a third branch of Indo-Iranian, agreeing generally with Indo-Aryan, but being situated on the Iranian side of some of the isoglosses which, taken as a whole, constitute the borderline between Indo-Aryan and Iranian' (1961:139). The recent work of Mrs. D.I. Ėdel'man (1965), a useful description, contributes nothing new to the debate and neglects voluntarily the historical and comparative aspects in favor of a consideration of the structural differences.[3] We indicate finally the valuable

[2] We have not been able to see Eric P. Hamp's article (1966).

[3] The bibliography presented (200–2) could not be exhaustive. I refer the reader, however, to the article by G. Morgenstierne (1961), the article by V.V. Ivanov, 'Problema jazykov *centum:satəm*' (*VJa* 1958.12–23) and, above all, the article by Z. Rysiewicz, 'Zagadnienie palatalnych w językach

bibliography compiled by Schuyler Jones (1966) whose first volume comprises three parts: General reference books (nos. 1–19), Nuristan (20–280; cf. E. Benveniste, *Le Nouristan. Civilisation iranienne*, 240–3, Paris, 1952), the Kalash Kafirs of Chitral (281–300); a map of Nuristan, due to Lennart Edelberg, completes the work.

3.3 *Yaġnābī*

Our knowledge of Yaġnābī, for a long time very meager, has been considerably enriched. Although C. Salemann's printed study has never been published, and the notes assembled by R. Gauthiot at the time of his voyage with H. F. J. Junker in 1913 have been lost, E. Benveniste has at least been able to publish a portion of the first, copied carefully by Gauthiot and found among his papers after his death (September 11, 1916, as a result of a war injury). What is involved is a vocabulary with a German translation (here and there Russian) which is cut short in the middle of the letter *k*[4] (1955; for *kafas*, see the correction made in BSL 54/2.81, 1959). The materials collected in the area by M.S. Andreev and E.M. Peščereva in 1924 and 1927 have been published by V. A. Livšic and A.K. Pisarčik (Andreev and Peščereva 1957); it is a question here of fifty tales, some proverbs, and poems (13–312), to which the editors have added an exhaustive lexicon (begun incidentally by Andreev, who died in 1948) with references to Sogdian — of which Yaġnābī is the sole survivor — and to the Pamir dialects; and a Russian-Yaġnābī index (371–391). For his part, A. Chromov has contributed some comparative lexicological materials (1966), emphasizing the considerable influence exerted by Tājik (notably in phonetics, the formation of nouns, and phraseology). In addition, a few tales have been published by S.I. Klimčickij (1940a) who had already given, in 1937, in two brief articles, some samples of his findings (see also, by the same author, the brief note devoted to the inhabitants of Yaġnāb and to their language, 1940c). The phonetic analysis has been made by V.S. Sokolova (1953: II.61–79) who has outlined briefly, with A. Grjunberg, the historical account of research done (1962:129–31, expeditions of 1947 and 1952 directed by K.K. Kurdoev and M.N. Bogoljubov). The latter has devoted his thesis to Yaġnābī (Leningrad, 1956), then an excellent monograph, the first at that time (1966; cf. also Oranskij 1963:164–6). Relations with Sogdian, which deserve a systematic investigation, have been presented by M.N. Bogoljubov (1958:837) and several points have been elaborated upon; E. Benveniste (1966a) indicates a Yaġnābī-Buddhist Sogdian association in the Sogd. particle *'štn* (which, like *'skwn*, constitutes the imperfect forms of verbs) and the Yaġnābī verbal affix *-išt* which is jointed to the present and to the preterite. I. Gershevitch, on the other hand, has compared Sogd.-Yaġnābī *nīst-* 'to sit' (past

dardyjskich' (*Studia językoznawcze*, 285–92, Wrocław 1956), in which, with great penetration, the late Polish linguist studies to what degree the facts furnished by the Dardic languages in a general sense are able to explain the palatalization of the earlier 'gutturals' in Indo-Iranian.

[4] The original by Salemann did not go any further, cf. Geiger, *Grundriss der iran. Phil.* I/2.289.

stem) with Bactrian *vioτo* (inscription of Surkh-Kotal), cf. Skt. *niṣad-* 'to sit down' (1966).

3.4 *Pamir Languages*

Before considering them individually, we call attention to the works which concern the group as a whole. The inventory of research is given, briefly, by Sokolova-Grjunberg (1962:118–29) and D.I. Ėdel'man (1964), the distribution of languages and their principal characteristics by I.M. Oranskij (1960:333–8, 1963:158–63), to which we might add Lawrence Krader's *Peoples of Central Asia* (Bloomington and The Hague, 1966:40–3, bibliography 279–303). A comparative dictionary has been procured by Šāh 'Abdullāh Badaxšī (1960) which gives, in columns, the Pašto-Persian-Šuġnī-Sanglēčī-Waxī-Iškāšmī-Munǰī correspondances; the materials derive in part from personal investigations (cf. Badaxši 1942–43) and are often valuable — in particular for the Munǰī — in spite of the lack of transcription.[5]

Numerous studies have introduced Pamir terms. We cite those by I. Gershevitch (1948), those by E. Benveniste 1) on the forms of *talqān, talxān*, 'a kind of broad, thin cake made from the grains of wheat or barley toasted or ground', borrowed from Eastern Turkic *talqan* 'ground and toasted barley', itself of Iranian origin, cf. Persian *talxān* 'dough made of toasted and ground wheat' (Benveniste 1948:181); 2) on the names for 'hammer', the Waxī type *bōleqa*, Sanglēčī *baləkē* next to Šuġnī *pulk*, Waxī *pulk*, Munǰī *putk* (as in Persian), which gives evidence of a double tradition, that of the Iranian *pulk*, and that of the Turkic *bolqa*, borrowed from Iranian and reintroduced into it by way of this detour (Benveniste 1948:181–2); and 3) on the Indo-Iranian *yat-* 'to attain its natural place' which has been conserved in Yaġnābī, Šuġnī, Sariqōlī, and even — G. Morgenstierne's suggestion — in Waxī *ŷat* and Sangl.-Iškāšmī *īd-, īt-* 'to arrive' (Benveniste 1964:24–5); finally the study of the names for 'dragon' made by G. Morgenstierne (1964), in particular on the type represented by Šuġnī *devūsk* (feminine) which should be the Iranian **ati-buga-čī/-čā*, and the Šuġnī *saŷ* 'snake', Rōšānī *sāw*, also Šuġnī *sāŷd* 'serpent, dragon', indicating an Iran. **sušna*, equivalent to the *Śuṣṇa-* of the Vedic mythology whose significance is thus made explicit.

3.4.1 *The Šuġnī-Rōšānī* Group. V.S. Sokolova has proposed a descriptive classification of this group (1963) which includes Šuġnī, Rōšanī, Xūfī, Bartangī, Orōšōrī, and Sariqōlī. Rōšānī, Bartangī, Orōšōrī, and Sariqōlī are distinguished from Šuġnī by many traits (alternance *d/g*, for example), and form two subgroups: Rōšānī-Bartangī and Orōšōrī. Bartangī has the vowels *ī ē ö ā ō ū i a u*, Rōšānī has in addition *ů* and *o*, but does not have *ö*. There are differences in the formation of the plural and tenses,

[5] The Tuxārī words given by the same author in the journal *Kābul* 100.73 ff. (June-July 1939) are from Badaxšān (= Toxāristān!). Cf. the comparativists' warning, given by G. Morgenstierne (1942: 260–1).

in the compound verbs, the personal endings, the suffixes (three postpositions the equivalent of a locative in Šuġnī: *-andi(r)*, *-and*, *-ard*, as opposed to two in Rōšānī: *-andi*, *-ari*, and only one in Bartangī: *-indēr*), the conjunctions and enclitics, and likewise in lexicon. R.Ch. Dodychudoev has taken up the delicate problem of the representation in Šuġnī-Rōšānī of the Iranian group *rt* (1964). After having reviewed and discussed the hypotheses of W. Geiger, H.F.J. Junker, and G. Morgenstierne, he proposes a new one, based on the comparison of the Šuġnī, Rōšānī, Bartangī, Orošōrī, Xūfī, Yazgulāmī, and Sariqōlī dialects, which can be summarized as: a) **-ṛt-* > **-ərd-* > **-ūd'-* *-ud-*; b) **-ṛtaka-* > **-ərdaka* > **-ūd'ak* > **ūd'ǰ̦* > *-ūg'ǰ̦* > *-ūγ̌ǰ̦* [cf. D. Gary Miller 1968]. The verbal system has been studied by N. Karamchudoev (1962) who pays particular attention to the forms of past tenses constructed with the aid of the participle in **dp* (probably from the old *-ta*, *-ka*); tables order the regular and irregular verbs; the preverbial forms are also studied (*ni-*, *ra-*, *in-*, *zi-*, *bi-*, *par-*, *wi-*, *nix̌-*, *fi-*, *di-*, *pa-*, *pi-*, *a-*, *x̌i-*); and in conclusion the author indicates the differences between Bartangī and Šuġnī. We have not been able to see A.K. Pisarčik's articles on *ro* and *lo* used as an apostrophe in this group (1949).

3.4.1.1 *Šuġnī.* Based on a Soviet model tested and applied to several of the Iranian languages, I.I. Zarubin has published a large volume (1960) which contains a series of texts with translation (9–81), a Šuġnī-Russian lexicon (85–288), and a Russian-Šuġnī index which greatly facilitates research (289–386). We owe to D. Karamšoev the first description of Bājuī, a Šuġnī dialect (1963b); the copious work includes sections on phonetics (8–89) where a great deal of space is devoted to experimental phonetics (kymograms), on morphology (90–240), on syntax (241–61), followed by a comparison with Šuġnī proper (262–85), tables of verbs (286–300), and texts — 909 sentences and 11 short tales (301–63). This general study — unfortunately without a lexicon — was preceded by two specific studies: a brief description of the dialect (1962) where special attention is given to the expression of gender (thus, the masculine suffixes *-bek*, *-šo*, *-māmad*, *-ali*, the feminine suffixes *-begim*, *-mo*, *-siltōn*, *-xotun*, *-bāxt*), and an examination of vocalic modifications (1963a). For his part, G. Morgenstierne — who has an etymological lexicon of Šuġnī in preparation — has compared the demonstrative pronouns with those of other Pamir languages (1942:258–60) in an article whose conclusions deserve to be cited: 'there can be little doubt that the two-case system of the modern Pamir languages goes back to an earlier three-case system' (259).

3.4.1.2 *Rōšānī* and *Xūfī.* Two works should be indicated, which complement each other: the collection of Rōšānī texts published by A.K. Pisarčik (1954) and the volume of V. S. Sokolova (1959) which is of the type described earlier — Rōšānī and Xūfī texts, with Russian translation (10–104), followed by an exhaustive lexicon (from which any etymological or historical consideration has been intentionally excluded: the borrowed vocables are not distinguished from the native ones, 105–304) and by a Russian-Rōšānī and Xūfi index (305–34).

3.4.1.3 *Bartangī.* A parallel, yet less voluminous work by the same linguist (Sokolova 1960): texts (13–64), a copious lexicon with phraseology, giving the Rōšānī equivalents (65–181), and a Russian-Bartangī index (182–95). We thus have, happily completed, the work published by I.I. Zarubin in 1937: *Bartangskie i rušanskie teksty i slovar'*.

3.4.1.4 *Sariqōlī.* If one does not take into account G. Morgenstierne's report (1965) on the sentences studied formerly by J. Biddulph, the only important contributions have been made by T. Nina Pachalina, who has had the courage and strength to make field investigations, and who has magnificently enriched our prior knowledge of this language that we owed to R.B. Shaw (1876) and W. Geiger (1901). One of the first articles which characterized the Sariqōlī (1963a) groups the dialects of Varšidē, Tiznēf, Baldir, Vačā, Marjóng, Tyng, Kičiktíng, Byryngsól and Kugušlúk. Vowels: *i e u o ÿ ə a* (ε); consonants: *p b t d k g q c z č ǰ s x̌ γ̌ f v θ ъ x γ š ž w y m n l r h.* There follows a text of Tobildi Ušur of Varšidē, with translation. In addition, three popular poems with translation and grammatical notes (1963b); then a study of the place of Sariqōlī among the languages of the Šuġnī-Rōšānī group (1963c; available as well in an English version following the Moscow Congress in 1960); some colloquial texts (1965); a study of the expression of the attribute (prepositions or suffixes), the prepositions, and postpositions (1966b), all this crowned by an imposing volume (1966a) which includes phonetics, where the dialectal differences are carefully noted (6–18), morphology (19–71), syntax (72–88), and texts with translation (91–238) — unfortunately it lacks a lexicon and an index.

3.4.1.5 *Yazgulāmī*, still spoken by some two thousand people from the valley of the Yazgul, an affluence of the Panǰ, belongs to the Šuġnī-Rōšānī group, but its position in it is difficult to determine. We are better acquainted with it today, thanks to Mrs. D.I. Ėdel'man and Mrs. V.S. Sokolova, who have greatly enriched the information collected by G.A. Arandarenko (1889) and M.S. Andreev (1904).[6] The former has studied its verbal system in a strictly descriptive manner (Ėdel'man 1963b); then she has produced a veritable manual of it (1966), constructed according to the ordinary scheme, but in which much attention is given to structural matters: phonetics (12–23), morphology (24–106), syntax (107–24), lexicon (125–33), and texts with translation (139–217). The same linguist has edited, with grammatical notes, a tale of Alexander (1963c). V.S. Sokolova, for her part, has sought to elucidate the dialectal situation of the language, by introducing all possible elements of comparison (historical analysis of the vocalic and consonant system, formation of the plural, infinitive, prefix *x̌a-*, gerund in *-arm*, attributive in *-i*, lexicon). She concludes her study with a Yazgulāmī-Šuġnī group in which can be clearly distinguished, on the one hand Yazgulāmī, and on the other a group composed of Sariqōlī, Orošōrī-Bartangī, Rōšānī-Xūfī, and Bāǰūī-

[6] On the inhabitants of Yazgul, consult N.A. Kisljakov, 'Jazguljamcy (ėtnografičeskij očerk)', *Iz. vsesojuznogo geograf. ob-va* 80/4 (1948), and L.F. Monogarova, 'Jazguljamcy zapadnogo Pamira', *Žurn. sovetsk. ėtnografija* 1949/3; Sokolova and Grjunberg have also cited (1962:128) the thesis of L.F. Monogarova (Moskva 1951), devoted to the same subject.

Šuġnī (Sokolova 1967). One chapter of her *Očerki* is devoted to Yazgulāmī as well (1953:II.176–208).

3.5 *Waxī*

Since R.B. Shaw's celebrated publication in 1876, Waxī has been the object of numerous investigations, which V.S. Sokolova mentions in her study (1953:II.209–29). The principal contribution is that made by D.L.R. Lorimer (1958) whose copious manuscript, composed of the notes that he collected in Hunza and Yarxun (1935 and 1921), i.e. outside of Waxān proper, has been reproduced in handwritten form (which certainly does not facilitate the reading of it). The first volume contains a meticulous grammatical description (all possible phonetic groups are inventoried and the list of verbs, with their principal forms, includes not less than 280 entries) and texts with translation (7 stories and 238 single sentences); the second volume, a very rich glossary as well as an English-Waxī index. Although this 'exterior' dialect differs from the Waxī at the sources of the Oxus, contaminated as it has been by the Burušaskī and Indo-Aryan, we have in it an invaluable documentation.[7] We also cite the studies made by M.N. Bogoljubov on the etymology of the auxiliary verb *tej-:tu-* 'to be' (1947) and that made by E. Benveniste on the words common to Waxī and Burušaski (1948: 177–80).

3.6 *Iškāšmī-Sanglēčī*

This is, with the Sariqōlī, the special field of interest of T.N. Pachalina to whom we owe colloquial texts (1956) and a work entirely devoted to this language (1959): phonetics (7–36, with the results of experimental research), morphology (37–62), syntax (63–7), texts (68–164: 643 sentences, 16 narrations, and 1 poem) to which the author has added those found by I.I. Zarubin in 1915 (165–75), finally a lexicon (176–255). In the previously cited article by E. Benveniste, one finds a note relative to *γənän* 'three- or four-year-old horse' = Turkic *γunan*, which derives from the Mongol *γunan* 'three-year-old animal' (1948:180).

3.7 *Munǰī*

Recent publications are rare. I.M. Oranskij has devoted a note to Munǰī in his two works (1960:338–9 and 1963:163–4). This dialect appears in the dictionary of Badaxšī (1960), from which G. Morgenstierne has taken the trouble to extract all the new words (1966).

3.8 *Parāčī*

Same remark. Besides Oranskij's two notes (1960:339–40 and 1963:167–8), we can

[7] Cf. in particular the review by G. Morgenstierne, *BSOAS* 23.151–3 (1960).

but indicate the brief study on the distribution of Parāčī made by M.N. Kohzad (1957).

3.9 *Ōrmuṛī*

Same remark. However, we will soon be able to add to Oranskij's notes (1960:339-40 and 1963:168–70), the complete lexicon and the description which Ch.M. Kieffer has in preparation.

3.10 *Balōčī*

G. Morgenstierne has procured some excellent reports on the group as a whole (1947a). J. Elfenbein has developed his article in the Encyclopedia of Islam (1959) into a solid monograph (1966). In it he describes the six principal groups of Balōčī, distinguished according to various criteria (17 are phonological, 10 morphological, 18 lexical, and 1, the 'passive construction', syntactical). From a chronological point of view, he seeks to establish that the periphery is more conservative than the center, which is, incidentally, a general phenomenon. He tries, on the other hand, to determine the origin of the Balōčīs (southeast shores of the Caspian Sea) and the paths of their migrations to the south and the east;[8] there follow nine short texts with translations, and a glossary of important words. We must also mention V.A. Frolova's study (1960) which includes a good bibliography (68–69), and those of Mrs. Sokolova (1950:5–10, 1953:I.7–77, and 1957). The latter has particularly studied, in collaboration with A. Grjunberg, the Balōčī of Merv in Russian Turkestan (where there are about 10,000 speakers in the districts of Yolotan, Bayrām 'Alī, and Kuibyšev), which belongs to the group called occidental or southern, but possesses certain individual characteristics: no aspirated *h* in any position, **-xt-* > **-ht-* > *-t-* (southern *-tk-* < **-kt-*, etc.), infinitive derived from the preterit, no opposition between transitive and intransitive constructions, etc. (Sokolova and Grjunberg 1962:144–7). Previous to this, S.N. Sokolov had given a careful, detailed description of this dialect (1956), while I.M. Oranskij — who devotes a brief chapter of his general work to Balōčī (1963:141–5) — has compared Balōčī and Parja, called 'afgon' (1964). G. Morgenstierne has contributed a number of new findings (1948a): notes on phonetics, nouns and pronouns, verbs, 'passive construction' (254–61), texts with translation (261–82), kinship terms compared with those of Brāhuī and with four modern Indo-Aryan dialects, finally a valuable account of Balōčī words 'from the Makran Gazetteer, etc.' (288–91). B. Spooner has published with great care the materials which he collected in Persian Baločistān: grammatical and lexical introduction organized in 12 grammatical and semantic sections (1967; cf. by the same author '*Kūch a Balūch* and *Ichthyophagi*', in

[8] Some linguistic notes on this subject can be found in R.N. Frye (1961). On Balōčistān, see also the work by M.G. Pikulin, 'Beludži', *Izd. vost. lit.* (Moscow 1959), which contains an excellent bibliography.

Iran 2.53–67, 1964). The lexicon of Merv has been systematically rearranged by J. Elfenbein, who has taken into consideration all published texts, and he indicates etymologies and borrowings when possible (1963). We owe to him as well the publication of a text with translation (1961). I.I. Zarubin has, for his part, published some tales (1949, as a continuation of the publication of 1932). Among the studies which indirectly treat Balōčī, we recall those by I. Gershevitch on *pis* (1964a:2, fn. 2), on chronological adverbs (1964b), and by E. Benveniste, who notes that *duskīč* (cf. Morgenstierne 1948a:283 and Elfenbein 1963:33) ought, in L. Dames' text, to signify 'sister of the woman', cf. Old Persian *duxši-* 'royal princess', etc., and is therefore without relation to the name for 'girl' (Benveniste 1966b:49; see also J. Duchesne-Guillemin, *Muséon* 59.571–5, 1946). We call attention finally to the minor publications indicated by I. Afšār (1961, nos. 4039–4041) and the linguistic desiderata pointed out by M.B. Emeneau (1964) to which we will return.

3.11 *Xorāsān*

This region, a systematic exploration of which remains to be made, has revealed no dialect which is not of the Persian type. This is true of *Sīstānī*, which has been more or less heavily influenced by *Balōčī* and which is still relatively unknown. G. Morgenstierne has published the materials which come from Sir George Grierson, collected for the Linguistic Survey of India but not included in it (1948a:291–2). In addition, he has reviewed all those materials published by Jan W. Weryho (1962, where, curiously, this aid is not mentioned), whose study includes a succinct characterization of Sīstānī, about forty poems of diverse genres (with translation), and a lexicon. A.L. Grjunberg, for his part, has given the results — seventy-four sentences with grammatical commentary — of an investigation of the Sīstānīs who had immigrated to Saraxs, in Turkmenistan (1963b). Finally, we owe to I. Afšār one hundred Sīstānī words, to M. Poršād, songs of Zabol, while R.N. Frye has published the *Zābolī* poem which we had recorded there together (Afšār 1961:nos. 4099–4101; cf. also Frye, 1952).

As Persian and its variants are not being considered here, we will limit ourselves to a reference to I. Afšār (1961:nos. 4054–4072) and indicate two particularly interesting works: one by Adīb Ṭūsī on the language of Noqān, an old quarter of Mašhad, which includes a phonetic analysis, a study of personal pronouns, and a glossary in transcription (1962: 'Loġāt-e noqānī', *RFLTiz* 14.1–41, 1341), and another on the phonology of the Persian of Qāen by R. Zomorrodiān (1967–68), the translator of André Martinet.

3.12 *Baškardī*

This dialectal group of South East Persia has for a long time been known through the research of E.A. Floyer, *Unexplored Baluchistan* (London, 1882, 467f.) which G.

Morgenstierne has brought to the attention of Iranists (1948a:253–4; note that the essential part of the linguistic materials collected by Floyer has been lost). In 1956, a long sojourn allowed I. Gershevitch to study Baškardī closely and to extablish the existence of two groups, northern and southern, which separate the isoglosses (e.g. *-t-* > *-r-* and *w* > *gw-* as against *-t-* = *-t-*, *-k-* > *-x-* and *rty* > *š*). Our colleague in Cambridge has given twenty words in a preliminary account of his trip (1959), and others are scattered throughout various studies: thus *ǰag*, *ǰax* > Old Iran. *yakā* which designates the tree named *Dalbergia sissoo* Roxb. (1957:318); *ǰān*, *ǰōn* 'body' (1962a:82); *xāk* 'ground on which one walks or sits', *bǎhr*, *bohr* 'spade', *nǎvak* (N Bašk. *nox*, *nűög*) 'hollowed-out tree-trunks used for irrigation purposes', *dor* 'udder', *dərāyén*, *drā'én* 'hail', *pāxwavés* 'bare-foot', *res* 'sun, day' (*e* < *au*), etc. (1962b:77–80, 83–4); *pīštom-pạra'uš*, *pas-para'-uš* 'four days hence', *pester* 'before', *ka* 'somebody', *pa* 'afterwards', *yāhmōn* 'sky', *čehm* 'eye', *gohort* 'big' (cf. Kermānī *gohort*), etc. (1964a:2, 11–12); also chronological terms (1964b); and some isolated terms generously communicated by I. Gershevitch to others, while waiting to publish all of his materials (thus, e.g., *šen-* 'to separate, tear asunder' is cited as *ben'-* by R.E. Emmerick, *Saka grammatical studies*, 103, London, 1968).

3.13 *Biyābānak*

W. Ivanow has shown in 1926 and 1930 a considerable interest in *Xūrī* and in the dialects of the other oasis of Dašt-e Kavīr. R.N. Frye has given a note on *Farvī* or *Farrōxī* (1949b, cf. also 1952 and a 'comparison' of Xūrī and Balōčī in *Mehr* 8.142–4, 217–21, cited by Afšār 1961:no. 4040). The materials have not been collected in the field, except for those of S̱. Kīā who has noted a phonetic trait (Farvī *g* = Persian *b*, for example *gā*: *bād* 'wind'), given twenty-four Farvī words, 1 Xūrī, as well as some interesting terms of other modern dialects and some less successful relations with Old and Middle Iranian (1954). We will note equally the Xūrī poem published by Moḥ. ʿAmīnī in *Yağmā* 7.186–7 (cited by Afšār 1961:no. 4042). In 1951 and above all in 1959, we conducted research at Xūr and in the surrounding area (Čāhmalek, Farrōxī in the Northeast, Čupānān, Garmāb, Irāǰ in the Southwest, etc.) which will be the subject of a monograph and from which, up to now, we have only extracted the terms relative to the palm tree (Redard 1962) and certain others concerning the camel (1964).

3.14 *Central Persia*

Despite the currently used designation, the central dialects do not represent any real unity. The actual dialects are close to varieties of Persian, and the distinction is not always easy to establish. In principle, the dialects are still spoken in the villages and by certain urban communities (Jews and Parsis). Note a general review by Sokolova and Grjunberg (1962:132–4) and Oranskij (1963:151–4).

3.14.1 *Gabrī* (*Yazdī*, *Kermānī*). The dialect of the Zoroastrian community of Yazd and Kermān has been studied by W. Ivanow, *The Gabri dialect spoken by the Zoroastrians of Persia* (Rome, 1940); this is a collection of articles appearing earlier in *RSO*. To this work has been added the excellent dictionary compiled by J̌. S. Sorūšiān (1956), and several articles inventoried by I. Afšār (1961:4087–4089 = contributions by Ḥ. Šakīhā, K. Kešāvarz, and S. Nafīsī in Pašutan's first volume; for Yazdī, cf. Afšār 1961:4238–4249). Although it concerns Persian, we will note here the dictionary of Kermānī published by Manūčehr Sotūdeh (1956), and the study on the phonetics and the verbal system of this same language by Nāṣer Baqāī: 'Fārsī Kermān', *RFLTiz* 15–19, 1342–1346 (1963–67).

3.14.2 The *Nāīnī* and the *Anārakī* languages have been discussed in the research mentioned under 3.13. There are two minor references to *Kāšanī* and *Nāṭanzī* by I. Afšār (1961:nos. 4152–4153).

3.14.3 *Sedehī* (Sedeh is situated west of Isfahān), once explored by Žukovskij, has attracted the attention of B. Farahvašī, who has outlined the verbal system, which is quite close to that of Persian (1962).

3.14.4 *Vafsī*, *Āštīānī*. Certain dialects are spoken between Hamadān and Sāve, in the Tafreš area, which appear to have made the transition between the central dialects and the Tālešī group (below). Vafsī, Āštīānī, notably, have been studied by M. Moġdam (1949), whose work concerned, in addition to these, the dialects of the Amore district, that of the Zand black-tenters, the Gypsy dialect, and the Xalaǰ and Turki dialects (1949). The study has been taken up again for Āštīānī by S̱. Kiā, who began by publishing a lexicon of it (1956). L.P. Elwell-Sutton has studied Vafsī and he gives a preliminary view of the rich materials he has collected (1963a).

3.15 *Semnānī and Surrounding Dialects*

Our knowledge of the lexicon has been notably enriched thanks to Manūčehr Sotūdeh's dictionary which deals with the group of Semnānī, Sorxeī, Lāsgerdī, Sangesarī, and Šāmerzādī, and which thus facilitates a comparison (1963). By the same author, we note the Semnānī proverbs published in *FIZ* 2.80–92 (Afšār 1961:no. 4095, cf. also 4069–4098), and the Firūzkūhī proverbs (northeast of Semnān) with Persian translation, but without any commentary (1964). Here again, we owe two important articles to G. Morgenstierne. The first, devoted to Semnānī (1958b), comprises a phonological study vocalism (*i e ä a ȧ ə o u*), some remarks on final vowels, gender, nouns, and pronouns, verbs (with list), a vocabulary, and some texts: two songs, two tales, and two letters, to which G. Morgenstierne has added a poem and two other texts with commentary (Add. Notes). The other article (1960:73–121, 139–40) combines notes on the phonetics and morphology of Semnānī (73–93, with texts), Biyābunekī (93–100, with a text), Aftarī (100–7; also Afdarī), Sangesarī (107–8), Šāmerzādī (108–9), and Sorxeī (109); finally the author has established a comparative vocabulary, distributed semantically (109–21); an additional note is accompanied by two drawings: millstone and feeder, interior of water-mill (139–40). The verbal morphology of the dialect of Sangesar (about 18 kilometers to the north of Semnan) has been the subject of G.L. Windfuhr's thesis (1965) which is based upon materials collected in the area in 1961, and which treats with clarity and rigor the problems studied by V.A. Žukovskij in 1888 and A. Christensen in 1935; provided with excellent indexes, it is an exemplary contribution to the dialectology of Modern Iranian. A. Christensen groups Sangesarī and Lāsgerdī with Semnānī, but not Šāmerzādī (Contributions I 8, note 2); nevertheless, this difficult question can and should be reconsidered.

3.16 *Caspian Dialects*

One will find a general review and a history of research in Sokolova and Grjunberg (1962:132–4) and Oranskij (1963:151–4). T.N. Pachalina and V.S. Sokolova have given a brief but substantial characterization of *Gīlakī* (1957a) and *Māzandarānī* (1957b). The phonetics of these two dialects has been studied by V.S. Sokolova's collaborator, V.I. Zav'jalova (1956); after having recalled the essays by Beresine (1853), G. Melgunov (1868) and A. Christensen (1930), she describes the articulation and defines the respective phonemic systems: while Gīlakī and Māzandarānī each have the same twenty-one consonants (*p b t d k g č ǰ m n f v s z j x γ h š l r*), they differ in regard to vocalism: Gīlakī *i ī e ə a u ū o ȧ*, Māzand. *i e ε a u o*. To this group ought to belong the language of the translation (probably from the eighteenth century) added to a manuscript of Qor'ān, belonging to the library of the Grand Loge in Edinburgh, and studied by L.P. Elwell-Sutton (1963b). The latter presents its phonetics, case-endings, pronouns, numerals, pre- and postpositions, the indeclinables, verbs (with a short note on the syntax, 123), and vocabulary (nos. 1–74: verbs; 75–320: nouns, adjectives, etc.).

3.16.1 *Gīlakī.* Manūčehr Sotūdeh has given us an admirable dictionary, very carefully composed (1954). He has also published, in transcription, a glossary of the dialect of 'Alī Ābād-e Faryam, a village in Sāri (1962a), and the dialect of Sabsalīr (1962b, with an indication of the fourteen villages where this dialect is spoken). I. Afšār notes several articles by M. Sotūdeh as well: the winds of Gīlān, the names of fish (which have also been studied by S. Nafīsī, *Ibid.*), then songs and poems published notably by Sotūdeh and E. Serāǰ (Afšār 1961:nos. 4183–4211); L. Mobašarī, for his part, published a collection of songs with musical notation (Āhanghā 1959). Gīlakī is represented in the poems found in five pages of an 1891 manuscript and edited by M. Mohaqeq (1959). Finally, F. Mačiānī has devoted four articles to his maternal language (Mačīān is a village of Rudsar): phonetics, stories, names of the months, and a glossary in transcription (1964–65).

3.16.2 *Māzandarānī* has been almost abandoned. Besides the texts — songs, verses, proverbs — that I. Afšār records (1961: nos. 4214–4230), it is necessary to mention the Gorgānī lexicon procured by S̱. Kīā (1951), who had already published — another indication of 'old Māzandarānī' — a Ṯabarī lexicon (*Īrān Kūde* 9, Tehran 1316/1937; cf. also W. B. Henning 1954:158).

3.17 *Dialects of Azerbaidjan*

The progressive establishment of Turkish tribes in Iranian Azerbaidjan (eleventh-sixteenth centuries) has been studied by A. Kasravī (1946, 3rd ed. reproducing the second of 1317/1938 which is also the best). This has profoundly altered the linguistic picture of a region whose common language — if you disregard the Persian imported by the administration and the schools — is today a Turkic dialect, aptly described by Vincent Monteil (*JA* 244.1–77, 1956). In the article *Tāt* of the Encyclopaedia of Islam, Vl. Minorsky noted the survival of Iranian dialects. He was also the one who initiated the investigation of the 'Nachlass' of Emil Baer, who disappeared in Germany at the end of World War II without publishing any of the materials which he had collected in Northwest Iran other than some preliminary reports, summarily presented in the *Actes* of the International Congresses of Orientalists in Rome in 1935, and in Brussels in 1938. Laborious and fruitless (cf. Henning 1954:167, fn. 1), these investigations finally made it possible for me to see various manuscripts, the most important of which I will mention here, for it is unlikely that permission to publish them will ever be granted by the family: a) Glossar des Dialektes von Harzandi, b) Vollständiges Questionnaire mit Aufnahmen aus 19 Orten von Nordwestiran, c) Prolegomena zur ersten Monographie über Dialektforschung in NW Iran, d) Prolegomena und Epilegomena zur iranischen Wortforschung.

In fact, it is W. B. Henning's article (1954) and, in Iran itself, the works of 'A. 'A. Kārang (1954 and 1955)[9] which will reveal the importance of the Iranian linguistic vestiges in Azerbaidjan. They are combined rather frequently under the name of Tātī, a name which should be reserved, however, for the dialects of the Tāts of the U.S.S.R., which will be discussed later.

3.17.1 Moving from south to north, one finds first, southwest of Qazvīn, *Tākistānī*, brought to light by a field investigation conducted in 1950 by W. B. Henning, who described its essential characteristics (survival of grammatical gender, pronominal

[9] We will note here the articles by Adīb Ṯūsī published in *RFLTiz*, poems in Āzarī dialect 8.240–57 (1335/1956); glossary of selected words 8.310–50 (1335/1956) and 9.361–89 (1336/1957); two odes with notes and index, in *nīme āẕarī* 'semi-āẕarī' 10.367–417 (1337/1957). I. Afšār has reviewed several publications which we have not been able to take into account here (1961: nos. 4004–4026).

system, formation of the preterite) and indicated its points of contact with other dialects, Semnānī, Tālišī, Gīlakī, and notably Ṯabarī (1954); Tākistānī appeared thus 'as the essential link, joining the Northern, Eastern and Southern groups' (1954:164). For his part, G. Morgenstierne contributed, in his study of the feminine nouns in *-a* (1962b), unpublished materials, among which appears *visite* 'husband's sister', given with no etymology and interpreted later by W.B. Henning as the final result of **visa^h^ duxtā*, cf. MIran. *visduxt* 'princess' which must have originally signified 'the daughter of the house' (1964). It is also necessary to mention the works of J̆. Āl Aḥmad on Ourāzān, the village of his ancestors, east of Ṯāleqān (1954); this monograph, which does not claim to be 'a study of dialectology or folklore', contains, nonetheless, a lexicon (43–52), followed by several sentences, with grammatical notes and tables of verbs. Elsewhere, the same author has produced a valuable collection of texts, coming primarily from Sagzābād (1958, with a map, drawings and photographs).

Tākistān belongs to the district of Rāmand, described by M. Sotūdeh, who had noted and used a manuscript of 1856, by an unknown author, and offering the most ancient Rāmandī materials that we are aware of (1955); in effect, there is, in this article of more than 50 pages, a descriptive list of the villages of the district with their local names (22–7), a glossary with a Persian translation (28–56), a translated and transcribed text (57–60), and an index of verbs (61–77). According to J̆. Āl Aḥmad, this manuscript, with which he was familiar, had been copied in Teheran and its writing was defective — he compares some of the facts which it contains with his own discoveries (1964). To M. Sotūdeh we owe a list of 150 words and a quatrain from Xū'īn, a village situated about 60 km southwest of Zanj̆ān (1958). Finally, this group has been the object of a study by E. Yar-Shater (1962) which deals notably with gender, declension, postpositions and the 'passive construction'. This same scholar has published the results of a brief investigation conducted in the two villages of Alvir and Vidar, northwest of Sāveh, in the heart of the Turkic area (1964): grammatical notes on the gender, number, and cases, pronouns and verbs, as well as three Alvin texts and two Vidari texts with English translation.

In Azerbaidjan proper, it is possible to distinguish:

3.17.2 *Harzanī*, discovered by E. Baer (cf. 3.17 above), then studied by 'A.'A. Kārang (1954) and by M. Mortaẕavī first in a short article (1954, concerning the cases and giving a transcribed text with a Persian translation), then in a more extensive work, devoted primarily to the verb (1962–63): infinitives ending in *-re*, *-te*, and *-de* (437–88: index of the important verbs), present and present participle, 'transitive construction', and phonological inventory. Best known is the variety spoken in the village of Galin-qaya, previously noted by C.F. Lehmann-Haupt who spent a night there in 1898 and recorded some of its words (*Armenien, einst und jetzt* 1.185f., 1910; cf. Henning 1954:167); Vl. Minorsky contributed seven words in a previously mentioned article (cf. 3.17), while A. Kasravī presented seventeen sentences and several words (1946:62–4). W.B. Henning has been able to make use of the material collected by M. Navvābī and to describe the dialect (1954:168–73): nominal inflection, case, verbal stems (there are three, for the present, preterite, and subjunctive, plus another for the 2nd person singular of the imperative; the present is formed from the preterite). He concludes that Harzanī is 'most closely related to Tālišī, also related to Zaza', and is probably 'a dislocated language' which 'had its home to the south-east of Tāliš' (1954:175). The dialect of Galin-qaya was the subject of a monograph by Y. Żokā (1957), which contains the phonological inventory, a glossary, several verbs, proverbs, and a text, as well as some excellent grammatical remarks on the plural, genitive, personal pronouns (note *čaman osbəm* 'my horse'), and the comparative ending in *-rax: čok* 'good', *čokrax* 'better'.

3.17.3 The dialect of certain villages of Qarağa-dāγ, to the northeast of Tabrīz, such as Karīngān, about which we have only the brief but solid study by Y. Żokā (1954).

3.17.4 The dialects of Xalxāl, at the eastern fringe of Azerbaidjan, marking the transition between Tālišī and Tākestānī, to which ʿA. ʿA. Kārang was the first to have drawn attention (1955), not considering the unpublished or lost materials of E. Baer. The best known variation is that of Šāhrūd, to which probably belong the few words presented by A. Kasravī (1938:61–2, cf. Henning 1954:166). E. Yar-Shater has devoted a study to Šāhrūdī (1959: phonology, morphology, texts) which he presented to the 24th International Congress of Orientalists in Munich, in 1957 (cf. 'Preliminary information', *Akten* ..., 458–60, Wiesbaden, 1959). It is also to him that we owe the first material on the neighboring dialect of Kajal (1960).

3.18 *Tātī*

As has been remarked (3.17), the name *Tātī* should be reserved for the language of the Tāts, those Iranians established within the confines of the Eastern end of the Caucasus (probably ever since the pre-Islamic epoch), and descended from ancient military colonies originating from the southwest of Persia. Some are Jews and are located in the cities and scattered villages of Daghestan; the others are Moslems, installed in the islet of Apchiron and in the northern cantons of the Socialist Republic of Azerbaidjan. There is a dialectal division which corresponds to this religious division. The Judeo-Tātī, once studied by V.F. Miller (*Materialy dlja izučenija evrejsko-tatskogo jazyka*, St. Petersburg, 1892), has had more success than the Muslim Tātī, since it has become one of the literary languages of Daghestan.

General communications on the subject of the dialects as a whole may be found in I.M. Oranskij (1963:145–8), while M. Hağyjev notes the main stages of research (1962, with a Russian summary). On Judeo-Tātī, there is the article by R.O. Šor on consonantism (particularly the emphatic consonants), which, unfortunately, we have not been able to see (*Jazyki Severnoga Kavkaza i Dagestana* II, 127–39, Moscow-Leningrad, 1949). Our knowledge of Muslim Tātī, still sketchy, has, however, progressed, thanks to V. S. Sokolova, who has carefully studied its phonetic system (1950: 20–8 and 1953:I.122–47), and above all to A. L. Grjunberg. The latter, in an article on interlinguistic influences (1961b), takes his examples from Tātī, whose verbal system he presents in a thorough manner (1963a); he distinguishes first, four groups of verbs: ending in *-ist-*, *-ўst-*, *-ust-*, in *-ir-* (infinitive in *-idän*, *-idan*), in *-un-*, and finally in *-xt-*, *-št-*, *-st-*, *-n-*, *-r-*; he then discusses inflection (for person, tense, and mood), and verbal nouns (infinitive, participle, gerundive, nomina agentis, absolutive); there follow some sentences with translation collected in 1956 at Dahkušču (about fifty) and at Afrudža (about forty), a valuable complement to the texts published by B. V. Miller (1945). A. L. Grjunberg has crowned these diverse studies by a fundamental work for which the material was collected during a systematic investigation conducted in diverse localities in the northeast of Azerbaidjan (1963c). After recalling what is known about the Tāts and mentioning the progressive disappearance of Muslim Tātī before Turkic (there are now only about 20 to 30 thousand speakers), Grjunberg gives an excellent description of this dialect. The phonetic part is brief (9–17), claiming only to complete the work of Mrs. Sokolova. The morphology is detailed, rich in examples (18–106); it will be noted that in Tātī — as in the Caspian dialects — the construction of the epithetic adjective is distinct from that of the determinant substantive: the adjective is affected by an enclitic suffix *æ* and placed after the substantive (*xúb-æ xunæ* 'good house'). In the verbal system, there is a present and an imperfect tense newly formed from the infinitive; the first assumes all the functions of the earlier present which has taken on the modal function of a conditional, the second the function of a durational past (comparable to the Persian preterite), the earlier imperfect now marking only the habitual action in the past and the unreal past. Several pages are devoted to the constitution of the clause and the complex sentence (106–11). One chapter treats the lexicon (112–22) and outlines the formation of the Tātī vocabulary where, to the words coming from earlier sources, may be added numerous borrowings from Persian, Arabic, and Turkic. The volume ends with a collection of texts (123–209), all translated, and with a colored map of the region explored; we regret the absence of a lexicon or at least of an index, which would have been very useful.

Nevertheless, it is possible to present a clearer picture of the place of Muslim Tātī among the Iranian dialects. Affinities with the Caspian dialects are evident, but even greater is the relationship with Persian of which Tātī may only be a dialectal variation, as has been remarked by A. L. Grjunberg himself (1961a).

3.19 *Gūrānī*

Our knowledge of *Gūrānī* — a group of dialects spoken principally in the mountains of Zagros — has increased considerably, thanks to M. Mokri and D.N. MacKenzie. To the former we owe the publication (with translation and commentaries, but without transcription) of a poem by Cheikh Amir, one of the great 'Seers' (*dīda-dār*) of the sect of Ahl-e Ḥaqq (to which M. Mokri has devoted several important works); this text, established on the basis of six manuscripts belonging to the editor, includes 52 verses, each with 3 hemistiches of 10 syllables and a title of 5 syllables which is repeated in the second half of the first hemistich (Mokri 1956). The same author has edited the first book of a manuscript (also in his possession) entitled *Daftar-i Xazāna-yi Pirdīwarī*, 'the book of the Treasury of Pirdīwar', which sets forth the doctrine of the Gurania; the text — untranscribed — is accompanied by a translation with commentary, abundant grammatical notes, glossaries, and an index (1967). For his part, D.N. MacKenzie has edited 16 of the lyrical poems in Gurani that appear on folios 8b–54b of manuscript Or. 6444 of the British Museum (1965), of which E.B. Soane had published forty couplets in 1921, unfortunately in a very uncertain form; after having reviewed what is known of the dialects of the Gurani group, and the importance of the literature to which Vl. Minorsky had called attention previously (*BSOAS* 11.75–103, 1943), MacKenzie gives a complete list of the poems contained in the manuscript, publishes 16 examples of them in transcription — and with an annotated translation; all this is followed by a valuable index (275–83).

Two dialects have been described by MacKenzie:

3.19.1 *Bāǰalānī*, according to notes collected in 1955 at Ārpačī, a Šabak village of Bāǰalānistān, northeast of Mosul (1956): MacKenzie comments on the noun, pronoun, adjective, verbs (with paradigms), followed by several sentences, numerals, and a vocabulary.

3.19.2 *Hawrāmānī* — the district of Hawrāmān (Awroman) is situated in the western part of the Iranian province of Kurdistan (Ardalān) — about which we already had the reports by J. de Morgan, A.M. Benedictsen, and O. Mann (MacKenzie 1966). MacKenzie had the opportunity of working, in London, in 1957, with an excellent informant from Nawsūda, the main village of the district of Lahon, which resulted in an exhaustive description of this dialect, which is, without a doubt, the oldest and best preserved of the group. The phonology (7–12) notes the existence of 10 vowels, 2 semi-vowels, and 26 consonants — a system which is very close to that of the surrounding Kurdic dialects of Suleimaniye and Sina; the morphology is treated in detail (13–57); several notes on the syntax (58–9) are followed by texts with translation (60–85; 162 sentences, 6 proverbs, 3 narratives, and 8 couplets), by an English-Hawrāmānī index which includes O. Mann's material (115–40) and addenda (141) which report some verification made in 1964.

3.20 *Lurī*

I.M. Oranskij gives a brief introduction to the dialects of this group — mainly Lurī and Baxtīārī (1963:139–40), and I. Afšār notes some minor works (1961:nos. 4033–4038 and 4212–4213; for Xūzestān: Dezfūlī, etc., see also nos. 4077–4084). J.M. Unvala has assembled in a volume his contribution to volumes XI and XII of *Indo-Iranica*, presenting the lexicographical material he had collected from 1927 to 1939 at Susa, where he was a member of the French Archaeological Mission then directed by R. de Mecquenem (1959). There he was able to question the laborers, mainly Lurs and Arabs; in addition, working from September to December at Nehāvend, under the direction of G. Contenau, he recorded the vocabulary of the Laks workers, or Little Lurs, as they are called. The glossary — preceded by grammatical notes (5–11) — contains 657 entries, distributed in word classes (adverbs, prepositions, adjectives, etc.) and in semantic groups (animals, time, cereals, diseases, etc.); in the appendix are dialectal expressions and Lurī names; this is completed by an index (57–73); the Lurī, Dezfūlī, Lakī, Lurī Nehāvendī words are occasionally accompanied by their equivalents in other dialects; we will also note a plate representing the plough and its parts, clumsily drawn (2A, with terminology). Since then, the Lurī vocabulary has been reviewed by ʿA. Ḥaṣūrī whose Report (1964) is above all a collection of words presented in transcription, with Persian translation, and followed by some sentences (66–75), and by H. Īzadpanāh, who has produced a dictionary, illustrated by several technical designs, whose intention is more valuable than its realization (1964). We owe G. Morgenstierne some elements, collected on location, March 16, 1957, of the dialect *Kurdšūlī*, from the name of a small tribe which has its winter quarters at Qaṣr-e Dašt near Sīvand; they are not considered to be Lurs, but include the Baxtīārī and the Manassanī, and several words which have been collected show 'the essential Lurī character of their dialect' (1960:133–4). On the unpublished study by W. Ivanow, concerning the Lurī of Famur, see 3.21 below.

3.20.1 Our knowledge of *Baxtīārī* has been increased thanks especially to D.L.R. Lorimer, who produced an excellent phonetics of it in 1922 (London). Following the publication of texts collected mainly in 1914, he presented a series of popular poems of the Baxtīārs in the southeast of Persia (1954)[10] and a savory 'Story of the guest and the householder' of the same origin (1964, with a prefatory note on the Baxtīārs and on his previous works). We also note the 182 proverbs published with an introduction and transcription by B. Dāvarī, who adds an untranscribed poem by Ḥ. Ḥ. Pažmān-e Baxtīārī (1964).

3.21 *Fārs*

The dialects of the Fārs, to the extent that they are known to us, would appear to belong to the principal one among them, Persian (*Fārsī*), but it is often difficult to

[10] The last text of the series was published in 1963 under the direction of D.N. MacKenzie, D.L.R. Lorimer having died in February 1962; it should be noted that he has bequeathed to the School of Oriental and African Studies of London rich unpublished materials, which also deal with Baxtīarī.

distinguish between what has been borrowed from Persian and what belongs to the early sources in the southwest. Besides the indications given by I. Afšār (1961: nos. 4121–4147 mainly concerning the Šīrāzī, Kāzerūnī, and Lārī dialects; see also nos. 4050–4053 concerning J̌ahrom), I. M. Oranskij has produced a brief summary (1963: 154–8). A collection of songs, with the music, transcription, and commentary, has initiated an Iranian series devoted to popular songs (Āhanghā 1956). Without being able to give a complete account of it, I nevertheless refer here to a manuscript by W. Ivanow which I saw in Teheran, at the home of the author, in October-November 1959. It contains 101 typed pages, is entitled 'Notes on some dialects spoken in the province of Fars' and contains a revised version of the material collected in 1928. Here is a summary of it: 'A. Introduction. 1. Distribution of ethnic groups and their languages, 2. The nature of the Persian dialects spoken in Fars. B. 1. Dialects of the Kazeruni group: Phonology, Morphology, Vocabulary'; there follows (74–101) a chapter 'On the Luri dialect spoken in Famur', with a text of 9 pages transcribed and translated.

3.21.1 *Sīvandī* has yet to be described exactly; to the studies by Cl. Huart, V.A. Žukovskij, F.C. Andreas and A. Christensen, and O. Mann, G. Morgenstierne has added some notes on the phonetics and morphology (1960:134–9, material collected in 1954 and 1957).

3.21.2 We owe to the same scholar information on *Kondāzī*, from the name of a small village situated about 30 km northwest of Sīvand, unknown until then (1960: 121–3): some substantives (like *rāšt* 'ashes', *šeš* 'louse', *duft* 'daughter') and a series of verbs attest to its membership in the Fārs group.

3.21.3 The same can be said for *Davānī* from Davān, a village 8 km north of Kāzerūn (1960:123–9, and additional note, 139). For *Kāzerunī*, properly speaking, besides the unpublished notes of W. Ivanow mentioned above (3.21), I can only call attention to the study by Adīb Ṯūsī (1959) which, unfortunately, we have not been able to see since the edition of the journal of Tabriz, where it appeared, is missing from our collection.

3.21.4 *Šīrāzī* no more belongs here than Mašhadī or Kermānī, all varieties of Persian. There did exist, however, a Šīrāzī, properly speaking, which is still relatively unknown. Adīb Ṯūsī has published three of its texts taken from the Dīvān of Šāh dāʿī-allāh-e šīrāzī (*RFLTiz* 17.149–82, 1344/1965). From the same author, as well as from the work of ḪāfeẒ and Saʿdī, Māhīār Navābī has drawn dialectal forms which have made it possible for him to outline the history of Šīrāzī up to the ninth century H. [= fifteenth A.D.] (Ṯūsī 1959:77–90). The study appeared in English without any notable revisions, in the *Unvala memorial volume*, 169–80 (Bombay, 1964). It is necessary to mention finally the Judeo-Šīrāzī about which we have only some notes taken in March, 1957, by G. Morgenstierne (1960:129–32: remarks on the phonetics and the lexicon) — interesting in many regards (thus *teš* 'louse' which must come from a form in Fārs **θišā-*) — and a page on the verbs which is purely of the type in Fārs.

3.21.5 The dialects of Lārestān (southeast of Shiraz) form a group apart, and it is legitimate to speak of one *Larī* or *Larestānī* dialect. A perspective was provided by A.A. Romaskevič (1945a), who produced a history of the research which has been done, and gives the essential parts of the phonetics, of nominal and verbal morphology, a note on the syntax (60–1), an excellent selection of transcribed and translated texts (61–82), and a short lexicon (82–6). The vocabulary is better known now thanks to the dictionary of A. Eqtedārī (1955), to whom we owe the publication of Lārī proverbs as well (*FIZ* 2.233–53, cited by Afšār 1961: no. 4214, which we have not been able to see), and of *Fišvarī* texts, from the name of a village in Lārestān (1963:72–91, a letter with annotated transcription).

3.22 *Ossetic*

The importance of this language and the works which have been devoted to it during the last quarter century is such that it should be treated separately in this article, as were Kurdic, Tāǰik, and Pašto. In order to maintain a certain equilibrium, we have been forced to restrict ourselves to the essentials, and to only those publications which have been accessible.

3.22.1 *General.* Concerning the Ossetic dialects, several succinct indications are given by W.K. Matthews (1951:102–3, 127), R.I. Avanesov and V.G. Orlova (1953), I.M. Oranskij (1960:310–13, bibliography 441–2; 1963:127–34). V.I. Abaev has presented two reports on the state and the goals of research (1939, 1957); M.I. Isaev has reviewed a certain number of non-Soviet publications (1957). The survey by Dietrich Gerhardt, 'Alanen und Osseten', in *ZDMG* 9.33–51 (1939) has not, unfortunately, been completed, at least to our knowledge. The history of research has been traced by M.I. Isaev (1960a: principal stages of linguistic studies of Ossetic), while N.Ch. Kulaev (1949, on the Finnish scholar, A.J. Sjögren) and R.K. Sikoev (1961) have reviewed the pioneers of Ossetic studies. Concerning the present master of the discipline, V.I. Abaev (= Vaso Abajty), consult the notes of his student M.I. Isaev (= Mäxämet Isajty) (1958, bibliography 407–14; 1960b, bibliography 22–8) and of Z.N. Baneev (1960); finally, I.M. Oranskij reports on the development of centers of research in the North Ossetic ASSR and in South-Ossetic Autonomous Region (Georgian SSR) in the years of Soviet power (1968:13, 29–30, bibliography 41, fn. 15).

3.22.2 *Collections.* Three fundamental works assemble previously published, or unpublished monographs. V.I. Abaev has thus completed an admirable collection of articles on the language and folklore (1949). We should mention here the linguistic introduction to the history of the Ossetic people (9–15), a glance at the history of the language (30–1), an outline of the general characteristics of modern Ossetic (95–108 [= *Jafetičeskij sbornik* (1932) 7.57–80] on phonetics, morphology, lexicon, semantics, syntax), the study of the ethnic denominations *Iron*, *Allon* (245–7 [= *Jafetičeskij sbornik* (1927) 5.105–8]), and the article entitled '150 ans de la vie d'une langue' (509–11 [= *IzvJOsNII* (1935) 2.235–8]). In his 'Etudes ...' (1959), E. Benveniste presents two articles published in the *BSL* (1956a, 1956b, with some corrections) and three others, which are new: morphology and lexicology of verbs (73–92), prefixes and suffixes (93–113), remarks on the traditional vocabulary (115–43), complete with additions and corrections (145–6), and an index of Ossetic and other words studied (147–63). Some important reviews of this work have been written, especially the one by V.I. Abaev (*VJa* 1960.141–5), H.W. Bailey (*JRAS* 1961.53–6), M. Mayrhofer (*BiOr* 1961/18.272–5) and R. Bouda (*Kratylos* 1961/6.48–52); it has been translated into Russian under the direction of K.E. Gagkaev (*Očerki po osetinskomu jazyku*, Moscow, Izd. Nauka, 1965), and this translation includes, in addition, a preface (5–20) in which V.I. Abaev suggests a good number of etymologies and interpretations which differ from E. Benveniste's (some had already been mentioned in the review cited above). Finally, G. Achvlediani has assembled a series of articles which appeared from 1923 to 1960 (1960a, cf. M.I. Isaev, *VJa* 1962.143–5 and N. Kulaev, *IzvSOsNII* 1962/23.159–63). Following the history of the development of Ossetic as a literary language (the concern of Ivan Jalguzidze, Daniil Čonkadze, etc.), there is a study of the dialectology, another on historical and descriptive phonetics, and, finally, etymologies.

3.22.3 *Grammars.* M.I. Isaev has translated the grammar prepared, in 1903, by Wsewolod Miller,[11] with a preface and supplements by V.I. Abaev (B.V. Miller 1962). We are indebted to the latter for providing us with the most efficient instrument for an initiation into Ossetic: Abaev's grammar first appeared in his dictionary (1950), then, in a second edition, in the dictionary of Bigulaev-Gagkaev (1952) and, finally, in a third edition, revised and augmented by several texts (1959a), which also appeared in the new edition of the Bigalaev-Gagkaev dictionary (1962); the English translation published by Steven P. Hill (Abaev 1959a) is based on the editions of 1952 and 1959; it is good, in spite of certain mistakes noted by L. Zgusta, *AO* 1966/34.446–54. The same scheme, but more richly illustrated, has been adopted for the grammar published under the direction of G.S. Achvlediani (Abaev-Cagaeva 1963), of which only the first volume has appeared, devoted to phonetics and morphology; the introduction, primarily historical, was written by Abaev, phonetics and a general treatment of morphology by Isaev, while A.Dz. Cagaeva deals with the substantives, adjectives, and adverbs, N.Ch. Kulaev the declension, numerals, pronouns, conjunctions, post-, and prepositions, T.Z. Kozyreva verbs, A.T. Agnaev the particles, and T.A. Guriev interjections. For his part, K.E. Gagkaev presented an excellent outline of the system of the language (1952), then a study of Ossetic-Russian grammatical parallels in the

[11] 'Die Sprache der Osseten', *Grundriss der iran. Phil.*, 1/6.111 pp.

lexicon, phonetic system, and morphology (1953). We are indebted to N.K. Bagaev for a description of modern Ossetic (1965, vol. 1: phonetics and morphology). For the Digor grammar of M.I. Isaev, see p. 128.

3.22.4 *Terminology.* With the growth of Ossetic as a literary and official language came the publication of manuals and the fixing of a scientific terminology. We do not possess anything similar for Persian, in spite of certain isolated attempts (e.g. Yār-Šāṭer 1957:47–8). The literary-scientific terminology of Tājik has been the subject of a dictionary which might serve as a model.[12] N.Ch. Kulaev has provided the basis (1960) for a linguistic terminology of Ossetic, and reports on the work in progress in northern Ossetic (1961b).

3.22.5 *Ossetic, Iranian, and Indo-European.* The position of Ossetic among the Iranian languages and in the Indo-European family has been the subject of numerous observations, which cannot be treated here exhaustively. The only general study is that by Abaev (1965) which, developing a previous article (1962), presents an entire series of lexical isoglosses (e.g. *laesaeg* 'salmon', Germ. *Lachs* 'id.'), phonetic isoglosses (thus *f* in Ossetic and Germanic), and grammatical isoglosses (as the use of the genitive in Ossetic and Slavic), to which are added mythological parallels (on the Nartic epic). Elsewhere the same author has inventoried the Old Persian elements in Ossetic (1945:138–43), and compared Vedic *arí-* with Ossetic *aecaegaelon* (1958b). H.W. Bailey has studied, on several occassions, the words and morphological elements which attest the importance of the connection of Ossetic with the Khotanese and other Eastern Iranian languages (1945; suppl. 1948, I:329–32; corrigenda 1948, II:125 in regard to Dig. *faedzaexsun* 'to entrust', 135–6 on the subject of Dig. *Asi* 'Balkaria'). Among the 'Irano-Indica' (1948), we note the study of the Ossetic Dig. *fazae* ,Iron *faz* 'back surface' < MIran **pāza-* (I:325, II:136), *rae* < Iran. **fra-*, *toenoeg* 'thin' (II:124), *sor* 'dry' (II-136–8). In 'Iranian *arya-* and *daha-*' (1959b and suppl.) Dig. *äldār*, *ärdār*, Iron *äldār* < *aryadāra-* 'owner of wealth' (74–5), Iron *āryn:ārd* 'find, get', Dig. *jerun:ird*, etc. (82–3), Dig. *irä*, *iriston* (97–8), *ar-* 'to attack' (105–6), Oss. *läg* 'man' < Alan **dahaka*, cf. perhaps Gr. δοῦχος? (108), Oss. *älγin* 'avaricious' < **arganya-* (Suppl. 88) are studied, among others. Finally, in the 'Indagatio' (1960), we note the derivatives of the base *vazd-* 'nourish' (62ff.), Dig. *od*, *ŭod* 'soul, life', etc. (71ff.), Oss. *ärzät* 'ore' (75ff.). It should be noted, on the other hand, that E. Benveniste rejects the equation *Eltaγan* = *Vṛθragna* proposed by G. Dumézil, in *Mélanges H. Grégoire*, 223f. (1949) (see also Dumézil, *JA* 1956:353), and that I. Gershevitch relates the form of the inscription of Surkh Kotal πορογατο < OIran. **pari-kan-* to the Oss. *faelgaetaeg* < **pari-kaθa-ka-* (1966:100, fn. 15).[13]

[12] R. Hodizoda, M. Šukurov, and T. Abdujabborov, 'Lughati istilohoti adabiëtšinosi', *Našriëti 'Irfon'*, 184 p. (Dušanbe, 1964).

[13] Other Iranian Languages' is regrettably incomplete. The concluding section was sent from Iran but never received by the editors; it will appear elsewhere.

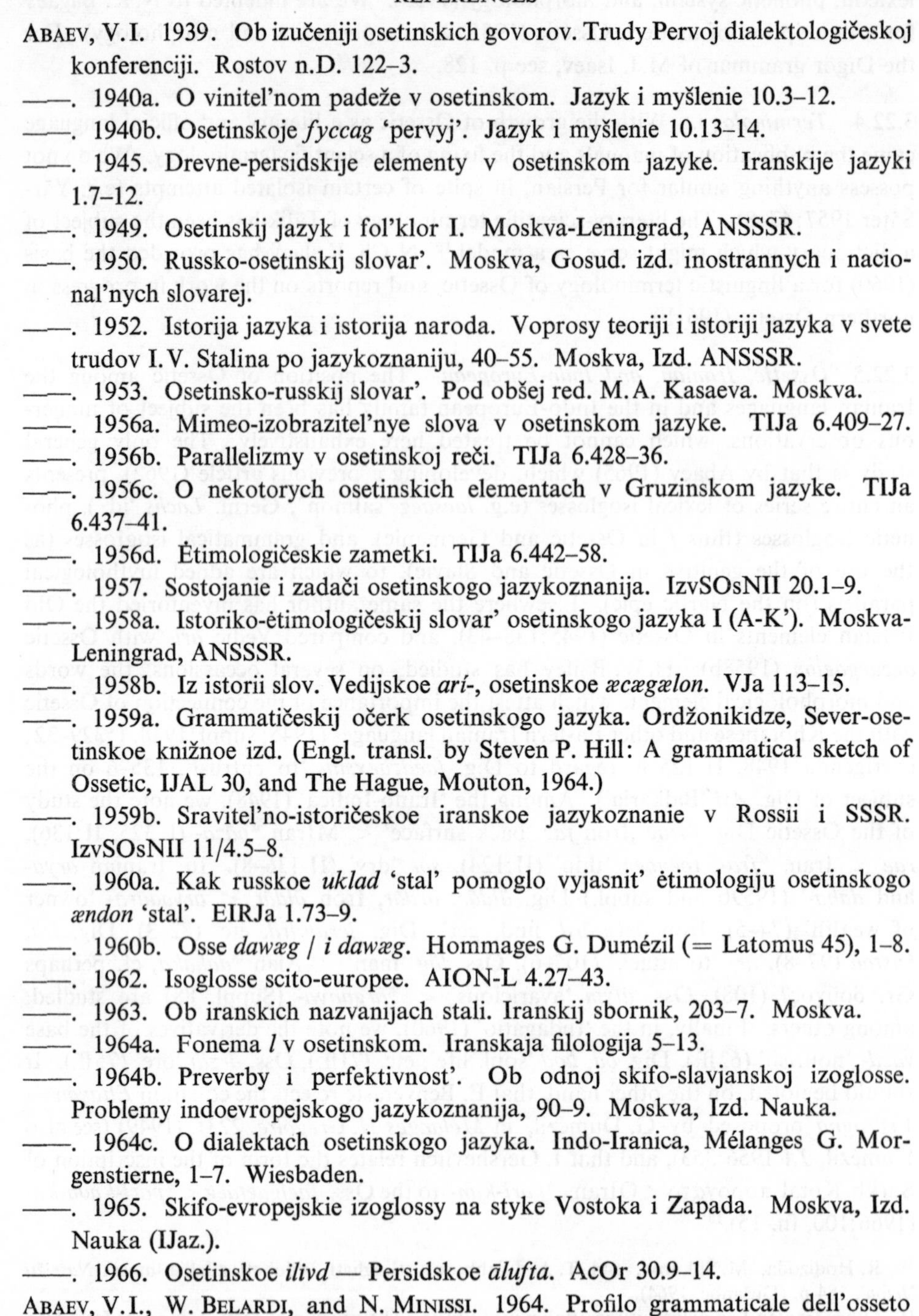

REFERENCES

Abaev, V. I. 1939. Ob izučeniji osetinskich govorov. Trudy Pervoj dialektologičeskoj konferenciji. Rostov n.D. 122–3.

——. 1940a. O vinitel'nom padeže v osetinskom. Jazyk i myšlenie 10.3–12.

——. 1940b. Osetinskoje *fyccag* 'pervyj'. Jazyk i myšlenie 10.13–14.

——. 1945. Drevne-persidskije elementy v osetinskom jazyke. Iranskije jazyki 1.7–12.

——. 1949. Osetinskij jazyk i fol'klor I. Moskva-Leningrad, ANSSSR.

——. 1950. Russko-osetinskij slovar'. Moskva, Gosud. izd. inostrannych i nacional'nych slovarej.

——. 1952. Istorija jazyka i istorija naroda. Voprosy teoriji i istoriji jazyka v svete trudov I. V. Stalina po jazykoznaniju, 40–55. Moskva, Izd. ANSSSR.

——. 1953. Osetinsko-russkij slovar'. Pod obšej red. M. A. Kasaeva. Moskva.

——. 1956a. Mimeo-izobrazitel'nye slova v osetinskom jazyke. TIJa 6.409–27.

——. 1956b. Parallelizmy v osetinskoj reči. TIJa 6.428–36.

——. 1956c. O nekotorych osetinskich elementach v Gruzinskom jazyke. TIJa 6.437–41.

——. 1956d. Ėtimologičeskie zametki. TIJa 6.442–58.

——. 1957. Sostojanie i zadači osetinskogo jazykoznanija. IzvSOsNII 20.1–9.

——. 1958a. Istoriko-ėtimologičeskij slovar' osetinskogo jazyka I (A-K'). Moskva-Leningrad, ANSSSR.

——. 1958b. Iz istorii slov. Vedijskoe *arí-*, osetinskoe *æcægælon.* VJa 113–15.

——. 1959a. Grammatičeskij očerk osetinskogo jazyka. Ordžonikidze, Sever-osetinskoe knižnoe izd. (Engl. transl. by Steven P. Hill: A grammatical sketch of Ossetic, IJAL 30, and The Hague, Mouton, 1964.)

——. 1959b. Sravitel'no-istoričeskoe iranskoe jazykoznanie v Rossii i SSSR. IzvSOsNII 11/4.5–8.

——. 1960a. Kak russkoe *uklad* 'stal' pomoglo vyjasnit' ėtimologiju osetinskogo *ændon* 'stal'. ĖIRJa 1.73–9.

——. 1960b. Osse *dawæg* / *i dawæg*. Hommages G. Dumézil (= Latomus 45), 1–8.

——. 1962. Isoglosse scito-europee. AION-L 4.27–43.

——. 1963. Ob iranskich nazvanijach stali. Iranskij sbornik, 203–7. Moskva.

——. 1964a. Fonema *l* v osetinskom. Iranskaja filologija 5–13.

——. 1964b. Preverby i perfektivnost'. Ob odnoj skifo-slavjanskoj izoglosse. Problemy indoevropejskogo jazykoznanija, 90–9. Moskva, Izd. Nauka.

——. 1964c. O dialektach osetinskogo jazyka. Indo-Iranica, Mélanges G. Morgenstierne, 1–7. Wiesbaden.

——. 1965. Skifo-evropejskie izoglossy na styke Vostoka i Zapada. Moskva, Izd. Nauka (IJaz.).

——. 1966. Osetinskoe *ilivd* — Persidskoe *ālufta*. AcOr 30.9–14.

Abaev, V. I., W. Belardi, and N. Minissi. 1964. Profilo grammaticale dell'osseto letterario moderno. AION-L 6.49–68.

Abaev, V. I., and A. Dz. Cagaeva [et al.]. 1963. Iron ævzadzy grammatikæ, I. — Grammatika osetinskogo jazyka, I. Fonetika i morfologija. Pod redakciej G. S. Achvlediani. Ordžonikidze, Severo-oset. knižnoe izd.

Abaev, V. I., and M. I. Isaev. 1962. Istorija izučenija osetinskogo jazyka v Rossii i SSSR. (Dorevoljucionnyj period: Abaev; Sovetskaja ėpocha: Isaev). Očerki po istorii izučenija iranskich jazykov, 84–99. Moskva, Izd. ANSSSR.

Achvlediani, G. S. 1948. L'élément énigmatique *d* dans ossète *dän*, *dä*. SANGruz 1.79–82.

——. 1960a. Sbornik izbrannych rabot po osetinskomu jazyku I. TTbilU, Trudy kaf. obščego jazykoved. 5.

——. 1960b. Ossetica-Georgica. IzvSOsNII 22.29–40.

——. 1963. Preverbnyj tmezis v osetinskom jazyke. KSINA 67.11–15.

Afšār, Iraǰ. 1955. Bibliographie de l'Iran, 1954 ss. Tehran, Ibn-e Sina and Iran Book Club.

——. 1961. Index Iranicus. Répertoire méthodique des articles persans concernant les études iranologiques, publiés dans les périodiques et publications collectives. I, 1910–1958. Tehren (Groupe bibliogr. national iran. 3).

——. 1964. Fehrest-nāme-ye ketābšenāsīhā-ye Irān (A bibliography of bibliographies on Iranian studies). I. Tehran, Fac. of letters, 1342.

Agnaev, A. T. 1964. Kriterii vydelenija častic v osetinskom jazyke. IzvSOsNII 24.122–30.

Āhanghā. 1956. Āhanghā-ye maḥallī-ye manāṭeq-e ǰonūb-e Īrān, I. Tehran, Edāre-ye honarhā-ye zibā-ye kešvar, 1335.

——. 1959. Āhanghā-ye maḥallī-ye Gīlān. Tehran, Edāre-ye honarhā-ye zibā-ye kešvar, 1338.

Āl Aḥmad, J̌alāl. 1954. Ourāzān. Tehran, Dāneš, 1333.

——. 1958. Tāt-nešīnhā-ye Bolūk-e Zahrā. Tehran, Dāneš, 1337.

——. 1964. Ešāre-ī besiār dīr āmade bar 'lahǰe-ye Rāmand'. FIZ 12.323–9, 1343.

Andreev, M. S., and E. M. Peščereva. 1957. Jagnobskie teksty, s priloženiem jagnobsko-russkogo slovarja, sost. M. S. Andreevym, V. A. Livšicem i A. K. Pisarčik. Moskva, ANSSSR.

Andronikašvili, M. K. 1966. Očerki po iransko-gruzinskim jazykovym vzaimootnošenijam, I. Tbilisi, Izd. Univ. (in Georgian).

Apor, Éva. 1963. Ossetic material among the literary remains of Bernard Munkácsi. AOH 16.225–40.

Aslanov, M. G. 1962. Očerednye zadači izučenija afganskoj toponimiki. Toponimika Vostoka, 142–5. Moskva.

Avanesov, R. I., and V. G. Orlova. 1953. Voprosy izučenija dialektov jazykov narodov SSSR. VJa 5.30–47.

Axvlediani = see Achvlediani.

Badaxšī, Šāh 'Abdullāh. 1942–43. Tadvin-e loġāt-e navāḥi-ye Pāmīr. Āriānā 1/12.7–10; 2/2.20–3.

——. 1960. Da Afġānistān da dzīno žəbo au lahǰo qāmūs. Paṣtū Ṭūlana da loġātū čāng. Kabul 1339.

Bagaev, N.K. 1957. Grammatika osetinskogo jazyka, I. Fonetika i morfologija, II. Sintaksis. Ordžonikidze.

——. 1963. Iron ævzadžy orfografion dzyrduat. Ordžonikidze, Cægat Irystony cinguytu rauagъdad.

——. 1965. Sovremennyi osetinskij jazyk. I. Fonetika i morfologia. Ordžonikidze, Severo-oset. knižnoe izd.

Bailey, H.W. 1945. Asica. TPhS 1–38; Supplementary note in TPhS 202–6 (1946).

——. 1948. Irano-Indica. I = BSOAS 12.319–32; II = 13.121–39 (1949).

——. 1950. L'accento in osseto digoron. RL 1.58–66.

——. 1958. *Arya.* BSOAS 21.522–45; II = 23.13–39 (1960); III = 24.470–83 (1961); IV = 26.69–91 (1963).

——. 1959a. Ambages Indoiranicae. AION-L 1.113–46.

——. 1959b. Iranian *Arya-* and *Daha-*. TPhS 71–115; Supplementary note in TPhS 87–88 (1960).

——. 1960. Indagatio indo-iranica. TPhS 62–86.

Bailey, H.W., and Alan S.C. Ross. 1961. Path. TPhS 107–42.

Balkarov, B.Ch. 1965. Adygskie ėlementy v osetinskom jazyke. Nal'čik, Kabardino-balkar. knižnoe izd.

Baneev, Z.N. 1960. V.I. Abaev i voprosy istorii Osetii. IsvJOsNII 10.30–48.

Barr, Kaj. 1949. Sur le développement du système verbal en iranien occidental. Actes 21e Congr. orient., 158–62. Paris.

Barth, F., and G. Morgenstierne. 1958. Vocabularies and specimens of some S.E. Dardic dialects. NTS 18.118–36.

Bausani, A. 1951. Les études d'iranistique et turcologie en Italie depuis 1941. AO 19.85–93.

Benveniste, E. 1948. Mots voyageurs en Asie centrale. JA 236.177–88.

——. 1952. Les langues de l'Afghanistan. La civilisation iranienne, 237–40. Paris, Payot.

——. 1954. Expression de 'pouvoir' en iranien. BSL 50.56–67.

——. 1955. Un lexique du yagnobi. JA 243.139–62.

——. 1956a. Etudes sur la phonétique et l'étymologie de l'ossète. BSL 52.6–59.

——. 1956b. Analyse d'un vocable primaire: indo-européen *bhāghu- 'bras'. BSL 52.60–71.

——. 1957–58. Mots d'emprunt iraniens en arménien. BSL 53.55–71.

——. 1959. Etudes sur la langue ossète. Paris (Coll. Société de linguistique 60). (Russ. transl. by K.E. Gagkaev: Očerki po osetinskomu jazyku. Moskva, Izd. Nauka, 1965.)

——. 1960. Les noms de l''oiseau' en iranien. Paideuma 7.193–9 (Festg. H. Lommel).

——. 1964. La racine *yat-* en indo-iranien. Indo-Iranica, Mélanges G. Morgenstierne, 21–7. Wiesbaden.

——. 1966a. Le verbe *stā-* comme auxiliaire en iranien. AcOr 30.45–9.

——. 1966b. Titres et noms propres en iranien ancien. Paris, Klincksieck (Trav. Inst. ét. iran. Univ. Paris 1).
BIGULAEV, B.B. 1952. Kratkaja istorija osetinskogo pis'ma. Dzaudžikau.
BIGULAEV, B.B., and V. MAMSUROV. 1941. Russko-osetinskij slovar'. Ordžonikidze, Severo-oset. knižnoe izd.
BIGULAEV, B.B., K.E. GAGKAEV, N.CH. KULAEV, and O.N. TUAEVA. 1952. Osetinsko-russkij slovar', pod obšej redaciej A.M. Kasaeva. S priloženiem grammatičeskogo očerka osentinskogo jazyka V.I. Abaeva. Moskva, Gosud. izd. inostr. i nac. slovarej. — 2- oe dopolnennoe izdanie. 1962. Ordžonikidze, Severo-oset. knižnoe izd.
BOGOLJUBOV, M.N. 1947. K etimologiji vachanskogo vspomogatel'nogo glagola *tej-:tu-* 'byt'. IzvAN 6.339–40.
——. 1948. Obzor pomeščennych v Učen. zap. vojen. instituta inostrannych jazykov iranskich rabot. Sovetsk. Vostokoved. 5.329–31.
——. 1954. K istorii modal'no-vremennych otnošenij v iranskich jazykach. LGU, naučnaja sessija 1953/54 g. Tezisy dokladov po sekcii vostokoved. nauk, 27–9. Leningrad.
——. 1958. Sogdo-jagnobskie dialektologičeskie otnošenija. Materialy pervoj vsesojuznoj naučnoj konferencij vostokovedov. Taškent.
——. 1960. Iranskoe jazykoznanie v Leningrade (1917–57). UZIV 25.303–18.
——. 1966. Jagnobskij jazyk. Jazyki narodov SSSR 1. Indoevropejskie jazyki 342–61.
CABOLOV, R.L. 1964. Sostavnye glagoly v osetinskom jazyke. IzvSOsNII 24.113–21.
CAGAEVA, A.DZ. 1960. Iz toponimiki i gidronimiki zapadnoj osetin. IzvSOsNII 22.121–33.
——. 1961a. Nekotorye osobennosti stur-digorskogo govora (Nekotorye itogi dialektologičeskoj komandirovki v Irafskij rajon Severo-Osetinskoj ASSR, 1955 g.). IzvSOsNII 23.64–73.
——. 1961b. Materialy po toponimike i gidronimike Osetii. IzvSOsNII 23.74–106.
——. 1964. Toponimičeskie nazvanija osetin; ich struktura. IvzSOsNII 24.74-83.
CHROMOV, A. 1966. Novye materialy po leksike jazyka jagnobcev. AcOr 30.129–35.
DĀVARĪ, BAHRĀM. 1964. Ẕarbolmašalhā-ye baxtiārī. Tehran, Ṯahūrī, 1343.
DEETERS, G. 1965. Ein weiterer Beleg des osteuropäischen Wanderwortes für 'Buch'. IF 70.53–6.
D'JAKOV, A.M. 1963. Jazyki i pis'mennost' narodov Južnoj Azii. Narody Južnoj Azii. Moskva, ANSSSR (Iranskie jazyki, p. 40).
DODYCHUDOEV, R.CH. 1964. Ob otraženii drevneiranskoj gruppy *rt* v šugnanskom jazyke. Iranskaja filologija 57–61, tab.
DUCHESNE-GUILLEMIN, J. 1964. Sui dialetti iranici. AGI 49.105–17.
DUMÉZIL, G. 1948. Loki. Paris, G.P. Maisonneuve (Germ. transl. Darmstadt 1959).
——. 1956. Noms mythiques indo-iraniens dans le folklore des Osses. JA 244.349–67.

——. 1958. L'épopée Narte. La Table Ronde 132.42–55. Paris.

——. 1963. Caucasique du Nord-Ouest et parlers scythiques. AION-L 5.5–18.

——. 1968. Mythe et épopée. L'idéologie des trois fonctions dans les épopées des peuples indo-européens. Paris, Gallimard.

DZAGUROV, G.A. 1964. K voprosu o sposobnosti osetinskich glagol'nych fraz prinimat' paredžnye okončanija. IzvSOsNII 24.102–12.

ĖDEL'MAN, D.I. 1963a. O edinoj naučnoj transkripcii dlja iranskich jazykov. Moskva-Leningrad, Komissija po unificirovannoj fonetičeskoj transkripcii (UFT) dlja jazykov narodov SSSR.

——. 1963b. Glagol'naja sistema jazguljamskogo jazyka. Iranskij sbornik ... I.I. Zarubina, 95–120, 2 pl.

——. 1963c. Jazguljëmskaja legenda ob Aleksandre (s priloženiem grammatičeskich svedenij). KSINA 67.55–61.

——. 1963d. Problema cerebral'nych v vostočno-iranskich jazykach. VJa 67–81, 10 pl.

——. 1964. Sovremennoe sostojanie izučenija pamirskich jazykov. VJa 128–33.

——. 1965. Dardskie jazyki. Moskva, Izd. Nauka.

——. 1966. Jazguljamskij jazyk. Moskva, Izd. Nauka.

EFIMOV, V.A. 1964. Ličnye glagol'nye formy v jakaulanskom dialekte chazara (Itogi polevoj raboty). Indijskaja i iranskaja filologija, 17–39, tab.

——. 1965. Jazyk afganskich chazara. Jakaulangskij dialekt. Moskva, Izd. Nauka (Jazyki narodov Azii i Afriki).

EILERS, W. 1954. Der Name Demawend. AO 22.267–374; Zusatznoten, 24.183–224 (1956).

EILERS, W., and M. MAYRHOFER. 1962. Kurdisch *būz* und die indogermanische 'Buchen'-Sippe. Zugleich ein Beitrag zur Ulme und allgemeinen Pflanzennamenkunde. Mitteil. Anthrop. Ges. Wien (= Festschr. Franz Hančar) 92.61–92.

ELFENBEIN, J. 1959. Balūčistān, B. Language. EI I.1006–7.

——. 1961. A Balūčī text, with translation and notes. BSOAS 24.86–103.

——. 1963. A vocabulary of Marw Baluchi. AION-L, Quaderni 2.

——. 1966. The Baluchi language: a dialectology with texts. London, RAS-Luzac (RAS Monographs, 27).

ELWELL-SUTTON, L.P. 1963a. The Vafsi dialect (North-Western Persia). Trudy 25. Kongr. vostokovedov II.314–19.

——. 1963b. An eighteenth century (?) Caspian dialect. Mélanges Henri Massé, 110–40. Tehran 1342 (Publ. Univ. 843).

EMENEAU, M.B. 1964. Linguistic desiderata in Baluchistan. Indo-Iranica, Mélanges G. Morgenstierne, 73–7. Wiesbaden.

EQTEDĀRĪ, AḤMAD. 1955. Farhang-e Lārestānī. FIZ 1334.

——. 1963. Lahǰe-ye fīšvarī. FIZ 11.71–91, 1342.

FARAHVAŠĪ, BAHRAM. 1962. Tahlīl-e sīsrem-e feʿl dar lahǰeh-ye sede-ī. RFLTan 10.311–23, 1342.

FARHĀDĪ, A.G.R. 1967. Languages. The Kabul Times Annual, 83–5. Kabul.
FREJMAN, A.A. 1946. Zadači iranskoj filologiji. IzvAN 5.374–86.
——. 1951. Stalinskoje učenije o jazyke i iranskoje jazykoznanije. IzvAN 10.50–65.
FROLOVA, V.A. 1960. Beludžskij jazyk. Moskva, Izd. Vostočnoj literat. (Jazyki zarubežnogo Vostoka i Afriki).
FRYE, R.N. 1949a. Report on a trip to Iran in the summer of 1948. Oriens 2.204–11.
——. 1949b. Note on Farvī, a dialect of Biyābānak. Oriens 2.212–15.
——. 1952. Notes on a trip to the Biyabanak, Seistan and Baluchistan. Indo-Iranica 6.1–6.
——. 1961. Remarks on Baluchi history. CAJ 6.44–50.
GAÁL, L. 1960. Ursprung des ossetischen Verbalpräfixes *ra-*. AOH 11.145–60.
GAGKAEV, K.E. 1952. Očerk grammatiki osetinskogo jazyka. Dzaudžikau, Gosud. izd. Severo-oset. ASSR.
——. 1953. Osetinsko-russkije grammatičeskije paralleli. Leksikon, fonetika i morfologija. Dzaudžikau, Gosizdat Severo-oset. ASSR.
——. 1956. Sintaksis osetinskogo jazyka. Ordžonikidze, Severo-oset. knižnoe izd.
——. 1961a. Iz oblasti stilistiki i semantiki osetinskogo jazyka. IzvSOsNII 23.5–44.
——. 1961b. Aleksandr Arnol'dovič Frejman kak redaktor 'Osetinsko-russko-nemeckogo slovarja' Vs. F. Millera. IzvSOsNII 23.143–50, portr.
——. 1964. Sostav i funkcii osetinskich ličnych imen. IzvSOsNII 24.53–73.
GAGLOEVA, Z.D. 1962. Osetinskie familii v Jugo-Osetii. IzvJOsNII 2.40–6.
GERSHEVITCH, I. 1949. Iranian notes. TPhS 1948. 61–8.
——. 1952. Ancient survivals in Ossetic. BSOAS 14.483–95.
——. 1955. Word and spirit in Ossetic. BSOAS 17.478–89.
——. 1957. Sissoo at Susa (OPers. *yakā-* = *Dalbergia sissoo* Roxb.). BSOAS 19.317–20, pl.
——. 1959. Travels in Bashkardia. Journal of the Royal Central Asian Society 46.213–24.
——. 1962a. The Sogdian word for 'advice', and some Muγ documents. CAJ 7.77–95.
——. 1962b. Outdoor terms in Iranian. A locust's leg. Studies in honor of S.H. Taqizadeh, 76–84. London.
——. 1964a. Dialect variation in early Persian. TPhS 1–29.
——. 1964b. Iranian chronological adverbs. Indo-Iranica, Mélanges G. Morgenstierne, 78–88. Wiesbaden.
——. 1966. The well of Baghlan. AM 12.90–109.
GRJUNBERG, A.L. 1961a. O meste tatskogo sredi iranskich jazykov. VJa 106–14.
——. 1961b. K voprosa o jazykovom vzaimodejstvii (na materiale jazyka severo-azerbajdžanskich tatov). KSINA 40.11–23, fig.
——. 1963a. Sistema glagola v tatskom jazyke. Iranskij sbornik ... I.I. Zarubina, 121–49.
——. 1963b. Seistanskij dialekt v Serachse. KSINA 67.76–86.

——. 1963c. Jazyk severoazerbajdžanskich tatov. Leningrad, Izd. ANSSSR.

GURIEV, T. A. 1961. Neskol'ko zamečanij o proischoždenii ėtničeskogo termina *ir*. IzvSOsNII 23.122–5.

——. 1962. Vlijanie russkogo jazyka na razvitie osetinskoj leksiki. Ordžonikidze, Severo-inst. knižnoe izd.

HAĞYJEV, M. 1962. Tat dilinin öjrənilməsi tarichindən. IzvANAzerb 83–7.

HAMP, ERIC P. 1966. Notes on Kafir phonology. Shahidullah presentation volume, ed. by Anwar S. Dil. Pakistani Linguistics Ser. 7.

HARMATTA, JÁNOS. 1952. Studies in the language of the Iranian tribes in South Russia. AOH 1.261–314 (1950–52) = Magyar-Görög tanulmányok 31.

——. 1953. Three Iranian words for bread. AOH 3.245–83.

ḤAṢŪRĪ, ʿALI. 1964. Gozāreš-e gūyeshā-ye lorī. Tehran, Ṭahūrī (Zabān va farhang-e Irān 28).

HENDERSON, E. J. A.,, 1949. A phonetic study of Western Ossetic (Digoron). BSOAS 13.36–79; [cf. M.I. Isaev, Zametki ... AO 26.279–83 (1958)].

HENDERSON, E. J. A. and H. W. BAILEY. 1950. Digoron word-list. BSOAS 13.381–8.

HENNING, W. B. 1954. The ancient language of Azerbaijan. TPhS 157–77.

——. 1964. The survival of an ancient term. Indo-Iranica, Mélanges G. Morgenstierne, 95–7. Wiesbaden.

IMOTO, EIICHI. 1960. Īrāngo no hōgenteki bunpu. HKN 3.43–54.

IRON ... 1964. Iron ævzadžy æmbaryngænæg dzyrdwat. Dzyrdwat arazyny soejrag æghdæuttæ æmæ dzyrdtæ æbaryn kænyny cævittontæ. Bærnon redaktor Gæbæraty N. Ja. Cxinval, GSSR, Zonædty akad. Xussar Irystony zonad-irtasæg inst.

ISAEV, M. I. 1954a. O vokalizme osetinskogo jazyka. TIJa 3.227–49.

——. 1957. Poslednie zarubežnye trudy ob osetinskom jazyke. VJa 108–10.

——. 1958. V.I. Abaev kak krupnejšij iranist-osetinoved. IzvJOsII 9.396–414.

——. 1959. Očerk fonetiki osetinskogo literaturnogo jazyka. Ordžonikidze, Severooset. knižnoe izd.

——. 1960a. Osnovnye ėtapy naučnogo izučenija osetinskogo jazyka. IzvJOsNII 10 5–29.

——. 1960b. Slavnyj put' učenogo. IzvJOsNII 22.5–28.

——. 1963. K voprosu o količestvennoj charakteristike osetinskich glasnych. KSINA 67.16–21.

——. 1964a. K voprosu o dialektnom členenii osetinskogo jazyka. Iranskaja filologija. Trudy ... 1962, 33–41. Leningrad.

——. 1964b. Očerki po frazeologii osetinskogo jazyka. Ordžonikidze, Severo-oset. knižnoe izd.

——. 1966. Digorijskij dialekt osetinskogo jazyka. Moskva, Izd. Nauka.

ISAEV, M. I., A. A. KERIMOVA, L. A. PIREJKO, and D. I. ĖDEL'MAN. 1964. Voprosy sostavlenija opisatel'nach grammatik iranskich jazykov. IzvSOsNII 24.92–101.

ĪZADPANĀH, ḤAMID. 1964. Farhang-e Lorī. Tehran 1343 (Anǰoman-e Farhang-e Īrān-e bāstān, 2).

JOKI, A. J. 1962. Finnischugrisches im Ossetischen? Comment. Fenno-Ugr. in hon. Paavo Ravila, 147–70. Helsinki. [Cf. K. H. Menges, Zur Frage der Beziehungen zwischen den Finnougriern und Osseten. UAJb 36.183–4 (1964).]

JONES, SCHUYLER. 1966. An annotated bibliography of Nuristan (Kafiristan) and the Kalash Kafirs of Chitral, I. HFM 41/3. København.

KARAMCHUDOEV, N. 1962. Nekotorye svedenija o glagol'nych osnovach bartangskogo jazyka v sopostavlenii s šugnanskim. IzvANTadž 3/30.36–56.

KARAMŠOEV, D. 1962. Imena v badžuvskom dialekte šugnanskogo jazyka. Izv-ANTadž 3/30.17–35.

——. 1963a. O nekotorych izmenenijach glasnych v badžuvskom dialekte šugnanskogo jazyka. KSINA 67.62–72.

——. 1963b. Badžuvskij dialekt šugnanskogo jazyka. TIJa (Dušanbe) 16.

KĀRANG, ʿA. ʿA. 1954. Tātī va harzanī. Tabriz 1333.

——. 1955. Xalxālī, yak lahǰe az āżarī. Tabriz 1334.

KASAEV, A. M. Osetinsko-russkij slovar'; see Bigulaev, et al. 1952.

KASRAVĪ, AḤMAD. 1946. Āżarī yā zabān-e bāstān-e Āżarbāījān. Tehran, 2nd ed. 1325.

KHĀNLARĪ = see XĀNLARĪ.

KĪĀ, ṢĀDEQ. 1951. Vāženāme-ye gorgānī. Tehran (Publ. Univ. 133).

——. 1954. Yāddāštī dar bāre-ye gūyeš-e farvīgī. RFLTan 2.34–41. 1333.

——. 1956. Gūyeš-e Āštiān I. Važenāme. Tehran 1335 (Publ. Univ. 384).

KIEFFER, CH. M. 1965. Notes de dialectologie afghane, 1. De quelques noms de champignons. Bern, roneogr. (24 p.)

KIEFFER, CH. M., and G. REDARD. 1967. La fabrication des chaussures à Bāmyān. Notes de dialectologie afghane. AcOr 31.47–53, 7 pl.

KLIMČICKIJ, S. I. 1940a. Jagnobskja skazka. TTadžAN 9.94–103.

——. 1940b. Sekretnyj jazyk u jagnobcev i jazgulemcev. TTadžAN 9.104–17.

——. 1940c. Jagnobcy i ich jazyk. TTadžAN 9.137–9.

KLIMOV, G. A. 1963. O leksike osetinskogo proischoždenija v svanskom jazyke. Ėtimologija, 180–6. Moskva, Izd. ANSSSR.

KOHZAD, MOHAMMED NABI. 1957. The distribution of the Parachi language. Afghanistan 2.39–41.

KOZYREVA, T. Z. 1959. O kategorii zaloga v osetinskom jazyke. IzvSOsNII 21.37–44.

——. 1961. Leksika osetinskogo jazyka s točki zrenija ee istoričeskogo proischoždenija. IzvSOsNII 23.45–63.

——. 1964. Iz istorii osetinskoj leksikografii. IzvSOsNII 24.143–56.

KUCHTINA, T. I. 1965. Bibliografija Afghanistana. Literatura na russkom jazyke. Moskva, Izd. Nauka.

KULAEV, N. CH. 1949. A. J. Šegren [Sjögren]. Odin iz pervych issledovatelej osetinskogo jazyka. Uč. zap. Severo-oset. gos. ped. inst. im. K.L. Chetagurova. 18. 217–19. Dzaudžikau.

——. 1958. Mestoimenie v sovremennom literaturnom osetinskom jazyke. Ordžonikidze, Severo-oset. knižnoe izd.

——. 1959. Sojuzy v sovremennom osetinskom jazyke. Ordžonikidze, Severo-oset. knižnoe izd.

——. 1960. Osetinskaja grammatičeskaja terminologija. IzvSOsNII 22.183–9.

——. 1961a. K voprosu o probleme padežej v osetinskom jazyke. Voprosy sostavlenija opisatel'nych grammatik. Sbornik statej, 245–52. Moskva, Izd. ANSSSR.

——. 1961b. O sostojanii razrabotki lingvističeskoj terminologii v Severo-osetinskoj ASSR. Vopro. terminologii, 166–9. Moskva, Izd. ANSSSR.

——. 1961c. O predlogach v osetinskom jazyke. IzvSOsNII 23.113–21.

——. 1964. Dve sistemy sčeta v osetinskom jazyke. IzvSOsNII 24.157–65.

Lewy, Ernst. 1954. Studien über den Bau der Sprachen, 2. Bemerkungen über den ossetischen Akzent. Lexis 4.70–8.

Ligeti, L. 1964. Mongol'skie ėlementy v dialektach chazara v Afganistane. KSINA 83.5–22.

Lorimer, D.L.R. 1954. The popular verse of the Bakhtiari of S.W. Persia. BSOAS 16.542–55, 17.92–110 (1955), 26.55–68 (1963).

——. 1958. The Wakhi language. 2 vols. London, School of Oriental Studies.

——. 1964. A Bakhtiari Persian text. Indo-Iranica, Mélanges G. Morgenstierne, 129–33. Wiesbaden.

MacKenzie, D.N. 1956. Bājalānī. BSOAS 18.418–35.

——. 1965. Some Gorānī lyric verse. BSOAS 28.255–83, 2 pl.

——. 1966. The dialect of Awroman (Hawrāmān-ī Luhōn). HFSkr. 4/3. København.

Mačīānī, M. Farzpūr. 1964–65. Zabān o farhang-e māčīān. RFLTiz 16.277–96, 451–70; 17.109–28, 261–84, 1343–1344.

Matthews, W.K. 1951. The languages of the U.S.S.R. Cambridge, Univ. Press, with 13 figs., 5 maps.

Mayrhofer, Manfred. 1964. Ueber Kontaminationen der Sippen von ai. *takṣ-*, *tvakṣ-*, **tvarś-*. Indo-Iranica, Mélanges G. Morgenstierne, 141–8. Wiesbaden.

Meid, Wolfgang. 1961. Lat. *volcānus* — osset. *wärgon*. IF 66.125–31.

Miller, B.V. 1945. Tatskie teksty. Materialy po govoram tatov Sovetskogo Azerbejdžana. Iranskie jazyki 1.107–26.

——. 1946. Trudy russkich učenych v oblasti iranskogo jazykoznanija. UZMU 107.71–85.

——. 1948. O suffikse *i* imen suščestvitel'nych v talyškom jazyke. Jazyk i myšlenie 11.237–46.

——. 1951. K voprosu o klassifikacii iranskich jazykov. Tezisy dokladov naučnych sotrudnikov Inst. ėtnogr., Inst. ist. mat. kul't., Inst. ist., Inst. jazykozn, 19–23. Moskva, ANSSSR.

——. 1953. Talyšskij jazyk. Moskva, ANSSSR.
——. 1962. Jazyk osetin. Perevod s nemeckogo M. I. Isaeva. Redakcija, predislovie i primečanija V. I. Abaeva. Moskva-Leningrad, ANSSSR.
MILLER, D. GARY. 1968. *rt*-clusters in Avestan. Lg. 44.274–83.
MOǦDAM, MAHMAD [MOǦADDAM]. 1949. Gūyešhā-ye Vafs va Āštiān va Tafreš. Tehran 1318 [sic] (Irān kūde 11).
MOḤAQEQ, MEHDĪ. 1959. Aš'ārī be lahǰehā-ye maḥallī. FIZ 7.247–52, 1338.
MOKRI, MOHAMMAD. 1956. Cinquante-deux versets de Cheikh Amīr en dialecte gūrānī. JA 244.392–415.
——. 1967. Le Chasseur de Dieu et le mythe du Roi-Aigle (Dawara-y Dāmyārī). Wiesbaden, Harrassowitz.
MORGENSTIERNE, G. 1941. Iranian research in the North. Le Nord 133–46. [Cf. also Tārīx-e tahavvol-e zabānhā-ye īrānī va moǰāhedāt-e dānešmandān-e skāndīnāvī dar bare-ye reštehā-ye moxtalef-e īrān-šenāsī. RFLTan 4.43–52, 1336/1957.]
——. 1942. Iranica. NTS 12.258–71.
——. 1945. Indo-European *k*' in Kafiri. NTS 13.225–38.
——. 1947a. Baluchi language. Encycl. Britann. 2.1013 (also in 1957 ed.).
——. 1947b. Metathesis of liquids in Dardic. Festskr. til Olaf Broch, 145–54. Oslo.
——. 1948a. Balochi miscellanea. AcOr 20.253–92.
——. 1948b. The development of *r* + sibilant in some Eastern Iranian languages. TPhS 70–80. Additional notes in TPhS 207 (1950).
——. 1949. The language of the Prasun Kafirs. NTS 15.188–334, 1 pl.
——. 1950. Ættetradisjon hos Kafirene i Hindukusj. MM 155–62.
——. 1951. Linguistic gleanings from Nuristan. NTS 16.117–35.
——. 1953. The personal pronouns first and second plural in the Dardic and Kafir languages. Indian Linguistics (Grierson commemoration vol.) 5.357–62.
——. 1954. The Waigali language. NTS 17.146–324.
——. 1956. Distribution of Indo-European features surviving in modern languages. For Roman Jakobson, 367–71. The Hague.
——. 1957. 'Mushroom' and 'toadstool' in Indo-Iranian. BSOAS 20.451–7.
——. 1958a. Neu-iranische Sprachen. Handbuch der Orient. 1. Abt., 4. Bd, 1. Abschnitt. Leiden-Köln (reprinted 1967).
——. 1958b. Notes on Sämnani. NTS 18.91–117. Additional notes in NTS 18. 162–70.
——. 1960. Stray notes on Persian dialects. NTS 19.73–140, 3 maps, 2 fig.
——. 1961. Dardic and Kāfir languages. EI II.138–9.
——. 1962a. Iranian feminines in *čī*. Indological studies in honor of W. Norman Brown, 160–4. New Haven, Conn.
——. 1962b. Feminine nouns in *-a* in Western Iranian dialects. A locust's leg, Studies in honor of S. H. Taqizadeh, 203–8. London.
——. 1964. An ancient Indo-Iranian word for 'dragon'. Unvala memorial volume, 95–8. Bombay.

——. 1965. J. Biddulph's Sarikoli sentences. AcOr 29.71–3.

——. 1966. Notes on the Pashto Ṭolana vocabulary of Munji. AcOr 30.177–88.

——. 1969. Irano-Dardica. Wiesbaden, Harrassowitz.

MORISON, G. 1951. Ossetic family and personal names. RL 2.75–88 [publ. 1952].

MORTAẒAVĪ, MANŪČEHR. 1954. Nokte-ī čand az zabān-e harzanī RFLTiz 6.304–14, 1333.

——. 1962–63. Feʿl dar zabān-e harzani. RFLTiz 14.453–88, 15.61–97, 1341–1342. Also separ., Tabriz 1342/1963, with errata.

MOŠĀR, XĀN BĀBĀ. 1958. Fehrest ketābhā-ye čāpī fārsī, I. Tehran, B.T.N.K., 1337.

NADEL', BEN'JAMIN. 1963. Sledy frakijskogo substrata v iranskich dialektach Severnogo Pričernomor'ja (K probleme kimmerijskogo jazyka). RO 26.107–22.

NÉMETH, J. [NEMET]. 1959. Eine Wörterliste der Jassen, der ungarländischen Alanen. ADAW 1958/4.

——. 1960. Spisok slov na jazyke jasov, vengerskich alan. Perevod s nemeckogo i primečanija V.I. Abaeva. Ordžonikidze, Severo-oset. naučno-issled. inst.

ONEY, E.R. 1959. A note on present dialect studies in Iran. GL 4.33–7.

ORANSKIJ, I.M. 1960. Vvedenie v iranskuju filologiju. Pod red. A.A. Frejmana. Moskva, Izd. vost. lit.

——. 1963. Iranskie jazyki. Moskva, Izd. vost. lit. (Jazyki Zarubežnogo Vostoka i Afriki).

——. 1964. Dva indoarijskich dialekta iz srednej Azii. Indijskaja i iranskaja filologija 3–16.

——. 1968. Old Iranian philology and Iranian studies. Fifty years of Soviet oriental studies (Brief reviews), ed. by B.G. Gafurov, Y.V. Gankovsky. Moscow, Nauka, Central Department of Oriental Literature.

PACHALINA, T.N. 1956. Iškašimskie razgovornye teksty. TIJa 6.113–32.

——. 1959. Iškašimskij jazyk. Očerk fonetiki i grammatiki. Teksty i slovar'. Moskva, Izd. ANSSSR.

——. 1963a. K charakteristike sarykol'skogo dialekta. Iranskij sbornik ... I.I. Zarubina, 81–94.

——. 1963b. Obrazcy sarykol'skoj narodnoj poėzii (s perevodom i grammatičeskim kommentariem). KSINA 67.46–54.

——. 1963c. Sarykol'skij dialekt i ego otnošenie k drugim dialektam šugnano-rušanskoj jazykovoj gruppy. Trudy 25. Kongr. vostokovedov II.305–12, fig., tab.

——. 1965. Colloquial texts in Sarikoli. AcOr 29.61–70.

——. 1966a. Sarykol'skij jazyk (issledovanie i materialy). Moskva, Izd. Nauka.

——. 1966b. Osobennosti upotreblennija prepozitivnych služebnuch ėlementov pri opredeljaemom imeni v sarykol'skom jazyke. AcOr 30.189–94.

PACHALINA, T.N., and V.S. SOKOLOVA. 1957a. Giljanskij jazyk. Sovremennyi Iran, 75–82. Spravočnik.

——. 1957b. Mazenderanskij jazyk. Sovremennyi Iran, 82–8. Spravočnik.

PEJSIKOV, L. S. 1964. Transpozicija kak sposob slovoobrazovanija v iranskich jazykach. Iranskaja filologija 14–26.

PETROV, V. P. 1962. Do metodyky doslidžennja vlasnych imen v epihrafičnych pam'jatkach Pivničnoho Pryčornomor'ja. Pytannja toponimiky ta onomastyky, 109–18. Kyjiv, Vyd. ANURSR.

PIREJKO, L. A. 1961. Ėrgativnaja konstrukcija v kurdskom i talyšskom jazykach. Opyt sravnitel'noistoričeskoj charakteristiki. KSINA 30.86–94.

PISANI, V. 1948. Russo *choróšij*. Acme 1.356.

PISARČIK, A. K. 1949. Terminy obraščenija *ro* i *lo* v šugnano-rušanskoj gruppe jazykov v verchov'jach Pjandža. IzvANTadž 15.

——. 1954. Rušanskie teksty. Stalinabad-Leningrad.

RAJĀ'Ī, AḤMAD 'ALĪ. 1964. Lahǰe-ye boxārā'ī. Mašhad 1342–1343 (Publ. Univ. 8).

RĀST, N. 1953. Fehrest-e mā'xaž-e zabānhā u lahǰehā-ye īrānī. FIZ 1.1–40, 1332.

REDARD, G. 1954. Panorama linguistique de l'Iran. Asiat. Stud. 8.137–48 (Festg. Abegg).

——. 1959. Projet d'un Atlas linguistique de l'Iran. Akten 24. Intern. Orient.-Kongr., 440–4. Wiesbaden.

——. 1962. Le palmier à Khur. Notes de dialectologie iranienne, I. A locust's leg, Studies in honor of S. H. Taqizadeh, 213–19. London, 8 pl.

——. 1963. L'Atlas des parlers iraniens (1957–60). Trudy 25. Kongr. vostokovedov II. 294–6; (1960–63): Proceed. of the 26th Intern. Congr. of Orient., New Delhi (in press); (1957–67): Atti Convegno Intern. 'Gli Atlanti linguistici: problemi e risultati', Roma, Accad. Naz. Linc. (in press).

——. 1964. Notes de dialectologie iranienne II: Camelina. Indo-Iranica, Mélanges G. Morgenstierne, 155–62. Wiesbaden.

ROMASKEVIČ, A. A. 1945a. Lar i ego dialekt. Iranskie jazyki 1.31–86.

——. 1945b. K voprosu o žargone iranskich dervišej. Iranskie jazyki 1.141–4.

ROZENFEL'D, A. Z. 1956. K voprosy o pamirsko-tadžiksich jazykovych otnošenijach. (Na materialach vandžskich govorov.) TIJa 6.273–80.

——. 1963. Tadžikskie govory sovetskogo Badachšana i ich mesto sredi drugich jazykov na Pamire. VLU 18.107–12, tab.

SANAKOEV, P. A. 1955. Guyrdziag-Iron dzyrduat. Gruzinsko-osetinskij slovar'. Stalinir, Chussar iryst. paddzachadon rauag'dad (1st ed. 1940).

SIKOEV, R. R. 1961. Pervye svedenija ob osetinskom jazyke (I. A. Gjul'denštedt, Ja. Rejnegs, Ju. Klaprot). IzvSOsNII 23.126–32.

SOKOLOV, S. N. 1956. Grammatičeskij očerk jazyka beludžej Sovetskogo Sojuza. TIJa 6.57–91.

SOKOLOVA, V. S. 1950. Novye svedenija po fonetike iranskich jazykov (Predvaritel'noje soobščenije). Iranskie jazyki 2.5–28.

——. 1953. Očerki po fonetike iranskich jazykov. 1. Beludžkij, kurdskij, talyšskij, tatskij jazyki, 2. Osetinskij, jagnobskij i pamirskije jazyki. Moskva, Izd. ANSSSR.

——. 1957. Beludžskij jazyk. Sovremennyi Iran, 88–93. Spravočnik.

——. 1959. Rušanskie i chufskie teksty i slovar'. Moskva, Izd. ANSSSR.
——. 1960. Bartangskie teksty i slovar'. Moskva-Leningrad, Izd. ANSSSR.
——. 1963. K utočneniju klassifikacii šugnano-rušanskoj gruppy pamirskich jazykov. Iranskij sbornik ... I.I. Zarubina, 71–80.
——. 1967. Genetičeskie otnošenija jazguljamskogo jazyka i šugnanskoj jazykovoj gruppy. Moskva, Izd. Nauka.
SOKOLOVA, V.S., and A.L. GRJUNBERG. 1962. Istorija izučenija bespis'mennych iranskich jazykov. (Iranskie jazyki vostočnoj gruppy — I. ja. zapadnoj gruppy). Očerki po istorii izučenija iranskich jazykov, 118–47. Moskva, Izd. ANSSSR.
SOKOLOVA, V.S., R.L. NEMENOVA, JU.I. BOGORAD, V.A. LIVŠIC, and A.I. FARCHADJAN. 1952. Novye svedenija po fonetike iranskich jazykov. TIJa 1.154–92.
SORŪŠĪĀN, ǏAMŠĪD SORŪŠ. 1956. Farhang-e Behdīnān. FIZ 1335.
SOTŪDEH, MANŪČEHR. 1954. Farhang-e Gīlakī. Tehran, Anǰoman-e īrānšenāsī, 1332.
——. 1955. Moqaddame-ye bar risāle-ye loġāt-e ahālī Rāmand [inside: risāle-ye loġāt 'fars qadīm' a.R.]. FIZ 3.22–77, 1334.
——. 1956. Farhang-e Kermānī. FIZ 1335.
——. 1958. Xū'īnī, yakī az laǰehā-ye āżarī. FIZ 6.324–7, 1337.
—. 1962a. Lahǰe-ye 'Alī Ābād-e Faryam. FIZ 10.437–70, 1341.
——. 1962b. Lahǰe-ye sab-salīrī. FIZ 10.471–7, 1341.
——. 1963. Farhang-e Seminānī, Sorxe'ī, Lāsgerdī, Sangesarī, Šahmīrzādī. Tehran 1342 (Publ. Univ. 883).
——. 1964. Maṣalhā-ye fīrūzkūhī. FIZ 12.243–66, 1343.
SPOONER, BRIAN. 1967. Notes on the Baluchī spoken in Persian Baluchistan. Iran 5.51–71.
SZEMERÉNYI, O. 1959. Iranian Studies I. KZ 76.60–77.
TOKAZOV, CH.A. 1964. Modal'nye slova v osetinskom jazyke. IzvSOsNII 24.84–91.
TURČANINOV, G. 1948. Epigrafičeskije zametki, V. K datirovke drevneosetinskoj Zelenčukskoj nadpisi. IzvAN 7.80–1; VI. Ešče raz o drevneosetinskoj Zelenčukskoj nadpisi. EV 12.48–51 (1958).
ṬŪSĪ, ADĪB. 1959. Lahǰe-ye kazerūnī qadīm. RFLTan 11.1–18, 1338.
UNVALA, J.M. 1959. Contribution to modern Persian dialectology. The Lurī and Dizfūlī dialects. Calcutta, Iran Society.
VERNADSKY, G., and DZ. DZANTY. 1956. The Ossetian tale of Iry Dada and Mstislav. JAF 69.216–35.
VOEGELIN, C.F. and F.M. 1965. Languages of the world: Indo-European, 10. The Iranian sub-branch of the Indo-Iranian branch. AnL 7/8.190–218.
VOGT, HANS. 1944. Le système des cas en ossète. NTS 4.17–41 (publ. 1948).
WERYHO, JAN W. 1962. Sīstānī-Persian folklore. IIJ 5.276–370.
WIKANDER, STIG. 1948. Problèmes irano-arméniens. SL 2.48–53.
WILBER, DONALD N. 1956a. Annotated bibliography of Afghanistan. Behavior Sciences Bibliographies, 9. New Haven.

——, ed. 1956b. Afghanistan. New Haven, Human Relations Area Files (with a chapter on languages by Charles A. Ferguson).

WINDFUHR, Gernot L. 1965. Verbalmorpheme im Sangesari. Ein Beitrag zur neuiranischen Dialektkunde. Diss. Hamburg.

XĀNLARĪ, P. N. 1959. Tarḥ-e ejmālī barāye taḥqiq dar lahjehā-ye mahall-e Īrān. Soxan 10.565–75, 1336.

YĀR-ŠĀṮER, EḤSAN, see Yar-Shater, E.

YAR-SHATER, E. 1957. Zabānhā va lahǰehā-ye īrānī. RFLTan 5.11–48, 1336.

——. 1959. The dialect of Shāhrud (Khalkhāl). BSOAS 22.52–68.

——. 1960. The Tāti dialect of Kajal. BSOAS 23.275–86.

——. 1962. The Tāti dialects of Rāmand. A locust's leg, Studies in honor of S.H. Taqizadeh, 240–5. London.

——. 1964. The dialects of Alvir and Vidar. Indo-Iranica, Mélanges G. Morgenstierne, 177–87. Wiesbaden.

ZARUBIN, I. I. 1949. Beludžskie skazki II. Moskva-Leningrad (I. Trudy Inst. vost. ANSSSR, 1932).

——. 1960. Šugnanskie teksty i slovar'. Moskva-Leningrad, Izd. ANSSSR.

ZAV'JALOVA, V. I. 1956. Novye svedenija po fonetike iranskich jazykov. Giljackij i mazanderanskij jazyki. TIJa 6.92–112.

ZGUSTA, L. 1960. Ossetic words recorded by Svatopluk Čech (1846–1908). AO 28.91–100. [Russ. transl. IzvSOsIIN 23.133–42 (1961).]

——. 1965. Zu den Subsystemen des Sprachsystems: eine scheinbare Unregelmässigkeit der ossetischen Deklination. Symbolae Kuryłowicz, 379–82. Wrocław-Warszava.

——. 1967. Studies in Ossetic onomasiology. AO 35.407–51.

ŻOKĀ, YAḤYĀ. 1954. Gūyeš-e Karīngān. Tehran, Dāneš, 1332.

——. 1957. Gūyeš-e Galin-Qaye: 'Harzandī'. FIZ 5.51–92, 1336.

ZOMORRODIĀN, REẔĀ. 1967–68. Fōnōlōžī-ye lahǰe-ye Qāen [qāin]. RFLMed 3.68–77, 1346; Tatbīq-e fōnōlōžī bar lahǰe-ye Qāen. RFLMed 3.315–22, 1346.

B

ARMENIAN

DIACHRONIC ARMENIAN

ROBERT GODEL

1. As de Saussure remarks, 'Etymology is neither a distinct discipline nor a division of evolutionary linguistics. It is only a special application of the principles that relate to synchronic and diachronic facts' (*Course in general linguistics*, transl. from the French by Wade Baskin, New York, 1959: 189). But it is also the basis of comparative and diachronic studies, especially in the case of marginal or isolated idioms, such as the Anatolian Indo-European languages, or Albanian, Tokharian and Armenian. In such cases, the philologist's proceeding is, so to speak, circular: in proposing a new etymology he does apply his knowledge of the language; but at the same time he has to question this knowledge, in view of the new evidence that may arise from the word he is dealing with. Thus, etymology, historical phonology, and morphology are so interconnected that treating each one separately may seem artificial. Practically, however, the division involves no difficulty; and it allows for a clearer statement of the problems.

Regarding Armenian, most of the etymological research had been completed toward the end of past century. Its results were submitted to sharp scrutiny by H. Hübschmann in the first volume of his Grammar, the only one he published; death prevented him from carrying out his plan. A great part of this volume is dedicated to the foreign components of the Classical Armenian lexicon. Only after sifting and listing separately the Iranian, Syriac and Greek loans does Hübschmann discuss the etymologies of the genuine, or presumably genuine, Armenian words. The list amounts to 438 items, many of which, however, are declared dubious. Meillet's *Esquisse*, first edited in 1903, can be regarded as a successful attempt to supplement Hübschmann's epoch-making work.

Almost forty years later, Ajarian published the seventh and last volume of his *Armenian root dictionary* (*Hayerēn armatakan bar̄aran*), a monumental, encyclopedic work, in which all Indo-European etymologies ever suggested for Armenian words are recorded and discussed, with the addition of many personal suggestions. As a dictionary of Armenian, Ajarian's work has a particular value, owing to his extensive knowledge of the classical literature as well as of the modern dialects. Unfortunately, it had to be edited from photographed handwriting. A printed and, if possible, up-dated edition would be helpful.

In spite of — or, perhaps, by reason of — the difficulties involved, Armenian etymology has been ever since an attractive sport for comparativists, not to speak of amateurs. A number of new contributions have been made in the course of the last thirty years, by Dumézil, Frisk, Pisani, Van Windekens, Bolognesi, Čop, Hamp, and others. Solta (1960) gives a convenient survey of the results of etymological research up to 1952. In fact, his purpose is rather to determine the dialectal position of Armenian by tracing lexical isoglosses. This particular concern may account for some inconsistency in his ideas about regular sound change and morphology, not to mention his too frequent resorting to 'Sprachtabu'. This assertion must be substantiated by at least a few instances. Arm. *unkn* 'ear', *kʻirtn* 'sweat' are respectively traced back to IE **usonqom*, **swidrom* (54, 61), as if Arm. *-n* could ever be the reflex of IE **-om*. Arm. *mēǰ* 'middle' is supposed to contrast with Skt. *mádhya-*, Lat. *medius*, etc. 'durch die dehnstufige Bildung' (72), which apparently means that Arm. *ē* < IE **ē* (On *mēǰ* < **medhyo-* and similar developments, see Pedersen 1905:205, 1906:404). Arm. *yli* 'pregnant' (Meillet, *REArm* 10.184 [1930]; 1936:48) has nothing to do with the Armenian representatives of IE **plē-* (Arm. *li* 'full'; *lnul* 'to fill', 93–94), etc. These and other weak points, however, are balanced by accurate references, a sense of the obscurity of the matter, and an earnest attempt to operate with reliable data only.

In this last respect, Mann's book (1963) is the exact opposite of Solta's study. 'The position of Armenian as an Indo-European study' he writes in his Preface, 'is little better today than it was at the turn of the century. Haphazard and piecemeal, and often highly speculative, much of the etymology, and its attendant phonology, does not stand up to scrutiny. The present study, imperfect though it is, makes an attempt to reduce most of the Armenian radical lexique, disguised by complicated sound-changes without parallel, to consistent phonological rules'. Unfortunately, this attempt has resulted in a failure, perverted as it was at the outset by a double prejudice: Mann overrates the Indo-European portion of the Armenian lexicon; on the other hand, he passes a strangely disparaging judgment on the methods and achievements of modern comparative philology, from 1900 onward.

I need not repeat here the relevant criticisms of the reviewers (Dressler 1964b, Benveniste 1965b). I would rather call attention to the original planning of this 'Historical Phonology'. In fact, it is no more than a collection of etymologies. A very large one, to be sure, since the author presumes to provide Indo-European prototypes for more than 1500 Armenian words, but the reader will search in vain for any hint at the chronology of the facts. The latest sound changes are mixed up with the earliest ones. Let us give one example of this method. In the evolution of simple vowels at least three successive stages have to be distinguished:

1. IE **e* > Arm. *e*; **o* > *o*; **ĭ*, **ē* > *i*; *ŭ*, **ō* > *u*
2. Before *n* or *m*, Arm. *e* > *i*; *o* > *u*
3. In non-final (unstressed) syllables, Arm. *i* and *u* are dropped.

In Mann's book, all three stages are put on one level, and thus appear contemporary: 'IE *e* before *m*, *n* is lost in non-final syllables' (§ 14); 'IE *ē* disappears in unstressed penultimate syllables' (§ 20); 'IE *i* disappears in non-final position by syncope' (§ 23), etc.

To close this survey, something must be said on the recent contributions of philologists from the Soviet Republic of Armenia. The latest reports on the progress of linguistics in Armenia (Karibian 1967, Tumanian 1967) seem to imply that comparative philology does not, as yet, keep up with grammar, dialectology, and other branches of linguistic science. Indeed, etymological notes or studies sometimes appear in the local reviews: *Patma-banasirakan handes*; *Lraber* (formerly *Teğekagir*) *hasarakakan gitut'yunneri*, issued by the Academy of Sciences at Erivan; but they usually bear the stamp of outdated methods ('Wurzeletymologie'). In the last chapter of his *History of the Armenian language*, Kapantsian gives a list of about 300 words, for which Indo-European prototypes can be stated with some confidence (Kapantsian 1961:300–57). Significantly enough, he keeps to Hübschmann's selection; for, in his opinion, 'most of the new etymologies recorded by Ajarian in his *Root dictionary* do not stand up to critical examination' (1961:358).

The present state of Armenian etymology is somewhat anarchic. Hübschmann's and Meillet's sound principles, though partly criticized, still hold good; but they leave room enough for free experiments. Even Ajarian, a faithful disciple of Meillet's, often had his own ways of searching for new etymologies. One example will show the range of variation allowed to earnest philologists. According to Meillet, Arm. *ert'am* 'I go', like Gk. *érkhomai*, is derived from the IE root **ser-*, with the addition of **th* (**ser-th-*) instead of **kh* (**ser-kh-*) (Meillet 1936:135, 143). This derivation, unsatisfactory though it is (Pedersen 1906:344 termed it 'kaum möglich'), has not been seriously challenged, for want of a better one. Now, *ert'am* has lately been paralleled with Skt. *trấyati*, Lat. *in-trāre* (Barton 1963): the initial **tr* cluster should not have undergone the same change before *a* (**trā-* or **trā-ye-* > *ert'a-*) as before *e* (**treyes* > *erek'* 'three'). As long as no evidence to the contrary is given, this etymology, though supported by no parallel as yet, cannot be simply dismissed. Various attempts, none of which seems to me quite convincing, have been made about *astuac* 'god' (Heubeck 1953, Pisani 1961), *erkink'* 'heaven' and/or *erkir* 'earth' (Dumézil 1938d, Essabalian 1942, Pisani 1951b, Knobloch 1961), and *hariwr* 'hundred' (Van Windekens 1947a, Hamp 1955, Pisani 1964).

In view of this state of affairs, Mann's violent reaction is not so surprising; but reverting to the theories of pre-Hübschmannian scholars (Windischmann, Müller, Bötticher) is not the right way out of the mess. He is not entirely wrong, however, in asserting that the position of Armenian in comparative studies is 'little better today than it was at the turn of the century' (see also Scardigli 1961). Nay, it is even worse in a sense; for the progress of Iranian philology had the unexpected consequence that quite a few words, commonly regarded as genuinely Armenian, turned out to be actually Iranian loans: so *gan* 'whipping', *mēg* 'mist', *mēz* 'urine' (Benveniste 1958:60–2); *mah* 'death', *seaw* 'black' (Bolognesi 1960a:17–9, 23–4); *samik'* 'yoke-pegs', *sast* 'rebuke', and even, possibly, *surb* 'sacred, holy' (Benveniste 1964:2–3).

Yet, comparative philology cannot do without a certain number of reliable etymologies. In the case of Armenian, this amount can still be increased not only by the recovering of unduly neglected parallels (Benveniste 1967a), but also by the acknowledgement of new discoveries, e.g. the derivation of *sartnul* 'to startle, be commoved' from *sirt* 'heart' (Pisani 1934:189 — recorded by Solta 1960:205–6), and the equation Arm. *argand* 'womb': OSl. *grqdĭ* 'breast' (Pedersen 1949 — recorded by Solta 1960: 406–7, Kapantsian 1961:358–9, Mann 1963:§§124, 140). To this I would add the paralleling of Arm. *lkti* 'youth (in the pl. only), unruly, shameless', *lknel* 'to act in a rash, shameless way' with Skt. *yúvan-*, Lat. *iuuenis, iuuāre* (Dumézil 1938b); of Arm. *himn* 'foundation' with Lat. *sēmen*, the link being supplied by Hitt. *sai-*, *siya-* 'to plant', *samana-* 'foundation' (Laroche 1963); and of Arm. *očʿ* 'no, not' with Gk. *ouki* (Cowgill 1960; cf. Pisani 1951a:166). If Cowgill is right in his deductions, the unusual development **ou-kʷid* > **okʷi* > *očʿ*, as against **loukʷo-* > **louk̂o-* > *loys*, etc. can be explained by the fact that the prototype was a compound word.

A number of non-controversial etymologies are in need of revision. The following are genuine Armenian words, the Indo-European origin of which has never been questioned: *akn* (pl. *ačʿkʿ*) 'eye'; *elungn* 'fingernail'; *kṙunk* 'crane'; *leard* 'liver'; *lsel* (aor. *luay*) 'to hear'; *unkn* (pl. *akanǰkʿ*) 'ear', etc. No semantic difficulty is here involved, but the Armenian word-forms are puzzling. Even such commonplace parallels as Arm. *heriwn* 'awl': Gk. *perónē*; *ji* 'horse': Skt. *háya-*; *nor* 'new': Gk. *ne(w)arós* still require a more accurate explanation, accounting for every particular. Telling suggestions have been made concerning *vecʿ* 'six' (< **useks*, Pisani 1934: 36); *ayr* (G. *aṙn*) 'man, husband' (Bonfante 1937, Hamp 1967); *tēr* (G. *teaṙn*) 'lord' (Pisani 1951a:64–5); *nēr* (G. *niri*) 'sister-in-law on husband's side' (Pisani 1966, Hamp 1967). *-k-* in *akn* might be a regular development of *kʿ* before *-n* (Winter 1960:31). Further research in this line would prove more helpful than increasing the store of bare etymological speculation.

Etymology today is no longer what it often was in the last century. The current requisites are involved in de Saussure's definition: 'Etymology is mainly the explaining of words through the historical study of their relations with other words' (*op. cit.* p. 189). The explaining of a word demands more than the bare application of phonological rules: morphology and semantics deserve no less attention. But Armenian etymology will scarcely progress as long as it has to rely on such scanty information as is supplied by dictionaries (Benveniste 1964, Winter 1966:210). Monographs on Armenian basic words or word families, as well as special lexica, such as are available for Greek or Latin writers, would certainly enlighten the semantic features and connections of many a word and, on occasion, give a clue to the right etymology. Unfortunately, not much work has been done to this effect, so far. According to all dictionaries, Arm *ənkenul* means 'to throw'. Any tentative etymology (e.g. Frisk 1944) can be made consistent with so vague a datum. I happened to notice that in classical literature this verb also occurs with a different, probably the original, meaning: 'to cause to fall, pull down'. This points to a connection with *ankanel* 'to fall':

ənkenul is derived from the old causative verb, well preserved in Germanic (Ger. *senken*, Engl. *sench*), and the primitive stem *ənke-* can be safely traced back to IE *$song^w$-eye-* (Godel 1965:26).

2. Although systematic studies on diachronic phonology are not wanting, the latest ones (not to speak of Mann's bold attempt) still appear tentative, correcting or supplementing, but not altogether replacing, earlier reports (Pedersen 1905, 1906; Grammont 1918; Meillet 1936).

Most of the problems have been re-examined by V. Pisani (1951a) with special regard to chronology and to the dialectal affinities of Armenian. Pisani often questions Meillet's statements, mainly on the strength of the large materials brought to light by Pedersen. The following are his main points.

Proto-Armenian, though belonging in the *satəm* area, had two sets of postpalatal stops: velar and labio-velar (see also Bonfante 1937:25). The voiceless labio-velar was palatalized, not only in coalescing with *y*, as Meillet thought, but also before front-vowels, just like the aspirated voiced. The rules of change are, therefore:

IE *g^w > Arm. *k*
*g^wh > *g*; before *e*, *i* : *ǰ*
*k^w > *k*ʻ; before *e*, *i* : *č*ʻ
(*k > *k*ʻ)

While Meillet (1936:52; cf. Minshall 1955) regarded Arm. *ǰ* as the regular reflex of **y* after a resonant, Pisani holds these clusters to have resulted in metathesis: **alyo-* > *ayl* 'other'; **plānyo-* > *layn* 'wide, broad', etc., and he tries to explain away Meillet's cogent evidence. (On *olǰ* 'whole, safe'; *munǰ* 'silent', see also Pisani 1934: 180–2.) I would point out that in the words brought forth by Meillet (*sterǰ* 'sterile'; *anurǰ* 'dream'; *kamurǰ* 'bridge'; *olǰ*; *munǰ*), the preceding vowel is never *a*; on the contrary, the most unquestionable instance of metathesis (*ayl*) occurs after *a*, in agreement with the clearest occurrences of epenthesis, either palatal (as in *ayr*, *jayn*) or labial (as in *awj*, *awr*, *artawsr*). So, the contrast between *ayl* < **alyo-* and *sterǰ* < **steryo-*, *olǰ* < **olyo-*, etc. may well be regular.

The issue of final nasals, involving morphological problems, is discussed at length. Here again, Pisani disagrees with Meillet. Starting from the assumption that Proto-Armenian had both *-*m* and *-*n*, he posits the following rules:

IE *-*m* (in monosyllabic words) > Arm. -*n* : **dōm* > *tun* 'house'
*-*m* (in polysyllabic words) dropped : **yugom* > *luc* 'yoke'
*-*n*, like -*r*, -*l*, is preserved.

Consequently, in Armenian nouns, -*n* is either an extension to the nominative-accusative of the *-*en* suffix, originally restricted to the oblique cases, e.g. in *jeṙn*, G. *jeṙin* 'hand', as against Skt. *ās*, G. *ās-n-aḥ*, etc. (so also Van Windekens 1943c); or it is the reflex of a nominative ending *-*ēn*, *-*ōn*, e.g. in *gaṙn*, G. *gaṙin* 'lamb'; *erdumn*, G. *erdman* 'oath'. The latter explanation had already been offered by Scheftelowitz (1905:53), whose not very illuminating study seems to have escaped Pisani's notice. The Italian scholar does not consider the third possibility, namely Arm. *-n* < *-*no*, *-nā*, as in *beṙn* 'load', *harsn* 'bride' (Pedersen 1905:216–17; E. Lidén, *GUÅ* 12:31 [1906]). Anyhow, Armenian has no traces at all of the Indo-European singular accusative ending. Meillet thought it to have survived in *jeṙn*, *otn*, *duṙn* (1936:83–4), but this interpretation seems contradicted by *akn* 'eye', an ancient neuter.

On the Armenian consonant-shift, Pisani keeps close to Pedersen's views, to which he adds personal suggestions. Like IE *y*, but of course at a later stage, the Proto-Armenian reflex of intervocalic *t* dropped: *pətr̥bhi* > *hayarb(i)* > *harb* (a retort to Meillet, 1936:81, last line), except in final syllables, where it yielded *-y* or *-w* according to the nature of the following vowel:

bhəti- > *bay* 'verb' (= Gk. *phátis*)
bhereti > *berey* > *berē* 'brings'
bherato > *beraw* 'was brought'

Regarding *beraw*, Pisani is apparently unaware that the same development (*-aw* < *-*āto*) had been previously conjectured by Kerns (1939:30). Anyhow, since both *-y* and *-w* have been lost after *-u*, his rule does not allow for any decision as to the original stems of *aṙu* 'brook, stream' (< *sruti-* or *sruto-* ?), *č'u* 'departure', *lu* 'hearing', though *-*ti* is more likely, on semantic grounds. Non-initial *-t*, however, is preserved as a dental stop (*t'*) after Proto-Arm. *au*, *ou*: *awt'* 'place for passing the night in'; *erewoyt'* 'appearance' (*-oyt'* < *-*ou-ti-*).

Concerning the puzzling sound-change *dw-* > *erk-* (*dwō* > *erku* 'two'), Pisani remains sceptical; he still believes that *dw* would have regularly developed to Arm. *k* (as in *melk* 'soft' < *meldwi-*). New evidence for either rule would be highly welcome. Speculation on *erkink'* (Essabalian 1942), *nerkanel* 'to dye' (Belardi 1950a), or even *erkn* (pl. *erkunk'*) 'pains of childbirth' (Frisk 1944:11) are weak support to the traditional view. In my opinion, the only new etymology worth recording is *serkean* 'of today (adj.)' < *k̂e-dwi-* (Dumézil 1938d:48).

Pisani's study is the latest comprehensive attempt to improve the traditional doctrine. Winter's approach, in comparison, appears rather revolutionary. He was first arrested by the problem of the Armenian aspirated voiceless stops (1954), in connection with the lack of the expected nasal in *arcat'* 'silver' (< *arĝn̥to-*, presumably), and in the 1st pl. endings *-ak'*, *-(c')uk'*. By paralleling this with the dropping of a nasal before *s*, he came to the conclusion that Arm. *p'*, *t'*, *k'* had been spirants at that time, without heeding that *k'* should then have merged with *x*. Later on, he partly corrected this error (1962:254). His subsequent studies deal with the evolution of Indo-European voiceless stops in various environments (1955), and of consonant clusters (1962). He succeeds in formulating more consistent rules of sound-change, still maintaining that *p'*, *t'*, *k'*, as the earliest Armenian reflexes of IE *p*, *t*, *k*(ʷ), were originally spirants, and admitting divergent developments for initial *p (> *pʻ*: *h*/*Ø*), **kʷ* (> *kʻ* : *h*/*Ø*), and even **t* (> *tʻ* : *h*). His suggestion of *-u-* anaptyxis in *kṙunk* 'crane' (< **kᵘṙunk*), *srunkʻ* 'legs', as well as before a nasal in the *-nu-* conjugation, and in the derivatives of the *-umn* type (1962:260), is particularly attractive.

Divergent sound-change, however, cannot be totally eliminated. In view of the contrary developments of **-ntV* in *arcatʻ*, as against *drand* 'doorway', or of **-nkʷV* in *yisun* 'fifty', as against *hing* 'five', etc., there is apparently no other escape than ascribing the differences to dialectal variety (Winter 1962:256 and fn. 5). In a later study (1966), Winter offers a systematic argument of this thesis, resulting in a tentative outline of four Early Armenian dialects. No less than sixteen dialectal features are sifted on the ground of conflicting sound-change, and clustered according to their partial co-occurrence in Armenian words. The evidence, as can be expected, is scarce, and partly objectionable; the presumed change of **t*- to Arm. *h*-, e.g., is warranted by one example only: *hiwsn* 'carpenter', together with the related verb *hiwsel* 'to weave'. I do not believe that the paralleling of *hiwsn* (< **tetk̑ōn*, allegedly) with Gk. *téktōn* will be readily accepted by strict comparativists.

Yet, Winter's sketchy study can be hailed as the first systematic attempt to tackle a problem that has been almost ignored so far, maybe as a consequence of Meillet's negative statement (Meillet 1936:9). To my knowledge, Scheftelowitz first asserted the existence of dialectal variants in Classical Armenian; but except for the doublets *čʻogay*: *čʻokʻay* 'I went'; *tʻaṙamel*: *tʻaršamel* 'to wither', all his evidence is delusive (Scheftelowitz 1905:18–19). Fifty years later, the question was raised again by Bolognesi (1954a:149–51, 1960:28–30), Bănăţeanu (1961:99–100), and Feydit (1963 pass.). There is certainly no ground for a priori denying the possibility of dialectal variety in fifth century Armenian, and earlier. But the only available linguistic material consists of classical literature, which at first sight does not reveal more than stylistic differences: the literary idiom (*grabar*) looks very much like a 'koinè', and there is no hope of new discoveries that would bring to light archaic or dialectal texts. In view of this situation, Winter's essay seems to me premature, and I would advocate a more cautious approach to the whole problem.

As a rule, dialectal diversity ought to be appealed to only in such cases as do not allow for another explanation. Orthographic variation is one to be taken into account for *ew*/*iw*/*eaw* in *ewtʻn*, *eawtʻn* 'seven', as in *gewł*, *giwł*, *geawł* 'village', and all similar instances. Initial *h*/*Ø* alternation in *hogi*/*ogi* 'spirit', or in *haycʻ* 'asking, searching' beside *aycʻ* 'visit', etc. may reflect either a dialectal isogloss (Bolognesi 1954:150), or a dropping of *h*- in close juncture (Jerejian 1953). On the other hand, the occurrence of an aspirated voiceless stop, instead of a voiced, in the same environment (e.g. after a resonant) is very likely to be a dialectal feature. Leaving aside *arcatʻ*, a much hackneyed, but suspicious, example, I would rather contrast *šołokʻ-ortʻ* 'flatterer' with *ors-ord* 'hunter', *gn-ord* 'purchaser', etc. Thus, *małtʻel* 'to wish', as a dialectal variant of **małdel*, could be brought into agreement with its Slavic, Baltic, Germanic, and Hittite cognates, all of which reflect IE **meldh-*. Anyhow, Classical Armenian can hardly have grown out of a mixture of dialects; traces of dialectal diversity, if preserved, are very likely limited to lexical particulars. A definitive statement on the dialect issue must be left to the future.

In the meantime, there is still much to be done in order to improve our imperfect knowledge of Armenian diachronic phonology — I mean, to simply set up the rules of sound-change from late Indo-European to Classical Armenian. Searching for traces of laryngeals in Armenian, (e.g., Austin 1942, Polomé 1950, Winter 1960) seems to me somewhat presumptious, when many more trivial problems still await a solution.

Some arise from the Classical Armenian spelling. The relevancy of Mesrop's alphabet to the phonemic pattern of the language cannot be questioned; each letter represents one phoneme, except probably *v* and *w*, which stand in complementary distribution (Pisani 1951a:186). The relevant features of the consonants can be described to a high degree of certainty; (on the three sets of stops and affricates, see Vogt 1958, Benveniste 1959:46–56, Bolognesi 1960a:20–1). Some orthographic rules, however, are puzzling. In view of such regular paradigms as *gir* 'letter, writing', G. *groy*; *marmin* 'body', G. *marmnoy*, etc., one would expect the genitive forms of *tʿiw* 'number, figure', *aniw* 'wheel', to be **tʿwoy*, **anwoy*. Instead, we find *tʿuoy*, *anuoy*. Not that *w* clusters were avoided; such clusters actually occur in the inflection of polysyllabic nouns ending in *-i* (< **-iyo-*): *ordi* 'son', G. *ordwoy*; *tʿzeni* 'olive-tree', G. *tʿzenwoy*, etc. Since the latter genitive forms have admittedly developed from **-iwoy* (**ordioy* > **ordiwoy* > *ordwoy*), the contrast with *anuoy* < **aniwoy* is amazing. Another issue is that of /ə/. This phoneme (if it really is a phoneme) mostly occurs between consonants, but in this case it is never written, so that the rules of its occurrence in Classical Armenian are unknown. The usual practice among Armenologists (so Jensen 1959) consists in transliterating the Armenian words, and in applying to the classical language the current rules of pronunciation: [gəro], [tʿəvo], [anvo], [ordvo]. There is evidence for a rather late development of [ə] in or before consonant clusters (Bolognesi 1954a:134–5, 141–8); but this does not account for the reduction of *-iw-* to *-u-* instead of *-(ə)w-*. In both cases, the syllabic structure of Classical Armenian is at issue.

Philologists make light of these difficulties. Feydit alone thoroughly discusses the problems of spelling. But his theory is far from offering a solution; in Mesrop's times, he believes, the Armenian vowels, diphthongs, and consonants were uttered in various ways on different dialectal areas, and the alphabet was devised so as to answer this variety, each letter or group of letters taking on different values according to the local pronunciation, e.g. *p* : [p], [bh], [b]; *o* : [o], [wo], [we]; *oy* : [oy], [uy], etc.

Since moot points still subsist in the phonological system of Armenian, it is no wonder that the prehistory of this system remains gloomy. Years of painstaking research failed to remove every doubt or disagreement as to the rules and the chronology of sound-changes, which seem to be more intricate than in most of the cognate languages. Our understanding of the prehistoric evolution, however, would perhaps improve by a more systematic approach to the problems, i.e. by giving up, as Winter does, the atomistic method which was unavoidable in the first period of research. There are no haphazard changes, and in stating one particular development, one has to make sure that it does not conflict with that of correlated phonemes or clusters, or else, that it does not belong in the same phasis of the evolution.

Scholars do not quite agree as to the fate of Indo-European stop + **y* clusters. There is positive evidence for **ky* > *čʿ* (*čʿu* 'departure' < **kyuti-*) and **dhy* > *ǰ* (*mēǰ* 'middle' < **medhyo-*). But what about the Armenian reflexes of **ty*, **dy*, **k̂y*, etc.? They are, to a certain extent, predictable; they will probably appear as affricates, voiced or voiceless, according to the regular development of the initial stops. Pisani was therefore mistaken when he traced Arm. *munǰ* 'silent, mute' back to IE **mundyo-* (Pisani 1934:182). Later, he changed his mind: **dy* and **ĝy* should have merged into *č* (1951a:178; cf. 1966:231–2 [*karč* 'short' < **gr̥dyo-*]). But did the clusters with voiced and those with aspirated voiced really result in the same phonemes? Scheftelowitz (1904:287) had admitted a change of **dy* to *c*, which seems to me more in agreement with morphological facts (Godel 1965:24–6). If Pisani's conjecture about a merger of **dy* and **ĝy* is valid, as I believe, though positive evidence for **ĝy* is still wanting, then **ĝhy* may very likely have undergone the same change as **dhy*, yielding *ǰ*. Arm. *iǰanel* (aor. 3rd sg. *ēǰ*) 'to go down' has long been paralleled with Gk. *oikhomai* (Scheftelowitz 1904:311, 1905:60; Pedersen 1906:425). Whether the root is **oiĝh-* or **oigh-* (the latter has been preferred because of Lit. *eigá* 'going, course'), *ǰ* is no regular match to Gk. *kh*. Pisani's construction of *ēǰ* (1951a:67) is untenable. On morphological grounds, **oigh-ye-* would be a better solution. Finally, *lucʿanel* 'to kindle' seems descended from **louk̂-ye-* (cf. *loys* 'light'). This leads to surmising a similar change of **ty* to *cʿ*. Anyhow, the evidence for **ty* > *čʿ* is not unobjectionable: *kočʿel* 'to call' < **gʷot-ye-*, cf. Got. *qiþan*, Lat. *uetare* (Meillet 1936:108; Mann 1963:§91, adds *plpčʿal*, a blunder, instead of *plpǰal* 'to bubble' < **bulbulya-*). So we can tentatively posit the following rules:

IE **ty* >	Arm. *cʿ* (?);	**k̂y* > *cʿ*;	**ky* > *čʿ*
**dy* >	*c*;	**ĝy* > *c* (?);	**gy* > *č* (?)
**dhy* >	*ǰ*;	**ĝhy* > *ǰ*;	**ghy* > *ǰ* (?)

The Indo-European diphthongs were preserved in the earlier phasis of Proto-Armenian, with the exception of **oi* and **eu*, which respectively merged with **ei* and **ou*. In a later stage, after the change of **ou* to *oy*, and the appearance of *w* as the reflex of closing stops (*arawr* < **arətrom*; *ewtʿn* < **septn̥*; **owtʿ* < **optō*) or of *m* (**anown* < **°nomn̥*) a new system was established, with /y/ and /w/ alternately functioning as consonants (before vowels) or the second part of diphthongs (before consonants). (The condition of final /*y*/, /*w*/ raises a particular question.) This system continues in Classical Armenian, save that **ey* changed to *ē*, and **ow* (C) to *u*, thus merging with Proto-Armenian *u* (< **ŭ*, *ō*). Antevocalic and final **ow* is written *ov*. Summing up the evolution, we get the following table:

IE	*ai	*ei *oi	*eu *ou	*au
Pr. Arm. I	ai	ei	ou	au
Pr. Arm. II	ay	ey	oy	aw ew/iw ow
Cl. Arm.	ay	ē	oy	aw ew/iw u (-ov(V))

(Cf. Bolognesi 1951a). The rules and the chronology of many sound-changes, and above all the puzzling developments of IE **w*, ought to be revised within this framework, in connection with the successive systems of diphthongs in Proto-Armenian.

Discussing these problems has taken me away from my present purpose. But I could not help insisting upon the necessity of restating the main lines of diachronic phonology by grouping together scattered facts, and locating them, as far as possible, in a chronological framework. I do not disregard the difficulties that have to be overcome. The rules of vowel contraction, e.g., have not been clearly elicited so far. Little is known about the origins of *pʿ*, *tʿ*, *č*, *x*, *š*, insofar as these phonemes occur in genuine Armenian words; and there is no agreement as to the Armenian reflexes of **sp*, **sk*. The old fancy of Arm. *t*, *k* reflecting IE **t*, **k* is almost abandoned, though still strongly upheld by Mann (1963:§§81 and Note 1; 113); but the deep-rooted belief in a relation of *pʿoytʿ* 'zeal, care' with Gk. *speúdō*, *spoudḗ*, etc. remains unshaken (Pisani 1951a:72, Bolognesi 1954a:150, Solta 1960:341–2, Kapantsian 1961:356, Mann 1963:§165), in spite of Pedersen's opposition (1905:200). In view of *šogi* 'damp, vapor' beside *hogi*, *ogi* 'spirit' (**p*-), and of *šołal* 'to shine, glitter' beside *pʿołpʿołel* 'id.', *pʿayl* 'shine, brightness' (**ph*-), one is tempted to regard *š* as a regular reflex of **sp*, and to substitute *šoyd* 'quick, prompt' for *pʿoytʿ* as a parallel to the Greek words quoted above. If this surmise turned out to be right, Arm. *gišer* 'night' would be a perfect match to Gk. *hespéra*, Lat. *uesper*. More evidence is of course wanted.

3. Less numerous studies have been devoted to morphology. A most embarrassing issue is the origin of the *-kʿ* endings in nominal and verbal inflection. This morpheme occurs as a plural marker in the nominative (*mard* 'man': pl. *mardkʿ*) and instrumental (*mardov*: pl. *mardovkʿ*) of all nouns, pronouns, and adjectives, and in all the 1st and 2nd persons of verbs (*beremkʿ* 'we bring', *berēkʿ* 'you bring'; aor. *berakʿ*, *berēkʿ*;subj. *bercʿukʿ*, *berǰikʿ*, etc.). Since nearly all the underlying Indo-European forms ended in *-*s* (Pl. N. *-*ōs*, *-ās*, etc.; Instr. *-*bhis*; 1st pl. *-*mes*), a development of *-s* to *-h* > *-kʿ* may be supposed to have taken place in the cases in question, while final *-*s* was lost elsewhere. This is the most widespread opinion (Pedersen 1905:209–27, Grammont 1918:227–9, Meillet 1936:69–70, Pisani 1951a:66). Haas, however, tried another solution by supposing *-kʿ* to have originated in plural forms ending in *-*wes*, *-*wōs*, etc., in which *w* should have been devoiced by the following *s* (as in *kʿsan* 'twenty' < **wik̑m̥tī*). Hence, regularly: *-*wVs* > *-*whVs* > *-*wh* > *-kʿ*. This rule could hardly be stated in terms of chronology, since *w* is in turn IE **w*, or a Proto-Armenian glide (*dukʿ* 'you' < **tu-w-es*; *-ikʿ* < *-*i-w-ōs*, in *ordikʿ* 'sons', etc.), or a development of **p*, **bh*, or **m* (Haas 1940).

Van Windekens revives Junker's derivation of *-k'* from the Indo-European enclitic particle **kʷe*; starting from its generalizing, collective value (Gk. *hós te*; Lat. *quisque*), one may conceive a semantic change to a plural meaning, first in nouns (but why in the nominative and instrumental only?), and later, analogically, in verbs (Van Windekens 1943b:38–41). Here too a chronological question arises; since there is no trace of the final syllable vowel in *mardk'* (IE **mr̥tōs*), *mardovk'* (IE **mr̥tobhis*), etc., it must be admitted that they had dropped before the addition of **kʷe* (or *k'*), a conclusion which is not quite consistent with the archaic stamp of Lat. *quisque.*

Reichenkron started a new way by dividing the problem: *-k'*, as a nominal morpheme, should have spread out of three sources, namely *kanayk'*, the plural of *kin* 'woman' (supposed to be identical to Gk. *gunaîkes*), the particle **kʷe*, and a few ancient dual forms (*ač'k'* 'eyes', *akanǰk'* 'ears'); as a verbal morpheme, it should have first appeared in the 1st plural, as the result of a blending of the 1st dual pronoun **wĕ* with the original ending (**-mes*) (Reichenkron 1961). He may be right in supposing that the *-k'* endings have developed separately in nominal and verbal inflection; but neither *kanayk'* (Pisani 1951a:182–3, Van Windekens 1964), nor *ač'k'*, *akanǰk'*, is a more primitive instance of *-k'* than any regular plural nominative. The remainder of the argument is merely hypothetical. None of these new speculations has found acceptance; and Solta, who repells the traditional view, falls back upon the hypothesis of a non Indo-European 'kollektives k-Formans' (Solta 1963:104).

New light has been thrown on the prehistory of the Armenian verb. While the aor. 3rd sg. *ed* 'put, placed', *et* 'gave' can be exactly paralleled with Ved. *ádhāt*, *ádāt*, this is not the case with the 1st sg. *edi*, *etu*, where one syllable must have been lost. These Armenian paradigms, however, are not isolated; apart from Ved. *ádhāsam*, *áyāsam*, etc., there are closer Old Slavic parallels: *děchŭ* (< **dhēsom*), 3rd. sg. *dě* (< **dhē(s)t*); *dachŭ* (< **dōsom*), 3rd sg. *da* (< **dō(s)t*). Albanian, too, has *dašë* 'I gave', 3rd sg. *dā*. Thus, Armenian shows traces of sigmatic aorists, at least in these archaic forms. Furthermore, the proportion *edi* : *ed* = *beri* : *eber*; *lac'i* : *elac'* etc. gives a clue as to the origin of the 1st sg. ending *-i*; it has very likely been abstracted from *edi* (Bonfante 1942). Another Slavic-Armenian isogloss has been detected in the similar derivation (**-ā-ske-*) of the Old Slavic imperfect in *-achŭ*, *-aše* ... and of the Armenian *-ac'-* aorist (*gitac'i*, from *gitem* 'I know'; *gorcec'i*, 3rd. sg. *gorceac'*, from *gorcem* 'I make', etc.) (Karstien 1956). In Armenian, however, *-c'-* also occurs without *-a-* (*lc'i* < **lic'i* 'I filled'; *lac'i* 'I cried'; *hatuc'i* 'I paid'), and vice versa (*nstay* 'I sat'; *luay* 'I heard'). Besides, the Old Slavic imperfect shares one semantic feature only with the Armenian aorist: both are past tenses, but they belong in quite different tense systems, neither of which, as Karstien remarks, allows for a guess as to the original use of the **-ske-* morpheme.

The Armenian imperfect is regularly derived from the present tense: *berem* (and *berim*): *berei, bereir, berēr* ...; *lam* : *layi, layir* ...; *lnum* : *lnui, lnuir* .... This regularity seems to have come about as a result of analogical levelling. Meillet, however, thought that the new imperfect (the ancient one having been shifted to the aorist) had developed from a compound tense, save for the 3rd sg. (*berēr* < **bheretor*), a relic of the Indo-European medio-passive; *ei* 'I was', instead of **i* (< *ēsṃ*) should have been remodelled on *berei* (Meillet 1936:126–7). This view was first criticized by Kerns, who turned the question by taking *ei* as the model for all other imperfect forms, and by tracing it back to an *-*ī*- optative with full grade of the root, as in Gk. *eiēn*: *ei* < *esīm* (Kerns 1939). He then explained the development of the whole paradigm from the active form *berei* (< **beresim*, *beresis* ...), the passive form *bereir*, and the surviving 3rd sg. *berēr* (< **bheretor*), through a new distribution of these forms. This would account for the lack of diathetic marks in the Armenian imperfect. The 1st pl. *bereakʿ*, with -*a*- from the aorist (*berakʿ*), should have been substituted to **bereikʿ*, to avoid confusion with the 2nd pl. The weak point in Kerns' argument is his assumption that long vowels are preserved in the last syllables of disyllabic words; holding *edi* to reflect **edhēm*, he is compelled to ascribe the 3rd sg. to analogy (*beri* : *eber* = *edi* : x; x = *ed*). Yet, he certainly took a step toward the right solution. Evangelisti, relying on a similar shift from optative to imperfect in Tokharian (previously pointed out by Kerns, too) and in Iranian, succeeded in setting up a Proto-Armenian paradigm more in agreement with the rules of sound-change: *ei* < **es-ı̑y-ṃ*; *eir* < **es-ı̑-ro*; *ēr* < **és-ī-r* ... (Evangelisti 1955).

Thus, some difficult problems of Armenian verb inflection have been cleared up. An outline of the Proto-Armenian verb system is perhaps still premature. My own study on this topic (Godel 1965) does not claim to be more than a tentative sketch. Karagulyan's study (1961) is a compilation work.

H. Frisk once called for 'eine philologisch vertiefte Wortbildungslehre' of Classical Armenian (Frisk 1944:7). Indeed, word derivation is probably that part of a language which best preserves traces of its whole background. This particular field of diachronic Armenian, however, has not been systematically explored so far. Aside from Meillet's article on Armenian compound words (Meillet 1962:159–84), few studies, such as Bolognesi's excellent paper on the *t*- prefix, are worth mentioning, let alone bare lists of suffixes and composition patterns, such as are to be found in grammar books.

The Classical Armenian lexicon yields materials from successive morphological layers. The earliest one consists of survivals of Indo-European morphology, e.g. root derivates in *-*ti*- (*bay*, *bard*, *awtʿ*, etc.) and in *-*me*/*on*- (*himn*, *sermn*, *erdumn*, etc.). The latest layer represents the Arsacian period (66–387 AD), when a number of new suffixes, abstracted from Iranian loanwords, were added to Armenian words or stems, and thus became part of the derivation system of Classical Armenian: -*ak*, -*akan*, -*agoyn*, -*oy*(*kʿ*), -*uhi*, -*uk*, etc. Up to now, both the Indo-European relics and the Iranian loanwords and morphemes (see below, p. 154) have drawn the attention of comparativists. It would be worthwhile to explore henceforth the intermediate layers, and to reconstruct, as far as possible, an earlier state of Proto-Armenian morphology. Indo-European suffixes, such as those quoted above, mostly occur in expanded forms: *oytʿ* < *-*ou-ti*-; -*awtʿ* < *-*au-ti*- (?); -*umn*; -*awn* (*paštawn*, G. *paštaman* 'worship', from an Iranian stem). The Armenian reflexes of old Indo-European words or verb stems fairly often show suffixes unknown in all cognate languages, e.g. *-s-* (< **-k̂-* or **-k-*) in *lsel* (< **lusel*; cf. aor. *luay*) 'to hear', from IE **k̂lu-*, and *busanel* (aor. *busay*) 'to grow', from IE **bheu-*; *-k* in *bok* 'barefoot' (Cf. OSl. *bosŭ*; OHG *bar*), *šēk* 'of a bright reddish color' (Cf. Skt. *çvetá-*; OSl. *světŭ*; Ags. *hwīt*); *-or* in *nor* 'new' < **new-or(o)* (Cf. Gk. *ne(w)os*, Lat. *nouus*, etc., and, on the other hand, Arm. *glor* 'round'; *molor* 'erring'; *stor* 'down, low', etc.). A careful study of these marginal word patterns, dating from a more or less remote stage of Proto-Armenian, would perhaps contribute valuable insights into the prehistoric evolution of the language and its connections with other Indo-European dialects.

Let us consider, in this respect, Arm. *ardiwn* 'action, achievement, production' (mostly used in the plural). According to Ajarian (1926–35, I:653–4), it is derived from *ard* 'shape, ornament' with the same suffix as in *šaržiwn* 'movement', *hnč'-iwn* 'utterance', etc. It may be objected that *-iwn* regularly occurs in verb derivates (action nouns). Furthermore, the semantic connection is obscure. Let us try another analysis: *ar-diwn*, i.e. the verb root *ar-* (*aṙnel*, aor. *arari* 'to do'), plus the compound suffix **-ti-on*. According to a well known rule, **t* after a resonant had to yield *d*. This suffix is documented in only three Indo-European dialects: Celtic (Old Irish), Italic (Latin and Oscan-Umbrian), and Armenian. But, while Latin and Old Irish share several morphological features, Armenian belongs in a different dialectal area. Besides, **-tion-* has been detected, so far, only in the widespread abstract noun suffix *-ut'iwn* (Pedersen 1905:220). Since this morpheme may be viewed as an expansion of *-oyt'*, as Meillet suggests (1936:80), the connection with Italic and Celtic lacks weight; for an isogloss cannot be drawn without regard to chronology, and *-ut'iwn*, if derivated from Proto-Armenian *-oyt'*, will by no means go so far back as Lat. *ratio*, *mentio*, or OIr *toimtiu*. But this is not the case with *ardiwn*, a primary derivate, with a stem identical to the bare root *ar-*, not to the aorist stem *arar-*, as is the rule for later derivates (*arar-ič'* 'creator'; *arar-ac* 'creature', etc.). Thus, the occurrence of **-tion-* in Armenian, as well as in Celtic and Italic, becomes more significant.

I dare not say to what extent a systematic study of Proto-Armenian word derivation would be fruitful, or even feasible. Anyhow, a closer examination of morphological data would help etymological research, and at least preclude mistakes. Paralleling Arm. *cameli* 'jaw' with Gk. *gamphēlḗ* 'jaw (of wild beasts)' (Solta 1960:254) does not make sense, because the latter, save for its possible relation with *gómphos*, is an isolated word, while *cameli* belongs in a class of regular, predictable derivates. Consequently, if any relation holds between *cameli* and Gk. *gamphēlḗ*, it is only through *camel* 'to chew', presumably a denominative verb from a Proto-Armenian noun **cam*. Meillet long ago equated Arm. *ełanim* 'I am being, I become' with Gk. *pélomai* (Meillet, *MSL* 10.282 [1897–98]). This equation, rejected by Pedersen (1906:388), and apparently by Meillet himself, who did not maintain it in his *Esquisse*, is taken over by Solta, on Ajarian's authority (Solta 1960:87). But it proves delusive as soon as the primitive paradigm is reconstructed: *linim*, aor. *elē*; subj. *elēcʿ*, *licʿis* .... Obviously *elanim*, like other analogical forms, has been derived from the aorist in late Proto-Armenian (Godel 1953).

4. Studies on syntax, with few exceptions (Benveniste 1952, Meillet 1962), do not belong in diachronic Armenian. The last part of this report will therefore be devoted to the connections of Armenian with other languages within the Indo-European family, on the one hand, and within its geographic area (Asia Minor and Caucasus) on the other.

The dialectal position of Armenian does not appear very different today from what it was thought to be before World War II (Porzig 1954, Solta 1960, Schmitt 1962). Greek-Armenian significant isoglosses have been pointed out long ago (Meillet 1936:142–3, Bonfante 1937; cf. Porzig 1954:155–7). Some include Baltic and Slavic and/or Albanian, too (Porzig 1954:171–2, 179–81). On the other hand, Armenian has lexical connections with Indo-Iranian, especially Vedic. Even after discarding the Iranian words that were formerly mistaken for genuine Armenian (see above, p. 141) there is a residue of Indo-European Lexicon peculiar to these languages (Porzig 1954: 161–2; Arm. *mēg* 'mist' is a loan from Iranian; but *sxalel* 'to err', Skt. *skhalati*, and perhaps *surb* 'holy', Skt. *çubhrá-* may be added, the latter in spite of Benveniste's doubt). There is no cogent reason for ascribing the Armenian words to the cultural influence of a Proto-Aryan people on the Proto-Armenians, as Porzig does, rather than to a common descent. Concerning Tokharian (Van Windekens 1943a and c, 1944, 1961), no particularly close relations with Armenian have been evinced.

The most debated problem remains the position of Armenian with regard to Phrygian (with or without Thracian), and the Anatolian languages. According to Herodotus' and Eudoxus' testimonies, Armenians and Phrygians were near cognates. The linguistic evidence, however, does not strongly support this view, which is nevertheless upheld by Bonfante (1946) and, with particular obstinacy, by Haas (1939, 1961; see also the Appendix to *Die phrygischen Sprachdenkmäler*, Sofia, 1966). For the time being, the opposite opinion seems safer, unless one chooses to leave the question open (Austin 1942, Solta 1963:80–2, Dressler 1964a, Heubeck 1967). As to the relation of Armenian with Hittite, advocated by Austin, it is firmly questioned by Kerns and Schwartz (1942), Pedersen (1945:5–7) who asserts the Phrygian-Hittite cognation, as well as by Kammenhuber (1961:38–42, 55–9), who denies it. A chapter in Kapantsian's book is dedicated to the Hittite components of Armenian (Kapantsian 1961:147–219); but it has to be discussed in connection with the author's theory on the origin and growth of the Armenian language. Anyhow, the Armenian-Hittite affinity does not seem to involve more than a few inherited Indo-European words (Porzig 1954:188, Laroche 1963), and possibly Hittite loans in Armenian. In the latter case, however, one has to inquire as to when and how the borrowing should have taken place (Schultheiss 1961; on Arm. *išxan* 'prince', Hitt. *išha-*: Kammenhuber 1961:56, fn. 2).

As soon as they settled in their historical territory in the South of Caucasus, the Armenians came into contact with nations speaking non-Indo-European languages, which may be supposed to have perceptibly affected the further evolution of their own idiom. Meillet's statement (1936:12), cautious though it is, has to be revised; evidence for lexical borrowings on both sides, but especially Lazo-Mingrelian and Georgian loans in Armenian, has been produced by H. Vogt (1938), who does not exclude, however, the presence of loanwords from some unknown language both in Armenian and in Western K'art'vel languages (cf. Treimer 1957–58:279–81). As for the structural analogies on the phonological and grammatical levels, which at first sight seemed very striking, they now appear to be the result of somewhat divergent developments (Vogt 1961). Further research on the relation of Armenian with the modern neighboring languages will doubtlessly yield positive results; the lateness of the linguistic data is compensated by plenty and variety.

Yet it is also advisable to inquire about the possible connections of Armenian with Urartean and Hurrian, and through the latter, with Accadian and Sumerian, to quote only those ancient non-Indo-European languages for which written evidence is available. Such connections, belonging to a remote past, will not be easily elicited; but there is such an enormous number of radical words of unknown origin in Armenian, that parallels may be fairly sought in any language that was ever spoken in that part of the Near East. One must not be too sanguine as to the result; neither did Armenian forward the decipherment of the Urartean inscriptions, nor did the latter throw much light on the dim portion of the Armenian lexicon.

Pioneer work in this field has been achieved by G. Kapantsian, from 1931 onward. His earlier publications are unknown to me; but his *History of the Armenian language*, edited after his death by the Academy of Sciences in Erivan (1961), offers the most elaborated version of his theory, which I briefly sum up. Reviving P. Kretschmer's parallel: *Hayasa* = *Hay* 'Armenian' (1961:29), Kapantsian locates the Armenians' home, toward the fifteenth century B.C., in the land of Hayasa-Azzi, in the North Eastern quarter of Asia Minor, between Sivas, Erzerum, and the Black Sea. They spoke a language of the 'Asianic' type, but they also had intercourse with their Eastern neighbors, the ancestors of the Lazo-Mingrelians. Later on, they moved East- and Southwards, settled in Urartu, and came into closer contact with the Hurrians. Consequently, as against the prevailing opinion, Armenian must be viewed as an actual 'Mischsprache'; its basic lexicon and grammar (derivational morphemes, reduplicated forms) has grown out of Asianic, South Caucasian, and, to a lesser extent, Hurrian and Urartean materials, which were never wholly superseded by the Indo-European dialect of the later invaders. This theory reminds us of N.J. Marr's ideas, which had prevailed in the Soviet Union up to 1950, and were then rejected as 'unhistorical', as Kapantsian himself acknowledges (1964:28). His most shocking mistake, however, is his ignoring the Indo-European origin of Hittite, and including it in the 'Asianic group', together with Hurrian and Urartean. This error has been pointed out by the editor in the Preface (1961:7–8) and elsewhere (217 and 223 fn.). Nevertheless, the Academy did not hesitate to publish the book, for the sake of the amount of material it contains, and of the new prospects it seems to open. Kapantsian's previous studies, it must be granted, had already been felt stimulating even by those who did not approve the theoretical basis (Bănăţeanu 1961). As a pioneer, he proceeded boldly; what he aimed at was accumulating as much comparative data as he could. Further research in his line will have, first of all, to check these data and to apply more rigorous criteria in valuing the probability of the equations, a number of which have to be discarded without delay: e.g. Arm. *bargawač* 'thriving', *manawand* 'chiefly', *tagnap* 'haste, panic', listed among the Armenian-Hittite words (150–1, 200), are unmistakably Iranian (Bailey 1956:94, 107–8; Benveniste 1964:27–8).

I do not venture going farther on ground hardly accessible to Indo-Europeanists. I would insist, however, upon one methodical requisite of such investigations. In paralleling Armenian words with Urartean, Hurrian, and even Hittite, Kapantsian relies on approximate phonological similarity; a criterion which, in the case of Armenian, may be particularly misleading. For, whether the non-Indo-European words or features in Armenian are traces of a substratum, or the result of intercourse and borrowing, they certainly have gone through some phases of the Proto-Armenian evolution. Now, it is impossible to guess how Kapantsian figures out the phonological process; does he hold the sound-changes that affected the Indo-European dialect to be previous to the first contact with the 'Asianic' languages? Or does he believe that a Hittite or Hurrian word, in Armenian mouths, did not alter in the same way as an Indo-European one, so that it would, e.g. preserve its initial *p*- while **patēr* changed to *hayr*? If Arm. *-uni*, in family names (*Amatuni*, *Slkuni*, etc.), is the same morpheme as Urartean *-uni*, in toponyms and patronymics (142; cf. Bănăţeanu 1961), how did it happen that neither the unstressed *-u-* nor the final *-i* was ever dropped? Scholars slowly become conscious of these problems (Treimer 1957–58:281). A systematic, if not quite successful, attempt has been made to determine the phonological stage Proto-Armenian had reached before receiving Hittite loanwords (Schultheiss 1961: 231–4).

I alluded above (p. 141) to the progress of Iranian philology. Since Hübschmann's and Meillet's days, many Middle Iranian texts have come to light, and an ever increasing number of loans from Parthian (and also Middle Medic, according to Perikhanian 1967) are being detected in Classical Armenian. Valuable studies have been contributed by Wikander (1948a and b), Pagliaro (1950), Belardi (1950a and b, 1962), Bolognesi (1951a, 1960, 1961, 1962), Bailey (1956, 1965), Benveniste (1958, 1961, 1963, 1964), Szemerényi (1966), with equal benefit for both Armenian and Iranian philology; for, while sparing the former useless etymological speculation, they sometimes supply the latter with phonological and semantic data that would not be so easily gained from obscure Parthian texts.

In conclusion: Armenian may, at first sight, appear as a rather narrow department in comparative philology. But I hope that, to the readers of this survey, it will prove more interesting than other cognate languages, on account of its quite peculiar evolution, and of its manyfold connections with various idioms. The result of research in the course of the last thirty years, though not impressive, must not be underrated, in view of the small number of Armenologists — I mean such as are earnestly engaged in comparative studies. More will be achieved in the future, provided Armenian philology does not come short of the application of the current methods that prove so effective in the diachronic study of Indo-European languages.

The selected bibliography covers the period from 1936 (2nd edition of Meillet's *Esquisse*) through 1967. Earlier studies, however, have been included, for reasons that the readers of the above report will easily understand. General works on comparative philology, as well as etymological dictionaries have not been recorded.

REFERENCES

AJARIAN [AČARYAN], H. 1926–35. Hayerēn Armatakan Bararan [Armenian root dictionary]. Erivan.
AUSTIN, W. M. 1942. Is Armenian an Anatolian language? Lg 18.22–5.
BAILEY, H. W. 1956. Armeno-Indoiranica. TPhS, 88–126.
——. 1965. Iranian in Armenian. REArm, Nouv. sér. 2.1–3.
BĂNĂŢEANU, VLAD. 1961. Urartean suffixes in Classical Armenian. RLing 6.85–107.
BARTON, CH. R. 1963. The etymology of Arm. *ertʿam*. Lg 39.620.
BELARDI, WALTER. 1950a. Arm. *nerkanem*; *pʿayt* e *paytʿem*. RL 1.147–9.
——. 1950b. Arm. *kox*. RL 1.255–7.
——. 1962. Sull'origine delle voci armene antiche composte con *pat-*. RL 5.149–69 (= HA 75.613–30 [1961]).
BENVENISTE, EMILE. 1952. La construction passive du parfait transitif. BSL 48.52–62. [Repr. in Problèmes de linguistique générale, 176–86, Paris, 1966].
——. 1958. Mots d'emprunt iraniens en arménien. BSL 53.55–71.
——. 1959. Sur la phonétique et la syntaxe de l'arménien classique. BSL 54.46–68.
——. 1961. Remarques sur les composés arméniens en *-pet*. HA 75.631–40.
——. 1963. Interférences lexicales entre le gotique et l'iranien. BSL 58.41–57.
——. 1964. Eléments parthes en arménien. REArm Nouv.sér. 1.1–39.
——. 1965a. Arménien *aregakn* 'soleil' et la formation nominale en *-akn*. REArm, Nouv.sér. 2.5–19.
——. 1965b. Review of Armenian and Indo-European, by Stuart E. Mann. BSL 60.36–9 (= REArm Nouv.sér. 3.387–9).
——. 1967. Une correspondance indo-européenne en arménien. REArm Nouv.sér. 3.7–10.
BOLOGNESI, GIANCARLO. 1948a. Sul prefisso *t-* in armeno. RSO 23.82–6.
——. 1948b. Etimologie armene. ASGIM 1.22–4.

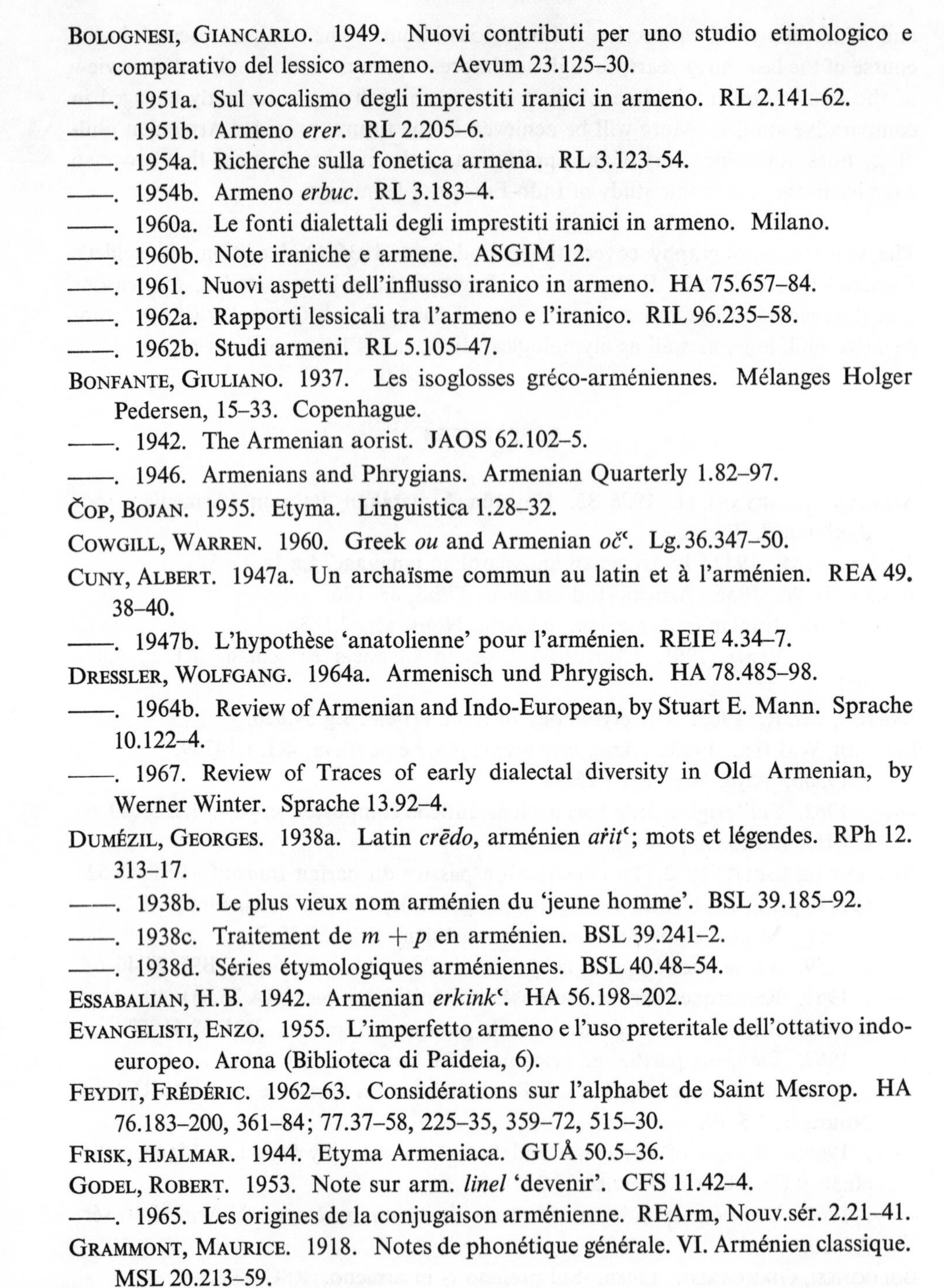

Bolognesi, Giancarlo. 1949. Nuovi contributi per uno studio etimologico e comparativo del lessico armeno. Aevum 23.125–30.

——. 1951a. Sul vocalismo degli imprestiti iranici in armeno. RL 2.141–62.

——. 1951b. Armeno *erer*. RL 2.205–6.

——. 1954a. Richerche sulla fonetica armena. RL 3.123–54.

——. 1954b. Armeno *erbuc*. RL 3.183–4.

——. 1960a. Le fonti dialettali degli imprestiti iranici in armeno. Milano.

——. 1960b. Note iraniche e armene. ASGIM 12.

——. 1961. Nuovi aspetti dell'influsso iranico in armeno. HA 75.657–84.

——. 1962a. Rapporti lessicali tra l'armeno e l'iranico. RIL 96.235–58.

——. 1962b. Studi armeni. RL 5.105–47.

Bonfante, Giuliano. 1937. Les isoglosses gréco-arméniennes. Mélanges Holger Pedersen, 15–33. Copenhague.

——. 1942. The Armenian aorist. JAOS 62.102–5.

——. 1946. Armenians and Phrygians. Armenian Quarterly 1.82–97.

Čop, Bojan. 1955. Etyma. Linguistica 1.28–32.

Cowgill, Warren. 1960. Greek *ou* and Armenian *oč'*. Lg. 36.347–50.

Cuny, Albert. 1947a. Un archaïsme commun au latin et à l'arménien. REA 49. 38–40.

——. 1947b. L'hypothèse 'anatolienne' pour l'arménien. REIE 4.34–7.

Dressler, Wolfgang. 1964a. Armenisch und Phrygisch. HA 78.485–98.

——. 1964b. Review of Armenian and Indo-European, by Stuart E. Mann. Sprache 10.122–4.

——. 1967. Review of Traces of early dialectal diversity in Old Armenian, by Werner Winter. Sprache 13.92–4.

Dumézil, Georges. 1938a. Latin *crēdo*, arménien *aṙit'*; mots et légendes. RPh 12. 313–17.

——. 1938b. Le plus vieux nom arménien du 'jeune homme'. BSL 39.185–92.

——. 1938c. Traitement de $m + p$ en arménien. BSL 39.241–2.

——. 1938d. Séries étymologiques arméniennes. BSL 40.48–54.

Essabalian, H.B. 1942. Armenian *erkink'*. HA 56.198–202.

Evangelisti, Enzo. 1955. L'imperfetto armeno e l'uso preteritale dell'ottativo indoeuropeo. Arona (Biblioteca di Paideia, 6).

Feydit, Frédéric. 1962–63. Considérations sur l'alphabet de Saint Mesrop. HA 76.183–200, 361–84; 77.37–58, 225–35, 359–72, 515–30.

Frisk, Hjalmar. 1944. Etyma Armeniaca. GUÅ 50.5–36.

Godel, Robert. 1953. Note sur arm. *linel* 'devenir'. CFS 11.42–4.

——. 1965. Les origines de la conjugaison arménienne. REArm, Nouv.sér. 2.21–41.

Grammont, Maurice. 1918. Notes de phonétique générale. VI. Arménien classique. MSL 20.213–59.

Gray, Louis H. 1945. The Armenian plural termination *-k'*. Word 1.304.

HAAS, OTTO. 1939a. Über die phrygische Sprachreste und ihr Verhältnis zum Armenischen. HA 53.225–35.
——. 1939b. [Gr.] *akoúō* - [arm.] *ansam*. HA 53.235–6.
——. 1940. Das armenische Pluralzeichen -*k*ʻ. HA 54.96–106.
——. 1961. Zur Vorgeschichte der armenischen Sprache. HA 75.563–612.
HAMP, ERIC P. 1955. Armenisch *hariwr*. KZ 72.244–5.
——. 1967. Three Armenian etymologies. REArm, Nouv. sér. 3.11–16.
HEUBECK, ALFRED. 1953. Εσϝεδιυς Ασπενδος et Asitawandas ou Azitawadda d'Azitawandi. L'origine de l'arménien *astuac*. NClio 5.322–5 (= BNF 4.122–5).
——. 1967. Review of Die phrygischen Sprachdenkmäler, by Otto Haas. Gnomon 39.579–83.
HÜBSCHMANN, HEINRICH. 1897. Armenische Grammatik. I. Teil, Armenische Etymologie. Leipzig (Bibliothek indogermanischen Grammatiken, 6). Repr. 1962. Darmstadt, Wissenschaftliche Buchgesellschaft.
JENSEN, HANS. 1959. Altarmenische Grammatik. Heidelberg, Carl Winter.
JEREJIAN, ARMEN V. 1953. The *h*-/zero alternation in Classical Armenian. Word 9.146–51.
KAMMENHUBER, ANNELIES. 1961. Zur stellung des Hethitisch-Luwischen innerhalb der idg. Gemeinsprache. KZ 78.31–75.
KAPANTSIAN [ǦAPʻANCʻYAN], GRIGOR. 1961. Hayocʻ lezvi patmutʻyun (Hin šrǰan) [A history of Armenian language (ancient period)]. Erivan, Izd. Akad. Nauk Armjanskoj SSR.
KARAGULYAN, TEREZA A. 1961. Hin hayereni xonarhman hamakargi cagumə [The Origin of Classical Armenian conjugation system]. Erivan, Izd. Akad. Nauk Armjanskoj SSR.
KARIBIAN [ǦARIBYAN], A. S. 1967. Sovyetahay lezvabanut'yan nəvačumnerə [The Conquests of Soviet Armenian linguistics]. Patma-banasirakan handes 2–3.73–86. Erivan.
KARSTIEN, H. 1956. Das slavische Imperfekt und der armenische -*acʻe*- Aorist. Festschrift für Max Vasmer, 211–29. Wiesbaden, Harassowitz.
KERNS, J. A. 1939. The imperfect in Armenian and Irish. Lg. 15.30–33.
KERNS, J. A., and BENJAMIN SCHWARTZ. 1942. On the placing of Armenian. Lg18.226–8.
KNOBLOCH, JOHANN. 1961. Zu armenisch *erkin* 'Himmel', *erkir* 'Erde'. HA 75.541–4.
LAROCHE, EMMANUEL. 1963. Etudes lexicales et étymologiques sur le hittite. 6. *siya*- et *samana*. BSL 58.73–7.
MANN, STUART E. 1963. Armenian and Indo-European. Historical phonology. London, Luzac and Co.
MEILLET, ANTOINE. 1936. Esquisse d'une grammaire comparée de l'arménien classique, 2nd. edition. Vienne, Imprimerie des PP. Mékhitaristes.
——. 1962. Etudes de linguistique et de philologie arméniennes. I. Recherches sur la syntaxe comparée de l'arménien. Lisboa, Bibl. arménienne de la Fondation Calouste Gulbenkian.

Minshall, R. 1955. Initial Indo-European */y/ in Armenian. Lg 31.499–503.

Pagliaro, Antonino. 1950. Armeno *p'ol harkanel.* RL 1.252–3.

Pedersen, Holger. 1905. Zur armenischen Sprachgeschichte. KZ 38.194–240.

——. 1906. Armenisch und die Nachbarsprachen. 1. Vorbemerkungen über das armenische Lautsystem. KZ 39.334–442.

——. 1945. Lykisch und Hittitisch. Kobenhavn, Det Kgl. Danske Videnskabernes Selskab.

——. 1949. V.sl. *gradĭ.* LPosn 1.1–2.

Perikhanian, Anahit. 1967. L'inscription araméenne du roi Artašēs trouvée à Zangezur (Siwnik'). REArm, Nouv.sér. 3.17–29.

Pisani, Vittore. 1934. Armeniaca. KZ 61.180–9.

——. 1944. Armenische Studien. I. Zur armenischen Etymologie. KZ 68.157–77.

——. 1948. La palatalizzazione armena. ASGIM 1.15–21.

——. 1951a. Studi sulla fonetica dell'armeno. RL 1.165–93, 2.47–74.

——. 1951b. *Uxor.* Milano, Ricerche di morfologia indoeuropea 5–6.

——. 1961. Der Gott als 'Verteiler' und arm. *astuac.* HA 75.549–62.

——. 1964. Armenisch *hariwr*; ein Versuch. HA 78.189–92.

——. 1966. Armenische Miscellen. Sprache 12.227–36.

Polomé, Edgar. 1950, 1952. Réflexes de laryngales en arménien. Annuaire de philologie et d'histoire orientales et slaves 10.539–69, 12.669–71. Université Libre de Bruxelles.

Porzig, Walter. 1954. Die Gliederung des idg. Sprachgebietes. Heidelberg, Carl Winter.

Reichenkron, Günter. 1961. Armeniaca. b) Das altarmenische Pluralzeichen *-k'.* HA 75.1034–44.

Scardigli, P. G. 1961. Aspekte der armenischen Etymologie. HA 75.641–56.

Scheftelowitz, J. 1904. Zur altarmenischen Lautgeschichte. I. Beiträge zur Kunde der idg. Sprachen (Bezzenberger's Beiträge), 28.282–313.

——. 1905. Zur altarmenischen Lautgeschichte. II. Bezzenberger's Beiträge, 29.13–71.

Schindler, Jochem. 1966. Hethitisch *liššu* 'Leber'. Sprache 12.77–8.

Schmidt, K. H. 1964. Desaffrizierung im Armenischen? MSS 16.89–93.

Schmitt, Rüdiger. 1962. Review of Die Stellung des Armenischen im Kreise der idg. Sprachen, by G. R. Solta. Kratylos 7.149–55.

Schultheiss, Tassilo. 1961. Hethitisch und Armenisch. KZ 77.219–34.

Schwyzer, Eduard. 1946 [1930]. Ein armenisch-griechisches Nominalsuffix. MH 3.49–58.

Solta, Georg R. 1960. Die Stellung des Armenischen im Kreise der idg. Sprachen. Eine Untersuchung der idg. Bestandteile des armenischen Wortschatzes. Wien, Mechitaristen Buchdruckerei.

——. 1963. Armenische Sprache. Handbuch der Orientalistik, Erste Abteilung. Band 7.

SZEMERÉNYI, OSWALD. 1966. Iranica II Nr. 27–31. Sprache 12.221–6.

TREIMER, KARL. 1957–58. Stand genetischer Probleme. Lingua 7.274–97.

TUMANIAN, E. G. 1967. Armjanskii jazyk. Sovetskoe jazykoznanie za 50 let, 158–70. Moskva, Izd. Nauka.

VOGT, HANS. 1938. Arménien et Caucasique du Sud. NTS 9.321–38.

——. 1958. Les occlusives de l'arménien. NTS 18.143–59.

——. 1961. Arménien et géorgien. HA 75.531–40.

WIKANDER, STIG. 1948a. Problèmes irano-arméniens. SL 2.48–53.

——. 1948b. Notes irano-arméniennes. Extract from Le Monde Oriental, 36. Uppsala.

VAN WINDEKENS, ALBERT J. 1943a. Les effets de l'intonation en tokharien et en arménien. Muséon 56.129–36.

——. 1943b. Note sur deux difficultés de la grammaire comparée arménienne. REIE 3.30–41.

——. 1943c. L'origine de la nasale dans arm. *otn*, *jeṙn*. REIE 3.175–7.

——. 1944. Neue Studien zur Wortkunde des Tokharischen und des Armenischen. KZ 68.218–21.

——. 1947a. Arménien *hariwr*. REIE 4.14–26.

——. 1947b. Recherches sur la morphologie comparée de l'arménien. REIE 4. 315–20.

——. 1961. Sur trois mots arméniens [*bir*; *kamurǰ*; *holm*]. HA 75.545–8.

——. 1964. Essai de solution d'un vieux problème: la formation d'arm. *kanai-* = gr. γυναι - 'femme'. HA 78.185–90.

WINTER, WERNER. 1954. Problems of Armenian phonology. I. The phonetic value of Old Arm. *p*ʻ, *t*ʻ, *k*ʻ. Lg 30.197–201.

——. 1955. Problems of Armenian phonology. II. The representation of IE *p*, *t*, *k* (k^w) in Armenian. Lg 31.4–8.

——. 1960. Armenian evidence for Proto-Indo-European laryngeals. Evidence for laryngeals, ed. by W. Winter, 27–41. Austin, The University of Texas.

——. 1962. Problems of Armenian phonology. III. Consonant clusters. Lg 38. 254–62.

——. 1966. Traces of early dialectal diversity, ed. by Henrik Birnbaum and Jaan Puhvel, 201–11. Berkeley and Los Angeles, University of California Press.

SYNCHRONIC ARMENIAN

M. J. CONNOLLY

Modern Armenian is customarily divided into two areas, Eastern and Western, each of which has a standing literary and scholarly tradition. These two major dialects differ markedly from one another in phonology and grammatical system yet are, for the most part, mutually intelligible. With the term EASTERN ARMENIAN (*arewela-hayerēn* or less accurately *ṙusahayerēn* 'Russian Armenian') one refers generally to the *um*-dialect (explained below), which is spoken by Armenians within the Soviet Union, in Iran and India. Western Armenian (*arewmtahayerēn*) is then used to fill in the remaining areas, namely Armenian colonies throughout the Levant, in France, the United States, South America, and elsewhere. The terms are indeed at times unsuitable for precise linguistic demands, but are in such common use by Armenologists and Armenian scholars that they cannot be successfully avoided.

In addition to the above-mentioned living languages, one will often encounter traces of Classical Armenian (*grabar*, as it is referred to by native grammarians), the Indo-European language which flourished during and after the fifth century A.D., and from which the modern dialects are customarily derived. Apart from ecclesiastical and quasi-archaic usages, however, Classical Armenian exercises little influence on the state or development of Modern Armenian, due undoubtedly in part to the fact that the former is of an inflexional type, whereas the latter is developing in what may be termed an agglutinative manner.

To illustrate a typological distinction between the types of literary Armenian, let us consider the formation of the present tense from a stem {*seyr-*} 'to love':

Classical: *sirem* {seyr-é-m}
= stem — theme — 1 sg.
Eastern: *sirum em* {seyr-úm + e-m}
= stem — gerund (≦ loc. case?) + 'be' — 1 sg.
Western: *kə sirem* {kə + seyr-é-m}
= particle + stem — theme — 1 sg.

This formational type continues throughout the remaining persons of the present tense and also into the past tense of the present system (imperfect): *sires/sirum es/kə sires* etc.; *sirēi/sirum ēi/kə sirēi* etc. The Eastern dialect also has a form *ksirem* [kəsirém] which functions as a future tense. In both Eastern and Western Armenian the Classical present (*sirem*) is a subjunctive. Further, due to the phonology of Western Armenian, the form *kə sirem* is pronounced [gəsirém] in most of those subdialects.

It is precisely the above feature of present tense formation which is used as an archetype for the more scientific classification of Armenian dialects (following Ačaŕyan 1909), which distinguishes a type in *-um* (*sirum em*), a type in *kə-* (*kə sirem*), and a subordinate type in *-el* (based on infinitival *-l* plus copula, and thus parallel to the *-um* types). To these Ačaŕyan's student A. Łaribyan later added a fourth group using similar classification. The distinction, it may be argued, provides little more satisfaction than the Indo-Europeanist's *centum/satəm* or similar dichotomies. Such is true to the extent that few such arbitrary or coincidental features (even with geographical orientation) will hold across the board, yet it is precisely upon this basis that much useful work in Armenian dialectology has been carried out for over a half-century now.

The first significant work in Armenian dialectology, a field which has developed tangible results although employing even to this day what would be considered by Western linguists as an old-fashioned descriptive technique, was carried out before the turn of the century by K. Patkanjan (1869, 1875) and L. Msereancʿ (1897–1901). Thereafter H. Ačaŕyan, a student of A. Meillet, produced an extensive series of dialect studies in addition to his epic works on Armenian etymology and general grammar. At present the undisputed dean of Armenian dialectology is Academician A. Łaribyan, whose talent for collation and proper organization of data has led to a synthesizing tendency in the aims and methods of dialect studies. Thus when a seemingly interminable controversy arose on the pages of the journals *Patma-banasirakan handes* (1958 ff.) and *Voprosy jazykoznanija* (1959 ff.) about the nature of diachronic Armenian consonantism, the descriptive data furnished by Łaribyan (who had recently introduced a sevenfold typology of the dialects (1953) with threefold morphological regrouping) and his colleagues proved central to the entire discussion, drawing the attention of the entire linguistic world to the quality of the analyses in this previously little-recognized area. The work is continuing in the same thorough format in a series from the Armenian Academy of Sciences entitled *Hayereni barbaŕner* (Armenian dialects), several titles of which are included in the appended bibliography, along with some of the more outstanding dialect studies.

At its inception in the fifth century A.D., the Armenian alphabet was most probably phonemically based, since all evidence points to a relative one-to-one correspondence of sound and letters. Due to later sound changes in the language, however, the historical orthography is in many ways inadequate. In order to produce the modern pronunciation from a transcription of the standard orthography (= the classical writing with the addition of two characters: *ō* [< *aw* in certain contexts] and *f*), a fairly complex mechanism is required, which may be roughly summarized in the following partially ordered rules:

1. *iw* → /yu/ // ___C (except before morpheme boundary: *xačʿiwn* = /xačʿivn/, but *-utʿiwn* = /utʿyun/)
2. a. *e* → /y/ // ___ $\left\{\begin{matrix} \bar{o} \\ a \end{matrix}\right\}$
   b. → /ye/ // #___
   c. → /e/
3. a. *o* → /u/ // ___yC
   b. → /vo/ // #___ (unless immediately followed by /v/!)
   c. → /o/
4. $\left\{\begin{matrix} w \\ v \end{matrix}\right\}$ → /v/
5. a. u → /v/ // ___V
   b. → /u/
6. a. y → Ø // #...___# (where context is non-substantival and/or contains more than one V)
   b. → /h/ // #___ (as well as after certain internal boundaries: *anyapal* 'immediately' = /anhapağ/)
   c. /y/
7. various low-level phonetic adjustments, varying with speaker, such as loss of final *-h* and devoicing of stops intervocalically as well as after *r*, *n*, and *l*.

The problem of attaining near universal literacy is considerably hindered under such circumstances, and misspellings commonplace, since the spoken language cannot, of course, be written out properly without orthographic training and drill. One method employed in the Western Armenian tradition, which still clings to the classical orthography, is to introduce spelling-pronunciations, such that *ē* and *ō* are pronounced more close than the corresponding *e* and *o*, *v* is given the value of a long or doubled /v/ versus simplex *w*, *xačʿiwn* is pronounced /xačʿyun/ etc. Such methods neither remove all the difficulties (one is still left with problems like whether /hayt/ 'visible' is to be written *hayt* (incorrect) or *yayt*) nor provide a reasonable substitute for rote memorization. Orthographic reform, anathematized by many tradition-conscious Armenians, would seem the only likely alternative.

This course of action was undertaken in 1922 with a series of orthographic reforms parallel to the Soviet Russian situation of 1917 — a tradition-based morphophonemic spelling. The multivalent letters were allowed to represent only one phonemic value, and linear distribution in diphthongs restated to correspond to actual phonological shape (*iw* > *yu*, *ea* > *ya*, *eō* > *yo*, (#)*o*- > *vo*, (#)*e*- > *ye*, etc.). In 1940 a bow to tradition was made and the distinctions *e*/*ē*, *o*/*ō* reintroduced in initial position, thus tolerating one small and almost typically Armenian ambivalence:

a. $\begin{bmatrix} e \\ o \end{bmatrix} \rightarrow \begin{bmatrix} /ye/ \\ /vo/ \end{bmatrix}$ // #___

b. $\rightarrow \begin{bmatrix} /e/ \\ /o/ \end{bmatrix}$

In going from speech to script the slight irregularity is taken care of by a simple rule that initial /ye/ and /vo/ are written with *e-* and *o-* respectively, elsewhere with *-ye-* vs. *-vo-*, further that initial /e/ and /o/ are written *ē-/ō-*, elsewhere *-e-/-o-*. The resultant Soviet Armenian orthography is thus a most efficient pedagogical vehicle for the reading and writing of Armenian.

In the field of lexicology (Gasparyan 1967), Armenian is continuing well in an almost enviable tradition. The compendious dictionaries of the classical and modern language from the last century are being fully utilized and improved. S. Malxasyancʻ (1944–45) produced a four volume *tolkovyj slovarj* for Armenian which represents a monumental linguistic undertaking. Numerous essays (e.g. Petrosyan 1960) have pointed out the major shortcomings in the Malxasyancʻ' work, and due to these helpful discussions a new dictionary, also in four volumes, is being prepared (*Hayereni bacʻatrakan bararan* 1969) under the collaboration of several associates in the Armenian Academy of Sciences.

Nor has there been any lack of specialized and multilingual dictionaries for school and professional use. In 1969 a linguistic dictionary (*Lezvabanakan bararan* 1969) was announced, which treats not only Western and Soviet terminology as received by the Armenians, but also native adaptations and calques, successfully developed and employed by scholars like M. Abełyan and E. Ałayan. One very useful item for advanced linguistic and stylistic studies is the recently issued dictionary of Armenian synonyms (Sukʻiasyan 1967). To date this author knows of no reverse-alphabetized dictionary. There are also some very good studies on foreign words in modern Armenian (Ačaṙyan 1951, Kusikjan 1964, Łazaryan 1955), a topic which is of considerable assistance in the prescription of the literary language. The fundamental tasks of Armenian lexicology have been admirably accomplished.

At the head of general Armenian grammars stands the nearly completed multi-volume grammar by H. Ačaṙyan (1952–67), which brings in typological comparisons from an asserted 562 languages as well as Classical, Medieval, and dialect Armenian. Ačaṙyan's *Complete grammar* is a veritable masterpiece of description, presentation, and comparison, to which Armenian studies can point with considerable pride. In the nineteenth century there were several good introductory pedagogical grammars for modern Armenian, the more significant of which are listed in the selected bibliography. In this century all notable grammars, with the exception of two (Abeghian 1936, Movsessian 1959) tend toward the treatment of only one of the literary languages; (we exclude here from discussion the grammars of Classical Armenian by Meillet, Jensen, A. Abrahamyan, Ałayan, et al.). For the Western dialect, one must note that Kogian (1949) is primarily for reference, Gulian (1902) is in the tradition of the Gaspey-Otto-Sauer method and shares in that system's shortcomings, and that the most suitable grammar is that of Feydit (1948) for pedagogical purposes. The conversational grammar of Fairbanks (1958), while well-researched, is fraught with misprints and offers an ideolectal Armenian style, thus rendered unfit for use without a skilled teacher. The short grammars of Eastern Armenian by Łaribyan (1965) and

Sevak (1967) are most useful and authoritative, but are in Russian and Armenian. A section of Movsessian (1959) is devoted to a survey of Eastern Armenian (old orthography!), but otherwise Westerners have to rely on Fairbanks and Stevick (1958), which shares the same drawbacks as its companion Western grammar (mentioned above), or on mimeographed grammars in circulation from university departments such as at Columbia or the University of California. In order to fill the existing gap, this author is in the process of completing a translation and adaptation of Łaribyan's *Kratkij kurs armjanskogo jazyka* (1965). There is an excellent, well-organized sketch of modern Armenian grammar by È. Tumanjan (1966) containing few misprints.

The modern school in Soviet Armenia is becoming increasingly aware of outside trends in general linguistics through Russian publications, and it would seem that their incorporation is currently taking hold. The linguistic historian and theoretician Ē. Ałayan has shown in a recent study on declension and conjugation (1967b) that modern structural methods can be well applied to the data of modern Armenian and synthesized with the traditional school of theory, for which M. Abełyan (esp. 1931) is the standard referential point. The Russian works of E. Atayan (*Problemy i metody strukturaljnogo sintaksisa*, Erevan, 1962 and *Ponjatie elementarnoj sintaksičeskoj struktury*, Erevan, 1964), S. K. Šaumjan (esp. *Strukturnaja lingvistika*, Moskva, 1965), and Ju. Apresjan, along with the modern mathematical-structural classics in Russian or translated into Russian (e.g. the collections *Novoe v lingvistike*), constitute the leading influences on current Soviet Armenian general linguistics.

Determination of the number of cases in the modern language is a problem which illustrates the type of recourse to linguistic theory prevalent in Armenian studies. The first thorough Westerner's grammar of Armenian (Schröder 1711) distinguished ten cases for the nominal system (employing an archaic paradigm):

anvanakan (*ułlakan*)	— nominative
seṙakan	— genitive
trakan	— dative (w. prefixed and unprefixed forms)
haycʿakan	— accusative
kočʿakan	— vocative
aṙołakan (*bacʿaṙakan*)	— ablative
patmakan	— narrative
nergoyakan	— locative (commorative)
gorciakan	— instrumental
šrǰakayakan	— circumlative

Of these forms the vocative is indistinct from the nominative, and the prefixed dative, narrative, and circumlative are essentially another case with preposition. The situation in modern Eastern Armenian can be even more significantly reduced, since, similar to the Slavic pattern, the direct object form is identical with the nominative for inanimates and with the dative for animates:

Es sirum em ays nkarə (nom.) 'I like this picture'
Es sirum em ays erexayin (dat.) 'I like this lad'

Further, the dative in nouns and adjectives is the same as the genitive with the addition of the definite article, although in the pronouns these cases remain distinct; a locative in *-um* is found for inanimates in Eastern Armenian. On this basis, M. Abełyan (1908, 1931) opted for five cases (nominative, dative, ablative, instrumental, and locative), using strict formal argumentation; other scholars (Sevak 1939–47) have preferred to retain the genitive and accusative, while Ē. Ałayan (1967b) has reasoned on distributional and structural grounds to the linguistically most acceptable complement of six cases: nominative, genitive, dative, ablative, instrumental, and locative.

In the special fields of phonology, morphology, and syntax there are publications of reasonable quality on the specific classes of elements and categories for each subdiscipline. For those who do not read Armenian, È. Tumanjan's treatise on articles (1963) is recommended as an outstanding example. The titles of other entries in the appended bibliography are self-explanatory.

While outside interest in Armenian has been primarily diachronic and will inevitably continue on this plane, the descriptive accomplishments in Armenian linguistics, especially by Soviet scholars, have been outstandingly thorough and painstaking. One observes an encouraging occupation with Armenian literature, a type of modern-day philology, which serves to concretize findings. Armenian synchronic linguistics is currently approaching a new threshold of renewed structural orientation as is evident in the line between M. Abełyan, an outstanding pioneer of linguistic method, and Ē. Ałayan, a scholar who could be placed among the foremost Western linguists. In Europe F. de Saussure's student R. Godel (Geneva) and F. Feydit (Paris) are both significantly forwarding the work of descriptive Armenian studies among their colleagues.

Armenian is rich in features typologically interesting for the descriptive and general linguist; a well-paved way lies open for future generative (transformational), mathematical (Melkumjan 1965, Motalova 1967), and structural studies on the data of Armenian.

SELECTED BIBLIOGRAPHY

The selected bibliography is intended to provide references to the more accessible fundamental books and articles on the various aspects of Armenian synchronic studies. Several grammars of the classical language are also included, since these are one of the prime sources for good linguistic description of Armenian. Incomplete references, of which there are hopefully few, are of presently inaccessible works consulted before the inception of this survey. Transcription is essentially that prescribed for the new series of the *Revue des Études Arméniennes* (Paris, 1964ff.). The individual Armenian surnames are cited in their most common form, for which it should be noted that the standard ending *-ean(c')/-yan* etc. is variously handled by publishers and cataloguers. Armenian titles have been parenthetically given in translation in a Western language, the choice thereof often being founded on publishers' secondary titles.

ABEGHIAN, A. 1936. Neuarmenische Grammatik. Berlin.
ABEŁYAN, M. 1892. Hayocʻ lezui ułagrutʻiwn (Orfografija armjanskogo jazyka). Tiflis.
——. 1906. Ašxarhabari kʻerakanutʻiwn (Grammatika novoarmjanskogo jazyka). Vałaršapat.
——. 1908. Ašxarhabari holovnerə (Padeži novoarmjanskogo jazyka). Vałaršapat.
——. 1909. Haycʻakan holovə mer ašxarhabarum (Viniteljnyj padež v našem novoarmjanskom jazyke). Vałaršapat.
——. 1912. Ašxarhabari šarahyusutʻiwn (Sintaksis sovremennogo armjanskogo jazyka). Vałaršapat.
——. 1931 (1965). Hayocʻ lezvi tesutʻyun (Teorija armjanskogo jazyka). Erevan.
——. 1933. Hayocʻ lezvi tałačʻapʻutʻyun (Metrika armjanskogo jazyka). Erevan.
——. 1936. Grabari kʻerakanutʻyun (Grammatika drevnearmjanskogo jazyka). Erevan.
ABRAHAMYAN, A. 1953. Hayereni derbaynerə ev nrancʻ jevabanakan nšanakutʻyunə (Pričastnye formy armjanskogo jazyka i ix morfologičeskoe značenie). Erevan.
——. 1958a. Grabari jeřnark (Učebnik po grabaru [drevnearmjanskomu jazyku]). Erevan.
——. 1958b. Žamanakakicʻ hayereni krknaserutʻyan erevuytʻi šurjə (O javlenii glagoljnoj dvuzalogosti sovremennogo armjanskogo jazyka). IzvANArm 5.81–9.
——. 1962a. Bayə žamanakakicʻ hayerenum I (Glagol v sovremennom armjanskom jazyke). Erevan.
——. 1962b. Žamanakakicʻ hayereni bayakan demkʻi harcʻer (Voprosy kategorij glagoljnogo lica v sovremennom armjanskom jazyke). IzvANArm 2.31–48.
——. 1962c. Žamanakakicʻ hayereni bayakan demkʻi (u tʻvi) imastayin ev kiřakan ařanjnahatkutʻyunnerə (Osobennosti značenij i upotreblenija glagoljnogo lica v sovremennom armjanskom jazyke). IFŽ 3.141–56.
ABRAHAMYAN, S. 1953. Ardi hayereni paymanakan kam entʻadrakan ełanakə (Uslovnoe ili položiteljnoe naklonenie sovremennogo armjanskogo jazyka). IzvANArm 9.75–90.
——. 1956. Ardi hayereni deranunnerə (Mestoimenija sovremennogo armjanskogo jazyka). Erevan.
——. 1959. Žamanakakicʻ hayereni čʻtʻekʻvoł xoskʻi maserə (Neizmenjaemye časti reči sovremennogo armjanskogo jazyka). Erevan.
——. 1960. Naxadasrutʻyan tesaknern əst bnuytʻi žamanakakicʻ hayerenum (Tipy predloženij po xarakteru v sovremennom armjanskom jazyke). VJaStArm I. 84–124.
——. 1962a. Naxadasrutʻyunə ev nra pʻoxharaberutʻyunnerə xoskʻi mej žamanakakicʻ hayerenum (Predloženie i vzaimootnošenija predloženij v reči v sovremennom armjanskom jazyke). IFŽ 1.42–61.
——. 1962b. Žamanakakicʻ hayereni šarahyusutʻyan mi kʻani harcʻer (Nekotorye voprosy sintaksisa sovremennogo armjanskogo jazyka). Erevan.

AČAŘYAN, H. (= ADJARIAN). 1901a. K'nnut'iwn Łarabałi barbařin (Issledovanie garabagskogo dialekta). Vałaršapat.
——. 1901b. Lautlehre des Van-Dialektes. ZAPh I.74–86, 121–38.
——. 1909. Classification des dialectes arméniens. Paris.
——. 1911a. Anyōd bařer (Unartikulierte Wörter). Yušarjan, edited by N. Akinean et al., 289–90. Wien.
——. 1911b. Hay barbařagitut'iwn (Armjanskaja dialektologija). Moskva.
——. 1925. K'nnut'yun Nornaxiǰewani (Xrimi) barbaři (Issledovanie novonaxidževanskogo dialekta). Erevan.
——. 1926. K'nnut'yun Marałayi barbaři (Issledovanie maragaskogo dialekta). Erevan.
——. 1935. K'nnut'iwn agulisi barbaři (Issledovanie agulisskogo dialekta). Erevan.
——. 1940. K'nnut'iwn Norǰułayi barbaři (Issledovanie Novodžugajskogo dialekta). Erevan.
——. 1947. K'nnut'yun hamšeni barbaři (Issledovonie xemšinskogo dialekta). Erevan.
——. 1951. Ewropakan p'oxařeal bařer hayereni meǰ (Parole europee prese nella lingua armena volgare). Wien.
——. 1952. K'nnut'yun Vani barbařin (Issledovoanie vanskogo dialekta). Erevan.
——. 1952–67. Liakatar k'erakanut'yun hayoc' lezvi I–VI (Polnaja grammatika armjanskogo jazyka). Erevan.
——. 1953. K'nnut'yun artiali barbaři (Issledovanie ardialjskogo dialekta). Erevan.
AŁAYAN, Ē. 1952. Jazykoznanie v armenii. VJa 5.110–16.
——. 1954. Mełru barbařə (Megrinskij dialekt). Erevan.
——. 1958–61. Hay lezvabanut'yan patmut'yun I-II (Istorija armjanskogo jazykoznanija). Erevan.
——. 1958. Nor hayeren barbařneri ařaǰac'man harc'i masin (K voprosu o voznikovenii armjanskix dialektov). IFŽ 2.211.
——. 1959. Vvedenie v jazykoznanie. Erevan.
——. 1960. O genesize armjanskogo konsonantizma. VJa 4.37–52.
——. 1963a. Bayakazmut'yunə žamanakakic' hayerenum (Obrazovanie glagola v sovremennom armjanskom jazyke). IzvANArm 5.19–30.
——. 1963b. Bayi jevabanakan karuc'vack'ə žamanakakic' hayerenum (Morfologičeskaja struktura glagola v sovremennom armjanskom jazyke). IFŽ 3.239–69.
——. 1964. Grabari k'erakanut'yun I (Grammatika drevnearmjanskogo jazyka). Erevan.
——. 1966. Žamanakakic' hayereni holovnerə (Padeži sovremennogo armjanskogo jazyka). IFŽ 4.117–40.
——. 1967a. Lezvabanut'yan neracut'yun (Vvedenie v jazykoznanie). Erevan.
——. 1967b. Žamanakakic' hayereni holovumə ev xonarhumə (Sklonenie i sprjaženie v sovremennom armjanskom jazyke). Erevan.
ALEK'SANYAN, Z. 1964. Paraga erkrordakan naxadasut'yunnerə žamanakakic' hay-

erenum (Pridatočko-obctajateljstvennye predloženija v sovremennom armjanskom jazyke). EArmS 9.297–337.

ALLEN, W. 1950. Notes on the phonetics of an Eastern Armenian speaker. TPhS 180–206.

ANDONIAN, H. 1966. Modern Armenian. New York.

ARAK'ELYAN, V. 1944. Grabari holovneri imastakan nšanakut'yunnerə (Smyslovye značenija padežej drevnearmjanskogo jazyka). Erevan.

——. 1952. Hayereni očabanut'yan mi k'ani xndirneri masin (O nekotoryx stilističeskix voprosax armjanskogo jazyka). IzvANArm 2.37–55.

——. 1955. Žamanakakic' hayereni hnč'yunabanut'yun (Fonetika sovremennogo armjanskogo jazyka). Erevan.

——. 1957. Žamanakakic' hayereni holovneri ev holovakan kapakc'ut'yunneri imastayin aṙumnerə (Smyslovye žnacenija padežej i predlogov sovremennogo armjanskogo jazyka). Erevan.

——. 1958–64. Hayereni šarahyusut'yun I-II (Sintaksis armjanskogo jazyka). Erevan.

——. 1959. Neracut'yun hayereni šarahyusut'yan (Vvedenie v sintaksis armjanskogo jazyka). Erevan.

——. 1964. Hay grakan lezvi ev barbaṙneri p'oxharaberut'yan harc'i šurjə (K voprosu o vzaimootnošenii armjanskogo literaturnogo jazyka i dialektov). IFŽ 3.139–56.

——. 1967. Hayereni parberuyt'ə (Armjanskij period). Erevan.

ARAMJAN, A. 1958. Obščie dannye èksperimentaljnogo issledovanija glasnyx zvukov armjanskoj reči. IzvANArm 2.55–74.

——. 1960. Nekotorye voprosy fonetiki i fonologii v russkom i armjanskom jazykoznanii. VJaStArm I.315–36.

——. 1962. Žamanakakic' hayereni jaynavornerə (Glasnye sovremennogo armjanskogo jazyka). Erevan.

——. 1963. Jaynordneri usumnasirman harc'i šurjə (K voprosu ob izučenii sonantov). IzvANArm 1.17.

ASATRYAN, A. 1959. Bayi seṙerə žamanakakic' hayerenum (Rody glagola v sovremennom armjanskom jazyke). Erevan.

——. 1962. Urmiayi (Xoyi) barbarə (Urmijskij [xojskij] dialekt). Erevan.

——. 1966. Loṙu xosvack'i hnč'yunakan ev jevabanakan aṙanjnahatkut'yunnerə (Fonetičeskie i morfologičeskie osobennosti Lorijskogo dialekta). IFŽ 3.193–202.

——. 1967. Loṙu barbaṙə (Lorijskij dialekt). Erevan.

ASMANGULYAN, H. 1962. Hayereni bayi xonarhman jeveri hamakargi harc'i šurjə (K voprosu o sisteme form sprjaženija armjanskogo glagola). IFŽ 2.151–62.

AYTƏNEAN, A. 1866. K'nnakan k'erakanut'iwn asxarhabar kam ardi hayerēn lezui (Critical grammar of modern Armenian). Wien.

——. 1883. K'erakanut'iwn ardi hayerēn lezui (Grammar of modern Armenian). Wien.

BABASYAN, A. 1963. T'vi k'erakanakan kategorian hayerenum (Kategorija grammatičeskogo čisla v armjanskom jazyke). Erevan.

BADIKYAN, X. 1966. Šaradasut'yan k'erakanakan derə žamanakakic' hayerenum (Grammatičeskaja rolj porjadka slov v sovremennom armjanskom jazyke). IFŽ 1.198–207.

BAGRATUNI, A. 1852. Hayerēn k'erakanut'iwn i pēts zargac'eloc' (An Armenian grammar for advanced students). Venezia.

BAHAT'REANC', A. 1879. K'erakanut'iwn ašxarhik lezui (Grammar of the secular language). Tiflis.

BALDASARYAN-T'AP'ALC'YAN, S. 1958. Mšo barbařə (Mušskij dialekt). Erevan.

BAŁRAMYAN, R. 1960a. Dersimi barbařayin k'artezə (Dialektnaja karta Dersima). Erevan.

——. 1960b. Erkaki t'vi mnac'ordner hayereni barbařnerum (Perežitki dvojstvennogo čisla v armjanskix dialektax). IFŽ 1.191–200.

——. 1964a. Jaynavorneri nerdasnakut'yan ōrenk'ə barbařnerum (Zakon garmonizma glasnyx v armjanskix dialektax). IzvANArm 12.61–72.

——. 1964b. Šamaxi barbařə (Samaxinskij dialekt). Erevan.

BARSEŁYAN, H. 1953. Ardi hayereni bayi ev xonarhman tesut'yun (Teorija glagola i sprjaženija glagola sovremennogo armjanskogo jazyka). Erevan.

——. 1964. Hatuk anun (Sobstvennoe imja). Erevan.

BELECKAJA, I. 1964. Vzaimosootvetstvija glagoljnoj formy *past indefinite* s nekotorymi vido-vremennymi formami armjanskogo jazyka. EArmS 9.339–51.

BITTNER, M. 1911. Einige Kuriosa aus dem armenischen Dialekte der Walachei und der Moldau. Yušarjan, edited by N. Akinean et al., 361–8. Wien.

Č'ALəXEAN, V. 1885. K'erakanut'iwn haykaznean lezui (Grammar of the Armenian language). Wien.

Č'AMČ'EANC', M. 1826. K'erakanut'iwn haykaznean lezui (Grammar of the Armenian language). Tiflis.

CIRBIED, J. 1823. Grammaire de la langue arménienne. Paris.

DAŁBASEAN, Y. 1913. Arewelahay ašxarhabari k'erakanut'iwnə (Grammar of modern Eastern Armenian). Tiflis.

DANIELYAN, T'. 1964a. Malat'iayi barbaři holovumn u xonarhumə (Sklonenie i sprjaženie v malatijskom dialekte). IFŽ 2.135–48.

——. 1964b. Malat'iayi barbaři hnč'yunabanut'yunə (Fonetika malatijskogo dialekta). IzvANArm 5.41–54.

DAVT'YAN, K. 1966. Leřnayin Łarabałi barbařayin k'artezə (Dialektnaja karta nagornogo Karabaxa). Erevan.

DAWIT'-BĒK, M. 1930. Arabkiri gawařabarbařə (Arabkir dialect). Wien.

DIRR, A. 1912. Praktisches Lehrbuch der ostarmenischen Sprache. Wien.

ĒLOYAN, S. 1959. Žamanakakic' hayereni acanc'neri ařajac'man ułineri masin (Puti obrazovanija affiksov sovremennogo armjanskogo jazyka). IFŽ 4.46–68.

——. 1960. Hayereni miǰacanc'nerə (Infiksy v armjanskom jazyke). VJaStArm I. 190–6.

——. 1963. Acanc'nerə žamanakakic' hayerenum (Affiksy v sovremennom armjanskom jazyke). Erevan.

FAIRBANKS, G. 1958. Spoken West Armenian. New York.

——, and E. STEVICK. 1958. Spoken East Armenian. New York.

FEYDIT, F. 1948. Manuel de la langue arménienne (Arménien occidental modern). Paris.

——. 1951. Phéonomes d'influence reciproque entre le cas et la determination dans le domaine de l'arménien (resumé). BSL XLVII/1.xxxii-xxxiv.

——. 1952. Les articles en arménien modern occidental. Pazmaveb CX/7–9.171–9.

——. 1954. Remplacement du signe zéro dans le parfait arménien (resumé). BSL L/1.xxvi-xxvii.

——. 1956. Cambiamenti di struttura del verbo armeno. Tempi, modi, e aspetti in armeno. Pazmaveb CXIV.4–8.

——. 1960a. Problèmes et utilité de la dialectologie arménienne. Communications et rapports du premier Congrès International de Dialectologie, edited by A. van Windekens. I.146–53.

——. 1960b. Relatives 'intellectuelles' et relatives 'populaires' en arménien. BSL LV/1.xxxvi-xxxviii.

FINCK, N. 1902. Lehrbuch der neuostarmenischen Literatursprache. Marburg.

GABRIELEAN, M. 1912. Aknay gawaṙabarbaṙə ew ardi hayerēn (Der Dialekt von Akyn und die neuarmenische Literatursprache). Wien.

GALSTYAN, S. 1967. Hayoc' lezu (Armjanskij jazyk). Erevan.

GAREGINYAN, G. 1960. Sałkapi ev deranvan xosk'i masayin haraberak'anut'yan harc'i šurǰə (Po voprosu sootnošenii sojuza i mestoimenija v sovremennom armjanskom jazyke). VJaStArm I.145–72.

——. 1963. Šałkapnerə žamanakakic' hayerenum (Sojuzy sovremennogo armjanskogo jazyka). Erevan.

GASPARYAN, G. 1967. Hay baṙaranagitut'yan patmut'yun (Istorija armjanskoj leksikografii). Erevan.

GAZANČEAN, Y. 1895. Ewdokioy hayoc' gawarabarbaṙə (Dialect of Evdokia). Wien.

——. 1924. Nor k'erakanut'iwn ardi hayerēn lezui (New grammar of the modern Armenian language). Constantinople.

GODEL, R. 1945. Formes et emplois du redoublement en turc et en arménien modern. CFS V.5–16.

——. 1953. Note sur arm. *linel* 'devenir'. CFS XI.42–4.

GRIGORYAN, A. 1948. Sovetahay barbaṙagitut'yan met'odakan mi k'ani harc'er (Nekotorye metodičeskie voprosy sovetskoj armjanskoj dialektologii). Erevan.

——. 1957. Hay barbaṙagitut'yan dasəntac' (Učebnik armjanskoj dialektologii). Erevan.

GULAKYAN, B. 1965. K voprosu o fonologičeskoj sisteme armjanskix glasnyx. IFŽ 1.219–28.

GULIAN, K. 1902 (1954). Elementary Modern Armenian grammar. Heidelberg, repr. New York.

GYULBADAŁYAN, S. 1964. T'vakan anunə žamanakakic' hayerenum (Imja čisliteljnoe v sovremennom armjanskom jazyke). Erevan.

HAMP, E. 1963. Notes on Eastern Armenian Phonemics. AO XXXI.398–400.

Hayereni bac'atrakan bar̄aran I. 1969. Erevan.

HAYRAPETYAN, V., and G. HOVHANNISYAN. 1967. Žamanakakic' hayereni bałajayneri kinor̄entgenologiakan met'odov hetazotut'yan porjic' (Iz opyta kinorentgenologičeskogo analiza soglasnyx sovremennogo armjanskogo jazyka). IFŽ 1.38–53.

HOVSEP'YAN, N. 1966. Ozmi barbar̄i mi k'ani ar̄anjnahatkut'yunneri masin (O nekotoryx osobennostjax vozmskogo dialekta). IFŽ 2.226–38.

J̌AXJ̌AXEAN, M. 1837. Bar̄agirk' i barbar̄ hay ew italakan (Dizionario armeno-italiano). Venezia.

JENSEN, H. 1959. Altarmenische Grammatik. Heidelberg.

J̌UHARYAN, T'. 1956. Bayi usuc'man himnakan harc'er (Osnovnye voprosy obučenija glagolu). Erevan.

KAINZ, C. 1891. Praktische Grammatik der armenischen Sprache für den Selbstunterricht. Wien.

KOGIAN, S. 1949. Armenian Grammar (West Dialect). Wien.

KOSTANYAN, H. 1957. Aknarkner verǰin tasnamyaki sovetahay ar̄jaki lezvi ev oči masin (Očerki o jazyke i stile sovetsko-armjanskoj prozy poslednego desjatiletija). Erevan.

——. 1958. Lingvističeskie i armjanovedičeskie raboty v Institute Jazyka AN ArmSSR. VJa 6.119–22.

K'OSYAN, V. 1962. Acakani bar̄akapakc'ut'yunnerə žamanakakic' hayerenum (Slovosočetanija imen prilagateljnyx v sovremennom armjanskom jazyke). IFŽ 2.92–104.

——. 1963. Goyakani bar̄akapakc'ut'yunnerə acakan lrac'umov (Slovosočetanie suščestviteljnogo s prilagateljnym dopolneniem). IzvANArm 9.29–40.

KUSIKJAN, I. 1964. Izmenenija v slovarnom sostave literaturnogo armjanskogo jazyka sovetskogo perioda. Moskva.

K'YURK'ČYAN, A. 1961. əndhanrakan makbaynerə hayerenum (Narečija obščego značenija v armjanskom jazyke). IFŽ 3–4.195–209.

ŁAP'ANC'YAN, G. 1939. əndhanur lezvabanut'yun I (Obščaja lingvistika). Erevan.

ŁARIBYAN, A. 1947. Hayoc' lezvi met'odika (Metodika armjanskogo jazyka). Erevan.

——. 1953. Hay barbar̄agitut'yun (Armjanskaja dialektologija). Erevan.

——. 1954a. Bližajšie zadači armjanskoj dialektologii. IzvANArm 7.57–70.

——. 1954b. Hayoc' lezvi dasavandman met'odika (Metodika prepodavanija armjanskogo jazyka). Erevan.

——. 1954c. Hayocʻ lezvi kʻerakanutʻyun (Grammatika armjanskogo jazyka). Erevan.

——. 1958a. Hay barbaṙagitakan hetazotutʻyunneri himnakan ardyunkʻnerə sovetakan Hayastanum (Osnovnye itogi naučno-issledovateljskix rabot po armjanskoj dialektologii v sovetskoj Armenii). IFŽ 1.18–39.

——. 1958b. Hay barbaṙneri cagman harcʻi surj (K voprosu o proisxoždenii armjanskix dialektov). IFŽ 3.240–66.

——. 1958c. Hayereni norahayt barbaṙneri mi nor xumb (Novaja gruppa novootkrytyx armjanskix dialektov). Erevan.

——. 1958d. Novaja gruppa dialektov armjanskogo jazyka. VJa 6.95–101.

——. 1961. Naučnye dostiženija armjanskoj dialektologii. IFŽ 1.36.

——. 1964. O morfologii glagola armjanskix dialektov. Problemy sravniteljnoj filologii, edited by N. Alekseev. Moskva.

——. 1965. Kratkij kurs armjanskogo jazyka. Erevan.

——. 1966. Hay lezvabanutʻyan xošoraguyn nerkayacʻucʻičʻə (Krupnejšij predstavitelj armjanskogo jazykoznanija). IFŽ 2.

——. 1967. Hayocʻ lezvi kʻerakanutʻyan avanduytʻayin harcʻeri masin (O padežnyx tradicijax v armjanskoj grammatike). IFŽ 1.8–94.

ŁARIBYAN, A., and G. PARIS. 1957. Hayocʻ lezvi kʻerakanutʻyan, ułłagrutʻyan ev ketadrutʻyan ułecʻuycʻ (Spravočnik po grammatike, orfografii i punktuacii armjanskogo jazyka). Erevan.

LAUER, M. 1869. Grammatik der classischen armenischen Sprache. Wien.

LAVROV, V. 1899. Kratkij samoučitelj armjanskogo jazyka. Tiflis.

ŁAZARYAN, S. 1955. Žamanakakicʻ hayocʻ lezun ev ṙusereni derə nra harstacʻman u zargacʻman meǰ (Sovremennyj armjanskij jazyk i rolj russkogo jazyka v ego obogaščenii i razvitii). Erevan.

Lezvabanakan baṙaran (Lingvističeskij slovarj). 1969. Erevan.

MAKʻSUDEAN, M. 1911a. Le parler armenien d'Akn. Paris.

——. 1911b. Zeytʻuni barbaṙi jaynakan drutʻiwnə (Die phonetische Stellung des Zeytoun-Dialektes). Yušarjan, edited by N. Akinean et al., 319–23. Wien.

MAKʻSUDYAN, L. 1962. Naxnakan ditołutʻyun hayocʻ lezvi baṙakazmutʻyan jevakan matematikakan modeli karucʻman masin (Predvariteljnoe zamečanie po voprosu postroenija formaljno-matematičeskoj modeli slovoobrazovanija armjanskogo jazyka). IzvANArm 4.71–6.

MALXASYANCʻ, S. 1910. Haycʻakan holovə asxarhabarum (Viniteljnyj padež v armjanskom jazyke). Tiflis.

——. 1944–45. Hayeren bacʻatrakan bararan I-IV (Tolkovyj slovarj armjanskogo jazyka). Erevan.

MARGARYAN, A. 1955. Ardi hayereni kaperə (Predlogi i poslelogi sovremennogo armjanskogo jazyka). Erevan.

——. 1964. Harakatarn u ancʻyali harakatarə bayakan žamanakner en (Formy 'harakatar' i 'ancʻyali harakatar' — glagoljnye vremena). IFŽ 2.183-92.

——. 1966. Hayereni ankanon bayeri zargacumə (Razvitie nepraviljnyx glagolov armjanskogo jazyka). Erevan.

MEILLET, A. 1913. Altarmenisches Elementarbuch. Heidelberg.

MELIK'-T'ANGEAN, N. 1893. Ašxarhabari k'erakanut'iwnə (Grammar of modern Armenian). Šuši.

MELK'ONYAN, S. 1962. Paymani paraga erkrodakan naxadasut'unner ardi hayerenum (Predatočnye uslovnye predloženija v sovremennom armjanskom jazyke). IzvANArm 7.53–60.

MELK'ONYAN, V., and V. HAYRAPETYAN. 1965. Hayoc' lezvi bałajaynneri spektral usumnasirut'yan miǰoc'neri harc'i masin (K voprosu o spektraljnom analize soglasnyx zvukov armjanskogo jazyka). IzvANArm 12.27–36.

MELKUMJAN, M. 1965. Isxodnye dannye i statistiko-kombinatornoe vydelenija paradigmy pervogo morfologičeskogo tipa v armjanskom jazyke; Statistiko-kombinatornoe vydelenie paradigmy vtorogo morfologičeskogo tipa v armjanskom jazyke. Statistiko-kombinatornoe modelirovanie jazykov, edited by N. Andreev, 123–36, 253–6. Moskva.

MKRTČ'YAN, H. 1952. Karno barbařə (Karinskij dialekt). Erevan.

——. 1966. 'Um' cyułi mi barbar 'kə' cyuli miǰavayrum (Dialekt vetvi 'um' v srede dialektov vetvi 'kə'). IFŽ 1.239–46.

MOTALOVA, L. 1967. Smyslovoe vosprijatie mira v poème A. Isaakjana 'Abulala Maari' i ego otraženie v russkom perevode V. Ja. Brjusova. AO XXXV/3.372–7.

MOVSESSIAN, L. 1959. Armenische Grammatik. Wien.

MSEREANC', L. 1897–1901. Ètjudy po armjanskoj dialektologii I-II. Moskva.

——. 1899. Hayeren barbařaxosut'iwn (Armenische Dialektologie). Wien.

MURADYAN, A. 1967. Hay k'erakanakan terminabanut'yan kazmavarum (Obrazovanie armjanskoj grammatičeskoj terminologii). IFŽ 1.125–33.

MURADYAN, H. 1960. Karčevani barbařə (Karcevanskij dialekt). Erevan.

——. 1962. Šataxi barbařə (Šataxskij dialekt). Erevan.

——. 1967. Kak'avaberdi barbařə (Kakavaberdskij dialekt). Erevan.

MURVALYAN, A. 1955. Hayoc' lezvi bařayin kazmə (Slovarnyj sostav armjanskogo jazyka). Erevan.

——. 1959. Hayoc' lezvi drajvacabanut'yun ev bayakazmut'yun (Armjanskaja frazeologija i glagoljnye obrazovanija). Erevan.

ŌHANYAN, H. 1962. Acakan anunə žamanakakic' hayerenum (Imja prilagateljnoe v sovremennom armjanskom jazyke). Erevan.

PALASANEAN, S. 1870. əndhanur tesut'iwn arewelean nor grawor lezui hayoc' (Obščaja teorija novovostočnoarmjanskogo literaturnogo jazyka). Tiflis.

——. 1906. K'erakanut'iwn mayreni lezui (Grammatika rodnogo jazyka). Tiflis.

P'AŠAYAN, A. 1963. Svediayi barbaři masin (O svedijskom dialekte). IFŽ 4.159–74.

——. 1964. Svediayi barbaři jevabanut'yun (Morfologija svedijskogo dialekta). IzvANArm 9.59–70.

PATKANJAN, K. 1864. Issledovanie o sostave armjanskogo jazyka. Sankt Peterburg.

——. 1869. Issledovanie o dialektax armjanskogo jazyka. Sankt Peterburg.

——. 1875. Materialy dlja izučenija armjanskix narečij. Sankt Peterburg.

PETERMANN, J, 1872. Brevis linguae armeniacae grammatica. Karlsruhe.

PETOYAN, V. 1954. Sasuni barbaṙə (Sasunskij dialekt). Erevan.

PETROSYAN, H. 1960. Orosyali u anorosi anji u iri aṙumnerə hayerenum (Kategorii opredelennosti i neopredelennosti, lica i predmeta v armjanskom jazyke). Erevan.

POŁOSYAN, A. 1965. Hadrutʿi barbaṙə (Gadrutskij dialekt). Erevan.

POŁOSYAN, P. 1959. Bayi ełanakayin jeveri očakan kirarutʿyunnerə ardi hayerenum (Stilističeskie upotreblenija ličnyx form glagola v sovremennom armjanskom jazyke). Erevan.

RIGGS, E. 1856. A Grammar of the Modern Armenian language as spoken in Constantinople and Asia Minor. Constantinople.

ŠAHABAZYAN, T. 1958. Hayocʿ lezvi dasavandman metʿodika (Metodika prepodavanija armjanskogo jazyka). Erevan.

——. 1963. Arevmtahay ašxarhabari arajacʿumə (Voznikovenie armjanskogo ašxarabara). Erevan.

ŠARABXABYAN, P. 1960. Grabari sałkapnerə (Sojuzy drevnearmjanskogo jazyka). Erevan.

SARGSEANCʿ, S. 1883. Agulecʿocʿ barbaṙə (Aguliskij dialekt). Moskva.

SCHRÖDER, J. 1711. Thesaurus linguae armeniae antiquae et hodiernae... Amsterdam.

SEVAK, G. 1939. Xoskʿi maseri usmunkʿə (Učenija o častjax reči). Erevani petakan hamalsarani gitakan ašxatutʿyunner XI.

——. 1939–47. Žamanakakicʿ hayocʿ lezvi tesutʿyun I-II (Teorija sovremennogo armjanskogo jazyka). Erevan.

——. 1959. Hay barbaṙneri cagman harcʿi šurjə (K voprosu o proisxoždenii armjanskix dialektov). IFŽ 1.224–45.

——. 1964. Hayocʿ lezvi šarahyusutʿyun (Sintaksis armjanskogo jazyka). Erevan.

——. 1967. Žamanakakicʿ hayocʿ lezvi dasəntʿacʿ (Kurs sovremennogo armjanskogo jazyka). Erevan.

ŠILAKADZE, I. 1962. Aspekʿtis kategoria somḫursi (Kategorija aspekta v armjanskom jazyke). TTbilU 99/3.173–211.

SOLTA, G. 1963. Die armenische Sprache. Armenisch und Kaukasische Sprachen, edited by B. Spuler, 80–128. Leiden.

SOMALEAN, S., ET AL. 1936. Nor baṙagirkʿ haykaznean lezui (New dictionary of the Armenian language). Venezia.

STEVICK, E. 1955. Syntax of colloquial East Armenian. Ph.D. dissertation, Cornell University.

SUKʿIASYAN, A. 1963. Hamaṙot aknark sovetakan šrjani hay-ruseren əndhanur baṙaranagrutʿyan (Kratkij očerk obščej armjano-russkoj leksikografii sovetskogo perioda). IzvANArm 12.43–56.

——. 1967. Hayocʻ lezvi homanišneri bařaran (Slovarj sinonimov armjanskogo jazyka). Erevan.

TʻASEAN, B. 1963. Lezuakan harcʻer (Voprosy jazykoznanija). Cairo.

TER-MARTEVOSJAN, A. 1939. Kratkij sravniteljnyj obzor strukturnyx osobennostej russkogo i armjanskogo jazyka. Baku.

TIROYAN, A. 1927. Grammatica della lingua Armena Moderna. Venezia.

TOMSON, A. 1890. Istoričeskaja grammatika sovremennogo armjanskogo jazyka goroda Tiflis. Sankt Peterburg.

TORBIÖRNSSON, T. 1945. Armenisk akcentering. Hum. Vetnes.-Samf. i Uppsala Årsbok 85–96.

TʻUMANEAN, Y. 1910. Hayocʻ ašxarhabar lezui hamařōt kʻerakanutʻiwn (Kratkaja grammatika sovremennogo armjanskogo jazyka). Tiflis.

TUMANJAN, E. 1955. Privraščenie artiklja v fleksiju dateljnogo padeža v novoarmjanskom jazyke. VJa 5.93–9.

——. 1963. Artikli v sovremennom armjanskom jazyke. Erevan.

——. 1966. Armjanskij jazyk. Jazyki narodov SSSR, edited by V. Vinogradov et al., I.562–98. Moskva.

——. 1967. Armjanskij jazyk. Sovetskoe jazykoznanie za 50 let, edited by F. Filin et al., 158–70. Moskva.

TʻUMAYEAN, K. 1930. Marzuani gawařabařə (Marzvan dialect). Wien.

VAHANYAN, G. 1956. Hayocʻ lezvi očabanutʻyan jeřnark (Posobie po stilistike armjanskogo jazyka). Erevan.

VANCʻEAN, G. 1891. Dprocʻakan kʻerakanutʻiwn (School grammar). Tiflis.

——. 1906. Patmakan kʻerakanutʻiwn arewelahay lezui (Istoričeskaja grammatika vostočnoarmjanskogo jazyka). Tiflis.

XAČʻATRYAN, A. 1966. Hayereni ʻəʼ jaynavori hnčʻuytʻaynutʻyan harcʻə (O fonologičeskoj funkcii glasnoj ʻəʼ v armjanskom jazyke). IFŽ 4.141–50.

XAČʻERYAN, L. 1959. Paraga erkrordakan naxadasutʻyunneri usmunkʻə hay kʻerakanagitutʻyan meǰ (Učenie o pridatočnom obstojateljstvennom predloženii v armjanskoj grammatičeskoj nauke). IFŽ 2–3.218–31.

ŽARBEDŽJAN, S. 1964. Značenie i upotreblenie prošedšix vidovremennyx form v sovremennom armjanskom jazyke. VJaStArm II.293–378.

PART TWO

ALTAIC LANGUAGES

ALTAIC LANGUAGES

AN OVERVIEW

The present volume of our series *Current Trends in Linguistics* is, as its name implies, intended to deal precisely with linguistics in the countries of and about the languages of 'South West Asia and North Africa', and these brief remarks will survey only the Altaic languages spoken within these confines at the present time. In the first place, we may further delimit the rather uncustomary expression 'South West Asia' to mean for our purposes that portion of the Asian, or better Eurasian land-mass, which is neither a portion of South East Asia (whose western bounds would lie at India), nor of India that sub-continent itself, nor further of the People's Republic of China on the mainland, and of course, not of the Soviet Union — obviously, since earlier volumes of this series, specifically Volume One, 'Soviet and East European linguistics', and Volume Two, 'Linguistics in East and South East Asia', have included treatments of the Altaic languages spoken over these territories. For our needs, North Africa, meaning Egypt and the countries west of it, or indeed the Near East south of the Anatolian plateau itself, do not enter into it. Though this area is not now the homeland nor even the extended range of peoples speaking Altaic languages, the Turks and Mongols of the Ilhan dynasty in Persia invaded Syria and Egypt in the thirteenth century; Turks founded the Mamaluke dynasty in Egypt in the same century; and Turks conquered Egypt as part of the grand Ottoman Empire in more recent centuries. In the present day, though scattered archeological remains report the *quondam* presence of Mongols in Anatolia, in Egypt and North Africa even Turks live only as minority groups and constitute no political or social force in these countries.

Linguistically, Turkish of modern Turkey, as the southwesternmost projection of a population mass still having its center in the southern and central Russian steppes, presents the same sort of linguistic isolation and divergence that the non-Indo-European Hungarians (or indeed the Finns) do amid the other nations of Europe. The more one follows this down and outward (that is, south and westward) thrust in reverse to its point of presumed origin, the more trace one sees in the history of Persia (Iran) and Afghanistan (even of India, here quite beyond our scope) of the tremendous force once exerted by nations speaking Altaic languages. Since knowledge of such kingdoms as the Ilhan (Mongol) dynasties of Persia and the Moghols of India should be a commonplace to most readers, it will not be dwelt on here. The realities of present-day Altaic-speaking groups are the mute witness to the glories of past economic powers and political realms.

G. Doerfer, a leading scholar of the Turco-Mongolian languages, and particularly of their Iranistic connections (and the author of a far-ranging four-volume handbook of Turkic and Mongolian elements in Persian, surely one of the more significant Altaistic publications of recent decades) gives a penetrating up-to-date analysis of the modern linguistic situation *vis-à-vis* Turkic and Mongolian studies in modern Iran and Afghanistan. His article is of merit for the specialist as well as the more generally-oriented non-specialist, in particular as he reports there his findings of a hitherto unsuspected seventh grouping of Turkic languages, the Khalaj, in Iran. An expedition conducted on-the-spot studies in 1968.

Most numerous of the Turkic groups outside Turkey or the USSR are, first, the Azerbaijani of northwestern Persia. Though politically and administratively bound to Persian as the national language, this Turkic language, of the closest possible relationship to Soviet Azerbaijani, continues to be spoken by millions of Iranian inhabitants. M. Ilhan Başgöz (Indiana University) travelled freely among them during the summer of 1967, collecting folkloristic material for his own research in this subject. On the basis of speech material from informants from this area who were students at Indiana University in past years, F. W. Householder was able to compile a structural grammar (*Basic course in Azerbaijani*, 1965), and speakers of this language are still to be found from time to time as students in American universities. Second in number, and also forming a sizeable group outside Turkey and the U.S.S.R., are undoubtedly the Uzbeks of Afghanistan, whose over-all position is similar to that of the Turks in Iran. Though politically subservient to Pashto, the use of their native Uzbek by these million or more speakers (figures are not easy to come by) continues unabated, and remains closely tied to the Uzbek of neighboring Uzbekistan. It may perhaps further be mentioned that Alo Raun's book, *Basic course in Uzbek*, structured similarly to the Azerbaijani book by Householder, appeared in 1969. In addition, several Uzbek-speaking students, residents of Afghanistan, have attended Indiana University in the last three years, where their presence has been a great assistance in the further study of this language by Ilse Cirtautas, who will also publish additional materials on Uzbek.

Although directing attention to those interesting and sizeable groups of Turkic speakers outside the U.S.S.R. and Turkey, one must give greatest prominence to the present-day Turkish Republic, home to at least 25 million native Turks, out of the present population numbering upwards of 30 million (this figure, however, including Turkish citizens of other national origin). As Hazai points out in his informative survey, Turkish was among the first 'Oriental' (as they are called) languages given regularly from chairs in old-line European universities, and the obvious and continuing importance of Turkey as a major country in the Middle East — indeed an economic and political power there — cannot be slighted. Hazai has given a good over-all picture of the linguistic work conducted by native Turkic scholars on their language in the past decades.

Turkey presents something of a special case, however, because of its unique, and practically unprecedented instance of language and alphabet reform, a reform still so recent in history that thousands of adults experienced the change-over and still remember it (1928) and its later developments. Though an enormous and beautiful literature of subtlety and complexity (as anyone who has tried to read Sufi poets will say) existed among the Turkish *literati*, steeped in their Arabic and Persian education and usage, the pre-reform literacy rate in Turkey could hardly have been one per cent. Realizing that drastic measures were necessary to Westernize, secularize, nationalize, and update Turkey, and to educate the broad masses, the change from Arabic to Latin script was begun. This script change in itself brought with it many problems of creating textbooks, standardizing usage and forms, re-training clerks, teachers and others (for years many persons continued to write privately in Arabic script, and left the work of re-transcribing into the official Latin letters to a clerk, typist or to the typesetter). One should not be misled by the obvious external sign of script reform into thinking that it was merely a question of substituting one writing system for another. Indeed not! The script reform was only part of a broader program, expressing Turkish nationalism and the search for a national identity, to reformulate the modern Turkish language by purging, eliminating, or at least greatly reducing the huge stock of Arabic and Persian learned words in use as part of written Turkish. Things had gone so far that in some paragraphs of this style scarcely a native Turkish noun or abstract word was to be found; in fact, it was admissible to consider as part of the Turkish literary vocabulary any Arabic or Persian word, however rare. It would be virtually the same if English writers were allowed absolutely free use of French and German words in their compositions, indeed, if they strove to make them as French or German as possible with an underlying English structure. Such a system would not fluster a university teacher or student of European languages, but the average businessman or even professional man who might want to read a little poetry or some novels does not know any French or German beyond isolated words and would therefore be incapable and uninterested.

Fascinating though these stories and events are, and tempting though it is to digress and give even a summary history of the stages of reform, the creation and resurrection of new and old words, one can do little better than to refer the general reader to Uriel Heyd's book, *Language reform in modern Turkey* (Jerusalem, 1954, 116 pages, appearing as No. 5 of the *Oriental Notes and Studies*, published by The Israel Oriental Society). This excellent, very readable, and even entertaining monograph sets the language and script reform in its proper perspective as part of the entire post-1905 history of Turkey, discusses the puristic movements and their successes and failures, the conscious coining of neologisms, the work of the linguistic societies and committees, and the entire picture of Turkish and foreign elements in the vocabulary. Although his book is now getting close to 15 years old, the language issue is no more 'dead' in Turkey than it is in Norway, though a number of differing political factors make the Norwegian case different. The entire topic of script reform history and language issues could be given a useful and profitable treatment, but at the present time, we can only point in this direction and hope that in the second cycle of these volumes this wish may come to fruition.

An only natural outcome of introducing a modern educational system into Turkey was the rise and development of modern Western European languages taught in the schools. Prior to the second World War, German and French were given in the junior and senior high schools (*orta okul, lise*), and in Ankara one school even gave Latin in the 1940's. English was accepted to fulfill the high school requirements. Emphasis in the lower schools was definitely on French until the second World War. However, some schools of American backing were also operating, as Roberts College, the Tarsus American college, and others.

Under Premier Menderes, six colleges were established where English was the sole language of instruction, except for study of Turkish language and literature, of course, at Konya, Eskişehri, Izmir, and elsewhere, which still continue. The various military schools used French and German before the War, but have now gone over to English as the chief foreign language studied. Widespread private English instruction, supported by such American agencies as AID, has gone on, along with extracurricular English study supported by schools in evening study courses. After 1945, one can definitely state that English became the number one foreign language studied in Turkey.

Some typical statistics, taken from the government handbook for 1959–60 which happens to be at hand, reveal that those studying English in state schools (that is, exclusive of all private schools and programs) numbered about 250,000 in the junior high schools, about 59,000 in the high schools, about 58,000 in the technical schools, in the higher institutes about 52,000, and in the universities around 15,000.

JOHN R. KRUEGER

TURKISH

G. HAZAI

Studies in the Turkish language have a tradition centuries old in Europe. Apart from some minor records and glosses from the early period which were mostly looked upon as curiosities at the time, the first pioneers who also wanted to study the language as a whole may be found in the sixteenth and seventeenth centuries. The credit for this beginning (namely the creation of the very first grammars and dictionaries, the number of which kept increasing over the centuries to result in an extensive grammar and dictionary literature by the nineteenth century), goes to missionaries, learned envoys and travellers. Their works formed a solid basis for all those scholars who concentrated their investigations in the Turkish language on the ever-changing problems and methods of modern linguistics that took shape in the last century.

It was not until the twentieth century, the period of the Turkish Republic, that linguistics in Turkey came into existence. Emerging from the ruins of the Ottoman Empire which has also hamstrung the country's intellectual life, the young, independent state aimed at modernizing the country, and also bringing intellectual life into line with the universal progress. Among the most difficult tasks were those concerning science and scholarship. Here, to be sure, there were but few antecedents to rely on, and this meant that work had to start with the very fundamentals.

Such are, then, the antecedents of the birth of Turkish linguistics. However, the conditions and circumstances of its emergence are somewhat different from those of any other branch of Turkish science and scholarship. Due to the particular historical circumstances, it had to face important tasks at the very moment of its birth. Kemal Atatürk, the far-sighted president of the Republic, placed primary emphasis on the cause of linguistic reform, which was a key issue of social development and had for some decades been adopted by the intelligentsia. Script reform was put first on the agenda of the Republic. It was followed by a language reform, that is, a 'Turkization' of the language in order to get rid of foreign elements, mainly Arabic and Persian, in an effort to make the language more understandable to the people. These reforms formed a major objective of the intellectual endeavors of society for long years or rather decades to come. Undoubtedly, these circumstances played an exceedingly positive role in developing Turkish linguistics, in setting up its institutions, in providing for financial and manpower resources, and naturally in starting several important linguistic undertakings, even if opinions about the final outcome of the language reform differ considerably both inside and outside Turkey. On the primary initiative of the state and Kemal Atatürk, linguistics assumed the role of 'the first branch of science' in Turkish scientific life for a long time.

These circumstances, which thus determined the development of the over-all structure and individual branches of linguistics, should be kept in mind when considering the present situation.

The fact that linguistics in Turkey was born and gained strength in the twenties and thirties of this century (now largely independent of the historical conditions explained above), determined the program and methodology of the initial stage as well as the subsequent periods. Turkish linguists, who became closely related mainly with German and Hungarian schools of Turkish studies, made their start with an essentially new grammatical program, and are still engaged in its realization, although the scope of their subject fields has widened considerably in the course of time.

The fact of uneven development, a world-wide phenomenon in research and application of methods, that is, in realizing the conceptions of general linguistics, is perhaps one of the most important features of universal linguistics today. Naturally, this phenomenon may well be observed in the relationship between general and Turkish linguistics. Besides improving their methodological means and tools, Turkish linguists even now place historical linguistics at the center of their work. They do so with good reason however, since there still remains a sea of problems to be solved.

This brief outline is adapted to these facts. Consequently, in analyzing diachronic and synchronic linguistics, the former is given priority in both order and size.

The afore-mentioned circumstances make it obvious that the discipline of general linguistics is poorly represented in Turkish linguistics, and thus its output in the professional literature is rather slight. All the more space should, therefore, be devoted to other linguistic disciplines.

As has been shown by general works, handbooks and bibliographies published during the last decade, Turkic studies have now reached the period of their first major recapitulation.[1] Turkey herself is also an active participant in this development since, above and beyond some broader international undertakings, she also sums up the results of the past few decades within a narrower range.

During the past few years, a good number of handbooks have been published in an

[1] J. Benzing, 1953. *Einführung in das Studium der altaischen Philologie und der Turkologie.* Wiesbaden, O. Harrassowitz; *Philologiae Turcicae Fundamenta.* [1–2.] 1959–64. Wiesbaden, Fr. Steiner; *Handbuch der Orientalistik*, Erste Abteilung: Der Nahe und der Mittlere Orient, Fünfter Band: Altaistik, Erster Abschnitt: Turkologie. Herausgegeben von B. Spuler. 1963. Leiden-Köln, E.J. Brill; D. Sinor. 1963. *Introduction à l'étude de l'Asie Centrale.* Wiesbaden, O. Harrassowitz; N. Poppe. 1965. *Introduction to Altaic linguistics* (Ural-Altaische Bibliothek 14). Wiesbaden, O. Harrassowitz; K.H. Menges. 1967. *The Turkic languages and peoples.* An introduction to Turkic studies. Wiesbaden, O. Harrassowitz; R. Loewenthal. 1957. *The Turkic languages and literatures of Central Asia* (Central Asiatic Studies 1). 's-Gravenhage, Mouton; *Sovietico-Turcica.* Beiträge zur Bibliographie der türkischen Sprachwissenschaft in russischer Sprache in der Sowjetunion 1917–57. Herausgegeben von G. Hazai. 1960. Budapest, Verlag der Ungarischen Akademie der Wissenschaften.

attempt to give a more general outline of the individual groups of problems. The first two parts of A. Caferoğlu's (1958–64) handbook on the history of the Turkic languages, a major work planned to consist of four volumes, which were first published prior to World War II, appeared in a revised and enlarged edition, including the results of recent literature in the field. The work presents the history of the origins and development of Turkic languages against a historical or cultural-historical background. It also offers a critical review of the problems related to the prehistory of these languages where no linguistic records are available. It deals with the problems of Altaic or Ural-Altaic linguistic relations, and, in a historical section, it also treats the relics of old Turkic languages and writings, as well as the interrelationship between individual groups. Thus the author essentially follows the line of the 'external history' of Turkic languages, and — even if he touches upon some internal problems of the language — he does not aim at a thorough examination of historical grammar. Naturally, it will not be until the publication of the later volumes that the work can give a full picture of problems concerning all the contemporary Turkic peoples and languages, and in particular the development of more recent periods.

Among the syntheses of the history of language, mention has to be made of M. Ergin's (1962b) work which, in fact, was supposed to be a historical grammar. The author's explanation of his purpose gives a clear picture of the character of his work: 'The book is not a static, descriptive grammar of a certain period of the Western Turkish language, but a historical comparative grammar of all Western Turkic languages.'

Another manual by M. Ergin (1962a) is, to some extent, in close connection with the former. Adopting a rather practical (palaeographical, metrical, etc.) approach to the problems, the book is meant to be an introduction to the study of works written in the old Turkish literary language.

F. Timurtaş's manuals (1962b, 1964a) serve the same purpose, although they contain several details relating to the history of language as well.

With its peculiar methodology, A. C. Emre's (1949) comparative Turkic grammar, only the phonetic part of which has so far appeared, did not evoke too much response from the Turkish scholars.

A. Dilâçar's (1964) handbook is of a different type. Divided into languages and problems, it focuses its attention on literature rather than on actual linguistic problems. The book, in fact an informative handbook or reference-book, does not express original opinions which would contribute to the solution of the groups of problems which actually form its framework. Its most important part is a large bibliography which gives invaluable information to non-Turkish scholars.

S. Çağatay's (1963a) anthology, a manual of Ankara University, is meant to provide an introduction to comparative historical studies of the language, first of all the studies of the records of ancient Turkic languages. Of similar character are F. İz's anthologies (1964a, 1966) which furnish a very useful basis for researchers in

Anatolian and Rumelian Turkish, although they are within much narrower compasses and are not specifically linguistic works.

I would like to begin the review of historical works with those Turkic languages or linguistic relics and records which go beyond the sphere of Anatolian and Rumelian Turkish in the diachronic sense, too. This is the exact field of comparative Turkic linguistics which is based on systematic studies in both the old Turkic linguistic records and the material of contemporary Turkic languages.

As far as linguistic records are concerned, mention should be made first of all of the unparalleled publishing activity of the Türk Dil Kurumu which (later on and to a smaller extent) was followed by other Turkish institutions, too. Founded by Kemal Atatürk and relying even now on the resources of that statesman's material endowment, the Türk Dil Kurumu, led by defined conception, has always regarded the editing and scholarly treatment of ancient Turkic linguistic records and publishing them in facsimile as its most important task. As a result of these activities, rich historical material has appeared which even today forms a solid basis for international research. These activities covered equally the Karakhanide, Kipchak, Oghuz, Khwarezmian, and Chaghatai records. Among the works thus published and treated are such treasure-troves of Turkish historical linguistics as the *Ḳutadġu bilig*, *Kāšġarī's dictionary*, *Nahdžu'l-farādīs*, and so forth. This wide-ranging activity may well be seen in our bibliography.

It seems to be appropriate to review the other related works by language groups.

Notwithstanding that the material of old Turkic inscriptions have not been at the center of interest, a number of studies have been devoted to their interpretation to clear up certain problems. Here I refer to works by Talât Tekin (1957, 1963, 1964, 1966) and O. N. Tuna (1957, 1960) which offer new interpretations of certain passages; moreover, they also contain several new conceptions as regards the universal interpretation.

More activity is evident in the field of ancient Uighur written material which, through R. R. Arat, S. Çağatay, A. Temir, and Şinasi Tekin, was closely associated with the Berlin school, with W. Bang-Kaup and his circle.

R. R. Arat, one of the most outstanding personalities of Uighur studies, edited several Uighur texts during his activities in Turkey (1961, 1964a and c, 1965a). Published shortly after his death, his Uighur anthology (1965b) is also of great importance. Although it is of a literary character, the work was a considerable addition to the Uighur linguistic literature, since it not only gave new interpretations of certain texts but also included a number of new texts.

The edition of two important Karakhanide records, the *'Atabatu'l-ḥaḳā'iḳ* and the *Ḳutadġu bilig*, is also linked with the name of R. R. Arat (1947–59, 1951). Death prevented him from completing his works in this field. Another valuable work he left behind is the translation of *Bābur-nāme* which constitutes an important addition to its interpretation (1943–46).

Some text editions are also connected with other scholars in this field. S. Çağatay published two passages of the well-known Uighur translation of the Buddhist work Suvarṇaprabhāsa (1947–48), while Şinasi Tekin, in addition to some minor publications, undertook the edition of *Ḳuanši im pusar* (1960). Both devoted several studies to certain details of Uighur grammar. Studies by A. Temir also belong to this field (1946, 1948, 1956).

More than one scholar was engaged in editing Kipchak linguistic records. Both the edition and interpretation of the *At-tuḥfat az-zakīya fi'l-luġat at-turkīya* are linked to two scholars, B. Atalay (1945, 1948) and T. Halasi-Kun (1947–49), if, from a historical point of view, we consider the dispute between them to have been closed and we restrict ourselves to what has proved to be of lasting value. The editing and analysis of other linguistic relics were undertaken by A. İnan (1950, 1952a and b, 1953, 1956a, 1960, 1967) who, moreover, devoted many other studies to the problems of the development of the Central Asiatic literary language, and thus to the problems of the origins of 'mixed language' linguistic records.

J. Eckmann (1956, 1958a, 1959b, c, d, and e, 1959–64, 1960b, 1962a, 1963) started the systematic study of Khwarezmian and Chaghatai linguistic records. His works ranged from the philological approach and the publication of material to systematic studies in certain grammatical details which also led him to highly scholarly syntheses. Some studies by A. İnan (1946a, 1957, 1962) also deal with the problems of the Chaghatai period.

With the wide-ranging activities related to the investigation and editing of linguistic relics demanding attention, studies in the contemporary Turkic languages (such as the material explored and research results achieved by Turkic studies in foreign countries, primarily in the Soviet Union, as well as their additions to the body of knowledge) were to some extent pushed into the background. There are only two scholars, A. Caferoğlu and S. Çağatay, who concern themselves with this field. It is conceivably due to their mother tongue that they are so much interested in the problems of those languages. They have published several treatises, mainly historical. At the same time, S. Çağatay (1951, 1961b and c) is the author of some anthologies which will make the studies of those languages easier. It is regrettable, however, that these studies cannot become deeply rooted in the young generation of linguists.

Comparatively less attention is being paid to investigations into the concrete problems of comparative linguistics. Deserving special mention among the works in this field is R. R. Arat's treatise concerning the classification of Turkic languages, which, even though its final conclusions differ markedly from generally held opinions, gives evidence of very thorough examination of the subject matter. A. Dilâçar's two minor papers are also related to this topic.

Besides some relevant articles by R. R. Arat, the literature of comparative studies has mainly been enriched by S. Çağatay, Z. Korkmaz, M. Mansuroğlu, and Talât Tekin. Their works, even if not systematically, cover the fields of historical phonetics, morphology, and vocabulary. However, the material is not voluminous, since the related problems are not at the very center of interest of contemporary Turkish linguists. What really attracts them is the history of their mother tongue, particularly the investigation of well-documented and thus much more palpable periods. It is easy to understand that the greater part of the scholars' activities is concentrated on this field. This, further, is the very sphere where they are indebted to international science for many works.

The history of the Turkish language seems to be the only idiom within the family of Turkic languages which is very well documented with written material. From the thirteenth century up to now, an immense number of records covers the history of eight centuries practically without gap. Naturally, this material also includes thousands of barriers for those who venture to 'make out' the language.

Turkish science has made a big step forward in systematizing and preparing this material for further philological works. Step by step, the most important collections take shape, and become known as they are gradually cataloged. Obviously, we are still far from having a picture of the material in full, or even of the most valuable items of the material.

These circumstances more or less determine the further phases of investigations, first of all the linguistic selection of relics. This work is indispensable although it has not yet been emphasized adequately. Namely, it is beyond doubt that the individual items of this immense linguistic material are not of the same value for the historical investigations of language. The material should undergo a selection which would single out those records, mainly prosaic, in which the Turkish idiom is predominant over an alien literary language, full of Arabic and Persian elements, which was different from the spoken language and was destined to comply with the literary taste of a narrow stratum in a certain period. The history of the currently-spoken idiom together with its regional variants may be cleared up only by the aid of the aforementioned groups of linguistic relics. To make this statement even clearer, it may also be put this way: when analyzing the available texts, it should be decided which of them is really linguistic and which only a literary relic.

Both Turkish and European research is even now in great need of this selection, which is considered to be a prerequisite to linguistic investigations, as well as to investigations of several other details, for example, the linguistic examination of manuscript copies as such.

Records in Arabic script are, naturally, not the only sources for the history of the Turkish language. The so-called transliterated linguistic records, 'explored' at the beginning of this century, which have rightly been brought into the focus of research work over the past two decades, became the indispensable sources of investigations into linguistic history. It is clear that while the records in Arabic script give helpful information for research work in historical morphology and syntax, the same sources, not counting the modest potentialities of vocalized texts, fail to unveil the problems of phonology. Researches into texts transliterated into Roman, Greek, Cyrillic, Georgian, etc. alphabets can mainly be expected to give a satisfactory answer to phonological and morphophonological questions.

This particular distribution of the material is, understandably enough, mirrored by the changes in the researchers' interest. Turkish scholars restrict their interest to material in Arabic script only, while their European colleagues are concerned with transliterated texts. At the stage of exploring and presenting the material this 'natural division of labor' has certain advantages, too. It is obvious, however, that the synthesis requires the joint consideration of conclusions and lessons drawn from the two bodies of linguistic records. This holds good for the preparatory stage as well.

Over the past few decades, the interest of research work in linguistic records has constantly been commanded by the works of the Old Turkish (Old Osman) period. This is a traditional line of research work which rightly tends to get the best out of records written in the purer Turkish language of the early centuries, thus giving invaluable data to research work in the history of the Anatolian and Rumelian Turkish, as well as to the comparative Turkic studies. This endeavor, which by itself can hardly be blamed, is also peculiarly mirrored by historical research, and explains the origins of the 'unexplored region' that has long existed in our knowledge concerning the period between the earliest and most recent centuries.

From the viewpoint of analysis, the linguistic records being dealt with now show a variegated picture as regards the actual method of work.

Some of the scholars are only interested in philological works pertaining to the manuscript, and thus they refrain from linguistic evaluation. Others, however, subordinate philological work to historical linguistic studies.

The Türk Dil Kurumu also played a pioneering role in publishing linguistic records of Anatolian and Rumelian Turkish. In cherishing this tradition a prominent part was taken by the outstanding linguist-philologist, A. S. Levend, who, as secretary-general and then president of the Society, particularly encouraged this activity.

A great deal of important linguistic relics appeared in facsimile editions by the Society, among others, *Yūsuf u Zalīḫā* by Šayyād Ḥamza, *Vasīlatu'n-nadžāt* by Sulaymān Čelebi, *Manṭiku't-ṭayr* by Gülšahrī, *Kitāb-i Dede Ḳorḳud*, Barġamalï Kadrī's *Muyassiratu'l-ulūm*, and so forth.

Several facsimile editions and philological text studies have also been published by the Istanbul and Ankara universities. İ. H. Ertaylan edited facsimiles of *Bahdžatu'l-ḥada'iḳ* and *Tabī'atnāme* (1960a and e), as well as works by Aḥmad-i Dā'ī (1952) to mention only the most outstanding. A. Karahan (1966) made a remarkable contribution to this work by his philological edition of Fiġānī's Divan, while the edition of Mehmed's 'Išḳ-nāma is due to S. Yüksel (1965).

Mention should be made here of the historical sources, published by the Türk Tarih Kurumu, which may also serve the purposes of linguistic history.

Naturally, the circle of scholars who also aim at a linguistic historical approach is rather narrow since the literary historians will not go beyond the philological work, and justifiably so considering their particular subject field.

Among the scholars engaged in the historical evaluation of linguistic records, I would like to refer first of all to M. Mansuroğlu. This linguist left us an invaluable legacy with his several published works, as well as with his solid, purposeful program and method (Mansuroğlu 1945, 1946a, b and c, 1947, 1952, 1954a and b, 1956a, b and c, 1957b, 1958a). The philological and linguistic treatment of the Old Anatolian Turkish texts, strictly speaking the written records of the Saljuk period, such as works by Džalāladdīn Rūmī, Sultān Valad, Dahhānī, Aḥmad Faḳīh, and Šayyād Ḥamza, is also linked with his name. His untimely death, which struck at the most creative period of his career, was a great loss to science.

Several other works in the field of linguistic records must also be mentioned. S. Buluç contributed to the philological interpretation and linguistic evaluation of the *Bahdžatu'l-ḥadā'iḳ* (1954, 1956a and b). The linguistic treatment of the *Dede Ḳorḳud* is due to M. Ergin (1958–63). V. Kılıçoğlu (1956) undertook the treatment of Sabundžu-oğlu Šarafaddīn's *Džarrāḥiya-i ilḫāniya* which as a non-literary text was very important for linguistic investigation. Z. Korkmaz and S. Olcay (1956) wrote a minor monograph on Fużūlī's language. Z. Korkmaz's treatise, giving a linguistic representation of individual items of the Turkish manuscript corpus, as well as her paper on the interpretation of *Ḳābūs-nāme*, which she edited, also deserve special mention (1966a, 1967a). In monograph form S. Olcay (1965) treated the translation of the *Tazkiratu'l-avliyā* by Abu'l-Layṣ Samarḳandī. As regards the group of linguistic records in Arabic script, his work was the first relating to the sixteenth century and was the earliest sign of the widening circle of research work which had thus far been restricted to the problems of the Old Turkish. F. K. Timurtaş (1958, 1960–61, 1963, 1964b) undertook the treatment of Šayḫī's works. One of these studies treated the Ḫarnāme; in a monograph, which at the same time was a philological text edition, he dealt with the language of the poet's Ḫusrav u Šīrīn, and another study of his offered a survey of the language of Šayḫī and his contemporaries.

From the methodological point of view, these linguistic works give a variegated picture. They truly reflect the various conceptions of authors, but the way in which they show the authors' position on the road from philology to linguistics is perhaps even more important. However, due to the philological starting point of these works and to the more convenient comparison with the present state of language, less attention was paid to the representation of linguistic relics in such a way as to give a synchronic historical cross-section so that linguistic structure could unambiguously be recognized. This, in turn, overshadows the grammatical interpretation which should be independent of other historical cross-sections.

Obviously, both the philological text editions and the treatment and presentation of linguistic records add a great deal to our knowledge. Considering however that not less than a century has elapsed since the publication of M. Wickerhauser's 'Saljuk poems', and almost seventy years since Vámbéry's work which was epoch-making in view of monographic studies, it seems just to weigh the relevant works of Turkish and European linguistics, as a whole, from the point of view of objective possibilities and tasks. And, unfortunately, this weighing does not always yield positive results. This is also shown by the fact that, if we only think of some periods which have not been explored at all, there is still no basis for the writing of a much-advocated historical grammar.

However, this is not to imply that scholars have refrained from studying problems of historical grammar altogether. Even if the number of such studies is comparatively small due to some objective circumstances as explained above, several authors are engaged in analyzing the explored grammatical material from this aspect. S. Çağatay (1947–48) devoted a major treatise to some problems of Old Turkish. In some of their papers, J. Eckmann and H. Eren dealt with the problems of historical phonetics, while D. Aksan treated historical semantics. Of particular value are treatises by Z. Korkmaz (1958a, 1959a and b, 1960a and b, 1961a, b and c, 1962, 1964b, 1965b, 1966b, 1967b) which, in connection with some comparative studies, furnish useful data on the history of Anatolian and Rumelian Turkish. Furthermore, as has been mentioned before, M. Ergin attempted to write a synthesis of historical grammar, though within the compasses of a university manual.

One of the most significant undertakings of Turkish linguistic history is the publication of a four-volume historical dictionary by the Türk Dil Kurumu.[2] The start and consequently the method were determined by the neologist movement and by its demand on words. The work of collecting was, therefore, meant to meet that demand. During the work they examined the vocabulary of 160 linguistic relics from which they singled out the Turkish words. At the initial stage the philological and historical considerations were of secondary importance, but in the subsequent volumes they gained more and more ground. Although still based on modern orthography, they contain accurate philological references to the source; moreover, they also include the variants of entry words in Arabic script. The consideration of the content also adds to the value of the dictionary. The improvement of the method considerably increased its usability. Despite its shortcomings, the dictionary makes exceedingly rich material available for historical investigation.

The new edition of the dictionary, three volumes of which have so far appeared, shows a new editorial policy.[3] Material from 67 further linguistic relics was added and some of the shortcomings of the original edition (e.g. alphabetical order in the individual volumes) were eliminated.

The prime movers of both versions of the dictionary, which according to the plans of the Türk Dil Kurumu are considered to be preparation for a universal Turkish historical dictionary, were Ö. A. Aksoy and D. Dilçin.

The increase in the amount of linguistic material furnished a good basis for investigations into the history of vocabulary and etymology. The influence of Western, more precisely, the French and German languages on Turkish is dealt with in monographs by E. Esenkova (1959) and Y. Önen (1955). A. Tietze's (1952) study offers a

[2] *Türkiye Türkçesi tarihî sözlüğü hazırlıklarından. XIII. yüzyıldan günümüze kadar kitaplardan toplanmış tanıklariyle tarama sözlüğü*, 1–4. 1943–57. Istanbul-Ankara, TDK.

[3] *Onüçüncü [XIII] yüzyıldan beri Türkiye Türkçesiyle yazılmış kitaplardan toplanan tanıklariyle tarama sözlüğü*, 1–3. 1963–67. Ankara, TDK.

carefully elaborated picture of the phonetic questions of words of Western origin. It was he who undertook a thorough study of the layers in the vocabulary of the Anatolian dialect. His other treatises (1955, 1957, 1958b) are concerned with the problems of Greek, Slavic, and Arabic loanwords, respectively, and with the theoretical problems of the historical division of Turkish vocabulary. The monograph, so far perhaps the most important in both depth and dimension among the works on Turkish vocabulary, which treats the problems of 'lingua franca' or rather its Mediterranean elements with deep insight, bears the names of H. and R. Kahane and A. Tietze (1958).

The attention of H. Eren, one of the most industrious scholars of etymology, has been primarily attracted by the inherently Turkish layer of vocabulary, although his studies also touch upon the problems of loanwords. He treats his subject with a broad comparative method. H. Eren is now engaged in compiling a voluminous Turkish etymological dictionary.

Turkish dialectological studies have made a great step forward during the past two or three decades. Following the pioneering studies of I. Kúnos at the end of the last century, investigations carried on by T. Kowalski and M. Räsänen again laid stress upon the Anatolian and Rumelian dialects, but only suggest the possibilities of this exceedingly rich and valuable material.

It was A. Caferoğlu, professor at Istanbul university, who took the initiative. Started in the early forties, his vast undertaking attempts a systematic survey of Turkish dialects. Up to 1951 no less than nine volumes of dialect material were published. Based primarily on prosaic and lyrical material of folklore, the anthologies, in fact, cover the whole territory of the Turkish language, except Rumelia. However, Rumelia, too, is included in the program: the author and his co-workers carry on investigations in this field and certain reports on their preliminary studies have already been published.

The anthologies — though some authors criticise the methods of collecting and phonetic recording — render it possible to survey the broad field of Turkish dialects and to give a clear-cut view of the possibilities of research. The material unambiguously shows that dialectological researches may open up new vistas for investigations into the history of Oghuz languages. Considering the broad dialectal network of the immense language territory and the demands of research, however, the nine-volume material — as the author, too, has always emphasized — may only be the first step.

A. Caferoğlu's dialectal collection represents the individual dialects in Turkey in texts, and thus, as any other dialectal text, can only give a partial view of the linguistic system. In this field too, it was A. Caferoğlu who took the initial step. His treatise (1950) aimed to describe the peculiarities of the dialects of Eskişehir, which already shows one dialect as a whole with a wide range of phenomena characteristic of it. It was the opening of the second phase of dialectological research.

Naturally this work was followed by further analyses of phenomena affecting the whole network of dialects. The comprehensive study which, on the basis of the recent research results, examined the Turkish dialects was also published by the Nestor of Turkish dialectology.

J. Eckmann's methodologically exemplary studies (1950b, 1960a, 1962b) gave evidence of the extension of dialectological investigations in Istanbul. Describing the dialects of Razgrad and Dinler, Eckmann added to the study of Rumelian Turkish dialects. He also devoted several treatises to the historical explanation of certain dialectal categories. His historical explanations refer to the fact that dialectal material is widely-used in research work. Eckmann's study (1948, 1950a and c, 1953a) in the Karamanli dialect quickly leads to the domain of historical dialectological investigations. It examines the language of the orthodox Karamanli records written in Greek letters, thus making it possible that this type of language may be determined from a historical linguistic aspect. In another paper, with M. Mansuroğlu as co-author (Eckmann 1959), he gave a preliminary report on the findings of a dialectological study-trip to Rumelia. As another result of the same study-trip, M. Mansuroğlu (1960) described the Edirne dialect in a paper that appeared in the year of the author's death.

There are two important monographs in the field of early Turkish dialectology. Ö. A. Aksoy (1945–46) covers the Gaziantep and K. E. Ünsel (1945) describes the Urfa dialect. Of these two works, Ö. A. Aksoy's study is more voluminous and solid: his texts, vocabulary and observations on the peculiarities of the dialect — even though the methodological basis of the survey that he gives is at variance with the traditional one — are valuable contributions to Turkish dialectology.

Deserving special attention among other dialectological monographs are Z. Korkmaz's excellent works which are characterized by an extended scope in collecting material and by concentration upon dialectal structure (1956, 1963a, 1964a, 1965a). The author's dialectological field studies took place in South-Western and Middle Anatolia. Naturally, as a woman, she more easily succeeded in getting in touch with the female members of Mohammedan families who may well be looked upon as vitally important informants of Turkish dialectology. The adoption of circumspect dialectological methods resulted in good performance. The rich and valuable text material furnished a solid basis for analytical description which, in turn, facilitated a more detailed analysis of dialectal peculiarities. This, however, does not imply a phonological and structural analysis. Her objective is to give a painstakingly accurate description of dialectal phonetics and to show in detail other dialectal peculiarities differing from the norms of the standard language. These works, products of the 'second phase' of Turkish dialectology, already suggest further possibilities.

An interesting 'by-product' of Z. Korkmaz's study is the demonstration of the occurrence of primary long Proto-Turkic vowels in certain Anatolian dialects, an important discovery for the comparative Turkic linguistic studies (1953).

The publication of the six-volume dictionary of Turkish dialects was an important event in dialectological studies.[4] Motivated by the neologist movement, the Türk Dil Kurumu took the initiative in this case, too. Making use of printed sources and by means of lists of collections, the work of collecting started with a very large number of themes. The collectors were recruited from among the representatives of the village intelligentsia. Obviously, this approach implied certain shortcomings at the very beginning; thus, for example, the consistent enforcement of unified requirements of methodology — to insure phonetic recording or to exert appropriate supervision — was impossible. Despite all contingencies the heroic work resulted in the collection of an immense quantity of dialectal words which greatly increased the body of knowledge relating to Turkish vocabulary, and furnished an important source for the historical study of Turkish words. The dictionary consists of four basic volumes (one of them being a supplement), a 'folklore booklet' and a useful index which facilitates retrieval by subject fields and also helps to meet the methodological requirements (e.g. gathering together the historically related or coherent words) which were ignored during the work of collecting.

This undertaking of the Türk Dil Kurumu is still going on under similar circumstances. The result of this collection was the new volumes[5] which not only give the new material, but also include the material of the former series. The first two volumes cover the letters A and B and thus the completed work promises to be even more comprehensive.

H. Z. Koşay's dialectal dictionary (with O. Aydın 1952), which is the continuation of one of the author's earlier works started in the thirties, surpasses the Türk Dil Kurumu's undertaking in many respects. The collection, treatment, and presentation of the material, though much smaller in size than the former, was based on a more reliable methodology. Since the dictionary covers an essentially different vocabulary from that of the Türk Dil Kurumu, it is — as the author puts it — destined to complement the other one. The work is more accurate and careful both as regards semantic explanations and the definition of the scope of usage. The author's ethnographic knowledge also comes into useful display.

Dialectological investigations may look back upon considerable results achieved over the past few decades. However, considering the tasks and possibilities, they have hardly gone beyond the initial stage. It is clear enough that the preparation of the Turkish linguistic atlas should be put on the agenda as soon as possible. There is also a lot to do in the monographic representation of dialects. No less important are the tasks or fewer the possibilities than in the field of Anatolian vocabulary, where the extension and methodological improvement of lexicological efforts seem to be the next step forward. And time mercilessly presses for their realization, because without these advances the tasks which can now be completed will be nearly impossible to carry out in the future. And if this were to happen, it would mean the loss of exceedingly valuable linguistic sources, which would later serve as perhaps the only reliable

[4] *Türkiyede halk ağzından söz derleme dergisi*, 1–6. 1939–57. Istanbul-Ankara, TDK.

[5] *Türkiye'de halk ağzından derleme sözlüğü*, 1–3. 1963–67. Ankara, TDK.

basis for the complex study of Turkish, Azerbaijan, and Turkmenian dialectal material, and also for studying Oghuz dialectological and historical problems from a new point of view. In fact, Turkish dialectology forms one of the keys to this sphere of problems. It is only Turkish linguistics that is really destined to solve these important problems, and international linguistics rightly expects it to do so.

During the last decades there have been only two scholars in Turkey who concerned themselves with onomatology: A. Caferoğlu (1951–53, 1958b, 1961b, 1962a, 1964b and c) and H. Eren (1950c, 1953b, 1955, 1965a) were led to this field first of all by their dialectological and etymological studies. They both have written several papers. A. Caferoğlu analyzes some problems from the broader point of view of general Turkic studies. The merit for the first attempt to summarize certain peculiarities of place names goes to H. Eren (1965b).

As has been referred to at the beginning of this paper, historical language studies have priority in the program of linguistics. Dialectology — whose birth is due to other motivations and reasons — is also closely related to the former. These two disciplines virtually captivate the interest of scholars completely, and clearly these two disciplines overshadow grammatical studies. It is precisely this latter field where uneven development of methodology is perhaps most clearly to be observed. Turkic studies in Turkey — and in this respect its European counterpart is in a similar position — are still far from the advances achieved by general linguistics during several decades in forming grammatical concepts. Studies adopting a generative grammatical approach[6] have not yet prompted too much response since linguistic research is generally characterized by a pre-phonological state.

Such a pre-phonological conception can be observed in Banguoğlu's (1959b) phonetics which is meant to form the first volume of a major grammar. He has also written several more specialized papers (1956, 1957) reflecting the traditional grammatical conception. Mention should be made here of A. C. Emre's (1945) grammatical treatises, too, and also of his grammar which, however, do not give a synchronic description; the author even includes historical language facts in his 'tableau'.

T. N. Gencan's grammar (1966), too, was published at the initiative of the Türk Dil Kurumu. The work — the author claims — is patterned after the *Grammaire Larousse du XXe siècle.*

This survey of the state of grammatical researches closes by mentioning studies by Z. Korkmaz, M. Mansuroğlu, and A. Tietze. The works of these very scholarly linguists have greatly added to the body of Turkish grammar.

The two great undertakings of Turkish lexicography — historical and dialectal dictionaries initiated by the Türk Dil Kurumu — have already been dealt with. There

[6] R.B. Lees. 1961. *The Phonology of Modern Standard Turkish.* UAS 6. Bloomington, Indiana University; R.B. Lees. 1962. 'A compact analysis for the Turkish personal morphemes'. *American Studies in Altaic linguistics*, edited by N. Poppe. UAS 13.141–76. Bloomington, Indiana University; R.B. Lees. 1966. 'Turkish harmony and the phonological description of assimilation'. *TDAYB* 279–97; R.H. Meskill. 1966. *A transformational analysis of Turkish structure.* 's-Gravenhage, Mouton.

are however still other works of the Türk Dil Kurumu in the lexicographical field to be mentioned.

An explanatory dictionary, edited by the Society, the *Türkçe sözlük*, was first published in 1944, and has had four enlarged editions up to now (Ağakay 1966). In the meantime both its entries and explanations have been augmented and improved. It is true, in turn, that the dictionary, in fulfilling the task of a synonymic dictionary, became somewhat subordinate to the neologist endeavor. It contains a number of neologisms whose fat still remains to be seen. At the same time it omitted foreign — Arabic, Western, etc. — elements which now form an organic part of the standard language, and the problem of their replacement may also be solved only in the unforeseeable future. Thus the material of the dictionary does not reflect a completely true image of the spoken language. In spite of this, however, the *Türkçe sözlük* seems to be a very serious undertaking by Turkish linguists and is an important step toward a Turkish Larousse.

The smaller dictionary of synonyms (Ağakay 1956), published by the Türk Dil Kurumu, is also designed to serve the purpose of language reform, and so are a number of terminological dictionaries which, on the basis of Turkish vocabulary, are to meet the demands of professional terminology emerging day by day from the different branches of science and technology.

The Türk Dil Kurumu also undertook the preparation of orthographic dictionaries along with the not too popular task of 'putting orthography in order'. As the most recent product of a several decades-old undertaking of the Türk Dil Kurumu, the *Yeni imlâ kılavuzu*, which like its antecedents created great interest among linguists, is in fact a new edition of the orthographic dictionary published originally under a different title.[7]

As far as can be judged from the current printed publications, unfortunately the normalizing efforts of the Türk Dil Kurumu, which have not been adequately supported by the state in the fields of education and publishing, did not meet with resounding success.

Published by the Türk Dil Kurumu, Ö. A. Aksoy's (1965) book of proverbs and phrases — though it is not a dictionary in the narrow sense of the word and goes far beyond the usual boundaries of linguistics — is also very valuable. This rich phrasebook should certainly be registered.

Dictionaries by F. Devellioğlu (1962) and M. N. Özön (1965) are aimed at facilitating the reading of old literary works, and give a practical explanation of the vocabulary of old literary language.

The new edition of Redhouse's well-known dictionary gives a scientific mapping of the vocabulary of old and new literary language. This major undertaking, which ultimately was directed by A. Tietze, appeared in 1968 as the *New Redhouse Turkish-English dictionary* (Istanbul, Redhouse Press).

[7] *İmlâ Kılavuzu*. 1962. Ankara, Türk Dil Kurumu.

As another significant contribution to Turkish lexicography, the undertaking hallmarked by Redhouse's name was designed to produce a modern English-Turkish dictionary[8] on the basis of a wide-ranging vocabulary. Its subsequent editions, published at short intervals, show that the joint efforts of outstanding scholars for more than a decade have brought good results.

It would take a lot of space to dwell at length upon other bilingual dictionaries. It will suffice here to mention two more dictionaries which, although they were published by Western publishers, are related to Turkey through their authors. I refer here to the English-Turkish and Turkish-English dictionary by F. İz (1952) and H. C. Hony (1946), and to the Turkish-German dictionary by Fr. Heuser (1962) which won renown in the world of science.

Studies dealing with the theoretical and practical problems of language reform have grown into a sizeable literature. It shows that the neologist movement, directed by Kemal Atatürk's new conceptions, has for a long time engaged the greater part of linguists' activities, even if it is past its youthful days. It is impossible to give even a comparatively full account of this exceedingly variegated and ramified literature within the narrow compasses of this modest recapitulation. It is even more difficult to take a stand on the most widely debated questions. All go beyond the limits of linguistics and lead to the study of the relationship between language and society where the success or failure of every conscious intervention is the result of complex tendencies prevailing in the linguistic community.

We have already referred to some of the positive effects of the neologist movement on linguistics. We have outlined those undertakings of historical language and dialectological research — the publication of linguistic relics, historical and dialectal dictionaries — which were inspired and encouraged essentially by the language reform and by its most important agency, the Türk Dil Kurumu. However, it should be underlined once more that with all these the Society rendered invaluable service to the cause of Turkic linguistic studies.

From the literature on the problems of language reform I would like to refer only to the most significant general works. First of all, there is A. S. Levend's monograph (1960b) which is not restricted to the most recent tendencies but covers the whole of the century-old problem. It is an important addition to the history of the Turkish literary language. Whereas Z. Korkmaz's (1963b) work analyzes the significance of the language reform and its place among the Turkic languages, Ö. A. Aksoy's (1964) book treats the practical problems involved in the reform.

Naturally, papers on the problems of the language reform formed the basis of more than one collection of essays. These show the readers the very nucleus of current debates. With the outsider's objectivity in mind, may I be permitted to mention the works of two foreign authors for the sake of orientation. Here I refer to U. Heyd and K. Steuerwald's monographs dealing with the Turkish language reform.[9] The

[8] *Yeni Redhouse lûgati. İngilizce-Türkçe*. 1958. Istanbul.

two works essentially represent two different poles of evaluating the reform, but it is precisely on this account that they help in forming an objective opinion.

However, it will be the language itself that will give the final reply to all the questions. And the language, independently of any radical purism or excessive conservativism, will — as it seems today — justify the linguistic renewal.

Our task was to give an account of two decades of Turkish linguistic investigations. Finally I would also like to sum up those bibliographical sources which make orientation easier and facilitate a full survey of the material.

Current Turkish linguistic literature is now covered by several bibliographical publications. Two excellent bibliographical tools of the Millî Kütüphane, *Türkiye Makaleler Bibliyografyası* and *Türkiye Bibliyografyası*, being of the nature of national bibliography, cover the whole material. In quarterly issues, the former registers the books, and the latter includes the papers, articles published in journals, memorial volumes, proceedings of conferences, congresses, and material in other irregular periodicals. Since it takes a lot of time to meet the requirement of completeness, the issues are generally one year late. Summaries by the outstanding Turkish bibliographer, S. N. Özerdim, published in the yearbooks of the Varlık Publishing House (*Varlık Yıllığı*), offer a selective view of certain fields and events of Turkish linguistics. As regards the current literature of Turkish linguistics outside Turkey, the inquirer should consult the well-known bibliographical sources of linguistics. The systematic bibliographical coverage of onomatology, one of the related subject fields, is to be found in the volumes of *Onoma*, edited by A. Caferoğlu within the framework of the renowned international undertaking.

Unfortunately, retrospective bibliographies are wanting. Their lack is, to some extent, made up by the regular lists of publications of the Türk Dil Kurumu,[10] which not only register the more recent publications but also give a general survey of the publishing activities of several decades. A similar series of the Türk Tarih Kurumu,[11] which deals with some of the related fields — historical sources which can also be considered as linguistic records — is also of great importance. The linguistic publications of Ankara University can be run down with the aid of Yeşiloğlu's bibliography (1958).

It is also a good thing that bibliographical activities show interest in personal (bio-) bibliographies, that is, in bibliographic recording of the complete works of outstanding Turkish linguists (R. R. Arat, A. Caferoğlu, M. Mansuroğlu). At the initiative of the Türk Dil Kurumu, similar attention is being paid to the works of the foreign representatives of Turkic studies. The same interest is shown in the history of linguistics: the works and achievements of the most outstanding linguists of the past are commemorated by the Türk Dil Kurumu in the form of minor monographs.

[9] U. Heyd. 1954. *Language reform in modern Turkey*. Oriental Notes and Studies Published by the Israel Oriental Society, No. 5. Jerusalem 1954; K. Steuerwald. 1963–64–66. *Untersuchungen zur türkischen Sprache der Gegenwart*, 1–3. Berlin-München-Zürich, Langenscheidt.

[10] *Türk Dil Kurumu yayınları*, 1933–1967. 1967. Ankara, TDK.

[11] *Türk Tarih Kurumu yayınları*, 1933–1967. 1967. Ankara, TTK.

Their registration here, however, would go beyond the narrow compasses of this paper, and this task is already very well performed by the above mentioned list of the Türk Dil Kurumu's own publications.

REFERENCES[12]

ACAROĞLU, M. T. 1954. Louise-Noëlle Malclès, Türk dilinin bibliyografya kaynakları. TD 36.721–4.

AĞAKAY, M. A. 1953. İkizlemeler üzerine. TD 16.189–91; 17.268–71.

——. 1954. Türkçede kelime koşmaları. TDAYB 97–104.

——. 1956. Türkçede yakın anlamlı kelimeler sözlüğü. Ankara, TDK.

——. 1962. Fransızca-Türkçe sözlük. Ankara, TDK.

——. 1966. Türkçe sözlük. Ankara, TDK.

AKARSU, B. 1955. Wilhelm von Humboldt'da dil-kültür bağlantısı. Istanbul, İÜ.

AKSAN, D. 1961. Anlam alışverişi olayları ve Türkçe. TDAYB 207–73.

——. 1965. Türk anlam bilimine giriş — anlam değişmeleri. TDAYB 167–84.

AKSOY, Ö. A. 1945–46. Gaziantep ağzı, 1–3. Istanbul, TDK.

——. 1959. Şeyẖ Aḥmed ve Naẓmü'l-leāl. TDAYB 205–48.

——. 1960. Dürrü'n-nizām ve Nazmü'l-cevāhir. TDAYB 145–71.

——. 1964. Dil üzerine. Düşünceler, düzeltmeler. Ankara, TDK.

——. 1965. Atasözleri ve deyimler. Ankara, TDK.

AKYÜZ, K. 1959. Paris Millî Kütüphanesinde ilk Türkçe-Fransızca ve Fransızca-Türkçe yazma eserler. TDAYB 249–92.

ALPARSLAN, A. 1960. Ahmedî'nin yeni bulunan bir eseri. 'Mirkat-i edeb'. İÜEFTDED 10.35–40.

ANHEGGER, R., and H. İNALCIK. 1956. Kānūnnāme-i sultānī ber muceb-i 'örf-i 'Osmānī. Ankara, TTK.

ARAT, R. R. 1943–46. Gazi Zahirüddin Muhammed Babur. Vekayi. Babur'un hatıratı, 1–2. Ankara, TTK.

——. 1946–51. Atabetü'l hakayık'ta *g* ve *ġ* seslerine dair. TM 9.65–72.

——. 1947–59. Ḳutadġu bilig, 1–2. Istanbul-Ankara, TDK-TTK.

——. 1951. Edib Ahmed b. Mahmud Yükneki. Atebetü'l-Hakāyık. Istanbul, TDK.

——. 1951–53. Türk şivelerinin tasnifi. 10.59–138.

——. 1953a. Türkçe metinlerde *e/i* meselesine dair. RO 17.306–13.

——. 1953b. Bir yazı nümûnesi münasebeti ile. [1.] 60. doğum yılı münasebetiyle Fuad Köprülü armağanı, 17–29. Istanbul, AÜ.

12 Covering the literature from 1945 up to the end of 1966, the bibliography does by no means aim at completeness. Works written prior to 1945 are registered only if further volumes of the particular work or its series were published later. In the case of works with several editions, only their last edition is included. Works translated from foreign languages are not registered. Included are, however, those works by foreign authors who lived in Turkey for a longer period and which were published during their stay there. Similarly, the bibliography includes the works of Turkish scholars who have left the country.

ARAT, R. R. 1955a. Gramer ıstılahları hakkında. TD 44.479–88.
——. 1955b. Türkçede kelime ve eklerin yapısı. TD 43.396–400.
——. 1961. Zu einer Schriftmusterhandschrift. UAJb 33.205–17.
——. 1962. Bir yazı nümûnesi münasebeti ile. 2. İÜEFTDED 12.121–38.
——. 1964a. Brüchstücke eines Gebetsbuches. SO 28/9. Helsinki, Societas Orientalis Fennica.
——. 1964b. Der Herrschertitel 'Iduq-qut'. UAJb 35.150–7.
——. 1964c. Eski Türk hukuk vesikaları. TKA 1.5–53.
——. 1964d. Türkçede cihet mefhumu ve bunun ile ilgili tâbirler. TM 14.1–24.
——. 1964e. Zahl der Türken und ihre Siedlungsgebiete. CT 1.35–43.
——. 1965a. Among the Uighur documents, 2. UAJb 36.263–72.
——. 1965b. Eski Türk şiiri. Ankara, TTK.
ARATAN, E. U. 1965. Kâşgar ağzından derlemeler. Ankara, TKAE.
ATALAY, B. 1945. Et-tuhfet-üz-zekiyye fi-l-lûgat-it-türkiyye. Istanbul, TDK.
——. 1946. Bergama'lı Kadri. Müyessiret-ül-ulûm (Muyassıratu-'l-ʿulūm). Istanbul, TDK.
——. 1948. Ettuhfet-üz-zekiyye çevirmesi'nin tenkidi dolayısiyle. AÜDTCFD 6.87–126.
——. 1949. Eş-şüzur-üz-zehebiyye ve-l-kıta-il-ahmediyye fi-llûgat-it-türkiyye. Istanbul, TDK.
——. 1950. Mirza Mehdi Mehmet Han. Seng-lâh. Lûgat-i Nevaî. Istanbul, TDK.
ATEŞ, A. 1947. Varaka ve Gülşah mesnevisinin kaynakları. İÜEFTDED 2.1–19.
——. 1954. Süleyman Çelebi. Vesîletü'n-necât. Mevlid. Ankara, TDK.
——. 1958a. Anadolu kütüphanelerinden bazı mühim Türkçe el yazmaları. İÜEFTDED 8.90–108.
——. 1958b. Şark Türkçesi ile eski bir şiir ve bir risale. Jean Deny armağanı 25–30. Ankara, TDK.
——. 1964. Ubeydullah Han'ın bilinmiyen mensur bir eseri. TDAYB 127–47.
——. 1966. Arapça yazı dilinde Türkçe kelimeler (X. yüzyıla kadar). Reşid Rahmeti Arat için 26–31. Ankara, TKAE.
AYYUBİ, N. A. 1965. Önemli bir Türkçe sözlük. TDAYB 65–101.
BANGUOĞLU, T. 1956. Türkçede tekerrür fiilleri. TDAYB 111–23.
——. 1957. Türkçede benzerlik sıfatları. TDAYB 13–27.
——. 1958. Kâşgari'den notlar: 1. Uygurlar ve Uygurca üzerine. TDAYB 87–113.
——. 1959a. Kâşgari'den notlar: 2. Oğuzlar ve Oğuzeli üzerine. TDAYB 1–26.
——. 1959b. Türk grameri. 1. bölüm. Sesbilgisi. Ankara, TDK.
——. 1960. Oğuz lehçesi üzerine. TDAYB 23–48.
——. 1964. Eski Türkçe üzerine. TDAYB 77–84.
BAŞGÖZ, İ. 1960. Dede Korkut'ta yanlış okunan bazı kelimeler. TD 104.442–4.
BAŞKAN, Ö. 1958. Some phonological remarks with special reference to Turkish phonemics. Litera 5.25–55.
BATTAL-TAYMAS, A. see Taymas, A. B.

BAYDUR, S.Y. 1953. Dilimiz ve Yunan-Lâtin asıllı kelimeler. TDAYB 93–121.

——. 1964. Dil ve kültür. Ankara, TDK.

BULUÇ, S. 1946. Diyalektoloji. 1. Almanya ve Fransa'da diyalekt araştırmalarına toplu bir bakış. İÜEFTDED 1.171–9.

——. 1954. Eski bir Türk dili yadigârı. Behcetü'l-ḥadā'iḳ fī mev'iẓeti'l-ḫalā'ik. İÜEFTDED 6.119–31.

——. 1956a. Behcetü'l-ḥadā'iḳ fī mev'iẓeti'l-ḫalā'iḳ'den örnekler. İÜEFTDED 7.17–44.

——. 1956b. Şeyyâd Hamza'nın beş manzumesi. İÜEFTDED 7.1–16.

——. 1963. Behcet-ü'l-ḥadāi'iḳ fī mev'iẓet-i'l-ḫalā'iḳ'ten derlenmiş koşuklar. TDAYB 161–201.

——. 1964. Bir eserin iki yazma nüshası. TM 14.151–97.

——. 1966. Kerkük Hoyratlarına dair. Reşid Rahmeti Arat için 142–54. Ankara, TKAE.

CAFEROĞLU, A. 1940. Anadolu dialektolojisi üzerine malzeme. 1. İstanbul, İÜ.

——. 1941. Anadolu dialektolojisi üzerine malzeme. 2. Istanbul, İÜ.

——. 1942. Doğu illerimiz ağızlarından toplamalar. 1. Istanbul, TDK.

——. 1943. Anadolu ağızlarından toplamalar. Istanbul, TDK.

——. 1944. Sivas ve Tokat illeri ağızlarından toplamalar. Istanbul, TDK.

——. 1945. Güney Doğu illerimiz ağızlarından toplamalar. Istanbul, TDK.

——. 1946a. Ahmet Mithat Efendi ve Türkçemiz. İÜEFTDED 1.2–8.

——. 1946b. Anadolu dialektolojisine dair bir deneme. TDB Seri 3/6–7.561–8.

——. 1946c. 1945 yılı Kuzey Doğu Anadolu gezisinden. İÜEFTDED 1.65–80.

——. 1946d. Kuzey Doğu illerimiz ağızlarından toplamalar. Istanbul, TDK.

——. 1946e. 'Küçük, çocuk, enik' kelimelerinin morfolojik ve semantik değişmelerine dair. TDB Seri 3/10–11.6–12.

——. 1946f. Niğde ağızlarından örnekler. İÜEFTDED 1.150–62.

——. 1948a. Çağatay Türkçesi ve Nevaî. İÜEFTDED 2.141–55.

——. 1948b. Orta-Anadolu ağızlarından derlemeler. Istanbul, İÜ.

——. 1948c. Terekeme ağzile hudutboyu saz şairlerimizden Kurbanî ve şiirleri. İÜEFTDED 3.87–106.

——. 1950. Eskişehir ağızları üzerine bir deneme. İÜEFTDED 4.15–33.

——. 1951a. Anadolu illeri ağızlarından derlemeler. Istanbul, İÜ.

——. 1951b. [1953] Azeri şivesinde *nohur* ve *lap* kelimeleri. RO 17.180–3.

——. 1951–53. Türk onomastiğinde 'at' kültü. TM 10.201–12.

——. 1952a. Erkilet çerçilerinin argosu 'Dilce'. İÜEFTDED 4.331–44.

——. 1952b. Recherches sur la dialectologie de Turquie. Orbis 1.509–11.

——. 1953a. Anadolu abdallarının gizli dillerinden bir iki örnek. 60. doğum yılı münasebetiyle Fuad Köprülü armağanı 77–9. Istanbul, AÜ.

——. 1953b. Azerbaycan dil ve edebiyatının dönüm noktaları. Ankara, Azerbaycan Kültür Derneği.

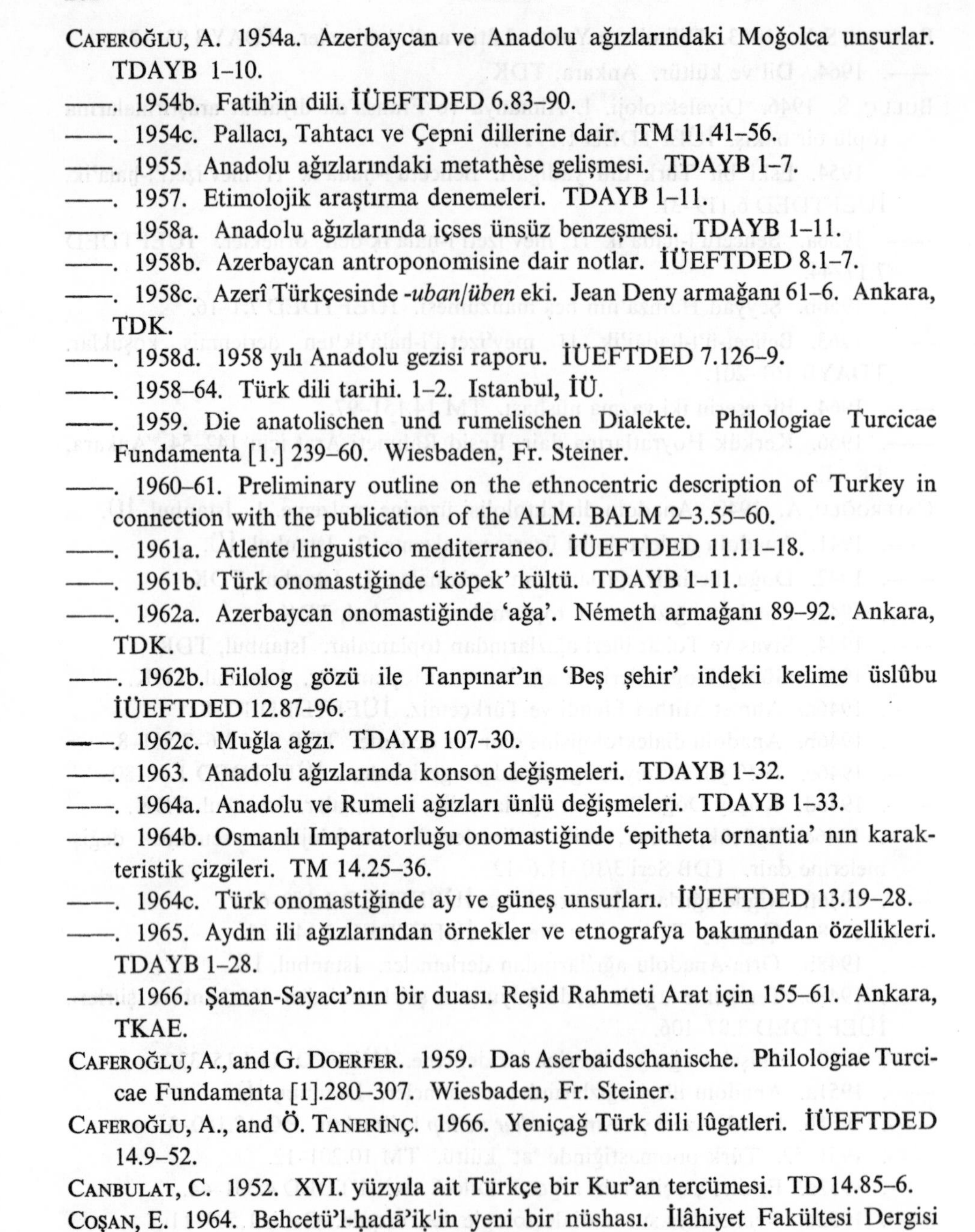

CAFEROĞLU, A. 1954a. Azerbaycan ve Anadolu ağızlarındaki Moğolca unsurlar. TDAYB 1–10.

——. 1954b. Fatih'in dili. İÜEFTDED 6.83–90.

——. 1954c. Pallacı, Tahtacı ve Çepni dillerine dair. TM 11.41–56.

——. 1955. Anadolu ağızlarındaki metathèse gelişmesi. TDAYB 1–7.

——. 1957. Etimolojik araştırma denemeleri. TDAYB 1–11.

——. 1958a. Anadolu ağızlarında içses ünsüz benzeşmesi. TDAYB 1–11.

——. 1958b. Azerbaycan antroponomisine dair notlar. İÜEFTDED 8.1–7.

——. 1958c. Azerî Türkçesinde *-uban/üben* eki. Jean Deny armağanı 61–6. Ankara, TDK.

——. 1958d. 1958 yılı Anadolu gezisi raporu. İÜEFTDED 7.126–9.

——. 1958–64. Türk dili tarihi. 1–2. Istanbul, İÜ.

——. 1959. Die anatolischen und rumelischen Dialekte. Philologiae Turcicae Fundamenta [1.] 239–60. Wiesbaden, Fr. Steiner.

——. 1960–61. Preliminary outline on the ethnocentric description of Turkey in connection with the publication of the ALM. BALM 2–3.55–60.

——. 1961a. Atlente linguistico mediterraneo. İÜEFTDED 11.11–18.

——. 1961b. Türk onomastiğinde 'köpek' kültü. TDAYB 1–11.

——. 1962a. Azerbaycan onomastiğinde 'ağa'. Németh armağanı 89–92. Ankara, TDK.

——. 1962b. Filolog gözü ile Tanpınar'ın 'Beş şehir' indeki kelime üslûbu İÜEFTDED 12.87–96.

——. 1962c. Muğla ağzı. TDAYB 107–30.

——. 1963. Anadolu ağızlarında konson değişmeleri. TDAYB 1–32.

——. 1964a. Anadolu ve Rumeli ağızları ünlü değişmeleri. TDAYB 1–33.

——. 1964b. Osmanlı Imparatorluğu onomastiğinde 'epitheta ornantia' nın karakteristik çizgileri. TM 14.25–36.

——. 1964c. Türk onomastiğinde ay ve güneş unsurları. İÜEFTDED 13.19–28.

——. 1965. Aydın ili ağızlarından örnekler ve etnografya bakımından özellikleri. TDAYB 1–28.

——. 1966. Şaman-Sayacı'nın bir duası. Reşid Rahmeti Arat için 155–61. Ankara, TKAE.

CAFEROĞLU, A., and G. DOERFER. 1959. Das Aserbaidschanische. Philologiae Turcicae Fundamenta [1].280–307. Wiesbaden, Fr. Steiner.

CAFEROĞLU, A., and Ö. TANERİNÇ. 1966. Yeniçağ Türk dili lûgatleri. İÜEFTDED 14.9–52.

CANBULAT, C. 1952. XVI. yüzyıla ait Türkçe bir Kur'an tercümesi. TD 14.85–6.

COŞAN, E. 1964. Behcetü'l-ḥadā'iḳ'in yeni bir nüshası. İlâhiyet Fakültesi Dergisi 12.159–61.

ÇAĞATAY, S. 1945. Altun Yaruk'dan iki parça. Ankara, AÜ.

——. 1947–48. Eski Osmanlıca'da fiil müştakları. AÜDTCFD 5.353–68, 525–52; 6.27–47.

ÇAĞATAY, S. 1951. Karaçayca bir kaç metin. AÜDTCFD 9.277–300.
——. 1953. Die Ädige-Sage. UAJb 25.243–82.
——. 1954. Türkçede *ñ* - *ġ* sesine dair. TDAYB 15–30.
——. 1957. Einige Ellipsen in Türk-Dialekten. UAJb 29.231–9.
——. 1958. Kazan lehçesinde *indi*. Jean Deny armağanı 71–5. Ankara, TDK.
——. 1960. Zur Wortgeschichte des Anatolisch-Türkischen. UAJb 32.78–87.
——. 1961a. Die Bezeichungen für Frau im Türkischen. UAJb 33.17–35.
——. 1961b. Kazakça metinler. Ankara, AÜ.
——. 1961c. Nogay atasözlerinden bir kaç örnek. TDAYB 47–51.
——. 1962a. Kazan lehçesinde bazı tekitler. Németh armağanı 103–10. Ankara, TDK.
——. 1962b. Türkçede 'kadın' için kullanılan sözler. TDAYB 13–49.
——. 1963a. Türk lehçeleri örnekleri. VIII. yüzyıldan XVIII. yüzyıla kadar yazı dili. Ankara, AÜ.
——. 1963b. Türkçede *ki* < *erki*. TDAYB 245–50.
——. 1964. Über die Bezeichnung der Frau im Türkischen. 2. UAJb 35.158–63.
——. 1965. Reşid Rahmeti Arat. 15.V.1900–29.XI.1964. Belleten 113.177–93.
——. 1966. Pekiştirilen fiiller. TDAYB 39–50.
ÇAĞDAŞ, K. 1954. Huent-Tsang biografisinin Uygurca tercümesinde geçen Sanskrit kelimelerin izahı. AÜDTCFD 12.127–32.
ÇAĞDAŞ, K., and N. M. ÇETİN. 1964. Ahmedî'nin 'Mirkatü'l edeb' i hakkında. TM 14.217–30.
DEMİRTAŞ, F. K. 1948a. XVII asır şairlerinden Edirneli Güftî ve 'Teşrîfât-üş-süerâ' sı.2.193–221.
——. 1948b. Harname. İÜEFTDED 3.369–87.
——. 1951. Fâtih devri şairlerinden Cemâli ve eserleri. İÜEFTDED 4.189–213.
DEMİRTAŞ, F. K. see also TİMURTAŞ, F. K.
DEVELLİOĞLU, F. 1959. Türk argosu. Ankara, TDK.
——. 1962. Osmanlıca-Türkçe ansiklopedik lûgat. Ankara.
Dil dâvası. 1952. Ankara, TDK.
Dil devrimi üzerine. 1967. Ankara, TDK.
DİLÂÇAR, A. 1948. Azerî Türkçesi. TDB Seri 3/12–13.57–80.
——. 1953a. Batı Türkçesi. TDAYB 73–92.
——. 1953b. Cumhuriyet devrinde harf devrimi hakkında yayımlanan eserlerden görebildiklerimiz. TD 23.736–7.
——. 1953c. Türkiye Türkçesi sözlüklerinden seçme eserler. TD 22.677–80.
——. 1954a. Lehçelerin yayılma tarzı ve Türk dil ve lehçelerinin tasnifi meselesi. TDAYB 39–58.
——. 1954b. Türk dili ve lehçelerinin yeni bir tasnifi. TD 28.182–5.
——. 1957. Türk lehçelerinin meydana gelişinde genel temayüllerin koyulaşması ve körlenmesi. TDAYB 83–93.
——. 1964. Türk diline genel bir bakış. Ankara, TDK.

Dilbilgisi sorunları. 1967. Ankara, TDK.
Dilbilim terimleri sözlüğü. 1949. Ankara, TDK.
DİLÇİN, D. 1946. Şeyyad Hamza. Yusuf ve Zeliha. Istanbul.
——. 1957. Arap alfabesine göre Divanü Lûgat-it-Türk dizini. Ankara, TDK.
DİLEMRE, S. A. 1952. Gramer dâvası ve 'linguistique statique'. TD 15.123–30.
——. 1953. Türkçenin tarihsel tabiatı. 'L'indo-touranien'. TDAYB 149–59.
DİZDAROĞLU, H. 1963. Türkçede fiiller. Ankara, TDK.
DOLU, H. C. 1952. 'Yûsuf hikâyesi' hakkında birkaç söz ve bazı Türkçe nüshalar. İÜEFTDED 4.419–45.
——. 1953. Sultan Hüseyin Baykara adına yazılmış Çağatayca manzum bir Yusuf hikâyesi. İÜEFTDED 5.51–8.
——. 1954. Dâstân-ı Varka ve Gülşâh'ın fiil çekimi. TDAYB 221–31.
DURAN, S. 1956. Türkçede cihet ve mekân gösteren ek ve sözler. TDAYB 1–110.
ECKMANN, J. 1948. Karamanlıca *-işin*-li gerundium hakkında. TDB Seri 3/12–13. 45–52.
——. 1950a. Anadolu Karamanlı ağızlarına ait araştırmalar. AÜDTCFD 8.165-200.
——. 1950b. Razgrad Türk ağzı. Türk dili ve tarihi hakkında araştırmalar 1.1–25. Ankara, TTK.
——. 1950c. Yunan harflı Karamanlı imlâsı hakkında. Türk dili ve tarihi hakkında araştırmalar 1.27–31. Ankara, TTK.
——. 1951–53. Kelime ortasındaki *b*, *p*, ve *m*-nin türemesi. TM 10.313–20.
——. 1953a. Karamanlı Türkçesinde *-maca* ekli fiil şekli. TDAYB 45–8.
——. 1953b. Türkçede *-raq*, *-rek* ekine dair. TDAYB 49–52.
——. 1954a. Bolmasa kelimesine dair. TDAYB 33–8.
——. 1954b. Terekeme ağzında *-mamaca* eki fiil şekline dair. Azerbaycan Yurtbilgisi 37.16–7.
——. 1955. Türkçede *D*, *T* ve *N* seslerinin türemesi. TDAYB 11–22.
——. 1956. Nehcü'l-feradis. 1. Tıpkıbasım. Ankara, TDK.
——. 1958a. Çağatay dili hakkında notlar. TDAYB 115–26.
——. 1958b. Einige gerundiale Konstruktionen im Karachanidischen. Jean Deny armağanı 77–83. Ankara, TDK.
——. 1959a. Ahmet Caferoğlu'nun eserleri. İÜEFTDED 9.1–18.
——. 1959b. Çağataycada yardımcı cümleler. TDAYB 27–58.
——. 1959c. Das Chwarezmtürkische. Philologiae Turcicae Fundamenta [1]. 113–37. Wiesbaden, Fr. Steiner.
——. 1959d. Das Tschagataische. Philologiae Turcicae Fundamenta [1].138–60. Wiesbaden, Fr. Steiner.
——. 1959e. Eine ostmitteltürkische interlineare Koranübersetzung. UAJb 31.72–85.
——. 1959–64. Çağatay dili örnekleri. 1–4. İÜEFTDED 9.33–64; 10.65–110; 12.157–74; 13.43–74.

ECKMANN, J. 1960a. Dinler (Makedonya) Türk ağzı. TDAYB 189–204.
——. 1960b. Küçük Çağatay grameri. İÜEFTDED 10.41–64.
——. 1960c. Mecdut Mansuroğlu (1910–1960). İÜEFTDED 10.5–16.
——. 1962a. Çağataycada isim-fiiller. TDAYB 51–60.
——. 1962b. Kumanova (Makedonya) Türk ağzı. Németh armağanı 111–44. Ankara, TDK.
——. 1963. Nehcü'l-feradis'in bilinmiyen bir yazması. TDAYB 157–9.
——. 1964. Memlûk Kıpçakçasının oğuzcalaşmasına dair. TDAYB 35–41.
ECKMANN, J., and M. MANSUROĞLU. 1959. 1959 yılı Trakya dialektoloji gezisi raporu. İÜEFTDED 9.113–18.
ELÇİN, S. 1966. Tuz-ekmek hakkı deyimi üzerine. Reşid Rahmeti Arat için 164–75. Ankara, TKAE.
ELGİN, N. 1964. Dâvûd-i Halvetî'nin 'Gülşen-i tevhid-i'. İÜEFTDED 13.91–8.
ELÖVE, A. U. 1953. 'Bıldır, bir yıldır' kelimeleri üzerine. TD 53.309–13.
——. 1956. Türkçede yumuşak ve kaba *L* konsonları. TD 56.484–89.
——. 1958a. Bir yazı meselesi üzerine. TDAYB 69–85.
——. 1958b. *Da/de* üzerine bazi düşünceler. TD 81.454–7.
——. 1961. Bir Uygurca yazı. TDAYB 311–17.
EMRE, A. C. 1945. Türk dilbilgisi. Istanbul, TDK.
——. 1946a. Türkçede bulanık *e/ė* fonemi. TDB Seri 3/6–7.487–97.
——. 1946b. Türkçede uzun vokaller (ünsüller). TDB Seri 3/10–11.1–5.
——. 1946c. Yakutça'da fonetik degişmeler. TDB Seri 3/8–9.1–12.
——. 1949. Türk lehçeleri mukayeseli grameri. 1. Fonetik. Istanbul, TDK.
——. 1955a. Türkçede cümle. 1. Ünlemden cümleye. TDAYB 105–80.
——. 1955b. Türkçede cümle. 2. İsim cümlesi. TDAYB 23–58.
——. 1960. Le problème de la parenté des langues turques et indo-européennes. Ankara.
EREM, T., and N. SEVİN. 1947. Milletlerarası fonetik işaretleriyle konuşma dilimiz. Istanbul.
EREN, H. 1946–51a. Etimoloji araştırmaları. TM 9.95–6.
——. 1946–51b. Türkçe qarman kelimesi hakkında. TM 9.97–8.
——. 1948. Sibirya Türk dillerinde Moğol unsurları. TDB Seri 3/12–13.35–43.
——. 1949. İkiz kelimelerin tarihi hakkında. AÜDTCFD 7.283–6.
——. 1950a. Çağatay lûgatleri hakkında notlar. AÜDTCFD 8.145–63.
——. 1950b. Dede Korkut kitabına ait notlar. *Pay dilemek, pay vermek.* Türk dili ve tarihi hakkında araştırmalar 1.33–7. Ankara, TTK.
——. 1950c. Türk yer adları hakkında araştırmalar. *Ören.* Türk dili ve tarihi hakkında araştırmalar 1.39–43. Ankara, TTK.
——. 1951–53. Onomatopée'lere ait notlar. TM 10.55–8.
——. 1952a. Etymologische Untersuchungen. 1–2. UAJb 24.132–3.
——. 1952b. Zurufe an Tiere bei den Türken. UAJb 24.134–7.
——. 1953a. Türk dillerinde metathèse. TDAYB 161–80.

EREN, H. 1953b. Türk *onomastique*'i hakkında. 60. doğum yılı münasebetiyle Fuad Köprülü armağanı 127–9. Istanbul, AÜ.

——. 1954. Etimoloji araştırmaları. TDAYB 31–2.

——. 1955. *Kimek* ve *İmek* boy adları hakkında. TD 45.541–3.

——. 1956. Türkçe *istabur* kelimesi üzerine. TDAYB 145–52.

——. 1958a. Türkçe *folluk* kelimesi üzerine. TDAYB 13–15.

——. 1958b. Türkçe *gök* kelimesinin türevleri. Jean Deny armağanı 85–9. Ankara, TDK.

——. 1959a. Türkçede *-MM-* > *-MB-* dissimilation'u. TDAYB 95–103.

——. 1959b. *Üveyik*. TDAYB 105.

——. 1960a. Anadolu ağızlarında Rumca, İslâvca ve Arapça kelimeler. TDAYB 295–371.

——. 1960b. Enigmes populaires turques de Chypre. AOH 11.104–14.

——. 1961. Anadolu'da Kafkasya Türkleri. TDAYB 319–57.

——. 1964. Kıbrıs'ta Türkler ve Türk dili. TDe 1.1–14.

——. 1965a. Türk yer adları. Sökü. TDAYB 149–53.

——. 1965b. Yer adlarımızın dili. TDAYB 155–65.

——. 1966. Osmanlı kanunnamelerinin dili üzerine. 1. *Gönül*. Reşid Rahmeti Arat için 172–5. Ankara, TKAE.

ERGİN, M. 1948. Câmi-ül-meâni'deki Türkçe şiirler. İÜEFTDED 3.539–69.

——. 1950. Bursa kitaplıklarındaki Türkçe yazmalar arasında. İÜEFTDED 4.107–32.

——. 1951. Kadı Burhaneddin divanı üzerinde bir gramer denemesi. İÜEFTDED 4.287–327.

——. 1954a. Dede Korkut kitabı hakkında. TD 29.267–9.

——. 1954b. Türkçe bir bütündür. TD 32.456–9.

——. 1958–63. Dede Korkut kitabı. 1–2. Ankara, TDK.

——. 1960–61. Türkoloji çalışmaları. 2. Tez çalışmaları. İÜEFTDED 10.133–60, 11.109–28.

——. 1961. R. Rahmati Arat'ın eserleri. İÜEFTDED 11.1–10.

——. 1962a. Osmanlıca dersleri. Istanbul, İÜ.

——. 1962b. Türk dil bilgisi. Istanbul, İÜ.

——. 1965. Reşid Rahmeti Arat. TK 27.143–58.

——. 1966. Reşid Rahmeti Arat. Reşid Rahmeti Arat için IX–XIV. Ankara, TKAE.

ERGİN, M., and A. TEMİR. 1966. Reşid Rahmeti Arat'ın eserleri. (1918–1965.) Reşid Rahmeti Arat için XV–XXXIII. Ankara, TKAE.

ERÖZ, M. 1966. Ege bölgesinde yer (köy ve şehir) adları. Reşid Rahmeti Arat için 176–88. Ankara, TKAE.

ERTAYLAN, İ. H. 1945a. Risâle-i Hüseyin Baykara. Istanbul, İÜ.

——. 1945b. Varaka ve Gülşah. İstanbul, İÜ.

——. 1946a. Divan-i Sultan Hüseyn Mirza Baykara 'Hüseyinî'. Istanbul, İÜ.

Ertaylan, İ. H. 1946b. Yeni ve değerli bir dil ve edebiyat belgesi. Tarikatname. İÜEFTDED 1.235–44.

——. 1948. VII.H./XIII.M. asra ait çok değerli bir Türk dili yadiğârı. Behcet ül-hadâik fi mev'izet ül-halâik. İÜEFTDED 3.275–93.

——. 1952. Ahmed-i Dâ'î. Hayatı ve eserleri. Istanbul, İÜ.

——. 1960a. Behcetü'l-hadayık. Istanbul, İÜ.

——. 1960b. Hatiboğlu. Bahrü'l-hakayık. Istanbul, İÜ.

——. 1960c. İâhi divanı. Istanbul, İÜ.

——. 1960d. Lûtfi divanı. Istanbul, İÜ.

——. 1960e. Tabiatname. Istanbul, İÜ.

——. 1960f. Tarih-i Edirne. Hikâyet-i Beşir Çelebi. Istanbul, İÜ.

——. 1960g. Tercüme-i kaside-i Bürde. Istanbul, İÜ.

——. 1960h. Yusuf ile Züleyha. Istanbul, İÜ.

——. 1961. Sinan Paşa. Maarifname. Istanbul, İÜ.

Esenkova, E. 1959. Türk dilinde Fransız tesiri. Istanbul.

Eyİce, S. 1964. İstanbul'un mahalle ve semt adları hakkında bir deneme. TM 14. 199–216.

Fuad Köprülü'nün ilmî neşriyatı. 1953. 60. doğum yılı münasebetiyle Fuad Köprülü armağanı XXV-L. Istanbul, AÜ.

Gatenby, E. V. 1954. Material for a study of Turkish words in English. AÜDTCFD 12.85–144.

Gencan, T. N. 1954. Sıfat birlikleri. TDAYB 181–7.

——. 1966. Dilbilgisi. Istanbul, TDK.

Genceî, T. 1948. Tebrizli Te'sir'in Türkçe şiirleri. İÜEFTDED 3.116–28.

Göğüş, B. 1962. Türkçede bileşik kelimelerin oluşumu ve nasıl yazılması gerektiği. TDAYB 245–64.

Gökberg, M. 1960. Die Entwicklung des Türkischen im Rahmen der türkischen Kulturgeschichte. Felsefe Arkivi 5.7–18.

Hacıemİnoğlu, M. N. 1961–62–64. Sa'lebi'nin Kısasu'l-enbiyâ'sının tercümesi üzerinde bir gramer denemesi. İÜEFTDED 11.47–66; 12.185–204; 13.99–122.

Halası-Kun, T. 1947–49. Philologica. 1–3. AÜDTCFD 5.1–37; 7.415–65, 603–44.

——. 1950a. Avrupa'daki Osmanlı yer adları üzerine araştırmalar. Peşte, ازژدرهس Türk dili ve tarihi hakkında araştırmalar 1.63–104. Ankara, TTK.

——. 1950b. Orta-Kıpçakça *q-*, *k-* > *0* meselesi. Türk dili ve tarihi hakkında araştırmalar 1.45–61. Ankara, TTK.

Hatİboğlu, V. 1963. Kelime grupları ve kuralları. TDAYB 203–44.

——. 1964. Türk dilinin imlâsı. TDe 1.51–69.

Heuser, Fr. 1962. Heuser-Şevket. Türkish-Deutsches Wörterbuch. 5. verbesserte Auflage. Wiesbaden, O. Harrassowitz.

Hony, H. C., and F. İz. 1946. A Turkish-English dictionary. Oxford, University Press.

İnalcık, H. 1954. Fatih devri üzerinde tetkikler ve vesikalar. 1. Ankara, TTK.

İNALCIK, H. see Anhegger, R.

İNAN, A. 1946a. Çağatay yazı dilinin kuruluşu tarihine dair düşünceler. TDB Seri 3/6–7.531–43.

——. 1946b. *Isırğa- sırğa* sözünün etimolojisi. TDB Seri 3/13–15.

——. 1946–51. Güvey. TM 9.139–44.

——. 1948. Dilin özleşmesi. TDB Seri 3/12–13.7–10.

——. 1950. Kutup'un Husrev ve Şirin'inden örnekler. TDB Seri 3/14–15.5–28.

——. 1952a. Eski Kuran tercümelerinin dili meselesi. TD 7.19–22; 9.14–16.

——. 1952b. Eski Türkçe üç Kur'an tercümesi. TD 6.12–15.

——. 1953a. Fatih devrinde Türkçe. TD 20.506–9.

——. 1953b. XIII-XV. yüzyıllarda Mısır'da Oğuz-Türkmen ve Kıpçak lehçeleri ve 'Halis Türkçe'. TDAYB 53–71.

——. 1956a. Karışık lehçelerle yazılan Türkçe eserler. TD 53.273–5.

——. 1956b. Türk etnolojisini ilgilendiren birkaç terim-kelime üzerine. TDAYB 179–95.

——. 1957. Ebülgazi Bahadır Han ve Türkçesi. TDAYB 29–39.

——. 1958a. *Börü = kurt* ve *yok = hayır* kelimeleri üzerine. TD 84.606–8.

——. 1958b. İslâmdan sonra Türkçe adlar. TD 82.491–4.

——. 1958c. Kayıtbay'ın Türkçe duaları. Jean Deny armağanı 91–4. Ankara, TDK.

——. 1958d. *Tarla* ve *darı* kelimeleri üzerine. TD 86.102–3.

——. 1960. Kur'an'in Eski Türkçe ve Oğuz-Osmanlıca çevrileri üzerine notlar. TDAYB 79–94.

——. 1962. Şeybanlı Özbekler çağına ait bir Çağatayca Kuran tefsiri. TDAYB 61–6.

——. 1964a. Kazak ve Kırgız yazı dillerindeki dudak benzeşmesi meselesi. TDAYB 67–76.

——. 1964b. *Yasa, töre ~ türe* ve *şeriat*. TKA 1.104–10.

——. 1967. Türk yazı dili tarihinden notlar. TK 57.653–9.

İZ, F. 1964a. Eski Türk edebiyatında nesir. Istanbul, İÜ.

——. 1964b. Makale-i Zindancı Mahmud Kapudan. TM 14.111–50.

——. 1966. Eski Türk edebiyatında nazım. Istanbul, İÜ.

İZ, F., and H.C. HONY. 1952. An English-Turkish dictionary. Oxford, The Clarendon Press.

KAFESOĞLU, İ. 1958. Türkmen adı manası ve mahiyeti. Jean Deny armağanı 121–33. Ankara, TDK.

——. 1966. Tarihte 'Türk' adı. Reşid Rahmeti Arat için, 306–19. Ankara, TKAE.

KAHANE, H. and R., and A. TIETZE. 1959. The lingua franca in the Levant. Turkish nautical terms of Italian and Greek origin. Urbana, University of Illinois Press.

KARAHAN, A. 1948. XVI. asır divan şairlerinden Figanî ve şiirleri. İÜEFTDED 3.389–410.

KARAHAN, A. 1952–53. Tercüme edebiyatından nümûneler üzerinde çalışmalar. İÜEFTDED 4.345–71, 5.59–84.

——. 1953. Hakânî'nin Kırk hadîs tercümesi. TD 16.199–203.

——. 1966. Kanunî Sultan Süleyman çağı şairlerinden Figanî ve divançesi. Istanbul, İÜ.

KARAMANLIOĞLU, A. F. 1962. Kıpçaklar ve Kıpçak Türkçesi. İÜEFTDED 12.175–84.

——. 1966. '*Silik*' sözü üzerine. Reşid Rahmeti Arat için 320–2. Ankara, TKAE.

KILIÇOĞLU, V. 1953a. '*-dir*' eki meselesi. TD 24.802–4.

——. 1953b. Türk gramerinde yeni araştırmalar. TD 18.372–8; 22.655–62.

——. 1953c. Türk gramerinde yeni araştırmalar. TDAYB 181–96.

——. 1954a. Dilimizin bir meselesi. (Birleşik kelimelerde hece tasarrufu) TD 36. 715–9.

——. 1954b. Gerundiumların özellikleri ve '*-iser*' eki. TD 33.510–8.

——. 1954c. Şart kipi. TD 29.254–8.

——. 1956. Cerrahiye-i ilhaniye. Ankara, AÜ.

KIRZIOĞLU, M. F. 1962. Lehce-i Erzurum yazmasındaki halk sözleri. TDAYB 195–244.

KORKMAZ, Z. 1953. Batı Anadolu ağızlarında asli vokal uzunlukları hakkında. TDAYB 197–203.

——. 1956. Güneybatı Anadolu ağızları. Ses bilgisi. (Fonetik.) Ankara, AÜ.

——. 1958a. Türk dilinde *-ça* eki ve bu ek ile yapılan isim teşkilleri üzerine bir deneme. TDAYB 41–68.

——. 1958b. İzmir kitaplıklarında Eski-Anadolu Türkçesine ait birkaç değerli yazma. Türk Kütüphaneciler Derneği Bülteni 8.40–51.

——. 1959a. Türkçede *-acak/-ecek* gelecek zaman (futurum) ekinin yapısı üzerine. AÜDTCFD 17.159–68.

——. 1959b. Türkiye Türkçesinde 'iktidar' ve 'imkân' gösteren yardımcı fiiller ve gelişmeleri. TDAYB 107–24.

——. 1960a. Türk dilinde *+ça* eki ve bu ek ile yapılan isim teşkilleri üzerine bir deneme. AÜDTCFD 17.275–358.

——. 1960b. Türkçede ek yığılması olaylarının meydana gelişi üzerine. TDAYB 173–80.

——. 1961a. Türkçede *ok/ök* kuvvetlendirme (intensivum) edatı üzerine. TDAYB 13–29.

——. 1961b. *uçun* ~ *üçün* ~ *için* v.b. çekim edatlarının yapısı üzerine. TDAYB 31–5.

——. 1961c. Zur Ableitung der türkischen Postposition *uçun* ~ *üçün* ~ *için* usw. UAJb 33.98–100.

——. 1962. Türkçede eklerin kullanılış şekilleri ve ek kalıplaşma olayları. Ankara, AÜ.

——. 1963a. Nevşehir ve yöresi ağızları. 1. Ses bilgisi. Ankara, AÜ.

Korkmaz, Z. 1963b. Türk dilinin tarihi akışı içinde Atatürk ve dil devrimi. Ankara, AÜ.

——. 1964a. Bartın ve yöresi ağızları üzerine. TDe 1.103–41.

——. 1964b. Eski Anadolu Türkçesi'ndeki *-van/-ven, -vuz/-vüz* kişi ve bildirme eklerinin Anadolu ağızlarındaki kalıntıları. TDAYB 43–65.

——. 1965a. Bartın ve yöresi ağızlarındaki lehçe tabakalaşması. TDe 2.227–49.

——. 1965b. Türkiye Türkçesindeki *-madan/-meden* < *-madın/-medin* zarf-fiil (gerundium) ekinin yapısı üzerine. TDe 2.259–69.

——. 1966a. Ḳābūs-nāme ve Marzuban-nāme çevirileri kimindir? TDAYB 267–78.

——. 1966b. Türkçedeki *-arak/-erek* zarf-fiil (gerundium) ekinin yapısı üzerine. Reşid Rahmeti Arat için 331–5. Ankara, TKAE.

——. 1967a. 15 inci yüzyıldan çeviriler (Mercimek Ahmed'in Ḳābūs-nāme çevirisinin ikinci basılışı dolayısiyle). TD 188.664–7.

——. 1967b. Türkçede *-ᵒl* eki (*al/el, ıl/il, ul/ül; sal/sel*). TD 181.24–32; 187.514–9; 188.635–42.

Korkmaz, Z., and S. Olcay. 1956. Fuzulî'nin dili hakkında notlar. Ankara, AÜ.

Koşay, H. Z. 1953. Kara Kırgızlarda ehli hayvanlar ile ilgili kelimeler. 60. doğum yılı münasebetiyle Fuad Köprülü armağanı 127–9. Istanbul, AÜ.

——. 1957. Dil mukayeselerine göre Basklarla Türklerin temasları, göç yolları ve zamanı hakkında. Belleten 84.521–60.

——. 1959. Bask dili ve Türkçe arasındaki münasebetlere dâir yeni deliller. Belleten 92.541–3.

——. 1962. Türkiye halk dilindeki yemek adları. Németh armağanı 289–317. Ankara, TDK.

Koşay, H. Z., and O. Aydın, 1952. Anadilden derlemeler. 2. Ankara.

Kutluk, İ. 1947. Kültür ve dil tarihimizin yeni vesikası. Attar'ın Esrarnâme tercümeleri. İÜEFTDED 2.125–32.

Levend, A. S. 1948. Atayi'nin Hilye-tül-efkâr'ı. Ankara.

——. 1952a. Bilinmiyen eski eserlerimizden: Ahmed Rıdvan'ın Leylâ ve Mecnun'u. TD 7.13–18.

——. 1952b. Bilinmiyen eski eserlerimizden: Halife'nin Leylâ ve Mecnun'u. TD 8.7–11.

——. 1952c. Eski edebiyatımızın dili. TD 11.609–11.

——. 1952d. Kadimi'nin Leylâ ve Mecnunu. TD 9.21–6.

——. 1952e. Larendeli Hamdi'nin Leylâ ve Mecnun'u. TD 13.12–17.

——. 1953. ʿAşıḳ Paşa'nın bilinmiyen iki mesnevisi. Faḳrnāme ve Vasf-i ḥāl. TDAYB 205–55.

——. 1954. ʿĀşıḳ Paşa'nın bilinmiyen iki mesnevisi daha. Hikâye ve kimya risalesi. TDAYB 265–76.

——. 1955a. ʿĀşıḳ Paşa'ya atfedilen iki risale. TDAYB 153–63.

——. 1955b. Feyżī'nin bilinmiyen Ḫamse'si. TDAYB 143–52.

LEVEND, A. S. 1956a. Ġazavāt-nāmeler ve Mihaloğlu Ali Bey'in Ġazavāt-nāmesi. Ankara, TTK.

——. 1956b. Nevā'ī'nin Arapça sözlüğü. TDAYB 239–45.

——. 1957a. Gülşehrī. Manṭıḳu'-ṭ-ṭayr. Ankara, TDK.

——. 1957b. Nevai'ye atfedilen bir eser: Muamma-yi esma-i hüsna. TDAYB 189–93.

——. 1958a. Nevā'ī adına basılmış bir eser. Jean Deny armağanı 163–9. Ankara, TDK.

——. 1958b. Nevā'ī'ye atfedilen Esmā-i ḥüsnā. TDAYB 211–15.

——. 1958c. Türkiye kitaplıklarındaki Nevai yazmaları. TDAYB 127–209.

——. 1959. Attar ile Tutmacı'nın Gül ü Husrev mesnevileri. TDAYB 161–203.

——. 1960a. Tutmacı'nın Gül ü Husrev mesnevisinde dil özellikleri. TDAYB 49–77.

——. 1960b. Türk dilinde gelişme ve sadeleşme evreleri. Ankara, TDK.

——. 1961a. Tarih boyunca Türk dili. Ankara.

——. 1961b. Türk edebiyatında manzum atasözleri ve deyimler. TDAYB 137–46.

——. 1962. Siyaset-nameler. TDAYB 167–94.

——. 1964. Lâmiî'nin Ferhad ü Şirin'i. TDAYB 85–112.

——. 1965a. Celili'nin Husrev-ü Şirin'i. TDAYB 103–27.

——. 1965b. Tarih boyunca Türk dili. TDAYB 129–47.

——. 1965–67. Ali Şir Nevaî. 1–4. Ankara, TDK.

——. 1966. Ahmet Rızvan'ın Hüsrev ü Şirin'i. TDAYB 215–58.

MANSUROĞLU, M. 1945. En eski Anadolu Türkçesine ait bazı metinler. İstanbul Dergisi 39.4–5.

——. 1946a. Anadoluda Türk dili ve edebiyatının ilk mahsulleri. İÜEFTDED 1.9–17.

——. 1946b. Anadolu Türkçesi (XIII. yüzyıl). Şeyyad Hamza'nın Doğu Türkçesi ile karışık bir manzumesi. TDB Seri 3/8–9.16–29.

——. 1946c. Anadolu Türkçesi (XIII. asır). Şeyyat Hamzaya ait üç manzume. İÜEFTDED 1.180–95.

——. 1947. Anadolu Türkçesi (XIII. asir). Dehhanî ve manzumeleri. Istanbul, İÜ.

——. 1948. Türkçede zamir çekimi. İÜEFTDED 3.501–18.

——. 1951. Anadolu'da Türk yazı dilinin başlama ve gelişmesi. İÜEFTDED 4.216–29.

——. 1951–53. Türkçede *-gu* ekinin fonksionları. TM 10.341–8.

——. 1952. Calāladdīn Rūmī's türkische Verse. UAJb 24.106–26.

——. 1953. Türkçede *-mış* ekinin fonksionları. 60. doğum yılı münasebetiyle Fuad Köprülü armağanı 345–50. Istanbul, AÜ.

——. 1954a. Drei Gedichte Şayyād Ḥamza's. UAJb 26.78–89.

——. 1954b. Mevlâna Celâleddin Rumî'de Türkçe beyit ve ibareler. TDAYB 207–20.

——. 1954c. Réformes et débats linguistiques en Turquie. Orbis 3.395–9.

MANSUROĞLU, M. 1954d. The rise and development of written Turkish in Anatolia. Oriens 7.250–64,

——. 1955a. On some titles and names in Old Anatolian Turkish. UAJb 27.94–102.

——. 1955b. Türkçede cümle çeşitleri ve bağlayıcıları. TDAYB 59–71.

——. 1956a. Ahmet Fakih. Çarhnâme. Istanbul, İÜ.

——. 1956b. Şeyyad Hamza'nın Doğu Türkçesine yaklaşan manzumesi. TDAYB 125–44.

——. 1956c. Şeyyad Hamza'nın üç manzumesinin tıpkı basımı. İÜEFTDED 7.108–14.

——. 1956d. Türkçede *-taçı* ekinin fonksionları. İÜEFTDED 7.105–8.

——. 1957a. Das geschlossene *e* im karachanidischen Türkisch. UAJb 29.215–23.

——. 1957b. Şeyyad Hamza'nın beş manzumesi. Oriens 10.48–70.

——. 1958a. Sultan Veled'in Türkçe manzumeleri. Istanbul, İÜ.

——. 1958b. Türkçede *-gay*/*-gey* eki ve türemeleri. Jean Deny armağanı 171–83. Ankara, TDK.

——. 1958c. Türkiye Türkçesinde birleşim ve yazılışları üzerinde. TDAYB 28–43.

——. 1959a. Das Altosmanische. Philologiae Turcicae Fundamenta. [1.] 161–82. Wiesbaden, Fr. Steiner.

——. 1959b. Das Karakhanidische. Philologiae Turcicae Fundamenta [1.] 87–112. Wiesbaden, Fr. Steiner.

——. 1959c. Türkiye Türkçesinde ses uyumu. TDAYB 81–93.

——. 1960a. Edirne ağzında yapı, anlam, deyim ve söz dizimi özellikleri. TDAYB 181–7.

——. 1960b. Türkiye Türkçesinde söz yapımı üzerinde notlar. İÜEFTDED 10. 5–24.

——. 1962. In connexion with the language of the *Sarḥu'l-Manār*, an Old Anatolian Turkish manuscript. Oriens 15.315–24.

MANSUROĞLU, M. see Eckmann, J.

MAZIOĞLU, H. 1964. Geçmişin Türkçesinden örnekler. TD 145.25–30.

OLCAY, S. 1961. Yarkent ağzından örnekler. AÜDTCFD 19.31–65.

——. 1965. Ebu'l-Leyṣ Semerḳandī. Tezkiretü'l-Evliya (tercümesi). İnceleme-metin-indeks. Ankara, AÜ.

OLCAY, S. see Korkmaz, Z.

ONAN, N.H. 1949. Şeyyad Hamza'nın iki yeni gazeli dolayısiyle. AÜDTCFD 7.529–34.

ONAT, N.H. 1944–51. Arapçanın Türk diliyle kuruluşu. 1–2. Istanbul, TDK.

——. 1946–48. Türkçeden Arap diline geçmiş din ve kültür kelimelerinden. TDB Seri 3/6–7.488–529; 12–13.I–XIV.

——. 1953. '*Yavuz*' ve bununla ilgili bazı kelimelerimizin Arap diline geçmiş şekilleri. TDAYB 123–48.

ONAY, T. 1946. Dastan-ı Ahmet Harami. Istanbul, TDK.

Onbirinci [XI] Dil Kurultayına sunulan Türk Dil Kurumu çalışmaları. 1932–1966. Ankara, TDK.

Onüçüncü [XIII] yüzyıldan beri Türkiye Türkçesiyle yazılmış kitaplardan toplanan tanıklariyle tarama sözlüğü, 1–3. 1963–1967. Ankara, TDK.

ORKUN, H. N. 1948. Kara-yüs yazıtının yeni çözümü. TDB Seri 3/12–13.53–5.

ÖNDER, A. R. 1958. İç Anadolu ağzı. 278–82.

ÖNEN, Y. 1955. Deutsches im Türkischen. Studien zu Fragen der Sprachberührung. Ankara, AÜ.

ÖNERTOY, O. 1964. D.T.C.F. Türk Dili ve Edebiyatı Bölümü çalışmaları. TDe 1.149–64.

ÖZDARENDELİ, M. N. 1954. Türkçede uzun ünlüler. TD 54.348–54.

ÖZERDİM, S. N. 1950. F. Köprülü'nün yazıları. 1908–1950. Türk dili ve tarihi hakkında araştırmalar 1.159–248. Ankara, TTK.

ÖZERGİN, M. K. 1960. Ahmed Paşa'nın tarih manzumeleri (855–896/1451–1491). İÜEFTDED 10.161–84.

ÖZÖN, M. N. 1965. Büyük Osmanlıca-Türkçe sözlük. Istanbul, İnkılâp ve Aka Kitapevleri.

PEKOLCAY, N. 1954a. Ahmed'in *Mevlid* isimli eseri. İÜEFTDED 6.65–70.

——. 1954b. Süleyman Çelebi'nin mevlidi metni ve menşei meselesi. İÜEFTDED 6.39–64.

RÁSONYİ, L. 1963. Türklükte kadın adları. TDAYB 63–87.

——. 1964. Türk özel adlarının kaynakları. TDe 1.71–101.

——. 1966. Macarca 'gyermek' kelimesi ve 'ermyak' adı. Reşid Rahmeti Arat için 382–7. Ankara, TKAE.

ŞEHSÜVAROĞLU, B. N. 1964. Esref bin Muhammed. Hazâ'inü'-saâʿdât. 1460 (H. 864). Ankara, TTK.

SILACI, E. 1967. Redhouse' in hayatı ve eserleri. Yeni Ufuklar 67.214-17.

TANERİNG, O. see Caferoğlu, A.

TANSU, M. 1963. Durgun genel ses bilgisi ve Türkçe. Ankara, TDK.

TARLAN, A. 1948-51. Fuzulî'nin bilinmiyen kasideleri. İÜEFTDED 3.193–209, 411–27; 4.257–64.

TAYMAS, A. B. 1954. Kırımlı filolog-şair Bekir Çobanzade'yi tanıtma tecrübesi. TDAYB 233–63.

——. 1955. Seyf Sarayî'nin Gülistan tercümesini gözden geçiriş. TDAYB 73–98.

TAYMAS, A. [B.], and H. EREN. 1950. İbn Mühenna lûgati hakkında. Türk dili ve tarihi hakkında araştırmalar 1.127–58. Ankara, TTK.

TEKİN, ŞİNASİ 1958. Palatogramme türkischer Laute. ZPhon 11.198–205.

——. 1959. Altun Yaruk'un Çincesinin Almancaya tercümesi dolayısiyle. TDAYB 293–306.

——. 1960. Kuanşi im pusar. (Ses işiten ilâh). Ankara, Atatürk Üniversitesi Erzurum.

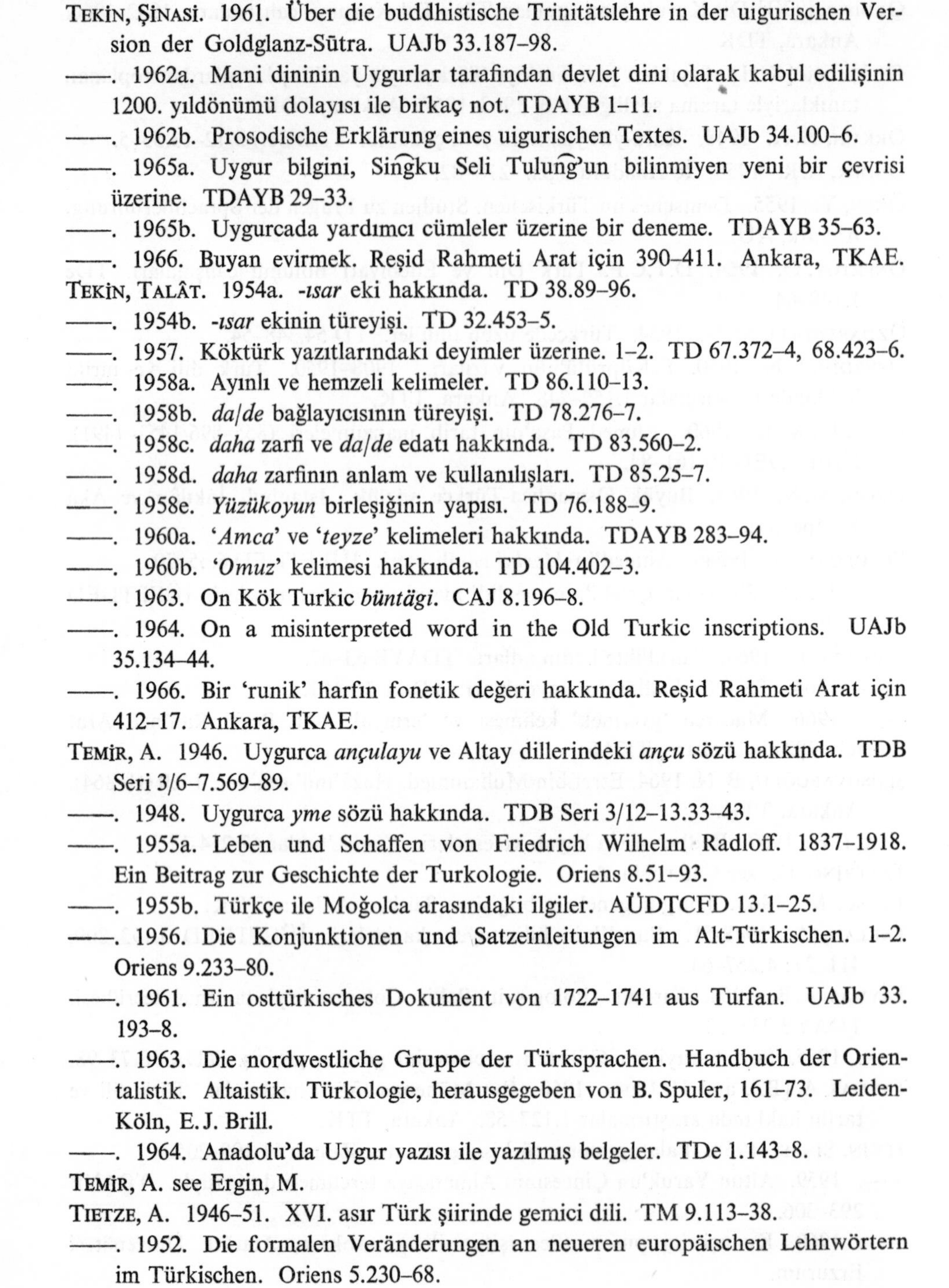

Tekin, Şinasi. 1961. Über die buddhistische Trinitätslehre in der uigurischen Version der Goldglanz-Sūtra. UAJb 33.187–98.

——. 1962a. Mani dininin Uygurlar tarafından devlet dini olarak kabul edilişinin 1200. yıldönümü dolayısı ile birkaç not. TDAYB 1–11.

——. 1962b. Prosodische Erklärung eines uigurischen Textes. UAJb 34.100–6.

——. 1965a. Uygur bilgini, Singku Seli Tulung'un bilinmiyen yeni bir çevrisi üzerine. TDAYB 29–33.

——. 1965b. Uygurcada yardımcı cümleler üzerine bir deneme. TDAYB 35–63.

——. 1966. Buyan evirmek. Reşid Rahmeti Arat için 390–411. Ankara, TKAE.

Tekin, Talât. 1954a. *-ısar* eki hakkında. TD 38.89–96.

——. 1954b. *-ısar* ekinin türeyişi. TD 32.453–5.

——. 1957. Köktürk yazıtlarındaki deyimler üzerine. 1–2. TD 67.372–4, 68.423–6.

——. 1958a. Ayınlı ve hemzeli kelimeler. TD 86.110–13.

——. 1958b. *da/de* bağlayıcısının türeyişi. TD 78.276–7.

——. 1958c. *daha* zarfı ve *da/de* edatı hakkında. TD 83.560–2.

——. 1958d. *daha* zarfının anlam ve kullanılışları. TD 85.25–7.

——. 1958e. *Yüzükoyun* birleşiğinin yapısı. TD 76.188–9.

——. 1960a. '*Amca*' ve '*teyze*' kelimeleri hakkında. TDAYB 283–94.

——. 1960b. '*Omuz*' kelimesi hakkında. TD 104.402–3.

——. 1963. On Kök Turkic *büntägi*. CAJ 8.196–8.

——. 1964. On a misinterpreted word in the Old Turkic inscriptions. UAJb 35.134–44.

——. 1966. Bir 'runik' harfın fonetik değeri hakkında. Reşid Rahmeti Arat için 412–17. Ankara, TKAE.

Temir, A. 1946. Uygurca *ançulayu* ve Altay dillerindeki *ançu* sözü hakkında. TDB Seri 3/6–7.569–89.

——. 1948. Uygurca *yme* sözü hakkında. TDB Seri 3/12–13.33–43.

——. 1955a. Leben und Schaffen von Friedrich Wilhelm Radloff. 1837–1918. Ein Beitrag zur Geschichte der Turkologie. Oriens 8.51–93.

——. 1955b. Türkçe ile Moğolca arasındaki ilgiler. AÜDTCFD 13.1–25.

——. 1956. Die Konjunktionen und Satzeinleitungen im Alt-Türkischen. 1–2. Oriens 9.233–80.

——. 1961. Ein osttürkisches Dokument von 1722–1741 aus Turfan. UAJb 33. 193–8.

——. 1963. Die nordwestliche Gruppe der Türksprachen. Handbuch der Orientalistik. Altaistik. Türkologie, herausgegeben von B. Spuler, 161–73. Leiden-Köln, E. J. Brill.

——. 1964. Anadolu'da Uygur yazısı ile yazılmış belgeler. TDe 1.143–8.

Temir, A. see Ergin, M.

Tietze, A. 1946–51. XVI. asır Türk şiirinde gemici dili. TM 9.113–38.

——. 1952. Die formalen Veränderungen an neueren europäischen Lehnwörtern im Türkischen. Oriens 5.230–68.

TIETZE, A. 1953a. Die Wiederholung mit verändertem Wortbeginn im Türkischen. UAJb 25.92–108.
——. 1953b. XVI. asır Türk şiirinde gemici dili. Nigârî, Kâtibî, Yetîm. 60. doğum yılı münasebetiyle Fuad Köprülü armağanı, 501–22. Istanbul, AÜ.
——. 1955. Griechische Lehnwörter im anatolischen Türkisch. Oriens 8.204–57.
——. 1957. Slavische Lehnwörter in der türkischen Volkssprache. Oriens 10.1–47.
——. 1958a. Der freistehende Genitiv im Türkei-Türkischen. UAJb 30.183–94.
——. 1958b. Direkte arabische Entlehnungen im anatolischen Türkisch. Jean Deny armağanı 255–333. Ankara, TDK.
——. 1959. Die Eingliederung der wörtlichen Rede im Türkischen. WZKM 55. 89–121.
TIETZE, A. see Kahane, H. & R.
TİMURTAŞ, F.K. 1958. Şeyhî'nin 'Husrev ü Şirin'i. Jean Deny armağanı 335–48. Ankara, TDK.
——. 1960–61. Şeyhî ve çağdaşlarının eserleri üzerinde gramer araştırmaları. [1.–] 2. TDAYB 95–144, 53–136.
——. 1961. Şeyhî'nin eserleri. İÜEFTDED 11.99–108.
——. 1962a. Bâkî'nin Kanunî Mersiyesi'nin dil bakımından izahı. İÜEFTDED 12.219–32.
——. 1962b. Osmanlıca. 1. Eskiyazı, gramer, metinler. Istanbul, İÜ.
——. 1963. Şeyhî'nin Husrev ü Şirin'i. Istanbul, İÜ.
——. 1964a. Osmanlıca grameri. Eski yazı ve imlâ – Arapça – Farsça – Eski Anadolu Türkçesi – Aruz. Istanbul, İÜ.
——. 1964b. Şeyhî'nin Harnâme'si üzerinde dil araştırmaları. TKA 1.254–81.
TOĞAN, Z.V. 1964. Zimahşeri'nin Doğu Türkçesi ile 'Mukaddimetü'l-edeb'i. TM 14.81–92.
TUNA, O.N. 1948–50. Türkçede tekrarlar. İÜEFTDED 3.129–447, 4.35–82.
——. 1957. Bazı imlâ gelenekleri, bunların metin incelemelerindeki önemi ve Orhon yazıtların'da birkaç açıklama. TDAYB 41–81.
——. 1960. Köktürk yazılı belgelerinde ve Uygurcada uzun vokaller. TDAYB 213–82.
——. 1961. Kelimeler arasında. 1–4. TD 112.212–4, 114.398–401, 116.547–50, 117. 642–4.
TURAN, Ş. 1954–57. İbn Kemal. Tevârih-i Âl-i Osman. VII. Defter. [1–2]. Ankara, TTK.
Türk Dil Kurumu yayınları. 1933–67. 1967. Ankara, TDK.
Türk Dil Kurumu çalışmaları, XI Dil Kurultayına sunulan, 1932–1966. Ankara, TDK.
Türk dili için. 1–5. 1966–67. Ankara, TKAE.
Türk diyelekleri çevriyazı sistemi. 1945. Istanbul, TDK.
Türk Tarih Kurumu yayınları. 1933–1967. 1967. Ankara, TTK.
Türkiye Türkçesi tarihî sözlüğü hazırlıklarından. XIII. yüzyıldan günümüze kadar

kitaplardan toplanmış tanıklariyle tarama sözlüğü. 1–4. 1943–57. Istanbul-Ankara, TDK.
Türkiye Türçesiyle yazılmış kitaplardan toplanan tanıklariyle tarama sözlüğü, XIII yüzyıldan beri 1–3. 1963–67. Ankara, TDK.
Türkiyede halk ağzından söz derleme dergisi. 1–6. 1939–57. Istanbul-Ankara, TDK.
Türkiye'de halk ağzından derleme sözlüğü. 1–3. 1963–1967. Ankara, TDK.
Türkoloji çalışmalarına toplu bir bakış ve ödevlerimiz. 1960. TDAYB 1–21.
UNAT, F. R., and M. KÖYMEN. 1949–57. Mehmed Neşrî. Kitab-i Cihan-numâ. (Neşrî tarihi). 1–2. Ankara, TTK.
UYGUN, R. 1960. Kırım-Türk yazı dilinin tarihçesi. TDAYB 373–9.
UZLUK, F. N. 1954. Seyf-i Serâyi. Gülistan tercümesi. Ankara, TDK.
——. 1961. XIV. yüzyıl mevlevi şairlerinden Eflâkî Dede'nin 600. ölüm yıldönümü dolayısiyle Ahmet Eflâkî Dede. TDAYB 275–304.
——. 1962. Karaman-oğulları hakkında iki ağıt. TDAYB 67–99.
——. 1963. Taş yazıtlarda Türkçe vakfiyeler, Arapça yazıtlarda Türkçe söz ve şiirler. TDAYB 251–67.
ÜÇOK, N. 1947. Genel dilbilim. Ankara, AÜ.
——. 1951. Fonemlerin özellikleri üzerine bir deneme. AÜDTCFD 9.363–80.
ÜLKÜTAŞIR, M. Ş. 1946. Büyük Türk dilcisi Kâşgarlı Mahmut. Istanbul, TDK.
——. 1948. XI. yüzyıldan günümüze kadar yazılmış başlıca sözlüklerimiz. TDB Seri 3/12–13.45–55.
——. 1965. Besim Atalay (1882–27. XI. 1965). TK 38.194–5.
[ÜNSEL], K. E. 1945. Urfa ağzı. Istanbul, TDK.
Yeni imlâ kılavuzu. 1967. Ankara, TDK.
Yeni Redhouse lûgati. İngilizce-Türkçe. 1958. Istanbul.
YEŞİLOĞLU, A. 1958. Ankara Üniversitesi Dil ve Tarih-Coğrafya Fakültesi yayınları bibliyografyası. 1935–1956. Ankara, AÜ.
YÜKSEL, S. 1965. Mehmed. Işk-nâme. Ankara, AÜ.

IRANO-ALTAISTICA: TURKISH AND MONGOLIAN LANGUAGES OF PERSIA AND AFGHANISTAN*

GERHARD DOERFER

Persia and Afghanistan, at least since the period of the Mongol Empire (thirteenth century), are among the countries with the most variegated mixtures of languages; in this respect they resemble the Caucasus region. Since many smaller tribes (language communities) live in barely accessible deserts or mountainous regions, the exploration of these languages offers exceptional difficulties. Furthermore, since the Iranian nations (especially the Persians, less so the Afghans) lived for many centuries under Altaic (Turkish or Mongol) domination, too intensive a preoccupation with the languages of their former dominators does not always seem very desirable to them. From these facts special linguistic problems arise.

As to the distribution of Altaic nations in the area, please see pp. 179–82 of this book (Krueger); it is dealt with, above all, in the articles (and the maps subjoined to these articles) of Jarring 1939, Ligeti 1954a, Schurmann 1962 (Afghanistan), and Field 1939, Mason 1945, Menges 1951, Monteil 1956 and 1966, Caferoğlu and Doerfer 1959, Bazin 1959, Ivanov 1961, Oberling 1964 (Persia). A *Linguistic atlas of Persia* is being prepared by G. Redard (University of Bern). Indications as to the ethnic composition of the towns and villages of Persia are to be found in Razm-Ārā 1949 sqq.; based upon this information, a very precise ethnic map would be feasible. On the whole, the Altaic-speaking nations live in the northern parts of the area.

In the following chapters, I will give a survey of the exploration of Altaic languages in the area settled and dominated by Iranian (Perso-Tajik and Afghan) nations, beginning with Persia.

1. AZERBAIJANI

Of the Turkish languages of Persia, Azerbaijani is the most important numerically. Foy (1903–04) may be regarded as the proper founder of Irano-Azerbaijanistics

* I prepared this article with the aid of a grant as an Asian Studies Research Fellow, when in Bloomington, Indiana (Department of Uralic and Altaic Studies), in 1966 and 1967. For this favor I owe my special thanks. I am grateful, furthermore, to Professor Yar-Shater (Columbia University, New York), Professor M. Š. Širəlijev (Akademija Nauk Azerbajdžanskoj SSR, Institut literatury i jazykoznanija), and Dr. W. Brands (Fulda) for kind information, to Dr. Abbas Zaryab (Library of the Senate, Teheran), and to the Faculty of Letters of Tebriz for kindly placing at my disposal books not obtainable outside Persia.

(though there do exist some rather inadequate studies by Radloff, Vámbéry, and others). One may affirm that Turcology, until today, has not gone very far beyond his discoveries. Scholarly production in this field after the Second World War has been very scarce. There exist some moderately extensive articles. Monteil 1956 offers some texts (8–43), a glossary (44–70), and a list of some verbal forms (71–7); on the whole, this is not a bad work. It is based on materials gathered in Zendjân (300 km NW of Teheran), February 1950 till May 1952, but has many gaps; only a small part of the grammar has been dealt with. Even less extensive is de Planhol's article (1961); it deals with 87 terms for animals, plants, and tools in the dialect of Lighwan, south of Tebriz. In 1959 Caferoğlu and Doerfer wrote a summary sketch based on the material accessible at that time (Foy, Szapszał, Ritter, and others). This article gives a general survey, but, on the whole, must be regarded as insufficient. Since all Azerbaijani dialects had to be described (even those of the Soviet Union and of Turkey), and since only a few pages were at the authors' disposal, the Irano-Azerbaijani dialects were dealt with in a very superficial way. Better, and relatively voluminous, is Householder's book (1965). Its disadvantage is that it describes only the dialect of Tabriz, somewhat modified so as to be understandable to all Azerbaijanis (i.e. it presents a kind of artificial language). The grammatical description is rather precise and correct, but, all in all, the book was not written for scholarly but for practical purposes ('for the U.S. Armed Forces'); thus it is not a deep study, neither structuralistic. nor mentalistic, nor comparative.

Consequently, a complete (structural and comparative) study of the Irano-Azerbaijani dialects remains a desideratum. In Soviet studies, normally only the Azerbaijani dialects of the Soviet Union are dealt with, not those of Persia, though sporadically forms of the Tebriz dialect are mentioned in Širəlijev 1942–43, 1962, 1965, Hüsejnov 1958, Rəhimov 1965, Rüstəmov 1965, and others (the same holds true for von Gabain 1963).

Furthermore, there are some studies of Azerbaijani loanwords in Persian: besides some smaller articles by Caferoğlu (1951–52, 1954) and Ligeti (1957b), there is the voluminous book of Zərinəzadə 1962 (containing 436 pages). Here, about 600 loanwords have been dealt with (some of which, however, are not of Azerbaijani origin, as e.g. *tovāčī* 'inspector of the army' which goes back to the Mongol period; in general the Azerbaijani elements in Persian have not always been very carefully separated from those of Chaghatai and West Mongolian origin. Even in a comparative linguistic respect the book is insufficient, inasmuch as modern Azerbaijani and Persian forms have simply been compared, although Azerbaijani loanwords came into Persian as early as the sixteenth and seventeenth centuries). Finally, Doerfer 1963–67 may be mentioned, in which Altaic elements in Persian, including Azerbaijani ones as well, have been studied (about 50 Seljuk words before the Mongol period, 400 Mongolian, 350 Chaghatay, 600 Azerbaijani, these last derived not only from Persian sources, but also from notices in works by European travelers of the seventeenth and eighteenth centuries). Finally, we should mention two interesting articles by Bodrogligeti (1968a and b), dealing with a seventeenth-century Azerbaijani glossary, and one by Householder (1962) about Azerbaijani onomatopes.

Considering the fact that there are about 3 million Azerbaijanis in Persia, works dealing with Azerbaijani spoken in Persia are surprisingly few.

2. QASHQAI AND AYNALLU

But, as is well known, everything is relative. Even less than Azerbaijani have the Turkish languages of Southern Persia, those of the Qashqais and the Aynallus, been explored. As a matter of fact, the older material (Romaskevič, Sir A. Stein), already embodied in Kowalski 1937, has remained nearly the only source of our knowledge of these dialects. Afterwards, several scholars did visit these tribes (Garrod 1946, Menges 1951, Ullens de Schooten 1954), but have not yet published any linguistic material. The studies by Caferoğlu and Doerfer 1959 and von Gabain 1963 are rather poor.

There are some controversies about the linguistic affiliation of the Qashqai-Aynallu group. Kowalski (1937, 1967) regarded it as Azerbaijani (so did Caferoğlu and Doerfer 1959 and von Gabain 1963), whereas Menges (1951:278) informs us 'certain Qašqā'ī dialects exhibit a greater similarity with Osman-Turkic than with Āzerbājdžānian'. But he surely is right when he adds that Osman-Turkish and Azerbaijani actually are only dialects of *one* language.

3. SMALLER TURKISH-SPEAKING GROUPS OF PERSIA

Other Turkish groups in Persia have been explored even less; e.g. the Salchuq, cf. Menges (1951:279) 'In the prov. of Kirmān, S and SW of the city, Turkish-speaking tribes (Sałčuq) were reported to me'; he did not have the opportunity to study their language. The dialects of the Turkmens of Persia, too, are almost unknown; Bazin 1959 does not deal with them, Menges only mentions their existence, without giving samples (1951:278; by the way, it also is unclear, p. 279, whether Turks are to be found in Baluchistan and Mekran).

4. KHALAJ

Though there exists some material about Khalaj, the position of this idiom among the Turkish languages was unknown until recently. Minorsky (1940:417) qualified it as 'the dialect which struck me by its unusual features'; he says 'their aberrant dialect is quite remarkable' (418). He gave some samples (single words and short sentences, 418–24) and a brief grammatical sketch of Khalaj. (The rest of his article was dedicated to historical investigations.) In the same year, Muġaddam published a study about several Persian dialects of the region S and SW of Sāwä, in which he included some Azerbaijani material and 290 Khalaj words; as a matter of fact, he noted (22) that a further study of Khalaj would be worthwhile, but, not being a Turcologist, he (like Minorsky) was unable to realize the relevance of the language and to define its position among the Turkish languages. Menges (1951:278–9) qualified Khalaj ('in diaspora in the districts of Sulṭānābād and Sāva, SW of Tehrān') as 'Āzerbājdžān-Turkish'; he informs us that it 'will probably be investigated by Dr. Borecký of Tehrān University (formerly at Prague University)'. To my knowledge, Mr. Borecký has never published anything about this topic. Minorsky's article has found no echo in Turcology, though there were to be discovered some remarkable features of Khalaj even in these few lines: words like *kön-* 'to burn', *daγ*, *daγïl* (< *daγ ol*) 'is not' prove clearly that Khalaj is a continuation of al-Kāšġarī's Arghu language. Minorsky's article has been cited in some works, but only as a historical source (Köprülü 1950, Schurmann 1962:42–3, 415), and Muġaddam's book has been completely ignored (Iranica non leguntur).

According to a letter to the author (May 3, 1967), László Szimonisz (Bloomington) stayed in Southern Iran, in the regions of Isfahan and Shiraz in July and August of 1965. Up to this time, he has not published the materials he gathered there, of which he possesses, it is true, but very few. According to him, some words seem to reveal some similarity with Qïpchaq-Turkish. He was told of two villages near the town of Riżā-Šāh (90 km S of Teheran, on the way to Isfahan [i.e. N of the region of the Khalaj]); in one of them Chaghatai or Uighur Turkish (Eastern Turkish) is spoken, in the other Qïpchaq Turkish. The informant belonged to the tribe of 'Semerkant' and spoke Chaghatai; his numeral system resembled very much that of the (ancient Turkish) Orkhon inscriptions. It is possible that the material designated by Szimonisz as 'Eastern Turkish' or 'Chaghatai' is Khalaj, too.

According to Garrod (1946:294–6) and Ivanov (1961:30–3), Khalaj live among the Qashqai in Southern Iran; they are said to have immigrated there from Khalajistān (near Sāwä), but it is unclear whether they still speak Khalaj or have been assimilated by their Qashqai-speaking neighbors (the latter seems more likely: Garrod says the dialect of the Amaleh tribe of the Qashqai 'differs [only] slightly from that of the Khalaj' [296]). Using primarily Muġaddam's materials, the author of this article has proved (1968) that Khalaj is neither Azerbaijani, nor Eastern Turkish (nor Tuvinian), but an autonomous subgroup of the Turkish group of languages. Khalaj is a very archaic idiom, in many features the most archaic of all living Turkish languages, and has preserved many features to be found elsewhere only in the far east of the Turkish linguistic area, in Tuvinian (e.g. ancient Turkish *-d-* has been preserved). That is to say, there exist seven Turkish subgroups: (1) Chuvash, (2) Oghuz (Southwestern), (3) Qïpchaq (Northwestern), (4) Uighur or Chaghatai (Southeastern), (5) South-Siberian (Northeastern), (6) Yakut, (7) Khalaj.

5. UZBEK OF AFGHANISTAN

The (numerically) most important Turkish group in Afghanistan are the Uzbeks. The best older study is that of Jarring 1938, who may be regarded as the founder of Afghano-Turcology. Several other works are based on his materials (texts), such as Menges 1946–49 which is but an augmented review of Jarring 1938, which gives a sketch of Afghano-Uzbek grammar. Unfortunately, the encyclopaedias (Grundrisse) of Turcology (Wurm 1959, von Gabain 1963) give even less consideration to Afghano-Uzbek than they do to Irano-Azerbaijani; and more recent works on this topic do not exist. An intensive and thorough study of this very important group (according to Jarring 1939, from 200,000 to 800,000 speakers; according to Schurmann 1962, from 500,000 to 1,000,000) is an urgent necessity. Ligeti 1954 tells us he has gathered Uzbek material, but he has not published anything up to this date (October 1967).

Some works do exist about the influence of Turkish (Chaghatai, or Ancient Uzbek) on Afghan: Aslanov 1947, Ramstedt 1952. The basic fault of Ramstedt's article is that he did not realize that the 'Turkish' elements in Afghan have come entirely via Tajiko-Persian, i.e., are not to be derived directly from Turkish. Spies 1956 had already noticed this fact; cf. also Doerfer 1963–67, passim. (The same, by the way, holds for the 'Turkish' loanwords in the Indian languages, more correctly: 'originally Turkish, but directly Tajiko-Persian').

6. SMALLER TURKISH-SPEAKING GROUPS OF AFGHANISTAN

In Afghanistan live abundant smaller Turkish-speaking groups. Based on older material, Jarring gave a survey of them in 1939, without, unfortunately, adding language samples (Turkmens; Qïpchaqs, which may be an Uzbek tribe; Qazaq; Qirghiz; Qaraqalpaq; Qarluq, who perhaps speak Uzbek, or an archaic language too, but about which no precise information exists; New Uighurs in the East; furthermore the already Iranized Chaghatai Turks, and Qïzïlbashes). Cf. also Ligeti 1954a (reporting about Turkmens and Qïpchaq-Uzbeks, the latter speak a NW dialect); the author has not published his materials. Schurmann 1962 reports, without giving samples, about Turkmens and Qazaqs; furthermore, in his Ethnographic Map of Afghanistan some Qaraqalpaqs are recorded S of Mazār-i Šarīf, and Qïrghïzes in the NE of Afghanistan. About the Qïzïlbashes he tells us the same as Jarring: 'all speak Persian' (109–10). The only language material of a smaller Turkish-speaking group of Afghanistan is that of Ligeti 1957a; he has proved that at least a part of the Qïzïlbashes, namely the Afshars, are bilingual: besides Tajik they speak their native Azerbaijani dialect; this dialect, to be sure, has changed its original Turkish features enormously under Iranian influence, e.g. the non-Iranian vowels *ö*, *ü* have become *e*, *i*. Ligeti gives a little phonology (a primarily historical comparison with other Turkish languages, above all with the other Azerbaijani dialects), and a survey of the verbal forms of Afshar; however, he gives neither texts nor further grammatical indications.

7. MOGHOL

Moghol (a Mongolian idiom) is the best explored of all Altaic languages of Afghanistan. The first study (by Leech) dates from 1838 and contained relatively ample lexical material and some texts. Von der Gabelentz and Fleischer used it for some grammatical interpretations (1866), unfortunately basing their work on a bad edition. After Ramstedt gathered some Moghol material (Manggut) in 1906, the exploration of this language actually stopped for a long time. Jarring (1939:79–81) still revealed some unclear notions of the Moghol tribes; and the description of Moghol in the comparative grammars of Mongolian by Sanžeev 1953 and Poppe 1955 is based exclusively on Ramstedt's materials. But recently Moghol has become the object of more intensive exploration. In 1954 an article by Iwamura and Schurmann appeared, reporting on the results of an expedition undertaken in the same year in Northern Afghanistan; some language samples were subjoined. Also in 1954a Ligeti published the report on his 1936–37 voyage; the author informed his colleagues about having gathered material both from the Marda and the Manggut tribes, but still other dialects must exist which he could not investigate. His materials are said to consist of 4000 words, some sentences and smaller texts, as well as some texts written by a Moghol poet. He promised to edit the linguistic materials as soon as possible. In the same journal (1954b) a study about Leech's material also appeared, with some grammatical notes and constantly comparing Leech's material with that gathered by Ligeti himself in the 1930's. Thus Ligeti published some of his Marda and Manggut words, namely those which, by chance, appeared in Leech's article, too. Several articles about the Japanese expeditions of 1954 and 1955 have been published: Iwamura 1956 (a and b) and Umesao 1956; however, all remain inaccessible to me. Nevertheless, Iwamura's edition (1961) of a larger Moghol (Marda) manuscript dating from 1835 was extremely important; the author not only transcribed the original and provided an alphabetical glossary to it, but he also added some good grammatical notes. In the same year Poucha published an article (based only on Ramstedt's material) proving the very marked Iranization of Moghol and characterizing it as an Iranian-Mongolian mixed language to be sure, with prevailingly Mongolian features. Schurmann 1962 offered very little new material in a linguistic respect (with the exception of some ethnological and administrative terms). But Ligeti's article about a West Middle Mongolian text (1962, and also his notes to this article, 1964a) gave many comparisons with Moghol, and thus offered new Moghol material. Based on the older works, mainly on Ramstedt 1906 (in some cases also on Ligeti 1954b and Iwamura and Schurmann 1954), a concise Moghol grammar by Pritsak appeared in 1964. This work is meritorious as an over-all survey but, as the author himself remarks (160), is based on insufficient material. He quite correctly says 'Es ist sehr zu bedauern, daß LIGETI bis auf kleine Glossen seine Schätze noch immer nicht veröffentlicht hat. Denn solange das nicht geschehen ist, kann keine erschöpfende und zuverlässige Darstellung des Mogholischen erfolgen.' Pritsak's saying holds true even today, though in the meanwhile (not to mention Iwamura 1961, which was not considered by Pritsak) two more studies have appeared (Ligeti 1964b and c) in which the author presented rather ample lexical material; 1964b was intended to prove that Moghol has preserved proto-Mongolian long vowels (see below). For the present, we are waiting for the publication of Ligeti's materials.

We still may mention some important works about Hazāra which, to be sure, is (as against the older supposition) a Tajik, i.e. an Iranian, dialect, but which has borrowed (or preserved?) numerous Mongolian words: Ligeti 1964c, Efimov 1965.

I should like to mention now some characteristic features of Irano-Altaistics. These are throughout merely negative and the following remarks will be not so much information on results and successes but an indication of what remains to be done.

8. THE IRANIAN INFLUENCE ON THE ALTAIC LANGUAGES OF THE AREA HAS NOT YET BEEN ADEQUATELY CONSIDERED

Generally speaking, there is no systematic description of the mutual correlations of Iranian (Persian and Afghan) and Altaic (Turkish and Mongolian) languages. Even the Altaico-Iranian manner of borrowing (Altaic loanwords in Iranian languages), about which some voluminous works do exist (Zərinəzadə 1962, Doerfer 1963–67, Ligeti 1964c, Efimov 1965, Telegdi 1966, Doerfer 1967), has not been sufficiently explored. Even less is known of the Irano-Altaic manner of borrowing. It would be reasonable to form a department to study the problem of the correlation between Altaic and Iranian languages and cultures. Normally, departments are occupied only with single and separate problems of Iranistics, or Altaistics, or Sinology, or Africanistics, etc., acting as if these languages (and the civilizations connected with them) were lying in drawers not to be opened. Compartmentalization has been the approach of the philosophers of civilizations, too (Spengler, Toynbee). But there are not only cultures (and languages), there are also communication and correlation of cultures (and languages). All of us live on one earth which, in itself, has no frontiers. And these correlations should be explored; such a study would enrich our knowledge of the structure and development of human civilization and the formation of human language. To be sure, Irano-Altaistics would not be simply an accumulation of Iranistics and Altaistics but a close junction of them which would be a completely new thing; (the whole is more than the sum of its parts). But I am afraid that such a plan would not be acceptable to the compartmentalized thinking of administrative officials and authorities.

To be sure, there are found sporadic remarks about the influence of Iranian on the Irano-Altaic languages, cf. Kowalski 1938 (see Menges 1946–49:680), who explains the long vowels in Uzbek (mainly *ā*, seldom *ō*, never other vowels) as a phenomenon of Iranization (and he is completely right); Kowalski (1937:1, 66) remarked on the Iranian influence on Qashqai and Aynallu, Ligeti (1957:109 and 1964b:1) on Moghol and (1957:111) on Afshar, Poucha 1961 (passim) and Ramstedt (1906:50) on Moghol, Menges 1933 (passim) on Uzbek and Qïpchaq-Uzbek of Afghanistan. As a matter of fact, all Irano-Altaic speakers are bilingual. Most of them speak, besides their native language, Tajiko-Persian and some speak Afghan; this holds true especially for the smaller peoples, such as the Afshars and the Moghols, but even the larger ones are not exempt from Iranian influence. But though this fact of strong Iranization is fairly well known, it actually is given too little consideration. There are occasions when this fact is not mentioned at all (or maybe not realized) as in Jarring 1938, Poppe 1955, Pritsak 1964. Pritsak, e.g., has not noted that the dropping of Middle Mongolian *h-*, a characteristic of Moghol, is a result of Iranization (both Afghan and Afghano-Tajik have *h* > zero, cf. Doerfer 1963), nor did he note (166) that the consonant scheme of Moghol is completely identical with that of Afghano-Tajik. Poppe (18) did not realize that in Moghol *qï*, *γï* is not to be explained as a case of preservation of Proto-Mongolian *ï*, but that simply *i* after *q*, *γ* has become *ï*. Thus *ï* is the same phoneme as *i* of which it is only a variant, just as in Tajik (where *ï* originally never existed: it is not an Indo-European or Iranian vowel) and as in the Tajik-Uzbek dialects. Unless one considers this Iranian influence, false conclusions are easily reached even in the Altaic field. But even those scholars who did realize that there was Iranian influence did not always pay regard to it. Ligeti, e.g., tries to prove that Moghol has preserved Proto-Mongolian long vowels (1964b, and even in 1954b: 151–2). But it can easily be shown, on the basis of a comparison of the Moghol vowel structure with that of the local Tajik dialects, that these long vowels are secondary: the only long vowel to be found in original Mongolian words of Moghol is *ā̊*, which in Tajik, as a rule, is also long (more precisely, nonreduceable). As a more detailed instance, I only refer to the items alleged by Ligeti as a proof of 'preservation' of Proto-Mongolian **ǟ* in non-first syllables. Of 15 items, 13 are **ǟ* > *ā̊* before *n* (normally, Mongolian *ä* becomes *a* in Moghol); we sometimes find variants: nasalized *-ā̊* ~ *ā̊n*. But this can be explained more simply as an influence of the local Tajik dialect, where (cf. Efimov 1965: 16, 17, 20) both *-ā̊n* and *-an* have become (via nasalized *-ā̊*) *ō*: *ā̊* and *a* before *n* develop in the same way. And that is precisely the reason why, in Moghol too, we find both **aman* 'mouth' > *ā̊mā̊n* and **dörbän* 'four' > **dȯrban* > *du̇rbā̊n*. The system of sounds of the Irano-Altaic dialects is inexplicable without a consideration of the Iranian system and the influence of this system on the Altaic sounds. A precise phonological study and comparison of these sound systems, therefore, remains a desideratum. (The author of these lines has an article in preparation, called 'Das Vokalsystem der irano-altaischen Sprachen'; for the present cf. Doerfer 1966:98 and Menges 1945.)

9. NATIVE PUBLICATIONS ARE SCARCE

The Iranian peoples living in Afghanistan do not seem to be very interested in the Altaic languages of their area; at least they have not published anything about this topic (with the exception of some older material published by Iwamura 1961). An inspection of Akram 1947, Wilber 1956, *Bibliography* 1956 gives no results in this respect. Nor did the Linguistic Institute of Kabul answer my questions in this matter, so that we may suppose that even today nothing has been undertaken in this field.

The situation is somewhat different in Persia, cf. Yar-Shater's article in this book, pp. 669–89. Examining Afshar 1961, chapter 'dialect', headword 'Āzarbāiǧān', we find 23 items (No. 4004–4026), a rather significant figure. One must consider that in modern Persian the term 'Āzarī' normally does not mean Azerbaijani (Turkish), but it denotes the old Iranian dialect spoken in Azerbaijan before the arrival of the Turks and, gradually, superseded by Azerbaijani Turkish, though still spoken in some villages even today; cf. e.g. Qazwīnī 1928, article (141–8) Āẕarī yā zabān-i bāstān-i Āẕarbāigān (Azeri, or the ancient language of Azerbaijan), also Mortażavī in Arẕangī 1959:i-xiv, etc. Most of the articles mentioned in Afshar No. 4004–4026 actually refer to the Iranian Azeri dialect. In some cases, the author's viewpoint is that the contemporary Turkish Azerbaijanis in a sense illegally inhabit the area (as proof of this is, inter alia, the designation of Turkish Azerbaijani: zabān-i kunūnī-yi Āzarbāiǧān 'the language of Azerbaijan of this age'). A strong national tension reveals itself, which is quite understandable: since the eleventh century (period of the Seljuks) Persia has been governed by Altaic dynasties (after the Seljuks: the Khwarezm Shahs, the Mongols, Timur and his successors, the Safevids and Kajars which supported themselves on Azerbaijani armies). Not until Reżā Šāh, founder of the present dynasty, was the Turks power suppressed. After the Second World War there was almost an autonomous Azerbaijani-Turkish government in Azerbaijan (1945–46). Azerbaijani was the official language; scientific works were published in Azerbaijani at this time which are inaccessible today (Monteil 1956:3). Afterwards Azerbaijan was reincorporated into the Persian state, which proved a rather uncomfortable time for many Azerbaijanis. Generally, preoccupation with Turkish themes is not very popular in Persia, as a result of these inherited national tensions. An attempt at reconciliation, such as that of Muġaddam (1940:164–78) was insufficient (the author 'proved' that Azerbaijani Turkish, which he called turkī, was a Persian dialect [turkī yak gūyiš-i īrānīst] and cognate to the Indo-European languages, e.g. Azerbaijani *ertä* 'early' = Latin *aurora*, and other such nonsense).

Let us review the Iranian publications. Muġaddam 1940 is the result of a trip to the territory between Qum and Hamadān, undertaken in 1939. The author gathered material of six local Iranian dialects; further, as already mentioned, of (Turkish) Khalaj, and, finally, of the Azerbaijani dialect of the region. The main part of his book (which contains 184 pages) is a glossary of the eight idioms (26–109), arranged in systematic order (relatives, body parts, animals, etc.), and 157–64 give some notes on Azerbaijani. The Azerbaijani material contains about 400 words; though not very ample, it reveals some interesting features of the local dialect. Aržangī 1959 (xiv + 68 pp.) deals with 'the phrases, locutions, and sayings common to Persian and Azerbaijani'. It is a good proof that Persian and Azerbaijani, as spoken in a common area, have greatly converged in their modes of expression (normally, the Persian element would have been the active one). The book is written in a fair Tabriz dialect, not in written language (cf. e.g. *tüšdüla* 'they fell' instead of *düšdülär*); the Turkish words are transcribed in Latin letters with diacritical signs, rather precisely. Kārang 1962 is a small (52 pp.) descriptive grammar of 'turkī-yi āẕarī' (Azerbaijani Turkish), or 'zabān-i turkī-yi Āẕarbāiǧān' (the Turkish language of Azerbaijan; this marks a certain progress in terminology). It is written throughout in Arabic script; even its terminology and the order of the material corresponds exactly to that of Arabic grammar; the language is Azerbaijani written language, not dialectal. This book is not bad, but sometimes the material has been pressed too much into the Procrustean bed of Arabic linguistics, so that, e.g., the Turkish gerund (converb), a category not existing in Arabic, has not been mentioned at all. Bahrangī 1966 is a short article dealing with predicative endings in modern Azerbaijani.

So much for the works accessible to me. They are, fortunately, the most voluminous ones, since they are primarily books. The articles, e.g. those of the journal *Našrīya-yi Dāniškada-yi Adabīyāt-i Tabrīz* (Journal of the Department of Literature of Tebriz), are, as can be seen from the bibliography, rather small, cf. Daulat-Ābādī (= Afshar 1961, No. 4013–4015), Māhyār Nauwābī, Bahrangī, Iqbāl.

There are, all in all, 11 native Persian works about Azerbaijani, a language spoken by several millions of inhabitants, the most important language of the country except for Persian.

10. MANY DIALECTS HAVE NOT BEEN EXPLORED

On the linguistic map of Persia and Afghanistan many white spots are to be found. Azerbaijani of Persia, e.g., has been much less investigated than that of the Soviet Union. Whereas Sə'dijev 1960 contains 1442 Soviet Azerbaijani items, the greatest part of the alleged works being written after the Second World War (at least 1000), the stock of works dealing with Persian Azerbaijani (leaving aside books in which Persian Azerbaijani is mentioned only en passant, such as Hüsejnov 1958, or mere loanword studies) is remarkably small: 7 West-European-American and 11 Persian works. M. Š. Širəlijev informs me (letter, September 30, 1967): 'Meines Wissens ist nach dem 2. Weltkrieg bei uns über die Sprache der Aserbeidschaner in Iran noch keine Arbeit geschrieben worden.' Let us insert here a positive and a negative list.

A. *Languages sufficiently* (*though not completely*) *investigated.*

(1) Azerbaijani of Iran and Afghanistan. These dialects are, without any doubt, the best explored Altaic idioms of the area, especially if one considers the older material

(dating from the time before the Second World War). The Tabriz dialect, above all, is fairly well known. Of the other dialects, however, many have not been studied, e.g. there is no description of the dialects (probably Azerbaijani) of the Gündüzlü and Aghach-Eri in South Persia, cf. Oberling 1964.

(2) Qashqai and Aynallu. To be sure, it has been investigated just enough for us to have some idea of its structure; as a matter of fact, Caferoğlu and Doerfer (1959: 302) were not even able to make up a complete scheme of predicative endings, etc. It seems very probable that there exist many more dialects of this language (these languages) than have been known up to now.

(3) Khalaj. Only its phonology is moderately clear; for this aim, the scanty word material is sufficient. Its morphology is almost unknown. Unknown, too, is the idiom of the Khalaj living among the Qashqai, cf. Garrod 1946: 294–6. There is no doubt that also among the Khalaj of Khalajistan (S of Sāwä) exist dialects (cf. 'house' in Muġaddam and in the dialect of Kundürüd *häv*, in Paugird *höv*; 'water' is *su* in Muġaddam and in Kundürüd, in Ḫurakābād it is *suf*), but we know very little of them. It is typical that the first works about Khalaj appeared in 1940, and that only in 1967 was it realized that it is a special language group, not a language or dialect.

(4) Uzbek of Afghanistan. Complete details are not known about its dialects, but it may be that the language is rather monolithic. In recent years, no further investigations have been published (though material has been gathered).

(5) Moghol. This has been relatively well explored, and fairly rich material exists; on the other hand, even Ligeti admits to not having been able to investigate all dialects.

B. *Languages not (or quite insufficiently) investigated.*

(1) Salchuq in the Persian province of Kirmān (= Azerbaijani?).
(2) Turkmen, both of Persia and Afghanistan.
(3) Turkish dialects of Baluchistan and Mekran (?).
(4) a Qïpchaq dialect in Persia (Szimonisz).
(5) an Uighur dialect in Persia (= Khalaj?, Szimonisz).
(6) Qïpchaq-Uzbek of Afghanistan.
(7) Qazaq of Afghanistan.
(8) Qïrghïz of Afghanistan.
(9) Qaraqalpaq of Afghanistan.
(10) Qarluq of Afghanistan (= Uzbek?).
(11) Uighurs of Afghanistan.
(12) Chaghatai of Afghanistan (= Uzbek?).

Thus, we find 5 sufficiently (it would be better to say moderately) well-known dialects, and 12 (almost) unknown dialects, and of some of the latter we do not know whether they even exist at all.

11. MUCH MATERIAL HAS NOT YET BEEN PUBLISHED, THOUGH GATHERED A LONG TIME AGO

The most striking case is that of Ligeti's Moghol material. In 1936–37 this scholar traveled over the area and gathered his texts, in 1954 he wrote a note announcing the immediate publication of his materials, but up to today (October 1967), i.e. 30 years after his exploration, nothing has been published. Nor did Ligeti publish his Afghano-Uzbek materials; nor Menges his Qashqai texts gathered in 1950. According to the specimens he placed at my disposal (in a letter of December 3–7, 1956), for publication in Caferoğlu and Doerfer 1959 (which was only partly possible), and according to his further information on Qashqai grammar, his materials are highly interesting and important. Perhaps the author of this article should take the initiative and publish this letter (which contains about two printed pages of texts); Menges writes to me (March 29, 1967): 'Mit Qašqajī-Material kann ich immer noch nicht dienen. Ob ich da so bald dazu komme, weiß ich auch nicht.' Szimonisz, too, has not yet published his brief materials (letter of May 3, 1967), nor has Borecký edited Khalaj material (announced in Menges 1951:278–9). Finally, Schurmann (1962:13) writes: 'In the late 1940's, an American named MacKenzie, then teaching in Kabul, was reputed to have come across some Mongol settlements in the Turkestan region [= Maimanā and Qundūz-Baġlān regions, according to p. 49]. He made some photographs and compiled a small vocabulary. However, although he communicated his discoveries to a number of scholars, none of his material has been published, to my knowledge.'

I wish to urgently exhort these scholars to publish their materials; science is based on communication. Materials concealed in one's writing desk are good for nothing and nobody. To publish some single parts (which, by chance, were of interest to the author), without giving the total material, is almost useless: Nobody, basing himself only on some details of a language and not knowing its complete structure, can earnestly and sufficiently judge a linguistic problem. In science, there are priorities. First of all, those works have to be published which are reproductions of materials gathered *in situ*; they are the basis of studies for other scholars, too. And all the other publications (though they may be much less tedious than a publication of texts) have to come second.

12. A SYSTEMATIC DESCRIPTION OF AN IRANO-ALTAIC LANGUAGE DOES NOT AT PRESENT EXIST

There are to be found some works which might be called exceptions to this rule, such as Foy 1903–04, Ramstedt 1906, Pritsak 1964, Householder 1965, but they, too, are absolutely insufficient, being based on too little material. In Ligeti's articles about Moghol, e.g. some word material has been published (1954b, 1962, 1964a, b and c).

But this was done, so to say, en passant and with the author's left hand. Ligeti has taken the third step before the first. The normal procedure should be: (1) publication of texts; (2) on investigation of these texts, the production of a complete descriptive grammar; and based on this (3) one may dare to write comparative and reconstructive studies, dealing with the history (or even prehistory) of the given language. Ligeti published the comparative studies at once, but nobody knows the whole of his materials. The same holds true for other works, not only for Ligeti's: there is an abundance of scattered and dispersed material (a great part of which is unpublished). This material is hardly utilizable, since it is not written in a systematic form.

Leaving aside this rather quantitative viewpoint, the materials have not been published, up to now, in a way corresponding to modern linguistic requirements. There exist no experimental-phonetic transcriptions, neither in visible speech, nor on tape recordings, nor in any other form. The exactness of the transcription, consequently, depends exclusively on the explorer's ear. Now, some reports seem to be quite reliable, e.g. Ligeti's, but others seem to reproduce neither phonetic nuances, nor phonemic values, such as Iwamura and Schurmann 1954 (where no difference is made between the normal *u* and *ů*, high-mixed-narrow-round). Furthermore, no modern linguistic study has been made, neither phonological, nor a structuralist description of morphology and syntax. As insufficient material has been gathered, a stylistic-mentalistic investigation à la Spitzer, which demands an exceptionally intensive knowledge of a language, has been impossible. (The author regards structuralist and mentalistic studies as enjoying equal rights.) And, finally, there is no comparative description of the totality of the Irano-Altaic languages, whether within the Altaistic scope, or whether considering the correlations with the Iranian neighbor languages.

And yet this situation has an advantage: here is a white spot on the map of linguistics, and we may look forward to many future explorations.

BIBLIOGRAPHY

The asterisks denote works not obtainable by me.

AFŠĀR, ĪRAĞ. 1961. Fihrist-i maqālāt-i fārsī, ğild-i auwal: 1328 q. 1338 š. Tehran. (also titled: AFSHAR, IRAJ. Index Iranicus I. 1910–58).

——. 1954–66. Kitābhā-yi Īrān I-XI. Tehran.

AKRAM, MOHAMMED. 1947. Bibliographie analytique de l'Afghanistan 1. Ouvrages parus hors de l'Afghanistan. Paris.

ARŽANGĪ, HŪŠANG. 1959. Ta'bīrāt wa iṣṭilāḥāt wa amṣāl-i muštarik-i fārsī wa āzarbāiğānī. RFLTiz 9.73–108, 182–200; 10.80–93 (according to Afshar 1961, No. 4010, but my copy: xiv + 68 pp., dating from 1959).

*ASLANOV, M.G. 1947. Borrowings from the Turkic languages in Pushtu. Trudy Moskovskogo Instituta Vostokovedenija.

*Bahrangī, Ṣamad. 1963. Paswand dar zabān-i kunūnī-yi Āzarbāiğān. Rāhnumā-yi Kitāb 6/3.220–3 (information from Yar-Shater).

——. 1966. Māżī wa mużāriʿ dar ğarayān dar zabān-i kunūnī-yi Āẕarbāiğān. FIZ 13.72–6. Tehran.

Bazin, Louis. 1959. Le Turkmène. Philologiae Turcicae Fundamenta I.308–17. Aquis Mattiacis.

Bibliography of Russian Works on Afghanistan. 1956. Central Asian Research Centre (66 King's Road, London, S.W. 3).

Bodrogligeti, A. 1968a. On the Turkish vocabulary of the Iṣfahān anonymous. AOH 21.15–43.

——. 1968b. Lexical features of a 17th century Azeri glossary. Paper read at the one hundred and seventy-eighth meeting of the American Oriental Society. Berkeley.

Caferoğlu, Ahmet. 1951–52. Azerî şivesinde nohur ve lap kelimeleri. RO 17. 180–3.

——. 1954. Azerbaycan ve Anadolu ağızlarındaki Moğolca unsurlar. TDAYB 1–10. Ankara.

——, and Gerhard Doerfer. 1959. Das Aserbeidschanische. Philologiae Turcicae Fundamenta I.280–207. Aquis Mattiacis.

*Daulat-Ābādī, Azīz. Zabān-i kunūnī-yi Āzarbāiğān. Muʿallim-i Imrūz 2.120–6, 159–68 (= Afshar 1961, No. 4013).

*——. Manša'-i yak żarb al-maṯal-i Āẕarbāiğān (Gövdüš a dïgïrlanïb duvaġïn tapdï). Muʿallim-i Imrūz 4.196–7 (= Afshar 1961, No. 4014).

——. Zabān-i kunūnī-yi Āẕarbāigān. RFLTiz 6.488–92 (=Afsher 1961, No. 4015).

De Planhol, Xavier. 1961. Contributions à la dialectologie rurale de l'Azeri (Notes lexicographiques par Louis Bazin). JA 249.411–25.

Doerfer, Gerhard. 1959. Prolegomena zu einer Untersuchung der altaischen Lehnwörter im Neupersischen. CAJ 5.1–26.

——. 1963. Review of Iwamura 1961. OLZ 58.502–4.

——. 1966. Zur Verwandtschaft der altaischen Sprachen. IF 71.81–123.

——. 1963, 1965, 1967. Türkische und mongolische Elemente im Neupersischen 1, 2, 3. Wiesbaden.

——. 1967. Türkische Lehnwörter im Tadschikischen. Wiesbaden.

——. 1968. Das Chaladsch — eine archaische Türksprache in Zentralpersien. ZDMG 118.79–112.

Efimov, V. A. 1965. Jazyk afganskix xazara. Moskva.

Field, Henry. 1939. Contributions to the anthropology of Iran. Anthropological Series, Field Museum of Natural History 29/1. Chicago.

Fleischer, H. see von der Gabelentz, H. C.

Foy, Karl. 1903, 1904. Azerbajğanische Studien mit einer Charakteristik des Südtürkischen. MSOS, Westasiatische Studien 6.126–93, 7.197–265.

GARROD, OLIVER. 1946. The Qashqai tribe of Fars. Journal of the Royal Central Asian Society 33.293–306. London.

HOUSEHOLDER, FRED W., JR. 1962. Azerbaijani onomatopes. American studies in Altaic linguistics. UAS 13.115–21.

HOUSEHOLDER, FRED W. JR., with MANSOUR LOTFI. 1965. Basic course in Azerbaijani. UAS 45. Bloomington and The Hague.

HÜSEJNOV, AZER. 1958. Azərbajǧan dialektologijasy. Baky.

*IQBĀL, ʿABBĀS. Zabān-i turkī dar Āẕarbāiǧān, Yādgār 2/3.1-9 found in Aržangī. 1959).

IVANOV, M.S. 1961. Plemena Farsa. Kaškajskie, Chamse, Kuchgiluje, Mamasani. Trudy Instituta Etnografii 63. Moskva.

*IWAMURA, SHINOBU. 1956a. Hunting for the Genghis Khanid Mongols in Afghanistan. The Japan Quarterly 3:2.

*——. 1956b. Mogoru-zoku no tanuzete [In search of the Moghôls]. Sabaku to hyôga no tanken [Exploring deserts and glaciers], by Hitoshi Kihara, 77–104. Tokyo.

——. 1961. The Zirni manuscript, a Persian-Mongolian glossary and grammar. Kyoto.

IWAMURA, SHINOBU, and H.F. SCHURMANN. 1954. Notes on Mongolian groups in Afghanistan. Silver jubilee volume of the Zinbun-Kagaku- Kenkyusyo Kyoto University, 480-515. Kyoto.

JARRING, GUNNAR. 1938. Uzbek texts from Afghan Turkestan. LUÅ 34:2.

——. 1939. On the distribution of Turk tribes in Afghanistan. LUÅ 35:4.

KĀRANG, ʿABD AL-ʿALĪ. 1962. Dastūr-i zabān-i kunūnī-yi Āẕarbāiǧān. Tabrīz. (= Afšār 1962, No. 196).

KÖPRÜLÜ, M. FUAD. 1950. Halaç. İslâm Ansiklopedisi 5.114–16. İstanbul.

KOWALSKI, TADEUSZ. 1937. Sir Aurel Stein's Sprachaufzeichnungen im Äi̯nallu-Dialekt aus Südpersien. Polska Akademia Umiejętności, Prace Komisji Orientalistyczny 29. Kraków.

*LEECH, R. 1838. Epitome of the grammar of Brahuiky, the Balochky, and the Panjabi languages, with vocabularies of the Baraky, the Pashi, the Laghmani, the Cashgari, the Teerhai, and the Deer dialects. JASB 7/2.780–7. Calcutta.

LIGETI, LOUIS. 1954a. O mongol'skix i tjurkskix jazykax i dialektax Afganistana. AOH 4.93–117.

——. 1954b. Le lexique moghol de R. Leech. AOH 4.119–58.

——. 1957a. Sur la langue des Afchars d'Afghanistan. AOH 7.110–56.

——. 1957b. Az 'ajándék' két török-perzsa neve. MNy 53.157–9.

——. 1962. Un vocabulaire mongol d'Istanboul. AOH 14.1–99.

——. 1964a. Notes sur le vocabulaire mongol d'Istanboul. AOH 16.107–74.

——. 1964b. Les voyelles longues en Moghol. AOH 17.1–48.

——. 1964c. Mongol'skie èlementy v dialektax xazara v Afganistane. KSINA 83. 1–22.

*MĀHYĀR NAUWĀBĪ, YAḤYĀ. Zabān-i kunūnī Āzarbāiǧān. RFLTiz 5.110–28, 217–24;

6.95–112, 203–40, 315–58, 453–70 (= Afshar 1961, No. 4021). (Only vol. 5 was accessible to me.)

MASON, K., et. al. 1945. Persia. London.

MENGES, KARL. 1933. Drei özbekische Texte. Islam 21.141–94.

——. 1945. Indo-European influences on Ural-Altaic languages. Word 1/2.188–93.

——. 1946–49. Zum Özbekischen von Nord-Afghanistan. Anthropos 41–4.673–710.

——. 1951. Research in the Turkic dialects of Iran (Preliminary report on a trip to Persia). Oriens 4.273–9.

MINORSKY, V. 1950. The Turkish dialect of the Khalaj. BSOAS 10/2.417–37.

MONTEIL, VINCENT. 1956. Sur le dialecte turc de l'Azerbâydjân Iranien. JA 244.1–77.

——. 1966. Les tribus du Fârs et la sédentarisation des nomades. Paris and 's-Gravenhage.

MUĠADDAM, MAḤMAD. 1940. Gūyišhā-yi Wafs wa Āštiyān wa Tafraš. Īrān-Kūdä 11. Tehran. (= Afshar 1961, No. 4027).

NAUTĀŠ: see Razm-Ārā.

OBERLING, PIERRE. 1964. The Turkic tribes of southwestern Persia. UAJb 35.164–80.

POPPE, NICHOLAS. 1955. Introduction to Mongolian comparative studies. MSFOu 110.

POUCHA, PAVEL. 1961. Mongolische Miszellen, V, Die Sprache der Mogholen in Afghanistan und die Theorie der Mischsprachen. CAJ 6.27–43.

PRITSAK, OMELJAN. 1964. Das Mogholische. Handbuch der Orientalistik 1:5/2. 159–84. Leiden/Köln.

QAZWĪNĪ, MĪRZĀ MUḤAMMAD ḪĀN BIN ʿABD AL-WAHHĀB. 1928. Bīst maqāla-yi Qazwīnī. Bombay.

RAMSTEDT, G.J. 1906. Mogholica, Beiträge zur kenntnis der moghol-sprache in Afghanistan. JSFOu 23/4.1–60.

——. 1952. Marginal notes on Pashto etymology, ed. by Pentti Aalto. SO 17.

RAZM-ĀRĀ, ḤUSAIN-ʿALĪ. 1949 sqq. Farhang-i ǧuġrāfiyā'ī-yi Īrān. Tehran. 10 vols. (vol. 10 by Nautāš).

RƏHIMOV, MIRZƏ. 1965. Azərbajǧan dilində fe'l šəkillərinin formalašmasy tarixi. Baky.

RUSTƏMOV, R., and M.Š. ŠIRELIJEV. 1964. Azərbajǧan dilinin dialektoloži lüyəti. Baky.

RUSTƏMOV, R. 1965. Azərbajǧan dili dialekt və šivələrində fe'l. Baky.

ṢAFĀ, IBRĀHĪM. 1966. Intišārāt-i Īrān dar sāl-i 1343. Tehran.

SANŽEEV, G.D. 1953, 1963. Sravnitel'naja grammatika mongol'skix jazykov I and II. Moskva.

SCHURMANN, H.F. 1962. The Mongols of Afghanistan. 's-Gravenhage.

SƏ'DIJEV, S. 1960. Azərbajǧan dilčilijinə dair ədəbijjatyn bibliografijasy (Sovet dövrü). Baky.

ŠIRALIEV (ŠIRƏLIJEV), M. Š. 1941. K voprosu ob izučenii i klassifikacii azerbajdžanskix dialektov. Izvestija azerbajdžanskogo filiala Akademii Nauk SSSR 4. Baky.
*——. 1942–43. Azərbajğan dialektologijasy 1, II hissə. Baky.
——. 1947. Izučenie dialektov azerbajdžanskogo jazyka. IzvAN 6.431–6.
——. 1962. Azərbajğan dialektologijasynyn əsaslary. Baky.
——. 1965. The forms of the present tense in the Azerbaijanian dialects. UAJb 36.413–15.
SPIES, O. 1956. Review of Ramstedt 1952. IF 62/2.200–3.
TELEGDI, ZS. 1966. A propos d'une construction tadjik (Evolution interne et influence extérieure dans la formation d'un procédé syntaxique). Paper read at the 1st congress of Iranists. Tehran.
ULLENS DE SCHOOTEN, M. TH. 1954. Among the Kashkai. A tribal migration in Persia. Geographical Magazine 27.68–78. London.
*UMESAO, TADAO. 1956. Mogôru-zoku tankenshi [Account of an expedition to the Moghôls]. Tokyo.
VON DER GABELENTZ, H. C. 1866. Über die Sprache der Hazâras und Aimaks. ZDMG 20.326–35. See also H. Fleischer, Ergänzungen und Berichtigungen, 612–13.
VON GABAIN, ANNEMARIE. 1963. Die Südwestdialekte des Türkischen. Handbuch der Orientalistik 1:5/1.175–204. Leiden and Köln. Die zentralasiatischen Türksprachen, 139–60.
WILBER, DONALD N. 1956. Annotated bibliography of Afghanistan. Human Relation Area Files. New Haven.
WURM, STEFAN. 1959. Das Özbekische. Philologiae Turcicae Fundamenta I.489–524. Aquis Mattiacis.
ZƏRINƏZADƏ, H. H. 1962. Fars dilində azərbajğan sözləri (Səfəvilər dövrü). Baky.

ADDENDA

The necessity for addenda is a fact very characteristic of the rapid development of Irano-Altaistics. There are two reasons.

Whereas in the 1940's and 1950's publishing books about Azerbaijani was almost impossible in Persia, the tendency toward liberalism — so visible in the social field (land distribution, the foundation of numerous schools and infirmaries, etc.) — has recently been extended to national minorities. Thus, some books dealing with Azerbaijani have appeared in the 1960's. Although there are still relatively few, these may be the harbinger of an intensive preoccupation with Azerbaijani in the future. During my stay in Tehran, in 1969, and after intensive research, I have been able to discover the following native works about Azerbaijani:

ANONYMOUS. 1961. Ḫud-āmūz-i turkī yā mukālamāt-i rūz-marra-yi zabān-i turkī. Tabrīz. (A small Persian-Azerbaijani dictionary, 48 pp.)
FARZĀNA, M. A. 1966. Mabānī-yi dastūr-i zabān-i Āẕarbāiğān. Tabrīz. (A small

descriptive grammar, 120 pp., relatively modern, i.e. of a more Western type than, e.g., Kārang; perhaps the best native work on Azerbaijani, it is based on Muharrem Ergin's work: Osmanlıca dersleri, I, Türk dil bilgisi, Istanbul, 1958, 2nd ed. 1962.)

ǦĀD, S. M. (no indication of date or place of publication). Āẕarbāiǧān dilinə maḫṣūṣ ṣarf u naḥv. (A small grammar of the conventional type, 103 pp.)

ǦĀVĪD, S. 1965a. Ḫud-āmūz-i zabān-i āẕarbāiǧānī va fārsī. Tehran. (A kind of basic course, with practical lessons pp. 13–64, grammar 67–99, orthography 103–31, dictionary 135–84.)

——. 1965b. Āẕarbāiǧān dil bilgisindən yazī qāʿidələri. Tehran. (An extract from 1965a: pp. 103–31 + 96–9 + 194–5.)

ŠUʿĀR, MUHAMMAD RIŻĀ. 1968. Baḥṣī dar bāra-yi zabān-i Āẕarbāiǧān. Tabrīz. (This deals, inter alia, with Azerbaijani loanwords in Persian, pp. 39–44, and Persian loanwords in Azerbaijani, 139 pp.)

At the same time, Persia has become relatively open to foreigners' research. Thus, two expeditions to Khalajestan could be undertaken, in 1968 and 1969. These enabled me to write several works about Khalaj, this recently discovered and very important Turkic group of languages, now using tape-recorded materials far more precise than Minorsky's and Muġaddam's notes.

DOERFER, GERHARD. 1969. Das Chaladsch, eine neuentdeckte archaische Türksprache. XVII. Deutscher Orientalistentag vom 21 bis 27 Juli in Würzburg, 719–25. Wiesbaden.

——. Die Turksprachen Irans. TDK, Belleten 1969.1–23.

——. Khalaj materials. UAS (4 volumes, the first of which is in press.)

During the second expedition, I not only gathered the material for a linguistic atlas of Khalajestan (the first linguistic atlas of a Turkish group of languages) but also discovered a very interesting Azerbaijani dialect at Galūgāh, on the southeastern border of the Caspian Sea (in which ö > ä, ü > u). Furthermore, I discovered a new Oghuz (Southwestern) Turkish language, Khorasani, which may number as many as 800,000 speakers; (it is very characteristic of the situation in Persia that such a relatively important national group has not been discovered before now). This language is not Turkmen (as was formerly supposed, but it must be said that Turkmens do live in enclaves among the Khorasanis, and at several places, e.g. near Gurgān, in close settlements; for Turkmen of Persia, cf., e.g., Yusuf Azmun. 1966. Türkmen halk edebiyatı hakkında. Reşid Rahmeti Arat için, 38. Ankara). Khorasani is closer to Turkmen than to Azerbaijani. Thus the Southwestern group does not consist of three languages (Osman, Azerbaijani, Turkmen) but of four:

Osman, Azerbaijani	Western Oghuz	Eastern Oghuz	Khorasani, Turkmen

Cf. my article in TDK, Belleten. Contrary to Schurmann's opinion (1962:114), it seems to be possible that the Berberis (in Khorasan) also are not a Tajik minority but Turks (or even Mongols); but this problem has still to be investigated.

PART THREE

AFROASIATIC LANGUAGES

AFROASIATIC

AN OVERVIEW

Before a Brugmann or a Brockelmann can provide the scholarly world with a compendium which remains standard long after it is outdated, there must be several generations of scholars gathering and organizing data. This preparatory work largely remains to be done in the field of Afroasiatic.[1] The basic data — reliable descriptions, including dictionaries — are yet lacking for most languages. The work that has been done is thus forced to rely on very uneven evidence over broad areas (Tucker 1967: 655). The difficulties of comparison have been increased considerably by the disparity in dates of attestation, Semitic and Egyptian going back to 2000–3000 B.C. while Cushitic and Chadic are known only from modern times. Berber has some older records (Rössler 1958) but nothing comparable to Semitic or Egyptian. This problem is often raised (e.g. von Soden 1965:163) and has been countered with such examples as comparisons of Lithuanian and Sanskrit (Rössler 1951:104–5; cf. Hodge 1968b). Klingenheben holds a somewhat overly negative view in this respect, maintaining that we are unjustified in assigning to the proto-language anything which is not represented in the older periods (1956:255).

The field as a whole has been treated in two works by major scholars, one near the beginning of the period under review (Cohen 1947) and the other near the end (Diakonoff 1965). The most complete listing of Afroasiatic languages, accompanied by general discussion of the 'phylum', as it is there called, is that of the Voegelins (1964). This was based on Greenberg's earlier work (1955a, 1963) and also had the advantage of later consultation with him and others. An earlier and still very useful list is found in Cohen (1952).

A sober appraisal of the state of Afroasiatic scholarship was made by von Soden

[1] 'Afroasiatic' includes the languages known as Semitic, Egyptian, Cushitic, Berber and Chadic (see the respective chapters, Chadic being in Volume 7). This term, introduced by Greenberg (1952), has largely replaced Hamito-Semitic in American usage and to some extent elsewhere. Hamito-Semitic, as well as the less common Semito-Hamitic, are still widely used. More recently Erythraic has been proposed by Tucker and Bryan (1966:2) as a meaningful and non-controversial alternative. A popular account of the current state of the field is found in Hodge (1968b). A summary of Soviet work is given by Sharbatov (1967). Afroasiatic is here referred to as a 'family' with 'branches', comparable to Indo-Hittite. This is perhaps premature, and the term 'phylum' for Afroasiatic and 'family' for Semitic, Egyptian, etc. is in some respects more appropriate to our present state of knowledge (Voegelins 1964; Polotsky 1964:122: 'stock' or 'phylum').

(1965). Primarily a review article (of Castellino 1962; see below), he is highly critical of the type of work being done. His points are generally well taken and the most important ones cannot reasonably be controverted. His plea for sound methodology combined with proper knowledge of the sources should be underlined (von Soden 1965:162; a previous statement by Cohen 1951). It also cannot be too strongly stressed that solid results must await the detailed analysis of the individual branches and reconstructions of proto-Cushitic, proto-Chadic, etc. (cf. von Soden 1965:164). Nor is this situation in any way peculiar to Afroasiatic. Dalby's remarks on African languages could well be said of any comparative linguistics: 'The first task in the comparative study of African languages is to establish the closest and most coherent groupings on a scientific basis, i.e. groupings for which regular sound-correspondences and reconstructed common-forms may be postulated. Only when this is done will it be possible to examine any remoter levels of relationship, on the basis of these immediate groupings.' (Dalby 1966:179).

It would follow from this quotation that the study of Afroasiatic is not at this point possible, considering the fact that the study of the most closely related groups has been done only in part. As a matter of fact both of history and of methodology the procedure has been quite different from both von Soden's and Dalby's ideal. All along the way the larger picture has been kept in mind, that is, comparisons between the branches have been made despite meagre information on the branches themselves as linguistic entities. The sequence of scholarly activity actually being followed is more like this: 1) Original hypothesis of relationship based on available data. 2) Closer analysis of these data for 'proof' of relationship. 3) Further collection of data to furnish information on all languages involved. 4) Analysis of new and old data, setting up sound correspondences first for smaller groups and eventually for the family as a whole. In the period with which we are concerned three main trends may be seen. The first is the use of broad techniques for the setting up of hypotheses of relationship. The second is the effort to establish sound correspondences (on a broad or narrow scale) among the various branches. The third is the investigation of similar morphologic and syntactic features. Most of the work done on the second and third of these has not been basically different from that of the previous fifty years. Only very recently have definite steps been taken to put sound correspondences on a firmer basis by working on the internal relationships of the branches, especially Cushitic and Chadic.

The hypothesis of relationship was at first supported mainly by morphologic features — pronouns, noun affixes, verbs affixes. Given approximately two hundred languages with data on them ranging from short word lists to thousands of bibliographic entries, some new kind of survey technique appeared to be in order. This Greenberg sought to furnish. Beginning with a general article critical of past work in the African field, including Afroasiatic (1948), he continued in a series of articles (reprinted 1955a), one of which was specifically concerned with this group of languages. Using basic word lists as the primary source of data he revised previous estimates of what languages belonged to the Cushitic and Chadic branches and how they should be grouped within these branches. This he put into a total frame, which he renamed Afroasiatic along the way, consisting of five sub-groups. The renaming was primarily to avoid the term 'Hamitic' being abstracted from 'Hamito-Semitic' (Greenberg 1955b: fn. 4). The non-existence of Hamitic has been stressed by Cohen (1953) who had difficulty seeing how scholars could still hold to a concept he had shown to be fallacious as early as 1924 (as done, e.g., by Rössler 1950:461). The concept of five branches was not new, though many scholars omitted Chadic or included Hausa with uncertainty as to its position (Cohen 1947, Rössler 1950, Friedrich 1952). The Africanist attitude, on the other hand, was expressed by Westermann, who considered the five branch hypothesis to be the generally accepted view (1952:255). Chadic as a group, not just Hausa, had been previously proposed by Delafosse, Lukas, and Meek, as Greenberg noted (1948:26).

Using his survey technique Greenberg re-examined the data and presented, for the first time, a comprehensive statement of the Afroasiatic hypothesis. The essential reasonableness of his presentation has made it the working hypothesis of many scholars. The division into five did not imply that these were co-ordinate. They were rather to be understood as five groups of languages about which insufficient was known to relate them in any more precise manner (Welmers 1963:412–13; Polotsky 1964:122). As a hypothesis, it should be considered along with his general statements on methodology, such as the essay on the genetic relationship of languages (Greenberg 1957) or his remarks (Greenberg 1954) in reviewing Westermann and Bryan. From the statistical point of view he feels that the hypothesis is justified, having found 11 out of 1000 items represented in all five branches (Greenberg 1953b). A critique of his methods has been made by Winston (1966). Aware of the preliminary nature of Greenberg's conclusions he is still critical of the tolerance of inaccuracy inherent in the method. Despite this he admits the usefulness of the results. He also points out the fact that morphological data used in establishing genetic relationships furnish phonologic data (sound correspondences — see below).

Another technique for the preliminary classification of Afroasiatic languages was suggested by Tucker. Here the aim 'is to explore the possibilities of using patternings in the pronominal and conjugational systems as criteria in classification' (1967:655). Using Cushitic as a testing ground he shows that a reclassification of these languages may be made on this basis. Further work will check the hypothesis, but it appears to be a useful tool for the purpose it is meant to serve. It is interesting to note in this connection the results obtained by Pilszczikowa comparing Chadic pronouns (1960) and those of Newman-Ma working on sound correspondences (1966). Of Pilszczikowa's two groups, one is mostly Plateau-Sahel in Newman-Ma terminology. Group two is mixed but has only one Plateau-Sahel language.

The second trend, the effort to establish sound correspondences, may be considered as belonging more to the next phase of the study of Afroasiatic, the 'proof' of the hypothesis. Technically speaking the setting up of such correspondences should provide the final 'establishment' of relationships, but data are as yet insufficient for efforts in this area to be considered definitive. The major work is that of Cohen (1947). This contains an historical bibliographic survey of previous work on Afroasiatic, a chapter on morphology and a commendable attempt to set up sound correspondences between the four branches postulated (Semitic, Egyptian, Berber, Cushitic). Hausa is included but is not accorded a 'branch' and few words are cited. No other Chadic examples are given, though Lukas' proposal to include Hausa with other Chadic languages is mentioned. The list itself consists of 521 entries, organized phonetically, with the suggested sound correspondences given. It took advantage of all earlier work and has not been replaced as the basic reference set of proposed Afroasiatic cognates. It was somewhat severely criticized by Hintze (1951, who adds valuable bibliography), less so by Leslau (1949), Brockelmann (1950) and Cantineau (1948). All reject many of his proposed etymologies. Brockelmann estimated 188 go back, 'with more or less certainty', to the proto-language (1950:60). Cantineau felt that a sound residue was left after the most stringent criticism (1948:179). Cohen himself appeared to have second thoughts as to what he had accomplished (1951:310). Nevertheless, despite the shortcomings inherent in such a pioneer work, it is still rewarding to study. It is rather singular to find that in doing independent comparative work, often with sources unavailable to Cohen, one may turn up possible etymological sets which fit Cohen's sound correspondences even where his own examples do not appear to be valid. Leslau (1949) pointed up the danger of loanwords, as he also did later (1958) in bringing his expertise in the Cushitic-Ethiopic area to bear on etymologies proposed by Hohenberger and Greenberg. A large part of the problem is due to the proximity of Cushitic to the Semitic languages of Ethiopia and the spread of Arabic over the present-day Afroasiatic speech area (cf. Rundgren 1955:10–12). Few proposed lists have been free of suspects.

An important over-all discussion of Afroasiatic is that found in Diakonoff (1965). This work is an excellent general survey, including both phonology and morphology. Although not a large book it is the only real discussion of the field as a whole, at the same time being full of insights and suggestions. In the field of phonology it has advanced little beyond Cohen (1947). The latter's proto-phonemes were, as he himself said (1947:68), those previously hypothesized for proto-Semitic. Diakonoff accepts this but adds two. One is a glottalized /p'/. Possible support for this (or at least for another voiceless labial) has come from Greenberg (1958), Illič-Svityč (1966), and Dolgopoljskij (1966) (see below). The other is a sibilant /s̱/, set up to account for the various sounds used for pronominal and causal morphemes: Akk. /š/, Heb. /h/, Aram /ʔ/, Ar. /s/. Most scholars have considered these differences to be due to the use of different morphemes in the various languages (e.g. Polotsky 1964:112; Rabin 1963:112; Rundgren 1955:151). Despite his proto-phoneme to account for them Diakonoff also refers to them as separate morphemes (1965:70, fn. 43).

Some general observations may be made on the correspondences proposed. Fairly good equations have been set up for such sounds as /p t k b d g s r l m n y w ʔ/.

It is not that these regularly yield the same sound in each daughter language, but rather that some promising sets of words with these sounds may be found, representing several or all the branches. Diakonoff points out (1965:37) that many triconsonantal roots contain /r l m n w y ʔ/, tying this in with his sonant theory (see below). It is significant that sounds such as /ḥ ʿ r ṭ ḍ ṣ θ̣ ð̣/ are among those more difficult to relate, and even /θ ð q/ are not easy. It is also significant that most of the first list may be illustrated by pronouns, noun affixes (such as /m-/, /-t/, /-w/, /-y/) and verb affixes (/s-/ causative, /n-/, /t-/). The third list includes very few sounds which are or form part of (recognized) regular affixes. /ḥ-/ as prefix (Leslau 1962b) is the clearest exception.

There have been a number of less comprehensive essays, contributing to the stock of probable etymologies and establishing more firmly or more accurately selected sound correspondences. Egypto-Semitic studies are the most frequent, following a long-established tradition. Vergote (1945) gives a very useful list of Egypto-Semitic sound correspondences with numerous examples. It serves very well as a summary of the work done by the beginning of the period under review. An attempt to evaluate the Egypto-Semitic situation and put it on a solid footing was made by Vycichl (1958). A prolific writer and thoroughly versed in the field, he sifted through the etymologies hitherto proposed and presented a selected, annotated list. Of the 948 etymologies gathered by Calice and published in 1936 he says pessimists would reckon about 100 to be valid while even extreme optimists would not go much beyond 200 (1958:367). He sets up a point system for evaluating etymologies, using one number for form and another for meaning (cf. Cantineau 1948). With regard to form, 3 indicates that all consonants match, 2 there is one irregularity, 1 there are two irregularities, 0 three or more. On the meaning side, 3 indicates identity, 2 a meaning shift known in Afro-asiatic, 1 a shift known from other languages, 0 that the semantic connection is pure conjecture. Of 76 etymologies which he presents and rates, 59 are given 33. Despite such care equations such as Eg. *j*, Sem. ꜣ, *j*, *l*, *r*, *w* (read Eg. /ʔ/ Sem. /ʔ, y, l, r, w/) remain. Also given the set Eg. *d*, Sem. *d ð ṭ*, Vycichl points out that Eg. *jd* (read /ʔd/) could correspond to fifteen different Semitic roots (if all combinations occurred, 1958:368). Vycichl has also contributed to Cushitic-Egyptian and Berber-Egyptian comparisons as well as other aspects of Afroasiatic (see his bibliography 1958 and also below).

Among contributions to Egypto-Semitic etymologies may be mentioned those of Lacau (1954), Müller (1961 — primarily Ethiopic Semitic), Leslau (1962a — mainly Ethiopic Semitic) and Ward (1961, 1962). Two articles by Hodge (1966, 1969) took sound correspondences as the starting point. A third (1968a) included a number of proposed etymologies with stress on the vowels rather than the consonants. One of these (1966) attempted to establish by numerous examples three correspondences between Egyptian and Hausa: Eg. /ꜣ/ Ha. /r/, /l/; Eg. /q/ Ha. /k'/; Eg. /ğ/ Ha. /s'/. Eg. /ꜣ/ — Sem. /r/ ~ /l/ (and sometimes /n/) was a well-established correspondence. However, /ꜣ/ was also equated with Sem. /ʔ/ (e.g. Vergote 1945:128; Cohen 1947:76–8;

Vycichl 1958:371). Rössler stated categorically that the /ꜣ/ — /r/ correspondence was the only possible one (1964:213). One of Hodge's purposes (1966)[2] was to stress this same fact, allowing also for /l/ and /n/ but definitely rejecting Eg. /ꜣ/ — other language /ʔ/. The Egyptian sound represented by single reedleaf (transcribed ỉ and by many as *j* [= i̯] was to be interpreted consistently as [ʔ]. This is used as a working hypothesis in all articles (1966, 1968a, 1969). Only two etymologies raise any serious doubts (those for /ꜣ č p/ 'load' and /z ꜣ b/ 'jackal'). The second article (1969) follows up the Eg. /ğ/ Ha. /s'/, endeavoring to find correspondences to Eg. /ğ/ among the emphatics of Semitic, Berber and Cushitic and the glottalized consonants of Chadic. No neat pattern emerged, but apparent groups of related words were found. Rössler (1964) offers a number of proposed etymologies, some illustrating new sound correspondences. His lists include words represented in Semitic-Cushitic-Chadic-Berber (205), Semitic-Cushitic (208), Semitic-Egyptian (213), and Cushitic-Berber (207). One of his main theses is the Semitic character of Berber.

It is clear from the above that no reliable over-all set of correspondences has been established. Diakonoff's table 'main Phonetic Correspondences in Semito-Hamitic' (1965:26–8) illustrates the still uncertain state of affairs. It follows that phase 3), the collection of further data, is the most necessary task at hand. While it is left to the articles on the individual branches to indicate advances in our knowledge of these, some of the broader implications are mentioned here. The best example of internal comparative work on a branch, that of Newman-Ma on Chadic (1966), contains no discussion of Afroasiatic as a whole. Using their list of proto-Chadic forms a few suggestions of possible related words, mostly Egyptian, were made by Hodge (1968a). While Newman-Ma aimed at the internal sound correspondences of most of Chadic, another article, that of Illič-Svityč, had a more limited aim. Building upon an earlier study by Greenberg (1958), Illič-Svityč (1966) reconstructed the labials of Chadic and then related these to Afroasiatic as a whole. Greenberg had shown that one Chadic group had six labials compared to the proto-Semitic three /p b m/. He concluded that /f/ (Chadic and Egyptian) was a separate Afroasiatic phoneme and that there may have also been an /ᵐb/ phoneme. The third distinction maintained by Chadic he left an open question. Illič-Svityč confirms Greenberg's /f/ but considers /ᵐb/ a combination including a prefix /m-/. Another article of Greenberg's (1965) gives further evidence for */ᵐb/ as a unit phoneme in the proto-language.

Dolgopoljskij's article (1966) is a study of labials and dentals in Cushitic, with their analogues in other Afroasiatic. He finds the three-way distinction reflected by Egyptian /f p b/ (reconstructed by him */p/, */p'/, */b/) to exist in Cushitic as well as Chadic. (We have noted that one of Diakonoff's departures from Cohen's list of protophonemes was the addition of /p'/; see above.) All three articles, Newman-Ma (1966), Illič-Svityč (1966) and Dolgopoljskij (1966) are efforts to take the next step following Greenberg's statement of the hypothesis, that is, the setting up of sound

[2] Originally presented as a paper at the Fourth West African Languages Congress, Ibadan, March 1964, and therefore written independently of Rössler.

correspondences for the individual branches. As such they represent more of a breakthrough in the study of Afroasiatic than any others in the period under consideration. Nevertheless, they are to some extent still analyses based on inadequate data, though field work (such as that of Hoffmann, Jungraithmayr, Newman and Ma in Chadic) is moving the study of Afroasiatic closer to the next phase. It is not implied that the three articles mentioned above are the only recent contribution to this aspect of Afroasiatic. That of Rössler on Berber */b/ should also be mentioned. This, though less extensive, also presents an internal set of correspondences essential to broader comparison.

At least as much effort has gone into the study of comparative morphology as has been spent on comparative phonology. When von Soden delivers his indictment of the field (1965), it is primarily directed against studies in comparative morphology. In Afroasiatic the phonology is recalcitrant; the morphology, on the other hand, offers some striking surface similarities. From Benfey's study of Semitic and Egyptian in 1944 to the present, morphologic features have been used as prime classificatory evidence. Descriptions of the family generally begin with a list of such features. Cohen gives verb forms, both prefix and suffix along with pronouns suffixed to noun and verb as being proof of relationship (1947:43–4). A comprehensive assessment of the morphologic features common to Semitic and Egyptian is given by Vycichl (1959a), along with phonologic data, in an effort to establish the position of Egyptian *vis-à-vis* Semitic. Most of Gordon's additions to Egypto-Semitic in his article of 1957 are morphological. Greenberg, in arguing for the inclusion of Chadic, lists morphologic features this group shares with others in the family, such as feminine *t*, connective *n*, noun plurals, etc. (1963:46–8). Many examples could be quoted from older literature.

Two separate aims may be distinguished in the study of morphology. One of these is classification, the other is reconstruction of the proto-language; they are often fused. A few scholars have stated their preference for the use of morphology for the purposes of determining linguistic relationship (Polotsky 1964:360, fn. 10; Rundgren 1961:110). Others have thought of morphology as a preliminary tool, used in lieu of better data (Tucker 1967; Diakonoff 1965:11). As noted earlier, morphologic features also provide data for sound correspondences, but the affixes so far identified have been phonologically restricted (see above). Relationship based on morphology alone would not provide anything like a full set of sound correspondences. It has served rather as a binder, to provide the 'proof' of relationship while awaiting the establishment of the family in phonologic detail.

The major motifs of the morphologic literature may be said to be: the nature of the root in the proto-language (how many consonants, the nature of the syllabic peak, nominal *vs.* verbal origin, root extensions); the verb (prefix conjugation, suffix conjugation, vowel patterns, 'derived' forms, aspect); the noun (affixes, vowel patterns, stem types); pronouns (personal, demonstrative, origin and relationships). On the whole these topics continue long-established areas of interest.

Discussions of the nature of the root have naturally been highly colored by the basic Semitic orientation of most scholars in the field. The 'root and pattern' system of Semitic, with a predominantly three consonant root and added vowel patterns, does not readily lend support to the theory of a proto-language involving roots with fixed vocalic or sonant components. Egyptian and Berber appear to support Semitic in this respect, while Cushitic and Chadic have a definitely different pattern. In the latter two the predominant root structure is of two consonants, with a fairly stable vowel system. If the hypothesis of relationship is correct, one must assume for most roots either a loss of a consonant in Cushitic and Chadic, a gain of one in the other three, or a mixture of both. All solutions have their proponents. Cohen (1947:58–9) believed that Semitic reflected the original pattern. Afroasiatic was, then, a kind of Semitic, from which the other languages diverged. Cantineau, reviewing Cohen, apparently accepted this, speaking of two, three and even four consonant roots, after the Semitic pattern (1948:180). This 'Semitic' position may be briefly (and slightly inaccurately) called the triliteral or triconsonantal theory, as it is assumed that most roots had three consonants. (All, however, recognize the small group of two consonant ones, such as /'ab/ 'father'.) The other position, to be more closely defined below, may be called the biliteral or biconsonantal one. There are, of course, those who straddle the fence, admitting to original three consonant roots, original two consonant roots, and to three consonant roots resulting from the addition of some affix to two consonant ones (so, apparently, Rössler 1950:463–4). The argument is often confined to Semitic; only discussions affecting the larger sphere are mentioned here. The strongest statement supporting the triliteral root has come from Rössler (1964). He argues that Semitic and Berber represent a more archaic stage in this respect and that the shorter roots of Cushitic and Chadic are due to loss under African (Rössler 'Guinea') influence. It is, in a sense, up to the proponents of the two-consonant theory to prove their point. This they have not yet done. To date the most that they can do is to construct a reasonable hypothesis. The major problems have been the determination of which two consonants were original and what was the nature of the third. If the latter was an affix, it must have been a morpheme. Both its shape and its meaning must be demonstrated in order to prove the hypothesis. In this respect several interesting observations have been made by Diakonoff (1965). He assumes an original biconsonantal root with a vowel or sonant peak. Verbal suffixes such as those found in Chadic (e.g. in Margi) may reflect 'the originally grammatical character of the third radical' (1965:37). Morphemic identification of a few third radicals in Semitic nouns is furnished by traces of 'grammatical classes', characterized by suffixes (1965: 55–6). He also refers to the CVC root type of Chadic (1965:38) and Cushitic (1965: 37) as being more original. Diakonoff's concept of a single vowel or a sonant as the syllabic peak (1965:30–7) is close to that of Gazov-Ginsberg, who argues for a monovocalism in proto-Semitic similar to that of Lehmann's concept of proto-Indo-European (Gazov-Ginsberg 1965).

A biconsonantal root is assumed by Hodge (1965, 1968a, 1969). In making comparisons of CVC roots with CCC roots, only two of the consonants are considered. In some cases the third consonant may reasonably be assumed to be an affix; in others it is unexplained. In one article (1968a) an effort was made to reconstruct a few proto-Afroasiatic CVC roots, relying on similarities of vocalization, particularly in Cushitic and Chadic. It is obvious that this is not a simple matter, as the vocalisms of these two are often different in what appear to be related words. However, both Diakonoff (1965) and Hodge (1968a) emphasize the fact that the vocalization is more stable than Semitic in general would lead one to believe. Diakonoff, as have others, holds Akkadian to be conservative in this respect.

The study of comparative Semitic raised a number of problems concerning the origin, nature, and interrelationships of the different verb forms. Several of these have been transferred to the larger sphere of Afroasiatic. In the family as a whole there are found two types of personal affixes to the verb: prefixes and suffixes. Semitic has both, as does Cushitic. Egyptian has only suffixes. Berber and Chadic primarily use prefixes — or reflect the prefix type, though some suffixes are also found. The discussions of the past twenty-five years have been efforts to identify which of the similar forms do in fact owe their similarity to common descent and which to convergence.

With a few exceptions scholars agree that the proto-language had at least one prefix conjugation. Rössler argues for two (1950:506), Klingenheben for one (1956:257). Thacker (1954:319) proposed a pre-Egypto-Semitic period where the forms which later developed into verbs were uninflected. Thacker's views are not as far from those of the others as would appear at first glance, and a somewhat similar concept is advanced by Castellino (1962:44–5). Vycichl on the other hand feels that the verb forms of the proto-language were Semitic in type, those of Egyptian and Berber being derivative (1953b:377). Discussions of the verb have also involved the semantics — aspect *vs.* tense, etc. The most extensive treatment of aspect, that of Rundgren (1959), is restricted in scope to Semitic, though some broader applications are discussed. A brief reference to Afroasiatic is made by him in his book on Hebrew aspects (Rundgren 1961:108–11). While he is inclined to view the Semitic aspectual picture as probably that of the proto-language, he stresses the fact that structures, not just individual forms (*losgerissene Formen*) must be compared. In other words, a comparative syntax must be developed.

The relationship of prefix verb forms with a doubled second radical having an imperfective (so-called 'present') meaning is one of the problems inherited from Semitic studies. Found in Akkadian and Ethiopic these verb forms were for many years classic examples of areal linguistics, believed to be 'relic' forms surviving at opposite ends of the speech area (Polotsky 1964:110; cf. Rundgren 1955:312). In 1950 Rössler connected these with forms in Berber and Cushitic. In 1952 Greenberg also argued for a proto-Afroasiatic origin of the geminate present, mainly on the Semitic and Berber evidence, though drawing on Chadic, Cushitic and Egyptian (!). Leslau (1953) questioned the Ethiopic evidence (one of the key witnesses) and also the South Arabic (where no gemination actually occurred, a long vowel being interpreted as representing it: *-VCC- > -V:C-; reply by Greenberg 1953a).

Rössler's discussion of the prefix form with double radical was part of an overall presentation of the Afroasiatic verbal system (1950). He felt that the extant forms justified projecting both prefix and suffix conjugations back into the proto-language, each conjugation having both a simple form and one with doubled middle radical. The suffix conjugation was represented by the Akkadian permansive, the West Semitic perfect, the Egyptian Old Perfective and suffix forms in Cushitic, Berber and Chadic. It was essentially stative (and nominal), while the prefix conjugation was used for actions (and was verbal). The suffix form with double middle radical was used for describing inherent qualities, the corresponding prefix form being durative (1950:466). He incidentally supports a basically triliteral root system (1950:464). His thesis is further developed in later articles, these being particularly directed to the theory that Berber is Semitic (1951, 1952, 1964). This last aspect of his work has not been generally accepted (Ullendorff 1961:22; Moscati 1959:19–21). His concept of the verb forms, continuing as it does ideas rooted in the Semitic tradition, has met with considerable approval. Brockelmann (1951:140), Friedrich (1952), Polotsky (1964:111) and Diakonoff (1965:23) have written favorably of at least some of his basic theses. Rundgren (1955) and Klingenheben (1956) are among those most critical of them (see also Cohen 1953).

The most thorough review of Rössler's hypotheses was made by Klingenheben (1956). Nearly thirty years before (1928:266) he had postulated a single conjugation, one with prefixes, for the proto-language. In 1956 he reasserts this, adding that a number of derived stems also go back to this period. The development of the suffix conjugation as well as all moods, aspects, etc., he considers to have developed secondarily in the daughter languages (1956:258). The article itself is devoted to a point by point refutation of Rössler's claims. For example, he denies the relevance of the Berber forms to the Akkadian geminate present, the connection between the Egyptian Old Perfective and the Akkadian permansive, maintains the secondary nature of the Ethiopic evidence and, incidentally, holds to a biliteral rather than a triliteral root system. On the whole Klingenheben writes very convincingly, but the argument so often depends on one's interpretation of the evidence that there will continue to be discussion on these issues for some time to come (cf. Diakonoff 1965:90, fn. 86). Nevertheless, he appears very much aware of the complexity of the situation and reveals a sound sense of linguistic realism. For example, he stresses the fact that verbal formations and constructions are constantly being made and reshaped, older forms being broken down or lost. Such a process is, of course, clearly seen in the language with the longest history, Egyptian. While he, like Rössler, has overstated his case, his views of the nature of linguistic change will undoubtedly outlast some of his conjectural detailed explanations. On the other hand, it should not be assumed that Rössler's theses have been entirely demolished. It is particularly hard to believe that the Egyptian Old Perfective and the Akkadian permansive do not reflect a common older form. One may also question Klingenheben's position on the Cushitic forms. The Bedauye non-verbal predication, composed of a noun, adjective or pronoun plus a set of suffixes related to the deictic determinative (Tucker-Bryan 1966:543) is taken by Rössler to be related to the Akkadian permansive and Egyptian Old Perfective, that is, the 'suffix conjugation' (Rössler 1950:493–4). Klingenheben (1956:234–7) feels that by pointing out its nominal character (noun plus copula) he has eliminated it for possible comparison with the permansive, etc. This would not seem to follow. The forms may not be related, but their nominal character does not disqualify them.

Castellino's is a more recent discussion of the Afroasiatic verb (1962) but is not so well knit. A stimulating book, offering ideas on many facets of the verb (and also pronoun — see below), it must nevertheless be used with care. Von Soden is, as noted above, highly critical of it (1965), not without reason. Thacker's work on the verb (1954), dealing almost exclusively with Semitic and Egyptian, has met with more favor for its contributions to the internal history of Egyptian than for his solutions of Afroasiatic problems. He assumes three original root types unassociated with any traditional verbal meanings, such as time, aspect, etc.: **qatl*, **qitl*, **qutl*.

The assumption of three vowels in the proto-language, in contrast to Diakonoff's more subtle analysis (1965:29–38; see above), is that most readily deduced from a traditional Semitic base. Discussions of the semantic values of /a i u/, particularly as stem formatives, are therefore nothing new. Vycichl attributes the causative/factitive meaning of the second form *qattal* (as distinct from the 'present' of the same shape) to the vocalization (1957:24). Castellino attempts to assign a meaning to each such 'characteristic vowel' of the root: '*-a-* marking the activity (with transitive meaning) in relation to an object; *-i-* marking what happens to the subject...; *-u-* indicating an intransitive state or condition affecting the subject' (1962:49, with references to earlier work).

Discussions of the verb have often included theories concerning the relationship of the noun to the verb, either with regard to specific forms (derivation) or the relative antiquity of the two. Rössler, for example, takes the nominal forms *qattal*, *qattāl* (the latter the agent noun pattern) to be derived from the verb (1950:477). Klingenheben assumes the opposite — that the verbs are derived from the nouns (1956: 249–50,257). A general survey of the noun is found in Diakonoff (1965:55–69). The major topics treated are gender, declension and plural formation. Gender and its formal representation have been treated at some length by Klingenheben (1951). The suffixes associated with it are generally identified with demonstrative elements, and further comment on them is made below. Semitic has declensional endings which might reasonably be attributed to an earlier stage, but there is little support from the other branches. Egyptian presumably did not have these endings, though this is inferred rather than attested, as the vowels are not written. The other branches are of such late attestation that any similar declensional forms which may appear there are very likely to be secondary.

The use of different vowel patterns to distinguish singular and plural, so well known in certain Semitic languages, exists to some extent in the other branches (Diakonoff 1965:66–9, who doubts their existence in the proto-language). One of these patterns, the main feature of which is the insertion of /a/ between the second and third consonants (sg. *qatl*, pl. *qatal*), has been traced by Greenberg in all five branches (1955b), a fact which he takes to be striking confirmation of the Afroasiatic hypothesis. A large number of noun stem patterns have been discovered to be common to Egyptian and Semitic (Vergote 1965; see EGYPTIAN). Vycichl has continued to publish on selected formations (e.g. the agent noun type *qattāl*, 1953c, 1957:14–15). He also believes he has identified a fossilized Berber suffix which corresponds to the Semitic nisbe (/-ī/ or /-iyy/, Eg. /-y/ 'pertaining to'; Vycichl 1952a; cf. Gordon 1957).

An increasingly important area of research has been the effort to identify morphemes which cut across the classification into nouns, verbs, etc. It is also an area in which speculation is often too little controlled. Again problems raised in Semitic are brought into the Afroasiatic field. Is an /s/ causative affix the same morpheme as an /s/ pronoun stem? Is the /t-/ 'she' prefix to the verb the same as the 'feminine' /-t/ nominal suffix and the /t/ of the independent pronoun? A number of scholars have considered such questions, usually in connection with the discussion of the pronominal system (personal, demonstrative). Among these have been Otto, Klingenheben, Rundgren and Castellino.[3]

Otto (1951), using Egyptian demonstratives as the basis for discussion, divides the morphemes into 1) local elements (near, far, simply deictic) and 2) nominal elements (determiner, number, gender). He sees in the Egyptian demonstrative pronouns elements identifiable both within Egyptian and related languages. /n/ and /d/ are described as having local reference; /t/ and /w/ are nominal formatives, /t/ being feminine and /w/ having both a nominalizing function and a plural function (perhaps separate suffixes /w_1/ and /w_2/). Egyptian and Berber share /a/ sg. *vs.* /i/ pl. elements, a local element Eg. /ʿ/ Ber. /γ/, an /n/ (Eg. neuter, Ber. pl.), and possibly deictic /p/. He is careful to point out that these are 'possibilities', not certainties. Klingenheben (1951) takes up the gender and number affixes. One of the points at issue is whether the two-gender (masculine and feminine) system, the prevailing one in Afroasiatic, goes back to the proto-language. Klingenheben feels that it does. He considers it possible that it eventually goes back to an earlier non-gender system but thinks that this is a pre-Afroasiatic stage and beyond our present powers of reconstruction (1951:79). Like Otto (and many earlier scholars) he attributes a number of the affixes to original demonstrative elements. Rundgren (1955), on the basis of an intensive study, especially of the Ethiopic evidence, considers /s/ ~ /š/, /t/ and /n/ to be basic elements found both in Semitic and other Afroasiatic. He is not, however, convinced of the existence of Afroasiatic as a proto-language from which the others are derived. These elements go back, in his opinion, to a 'Hamito-Semitic speech type, whether related or not'

[3] For a brief survey of older literature on the pronominals and demonstratives see Rundgren 1955:8–9.

(Rundgren 1955:333 tr.). Von Soden is very sceptical of these efforts to see common elements in the demonstratives and verbal affixes (1965:165). Nevertheless, it would appear that there is considerable support for relating them (cf. Diakonoff 1965:41, 70, 76–7). It is also likely that future work in this area will involve the study of semantic shift from one component of a 'pronoun' to another (see below). In support of von Soden's scepticism one may note that so far no one has formed a hypothesis setting up original forms, their meanings and patterns of combination, which would reasonably result in the extant forms. It does seem possible, however, that such a hypothesis will be possible in the near future. The forms hypothesized will undoubtedly turn out to be 'pre-gender' and will fall into the stratum which Klingenheben feels at present beyond our reach.[4]

It has long been recognized that the third person pronouns are demonstrative in origin, so that a sharp line may not be drawn between discussions of the demonstratives and those of the personal pronouns. Diakonoff has a short, sober appraisal of the latter (1965:69–77), dividing them into what we may paraphrase as independent subject pronouns, oblique pronouns, and suffix possessive pronouns. He believes that the original situation was more complex. Earlier writers had done a great deal of comparison and much detailed analysis of the forms. Castellino (1962) has presented a segmental analysis of the pronouns. Following Reinisch to a large extent, he not only assigns meaning to the various components but also suggests semantic shifting from one component to another (1962:15). Among earlier work on pronouns may be mentioned that of Vycichl, who usually centers the discussion on the Egyptian forms (1953a). His discussion of the Egyptian independent forms in /nt-/ (as /ntk/ 'you', /ntf/ 'he') involves the identification of the /n/ with a demonstrative stem and its use with syntactic constructions in other languages (1954b).

The entire area of comparative morphology is full of brilliant suggestions, along with a great many improbable analyses. The same data are used to support diametrically opposed views. One can but hope that some of these differences will be resolved and more generally accepted conclusions drawn on the basis of more intensive study of the individual branches. The internal reconstruction and other historical implications of such work will provide the foundation for a more sophisticated comparison of the morphologies involved. The morphologic studies which have been done show clearly that the establishment of sound correspondences is not enough to explain the relationships of forms and that comparative syntax and semantics must also be developed.

Comparative syntax has not been systematically treated, but some valid comparisons of selected structures have been made. Rundgren, in discussing the demonstrative and relative elements, notes striking syntactic parallelisms between Egyptian (including Coptic), Semitic and Berber (1955:298–311). Cazelles, taking note of the fact that the Egyptian Old Perfective was regularly compared with the Akkadian perman-

[4] Greenberg's observation (1948:28) is very interesting in this context: 'The genders of the Niger-Chad group, of at least probable Hamitic affiliation, are interpreted as an African class system.'

sive without reference to West Semitic, found what he felt was a syntactic usage of a Hebrew form parallel to the statives of the other two languages (1957). Here was a possible vestige in West Semitic of the suffix conjugation presumed (by some) to go back to the proto-language. Thacker has compared the use of the Egyptian verb *w n* 'to be' as an auxiliary with similar constructions in Semitic, showing these to be structurally comparable though not employing the same morphemes (1963). The parallels are convincing semantically, and material from other Afroasiatic languages may be added (e.g. Hausa). Vycichl (1963) has brought out an interesting parallel in the usage of the independent third person pronoun in Egyptian and Berber. In both languages it may serve as a second clause introducer (Vycichl: 'aber'). There is, however, no overall effort at comparative syntax.

Another motif frequently found in the literature, and going back well into the last century, is the ascription of linguistic similarities to substrata. Egyptian was often described as a mixture of Semitic and African features, caused by the mixing of peoples speaking different languages (see Polotsky 1964:123). It is certainly reasonable to consider all of the linguistic possibilities — substrata, adstrata, pidginizing, and creolizing — but the tendency now is to test the hypothesis that at least some of the similarities are due to inherited characteristics, that they are evidence that Egyptian is genetically related to the other languages. Vycichl, for example, illustrates the shift from the substratum to the relational concept (compare Vycichl 1954a, 1958:368, but 1959a:41–2).

Efforts have not been lacking to connect Afroasiatic with other language families. One may mention particularly the work of Homburger (1949), Mukarovsky (1966, q.v. for further bibliography), and Dolgopoljskij (1964). A useful bibliography of such studies, and also of Afroasiatic as related to Egyptian, is to be found in Korostovcev (1963:234–41).

BIBLIOGRAPHY

BROCKELMANN, C. 1950. Review of Essai comparatif sur le vocabulaire et la phonétique du chamito-sémitique, by Marcel Cohen. BiOr 7.58–61.

——. 1951. 'Die Tempora' des Semitischen. ZPhon 5.133–54.

CANTINEAU, J. 1948. Review of Essai comparatif ... by Marcel Cohen. BSL 44. 173–80.

CASTELLINO, G. R. 1962. The Akkadian personal pronouns and verbal system in the light of Semitic and Hamitic. Leiden, E. J. Brill.

CAZELLES, H. 1957. Un vestige de pseudo-participe en hébreu. GLECS 7.46–8 (1954-57).

COHEN, MARCEL. 1947. Essai comparatif sur le vocabulaire et la phonétique du chamito-sémitique. (Bibliotheque de l'école des hautes études, 248). Paris, Honoré Champion.

——. 1951. Langues chamito-sémitiques et linguistique historique. Scientia 86.304–10.

——. 1952. Langues chamito-sémitiques. Les langues du monde, ed. by A. Meillet and Marcel Cohen, 81–181. Paris, H. Champion.

——. 1953. Sémitique, égyptien, libyco-berbère, couchitique et methode comparative. BiOr 10.88–90.

DALBY, DAVID. 1966. Levels of relationship in the comparative study of African languages. AfrLS 7.171–9.

DIAKONOFF, I. M. 1965. Semito-Hamitic languages. (Also in Russian.) Moscow, Nauka.

——. 1967. Jazyki drevnej Perednej Azii. Moscow, Nauka.

DOLGOPOLJSKIJ, A. B. 1964. Gipoteza drevnejšego rodstva jazykovyx semej severnoj evrazii s verojatnostnoj točki zrenija. VJa 2.53–63.

——. 1966. Materialy po sravniteljno-istoričeskoj fonetike kušitskix jazykov: gubnye i dentaljnye smyčnye v načaljnom položenii. Moscow, Nauka.

FRIEDRICH, JOHANNES. 1952. Semitisch und Hamitisch. BiOr 9.154–7.

GAZOV-GINZBERG. 1965. The Semitic root and the general linguistic theory of monovocalism (in Russian, English summary). Semit. jaz. 2.200–4, 873. Moscow, Nauka.

GORDON, CYRUS H. 1957. Egypto-Semitica. RSO 32.269–77.

GRANDE, B. M. 1963. Kurs arabskoj grammatiki v sravniteljno-istoričeskom osveščenii. (Akademiya Nauk SSSR. Institut Narodov Azii). Moscow, Izdateljstvo Vostočnoj Literatury.

GREENBERG, JOSEPH H. 1948. The classification of African languages. AmA 50.24–30.

——. 1952. The Afro-Asiatic (Hamito-Semitic) present. JAOS 72.1–9.

——. 1953a. A reply. JAOS 73.167–8.

——. 1953b. Historical linguistics and unwritten languages. Anthropology today, ed. by A. L. Kroeber, 265–86. Chicago and London, University of Chicago Press.

——. 1954. Review of Languages of West Africa, by Dietrich Westermann and M. A. Bryan. Lg 30.302–9.

——. 1955a. Studies in African linguistic classification. New Haven, Compass Publishing Company.

——. 1955b. Internal *a*-plurals in Afroasiatic (Hamito-Semitic). Afrikanistische Studien Diedrich Westermann zum 80. Geburtstag gewidmet. Deutsche Akademie der Wissenschaften zu Berlin, Institut für Orientforschung, 26. Berlin, Akademie Verlag.

——. 1957. Essays in linguistics. (Viking Fund publications in anthropology 24). New York, Wenner-Gren Foundation.

——. 1958. The labial consonants of proto-Afro-Asiatic. Word 14.295–302.

——. 1963. The languages of Africa. (Indiana University Research Center publication 25). Bloomington.

——. 1965. The evidence for */^{m}b/ as a proto-Afroasiatic phoneme. Symbolae linguisticae in honorem Georgie Kuryłowicz, ed. by Adam Heinz, Mieczysław Karas, et al., 88–92. Wrocław, Warszawa, Kraków, PAN.

HINTZE, F. 1951. Zur hamitosemitischen Wortvergleichung. Bemerkungen zu M. Cohen, Essai comparatif. ZPhon 5.65–87.

HODGE, CARLETON T. 1966. Hausa-Egyptian establishment. AnL 8/1.40–57.

——. 1968a. Some Afroasiatic etymologies. AnL 10/3.19–29.

——. 1968b. Afroasiatic '67. Language Sciences 1.13–21.

——. 1969. Egyptian ǧ (I 10) amid Afroasiatic. American Oriental Society, Midwest Branch, Semi-centennial volume. Bloomington, Indiana University Press.

HOMBURGER, L. 1949. The Negro-African languages. London, Routledge and Kegan Paul Ltd.

ILLIČ-SVITYČ, V. M. 1966. Iz istorii čadskogo konsonantizma: labialjnye smyčnye. Jazyki Afriki, 9–34. Moscow, Nauka.

KLINGENHEBEN, AUGUST. 1928. Die Tempora Westafrikas und die semitischen Tempora. ZES 19.241–68.

——. 1951. Althamito-semitische nominale Genusexponenten in heutigen Hamitensprachen. ZDMG 101.78–88.

——. 1956. Die Präfix- und die Suffixkonjugationen des Hamitosemitischen. MIO 4.211–77.

KOROSTOVCEV, M. A. 1963. Vvedenie v egipetskuju filologiju. (Akademija Nauk SSSR, Institut Narodov Azii). Moscow, Izdateljstvo vostočnoj literatury.

LACAU, P. 1954. Egyptien et sémitique. Syria 31.286–306.

LESLAU, WOLF. 1949. Review of Essai comparatif sur le vocabulaire et la phonétique du chamito-sémitique, by Marcel Cohen. Lg 25.312–16.

——. 1953. The imperfect in South East Semitic. JAOS 73.164–6.

——. 1958. Observations of a Semitist on recent etymologies proposed by Africanists. Africa 28.324–8.

——. 1962a. Semitic and Egyptian comparisons. JNES 21.44–9.

——. 1962b. A prefix ḥ in Egyptian, modern South Arabian and Hausa. Africa 32.65–8.

MOSCATI, SABATINO. 1959. The Semites in ancient history. Cardiff, University of Wales Press.

MUKAROVSKY, HANS G. 1966. West African and Hamito-Semitic languages. WVM 8.9–36.

MÜLLER, W. W. 1961. Äthiopisches zur semitisch-ägyptischen Wortvergleichung. Muséon 74.199–205.

NEWMAN, PAUL, and ROXANA MA. 1966. Comparative Chadic: phonology and lexicon. JAfrL 5.218–251.

OLJDEROGGE, D. A. 1949. Xamitskaja problema v afrikanistike. SE 3.157–70.

——. 1952. Proisxoždenie narodov centraljnogo Sudana (Iz drevnejšej istorii jazykov gruppy xausa-kotoko). SE 2.23–38.

OTTO, EBERHARD. 1951. Über die Demonstrativa und Nominalbildung im Altägyptischen. ZDMG 101.52–66.

PILSZCZIKOWA, NINA. 1960. Le haoussa et le chamito-sémitique à la lumière de 'l'Essai comparatif' de Marcel Cohen. RO 24.97–130.

POLOTSKY, H. 1964. Semitics; Egyptian. The world history of the Jewish people, first series, vol. 1, At the dawn of civilization, ed. by E.A. Speiser, 99–111, 121–34. Tel-Aviv, Massadah Publishing Co.

RABIN, C. 1963. The origin of the subdivisions of Semitic. Hebrew and Semitic studies presented to G.R. Driver. Oxford, Oxford University Press.

RÖSSLER, OTTO. 1950. Verbalbau und Verbalflexion in den Semito-Hamitischen Sprachen. Vorstudien zu einer vergleichenden Semitohamitischen Grammatik. ZDMG 100.461–514.

——. 1951. Akkadisches und libysches Verbum. Or 20.101–7, 366–73.

——. 1952. Der semitische Charakter der libyschen Sprache. ZA 50.121–50.

——. 1958. Die Sprache Numidiens. Sybaris, Festschrift Hans Krahe, 94–120. Wiesbaden, Otto Harrassowitz.

——. 1964. Libysch-Hamitisch-Semitisch. Oriens 17.199–216.

RUNDGREN, FRITHIOF. 1955. Über Bildungen mit '*š*' und *n-t*-Demonstrativen im Semitischen. Uppsala, Almquist and Wiksells Boktryckeri.

——. 1959. Intensiv und Aspektkorrelation, Studien zur äthiopischen und akkadischen Verbalstammbildung. (Uppsala Universitets Årsskrift 1959:5.) Uppsala, Ab Lundequistska Bokhandeln.

——. 1961. Abriss der Aspektlehre. Stockholm, Göteborg, Uppsala, Almqvist and Wiksell.

SCHRAMM, GENE M. 1967. The correspondence of distinctive oppositions in distantly related languages. To honor Roman Jakobson, essays on the occasion of his seventieth birthday, 1769–74. The Hague, Mouton.

SHARBATOV, G. Sh. 1967. Semito-xamitskie jazyki. Sovetskoe jazykoznanie za 50 let, 391–403. Moscow, Nauka.

SODEN, WOLFRAM VON. 1965. Zur Methode der Semitisch-Hamitischer Sprachvergleichung. JSS 10.159–77.

SPEISER, E. A. 1964. Akkadian; Semites. The world history of the Jewish people, first series, vol. 1, At the dawn of civilization, ed by E.A. Speiser, 112–20, 135–41. Tel-Aviv, Massadah Publishing Co.

THACKER, T. W. 1954. The relationship of the Semitic and Egyptian verbal systems Oxford, Oxford University Press.

——. 1963. Compound tenses containing the verb 'be' in Semitic and Egyptian. Hebrew and Semitic studies presented to G.R. Driver, 156–71. Oxford, Oxford University Press.

TUCKER, A.N. 1967. Fringe Cushitic: an experiment in typological comparison. BSOAS 30.655–80.

TUCKER, A.N., and M.A. BRYAN. 1966. Linguistic analyses, the non-Bantu lan guages of north-eastern Africa. (Handbook of African languages.) London, Oxford University Press.

ULLENDORFF, EDWARD. 1958. What is a Semitic language? Or 27.66–75.

——. 1961. Comparative Semitics. Linguistica Semitica: presente e futuro, ed. by Giorgio Levi Della Vida, 13–32. (Studi Semitici 4.) Rome.

VERGOTE, J. 1945. Phonétique historique de l'égyptien: les consonnes. (Bibliotheque du Muséon, 19). Louvain, Bureaux du Muséon.

——. 1965. De verhouding van het Egyptisch tot de Semietische talen (with French translation: Le rapport de l'égyptien avec les langages sémitiques). (MKVA 27.4). Brussel.

VOEGELIN, C. F. and F. M. 1964. The languages of the world, African fascicle one. AnL 6/5.281–339.

VYCICHL, WERNER. 1951. Eine vorhamitische Sprachschicht im Altägyptischen. ZDMG 101.67–77.

——. 1952a. Die Nisbe-Formationen im Berberischen. AION-O 4.111–17.

——. 1952b. Ein Nomen actoris im Ägyptischen, Der Ursprung der sogenannten emphatischen Konjugation. Muséon 65.1–4.

——. 1953a. Die ägyptischen Pronominalendungen. Muséon 66.381–9.

——. 1953b. Über eine Klasse ägyptischer Verben ult. j. ZDMG 103.373–7.

——. 1953c. Neues Material zur Form des ägyptischen Nomen Agentis *qattāl*. OLZ 48.293–4.

——. 1954a. Notes sur la préhistoire de la langue égyptienne. Or 23.217–22.

——. 1954b. Der Aufbau der ägyptischen Pronomina *ntf*, *nts*, etc. Muséon 67.367–72.

——. 1955. Gab es eine Pluralendung *-w* im Ägyptischen? ZDMG 105.261–70.

——. 1957. Pi'elformen im Ägyptischen und im Koptischen. MIO 5.10–25.

——. 1958. Grundlagen der ägyptisch-semitischen Wortvergleichung. MDAIK 16.367–405.

——. 1959a. Is Egyptian a Semitic language? Kush 7.27–44.

——. 1959b. Studien der ägyptisch-semitischen Wortvergleichung. ZÄS 84.70–4.

——. 1959c. Ägyptisch-semitische Anklänge. ZÄS 84.145–7.

——. 1960. Gedanken zur ägyptisch-semitischen Sprachverwandtschaft. Muséon 73.173–6.

——. 1963. Ägyptisch *swt*, koptisch *ntof*, berberisch *netta* 'er' und 'aber'. Muséon 76.211–14.

WARD, WILLIAM A. 1961. Comparative studies in Egyptian and Ugaritic. JNES 20.34–41.

——. 1962. Some Egypto-Semitic roots. Or 31.397–412.

WELMERS, W. E. 1963. Review of The languages of Africa, by Joseph H. Greenberg. Word 19.407–17.

WESTERMANN, DIETRICH. 1952. African linguistic classification. Africa 22.250–6.

WINSTON, F. D. D. 1966. Greenberg's classification of African languages. AfrLS 7.160–70.

CARLETON T. HODGE

A

SEMITIC

THE SEMITIC LANGUAGES

AN OVERVIEW

If the articles which follow this overview are concerned principally with the Semitic languages themselves rather than with a description of serious language study carried on in the Near and Middle East, it is because very little significant scholarly activity dealing with language has taken place in that region in modern times, except for the productivity of a number of outstanding philologists and linguists at the Hebrew University and, much more recently, at the younger universities in Israel.

There was once, to be sure, a fairly long period of indigenous effort, beginning with the Syrian grammarians of the Byzantine period[1] and extending through the golden age of Islam, in which interesting — and even exciting — works were written which dealt with the three principal literary languages: Arabic, Hebrew, and Syriac. These studies were by no means produced in a vacuum; their production paralleled impressive achievements in the other academic disciplines then pursued. Although the grammars and grammatical sketches of this era were undoubtedly motivated largely by the rôle of these languages as the media of Sacred Writ, such motivation, it seems, imposed no serious limitation on the depths of insight gained.

With the decline of the centers of higher learning in Southwest Asia and North Africa, what was left of the mantle passed to Western Europe and the Renaissance. While interest in Arabic and Syriac lingered on for a while, the cultivation of the study of Hebrew grew with the rise of the Reformation for obvious reasons. But the great era of grammatical works dealing with Hebrew was over.

One of the consequences of the Renaissance was the rise of the institution of the Ghetto, and the enforced physical separation of the western Jewish communities had as one inevitable result the intellectual isolation of the people involved. Scholarship among the Jews was by no means abandoned, but it was limited in direction, and the narrowing physical and intellectual boundaries had a peculiar effect on interest in language. Up until this time, it seems that Jewish communities throughout the world spoke the same language as did their non-Jewish neighbors. But the growing eastward migration of Jews from Germany did not result in the replacement of Yiddish by a Slavic language any more than did the resettlement of Spanish Jews throughout

1 An example of their sophistication may be seen by checking citations in J. B. Segal's *The diacritical point and the accents in Syriac* (London, 1953).

the Ottoman Empire presage the demise of Ladino. On the contrary, the pre-existing Jewish communities by and large switched to the languages of the new settlers. While there was widespread polyglottism, especially among the men, this was accepted as a social norm and offered no academic stimulus.

It is true, of course, that there never had been any real cultivation of language studies among the Ashkenazic communities of the West, and this must be given due consideration in this account. But there was a great grammarian tradition in Spain prior to 1492; the trauma of the expulsion in that year was such, however, that the Sephardic community never really recovered intellectually.

Meanwhile, in the Christian West, the study of Hebrew rapidly developed into a tool of religious polemic. As local languages replaced Latin in the liturgies of the churches of the Reformation, Greek and Hebrew replaced it as languages of the primary theological sources.

These factors are not to be underestimated, since much of the stagnation in the field of Semitic linguistics can be accounted for by them. Growing awareness of and interest in the phenomenology of language during the seventeenth, eighteenth, and nineteenth centuries might have provided new impetus, but such was not the case.

Semitists of the nineteenth century were slow to absorb the progress made by their Indo-Europeanist colleagues. Ernest Renan planned to write a comparative grammar of the Semitic languages under the title *Histoire générale et système comparé des langues sémitiques* (Paris, 1855), but succeeded only in producing the first part, the general history, a work that can be characterized as charming but naive. Akkadian was as yet unknown to the western scholarly community, and reports reaching Paris of the survival of Aramaic as a colloquial idiom were scoffed at: 'Ni l'hébreu, ni l'araméen, ni même l'arabe n'ont produit d'idiome dérivé qui soit à ces anciens idiomes ce que le prakrit, le pali, l'hindoui, l'hindoustani sont au sanscrit, ce que les langues néo-latines sont au latin. Il n'y a pas de langues néo-sémitiques' (p. 458f.). This was apparently an article of faith for Renan, in as much as he declares that 'A l'inverse des langues indo-européennes, les langues sémitiques se sont enrichies et perfectionnées en vieillissant' (p. 427f.). The obvious counterexamples to this offered by the modern languages of Ethiopia were dismissed on the grounds of miscegenation (p. 438).

By 1877, William Wright was compelled to state: 'Besides the results of Indo-European philology, those as yet attained by Semitic grammarians seem scant and dwarfish. ... It was reserved for men of our own day to take a decided step in advance. Thanks to the studies of a Gesenius and an Ewald, a Roediger and an Olhausen, a Dillmann and a Noeldeke, the Comparative Grammar of the Semitic Languages is at last beginning to assume the proportions of a science ....'[2]

If this statement by Wright is to be justified by anything, then certainly the successful decipherment of Akkadian cuneiform provides this justification. It was established

[2] William Wright, *Lectures on the comparative grammar of the Semitic languages* (Cambridge, 1890).

by Edward Hincks in 1849 that Akkadian cunieform was a syllabic orthography and then, in 1851 by H. C. Rawlinson, that the characters were polyphonous in value and that the language was probably Semitic. On these bases, Akkadian was reconstituted with the help of the comparative method. By 1860, enough was accomplished to enable J. Oppert to publish a grammatical sketch of the language, and in 1889 F. Delitzsch published the first reference grammar of Akkadian that could be called a solid piece of work. But Assyriologists, on the whole, were and still are mainly interested in the Akkadian language as a tool for research in the ancient history of the Near East. As a consequence, the comparative method was taken up by them almost exclusively for the purpose of shedding more light on the meanings of Akkadian forms.

In more recent times, comparative studies were called upon again for a similar purpose. In 1930, following the French excavations at Ras Shamra, Syria, the previous year, a successful decipherment of the clay tablet inscriptions unearthed there was accomplished, apparently independently and simultaneously, by Hans Bauer, E. Dhorme, and Ch. Virolleaud, adding an additional ancient tongue, Ugaritic, to the semitistic repertory. The first grammatical description of Ugaritic was published in 1940 by Cyrus H. Gordon, followed in 1947, 1955, and 1965 by revised and enlarged editions.[3]

Interest in Arabic and Syriac was rekindled early in the nineteenth century as part of the growth of orientalia in general. In 1844–48, C. P. Caspari published his *Grammatica Arabica*, which later was to be translated into German and then into English.[4] For Aramaic, in spite of Renan's disclaimer, studies in the modern colloquials appear as early as 1868 with Nöldeke's *Grammatik der neusyrischen Sprache am Urmiasee und in Kurdistan* (Leipzig, 1868) and his classic *Mandäische Grammatik* (Halle, 1875). The colloquial Arabic dialects begin to appear in 1827 with M. Vasalli's *Grammatica della lingua maltese* (Valetta, 1827). Ethiopic studies begin amazingly early, with Hiob Ludolf's *Grammatica Aethiopica* in 1661, but were largely neglected until the nineteenth century. Even more amazing is the earliness of Isenberg's *Grammar of the Amharic language* (London, 1842).

For Hebrew, the first edition of Gesenius' *Hebräische Grammatik* was published in Halle in 1813. Its twenty-eighth edition, published in the same city by E. Kautzsch in 1909, was translated into English by A. E. Cowley the following year (Oxford, 1910). The most recent in this chain is that of G. Bergsträsser (Leipzig, 1918). These are solid, but old-fashioned, philological treatments. In 1922, Hans Bauer and Pontus Leander published their huge *Historische Grammatik der Hebräischen Sprache des Alten Testamentes* (Halle, 1922), which, despite its title, is not a historical grammar at all, but rather an attempt to bridge the gap between the language of the Bible and an *ad hoc* reconstruction of proto-Semitic.

[3] Cyrus H. Gordon, *Ugaritic manual* (Rome, 1965).
[4] The most recent edition is William Wright's *Grammar of the Arabic language*, edited by W. Robertson Smith and M. J. de Goeje (Cambridge, 1951).

For comparative Semitic, the standard reference is still Carl Brockelmann's mammoth *Grundriss der vergleichenden Grammatik der semitischen Sprachen* (in two volumes; Berlin, 1908 and 1913), a vast compilation of virtually all the data available half a century ago with practically no comparative reconstruction at all. Much more recently there appeared Sabatino Moscati's edition of *An introduction to the comparative grammar of the Semitic languages*,[5] a useful summary of the field. But perhaps the most convincing evidence of the lack of real progress is the fact that the only monograph dealing with comparative Semitic studies that can be termed a truly great contribution was produced not by a Semitist at all, but by an Indo-Europeanist: Jerzy Kuryłowicz's *L'Apophonie en sémitique* (Warsaw, 1961).

Wright's complaint of ninety years ago still stands, but his hopes for new breakthroughs would be more valid today than in his own time. Until recently, the terms linguist and semitist were almost mutually exclusive. I believe that this came about largely as a result of German philological dominance in Semitic studies which persisted after the decline of neogrammarianism during a period when there was no real activity of a linguistic nature in Germany. At the same time, linguistic efforts were largely anthropologically oriented, and philological data were shunned. Today's hopes rest on the existence of a few, all too few, universities where it is at last possible for a student to concentrate on general linguistics and Semitic studies at the same time.

GENE M. SCHRAMM

[5] Written jointly by Sabatino Moscati, Anton Spitaler, Edward Ullendorff, and Wolfram von Soden (Wiesbaden, 1964).

COMPARATIVE SEMITICS

EDWARD ULLENDORFF

When, in 1781, A. L. Schlözer[1] introduced the term 'Semitic' (based on the genealogical table in Genesis 10), he gave formal expression to a relationship between the languages spoken by the Hebrews, the Aramaeans, the Arabs, and other peoples, which had been recognized for a long time. Subsequently, the term 'Semitic' was used to characterize not only those members of the group that were known at the close of the eighteenth century but was also applied to some ancient languages (e.g. Akkadian, Ugaritic, etc.) to be discovered only in the nineteenth and twentieth centuries as well as to the modern forms of some of the 'classical' languages (e.g. Soqoṭri, Amharic, or the neo-Aramaic dialects).

While the officers of the King of Assyria (2 Kings 18) were able to speak Hebrew, Aramaic, and Assyrian, the Bible does not tell us whether they recognized any resemblances between these three tongues.[2] We may, however, doubt that such recognition obtruded upon their conscious minds, since the stimulus of such an awareness would probably derive from knowledge of a language of very diverse character — a rather unlikely contingency despite the existence of languages of fairly heterogeneous structure, such as Egyptian or the language of the Philistines, on the fringes of the Old Testament world.

It must remain perplexing that in the vast rabbinical literature matters of strictly linguistic interest occupy so negligible a place, especially as the continuing use, side by side, of Hebrew and Aramaic (the latter in its various dialects) might have offered a favourable field for comparative studies. Of course, there was no dearth, either in the Bible, Talmud, or Midrash, of facile etymologizing; but while it is easy to recognize isolated and random vocabulary resemblances, it requires intellectual endeavour of a different order to discern similarity of morphological structure.

It was only from the tenth century onwards that Jewish grammarians and exegetes, largely under the impulse of Arabic philology, began to give thought to the patent resemblances of Hebrew, Aramaic, and Arabic. This effort was at first directed at the elucidation of difficult scriptural passages but later on extended into the domain of morphology. 'And the highest stage is represented by scholars who systematically

[1] *Repertoire für Biblische und Morgenländische Literatur*, VIII.161 (1781).

[2] Cf. E. Ullendorff, 'The knowledge of languages in the Old Testament', Bulletin of the John Rylands Library, Manchester, 44.455–65 (1962).

compared the structures of Hebrew and Arabic by establishing the functional equivalents' (Polotsky 1964:99). Men like Saʿadia ben Yoseph, Yehuda ibn Quraysh, Menahem ben Saruq and others of that period laid the foundations of comparative Semitic studies. A millennium has thus passed since the inception of this discipline; and though there has naturally been progress, the advance has been halting and irregular, periods of stagnation alternating with forward thrust or occasionally even retrogression.

In the sixteenth and seventeenth centuries Christian theologians and orientalists compared the vocabularies and verbal paradigms of Hebrew, Aramaic, Arabic, and Ethiopic, but most of them still considered Hebrew as the 'original' language, and any deviations from its 'pure' type were in the nature of 'corruptions'. Polyglot Bibles, in particular, offered a fertile field for comparative Semitic studies and also furnished the data upon which exegesis and textual criticism could be based. Edmund Castell's *Lexicon heptaglotton* (comprising Hebrew, Aramaic, Syriac, Samaritan, Ethiopic, Arabic, and Persian) was a remarkable achievement, and Hiob Ludolf's great Ethiopian works, during the second half of the seventeenth century, marked a formidable advance in both substance and method. Ludolf's books repay close study even today; they were far ahead of their time, and their author must be reckoned among the greatest Semitists of any period.

While comparative Semitics possesses a long and chequered history, advance of a really decisive character did not occur until Bopp's epoch-making studies on the relationship of the Indo-European languages placed linguistic researches in general on a scientifically more secure as well as more fruitful basis. It is, perhaps, a curious facet of Semitic scholarship that methodological progress, notions of linguistic discipline, have almost invariably come from without, usually from the Indo-European side. But men like de Sacy, Gesenius, Ewald and others in the early nineteenth century were not slow to apply these new recognitions to the study of the Semitic languages. They laid the foundations for the remarkable progress which Semitic researches experienced throughout the last century, culminating in the polymathic genius of Theodor Nöldeke,[3] whose *Mandäische Grammatik* (Halle, 1875), among many other fundamental works, was a consummate achievement and the great model for this type of work.

This was the golden period of comparative Semitics, the era of the giants: Dillmann, Praetorius, William Wright, Brockelmann, Guidi. Meanwhile cuneiform had been deciphered, and Akkadian established itself as an important branch of Semitic studies. Others followed — such as South Arabian and Phoenician, as well as many of the modern forms of Arabic, Aramaic, and Ethiopic. This expansion of the available material was paralleled by a new understanding in depth; linguistic thinking was undergoing important changes: sound-laws and their status in linguistic development became part of the movement of scientific ascendancy, and the Semitic consummation

[3] 'whom all Semitists, whatever their speciality and their allegiance, acknowledge as The Master' (Polotsky 1964:108).

of this process was marked by Brockelmann's monumental *Grundriss* (1908–13), a work which has, over the past 60 years, exerted a profound influence and occupied a deservedly privileged position.

The establishment of Assyriology as an independent discipline and the rise of modern linguistic notions had gradually removed the study of Hebrew from the centre of Semitics which it had occupied for so long by virtue of its association with the Bible and theology. 'The greatest calamity that has befallen Hebrew is that in the divorce of Semitic studies from theology, Hebrew was assigned to the latter' (Polotsky 1964: 100).

During the present century comparative Semitic linguistics had to contend with strong centrifugal forces of three different types — in themselves not interrelated — which diverted interest into spheres largely divorced from linguistic study. In the first place, Assyriologists had always been inclined to look upon their subject as one that deserved, indeed demanded, to be studied with exclusive devotion, partly on account of a complex and non-Semitic writing system, a justified and even necessary concern with substrate languages and cognate civilizations, such as Sumerian, Hurrian, and Hittite, and partly because comparative Semitics seemed at times to obscure rather than to illuminate some of the features peculiar to Akkadian. Similar concern with their substrata, the Cushitic languages, would occasionally lure students of Ethiopian languages away from comparative Semitics into the even more hazardous alleys of comparative Hamito-Semitics.

The second tendency to desert diachronic Semitic studies arose from an interest in civilizations as a whole: Arabists with a concern for other Semitic languages gave way to *islamisants* who were bound to step outside the area of Semitics and seek contacts with other Islamic languages, such as Persian or Turkish, which had very disparate linguistic affiliations. Similarly, students of Syriac or Ethiopic frequently had an interest in Oriental Christianity and thus found a home in Armenian, Coptic, or Georgian researches rather than in comparative Semitics.

Thirdly and finally, the most serious threat to the comparative study of the Semitic languages did not originate from the rival attraction of related disciplines but from methodological considerations: a deep-seated revulsion from comparativism which appears to be a concomitant of contemporary linguistics. There can be no doubt that descriptive study must precede any comparative endeavour, for it is obvious that any sound historical examination can only succeed if the synchronic analysis has been properly done. Yet, comparative linguistics is a respectable occupation and answers a genuine human urge of inquiry, for — as Polotsky (1964:103) has said with characteristic felicity — 'the very existence of related languages constitutes a problem the legitimacy of which can hardly be denied'.

The history of Semitic studies has yet to be written. It would be a task of great fascination to survey what has been achieved and what remains to be done, and who have been the principal workers in this vast field of Semitics — from the time of Jerome or Saʿadia or Jonah ibn Janah to Albright, Driver, or Polotsky.

The traditional habitat of the Semitic languages is in western Asia, in particular Arabia, Mesopotamia, and Syria-Palestine. Whether the original home of the ancestor of these languages has to be sought in the Arabian peninsula or the Horn of Africa is within the realm of speculation and cannot be securely established. Apart from Arabia, the Fertile Crescent, and Ethiopia, areas of Semitic speech have been established outside this region by virtue of migration or conquest: Arab penetration throughout North Africa and on the islands of the Indian Ocean; Assyrians in Anatolia; or Phoenicians along the coasts and on the islands of the Mediterranean. Phoenician was even used at Karatepe in Cilicia where the author of the royal inscriptions appears to have been 'accustomed to the use of Phoenician for lapidary purposes'.[4] Aramaic gained an astonishing diffusion as a lingua franca, from Afghanistan to Egypt.

There is no dearth of attempts at grouping and classifying the Semitic languages. Classification[5] is harmless, unobjectionable, and at times even useful, if confined to describing present-day habitat and the prevailing geographical circumstances, but it is apt to obscure and confuse if intended to explain genetic connexions. In pressing some features for special consideration one is bound to neglect others that might materially affect the over-all picture. The value of linguistic classification schemes is purely pragmatic and calls for countless qualifications and contingent allowances, for it is comparatively easy to lump together any two languages and show the special affinities they bear.

In speaking — as we customarily do — of North-East Semitic (the languages of Mesopotamia), North-West Semitic (Syria and Palestine), and South-West Semitic (the languages of Arabia and Ethiopia) we are simply reflecting the geographical facts, without drawing any genetic or typological inferences. Schemes of classification which identify and distinguish groupings within the Semitic area on the basis of specific bundles of isoglosses may derive support from structural, functional, and genetic criteria. But not only does the position of, say, Ugaritic or South Arabian remain the object of scholarly disagreement, as indeed do the common features which have been postulated for Akkadian and Ethiopic on the grounds of *iparras* — *yəqattəl*, but the entire framework of comparison and the testing of affinities on the statistical, typological, and historical plane present formidable problems which will require more detailed methodological probing than they have hitherto received. On the whole, it may however be claimed that the rough geographical division indicated above corresponds tolerably well to the distribution of gross linguistic features.

Akkadian is the North-East Semitic language which was spoken in Mesopotamia in the two and a half millennia before the Christian era and which had replaced the non-Semitic Sumerian. The latter has, however, exerted a strong influence on the phonetic and phonological system of Akkadian (especially the loss of the laryngals) as well as upon its syntax. Akkadian diverges markedly from the usual Semitic two-

[4] Cf. A. M. Honeyman, 'Phoenician inscriptions from Karatepe', *Muséon* 61.56 (1948). See also S. Moscati, *Il mondo dei Fenici* (Milan, Il Saggiatore, 1966).
[5] Cf. Edward Sapir, *Language* (1921), Chapter VI.

tense plan. In the course of its long history it has developed a number of dialects and readily distinguishable linguistic phases.

The North-West Semitic languages of the Syro-Palestinian region make their first attested appearance in the second millennium B.C., largely in the form of the pseudo-hieroglyphic inscriptions of Byblos, the proto-Sinaitic inscriptions, and the so-called 'Canaanite' glosses in the Tell Amarna letters. Amorite is represented by certain sentence-type proper names and by some of the linguistic peculiarities of the Akkadian texts of the period of the First Babylonian Dynasty, and especially the Mari texts. Ugaritic, the language of the epigraphic material discovered at Ras Shamra from 1929 onwards, must however be considered the principal manifestation of second millennium North-West Semitic. It has profoundly influenced the study of the Old Testament, and 'the addition of Ugaritic to the repertoire of the Semitic languages' marks 'the most important change in the status of Semitics since Brockelmann's *Grundriss*'.[6]

Towards the end of the second millennium B.C. 'the distinction between Canaanite and Aramaic may properly be introduced', for 'Canaanite represents the non-Aramaic linguistic manifestations of the Syro-Palestinian area' from that time onwards (Moscati, Spitaler, Ullendorff, and von Soden 1964:9). The best attested, most longevous, and most elaborately studied of this group of languages (or, for that matter, of any Semitic language) is, of course, Hebrew. With a millennium of Biblical literature preceding the Christian era, 1500 years of rabbinic writings as well as exegetical, poetic, and philosophical works, and nearly a century of modern revival, Hebrew still presents many problems to the linguist (Ullendorff 1963:11–16). Its position within the Semitic languages is not as unambiguous as might be supposed, its tense system is far from having yielded all its secrets, and its syntax still awaits comprehensive treatment for the whole of its long history. Recent endeavours in the descriptive analysis of Israeli Hebrew show considerable promise.[7]

Phoenician and Punic have already been referred to, while Moabite — represented by the ninth century inscription of King Mesha — may possibly be a Hebrew dialect of the central Palestinian type.[8]

Aramaic is attested over a wide area of the ancient Near and Middle East and in a variety of dialectal forms; it has survived in several isolated communities to this day. Classical or Imperial Aramaic (of which the Biblical Aramaic of the books of Ezra and Daniel is a prominent type) is the language that was employed under the Assyrian, Babylonian, and Achaemenian empires about the middle of the first millennium B.C.

West Aramaic is represented by Nabataean and Palmyrene — both languages that were used by Arab populations — as well as Jewish Palestinian Aramaic, the language

[6] C.H.Gordon, *Ugaritic textbook* (Rome, 1965), p. 2. See also E.Ullendorff, 'The position of Ugaritic within the framework of the Semitic languages', *Tarbiz* 24.121–5 (1954–55).

[7] Cf. Haiim B.Rosén, *Ha'ivrit še'lanu* (Tel Aviv: Am-Oved Ltd., 1955); and *A textbook of Israeli Hebrew* (University of Chicago Press, 1962).

[8] See S.Segert, *AO* 29.197–267 (1961).

spoken in Palestine at the time of Jesus and during the first Christian centuries. Samaritan Aramaic and Christian Palestinian Aramaic belong to the same western group, but their literary documents cannot compare in extent and diversity with those of Jewish Palestinian Aramaic. An interesting survival of western Aramaic may be encountered in the Anti-Lebanon village of Maʿlula.[9]

The principal East Aramaic language is Syriac, originally the tongue of Edessa, which developed a rich Christian literature and is attested in two slightly differing forms (mainly of a phonetic character) of the Western Jacobites and the Eastern Nestorians. The linguistic distinctions correspond to certain ecclesiastical differences. Other representatives of Eastern Aramaic are Babylonian Aramaic, the language of the Babylonian Talmud, and Mandaean, the language of the Gnostic sect of Mesopotamia.[10] Modern survivals of East Aramaic are found near Lake Urmia and in the neighbourhood of Mosul. These modern Aramaic dialects have recently been subjected to some excellent linguistic investigations, carried out with exemplary method and profound knowledge of the subject.[11]

In turning to the South-West Semitic region we encounter three main representatives: Arabic, the South Arabian languages, and the Ethiopian languages. The position of South Arabian *vis-à-vis* the other two groups is still not securely established; and it seems safer, for present purposes, to assign it an independent place among the South-West Semitic languages. That South Arabian conquerors carried their language(s) and script to Abyssinia cannot be seriously questioned, but from a descriptive point of view it has been noted by some scholars that Old South Arabian is in several respects in agreement with classical Arabic and at variance with Ethiopic — just as the opposite is true in other cases.

'Proto-Arabic' is the term by which we describe the languages of the epigraphic material which precedes the formal attestation of classical Arabic. The conventional sub-division is into Liḥyanite, Ṣafaitic, and Thamudic.

Classical Arabic — the Arabic *par excellence* — came to replace Aramaic as the lingua franca over most parts of the Semitic region and, indeed, well beyond it as far as the shores of the Atlantic. It owes its linguistic crystallization to pre-Islamic Arabic poetry and to the Qur'an, while its geographical diffusion and long survival are the result of the Islamic conquests of the seventh century A.D. The Arabs thus fashioned a supra-tribal means of communication which, transcending their tribal dialects and ordinary modes of speech, became a most powerful symbol of Arab unity as well as one of the great languages of the world.

[9] Cf. A. Spitaler's model treatment in his *Grammatik des neuaramäischen Dialekts von Maʿlula* (Leipzig, 1938).

[10] Apart from Nöldeke's masterly grammar (already referred to), we now possess E.S. Drower and R. Macuch, *A Mandaic dictionary* (Oxford, 1963), and R. Macuch's *Handbook of classical and modern Mandaic* (Berlin, 1965).

[11] See in particular H.J. Polotsky, *JSS* 6.1–32 (1961); Konstantin Tsereteli, *Materials on Aramaic dialectology*, vol. I: *The Urmia dialect* (Tbilisi, 1965; Aramaic text and Russian translation); Irene Garbell [died 1966], *The Jewish neo-Aramaic dialect of Persian Azerbaijan* (The Hague: Mouton, 1965).

'High Arabic', largely the result of a process of systematization by Arab grammarians, combines 'artificiality and vigorous vitality in a most extraordinary manner' (Polotsky 1964:106). While colloquial Arabic appears in a large number of regional dialects which, at the opposite ends of the spectrum, may become mutually unintelligible, the force of politico-religious consensus and tradition has effectively debarred these spoken forms of the language from literary use.

Epigraphic or Old South Arabian is the language, dialectally variegated, of the ancient South-West Arabian city-states (approx. eighth century B.C. to sixth century A.D.), whose vast inscriptional resources have been unearthed during the past 150 years. Although the absence of vowel notation and of certain morphemes that are unlikely to occur in this lapidary style has unhappily placed marked limitations upon our knowledge of the language, scholars like Ryckmans, Beeston, Höfner, and others have greatly enhanced our understanding of Sabaean, Minaean, Qatabanian, Ḥaḍrami, and Awsanian. As far as can be judged from the appearance of the consonantal skeleton, these dialects are likely to have remained within the range of mutual intelligibility.

The modern South Arabian languages, Soqoṭri, Meḥri, and Šḫawri, are often held to be the continuation and development of the ancient speech forms, but investigations are insufficiently advanced to allow us to be certain about this. Most of the material at our disposal is owed to the labours of the Vienna South Arabian Expedition at the turn of the century. By now we are in pressing need of fresh material based on the whole gamut of modern technical equipment. The task is urgent in view of the increasing pressure and encroachment of Arabic. In 1967, T. M. Johnstone of London University carried out field work on the island of Soqoṭra; publication of his material is eagerly awaited.

Ethiopic (Geʿez) is the language which evolved on Ethiopian soil as a result of the South Arabian penetration into the horn of Africa. It makes its epigraphic appearance in the first few centuries A.D., particularly in the great Aksum inscriptions. Thereafter it became the vehicle of an extensive Christian literature reaching up to modern times. As a spoken language Ethiopic has long since been replaced by a plethora of modern Semitic tongues[12] which have been subjected to the impact — varying in extent — of a number of Cushitic substrata. The results of this influence have been particularly marked in the spheres of their sound and sentence structure.

'Ever since the days of Hiob Ludolf (1624–1704) the Semitic languages of Ethiopia have been fortunate in the men whom they attracted' and who produced 'works of which Semitic linguistics can be proud. The field is inexhaustible and exceptionally fascinating' (Polotsky 1964:107). More, perhaps, than in any other area of Semitics the study of the Ethiopian languages has married the best of contemporary linguistic methods to raw material of remarkable variety and range.

[12] Among which the most important are: Tigre and Tigriña in the north, and Amharic, Harari, and Gurage in the south. Cf. W. Leslau, *An annotated bibliography of the Semitic languages of Ethiopia* (The Hague: Mouton, 1965). Also: E. Ullendorff, *The Semitic languages of Ethiopia* (London, 1955).

The Semitic languages which have been briefly mentioned in the foregoing survey exhibit a relationship sufficiently close to each other to assume that at one time they must have constituted one single language which, in the course of time and by virtue of geographical separation, became so differentiated as to turn into a number of distinct tongues. By using the artificial concept 'Proto-Semitic' we simply refer to the ensemble of features, or isoglosses, which an examination of the historically attested Semitic languages leads us to regard as common property of the Semitic group in its most ancient phase (cf. Moscati, Spitaler, Ullendorff, von Soden 1964:15). Newly discovered Semitic languages or fresh recognitions should keep the Proto-Semitic working hypothesis in constant flux and ever ready to accommodate changes and altered dispositions. The basic concepts must at all times remain flexible enough to prevent the imposition of a Procrustean framework upon what are bound to remain hypothetical reconstructions. 'The notion of "primitive unity" has to be taken with a grain of salt; it is, in fact, as chimeric as would be that of the First Semite' (Polotsky 1964:109).

The measure of affinity between the Semitic languages is such as to liken Semitic to the Romance, Germanic, or Slavonic divisions rather than to Indo-European. The latter might possibly be compared to Hamito-Semitic. This larger grouping comprises — apart from Semitic — Egyptian, Berber, and Cushitic. It would not, however, be right to juxtapose Hamitic with Semitic, for there does not exist a Hamitic 'family' comparable to the Semitic one. The internal relationship between Egyptian, Berber, and Cushitic is — according to Polotsky, the most profound connoisseur of this domain — 'quite obscure' (Polotsky 1964:122–3). Polotsky does not rate the chances of progress in comparative Hamito-Semitic linguistics very high, partly in view of the nature of the material and partly because, apart from Egyptian, none of the African members of the stock is known from sources earlier than the nineteenth century (*Ibid.*).

One competent Semitist has recently arrived at the conclusion that the Hamitic languages are, in fact, African languages which have acquired certain Semitic phonological, morphological, and lexical forms. In other words: some African languages became Hamitic when they were exposed to the impact of a strong Semitic superstratum (Garbini 1965:13). However, the similarities are such as can hardly be accounted for by the assumption of borrowing, acquisition, or contagion. 'Although it is not (and perhaps cannot be) established that even whole grammatical paradigms are immune in this respect, it is safer to assume that languages sharing fundamental morphological elements owe them to common origin rather than to borrowing' (Polotsky 1964:122).

One of the most difficult tasks for the linguist is the establishment of the identity of a language in precise rather than impressionistic terms. If such descriptive and unambiguous identification is difficult for one single language, this is a fortiori the case where a whole group of languages, such as Semitic, is concerned. We can usually recognize a Semitic language when we meet one; yet such recognition is not tantamount to ability to describe it in terms that would commend themselves to a linguist.

While it may be easy to recognize, from experience, a Semitic language of the 'orthodox' type represented by, say, Arabic or Ethiopic or Ugaritic, where the Semitic characteristics are most fully and most clearly developed, the position may be very different with regard to modern Hebrew or Amharic or Soqoṭri. In the latter cases our historical knowledge of genetic relationships would decide the matter, but we might well have grave doubts if we were ignorant of the genealogical circumstances. This is particularly true when we observe the abandonment of much of the common Semitic vocabulary, the surrender of many of the accepted phonological notions, the well-nigh complete disintegration of Semitic syntax, and considerable inroads even into the 'système fermé'[13] of the morphology. In other words: it would be a diachronic rather than a synchronic descriptive approach that would determine classification; we would be guided by our knowledge of historical ramifications and not by typological analysis.

The frequently canvassed view that the Semitic languages stand in such proximity to one another that their affinity can be observed 'at a glance' may be defended in connexion with some of the so-called classical languages; but the relationship between, for instance, Gurage and Phoenician, or Mandaean and Akkadian can scarcely be considered patent or obvious.

It has become a commonplace that one of the most characteristic traits of the Semitic languages lies in the special relationship between consonant and vowel (references in Ullendorff 1958:69). It must not, however, be supposed that the relative importance of consonant *vis-à-vis* vowel is expressed in numerical terms. Statistical samples have shown (*Ibid.*) that the ratio between consonants and vowels in Semitic languages does not markedly differ from that attested for many Indo-European languages.

On the other hand, the claim that meaning in Semitic reposes 'entirely' in consonants has, on the face of it, a good deal to commend it, although the use of 'entirely' is hardly justified. I take it that 'meaning' in this context stands for primary semantic distinctions, for modifications, most often of a grammatical nature, brought about by vowels (Kuryłowicz 1962, Petráček 1960–64) convey meaning-variants and are thus at least of secondary semantic significance. Yet, internal vowel changes, indicative of grammatical rather than lexical distinctions, occur in Indo-European languages as well: *sing*, *sang*, *sung* or *give*, *gave* or *goose*, *geese* or *Vater*, *Väter*, etc. It seems, therefore, impossible to define, unequivocally, the identity of a Semitic language in terms of

consonants = carriers of 'Wurzelbedeutung' (Bergsträsser 1928:6); and
vowels = modifiers.

This special relationship between vowel and consonant appears to be restricted to the area of the verb and direct verbal derivatives. Bergsträsser himself concedes (*loc. cit.*) that in many nouns the relationship between consonant and vowel does not

[13] Cf. A. Meillet, *Linguistique historique et linguistique générale*, p. 84 (Paris, 1948),.

differ significantly from that obtaining in many non-Semitic languages: e.g. Hebrew *'ab* 'father' – *'eb* 'bud' – *'ob* 'bag'. In Akkadian *pu* 'mouth', Hebrew *pe*, Ethiopic *'af*, vowels form an integral part of the semantic pattern — quite indistinguishable from their role in Indo-European languages.

Instances of this type are not confined to biconsonantals; among triconsonantals (though their number is smaller in this connexion) one might mention:

Arabic	*jimāl*	'camels'	—	*jamāl*	'beauty'
Hebrew	*ḥäräb*	'sword'	—	*ḥoräb*	'drought'
Ethiopic	*sämun*	'week'	—	*sämen*	'north'

Closely bound up with the relations between consonant and vowel is the question of triliterality. Yet even this much-canvassed characteristic cannot be accepted, simpliciter, as a safe and unequivocal trait in the Semitic identity card. In the first place, triconsonantal morphemes are, it appears, quite widespread in Indo-European and other languages. And, secondly, while it is true to say that triconsonantal elements (either owing to *Systemzwang* or other causes) are predominant in most Semitic languages in their fully developed form, there are significant exceptions which upset any attempt at discovering a uniform pattern. Quite apart from the preponderance of biradicals in the Cushitic languages, there exist notable biconsonantal areas also in such languages as Akkadian,[14] Amharic, modern South Arabian, etc.

The biconsonantals are, perhaps, a suitable point from which a beginning may be made in setting out a number of characteristic elements which, in their cumulative effect, are likely to determine positively rather than negatively, the Semitic identity. It is probably widely accepted nowadays, on what must be considered cogent evidence, that historically many triconsonantal words represent, in fact, extensions of originally biconsonantal elements. There exist certain simple bases which run through a large number of 'roots' common to many Semitic languages, such as *fl* (or *fr*) 'to divide', *qt* – *qd* 'to cut', etc.[15] These bases were apt to be expanded, and the third consonant, in initial, medial, or final position, came to act as a modifier:

(a) initial:	*rḥm*	'to have compassion'
	nḥm	'to console'
(b) medial:	*šdf*	'to scorch'
	šzf	'to make brown, burn'
(c) final:	*zry*(*h*)	'to scatter'
	zr'	'to sow'

In the geminate type of the Semitic verb (i.e. identical second and third consonants) the device of gemination appears to have been employed to create triconsonantals

[14] Cf. W. von Soden, *Grundriss der Akkadischen Grammatik* (Rome, 1952) (Pontificium Institutum Biblicum), §§50, 51, 73.

[15] Cf. W. Wright, *Lectures on the comparative grammar of the Semitic languages* (Cambridge, 1890), p. 32; G. R. Driver, *Problems of the Hebrew verbal system* (Edinburgh, 1936), chapter II.

from original biconsonantals (such as Arabic *mdd* 'to stretch', *frr* 'to escape', etc.). That this is not mere speculation may be inferred from the fact that Semitic otherwise shuns identical consonants in verb morphemes (see below). It would thus appear that the original semantic connotation reposed in two radicals and that the third acted merely as a modifier.

Of exceptional importance in the determination of the Semitic *Sprachtypus* must clearly be 'the presence of definite, specifically Semitic, patterns of root morphemes, not occurring anywhere else, and their behaviour in relation to inflectional and derivative morphological elements' (Tsereteli 1967:7). The structural constitution of the Semitic root morphemes is obviously of crucial importance,[16] and the manner of their combination with affixal morphemes, as well as the structure of the latter, add up to a unique phenomenon, in both substance and performance, which in this constellation is highly unlikely to be repeated anywhere else.

It is a remarkable, and presumably unique, characteristic of the Semitic verbal root morpheme that it excludes identical and homorganic consonants in positions one and two. Thus *bbx* as well as *bmx* are impossible. While *xdd* occurs, *xdt* does not (cf. the observations on geminate verbs above); in other words: in positions two and three identical consonants are admitted, but homorganic ones are not. In positions one and three, there is a marked, but not consistent, shunning of identical and homorganic consonants (Greenberg 1950:162).

Again, while it is possible to demonstrate that neither the much vaunted laryngals nor the emphatic consonants (or possibly glottalized ejectives) are an exclusive possession of the Semitic languages, it is important to appreciate that the crucial factor relates to their phonological function and their behaviour in specific environments (cf. Tsereteli 1967:5).

Equally crucial is the role of internal flexion in Semitic where — as Petráček (1960–64) and Kuryłowicz (1962) have shown — apophony possesses a most pertinent morphological character. It is embodied in the phonological network of the language and produces, by contrastive vocalic patterns, a highly integrated paradigmatic system that has become the principal instrument of Semitic morphology (e.g. *yaqtulu* : *yuqtalu*; *qatala* : *qutila*; broken or internal plurals, etc.). Again, it is necessary to consider the system as a whole, for there is little doubt that individual features can be paralleled elsewhere.

Though vocabulary is a notoriously unstable factor and exposed to borrowings, changes, loss, and above all to purely fortuitous resemblances, yet well-distributed sectors of common stock still offer a ready, if not always completely reliable, guide to the establishment of relations of the more obvious type. While correspondence between the structural units of languages under comparison must remain the chief criterion for language grouping, lexical resemblances cannot be rejected out of hand. 'Here not the quantity of cognate items is important but their character' (Tsereteli

[16] Cf. von Soden, *loc. cit.*; B. Landsberger, *Islamica*, II:361–5 (1926); *idem*, *XIX Congr. Int. Or.*, 450ff.

1967:10). Clearly of particular significance are terms of relationship and similar basic notions (*'b* 'father', *'m* 'mother', *'ḫ* 'brother', *ym* 'sea', *dm* 'blood', etc.), pronouns, inflectional morphemes, some verbs, etc.

Statistical studies can also render much help in the determination of the Semitic *Sprachtypus*; and it seems that the full resources in this sphere have barely been tapped. Statistical samplings and calculations are often a salutary corrective to mere impressions (which occasionally turn out to have been erroneous) and may also throw into sharp relief common features which had not previously been recognized as significant. As examples in the phonological sphere I would mention J. Cantineau's studies in classical Arabic and Hebrew. Also, statistical work has proved that the general assumption that the prepalatals in Tigriňa are borrowed from Amharic cannot be maintained.[17] Similarly, a statistical study of the Ethiopic verb, by M. Cohen and some of his pupils,[18] has brought to light some interesting facts. This method may be employed with advantage to test common features, real or alleged, between Semitic and other language groups.

Finally, the most fundamental criterion of Semitic linguistic identity remains the interaction of the Semitic linguistic system as a whole — rather than the existence or absence of individual features in individual languages. What counts in the last resort are the operating rules of the over-all structure and the mutual relations of its parts and constituent elements.

REFERENCES

Bergsträsser, Gotthelf. 1928. Einführung in die semitischen Sprachen. Munich, Max Hueber.

Brockelmann, Carl. 1908–13. Grundriss der vergleichenden Grammatik der semitischen Sprachen. Vol. I: 1908; vol. II: 1913. Berlin, Reuther & Reichard.

Cohen, Marcel. 1947. Essai comparatif sur le vocabulaire et la phonétique du chamito-sémitique. Paris, Librairie Ancienne Honoré Champion.

——. 1952. Langues chamito-sémitiques (Les Langues du Monde, 2nd ed.). Paris, Centre Nationale de la Recherche Scientifique.

Fronzaroli, Pelio. 1966. Su alcuni problemi di tipologia morfologica in semitico. RALinc 21.210–23.

Garbini, Giovanni. 1965. La semitistica: definizione e prospettive di una disciplina. AION 15.1–15.

Greenberg, Joseph H. 1950. The patterning of root morphemes in Semitic. Word 6.162–81.

Hintze, Fritz. 1951. Zur hamitosemitischen Wortvergleichung. ZPhon 5.65–87.

[17] H. J. Polotsky, *JAOS* 67.143–4 (1947); E. Ullendorff, *The Semitic languages of Ethiopia* (London, 1955), 130–2.

[18] *RSEt* 9.41 ff. (1950).

KURYŁOWICZ, JERZY. 1962. L'Apophonie en sémitique. Wroclaw-Warsaw-Krakow, PAN, and The Hague, Mouton.
MOSCATI, SABATINO, ANTON SPITALER, EDWARD ULLENDORFF, and WOLFRAM VON SODEN. 1964. An introduction to the comparative grammar of the Semitic languages. Wiesbaden, Otto Harrassowitz.
NÖLDEKE, THEODOR. 1926. Semitic languages. Encylopaedia Britannica. 13th ed., vol. 24. London and New York.
PETRÁČEK, KAREL. 1960–64. Die innere Flexion in den semitischen Sprachen. AO 28.547–606; 29.513–45; 30.361–408; 31.577–624; 32.185–222.
POLOTSKY, H.J. 1964. Semitics and Egyptian. The world history of the Jewish people, vol. I, ed. by E.A.Speiser, 99–111, 121-34. London, W.H.Allen.
RABIN, C. 1963. The origin of the subdivisions of Semitic. Hebrew and Semitic Studies presented to G.R.Driver, ed. by D.Winton Thomas and W.D.McHardy, 104–15. Oxford, Clarendon Press.
TSERETELI, GEORGE V. 1967. The problem of the identification of Semitic languages. XXVII Int. Congress of Orientalists; papers presented by the U.S.S.R. Delegation, 1-12. Moscow.
ULLENDORFF, EDWARD. 1958. What is a Semitic language? Or 27.66–75.
——. 1961. Comparative Semitics. Linguistica Semitica: Presente e Futuro, ed. by G.Levi Della Vida, 13–32. Rome, Università di Roma, Centro di Studi Semitici.
——. 1963. Old Testament languages. A companion to the Bible, 2nd ed., ed. by H.H.Rowley, 11–18. Edinburgh, T. & T.Clark.

AKKADIAN

ERICA REINER

THE EMERGENCE OF AKKADIAN GRAMMAR

In 1855, the first Akkadian glossary, the *Lexique de l'inscription assyrienne de Behistoun* was published (F. de Saulcy, *JA* 1855.109–97), only a few years after the definitive decipherment of the third column (i.e. the Babylonian version) of Darius' inscription at Bisutun; in 1955, the first volume (letter Ḫ) of the Assyrian Dictionary of the Oriental Institute of the University of Chicago (= *CAD*) went to press. In those one hundred years, the task of deciphering cuneiform writing, the discovery of Mesopotamian civilization, and the establishment of the place of Akkadian as a member of the Semitic language family has been largely accomplished.

Although a convenient starting date to summarize work on Akkadian would be the year 1952, both to stay within the scope of the present volume, and to acknowledge, as an important milestone, the publication in that year of the *Grundriss der akkadischen Grammatik* by Wolfram von Soden,[1] we must, in order to understand the evolution of the present state of Akkadian studies, look back into the nineteen-twenties in order to assess the contributions to, and the influence on, all further research on Akkadian by Benno Landsberger.

After the first triumphant days when the understanding of Akkadian texts was first achieved, and when grammar and vocabulary of this newly discovered Semitic language was interpreted after the model of the other Semitic languages — mainly Arabic and Hebrew — Benno Landsberger (1926) was the first to issue a programmatic statement, to emphasize that the measures and models for the understanding of Babylonian culture have to be found in that culture itself, through the search for its *Eigenbegrifflichkeit.* In this now classical article (reprinted in 1965) he stated the

[1] It should be said, at this conjuncture, 'the theses and results of which could henceforth not be ignored'; unfortunately, that has not been the case in general, except for the small school of von Soden's entourage, and instead, many workers in the field have operated as if this grammar did not exist. Only in the last few years have publications in the field of Assyriology shown the assimilation of the *GAG* and used it as the background for their own assertions. Thus, von Soden's plaint (1961a: 34): 'In der Assyriologie verbreitete sich ... die noch heute durchaus nicht ausgestorbene Vorstellung, dass man akkadische Texte auch ohne eindringende grammatische Studien übersetzen könne; an die Stelle exacter grammatischer Analyse tritt das Raten' has been valid for many years after he established the basis for 'exact grammatical analysis'.

principle that the Akkadian language cannot be analyzed according to some other grammatical model, but has to be discovered, by the heuristic method, from Akkadian itself.

The ideas of Landsberger have ever since the cited article determined the approach to Akkadian studies — speaking here of course only of the high quality and significant works. Specifically, they are reflected in and form the basis of the major work on Akkadian grammar, the *Grundriss der akkadischen Grammatik*, by W. von Soden, published in 1952.

Strangely enough, Landsberger himself has never again formulated in a comprehensive way in writing his analysis of the Akkadian language; however, during his years of teaching at the University of Leipzig (Germany),[2] from 1919 to 1935, he has influenced the thinking of the Assyriologists he trained there, so that much of the writing of these scholars may be considered the outgrowth and systematization of his teachings in the field of Akkadian, Sumerian, and also general Semitic. Landsberger himself continued to publish occasional articles on linguistic and philological topics, apart from the numerous specific points solved *en passant*, often in footnotes, in his many articles on other topics of Mesopotamian civilization. Some of the specifically linguistic articles are Landsberger 1924 and 1938.

The only systematic presentation of Akkadian grammar by Landsberger himself was published as a grammatical sketch included in G. Bergsträsser's *Einführung in die semitischen Sprachen* (München, 1928). Although written by Bergsträsser, the acknowledgment in the foreword makes it clear that the organization as well as the ideas of this grammatical sketch (Chapter 2, pp. 20–8) stem from Landsberger. Consonant with the neogrammarian approach still favored by Semiticists of that period, also illustrated by the fact that Chapter 1 of the book is devoted to proto-Semitic (*Ursemitisch*), the sketch begins with a discussion of Akkadian phonology as resulting from loss, contraction, assimilation and dissimilation from the proto-Semitic prototype, or contrasted with similar rules in other Semitic languages.

The discussion of the verb incorporates Landsberger's major discoveries for Akkadian: the recognition of the category of *Aktionsart* which, in contrast to the subjective category of aspect, is an objective category, referring to the way in which the action takes place (e.g. durative, punctual, iterative, etc.); that of a three-way tense distinction which besides the so-called 'present' and the so-called 'preterite' includes an infixed tense (formerly identified with a *t*-infixed stem of other Semitic languages)

[2] Thus was continued the Assyriological tradition of the University of Leipzig, since Landsberger's predecessor there, Friedrich Delitzsch (1850–1922), is perhaps the only single scholar who must be mentioned in connection with the development of cuneiform studies, as author not only of numerous books and articles, but also of a chrestomathy with sign lists, *Assyrische Lesestücke* (1st ed. 1876), in subsequent editions (3rd ed. 1885, 4th 1900, 5th 1912) enlarged with paradigms and glossary, of a grammar, *Assyrische Grammatik* (1st ed. 1889), and the *Assyrisches Handwörterbuch* (1896), the first comprehensive dictionary, with citations and references, for which he abandoned after three fascicles (1887–90) his first ambitious project, the *Assyrisches Wörterbuch*, that was to be a thesaurus of all published material.

to which later the name 'perfect' was to be given, and that of a 'modus', corresponding (morphologically) to the 'energicus' in other Semitic languages, which functions in Akkadian to indicate movement hither, in contrast to verb forms lacking this ending which then, for the same verb, indicate movement thither. To this he gave the name 'ventive' (Landsberger 1924), though for a while after that the terms 'terminative' and 'allative' were also used. Landsberger also discovered that verbs may be classified, according to the vowel alternation of the verb stem, into *Bedeutungsklassen* (for this see now Aro 1964). A further new insight into verb morphology gained at that time was the recognition of the formation of the present tense with the gemination of the second radical;[3] this gemination, long disregarded or denied by Semitists, was systematically treated by Greenberg as late as 1952 (see also below op. 289). It is presumably due to the caution of Bergsträsser, himself a Semitist, that the gemination of the second radical of the verb in this tense is written in parentheses, and is called, in the preceding phonetic section, secondary gemination after stress; nevertheless, although the repeated consonant is in parentheses, it is in this sketch that Akkadian present forms are written with geminated consonant for the first time.

While Landsberger furnished the insights, it needed the systematic mind of a student of Landsberger's, determined to provide the field of Akkadian with long-needed tools, to produce the basic grammar, under the significant title *Grundriss*. Von Soden's determination to produce, personally, the basic tools for the student first bore fruit in the form of a list of signs and their values: *Das akkadische Syllabar* (1948a); this was followed by the *Grundriss* in 1952, and by the *Akkadisches Handwörterbuch* (= *AHw.*), in process of publication since 1959 (now including A-M); the second edition of the *Syllabar* in 1967 contains several observations of principle on grammar (primarily on phonetics and phonology), and the second edition of the grammar, scheduled to appear in 1969, will contain additions and corrections.

The *Grundriss* supersedes all previously published comprehensive grammars, grammatical sketches, and dialect monographs of Akkadian and its dialects (see p. 279; special mention should be made of Nougayrol 1952, an excellent grammatical sketch, with bibliography including studies on stylistics and metrics). However, partly because of the *Grundriss*' comprehensiveness and complexity, ill-suited for beginning students, and partly because of its being in German, new editions (simple photomechanic reproductions or more or less extensively revised versions) of earlier grammars and newly written grammatical sketches or grammars more properly addressing the beginner have continued to appear, the latter usually following the achievements of von Soden (Lancelotti 1962, Borger 1963, Lipin 1964, Nowicki 1964) or, a less happy choice, those of Ungnad 1949 (Ryckmans 1960). Several of these, especially Ungnad 1964, Oberhuber 1967, have made real contributions to Akkadian grammar, either by new insights, or by incorporating material adduced in reviews of *GAG* as well as published by von Soden himself since 1952, while Borger 1963 has, for his textbook,

[3] I have called this (Reiner 1966) the infixed morpheme 'length'; the similar German name *Längung* was used by Edzard (1965) in reference to the homophonous derivational morpheme.

excerpted *GAG* for the benefit of the beginner, and provided an appendix in which the specially Assyrian dialect features have been brought together from diverse paragraphs of *GAG*, as well as a terminological concordance with earlier grammars. So far only one such grammar (Reiner 1966) has deliberately dissociated itself from the historical approach of *GAG* and made an attempt at a taxonomic, descriptive analysis, naturally, however, still within the traditional presentational framework, as well as at a generative approach to some sections of Akkadian grammar.

Two recently revised grammars deserve special mention: Ungnad 1964 and Oberhuber 1967. A. Ungnad wrote his *Babylonisch-Assyrische Grammatik* in 1906, accompanied by, or rather, as stated in the Foreword, to accompany his *Übungsbuch*, destined for the student who wanted to teach himself Akkadian. For pedagogical reasons, Ungnad stated, he adduced complete paradigms, i.e. filled in hitherto not attested forms. In the verbal paradigm, the sequence of persons was in this edition 1, 2, 3; in the second edition (1925), this sequence was changed to conform to that of Hebrew, to 3, 2, 1.

Ungnad prepared a third edition under the title *Grammatik des Akkadischen* which went to press ca. 1945. Ungnad's death and the destruction of the typeset delayed the publication, supervised by M. San Nicolò, until 1949. The organization and content of this edition is substantially the same as the earlier ones, that is, the change of focus stimulated by Landsberger is not apparent in even the 3rd edition of this grammar, which remained, for teaching purposes, the standard textbook not only until the publication of *GAG* but, certainly in the majority of non-German universities, even to this day, or the publication of the completely revised 4th edition in 1964. The reasons for this ready acceptance are above all the compactness of the grammar (3rd edition: 87 pages text, 26 pages paradigms, and an Übungsbuch of 43 pages with a glossary of 42 pages), and the general trust of Assyriologists in the competence and good judgment of Ungnad, a leading Assyriologist of the first half of this century.

Ungnad's grammar is a typical neogrammarian (or neophilologist) grammar, that is, it is divided into Phonetics (*Lautlehre*), Morphology (*Formenlehre*), and Syntax (*Satzlehre*); the morphology in turn is divided according to parts-of-speech categories, beginning, as all Semitic grammars, with the pronouns, and continuing with nouns, verbs, and particles. Grammatical facts are described in terms of sound laws, operating either from Common Semitic (or some reconstructed protoform) to Akkadian, or within Akkadian, conditioned by phonetic environment. Although some of the examples have since proven to be incorrect, the phonetic laws which they illustrate need no revision, insofar as they are based on a standard historical phonology.

Perhaps the basic difference between this grammar, as also its precursors and followers, and any taxonomic, traditional grammar of better-studied languages (e.g. Old Church Slavonic, Latin, Gothic, etc.) is the frequency of loose or qualified statements. A sound change occurs 'almost always', 'often', 'occasionally', 'rarely', 'mostly', 'in very few cases', and the like. This shows that the sound laws and their apparent exceptions had not as yet been sorted out; certainly no such refinement as the exceptions to the sound laws organized in their turn into subsidiary, conditioned sound laws is evident. A greater scepticism might even suggest that what is described is not the sound changes as they actually occur, but the sound changes postulated on the basis of some standard examples, usually in accordance with sound changes observable in other Semitic languages, with the resulting picture that a certain historical trend is described, with a great number of unexplained occurrences floating around from phonology to morphology.

Among the special merits of Ungnad's grammar (third edition) is the special distinction of data referring to the Assyrian dialect, which are always so labeled, and an awareness of late phonetic developments deduced from Greek transcriptions of Akkadian words in the Neobabylonian period, the investigation of which was begun by Ungnad and furthered by Röllig 1960.

A complete revision of Ungnad 1949 was undertaken by Lubor Matouš, keeping the format and conciseness of the former editions but revising the presentation and interpretation of the linguistic data in accordance with von Soden's *Grundriss* (Soden 1952a), and including data published in recent years, and even unpublished, such as the dissertations Deller 1959 and Hecker 1961. This edition is an admirable tool for the student, even though it omits the reading exercises and glossary of the previous editions so as to enlarge the grammar proper by one-third (133 pages). However, the twofold aim of this grammar, to build a concise grammar in the manner of Ungnad 1949 on the foundations of Soden 1952a on the one hand, and to keep it *à jour* by presenting every novelty gleaned from all sources on the other, results in a mixture of solid grammatical data and various conjectures equally presented as facts. Therefore, the user must think of it in terms of its being an abridged *GAG* where, due to the abridgment, debatable interpretations are presented as immutable facts, apart from the fact that views unknown to Ungnad, and perhaps unacceptable to him, become attributed to him (D'jakonov 1966:184). Some of these debatable points, mainly on the distinction between writing and phonology and the verb system, two topics that I touch below, p. 283ff., have been raised in the only review so far (D'jakonov 1966), that has evaluated the grammar in its entirety rather than raised small points of detail.

The third, revised edition (Oberhuber 1967) of Bruno Meissner's *Die Keilschrift* (Sammlung Göschen, 1913) contains a completely revised chapter on Akkadian (Chapter V: 'Die akkadische Sprache'), based on von Soden's *GAG*; in order to look up-to-date, but without the space to make the customary cautionary remarks, suggestions of von Soden hardly proven or confirmed are presented as facts, such as the existence of *o* and *ü*, also of schwa and syllabic sonorants. Although some of Meissner's quaint formulations are eliminated, here and there they have slipped through, such as 'geht im Assyrischen der [Zischlaut] gern in l über' (§70/5, p. 89); on the other hand, the liberal sprinkling of such terms as 'Phonem' in contexts where they do not belong shows a lack of assimilation of linguistic categories and terminology. In the description of pronoun, noun, and verb (the sequence customary in Akkadian grammars), the author follows closely von Soden's *GAG*, albeit with minor slips and inconsistencies; certain phenomena, also appearing in *GAG* (§102g) that have since been explained in a different and more convincing fashion (Kraus, *RSO* 32.103–8), are here adduced to strengthen an atomistic interpretation of inflected verb forms (such as the written form *i-din-nam* = /iddinam/ explained as *i-din-am*, from a biradical base *din*), in §112.

Certain new ideas are introduced, such as that of an augment (*Wurzeldeterminativ*) *l* in the verb **lq'* < **lqḥ*, 'proven' by Hebrew, not by Akkadian ('wie zwar nicht das Akkadische, wohl aber das Hebräische mit seinem Imperativ ... beweist'). Verbs which before Landsberger's teaching, and on the basis of Semitic comparison, were considered mediae infirmae, but since then as 'hollow roots', i.e. roots consisting of a long vowel between two consonantal radicals, are again reinterpreted as 'triconsonantal', the long vowel being the reflex of short vowel plus laryngeal; this is a structural view singularly correct, whether because of the authority of Saussure which is referred to, or because of the equally adduced Common Semitic pattern. The same analysis is applied to the so-called tertiae infirmae. It is regrettable that the author does not usually draw the phonological or morphological consequences implicit in his statements.

As a result of the plea of von Soden in connection with the preparation of his *Grundriss*, and often upon his instigation or even under his supervision as doctoral dissertations or *Habilitationsschriften*, a number of grammars on different dialects of Akkadian began to appear in the fifties. Previous to this period, there existed smaller monographs on some periods of Akkadian (K. Tallqvist, *Die Sprache der Contracte Nabû-nâ'ids*, Helsinki, 1890, on Neobabylonian; S. C. Ylvisaker, *Zur babylonischen und assyrischen Grammatik*, Leipzig, 1912 [= *Leipziger Semitistische Studien* V/6], on the differences between the Babylonian and Assyrian letters in the royal letter archives of the late Assyrian kings; Lewy 1921, on Middle Assyrian; S. J. Bloch, 'Beiträge zur Grammatik des Mittelbabylonischen', *Or* 9 [1940], 305–47; G. Goossens, 'L'accadien des clercs d'Uruk sous les Séleucides', *Muséon* 55 [1942], 61–86) and on the so-called 'peripheral dialects', i.e. Akkadian written outside the native soil, by peoples speaking another Semitic or a non-Semitic language (of these, the studies on the El Amarna letter archive are relevant not so much for Akkadian studies, but for the Canaanite branch of West Semitic, and need not be mentioned here). The Akkadian of the Hittite archives was studied by R. Labat, *L'akkadien de Boghaz-Köi* (Bordeaux, 1932); the Akkadian written in Nuzi by Hurrian speakers by M. Berkooz, *The Nuzi dialect of Akkadian* (Philadelphia, 1937) (= *Language Dissertations* Nr.23), by C. H. Gordon, 'The dialect of the Nuzu tablets', *Or* 7 (1938), 32–63 and 215–32, and by A. Goetze, 'Some observations on Nuzu Akkadian', *Lg* 14 (1938), 134–43.

Beginning with the fifties, not only grammars of such 'peripheral dialects' were published, such as Finet 1956, Meyer 1962, Salonen 1962, but grammars of different periods of Akkadian, viewed synchronically.

For Old Akkadian, there is Gelb 1961a; for Old Assyrian, the still unpublished dissertation Hecker 1961; for Middle Babylonian, Aro 1955; for Neo-Assyrian, the still unpublished Deller 1959, material from which has been utilized by Deller in a number of articles, such as, for early Neo-Assyrian, 'Zur sprachlichen Einordnung der Inschriften Aššurnaṣirpals II. (883–859)', *Or* 26 (1957), 144–56, and 'Assyrisches Sprachgut bei Tukulti-Ninurta II. (888–884)', *Ibid.*, 268–72; see also Deller 1962a, b, c. Peripheral dialects have been studied by Aro 1956, Matouš 1956a, and there are the unpublished dissertations Zinkand 1958, Swaim 1962, and Giacumakis 1963.

A general criticism that can be directed at most of these dialect studies is that brought forward by Gelb (1957:199) and Aro 1957, namely that not all of the features discussed reflect the dialect investigated, since the provenience of the particular group of texts may be varied. A further criticism that applies to most such dialect grammars is that they do not describe the dialect itself, bnt only the specifically dialect features, i.e. those which differ from the standard language, for which as a rule von Soden's *GAG* serves as the standard, or else that the features of the standard dialect and that of the dialect investigated are treated as a whole and thus the specific dialect features do not clearly emerge (see Edzard 1964). Curiously, no monograph on Old Babylonian, considered the classical dialect, has yet appeared, although several are said to be in preparation.

In the field of lexicography, the currently progressing publication of two dictionaries represent a major turning point. The difference in approach of coverage between the *AHw.* and the *CAD* has been summarized by Oppenheim 1966, while the respective problems confronting both enterprises have been stated by von Soden 1959a. It is to be hoped, with Oppenheim 1966, that instead of discouraging lexical research, the publication of the two dictionaries 'will be a stimulus to the younger Assyriologists to turn to the fascinating pursuits of lexicography'.

Concentration on lexicographic work by those involved in the publication of the two dictionaries has yielded, as a by-product, short notices or medium-sized articles on new or more correct readings of individual words, new semantic interpretations, often connected with etymological attributions, and even discovery of grammatical patterns, for Akkadian alone as well as some related to those of other Semitic languages, in a great number of articles that cannot be enumerated here. While the collaborators on the *CAD*, pressed by other duties, often do no more than give the new reading and translation of a particular word in citations under some other keyword, leaving for a subsequent volume in which the appropriate entry will appear the proof or justification for such new interpretations, von Soden more regularly publishes such findings of his; at first, before publication of the *AHw.* began, in a series of articles titled 'Zum akkadischen Wörterbuch', in *Or* 15–27 (1946–58); now, starting with *Or* 35 (1966), on Aramaic words in Neo-Assyrian and Neobabylonian, as well as in other periodicals, mainly *AfO*. On the other hand, the lexicographical contributions of Landsberger are largely conceived independently from the *CAD*.

Since the beginning of the publication of these dictionaries, research has been stimulated not only in the field of lexicography — in semantic analysis as well as etymology and the problem of loans — but also in morphology itself, as the dictionaries record forms to which hitherto not enough attention has been given; see e.g. Oppenheim 1957, Kienast 1957a and 1961a.

On the many recent contributions to Akkadian grammar and philology, I refer to the list of References, and will attempt here only to mention the more significant ones arranged under topical subheadings, insofar as the often intersecting subject matters permit, and will then select for discussion a small number of current topics that are of methodological significance.

In the field of writing (often intersecting with phonology and/or morphology), Goetze 1958, Deller 1962a and b, Gelb 1961b may be singled out.

In the field of phonology and morphophonemics, Haudricourt 1953, Matouš and Petráček 1956b, Soden 1956, 1957b, Goetze 1958, Aro 1959, Soden 1959b and c, Knudsen 1961, 1965, Reiner 1964, and Deller and Parpola 1967.

In the field of morphology, Kienast 1957a and 1961a, Lewy 1959, Meyer 1964, and Edzard 1965.

In the field of syntax and semantics, Meek 1946 and 1950, Lewy 1960, Jacobsen 1960 with the rejoinder Soden 1961b and the surrejoinder Jacobsen 1963, Aro 1961 with the additions Deller 1962c and Frankena 1965, Rowton 1962, Aro 1963, Reiner 1965, Fleisch 1966, Buccellati 1968.

On the other hand, a number of articles whose titles suggest morphological treatments are in reality lexical investigations, usually in the area of lexical derivatives, due to the fact that derivational patterns in Akkadian, as in other Semitic languages, belong to morphology. Such studies are: Soden 1939b, Oppenheim 1940, 1942, 1947, Finet 1965.

Others, based on morphological problems, are likewise either lexical or syntactical studies, such as Oppenheim 1933 and 1935, Ungnad 1937, Soden 1939a, Edzard 1965.

Little has been done in metrics, thus Böhl 1958 and 1960 ought to be mentioned; comparative lexicography is represented by Leslau 1944 and 1962.

The existence of ancient Sumero-Akkadian grammatical paradigms has given rise to contrastive studies on the Sumerian and Akkadian verbal system, by Jacobsen 1956, and Soden 1965; for a general contrastive presentation see Falkenstein 1960, and earlier Poebel 1932. See also Lambert 1964.

The results of the new view on Akkadian grammar as exemplified in *GAG* were for the first time incorporated in a comparative Semitic grammar in Moscati *et al.* 1964 (for criticism see especially Deller 1965) as well as in Kuryłowicz 1961 and D'jakonov 1965.

LINGUISTICS AND PHILOLOGY

The distribution of scholars of Akkadian in universities and research institutions and the titles they hold there makes it immediately apparent that their responsibilities, if not alone their interests, lie in the field of philology, not in linguistics *per se*.

Polotsky (1964:101) writes, in reference to the discipline of the so-called 'Semitic Philology': 'In a field where both workers and academic posts are relatively few, there are practical reasons against carrying the distinction between linguistics and philology to the full length demanded by theoretical considerations.'

The interaction of the study of Akkadian and other languages of the Semitic family is also judged insufficient by Polotsky: 'There is no lack of factors which tend to make of technical Akkadian philology (as distinct from Assyriology in general) just another watertight compartment within Semitics, engrossed in its own narrow problems and lacking all interest in anything outside the "cuneiform" world. There is certainly enough day-to-day work to keep the student of Akkadian busy. The extra-Semitic connections within the "cuneiform" world are at least as numerous as, and hardly less important than, the Semitic ones. ... Moreover, after the study of Akkadian had, in its early stages, received a good deal of substantial help from the other Semitic languages, the prejudiced interference of Comparative Semitics had, in some cases, undeniably stood in the way of understanding peculiar features of Akkadian. The consequence of this experience was a revulsion from comparativism and the conviction that the time had come for the study of Akkadian to stand on its own feet. ... There arose a school in the linguistic study of Akkadian which made a point of avoiding the misleading associations of traditional Semitic grammar. It deliberately turned to other branches of linguistics for categories and technical terms and used them as tools to describe and analyze Akkadian grammar in terms adequate to its own system. ... The synchronic analysis of Akkadian would seem to have reached a stage where communion with General Semitics may become fruitful for both sides. Without such communion Comparative Semitic Linguistics is doomed.' (1964:103).

While Polotsky is both too harsh in regarding Assyriologists 'engrossed in [their] own narrow problems' and too generous in positing that the anti-comparativist tendencies have created a school which analyzed Akkadian grammar 'in terms adequate to its own system', which I can see reflected only in the writings of Landsberger, Goetze, and Speiser, he has pointed out the deficiencies of Akkadian philology as well as at least some of their causes.

One of the concomitant circumstances of the philological and 'cuneiform' orientation of Assyriologists is that numerous discussions on points of grammar appear, not in independent articles, but in so-called 'philological commentaries' appended to text editions. At least initial observations and reinterpretations of linguistic data are found thus scattered in various Assyriological publications; however, as the phenomena observed increase in number, or the new interpretation becomes crystallized in the mind of the scholar, usually a special study will be devoted to them. Hence, I have not included in my survey and bibliography the purely philological articles even if they contain important linguistic observations.

This is justified insofar as the philological orientation has as its consequence that the linguistic observations are restricted to the form occurring in the text, and perhaps some other sporadic examples known to or for some reason specially interesting the philologist. Hence, the lack of systematization precludes the classification of such notes under a heading 'grammatical studies' or the like.

Also the reviews of books on grammar — general works or dialect grammars — rarely state criticism relevant to methodology or affecting the general linguistic or specially Akkadian structure of the book, but rather operate on the philological level, correcting mistakes in individual examples or in the interpretation of some grammatical feature, or else contribute further examples, corroborating or contradicting the statements of the author.

SPECIAL PROBLEMS

I would like to single out a few topics which are currently debated in the field of Akkadian, illustrate the prevailing approaches by a rather more detailed discussion of these, and finally point out the need for a new and more confident attitude.

Perhaps it is the publication of Soden and Röllig 1967 that has brought into focus the problem of the relation of the writing to the language. To pose the problem in the briefest form: when a word is written with an unusual spelling, some scholars reinterpret the spelling, i.e. assign new readings to the cuneiform sign to obtain the postulated grammatical form, while others reinterpret the word, i.e. deduce from the spelling conclusions in the area of phonology or morphology.

This problem arises from the discrepancy between the written image and the linguistic form postulated on the basis of the assumed semantics, the normalized grammar of Akkadian, and comparative evidence. In order to obtain a normalized form, the current trend is to reinterpret the spelling, and only where this is not feasible, to reckon with phonetic reinterpretations of the grammatical form gained by the above criteria, an attitude criticized by D'jakonov (1966:185). These two types of revisions and reinterpretations result in an interesting re-evaluation of the grammar of Akkadian which at present is only at its beginnings.

For instance, while in the early days of Assyriology it was generally accepted that Akkadian had lost some consonants of the Proto-Semitic inventory, specifically the laryngeals and the interdental continuants, a number of recent articles (Soden 1956b, 1959b, 1968) have reintroduced into the Akkadian inventory a number of these, along with others conjectured from the Sumerian inventory, though restricted to particular lexical items. Similarly, vowels other than the traditionally postulated *a*, *e*, *i*, *u* have been assumed for sporadic instances on the basis of spelling differences (Soden 1948b). Both the additional consonants and vowels have found their way into at least one dictionary, the *AHw.*, if not as initial letter in the alphabetic order, at least in citation forms under the normalized entry or as variants listed after the normalized entry, e.g. the consonant *ʿayin* in the form *ʿadānum* listed under A, and the vowel *o* in the form *mommonnu-* (and *qorbu*) cited under *mamma(n)nu*. However, only to a limited extent have they been used in the values listed for the pertinent cuneiform sign (e.g. the value *kot* beside the value *kat*) in Soden 1967.

From a methodological point of view, transcription with a letter such as [ʿ] or [o], just as similar notations for a diaphoneme, is a possible way of indicating a spelling variation (in this case, between nothing and *ḫ*, and between *a* and *u*), but nothing more than the spelling variation, and may not correspond to any phonological or morphological reality unless additional and independent information corroborates such assumptions. The introduction of hitherto unrecognized vowel and consonant letters, being not mere graphic transliterations but claiming to be phonetic transcription, into the transcription of Akkadian texts needs special discussion about their predictability, i.e. their distinctiveness in differentiating morphemes. If, after such a special discussion, the claim of being a phonetic transcription is justified, further predictions about the phonology and morphophonemics may then be made. In the contrary case, there seems little point in revising our transcription, since, on the one hand, the phonetics of a dead language cannot be recaptured, and on the other, even insufficiently normalized readings sufficiently indicate, in the linguistic context in which they appear, which morphological form stands in the text. After all, it is the context which enables modern Assyriologists, and not only the ancients, to correctly read and interpret cuneiform texts, provided their language is known. Moreover, one has to differentiate, in recording spelling differences, between synchronic variation and diachronic linguistic change.

The continually spreading influence of linguistics, especially of the structural and, in Europe, of the functional school, has affected the approach of some, especially Scandinavian, Assyriologists to matters of Akkadian phonology and, to a lesser extent, morphology and syntax. Especially when investigating the relation of the spelling to the language such questions as whether a particular spelling represents a phoneme, on the phonological level, or an allophone, as the phonetic realization of some phoneme, are asked and answered. These answers, however, are less informative than they could be were the authors more consistent and rigorous in using the criteria and terminology evolved by linguistic theory. Methodological deficiency keeps these ostensibly phonological studies within a framework within which problems concerning dead languages can hardly be intelligently presented, let alone solved with any degree of finality.

The common procedure is to collect different spellings for one word or for a small group of words exhibiting the same type of spelling variation. Of the different spellings, one is taken to represent the phoneme under discussion, and the other or others, its variant or allophone. Conclusions are drawn in terms of phonetic variants. The shortcomings of this method may be seen primarily in the lack of relating the observations on the behavior of a particular item to the system as a whole by neglecting to put the relevant questions and provide answers in an orderly manner. When the questions, what is to be considered a phone, allophone, phoneme, variant and why, are not answered by the author, and the terms phone, allophone, phoneme, variant are used at variance with their rigorous linguistic acceptation, the terminology does not convey the maximal information that it could convey and thus is not used for the purpose for which it has been created. It is consequently up to the reader to find out for himself whether the terms are used in the customary linguistic acceptation or in a less informative and rigorous fashion. Hence such studies are useful only concerning the word or words that are used as examples or illustrations, and do not have the necessary predicting power concerning the general structure of the system of the language. For instance, spelling variation may indicate, depending on other information, not only that there existed a sound 'in between' the two for which the variation is documented, but also that the difference between the two which the variation refers to has been neutralized, i.e. not only can we increase the phonological inventory in this fashion, but also decrease it. The additional information needed in most cases comes from etymology, i.e. morphological factors, and thus it is reasonable to assume that investigations dealing on the surface with the elements of phonology in reality have to do with, and are applicable to, the elements of morphophonology, not to phonemes, but to morphophonemes (units whose alternants can be predicted in terms of morphological environment).

Since morphophonemes are ultimately realized as phones, particular instances of the realization of such morphophonemes reflected in spelling variants may in fact be considered to reflect allophones or free variants in the spoken utterance onto which the written text is projected. But such assumed allophones or free variants should eventually be assigned to a phoneme whose existence is established from the phonological analysis of the language (or rather of a particular dialect of it) as a whole; if the terms allophone and variant are more loosely used, as e.g. with reference to one phoneme being the allophone (*sic*!) of another phoneme, without specifying whether there actually exist such two different phonemes in the language, the phonological facts are further obscured. The customary atomistic investigation of such phenomena constantly obliges the reader versed in the formal analysis of languages to extract information relevant for him from the data adduced and not from their interpretation, without being given the assurance that all pertinent data have been collected. For the less versed reader, the picture resulting must be one of more or less complete randomness.

If it seems, as is reasonable to assume in the case of a dead language, that actual phonetic realizations of the smallest units are not recapturable, either because the written evidence itself is not sufficient, or because it is likely that there was no reason to change the orthography, at least not in all words that might exemplify one and the same phenomenon, it is more prudent to stay on the level of analysis — presumably that of morphophonemics — where there is sufficient information to arrive at a complete picture.

In the study of morphology, the verb has been the subject of primary interest. Many of the studies to be discussed are, however, dealing less with morphology *per se*, but with the syntactic-semantic interpretation of verb roots, stems, and inflectional forms. Whether morphologically or syntactico-semantically oriented, these studies have usually been motivated by the perplexing difference in verb morphology between Akkadian and all other Semitic languages, and have aimed at explaining the origin and function of the other Semitic verbal systems or the proto-form and proto-function from which both the Akkadian and the other Semitic systems could have been derived as much as the form and function of the Akkadian verb forms themselves.

Before delineating the most discussed problems, a brief statement on the Akkadian verb itself may be helpful. The Akkadian verb has one 'suffix-conjugation', i.e. a conjugation in which the actor marker is expressed by suffixes, which is called 'permansive' or 'stative'. It has two 'prefix-conjugations', one with a single stem-vowel appearing between the three root consonants (= radicals), and one with two vowels; the former is called preterite, the latter present. Suffixed endings on the verb are a vowel /u/ marking the subjunctive mood and the string /am/ marking the so-called ventive. A /t/ morpheme infixed after the first radical forms another conjugational set for one 'prefix-conjugation' in both the subjunctive and the ventive moods. Other features of the Akkadian verbal system, namely, the stem modifications operating either on the middle radical or by means of prefixes, and two secondary modifications operating on all stems, both simple and modified, by means of a /t/ or a /tn/ infix (see Edzard 1965, and below p. 289) are not relevant in this connection.

Formally, the 'suffix-conjugation' of the Akkadian verb corresponds to the West Semitic perfect, while the first type of 'prefix-conjugation' (the preterite) corresponds to the indicative (restricted in West Semitic to the imperfect), and the /am/ ending to the 'modus energicus'. The formal criteria involved thus provide no West Semitic parallel either for the Akkadian present, or for the extension of the moods with /u/ and /am/ ending for other tenses. Furthermore, to the West Semitic dichotomy of perfect and imperfect correspond in Akkadian not only three tenses (present, preterite, and perfect) but a fourth category, the stative of the suffix-conjugation. Hence, the first problem of analyzing the Akkadian verbal system is to find meaning or function categories for the various tense forms. Landsberger solved this (see above p. 275) by postulating differences in *Aktionsart*: stative, fientic-durative, and punctual, while the 'perfect tense' was taken to operate only in the *consecutio temporum*. This view was challenged by Rundgren whose first contribution to the question (1955), itself intended as refutation of Rössler 1950, aroused strong reaction from the Assyriological side (Soden 1957c, Kienast 1957b) and brought about several subsequent studies by Rundgren both in the domain of Semitic as a whole and of Hebrew in particular. Rundgren's position (excellently summarized by Aro 1960) is that the basic distinction in every Semitic verbal system, including Akkadian, is that of a binary aspect, from which developed, secondarily and in diverse manner, the 'tempora' of the individual languages. Since aspect distinction is essentially binary, the three-way tense opposition of Akkadian cannot be original.

Von Soden's answer to Rundgren (Soden 1957c) contains the important postulations that (a) the 'present' of Akkadian (to be compared, as heretofore, with the South-

Arabic-Ethiopic indicative as well as with analogous forms surviving in West Semitic), formed by means of gemination of the second radical, is to be considered Proto-Semitic, and (b) Common Semitic had two prefix-conjugated tenses, reflected in the West Semitic imperfect and jussive which are to be considered two different tenses, and thus there was in Semitic originally a three-way tense distinction (*Dreistufigkeit*) consisting of preterite, imperfect, and perfect, and this was enlarged in Akkadian to a four-way distinction (*Vierstufigkeit*) by the creation of the *t*-perfect. For the secondary extension of this *t*-perfect see the views of D'jakonov 1966.

Kienast 1957a, while arguing for a particular interpretation of the Semitic **yaprus*-form and its 'moods' formed by vocalic suffixes (i.e. the indicative with *-u*, the purposive with *-a*, and the jussive with zero, or rather, the two first-mentioned moods formed from the endingless jussive) which does not concern us here, contains a helpful comparative chart of languages and forms from which actual attestations and their overlapping in individual languages may be easily read off. The table shows the *Dreistufigkeit* of the verbal system which has been claimed by all mentioned scholars apart from Rundgren, and its reinterpretation or enlargement in various ways in the individual languages. The maximal system is represented by the union of Akkadian with Arabic, while no language possesses all the formal categories shown on the chart.

It is also clear that the verbal systems which show maximally divergent forms (Akkadian and Ethiopic) are based on three different forms (*ya-prus*, *paras*, and *i-parras*), derivable from one basic form. The base form is the stem with zero-grade (to borrow the terminology of Indo-European, applied to Semitic by Kuryłowicz 1961), e.g. *prus*. This zero-grade stem is either prefix-inflected for person (as in Akkadian *i-prus*), or it is suffix-inflected for the categories gender and number (as in the imperative *purus*, fem. *purs-i*, pl. *purs-a*).

The full grade, with vowel /a/ between the first and second radical is CaCVC, e.g. *paras*; the lengthened grade is formed from the full grade by gemination (or lengthening) of the second radical: CaC_aC_aVC, e.g. *parras*. The non-zero grade also has both a prefix- and a suffix-conjugation: the prefix-conjugation *i-parras* is concomitant with the lengthened grade (in Akkadian and Ethiopic); the suffix-conjugation CaC(V)C-*āku* is concomitant with the full grade (in all Semitic languages). Since the lengthened grade is the base not only for the present *i-parras* but also for the intensive stem and for certain nominal pluralizations, it may be interpreted in the verbal system as a durative.

In contrast to the morphological maximal system that the mapping of every form shows, Rundgren's arguments may be summarized, in the end, as interpretations of terminology. Since for every Semitic language there is, minimally, a three-step system (*Dreistufigkeit*), such a development can be envisaged only as resulting from repeated binary cuts. Rundgren chooses the first binary distinction as stative and fiens, and the second as the division of the stative in Akkadian and the fiens in West Semitic into 'constative' (with others: punctual) and 'cursive' (durative), while the lexical imperfect-perfect (or the grammatical imperfective-perfective) opposition is only secondary, depending on which (semantic) element is unmarked.

There would be no interest for the Assyriologist to enter into the theories underlying Rundgren's scheme were it not that he supports his argument with examples from Akkadian. Thus, any future study on the function of the Akkadian tenses will have to consider and if needs be refute Rundgren's syntactic and semantic interpretation of the respective verb forms.

One of the reasons for the possibility of operating with the Akkadian stative as a relevant category for the study of aspect is the discovery in recent years of functions of this conjugation not merely in a 'stative' but also in a transitive meaning. Of the two studies recently published on the subject, Haldar 1963–64 has been definitely refuted by Soden 1964, who made this case a case of principle to warn non-Assyriologists of unreliable example collections. Hence, the allegations of Haldar that the stative is used as a fiens and the present and preterite as stative need not be further discussed. The other study on the stative, Rowton 1962, gives a great number of examples to support the view that there exists 'the tendency of the permansive to become a perfect' and hence this permansive may be the possible origin of the West Semitic perfect.

The heated discussions on the question how and why the differentiation of the three grades took place are due to a large extent to terminological differences and to the assumption that the underlying form from which the other forms may be derived has to have a priority in time too. This assumption, which is the unavowed basis for many misunderstandings not only between the philologist and the linguist, but between philologists themselves, is reflected in many disagreements on the 'origin' of some form or other, a typically unsolvable question, since the establishment of a base form or underlying form for a diasystem is not necessarily a backward projection into time.

Thus, all theories on the 'origin' of the form *i-parras* are essentially equivalent and thus correct; it is the labels (asterisks, Proto-Semitic, etc.) that cause the differences and disagreements. It is thus not incorrect to say that *i-parras* (in Akkadian and Ethiopic) is derived from *i-paras*, i.e. from the base of the West Semitic perfect (*paras* or *qatala*) with, on the one hand, a shift from suffix-conjugation to prefix-conjugation, and, on the other, gemination of the second radical. It is the phonetic arguments for this gemination (shift of stress bringing about gemination) that were found unacceptable by some, while the question of the priority or 'originality' of the forms *i-parras* (parallel or not to Ethiopic *yeqattel*) results, as said above, from the confusion of underlying form with chronology. For this question of chronology we should note the moderate and agnostic view of Aro: 'Wir sind daher nicht imstande, kategorische Aussagen über das Verbformensystem des Ursemitischen zu machen.' (1960:18), and '... so sieht der Rez[ensent] keinen Grund, warum die semitischen Verbformen in alle Ewigkeit unfähig bleiben sollten, relative Zeit zum Ausdruck zu bringen, wenn sie auch von Hause aus wenig mit relativer Zeit zu tun gehabt hätten.' (1960:20); see also Aro 1964:185ff.

It is of course permissible to operate with chronology and project some forms into time on the basis of comparative evidence, not only on imaginary development of functions. This has been done by Greenberg 1952, in the same year that von Soden's *GAG* was published, that is, at a time when the gemination of the second consonant in the present was not yet a textbook truth. Hence he had to justify this gemination for the Semitists. Greenberg states his case as follows: 'From the very beginning, unfortunately, certain irrelevancies have obscured the real issues. One is that of the relative priority of the Akkadian present [i.e. *iparras*] and the Akkadian preterite [i.e. *iprus*]. Proponents of the identification of the Ethiopian imperfect indicative [i.e. *yeqattel*] and the Akkadian present, in positing these forms as proto-Semitic, sought to derive the Akkadian preterite (= West Semitic imperfect) from the present by elision of the *a* which occurs before the geminated second consonant (*iqtVl* < *iqat*(*t*)*Vl*). Since it would be easier to carry out this derivation if gemination did not occur in the present, its existence was usually denied by those who took this point of view. Their opponents derived the present from the preterite by the opposite process of intercalation. ... For this group of scholars, also, it was more convenient to deny the reality of the gemination in the present. Speculation of this type is as fruitless and outdated as the 19th century discussions concerning the relative age of the noun and verb in Semitic. I shall maintain that proto-Semitic had both a preterite ... and a present.'

Aside from this debate on the verb which is largely comparatively oriented, the first attempt to treat the Akkadian verb as a set of structural oppositions is Edzard 1965. Edzard examines the syntagmatic distribution of the affixes by which the verb stems are derived and their relation to the functional categories that the derived stems represent in terms of 'privative oppositions'. The examples are predominantly Old Babylonian, with the verb stems contrasted by pairs. Two graphs with a lattice structure illustrate the interconnection of the privative oppositions, stems with an affix being the marked, those lacking the affix the unmarked member of each pair.

Edzard's merit is to have presented a full analysis of, and made graphic, the distribution of the stem-derivational devices, which may be summarized in the 3×3 matrix:

$$\begin{bmatrix} \emptyset \\ \text{ŠA}(\{(\text{TA(N)}), \text{TA}_2\}) \\ \text{NA(TAN)} \end{bmatrix} \text{R}_1 \begin{bmatrix} (\text{TA(N)}) \\ \emptyset \\ \emptyset \end{bmatrix} \text{R}_2 \begin{bmatrix} (:) \\ \emptyset \\ \emptyset \end{bmatrix} \text{R}_3$$

The field of syntax has been least explored by scholars, except for the works mentioned p. 281, and for occasional studies on detail, usually embedded in a philological, lexical, or at best morphological study. Two recent studies are of particular interest to me personally: the syntactical study Soden 1960, in which von Soden examines an 'ungrammatical' Akkadian syntagm, gave the occasion for a restatement in terms of generative grammar by Reiner 1965 (as yet unpublished). While von Soden compared this construction to the Arabic 'improper annexation', Reiner 1965 derives it, by explicit transformation rules, from a relative clause considered the underlying string of this nominal compound.

Von Soden proposed two alternative explanations, with a slight preference for the second one, it seems; mine, partly in Reiner 1966:125–7, more rigorously formulated in 1965, is likewise a double one, and not so different from the von Soden solution.

The starting point of Reiner 1965 is the comparison of different Akkadian solutions for translating the same Sumerian construction type in a bilingual list. One solution — disregarding here simple Akkadian glosses — may be termed compounding, the other, periphrasis.

The examples of compounding include typical nominal compounds, two nouns in a genitival relation; the noun in the genitive is preceded by either the wh-word *ša*, or a noun denoting a person, such as *awīlum* 'man', *bēlum* 'master', in the bound form, or an active participle in the bound form. The periphrasis consists of a relative clause introduced by the wh-word *ša*. I take the relative clause as the underlying string of the nominal compound. The derivation can be stated in five rules:

1. $W_{have, know} \rightarrow \{N_{person}, wh\}$
2. $W_{vt} \rightarrow W_{part} / \_\_\_\_ \#$
3. $W_{vx} \rightarrow W_{adj} + a(m)$
4. $N_x \rightarrow N_{gen}$
5. 1–2–3–4–5 $\rightarrow$ 3–4–2

(Symbols: W = 'word'; N = 'noun'; wh = 'wh-word, i.e. *ša*'; vt = 'verb transitive'; part = 'participle'; vx = 'verb (neither 'have' or 'know' nor -*šu*- less vt)'; adj = 'adjective'; gen = 'genitive'.)

Since the 'ungrammatical syntagm' involves compounds whose first element ends in *am*, the first two rules do not pertain to the argument, and we need to consider only rule 3, whose output is adjective plus *am*, from a verb which is the predicate of an underlying relative clause consisting of wh, N_x, W_{vx}.

The two possibilities, namely either intransitive or transitive verb in the underlying relative clause, are the alternatives that are expressed by von Soden (1960:163ff.) in reference to the regens of the compound as 'an adjective proper' and a 'verbal adjective' respectively, since the passive verbal adjective is the transformation of the transitive verb, and the 'adjective proper' that of the intransitive verb, just as in English. Analysis of the underlying string of such a construction as *sakpam ilim* 'rejected by god' as *ša ilum iskipušu* 'who god + Nom rejected + Acc' i.e. 'whom god rejected' provides us with the accusative which appears in the shape -*šu* with verbs but in the shape *am* with adjectives; this solution therefore requires only finding the adjective corresponding to the transitive verb *sakāpu* 'to reject', since the accusative element can be transferred directly from its occurrence in the relative clause to the compound. (Such an accusative element indeed appears overtly with the noun in the relative clauses which have intransitive verbs as predicate). On this, the syntactic level, we can surely opt for von Soden's first explanation (1960:170), according to which the ending *am* is in fact an accusative ending.

The second solution is on the morphophonemic level. The Akkadian translation may be a compound with an active participle as first element, as e.g. *ākil karṣī* 'calumniator' (literally 'eater of calumny'), from an underlying relative clause *ša karṣī īkulu* 'who ate calumny', or one with a passive participle (= adjective) as first element, as e.g. **akil išātim* 'eaten by fire', from an underlying relative clause *ša išātum īkulušu* 'who fire + Nom ate + Acc', 'whom fire ate'. An important syntactical distinction — active *vs.* passive — is carried by the sole feature of length in the first syllable of the participle if it is active (*ākil*) *vs.* lack of length if it is passive (or verbal adjective) (*akil*). In the cuneiform writing system, the two forms are homographous. The typical phonemic shape of the adjective, no vowel between second and third radical (e.g. *akl-*), is obscured by the phonetic — or graphic — requirement that a vowel appear between them if these two consonants are not followed by an inflectional vowel. The cluster typical of the adjective can be maintained only if the consonants are not in final position — in this particular case, *aklam išātim*, if they are followed by the ending *am*, which then would simply be homophonous with the accusative ending. This morphophonemic solution is consonant with von Soden's second proposal, to see in the ending *am* an original bound form ending.

The methodological point to be made is precisely that, using an explicit and formalized analysis, the solutions suggested take a form which is clearer and more easily susceptible to evaluation. Moreover, the two solutions are in reality not alternative ones, but are both valid, although on a different level of linguistic hierarchy. Von Soden's first solution, comparable to my syntactic one, is more deeply embedded in the structure, and thus of a higher order, than von Soden's second, comparable to my morphophonemic solution, which pertains to rules that specify actual phonological or graphic realization and thus are on a much lower level.

The recent article of Giorgio Buccellati (1968), that may be called a morphosyntactic study, deserves particular attention because, although presented in conservative philological form and terminology, it could be called an analysis of the deep structure of a surface morphological category — the stative — in terms of its derivational history. Buccellati analyzes the stative as a nominal sentence with subject and predicate. If we accept his analysis, i.e. a tree derivation with optional, and under certain constraints obligatory, morphological fusion of subject and predicate (or NP and VP), we must reverse the categories of subject and predicate he assigns to the elements of the stative and to the phrases underlying them, for the following reasons: In Buccellati's analysis, the stative is composed of 'a noun (as predicate) and a pronominal element (as subject)' (1968:3). If we analyze the stative as consisting of two morphemes, a nominal morpheme (noun or adjective base) and a pronominal affix morpheme, as does Buccellati, we have to assign the syntactical functions of these two morphemes not as he does, but in the reverse way, namely, take the nominal morpheme as subject and the pronominal affix as predicate (see also Aro 1964:197). This results from the syntactic analysis of the corresponding deep structure, in which the noun and adjective of the underlying sentence is not in the predicative state but in the non-predicative state, and consequently it is not the noun but the pronoun which is the predicate of the underlying sentence. Only the pronoun can be predicate of the sentence because (a) the marked non-predicative forms are the nouns and adjectives, e.g. in the examples *šarrum dannum anāku, šarrum ša in šarrī šūturu anāku,* with the marker *-um* on the subject; and (b) if we substitute for the pronoun a part of speech which distinguishes between predicative and non-predicative state, the predicative state is obligatory, e.g. *šarrum dannum dan,* or *šarrum dannum šar*[4] and not, as Buccellati's analysis would require, **šar dan dannum,* **šar dan šarrum.* When the noun is determined by a genitive, the ensuing sequence noun plus genitive behaves as a compound in which the distinction between predicative and non-predicative state is neutralized, e.g. *šar mātim anāku,* and Buccellati's analysis is not contradicted. But, in the same sentence, when the noun is determined by an adjective or by a following *ša* (in turn followed by a genitive or a relative clause), the marker of the non-predicative state *-um* appears with it, as in the above-cited examples *šarrum dannum anāku, šarrum ša in šarrī šūturu anāku,* and thus cannot be considered the predicate of the sentence.

The respective assignment of the subject and predicate is not affected by inversion, which is permissible if the predicate is a free form. Since this free form of the pronoun merges the predicative and non-predicative forms, sentences which have a pronominal predicate are not overtly marked for predicate, and may thus, in the absence of overtly marked subject, have given rise to the interpretation of Buccellati.

In this connection, I would like to make a plea for the preservation of the distinction, established likewise by Landsberger but in this case without followers, between stative and predicative, lumped together in von Soden's *GAG* as well as in the works cited by Buccellati 1968. Although the desinences of both categories are the same, the term stative should be rightly used only for 'statives' of durative verbs which form a stative of the type *paris,* while forms such as *dan* and *šar* represent the predicative state of adjectives and nouns. The morphophonemic difference between *dan* (morphophonemic *dan:*) and *ṣalil* has been expressed in Reiner 1966:43 in terms of a (phonotactic) difference between long and geminated consonant, which difference is concomitant with the lexical opposition nominal stems *vs.* verbal stems, hence the two labels 'predicative' (for nominal stems) *vs.* 'stative' (for verb stems).

PROBLEMS AND DESIDERATA: A PROJECTION AND A PLEA

Future progress in Akkadian studies, such as compiling grammars for various periods and geographical dialects of the language, so far as possible, as well as a historical grammar and a comparatively oriented one (Moscati *et al.* 1964 is superficial and hence mostly incorrect; D'jakonov 1965, although of equally modest volume, con-

[4] Constructed examples, actually attested e.g. *awīlum šû sar* 'that man is guilty' (Codex Hammurapi §13), *šāyimānum šarrāq* 'the buyer is a thief' (*ibid.* §10).

tains a much larger amount of information, but, since it includes Hamitic languages as well, still does not cover sufficient Akkadian material) should be greatly facilitated by the availability of such essential tools as the new edition of the syllabary Soden 1967, the forthcoming reprinting, with additions and corrections, of Soden 1952a, and not least by the progressive publication of the two dictionaries. To make maximum use, however, of these tools, for linguistic and philological purposes both, Assyriology needs to outgrow a number of children's diseases.

One of them may be stated in anthropological terms, as consisting of an excessive romantic admiration for this ancient culture, or conversely of a contempt of its primitive and barbaric ways. Both attitudes of course hinder an objective, sympathetic appraisal of what the documents written by Mesopotamians actually do say. While these attitudes are not without bearing on linguistic matters, the other children's disease more directly affects the interpretation of cuneiform texts, linguistically as well as philologically.

Students of Assyriology are impeded by the image they have perhaps not created, but allowed to perpetuate, that Akkadian is something special, something more than an ordinary language. Since it is written with special characters which have to be painfully learned and whose combinations seem inexhaustible, every text takes on the character of a puzzle, of a secret code to be deciphered, and hence acquires either a kind of mystique — it remains, ultimately, elusive and unattainable — or a pompous and pedantic apparatus to justify a reading or an interpretation. In fact, there remains nothing to be 'deciphered', and this holds for newly discovered texts as much as for long-known ones. In spite of the polyvalence of the cuneiform syllabary, there is normally only one correct reading for each group of signs, whether the unit be a word or a phrase; in those cases where there is actual ambiguity, it cannot be solved from internal evidence alone, just as ambiguous constructions in any language, including English. To take an example, if sign A has as possible values the syllables *ur*, *liK*, *DaŠ*, and sign B the syllables *kur*, *laD*, *maD*, *naD*, *ŠaD* (K stands for an element of the set whose elements are {g, k, q}, abbr. K ∈ {g, k, q}, similarly Š ∈ {z, s, ṣ, š}, D ∈ {d, t, ṭ}), the combination AAB, representing one word, will be read, of all possible $16.16.22 = 2^9.11 = 512.11 = 5632$ combinations, uniquely and unequivocally as *lik-taš-šad*, because of these 5632 combinations 5631 will be eliminated on graphemical, phonological, morphological, and lexical grounds. The reduction of the possibilities may be illustrated as follows.

Spelling rules exclude any form beginning with *ur-ur*, *liK-ur-*, or *DaŠ-ur-*, because within one word (C)VC-VC sequences do not normally occur; consequently, the second syllable cannot be *ur*. The sequence *ur-liK-* is excluded on the basis of root-incompatibility (and phonotactics: the cluster /rl/ does not occur in Akkadian). Forms beginning with *liK-liK-* or *Daš-Daš-* and followed by one of the values of sign B are excluded on morphological grounds, and similarly *DaŠ-liK*-B is excluded because any resulting form would represent a root with four consonantal radicals, and none of the few such roots known in Akkadian fits the available combinations, not only lexically but morphophonologically (quadriliteral roots have a liquid as second radical which clusters with the third).

These sequences eliminated, only *ur-DaŠ*-B and *liK-DaŠ*-B are possible sequences. It remains now to select a value for sign B; the graphemic practice that a sign with a value ending in a particular consonant is followed by a sign whose value begins with the same consonant selects for sign B the value *ŠaD*, even before testing whether any other value would yield a correct grammatical form (it would not). The choice between *ur-DaŠ-ŠaD* and *liK-DaŠ-ŠaD* is determined by dictionary look-up (depending on the arrangement of the dictionary, either under the roots *rŠD* or *KŠD*, or under the infinitives *raŠāDu* or *KaŠāDu*, the first D being analyzed as the grammatical morpheme {D} (i.e. /t/ with possible allomorphs *d* or *ṭ*). Between the two morphologically correct forms *urtaŠŠaD* and *liKDaŠŠaD*, the choice is determined by syntax and semantics. To take the latter form, with more, to be exact 36, possibilities, the choice still is between only 28 roots, since roots of the composition *qŠṭ*, *qṣ*{*t*, *d*}, {*k*, *g*} *ṣṭ* are excluded on the basis of root incompatibility. Upon checking the lexicon in twelve places under the three letters of the alphabet *g*, *k*, *q*, the root *kšd* is chosen, of which *liktaššad* is a grammatical form.

To take a parallel from English, if English *gaol* were read according to the possible pronunciations of each of the constituent letters, *g* having five readings, *a* 10, *o* 9, and *l* 4, one could say that the string *gaol* could have 5.10.9.4 = 1800 readings, but in fact, has only one actual pronunciation (corresponding to two possible spellings: *gaol* and *jail*), determinable only by dictionary look-up, similarly to the Akkadian string. If Akkadian dictionaries were arranged according to signs, the reading of the string of cuneiform signs would be as directly given as it is in an English dictionary.

On the other hand, if the cuneiform sign A has the values *me* and *šib*, and sign B the values *ki* and *qi*, no decision can be made for AB between the two possible readings *meki* and *šibqi*, two nouns with similar meaning 'instruction' and 'instructions, plan' (see von Soden, *ZA* 49.176f.), a situation comparable to the ambiguity of English *read* in *they read*, which may be pronounced [rīd] or [red], i.e. taken as present or past tense. Thus neither in the case of *liktaššad* nor in that of *meki*/*šibqi* is anything like deciphering involved, although the previous lengthy illustration might perhaps suggest that the choices between sign values are conscious logical deductions. In fact, no more deciphering is needed in this case than in the case of English (handwritten) *hoU*/*Nse*, with a third letter permitting both *u* and *n* as reading; just as the reader does not consciously try *honse* only to reject it in favor of *house*, the reader of cuneiform signs will come up with the correct reading *liktaššad* of the sign sequence without first trying other possibilities — provided he is familiar with the grammar and lexicon of Akkadian.

This brings me to the second point: obviously, no reading is possible without knowledge of the language. And the Assyriologist often suffers from another children's disease: timidity and lack of confidence in his mastery of Akkadian. Thus, in publications of cuneiform texts, although no such extremes are encountered as the above deduction to justify any particular reading, it is nevertheless common that the readings (i.e. the giving of interpretive values) of more rarely occurring words are justified by the text editor by offering his reader a selection of forms, in a similar and sometimes only slightly less absurd way than the one exemplified on *liktaššad.* I put this practice on the score of timidity and insecurity, because to my mind it indicates that the editor of the texts is not sure of either his competence or that of his reader, since he assumes that his interpretation could and would be doubted. In order to support and substantiate his reading, i.e. interpretation (as well as his translation, since correct translation implies correct reading, if not always the converse), the philologist-editor may draw upon his own files and/or memory to cite grammatical and semantic parallels, but too often he takes the shortcut of citing the existing dictionaries. Now, if the parallels are rare and just as unusual as the passage in whose support they are adduced, such citations are welcome and informative. If, however, the text portion to be 'elucidated' is quite ordinary, it is either an insult to the reader, or betrays the editor's own lack of familiarity with its ordinariness to cite parallels, especially when the available dictionaries or glossaries give ample evidence for its occurrence. It may seem that the choice between what is 'ordinary' and what is unusual, i.e. to be commented upon, is a subjective one; examples show, however, that decisions may be made on the basis of frequency or of published material available in dictionaries.

The fear of commitment in matters of lexicon and semantics is paralleled by that in matters of morphology and writing. Often, needlessly, standard forms are explicated, usually with reference to the standard grammars, where the reader, assuming that his Akkadian grammar was as shaky as that of the philologist-editor, would turn in the first place. In regard to writing, in the reading of partially broken signs and in the practice of the apparatus criticus, much that is superfluous and redundant is marked and commented upon.

These practices, to which even the confident Assyriologist feels himself compelled to conform to the prevailing 'scholarly' standards, take much time and energy that would more profitably be invested in studying genuinely problematic matters of language and philology. In my opinion, the above-sketched attitude is the reason why Akkadian studies have not attained the level of such fields as Romance philology or Slavic linguistics, and will hardly arrive there unless the new generation rejects it and turns its endeavors to more substantial matters. It is my hope that the 'current trends' will soon be replaced by 'new trends' as Assyriology moves, after its 'heroic age' and its data-collecting phase, into a re-evaluation phase for which its achievements to date make it eminently qualified.

REFERENCES

AHw. Akkadisches Handwörterbuch. 1959-. Unter Benutzung des lexikalischen Nachlasses von Bruno Meissner (1868–1947) bearbeitet von Wolfram von Soden. Wiesbaden, Harrassowitz.

Aro, Jussi. 1953. Abnormal plene writings in Akkadian texts. SO vol. 19, part 11.

——. 1955. Studien zur mittelbabylonischen Grammatik. SO vol. 20.

——. 1956. Remarks on the language of the Alalakh texts. AfO 17.361–5.

——. 1957. Review of L'accadien des lettres de Mari, by A. Finet. OLZ 52.128–31.

——. 1959. Die semitischen Zischlaute (*ṯ*), *š*, *ś* und *s* und ihre Vertretung im Akkadischen. Or 28.321–35.

——. 1960. Review of Intensiv und Aspektkorrelation, by F. Rundgren. SO 25/4. 14–22.

——. 1961. Die akkadischen Infinitivkonstruktionen. SO vol. 26.

——. 1963. Präpositionale Verbindungen als Bestimmungen des Nomens im Akkadischen. Or 32.395–406.

——. 1964. Die Vokalisierung des Grundstammes im semitischen Verbum. SO vol. 31.

Bar-Am, Moshe. 1938. The subjunctive in the Cappadocian texts. Or 7.12–31.

Böhl, F. M. Th. de Liagre. 1958. Bijbelse en Babylonische dichtkunst. Een metrisch onderzoek. JEOL 15.133–53.

——. 1960. La métrique de l'épopée babylonienne. Gilgameš et sa légende, ed. by P. Garelli, 145–52. Paris, Librairie C. Klincksieck. (Excerpt from Böhl 1958.)

Borger, Rykle. 1963. Babylonisch-assyrische Lesestücke. Heft I: Elemente der Grammatik und der Schrift. Rome, Pontificium Institutum Biblicum.

Bravmann, M. M. 1947. The plural ending *-ūt-* of masculine attributive adjectives in Akkadian. JCS 1.343.

Buccellati, Giorgio. 1968. An interpretation of the Akkadian stative as a nominal sentence. JNES 27.1–12.

CAD. The Assyrian dictionary of the Oriental Institute of the University of Chicago. 1956–. Chicago and Glückstadt, J. J. Augustin Inc.

Castellino, Giorgio. 1962. The Akkadian personal pronouns and verbal system in the light of Semitic and Hamitic. Leiden, Brill. (Reviews by Dietz Otto Edzard, BiOr 21.190–4 [1964] and Wolfram von Soden, JSS 10.159–77 [1965].)

Deller, Karlheinz. 1959. Lautlehre des Neuassyrischen. University of Vienna Dissertation.

——. 1962a. Zweisilbige Lautwerte des Typs KVKV im Neuassyrischen. Or 31.7–26.

——. 1962b. Studien zur neuassyrischen Orthographie. Or 31.186–96.

——. 1962c. Zur Syntax der Infinitivs im Neuassyrischen. Or 31.225–35.

DELLER, KARLHEINZ, M. DAHOOD, and R. KÖBERT. 1965. Comparative Semitics. Some remarks on a Recent Publication. Or 34.35–44.

DELLER, KARLHEINZ, and SIMO PARPOLA. 1967. Progressive Vokalassimilation im Neuassyrischen. Or 36.337–8.

D'JAKONOV, I. M. 1965. Semito-Hamitic languages. An essay in classification. Moscow, Nauka.

——. 1966. Review of Grammatik des Akkadischen, by A. Ungnad. VDI 1966/3. 183–90.

——. 1967. Jazyki drevnej perednej Azii. (Chap. VI: Akkadskij jazyk drevnej stupeni. Priloženie k gl. VI: Akkadskij jazyk srednej stupeni.) Moscow, Nauka.

EDZARD, DIETZ OTTO. 1964. Review of Untersuchungen zur Schrift und Sprache des Altbabylonischen von Susa, mit Berücksichtigung der Mâlamir-Texte, by Erkki Salonen. BiOr 21.194–5.

——. 1965. Die Stämme des altbabylonischen Verbums in ihrem Oppositionssystem. Studies in honor of Benno Landsberger, ed. by Hans G. Güterbock and Thorkild Jacobsen, 111–20. Chicago, University of Chicago.

FALKENSTEIN, ADAM. 1960. Kontakte zwischen Sumerern und Akkadern auf sprachlichem Gebiet. Genava, NS 8.301–14.

FINET, ANDRÉ. 1956. L'accadien des lettres de Mari. Bruxelles, Académie Royale de Belgique.

——. 1965. La valeur adverbiale du superlatif *maḫrûm-ma* dans la syntaxe de Mari. RA 59.73–6.

FLEISCH, HENRI, S. J. 1966. Phrase relative en accadien. MUSJ 42.247–84.

FRANKENA, R. 1965. Review of Die akkadischen Infinitivkonstruktionen, by J. Aro. BiOr 22.173–4.

GEERS, FREDERICK W. 1945. The treatment of emphatics in Akkadian. JNES 4.65–7.

GELB, IGNACE J. 1955. Notes on von Soden's Grammar of Akkadian. BiOr 12.93–111.

——. 1957. Review of L'accadien des lettres de Mari, by A. Finet. Lg 33.197–204.

——. 1958. Lexicography, lexicology, and the Akkadian dictionary. Miscelánea Homenaje a André Martinet 'Estructuralismo e Historia', ed. by D. Catalán, vol. 2.63–75. Universidad de la Laguna (Canarias).

——. 1961a. Old Akkadian writing and grammar. (Materials for the Assyrian Dictionary, 2.) 2nd ed. Chicago, University of Chicago.

——. 1961b. WA = *aw*, *iw*, *uw* in cuneiform writing. JNES 20.194–6.

GIACUMAKIS, GEORGE JR. 1963. The Akkadian of Alalakh. Brandeis University Dissertation. Abstract: Linguistics 13.110–11 (1965). (Mouton, 1970).

GOETZE, ALBRECHT. 1936. The *t*-form of the Old Babylonian verb. JAOS 56.297–334.

——. 1937. The sibilant in Old Babylonian *naẓārum*. Or 6.12–18.

——. 1938. Some observations on Nuzu Akkadian. Lg 14.134–43.

——. 1942. The so-called intensive of the Semitic languages. JAOS 62.1–8.

GOETZE, ALBRECHT. 1945. The Akkadian dialects of the Old-Babylonian mathematical texts. Mathematical cuneiform texts, ed. by Otto Neugebauer and Abraham Sachs, 146–51. (American Oriental Series, 29.) New Haven, American Oriental Society.

——. 1946a. Number idioms in Old Babylonian. JNES 5.185–202.

——. 1946b. Sequence of two short syllables in Akkadian. Or 15.233–8.

——. 1946c. The Akkadian masculine plural in *ānū/ī* and its Semitic background. Lg 22.121–31.

——. 1947a. The Akkadian passive. JCS 1.50–9.

——. 1947b. Short or long *a*? (Notes on some Akkadian words). Or 16.239–50.

——. 1958. The sibilants of Old Babylonian. RAss 52.137–49.

GOOSSENS, GEORGE. 1942. L'accadien des clercs d'Uruk sous les Séleucides. Muséon 55.61–86.

GORDON, CYRUS H. 1938. The dialect of the Nuzu tablets. Or 7.32–63, 215–32.

GREENBERG, JOSEPH H. 1950. The patterning of root morphemes in Semitic. Word 6.162–81.

——. 1952. The Afro-Asiatic (Hamito-Semitic) present. JAOS 72.1–8.

——. 1960. An Afro-Asiatic pattern of gender and number agreement. JAOS 80.317–21.

HALDAR, ALFRED. 1963. The Akkadian verbal system. 1. The *paris* form. Or 32.246–79.

——. 1964. The Akkadian verbal system. 2. The *iprus* : *iparras* forms. Or 33.15–48.

HAUDRICOURT, ANDRÉ. 1953. La valeur de *š*, *z*, *s* dans le syllabaire cunéiforme. GLECS 6.37–8.

HECKER, KARL. 1961. Die Sprache der altassyrischen Texte aus Kappadokien. Dissertation Freiburg in Breisgau. (To appear in the series Analecta Orientalia, 44. Rome, Pontificium Institutum Biblicum.)

HEIDEL, ALEXANDER. 1940. The system of the quadriliteral verb in Akkadian. (Assyriological Studies 13.) Chicago, University of Chicago Press. (Review by Albrecht Goetze, JNES 4.246–9 [1945]; rejoinder: ibid. 249–53; surrejoinder: Goetze, ibid. 253; Review by Wolfram von Soden, ZA 49.330–3 [1950].)

HYATT, J. PHILIP. 1941. The treatment of final vowels in Early Neo-Babylonian. (Yale Oriental Series, Researches, 23.) New Haven, Yale University Press.

JACOBSEN, THORKILD. 1956. Introduction to the Chicago grammatical texts. Materialien zum Sumerischen Lexikon, ed. by B. Landsberger, vol. 4.1*–50*. Rome, Pontificium Institutum Biblicum.

——. 1960. *Ittallak niāti*. JNES 19.101–16.

——. 1963. The Akkadian ablative accusative. JNES 22.18–29.

JUCQUOIS, GUY. 1966. Phonétique comparée des dialectes moyen-babyloniens du nord et de l'ouest. (Bibliothèque du Muséon, 53.) Louvain, Institut Orientaliste.

KAPLAN, G. CH. 1965. K fonetike sredneassirijskogo dialekta akkadskogo jazyka. [The phonetics of the Middle Assyrian dialect of Akkadian.] Semit. jaz. 2/2. 186–200.

KIENAST, BURKHART. 1957a. Verbalformen mit Reduplikation im Akkadischen. Or 26.44–50.

——. 1957b. Erwägungen zu einer neueren Studie über semitische Demonstrativa. Or 26.257–68.

——. 1960. Das Punktualthema *japrus und seine Modi. Or 29.151–67.

——. 1961a. Weiteres zum R-Stamm des Akkadischen. JCS 15.59–61.

——. 1961b. Satzeinleitendes *mā* im älteren Akkadischen. ZA 54.90–9.

——. 1963. Das System der zweiradikaligen Verben im Akkadischen (Ein Beitrag zur vergleichenden Semitistik). ZA 55.138–55.

——. 1967. Zu den Vokalklassen beim akkadischen Verbum. Heidelberger Studien zum Alten Orient, ed. by D.O. Edzard, 63–85. Wiesbaden, Harrassowitz.

KIFIŠIN, A. G. 1965. Assiriologičeskie zametki. Reljativnaja forma *ša* ... *-šu* v akkadskom jazyke. [The relative form *ša* ... *-šu* in Akkadian.] Semit. jaz. 2/2. 786–92.

KLAEK, A. 1962. Struktura gramatyczna akkadyjskich nazw osobowych. SprOKr-PAN 78–9.

KNUDSEN, EBBE E. 1961. Cases of free variants in the Akkadian *q* phoneme. JCS 15.84–90.

——. 1965. Notes on two grammars of Susa Old Babylonian. AcOr 28.347–53.

KURYŁOWICZ, JERZY. 1961. L'apophonie en sémitique. Wrocław, Polska Akademia Nauk.

LAMBERT, MAURICE. 1964. La fonction relative dans les langues mésopotamiennes, II En accadien. GLECS 10.139–42.

LANCELOTTI, ANGELO. 1962. Grammatica della lingua accadica. (Analecta Hierosolymitana 1.) Jerusalem, Franciscan Press.

LANDSBERGER, BENNO. 1924. Der Ventiv des Akkadischen. ZA 35.113–23.

——. 1926. Die Eigenbegrifflichkeit der babylonischen Welt. Islamica 2.355–72. (Reprinted 1965. Wissenschaftliche Buchgesellschaft, Darmstadt, in the series Libelli, vol. 142.)

——. 1938. Die Gestalt der semitischen Wurzel. Atti del XIX Congresso Internazionale degli Orientalisti 1935, 450–2. Roma, Tipografia del Senato.

LESLAU, WOLF. 1944. Vocabulary common to Akkadian and South-East Semitic (Ethiopic and South Arabic). JAOS 64.53–8.

——. 1962. Southeast Semitic cognates to the Akkadian vocabulary, I. JAOS 82.1–4.

LEWY, JULIUS. 1921. Untersuchungen zur akkadischen Grammatik I. Das Verbum in den altassyrischen Gesetzen. (Berliner Beiträge zur Keilschriftforschung, vol. 1, part 4.) Berlin.

——. 1922. Studien zu den altassyrischen Texten aus Kappadokien. Berlin.

——. 1946. Studies in Akkadian grammar and onomatology. Or 15.361–415.

——. 1959. Old Assyrian *izêzum* and its implications. Or 28.351–60.

——. 1960. Grammatical and lexicographical studies. Or 29.20–45.

LIPIN, L. A. 1962. Èlementy aggljutinacii v akkadskom jazyke po materialam ličnych mestoimenij. [Elements of agglutination in the Akkadian personal pronouns.] Trudy XXV Kongr. vostokovedov, I, part 1.213–19. Moscow.

——. 1964. Akkadskij jazyk. Moscow, Nauka.

MATOUŠ, LUBOR. 1952. Základy akkadské gramatiky (mimeographed). Prague, Státní pedagogické nakladatelství.

——. 1956a. Les textes accadiens d'Ugarit. AO 24.375–82.

MATOUŠ, LUBOR, and KAREL PETRÁČEK. 1956b. Beiträge zur akkadischen Grammatik. I. Die Liquiden in ihrem Verhältnis zum Vokal im Assyrischen. AO 24.1–14.

MEEK, THEOPHILE J. 1946. The asyndeton clause in the Code of Hammurabi. JNES 5.64–72.

——. 1950. The explicative pronoun *šu*/*ša* in the Code of Hammurabi. AO 18/4.78–81.

MEISSNER, BRUNO. 1913. Die Keilschrift. Berlin, Sammlung Göschen. (1967. Third edition revised by K. Oberhuber. Berlin, Sammlung Göschen.)

MEYER, LÉON DE. 1962. L'accadien des contrats de Suse. Leiden, Brill.

——. 1964. De nominale woordvorming in het Oudbabylonisch der Susa-oorkonden. OGand 1.105–29.

MOSCATI, SABATINO (ed.), A. SPITALER, E. ULLENDORFF, and WOLFRAM VON SODEN. 1964. An introduction to the comparative grammar of the Semitic languages. Wiesbaden, Harrassowitz.

NOUGAYROL, JEAN. 1950. La détermination et l'indétermination du nom en accadien. GLECS 5.73–6, 78.

——. 1952. Langues et écritures sémitiques. 1. Sémitique oriental ou Accadien (Langue — écriture). Dictionnaire de La Bible. Supplément, fasc. 25.259–84.

NOWICKI, PAWEL. 1964. Pismo klinowe. Język akkadycki. Zagadnienia podstawowe (mimeographed). Warszawa, Akad. Teologii Katolickiej.

OBERHUBER, KARL. 1967. Die Keilschrift. Berlin, Sammlung Göschen. (Completely revised, 3rd ed., of B. Meissner, Die Keilschrift. Berlin, Sammlung Göschen. 1913.)

OPPENHEIM, A. LEO. 1933. Die Rolle der *t*-Formen im Codex Hammurapi. WZKM 40.181–220.

——. 1935. Die mittels *t*-Infixes gebildeten Aktionsarten des Altbabylonischen. WZKM 42.1–30.

——. 1940. Une nouvelle forme du pronom démonstratif en néo-babylonien. Or 9.221–2.

——. 1941. Idiomatic Akkadian (lexicographical researches). JAOS 61.251–71.

——. 1942. The Neo-Babylonian preposition '*la*'. JNES 1.369–72.

——. 1947. Deictic *-ka*, *-kunu* in Neo-Babylonian. JCS 1.120–1.

——. 1957. An 'etymology' for *andinānu*. AfO 18.278.

——. 1966. Review of Akkadisches Handwörterbuch, by Wolfram von Soden. JNES 25.143–4.

POEBEL, ARNO. 1932. Das appositionell bestimmte Pronomen der 1. Pers. sing. in den westsemitischen Inschriften und im Alten Testament. (Assyriological Studies 3.) Chicago, University of Chicago.

——. 1939. Studies in Akkadian grammar. (Assyriological Studies 9.) Chicago, University of Chicago.

——. 1947. Miscellaneous studies. (Assyriological Studies 14.) Chicago, University of Chicago.

POLOTSKY, HANS J. 1964. Semitics. At the dawn of civilization, The world history of the Jewish people, ed. by E.A. Speiser. First Series: Ancient times. vol. 1. B. Netanyahu, general editor. London, W.H. Allen.

RAVN, OTTO E. 1941. The so-called relative clauses in Accadian or the Accadian particle *ša*. Copenhagen, Nyt Nordisk Forlag, Arnold Busck. (Review by Albrecht Goetze, JCS 1.73–80 [1947].)

——. 1949. Babylonian permansive and status indeterminatus. AO 17/2.300–6.

REINER, ERICA. 1951. Un aspect de la proposition relative accadienne. RA 45.25–9.

——. 1964. The phonological interpretation of a sub-system in the Akkadian syllabary. Studies presented to A.L. Oppenheim, ed. by Robert D. Biggs and John A. Brinkman, 167–80. Chicago, University of Chicago.

——. 1965. An Ancient Babylonian transformation. Paper presented to LSA Annual Meeting.

——. 1966. A linguistic analysis of Akkadian. (Janua Linguarum, Series Practica, 21.) The Hague, Mouton.

RÖLLIG, WOLFGANG. 1960. Griechische Eigennamen in Texten der babylonischen Spätzeit. Or 29.376–91.

RÖSSLER, OTTO. 1950. Verbalbau und Verbalflexion in den semito-hamitischen Sprachen. ZDMG 100.461–514.

——. 1951. Akkadisches und libysches Verbum, I-II. Or 20.101–7, 366–73.

ROWTON, MICHAEL B. 1962. The use of the permansive in Classic Babylonian. JNES 21.233–303.

RUNDGREN, FRITHIOF. 1955. Über Bildungen mit *š*- und *n-t*-Demonstrativen im Semitischen. Beiträge zur vergleichenden Grammatik der semitischen Sprachen. Uppsala, Almqvist & Wiksells Boktryckeri AB.

——. 1959a. Intensiv und Aspektkorrelation. Studien zur äthiopischen und akkadischen Verbalstammbildung. Uppsala, UUÅ 1959.5.

——. 1959b. Akkadisch *utlellūm* 'sich erheben'. Or 28.364–9.

——. 1963. Erneuerung des Verbalaspekts im Semitischen. Funktionell-diachronische Studien zur semitischen Verblehre. (ASLU 1:3.) Uppsala.

RYCKMANS, GONZAGUE. 1960. Grammaire accadienne, 4e éd. revue par P. Naster. (Bibliothèque du Muséon, vol. 6.) Louvain, Université de Louvain.

SALONEN, ERKKI. 1962. Untersuchungen zur Schrift und Sprache des Altbabylonischen von Susa, mit Berücksichtigung der Mâlamir-Texte. SO vol. 27, part 1.

SIEVERS, EDUARD. 1929. Beiträge zur babylonischen Metrik. ZA 38.1–38 [mit Nachwort von H. Zimmern].

Soden, Wolfram von. 1932. Der hymnisch-epische Dialekt des Akkadischen. ZA 40.163–227.

——. 1933. Der hymnisch-epische Dialekt des Akkadischen. ZA 41.90–183, 236.

——. 1939a. Die akkadische Adverbialisendung *-attam*, *-atti*. ZA 45.62–8.

——. 1939b. Nominalformen und juristische Begriffsbildung im Akkadischen: die Nominalform *QUTULLĀ'*. Symbolae ad Iura Orientis Antiqui Pertinentes Paulo Koschaker Dedicatae, ed. by J. Friedrich, J. G. Lautner, and J. Miles, 199–207. (Studia et Documenta 2.) Leiden, Brill.

——. 1942. Aufgabe und Methode des akkadischen Sprachunterrichts (Zu P. Naster: Chrestomathie accadienne). OLZ 45.345–53.

——. 1948a. Das akkadische Syllabar. (Analecta Orientalia, 27.) Rome, Pontificium Institutum Biblicum.

——. 1948b. Vokalfärbungen im Akkadischen. JCS 2.291–303.

——. 1950. Verbalformen mit doppeltem *t*-Infix im Akkadischen. Or 19.385–96.

——. 1951a. Zur Aufgabe und Terminologie einer neuen akkadischen Grammatik. Compte Rendu de la Seconde Rencontre Assyriologique Internationale, 75–80. Paris, Imprimerie Nationale.

——. 1951b. Zum akkadischen Wörterbuch, 41–9. Or 20.151–66. [41. Zu einigen seltenen vierradikaligen Verben.]

——. 1951c. Zum akkadischen Wörterbuch, 50. Or 20.257–66. [Ingressiv-durative N-Stämme von Verben mediae geminatae.]

——. 1952a. Grundriss der akkadischen Grammatik. (Analecta Orientalia, 33.) Rome, Pontificium Institutum Biblicum.

——. 1952b. Unregelmässige Verben im Akkadischen. ZA 50.163–81.

——. 1956. Zum akkadischen Wörterbuch, 81. *l* statt *n* in altassyrischen Wortformen. Or 25.241–3.

——. 1957a. Grundsätzliches zum Akkadischen Wörterbuch. OLZ 52.485–92.

——. 1957b. Zur Laut- und Formenlehre des Neuassyrischen. AfO 18.121–2.

——. 1957c. Review of Über Bildungen mit *š*- und *n-t*-Demonstrativen im Semitischen, by F. Rundgren. BiOr 14.204–8.

——. 1959a. Das Akkadische Handwörterbuch. Probleme und Schwierigkeiten. Or 28.26–33.

——. 1959b. Assyriologische Miszellen. WZKM 55.49–61. [2. Akk. *abarša* und der sum. Laut *ř*. 51–3; 4. *dakāku* I und II und die Wurzelvariabilität beim schwachen Verbum im Akk. 54–5.]

——. 1959c. Aramäisches *ḥ* erscheint im Spätbabylonischen vor *m* als *g*. AfO 19. 149.

——. 1960. Status rectus-Formen vor dem Genitiv im Akkadischen und die sogenannte uneigentliche Annexion im Arabischen. JNES 19.163–71.

——. 1961a. Akkadisch. Linguistica Semitica: presente e futuro, ed. by Giorgio Levi Della Vida. (Studi Semitici 4.) Rome, Centro di Studi Semitici, Istituto di Studi del Vicino Oriente — Università.

SODEN, WOLFRAM VON. 1961b. Zum Akkusativ der Beziehung im Akkadischen. Or 30.156-62.

——. 1961c. Die Zahlen 20 bis 90 im Semitischen und der Status absolutus. WZKM 57.24–8.

——. 1964. Zu A. Haldar, The Akkadian verbal system. Or 33.437–42.

——. 1965. Das akkadische *t*-Perfekt in Haupt- und Nebensätzen und sumerische Verbalformen mit den Präfixen *ba-*, *imma-* und *u-*. Studies in honor of Benno Landsberger, ed. by Hans G. Güterbock and Thorkild Jacobsen, 103–10. (Assyriological Studies 16.) Chicago, University of Chicago.

——. 1966. Aramäische Wörter in neuassyrischen und neu- und spätbabylonischen Texten. Ein Vorbericht. Or 35.1–20.

——. 1968. Die Spirantisierung von Verschlusslauten im Akkadischen: Ein Zwischenbericht. JNES 27.214–20.

SODEN, WOLFRAM VON, and WOLFGANG RÖLLIG. 1967. Das akkadische Syllabar. 2nd rev. ed. (Analecta Orientalis 42.) Rome, Pontificium Institutum Biblicum.

SOUČEK, VLADIMÍR. 1956. Die Probleme der alt-akkadischen Dialektologie. AO 24.634 (abstract).

SPEISER, EPHRAIM A. 1936. Studies in Semitic formatives. JAOS 56.22–46.

——. 1947. A note on the derivation of *šumma*. JCS 1.321–8.

——. 1952. The 'elative' in West-Semitic and Akkadian. JCS 6.81–92.

——. 1953. Comments on recent studies in Akkadian grammar. JAOS 73.129–38.

——. 1954. The terminative-adverbial in Canaanite-Ugaritic and Akkadian. IEJ 4.108–15.

——. 1964. The syllabic transcription of Ugaritic [ḫ] and [ḥ]. BASOR 175.42–7.

SWAIM, GERALD GORDON. 1962. A grammar of the Akkadian tablets found at Ugarit. Brandeis University Dissertation.

THUREAU-DANGIN, FRANÇOIS. 1933. Observations sur la graphie des sifflantes dans l'écriture cunéiforme. RAss 30.93–6.

——. 1946. Les graphies rompues en Akkadien (Mededeelingen en Verhandelingen van het Vooraziatisch-Egyptisch Gezelschap 'Ex Oriente Lux', 8), 15–18. Leiden, E. J. Brill.

UNGNAD, ARTHUR. 1937. Die *t*-Form des akkadischen Verbs. Or 6.252–5.

——. 1949. Grammatik des Akkadischen. 3rd rev. ed. München, Biederstein Verlag.

——. 1964. Grammatik des Akkadischen. Völlig neubearbeitet von Lubor Matouš. Vierte Aufl. der Babylonisch-Assyrischen Grammatik Arthur Ungnads [1906[1]; 1925[2]; 1949[3]]. München, C. H. Beck.

WINCKWORTH, C. P. T. 1950. Some notes on Late-Babylonian orthography. Essays presented to S. A. Cook, ed. by D. Winton Thomas, 67–71. London, Taylor's.

YLVISAKER, SIGURD. 1912. Zur babylonischen und assyrischen Grammatik. (Leipziger Semitistische Studien, vol. 5, part 6.)

ZINKAND, JOHN MULLER. 1958. A study of the morphology of Ugaritic and Akkadian. Brandeis University Dissertation.

HEBREW

CHAIM RABIN

1. BIBLICAL HEBREW

A. *The Corpus*

Apart from a small number of inscriptions, the linguistic investigation of Biblical Hebrew is necessarily based on the Hebrew Bible, the Old Testament. Until the twentieth century, the identity of this corpus was clear to everybody. The printed Bibles exhibited a text which was established on the basis of MSS and massoretic studies by Jacob Adoniah ben Ḥayyīm for the so-called Second Rabbinic Bible printed by Bomberg at Venice, 1524–25, and they differed only in the degree of freedom from printing errors and in certain features of systematization. The vocalization of this text was assumed to represent the results of the work of the massoretic school which culminated in the model codex of Aaron Ben Asher of Tiberias in the early tenth century A.D. The original codex was said to be kept at a synagogue at Aleppo, Syria, but was not accessible to scholars, and even its identity was doubted by some. From 1929 onwards, P. Kahle printed in the *Biblia Hebraica*, published by the Württembergische Bibelanstalt at Stuttgart, a Hebrew text based upon the Leningrad Codex B 19 A (with some corrections), and it became obvious that Jacob ben Ḥayyīm's vocalization was a late development and systematization of the original Ben Asher system. In 1958 N.H.Snaith edited for the British and Foreign Bible Society a text based upon medieval Spanish and Yemenite MSS. In 1948 the Aleppo Codex reached Jerusalem, and now could be used by scholars. Its identity with the original text of Aaron Ben Asher was confirmed, and small parts were published.[1] A complete diplomatic edition of what has remained of this text is still outstanding; a definitive text for linguistic analysis should also list all variants in a number of roughly contemporary MSS.

While it is clear that all future linguistic work ought to be done on the original

[1] M.H. Goshen-Gottstein, 'The authenticity of the Aleppo Codex', *Textus* (Jerusalem) 1.17–58 (1960), with photographs of Dt.28:17 to end. Id., *The Book of Isaiah*, sample edition with introduction (Jerusalem, 1965), prints Isaiah 2, 5, 11, 51. For list of extant parts of the MS, see I. Ben-Zvi, *Textus* 1.2–3. Cf. I.Yeivin, *Keter Aram Ṣovah-niqqudo u-ṭəʿamaw* (Jerusalem, J.L. Magnes Press of the Hebrew University, 1968).

form of the Ben Asher tradition now recovered, this does not mean that all grammars written up to date are obsolete. The differences mainly concern a small number of well-defined phonetic features, such as the indication of secondary stress and the coloring of the *shewa* as reduced *a*. On the other hand, the more detailed grammars contain discussions about certain grammatical forms which differ in the printed editions: such doubts are now settled by having authoritative texts.

The Hebrew text, as we have it, is made up of three layers: the basic consonantal skeleton corresponding to the way in which all but the latest texts of the Old Testament were spelled when originally composed or edited;[2] the matres lectionis *w* and *y* inserted from the fourth century B.C. onwards to mark *ī ē* (by *y*) or *ū ō* (by *w*) under certain circumstances; the punctuation or vowel-signs introduced since the eighth century, together and interlinked with a system of indicating pauses and musical cantillation, called the Accents. The notation of Punctuation and Accents of the Ben Asher school is only one system out of many. Even the system employed by Aaron Ben Asher's father Moses in the Codex of the Prophetic Books kept at Cairo differed in some respects. Another system employing the same signs is known under the name of Ben Naphtali.[3] Completely different signs based on a different phonemic analysis are found in the so-called Babylonian and Palestinian systems, each of which is known in several distinct sub-systems,[4] as well as in a system using the Arabic vowel-signs, employed by some Karaites. A completely different tradition of Hebrew pronunciation and grammar, current among the Samaritan community,[5] is represented by the Samaritan system of punctuation.[6] The phonetic interpretation of these sign-systems can only be assured by careful study of the present-day traditional

[2] Cf. F.M.Cross and D.N.Freedman, *Early Hebrew orthography* (New Haven, 1952); D.N. Freedman, 'The Massoretic Text and the Qumran Scrolls', *Textus* 2.87–102 (1962).

[3] The identity of this vocalization system is still under discussion. See P.Kahle, *Masoreten des Westens*, II, 45*–68* (Stuttgart, 1930); S.Morag, 'The vocalization of Codex Reuchlinianus', *JSS* 4.216–37 (1959); *The vocalization systems of Arabic, Hebrew and Aramaic*, Janua Linguarum XIII, 34, 38–41 (The Hague, 1962); 'Heʿarot lə-teʿur šiṭṭat ha-niqqud šel maḥzor Wormaizah', *Ləšonenu*, 29.203–9 (Jerusalem, 1964–65); L. Lipschütz, 'Kitāb al-khilaf' (English), *Textus* 4.1–29 (1964).

[4] For general information see P.Kahle, *Die hebräischen Bibelhandschriften aus Babylonien* (Giessen, 1928), *Masoreten des Ostens* (Leipzig, 1913), *Masoreten des Westens*, 2 vols. (Stuttgart, 1927–30); E.Würthwein, *Der Text des Alten Testaments*, 2nd ed. (Stuttgart, 1963), *The Text of the Old Testament* (Oxford, 1957). Cf. A.Murtonen, *Liturgical texts and psalm fragments provided with the so-called Palestinian punctuation* (Helsinki, 1958), with sketch grammar pp. 25–61. Detailed investigations are in progress as Jerusalem University theses by I.Yeivin (Babylonian) and Mrs. S.Bahat (Palestinian).

[5] Z. Ben-Ḥayyim, "Ivrit nosaḥ Šoməron', *Ləšonenu* 12.45–60, 113–26 (1941–42); *'Ivrit wa-ărāmit nosaḥ Šoməron*, I-II native philologists, III,1 texts in transcription (Jerusalem, 1956–57, 1960–61); A. Murtonen, *An etymological vocabulary to the Samaritan Pentateuch*; *a grammar of the Samaritan dialect of Hebrew* (Studia Orientalia Soc. Orient. Fennicae, XXIV, XXIX, Helsinki, 1960–64).

[6] F.Diening, *Das Hebräische bei den Samaritanern* (Stuttgart, 1938); P.Kahle, 'Die Lesezeichen bei den Samaritanern', *Haupt Memorial Volume*, 425–36 (Baltimore and Leipzig, 1926); Z.Ben-Ḥayyim, 'The Samaritan vowel system and its graphic representation', *AO* 22.515–30 (1954).

reading-pronunciations of Hebrew, a task which is still unfinished, and may soon become impossible to perform because these traditions are dying out.[7]

The linguistic reliability of this corpus has been questioned on several counts. It is widely claimed by Biblical scholars that part of the material in various books consists of late additions or has been substantially altered. Such changes would still have occurred before the second century B.C., however, and would thus affect only our view of the internal history of Biblical Hebrew. It is further believed, even by scholars who deny that there were late additions, that the Hebrew text underwent widespread corruption and alteration, including the introduction of late and corrupt linguistic features.[8] Restoration of the original text is sought through emendation either by conjecture or by reference to the ancient Greek, Latin, Syriac, and Aramaic versions, and to a lesser extent, to quotations in second to sixth century A.D. Rabbinic literature, to the Dead Sea Scrolls, and to Biblical manuscripts.[9] Thirdly, since the various punctuation systems and traditions are phonetic notations of the way Hebrew was pronounced in synagogues in the eighth to tenth centuries A.D., there is a wide field for assuming corruptions in oral reading-tradition during the over 1,000 years intervening between this and the date of the latest Biblical books, not to mention the more than 2,000 years between it and the ostensible date of the Song of Deborah (Judges 5). This corruption can either concern individual forms, or individual occurrences of forms; or it can be systematic, by incorporating the effects of phonetic and phonemic changes which took place long after Biblical Hebrew ceased to be spoken or at least to be taught in schools as a written language and after the last books were composed. All modern historical grammars assume such post-Biblical changes in Biblical Hebrew vocalization and consonantal sub-phonemic values. Some take this to have been a more or less rectilinear development; another school, headed by P. Sievers and P. Kahle, however, assumes that after a period of far-reaching phonetic alteration, especially as concerns the silencing of the laryngals and pharyngals, older features were restored through spelling pronunciation and under the influence of contemporary Arab efforts to safeguard the pronunciation of the Qur'ān.[10]

[7] Cf. A.Z. Idelson, 'Die gegenwärtige Aussprache des Hebräischen bei Juden und Samaritanern', *MGWJ* 57.527–45, 697–721 (1913 — also as separate brochure, Breslau, 1913); Y.F. Gumpertz, *Mivṭa'ey śəfatenu* (Jerusalem, 1953); S. Morag, *The Hebrew language tradition of the Yemenite Jews* (in Hebrew, Jerusalem, 1963). The Project on the Language Traditions of the Jewish Communities, at the Hebrew University of Jerusalem, is carrying on a large-scale program of recordings and analysis (Directors: S. Morag and D. Téné). Cf. A. Sperber, 'Hebrew phonology', *Hebrew Union College Annual* 16.415–82 (1941).

[8] Friedrich Delitzsch, *Lese- und Schreibfehler im Alten Testament* (Berlin and Leipzig, 1920), is still widely used as an aid to exegesis. The most widely used scholarly Bible edition, *Biblia Hebraica*, ed. by R. Kittel and P. Kahle (see above), gives in its critical apparatus not only emendations of meaning, but also many purely linguistic corrections which do not affect the meaning of the text.

[9] The Hebrew University Bible Project (Directors: M.H. Goshen-Gottstein, C. Rabin, S. Talmon) works at a systematic investigation and presentation of the variants from all sources; cf. the Sample Edition, fn. 1 above.

[10] Cf. P. Kahle, *The Cairo Geniza*, 2nd ed. (Oxford, 1959). Criticism by Z. Ben-Ḥayyim, *Studies in the traditions of the Hebrew language* (Madrid, 1954); E.Y. Kutscher, *Lašonenu* 29.48–58, 120–8 (1964–65), and *JSS* 10.21–51 (1965).

The sound-changes supposed to be involved do not, strictly speaking, constitute a part of the history of Hebrew, but are reflections of developments in Aramaic, the spoken language of Palestinian Jews in the third to eighth centuries, upon their Hebrew reading style,[11] or, in the case of the Kahle theory, of orthoepic theories designed for Arabic upon Hebrew orthoepics. Only lately, a further factor of uncertainty has been taken into account: the influence of Mishnaic Hebrew speech habits upon the pronunciation and vocalization of Biblical texts transmitted by Mishnaic Hebrew speakers for several centuries, and possibly even upon the vocabulary, by replacing obsolete words with such as were known to later Hebrew speakers.[12] Moreover, the Ancient Versions which are being used to emend the Hebrew text are no doubt themselves influenced in their choice of meanings and understanding of the grammatical constructions by Mishnaic Hebrew, with which the Greek versions, the Peshitta, and the Aramaic Targums are contemporary.[13] Aramaic and Mishnaic Hebrew influence is evident in the spelling of the Dead Sea Scrolls,[14] the Greek and Latin transliterations of proper names and single words in the Versions[15] and of continuous texts in the remnants of Origen's Hexapla (third century A.D.),[16] as well as in the Samaritan traditions.[17]

A descriptive analysis of even the earliest vocalized texts must thus be assumed to refer not to Biblical Hebrew itself, but to an altered reflection of it. This difficulty has been present in the mind of most of the more important recent researchers. One common reaction is the process of non-analysis: a proportion of forms (in grammars) or words (in dictionaries) is rejected as corrupt, and is either left unexplained or its emended substitute is analyzed instead. In the last thirty years, especially since H.S.Nyberg's *Hoseastudien* with its outspoken preface,[18] emendation is less and less resorted to; the tendency to preserve and explain to the fullest possible extent the forms in the actual Hebrew text is more pronounced among linguists than among

[11] Much as the older pronunciation of Latin in England imposed the results of English sound-changes upon the Latin graphemes.

[12] E.Y. Kutscher, *The language and linguistic background of the Isaiah Scroll* (in Hebrew, Jerusalem, 1959), Introduction.

[13] Cf. C.Rabin, *Textus* 6.20, fn. 74 (1968).

[14] Cf. Kutscher, *op. cit.*, passim.

[15] The literature on this subject is vast. Cf. especially A. Sperber, 'Hebrew based upon Greek and Latin transliterations', *Hebrew Union College Annual* 12/13.103–274 (Cincinnati, 1937–38); G. Lisowski, *Die Transkription der hebräischen Eigennamen des Pentateuchs in der Septuaginta* (Basel, 1940). Criticism by J.Barr, 'St. Jerome and the sounds of Hebrew', *JSS* 12.1–36 (1967).

[16] Cardinal J.Mercati, ed., *Psalterii Hexapli Reliquiae* (Rome, 1958); E.Brønno, *Studien über hebräische Morphologie und Vokalismus auf Grund der mercatischen Fragmente der zweiten Kolumne der Hexapla des Origenes* (Leipzig, 1943); W.E.Staples, 'The second column of Origen's Hexapla', *JAOS* 59.71–80 (1939); G.Mercati, 'Il problema della II^{a} colonna dell' Esaplo', *Biblica* 28.173–215 (1947).

[17] Ed. A.v.Gall, *Der hebräische Pentateuch der Samaritaner*, 5 vols. (Giessen, 1914–18); Z.Ben-Ḥayyim, 'La tradition Samaritaine et sa parenté avec les autres traditions de la langue hébraïque', *Mélanges de philosophie et de littérature juives* 3/5.89–128 (Paris, 1962).

[18] *Studien zum Hoseabuche* (Uppsala, 1935).

exegetists. This tendency has led to the discovery of many hitherto unsuspected forms, constructions, and words.[18a] While H. Birkeland gives a phonetic and phonological reconstruction of pre-587 B.C. Hebrew, as opposed to the same text in its Tiberian form now read in Bibles,[19] the only serious attempt to provide a linguistic analysis based solely upon such reconstructed living Biblical Hebrew has so far been undertaken by Z. S. Harris.[20]

The emendations to the Bible text are to be found in commentaries and lexica; there is, to my knowledge, no exhaustive list of the emendations suggested. The first attempt to provide the Bible text with an apparatus systematically listing the emendations, as far as approved by the editor, is the *Biblia Hebraica* of R. Kittel in its three editions. At various times projects were mooted to print a complete emended text, but none came to fruition. It can thus be said that the linguistic analysis of Biblical Hebrew still describes the language as fixed by Aaron Ben Asher about 900 A.D.

B. *Grammatical Description*

The pre-modern stage of Biblical Hebrew grammar is best represented by Gesenius' Hebrew grammar. Originally published by Friedrich Wilhelm Gesenius (1786–1842) in 1813,[21] it was revised by various hands in 28 editions, the last one by E. Kautzsch in 1909, from which an English translation was published by A. E. Cowley in 1910.[22] In this final form, it provides a well-nigh exhaustive catalogue of forms found in the Bible, classified into correct and corrupt, 'best usage' and late forms. The logical approach, with its universal, Latin-based categories, is dominant. Historical interpretations, as far as offered, were even in 1909 behind the contemporary achievements of comparative linguistics. The grammar is divided into phonology, accidence, 'syntax' describing the function of the forms taught in the accidence, and syntax of sentences. The second and third parts are still the most complete descriptions available, while the first and last parts are now of little practical value. Full as it is, the 28th edition of Gesenius does not completely supersede, in terms of its own period, the monumental grammars of H. Ewald, J. Olshausen, F. Boettcher, and E. König.[23] The last-named is notable for its systematic use of medieval Jewish grammarians, while its Syntax volume, though its antiquated descriptive matrix

[18a] Criticism: J. Barr, *Comparative philology and the text of the Old Testament* (Oxford, 1968).

[19] *Akzent und Vokalismus im Althebräischen*, Skrifter ... Norske Vidensk.-Ak., II, Hist.-filos. Kl., 1940,3 (Oslo, 1940), especially pp. 53–8.

[20] 'Linguistic structure of Hebrew', *JAOS* 61.143–67 (1941).

[21] *Hebräische Grammatik* (Halle, 1813). Gesenius also wrote *Ausführliches grammatisch-kritisches Lehrgebäude*, etc. (Halle, 1817).

[22] Gesenius' *Hebrew grammar*, Second English edition (Oxford, 1910, and reprints).

[23] H. Ewald (1803–75), *Kritische Grammatik der hebräischen Sprache* (Leipzig, 1827), from the 8th edition onwards called *Ausführliches Lehrbuch*, etc.; G. Olshausen (1800–82), *Lehrbuch der hebr. Sprache* (Braunschweig, 1861); F. Böttcher, *Ausführliches Lehrbuch*, etc., 2 vols. (Leipzig, 1866–68); E. König, *Historisch-kritisches Lehrgebäude*, etc., 3 vols. (Leipzig, 1881–97).

makes it hard to use as a description, is still indispensable to the research scholar on account of its wealth of material.

In 1918, two major grammars began to appear, which aimed not only to provide a more modern and autonomous description of the structure of Hebrew as then understood, but to use to the fullest the results of Semitic comparative linguistics. These are the *Hebräische Grammatik* of G. Bergsträsser[24] and the *Historische Grammatik der hebräischen Sprache* by H. Bauer and P. Leander.[25] Unfortunately neither was completed: Bergsträsser contains only phonology and the verb, though it does incorporate into the description of the latter a good deal of the matter found in Gesenius in the first part of the syntax; Bauer-Leander remained without the planned syntax. The description in Bergsträsser is along conservative lines, with extensive use of contemporary research, and most of his new concepts and classifications have become generally accepted in Hebrew linguistics. He still relegates a large proportion of forms found in the text to the category of scribal corruptions. There is a sustained effort to describe the forms of the Babylonian and Palestinian systems of vocalization along with the Tiberian. The grammar of Bauer and Leander contains a 90-page section by P. Kahle on the non-Tiberian vocalization systems, but in the body of the work takes account of these rather erratically. On the other hand, there is a much more consistent effort to establish the connections of each form with its reconstructed Proto-Semitic original, with extensive employment of the theory, maintained by Bauer, that Hebrew was a mixture of two distinct language strains (see below). The proportion of forms left unexplained as corrupt is rather smaller.

Two attempts at large-scale grammars with use of comparative data were also made in Hebrew: M. B. Sznejder's *Torat ha-lašon bə-hitpattəḥutah* (Grammar of Hebrew in its development)[26] and Z. Har-Zahav's *Diqduq ha-lašon ha-ʿivrit*.[27] Both contain much material, some of it not found in European grammars, and include Mishnaic Hebrew (see below) in their compass, but tend to obliterate the distinction between rules describing the actual state of affairs in Biblical Hebrew and rules designed to provide normative guidance for present-day Hebrew speakers. This distinction is carefully preserved in the little that has been published of the Hebrew grammar of D. Yellin,[28] planned on a large scale and based on an independent survey of the corpus.

Among the many grammars for academic teaching published in the period since 1918, the Swedish one by H. S. Nyberg stands out.[29] It describes just one type of Biblical Hebrew, the prose language of the period down to 587 B.C., and in this way

[24] *Hebräische Grammatik* = 29th ed. of Gesenius, but completely rewritten (Leipzig, 1918 and 1929).

[25] *Historische Grammatik der hebr. Sprache*, I (Halle, 1922).

[26] Vilna, 1922/23–1939.

[27] Six vols. (Tel Aviv, 1950–53).

[28] *Diqduq ha-lašon ha-ʿivrit* (Jerusalem, 1942), contains phonology (separately reprinted Jerusalem, 1963) and the noun; a classified list of Biblical nouns in *Toladot hitpattəḥut ha-diqduq ha-ʿivri*, 169–260 (Jerusalem, 1944–45).

[29] *Hebreisk Grammatik* (Uppsala, 1952).

is a first step towards the important future task of writing descriptions of Biblical Hebrew in its different periods on a synchronic level, the present type of grammar being rather a cross-section than a synchronic analysis.[30] It is also the first grammar to be based on the new type of text, viz. the third edition of the *Biblia Hebraica*. Its descriptive technique approaches the structural method.

The small-scale German grammar by R. Meyer[31] takes account, in its descriptive part, of the Dead Sea Scrolls, and in its historical part, of Ugaritic. The *Historical grammar* of A. Sperber[32] is a venture different from all other grammars in that it takes full account of parallel passages, ancient transcriptions, and the variants of MSS and old prints, mainly in order to establish the existence of two different types of Hebrew, which the author identifies as Northern and Southern.

The first scholar to apply structuralist methods to Biblical Hebrew, albeit rather cautiously and in a diachronic context, was H. Birkeland in 1940.[33] The following year, however, there appeared what has remained to date the most complete structuralist analysis of the language, by Z. S. Harris,[34] though on the morphology it is so brief as to be a demonstration of what can be done rather than a description. It is based upon eighth century B.C. texts reconstructed in a sixth century phonological form. Harris also incorporated some partial analyses of Hebrew in his *Methods in Structural Linguistics* (1951) and in a Hebrew article written the same year.[35] A structuralist description of the main grammatical features is given by H. B. Rosén as an appendix to his *Textbook of Israeli Hebrew*.[36] M. H. Goshen-Gottstein drew up a suggestive 'framework' for detailed structural description of Biblical Hebrew morphology.[37]

The main structuralist achievement in Biblical Hebrew is concentrated in phonology, this being a branch born out of the structuralist approach. Here, Harris's treatment of 1941 is followed by J. Cantineau's *Essai d'une phonologie de l'hébreu biblique*,[38] several studies of H. B. Rosén,[39] and one by C. Rabin.[40] An important contribution

[30] It is another problem whether such a grammar distinguishing the different *états de langue* could be written in practice. At present too many Biblical books still are of disputed date, quite apart from the debates as to which portions of datable books are later additions. It may well be that the application of refined methods of literary statistics will help to decide this last question; work in that direction is in progress in various countries. On the other hand, the undisputed corpus for each period is rather small for an effective structural analysis.

[31] G. Beer and R. Meyer, *Hebräische Grammatik*, 2 parts (Sammlung Göschen nos. 763–64a, Berlin, 1952–55).

[32] Leiden, 1966.

[33] See fn. 19.

[34] See fn. 20.

[35] 'Ha-śafah ha-ʿivrit lə-or ha-balšanut ha-ḥădašah', *Ləšonenu* 17.128–32 (1950–51).

[36] Chicago, 1962.

[37] 'Semitic morphological structures: the basic morphological structure of Biblical Hebrew', *Studies in Egyptology and Linguistics in honour of H. J. Polotsky*, 104–16 (Jerusalem, 1964).

[38] *BSL* 46.82–122 (1950).

[39] 'Remarques au sujet de la phonologie de l'hébreu biblique', *Revue Biblique* 60.30–40 (1953). See also fn. 42.

[40] 'Ha-tənuʿot ha-qəṭannot ba-ʿivrit ha-ṭavranit', *Sefer Ṭur Sinai*, 169–206 (Jerusalem, 1960).

to combinatory phonology is G. Schramm's *Graphemes of Tiberian Hebrew.*[41]

The phonological analysis of Biblical Hebrew is complicated by the fact that not only have the non-emphatic plosives (*p b t d k g*) each become divided into a plosive and a fricative (*f v θ ð x γ*), as in Aramaic, but also the short vowel series of Proto-Semitic (*i a u*) has split into three series: short (*i ε a ɒ u*), lengthened (*e*: *ɒ*: *o*:) and reduced (*ə*, realized in certain circumstances as reduced *ε a ɒ*), all linked in rather an involved manner with syllabic structure and position with relation to word stress. It appears in fact that of the three oppositions (*ə*/*ø*; short vowel/lengthened vowel; plosive/fricative) it is reasonable to recognize only two as distinctive, while the third is a set of conditioned allophones. This still leaves two further problems unsolved: the phonemic division of the five short-vowel phones, and the so-called Shewa medium, a collection of morphophonemic contexts in which it is impossible to decide by ordinary grammar rules whether the Tiberian vocalization sign serving impartially for *ə* and zero vowel is to be interpreted as the former or as the latter. Solutions vary greatly, from Birkeland, who recognizes only three short-vowel phonemes, but *ə* and Shewa medium as separate phonemes,[42] to Harris, who recognizes (as apparently does Birkeland) plosives and fricatives as separate series of phonemes, but also each of the reduced vowel graphemes as an independent phoneme,[43] or Rabin's view that all the short and reduced vowels represent two phonemes only.[44]

While in the field of phonology the strands of diachronic and synchronic facts have been successfully unravelled, this has proved much more difficult in the treatment of one of the central problems of Biblical morphology, the so-called tenses. Biblical Hebrew possesses two sets of two tenses each, 1. *wayyiqṭōl*/*wəqāṭal* mainly in clause-initial position, and 2. *qāṭal*/*yiqṭōl* in non-initial position, but also initial to a speech or paragraph. In addition it has modal forms of the *yiqṭōl* type, and predicative uses of the active participle and the so-called absolute infinitive *qāṭōl* by which these can alternate with 'tense' forms. In the latest books, set 1 is increasingly replaced by set 2. In each set the first member (viz. *wayyiqṭōl* and *qāṭal*) serves largely in narratives, and was until the nineteenth century regarded as a past tense, with the second members (viz. *wəqāṭal* and *yiqṭōl*) as present-future tense. The many apparent inconsistencies in actual Biblical usage already led H. Ewald to think of an aspect rather than tense function, and this view was convincingly developed by S. R. Driver,[45] who introduced the terms perfect/imperfect for the opposition, To some extent the factor of aspect or *Aktionsart* is now generally acknowledged to make up part of the function of the 'ten-

[41] Berkeley, 1964.

[42] *Op. cit.* (fn. 19 above), 55. This view was independently developed by H. B. Rosén, 'A marginal note on Biblical Hebrew phonology', *JNES* 20.126 (1961), who mentions that some medieval Hebrew grammarians also held the opinion that Shewa medium was a separate entity.

[43] *JAOS* 61.147 (1941). Criticism by J. Cantineau, *BSL* 46.116 (1950); I. Garbell, *Ləšonenu* 23.152–5 (1958–59); H. B. Rosén, *JNES* 20.124–6 (1961).

[44] *Op. cit.* (fn. 40, above), 203; on Shewa medium, 196–200.

[45] *A treatise on the use of the tenses in Hebrew* (Oxford, 1874), much revised in the third edition (Oxford, 1892, repr. 1969).

ses', though later scholars have reintroduced a considerable time-tense component.[46] To this extent the problem of the tense forms is shared with other Semitic languages. It is in the matter of the two apparently parallel series with their curious inversion of items that Hebrew is different, though there may be some similarity with Ugaritic. We still lack any synchronic study which would help us to decide whether the choice of series 1 or 2 depends mechanically upon a word order governed by factors that have nothing to do with tense meaning, or whether perhaps the tenses of series 2 have a meaning difference which led the Hebrew speaker to adopt a word order in which they, rather than series 1, could be employed in some cases. The work done has been diachronic, to establish the genetic links between the Hebrew tense forms and those of other Semitic and Hamitic languages, particularly with the Akkadian system of a preterite *ikšud*, a present *ikaššad*, and a permansive *kašid*. While there can be no doubt nowadays that *wayyiqṭōl*, which in fourteen conjugation types has either shorter forms than *yiqṭōl* or retraction of stress (e.g. *wayyə'bārɛk* as against *yəbā'rēk*), was originally quite distinct from *yiqṭōl*, and represents the same type as Akkadian *ikšud*, the interconnection of the other forms is still a matter of controversy, and *wəqāṭal* (which in some cases has advanced stress: *wəqāṭal'tī* as against *qā'ṭaltī*) is altogether unexplained.[47] H. Bauer[48] and G. R. Driver[49] relate the co-existence of the two series to the theory of Hebrew as a composite or mixed language.

The theory that the Hebrew language exhibits traces of what now would be called a fusion between the Canaanite spoken by the indigenous population and a 'younger' type of West-Semitic, which the Israelite conquerors brought with them, was first put forward by H. Bauer, who based upon it many of the explanations in his and P. Leander's grammar. An even more systematic and far-reaching use of this principle for explaining various difficulties in the structure of Hebrew was made by G. R. Driver

[46] Thus especially F. R. Blake, *A resurvey of Hebrew tenses* (Roma, 1951). Cf. C. F. Burney, 'A fresh examination of the current theory of the Hebrew tenses', *Journal of Theological Studies* 20.200–14 (1918–19); V. Christian, 'Das Wesen der semitischen Tempora', *ZDMG* 81.232–58 (1927); M. Sekine, 'Das Wesen des althebräischen Verbalausdrucks', *ZATW* 58.133–41 (1940–41); C. Brockelmann, 'Die "Tempora" im Semitischen', *ZPhon* 5.133–54 (1951); G. Janssens, 'De werkwoordelijke "tijden" in het Semietisch, en in het bijzonder in het Hebreeuws', *JEOL* 15.97–103 (1957–58); F. Rundgren, *Das althebräische Verbum: Abriss der Aspektlehre* (Stockholm, 1961); R. Meyer, 'Aspekt und Tempus im althebräischen Verbalsystem', *OLZ* 59.117–26 (1964); M. Sekine, 'Erwägungen zur hebräischen Zeitauffassung', *VT, Supplement* 9.66–82 (1963).

[47] This particular verb-form seems to exist only in Hebrew. The most common explanation offered for it is the principle of polarity. Cf. M. Lambert, 'Le vav conversif', *REJuiv* 26.47–62 (1893), esp. p. 53; G. R. Driver, *Problems of the Hebrew verbal system*, 85–92 (Edinburgh, 1936); C. H. Gordon, 'The accentual shift in the perfect with Waw consecutive', *JBL* 57.319–25 (1938); F. R. Blake, 'The Hebrew Waw conversive', *JBL* 63.271–95 (1944); E. S. Hartom (Artom), "Al ba'ăyat ha-nəginah šel he-'avar ha-məhuppakh lə-'attid ba-'ivrit', *Ləšonenu* 17.88–9 (1950–51). See also E. A. Speiser, 'The pitfalls of polarity', *Lg* 14.187–202 (1938).

[48] In Bauer-Leander, *Historische Grammatik* (see fn. 25), *passim*, and especially in H. Bauer, *Zur Frage der Sprachmischung im Hebräischen: Eine Erwiderung* 11–15, (Halle, 1924), Criticism by G. Bergsträsser, 'Mitteilungen zur hebräischen Grammatik', *OLZ* 26.253–60, 477–81 (1923).

[49] G. R. Driver, *Problems of the Hebrew verbal system*, 85–97 (Edinburgh, 1936).

in 1936 and by H. Birkeland in 1940.[50] Since it is undeniable that Hebrew in some important respects continues the Canaanite of the Tell-Amarna glosses, and that in the same and some additional features it closely resembles (and is the only well-known language which resembles) its Canaanite next-door neighbor, Phoenician, this mixed-language (Mischsprache) theory has actually the advantage of allowing us to assume that the Israelites did not entirely give up whatever language they spoke before. On the other hand, it has not proved possible to identify the non-Canaanite component thus obtained with any known Semitic language. G. R. Driver favored Aramaic, but it now is held by some that Aramaic itself may be a fairly late development out of a number of local dialects. At one time 'Amorite', the language of the West-Semitic proper names from Babylonia and Mari, was considered a possible candidate; it seems to the present writer that as the language of these names becomes better documented and known, its similarity to the non-Canaanite part of Hebrew dwindles. The key to the situation may well lie within Hebrew itself: we know that the pre-dynastic language of the north of Palestine, as exhibited by the Song of Deborah in Judges 5, was different from the classical literary language of the monarchic period after 1000 B.C., but we have at present no means of assessing how large the differences between the dialects spoken by the different Hebrew tribes really were, and what measure of levelling set the standard language apart from them. If indeed Mishaic Hebrew grew out of pre-exilic non-standard forms of speech (see below), the distance must have been large. The rather monotonous tax labels on the Samaria Ostraca (ninth century) offer two deviations from standard Hebrew: *yn* = *yēn* for ˈ*yayin* 'wine', and *št* = *šatt* for *šanah* (i.e. **šantu* for *šanatu*) 'year'. Among the pairs of synonyms or near-synonyms which make up the core of the poetic device of parallelismus membrorum that characterizes Hebrew and other early Semitic poetry, a significant percentage is common to Biblical Hebrew and to Ugaritic poetry,[51] and contains words which do not appear to have formed part of the normal Hebrew language;[52] this strongly suggests that literary Hebrew borrowed from neighboring literary languages. It is thus possible to surmise that some of the fusional character of Hebrew may be due to interdialectal borrowing and to continuous exposure to outside influence, rather than to what happened at the very moment the local Canaanite language was adopted by the Israelite settlers. It is to be noted that this still leaves the question of the former language of the Israelite immigrants wide open.

[50] G. R. Driver, *op. cit.*; H. Birkeland, *Akzent und Vokalismus im Althebräischen* (Oslo, 1940).
[51] H. L. Ginsberg, *Or* 5.171–2 (Rome, 1936); M. D. Cassuto, 'Sifrut kənaʿănit wə-sifrut miqra'it', *Tarbiṣ* 13.197–212 (Jerusalem, 1941–42), 14.1–11 (1942–43): 'Millim maqbilot bə-ʿivrit uvə-ugaritit', *Ləšonenu* 15.97–102 (1945–46); M. Held "Od zugot millim maqbilot ba-miqrā uvə-khitvey Ugarit', *Ləšonenu* 18.144–60 (1952–53); S. E. Loewenstamm, *Tarbiṣ* 25.470 (1955–56), 28.248–9 (1957–58); R. G. Boling, 'Synonymous parallelisms in the Psalms', *JSS* 5.221–55 (1960); S. Gevirtz, 'The Ugaritic Parallel to Jeremiah 8:23', *JNES* 20.41–6 (1961); *Patterns in the early poetry of Israel* (Chicago, 1962).
[52] Cf. G. R. Driver, 'Hebrew poetic diction', *VT, Supplement* 1.26–39 (1953); M. Z. Kaddari, 'Ha-tiqbolet ha-miqra'it mi-bəḥinah semanṭit', *Ləšonenu* 32.37–45 (1967–68); A. Hurvitz, *The poetic vocabulary of Biblical Hebrew*, unpublished M.A. thesis, Hebrew University, Jerusalem.

Another theory deserves to be mentioned here, proposed first by M.Z. Segal, and reaffirmed by A. Bendavid:[53] that the spoken language of the period 1200–586 B.C. was an early form of Mishnaic Hebrew, while the Biblical Hebrew of the texts was a written or official language. This theory, too, would seem to allow ample opportunities for the written language to absorb elements from the spoken form(s), and might thus account for 'mixed language' features. Another fairly obvious explanation for apparent inconsistencies in diachronic developments lies in the field of geographical linguistics: Palestine being a veritable crossroads, diffusional influences from various directions produced in the area a network of superimposed isoglosses by which its language agrees now with one now with another of the neighboring languages.[54]

C. *Lexicography and Semantics*

As for grammar, so for lexicography the work of F.W. Gesenius still dominates the scene. While his large-scale *Thesaurus* in Latin (1829–58) never saw a second edition, his German *Handwörterbuch* (1810–12) saw in 1915 its 15th edition, revised by F. Buhl after previous editions by various hands, in which extensive changes were made according to the scientific fashions of the times. There were also several English editions; the latest one, revised by F. Brown, S.R. Driver, and C.A. Briggs (Oxford 1907 and later corrected editions), is in effect an independent work.[55] Both streams of the Gesenius tradition offer etymology, notes on inflection and spellings, ample references to the text for the different meanings given, and suggestions for emendation. They include all proper names, with identifications and references, as well as notes on their meaning. Both also contain as a separate section a dictionary of Biblical Aramaic. There is no need to enumerate the many other nineteenth and twentieth century dictionaries, all of which contain some or all the features of the Gesenius group, but most are more overtly scholastic in character. The Hebrew-Hebrew Biblical dictionaries of the same period, though of great importance for the development of Modern Hebrew, have no independent scientific value; mention might be made of *Ha-Oṣar* (5 vols., Warsaw 1902–14) by S.J. Fünn (1818–90), and *Mišpaṭ ha-urim* (Vilna 1896, and many later editions) by Joshua Steinberg (1825–1908).

The first attempt to use the immense material added since 1920 by philological work in commentaries and articles, and the increase of our knowledge of other

[53] M.Z. Segal, *Diqduq ləšon ha-Mišnah*, 7 (Tel Aviv, 1935–36) (less definitely in his *Grammar of Mishnaic Hebrew*, Oxford, 1927, p. 11); A. Bendavid, *Ləšon ha-miqrā o ləšon ḥăkhamim?*, 69–73 (Tel Aviv, 1951) (this theory has disappeared from the 2nd ed., Tel Aviv, 1967). Polemics by M.B. Sznejder, 'He-hayətah ha-lašon hamiqra'it lašon mədubberet?', *Ləšonenu* 8.112–22. Cf. also R. Gordis, 'Studies in the relationship of Biblical and Rabbinic Hebrew', *Louis Ginzberg jubilee volume* (New York, 1945), English section, pp. 173–99.

[54] Cf. C. Rabin, 'The origin of the subdivisions of Semitic', *Hebrew and Semitic studies ... G.R. Driver*, 104–15 (Oxford, 1963).

[55] A revised edition, by G.R. Driver and D. Winton Thomas, is in preparation.

Semitic languages, especially Ugaritic, is contained in L. Koehler, *Lexicon in Veteris Testamenti Libros* (Leiden 1953), with explanations in German and English. It is on the same plan as the Gesenius dictionaries; documentation from the text is even more exhaustive; the etymological material is rich, but not always fully reliable. A special feature of this dictionary is the appearance of words restored by emendation in their proper alphabetic place.[56]

The third edition of this dictionary was completely rewritten by W. Baumgartner, who had been responsible for the Aramaic part of the original work, in conjunction with B. Hartmann and E. Y. Kutscher.[57] It omits the English explanations, rationalizes the etymology by concentrating on the languages which are geographically and genetically closest to Hebrew, but above all provides full information on the form of the word in Hebrew tradition: the different vocalization systems, the Samaritan pronunciation, the Dead Sea Scrolls, and the ancient transcriptions.

Another large-scale dictionary project, by S. E. Loewenstamm and J. Blau, got only to the ninth letter of the alphabet.[58] It provides a rather more detailed classification of meanings, and discussion of suggestions in learned literature. Also E. Ben-Yehuda's *Thesaurus totius hebraitatis*,[59] though covering all periods of the language, provides a complete Biblical Hebrew dictionary (without the proper names), less detailed than others in the distinction of meanings, but important in giving in its footnotes a conspectus of the renderings of medieval Jewish exegetes and lexicographers, and etymologies often different, and at times better, than those in Gesenius and Koehler.

None of the dictionaries that exist, including Baumgartner's, gives a complete survey of the views and arguments advanced in books and learned journals over the last half-century regarding the meaning and etymology of Biblical Hebrew words.

Although the Biblical corpus would seem to offer to the semanticist a field of work comparable to Latin and Greek, no discipline of Hebrew semantics exists which could be compared with the work done in those languages. One reason is no doubt the overestimation of etymology as a key to meaning,[60] another the pre-occupation with the theological meaning of Hebrew words and tendency to search for 'basic' meanings with religious implications. This latter tendency has been critically analyzed

[56] *Supplementum* (Leiden, 1958) contains additions and corrections and a German-Hebrew glossary. The South-Semitic etymologies were corrected and amplified by W. Leslau, *Ethiopic and South-Arabic contributions to the Hebrew lexicon* (Berkeley and Los Angeles, 1958).

[57] Lieferung 1, '-*ṭbḥ* (Leiden, 1967).

[58] *Oṣar ləšon ha-miqrā, Thesaurus of the language of the Bible*, 3 vols. (meanings in Hebrew and English, Jerusalem, 1957-60). Interspersed with a concordance.

[59] 16 vols. (Berlin, 1908-Jerusalem, 1958), in Hebrew, with meanings also in English, French, and German. Vols. 8–9 ed. by M. Z. Segal, 10–16 by N. H. Torczyner (Tur-Sinai), who published discussion of many entries in his *Ha-lašon wəha-sefer* (Jerusalem, 1948–51, 3 vols., 1st vol. revised 1954) and in articles in *Ləšonenu*.

[60] E.g. C. von Orelli, *Die hebräischen Synonyma der Zeit und Ewigkeit* (Leipzig, 1871); S. Levin, *Versuch einer hebr. Synonymik*, I (Berlin, 1894); W. Caspari, 'Ueber semasiologische Untersuchungen am hebr. Wörterbuche', *ZATW* 27.162–211 (1907); L. Palache, *Sinai en Paran*, 101–32 (Leiden, 1959), *Semantic notes on the Hebrew lexicon* (Leiden, 1959).

by J. Barr, *Semantics of Biblical language*,[61] which is still the main work in Biblical Hebrew semantics.[62]

A frequency list of Biblical vocabulary was published in 1882 by W. R. Harper.[63] It is in a form not convenient for statistical work, and its data have been used mainly for didactic purposes, or quoted selectively in the dictionaries. Computerized statistical analysis was hampered by the difficulties inherent in the Hebrew script, with its graphic separation of consonants and matres lectionis in one line and vowels in another,[64] but parts of the Bible have been prepared for the computer in various parts of the world, and a number of important research projects are in hand.

2. THE SECOND TEMPLE PERIOD

The Hebrew of the later books of the Bible differs markedly from that of the pre-Exilic corpus. There can be no doubt that Biblical Hebrew was no more a living (that is, spoken) language, and that the authors of this period wrote it by imitation, with varying degrees of influence from the language or languages they spoke.

This Late Biblical Hebrew can be best studied in the Books of Chronicles, where for a large part the text is parallel to portions of Samuel and Kings.[65] On the basis of these parallel sentences, the special language of Chronicles has been described by A. Kropat.[66] So far, this is the only attempt at systematic description of this type of language, though the facts are pretty well known, and can be found scattered in

[61] Oxford, 1961; cf. his *Biblical words for time* (London, 1962).

[62] Other studies: N. H. Torczyner, 'Vom Ideengehalt der hebräischen Sprache', *Oesterreichische Monatsschrift für den Orient*, 1916 (Hebrew version, "Olam u-viṭṭuyo bi-lšonenu', in N. H. Tur-Sinai, *Ha-lašon wəha-sefer*, I, 2nd ed. [Jerusalem, 1954], 343–62), and 'Millim u-mussagim bi-mqorot ləšonenu', *Ləšonenu* 16.34–8, 115–20 (1947–48); Th. C. Vriezen, 'de beteekenis der semasiologie voor exegese en Schriftbeschouwing', *Vox Theologica* 20.89–99 (Assen, 1950); G. Gerleman, 'Struktur und Eigenart der hebräischen Sprache', *Svensk Exegetisk Årsbok* 22/23.252–64 (1957–58); M. Z. Kaddari, 'Ziwwugey ha-šem (dvandva) bə-'ivrit miqra'it', *Ləšonenu* 30.113–35 (1965–66); 'Ha-tiqbolet ha-miqra'it mi-bəḥinah semanṭit', *Ləšonenu* 32.37–45 (1967–68); J. F. A. Sawyer, 'Root meanings in Hebrew', *JSS* 12.37–50 (1967); T. Donald, 'The semantic field of rich and poor in the wisdom literature of Hebrew and Akkadian', *Oriens Antiquus* 3.27–41 (1964). On the boundary of semantics lies T. Boman, *Hebrew thought compared with Greek* (London, 1960).

[63] *Hebrew vocabularies* (Chicago, 1882, 2nd edition same year). The higher figures are in round numbers. Only nouns above frequency 25 are given, while verbal roots, though only those above frequency 25 are mentioned, include actual verbs in various conjugations of much lower frequency.

[64] G. E. Weil, 'Méthodologie de la codification des textes sémitiques ... sur ordinateur', I, *IRHT* 13.115–33 (1964–65); G. E. Weil et F. Chenique, 'Prolégomènes à l'utilisation des méthodes de statistique linguistique pour l'étude historique et philologique de la Bible hébraïque et de ses paraphrases', *VT* 14.344–66 (1964). The difficulties with post-biblical texts are much greater, as in these (apart from poetry) no vowels appear, and the overwhelming occurrence of homographs necessitates punching the grammatical analysis of each word along with the text.

[65] The parallel texts are set out most conveniently in P. Vannutelli, *Libri synoptici Veteris Testamenti*, 2 vols. (Roma, 1931–34); a smaller parallel edition by A. Bendavid, I *Kings* (Jerusalem, 1965). Cf. also M. Rehm, *Textkritische Untersuchungen zu den Parallelstellen der Samuel-Königsbücher und der Chronik* (1937, Alttestamentliche Abhandlungen, XIII,3).

[66] *Die Syntax des Authors der Chronik* (Giessen, 1909, Beihefte zur *ZATW*, 16).

commentaries, grammars, and dictionaries.[67] An attempt to utilize these characteristics for dating texts of uncertain date from Psalms has been made by A. Hurvitz.[68] What is more difficult to agree on, is their interpretation: which is the substrate language that influenced Second-Temple Hebrew?

Until the end of the nineteenth century it was assumed as a matter of course that the spoken language of this period was Aramaic, this being then the speech of Babylonia, where the exiled had lived, the language which ultimately emerged as the written and spoken language after Hebrew had ceased to be used (see below), and the idiom in which are recorded the few sayings of Jesus in the Gospels which are not in Greek.[69] Mishnaic Hebrew, written in sources of the first century B.C. to the beginning of the third century A.D., was taken to be an artificial revival of written Hebrew, colored by heavy Aramaic influence. According to this view, the non-Biblical Hebrew element in the mixture was Aramaic. An even more extreme view is that the books in question were originally written in Aramaic, and subsequently translated into Hebrew, with many Aramaisms standing as evidence of this process.[70]

After some scholars had claimed on general grounds that Mishnaic Hebrew gave the impression of a natural, living language rather than the result of the influence of spoken Aramaic on the habits of people attempting to write Biblical Hebrew,[71] M. H. Segal in several works[72] demonstrated that the structure and features of Mishnaic Hebrew could not be reasonably accounted for by the theory of interaction, and must therefore be the literary crystallization of a spoken dialect or dialects that existed

[67] Not strictly linguistic, but useful collections of material are M. Löhr, 'Der Sprachgebrauch des Buches der Klagelieder', *ZATW* 14.31–50 (1894); H. Striedl, 'Untersuchungen zur Syntax und Stilistik des hebräischen Buches Esther', *ZATW*, 55.73–108 (1937).

[68] *Linguistic criteria for dating late psalms*, Hebrew University, Jerusalem, thesis (in press). Much interesting material and observation on this subject is also contained in E. Y. Kutscher's book on the Isaiah Scroll, mentioned below.

[69] Cf., however, H. Birkeland, *The language of Jesus* (Oslo, 1954).

[70] H. H. Howorth, 'Some unconventional views on the text of the Bible, VII, Daniel and Chronicles', *Proceedings of the Society of Biblical Archaeology* 29.31–8, 61–9 (1907); F. Zimmermann, 'The Aramaic origin of Daniel 8–12', *JBL* 57 (1938), 'The Aramaic provenance of Qohelet', *JQR* 36.17–45 (1945), 'Chronicles as a partially translated book', *JQR* 42.165–82, 387–412 (1951–52) and 'The question of Hebrew in Qohelet', *JQR* 40.79–102 (1949); R. Gordis, 'The original language of Qohelet', *JQR* 37.67–84 (1946), and 'The translation theory of Qohelet re-examined', *JQR* 40.103–16 (1949); H. L. Ginsberg, *Studies in Daniel* (New York, 1948), *Studies in Kohelet* (New York, 1950), and *Qohelet* (Hebrew, Tel Aviv 1961), esp. pp. 28–49.

[71] H. Graetz, Review of A. Geiger's *Lehrbuch der Sprache der Mischna*, *Literaturblatt des Orients* 5.822–7, 6.30–1, 54–9, 76–8, 86–90 (Supplement to *Der Orient*, Leipzig, 1844–5); S. D. Luzzatto, *Ibid.*, 7.830 seq., 8.1–5, 46–8, 55–7 (1846–47, 'Ueber die Sprache der Mischna'); Th. Nöldeke, *Encyclopaedia Britannica*, 9th edn. XXI,646, and *Die semitischen Sprachen*, 2nd edition, 25 (Leipzig, 1899).

[72] 'Mišnaic Hebrew and its relation to Biblical Hebrew and to Aramaic', *JQR*, Old Series, 20.647–737 (1908–9, also separately, Oxford, 1909); 'Hebrew in the period of the Second Temple', *International Journal of Apocrypha* 1910.79–82; 'Ləšon ha-Mišnah moṣa'ah wə-toləd oteha', *Madda'ey ha-Yahădut* 1.30–44 (Jerusalem, 1926); *A grammar of Mishnaic Hebrew*, 5–19 (Oxford, 1927); *Diqduq ləšon ha-Mišnah*, 4–17 (Tel Aviv, 1935–36). Cf. further A. Sperber, *OLZ* 534–5 (1929); R. A. Bowman, 'Arameans, Aramaic, and the Bible', *JNES* 7.65–90 (1948), esp. p. 82; W. Chomsky,

in the country. It has been variously pointed out[73] that reflections of Mishnaic Hebrew usage — as distinct from Biblical Hebrew and from Aramaic — can be discovered in the Septuagint (third century B.C. onwards), Samaritan Hebrew,[74] Jewish Aramaic, and Christian Palestinian Aramaic. It appears to the present writer that the discussion has been clinched in favour of Segal's view by the discovery, in 1951, of letters written by Simeon bar Kosba (Bar Kokheba) in 131–134 A.D. in Mishnaic Hebrew.[75] A private document like this would hardly by styled in a language of 'pious scholarship', while the motive of 'nationalism'[76] is excluded by the fact that the same Bar Kosba left also several letters in Aramaic.

The fact that, broadly speaking, the thesis of Mishnaic Hebrew being a natural language has been accepted by Israeli scholarship, and hesitantly, or not at all, by many scholars outside Israel, has vitally affected the emergence of an Israeli school of research in Second-Temple linguistics, affecting both the study of Hebrew and of Aramaic in their various manifestations. A contributory factor has been the immense growth in our information on this period since World War I, which also includes quite a number of inscriptions. The most sensational discovery of all, of course, was that of the Dead Sea Scrolls in 1947 and onwards, adding a whole and unsuspected new literature to the corpus of early Hebrew, supplemented by the finds at Murabbaʿat and in the caves near En Gedi, which belong to the Bar Kokheba period. It is significant that research in the language of the Scrolls — as distinct from research into their historical and religious significance — has been largely restricted to Israeli scholars. Among these, the outstanding work is E.Y.Kutscher's Hebrew book, *The language and linguistic background of the Isaiah Scroll* (Jerusalem 1959). It discusses practically every facet of phonetics, grammar, and lexicography, on the basic principle that the scroll represents a somewhat simplified adaptation by people whose spoken language was a heavily Aramaicized Mishnaic Hebrew. The linguistic, especially phonetic, peculiarities of other texts from this group have been described by M.H.Goshen-Gottstein[77] and by M.Martin,[78] with numerous discussions on

'What was the Jewish vernacular during the Second Commonwealth?', *JQR* 42.193–212 (1951–52); M.Grintz, "Ivrit ki-lšon ha-sefer wəha-dibbur bi-ymey bayit šeni ha-aḥăronim', *Eškolot* 3.125–44 (Jerusalem, 1958–59); E.Margaliot, 'Li-š'elat śəfat ha-dibbur bi-zman bayit šeni uvi-tqufat ha-Mišnah wəha-Talmud', *Ləšonenu* 23.49–54 (1958–59); K.Hruby, 'La survivance de la langue hébraïque pendant la période post-exilienne', *Mémorial du Cinquanténaire*, Écoles des langues orientales de l'Institut catholique de Paris, 109–20 (Paris, 1964).

[73] Summary in C.Rabin, 'The historical background of Qumran Hebrew', *Scripta Hierosolymitana* 4.144–61 (Jerusalem, 1958).

[74] Z.Ben-Ḥayyim, 'Traditions in the Hebrew language, with special reference to the Dead Sea Scrolls', *Scripta Hierosolymitana* 4.200–14 (1958).

[75] Edited by P.Benoit, J.T.Milik, R. de Vaux, *Les Grottes de Murabbaʿât*, 155–67 (Oxford, 1961); cf. Y.Kutscher, 'Ləšonan šel ha-iggərot ha-ʿivriyyot wəha-ăramiyyot etc.', II, *Ləšonenu* 26.7–23 (1961–62).

[76] Both terms from R.A.Bowman, *JNES* 7.82 (1948).

[77] 'Linguistic structure and tradition in the Qumran Documents', *Scripta Hierosolymitana* 4.101–37 (1958).

[78] *The scribal character of the Dead Sea Scrolls*, 2 vols. (Louvain, 1958).

points of detail contributed by many scholars over the years.[79] Among the discussions of the vocabulary of the Dead Sea Writings, two works call for special mention, H. Yalon's *Məgillot Midbar Yəhudah: Divrey lašon,*[80] in which the attribution of new meanings to numerous words in the Scrolls is used to re-interpret usages in Biblical and early Rabbinic texts; and M.Z. Kaddari's *Expressions of obligation and injunction in the Dead Sea Scrolls,*[81] an exhaustive treatment of a semantic field. Since the number of words found in the Scrolls that do not occur in the Bible is very small, but the use of the words frequently differs from the Biblical one in puzzling ways, this is almost a classic situation for the application of the field method.

A similar position in the research on the period is held by the Hebrew Book of Ecclesiasticus (Sirach). This book of the Apocrypha was until 1896 known only in its Greek (and derived) and Syriac versions, and from a few Hebrew quotations in Rabbinic works, etc. In that year the first fragment of the original Hebrew text came to light. Since then the Hebrew material has been steadily increasing in quantity, until finally the discovery by Y. Yadin of a fragment in a first century archaeological context at Massadah clinched the long-debated question of the genuineness of the Hebrew.[82] The Hebrew of the recovered portions of the book is late Biblical, with, however, a stronger admixture of Mishnaic features.[83] Since its author, Yeshuaʿ ben Sira or Simeon ben Yeshuaʿ, can be dated with great precision in the early years of the second century B.C., the book provides a valuable fixed point in reconstructing the history of the Hebrew language.

The type of language exhibited in Ecclesiasticus and other indices have led some scholars to the conclusion that at least during part of the Second Temple period we should not speak of an irregular and unstable transition between a decaying late

[79] Selection: R. Meyer, 'Zur Sprache von ʿAin Feschcha', *Theologische Literaturzeitung* 75.721–6 (1950); S. Morag, 'Ha-kinnuyim ha-ʿaṣma'iyyim lə-nistar, etc.', *Ereṣ Yisra'el* 3.160–9 (1954); M. Mansoor, 'Some linguistic aspects of the Qumran texts', *JSS* 3.40–54 (1958); J. Schreiden, 'Les caractéristiques linguistiques de l'hébreu Qumranien, etc.', *Le Muséon* 72.153–8 (1959); B. Jongeling, 'Les formes QṬWL, etc.', *RQ* 1.483–94 (1959); S. Segert, 'Die Sprachenfragen in der Qumran-Gemeinschaft', *Qumran-Probleme*, ed. by H. Bardtke, 315–39 (Berlin, 1963). Cf. C. Burchardt, *Bibliographie zu den Handschriften vom Toten Meer*, 2 parts, (Berlin, 1957–65 = *ZATW*, Beihefte 76 and 89).

[80] English title: *Studies in the Dead Sea Scrolls, philological essays (1949–52)* (Jerusalem, 1967).

[81] *Ha-ḥiyyuv bi-lšon ha-məgillot ha-gənuzot* [Semantic fields in the language of the Dead Sea Scrolls] (Jerusalem, 1968).

[82] For the earlier history of the discovery and the controversy, see G.H. Box and W.O.E. Oesterley, in R.H. Charles, ed., *Apocrypha and Pseudepigrapha*, I, 271, 275 (Oxford, 1913). To the editions enumerated there, add M.Z. Segal, *Ḥokhmat ben Sira* (Jerusalem, 1932–33), and *Ben Sira ha-šalem* (Jerusalem, 1953); J. Schirmann, 'Dappim nosafim mi-sefer Ben Sira', *Tarbiṣ* 29.125–34 (Jerusalem, 1959–60); Y. Yadin, *The Ben Sira Scroll from Masada* (Jerusalem, 1965).

[83] D. Strauss, *Sprachliche Studien in den hebräischen Sirach-fragmenten* (Zürich, 1900); M.Z. Segal, 'Ləšono šel Ben Sira', *Ləšonenu* 7.100–20 (1935–36); C.C. Torrey, 'The Hebrew of the Geniza Sirach', *Alexander Marx jubilee volume*, English section, 585–602 (New York, 1950). Bibliography by T. Ackroyd, *VT* 3.118, fn. 3 (1953). R. Sapan, *Comparative glossary of non-Biblical words in the Hebrew Ben Sira* (unpublished M.A. thesis, Hebrew University, Jerusalem). A.A. Di Lella, *The Hebrew Text of Sirach* (The Hague, 1966).

Biblical Hebrew and a rising tendency to write the Mishnaic colloquial, but rather of an, albeit short-lived, fixed literary language incorporating features of both.[84] One is tempted to include in the documentation preserved of this literary idiom also the early parts of the Jewish prayer-book; but although Jewish tradition dates the origin of these prayers very early, and confirmation of their existence has been forthcoming from the Dead Sea Scrolls,[85] the instability of the text and the impossibility to establish an *Urtext*[86] prevent any possibility of making more than general statements about linguistic character.

3. MISHNAIC HEBREW

The controversy, described in the previous chapter, as to the origins of Mishnaic Hebrew affects in practice only our view of the period before the destruction of the Second Temple, in 70 A.D. The linguistic analysis of Mishnaic Hebrew itself is solidly founded upon its literary remains. These, again, fall into two periods: the remnants of the Tannaitic period, ending shortly after 200 A.D., and the works written in the Amoraic period (200–500) and later. Tannaim and Amoraim are the designations of two groups of legal teachers: the former being those whose names are mentioned in the collections of the Mishnah, the Tosephta, and the Halakhic (legal) Midrashim; the latter, the teachers mentioned only in the Palestinian and Babylonian Talmuds and related Midrash works. It seems fairly certain, however, that Mishnaic Hebrew ceased to be spoken about 200 A.D., so that the Tannaitic literature represents the dicta of men still accustomed to spoken Hebrew, the later literature being to it in the same relation as the Hebrew writings of the Second Temple period to spoken Biblical Hebrew. It has long been realized that any description of Mishnaic Hebrew must be based on the earlier period, and principally upon the Mishnah itself.[87] The corollary, that the language of the later sources is worthy of being described for its own sake, is only now being drawn, and research on it is being done in Jerusalem.

This recognition of the different status of pre-200 and post-200 Mishnaic Hebrew

[84] Especially M. Sznejder, 'Ha-lašon ha-ʿivrit ha-safrutit', *Ləšonenu* 6.301–26, 7.52–73 (1933–35, 1935–36); J. Matmon-Cohen, 'Ha-ʿivrit aḥărey galut Bavel', *Ləšonenu* 6–9 (1933–39); cf. also C. Rabin, *Scripta Hierosolymitana* 4.153–6 (1958).

[85] Cf. S. Talmon, 'Maḥzor ha-bərakhot šel kat midbar Yəhudah', *Tarbiṣ* 29.1–20 (1959–60).

[86] Cf. I. Elbogen, *Der jüdische Gottesdienst in seiner geschichtlichen Entwicklung*, 41–2 (Leipzig, 1913); J. Heinemann, *Ha-təfillah bi-tqufat ha-tanna'im wəha-ămora'im*, 29–47 (Jerusalem, 1963–64). For the existence of a fixed *Urtext* argue L. Finkelstein, 'The development of the Amidah', *JQR* 16.1–43, 127–70 (1925–26); F. C. Grant, 'Modern study of the Jewish liturgy', *ZATW* 65.69 (1953); A. Mirsky, 'Məqorah šel təfillat Yoṣer', *Sefer ha-yovel lərabbi Ḥănokh Albeck*, 324–30 (Jerusalem, 1962–63), and 'Məqorah šel təfillat Šəmoneh-ʿeśreh', *Tarbiṣ* 32.28–39 (1963–64). C. Rabin, 'Lešon ha-təfillot', *Maḥănayim* 40.45–50 (New Year Issue 1959–60).

[87] Many dicta ascribed to Tannaim are recorded only in post-Tannaitic works. These in theory complement the early corpus, but ascriptions are often doubtful, and there is likelihood of alterations in the process of oral tradition. For the whole literature, see H. L. Strack, *Introduction to the Talmud and Midrash* (Philadelphia, 1931 and later reprints).

has not been acted upon so far in lexicography. Moreover, not only are both registered as one corpus, but there exists so far no dictionary of Mishnaic Hebrew alone. Either its vocabulary is listed together with the Aramaic material predominant in the Talmuds and some later Midrashim, mostly even together with the Targumic Aramaic vocabulary,[88] or it appears mixed with Biblical and post-Mishnaic material in dictionaries of Hebrew.[89] However, the Historical Dictionary project of the Hebrew Language Academy at Jerusalem is planning in 1968 or soon after to gather up its mechanographically-recorded Hebrew material for the entire Tannaitic period in the form of a joint concordance, to be made available for use by scholars on its premises.[90]

The problem of the optimal corpus for grammatical analysis, which we described above for the Bible, obtains with added force for the Tannaitic form of Mishnaic Hebrew. The Mishnah has been printed very many times, several editions being fully vocalized. From the seventeenth century onwards, this vocalization was more and more strictly patterned on the grammarians' rules abstracted from the Tiberian vocalization of the Bible, the same rules which were and still are used for vocalizing poetry and other texts printed with vowels. The same process took place in prayer-books. Also the consonant text, though much less consistently, was reshaped according to Biblical grammar rules. In this way, the difference in structure between Biblical and Mishnaic Hebrew was minimized and obscured. On the other hand, manuscripts of the Mishnah and the Talmud (which contains the Mishnah) were excessively rare, owing to the frequent public burnings of Talmud manuscripts by zealous Christian authorities in the Middle Ages. The earlier grammarians of Mishnaic Hebrew may thus be forgiven for thinking that the printed Mishnah texts they knew were a true representation of the language. All grammars up to and including those of M.H. Segal[91] therefore describe a Biblicized form of the language of the Mishnah, and their authors did not see any reason to hesitate to vocalize words and forms found in other

[88] Earliest: ʿArukh by Nathan of Rome (1101). The dictionaries now in use are: Jacob Levy, *Neuhebräisches und Chaldäisches Wörterbuch über die Talmudim und Midraschim*, nebst Beiträgen von H.L.Fleischer [the famous Arabist], 4 vols. (Leipzig, 1876–89); M.Jastrow, *A dictionary of the Targumim, the Talmud ... and the Midrashic literature* (London and New York, 1886–1903 and reprints); G.H.Dalman, *Aramäisch-neuhebräisches Wörterbuch zu Targum, Talmud und Midrasch* (Frankfurt a. Main, 1897–1901).

[89] Such as Ben-Yehudah's *Thesaurus*; Y.Gur (Grazowski), *Millon ʿIvri*, 2nd edition (Tel Aviv, 1947); R.Avinoam and M.H.Segal, *Compendious Hebrew-English dictionary* (Tel Aviv, 1938 and reprints), etc. There is as yet no dictionary with references to the vast and scattered literature on lexicographical details. (S.Lieberman alone is stated to have established the meaning of 2,500–3,000 Mishnaic Hebrew and Talmudic Aramaic words, cf. L.Prijs, *ZDMG* 117.269, fn. 1 [1967]). For Semantics, cf. Y.Kutscher, 'Bavu'ah (calque) šel ha-ăramit ba-ʿivrit', *Tarbiṣ* 33.118–30 (1963–64); G.B.Sarfatti, "Iyyunim ba-semanṭiqah šel ləšon Ḥazal uvi-drašotehem', *Ləšonenu* 29.238–44 (1964–65), 30.29–40 (1965–66); A.Bendavid, *Ləšon ha-miqrā u-lšon ḥăkhamim*, 2nd edition, 135–47 (Tel Aviv, 1967). Y.Kutscher, *Millim wə-toladotehen* (Jerusalem, 1960–61), though also touching on Modern Hebrew, is largely on Mishnaic Hebrew semantics.

[90] See fn. 124, below. Concordances by J.Kossovsky for the Mishnah (2 vols., Jerusalem, 1914–27, 2nd edn. 4 vols., Jerusalem, 1956–60) and the Tosephta (6 vols., Jerusalem 1932–61) are available in printed form.

[91] *A grammar of Mishnaic Hebrew* (Oxford, 1927); *Diqduq ləšon ha-Mišnah* (Tel Aviv, 1935–36).

works (where they were not vocalized in the printed editions) according to the principles they found applied in Mishnah prints.

A fully-vocalized manuscript of the Mishnah, the Kaufmann MS at Budapest, had been known, and had been used by some scholars who prepared critical editions of parts of the Mishnah. A photographic edition of it was edited by G. Beer (Hague, 1929). A partly-vocalized manuscript at Parma was also known. So were manuscripts from Yemen, vocalized in Babylonian pointing. It was largely the merit of Henoch Yalon, of Jerusalem, to penetrate gradually to the significance of all these odd, and yet hauntingly similar vocalizations, and furthermore to connect them with similar oddities in the traditional manner in which various Jewish communities, especially in the Orient, were accustomed to read their (unvocalized) texts. From the 1930's onward he began to present in a number of articles the forms of Mishnaic Hebrew as it had been before the seventeenth-century Biblicizing process, and as we may assume it to have been handed down originally, save for accidents of tradition.[92] In 1938, E. Porath published classified grammatical forms from early manuscripts of Tannaitic texts with Babylonian pointing.[93] The linguistic importance of the manuscripts is taken into account in J. N. Epstein's monumental work on the Mishnah text.[94] In 1952–59, a new standard Mishnah edition was published by the national (Jewish Agency) publishing house Mosad Bialik, with a commentary by H. Albeck (Professor of Talmud 1936–56), and vocalized, 'at hand of oral traditions, old manuscripts and old prints', by H. Yalon, who subsequently published the principles guiding him in this work in an article and a book.[95] The vocalization of the Albeck-Yalon Mishnah is a compromise between the phonetic principles of normalized Tiberian pointing (from which the MSS often deviate) and the pure and original Mishnaic forms as recovered by Yalon and his school. The phonology and accidence of the recovered Mishnaic Hebrew is nowadays well established in most details, and currently taught in Israel and elsewhere and utilized in published research, foremost in that of E. Y. Kutscher,[96] but the revolution has not yet been brought to its logical conclusion in the form of a new systematic grammar.

The question of linguistic borrowing is a particularly important one for Mishnaic Hebrew, especially as concerns the influence of Aramaic, in view of the theory long held that Mishnaic Hebrew actually was formed through Aramaic influence upon Biblical Hebrew (see above). Of the many similarities with Aramaic there can be no doubt, but it is not easy to establish which of these are due to the effect of contract of

[92] See Y. Kutscher, in S. Liebermann *et al.*, eds., *Henoch Yalon jubilee volume* (Jerusalem, 1963), pp. 20–1, bibliography pp. 37–50.

[93] *Mishnaic Hebrew as vocalised in the early manuscripts of the Babylonian Jews* (in Hebrew, Jerusalem, 1938).

[94] *Mavō lə-nosaḥ ha-Mišnah* (Jerusalem, 1947–48, 2nd edition, 1964).

[95] 'Nimmuqim lə-mišnayot mənuqqadot', *Ləšonenu* 24.15–39, 157–66, 253 (1959–60); *Mavō lə-niqqud ha-Mišnah* (Jerusalem, 1963–64); 'He'arot wə-tiqqunim', *Ləšonenu* 29.59–62 (1964–65).

[96] E. Y. Kutscher, 'Mischnisches Hebräisch', *Rocz. Orient.* 28.35–48 (1964); 'Mittelhebräisch und Jüdisch-Aramäisch im neuen Köhler-Baumgartner', *Hebräische Wortforschung, Festschrift ... W. Baumgartner*, 158–75 (Leiden, 1967).

fully-formed Aramaic with fully-formed Hebrew, which ones may be due to a northern origin of the parent dialects of Mishnaic Hebrew, in an area where they had common isoglosses with Aramaic,[97] and which are the result of parallel development of Middle Aramaic and Middle Hebrew. It is now widely recognized that the Jewish, and probably also other Western-Aramaic, dialects were strongly affected by Hebrew, and that therefore facts adduced as Aramaic influence must be carefully sifted, as the influence may have been from early Mishnaic Hebrew upon Aramaic. Already Th. Nöldeke advised caution[98] with regard to E. Kautzsch's careful study *Die Aramaismen im Alten Testament*, I (Halle 1902). From this point of view, M. Wagner's comprehensive work[99] is rather to be considered a retrogressive step; even if it does try to judge each proposed borrowing on its own merits, it is much too liberal in quoting proposals that would better be forgotten, and does not distinguish (as Kautzsch does) between words attested before the First Exile and those which may reasonably be assumed to have come into Hebrew after that date. Moreover, it seems methodically wrong to treat Aramaic influence on post-Exilic Biblical texts as a feature of Biblical Hebrew. If one assumes that Aramaic was the spoken language of that period, then these are not borrowings, but slips betraying the linguistic background of the writers; if one believes that the authors spoke for the most part a form of Mishnaic Hebrew, then these 'Aramaisms' are likely to have penetrated because they were current at the time in Mishnaic Hebrew. In either case the post-Exilic Aramaisms should be treated in conjunction with the Aramaic elements in Mishnaic Hebrew, and not in isolation.[100]

While Persian influence is small,[101] that of Greek — which includes Latin words that came through Greek — is very large in Mishnaic Hebrew.[102] After some earlier collections, the material for Mishnaic, Talmudic, and Midrashic literature in Hebrew and Aramaic was gathered by S. Krauss,[103] and that for the Mishnah alone by H.

[97] E.g., cf. C. H. Gordon, 'Hašpaʿah ṣəfon-Yiśrə'elit ʿal ha-ʿivrit šellə'aḥar galut Bavel', *Ereṣ Yiśra'el* 3.104–5 (Jerusalem, 1954).

[98] In his review, *ZDMG* 57.412–20 (1903).

[99] Max Wagner, *Die lexikalischen und grammatikalischen Aramaismen im alttestamentlichen Hebräisch* (Berlin, 1966, Beihefte zur *ZATW*, 96).

[100] For Aramaic loanwords in Mishnaic Hebrew, see S. Mannes, *Ueber den Einfluss des Aramäischen auf den Wortschatz der Mišnah* (Erlangen thesis, Posen, 1899); H. Albeck, *Mavō la-Mišnah*, 130–52 (Jerusalem, 1959); A. Bendavid, *Ləšon ha-miqrā u-lšon ḥăkhamim*, 2nd edition, 64–74, 127–35 (Tel Aviv, 1967).

[101] For Old Persian words in Biblical Hebrew, see J. Scheftelowitz, *Arisches im Alten Testament* (Berlin, 1901). Cf., however, the caution in M. Ellenbogen, *Foreign words in the Old Testament*, viii-ix and *passim* (London, 1962). For Mishnaic Hebrew and Jewish Aramaic loans from Middle Persian, cf. S. Telegdi, 'Essai sur la phonétique des emprunts iraniens en Araméen talmudique', *JA* 226.177–256 (1935), with extensive list of words.

[102] Cf. R. H. Gundry, 'The language milieu of 1st-century Palestine, etc.', *JBL* 83.404–8 (1964); V. Colorni, *L'uso del greco nella liturgia del giudaismo ellenistico*, etc. (Milano, 1964, Estr. *Annali di Storia del Diritto* 8 (1964)).

[103] *Griechische und lateinische Lehnwörter im Talmud, Midrasch und Targum* (Berlin, 1898–1900). For a summary of the criticism, see Rosén, fn. 108 below.

Albeck,[104] with important corrections and valuable background provided by S. Lieberman's two magistral studies.[105] The existence of a further large body of loan-translations was demonstrated by A. Bendavid.[106] On the other hand, the Talmudic dictionary of M. Jastrow[107] goes to great lengths in searching for internal Hebrew or Aramaic etymologies for words assumed by others to be Greek borrowings. The discussion of this question is impeded by the large variety of spellings of many of these words in the manuscripts, and the absence of critical editions. H. Rosén rightly points out[108] that the theoretical basis of the investigation has never been worked out.

4. MEDIEVAL HEBREW

Though we have no clear idea of the process or of the exact chronology, the evidence on the whole goes to show that Hebrew ceased to be spoken in Palestine about 200 A.D.,[109] having been abandoned by the Jewish communities outside their homeland in all probability centuries before that. During the following 1700 years, Hebrew served most, and from about 1000 A.D. probably all, Jewish communities as a language of prayer and Bible reading, and was thus passively understood more or less, at least by men. However, at all times there were large groups in the Jewish diaspora to whom Hebrew also was a language (and often the only language) for written expression in serious writing, poetry, and even private correspondence. The body of literature produced in Hebrew during the Middle Ages is in the same order of size as that of medieval Latin, the position of which it paralleled,[110] though with the difference that the knowledge of writing and of the written language was far more wide-

[104] *Op. cit.* (fn. 100 above), 203–15; for the Tosephta see M.S. Zuckermandel's edition (reprint Jerusalem, 1937), Glossar, pp. XLIX-LXLIV. Cf. P. Joüon, 'Mots grecs de l'araméen d'Onkelos ou de l'hébreu de la Mishna qui se trouvent aussi dans les Evangiles', *Recherches des Sciences réligieuses* 22.463–9.

[105] *Greek in Jewish Palestine* (New York, 1942); *Hellenism in Jewish Palestine* (New York, 1950); both together in *Yəwanit wə-yawnut bə-Ereṣ Yiśra'el* (Jerusalem, 1962).

[106] See reference in fn. 89, above.

[107] See fn. 88, above.

[108] 'Palestinian *koinē* in rabbinic illustration', *JSS* 8.55–72 (1963).

[109] E. Ben-Yehudah, *'Ad ematay dibbəru 'ivrit*? (New York, 1919), and *Thesaurus Totius Hebraitatis*, Prolegomena vol., 83–254; S. Morag, "Ad ematay dibbəru 'ivrit?', *LLA* 67/68.3–10 (1966–67); A. Bendavid, *Ləšon ha-miqrā u-lšon ḥăkhamim*, 2nd edition, 153–65 (Tel Aviv, 1967). W. Chomsky, *Hebrew: The eternal language*, 206–27 (Philadelphia, 1957) (less forcibly in the Hebrew edition, Jerusalem, 1967, 243–53) and others indeed claim that 'Hebrew never died', meaning thereby its continued use as a written language, and its occasional use as an emergency vehicle of oral communication or in certain religious situations, cf. C. Roth, *Personalities and events in Jewish history*, 136–42 (Philadelphia, 1953), for a collection of sources. S. Federbush, *Ha-lašon ha-'ivrit bə-Yiśra'el uva-'ammim* (Jerusalem, 1967), a somewhat naive but useful collection of source-material, even manages not to mention the cessation of Hebrew speech at all. While this seems a purely terminological difference of opinion, M. Zulay, *Məlilah* 1.73 (Manchester, 1944), thinks it likely that Hebrew was still spoken in some circles as late as the sixth century.

[110] For this diglossia situation, cf. Max Weinreich, 'Inveynikste tsveyšpraxikeyt in Aškenaz biz der Haskole', *Di Goldene Keyt* 35.3–11 (1959); C. Rabin, *Gorəmim sociologiyyim bə-tolədot ha-lašon ha-'ivrit* (New York, 1967) and 'Ḥiyyutah šel ha-'ivrit bi-ymey ha-benayim', *LLA* 123.14–18 (1961).

spread amongst Jews than among Christians.[111] Some of the literatures comprised in this vast development introduced considerable numbers of new words into the language, changed the syntax, and in some cases even the grammar. Thus the period immediately following the cessation of spoken Hebrew[112] and until the eleventh century saw a type of religious poetry, the Piyyuṭ, which not only created thousands of new words, but also consistently treated triliteral roots containing the 'weak' elements *w*, *y*, and *n* as biliteral roots[113] and introduced some revolutionary changes in the syntax. Yet, apart from lists of these phenomena drawn up by a historian of literature in 1855,[114] this language has not been investigated by anyone; of a planned dictionary only a specimen appeared.[115] This apparent neglect was a result of the attitude accepted in linguistics during the nineteenth and early twentieth centuries, that only living, spoken languages were suitable for linguistic investigation. Even the revival of spoken Hebrew, and the absorption of many of these linguistic innovations of the Middle Ages into the modern language, only slowly produced a change towards greater interest in the structural phenomena of the intervening periods (as distinct from a purely practical interest in their vocabulary).

The nearest to a full linguistic description is M. H. Gottstein, *Syntax and vocabulary of Medieval Hebrew as influenced by Arabic*,[116] which describes the language of the translations made in Provence and Italy from the Arabic between 1150 and 1400[117] and of Hebrew works influenced by them. The vocabulary of this literature is largely listed in E. Ben-Yehudah's *Thesaurus*, and its terminological component at greater length by J. Klatzkin,[118] both unfortunately without the Arabic equivalents which would make the meaning clear beyond contextual guesswork. The processes, especially loan translation, by which the Arabic terminology was reproduced in Hebrew, were examined by G. B. Sarfatti.[119]

111 For surveys of this literature, see C. Rabin, 'Hebrew literature', in the *Encycl. Britannica* (1955 onwards) and bibliography *Ibid.* at end; S. W. Baron, *A social and religious history of the Jews*, vols. 6–8 (Philadelphia, 1958).

112 For this dating, see J. Schirmann, 'Hebrew liturgical poetry and Christian hymnology', *JQR* 44.123–61 (1953); cf. A. Mirsky, *Rēšit ha-piyyuṭ* (Jerusalem, 1965).

113 In other words, in the past tense it reduced such roots in all conjugations to forms resembling the *Qal* of mediae *w/y* verbs, e.g., both *biṭṭa'* and *hibbiṭ* (*nbṭ*) appear as *baṭ*. Similarly the nouns *gin* 'protection' (*gnn*), *ṭif* 'speech' (*nṭp*), etc.

114 L. Zunz, *Die synagogale Poesie des Mittelalters*, 2nd edition, 379–453 (Frankfurt am Main, 1920).

115 J. Kena'ani, *Millon konkordanṣiyoni li-lšon ha-piyyuṭim* (Jerusalem, 1930–31), 46 pp. Cf. his 'Me-oṣar ləšono šel ha-Qalir', *Ləšonenu* 10.21–9 (1938–39); M. Zulay, 'Meḥqarim bi-lšon piyyuṭey Yannay', *Yədi'ot ha-Makhon lə-ḥeqer ha-širah ha-'ivrit* 6.161–248 (Jerusalem, 1944–45). Kena'ani includes material from the Piyyuṭ in his general Hebrew lexicon *Oṣar ha-lašon ha-'ivrit* (Jerusalem, 1960 onwards), but without individual references.

116 Jerusalem thesis (1951, Hebrew). Cf. also C. Rabin, 'R. Avraham bar Ḥiyya u-tḥiyyat ha-'ivrit ba-me'ah ha-XI', *Məṣudah* 3/4.158–70 (Leeds, 1945), and *The development of the syntax of post-Biblical Hebrew*, Unpublished thesis, Oxford university, 1943.

117 Cf. M. Steinschneider, *Die hebräischen Uebersetzungen des Mittelalters* (Berlin, 1893, reprint Graz, 1956).

118 *Thesaurus philosophicus linguae hebraicae*, 4. vols. (Berlin, 1928–33), with meanings in German.

119 *Mathematical terminology in the Hebrew scientific literature of the Middle Ages* (Hebrew, with English summary, Jerusalem 1968).

The type of language from which the translators started out was that used in France and Germany, with local variations, from ca. 900 onwards, itself mainly developed out of late Mishnaic Hebrew. One of the outstanding representatives of that idiom was Solomon ben Isaac, commonly referred to by the abbreviation Rashi, of Troyes (ca. 1040–1105), and particularly his commentaries to the Bible and the Talmud (the French equivalents, in Hebrew characters, in these commentaries are an early document of French). I. Avinery, in a kind of linguistic encyclopedia to this one writer,[120] has so far published a dictionary of his innovations in words and meanings, an alphabetical list, with a wealth of documentation, of selected items from his syntax, and a glossary of idioms and proverbs. While a systematic descriptive analysis of Rashi's language would raise many methodological problems, because of the complicated way in which the wording of the sources he interprets is interwoven with his own comments, such an analysis is possible with others, containing more independent material. A beginning has been made with the ethical treatise *Sefer Ḥasidim*, compiled at Regensburg about 1200,[121] in an article[122] and two unpublished M.A. theses at Jerusalem.[123]

The Academic Dictionary which is being prepared, under the editorship of Z. Ben-Ḥayyim, by the Hebrew Language Academy at Jerusalem,[124] will, when completed, fill this lacuna completely from the lexical point of view, and to a large extent also as concerns grammar. It is being prepared by concordantial treatment of the entire literature with the help of a computer, and planned to give references for each word and each meaning at intervals of 30 years.

Meanwhile, especially at Israeli universities, an increasing number of students turn to syntactical and other studies in various periods of medieval literature. Several doctorates are being written in this field. In contrast to the *Encyclopaedia Judaica* of 1928–34,[125] where the article on the Hebrew language, written by N. H. Torczyner (later Tur-Sinai), covered in effect only Biblical and Mishnaic Hebrew, the new *Encyclopaedia Judaica* to be published at Jerusalem will cover the entire history of the language in at least its main periods.

5. THE TRANSITION TO MODERN HEBREW

The modernization of Hebrew may be said to have begun in the sixteenth century.

[120] *Hekhal Rashi* (Tel Aviv, 1940 onwards; published by the author). Four volumes have appeared so far, including also a glossary of Rashi's word explanations and a classified list of his grammatical remarks.

[121] Selections in Dutch translation by M. A. Beek (Amsterdam, 1954); a complete English translation is due to be published by Routledge and Kegan Paul, London.

[122] C. Rabin, 'The tense and mood system of Ashkenazi Medieval Hebrew', *Fourth international congress of Jewish studies*, II, 113–16, 188 (Jerusalem, 1968; Hebrew, with English summary).

[123] M. Azar, *A glossary of verbs in Sefer Ḥasidim*; S. Kogut, *The conditional clause in S. Ḥ.*

[124] Z. Ben-Ḥayyim, 'A Hebrew dictionary on historical principles', *Ariel*, no. 13 (Jerusalem, 1966); 'Min ha-ʿăvodah ba-millon ha-hisṭori', *Ləšonenu* 27/28.170–8 (1963–64); *Sefer ha-məqorot*, I (Jerusalem, 1962–63).

[125] Only the vols. *A* - *Lyra* appeared (Berlin).

In 1574 there appeared at Mantua *Mə'or 'enayim* by Azariah de' Rossi, the first Hebrew book to use scientific sources in a modern way. Also at Mantua, Judah Sommo (1527–92) published the first Hebrew play.[126] Elijah Levita, a German scholar living in Italy (ca. 1468–1549), wrote a Judaeo-German-Hebrew dictionary,[127] thus for the first time facing the challenge of expressing in Hebrew all that could be said in a living contemporary language. In the following centuries, a small trickle of works tried to explain modern sciences to the Jewish public in Hebrew, and the authors of legal and ritual opinions (Responsa) increasingly dealt with modern objects and institutions, often naming them in German etc. in Hebrew characters, but quite frequently also creating for them new Hebrew words or combinations, many of which are still current.[128] The first attempts at Hebrew newspapers were made by Isaac Lampronti of Ferrara (1679–1756),[129] and by Moses Mendelssohn at Dessau in 1750,[130] the first properly-established weekly began to appear in Russia in 1856.[131] From ca. 1775 onwards modernization made rapid strides in the Enlightenment (Haskalah) movement, which soon also went in for language reform, viz. the use of purest Biblical Hebrew to express all modern ideas.[132] The first contemporary play appeared in 1821 at Breslau,[133] the first novel 1853 in Lithuania, by Abraham Mapu, who also in 1858 began to publish the first contemporary, 'realistic' novel.[134] In 1884, S.J. Abramovich (Mendele Mokher Sefarim) inaugurated a new era by translating his own Yiddish contemporary stories into a Hebrew mixed of Biblical and Mishnaic elements, which became the basis of Modern Hebrew.[135]

[126] *Ṣaḥut bədiḥutā də-qiddušin*, ed. H.Schirmann (Jerusalem, 1945–46); cf. H.Schirmann, 'Eine hebräisch-italienische Komödie des 16. Jahrhunderts', *MGWJ* 75.97–118 (1931).

[127] *Šəmot dəvarim*, with Latin equivalents by P.Fagius (Isny, 1541–42). A similar dictionary by J.Rodrigues Moreira, *Kehilath Jahacob* (London, 1772–73, equivalents in English and Spanish). Cf. C.Rabin, ''Ivrit mədubberet lifney 125 šanah', *LLA*, no. 137 (1963).

[128] Cf. N.Shapira, 'Ha-lašon ha-tekhnit ba-sifrut ha-rabbanit', *Ləšonenu*, 26.109–16 (1961–62), and ''Al ha-kohal wəha-yaš bi-mqorot 'ivriyyim', *Ləšonenu* 20.62–4 (1955–56); M.Doron, *Words for new inventions and institutions in 17th–18th century North-West German Responsa collections* (Unpublished M.A. thesis, Hebrew University, Jerusalem).

[129] In 1715 at Venice, under different names for each issue, dealing mainly with religio-legal controversies of the day.

[130] *Qohelet* (*sic*!) *musar*, an imitation of the London *Tatler*. Only two weekly issues appeared. This was followed by a literary quarterly, *Ha-mə'assef*, which appeared irregularly in various places in E.-Germany, 1784–1829.

[131] *Ha-Maggid*, at Lyck (East-Prussia), 1856–90. The first dailies appeared at St. Petersburg and Warsaw in 1886.

[132] Cf. J.Kena'ani, 'Ḥiddušey lašon bi-tqufat ha-haskalah', *Ləšonenu* 5.59–72 (1932–33); D. Patterson, 'Some linguistic aspects of the nineteenth-century Hebrew novel', *JSS* 7.309–24 (1962).

[133] David Zamoscz, *To'ar ha-zəman* (Dyhernfurth, 1821); cf. C.Rabin, *s.v.* 'Zamoscz' in the *Enciclopedia dello Spettacolo*, and *Məlilah* 5.216–17 (Manchester, 1955–56).

[134] Cf. D.Patterson, *Abraham Mapu* (London, 1964); I.Carmiel, *Non-Biblical words in Mapu's writings* (Unpublished doctoral thesis, Leeds, England).

[135] For basic facts on Modern Hebrew literature, see J.Klausner, *History of Modern Hebrew literature* (London, 1932); S.Spiegel, *Hebrew reborn* (New York & London, 1930); S.Halkin, *Modern Hebrew literature, trends and values* (New York, 1950); D.Patterson, *The Hebrew novel in Czarist Russia* (Edinburgh, 1964).

In spring 1879 Eliezer Ben-Yehudah (Perelman) published from Paris in a Hebrew quarterly appearing in Vienna an article entitled 'A burning question',[136] in which he advocated speaking Hebrew as part of a plan for Jewish resettlement in Palestine. From 1881, he worked in Palestine for the revival of spoken Hebrew and for the creation of the vocabulary necessary for a modern language, both by searching the ancient and medieval sources and by inventing new words.[137] For the former purpose, Ben-Yehudah undertook the labour of compiling *Thesaurus totius hebraitatis*, a dictionary based upon sources from all periods, continued after his death by M.Z. Segal, and for the last eight volumes by N.H.Tur-Sinai.[138] For the latter activity, after an abortive attempt in 1890, a Language Committee (Waʿad ha-lašon) was constituted in 1904, and functioned until 1953, when it was replaced by the official Hebrew Language Academy (Ha-ăqademiyyah la-lašon ha-ʿivrit).[139]

Owing largely to the foundation of agricultural and urban settlements by new Jewish immigrants from Eastern Europe since 1881, and the adoption of Hebrew as the language of instruction by the new schools, Hebrew spread rapidly as the language of everyday life, and held undisputed sway in the community that grew and consolidated itself in Palestine to its present size of 2¼ millions and to the establishment of the state of Israel, where Hebrew became established as the official language (with Arabic as the recognized minority language).[140]

While this historical sequence is known in its general outline, many details even on the factual level remain uninvestigated, not to mention the sociological and psychological aspects of its development. None of the language states of this period has been linguistically analyzed.

[136] Reprinted in I.Ben-Avi, ed., *Yiśra'el lə-arṣo wəli-lšono*, I, 3–13 (Jerusalem, 1928–29). B.Y.'s life is described, rather romantically, by R.St.-John, *Tongue of the prophets* (New York, 1952 and reprints). Complete bibliography by J.Kenaʿani, *Mizraḥ u-maʿărav*, 3 (in 5 issues, Jerusalem, 1928–29). Cf. W.Chomsky, *Hebrew: the eternal language*, 231–44 (Philadelphia, 1957); C.Rabin, *The revival of Hebrew* (20 pp., Jerusalem, 1958). No serious study of B.Y.'s work or of the Revival has yet appeared. See also C.Rabin, *Gorəmim sociologiyyim bə-toládot ha-lašon ha-ʿivrit*, 14–15 (New York, 1967), and 'The revival of the Hebrew language', *Ariel* 25.25–34 (Jerusalem, 1969).

[137] Cf. R.Sivan, 'Ḥiddušey ha-millim šel E.Ben-Yəhudah', *LLA*, nos. 114–15 (Jerusalem 1960–61; also separately under the title '*Al Ḥiddušey millim* [Jerusalem, 1968]); N.H. Ṭur-Sinai, *The revival of the Hebrew language* (Jerusalem, 1960).

[138] 16 vols. and Introduction (Berlin, later Jerusalem, 1908-58; also published by Yoseloff, New York and London). Previously Ben-Yehudah had published a small Hebrew-Yiddish-Russian dictionary (Vilna, 1903).

[139] Cf. the booklet *The Academy of the Hebrew language* (Jerusalem, 1963). A sort of history of the Language Committee is S.Eisenstadt, *Śəfatenu ha-ʿivrit ha-ḥayyah* (Tel Aviv, 1967). Summaries of the discussions in *Zikhronot Waʿad ha-lašon* (1912–28) and *Zikhronot ha-Aqademiyyah* (since 1954), which also publish lists of the words approved or invented, according to subjects. Most of these lists also appeared in separate booklets. The periodicals *Ləšonenu* (since 1928) and the more popular *Ləšonenu La-ʿam* (since 1945) are only to a limited extent concerned with Modern Hebrew. Cf. also J. Klausner, 'Waʿad ha-lašon bə-šiššim šənot pəʿulato', *LLA* 33.1–8 (1952–53); *Leqeṭ təʿudot* (Jerusalem, 1969–70); R. Sirvan, 'Šəmonim šanah', *LLA* 204–5, 1970.

[140] Cf. R. Bachi, 'A statistical analysis of the revival of Hebrew in Palestine', *Scripta Hierosolymitana* 3.179–247 (1956).

6. MODERN HEBREW

As was to be expected, the attitude of those professionally occupied with language in the society toward reviving Hebrew was at first strictly normative, and concerned with teaching and preserving intact the language as they understood its structure to be. In practice this meant that the school grammars gave the rules of Biblical Hebrew, omitting the rare phenomena and such forms as were considered to have gone out of use, e.g. the 'consecutive' tenses *wayyiqṭol* for the past and *wəqaṭal* for the future. This was only slightly modified to allow for Mishnaic elements that had become common, such as the use of the participle as a present tense; but other Mishnaic forms in common use, such as the verbal nouns (as distinct from the Biblical infinitive), were not taught. The terminology and formulations were taken mainly from the medieval grammarians of Spain and Southern France. The schools taught a strict normalized Biblical spelling, and this was vocalized according to Biblical rules; indeed, the involved rules for the Tiberian vocalization took up the best part of grammar teaching in schools. At the same time publications for adults, which were printed without vocalization, used the more explicit Mishnaic and medieval spelling with frequent insertion of *w* to mark *u* or *o*, and *y* to mark *i* and sometimes *e*. This 'full' (plene) spelling was applied instinctively, there being no normative rules; only in April 1968 did the Language Academy decide to recommend to the government the adoption of a set of rules formulated by the former Language Committee in 1947.[141] The written language freely used Mishnaic and medieval forms and constructions that were not found in the school grammars, and as for syntax, there was only a minimal normative regulation. The rules of Biblical syntax were insufficiently established to be usable as a normative framework (and what was known in European scholarly works seems largely to have been ignored by the Hebrew teacher-grammarians), and in any case would have been inapplicable, as the sentence structure of Modern Hebrew resembles Mishnaic rather than Biblical Hebrew. Spoken Hebrew, of course, deviated from the norm to a much larger extent than published writing, and in many fairly obvious respects ran counter to the school rules.

The situation produced an orthoepic literature, which on the one hand berated the public for disregarding the grammar rules as established — and at times admitted that the time might have come to neglect certain rules, at least in speaking — and on the other hand enriched the normative framework by prescribing usages in the field of syntax, use of prepositions, idiomatic use of words, etc., which were not given in the school grammars, and had in fact only become actual by the development of the written and spoken language, with its mixture of Mishnaic, Aramaic, and medieval material and the strong European influence in syntax and idiom. The new prescriptions were

[141] A study of the various official and unofficial proposals for reforming the spelling of Hebrew, by Werner Weinberg (Hebrew), is shortly to be published (J. L. Magnes Press, The Hebrew University, Jerusalem).

based on investigations of the 'sources' (i.e. Biblical and Mishnaic literature),[142] on 'logic' and internal consistency, on aesthetic preferences, or on pedagogical considerations; the argument of 'best usage' in living or recent authors is hardly used, in contrast to orthoepic literature elsewhere. The earliest book of this type was published in 1908–9,[143] but the regulative activity became established as a recognized social institution in Hebrew-speaking Palestine through the personality and impressive learning of Isaac Epstein (1862–1943) from about 1910.[144] His mantle fell upon Isaac Avinery (b. 1900)[145] and Isaac Pereṣ (1899–1967),[146] with numerous other writers of lesser influence. Some of these published their prescriptions through semi-official channels in the form of brochures for language improvement printed by various ministries for their officials. *Wə-dayyeq* by J. Bahaṭ and M. Ron (Merḥaviah, 1959–60) obtained an authoritative position by being widely used in school teaching. A study of this literature appeared at Jerusalem in 1967.[147]

In a language but recently revived out of books, the clash of attitudes in normative discussion is in itself of fascinating interest, and the search of the orthoepists for enlightenment in the sources has brought to light many structural and idiomatic details that would otherwise have gone unnoticed. For the linguist, however, the orthoepist, by pointing his finger at linguistic corruption, unwittingly also produces invaluable evidence of the existence of certain tendencies in the spoken language at a time when we have no direct descriptions or texts of it.

Linguistic discussion of Modern Hebrew as such began only in the 1930s. It began with the problem of the co-existence in it of elements derived from Biblical Hebrew and Mishnaic Hebrew. While in the formative stages of living Hebrew, starting with Mendele Mokher Sefarim (see above, section 5) and Ben-Yehudah, the process of mixture was conceived of as enrichment of a basic Biblical stock by later elements, more sophisticated linguists realized that Biblical and Mishnaic Hebrew were two distinct linguistic systems, with rival means of expressing the same content, and their mixture produced a structural disturbance. The historian and literary historian J. Klausner (1874–1958) in a long series of essays[148] gradually arrived at the conclusion that living Hebrew should be based on Mishnaic Hebrew exclusively,

[142] Avinery (fn. 145, below) added as a supplementary 'source' the medieval Bible commentator Rashi (cf. fn. 120, above); since the latter's language is fairly Europeanized, this gives authority for some relaxation of the norm.

[143] A. J. Shapira, *Moreh Nəvukhey ha-lašon*, 2 vols. (Warsaw, 1908–9).

[144] Published in 1915 a Lausanne doctoral thesis on *La Pensée et la Polyglossie*. His normativist writings in the press, 1925–43, were reprinted as *Hegyoney lašon* (Tel Aviv, 1946–47).

[145] Much of his writing since 1930 is reprinted in his orthoepic encyclopaedia, *Yad ha-lašon* (Tel Aviv, 1964).

[146] His newspaper articles were reprinted, in revised form, in *'Ivrit ka-hălakhah*, 3 vols. (Tel Aviv, 1953–58), and in a 2nd edition in one volume (Tel Aviv, 1961). They show a constant development towards liberalism and recognition of the autonomy of the spoken language. Cf. fn. 160, below.

[147] M. Ben-Asher, *The emergence of normative grammar in Modern Hebrew* (Doctoral thesis, Hebrew with English summary, published Merḥaviah, 1969).

[148] Collected in *Ha-'ivrit ha-ḥădašah u-va'ăyoteha* (Tel Aviv, 1957).

this being the last stage at which the language had led a natural life. In 1937–38 he published a *Short Grammar of Modern Hebrew*,[149] in which the rules are entirely Mishnaic, with a number of modernizations and innovations derived from his own observation of contemporary usage. It must be stressed that the *Short Grammar*, like Klausner's own language, does not reflect contemporary written (or spoken) usage, but a Mishnaized version of it. Klausner even went so far as to translate a Biblical text into his version of Modern Hebrew.[150]

A. Bendavid, in 1951,[151] carefully analyzed the extent to which the two systems overlap and conflict, and Modern Hebrew — at least theoretically — has at its disposal two alternative ways of saying the same thing. He rejects the possibility of going back to an unmixed language, but demands that the mixture must be normatively regulated, by a body of scholars deciding in each case which of the alternatives should be used in practice.[152]

To describe the conflict of source systems, Bendavid uses the picture from Genesis 25:22 of Jacob and Esau 'struggling together' in Rebekkah's womb.[153] This metaphor is taken up by Z. Ben-Ḥayyim in a thoughtful essay on whether descriptive research in Modern, especially spoken, Hebrew is justified.[154] His claim is that this 'struggle' of systems denies Modern Hebrew the character of a consistent linguistic system in the Saussurian sense, and therefore makes structural investigation pointless. In the end the competitive elements will be restructured into a new system, but this process needs careful guidance by linguists competent to observe the direction of the true tendencies of the language, and in the meantime it is essential that people should learn and observe the traditional normative forms, with all their duplication, so that no form dies out before it is really ripe for obsolescence.[155]

H. B. Rosén, against some of whose earlier studies[156] Ben-Ḥayyim's essay is largely directed, gives the title 'The elements struggling together' to one of the chapters in his book *Ha-ʿivrit šellanu* ['Our Hebrew'] (Tel Aviv, 1955–56). For Rosén the struggle of systems is devoid of any reality: the restructuring has already taken place, the items taken over from the various strata have assumed new functions in an entirely different structural system, an *état de langue* which he names Israeli Hebrew ('Ivrit

[149] *Diqduq qaṣar šel ha-ʿivrit ha-ḥădašah.*
[150] *Sefer ʿAmos ʿim paršegen (paraphrazah ʿivrit)* (Tel Aviv, 1942–43).
[151] *Ləšon ha-miqrā o ləšon ḥăkhamim?* (Tel Aviv, 1951). The 2nd edition, entitled *Ləšon ha-miqrā u-lšon ḥăkhamim* (Tel Aviv, 1967), is in effect a new work.
[152] *Op. cit.*, 199. In the 2nd edition he proposes that the alternative words and forms might be used to mark different stylistic levels, while at the same time deriding the contention of various researchers in contemporary Hebrew that such stylistic differentiation had already taken place.
[153] *Ibid.*, 198. The Hebrew phrase *wayyitroṣəṣu* is much stronger than its rendering in the English Bible versions: it literally means 'they tried to crush each other', in the Vulgate *collidebantur*.
[154] 'Lašon ʿattiqah bi-mṣi'ut ḥădašah', *LLA*, no. 35/37.55 (1952–53); see also his clarification of his own attitude in 'Diqduq bəney adam', *Maśśā* III/19.2,9 (Tel Aviv, August 27, 1953).
[155] *Op. cit.*, 81–3.
[156] 'Tahălikhey lašon', *LLA*, nos. 25 (1951), 32 (1952), 62 (1956); cf. his "Al sṭandard wə-normah, etc.', *LLA*, nos. 38–41 (1953), *Siḥot ʿal lašon wə-hisṭoriah* (Tel Aviv, 1953), Review of Weiman (see below), *Tarbiṣ* 24.234–47 (1954–55), and Ben-Ḥayyim's rejoinder, *Tarbiṣ* 24.337–42.

Yiśrə'elit). This possesses the same structural autonomy as Biblical or Mishnaic Hebrew. Having thus rebutted any doubts about the justification of descriptive research on Israeli Hebrew, Rosén gives in 107 closely-packed pages a highly interesting exposition of its structure. In two other chapters he shows how linguistic elements which received no differentiated function in this restructuring are utilized as markers for stylistic levels. The type of language he analyzes is a fairly 'high' one; he himself identifies it as the speech of civil servants educated at highschool, when on duty. It does not include some almost universal colloquialisms, e.g. the series *oˈtanu otˈkhem oˈtam* 'nos, vos, eos' for normative *etˈkhem*.

In fact, Rosén suggests, the time has come to accept the forms of Israeli Hebrew as standard for the written language as well, instead of the vain attempt to impose upon the writer, and theoretically even upon the speaker, rules derived from the Sources but meaningless within the new language structure. He adduces examples to show that, applied to a different system of pronunciation, phonetic rules either create meaningless exceptions[157] or become part of morphology.[158] In his second book, *ʿIvrit ṭovah* (Jerusalem, 1957), he shows the degree of restructuring in syntax which has taken place in perfectly 'good Hebrew', unnoticed by the normativists — mainly, as he claims, because they only notice mistakes within the compass of a single word. He also produced a complete descriptive grammar in English;[159] though the material there is broken up into beginner's lessons, the linguist can easily survey Rosén's views on structure by using the index. In this book, the recognized normative rules are mentioned along with the forms described.

From 1952 to 1954, H. Blanc published in the literary weekly *Maśśā* 24 articles under the pseudonym Qablan, entitled 'Ləšon bəney adam', a phrase which might perhaps be rendered as 'How people really speak'. The tenor of this column is proclaimed by the title of the first article, 'Development or deterioration?'. With fine humor, Blanc argues for freeing Hebrew speech from the shackles of exaggerated normativism, and for applying instead modern linguistic methods and attitudes to find out what is really happening. He polemicizes with the normativists of the daily press and reacts to various publications.[160] The range of subjects discussed, in a discursive fashion, covers not only grammar and syntax, but also phonetics, semantics,

[157] E.g. the rule that the definite article *ha-* must be pronounced *he-* before *h*, *ḥ*, ʿ when these are followed by unstressed [a] written by the sign *Qamaṣ* (Gesenius §35h); when *Qamaṣ* still was pronounced [ɒ:], this was phonetic dissimilation, but now that it is indistinguishable from short [a] (*Pattaḥ*), the rule is meaningless and merely provides a number of exceptions, cf. *REJuiv*, NS 17.85–6 (1958).

[158] E.g. the alternations between *b-v*, *p-f*, *k-kh* in inflection, since the distinction of long and short vowels and the phone [ə], which conditioned these alternations, have disappeared, cf. 'Ḥălaqeha šel torat ha-lašon', *LLA* 66.17–20 (1955–56). (In contemporary Hebrew, [ə] is a facultative svarabhakti vowel.)

[159] *Textbook of Israeli Hebrew* (Chicago, 1962).

[160] Evidence of the effectiveness of his criticism may be seen in the fact that I. Pereṣ omitted for his *ʿIvrit ka-hălakhah* (see fn. 146 above), a number of items which Blanc had criticized when they first appeared in the daily press.

borrowing, and socio-linguistics. A shrewd observer, Blanc was the first to notice many features of Israeli Hebrew.

Blanc is also the only one so far to have published phonetic transcriptions of actual spoken Hebrew texts.[161] A large number of recorded and transcribed texts forms the basis of his exhaustive, but unfortunately hitherto only partly-published, course of Israeli Hebrew.[162] This course represents, to date, the most complete description of Israeli Hebrew, in its spoken variety.

The appearance of Rosén's *Our Hebrew* may be said to have concluded the preparatory period of the fight for recognition of contemporary Hebrew as a legitimate subject for linguistic research and the quest for method, a period to which we have to reckon also the attempts at linguistic description of this language undertaken outside Palestine, e.g. Weiman's.[163] This book roused a storm among teachers and writers,[164] but it appears that this public discussion itself cleared the air. A contributory factor may have been that the use of colloquial Hebrew in the dialogue, and at times even in the narrative, of stories and novels, which had begun as an aftermath of the 1948 War of Independence, along with other symptoms of revolt of the native-born youth against the culture of its parents,[165] had by 1955 come to be accepted. In academic circles, at any rate, research on contemporary Hebrew had come to stay, and entered a phase of academic respectability. Though discussion of the 'problems' of contemporary Hebrew had been part of the teaching program of the Department of Hebrew Language at Jerusalem since about 1950,[166] it was only in 1957 that Modern Hebrew studies were incorporated as an essential part of the syllabus. In 1959, the first Ph.D. thesis in the field of contemporary Hebrew was presented in the Department of Linguistics, A. Bar-Adon's *Children's Hebrew in Israel*, I; *The Verb* (549 pp.). This

161 'Israeli Hebrew texts', *Studies in egyptology and linguistics in honour of H. J. Polotsky*, 132–52 (Jerusalem, 1964) (written in 1955–56); 'Qeṭaʿ šel dibbur ʿivri-yiśrəʾeli', *Ləšonenu* 20.33–9 (1955–56). The specimen published by C. Rabin in *Maître Phonétique*, 1941.21, was a constructed text. The texts transcribed by D. Téné, E. A. Levenston, and P. Enoch are still unpublished.

162 *Intensive spoken Israeli Hebrew*, English Language Services, Inc. (Washington, D.C., 1960), with pre-recorded tapes. Only Books I and IV out of five have appeared.

163 The most important of these was R. W. Weiman, *Native and foreign elements in a language: A study in general linguistics applied to Modern Hebrew* (Philadelphia, 1950), the material for which was assembled by inquiries from Israelis studying in U.S.A. The criticism of this work, by M.H. [Goshen-] Gottstein, *Ləšonenu* 17.231–40 (1950–51); H. Blanc, *Word* 11.87–90 (1953); H. Rosén, *Tarbiṣ* 24.234–47 (1954–55), and the rejoinder to Rosén by Z. Ben-Ḥayyim, *Tarbiṣ* 24.337–42, considerably contributed to the emergence of a positive attitude to research into Israeli Hebrew. C. Rabin's Diploma thesis, *Prolegomena to a phonetic description of Palestinian Colloquial Hebrew* (School of Oriental Studies, London, 1938), remained unpublished, as no doubt did other investigations unknown to the present writer. It should be noted that the numerous practical books for teaching Modern Hebrew to foreigners published since the Revival, generally made some attempt to fit the traditional normative presentation to the facts of the language as each author himself handled it, and that much valuable descriptive material may lie hidden there.

164 The veteran writer and literary critic S. Zemach published an 8,500 word attack on the book in *Davar* (the daily representing the socialist Founding Fathers of Israel).

165 Cf. J. Melkman, ... *en een geslacht komt* ... (Inaugural lecture, Amsterdam, 1952).

166 The subject was first taught by Z. Ben-Ḥayyim.

also contains as an appendix a collection of samples of children's speech in a semi-phonetic transcription. Other Israeli universities followed suit. On the other hand, in most of the growing number of departments and courses of Modern Hebrew in universities outside Israel, teaching concentrates on literature and practical writing and speaking skill along normative lines, though in some places, such as M.I.T., the University of Texas, and the School of Oriental and African Studies in London, research on Israeli Hebrew is being done, and two teachers at the University of Paris, for instance,[167] have written a grammar which, while not specifically describing Israeli Hebrew, is based on material from actual texts, and gives an account of the phonetic and morphological features.

The above-mentioned works of Rosén (1955–56, 1962) and of Blanc (1960) go quite a long way in describing the phonetics and phonology of Israeli Hebrew as spoken by that part of the population whose parents came from Europe or America. The findings of this phase are summed up by W. Weinberg,[168] though not in the structuralist spirit of the authors named. Descriptions, involving the use of experimental phonetics, by D. Téné[169] and P. Enoch[170] are still unpublished, except for Téné's results on vowel length.[171]

The work done in morphology, apart from full descriptions, is of course largely concerned with tangible innovations, such as the introduction of nominal and adjectival compounds into a language which, like Semitic in general,[172] did not know composita;[173] the development of new suffixes, partly by borrowing, partly by metanalysis;[174] the spread of diminutive formations;[175] or the replacement of the imperative by the corresponding forms of the future tense.[176] On the other hand, there are only the beginnings — as far as published work is concerned — of detailed investigations of the restructuring of the inherited material. R. Sivan[177] deals with the exploitation of

[167] David Cohen and H. Zafrani, *Grammaire de l'hébreu vivant* (Paris, 1968).

[168] 'Spoken Israeli Hebrew: Trends in the departure from classical phonology', *JSS* 11.40–68 (1966).

[169] *Description phonologique d'un idiolecte* (Paris doctoral thesis, 1961).

[170] *Essai de phonétique comparée de l'hébreu et du français contemporain* (Besançon doctoral thesis, 1965).

[171] 'Ha-mešekh ha-nimdad šel ha-tənuʿot bə-ʿivrit', *Ləšonenu* 26.220–68 (1961–62). Note also C. Rabin, 'La chute de l'occlusive glottale en hébreu parlé et l'évolution d'une nouvelle classe de voyelles', *GLECS* 3.77–9 (1940); N. Pəladah, 'Šəkhiḥut ha-hăgayim bə-ʿivrit', *Ləšonenu* 23.235–42 (1958–59); J. Mansour, "Al haṭʿamat milləʿel ba-ʿivrit ha-mədubberet', *LLA* 106/107.99–105 (1959–60).

[172] Cf. C. Brockelmann, *Grundriss der vergl. Gramm.* etc., I, 481.

[173] M.Z. Kaddari, "Al herkəvey šem-to'ar ba-ʿivrit', *LLA* 159/160.195–206 (1964–65); M. Altbauer, *LLA* 65.3–7 (1955–56); C. Rabin, *Ləšonenu* 22.250–4 (1957–58); R. Mirkin, *Ləšonenu* 26.217–19 (1961–62).

[174] R. Mirkin, *LLA* 92.286–93 (1957–58).

[175] M. Altbauer, *LPosn*, 1949.189–98.

[176] H.B. Rosén, *Ha-ʿivrit šellanu*, 216–18; A. Bar-Adon, *Proceedings 9th International Congress of Linguists*, 760–1 (1964), and *JAOS* 86.410–13 (1966).

[177] *Patterns and trends of linguistic innovations in Modern Hebrew*, General Introduction and Part I: The Verb, Doctoral thesis, Hebrew University, Jerusalem, 1964.

the verbal patterns[178] in forming new verbs from a quantitative point of view, without really going into the question of functional shifts; M. Ben-Asher[179] investigates the increasing semantization of nominal patterns in official word formation; R. Mirkin[180] the widespread formation of the 'intensive' passive participle from non-verbal bases.[181] While the suggestions of Z. S. Harris's 'Componential analysis of a Hebrew paradigm'[182] have of course been absorbed into the analytical work of the 1950's, the pioneer publication of M. Shapiro and Y. Shvika on computer analysis of Hebrew morphology[183] is the first published result of research activities now carried on in a number of places, as is also research, still unpublished, in transformative analysis of Modern Hebrew morphology.

While the ordinary grammars written for schools and for teaching Hebrew to foreigners cannot be expected to reflect Israeli Hebrew, except in so far as they omit Biblical and Mishnaic Hebrew forms no longer current,[184] the syntax of present-day Hebrew is so different from that of previous periods that it cannot be described at all in terms borrowed from the latter, and even a syntax for schools must give some account of Hebrew as it is. To mention only the books most widely used in Israeli schools: those by M. Yo'eli[185] and M. Nahir,[186] though they concentrate entirely on parsing, give at least most of the examples in recognizable Modern Hebrew; I. Pereṣ[187] gives a wealth of examples from modern authors, and does mention some phenomena peculiar to Modern Hebrew (though not pointing them out as such); while J. Blau,[188] whose examples are mostly constructed, does discuss modern written Hebrew.

The grammars by Rosén (1962) and Blanc (1960), as well as Cohen and Zafrani,[189] of course deal systematically with syntax, on the basis of actual usage. U. Ornan's lectures on syntax appeared in a summarized form in 1965, and the first part of a

[178] I.e. the simple, 'intensive', causative (and intransitive-inchoative), and reflexive-reciprocal conjugations and their respective passives (Binyanim).

[179] 'Niṣṣul ha-mišqalim bə-ḥiddušey ha-Aqademiyyah la-lašon', *Baša'ar* 3.38–46 (Merḥaviah, 1960). Popular discussion: E. Horowitz, *How the Hebrew language grew*, 163–94 (New York, 1960); cf. also S. Rabinowitz, *Sefer ha-mišqalim* (New York, 1947).

[180] 'Mišqal məfo'al', *Ləšonenu* 32.140–52 (1967–68), extract from M.A. thesis, Hebrew University, Jerusalem.

[181] E.g. *məfor'aš* 'full of fleas' (*par'oš*), cf. German *verlaust*; *məmušqaf* 'spectacled' (*mišqafayim*, root *šqp*).

[182] *Lg* 24.87–91 (1948), cf. *Methods in structural linguistics*, 246–8, 314–24 (Chicago, 1951). A brief, but highly suggestive sketch of Hebrew structure is also given by Harris in 'Transfer grammar', *IJAL* 20.259–70 (1954).

[183] 'Nittuaḥ mechanographi šel ha-morphologiah ha-'ivrit', *Ləšonenu* 27/28.354–72 (1963–64).

[184] Some older forms generally omitted in the Modern Hebrew grammars, such as the 'consecutive' tenses, are, however, still used in set phrases and in certain styles.

[185] *Taḥbir 'ivri* (Tel Aviv, 1953–54, and reprints).

[186] *'Iqqərey torat ha-mišpaṭ* (Haifa, 1946–47).

[187] *Taḥbir ha-lašon ha-'ivrit* (Tel Aviv, 1943, and reprints).

[188] *Yəsodot ha-taḥbir* (Jerusalem, 1966).

[189] See fn. 167 above.

complete syntax in a provisional edition in 1968.[190] A contrastive English-Hebrew syntax has been prepared by E. A. Levenston.[191]

The following fields of the syntax of standard written Hebrew have been covered in published work or in theses that can be obtained:[192] *The nominal phrase ... with special reference to the prose of C. N. Bialik* by U. Ornan[193] is a transformational study; the pronoun *ka-zeh* 'such' and its agreement, by the same author,[194] developments in negation by M. Altbauer[195] and C. Rabin;[196] the expression of modality, by H. Maschler;[197] emphasis, by I. Pereṣ;[198] the nominal clause, by E. Rubinstein,[199] with use of generative techniques; the use of adverbial phrases as subject or predicate, by J. Blau;[200] the compound nominal clause (extraposition, nominativus pendens), by E. Rubinstein[201] and U. Ornan;[202] the relative clause, by I. Pereṣ,[203] S. Bahaṭ,[204] and the asyndetic relative clause by C. Rabin;[205] the conditional clause, by M. Ben-Asher;[206] and the concessive clause, by T. Vardy.[207] The language of the 1966 Nobel Prize winner, S. J. Agnon, which is pronouncedly traditional and un-Modern Hebrew[208]

[190] *Taḥbir ha-ʿivrit ha-ḥădašah* (Jerusalem, Aqademon publ. no. 185–65); *Taḥbir ha-ʿivrit ha-ḥădašah, Sikkumey harṣa'ot*, I: *Ha-mišpaṭ ha-pašuṭ* (Mahădurah ăraʿit, Jerusalem, 1968). See also his 'Nittuaḥ mechani wə-hora'at ha-taḥbir', *Ləšonenu* 23.243–58 (1958–59).

[191] *A scale-category description of the syntax of Israeli Hebrew* (doctoral thesis, University of London, 1966). In this connection one should also mention the pamphlet by S. Campus, *Noţiuni de sintaxa comparata Romîna-Ebraica* (Jaffa, [after 1961]), which, while by no means structuralist, yet contains much information not found in elementary textbooks.

[192] Jerusalem doctoral theses must be 'published' by statute, generally in cyclostyled form, and can be obtained by exchange or microfilm from the National and University Library, Jerusalem, or from the authors. M.A. theses are deposited in one copy in the same library, and may be consulted.

[193] Doctoral thesis, Hebrew University, Jerusalem, 1964. Part I: *Introduction and* [*syntax of the*] *article*, has been published as Technical Report no. 18 (Catalogue no. ED 011.644) by Educational Resources Information Center, Clearing-House for Linguistics (May 1965).

[194] 'Kazeh wə-khazot', *Ləšonenu* 32.46–52 (1967–68), cf. H. B. Rosén, *LLA* 62.27–34 (1954–55). Literally 'like-this', the pronominal part agrees in gender and number with the headword.

[195] *For Max Weinreich*, 1–5 (The Hague, 1964), on superfluous and double negations.

[196] *Ləšonenu* 22.246–57 (1957–58), on negation of present tense and verbal noun.

[197] *Ways of expressing modality in Modern Hebrew*, M.A. thesis, Hebrew University 1966.

[198] *Ləšonenu* 26.118–24 (1961–62).

[199] *The nominal sentence*, doctoral thesis, Hebrew University, Jerusalem, 1967 (Merḥaviah, 1968; in Hebrew).

[200] *Ləšonenu*, 20.30–40 (1955–56).

[201] *The compound nominal clause* (*Pəsuq ha-yiḥud*) *in Modern Hebrew*, M.A. thesis, Hebrew University, Jerusalem, 1965.

[202] 'Pirqey yiḥud', *Maʿălot* 6.46–59 (Tel Aviv, 1967–68, periodical publ. by the Secondary School Teachers Organization).

[203] *Mišpaṭ ha-ziqqah ba-lašon ha-ʿivrit lə-khol təqufoteha* (Tel Aviv, 1967), 197 pp, including a 60-page history of the Hebrew language.

[204] *The relative clause in Modern Hebrew*, M.A. thesis, Hebrew University, Jerusalem, 1964.

[205] *Trudi XXV m'eždunarodnovo kongressa vostokov'edov*, I. 379–81 (1962).

[206] *The conditional clause in Modern Hebrew*, M.A. thesis, Hebrew University, Jerusalem, 1965; *Haḥinnukh* 40.355–60 (1967–68).

[207] *The concessive clause in Modern Hebrew*, M.A. thesis, Hebrew University, Jerusalem, 1967.

[208] It is an artistic re-shaping of the highly-traditional yet yiddishized language of Hassidic stories of ca. 1725–1850. On Agnon see A. Brand, *Nostalgia and nightmare* (Los Angeles, 1968).

but has been exercising a powerful influence upon the style of younger novelists, has been partly investigated by J. Mansour[209] along moderately structuralist lines.

The latest major Hebrew dictionaries[210] cover fairly adequately the vast increase in vocabulary that has taken place in Hebrew since the revival in the 1880s;[211] but since they aim at enabling the user also to read traditional literature, they are not restricted to words or meanings actually current in any variety of contemporary Hebrew; nor do they represent satisfactorily the development of meaning. The Academic Dictionary[212] is planned to include developments up to 1948 (foundation of the State of Israel). A large-scale dictionary based on texts from the 1880's onwards, by M. H. Goshen-Gottstein,[213] will fill this gap. The Introductory Volume, setting out the method and discussing the features of the Modern Hebrew vocabulary, has appeared (Tel Aviv 1969). Since 1955, Goshen-Gottstein has been publishing a weekly feature, 'Ṭur ha-lašon', in the Friday number of the daily *Haaretz* (Ha-areṣ) which, while officially orthoepic in character, contains mainly discussions on the more recent formal and semantic developments of words. I. Avinery, *Gənazim məgullim* (Tel Aviv, 1968), a supplement to existing dictionaries from medieval and early modern literature, specializes in providing evidence for pre-modern occurrences of supposedly modern words or meanings.[214] R. Sivan has had since 1966 (167/168) a column, 'Me-ḥayyey ha-millim', in *LLA*, investigating the date and circumstances of the innovation of words now current; another column, by R. Mirkin, 'Lə-hašlamat he-ḥaser ba-millonim' (since *LLA* 175 [1967]), provides the earliest known attestations of new words, with appeals to the readers to supply earlier ones, if known. E. Y. Kutscher's *Millim wə-tolədotehen* (Jerusalem, 1961), previously mentioned, also provides details of the history of many modern words. Finally, D. Sadan, in numerous articles in *LLA* and elsewhere, discusses from literary quotations the way in which words and phrases reached the meaning they have in Modern Hebrew. A specific

[209] *'Iyyunim bi-lšono šel Š. Y. 'Agnon* (Tel Aviv, 1968; based on his doctoral thesis, Hebrew University, Jerusalem, 1964); *Bar-Ilan* 4/5 403–14 (Ramat-Gan, 1964–65); *Lašonenu* 30.113–35 (1965–66); *Haḥinnukh* 39.135–42 (1966–67). See also C. Rabin in *Lə-'Agnon Šay*, 217–36 (Jerusalem, 1958–59); in *Yuval Šay*, 13–25 (Ramat-Gan, 1957–58); B. De Vries, *Yuval Šay*, 77–82; M. Goshen-Gottstein, *Lə-'Agnon Šay*, 63–76.

[210] Thus A. Even-Šušan, *Ḥa-millon he-ḥadaš*, 2nd edition (Jerusalem, 1966 onwards), gives new words with references to literary sources; J. Kena'ani, *Oṣar ha-lašon ha'ivrit* (Jerusalem, 1960 onwards), marks new words by a siglum; R. Alcalay, *The complete Hebrew-English dictionary*, 4 vols. (Tel Aviv & Jerusalem, 1963–65; one volume edition, 1965); R. Sivan and E. A. Levenston, *The Megiddo modern dictionary* (Tel Aviv, 1965); R. Alcalay, *Millon 'ivri šalem* (1969–).

[211] It should be noted that only part of the new words were inaugurated by the Language Council, Academy, or other official bodies. At least an equal number are due to those who needed them for their everyday occupations, or to authors and poets. Cf. also I. Avinery, *Kibbušey ha-'ivrit bə-dorenu* (Merḥaviah, 1946).

[212] See above, section 4.

[213] The first three vols., out of a planned ten, are in press (Tel Aviv, Schocken Publishing Co.).

[214] See also his "Al 'iwwutey millonim', *LLA* 164/5 (1965–66).

chapter of vocabulary innovation, the agricultural terms of the 1880's, was investigated by H. Adar.[215]

The first frequency list of Modern Hebrew, by E. Rieger, appeared in 1935.[216] It was based on 200,000 running words, and lists the 2,017 words with frequencies above 10. One third is 'Sources' in Biblical and Mishnaic Hebrew, the rest mainly letters. Modern Hebrew literature is not represented. On this list, with rectifications for practical needs, was built the 1,000-word basic list now widely used in teaching foreigners.[217] A new list, based on one million running words from all types of recent prose writing, is being prepared by R. Balgur; the list for children's literature (200,000 running words) has been separately published in 1968.[218] So far, there is only one concordance to a modern Hebrew author, viz. the poems of C. N. Bialik (1873–1934).[219] This has been utilized for literary statistics, and work is in progress for obtaining frequency lists of other poets.[220]

Some aspects of children's vocabulary have been discussed by A. Bar-Adon.[221] Of special languages, only that of fishermen and sailors — which contains *lingua franca* elements — has been investigated.[222] The earliest dictionary of Israeli slang known to me appeared in 1949,[223] and there are many lists of slang in periodicals, the items of which are often difficult to check, as in educated Israeli Hebrew usage *sleng* also means substandard speech in general. The scientific approach to slang was initiated by R. Sapan's dictionary and treatise.[224]

Hebrew slang includes numerous Colloquial Arabic words, some of them already slang terms in Arabic.[225] The Palestinian Arabic loanwords in Israeli Hebrew are discussed in full by H. Blanc,[226] who also wrote on Yiddish influence.[227] The wide-

[215] *New words in agricultural terminology created during the "Bilu" period*, M.A. thesis, Hebrew University, Jerusalem, 1965.

[216] *Oṣar millot ha-yəsod šel ha-lašon ha-ʿivrit ha-šimmušit* (Jerusalem, 1935).

[217] I. Mehlman, H. B. Rosén, J. Shaked, *A foundation word list of Hebrew* (Jerusalem, 1960); cf. E. Rieger, *Modern Hebrew* (New York, 1953).

[218] *Rəšimat Millot ha-yasod lə-vattey ha-sefer* (Tel Aviv).

[219] A. Even-Šušan and Y. Segal, *Concordanṣiah lə-širat Ḥ.N.Bialik* (Jerusalem, 1960). Bialik's poems, except for one, were written before he came to settle in Palestine in 1924.

[220] Research Project, headed by D. Téné, under the auspices of the Institute of Jewish Studies, Hebrew University of Jerusalem.

[221] *LLA* 174 (1966–67). On his descriptive work, see above. Cf. also Y. Rivqa'i, *Ləšonenu* 4.279–94 (1931–32), 5.73–7, 243–75 (1932–33), and *ʿAl śəfat yəladenu ba-areṣ* (Tel Aviv, 1938).

[222] M. Altbauer, *LLA* 45/46.26–32 (1953–54); *Bollettino dell' Atlante Linguistico Mediterraneo*, 2/3.169–74 (1960–61); S. Morag and R. Sapan, *Ləšonenu* 31.289–98 (1966–67), a summary of work done for the Atlante Linguistico Mediterraneo, Venice.

[223] M. Fraenkel, *Qunṭres ləšon ha-ʿam* (Jerusalem, 1949), contains a wordlist with German equivalents, and a list with references to modern literature. On the other hand there is no clear delimitation between slang and normal idiom.

[224] *Millon ha-sleng ha-yisrə'eli* (Jerusalem, 1965 and 2nd edition), contains ca. 1000 items; *Darkhey ha-sleng* (Jerusalem, 1963). Cf. also C. Rabin, *GLECS*, 10.60–3 (1964).

[225] Cf. on *ḥătikhah* 'piece' > 'girl', A. Bar-Adon, *LLA* 140/141.250–64 (1962–63).

[226] *LLA* 53.6–14; 54/55.27–32; 56.20–6 (all 1954–55). Cf. also M. Piamenta, *LLA* 118.150–5 (1960–61).

[227] In U. Weinreich, ed., *The field of Yiddish*, II, 185–201 (The Hague, 1965).

spread English influence in loans and loan-translations has been extensively deplored in print, but scientific study of it is only beginning.[228] Very valuable for the earlier period is I. Chanoch-Garbell's doctoral thesis, *Fremdsprachliche Einflüsse im Modernen Hebräisch* (Berlin, 1930).

The semantic study of Israeli Hebrew is still in its infancy, though a great deal of work is in progress. The first study, and so far still the only treatment of Modern Hebrew semantics in general, was M. Altbauer, 'Gilguley Mašma'ut', *LLA* 84 (1957–58). Since then, there has been important research on the question of content-structure in the Hebrew root, by D. Téné,[229] and studies on formal differentiation as a result of semantic development in verbs, by M. Ben-Asher;[230] on abstract-concrete metonymy, by I. Pereṣ;[231] on secularization, by M. Gan,[232] and substantial inquiries on idioms, by R. Nir, R. Landau, and M. Moreshet.[233] The two extant semantically-arranged dictionaries[234] are not based on any type of Israeli Hebrew . A new 'Roget', by Z. Raday, began to appear in 1970, and several are said to be in preparation.[235]

BIBLIOGRAPHY

LLA entries refer to numbers; where no pages are indicated, the article comprises a whole number.

The bibliography includes only material of descriptive linguistic nature or relevant to the discussion on the justification of descriptive linguistics as applied to Israeli Hebrew. It does not include reviews (with a few exceptions) or unpublished theses. The latter, as far as known to the present writer, are enumerated in the body of the article.

English translations of Hebrew etc. titles enclosed in square brackets are by the bibliographer; those not enclosed in brackets are given somewhere in the original item.

[228] E.g. M. Altbauer on the semantic development in Hebrew of *puncture* > 'mishap' and *traffic* > 'traffic policeman', *LLA* 53.14–17 (1954–55); R. Sapan on loan-translations, *LLA* 77.134–9 (1956–57). The latest and fullest dictionaries of foreign words in Hebrew, D. Pines, *Millon 'ămami lo'azi-'ivri* (Tel Aviv, 1958), and R. Alcalay, *Lexicon lo'ăzi-'ivri ḥadaš* (Ramat-Gan, 1967), cannot be relied upon to give only words actually in usage, or the exact meaning a word has in Hebrew speech.

[229] *Ləšonenu*, 32.173–207 (1967–68).

[230] On *noda'* 'be known'/'become, be'; *yittakhen* 'is possible'; *nišqaf* 'look from afar'/'may happen', under the misleading title 'Hitpattəḥuyot ləšoniyyo', *LLA* 181.236–43 (1966–67).

[231] *LLA* 148 (1963–64).

[232] *LLA* 125.67–77 (1961–62).

[233] R. Nir, *Hebrew idioms and their place in the linguistic education of the secondary school pupil in Israel*, doctoral thesis, Hebrew University, Jerusalem, 1967 (in the press); R. Landau, *The bound phrase in Contemporary Hebrew: Its character, sources, and developmental trends*, M.A. thesis, Bar-Ilan University, 1967, with a computerized list of idioms recorded in Even-Šušan's dictionary, 1st edition; M. Moréšet, *LLA* 178/179 (1966–67).

[234] Z. Scharfstein, *Oṣar ha-millim wəha-nivim*, 3rd edition (Tel Aviv, 1963–64); N. Stutchkoff, *Thesaurus of the Hebrew language* (New York, 1968).

[235] We should note two works in the press, and likely to be published in 1969: a special number of *Ariel* (Jerusalem) on the revival and present state of Hebrew; and a symposium on the influence of the revival on the Hebrew language, held at the University of Texas, Austin, Spring 1967.

ALTBAUER, M. 1947–48. 'Gilguley mašmaʿut' [Shifts of meaning]. LLA 84.
——. 1949. O technice zdrobnień we współczesnej hebrajszczyźnie, La technique des formations diminutives et hypocoristiques dans l'hébreu moderne. LPosn 1949.189–98 (Polish with French summary).
——. 1953–54. Mi-ləšon dayyagey Yiśra'el [From the language of Israeli fishermen]. LLA 45/46.26–32.
——. 1954–55. Mi-gəvul el gəvul [Across language frontiers]. LLA 53.14–17.
——. 1955–56. ʿAl yəsodot taḥbiriyyim zarim bi-lšon yamenu [Foreign elements in contemporary Hebrew syntax]. LLA 65.3–7.
——. 1960–61. Della lingua dei pescatori israeliani. Bollettino dell'Atlante linguistico mediterraneo 2/3.169–74. Venice.
——. 1964. New negation constructions in Modern Hebrew. For Max Weinreich, 1–5. The Hague.
AVINERY, I. 1946. Kibbušey ha-ʿivrit bə-dorenu [The achievements of Modern Hebrew]. Merḥaviah.
——. 1959–60. Darkhey ezeh wə-zeh [Treatment of *ezeh* 'which', 'some', and *zeh* 'this, that']. Sinai 47.273–85.
BAR-ADON, A. 1962–63. Ḥătikhah — targum-šə'ilah me-ʿarvit [*ḥătikhah* 'girl', a calque from Arabic]. LLA 140/141.250–64.
——. 1963. Ləšono ha-mədubberet šel ha-dor ha-ṣaʿir bə-Yiśra'el kə-nośē lə-meḥqar [The spoken language of the younger generation in Israel as a subject for research]. Haḥinnukh 35.21–35. Tel Aviv.
——. 1964. Analogy and analogic change as reflected in contemporary Hebrew. Proceedings IX Int. Congress of Linguists, 758–64. The Hague.
——. 1966. New imperative and jussive formations in contemporary Hebrew. JAOS 86.410–13.
——. 1966–67. ʿIyyunim bə-oṣar ha-millim šel yaldey Yiśra'el [Studies in Israeli children's vocabulary]. LLA 174.
BEN-ASHER, M. 1960. Niṣṣul ha-mišqalim bə-ḥiddušey ha-Aqademiyyah la-lašon [The utilization of noun patterns in the innovations of the Language Academy]. Bašaʿar 3.38–46. Merḥaviah.
——. 1966–67. Hitpattəḥuyot ləšoniyyot [Linguistic developments]. LLA 181. 236–42.
——. 1967–68. Mišpaṭ ha-tənay eṣel ha-mədaqdəqim ha-normaṭiviyyim [The treatment of the conditional sentence in the writings of normative grammarians]. Haḥinnukh 40.355–60.
BEN-ḤAYYIM, Z. 1952–53. Lašon ʿattiqah bi-mṣi'ut ḥădašah [An ancient language in a new reality]. LLA 35/37.
——. 1953 (August 27). Diqduq bəney adam [Grammar as people use it]. Maśśā.
——. 1954–55. Lə-te'urah šel ha-ʿivrit kəše-hi mədubberet [On the description of Hebrew as a spoken language]. Tarbiṣ 24.337–42. Jerusalem.
——. 1966. A Hebrew dictionary on historical principles. Ariel 13. Jerusalem.

BLANC, H. 1952–54. Ləšon bəney adam [Language as people speak it]. 24 articles in Maššā from Oct. 16, 1952 to Dec. 2 1954.
——. 1954. The growth of Israeli Hebrew. Middle Eastern Affairs 5.385–92. New York.
——. 1954–55. La-yəsod ha-ʿarvi šeba-dibbur ha-yiśrə'eli [On the Arabic element in Israeli speech]. LLA 53.6–14, 54/55.27–32, 56.20–6.
——. 1955–56. Qeṭaʿ šel dibbur ʿivri-yisrə'eli [A short text of spoken Israeli Hebrew]. Ləšonenu 20.33–9.
——. 1956a. Dialect research in Israel. Orbis 5.185–90. Louvain.
——. 1956b. A note on Israeli Hebrew 'psycho-phonetics'. Word 12.106–13.
——. 1957. Hebrew in Israel: trends and problems. MEJ 11.398–9.
——. 1960. Intensive spoken Israeli Hebrew, Course with 114 pre-recorded tapes. Washington, D.C., English Language Services, Inc. Only Books I and IV published.
——. 1964. Israeli Hebrew texts. Studies in egyptology and linguistics in honour of H. J. Polotsky, 132–52. Jerusalem.
——. 1965. Some Yiddish influences in Israeli Hebrew. The field of Yiddish II, ed. by U. Weinreich, 185–201. The Hague.
CAMPUS, S. (after 1962). Noţiuni de sintaxa comparata Romîna-Ebraica. Jaffa.
CHOMSKY, N. 1954. Review of Modern Hebrew, by E. Rieger. Lg 30.180–1.
CHOMSKY, W. 1952. Hebrew: the eternal language. Philadelphia.
——. 1962. The growth and progress of Modern Hebrew. Essays in honor of Abraham A. Neuman, 106–27. Leiden.
——. 1967. Ha-lašon ha-ʿivrit bə-darkhey hitpattəḥutah [Hebrew in its trends of development — translation and revision of Hebrew: the eternal language]. Sifriyyat Dani lə-maddaʿ 76. Jerusalem, Reuben Mass.
COHEN, H. M. 1951. Schets der ontwikkeling van het Hebreeuws tot moderne omgangstaal. Amsterdam.
DE VRIES, B. 1958–59. Waw ha-məhappekh [*Waw* conversive — on the use of Mishnaic Hebrew in contemporary literary style]. Lə-ʿAgnon Šay 77–82. Jerusalem.
EITAN, E., see GOSHEN-GOTTSTEIN, M.
FRAENKEL, M. 1949. Qunṭres ləšon ha-ʿam. Handbook of Hebrew slang with vocabulary. Jerusalem.
GAN, M. 1961–62. Ben qodeš lə-ḥol [Secularization of words. LLA 125.67–77.
CHANOCH-GARBELL, I. 1930. Fremdsprachliche Einflüsse im modernen Hebräisch. Berlin.
——. 1955. The pronunciation of Hebrew in Israel. MPhon 104.26–9.
GOSHEN-GOTTSTEIN, M. 1953–54. Balšanut mivnit u-politikah ləšonit [Structuralist linguistics and language policy]. LLA 43.17–24.
——. 1956 (March 30). ʿAl balšanim, sofərim wa-ahăvat Yiśra'el [On linguists, writers, and charity – reply to S. Zemach]. Davar.

——. 1958–59. Ben sifrut mofet lə-diqduq normaṭivi [Literary classics and normative grammar]. Lə-ʿAgnon Šay 63–76. Jerusalem.

——. Ṭur ha-lašon, weekly column in the daily *Haaretz*.

GOSHEN-GOTTSTEIN, M., and E. EITAN. 1951–52. Ha-yəsodot lə-tiqquney lašon [The basis of orthoepic statements]. LLA 26.3–10.

GRUBER, R. 1950. Hebrew as she is spoke. Commentary 10.466–7.

HARRIS, Z. S. 1948. Componential analysis of a Hebrew paradigm. Lg 24.87–91.

——. 1954. Transfer grammar. IJAL 20.259–70.

KADDARI, M. Z. 1964–65. ʿAl herkəvey šem-to'ar ba-ʿivrit šel yamenu [On adjectival compounds in Contemporary Hebrew]. LLA 159/160.195–206.

KLAUSNER, J. 1933–34, 1938². Diqduq qaṣar šel ha-ʿivrit ha-ḥădašah [Short grammar of Modern Hebrew]. Tel Aviv.

KLAUSNER, S. Z. 1955. Phonetics, Personality and Status in Israel. Word 11.209–15.

KUTSCHER, E. Y. 1956. Modern Hebrew and 'Israeli' Hebrew. Conservative Judaism 10/3.28–45. Philadelphia.

——. 1957. The role of Modern Hebrew in the development of Jewish-Israeli national consciousness. PMLA 72/2.38–42.

——. 1961. Millim wə-toldotehen [Words and their history]. Jerusalem.

LAMBERT, W. E., M. ANISFELD, and G. YENI-KOMSHIAN. 1965. Evaluational reactions of Jewish and Arab adolescents to dialect and language variations. Journal of Personality and Social Psychology 2.84–90.

LEVENSTON, A. E. 1965. The translation paradigm: a technique of contrastive syntax. IRAL 3.221–5.

——. 1966. A classification of language differences [Hebrew-English]. IRAL 4. 199–206.

MANSOUR, J. 1959–60. ʿAl haṭʿamat milləʿel ba-ʿivrit ha-mədubberet [On stress shift to the penultimate in spoken Hebrew]. LLA 106/107.99–105.

——. 1964–65. Məqomo šel ha-nośē ben ha-mašlimim ba-pasuq mi-ṭipus P-N eṣel Š. Y. ʿAgnon [The position of the subject among the complements in the sentence-type V-S with S. J. Agnon]. Bar-Ilan 4/5.403–14. Ramat-Gan.

——. 1965–66. ʿAl yidduʿo šel ha-ṣeruf 'šəmo šel šem' bə-khitvey Š. Y. ʿAgnon [The determination in the syndetic genitive with proleptic pronoun in S. J. Agnon's works]. Ləšonenu 30.113–35.

——. 1966–67. Šinnuyim bi-lšono šel ʿAgnon bə-nosḥey 'Təmol šilšom' [Linguistic alterations in successive versions of Agnon's novel 'Təmol šilšom']. Haḥinnukh 39.135–42.

MEHLMAN, I., H. ROSÉN, and J. SHAKED. 1960. Rəšimat millot yəsod lə-hora'at ha-lašon ha-ʿivrit. A foundation word list of Hebrew. Jerusalem.

MIRKIN, R. 1957–58. ʿAl šaloš tofaʿot morphologiyyot ba-ʿivrit ha-ḥădašah [Three morphological phenomena in Modern Hebrew]. LLA 92.286–93.

——. 1961–62. *i* + šəmot ha-pəʿulah ba-ʿivrit ha-sifrutit ha-ḥădašah [*i* as prefix of verbal nouns in Modern Literary Hebrew]. Ləšonenu 26.217–19.

——. 1967. Lə-hašlamat he-ḥaser ba-millonim [Towards supplementing gaps in dictionaries]. Column in LLA since 1967.

——. 1967–68. Mišqal məfoʿal [The adjectival pattern $m\partial C_1uC_2C_2aC_3$]. Ləšonenu 32.140–52.

MORAG, S. 1957–58. ʿAśor šel ʿivrit [Ten years of Hebrew in the State of Israel]. LLA 98.

——. 1959. Planned and unplanned development in Modern Hebrew. Lingua 8. 247–63.

MORAG, S., and R. SAPAN. 1966–67. Mi-ləšon ha-dayyagim wə-yorədey ha-yam bə-yiśra'el [From the language of Israeli fishermen and sailors]. Ləšonenu 31.289–98.

MOREŠET, M. 1966–67. Gilguley mašmaʿut šel nivim wə-šel ṣerufey lašon še-məqoram ba-miqrā [Shifts in meaning of idioms and phrases from the Bible in Modern Hebrew]. LLA 178/179.

ORNAN, U. 1958–59. Nittuaḥ mekhani wə-hora'at ha-taḥbir [Mechanical syntactical analysis and the teaching of syntax]. Ləšonenu 23.243–58.

——. 1965. The nominal phrase in Modern Hebrew. Part I: Introduction and article. Educational Resources Information Center, Clearing-House for Linguistics, Catalogue no. ED 011.644. Jerusalem.

——. 1965. Taḥbir ha-ʿivrit ha-ḥădašah, ʿarəkhah ləfi harṣa'ot Š. Bittermann. Jerusalem.

——. 1967–68a. Kazeh wə-khazot [The development of the pronoun *ka-zeh* 'like this' > 'such']. Ləšonenu 32.46–52.

——. 1967–68b. Pirqey yiḥud [Chapters on the compound nominal clause]. Măʿālot 6.46–59. (Tel Aviv, Organization of Secondary School Teachers.)

——. 1967–68c. Taḥbir ha-ʿivrit ha-ḥădašah, I: Ha-mišpaṭ ha-pašuṭ [Modern Hebrew syntax, I: the simple sentence]. Provisional edition, Jerusalem.

PATAI, R. 1953–54. Phonology of 'Sabra' Hebrew. JQR 14.51–4.

PəLADAH, N. 1958–59. Šəkhiḥut ha-hăgayim bə-ʿivrit [Frequency list of Hebrew sounds]. Ləšonenu 23.235–42 (with introduction by C. Rabin).

PEREṢ, I. 1961–62. Lə-darkhey ha-hadgašah ba-ʿivrit ha-ḥădašah [Means of emphasis in Modern Hebrew]. Ləšonenu 26.118–24.

——. 1963–64. Hamḥašah wə-hafšaṭah [Shift from abstract to concrete and conversely]. LLA 148.

——. 1965 (December 10). Mədiniyut lašon wə-ḥeqer lašon [Language policy and linguistic research — against research into Israeli Hebrew]. Davar.

——. 1967. Mišpaṭ ha-ziqqah [The relative clause]. Tel Aviv.

PIAMENTA, M. 1960–61. Hašpaʿat ha-ʿarvit ʿal ḥiddušey Ben-Yəhudah [The influence of Arabic on Ben-Yehudah's word innovations]. LLA 118.150–8.

PLESSNER, M. 1931. Modernes Hebräisch. OLZ 34.803–8.

RABIN, C. 1940. La chute de l'occlusive glottale en hébreu parlé et l'évolution d'une nouvelle classe de voyelles. GLECS 3.77-9.

——. 1941. Hebrew [Specimen]. MPhon 1941.21.

——. 1957–58. Lə-ḥeqer ha-ʿivrit ha-sifrutit ha-ḥădašah [Contribution to the investigation of Modern Literary Hebrew]. Ləšonenu 22.246–57.

——. 1958 (September). Language revival: Colloquialism or purism? Jewish Frontier, Suppl. 11–15. New York.

——. 1957–58. Heʿarot balšaniyyot lə-vaʿăyat tirgum divrey Š. Y. ʿAgnon lə-loʿăzit [Linguistic observations on the problems involved in translating Agnon]. Yuval Šay, ed. by B. Kurzweil, 13–25. Ramat-Gan.

——. 1958–59. Hannaḥot yəsod lə-ḥeqer ləšono šel ʿAgnon [Some basic assumptions for research into the language of Agnon]. Lə-ʿAgnon Šay, 217–36. Jerusalem.

——. 1962. Sovremennï drevn'eyevreiskiy yazïk (Ivrit) k voprosu o razvitii yazïka v kontakte s drugimi yazïkami. Trudï XXV Meždunarodnovo Kongressa Vostokovedov I, 379–81. Moscow.

——. 1964. L'argot des étudiants en hébreu moderne. GLECS 10.60–3.

Rieger, E. 1935. Oṣar millot ha-yəsod šel ha-lašon ha-ʿivrit ha-šimmušit [The basic vocabulary of practical Hebrew). Jerusalem.

——. 1953. Modern Hebrew. New York.

Rivqa'i, Y. 1931–33. ʿAl ha-specifiyyut ha-ləšonit bəfi yəladenu ba-areṣ [On the specific features of the language of our Palestinian children]. Ləšonenu 4.279–94; 5.73–7, 243–75.

——. 1938. ʿAl śəfat yəladenu ba-areṣ [About the language of our children in Palestine]. Tel Aviv.

Rosén, H. B'. 1949–50. Ḥiddušey lašon še-lo mi-daʿat [Unwitting linguistic innovations]. LLA 11.17–20.

——. 1951–55. Tahălikhey lašon [Linguistic development processes]. LLA 25 (1951–52), 32 (1952–53), 62 (1954–55).

——. 1952. Remarques descriptives sur le parler hébreu-israélien moderne. GLECS 6.4–7.

——. 1952–53. ʿAl sṭandard wə-normah, ʿal tahălikhim u-šgi'ot [On standard and norm, developmental processes, and mistakes]. LLA 38.3–8, 40/41.3–11.

——. 1953–54. Siḥot ʿal lašon wə-hisṭoriah [Talks on language and history]. Tel Aviv (the preface is dated August 1951).

——. 1954–55. Diqduq ha-ʿivrit ha-yiśrə'elit [The grammatical treatment of Israeli Hebrew — review of Weiman]. Tarbiṣ 24.234–47 (the review was written in 1950).

——. 1955–56a. Ha-ʿivrit šellanu: dəmutah bə-or šiṭṭot ha-balšanut [Our Hebrew: its image in the light of linguistic methods]. Tel Aviv.

——. 1955–56b. Ḥălaqeha šel torat ha-lašon [The divisions of grammar]. LLA 66.17–20.

——. 1957. ʿIvrit ṭovah: ʿiyyunim bə-taḥbir ha-lašon ha-ʿnəkhonah' [Good Hebrew: studies in the syntax of 'correct' language]. Jerusalem.

——. 1958a. L'hébreu-israélien. REJuivNS 17.59–90.

——. 1958b. Sur quelques catégories à expression adnominale en hébreu-israëlien. BSL 53.316–44.

——. 1961. Syntactical notes on Israeli Hebrew: Determination, indetermination, and the definite article. JAOS 81.21–6.
——. 1962. Textbook of Israeli Hebrew. Chicago.
ROSÉN, ḤANNAH. 1955–56. Signono šel no'em [A stylistic analysis of speeches by D. Ben-Gurion]. Ha-ʿivrit šellanu, by H. B. Rosén, 283–308. Tel Aviv.
SAPAN, R. 1956–57. ʿAl kammah 'targumey šə'ilah' bi-lšon ha-ʿittonut [On some calques in newspaper Hebrew]. LLA 77.134–9.
——. 1963. Darkhey ha-sleng: tofəʿot mašmaʿut wə-ṣurah ba-ʿivrit ha-tat-tiqnit [The ways of slang: semantic and morphological phenomena in sub-standard Hebrew]. Jerusalem.
——. 1965. Millon ha-sleng ha-yiśrə'eli [Dictionary of Israeli Hebrew slang]. Jerusalem.
——. 1966-67. See Morag, S.
SHAHEVITCH, B. 1958–59. Pissuq bi-zmano: ʿal ha-pissuq ha-noheg bə-sippurey Š. Y. ʿAgnon [A comma in time: the punctuation in S. J. Agnon's stories]. Lə-ʿAgnon Šay, 281–8. Jerusalem.
SHAPIRO, M., and Y. SHVIKA. 1963–64. Nittuaḥ mekhanographi šel ha-morfologiah ha-ʿivrit [Mechanographical analysis of Hebrew morphology]. Ləšonenu 27/28. 354–72.
SIVAN, R. Me-ḥayyey ha-millim [The life of words]. Column in LLA since no. 167/168.
TÉNÉ, D. 1961–62. Ha-mešekh ha-nimdad šel ha-tənuʿot bə-ʿivrit [Measured length of Hebrew vowels]. Ləšonenu 26.220–68.
——. 1967–68. Ha'im tokhno šel ha-šoreš ha-ʿivri ʿarukh? [Is the Hebrew root content-structured?] Ləšonenu 32.173–207.
——. 1968. L'hébreu contemporain, in the volume Linguistique of the Encyclopédie de la Pleiade. Paris.
TSEVAT, M. 1953. Learned intention and free development. The Shane Quarterly 14.135–8.
TUBIELEWICZ, W. 1956. Vom Einfluss europäischer Sprachen auf die Gestaltung des modernen Hebräisch. RO 20.337–51.
TUR-SINAI, N. H. 1952. The revival of the Hebrew language and its problems. Civilization 2.33–8.
ULLENDORFF, E. E. 1957. Modern Hebrew as a subject of linguistic investigation. JSS 2.251–63.
VRIEZEN, T. C. 1956. De ontwikkeling van het moderne hebreeuwsch. Mededelingen der Koninkl. Nederlandsche Akademie der Wetenschappen, Afd. Letterkunde, NR, Deel 19, No. 3, 14 pp. Amsterdam.
WEIMAN, R. W. 1950. Native and foreign elements in a language: A study in general linguistics applied to Modern Hebrew. Philadelphia.
WEINBERG, W. 1965. Special bibliography: Spoken Israeli Hebrew. Hebrew Abstracts 10.18–32. New York.

——. 1966. Spoken Israeli Hebrew: trends in the departure from classical phonology. JSS 11.40–68.

ZELDNER, E. 1956. And it's all in Hebrew. MLJ 40.71–5.

ZEMACH, S. 1956 (March 9 and 16). Isfu yədekhem! [Hands off! — review of Rosen, Ha-ʿivrit šellanu]. Davar.

ARAMAIC*

EDUARD YECHEZKEL KUTSCHER

1. SCOPE

Aramaic (*A*)** is the only Semitic Language (*SL*) spoken today whose history can be traced back, as a living language, to about 1000 B.C. An outstanding account of the research on *A* during the last decades of the nineteenth century and the first decades of this century (until 1938) was made by a then very young scholar, F. Rosenthal, in 1939. This is still a standard work and will doubtless remain so for a considerable time. See reviews by H. L. Ginsberg (1942), E. Y. Kutscher (1942–43), and E. Littmann (1941).

Our paper begins where the Rosenthal (1939) study ends and will exceed this limit only for a few dialects.

2. DIVISION OF ARAMAIC

The accepted division of *A* (based on Rosenthal 1939) is as follows:

a) Old Aramaic (*OA*), consisting of *A* inscriptions found in the territory between India in the east, Egypt in the west, the Caucasus in the north, and Southern Egypt-Northern Arabia in the south. The *A* of the Nabataean (*N*) and Palmyrenean (*Pa*) inscriptions could be regarded as offshoots of *OA*, already exhibiting elements of Middle Aramaic (*MA*). To a certain extent this could also apply to the Targum of the Onqəlos type, as well as to the *A* of the Dead Sea Scrolls.

b) *MA*, which has two branches: the eastern, consisting of Syriac (*S*), Mandaic (*M*), the Aramaic of the Talmud Babli (*ATB*), the Gaonic Literature, and incantation texts found mainly in Nippur; and the western, consisting of Samaritan Aramaic (*SA*), Palestinian Christian Aramaic (*PCA*), and Galilean Aramaic (*GA*) (that is, the *A* portions of the Jerusalemite Talmud and of the Haggadic Midrashim).

c) Late Aramaic (*LA*), also with a western branch (Maʿlu:la) and an eastern one, surviving in and around Kurdistan, as well as in the Caucasus.

However, we shall adopt the division suggested by J. A. Fitzmyer (1966:19, fn. 60):

*Due to ill health, the author was unable to accomplish his original plan, which envisaged the inclusion of Middle-Late and Modern Aramaic. It is his intention to publish the complete material separately. This article was prepared with the aid of a grant from the American Philosophical Society for research on the Aramaic inscriptions.

**A list of abbreviations used in this article appears on p. 412.

a) Old Aramaic (*OA*), up to 700 B.C.
b) Official Aramaic (*OfA*), 700–300 B.C.
c) Middle Aramaic (*MA*), 300 B.C.–200 C.E.
d) Late Aramaic (*LA*) = *MA* of the previous division
e) Modern Aramaic (*MdA*) = *LA* of the previous division

3. OLD ARAMAIC

3.1 *The Material*

This has grown considerably, especially with the discovery of Sefîre (previously called Sujîn), stele II and III, which were first edited by A. Dupont-Sommer and Jean Starcky, who also re-edited stele I. The entire material plus introduction and extensive commentary was published by Fitzmyer (1967) in what is a comprehensive, clear and very solid work. Extremely useful are the appendix, the grammar of the Sefîre inscriptions, as well as the glossaries and the indexes. This reliable work leaves very little room for criticism. The earliest *A* inscription, from Tel-Hala:f (Donner and Röllig 1962–64: No. 231), yields very little linguistically.

Selections from the material (old and new) were treated by H. Donner and W. Röllig (1962–64) — Donner being responsible for *A* — and by J.J. Koopmans (1962). Both works have extensive bibliographies and commentaries, and the Donner-Röllig study includes translation and glossaries. Donner and Röllig stop short of the Dead Sea Scrolls, while Koopmans even has inscriptions in *GA*. Rosenthal (1967) offers a good selection of texts and glossary. Koopmans' is a reliable work, while the Donner-Röllig treatment is less satisfactory. The following instances will point up the difference between the two. In the ZKR inscription (Donner-Röllig I, II, no. 202; Koopmans no. 8) *ʾnh ... š ʿnh ʾnh*, Donner and Röllig are still inclined to consider *ʾš* as the Canaanite (*C*) relative pronoun! There is no indication that the structure of this clause is well known in *LA* (the second *ʾnh* employed as copula?). Nor is it indicated that (*bʿl*) *šmyn* is undetermined (a survival, for obvious reasons?). In regard to *wyʿnny*, there is no attempt to explain why not **wyʿnnny* (cf. *wyhnsnh* B 20); the defective spelling goes unnoticed. The same applies to *ʾḥṣlk* (instead of **ʾḥṣlnk*); there is no explanation of the root *mḥʾ* (instead of **mḥq* or **mḥʿ*, cf. the Arabic [*Ar*] cognate *mxḍ* and Hebrew [*H*] *mḥṣ*). Koopmans tackles nearly all of these problems and in addition furnishes a plausible explanation of the strange *w*(*ʾš*), *w*(*yʿnny*), etc. (which generally is explained as *waw consecutive*, as in *H*, a loan from *C*!?). Donner and Röllig are not aware of the problem.

References to other texts published since Rosenthal 1939 can be found with the help of I.N. Vinnikov (1958–65), Ch.F. Jean and J. Hoftijzer (1965) (see 3.3 below), J. Naveh (1964–65, 1965–66), and S. Segert (1967).

A brief outline of *A* was given by A. Diez Macho (1963), by H.L. Ginsberg (1966–67), and by E. Y. Kutscher (1950). In 1956 G. Garbini published a grammar of *OA* of the texts known up to that date. I do not think that Prof. Garbini, who wrote this work at the outset of his career, would use the same approach today; see, e.g., Fitzmyer (1967:147).

Meanwhile R. Degen's grammar (see 3.6, p. 360) has appeared: *Altaramäische Grammatik der Inschriften des 10–8 Jh. v. Chr.* (1969). This is a very satisfactory work, and Degen is to be recommended both for his knowledge of *A* and for his careful handling of the material. Only a few points call for criticism. I hope to publish soon an extensive review of this work in the *ZDMG*.

On the other hand, V. Christian's 'Die Stellung des Mehri innerhalb der semitischen Sprachen' (1944), is entirely unreliable. The author believes 'dass Mehri ... offenbar in ein näheres verwandschaftliches Verhältniss zum Aramäischen zu stellen ist' (p. 2). For Christian, *A* begins with *GA* and *SA*, he has no inkling of the existence of *OA*. He can therefore say that Mehri 'wie das Aramäische überhaupt nur dentale Verschlusslaute kannte' (5), but knows nothing of the situation in *OA*. His approach enables him to maintain, on the basis of *GA* and *SA*, that the phoneme /ʿ/ is missing in *A*, exactly as in Mehri, again disregarding the evidence in *OA* and *OfA* which decisively proves that the situation in *SA* is due to later internal development in *A*. (I propose to deal with *GA* elsewhere.) His further 'proofs' are all of the same order. It should be stressed that there remains practically no evidence of this alleged 'näheres verwandschaftliches Verhältniss' in the light of *OA* and *OfA*. It is a pity that E. Wagner (*Sprache* 12.252, fn. 3, 1966) should have been misled by this wholly unscientific approach, although it is true that Wagner dissociates himself from Christian's conclusions.

F. M. Cross, Jr. and D. N. Freedman 1952 contains a penetrating study of all the words to be found in *OA* (1952:21–34) which pertain to their particular problems. They conclude that (1952:31): 'The spelling of these inscriptions is characterized by the regular use of *matres lectionis* to indicate final vowels, the absence of medial vowel letters (although this was modified sporadically in the late eighth century in the spelling of foreign words), and the consistent representation of diphthongs by their consonantal element.' These conclusions will now have to be modified. There are at least three (?) clear-cut instances of medial vowel letters in the new Sefîre material: *rwḥ*, *ymwt*, *šybt* (Fitzmyer 1967:145). Add to these *šwrʾ* of ZKR inscription, *A* 1.17 — *ibid.* 1.10 *šr* — (overlooked by Cross and Freedman). Diphthongs are spelt defectively twice in the new Sefîre material (Fitzmyer 1967:146). In addition, they have not dealt with the demonstrative pronoun *ʾln*, which contains a contracted diphthong. This diphthong occurs uncontracted in the fragments of the Jerusalemite Targum published by P. Kahle (1930: e.g. 12). I believe that their conclusion concerning the regular use of final *matres lectionis* only applies to certain morphological patterns, e.g. the 3rd person masculine plural of the perfect (*qṭlw*), for obvious reasons (*qṭl* = 3rd person singular of the perfect, and can also represent other forms). But, for example, the defective spelling of the personal suffix in the 3rd person masculine singular of a masculine plural noun, e.g. *mlkwh* 'his kings', which in Elephantine (*E*) is generally spelt *mlkwhy* (=[*malḵo:hi:] in Biblical Aramaic [*BA*]), does not indicate that there was no vowel after the [h]. The suffix had a final vowel in Proto-Semitic (*PS*). Of course, it might have disappeared in *OA*. But then, how are we to account for its (re)appearance, e.g. in *OfA* (*E* and *BA*)?

Another example is that the suffix of the 1st person plural of the perfect in *E* is *-n*, once also in Sefîre (Fitzmyer 1967:73) *'mrn* 'we said'. Now in *E* not only do we find the spelling *-n'* (*ibid.*), and the final vowel of this morpheme is *PS*, but we discover that it survives in *OfA* (*E* and *BA*), as well as in other *A* dialects. The same applies to the final vowel of the independent personal pronoun, first person plural *'nḥn* and *'nḥnh* of *E* = [ʾᵃnaḥna:] in *BA*. How can we account for the emergence of this vowel except by assuming that it was original? Archaic spellings are able to survive a long time even where they clash with current pronunciation and established rules of spelling; e.g. spelling with *z* instead of *d*, *q* instead of ʿ in *E* (cf. Rosenthal 1939:69–70). Therefore all these and similar cases apparently reflect defective spellings of final vowels.

The whole material should be reviewed in this light and the knowledge of the situation in *E* will certainly be revealing.

J. Friedrich (1951) tried to show that the language of the Hadad and Panammu: inscriptions is not *A* but represents a new Northwestern *SL*, which he calls 'Jaudisch'. In order to deal with his critics, he returned to the subject in 1965, but his article (1965) only proved how weak his theory is. It emerges that those characteristics which distinguish the language of these inscriptions from *A* are mainly archaic features. These features disappeared both from the later *A*, as well as from other *SL*. In what follows, Friedrich's main points are refuted.

a) The morpheme of the masculine plural noun suffix, *-w* (=[u:]) of the nominative case and *-y* (*[i:]) of the oblique, is a *PS* trait (and survived only in Akkadian [*Ak*]).

b) Lack of the postpositive article is again an archaic feature which survived in proper nouns in *OA*, e.g. *bʿl šmyn* in ZKR, while in *OfA* the determined form [šəmayya:] 'heaven' occurs. In Sefîre, e.g., both the determined *'lhy'* and the undetermined *'lhn* 'goods' occur. These two characteristics then are not un-*A*, but Proto-*A*.

c) The same applies to the plural morpheme of the feminine *-t* as against [-a:n] in *A*. As is well known, this form represents a secondary development peculiar to *A*. But Sefîre has already turned up a few more instances of the archaic *-t* ending (Fitzmyer 1967:155) and several more have been found in the Hermopolis papyri (see below p. 368).

d) As regards the consonantal phonemes, Garbini (cited by Friedrich 1965) is certainly right: *PS* /ḍ/ > /q/ in these texts, as in Sefîre, *E*, etc., identifies the language absolutely with *A*. The other phonemes are irrelevant to our problem.

e) The plural suffix of the imperfect is *-w* ([*-u:]) and not *-wn* (=[u:n]). These very endings occur in *ATB*. To be sure, there they may represent a later development so that Friedrich here has a point. (But this feature could also be regarded as an archaism.)

f) Infinitive of Qal without prefixed [m-]. Here too Friedrich should have known that it occurs in Sefîre and elsewhere (Fitzmyer 1967:156; also in the Assur-letter and *E*: *l'mr*!).

g) The conjunction *p* (*p'*) has turned up in Sefîre and elsewhere in *A* (Fitzmyer 1967:189).

h) Vocabulary plays a minor role in this type of classification (strangely enough, he lists the good *A ntn* 'give', cf., e.g., *E* where it is also used in the perfect, as non-*A*!). Besides, the non-*A* words *hrg* 'kill', (')*gm* 'also', '*nk*(*y*) (?) 'I' could be *OA* material that disappeared from later dialects (e.g. the last two words can be found in Biblical Hebrew [*BH*] but did not survive in Mishnaic Hebrew [*MH*]!).

While these points then do not contradict the *A* character of these inscriptions (with possibly one exception), there *are* a few traits which definitively establish it as *A*:

1) Consonants, see above; 2) the feminine abstract ending -*w* [(u:]), e.g. *zkrw* 'remembrance' is only *A*; 3) present passive participle *qtyl* is mainly *A*; 4) the relative pronoun *zy* is *A*; 5) the demonstrative masculine pronoun *znh* is *A*, and apparently also the feminine *z'*.

H.L. Ginsberg (1957) adduces a few more points supporting the *A* character of this language, e.g. '*mattab* "throne" (spelt *mšb*) ...*hrpy*... to be read *harpī* (contrast, e.g., *H hirpā*.)'.

Thus, the conclusion to be drawn is that the language must be considered as archaic *A*. J.C. Greenfield (1967–68:359ff.) comes to the same conclusion, and most of his points are identical with those made above.

The other traits that are not dealt with in Friedrich's article do not contradict this conclusion. A good survey of these points and of the opinions of other scholars is that of S. Segert (1958b).

A is also treated by G. Garbini (1960). This work is rich in bibliography but not entirely satisfactory; (see my review 1965, which was perhaps a shade too severe). Moscati (1964) is very bad. Often even his paradigms are wrong (not due to misprints!). In §16.68 (1964:146) he mentions Syriac *qāber*. This form does not and cannot exist in Syriac, where [e] > [a] before [r]. But since Moscati uses the root *qbr* for the verbal paradigm in Syriac, there appears on p. 147 (§16.72) the incorrect form *qabber*, while four out of five forms are listed incorrectly in the Syriac column on p. 148, four out of five again on p. 149, three out of five on p. 150, etc. Comparative Semitists should at least know the elementary grammatical rules of the languages they are dealing with. On p. 104 (§13.8) he mentions '*antī* in *BA*, on p. 140 (§16.47) *qabartēn* in *BA*; these forms do not exist in *BA*. Moscati was apparently misled by the reconstructed (!) forms listed in Rosenthal's Grammar (see below and also my review 1966). But the bibliography of this volume is useful, as is that of G. Garbini (1966:59ff.). Another extensive review of Moscati (1964) was published by Dahood, Deller, and Köbert (1965).

C. Brockelmann dealt with *A* and *S* (1954:135–62), with many bibliographical references, and added a few linguistic remarks. However, I dissociate myself from his view (1953:136) that *yqḥw* 'they took' in Hadad 12 is a *C* loan, cf. *E*. As to *wyʿnny*, Koopmans' (1962) solution (see 3.1 above) is to be preferred. The article is disappointing.

H.B. Rosén (1959) believes that *zy* in the first line of the ZKR inscription is still a demonstrative pronoun (nominative) and not (yet) the relative pronoun. In view of *mlkyʾ ʾl zy mḥʾw* which he does consider a relative, his interpretation seems doubtful (in spite of his explanation). I am also very much in doubt concerning his explanation of *ʾšr* as relative pronoun (which is only *H*, but neither *A* nor *C*); it most probably means 'inscription', cf. Donner and Röllig (1962–64). H. Schuster also touches upon the problem of the relative pronoun in the *Landsberger* volume. He maintains (1965: 441) on the basis of the Panammu: inscription 1–2: *šḥth ʾzh hwt* 'Verderben ... das ... war' that 'durch den Absolutus *šḥth*' it is proven 'dass der relativische Passus attributiv zum Leitnomen steht und nicht untergeordnet ist [as, e.g., in *Ak* where the noun is in construct before the relative clause] durch das feminine Demonstrativum *ʾzh*, dass dieses mit dem femininen Leitnomen in Genus kongruiert'.

This is by no means certain. Schuster was misled by Donner and Röllig (1962–64) who failed to note that there is another, apparently more probable, reading: *ʾlh:* (translated: 'conspiracy') instead of *ʾzh:* (cf. Cooke 1903:175).

But he certainly is right concerning another point (Schuster 1965:442): 'die Verwendung von *zy/dy* in der Genitivverbindung beruht auf einer Lehnübersetzung aus dem Akkadischen.' Since this construction is generally considered to be *A* even by scholars of the stature of W. von Soden (see 3.4 below), I think it might be useful to adduce some support for this assumption.

The assumption of the *Ak* origin of this construction seems to be borne out by the following facts: 1) It does not occur in *OA* (as Schuster and others have also pointed out) except for one case (Schuster 1965:441, fn. 44) which can be interpreted differently. 2) As in other *SL*, *OA* (and sometimes even in *OfA*), the preposition *l-* seems to have been employed with an undetermined antecedent (Bauer and Leander 1927: 311f.), and perhaps also in the Bir-Rakab inscription, line 17–19, in *E*, where *brly*, etc., means 'a son of mine' (the later construction *zyl-* [di:l-] also occurs; see instances Leander 1928:123 i), or where we find *lʾ hwt ʾrq ldrgmn* 'it was not a field of Dargman' (Cowley 1923:No. 6, 1.7). Cowley's translation ('the field') fits neither the grammar (*ʾrq* is undetermined) nor the context. 3) On the weights, which also bear an *Ak* legend, we find *mnm* 15 *b zy ʾrqʾ* (15 double (?) minas of the country). This is the earliest attestation of this construction in *OA*. Not only does it parallel the *Ak* legend (*manē ... ša ... kaspi*) (cf. Cooke 1903:192, *Corpus Inscriptionum Semiticarum* II. 1–14) which in itself would be remarkable, but *zy* here is employed after an undetermined noun. Now *zy* as a relative pronoun goes back to a demonstrative pronoun, therefore of course, at least at its inception, it cannot have been employed with an undetermined antecedent. After an undetermined antecedent, only the construction with *l-* was possible (cf. *Ar*, *H*, e.g. *mizmo:r ləDa:wi:d*, 'a psalm of David' and the *A* instances quoted above). On these weights, dating back to the eighth century B.C., it is, to say the least, strange. Since it parallels in this respect the *Ak* legend, and considering the fact that the weights were found in *Ak*-speaking territory, in Nineveh, the conclusion is that it is a calque of the parallel *Ak* text (*Ak* does not possess the article). 4) The *Ak ša*, pure and simple, instead of the *A zy*, seems to have been used in Ne:rab as a 'free genitive': *š'gbr* (and probably) *ššnzrbn* 'of (belonging to) Abgar', etc. (Cooke 1903:186, 189) which seems to indicate that the native *zy* in this role was still felt to be strange.

M.M. Bravmann, in his highly interesting study on the 'Genetic aspects of the genitive in the Semitic languages' (*JAOS* 81.386ff., 1961), also deals with this construction. However, since he disregards *OA* and the possibility of *Ak* influence, his conclusions drawn from *BA* can scarcely be regarded as decisive.

In short, the *A* genitive construction *ša* is most probably a calque from *Ak*.

B. Landsberger has contributed several good observations to the interpretation of some *OA* inscriptions (1948:60–70). They of course were utilized by Donner and Röllig (1962–64) and Koopmans (1962) (why did the latter not mention the excellent explanation of *wrṣt bglgl* of Panammu:?). Especially important is his remark (Koopmans 1962:fn. 169): 'Der letzte König von Damaskus ist nicht Ra-ṣun-nu zu lesen, sondern ra-ḫi-a-nu, d.i. Raʿyān. Im *AT* (Altem Testament) wird sein Name in kanaanäischer Aussprache überliefert als *RṢYN*, das ist Raṣyān ...' This assumption has been proven correct by the spelling *rṣy'n* of the Dead Sea Scroll Isaiah (see Kutscher 1959:90 where the problem is discussed). The form as established by Landsberger therefore apparently indicates that at that time (eighth century B.C.) the *PS* /ḑ/ was a ready realized as /ʿ/. But in the parallel *OA* texts it is still the sign /q/ which is employed for the notation of the *PS* /ḑ/, apparently, because the phone had no sign of its own and its realization, as is generally assumed, at some (previous) time was close to that of /q/ (but not identical with it). This spelling /q/ occurs in the very root discussed (cf. Jean and Hoftijzer 1965) = *PS rḑy, H rṣy, OA rqy, LA rʿy*. Therefore, we are compelled to assume that the *OA rqy* already represents an historical spelling!

Incidentally, this hypothesis seems to be supported by *mḥ'w* of the ZKR inscription = *PS mxḑ* > *OA mḥ'* (< **mhʿ* by dissimilation, cf. *'a:ʿ* < **ʿa:ʿ* 'wood'), instead of **mḥq* (which seems to have penetrated early Biblical Hebrew (*BH*) — Song of Deborah — cf. Wagner 1966:74).

But, as Prof. M. Greenberg informs me, Dr. L. Levine has come across in *Ak* a spelling with /q/! The above interpretation, therefore, is at least dubious. Both spellings might represent an attempt to transliterate in *A* an unfamiliar phone.

K. Aartun (1959) tries to show that the definite article did not originate from [*'*a:*] or [*ha:], but from [*ya:']. He tentatively identifies this element with the *Ar* [ya:], but has difficulty in accounting for the loss of the final /'/ in *Ar*. In addition, he overlooks the fact that Ugaritic (*U*) too knows only [y] (= **ya:*). In spite of these (and other) difficulties, his hypothesis should not be rejected out of hand.

S. Segert (1958b: 578–84) also deals with the problem of the definite article. He believes the ['] to be *mater lectionis*, employed for the final [a:]. The newly edited fragments of Sefîre have again shown that this sign is nearly always used only for the article (cf. Fitzmyer 1967:147), and not to indicate the feminine ending [a:]. This fact, as well as the overwhelming majority of the cases in *E*, does seem to indicate the (originally) consonantal character of the [']. On the other hand, the Hermopolis papyri might be adduced to show that at that period at least the ['] was just a *mater lectionis*, despite the consistent spellings of *E* (i.e. ['] for the article, [h] for the feminine ending), which are, in general, contemporaneous with the Hermopolis papyri; cf. p. 368.

F. Rundgren (1955:128 ff.) could have dealt with the problem of *šmrg*, which apparently means 'became ill' of the Panammu: inscription. The root seems to be *PS mrḏ* = *A mrʿ* (Sefîre *mrq*, Fitzmyer 1967:48); for *PS* /ḏ/ = /g/, see Brockelmann 1928 s.v. *gḥk*. The problem is that since the *šapʿel* in A most probably goes back to *Ak* (cf., e.g., Speiser 1939), can we expect to find this form as early as this period (when, as yet, it does not seem to exhibit any trace of *Ak* influence)?

C. Rabin (1969) went thoroughly into the problem of 'The nature and origin of the šafʿel in Hebrew and Aramaic'. The material he marshalled is very impressive. He mentions *šmrg*, discussed above. I am inclined to agree with his statement that this is a loan-translation from *Ak* (1969:150, fn. 11), especially in view of the context (it occurred in the Assyrian camp).

His conclusion is that 'the šafʿels were thus borrowed by Aramaic, Hebrew and Arabic from a language that had also preserved as a separate phoneme the sibilant found in these three morphemes, and was geographically contiguous with the three languages named. It is suggested that this language was "Amorite"' (Non-Hebrew Section, 1969:138).

I am still dubious, in spite of his eloquent arguments. If we glance at his material we immediately realize that the overwhelming part of it comes from *S* or *PCA* (that was influenced by *S*). On p. 149, e.g. from among seventeen instances ten are to be found only in *EA*, while the others are common to other dialects as well. Considering that *S* was profoundly influenced by *Ak* in all the linguistic spheres, it would not be easy to explain away this fact. The cases of safʿel (and there are more than generally assumed) also fit into this picture: šafʿel is Babylonian, while safʿel is Assyrian ([š] > [s] in Assyrian). In addition, it could hardly be a coincidence that among the three roots that are employed in *BA* in the šafʿel two are undeniably *Ak*, and the third highly probably so, cf. Bauer and Leander (1927:92, i).

'Most Aramaic causatives with *š*- prefix seem to be loanwords from Akkadian', says Deller (Dahood, Deller, and Köbert 1965:41), and I am inclined to agree with him. This view, of course, does not exclude the possibility of analogical extension, e.g. [šaʿbed] 'to enslave'.

S. Segert, in his article on 'Ugaritisch und Aramäisch' (1965), treated the isoglosses between *U* and *A*. The results are indeed very meager. The only isogloss to be reckoned with is the fact that *PS* /ḏ/ > /d/ in both languages. All the other characteristics stressed by Segert are nearly always extremely doubtful or irrelevant to the problem.

3.3 *Dictionaries; Proper Nouns*

Jean and Hoftijzer (1965) contains the *A* material (besides *H* and Phoenician-Punic) down to *GA*. /ʾ/–/k/ was prepared and published during the lifetime of Jean, and included *U*, but after his death the fascicles were reissued by the publisher, edited by Hoftijzer who dropped the *U*. Hoftijzer's work is more satisfactory. Vinnikov (1958–65) is only concerned with *OA* and *OfA*, including proper nouns. His dictionary also serves as a concordance, since it lists, sometimes in extenso, all the occurrences. Both are accurate. S. Segert (1967:465) compared letter *q* in both and found a few more words in Vinnikov's dictionary, while 'the comparison for the letter *t* has shown practically complete agreement.' Neither of them as a rule indicates etymology, but sometimes both do include some such reference; Jean and Hoftijzer (1965) very often refers to articles dealing with the lexeme, and Vinnikov less so (1958–65). On the other hand, Vinnikov quite often quotes parallel passages from the Jewish Aramaic (*JA*) literature (sometimes very extensively), e.g. s.v. *ʾḥrn*. For example, both dictionaries mention (or hint at) the *Ak* origin of *ʾgr* 'wall' but not that of *ʾgwrʾ* 'temple'. It certainly would help to find e.g. under *gmḥ*, in Jean-Hoftijzer (Palmyrenean), the Greek translation of the lexeme from the parallel Greek inscriptions of Palmyra, as well as a reference to Nöldeke's and Hoffmann's articles dealing with its origin (*ZA* 9. 264, 329 [1894]). It is a pity that Jean and Hoftijzer were not consistent in indicating the pertinent literature. (For further discussion of *gmḥ*, see Eretz-Israel 8, *E.L. Sukenik memorial volume*, 273, Jerusalem, 1967, where *gmḥ*, *gwḥ*, *ku:k*, etc., are dealt with.) Yet in this respect there is still an important difference between the two works. Vinnikov does not include modern literature in his references (note *ʾwdys*, *ʾzd*, *ʾzt*, *ʾrdkl*, *ʾrṣtʾ*, *bdykr*, etc.) apparently because none was available to him, whereas Jean and Hoftijzer do. Also see *ʾpś* where the explanation of Lidzbarski is quoted but not that of Albright (this is a place name and therefore missing in Jean and Hoftijzer); see e.g. Donner and Röllig 1962–64: II.210. While *ʾnḥnn* in Vinnikov is of course a misprint (= *ʾnḥn*), it is strange that *by* and *bytʾ* are listed under two different headings. On the other hand, Hoftijzer lists *A mḥʾ* under the heading *mḥy*. These two lexemes differ both in meaning and etymology. One may hope that new editions of Jean and Hoftijzer (1965) and Vinnikov (1958–65) will remedy this situation. Otherwise, the early literature in particular will be lost to *A* lexicography.

M. Liverani, in his 'Antecedenti dell'onomastica aramaica antica' (1962), believes 'i dati concordi della lingua e della cultura mostrano una assai notevole continuità al tempo della formazione degli stati aramaici' (76). Landsberger's reading *Ra-ḫi-a-nu* (above p. 353) seems to have escaped Liverani's attention (67). He also does not indicate that one of the forms he adduces there, *Ra-ṣun-nu*, parallels that of the Septuagint of *H* [Rəsi:n]. Why should *Mtʿl* of Sefîre be 'ibrido semitico-hurrita'

(71)? The root *mtʿ* occurs in South-Arabic inscriptions, as H. Bauer had noted, and the name 'has been found to belong to a Dedanite king ... [and] occurs in a Nabataean inscription' (Fitzmyer 1967:25).

I do not understand the title of G.R. Driver's article 'Aramaic names in Accadian texts' (1957). It does not deal with *A* names in *Ak*, but with *Ak*, *P*, *Ar*, and Egyptian names in *A* texts. Neither do I believe that this kind of treatment, which covers several centuries, different geographical areas, and various languages, can be of real use to *A* linguistics, in spite of the author's extensive knowledge evidenced here.

3.4 *Aramaic in Other Languages*

A in *Ak*. In a very important article, von Soden (1966) discussed the lexicographical influence of *A* on *Ak*. The article was long overdue. Von Soden had stated (1952: §192b-c, §196b-c) that Aramaisms are already to be found in 'Neubabylonisch' (1000–625 B.C.) and in 'Neuassyrisch' (1000–600). As for 'Spätbabylonisch' (after 625) he said 'ist noch stärker aramaisiert als das Neubabylonische ... es bedarf als Mischsprache eigentlich einer eigenen Darstellung' (1952:§193a). (The paragraphs that deal with *A* traits in *Ak* can be traced conveniently by perusing §§192, 193, 196. Also see von Soden 1959:149.) However, I.J. Gelb (1955:97a), reviewing von Soden's volume, countered by saying: 'From my acquaintance with Late Babylonian texts, I can say that I could go through dozens of these texts without finding a single Aramaism.' Von Soden's article (1966) thus seems to go some way toward the solution of the problem of lexical Aramaisms in these texts. While I can concur from the viewpoint of *A* with most of his assertions, I must take exception to several points; see below.

The introduction, in which von Soden deals with methodological aspects of this difficult field, is very important. I agree with nearly all the points he makes there. The man who works in this field should be one who 'mit Lexicon und Grammatik des Akkadischen des 1. vorchr. Jahrtausends gut Bescheid weiss' (von Soden 1966:1) and 'ist es wichtig festzustellen, wann ein aramäischer Herkunft verdächtiges Wort in Keilschrifttexten zuerst auftaucht' (1966:3–4). Let me add that the same should apply to *A*. Especially concerning this second point, von Soden does not avoid the pitfalls that sometimes make problematic E.S. Rimalt's otherwise good article (1932). Rimalt overlooked entirely the *A* inscriptions; he therefore attributed traits that occur only in *LA* to the *Ak* influence on *A*, as does von Soden to a certain extent. Rimalt states, for example, that the construction *māršu ša* 'son of' results from the influence of *A*. He is not aware that this construction, so common in *A*, is missing in *OA*, and first appears only in the Behistun inscription where it parallels the *Ak* version. In *Ak* it is already found in Old Babylonian and Old Assyrian (von Soden 1952:§138j). Thus there is no reason to assume that *māršu ša* is a calque from *A*, especially since the *ša* genitive (without the proleptic suffix) is also practically non-existent in *OA* (see above 3.2 in dealing with Schuster). It is more probable that this characteristic, as some others, originated in *Ak* and penetrated *A*. The same holds true concerning his statement: 'im Alt- und Reichsaramäischen ... *n* an den folgenden ... Konsonanten ... nicht assimiliert wurde.' There is not even one safe case of non-assimilation to be found in *OA* (cf., e.g., Fitzmyer 1967:150). But since in the contemporary *Ak* texts it does exist (von Soden 1952:§32), the reverse explanation would seem to be true. See Kutscher (1965:37–9), and Ginsberg (1936:96-7).

Von Soden states that, regrettably, because of the lack of extensive collections 'die vielen aramäischen Personen, Götter- und Flurnamen in akkadischen Texten ausser Betracht lasse'; see his note to K. Deller in *Or* 34.473ff. (1965). Still, the article is a very important contribution to the research on *OA* and *OfA*. I generally agree with his statements, a few instances excepted. The root *gᵉḏa* (1966:9) does not have the meaning 'abschneiden' in *A*. What he has in mind is *gdd*! *hānā* (1966:6) is not *A*, only *S*; therefore it is at least problematic whether the Neo-Assyrian (before 600 B.C.) *ḫanniu* owes its existence to the *S hānā* (several hundred years later); in the *OA* and *OfA* inscriptions only *zn, znh, h' znh, dnh*, etc., are attested. Therefore *hn'*, despite its use as ideogram in Middle Persian, cannot be considered to be an early form (pace Rosenthal 1939:81). *Mâlatu* 'als Terminus für Gersten- und Dattelopferlieferung' (von Soden 1966:16) seems to have a quite close parallel in [məle:atka:] 'the gift (of your harvest)', Exod. 28:22. There is an instance of a 'Rückwanderer' in his list appearing in his second article (von Soden 1968:265): *sagānu* = *A səgana* < *Ak šaknu*. The proper *A* form, however, is **səgan*, determinate **signa:*, as shown by the Targum (Sperber's edition), e.g. in Jeremiah 20:1. The *Ak* form, therefore, seems strange. I am less convinced about **ḫarurtu* 'Gurgel' (1966:10).

Von Soden sometimes tends to view as *A* an *Ak* lexeme without attempting to prove that it is indeed an *A* loan in *Ak*, and not vice versa. *Egertu* 'Brief' (1966:8) has no known *A* etymology, and Aramaists used to look to *Ak* (and to other languages) for its origin. *Gurābu* 'Sack' (1966:9), too, has no *A* etymology; the same is true of *lūlītu* 'Pfeilspitze' (1966:11), and of *nibzu* 'Dokument' = *OfA nbz* (von Soden 1968:261). The fact that almost none of these lexemes is documented in *WA* does not favor von Soden's contention. On the other hand, he seems to be overly cautious as to '*nasīku* ... Aramäerscheich-fürst ... < *nsīkā* [read: *nəsīkā*, E.Y.K.]?' The *A* lexeme is attested in *Aḥi:qar*. '*Qu-ub-bal* ... Empfang der Quittung' < *A qbl*: 'Die Vokalisierung könnte auf ein Passiv deuten: wir kennen aber aram. Passiv des Puʿal Typus nicht' (1968:264). But we do. Exactly the same lexeme with exactly the same meaning is to be found in *S* (Brockelmann 1928:642a). The *qutta:l* pattern, as is well known, serves as a verbal noun (which is neutral as to the diathesis) of the Paʿel in *S*. He is certainly wrong in saying that *OA* does not have the assimilation of [n] (1966:17); the opposite is true (see, e.g., Fitzmyer 1967:150).

The same reservations in regard to von Soden's article also hold for that of Aro (1963:405–6). He says 'dass in n(eu)/sp(ät) B(abylonisch)', constructions like *ina muḫḫi imērē ša ina pān* PN 'betreffs der Esel, die zur Verfügung PN's stehen', i.e. where a prepositional expression used adverbially is preceded by *ša* 'wieder reichlicher (erscheinen) .... Es ist möglich, dass hier ein Einfluss des Aramäischen vorliegt', cf. Ezra 7:25. The trouble here, too, is that as far as I am aware in the *OA* inscriptions no clear-cut case is to be found of such a construction (which is very common in *LA*). This of course might be just coincidence. At any rate, *OfA* cannot serve as a basis for this assumption, since there the reverse is also possible.

A in *BH*. This field was also in need of a new approach, mainly because our knowledge of *OA* and *OfA* has grown tremendously since E.F. Kautzsch's work (see Rosenthal 1939:41–3). G.R. Driver tackled the problem of *A* in Biblical Hebrew (*BH*) in an important article (1953), which should be read carefully by every scholar interested in the problem, for he very clearly sets forth all the difficulties encountered working in this field. His main conclusions are: '(i) the *A* is by far the largest single extraneous element in the *H* language and (ii) the percentage of words found otherwise only in *A* is far higher in poetry than in prose' (1953:35). It is especially the second conclusion that will have to be considered carefully, and the material sifted (e.g. *mll* [1953:30] is not only poetic).

Driver is certainly right in saying: 'Many if not most of the supposed Aramaisms, at any rate of those found in the pre-exilic literature, possibly or probably descended from the old common Semitic stock on which the vocabularies of the several languages were based. *They may be called "Aramaisms" only in the sense that they cannot otherwise be traced except in Aramaic*' (1953:36) [my italics, E.Y.K.].

Finally, a resurvey of the whole field was undertaken by M. Wagner (1966). There is no doubt that a very great amount of work and scholarship went into the making of this volume, but the fruits are not entirely satisfactory.

Kautzsch lists as certain Aramaisms 153 lexical items, traceable to 122 roots (p. 99), more than 150 items assumed to be of *A* origin by different scholars, and 41 of these 150, from 33 roots, which he considers very likely Aramaisms (p. 111). Wagner lists about 350 lexemes (he actually numbers only 333, but more than 30 words can be added since several numbers have multiple items, e.g. 6, and about 15 lexemes can be subtracted, e.g. 256–64, these having been dropped in the process of printing the volume). The difference between this figure and the corresponding one in Kautzsch's work (153 + 41 [+110 according to others]) is quite startling, but the reasons for this discrepancy are not difficult to discover.

Wagner (1966) lists about ten lexical items found in Ben-Sira. This is not justified: 1) Ben-Sira, not being part of the Old Testament, has no place in this work. 2) Wagner used the Ben-Sira texts found in the Cairo Geniza, i.e. of the Middle Ages. The Ben-Sira fragments unearthed by Y. Yadin in the excavation of Massada, dating from the first century B.C., have shown that the text of Ben-Sira was to a very large extent changed by the scribes of the Geniza fragments. 3) Wagner includes proper nouns in his list, e.g. 74c–74n.

But the main reason for the inflation of the material is the latitude of his notion of Aramaisms. Driver points out that 'many if not most of the supposed Aramaisms ...

might be proved *gemeinsemitisch* if the sources were available for tracking them down; but whether such words came into Hebrew directly or through Aramaic would be an insoluble problem in the majority of instances unless their form betrayed them ... The description of most of these words, except the last (i.e. words which ... preserved their original *A* forms), as Aramaisms therefore is *rather a philological convenience than a demonstrable fact*' (1953:37–8; my italics, E.Y.K.). It is very much to be regretted that Wagner stretched the notion of Aramaism so far. He should have heeded the warning of B. Stade (referred to by Driver 1953:36, fn. 2): 'Not every word which *H* shares with *A* must necessarily be regarded as an Aramaism.'

Wagner (1966) lists, e.g., the *H* [ʾᵉno:š] as Aramaism, in spite of its clear-cut *H* form (*A* [ʾᵃna:š]), and in spite of the fact that the word is also found in *Ar*. This item is missing in Kautzsch's work (absent even in the list of suspected Aramaisms). An extreme case is that of the root *šḥr* 'to be black' and its derivates (304d-h). His argument leaves the reader speechless. He says, 'Da der Stamm nur exil[isch]/nachex[ilisch] belegt ist in Aram., aber gut beheimatet erscheint, kann ein A[ramaismus] in Betracht gezogen werden. Gewisse Bedenken erregt freilich der Umstand, dass erstens nicht alle hebräische Derr[ivate] aram[äische] Entsprechungen aufweisen ... und zweitens ein so alltägliches Begriff bloss Thr. 4,1 [postexilic! E.Y.K.] ... *ʿmm* ... zu Syn[onym] hat.' He thus cannot point to even one pre-exilic case where the notion 'black' has to be expressed and where another root is employed. And yet the root *šḥr* comes from *A*! It goes without saying that there is not a shred of evidence for his assumption.

On the other hand, some Persian loans are listed as Aramaisms, despite the fact that they are not attested in *A*, e.g. no. 9. Also words that are based on emendation of the *BH* text appear in his list, e.g. nos. 109a, 111. There are many instances where Wagner himself is very much in doubt (and always with reason) as to the *A* origin, e.g. [ʾaso:n]. To Wagner's list should be added *mille(ʾ)t* 'well', which was discovered in *GA* (Kutscher 1950:59). Also, the problem of *A* calques in *BH* (Wagner 1966:151; some of those listed there are *A*, e.g. [ʿᵉba:d]) deserves a more thorough treatment. I, for one, would add, e.g., [za·ka·r] Malachi 1:4; see my article on *A* calques in *H* (Kutscher 1963–64:118ff.). In that article, I also deal with what might be termed 'inverted calque'. *BH* employs the root *qwm* = 'to get up' and *ʿmd* = 'to stand'. In Late *BH*, at the height of the *A* influence, *ʿmd* carries both meanings (also in *MH*). Since *A* also uses only one lexeme for both meanings, it stands to reason that the change in *BH* indicates the influence of *A*, the content being *A* but the sign *H*.

I would suggest that a new edition of Wagner 1966 should carefully distinguish between early (poetic) Aramaisms as defined by Driver, and late Aramaisms existing only in later *BH*. The early Aramaisms should be divided into 1) those whose form betray them as Aramaisms (e.g. *mḥq*, no. 160a, *H mḥṣ*, see above 3.1), and 2) those whose *A* origin cannot be proven (e.g. *ʾty*). Also, those lexemes, mainly Persian, that are not attested in *A* but where *A* might have been the intermediary, should be listed separately. Another list should enumerate those Late *BH* lexemes, whose *A* origin is not definitely established. All this could be done by adding a short appendix to this otherwise good work.

I would like to add that the part dealing with grammatical Aramaisms seems to be more reliable than that treating lexical Aramaism.

3.5 *Gains*

I believe that one major gain from the new material was the discovery that *OA*, like *H*, had a special infinitive absolute (cf. Fitzmyer 1967:105); only the Targum Onqəlos (*TO*) and *S* were known to have an infinitive absolute in the Qal [maqta:l]. It was established beyond any doubt that *OA* also possessed an infinitive without prefixed *m-* for the Qal. This form should not be considered as a loan from *C*, since the *qəṭa:l* type is also employed as an infinitive in several *A* dialects (Maʿlu:la, *MdA* dialects of the East). In Sefîre there is one case which seems already to indicate the shift /d̲/ > /d/, and perhaps another indicating the shift /t̲/ > /t/ (Fitzmyer 1967:138). As to *Ktk*, see Degen (1967:56–60).

3.6 *Desiderata*

A great deal remains to be done in the field of *OA*. First of all, the texts should be re-edited with a short, mainly linguistic, commentary, which should not hesitate to point up the problems that are as yet unsolved. Fitzmyer (1967) took the first step in the right direction. The field cries out for a descriptive, historical, and comparative grammar. It is to be hoped that S. Segert's grammar which is scheduled to be published in the near future will fill this void. A grammar of *OA* by R. Degen has just appeared (cf. 3.2). The dictionaries, especially Jean and Hoftijzer (1965), should in, new editions, try to list the literature fully and develop into full-fledged etymological dictionaries. A special monograph should be devoted to the problem of a *C* substratum. In Sefîre, e.g., *ḥṣr* comes from *C* (cf. Baumgartner 1967:171), but, e.g., *lylh* is not *H* but *A*! J.C. Greenfield (1965–66:2–10) has collected a proportionately large number of idiomatic expressions in these inscriptions that 'have direct *H* equivalents'. He assumes them to be 'Idiomatic Aramaic', but I do not think that he intended to prejudge the issue of possible *C* influence (1964–65:15). The impact of *A* upon other languages, mainly upon *Ak* and *H*, should be treated comprehensively.

The impact of the *C* substratum upon *A* is dealt with by R. Stiehl (Altheim and Stiehl 1964:213–36). Her effort to establish the influence of the *C* substratum upon *OA* spelling is entirely unconvincing. I intend to deal with this problem (and the article by Miss Stiehl) elsewhere.

The influence of *A* upon *C* belongs to the following section (*OfA*), while speculations of *A* influences upon languages that predate the first millenium B.C. (before the appearance of *A* inscriptions), e.g. Mari, should be taken up in discussions of Northwest Semitic.

4. OFFICIAL ARAMAIC

4.0 *Preliminary Remarks*

Fitzmyer (1966:20, fn. 60a) says: '... the distinction [between Western and Eastern Aramaic] is clear in this phase [i.e. *LA*] of the language.' This statement is true as far as it concerns those traits that are generally considered to be the isoglosses that divide the two branches of *LA*, that is, '1) *l-* or *n-* as the prefix of the third person imperfect instead of the common *A y-*; 2) ... *e:* for common *A -ayya:* [and often for *-i:n*, E.Y.K.] as the ending of the masculine plural; 3) the loss of the determinative force of *-'a:* ...; 4) the elimination of *n-* bearing pronominal suffixes of the imperfect' (Ginsberg 1942:234, fn. 26). Ginsberg's notes, especially those pertaining to 3), should be read very carefully. Still, there remains little doubt that *Ak* was either the direct source, or the indirect one, emphasizing forms that may have existed in *A* but did not survive in *LA* of the West (especially concerning 1). However, Ginsberg's contention that 'it had not yet triumphed completely long after *Ak* had ceased to exercise any influence' is scarcely relevant, since the prefix *y-* occasionally crops up even much later in *ATB* (the incantation texts, and in Gaonic literature) which shows that it could be considered an archaism even in earlier times. It always takes time for a substratum (here = the *n-*, *l-* prefixes) to surface. On the other hand, the fact that there is no trace of the ending *-e:* in *OA* and — except for '*mm*' twice in Aḥi:qar — in *OfA* and even later, should make us wary of Ginsberg's assumption that it might be original in *A*.

To these four points should be added: 5) the syntagm *qti:l l-* employed in the East as perfect (later as preterit), unknown in the West. This syntagm is an offshoot of the *P* impact. For the time being, without thorough and reliable works on the syntax of the *LA* Western dialects, we prefer not to take into account the mainly syntactic features mentioned below.

But, as H. L. Ginsberg puts it in his review of Rosenthal 1939 (1942:232), '... official Aramaic was never absolutely uniform except in intention, and ... in course of time, especially after the destruction of the Achaemenian empire, became more and more colored by the spoken languages of the writers.' Perhaps we could phrase this statement a bit differently: *OfA*, originating in the territory of the (later) *A* dialects of the East (according to Ginsberg 1933:8), was unable to uproot the *A* spoken by Arameans coming from the territory of the (later) *A* dialects of the West.

The origin of quite a large part of the material in question can be safely traced to the East, despite the fact that the place of its discovery is Egypt in this respect. This is clear sometimes from the content (the Driver documents [1954], see below 4.1), sometimes from the historical context (the Behistun inscription), and sometimes from the local color (the story of Aḥi:qar). Also, it can be assumed that in a petition to a high official (e.g. Cowley 1923:30) an attempt would be made to imitate the *OfA* of the Eastern type, no matter where it was composed.

On the other hand, it may be assumed that in private letters there was less of a tendency to imitate *OfA* when the writers came from the West, and the same would apply to legal documents, which tend to be more conservative than other written material.

If, then, we are able to establish both that this material differs from the Eastern, and that its language is close to that of *OA* (coming from the West), we may tentatively assume that it represents a Western variety of *OfA*.

The 'new' *EA* features are, admittedly, not quite as clear-cut as those that divide the two branches of *LA* (see p. 361), since there was no escape from the all pervasive influence of *OfA*. Still, they cannot be disregarded. What should be decisive is the accumulation of these features, not their sporadic occurrence. Therefore, I would suggest dividing the material into two types: Western *OfA*, quite close to *OA*, and Eastern *OfA*.

The characteristics of the Eastern type of *OfA* are: 1) Excessive use of the genitive construction +*zy* (=[di:]). 2) In particular, the use of the proleptic suffix of the type [be:teh di:] (see 3.2) — both absent from *OA*. 3) An excessive use of the possessive pronoun *zyl-* (=[di:l-]) instead of the possessive suffix. 4) The object (often) precedes the infinitive. 5) The object (often) precedes the finite verb. 6) The subject (often) precedes the verb. 7) The syntagm *qəti:l l-* employed as perfect. 8) An excess of *Ak* and *P* loans and loan-translations. All these traits are absent in *OA*.

As to 1) and 2), see above 3.2. 4)-6) have been dealt with by Baumgartner (1927); concerning Sefîre, see also Fitzmyer 1967:168–9. Concerning 6), I do not agree with Fitzmyer; I found about 45 cases of the order of verb-subject against 15 of subject-verb (presumably this indicates that the subject is stressed), a ratio of 3:1. These traits apparently go back to the impact of *Ak* and *P* upon *OfA*, except possibly for 3), which already occurs in the Assur letter.

Again, as we have said, only an accumulation of these features due to the overwhelming influence of Eastern *OfA* can be considered decisive.

The following (important) texts dealt with by Rosenthal (1939) may therefore be considered to belong to Eastern *OfA*:

The Assur letter. Traits 1) (1. 14, 21[2]). 2) Absent. 3) (only once, l. 13). 4) No instance (i.e., no possibility of documentation). 5) Baumgartner (1927:129) 'nur Vorausnahme des Objekts'. 6) Baumgartner (*ibid.*) 'beide Stellungen gleich häufig'. 7) Absent. 8) One instance of *Ak* calque (11. 19, 20, see commentaries).

The Behistun inscription. Traits 1) (1. 25, 40) (paralleled by the *Ak* version!). 2) (e.g. 1. 5, 10, 28, apparently 23*, there also paralleled by *Ak*!). 3) (e.g. 5,20*). 4) The object always follows the infinitive (the same phrase), paralleling the *Ak* version. 5) The object generally follows, but sometimes precedes the verb, again apparently in accordance with the *Ak* version. 6) Passim. 7) Absent. 8) *Ak* *ʾlwk* 1. 23, *brtʾ* 1. 2, [*p*]*ḥtʾ* 1. 18. In addition, in Behistun, we can already observe 'the loss of the determinative force of (the definite article) [-ʾa:]', one of the characteristics of (Later) Eastern Aramaic, see above p. 363, cf., e.g. (*lmʿbd qrb* ...) *ʿbdw qrbʾ* = ('to join battle'

...) 'joined battle', 1. 2, but (*lmʿbd qrb* ...) *ʿbdw qrb* 1. 4; see also 1. 20 and 1. 29.

The *story* of Aḥi:qar. Traits 1) (l. 60) 2) (e.g. 1. 3, 47, 55, 63). 3) (1. 48, 61, 63). 4) (1. 63). 5) (ll, 21, 24, 29, 53, 61, 66). 6) (2, 19, 47, 51, 56, 61, 77). 7) Absent. 8) (*ṣbyt, bb, hykl, mt, šzb, knwtʾ, srys* — cf. Cowley 1923:index). Some of these *Ak* loans do not occur at all in Western *A*.

The petition of the Jews to Aršam (Cowley 1923:30). Traits 1) (1. 5, 6, 9–10, 10, 10–11, 11, 12, 26). 2) (1. 18–19). 3) (1. 20). 4) No instance. 5)-6) cf. Baumgartner 1927:129: '[Subject] viel häufiger vorausgestellt als im Altaram, vgl. namentlich Pap 1 [= Cowley 1923:30] ... Beim Object ... Vorliebe für Vorausnahme ... so 1' [= Cowley 30]. 7) Absent. 8) Both *Ak* (*ʾgrh* 'letter') and *P* (1.2 *bny bytʾ*, cf. Rosenthal 1939:81, Driver 1954:41 as well as 1.13: *lnpšhm ʿbdw*, cf. Driver 1954:83 = *P* calque).

A different picture appears in the legal documents. Baumgartner has already pointed out (1927:129) that as for the word order the evidence seems to be conflicting: 'In den Urkunden ... sind beim Subjekt die Belege für beide Stellungen ungefähr gleich zahlreich. Jedenfalls findet man es sehr viel häufiger vorausgestellt als im Altaram, vgl. namentlich Pap 1 (= Cowley 30). Nachgestellt wird es namentlich in 2 Fällen: im Eingang der Urkunde, *ʾmr qwnyh* ... und ähnlich bei der Nennung des Schreibers, *ktb plṭyh* .... Beim Object haben einzelne Texte eine Vorliebe für Vorausnahme desselben ... So auch ständig in der Grussformel *šlm* ... *yšʾl* ... Die meisten Texte lassen es folgen ... Beim Infinitiv dagegen ist umgekehrt die Vorausnahme etwas häufiger ... *Nach welchem Prinzip sich die Texte auf die beiden Lager verteilen, ist nicht ganz festzustellen*' [my italics, E.Y.K.].

I believe that we can solve this problem. It boils down to the difference between deeds, in which the wording does not change too easily, and administrative documents that try to keep as close as possible to the Eastern *OfA*. The very instances Baumgartner adduces, the opening and the closing sentences of the deeds that follow the word order verb-subject-object, prove our point. Since the framework of the deeds is apparently of *A* origin (no parallels were found, to the best of my knowledge, in the *Ak* deeds), it is not surprising that they preserved the West-Semitic (*OA*) word order. Within the deeds, of course, where the scribe had more leeway, other linguistic influences could assert themselves and the word order is therefore likely to be that of *OfA*.

Muffs, in his study (1969:196), deals with the legal aspect of the *E* papyri but has also handled well their linguistic aspect: 'My investigations into the N[eo] A[ssyrian] background of many terms and clauses used in the deeds (1969:179–92) has to be coordinated with Kutscher's studies concerning the syntactical orientation of the language of the deeds [see Kutscher 1954:243ff. and 1950:590–1]. While the content of the deeds points, at least in part, to a *NA* (political) milieu, the language of the deeds points to a Western milieu. I would suggest the following tentative synthesis of these two points of view:

'The indigenous legal tradition of second millenium Syria-Palestine (reflected in the deeds of Ras Shamra and Alalakh, and in contemporary West-Semitic legal loanwords into Egyptian) were taken over by the first millenium Aramean dynasties of the West ... thus, the Elephantine formulary, with its Western linguistic orientation, must be, at least in part, a reflex of the Old Aramaic formulary. These, then, are some of the historical implications of Kutscher's grammatical investigations.

'However, the strong *NA* component in the Elephantine formulary clearly indicates that this formulary is not simply a direct scion of the Old Aramaic one. Before it made its way to Egypt, it must have undergone a strong "Assyrianization" ... Although N[eo] B[abylonian], Egyptian and Persian elements were subsequently assimilated, the Elephantine formulary is based on Western ... tradition, with Reichsaramäisch (Eastern based) formulary based on Assyrian ones.'

I can wholeheartedly agree with this exposition by a legal scholar which confirms linguistic views that I have held for a long time. For a further very good instance of the survival of a formula phrase, see below.

On the other hand, the greeting formula, e.g. *šlm* ... *ʾlh yšʾl* 'the health ... may the God ... seek' (Cowley 1923:30 and in the letters), as this instance shows (petition to the *P* Aršama), is of course part and parcel of *OfA*, i.e. Eastern. This assumption is confirmed by the fact that this formula is paralleled exactly by the same introductory formula of the letters of the Neo-Babylonian, Neo-Assyrian, and Late-Babylonian periods, cf. E. Salonen 1967:78ff., especially 99–102.

We are, therefore, indeed entitled to maintain that the deeds are much closer in traits 4), 5), 6) to *OA* than Eastern *OfA*, since they seem to be descended from *A* of the territory of *OA* (Syria and Palestine), while of course they, too, are to a certain extent permeated by Eastern *OfA*.

As to the other traits, I found the following picture in Cowley 1, 5, 6, 8, 9, 10, 13, 14, 15, 20, 25, 28 — all of them deeds: 1) Quite frequently denoting material, and nearly always after an undetermined noun, which is indicative of its foreign origin. When the antecedent is undetermined we find the original construction + *l* as well, cf., e.g., *lḥn lyhw* Kraeling 1953:1,2, = 'a *lhn* of Yahu' (also e.g. 3,3,25; 12,1), Kraeling 2,2, = *lḥn zy yhw* (also, e.g. 4,2; 12,10; in No. 12 the scribe once employs the *l* construction and once the *zy* construction!). 2) 6 cases: 2, 6, 10; 15, 18–19, 30; 28, 3, 13. 3) This is an important point, since it goes a long way to prove our assumption of the *OA* origin of the legal documents. A certain legal phrase with slight variations occurs in nearly all these documents: *ʾnh wbr ly wbrh ly ʾḥ wʾḥh ly*, 'I and any son of mine and any daughter of mine, any brother and sister of mine', etc. (Cowley 6,12–13; Cowley's translation here 'my son' etc. is incorrect, but Cowley 8,12: 'son or daughter of yours' is accurate). This construction, as pointed out above, is in keeping with *H*, *Ar* (and Early *A*?) usage, since the noun is undetermined (cf. *Ar baytun li:* 'a house of mine'). The formula was more or less firm, but started crumbling at the end. Here we also find *P* loans *hngyt*, *hnbg*ʾ, etc. (see Cowley index). It is therefore very illuminating that in final position, although the noun is undetermined, we often find *zyl-* [di:l-], to wit, the independent possessive pronoun, which contains the relative pronoun (that originally could only be used with a determined noun, see above 3.2), cf. Cowley

8,12: *br wbrh lky w'yš zylky*'... any one belonging to you', 28,8: *br wbrh ly 'ḥ w'ḥh ly w'nš zyly* '... any dependent of mine', 43,9: *wbrh ly hngyt whnbg' zy l*[*y*] '... compatriot or partner of mine', but e.g. 25,10–11: *br wbrh lkm 'ḥ w'ḥh 'nth w'yš lkm*, while in Cowley 13, which in many respects is written carelessly, 1.8: *bny* (sic! = 'my sons') *wzr' zyly* '... my descendents', but Cowley 5,9: *lbr lh* 'a son of his'. The vacillation between the (old) *l* and (young) *zy*[*l*]- can also be discovered in predicative (and not attributive) use, e.g. Cowley 28, 5, 61 *lmbtḥyh* 'belonging to Mibṭaḥya: — instead of **zy mbtḥyh* and *lk yhwh* (Cowley 12) 'he belongs to you' — instead of *zylk yhwh*, but it is followed by *wzy bnyk* (and not **wlbnyk*). 4)-6) were dealt with above. 7) Absent. 8) There are, of course, *Ak* and *P* legal terms, loans and calques, which is not surprising, see above Muffs (1969).

It should also be mentioned that the particle *hn* 'if', when followed immediately by the verb, prefers (cf. *Ar*) the imperfect (see Kutscher 1954:234), which is also found in Sefîre (Fitzmyer 1967:171); incidentally, this might also be the reason for its use as future perfect in the apodosis of a condition (Fitzmyer 1967:170), since in all cases the conjunction *hnlhn* (=[*henla:hen]) precedes. (This usage also survives in *S*, Nöldeke 1898:§258.)

Another feature peculiar to the legal documents is the fact that the imperfect can be the direct object of another imperfect (without the relative pronoun). This also occurs in Sefîre (Fitzmyer 1967:172). It is scarcely a coincidence that exactly as in Elephantine (*E*) the verb *khl* figures dominantly in Sefîre as the governing verb, e.g. in *E wl' ykhl ... ygrnk*, 'nor shall ... be able to start against thee suit' (Kraeling 1953:3. 16–17), cf. in Sefîre *pl'khl l'šlḥ* 'then I shall not be able to raise'. (I am not convinced the second *l* equals the particle of negation; it might be the preposition-conjunction, as in *Ar*!). But again, it has to be admitted that *S* also has this feature (Nöldeke 1898:§§267, 368; one of the verbs listed by Nöldeke is *škḥ* 'to be able' = *khl*(!) in *E* and Sefîre). It is certainly no coincidence that *ykl* survived with this use not only in *SA*, but also in late *BH* where Aramaisms abound (Lamentations 4,14), as well as in *MH* (full of Aramaisms).

The *proverbs* of Aḥi:qar are somewhere in between, since some traits are of Western provenience, others Eastern (see below). 1) Only once, 1.84 (?). 2) Absent. 3) Absent. 4) Following the infinitive (one exception, 1.192). 5) Following the verb. 6) The subject apparently prefers to precede the verb. 7) Absent. 8) Apparently absent. But on the other hand, besides 6), we find a few more features of apparently Eastern origin: a) The dissimilation of emphatics, e.g. *hkṣr* < **hqṣr* (see Leander 1928:17), a phenomenon well known in *Ak* (and Mandaic) and also found sporadically in Western *A* (the Ne:rab inscriptions that also evidence this trait are already influenced by *Ak*, even the name *nrb* < *Ak ne:ribu* (root *'rb*!) (cf. Ginsberg 1936:96b). b) Particularly important is the plural ending [e:] of the noun, found twice in *'mm'* 'the peoples' (Leander 1928:102). c) The form of the ordinal *zy tlt'* 'the third' l. 92 (not recognized by Cowley!) is of a type found in *S* (Nöldeke 1898:§239, Ginsberg 1924–25:80) and Pa. Incidentally, this is the only trait which pinpoints the territory of origin of the proverbs (disregarding the time factor of course), since this construction is absent in all the other *LA* dialects. d) The fact that the infinitives of Paʿel and Hapʿel are formed by prefixed [m + *V] (see Leander 1928:51g) can point to *S* as well, but since this is the case e.g. in *GA*, the evidence is inconclusive. e) The use of *ʾyš* 'man', see below 4.2 regarding Bresciani and Kamil 1967. f) The employment of *ky* 'since, because', that occurs in *OA*, in the Adon letter, written in the West, but also once in the Assur letter (see Jean and Hoftijzer 1965).

How then are we to account for this apparent clash? We could always argue that the proverbs originated somewhere in the territory that lies between the Eastern and Western *A* territory (cf. the modern *A* dialect of Ṭur-ʿAbdin which shares some traits with the Modern Eastern group, some with the Western, see Jastrow 1967:x). But another solution is possible: proverbs keep wandering and it is therefore not surprising to find in them ingredients of many dialects.

It is impossible to deal here with the language of the letters of Cowley and of the ostraca. They more or less confirm the above picture, but the material requires a special study. As to the greeting formula, see above, p. 364.

These preliminary remarks were necessary to put into relief the gains achieved in the field by the discovery of new material. We can now proceed to the material itself.

4.1 *The Texts*

The most important discoveries were the texts published by Kraeling 1953, Driver 1954, Bresciani and Kamil 1966, and Bresciani 1960, as well as some shorter texts — the Adon letter and, especially, the ostraca published by Dupont-Sommer.

Kraeling 1953 (*Kr*)

The *Kr* volume comprises twelve legal documents preserved intact and five fragmentary texts. The work of Kraeling is in general well done. The historical introduction, the extensive commentaries and the glossary are all important.

These documents also fall into the category of Western *OfA*. Everything said above concerning Cowley 1923 (*Co*) also applies to them. Note especially the *l* construction (see 4.0 above).

The most important reviews and review articles to have been published about this volume are: Benveniste 1954, who is concerned here with only one aspect of the language of *Kr* and Driver 1954, i.e. the *P* loans; Cazelles 1955, reviewing both volumes; Couroyer 1954, dealing with Egyptian loans and loan-translations in *Kr* (see also his important remarks concerning Milik 1954a, pp. 251–3); Eilers 1954–58, also reviewing both volumes (see below p. 368); Ginsberg 1954; Kutscher 1954 (see also below); de Menasce 1954, on both volumes; Milik 1954a; Segert 1956, also on both volumes. Some of these articles do not deal with only the linguistic aspects of the new material.

While Benveniste's very important article only treats *P* loans and loan-translations, and Couroyer proceeds along the same line as to *Eg*, Eilers' approach is more general, but still important. (I am not, of course, qualified to express any opinion concerning the *quality* of works of Iranists.) However, Eilers does include a list of *P* proper nouns, as well as a list of *P* loans in both volumes. Ginsberg's notes help clarify several readings, while Kutscher deals with the problem of 'languages in contact' (the interpenetration of *A*, *Ak*, *Eg*, and *P* in the field of legal terminology, see below p. 389f.) Milik's notes, as usual, are very penetrating and revealing. De Menasce treats the Iranian element, while Segert tries to so use these texts that light is shed on *BA*.

Linguistically, except for new *Eg* (and *P*) loans, nothing really surprising has emerged. I would stress only one point: the form of the second person singular feminine (both of the perfect and the possessive suffix of the noun) is very often spelled 'incorrectly:' *-t*, *-k* (instead of *-ty*, *-ki*, normal to *Co*, see Kutscher 1954:236). Is this an archaism (of spelling) or an innovation, the vowel (which is still spelled [and not read] in *S*, but not in *LA*) having already been lost? *ʿṭyq* 'old' (instead of *ʿtyq*), that also occurs in Nisā, gives food for thought (note three occurrences in *Kr*).

Driver 1954 (*Dr*)

The *Dr* documents came out in two editions, the second shorter one being more reliable than the first unwieldy edition. Benveniste says (1954:299, fn. 5) in regard to the first edition: 'La présèntation matérielle de l'édition ... de format trop grand, peu maniable et inutilement coûteuse, grossie d'appendices d'une nécessité contestable ... ne laisse pas voir tout de suite que les documents comptent au total *moins de cent lignes*. Réédités en un format commode, avec la traduction et une annotation reduite à l'utile, ils tiendraient dans une mince brochure.' It might have been this view that prompted Driver to bring out the shorter edition in a small format. In this second edition, Driver of course could make use of the reviews of the first edition (*Dr*:vi). It comprises thirteen letters, apparently sent to Egypt from the East (Babylonia, Persia) in the late fifth century B.C. (*Dr*:10–12). It is impossible to establish Driver's indebtedness to those whose typescript he used in preparing the edition, i.e. E. Mittwoch, H.J. Polotsky, W.B. Henning, F. Rosenthal. Polotsky and Rosenthal were already outstanding Aramaists and Henning was an excellent Iranist, so their contribution must have been quite substantial. Driver might have indicated what he found in the typescript. (And, in the Preface, Driver does not mention that two letters, VII and VIII, had been previously edited by two other scholars.)

There is no doubt that the extensive commentaries (sometimes too extensive!) are helpful. But I cannot refrain from quoting Benveniste's view on the first edition again (1954:300, fn. 4): '... nous devons avertir que les notes relatives aux données iraniennes appellent bien des réserves. Il est probable qu'aucun des iranistes qui y ont contribué n'en approuverait la rédactione présente. Non seulement les inexactitudes matérielles abondent ... Un réviseur qualifié aurait récrit la plupart des remarques touchant à l'iranien, et n'eût surement pas laissé subsister la note de la p. 55 où gr.

κίταρις (= κίδαρις, sorte de tiare) est indentifié à la fois à av. *xšaθra-* et à hébr. *keθer.*' Eilers is also very critical of Driver's handling of the Iranian aspect (1954–56:331), as is also J. de Menasce (1954:161). I am therefore not inclined to accept the verdict of T. Jansma in *BiOr* 11.215 (1954) that it is a 'brilliant volume'. I should stress, however, that as far as I was able to check on the matter, Driver, in the second edition, took note of the criticism. (He was guided by Henning.)

While the historical introduction seems to be satisfactory, as do also the appendix and glossary, etc., the meagre paragraph (half a page, p. 19) on 'The Language of the Letters' is very disappointing. Driver does not seem to have grasped that the language of these letters is different from that in most of *Co* and of *Kr*. A good example of this shortsightedness is the fact that in No. VII he did not notice that in the construction *šmyʾ ly* (1.3) we have the first attestation in *OfA* of the *qəti:l l-* construction which is one of the characteristics of the Eastern branch of *LA* but is missing in the Western one; (this fact has been pointed out by Kutscher in his publication of this text in *Kedem* ([*H*] II.66–74, quoted very often by Driver). The *Dr* documents may thus be termed the most conspicuous representatives of Eastern *OfA*, the characteristics of which (see p. 361 above) are evidenced in the letters as follows: 1) Six attestations. 2) Two attestations. (But the construct, too, is comparatively rare, only 5–6 instances). 3) Very frequent; in letter no. 1 there are 9 attestations, and others are found in the other letters. 4) Absent, due probably to chance (there are only two instances of the opposite word order). 5) The object usually precedes the finite verb, but always *ydʿ tʿmʾ znh* 'is cognizant of this order' of (the final sentence of) the letters. 6) The subject nearly always precedes the verb. 7) The construction *qəti:l l-* occurs (see 4.0 above). 8) *P* loans (and a few *Ak*) are plentiful.

For reviews and review articles, see above concerning *Kr*. We must, however, mention Milik (1954) again. As usual, Milik has some important notes, but I must take exception to two of them which, because of their importance, should be dealt with here briefly. He says (1954:593): '*pyrmʾ* au lieu de *prymʾ* et *ʿylmy* au lieu de *ʿlymy* ... (indicate) une tendence à remplacer la form *qtil* par *qitl* au voisinage de *l*, *r* et des laryngales' (as in Qumra:n). His assumption concerning Qumra:n may be right, and it is paralleled by Middle Hebrew (*MH*) (see Kutscher 1963). But *ʿlymʾ* is, as we know from other *A* dialects, no *qaṭi:l* but a *qutayl* form! (cf. *TO* and *S*.)

Milik also says (p. 543): 'Dans *Gwzʾn* ... l'aleph comme mater lectionis me paraît tout à fait exclu pour cette époque.' But the spelling *ḥšyʾrš Co* 5,1 as against *ḥšyrš Co* 2,1 (but see Friedrich 1957:41, fn. 1) does show that a plene spelling with aleph at this period is entirely possible, especially in a proper noun. E. Y. Kutscher (1957) particularly stresses the importance of the constructions *qəti:l l-* (see above and below p. 377).

Bresciani and Kamil 1966 (*BrKa*)

Just as the *Dr* material is important because it is an excellent representative of Eastern *OfA*, so the material of *BrKa* is very important since it seems to be an outstanding representative of Western *OfA*. This fact was alluded to in the article by

Porten and Greenfield (1968; discussed below p. 370) and has been treated at length by Kutscher in his article (cf. p. 370). Considering the fact that Miss Bresciani is an Egyptologist and Mr. Kamil was known mainly as an Abyssinologist it must be stated that they acquitted themselves well. It is, however, strange that Miss Bresciani did not recognize a certain *A* phrase she had treated a few years earlier in the *Br* letters (see below p. 371).

The *BrKa* material comprises 8 letters: 1–6 and 8 written by the same scribe and sent by members of the same family; these are linguistically different from no. 7. There are no Jewish names (perhaps with one exception; contrast *Co*!). The time is the fifth century B.C.

Their Western *OfA* character becomes immediately clear. This is the picture that emerges when the above (4.0) traits are applied: 1) Absent. 2) Absent. 3) Absent. 4) There is no instance of infinitive + nominal object. 5) The accusative object generally follows the finite verb (no. 1-5:2; no. 2-about 10:0; no. 3-6:2; no. 4-3:1, etc.). 6) The subject generally follows the verb (no. 1-1:0; no. 2-0; no. 3-2:0; no. 4-1:0; no. 5-2:0). 7) Absent. 8) There are *Eg* loans, but no *P* and few *Ak* loans (except perhaps *ʾlp*, *gšr*? *tʿm*?; see index).

These traits would seem decisively to prove that the letters originated with people whose language was the Western type *OfA*. But there are some more traits which seem to clinch the matter: a) The spelling. Not only is the feminine ending [a:] spelled with *h* but, in nos. 1–6 and 8, also the endings of the status determinatus (instead of with ʾ). This fact immediately distinguishes these texts not only from the *E* texts (*Co* and *Kr*) and from *Dr* where the *h* is nearly always employed for the feminine ending and the ʾ for the status determinatus, but even from *BA*, where this division is not that clear-cut, but still very much in evidence. To be sure, this division also applies to *OA*. But on the other hand, this spelling is only present in the *LA* of the West: *SA* and to a large extent *GA* (see *Tarbiẕ* [*H*] 21.201), while *PCA* has adopted the *S* spelling along with the *S* script. In the Eastern *LA* dialects: *S*, *M*, and *ATB*, the ʾ practically dominates in both positions. b) In the feminine adjective and participle very frequently the ending is still the early *-t* and not the later *-h*. This ending occurs twice (three times?) in Sefîre (once in a proper noun), cf. Fitzmyer 1967:41. c) In keeping with the *OA* the [n] is assimilated except in one case (cf. also *BrKa* 1966: 368–9; Porten and Greenfield 1968; see above p. 357). d) As in the legal documents of *E* and Sefìer (see above p. 365) the root *ykl* is followed by the imperfect (and not by the infinitive (see 1,4; 5,5). e) Here, too, the conditional particle *hn* -*ʾn* is followed by the imperfect, see 4,9 (but 5,5 imperfect). f) Bresciani and Kamil are certainly right in assuming that '*ybl* possa essere passivo del peal e cosi anche *ywbl* in VII 5, con *scriptio plena*' (1967:382), but their other explanation is improbable, in view of *ywbl* (*ybl* active *paʿal* see, e.g. *Co* 12,3, Aḥi:qar 52). The imperfect pass. does not occur in *OfA* (perhaps in Aḥi:qar) but it is to be found in *OA*, in Sefîre, cf. Fitzmyer 1967:156 (Yuqtal). To be sure, there seem to be survivals in Palmyrene. g) *ʾš* 'man' (three times; *gbr* does not occur!) is to be found only in *OA* and *OfA* of the Western type, in the legal documents and proverbs of Aḥi:qar. It occurs only once in *Dr* (because of the alliteration with the following *bʾyš* 'harm'?).

There are a few more traits which separate the language of these letters from the other contemporary material, but since they cannot be localized we can disregard them here. One should, however, be mentioned: the contracted diphthongs (see also *BrKa* 1966:368 and Porten and Greenfield 1968:4). As mentioned above (3.2) these also occur in Sefîre and in *Kr*.

In short, these letters seem to represent a Western dialect of the *OfA*, while sharing, of course, with the other material some spelling and phonological traits with *A* (e.g. verbs tertiae aleph > tertiae yod, etc.)

To date I know of several reviews and review articles concerning *BrKa*. Of them all only Kutscher's is restricted to the linguistic aspect. See the review by Grelot (1967). His hypothesis (submitted hesitantly) to explain the assimilation of the *n* (see c above): 'le scribe était peut-être plus habitué à écrire des lettres en phénicien qu'à rédiger en araméen' (p. 434), is not acceptable, since there are quite a few words that are pure and simple *A*, for which this explanation is impossible. Besides, as shown above, there are a few more traits that are left unaccounted for (this thesis is rightly opposed by Porten and Greenfield 1968).

Nor does his view that 'l'hébreu et l'araméen n'emploient cette racine (i.e. *wbl*) qu'aux formes factitive' (p. 434) hold true for *A*; see the instances given in f) above. A few of his other remarks seem to be right, especially on *bʿn* being imperfect (and not participial), p. 436, (as the editors explain in the glossary!).

In his review (1971) E.Y. Kutscher points out the Western *OfA* traits of these letters and adds notes to the text (as well as a new interpretation of letter 1).

J.T. Milik's 1967 article, with its extensive indexes and glossaries, is important. As always, one cannot but marvel at the wide range of Milik's knowledge and his bold suggestions. The article merits very close scrutiny by all those interested in *A* scholarship, since it is not restricted to *OfA*. I do not, of course, accept his view (p. 550): 'Quant à la terminaison *-t* des féminines ... un cas frappant d'une Mischsprache ... araméenne et phénicienne'. As we have shown above (p. 369), *all* the traits found in these letters are also *A* traits. Many other suggestions in this wide-ranging article seem to be acceptable, e.g. Milik's explanation of *ʿrq ʾlp* as 'allez au devant du bateau' (554) which occurs often in the ostraca published by Dupont-Sommer (whose translation — 'Attache le bœuf' — seems to be less suitable because of the context, as well as the difficulty of defining the meaning of *ʿrq*, which is as yet unattested). As to the meaning suggested by Milik, compare *H brḥ*, *Ar brḥ*, as well as φεύγω in Classical and Modern Greek. The article must be read to appreciate the wealth of information and the author's sharpness of mind.

B. Porten and Jonas C. Greenfield have published a predictably solid article (1968). They too allude to the Western provenience of these texts without going into much detail.

Bresciani 1960 (Br)

Miss Bresciani had published previously — in 1960 — one more or less complete papyrus and the fragments of two others, which also date from the fifth century B.C. They are commented upon by J.A. Fitzmyer (1962); see also Naveh (1964–65).

One look at the papyrus I is enough to convince us that the scribe was trying to employ the Eastern *OfA*. The traits: 1) (verso 4). 2) Absent. 3) (verso 2). 4) No infinitive occurs. 5) Apparently only 1:3 (see recto 1 as against recto 3, verso 4,6). 6) Absent. 7) One instance (verso 6) went unrecognized by Miss Bresciani, but see Naveh 1964–65. 8) Miss Bresciani identified the *Ak tmly lbt* (verso 3), which strangely enough she did not identify later in *BrKa* 1, l. 6! In addition, the *n* is dissimilated (recto 3, verso 3). The status determinatus has the ending aleph (there is no instance of the feminine status absolutus).

A comparison with *BrKa* (see above p. 369) will put into relief all the salient points of Eastern *OfA* in this papyrus.

The Adon letter — sent by one of the kings of the Palestine seacoast to Pharaoh about 600 B.C. (but see Milik below) — was first edited by Dupont-Sommer. What seems to be, for the time being, the final edition, was prepared, with bibliographies and a good commentary, by J.A. Fitzmyer (1965), and is, as always, a competent work. Cf. also J.T. Milik (1967:555–6), who provides many new readings and restorations. Milik comes to the conclusion that the papyrus was sent from Tyre or from Sidon.

F. Vattioni's 'Il papyro di Saqqarah' (*Studia Papyrologia* 5.101–17, 1966) did not add anything substantial to our understanding of this papyrus.

Raymond A. Bowman published in 1944 parts of 'An Aramaic ... text in Demotic script'. In spite of many strange looking forms the language seems indeed to be *A*. A publication of the full text would be desirable.

Old texts newly edited. We have already given a short description of different chrestomathies (see 3.1). It was F. Rosenthal (1967) who dealt with the *Eg* material (pp. 10–16). The Assur letter was re-edited by A. Dupont-Sommer (1944–45), with a very extensive commentary and glossary. Incidentally, Mark Lidzbarski (the first editor) assumed the *'ḥz'* (1.14) is a long imperative (as in *H*). His suggestion should not be rejected out of hand, cf. *ptḥh ly 'rḥ'* in Sefîre, cf. Fitzmyer 1967:112. Worth mentioning are forms in this letter that had previously existed in *A* grammar but marked with an asterisk, e.g. *'zy* (1.6, 14, 2X) 'then', cf. *H 'ᵃzay* and later *OfA 'ᵉdayin'* (overlooked by Bauer and Leander 1927:§68b), *hny* 'they', feminine (1.12) which seems to be the transitional form between the *PS* (**hinna*) and the later *OfA* (*'inni:n*) (*BA*) — again disregarded by Bauer and Leander 1927:§38s. Why Dupont-Sommer reconstructs it as *hinnay* I do not understand. There are to be found two instances of *PS* /ṯ/ spelled with *t* (and not with *š*), i.e. *'ythm* (1.6, with contracted diphthong!) and *yhtb* (1.11) cf. above. It is strange that *Ak* /š/, which in Assyrian is supposed to be realized as [s], is always spelled with *š*, e.g. *Nbwšlm* = *Nabu:-Šallim* and even *Šrkn* (instead of

Srgn — Assyrian [k] often appears in *H* and *A* as [g]); there are many more instances (see glossary), which is surprising in a letter found in Assur (sent from Babylon).

Dupont-Sommer also re-edited the Bauer-Meissner papyrus in 1944.

H.L. Ginsberg retranslated the Proverbs of Aḥi:qar in *Ancient Near Eastern texts* (1955) and added a few interesting footnotes. A French translation with copious footnotes was supplied by P. Grelot (*RB* 68.178–93, 1961). His translation of *m[l]ṣṣ* 'maraude', on the basis of *Ar lṣṣ* 'être voleur' (p. 181, fn. 10), is impossible, since this *Ar* root is a loan from Greek via *A* (cf. S. Fraenkel's *Die aramäischen Fremdwörter im Arabischen*, 284, Leiden 1886).

C.H. Gordon returned to 'The cuneiform Aramaic incantation' (1940) after having published a comprehensive treatment of it (1937–9) to which Landsberger responded (1937–39). Note that actually this material already belongs to *MA*.

4.2 *Grammar*

Since Bauer and Leander (1927) and Leander (1928), no new scholarly grammars of the *OfA* in general and *BA* in particular have been published, while the wealth of the new material, as well as new insights and linguistic achievements, certainly warrant a new synchronic and diachronic treatment of the field. We have to keep in mind the fact that not only do these publications not cover the entire field (Leander 1928 does not treat syntax), but that they were written before the de Saussure, Trubetzkoy, and Bloomfield schools of linguistic science became dominant. Bauer and Leander (1927), a diachronic grammar, does not make full use of the wealth of material already available in *OA* and *OfA* (see two instances 4.1 above, regarding the Assur letter). Their diachronic approach is very conspicuous in 'reconstructing' the 'original' à la Brockelmann (and this is not mentioned here to belittle their excellent achievements). One work, Rosenthal 1961, deserves to be mentioned here, in spite of his own comment that 'very little, if anything, ... is new in this grammar' (p. 2). Of course, since it is a part of the *Porta Linguarum Orientalium* it could not be a new edition of Bauer and Leander 1927, therefore the strictures of Donner 1963:362 are not justified. (Other reviews: H.L. Ginsberg 1961, P. Nober 1961, A. Murtonen 1960–61, H. Michaud 1961.) Still, the user will be able to glean from it insights and information not yet available in Bauer and Leander (1927), especially thanks to the Short Bibliography (1961:72–5) and the glossary as well as the chapters dealing with foreign loans (1961: 57–9). I only wish Rosenthal had dropped the reconstructed forms, especially the feminine singular and plural (of the verb and noun and pronoun). I can imagine that if these forms proved to be a stumbling block to Moscati (above 3.2) they will play havoc with the young undergraduates for whom this volume is destined. In his paradigms one form should be corrected, e.g. *hitkətebtu:n* (p. 62, *hitpəʿel*), as well as kindred forms that are apparently incorrect (see Bauer and Leander 1927:31e[1]).

4.2.1 *Articles*; *Spelling*

J. Friedrich (1957) came to the conclusion that plene spelling with *aleph* in medial position in *A* dialects has to be attributed to *P* influence. He denies its occurrence in *OfA* (see p. 41, fn. 1).

His impressive arguments only carry weight if it can be shown 1) that this development could not have occurred independently in *A*; and 2) that it does not occur prior to the *P* domination. But both premises are wrong. M. Tsevat (1960:88) resoundingly establishes that: '(1) The *aleph* as a vowel letter has been in use since the fourteenth century. (2) It occurs in medial as well as in final position' (see *lʾ*, *zʾ* 1960:83–4, and especially *nbʾ* = *Nabu:* in Sefîre, 1960:86; as to final position, *lʾm* = *limmu*, in 682 and 680 B.C.! Regarding final position, he also mentions *pʾ* of Panammu:). This is not to deny that *P* might have accelerated a process that began in *A* (where the *matres lectionis waw* and *yod* marking long vowels are earlier to be found mainly in final position and not until later (exceptions in *OA*, see 3.2) in medial position. The same could be assumed concerning the *aleph*, whose occurrence as a *mater lectionis* in final position in *OA* no one denies.

4.2.2 *Phonology*

The laryngeals. As is well known, /ʿ/ and /ḥ/ weakened in *ATB* and in *M* and apparently were reduced to /ʾ, h/ (or zero). The same can be observed in the *A* logograms of Pehlevi. The reason obviously is the *Ak* and *P* substrata, respectively, to which these phonemes were alien. This process is bound to happen wherever Semites and non-Semitic peoples establish contact.

I therefore believe it had already taken place in those territories of the *P* empire where *A* was used by non-Semitic people. The first instance seems to occur in the *A* inscription found at Bahadirli, Asia Minor (fourth-third century B.C.), in which case we can scarcely assume that *A* was employed as a spoken language. There we read: *wʾyš zy yḥgh ltḥwmʾ znh qdm kbbh* 'A man who will move (?) this border(stone) before Kubaba (a deity).' The explanations advanced for *yḥgh* are scarcely satisfactory, see A. Dupont-Sommer (1964). But there seems to be a parallel in the ZKR inscription, B 18–20: *wm[n y]hgʿ nṣbʾ znh mn [qd]m ʾlwr* 'Whoever will move (?) this stela from the presence of ʾLWR (a deity)'! — *yhgʿ* also occurs in 1.10. Whatever the root of *yhgʿ* might be (*gwʿ* or *ngʿ*), there is no doubt as to its meaning. The similarity is striking. What happened was apparently the following: because of the weakening of /ḥ/ > /h/ — as in *ATB* and *M* — the scribe spelt an original /h/ with *ḥ* (hypercorrection), while the /ʿ/ > /ʾ/, or zero, and the grapheme *h* was used as *mater lectionis* of the preceding vowel (see Naveh 1964–65:193, fn. 37 of Kutscher).

An additional proof of the loss of a pharyngeal in *Ak* territory seems to be the *A* transliteration of *Ak* Arad-Nabû; see L. Delaporte's *Épigraphes araméens* (Paris, 1912), p. 26. But since /r/ can cause pharyngealization in *A* (see J.-J. Hess's article in *Zeitschrift für Semitistik und verwandte Gebiete* II.219, 1924), the /ʿ/ in the above name might be, after all, legitimate.

bgd kpt. 'Spirantization of /bgd kpt/ is an *A* development which, in all likelihood, was under way in the sixth century B.C.' (Rosenthal 1961:§15). Apparently it is possible to prove this. To be sure, E. A. Speiser has tried to update this process which he believes to be of Hurrian origin (see Speiser 1939:5, fn. 10), but this view can hardly be proved. However, if W. Eilers is right, as he seems to be, *Ak* transliterations ascribe it decisively to the sixth century B.C. He states (1940:70, fn. 6): 'In der Wiedergabe von altiranischen *x* schwankt das Babylonische und Assyrische ... zwischen *ḫ* und *k*, *letzteres selbstverständlich nur postvokalisch verwendet* [my italics, E.Y.K.]. Bezeichnend ist der Wechsel in den Schreibungen von Xerxes und Artaxerxes.' See Eilers 1935:207, fn. 5, where he mentions *ᵐAk-ši-ya-ar-šu*, but also *ᵐXi-ši-ʾ-ar-ši*; both mean Xerxes.

Eilers says 'selbstverständlich' since, as he explains further (1940:69–70, and also in 1934:90ff.), *Ak* by then was a dead language, written by *A*-speaking scribes who superimposed on the *Ak* their *A* pronunciation. See also the beginning of the note quoted from his *Beamtennamen* (1940). But what he states (1940:70) as to Greek transliterations of *Ak* is not relevant, see Kutscher 1965:31, 33–4. As to the origin of the double realization of /bgd kpt/, see the important article by Knudsen (1969; see 4.4.1 below, regarding *Ak*).

A. Spitaler (1952–54) deals with the problem of the so-called dissimilation of geminates, mainly by means of [n]. Obviously, he says, the term 'dissimilation of gemination' can only be employed where the phone used is not one of the radicals. He can only list five cases in *OfA*, e.g. [tindaʾ] (<[*tiddaʾ]), root = *ydʾ*. But in all the other cases — and there are many of them — the [n] is original (i.e. part of the root). Therefore the term non-assimilation of [n] would be preferable. What complicates the matter is the fact that very many of these cases appear both with assimilated [n] and without, e.g. [yintin] and [ytn] (= **yittin*) 'he gives'. Without denying in principle that assimilated and unassimilated forms can appear side by side, he prefers the solution that the unassimilated forms represent etymological spellings. He deals separately with those cases which he believes cannot be explained phonetically, e.g. [n] before /ʿ/, [hanʿa:la:] root *ʿll*, and which in his opinion go back to graphic analogy. Since, e.g., a geminated consonant could be spelled + [n], because of the etymological spelling, without the [n] being realized in speech, people concluded that the grapheme *n* in these cases indicated gemination and came to use it elsewhere too, where it was neither etymologically nor phonetically justified.

In spite of his seemingly convincing proofs, doubts linger on. *OA* does not know this etymological orthography, while *Ak* does know this kind of dissimilation (see Kutscher 1965:37–9; see 3.4 above). As noted above, it seems to have penetrated from *Ak* into *A*. The fact that among the *A* loans in *Ak* we also find [manḫal] = *A* [*manʿal]-root *ʿll* — see 3.4 above — does seem to indicate that the [n] was realized in speech! Would it, therefore, not be more plausible to assume that the dissimilation was indeed a phonetic reality, precisely in the phonetic conditions postulated by Spitaler? But since dissimilated and undissimilated forms were probably in use at least for some time simultaneously, this use was analogically extended to cases which did not warrant it on phonetic grounds (the same process, assumed by Spitaler to be a visual process, thus having taken place as a phonetic one).

Perhaps after all Bergman (1968) is right to assume that the frequency of this process in the root *ʿll* 'enter' was prompted by *npq* 'leave', though his premises are not correct.

H. Birkeland (1940:1–4) deals with the problem of stress in *A*. Birkeland may generally be right in his conclusions, but very often he bases his assumptions upon a kind of argumentation that is far from unproblematic. For example, he says: 'Es kann deshalb nicht zweifelhaft sein, dass -*ā* [the *A* postpositive article] und Kasusvokale einmal zusammen existiert haben' (1940:2). Why? Since this -*ā* 'gehört der Sprache ... schon der Zeit, da die Sprache eine Wüstensprache war. Nun haben arab(ische) Wüstendialekte noch mehrere Jahrhunderte n(ach) Ch(ristus) die kurzen Flexionsvokale bewahrt.' First of all, there is no internal *A* evidence whatsoever for this assumption (as to the problematic nature of the external evidence, see Huffmon 1965:116, fn. 23). And if the *Ar* is adduced as a proof, it should be pointed out that it is certainly no coincidence that *Ar* (of the sedentary Arabs) lost its case endings during the first century of its expansion (see Blau 1965:1–8).

In times of such expansion and transition from a nomadic to a sedentary way of life the structure of a language may very likely be revolutionized, as indeed happened to *Ar*. Therefore, it can be assumed that *A* lost its case endings during the time the Arameans settled in Syria (at the end of the second millenium B.C.). Also, it is scarcely a coincidence that the so-called Yaʾudic, which had preserved the case endings at least in the plural, does not yet possess the article. And his contention that *BA* /á:bi:/ (with penultimate stress) represents the original stress (as well as the penultimate stress of this form in *S*, *ATB*, and *M*) is scarcely acceptable. On the contrary! As Brockelmann has maintained, these forms reflect a regressive movement, from ultimate to penultimate stress, the outcome of which we can observe, e.g., in Maʿlu:la and other living *A* dialects (see, e.g., A. Spitaler in his grammar of Maʿlu:la, § 33: '... lässt sich die Zurückziehung des Akzents beim Syrischen gegen Ende der klassischen Periode feststellen.' As to the Western dialects, he says (*ibid.*), 'Jedenfalls ... darf man für beide Dialekte ein fortschreitendes Überwiegen der Pänultimabetonung voraussetzen, die dann im Maʿlu:la-Dialekt ihren Abschluss gefunden hat.' (See also Blake [1953] and Morag [1964] discussed below.)

4.2.3 *Morphology*

H. L. Ginsberg (1948:1–4) begins his *Studies in Daniel* with 'Linguistic notes on the Aramaic portion'. The (practically) four notes are indeed very interesting and very important. While F. Rosenthal, in his review in *JAOS* 69.137 (1949), says 'the *Studies* start with a short linguistic note which is the only weak part of the book', during the following two years it became clear that Ginsberg was proved wrong on one additional point, and it is with this point we shall deal. Ginsberg maintains that 'the *A* dialects have preserved feminine plural forms distinct from the masculine not only in the imperfect but also in the perfect of the verb. Only the *A* of Daniel seems to be an exception ... the ktibs *npqw* (5,5), *ʾtʿqrw* (7,8), and *nplw* (7,20)' ... (changed by the *qəre* into *nəpa:la:* etc.). Ginsberg continues: 'However, the feminine plural ending *ā* is ... Babylonian and targumic; whereas the Palestinian *A* dialects "use *ī*".' So he therefore believes the *waws* to be miswritten for *yods: nəpa:qi:*, etc.

This assumption sounded strange from the very beginning. Is it plausible that copyists living in Palestine, speaking *A*, should have miswritten *all* the instances of a form that they employed in their everyday speech? Indeed, Z. Ben-Ḥayyīm, in an excellent article (1951), proved him wrong. Ben-Ḥayyīm was able to show that the very basis of Ginsberg's emendation, '*A* dialects have preserved feminine plural forms distinct from the masculine', is simply incorrect. He pointed out that in nearly all cases where the feminine plural should be employed in *BA*, the *kətib* displays the masculine form, e.g. Dan. 7, 8, 17, 19, etc. Among fifteen instances, he found only two that, so it seems, look like the feminine, and showed that it is the *qəre* that changes these masculine forms into feminine ones. In addition, he decisively proved that the same applies to the *E* texts (cf. e.g. Aḥi:qar 1.151, 155, 157), to the texts of Palmyra (Tariff 1.17–18) and to Nabataean (e.g. *Corpus Inscriptionum Semiticarum* II, 205). This article (overlooked by Aramaists) must be read by everyone dealing with the language of our period.

H.L. Ginsberg (1959:143–5) returned to the subject. While he did not concede defeat concerning the forms of the imperfect (and Ben-Ḥayyīm had added one more instance), and strangely enough chose not to discuss *E, N*, and *Pa* in this regard, he concentrated upon the imperfect. There he may have scored one or two points. But in general, it must be emphasized that Ben-Ḥayyīm *grosso modo* is right. The consonantal text of *BA* does not distinguish in the plural between masculine and feminine in the verb (perfect and imperfect) and in the pronoun. The same seems to hold true concerning *E, N, Pa.* But since in the meantime new texts have been discovered, another survey would be desirable.

H.L. Ginsberg treated *BA* in Rosenthal 1967, where I was surprised to come across the following note to Dan. 5:5 *npqw:* 'perhaps read [nəpaqi:]', and Dan. 7:4 *mryṭw:* 'probably [məri:ṭi:]'. Since Ginsberg did not oppose Ben-Ḥayyīm concerning the perfect, obviously because of the impressive arguments marshalled by his opponent, what is the justification for these notes? In his notes to 7:8 and 7:20 he even drops the 'perhaps'.

F.R. Blake (1953:11–16) deals with several problems of *BA* phonology and morphology. I cannot, however, say that his interesting notes convincingly solve all the problems he discusses, especially No. 6: 'The Aramaic plural endings *-ôn* and *ên.*' The point merits a new approach. On the one hand, forms like [yədaʿto:n] *PTK* p. 21, line 8, also see *PTK* p. 23, 1.14, p. 26, 1.19 (but *PTK* p. 26, 1.18 [-tu:n]!) show that the ending *-to:n* is not only Eastern Aramaic (*EA*). On the other hand, the vocalization of *BA* (as will be shown elsewhere, see below, p. 403) is apparently based mainly upon

EA! The endings *-o:n, e:n* do not necessarily go back to *PS* **-o:n*, **e:n* (or a diphthong); they most probably represent, as in the other *SL*, **-u*(*n*), **-i*(*n*), which in *BA* can, when stressed, become [o][e]; but they can also stay unchanged, see Bauer and Leander 1927:§6, b', f', g'. The plene spelling is in keeping with the *MA* where it is not restricted to *PS* long vowels (*BA* underwent a spelling modernization; see Rosenthal 1939:69). This explanation of the plene spelling of these endings is supported by the fact that wherever the earlier ending [-om] is used in *BA*, the spelling is defective, while the [-on] ending, the common ending in *BA*, is spelled plene, as in *MA, LA* (see, e.g., Bauer and Leander 1927:§20g). This problem then should be tackled anew.

Other problems in Blake (1953) have been dealt with more satisfactorily: 7) The mixing of verbs tertiae *y* and ʾ; 8) The confusion between certain noun patterns; 9) The diphthong [ay]; 10) Hapʿel; 11) Passive forms.

J. Friedrich (1957–58) deals with an extremely important point touched upon several times above (see 4.0; 4.1). He correctly identified the syntagm *šmyʿ ly*, 'I have heard', *Dr* 7,3, with the *qəti:l l-* construction of *EA* (*S, ATB*, and *M*). He traces this construction to the influence of *P*, e.g. *mana: kartam* 'I have done' of the Behistun inscription (<'done by me', but see below). As a matter of fact, I also came to this conclusion in my review of *Dr* (1957:337) (which was published at the same time as Friedrich's article). But Friedrich confuses this construction with others, which are found in *A* dialects but have nothing to do with it.

As to the *P mana: kartam*, in a brilliant article (1952), E. Benveniste was able to show that this is not a passive construction, but a possessive one: **manā pus͜sa astiy* (*P*) = 'mihi filius est' = 'habeo filium', *manā krtam astiy* (*P*) = 'mihi factum est' = 'habeo factum'. The same then applies to *A šmyʿly* which therefore exactly parallels 'I have heard'! This construction only appears in *EA*, and not in Western Aramaic (*WA*), which is further proof of its *P* origin. (The territory of *EA*-speaking peoples was exposed to *P* rule and influence for about 1,200 years, from Cyrus to the Arab conquest; the *WA* territory only for about 200 years, from Cyrus to Alexander the Great.)

Entirely different from this construction is that referred to by Friedrich, who says that 'Im Neuwestaramäischen von Maʿlūla ... hat die passivische Ausdrucksweise die alte aktivisch-perfektische weitgehend ... verdrängt.' In Maʿlūla there is no *qəti:l l-* only *qəti:l* (passive participle which functions as if active). This use is to be found in both *EA* and *WA*. The replacement of the active participle by the passive one with 'active' force, mainly as a present perfect, seems to be a purely *A* trait (which incidentally influenced Late *BH*).

The third construction dealt with by Friedrich concerns the finite verb (and not the passive participle), e.g. instead of 'I gave' (*yhbt*), the deity, the king, or a high official says 'it was given by me' (*mny yhyb*), a kind of *passivum majestatis*. The first and the third construction are gone into at length in my paper (1969).

Morag (1964) has supplied us with the long overdue survey of the grammar of *BA* according to the Babylonian vocalization (see Rosenthal 1939:49–50). For the purpose of his study he was able to draw upon the texts published by H.L. Strack and P. Kahle (which were utilized by Bauer and Leander 1927) as well as two MSS and a number of fragments. While there are differences between the various MSS, a certain coherent picture, distinct from that of the *BA* of the Tiberian vocalization, does emerge. His main conclusion (1964:130) is: 'in the Babylonian MSS of *BA*, Targum Aramaic forms (i.e. of the Onqəlos type) sometimes break through.' Among these features are: 1) 'the tendency to have /o/ rather than /u/ as the vowel of imperfect' (p. 125); 2) 'the first pers.sing. of the perfect is formed by adding /-it/ to the third pers.masc.sing.' (p. 126); 3) '*qəṭalat* ... forms for the third pers.fem.sing. in the perfect of the simple stem (instead of *qiṭlat*, p. 126); 4) '*məquṭṭal* passive participles of the *paʿel* stem' (instead of *məqaṭṭal*, p. 127. See 3.3 p. 128). I would especially stress 2) and 3), since I have proved that they are identical with those of the *ATB* (Kutscher 1961–62) but are absent from the *WA* (as far as we know). See also Morag 1964:fn. 69. Therefore we may rephrase the dictum of Morag: 'In Bab MSS of *BA*, *EA* forms, as represented by *ATB* and *A* of the Targum Onqəlos type (which was transmitted and vocalized in Babylonia and therefore reflects to a large extent *EA* features), sometimes break through.' As a matter of fact, I intend to show elsewhere that the Tiberian vocalization of *BA* is also based to a large extent not upon *WA* but upon *EA*! Thus, the Babylonian vocalization only accelerates a tendency already discernible in the Tiberian vocalization.

4.2.4 *Syntax*

H.B. Rosén (1961) has tackled a very complicated problem. Bauer and Leander (1927) tried to present a clear-cut picture of the tense system of *BA* (including Daniel), but Rosén has no difficulty in exposing the many shortcomings of their presentation. He points to (1961:183) 'the use of a preformative tense ... not unlike the *Ak* preterite ... as a narrative tense (besides being the tense of the non-past)'. He denies that the 'perfect' (called 'nominal' by Bauer and Leander, 'stative' by Rosén) serves as a narrative tense (185). On the contrary, it is used to express 'anteriority' and its use as a perfect is 'clear in phrases where it stands alone' (187). The stative is used in the 'cleft sentence' (Jespersen's term) where the verb is the logical subject, as Rosén shows (following H.J. Polotsky's brilliant *Études de syntax copte*). But then 'we should ... expect to see [the preformative tense] precluded from use as a future or volitive ... Similarly, the participle fulfills the function of a narrative tense, yet at the same time it frequently has "present" meaning' (191). How can we account for this confusion? Rosén believes that (p. 192): 'It can be shown that there is a rather neat distinction in Daniel between (1) verbs whose narrative tense is the participle, whose future-volitive is preformative, and whose subordinative is a simple stative, and (2) verbs whose participle denotes a present, whose preformative tense is narrative... ... the first group [are] "point aspect" verbs ... the other class — the "linear" class.'

He sets up two separate tense paradigms (192):

LINEAR ASPECT VERB		POINT ASPECT VERB
Future-volitive	[lɛh^ɛwe: da:'ar]	[yippul]
Present	[da:'ar]	['i:tay na:pel]
Narrative-constative	[yədu:r]	[na:pel]
Subordinative	[h^awa: da:'ar]	[nəpal] (also perfect)

These seem to me to be the main points of this brilliant revolutionary article which cannot be summarized completely within this framework.

Still, his thesis needs a second hard look. According to his analysis, e.g., the root *khl*, 'can', 'to be able', has to be considered as a 'point class' verb! (e.g. 192). The root *ṣbʿ* 'to wet' is (196) in *hitqaṭṭal* 'point', but in *qaṭṭil* 'linear'. The verb occurs twice in parallel contexts (Daniel 4:12, 22) in the story of Nebuchadnezzar's dream and Daniel's interpretation of the same dream. Therefore, Rosén's interpretation scarcely makes sense concerning this root.

There seem to be other flaws in this construction. Still, I am very much impressed by his analysis of the function of the 'stative' and 'the preformative' (it immediately calls to mind the theory of H. Bauer on the genesis of the stative). No Semitist in general and no Aramaist in particular can disregard this article in any future work concerning *A* (and Semitic) tenses.

Takamitsu Muraoka's notes on *BA* syntax (1966) have little in common with Rosén's article published in the same journal (and does not mention him, in spite of the fact that Muraoka deals with the use of the participle, 1966:157–9). 'In many places (the) starting point of the discussion is *BL*', and indeed his notes sometimes boil down to the question of definition, e.g. 9:1 (p. 196). As to Dan. 2:38 ['ant hu: re:ša: di: dah^aba:] 'you are the head of gold', I fail to see how, by any definition of 'subject', 'it is possible to take *'ant* as the subject,' considering the preceding verses! Besides, in *BA*, as in all the *SL* that employ a copula, it always follows the predicate (this rule, which applies to *H* and *A* [and *Ak*!] but was unknown even to Th. Nöldeke, was expressly stated only concerning Geʿez, cf. Praetorius, 1886:§171), e.g. Dan. 2:28; 3:15; also cf. 5:13 ['ant hu: da:niyyel di: min bəne: ga:lu:ta:] 'You are that Daniel, one of the exiles', where there can be very little doubt as to the subject, also cf. Dan. 4:19. The problem of defining subject and predicate in identifying clauses arises only in nominal clauses of the type of *H* Gen. 42:6 [yo:sep hu: haššalli:ṭ] (The Revised Standard Version translation, 'Now Joseph was governor' is not correct; see The Jewish Publication Society of America's 'Now Joseph was *the* Vizier.'), but even in this case the above rule seems to apply!

I am in doubt about his treatment of *ne:mar*, Dan. 2:16 (p. 163). He prefers to see it as = 1st pers.(sing.!), as in *GA*. It should, however, be stated: 1) In *GA* it is nearly always employed for the first person singular and is very conspicuous even in the (Jerusalemite) Targum (Ginsberg 1933–34:382–3), in spite of the fact that the *H* text of the Bible must have been a restraining factor in this respect. 2) Only two instances are to be found in the participle, according to Dalman (see below), and these prove nothing. The speakers discuss their journey to Palestine (from Babylonia). At those times, obviously they did not travel alone! But the 'plural' form of the first person imperfect for the singular is sometimes accompanied by the pronoun of the first person singular *ʾnh*! (see Ginsberg 1933–34:382–3). Therefore, since the 'plural' instead of 'singular' only occurs in the imperfect, the reason obviously is not semantic (as assumed by Dalman and Muraoka) but morphological (which cannot account for the occurrence of this form in *BA*), as I intend to show elsewhere. 3) The entire note seems superfluous, since this explanation had been put forward by Dalman, p. 265, fn. 6 (cited by Muraoka 1966:164, fn. 3, who, however, by a *lapsus calami*, four times writes Nöldeke instead of Dalman — in the text, in fn. 3, below 7.4.4., as well as on p. 159, fn. 5).

I feel I must also take exception to Muraoka's last item (1966:167): 'In such a stage in the history of *A*, when the inflectional system has collapsed, we can properly question the legitimacy of arguing about "accusative" or "dative" in that language' (the latter never existed in any *SL* except Akkadian). There are several misconceptions in this small item, e.g. in spite of the fact that 'the inflectional system had collapsed' in *H*, we do distinguish between the accusative object, which when determined can be preceded by /ʾet/, and the dative object, preceded by other prepositions. The problem arises in *BA* since the preposition /l-/ can be employed to indicate that which corresponds both to the dative and accusative of certain languages. But Bauer and Leander are certainly right in showing that the distinction between these two cases *does* exist in *BA* (1927:100a): *qətalu: ləgabra:* 'they killed the man' loses the /l-/ when transformed into the passive, but not *ʾᵃmaru: ləgabra:* 'they spoke to the man'.

There are quite a few other points where, *pace* Muraoka, Bauer and Leander are right, while in other cases, e.g. 2.3, 7.1 (concerning Ezra 5:15) etc., he was able to improve on their findings.

On the other hand, he was able to show (pp. 152–5), e.g., that the strange assertion of Bauer and Leander that 'Die Gebrauchsweise dieser Verbindung (i.e. that of the genitive by means of [di:]) entspricht durchweg der des Stat. cstr.' does not hold water. Especially interesting is his explanation of [gob ʾarya:wa:ta:] 'a lion's den', as against [gubba: di: ʾarya:wa:ta:] 'the den of the lions' (but Dan. 6:17 seems to be an exception!). In short, some of his conclusions are valuable, others less so.

J.A. Fitzmyer has treated the syntax of *kl, klʾ* in the Aramaic texts from Egypt and in *BA* satisfactorily. He showed that *klʾ* has to be regarded 'as the emphatic state of *klʾ*' (the final /a:/ being the article and not an adverbial ending, 1957:178–83). The problem of the penultimate stress remains unresolved.

W.F. Stinespring, in an article on the active infinitive with passive meaning in *BA* (1962), set out to explain 'This striking and rather common phenomenon' (according to him, 16 occurrences). As a matter of fact this case is not an isolated phenomenon within the *SL*. In *Ar*, the infinitives are neutral as to diathesis 'as /qatluhu/ "his killing (another)" or "his being killed himself"' (Wright 1955:§201). Concerning *H*, see Bergsträsser 1929:55f. In *S*, the verbal substantive of the Paʿʿel is also employed for its passive-reflexive stem (Nöldeke 1898:§117). Therefore, I do not think that the *BA* usage presents a problem.

A closer look into the cases alluded to by Stinespring (1962:392, fns. 6, 7) revealed that there is even less of a 'problem' than I had thought. It turned out to be a case of analyzing *A* with an English looking-glass. In nearly all the occurrences the infinitive depends on a verb expressing command, and the subject of the infinitive is of course different from that of the governing verb. In English, these cases, when the subject of the infinitive is not mentioned, require a passive construction (infinitive or dependent clause), e.g. 'He ordered the house to be pulled down', but 'He ordered him to pull down the house'. The occurrences listed by Stinespring are of the first type, e.g. Daniel 2:12 [ʾᵃmar ləho:ba:da:] in the *RSV* '... commanded ... be destroyed', while in German: 'befahl ... umzubringen'. The same applies of course to *H* (*very* common), e.g. Leviticus 7:36 [ʾᵃšer ṣiwwa: ... la·tet la.hɛm] is translated into German as 'welches (der Ewige) geboten ihnen zu geben', but in English as 'these (the Lord) commanded to be given them'. The (only?) exceptions are to be found in Esther (!) 9:1, 14. This being the case, one only can wonder why there was a 'problem' in the first place.

J.G. Williams points out that the *A* impersonal plural of the verb 'serves as the predicate in a statement referring to a divine or royal decree or at least to some irresistible external power ...' (1964:182). Cf. the *passivum majestatis* in my article mentioned above (p. 377).

A. Spitaler believes, in a very interesting article (1962:112–14), that Ezra 5:10: [di: niktub šum gubraiya: di: bəra:še:hom] should be translated 'Was wir aufschreiben ... sind (aber nur) die Namen der Männer, die an ihrer Spitze stehen. Das einschränkende "nur" der deutschen Übersetzung wird vom Zusammenhang gefordert, dürfte aber bereits der analytischen aramäischen Konstruktion "das, was wir aufschreiben, sind ..." inhärieren, man denke an arab. *innamā* ... Die Berichterstatter wollen sagen, das sie ... nur eine beschränkte Anzahl (der Namen) aufnehmen, eben die der massgebenden führenden Persönlichkeiten.'

If he is right, this would be the first instance of a cleft sentence in *A*, cf. O. Jespersen (1937:83–6) and H. Paul (1937:285). On the cleft sentence in general, see H.J. Polotsky (1944:21–96; on *innama:*, 66–7). I knew of this construction in *ATB* (cf. M. Schlesinger 1928:221–4, especially 221 fn. and 223 fn., last line.). However, neither in *ATB*, nor in English, French, etc., does the relative clause begin the sentence.

Incidentally, Spitaler (1962:114, fn. 1) says: 'Der Sing. *šum* ist auffällig'. This is not an isolated case, cf. *Co* 30,13: *wmn ywmy mlk mṣryn*, where it may, of course, be a scribal error; but then we shall have to assume the same in the parallel text, *Co* 31,12 *wmn ywm mlky mṣryn*, apparently both to be translated 'Already in the days of the kings of Egypt'. One is reminded of *Ak be:l ḫubulli:šu* 'seine Gläubiger' (von Soden 1952:84 l). Also cf. Bauer and Leander 1927:§87, k.

F. Rundgren (1953:301–4) believes that there is no need to emend [(zi:wo:hi:) šəno:hi:] Daniel 5:6 '(the king's) color changed' to [ša:nayin ʿᵃlo:hi:]; cf. Geʿez, where 'every verb which has for Subject ... a member of the body ... has a Suff. Pron.

appended to it, ... having a Dative ... force' (Dillmann 1907:443), e.g. [yətfe:š-šəḥanni: ləbbəya] 'my heart rejoices (in me)'. Rundgren denies (1953:304–16) the existence of a root *hwk* 'to go' in *A*; forms like [yəha:k] of *BA* go back to **yihlak* (root *hlk*), which under the influence of the root *ʾty* 'to come' and perhaps because of velarization of the /l/ (! — E.Y.K.) > [yəha:k]. In spite of the impressive arguments of Rundgren, I do not think that this subject is now closed. Incidentally, he states, relying upon the Berliner (Sabioneta) edition of Targum Onqəlos (*TO*) (p. 306), 'kurzer Vokal in geschlossener, langer Vokal dagegen ... in offener Silbe steht' (e.g. [yəhak, yəha:ku:n]). It has to be stressed that this edition is utterly unreliable. Only the texts with Babylonian vocalization, e.g. Sperber's edition, are trustworthy. (In these texts the vocalization is indeed [yəha:k] as noticed by Rundgren.)

4.3 *Lexicography; Dictionaries*

Jean and Hoftijzer (1965) and Vinnikov (1958–65) were dealt with above. Here we should mention L. Koehler and W. Baumgartner (1958). W. Baumgartner, one of the best Hebraists and Aramaists of our times, was the editor of the *A* part. It is, with Brockelmann's *Lexicon Syriacum* (1928), the only etymological and comparative dictionary of any *A* dialect that can be considered satisfactory.

Baumgartner informs us about his task in the *Festschrift Otto Eissfeldt* (1947: 47–55), especially in his 'Introduction to the Aramaic Part, German and English' [xvi-xxiii) (the German text apparently has fuller references than the English). His works are a model presentation of the problems involved in such a work. The problem of the differences between Tiberian and Babylonian forms is discussed; (see 4.2 regarding Morag 1964). He evaluates the new material available since the last edition of Gesenius-Buhl, to be included in his dictionary, i.e. the new *OA*, *OfA*, and other *A* material. It is the first time that the *A* logograms of Pehlevi were included in any *A* dictionary. The problem of *Ak* and *P* loans is not neglected. The question of time and place of origin of Ezra and Daniel is touched upon (see 4.7 below), but the evidence is judged inconclusive.

I cannot refrain from mentioning one point which proves Baumgartner to be not only an excellent Aramaist, but also a modest and honest scholar. It was Baumgartner who tried to prove (1927:120ff., cf. Rosenthal 1939:66–7) that the differences between the *A* of Ezra and Daniel prove the earlier date of Ezra. Here (1947:xxxi) he admits that Schaeder's opinion is to be preferred! The question of Hebraisms and Canaanisms is not overlooked either. In short, Aramaists, especially those interested in comparative *A* lexicography, should make it their business to study carefully both articles of Baumgartner.

But — *dies diem docet* — Baumgartner certainly would not repeat (1947:52) 'dürfte die ... Schreibung *šmsyʾ* "Sonne" (Pehlevi logogram) doch wohl auf Zufall beruhen', since *Kr* 5,9 *smšʾ* has come to light. We also have little reason to assume

(1947:xxx) that *'l*, *l'mr* are not *A* (concerning *l'mr* see above 3.2, p. 351); *zkh* is most probably *Ak* (*Tarbiẓ* (*H*) 19, p. 125). I believe that [la:hen] is *A* [la:+hen] = [hen/'en+la:]>['ɛlla] in *A* dialects = 'except' (see 4.4.2 below).

How the newly discovered material can be put to good use in solving old cruces of *BA* vocabulary was shown by F. Rundgren (1957:400–4), who was able to prove convincingly the *P* origin of the *BA šršw*, Ezra 7:26. If A. Shaffer (1965:32–4) is right then [kirenzi] < [*kirezzi] in Nuzi 'proclamation' is etymologically related to *krz* 'to proclaim, announce' in *A*. As is well known, until H.H. Schaeder found a *P* etymology, *A krz* was thought to be of Greek origin (and was used to prove that the *A* of Daniel goes back to post-Greek times, see 4.6 below).

Still, some doubts remain. It is not only the time gap which is disturbing (more than one thousand years), but especially the fact that the form *kirenzi* is 'taken as dissimilated from **kirezzi*' (Shaffer 1963:33, fn. 6), which is certainly possible. (But see von Soden 1952:§32b: 'Die Nasalierung tritt ... nie ein in Silben, die mit ... *r* ... anfangen').

C.G. Tuland, in his article on 'Uššayyā' and 'Uššarnā' (1958) believes that the first word means 'subfoundation', the second '(building) material' (but the second scarcely fits Ezra 5:3, since *škll* means 'finish' and not 'prepare'). An attempt to solve the problem of *BA* ['ᵃdarga:zərayya:] was made by F. Rundgren (1963) and by P. Nober (1958). Rundgren believes *'ᵃdar-* to be a Medic form = 'thousand', the *A* word meaning something like χιλίαρχος. Nober's article deals mainly with *BA* ['adrazda:], which he identifies with Avestan [zrazda:] 'glaubenstreu' ... 'eifrig treu', 'herzenstreu'.

In a very interesting article, 'Das "Tor des Königs" im Buche Esther und verwandte Ausdrücke' (1964), H. Wehr was able to demonstrate that the phrase *tr' mlk'* in Daniel, *tr' ḥykl'* in Aḥi:qar, and its equivalents in *H* [ša'ar hammɛlɛk], as well as in *A*, *Ak*, and other Near Eastern languages, does not mean 'am Tore' but 'dass er im königlichen Palast weilte, seinen Aufenthalt unter den Beamten und Dienern [of the king] hatte' (p. 261) ... 'so kann nicht das Aussentor gemeint sein ... sondern die Tür im Innern ... des Palastes' (p. 256). 'Die Grenze zwischen "Palast Hof" and "Regierung" zerfliesst' (p. 257); therefore the above phrase can mean government. The provenience of this phrase is, as yet, unknown.

Legal scholars have discussed very extensively, within the framework of their researches into the *E* deeds and documents, the *A* legal terminology. My review article (1954) on *Kr* was the first attempt (since Rosenthal 1939) to deal with the linguistic implications of the *A* legal terms of *E* (see the evaluation by Muffs 1969:8ff., above p. 363). But Muffs (1969:6) was correct in pointing out that both I and the other scholars had overlooked the important statements of Lidzbarski in this connection. *A* legal terms I treated previously in *Tarbiẓ* (Kutscher 1945–46).

In my article in *JAOS* I tried to stress the importance of the fact that the *A* legal terms and phrases are, on the one hand, paralleled by *Ak* legal terms etymologically or semantically identical with the *A* terms, and on the other hand, that they equal semantically legal terms and phrases often occurring in Demotic, Greek, and even legal terms that turn up in other European languages. A good case in point is the term for 'capital'. In *Ak* it is expressed by [re:šu], [qaqqadu] 'head' (I am told that the same applies to Sumerian), and the word for 'head' can be found with this meaning in *BH*, *MH*, *A*, Demotic, Greek, Latin, Arabic, and German. 'The underlying notion (*chief* money, as against the interest) seems to be present in (all?) the languages concerned. Still, is it a coincidence that in all of them it worked that way? Would it not be less difficult to assume that the Greek which borrowed, e.g., *xrúsos* "gold" and *arrabo:n* "caution money" from the Semites goes back to a Semitic prototype' (p. 243). It is possible that *A* played the role of clearing house between Orient and Occident at this highly sensitive juncture. But, of course, both the problem of loans and, especially, of loan-translations requires a very careful approach with co-ordination of extra-linguistic factors. Three legal scholars, whose works appeared after the publication of my article, concerned themselves with this matter; they are J.J. Rabinowitz, R. Yaron, and Y. Muffs.

J.J. Rabinowitz, in *Jewish law: Its influence on the development of legal institutions* (1956) as well as in *Studies in legal history* (1958), traces the Jewish legal influence with the help of the legal terms. The same applies to his published articles (quite a few of which are listed in Muffs' volume, see below, p. 385). The documents and legal terms he treats occur mainly in *A* but also in such diverse languages as *Ak*, *H*, *Ar*, *S*, Demotic, Greek, and Latin.

There is no doubt that the sharp eye of Rabinowitz was indeed able to make important discoveries. But it has to be stated that nowhere can his statements be accepted at face value. The bulk of his material needs (and deserves) close scrutiny both in regard to the facts and in regard to the method employed. Rabinowitz nowhere clarifies the criteria that enable us to distinguish a loan-translation from the other possibility, a parallel process whereby identical conditions give rise to identical linguistic expressions.

To be sure, some of his suggestions have been confirmed independently by other scholars (at the same time, or previously: L. Blau, M. San-Nicoló, E.Y. Kutscher). But scholars would be more reluctant to agree with his other findings.

R. Yaron, professor of Roman law at the Hebrew University, in his review-article deals with 'I, the "similar-hence-dependent" fallacy; II, the time factor in comparison; III, proximate and remote influence; IV, law and language; V, the evaluation of evidence' (1959:308ff.). This is an important article concerning the methodology of tracing loan-translations in general and in the legal field in particular. He concludes his article with the following statement: 'The author's writings are very instructive for the reader who is able and willing to approach them critically. They are a source of error for him who is not.'

I too believe that some of Rabinowitz's suggestions are too bold, e.g. his identification of *prypt* of *Kr* with Greek ϑρεπτή (1956:37), without attempting to explain why the Greek ϑ should have been replaced in *A* by /p/. The same applies to the *P* loan *prtrk* (the title of a *P* high official!) in *Co*, which Rabinowitz equates with Greek πρωτάρχης! (1956:37). The danger of this method is pointed up by the fact that on the basis of the consonants we would have no difficulty linking *prtrk* with the Latin *praetoricius* 'ex-praetor'. (As to the problem of Greek loans in *E*, see 4.4.2 below.) *gwʾ* in *A* does not mean 'body', as Rabinowitz mistakenly states (1956:36). Nevertheless, we fully agree with Muffs (1969:10) that Rabinowitz 'called attention to many significant parallels and was able to interpret in their light many a difficult passage'.

R. Yaron has also produced some articles dealing with *E* law (and legal terms), as well as an *Introduction to the law of the Aramaic papyri* (1961, which also appeared in *H*. For particulars, see Muffs' bibliography). He is primarily a legal scholar. While I would not give blanket approval to Yaron's linguistic findings (see e.g. 1961:90, fn. 5, in regard to *pṣl*, concerning Greek loan-translations, see 4.4.2. below) I find myself in agreement with Muffs (1969:11) that 'Yaron's method is characterized by great care and reserve'. The linguist will find the last two chapters, on 'Some problems of comparison' and 'Sources and contacts', interesting.

Muffs is the last scholar to appear on this scene. He has a very good grounding in *H*, *A*, and *Ak*, and has made it his business to deal with the legal aspect of some *A* phrases of *E*; his work (1969) is mainly comparative. While I am not qualified to judge this volume on its legal merits, I am very much impressed by his achievements in tracking down genetic and semantic parallels of *A* legal terms. Especially Aramaists (as well as Akkadologists) interested in problems of 'languages in contact' (see 4.4 below) will profit from a careful reading of this important, well written volume. It is full of comparative material of *A*, *Ak* (and *H*) legal terms, and solidly done. As mentioned in 4.0 above, Muffs is in agreement with my basic attitude as to the role played by the *OfA* as a medium of transmission and distribution of legal terms. I should only like to sound a note of caution. Muffs says (1969:14): 'Thus, in a sense, the Aramaic formulary is the recipient of over two millennia of cuneiform legal experience; it is the culmination of many developments and inner-Assyriological trends, an amalgamation of various cuneiform traditions. As will be demonstrated in this study, every Aramaic term and clause is, to a very great degree, like a palimpsest: preceding stages of cuneiform legal history transpire through them. Hence, the Aramaic legal material can only be understood properly if all preceding *Vorlagen* — not merely the proximate ones — are thoroughly reinvestigated, philologically, legally, and historically.' These words are bound to create the impression that *all* the *A* legal terms go back, in one form or another, to *Ak*. This impression is strengthened by what Muffs has to say concerning the Neo-Assyrian analogies of *A* legal terms (1969:180ff.): 'According to Yaron, there is virtually no trace of Neo-Babylonian or Neo-Assyrian legal traditions in the *A* deeds'. But, he continues, a recent publication (by Deller) 'has enabled me to confirm the cuneiform origin of these *A* terms' and he presents a list of 12 items. More than half of these turn up in Neo-Assyrian (and not in the earlier *Ak*) sources. Now according to von Soden (1952:4k) concerning Neo-Assyrian (1000–600 B.C.): 'Im 7. Jahrhundert machen sich auch Einflüsse von seiten des gleichzeitigen Aramäischen stark bemerkbar *vor allem in den Urkunden*' (my italics,

E.Y.K.). Therefore the question arises: How do we know that *A* borrowed these terms and not the reverse? Muffs is aware of this possibility (see 1969:187, fn. 4), but his first example, *Ak egirtu* < *A 'grt'*, is a misnomer, since the term is certainly *not* of *A* origin (cf. Koehler and Baumgartner 1958:1048). It is therefore strange that he did not take this possibility into consideration when dealing with some of the terms brought to light by the recent publication by Deller.

Therefore, this particular aspect of his work should be reinvestigated in accordance with the guiding maxims set forth in regard to von Soden's study of *A* loans in *Ak* (see 3.4 above).

F. Rundgren (1958) believes that *raḥ(ḥ)i:qi:n*, Ezra 6:6, is a legal term, identical with the legal terms created from the root *rḥq* in *E*. Incidentally this case might serve as an excellent illustration of how difficult it very often is to decide what the ultimate origin of legal terms might be. While Nöldeke and Kraeling came out in favour of an Egyptian derivation, Rundgren denies it (as I did earlier); see also Yaron (1961a:103) who is undecided. Now Muffs has discovered the cognate *Ak re:qu* in Nuzi (1969:178), 'functionally and semantically identical with *A rḥq*' as employed in *E*.

4.4 *Languages in Contact*

4.4.1 *The Impact of Other Languages upon A*

Ak. It is at this period (about 700) that the *Ak* influence upon *A* makes itself felt. I know of no new work that tries to summarize the points of interference of *Ak* with *A* (cf. my article 1954:240ff.). The problem concerning legal terms has been treated especially by Muffs (4.3 above). The case of the genitive construction +*zy* (*dy*) has been alluded to above (3.2).

An important article on 'Spirantization of velars in Akkadian' was published by E. E. Knudsen (1969). He shows 'that there was a tendency towards spirantization all over the Akkadian speech area, both in space and time .... However, the state of evidence does not allow any other condition for this alternation than free variation in certain environments' (1969:147–8). The spirantization works according to two laws: 1) Dissimilation of velars; and 2) Assimilation to vowels (p. 149). The second law is close to that for *A* and *H*. 'As in Hebrew and Aramaic, /gg, kk, q/ were never spirantized' (p. 148). He closes his article with the sentence: 'Though circumstances were only parallel in part it is tempting to ask the question whether the Aramaic and Hebrew treatment of the *begadkefat* series might be traced back to Akkadian influence on Aramaic' (p. 155). It is a pity that Knudsen was unaware of Eilers' important discovery (p. 374 above) in which he pointed out a case where the rule seems to work exactly as in *A*. It would be interesting to have the comments of Knudsen as to whether he considers it, as Eilers does, to be a reflection of the *A* rule in *Ak*, or *Ak* proper. Regarding spirantization in *Ak* cf. von Soden's article in *JNES* 27.214–20 (1968).

Scattered remarks can no doubt be found in the works of various Assyriologists.

It would be especially worthwhile to scan the writings of B. Landsberger. Landsberger (1967a), e.g., is studded with comparative *A-Ak* material, but, as far as I was able to judge, it is of most significance to Late Aramaic studies. However, occasionally, there are to be found illuminating remarks concerning our period as well. Consider, for example, the following remark in Landsberger (1967b:48, fn. 86), where he explains *Ak* [ibašši] = Ger. 'wirklich' and continues: 'Augenfällig die Parallele mit hebräisch *i̯ēš* und biblisch-aramäisch *ītai̯* "wirklich"' (Brockelmann, *Grundriss* II.105 (=106)f.). We apparently can also add *E*, since *Co* 20,7 *'yty zy bpq*[*dwn*] *hp̄qdw* (*Co* p. 60: 'The construction is very awkward') is apparently best translated: 'Indeed, they are on deposit'. See also Rimalt (1932:119–20).

A. Goetze (1946) believes that the *A* (double) 'plurals *-ân-în* (*WA*) or *-ân-ê* (*EA*) [are] the closest analogue to the *Ak* plurals in *-ān-ū*' (p. 126). In my opinion, it might be an *Ak* loan.

P. According to H.H. Schaeder, 'Dareios I führte das Aramäische in Schrift und Sprache in die achaimenidischen Kanzleien ein', whereas Altheim and Stiehl (1963:78) maintain that 'Der Schriftverkehr wurde ... schon unter Kyros, ... auf Aramäisch geführt'. Be that as it may, the impact of *P* on *A* began in this period and in one form or another has continued to exert its influence upon *EA* until today. This interference during the course of 2,500 years should prove a fascinating topic not only for the Aramaist but also for the general linguist. In fact, I doubt very much whether a parallel case can be found, i.e. of two collateral languages, known to have been in contact for 2,500 years (both known pretty well during the time of their contact), let alone the existence of one special case of interference which can be shown to have transformed to a large extent the whole tense system of one language — the *qəti:l l-* construction in *EA* (p. 377 above). Especially scholars close to the Trubetzkoy school of thought (i.e. that the Indo-European languages may owe their common traits to contact established between the different languages of the 'Sprachbund', and not to a common ancestry), as represented, e.g., by V. Pisani (1966), should carefully study this piece of unparalleled evidence.

No doubt, the tense system and vocabulary as well as other fields were deeply affected, but the morphology, *grosso modo*, was able to withstand the onslaught of *P*. The first published occurrence of *qəti:l l-* is to be found in *Dr* (later it came to light elsewhere, see 4.1 above) which bristles with *P* loans. This volume gave new impetus to research in this field, as shown by the proportionately vast number of articles and, of course, by the commentary on *Dr* and the review articles (see 4.1 above).

P loans in *OfA* are also treated in several volumes that are not entirely devoted to this problem (see below).

More difficult than the tracing of *P* loans is the problem of loan-translations. There seems to be very little doubt that *A lnpšhm ʿbdw* of *Co* and *Dr* is of *P* origin (see Benveniste on *Dr*). It is therefore very interesting to note that according to R. Yaron (1961b:128) it managed very early to penetrate Demotic (possibly via *A*?). On the other hand, if Eilers is right (1954–58:335), then the same should apply to *A* [ṣəbu:]

which took its meaning (wish >) 'affair' from *P* and transmitted it to *H*. (But what about *Ak*? See *Dr*, p. 49 of the 2nd edition.)

Another case in point would be *A ʼḥr* = *Ak* [arki] < *P* [pasa:va] 'then', cf. Kutscher (1954:241). But the case of *P* [na:ma:] = *Ak* [šumšu] = *A šmh* (*ibid.*) proves how slippery this ground can be.

W. Wüst (1966) has close to nothing concerning *A*. E. Benveniste (1966) very often treats *P* loans in *A*, mainly in *E* and *S*. Very rich in this respect is W. Eilers (1940), who also discusses lexemes that are not relevant to his theme. Aramaists will certainly profit very much by carefully reading this work (see 4.2.2 above). His findings concerning *BA* are of course listed in Baumgartner's dictionary. But 'das bisher unbeachtete talmudische *pwrsy šmng*' (incidentally, Eilers vocalizes both lexemes, which should *not* be done, since the vocalization of the Talmudic dictionaries has no scientific base, the texts being unvocalized, see Baumgartner 1967:164, 172) is not 'unbeachtet', and it had been explained exactly, as < **pursišn-nāmaγ* by Eilers (1940:17–18), cf. S. Telegdi (1935) and M. Jastrow, *A dictionary of the Targumim, the Talmud Babli and Yerushalmi and the Midrashic literature*, p. 1147b, New York, 1903 (2nd ed., 1926).

In 1955:229, fn. 4., Eilers deals with *prmnkry*ʼ of *E*. Incidentally, in the same article (1955:225–6) he denies the existence of *A* loans in Elamite.

W. Eilers has posed the problem of the form of the name [Ko(:)rɛš] = Cyrus in *BH* and *BA* ('Kyros', 1964). In the *Old P* inscriptions it appears as *Ku-u-ru-u-š* in the nominative, which can be read both [Ku:ru:š] and [Kuruš] (p. 192). How, therefore, can we account for the *BH* and *BA* form? 'Vielleicht findet ein Kenner der jüdischen Tradition die Antwort darauf' says Eilers (p. 193, fn. 46). But there is no need for a 'Kenner der jüdischen Tradition'; *H* (and *A*) linguistics will suffice.

In *Ak* the form is ^{m}*Ku-raš*, etc. (194). The *u* is in all probability short (see below). In Greek, as shown by Eilers, the more correct form of the name is not Κῦρος but Κόρος. This is not surprising, since we know from Greek transliterations of *Ak* that *Ak* /u/ appears as *o* in Greek (A. Ungnad 1928). This transliteration decisively proves that the *u*'s of *P Ku-u-ru-u-uš*, *Ak* (and Elamite, 194, fn. 47) *Ku-raš*, is short.

If then it was the *Ak* form that was transmitted to the (*H*- and *A*-speaking) Jews, they had to treat it as a noun of the *quṭl* pattern > *qoṭɛl* [Korɛš] — the *w* being, as Eilers correctly observed (193), plene spelling to indicate in this (foreign) name the quality (not quantity) of the vowel. Furthermore, since in the Babylonian vocalization there is no *segol* vowel [ɛ], *quṭl* pattern > *qoṭal*. Indeed, it is the form [Koraš] that appears in this vocalization (cf., e.g., Sperber 1962:92 [Isaiah 44:28]).

But even assuming that it was *P* that transmitted the name, we are bound to arrive at the same result. As is well known, the Septuagint often transliterates the noun-pattern *quṭl* as **qoṭol*, cf., e.g., Brönno 1941:42; cf. also *Moloch* = [Molɛk] in the Massoretic vocalization. Consequently *P* [Kuruš] = Greek Κόρος and corresponds exactly to the (*quṭl* >) **quṭul* pattern. Since this pattern became **qoṭɛl* quite early (Hieronymus, fourth-fifth centuries C.E., no longer uses **quṭul*, cf. Kutscher 1959:50), it is no wonder that according to the Massoretic vocalization the name is [Ko(:)reš].

Demotic. Both Demotic loans and loan-translations have been discovered in *E*, see especially the review articles of *Kr* (and *Dr*), 4.1 above, as well as the discussion on legal terms (4.3 above). Yaron may even have come across a case of syntactic interference (1960:70) (the double negation).

How problematic this particular field is has been pointed out in 4.3 above (see discussion of Rabinowitz's Jewish Law). A further instance is that while I had believed a certain phrase in *Kr* to be paralleled by early *Ak*, Yaron (1961b:129) found an Egyptian parallel.

Luwian. A. Goetze (1962:55–7) has dealt with the names of *ḥlkyn* (no doubt, Cilicians) that appear in *Dr* no. 5, and a few others. They are, according to him, of Luwian origin.

Greek in *OfA*? As stated above in 4.3 (concerning Rabinowitz 1956), it does not seem likely that Greek loans have surfaced in *OfA*. Yaron (1957) attempted to identify two Greek loans and one loan-translation in *E*. In his *Introduction to the law* of the *Aramaic papyri* he states: 'The problem of Greek influence on the Elephantine papyri is difficult to answer with confidence. I have noted above that "a certain clause" may be of Greek origin; but I am far from categorical on this point ... other suggestions of Greek influence ... fail to carry conviction' (1961a:126). I am in agreement with his statement (*ibid.*), 'We have already mentioned the reference to Greek money ... and have denied it to be of any significance for the law' or, I would add, for Greek loans. As matters stand today, I would say that the presence of Greek loans in *OfA* is not impossible, but has as yet to be proven (*BA* presents a special case, see 4.6 below).

The alleged *qrplgs* = καρπολόγος 'tax-gatherer' (Elath, 5th century B.C.) (Glueck 1940), seems to be very doubtful (Albright: 'if correct', in Glueck 1940:9, fn. 12). Torrey (1941:15) offers a conjecture and reads *ḥmr blgn* 'bottled wine' (*lg* being of dubious origin, cf. *BH* and *U*).

C-H. Nobody has as yet tried to trace the impact of *C-H* upon *A*. To be sure, the symbiosis of both languages in the territory of Syria-Palestine during more than one thousand years has been noticed by scholars, but it is only one aspect of this symbiosis — the *A* element in *H* (and not *C*) — that was attended to. (See 3.4 above and below, p. 391.) However, there is no doubt that the impact of *C-H* upon *A* was far-reaching as well. J.C. Greenfield's article dealing with parallels between the style of Sefîre and *BH* is an important signpost in this respect. A case of a *C* loan in Sefîre has been mentioned in 3.6 above.

But there exists clear-cut evidence that this was not a one-way process. The very fact that the stock of consonantal phonemes of *A* is (synchronically) identical with that of *C-H* would in itself be a remarkable phenomenon. It would not be easy to find such a situation even concerning two dialects of the same language, let alone two collateral languages.

To be sure, the phenomenon of the double realization of /bgd kpt/, as well as the fact of dephonemicization of /ś/ and its eventual merging with /s/ — both phenomena shared by *H* and *A* — has been commonly put down to predominance of *A*, see, e.g., my 1965:24–35, 41 and 4.4.2 below. (Concerning /ś/ see Schramm 1964:19). However, this assumption (which should not be taken as proved) is out of the question as regards the consonantal phonemes of *OfA*. The *OA* inscriptions reveal an excess of four phonemes, i.e. *PS* /ḏ, ṯ, ṭ, ḏ̣/, over the *OfA*. In our period, as the spelling of *BA* clearly proves, these phonemes no longer exist. This also applies to *E* (and *Dr*), i.e. the fifth century B.C., as is convincingly shown by Schaeder, cf. Rosenthal 1939: 69–70.

Therefore, if during the centuries of its co-existence with *C-H A* has jettisoned those phonemes that were alien to *C-H*, I, for one, can think of only one reason — the fact that the *C-H* substratum was able to assert itself, imposing its phonemic set upon the *A* superstratum.

The fact that this happened only several centuries after these two languages established contact with each other does not create any problem. It takes time for a substatum to surface; see, e.g., Pisani (1966:140), whose explanation of this phenomenon is certainly acceptable even to those who do not see eye to eye with him concerning his general theory.

If, therefore, the whole tense-system of *MH* turns out to be strikingly similar to that of *LA*, *a priori* there is no telling how this situation came about. The more so, since, as revealed by *OA* and *OfA*, the tense system of *A* itself underwent remarkable changes (though not as far-reaching as that of *H*).

H. Though the time of origin of *BA* is not yet established (see 4.6 below), there is no doubt that its language is *OfA* (see Baumgartner in his preface to Koehler-Baumgartner 1958:xxxi). Therefore it must be treated in this context.

The influence of *H* upon *BA* has been dealt with most recently by Frank R. Blake (1951:81–98). The work is very disappointing. It is hard to understand how Blake could state (p. 82): 'Most words containing $\check{s}_2$, which in *A* in general is regularly written with *s*, usually appear in a Hebraized form with *ś*, e.g. *bśr* ("meat")'. Has he never seen *OA* and *OfA* texts, where the spelling with *ś* is exclusively the rule? It is amusing to note that both G. Garbini and S. Moscati assume the opposite, i.e. that the /ś/ in *H* is the result of *A* influence! (See, e.g., my 1965:40). 'The prevailing use of *h* (as *mater lectionis*) for absolute feminine singular ... is perhaps to be ascribed to *H* influence' (Blake 1951:83) — again a statement that clashes head on with the picture presented by *OA* and *OfA*. The same applies to his statements concerning *h* (p. 84).

Grammar also did not fare much better at Blake's hands. The noun-pattern of [gəze:rat] (p. 85) presents a problem in *H* too (cf., e.g., the explanation of G. Bergsträsser 1918:147 d, c); [la:hen] (p. 86) is *A* = [la: + hen], see 4.3 above; *maʿᵃba:d* (p. 87) is *A*; the *maqta:l* pattern serves as absolute infinitive in *TO* (incidentally, this very noun is found in *BH* and nobody doubts that it is a loan from *A*); *S* [zəʿo:ra:] (p. 88, fn. 3) represents a *PS quta:l* pattern; the /a:/ → /o:/ (assimilation), cf. Brockelmann, *Grundriss* I, p. 185. In short, Blake's treatment of his subject could hardly be termed satisfactory.

4.4.2 *The Impact of* A *upon Other Languages*

A in *Ak*, see 3.4 above.

A in *H*, see 3.4 above.

A in *C*. An attempt to trace *A* influence in *C* was made by Kutscher (1969). This influence is heralded by [Klmw] *br* [ḥy'] of the Klmw inscription (eighth century), cf. Rosenthal (1939:85). It is clearly visible in the *Ak* transliteration of the Phoenician *Ba-a-a-ti-il* (= *bayti-il*). Since in Phoenician the diphthongs are contracted, this form obviously represents an Aramaism, as W. F. Albright had already assumed. The noun *'pt'* 'female demon' apparently represents a mixed form: *H-C* participle of the hollow verb (and *H-C* root) + the *A* postpositive article. A form like *mnṣbt* < *mṣbt* 'stela', *nntn* 'they were delivered', can only be explained as the result of dissimilation of a geminated consonant, as in *OfA*. Since in *C* the root *ntn* 'give' does not exist (it is *ytn*), the explanation of Friedrich (1951:§58c) (analogical formation) is impossible. The fact that Punic employs only *š* for the genitive construction, instead of the earlier *'š l* (= *H šl*), e.g. *mnṣbt šbtb'l* 'stela of the house of *B'l*' also seems to go back to the *A* use of *zy* (*dy*) in this position. Possibly the Greek transliteration *ρυβαν = *rbtn* 'our mistress' reflects the *A* possessive suffix (with stress-lengthened vowel, as is usual in *C*-Punic).

In the domain of vocabulary too, there seem to be a few clear-cut cases, e.g. *amma* 'mother' < *A 'imma:*, *šmš* 'serve', the prepositions *gw* 'in', *ṣd* 'to'.

A influence in Punic is probably due to the assumed *C-H*-Punic koine (Milik).

A in *P*. Roland G. Kent (1953:§12) says: '... it is to be expected that the style of the (*P*) inscriptions should reflect the style of Aramaic; and it does.'

I believe this to be right, but the proofs he adduces do not bear out his contention. E.g. §312: '... at the first mention of a person ... of a place ... the name of that person or place should be followed by [nāma] ... These phrases are perhaps based on similar phrases in Aramaic'. As I have shown, this does not seem to be the case, since these phrases are alien to *A* of both the preceding and following periods. Therefore in *A* it is most probably of foreign origin (1954:240).

In Kent's Addenda, p. 217, the construction of the phrase 'Thus says Darius' in *P* is ascribed to *A* influence. A. Meillet and E. Benveniste (1931:14) assume it to be of *Ak* origin. Incidentally, their proof for *A* influence upon *P* (1931:14–15) is not convincing either.

W. Brandenstein and M. Mayrhofer (1964) do not anywhere discuss the *A* impact upon *P*, but they do believe that the inventor(s) of the *Old P* script 'machten sich alle Vorzüge der aram(äischen) Schrift zu eigen' (p. 18, differing with Kuryłowicz). W. Hinz (in his review in *ZDMG* 107.395, 1967) believes '*astiy* "ist" meint in Wirklichkeit nur *asti*', the spelling being influenced by *A*. He has words of praise for Mayrhofer (who supplied the lexicon) for use of the 'aramäische Quellen' (*Ibid.*).

Recently W. Eilers (1968) discussed four points of contact between *A* and *P*. His article is disappointing. He assumes that '*P 'ta-ya* (entspricht) im Syrischen ein *hau-də* jener, der'. This construction 'ist typisch für ... das Syrische' and also, according to

Eilers, for the 'Altaramäische des Achämenidenreiches'. Therefore he believes (p. 66) that *A* serves as a parallel 'wenn nicht gar das Vorbild für den achämenidischen Bau des Relativsatzes'. This is certainly not correct. The material gathered by Eilers from *OA* and *OfA* is irrelevant, since the demonstrative pronoun is not employed as a correlative (in contrast to that of *S*). However, the best argument against Eilers' conclusion is the following: In the *A* version of the Behistun inscription the *P* relative pronoun *ta-ya*, etc., is paralleled by the single *A* relative pronoun *zy* without any demonstrative pronoun as correlative, e.g. *wḥrʾ ZY* ʿ[*mh*] 'and the nobles who were with him' *Co* 253, 1.34, in the *P* version appears as [utā : martiyā : tyaišaiy : fratama : anušiya : āhata] 'and those who were his foremost followers' (Kent 1953:125, 48–9). However, where the antecedent is followed by a demonstrative (which nevertheless does *not* function as a correlative) e.g. *gbrʾ ZK ZY rb hwh* 'that man, who was in command' *Co* 253,45, is rendered in *P* [hauv : martiya : hya : avahyā : kārahyā : maθišta : āha] 'this man who was the chief of that army' (Kent 1953:126, 70); the *A* demonstrative pronoun *zk* corresponds to the *P* demonstrative [hauv], while *zy* is paralleled by *P* [hya]. This point by itself ought to dispose of material collected by Eilers from *OfA*, e.g. [baitā zāk zī] (1968:65), where he equates *zk zy* (*[ze:k zi:]) which, as pointed out above, does not function as correlative, with [ha-ya (=hya)], etc. Perhaps he should have compared it with *Ak*, in which, according to Rimalt (1932:107–8), the demonstrative pronoun can also be employed as correlative.

Eilers also deals with the 'passivische Ausdrucksweise der Achämenideninschriften' and its *A* parallel. Strangely enough, he does not seem to know either Friedrich's article (and my note) or Benveniste's trailblazing article, see above 377. The third parallel is 'der mit dem aram. *šəmēh* ... merkwürdig übereinstimmende Gebrauch von *P nāma*, namens, genannt'. Eilers does not mention that this construction, e.g. *bkndr šmh* 'at a (city) named Kundur' *Co* 251,12 appears not only in *P* as [Kud^{u}ruš : nāma] 'a town by name Kunduru' (Kent 1953:122, 65), but also in *Ak* as [ina Kundur šumšu] *Co* 255,12. Since this construction does not appear in *A* prior to this period, not in *MA*, there is no doubt that it is either a calque from *P* or from *Ak*, see Kutscher (1954:241).

On the ostraca of Nisa: we seem to find a lexeme that parallels the use *šəmēh* of *OfA*, pass.part. of *Pəʿal* of the root *qry* (<*qrʾ*) (a village 'called'), see Diakonov and Livšic 1960:76, no. 99. Since these ostraca originated in a community speaking an Iranian dialect, it seems to be a new expression reflecting the *P nā:ma* construction. This fact could then be taken as an indication of *P* origin (at least during the periods concerned) of this phrase.

The last item, the possible parallel of the double realization of /bgd kpt/ in Middle Persian, should be noted by Aramaists.

Aramaists will certainly be unhappy about the fact that O. Szemerényi (1966:204), who maintains 'that O[ld] P[ersian] *azdā* is a noun meaning "announcement, message, news"' and that 'this noun is also contained in OP *azdā-kara* "announcer" attested by the Elephantine papyri', seems to have overlooked the occurrence of *azdā:* in *BA* and the phrase *'zd yt'bd* of *E*, *Co* 37,8 (cf. *azd krdn* in Pehlevi, *krdn* = *'bd*). The Aramaist will wonder whether Szemerényi's explanation of *azda kušuvā* (1966:205) still stands in view of *'zd yt'bd*. Other items in this article that might interest the Aramaist are no. 9 *Hūža* 'Elam' (= *Šūša*) and no. 10 *H^vārazmiš*, cf. *ḥrzmy* in *E*.

A complete breakdown of communication between the Iranists and the field of *A* is signified by R. Schmitt (1967), 'Griechisches μανιάκης — ein iranisches Lehnwort'. It is regrettable that Schmitt, who cites Daniel 5:7 in the Septuagint, did not look up the *A* text. Had he done so, he would have found that the corresponding *A* lexeme is identical with that of the Greek. With the help of, e.g. Koehler and Baumgartner 1958, he could easily have established that a whole literature had sprung up dealing with this Iranian loan in *A* and Greek.

I, for one, would be very interested to find out whether the fact that the *P* phrase [ka:ra hya mana:] exactly parallels both *A ḥyl' zy ly* and *Ak* [uqu attûa] 'my army' is merely a coincidence. All three languages can express the same notion by means of the possessive suffix, but in the Behistun inscription they take recourse to the analytic construction, based in *A* and *P* upon the relative pronoun (also see 4.1 above, especially concerning *Dr*). Since both in *Ak* and *A* this use predates the *P* period (it occurs in the Assur letter, 4.0 above), the only question seems to be whether this use in *P* is of indigenous growth or a calque from *A* or *Ak*.

A in Elamite. W. Eilers (1955) believes that the Elamite [pir-ra-tam-ma] is not *A* [bi:rta:], but a *P* lexeme. Eilers states (p. 256) 'dass aramäische Fremdwörter im Elamischen überhaupt gänzlich zu fehlen scheinen'.

A in Demotic. I do not know of any article dealing with the question of *A* influence upon Demotic. Concerning possible loan-translations, see pp. 383–4; see also my article, 1954:141–2. However, reading E. Bresciani (1964:119), I came across the following instance: '*ktn* (XII, 32) "Baumwolle" zu verstehen (wie Stricker)?'

This is impossible, since 'cotton' ('Baumwolle') goes back to *Ar* [quṭn], see Löw 1924:241–2. This lexeme cannot be identified with the root *ktn* that in *SL*, including *A*, means 'linen', cf. Löw 1924:210, as well as von Soden (1959) where he discusses *kitû(m)* (p. 495).

W. Erichsen (1954) translates *ktn* (p. 569) 'Gewand', which he seems to identify with *gtn*; see *gtn* (p. 594) where he says 'ein Gewand, o.ä., öfter in den Listen der Mitgift'. Now both *ktn* 'linen' and *ktwn* (> Greek χιτών 'garment of linen') occur quite often in *E* (correctly identified by *Kr*, but not by *Co*), and, e.g., in a marriage document (*Kr* 7).

In Kutscher 1954:240ff., I point to a possible loan-translation from *A* (and possibly a few loans). This field should prove promising for a Demoticist also at home in *A*, like Miss Bresciani.

4.5 *The A Logograms of Middle Persian*

E. Herzfeld states that 'If we take into account the very archaic character of a considerable number of ideograms [of Middle Persian], we clearly see that the ideographic system of writing in Aramaic script and in Aramaic language must be an inheritance from Achaemenian times' (Rosenthal 1939:79). But how did the system arise? H. H. Schaeder tried to explain it in the following manner: 'der achämenidische Kanzleiverkehr einerseits auf Einsprachigkeit [i.e. *A*] des Schriftwesens, anderseits auf Mehrsprachigkeit [i.e. *P*, Egyptian, Elamite, *Ak* etc.] der Schreiber gestellt war. Sie mussten imstande sein, ... ein aramäisches Schriftstück unmittelbar, "vom Blatt weg", in die Sprache des Adressaten zu übersetzen' (Schaeder 1930:5–6; see Rosenthal 1939:67–8). In this way the scribes grew accustomed to reading silently one language while speaking another. Therefore, when eventually they switched over to *P*, they maintained this custom to a certain extent by retaining a part of the basic *A* vocabulary and transferring it to their written *P*.

Schaeder even believed that he was able to determine the exact tecnical term that was employed in *OfA* (and *H*) for this kind of 'vom Blatt weg' translation: *A* [məpa:raš] (*H* [məporaš]). He identifies this term with the *P* term [uzva:rišn] which he believes was used to denote the system of logograms (Rosenthal 1939:67–8; Schaeder 1930:1–14).

Consequently, Schaeder assumes that these logograms go back to the fifth-sixth century B.C. This view emerges clearly from a passage on p. 41. He could therefore draw upon these logograms to prove the early origin of *BA* (see 4.6 below).

In this respect, there is no doubt that Schaeder has overreached himself. After all, he himself had to admit that late forms, as known, e.g., from *M*, are to be found among the logograms, see, e.g., p. 52 fn. 1 and especially concerning Parsik, p. 40: 'Denn wenn in diesem auch *orthographische* [his italics] Neuerungen erscheinen, die der Entwicklung des babylonischen Aramäisch, bzw. seiner Orthographie, in nachchristlicher Zeit entsprechen, ... so bleibt doch der reichsaram., aus der achämenidischer Zeit stammende *Formenbestand* [his italics] *bis auf wenige Ergänzungen* [my italics, E.Y.K.] unangetastet.'

Therefore, I cannot agree with his statement (p. 41): 'Wenn sie [i.e. *'šty* instead of *šty* = "drank"] einerseits in Dan(iel) und im Jüd.-Aram., anderseits im Pahl. und im Syr. auftritt, so gehörte sie schon deren gemeinsammen Ursprung: dem babylonischen Aramäisch des 6/5 Jh. v. Chr. an'. Once the existence of late forms is admitted, there is no clear-cut time limit as to the terminus *ad quem*. Even in this special case, because of the occurrence of this form both in *EA* and *WA*, the time limit could be the destruction of the *P* empire in the fourth century B.C. Rosenthal, too, who is quite close to Schaeder's views, expressly states (1939:80–1) that infiltration of late forms is a possibility to be reckoned with.

But if that be the case, only those logograms that occur in *OfA* sources can safely be attributed to Achaemenian times, as I pointed out in my review of Rosenthal 1939, (1942–43:180).

Recently, Altheim and Stiehl (1963) vehemently attacked Schaeder's views. They disagree with him 1) concerning the time of origin of the *A* logograms; 2) concerning the way they arose; and of course 3) concerning the alleged 'technical term'. (See below p. 398.)

W.B. Henning (1958:21–40) also deals with the problem of the logograms.

As to 1), he also seems to believe that the *A* nucleus of the individual logograms ('Urideograms', in his words) reflect *OfA* (incidentally, he does not mention Schaeder in this context); 3) the alleged technical term is not discussed at all. As to 2), he believes that once the Iranians learned the art of writing in *A*, they were reluctant to give it up. *P* started easing out *A* only during the second century B.C. The painful transition from *A* to *P* was facilitated by the retention of a part of *A* lexicon as logograms, to avoid a radical break with the past.

To be sure, these original logograms underwent changes at the hands of the Iranian scribes during hundreds of years and therefore it is 'verkehrt ... späte Schriftformen ohne die nötigen Abstriche dem Aramäischen zuzuschreiben; eine Schreibung wie ḤZYTWN muss man zwiebelgleich auswickeln um das wirklich aramäische Urideogram (! E.Y.K.) ḤZY erkennen zu können' (1958:35–6). He then does not believe in the infiltration of *LA* forms; the difference between the logograms and their *OfA* parents is to be attributed to the Iranian scribes. (See instances below p. 398.)

Henning does not make sufficiently clear one important point: Why should this avoidance of a break with the past have been coupled with another (and probably greater) break: the *A* elements being read in *P*? How did this revolutionary change come about? I, for one, can hardly follow the line of his argument that culminates in his words: (p. 31) '... jeder, der sich heutzutage mit den Dokumenten der älteren mitteliranischen Zeit befasst, weiss ... dass es wesentlich leichter ist, die Ideogramme als einheimische Wörter zu verstehen; den Schreibern jener Zeit mag es nicht anders gegangen sein'.

With all due respect to the great Iranist Henning, I doubt whether the comparison is valid with respect to people who read texts in their native tongue (in spite of the difficulty of reading Pehlevi, in which 12 graphemes are homographs). To be sure, Altheim and Stiehl, who are opposed to his views, as they reject those of Schaeder, do agree with him on this point for obvious reasons (see below).

Altheim and Stiehl (see above), who devote a large part of their work to contesting both the thesis of Schaeder and of Henning (1963:1–71, 278–308), say (p. 304) '... *Übereinstimmungen* [between *OfA* and the logograms] *sollen nicht geleugnet werden* [my italics, E.Y.K.]. Aber sie beweisen nicht den unmittelbaren Zusammenhang zwischen dem Aramäisch der achaimenidischen Zeit und der ideographischen Schreibweise unter den Sasaniden. Sondern sie gehen darauf zurück, dass reichsaramäische (*OfA*) Bestandteile ... im schriftlichen Gebrauch oder auch innerhalb der lebendigen Sprache [! E.Y.K.] durch die Jahrhunderte sich erhalten hatten. *In allem Übrigen bieten die Ideogramme das Bild des späteren Ostaramäisch*' [my italics, E.Y.K.].

Consequently, it is not surprising that they do not accept Schaeder's theory concerning the genesis of the logograms, nor that they deny the existence of the alleged technical term. Contrary to Henning they believe that the forms are genuine *A* forms, but reflect the *LA* (*EA*).

But how do they propose to solve the problem of the appearance of these logograms? Here they disappoint the reader. 'Die neue Form des Ideogramms — neu sowohl, was die Ausgestaltung der aramäischen Maske angeht, als auch neu durch den Antritt einer iranischen Endung — begegnet erst mit den Sasaniden. Daraus ergibt sich, als Folgerung, dass sie Schöpfung einer bestimmten geschichtlichen Lage und einer bestimmten geschichtlichen Haltung war. Etwa derart, dass man die überkommene aramäische Schreibung, dieses Erbe einer langen und grossen (will sagen: der achaimenidischen) Vergangenheit nicht missen möchte, aber sich doch veranlasst sah, es mit den neuen nationalen Forderungen, die sich mit der Erhebung des sasanidischen Königshauses einstellten, zu vereinigen. So kam es zu der Schreibung aramäischer Masken, an die iranische Endungen anträten. In jenen Masken erhielt sich das Alte im schriftlichen Bild, musste aber nunmehr *unweigerlich* iranisch gelesen werden. Erst die Neuerung der Endung führte den Umschlag herbei' (1963:63).

Again, as I said concerning Henning (above, p. 395), no real explanation is forthcoming as to how this revolutionary change (1963:64: 'bedeutete eine Revolution'!) happened. Since Altheim and Stiehl know no way out, at this particular point they agree with Henning (p. 64) (as quoted above, p. 395).

Very recently, F. Rundgren, in an interesting review of H. N. Nyberg's *A manual of Pahlavi* (Rundgren 1967), gave a short synopsis of the Schaeder-Altheim and Stiehl-Henning debate. He believes, like Henning, that the change goes back to the activities of the Iranian scribes. From an imperfect like *yktlwn* the plural morpheme *-wn* was transferred to the perfect, *ktlw*>*ktlwn*, and also to the passive participle: *'byd*+*wn*. Now, while he might be right concerning the second case (see below p. 398), I cannot agree with him as to the first. Even if he does not believe that *LA* forms might be found among the logograms, he should have taken into consideration the fact that the morpheme -(*w*)*n* in the perfect already appears in one of the Aśoka inscriptions (third century B.C.), see Altheim and Stiehl 1963:27, 58.

It should be remembered that a form, e.g. *yb*<*yhb*, that until recently was only attested in *LA*, has been found in fifth century B.C. Persepolis (see Schmidt 1957:55ff., and Altheim and Stiehl 1963:17ff.). Therefore, I see no problem at all in the assumption that the *-wn* morpheme of the perfect had existed at least a century before its emergence in the Aśoka inscription, i.e. in the *OfA* of the fourth century B.C. Incidentally, there is practically no *A* material dating from this century, except that to be published by Cross (see *BA* 26.110–21, 1963).

Can these seemingly entirely divergent views be reconciled? I believe they can, since on certain facts everyone seems to agree. There seems to be a consensus, as shown above, that at least a certain number of these logograms go back to *OfA*, and that a number of the logograms are different from their *OfA* counterparts (see above p. 395). The main problem, therefore, boils down to the problem of quantity: How many early logograms managed to survive without undergoing change? And do those which did change reflect *LA* (as maintained by Altheim and Stiehl [1963] and Rosenthal [1939], and admitted even by Schaeder), or are they the outcome of various analogical processes, to be attributed to the Iranian scribes who no longer knew *A* (Henning, Rundgren, and Schaeder 1930:39)? It seems pretty clear that both views are correct. Altheim and Stiehl's view is borne out by many (but by no means all) of the instances they discuss.

To clinch the matter, I would like to introduce a source overlooked by the scholars, though H. L. Ginsberg has pointed out its importance (1942:237–8). This source is the *A* deeds preserved in the *ATB* and in the writings of the Geonim. They contain many *OfA* elements that managed to survive even about 1,500 years after the domination of *OfA*. We find, e.g., *hnpq* (Hapʿel of *npq*) 'to bring out' (*'p(p)q-* in *LA*); see my article in *Tarbiẕ* (*H*) 17.125–7. But this form also survived in a different garb: the verbal substantive occurs as *hnpwqy*.

In other words, the consonantal base did not change but the noun pattern is that of *LA* (*ATB*, *M*, and *Pa*) *ʾqṭwly* (=*ʾp*(*p*)*wqy*). This instance proves: 1) the possibility of survival of *OfA* in deeds, but also 2) that it was apt to change under the influence of *LA* (and, of course, entirely new elements could be introduced).

Considerable material can be found, e.g. in *The Book of Shetaroth* (*Formularies*) by R. Hai Gaon (1930).

It may be assumed that some of these changes are early (cf. the plural morpheme *-wn*, above p. 396). A case in point is the logogram *ykʿymwn* = [e:sta:tan] 'to stand' from the root *qwm*. The intrusive /ʿ/ is as yet unexplained, but it may be early. The form *ʾrʿm*, *PTK* (Kahle 1930:34) (root *rwm*, *ʾApʿel*) may perhaps be taken as a hint in this direction. In these texts, there is no trace of weakening of the pharyngeals. Does then this spelling reflect a literary tradition that goes back to *OfA*? The fact that in *SA* the root *qwm* is spelled with /ʿ/ is less conclusive (because of the weakening of the pharyngeals in *SA*).

Be that as it may, the *ATB hnpq*, *hnpwqy*, etc., convincingly show that the infiltration of *LA* into texts that attempted to maintain *OfA* is a distinct possibility. Therefore, when the switch to *P* was made, the scribes were probably using an *OfA* infiltrated by *LA*, and it was this *A* material which they transferred to *Middle P*.

Incidentally, a further point as to the importance of these Jewish *A* deeds for the *Middle P* logograms is provided by the logogram *ʾyk*, read *ku* 'that' (introducing direct speech). As far as my knowledge goes, it is only in these texts that *A ʾyk* is employed with the same meaning, cf. *The Book of Shetaroth* (Hai 1930), e.g., p. 22, 1.16–17: *śhdwtʾ dhwt bʾnpnʾ* ... *ʾyk pl*(*ny*) ... *ʾmrlnʾ*: 'Testimony that was before us ... how (= that) X ... said to us'.

To come back to our problem, the influence of Iranian scribes on the language is more than a mere probability. It would have been a miracle had these scribes been able to avoid analogical spelling, as outlined, e.g. (but probably overstated) by Rundgren. One instance should suffice. Altheim and Stiehl had to do a lot of explaining concerning the logograms that contain the base *qṭyl*. They believe (1963:43), e.g., that *ʿBYDWN* represents an /i/ perfect (of the first stem), third person plural. This is impossible for two reasons: a) in the *A* dialects this root has an /a/ perfect; and b) this is one of the few roots that have an /i/ imperfect in *A* dialects. As is well known (cf. *H*, *Ar*), a verb with an /i/ perfect cannot have an /i/ imperfect. Therefore, the only acceptable explanation seems to be that of Henning and Rundgren: *ʿbyd* (and others) is a passive participle, and the plural morpheme *-wn* was transferred from the imperfect (and perfect, see above p. 396) by the Iranian scribes.

To be sure, Schaeder (p. 39) rejects this solution, since among the roots concerned there are also to be found intransitive verbs 'von denen im Aram. ein Part. pass. nicht gebildet werden kann'. It can be shown, however, that all these intransitive verbs *do* possess a passive participle (or a *qaṭṭi:l* form which is employed as a present perfect, at least in some of the *A* dialects): *ʿryq*(wntn)? = *vire:xtan* (Ebeling 1941:73) <['arri:qa:] 'fugitivus' in *S*; *ytyb/p*(wntn) = *nišastan* (p. 78) <[yatti:ba:] 'sedens' in *S*; *qym*(wntn) = *xa:stan* (p. 82). Schaeder remarks (45): 'das Aramäische stimmt mit dem Iranischen nicht überein, insofern als *xa:stan* nur intr(ansitiv) "aufstehen" heisst, *qymun* aber hier nur Pa(ʿel) sein kann "zum Aufstehen bringen"'. Since the passive participle of this root, *qym*, is employed in *S*, *M*, and *ATB* in the construction *qṭyl l-*, (see, e.g., Nöldeke 1875:382, fn. 2) the problem does not exist. Also the suggestion of Nyberg (1923:219), that these forms are best taken as imperatives, fails to carry conviction, because of *ʿryq*. But *qym*(wntn) = *vira:stan* 'einrichten' (Ebeling 1941:65) might indeed be a Paʿel. All the other *qṭyl* bases do not present a problem, since they belong to transitive verbs (including *ydʿy*(tn) for *da:nistan* 'to know', the reading given by H.J. Polotsky, instead of *ḥwy*(tn) (1932:281, fn. 1), cf. Rundgren (1967:233).

Perhaps the view rejected by Nyberg (1923:223), that 'there is no reason at all why we should claim identical explanations for all the ideograms of the *nplwn* type', is correct after all.

To sum up: A certain number of the *Middle Persian* logograms were handed down during the centuries virtually unchanged, others changed under the impact of *LA*, others were reshaped by the Iranian scribes. It will be the task of future researchers to decide each case on its merits.

At this stage, I still believe that the scales are weighted in favor of Schaeder's hypothesis concerning the genesis of the system.

To be sure, H.J. Polotsky (1932) has shown convincingly that both the accepted translation of [uzva:rišn] 'explanation' and Schaeder's identification of it with the *A* root *prš* are incorrect. But he has also assumed a certain complicated connection between the *P* lexeme, translated by him 'unterscheiden, erkennen', and the *A* root *prš*. Altheim and Stiehl apparently overlooked this important article (nor is it mentioned by Rosenthal 1939). It must be admitted that Altheim and Stiehl's objections to Schaeder's view cannot be rejected out of hand, but their interpretation of the alleged 'technical term' is at best possible, not really decisive. Since they were unable to put forward another convincing solution, I believe Schaeder's view still stands as a working hypothesis, even if the matter of the identification of the *A* (and *H*) *prš* with the *P* [uzva:rišn] remains unresolved.

Incidentally, the process which Schaeder assumes was used in translation seems to be practically unavoidable in parallel situations. The late I. A. Abbady, who was the chief English-*H*, *H*-English translator for the British Mandate Government in Palestine, during which these two languages and *Ar* were accorded the status of official languages, was able to translate in this way. In fact, he told me that one of his Arab colleagues was fired because he was not up to this required skill.

In future, it would be useful if those trying to solve the riddle of the genesis of the *Middle P* logograms familiarized themselves with the views of Assyriologists as to the same problem in *Ak*: the genesis of Sumerian logograms in *Ak*.

Two more works dealing with the *P* logograms should be mentioned: E. Ebeling's *Das aramäisch-mittelpersische Glossar Frahang-I-Pahlavik im Lichte der assyriologischen Forschung* (1941) and H. F. J. Junker's *Das Frahang-I-Pahlavik in zeichengemässer Anordnung* (1955). W. Eilers closes his review of the latter (in *Oriens* 16.328–33, 1963), by saying that 'auch als Vorstudie [es] noch weit entfernt ist von der Publikation des *Frahang*, die wir einst erwarten'. Concerning Ebeling he thinks 'Ein Assyriologe von der Beschlagenheit Erich Ebelings hat diese Zusammenhänge [between the logograms and the field of Assyriology] ganz richtig gefühlt, doch im Einzelnen meist falsch gedeutet' (1933).

It is earnestly hoped that in the future scholars will also draw upon the Dead Sea Scrolls in which have been found some spellings identical with those of *Middle P* logograms, e.g. *r'yšh* 'Haupt' (Ebeling 1941:22), cf. *H r'yšyt* = [rē(')ši:t] (Kutscher 1959:132); *mzn'* 'Waage' (Ebeling 1941:43), which in *E* is spelt *mwzn'*, appears once in the Dead Sea Scrolls = *H mzn(ym)* (Kutscher 1959:141).

Schaeder (cited in Ebeling 1941:50–1) believes *ynsywn* 'nehmen' to be a mistake, and that it should have been *ynsbwn*. Since *nś'* (> *nsy* in *GA*) is employed with this meaning in *BA* and *Dr*, the emendation does not seem to be necessary.

H. S. Nyberg's *A manual of Pahlavi* (1964) is a new edition of his very important *Hilfsbuch des Pehlevi* (I=1928, II=1931). It contains about 300 logograms (the derivatives included, see Rundgren's [1967] review). We can only wait for the publication of the second volume where, it is to be hoped, Nyberg will clarify problems pertaining to the logograms. He remarks (1964:X, 10): 'The miswritten ideogram LṢT = the preposition *tar*, is throughout replaced by the correct form LṢD -*r*, found in the inscriptions, and not seldom also occurring in the MSS'. Is this assumption really necessary? The *BA* preposition *lṣd* turns up in *TO* as *lṣyt* (Koehler and Baumgartner, *A* section). Is it impossible to assume that both the early and late forms were absorbed by Pehlevi?

A collection of all the *Middle P* logograms prepared by an Iranist, Aramaist, and Akkadologist is an urgent desideratum.

4.6 *The Problem of BA*

Concerning the problem of *BA*, the time and place of its origin, Rosenthal (1939:60–

71) has given an excellent account of the long drawn out debate starting with G.R. Driver and finishing with H.H. Schaeder. Does the language of *BA* indicate a provenience from the (later) *EA* region or the *WA* one? Does the language represent early *A* (fifth-sixth century B.C.) or late (second century B.C.)?

In the wake of Schaeder, Rosenthal arrived at the conclusion that no decision in this respect is possible 'Somit war der alte "Sprachbeweis" ad acta gelegt' (p. 70).

H.L. Ginsberg, in his excellent review of Rosenthal (1939), does not accept this verdict, because (1942:231): '1. The particular Greek words in Dan. 3 are late. 2. The Grecism in 2:47 likewise precludes any dating before 320 B.C. and renders questionable any location beyond the extreme limits of Lagid expansion. 3. While the suffixes and pronouns ending in *n* instead of *ō* or *m* may have been in vulgar use long before they were admitted into literature, the fact is that at first they were not admitted at all and in the fifth century only sparingly. 4. As for the accusative particle **yat* (Dan. 3:12), its literary use is not only late but characteristic of the west and rare in the east. 5. It is further suggestive that the substitution of the masculine for the feminine of the third person plural perfect (in the Ktib of Dan.) also coincides with frequent Palestinian usage.'

As to 1. see below p. 401. 2. The phrase *mr' mlkyn*, Dan. 2:47 has since turned up in the Adon letter (sixth century B.C.). This fact then effectively disposes of Ginsberg's argument, see Fitzmyer's discussion (1965:44–6). 3. Ginsberg is inclined to disagree with Schaeder (on modernization of the spelling). In view of the archaic spellings in Nabataean, Schaeder's theory has to be considered a distinct possibility (see below, p. 401). 4. *yt* has turned up in *Kr*. To be sure, Ginsberg, in his review of *Kr* (1954:157) has made an attempt to explain this lexeme as being derived from the root **yty* 'to come': 'Though one may hesitate between taking *yth* as an imperfect — as against the perfect *khln pṣln* — or as a perfect backformed from an imperfect *yēṯē'* (*sic*!). It goes without saying that Aramaists will not be too impressed by his views, cf. Jean and Hoftijzer (1965:28–9). Moreover, the very fact that *yt* is recorded only once in *BA*, while *l-*, indicating the accusative, is quite frequent (see p. 127 of my article, mentioned below), indicates the East (where *yt* is rare) and not the West (where it is common). 5. May I be permitted to quote H.L. Ginsberg, *Studies in Daniel* (1948:3): 'we may say that from first to last the Aramaic dialects have preserved feminine plural forms distinct from the masculine not only in the imperfect but also in the *perfect* of the verb' (my italics, E.Y.K.). Thus we need not tackle this point (see above p. 373 f.).

In his *Studies in Daniel*, Ginsberg (1948:1–2) adduces a new loan-translation from Greek [ʿidda:n] 'time, season, year', Greek χρόνος 'time, year'. However, F. Rosenthal, in his review (1949:173), has shown that this case is far from convincing.

On the other hand, I have pointed out (1952:123–7) that the word-order of *BA* is of the Eastern type.

Still, *grosso modo*, the situation remains unchanged, even if it can be shown (as I intend to do elsewhere) that the vocalization of *BA* goes back to *EA*.

K.A. Kitchen in 'The Aramaic of Daniel' (1965) again took up the problem. His is clearly an apologetic attempt, but well done. He shows that in respect to the period of the language the famous verdict of G.R. Driver (Rosenthal 1939:61) '... the Greek words *demand* ... the Aramaic *permits* a date after the conquest of Palestine by Alexander the Great (332 B.C.)' no longer seems that impressive. He has marshalled all the evidence pertaining to the problem and handled it carefully. How successful he was can be realized from the review by H.H. Rowley (1966:112–16) — Kitchen's article is mainly directed against Rowley's *The Aramaic of the Old Testament* (1929). — Rowley's criticism boils down to two points:

1) He does not believe in the modernizing of the *A* of Daniel, without trying to refute the arguments of Schaeder. However, the Hermopolis papyri, I think, clearly point up the danger inherent in linguistic argumentation based practically only on spelling criteria (see above p. 400).

In these papyri, e.g., final [a:] is always spelled plene + *h*, both the final [a:] of the feminine and the [a:] of the definite article, which elsewhere at this time (fifth century B.C.) is nearly always spelled plene + ['], see above p. 369. On the basis of *this* spelling we should date the Hermopolis papyri nearly a thousand years later, since this type of spelling is dominant in *GA* and is the only spelling in *SA*. Therefore *today* we must be cautious when employing this type of argument in dating a text.

Rowley also makes no effort to explain why, e.g., Nabataean inscriptions of the first century B.C. should have preserved archaic spellings with *z* (for /ḏ/), while no trace of this spelling can be discovered in Daniel, admittedly written at least one hundred years earlier. Also, it would be difficult to date the language of the Genesis Apocryphon in the first century B.C. (see Fitzmyer 1966:14–17) without explaining why it should differ from *BA* in so many respects (see Fitzmyer 1966:17–25, and Kutscher 1957b:6–13).

Therefore, the only answer seems to be either the assumption of modernization (cf. Rosenthal 1939:68) or the assumption that *BA*, like the Hermopolis papyri, represents an aberrant type of *OfA*.

2) Rowley's argument that the Greek loans ψαλτήριον and συμφωνία as names for musical instruments occur in Greek several hundred years after the suggested date of Daniel also does not sound convincing. After all, if we assume Greek influence prior to Alexander, it is not the Attic dialect, or other dialects of Greece, that must be taken into consideration as the place of origin of these loans, but rather dialects of Asia Minor and/or those of the Greek isles. What do we know about the Greek of Asia Minor and of the Greek isles during the period in question? To the best of my knowledge, very little. As a parallel to my assumption, cf. the following statement: 'The curiosity of Latin military vocabulary that it preserves in *ballista* a Greek term that does not occur in our Greek texts is easily explained by Athenaeus' statement (8.362b) that βαλλίζω belongs to Sicily and Magna Graecia, whence the Romans will have borrowed the noun' (G. Shipp 1961:144). I therefore believe that the onus of proof (that these two Greek loans are late in Greek) rests upon Prof. Rowley.

On the other hand, the very fact that as of now no trace of Greek influence has been discovered in other semantic fields where it would be natural for it to surface, e.g. the names of officials, cf. Daniel 3:2 (and these names are *P* and *Ak*), cannot be easily explained away. The fact that the field of music is the only one where Greek influence has come to light, calls to mind Otto Jespersen's words (in his *Growth and structure of the English language*, 9th ed., 27): 'If all other sources of information were closed to us except such loan-words in our ... North-European languages as *piano*, *soprano*, *opera*, *libretto*, *tempo*, *adagio*, etc., we should still have no hesitation in drawing the conclusion that Italian music has played a great role all over Europe'. The influence of Italian upon English is otherwise small (142).

Therefore, while on the one hand the presence of Greeks in the Middle East before the Persian Empire is well attested (Kitchen has assembled all the relevant material, 1965:44–6) — but, I believe, was not strong enough to make itself felt in the Near Eastern languages prior to Alexander (see above p. 389) — Greek musicians might have been dominant enough to make their impact felt in those languages, as the Italian musicians did in English.

I believe that the explanation given by Rowley (1929:151) to account for the anomaly of the use of Greek loans only in the field of music is unconvincing, since the same could apply to the terms belonging, e.g., to the field of administration (the names of high officials).

The 'Sprachbeweis' then is neutralized, and other criteria should be used to date Daniel.

As to the solving of the problem of place of origin, i.e., to which is *BA* closer, Eastern *OfA* or Western *OfA* (see above 4.0), I believe that the *A* of the Dead Sea Scrolls might be usefully consulted.

Let us assume that further research uncovered in *BA* hitherto unnoticed linguistic traits (or traits which have not been adequately brought to bear upon the problem) that could by no means be attributed to *WA*; would not these new insights (and there are some in the domain of syntax) constitute a clear-cut proof of the Eastern provenience of *BA*?

It is here that the Qumra:n *A* may be destined to play a very important role. This material, *prima facie*, has to be considered to be of Western (Palestinian) origin. How then are we to account for the occurrence of *EA* elements in it, such as we find in the Genesis Apocryphon? 'Of course, we could assume that originally they had been common to both branches of Aramaic and eventually died out in the Western branch. But the solution seems to be much simpler. The centre of the Persian Empire being in the east, including the territory that was to become the domain of the (later) Eastern Aramaic, it was only natural that especially in the lexical field "Reichsaramäisch" should be coloured by the Eastern dialects. Therefore, words of Eastern origin should have been known to and used by people composing in *A* even in the West (the opposite is much less probable)' (Kutscher 1957b:14).

The third person feminine plural of the perfect has in the Genesis Apocryphon the ending [ʾ]=[*a:] (Fitzmyer 1967:161) like the Qere of *BA*. Ginsberg (1948:4) had pointed out correctly that this is an *EA* trait. — Indeed, I hope to be able to show elsewhere, that the vocalization of *BA* reflects *EA*! — Still, in this case we might argue that this form was originally at home also in *WA* and was eventually replaced by another. But it would be much more difficult to dispose in this way of the following point. According to A.S. van der Woude (1963:327), '*Status absolutus* und *status emphaticus* werden promiscue gebraucht, offenbar ohne Unterschied in Bedeutung'. There is not the slightest doubt that *WA*, i.e. *GA*, *SA*, and *PCA*, as established already by Th. Nöldeke (1904:48–9), does distinguish correctly between the different states, and it is only in the contemporary *EA* that these distinctions have broken down.

The above-mentioned solution (viz., that a certain trait was originally common to both branches) would not apply here, and only the second (the coloring of *A* everywhere by the Eastern branch) can be considered. But once we can prove that even texts that originated in Palestine (and, concerning the Targum of Job, as long as the opposite is not proved, this seems to be the case) could exhibit *EA* grammatical traits, the same could also hold true concerning *BA*. Therefore, even clear-cut *EA* lexical and grammatical elements in *BA* could not be regarded as decisive in this respect.

4.7 *Gains*

The chief gains of our period are, clearly, the discovery of the Driver documents which are essential in establishing the existence of both branches of *A* (Eastern and Western *OfA*) especially thanks to the *qtyl l-* construction (see above p. 377), the clarification to a certain extent of the problem of the P logograms (see above 4.5), and the excellent article of Ben-Ḥayyīm, establishing beyond doubt the fact that *OfA* had but one form for the perfect 3rd person plural. This possibly holds true for the imperfect as well. To be sure, fem. forms like *yhynqn* in Sefîre seem to indicate the fem. [*yuhayniqa:n]. Since they function as short imperfect (the so-called 'jussive'), where the parallel masculine form does drop the *n*, they indeed seem to contradict Ben-Ḥayyīm's thesis concerning *OA*. Very important concerning the terminus a quo of the double realization of /bgd kpt/ is Eilers' discovery (above p. 374). The lexical gains from the new texts also deserve to be mentioned.

4.8 *Desiderata*

We very much need a grammar of the texts of our period (including their greatly neglected syntax).

A new grammar of *BA* is also long overdue. The tasks of this new grammar are set forth very clearly by S. Segert (1958a). I can subscribe to all his points except two: 1) 'die aramäische Syntax in ihrer genuinen Gestalt ohne wesentliche fremde Einflüsse eigentlich nur im Mandäischen vorliegt' (1958a:132). Considering the fact that Mandaean seems to exhibit traces of spectacular *Ak* influence (cf., e.g., the weakening of the pharyngeals and laryngeals, the dissimilation of geminates by [n], cf., e.g., Ginsberg 1936:96–8), his statement today sounds strange; 2) 'für die letzte Phase des Bibeltextes noch mit der Heranziehung der arabischen Sprache ... zu rechnen [ist] besonders für die Aussprache der Laryngalen' (133). This view is based upon a famous theory of Kahle. However, his views concerning the influence of Arabic upon the Massorites can no longer be taken seriously, as was shown immediately after the discovery of the Dead Sea Scrolls by, among others, H. Yalon, Z. Ben-Ḥayyīm, and E.Y. Kutscher; cf., e.g., Kutscher 1959:34–6, 42, 352, 401–3.

Segert also rightly stresses the urgent need for an edition of the ostraca of Persepolis and Elephantine (1958a:129).

Several monographs on 'Languages in Contact' would also be very welcome (see 4.4 above). After all, this is the last *A* period in which the literary *A* more or less reflects the stage of the spoken language, which can scarcely be said of the following period, Middle *A*.

BIBLIOGRAPHY

Aartun, K. 1959. Zur Frage des bestimmten Artikels im Aramäischen. AcOr 24.5–14.

Altheim, F., and R. Stiehl. 1963. Die aramäische Sprache unter den Achaimeniden. I. Frankfurt am Main.

——. 1964. Die Araber in der alten Welt I. Berlin.

Aro, J. 1963. Präpositionale Verbindungen als Bestimmungen des Nomens in Akkadischen. Or 32.395–406.

Bauer, H., and P. Leander. 1927. Grammatik des Biblisch-Aramäischen. Halle-Saale.

Baumgartner, W. 1927. Das Aramäische im Buche Daniel. ZATW 45.81–133. Reprinted 1959 in his Zum Alten Testament und seiner Umwelt. Leiden.

——. 1947. Vom neuen biblisch-aramäischen Wörterbuch. Festschrift Otto Eissfeldt, ed. by J. Fück, 47–55. Halle an der Saale.

[——.] 1967. Hebräisches Wortforschung. Festschrift W. Baumgartner. Leiden.

Ben-Ḥayyīm, Z. 1951. Hannistaro:t ba'ᵃra:mi:t haqqadmo:ni:t. Eretz Israel I.135–9. Jerusalem.

Benveniste, E. 1952. La construction passive du parfait transitif. BSL 48.52–63.

——. 1954. Éléments perses en araméen d'Égypt. JA 74.297–310.

——. 1966. Titres et noms propres en iranien ancien. (Travaux de l'institut d'études iraniennes de l'Université de Paris 1.) Paris.

Bergman, B.Z. 1968. *Han'el* in Daniel 2:25 and 6:19. JNES 27.69–70.

Bergsträsser, G. 1918. Hebräische Grammatik I. Leipzig.

——. 1929. Hebräische Grammatik II. Leipzig.

BIRKELAND, H. 1940. Akzent und Vokalismus im Althebräischen. Oslo.

BLAKE, FRANK R. 1951. A resurvey of Hebrew tenses, with an appendix: Hebrew influence on Biblical Aramaic. Rome.

——. 1953. Studies in Semitic grammar V. JAOS 73.7–16.

BLAU, J. 1965. The emergence and linguistic background of Judaeo-Arabic. Scripta Judaica V. Oxford.

BOWMAN, RAYMOND A. 1944. An Aramaic religious text in Demotic script. JNES 3.219–31.

BRANDENSTEIN, W., and M. MAYRHOFER. 1964. Handbuch des Altpersischen. Wiesbaden.

BRAVMANN, M.M. 1961. Genetic aspects of the genitive in the Semitic languages. JAOS 81.386ff.

BRESCIANI, E. 1960. Papyri aramaici egiziani di epoca persiana presso il Museo Civico di Padova. RSO 35.11–24.

——. 1964. Der Kampf um den Panzer des Inaros. Wien.

BRESCIANI, E., and M. KAMIL. 1966. Le lettere aramaiche di Hermopoli. Atti della Accademia Nazionale dei Lincei, Memorie, Classe di Scienze morali, storiche e filologiche, Series VIII 12/5.357–428.

BROCKELMANN, C. 1928. Lexicon Syriacum. 2nd ed. Hallis Saxonum.

——. 1954. Handbuch der Orientalistik III. Semitistik 2–3.135–62. Leiden-Köln.

BRÖNNO, E. 1941. Einige Namentypen der Septuaginta. AcOr 19.33–64.

CAZELLES, H. 1955. Nouveaux documents araméens d'Égypte. Syria 32.75–100.

CHRISTIAN, V. 1944. Die Stellung des Mehri innerhalb der semitischen Sprachen. SWAW 222/3.

COOKE, G.A. 1903. A textbook of North-Semitic inscription. Oxford.

COUROYER, B. 1954. Termes égyptiens dans les papyri araméens du Musée de Brooklyn. RB 61.554–9.

[——.] See MILIK 1954a:251–3.

COWLEY, A. 1923. Aramaic papyri of the fifth century B.C. Oxford.

CROSS, F.M. JR. 1963. The discovery of the Samaria papyri. The Biblical Archaeologist 26.110–21.

——, and D.N. FREEDMAN. 1952. Early Hebrew orthography. New Haven.

DAHOOD, M., K. DELLER, and R. KÖBERT. 1965. Comparative Semitics. Some remarks on a recent publication (Review of Moscati 1964). Or 34.35–44.

DEGEN, R. 1967. Zur Schreibung des Kaška-Namens in ägyptischen, ugaritischen und altaramäischen Quellen. Die Welt des Orients IV. 48-60.

——. 1969. Altaramäische Grammatik der Inschriften des 10.-8. Jh. v. Chr. (Abhandlungen für die Kunde des Morgenlandes, 38/3.) Wiesbaden.

DIAKONOV, I.M., and V.A. LIVŠIC. 1960. Dokumenti iz Nisi. Moskva.

DIEZ-MACHO, A. 1963. Arameo. Enciclopedia de la Biblia I. col. 666–72. Barcelona.

DILLMANN, A. 1907. Ethiopic grammar. 2nd ed. enlarged and improved by C. Bezold.

DONNER, H. 1963. Review of Rosenthal 1961. OLZ 58.358–62.

——, and W. RÖLLIG. 1962–64. Kanaanäische und aramäische Inschriften. 3 vols. Wiesbaden.

DRIVER, G.R. 1953. Hebrew poetic diction. Congress Volume, Supplements to Vetus Testamentum I, 26–39. Leiden.

——. 1954. Aramaic documents of the fifth century B.C., transcribed and edited with translation and notes by G.R. Driver ... with help from a typescript by E. Mittwoch, W.B. Henning, H.J. Polotsky, and F. Rosenthal. Oxford, Clarendon Press. (Abridged and revised edition, 1957.)

——. 1957. Aramaic names in Accadian texts. RSO 32.41–57.

DUPONT-SOMMER, A. 1944. Mémoires présentés par divers savants à l'Academie des Inscriptions et Belles Lettres, Paris. XIV/2.1–42.

——. 1944–45. L'ostracon araméen d'Assour. Syria 24.24–61.

——, and L. ROBERT. 1964. La déesse de Hiérapolis Castabala (Cilicie). Bibliothèque archéologique et historique de l'institute français d'archéologie d'Istanbul XVI.7–15. Paris.

EBELING, E. 1941. Das aramäisch-mittelpersische Glossar Frahang I Pahlavik im Lichte der assyriologischen Forschung. Leipzig.

EILERS, W. 1934. Review of O. Krückmann, Babylonische Rechts und Verwaltungs-Urkunden aus der Zeit Alexanders und der Diadochen (Weimar, 1931). OLZ 37.90–100.

——. 1935. Das Volk der *karkā* in den Achämenideninschriften. OLZ 38.201–13.

——. 1940. Iranische Beamtennamen in der keilschriftlichen Überlieferung I. (Abhandlungen für die Kunde des Morgenlandes XXV/5.) Leipzig.

——. 1954–58. Neue aramäische Urkunden aus Ägypten. AfO 17.322–35, 18.125–7.

——. 1955. Altpersische Miszellen I. ZA N.F. 17.225–36.

——. 1964. Kyros. BNF 15.180–235.

——. 1968. Zum altpersischen Relativpronomen. Zeitschrift für vergleichende Sprachforschung 82.62–9.

ERICHSEN, W. 1954. Demotisches Glossar. Kopenhagen.

FITZMYER, J.A. 1957. The syntax of *kl*, *kl'* in the Aramaic texts from Egypt and Biblical Aramaic. Biblica 38.170–84.

——. 1962. The Padua Aramaic papyrus letters. JNES 21.15–24.

——. 1965. The Aramaic letter of King Adon to the Egyptian Pharaoh. Biblica 46.41–55.

——. 1966. The Genesis Apocryphon of Qumran Cave I. Rome.

——. 1967. The Aramaic inscriptions of Sefîre. Rome.

FRIEDRICH, J. 1951. Phönizisch-punische Grammatik. Rome.

——. 1957. Zur Bezeichnung des langen *ā* in den Schreibweisen des Aramäischen. Or 26.37–42.

——. 1957–58. Zur passivischen Ausdrucksweise im Aramäischen. AfO 18.124–5.

——. 1965. Zur Stellung des Jaudischen in der nordwestsemitischen Sprachgeschichte. Studies in honor of Benno Landsberger on his seventy-fifth birthday, 425–9. Chicago.

GARBINI, G. 1956. L'aramaico antico. Atti della Accademia Nazionale dei Lincei, Memorie, Classe di Scienze morali, storiche i filologiche, serie VIII, 7/5.239–84.

——. 1960. Il semitico di nord-ovest. Napoli.

——. 1966. Semitico nord-occidentale e aramaico. Linguistica Semitica: presente e futuro. Roma.

GELB, I.J. 1955. Review of von Soden 1952. BiOr 12.93–111.

GINSBERG, H.L. 1924–25. Minḥa ləDa:vi:d, David Yellin jubilee volume (*H*). Jerusalem.

——. 1933. Aramaic dialect problems. AJSL 50.1–9.

——. 1933–34. Notes on a Palestinian Targum. Tarbiz 5.381–3.

——. 1936. Aramaic dialect problems II. AJSL 52.95–103.

——. 1942. Review of Rosenthal 1939. JAOS 62.229–38.

——. 1948. Studies in Daniel. (Text and studies of the Jewish Theological Seminary of America, XIV.) New York.

——. 1954. The Brooklyn Museum Aramaic papyri. (Review of Kraeling 1953.) JAOS 74.153–62.

——. 1955. Proverbs of Aḥi:qar. Ancient Near Eastern texts, 427–30. 2nd ed. Princeton.

——. 1957. Akten des vierundzwanzigsten internationalen Orientalisten-Kongresses, München, 256–7. Wiesbaden.

——. 1959. Notes on some Old Aramaic texts. JNES 18.143–9.

——. 1961. Review of Rosenthal 1961. JBL 70.386–7.

——. 1966–67. Hahisto:riyya: šel ʿAm Yisra:ʾel (The history of the Jewish people) II, ed. by B. Mazar, 72–5, 319 (notes). Jerusalem.

GLUECK, N. 1940. Ostraka from Elath. BASOR 80.3–10.

GOETZE, A. 1946. The Akkadian masculine plural in *-ānū/ī* and its Semitic background. Lg 22.121–30.

——. 1962. Cilicians. JCS 16.48–57.

GORDON, C.H. 1937-39. The Aramaic incantation in cuneiform. AfO 12.105–17.

——. 1940. The cuneiform Aramaic incantation. Or 9.29–38.

GREENFIELD, J.C. 1965–66. Stylistic aspects of the Sefire treaty inscriptions. AcOr 29.1–18. (Previously published in Lĕšonénu 27/28.303–13.)

——. 1967–68. Dialect traits in Early Aramaic. Lĕšonénu 32.359–68.

GRELOT, PIERRE. 1967. Review of Bresciani and Kamil 1967. RB 74.432–7.

HAI, R. GAON. 1930. The Book of Shetaroth (Legal Formularies) (*H*), ed. by S. Assaf. Supplement to Tarbiz I/3. Jerusalem.

HENNING, W.B. 1958. Handbuch der Orientalistik I, IV. Iranistik, Abschnitt 1. Leiden-Köln.

HUFFMON, H.B. 1965. Amorite personal names in the Mari texts. Baltimore.

JASTROW, O. 1967. Laut- und Formenlehre des neuaramäischen Dialekts von Midin im Ṭur ʿAbdin. Bamberg.

JEAN, CH. F., and J. HOFTIJZER. 1965. Dictionnaire des inscriptions sémitiques de l'ouest. Leiden.

JESPERSEN, O. 1937. Analytic syntax. London.

JUNKER, H. F. J. 1955. Das Frahang I Pahlavīk in zeichengemässer Anordnung. Leipzig.

KAHLE, P. 1930. Masoreten des Westens II. Stuttgart.

KENT, ROLAND G. 1953. Old Persian. 2nd ed. New Haven.

KITCHEN, K. A. 1965. The Aramaic of Daniel. Notes on some problems in the Book of Daniel, by D. J. Wiseman, T. C. Mitchell and R. Joyce, W. J. Martin, and K. A. Kitchen, 31–79. London.

KNUDSEN, E. E. 1969. Spirantization of velars in Akkadian. *lišān mitḫurti.* Festschrift W. von Soden, ed. by W. Röllig and M. Dietrich, 147–55. Neukirchen-Vluyn.

KOEHLER, L., and W. BAUMGARTNER. 1958. Lexicon in Veteris Testamenti Libros. Leiden.

KOOPMANS, J. J. 1962. Aramäische Chrestomathie. 2 vols. Leiden.

KRAELING, EMIL G. 1953. The Brooklyn Museum Aramaic papyri. New documents of the fifth century B.C. from the Jewish colony of Elephantine. New Haven.

KUTSCHER, J. [= E. Y. Kutscher). 1945–46. On the terminology of documents in Talmudic and Gaonic literature. Tarbiz (*H*) 17.125–7; 19.53–9, 125–8.

——. 1950. Studies in Galilean Aramaic. Tarbiz (*H*) 22.53–63.

KUTSCHER, E. Y. 1942–43. Review of Rosenthal 1939. Kirjath Sepher (*H*) 19.171–81.

——. 1950. ʾAra:mi:t. Encyclopedia Biblica (*H*) I. Hierosolymis coll. 959–70.

——. 1952. Biblical Aramaic — Eastern Aramaic or Western Aramaic. World Congress of Jewish Studies, Summer 1947, I (*H*), 123–7. Jerusalem.

——. 1954. New Aramaic texts. JAOS 74.233–48.

——. 1957a. Review of Driver 1954. JBL 76.336–8.

——. 1957b. The language of the Genesis Apocryphon. Scripta Hierosolymitana IV.1–35.

——. 1959. The language and the linguistic background of the Isaiah Scroll (*H*). Jerusalem.

——. 1961–62. The research on the Aramaic of the Talmud Babli. Lĕšonénu (*H*) 26.149–83.

——. 1963. Mishnaic Hebrew. Henoch Yalon jubilee volume (*H*). Jerusalem.

——. 1963–64. Aramaic calques in Hebrew. Tarbiz (*H*) 33.118–30.

——. 1965. Contemporary studies in North-western Semitic. JSS 10.21–51.

——. 1966. Review of Moscati 1964. Asian and African Studies 2.192ff.

——. 1969. Two 'passive' constructions — Aramaic-Persian calques. Proceedings of the International Conference on Semitic Studies, 1965. Jerusalem.

——. 1971 The Hermopolis papyri. Qudem, Annual of Oriental Studies. Tel-Aviv University.

LANDSBERGER, B. 1937–39. Zu der aramäischen Beschwörung in Keilschrift. AfO 12.247–57.
——. 1948. Sam'al. Ankara.
——. 1967a. The date palm and its by-products according to the cuneiform sources. AfO, Beiheft 17, ed. by E. Weidner. Graz.
——. 1967b. Brief des Bischop von Esagila an König Asarhaddon. MKNA 28/6.
LEANDER, P. 1928. Laut- und Formenlehre des Ägyptisch-Aramäischen. Göteborgs Högskolas Årsskrift 34/4. Göteborg.
LITTMANN, E. 1941. Review of Rosenthal 1939. Or 10.397ff.
LIVERANI, M. 1962. Antecedenti dell'onomastica aramaica antica. RSO 37.65–76.
LÖW, I. 1924. Die Flora der Juden II. Wien and Leipzig.
MEILLET, A., and E. BENVENISTE. 1931. Grammaire du vieux-perse. 2nd ed. Paris.
MENASCE, J. DE. 1954. Mots d'emprunt et noms propres iraniens dans les nouveaux documents araméens. BiOr XI.161–2.
MICHAUD, H. 1961. Review of Rosenthal 1961. Syria 38.327–40.
MILIK, J.T. 1954a. Review of Kraeling 1953. RB 61.247–51.
——. 1954b. Review of Driver 1954. RB 61.592–5.
——. 1967. Les papyrus araméens d'Hermoupolis et les cultes syro-phéniciens en Égypt perse. Biblica 48.546–622.
MORAG, SH. 1964. Biblical Aramaic in Geonic Babylonia. Studies in egyptology and linguistics in honour of H.J. Polotsky, 117–31. Jerusalem.
MOSCATI, S. (ed.). 1964. An introduction to the comparative grammar of the Semitic languages, by S. Moscati, A. Spitaler, E. Ullendorff and W. von Soden. (Porta Linguarum Orientalium, Neue Serie VI). Wiesbaden.
MUFFS, Y. 1969. Studies in the Aramaic legal papyri from Elephantine. Leiden.
MURAOKA, TAKAMITSU. 1966. Notes on the syntax of Biblical Aramaic. JSS 11.151–67.
MURTONEN, A. 1960–61. Review of Rosenthal 1961. Abr Naharain 2.72–6.
NAVEH, J. 1964–65. Early Aramaic inscriptions. Lĕšonénu (*H*) 29.183–97.
——. 1965–66. Addenda to Early Aramaic inscriptions. Lĕšonénu (*H*) 30.157–60.
NOBER, P. 1958. 'Adrazda: (Ezdras 7:23). Biblische Zeitschrift N.F. 2.134–8.
——. 1961. Review of Rosenthal 1961. Biblica 42.245–6.
NÖLDEKE, TH. 1875. Mandäische Grammatik. Halle.
——. 1898. Kurzgefasste syrische Grammatik. 2nd ed. Leipzig.
——. 1904. Beiträge zur semitischen Sprachwissenschaft. Strassburg.
NYBERG, H.S. 1923. The Pahlavi documents from Avromān. MO 17.182ff.
——. 1964. A manual of Pahlavi I. Wiesbaden. (First edition: Hilfsbuch des Pehlevi, I=1928, II=1931, Uppsala.)
PAUL, H. 1937. Prinzipien der Sprachgeschichte. 5th ed. Halle-Saale.
PISANI, V. 1966. Entstehung von Einzelsprachen aus Sprachbünden. Kratylos XI. 125–41.
POLOTSKY, H.J. 1932. Aramäisch *prš* und das 'Huzvaresch'. Muséon 45.273–83.
——. 1944. Études de syntaxe copte. Cairo.

PORTEN, B., and JONAS C. GREENFIELD. 1968. The Aramaic papyri from Hermopolis. ZATW 80.216–31.

PRAETORIUS, F. 1886. Äthiopische Grammatik. Karlsruhe und Leipzig.

RABIN, C. 1969. The nature and origin of the šafʿel in Hebrew and Aramaic. Eretz-Israel 9 (W.F. Albright volume), 148–58 (Hebrew section), 138 (Non-Hebrew section, summary). Jerusalem.

RABINOWITZ, J.J. 1956. Jewish law: its influence on the development of legal institutions. New York.

——. 1958. Studies in legal history. Jerusalem.

RIMALT, E.S. 1932. Wechselbeziehungen zwischen dem Aramäischen und dem Neubabylonischen. WZKM 39.99–122.

ROSÉN, H.B. 1959. Zur Vorgeschichte des Relativsatzes im Nordwestsemitischen. AO 27.186–98.

——. 1961. On the use of the tenses in the Aramaic of Daniel. JSS 6.183–203.

ROSENTHAL, F. 1939. Die aramaistische Forschung seit Th. Nöldekes Veröffentlichungen. Leiden.

——. 1949. Review of Ginsberg 1948. JAOS 69.173–4.

——. 1961. A grammar of Biblical Aramaic. (Porta Linguarum Orientalium.) 2nd ed. Wiesbaden.

——, (ed.). 1967. An Aramaic handbook. 4 vols. Stuttgart.

ROWLEY, H.H. 1929. The Aramaic of the Old Testament. Oxford.

——. 1966. Review of Kitchen 1965. JSS 11.112–16.

RUNDGREN, F. 1953. Zum Lexicon des Alten Testaments. AcOr 21.301–45.

——. 1955. Über Bildungen mit *š*- und *n-t*- Demonstrativen im Semitischen. Uppsala.

——. 1957. Zur Bedeutung von *šršw* — Esra 7:26. VT 7.400–4.

——. 1958. Über einen juristischen Terminus bei Esra 6:6. ZATW 70.209–15.

——. 1963. Ein iranischer Beamtenname im Aramäischen. OS 12.89–98.

——. 1967. Review of Nyberg 1964. OS 16.226–34.

SALONEN, E. 1967. Die Gruss-und Höflichkeitsformeln in babylonisch-assyrischen Briefen. SO XXXVIII.

SCHAEDER, H.H. 1930. Iranische Beiträge I. Schriften des Königsberger Gelehrten Gesellschaft, geisteswissenschaftliche Klasse 6.199–296.

SCHLESINGER, M. 1928. Satzlehre der aramäischen Sprache des babylonischen Talmuds. Leipzig.

SCHMIDT, E.F. 1957. Persepolis. 2nd ed. Chicago.

SCHMITT, R. 1967. Griechisch μανιάκης — ein iranisches Lehnwort. Sprache 13. 61–4.

SCHRAMM, GENE M. 1964. The graphemes of Tiberian Hebrew. (University of California Publications, Near Eastern Studies II.) Los Angeles and Berkeley.

SCHUSTER, H.-S. 1965. Der Relativsatz im Phönizischen und Punischen. Studies in honor of Benno Landsberger on his seventy-fifth birthday, 431–48. Chicago.

SEGERT, S. 1956. Aramäische Studien I. AO 24.383–403.
——. 1958a. Aufgaben der biblisch-aramäischen Grammatik. Communio Viatorum 2.127–34.
——. 1958b. Aramäische Studien III-V. AO 26.561–84.
——. 1965. Ugaritisch and Aramäisch. Studia Semitica philologica necnon philosophica Ioanni Bakoš dicata, 215–26. Bratislava.
——. 1967. Contribution of Professor I.N. Vinnikov to Old Aramaic lexicography. AO 35.463–6.
SHAFFER, A. 1965. Hurrian **kirezzi*, West-Semitic *krz*. Or 34.32–4.
SHIPP, G.P. 1961. *Ballista*. Glotta 39.149–52.
SODEN, W. VON. 1952. Grundriss der akkadischen Grammatik. Rome.
——. 1959–. Akkadisches Handwörterbuch. Wiesbaden.
——. 1959–60. Aramäisches *ḥ* erscheint im Spätbabylonischen vor *m* auch als *g*. AfO 19.
——. 1966. Aramäische Wörter in neuassyrischen und neu- und spätbabylonischen Texten, Ein Vorbericht I (*aya-* **mūs*). Or 35.1–20.
——. 1968. Aramäische Wörter ... II (*n-z* und Nachträge). Or 37.261–71.
SPEISER, E.A. 1939. Progress in the study of the Hurrian language. BASOR 74.4–7.
SPERBER, A. 1962. The Bible in Aramaic III. Leiden.
SPITALER, A. 1938. Grammatik des neuaramäischen Dialekts von Maʿlūla (Antilibanon). Leipzig.
——. 1952–54. Zur Frage der Geminatendissimilation im Semitischen. Zeitschrift für indogermanische Forschungen 61.257–66.
——. 1962. *Al-Ḥamdu Lillāhi Llaḏī* und Verwandtes: Ein Beitrag zur mittel- und neuarabischen Syntax. Oriens 15.97–114.
STINESPRING, W.F. 1962. The active infinitive with passive meaning in Biblical Aramaic. JBL 81.391–4.
SZEMERENYI, O. 1966. Iranica II. Sprache 12.190–226.
TELEGDI, A. 1935. Essai sur la phonétique des emprunts iraniens en araméen talmudique. JA 226.177–256.
TORREY, CHARLES C. 1941. On the ostraca from Elath. BASOR 82.15–16.
TSEVAT, M. 1960. A chapter on Old West Semitic orthography. The Joshua Bloch memorial volume, 82–91. New York.
TULAND, C.G. 1958. Uššayyā' and 'Uššarnā. JNES 17.269–75.
UNGNAD, A. 1928. Zur Sprache des Spätbabylonischen. Mitteilungen der Altorientalischen Gesellschaft 4.220–5.
VINNIKOV, I.N. 1958–65. Slovar aramejskich nadpisey (A dictionary of the Aramaic inscriptions). Palestinsky Sbornik 3.171–216 (1958), 4.196–240 (1959), 7.192–237 (1962), 9.141–58 (1962), 11.189–232 (1964), 13.217–62 (1965).
WAGNER, M. 1966. Die lexicalischen und grammatikalischen Aramaismen im alttestamentlichen Hebräisch. Berlin.

WEHR, H. 1964. Das 'Tor des Königs' im Buche Esther und verwandte Ausdrücke. Islam 39.247–66.

WILLIAMS, J.G. 1964. A critical note on the Aramaic indefinite plural of the verb. JBL 83.180–2.

WOUDE, A.S. VAN DER. 1963. Das Hiobtargum aus Qumran Höhle XI. Supplements to VT 9.323–31.

WRIGHT, W. 1955. A grammar of the Arabic language I. 3rd ed. Cambridge.

WÜST, W. 1966. Altpersische Studien. München.

YARON, R. 1957. Two Greek words in the Brooklyn Museum Aramaic papyri. HUCA 28.49–51.

——. 1959. Jewish law in other legal systems of antiquity. JSS 4.308–31.

——. 1960. Aramaic marriage contracts: corrigenda and addenda. JSS 5.66–70.

——. 1961a. Introduction to the law of the Aramaic papyri. Oxford.

——. 1961b. Notes on Aramaic papyri II. JNES 20.127–30.

Abbreviations used in article

A Aramaic
Ak Akkadian
Ar Arabic
ATB Aramaic of the Talmud Babli
BA Biblical Aramaic
BH Biblical Hebrew
Br Bresciani 1960
BrKa Bresciani and Kamil 1966
C Canaanite
Co Cowley 1923
Dr Driver 1954
E Elephantine
Eg Egyptian
EA Eastern Aramaic
GA Galilean Aramaic
H Hebrew
JA Jewish Aramaic
Kr Kraeling 1953
LA Late Aramaic
M Mandaic
MA Middle Aramaic
MdA Modern Aramaic
MH Mishnaic Hebrew
N Nabataean
OA Old Aramaic
OfA Official Aramaic
P Persian
Pa Palmyrenean
PCA Palestinian Christian Aramaic
PTK Palestinian Targum, edited by Kahle (see Kahle 1930)
PS Proto-Semitic
S Syriac
SA Samaritan Aramaic
SL Semitic Language(s)
TO Targum Onqəlos
U Ugaritic
WA Western Aramaic

CLASSICAL ARABIC[1]

CAROLYN G. KILLEAN

The length of the bibliography which accompanies this article is misleading. There is really very little work on Classical Arabic that can be classified as linguistic in any modern sense of the term. However, if linguistics is given a broader interpretation, one which includes textual analysis, lexicography and stylistics, then there is a much larger field to survey. This situation is not very surprising. Classical Arabic has no native speakers. Its long history of written data and equally long tradition of native grammatical studies has not been very attractive to linguists primarily interested in language as oral communication and the description and comparison of phonological systems. Linguists trained in modern schools of analysis have regarded work in Classical Arabic as ancillary to their major efforts in the fields of comparative semitics and modern dialectology. Analysis of the structure of Classical Arabic has thus been left principally to the Arabist-philologists. Left alone in the field, they have produced some remarkably good works outside the mainstream of modern linguistic thought. They have carried on the tradition begun by the great German Arabists of the late nineteenth and early twentieth centuries. Some of these modern philological works will be discussed below for, without an understanding of their viewpoint and efforts, Classical Arabic linguistics will continue to suffer from a certain shallowness which encourages Arabists to ignore it.

In the brief survey which follows, works have been singled out for attention which seem particularly significant to a linguist in the general field of Classical Arabic studies.[2] The material is organized into two major sections — Descriptive and Dia-

[1] The title of this article refers to that linguistic entity more properly termed Literary Arabic (Rabin et al. 1957). In the divisions of the historical development of this language proposed in that excellent article, the title Classical Arabic is reserved for the first period of development of the literary idiom after the rise of Islam. This practice is entirely laudable and should be encouraged in future publications. Since, however, the use of the name Classical Arabic as a synonym for Literary Arabic is a long established tradition and is so used in most of the articles covered by this review, it will be retained in the following discussion.

[2] Bibliographical material for this article was drawn primarily from the following sources: *Bibliographie linguistique et complément des années précédentes*, par le Comité International Permanent des Linguistes, *Linguistic Bibliography*, Vol. I-XX (Utrecht, Spectrum, 1946–65); *1960–1967 Selected Bibliography of Arabic*, Educational Resources Information Center, Clearinghouse for Linguistics (Washington, Center for Applied Linguistics, 1967). Annotated bibliographical information on some linguistic works covering Arabic can also be found in the *Abstracta Islamica*, the second half of every volume of the *REIsl.* Bibliography on the older philological works in the field of Arabic, particularly

chronic Studies. In addition, two particularly important trends in this field have been singled out for special attention. One is the on-going attempt to formulate and describe those characteristics which separate Modern Literary Arabic as a linguistic entity from earlier stages of Classical Arabic. The other is the assessment of the long tradition of linguistic philosophy and methodology of the native Arab grammarians. A brief comment on the state of Arabic linguistics in the Arab world today closes this review.

1. DESCRIPTIVE STUDIES

1.1 *General Works*

For a concise, well-organized and well written introduction to Classical Arabic structure and the historical development of the literary language, the *Arabic language handbook* (Bateson 1967) can be recommended highly. Outdating the earlier attempt at such a structural sketch by Yushmanov (1938; in English 1961), an ambitious effort to treat both the diachronic and synchronic structure of Arabic simultaneously, Miss Bateson confines herself to generalizations which go far enough but not too far. Her presentation of the major points of Classical Arabic phonology, morphology and even, surprisingly, some syntax is given along the well-established lines of American structuralism.

In direct contrast to the format of Miss Bateson's description stands the introductory work of Father Henri Fleisch (1956) one of the most outstanding contributors to the field of Arabic linguistics and philology. Following the Sapir-Trubetskoy tradition of the French school of Arabic linguistics, Father Fleisch presents the synchronic structure of Arabic in process terminology, not, however, without frequent references to diachronic explanations. The work should be read in conjunction with its important review by Charles Ferguson (1958) in which some interesting counter analyses based on a Bloomfieldian approach to the subject are presented.[3]

Fleisch's latest major work (1961) abandons all pretext of being a modern linguistic analysis. Writing for Arabists, not linguists, Fleisch puts all his examples into Arabic script, draws heavily upon his knowledge of the works of the Arab grammarians of the early Middle Ages for comparison with his own analysis, and includes a mixture of synchronic, diachronic and comparative statements. The total effect is very good

---

the important German contributions, can be found in Brockelmann (1953–54), Rabin et al. (1957), and Wehr (1934).

[3] Of special interest to the student of linguistic history, the Ferguson-Fleisch confrontation mentioned above is only one example of a theoretical controversy which arose in several Arabic dialectology studies in the 1950's between these two competing schools of linguistic thought. For an interesting discussion of these differences as reflected in specific contrasting analyses of dialect phenomena, see Cantineau (1956), Smeaton (1956), and Ferguson (1957). Reflecting the changing scene in American linguistics, the modern student of generative-transformational linguistics finds himself in basic agreement with the French point of view in their arguments with the American descriptivists.

philology and an excellent summary of past philological work in the field. It is well worth the effort it requires for a student of Arabic linguistics to read it. So far, only the first volume covering the sound system and the noun has appeared. It is to be hoped that future volumes will contain, in addition to the full treatment of morphological data exhibited for the noun, an adequate treatment of the domain of Arabic syntactical studies.

1.2 *Phonological Studies*

Classical, and for that matter also so-called Modern or Contemporary Arabic, is a *Schriftsprache* as capable of as much difference in phonetic interpretation between countries as the ecclesiastical Latin of the Mass. (Mitchell 1960:374)

The largest amount of phonological research on Classical Arabic has been carried on by the French school of Arabic linguistics (1.1). The great Arabic dialectologist, Jean Cantineau, published a short, basically philological review of the Classical Arabic sound system in 1941. After revising his views in the light of the phonological principles of Trubetskoy, Cantineau (1946) established distinctive oppositions for 26 consonants and 3 vowels in Classical Arabic.[4] The recent work by Denz (1964) carries on this approach in phonology. Jakobson (1957) employs his new distinctive feature system of analysis to reduce Cantineau's numerous phoneme oppositions to 9 binary feature oppositions which cover the vocalic as well as the consonantal system of Arabic. This article illustrates what can be accomplished when modern linguistic theories are applied to Classical Arabic data. Unfortunately, it represents a good beginning but no Arabist-linguist has continued this line of development as yet.

Two phonological problems in the description of the sound system of Classical Arabic have been of special interest to linguists. One is the description of 'emphasis', i.e. velarization or pharyngalization in certain consonants and its effect on its environment. The title of Jakobson's article (1957) reflects his conviction that velarization, the *mufaxxama* of native Arab phoneticians, is equivalent to the flat feature of his flat/plain phonological opposition. A classical taxonomic phonemic approach to this same problem is presented by Nasr (1962). In addition, Ferguson (1956) in establishing the phonemic status of the velarized /l/ in Classical Arabic bases it on structuralist criteria. For additional studies, see Petraček (1952, 1956).

The second major interest in Classical Arabic phonology has been the phenomenon known as the root patterning of consonants. In discussing this phenomenon in its widest application to all Semitic, Greenberg (1950) draws heavily on Arabic for data. More restricted studies on this same subject and the related problems of metathesis and dissimilation of root consonants include Colin (1939, 1945–48), Chouemi (1961, 1965), Lecerf (1963), and Petraček (1964).

[4] Both of these important articles have been republished in Cantineau (1960).

Discussions of the synchronic status of stress phenomena in Classical Arabic have generally grown out of diachronic studies of dialect stress systems (2.5). For example, Mitchell (1960) proposes a prosodic analysis of Classical Arabic stress which would base prediction of stress exclusively in terms of syllable structure.

1.3 *Morphological Studies*

> The verb in Arabic is complex, but highly regular and symmetrical. The noun on the other hand has a simple case inflection but is generally unpredictable, almost chaotic in plural formations. (Ferguson 1958:318, in a review of Fleisch 1956)

Linguistic studies of the morphology of Classical Arabic have been carried on principally in connection with comparative studies or the preparation of textbooks. For general statements of the morphology of Classical Arabic, reference should be made to the works of Bateson (1967) and Fleisch (1956) mentioned above (1.1).

One refreshingly new approach is that taken by Schramm (1962). Taking as a base form the unmarked imperative stem of the verb, Schramm derives the entire system of Arabic verb stems through synchronic, generative morphophonemic rules. Aside from a few minor faults, the system is admirable, particularly in its ability to account in a regular way for the behavior of the stems derived from weak roots. In a summary concluding his presentation, Schramm predicts that comparisons between systems of ordered series of morphophonemic rules such as the one he has presented for the Arabic verb stems could be used to establish generic relationships between languages. This predication is being borne out as historical linguistics today turns to comparisons of rule correspondences as a new part of its methodology.

The linguistic nature of the formal binary division of the Arabic verb stem is still a subject of debate among Arabists and linguists. The question of whether this division represents a temporal contrast: past/non-past or an aspectual split: perfective/non-perfective has been resolved in different ways by different scholars. Recent articles in this controversy include those in Russian by Kovalev (1952, 1963; with Šarbatov 1960), and Chrakovskij (1965a, b, and c) as well as the recent work in German by Aartun (1963). The 'aspect-above-all' position of the French school of Arabists is presented clearly by Fleisch (1957b) and repeated by him (1961) in addition to a survey of past arguments on this question.

On the classification of the Arabic derived or augmented verb stems, several articles have proposed changes in the traditional system which is based only on increasing stem length. Better linguistic criteria are proposed by Ferguson (1958) in his review of Fleisch (1956) which include the syntactic/semantic notion of transitivity. Drozdik (1964) elaborates on this approach with more emphasis given to semantic over formal criteria. Less successfully, MacDonald (1963) returns, for pedagogical reasons, to the traditional symbolization for derived stems employed in general by Semitists. The recent study of the Arabic verb by Bulos (1965) should be considered only in conjunction with its review by Krotkoff (1967). Unseen by this author, but presumably also in this category, is the article in Russian by Belkin (1963).

Nominal Classical Arabic morphology has been barely touched on by synchronic linguistic analyses. Classical examples of post-Bloomfieldian methodology in the field of morphology are found in Trager and Rice (1954) and the brief additional remarks by Hamp (1959). This type of analysis is evident also in the recent work of Petraček (1965) on the plural suffixes of Arabic nouns.

The nominal declensions of Classical Arabic and their interesting interaction with the system of final vowels which mark case relationships are the subject of articles by Pellat (1951), Vycichl (1953, 1958), and, in particular, Rabin (1965) although the latter is principally diachronic in approach. Pellat (1960) presents a short note on the usage of collective nouns for the names of certain animals in Arabic.

1.4 *Syntactic and Semantic Studies*

> One phenomenon I encountered with all the informants, which may well be unique to work with a written language about which people have a reading knowledge but not a fluent speaking knowledge, was the reluctance of informants to declare a sentence completely unacceptable ... One informant repeatedly stressed to me that modern Arabic is everything that is in the ancient grammar books, plus some new structures — i.e. that there is no such thing as obsolescence in literary Arabic. (Lewkowicz 1967: 5–6)

The most significant trend for the future of Classical Arabic linguistics is the current rise in interest in syntactic studies following closely the rise and development of the generative-transformational school of linguistics in America. Recent applications of this theory to the data of Modern Literary Arabic (1.6) have been preceded by several earlier works in Arabic linguistics. Bravmann (1953) produced a study which was ten years premature in its observations and methodology. Attempting to analyse the syntax of some constructions long considered peculiarly Arabic in nature by the application of what he terms semantic or syntactic universals, Bravmann's terminology is vague and obscure but his theoretical viewpoint is familiar to those favoring the current transformational approach to the description of syntax. Some of the same syntactic constructions which puzzled Bravmann have received additional treatment by Pellat (1961), Mamedov (1963), and Snow (1965). The latter work represents an attempt to treat these constructions as optional stylistic transformations of basic kernel sentences in Arabic. Bishai (1965) carries on the more traditional American approach to syntax; divide, substitute and classify. This article will seem out of date and insignificant to those who favor the transformational analysis of syntax.

Semantic studies of Classical Arabic are limited to the field of lexicography. These works generally concentrate on the vocabulary of some major period (Wehr 1934) or literary work in Classical Arabic (Beck 1956). Inclining more to philology than to linguistics with the welcome exception of Wehr, only a few articles of this type have been included in this bibliography. Morabia (1964) has produced an interesting collection of data on the connotation of color adjectives in Arabic.

1.5 *Applied Studies*

The long history of written data in Classical Arabic has appealed to those interested in the new theory of lexicostatistics or glottochronology which arose in the 1950's. Samarrai (1959) announced results from such a study which he claimed supported the traditional myth of the naturally conservative nature of the Semitic languages. Hymes (1959) readjusted Samarrai's data to bring his results more into line with the established constant rate of morphemic loss postulated for all languages by this method. Satterthwait (1960) agreed with Hymes using data which he claims represents the dialect of Mecca in 632 A.D., i.e. the Koran. These studies support lexicostatistics for those who already believe it valid. They make no new converts of those who deny the scientific validity of its premises.

Pilot programs of machine translation of Arabic have been prepared by Cohen (1961), Frolova and Fitialov (1963) as well as Satterthwait (1963, 1965). The statistical techniques of information theory analysis have been applied to quantitative data on the verb stem formations of Arabic by Skalmowski (1964) with interesting if not wholly understandable results.

1.6 *Modern Literary Arabic*

> ... a written language, powerfully influenced by traditional norms, which nevertheless is required to express a multitude of new foreign concepts, not for one country only, but for many distributed over a vast geographical area. (Wehr 1961:IX)

One of the most significant trends in modern Classical Arabic linguistics is the attempt to characterize by lexicographical and other internal criteria, the nature of Modern Literary Arabic. In addition to the article on this subject by Hans Wehr in Rabin et al. (1957), the major work of Monteil (1960) is important for an introduction to the development of this stage of Classical Arabic.

Lexicography has been of vital importance in the attempt to describe Modern Literary Arabic. As early as the 1930's scholars were turning their attention to the problem of defining the nature of its lexicon (Wehr 1934, Mainz 1931). Several teams of scholars have collected lists of vocabulary actually in use on the printed page in the Arab world today and others have subjected these to frequency counts. Worth mentioning here are the works of Brill (1940), Pellat (1952), and Landau (1959). The pinnacle of all this work was reached with the publication in 1958 of the Arabic-German edition of Hans Wehr's excellent dictionary of Modern Literary Arabic. Its

English edition followed shortly thereafter (1961) with another excellent discussion of the nature of Modern Literary Arabic included in its introduction.

The processes of word derivation and borrowing that contributed to the development of this new era in Classical Arabic vocabulary are discussed in several other articles and a recent dissertation (Bielawski 1956, Lecomte 1961, 1964, Lecerf 1966, and Saʿid 1964). In addition, Arab authors have discussed these processes with a view to suppressing or changing some of them (see below under 3).

In addition to work on the lexicon of Modern Literary Arabic, other aspects of this modern form of Classical Arabic have been researched. Syntactic studies include several recent Ph.D. dissertations applying the Chomsky model of language description to various sectors of Modern Literary Arabic structure. Snow (1965) has been mentioned above (1.4). Killean (1966) has written phrase structure and transformational rules employing syntactic features to account, in particular, for the partitive nature of some Arabic noun phrase constructions. Lewkowicz (1967) concentrates on the transformational derivation of participles in Arabic from underlying verb phrases. Comparative analyses appear in the theses of Erickson (1965) and Becker (1964). In addition to these transformational approaches to the syntax of Modern Literary Arabic, the work by Borrmans (1961) is worthy of note. In an interesting collection of data taken from published sources, Borrmans exhibits the increase in constructional ambiguity which results from the influence of French syntax on Arabic writers.

Phonological studies are, if anything, rarer than syntactical analyses. Comparisons of the phonological systems of the modern dialects and Modern Literary Arabic are available in the following works: Alani (1963), Selim (1967), Al-Toma (1957), Mitchell (1960), and Harrell (1961). It is particularly significant that three of these works are by Arabs trained in linguistics in the United States. They represent one of the brightest hopes for the continuation of good phonological and syntactic studies in this field.

The following recent works in Russian have appeared in the U.S.S.R. since the date (1963) of Haim Blanc's excellent survey of this field (Vol. I, *Current Trends in Linguistics*, 377–83). From their titles alone, they are presumed to be works primarily concerned with the general field of Modern Literary Arabic.

Lexicography: Kariev (1965a and b), Nedospasova (1963), Panachi (1965), Ušakov (1963, 1965), Šagal' (1963a and b).

Structure: Belkin (1963), Romačev (1965), Šegal' (1965).

Besides interest in the structure of Modern Literary Arabic, another important concern of current linguistic investigation is the usage of this language form in the modern life of the Arab world. Bateson (1967) gives an excellent review of the situation. Ferguson (1959b) presents an outline of the *diglossia* nature of Arabic and compares it to other contemporary language situations, notably usages of Greek, Swiss German and Haitian Creole. Harrell (1961) discusses very briefly the structure and use of the oral form of Modern Literary Arabic which appears in Egyptian radio broadcasts. In the same monograph, Blanc (1961) includes data and a brief analysis of an interdialectal conversation in Arabic. A better study of this form of 'compromise' Arabic — neither fully Classical nor fully Colloquial in nature — is to be found in Bishai (1966). Further studies of this interesting problem include the articles of Shamosh (1951–52, in Hebrew), Belkin (1959, 1960), Šarbatov (1965), and Cachia (1967).

2. DIACHRONIC STUDIES

There are very few works in the field of historical and comparative studies in Classical Arabic which are accessible to a linguist without a good knowledge of Arabic. The following survey therefore is very brief and will be little more than an outline of those areas of concern which hopefully will be studied more fully by Arabist-linguists in the future.

2.1 *General Works*

An excellent survey of the development of Classical Arabic as a literary language is found in the new edition of the *Encyclopedia of Islam* (Rabin et al. 1957). A very brief summary of this appears in Bateson (1967). For a more detailed account of the external cultural history of Classical Arabic, the work of Fück (1950) is important for the Classical period while Monteil (1960) covers the modern era.

2.2 *Phonological Studies*

Diachronic studies of the internal linguistic development of Classical Arabic are rather rare. The fiction that Classical Arabic is a synchronic rather than diachronic unity contributes to this fact. There is no lack of historical data, for example, scribal errors, descriptions of pronunciation by Arab grammarians and such evidence as the transcription of foreign words, but there are only a few qualified linguists who know Arabic well enough to evaluate and interpret this data. In the field of phonological development, only a few studies are worth mentioning as yet. Magee (1950) has written a brief article on the evolution of the 'emphatic' consonants in Arabic. Martinet, in an excellent article (1959), discusses the palatalization of /g/ which occurs in Classical Arabic without the expected corresponding palatalization of /k/. For additional work in this field, see the contributions of Cantineau (1941), Blachère (1952), and Ružička (1950).

2.3 *Morphological Studies*

In the realm of comparative and diachronic morphology, the following studies are recommended. Wehr (1952) discusses the development and use of the superlative adjective or elative form in Arabic. In 1953, he turns his attention to the expression of negation in Arabic in comparison to other Semitic languages and the modern dialects. The form and development of the definite article in Arabic has been analyzed in studies by Pellat (1951), Gabučan (1963b), and in particular Ullendorff (1965). Kuryłowicz (1950) and, in particular, Rabin (1965) review the origins and present function of the diptote declension. Murtonen (1964) covers the formal patterns of the broken plural noun forms in Classical Arabic. This last work unfortunately lacks a bibliography and has not yet been assessed by scholars in the comparative field.

2.4 *Historical Dialectology*

Three major areas of concern are the basis of the majority of philological and linguistic works on the dialectology of Classical Arabic.

(1) The dialect situation in Arabic at the time of the formation of Classical Arabic.
(2) The origin of the *ʿArabiyya* or Classical Arabic itself.
(3) The stages of internal linguistic development in the literary language.

The following classification of articles takes into consideration that these areas tend to overlap within any single work on the subject of Classical Arabic historical development.

2.4.1 The best comprehensive studies of the dialect situation of the pre-Islamic Arab world are those of Rabin (1946, 1951; et al. 1957). His most extensive work is that of 1951. His collection of data on the Western Arabian dialects is limited but his methodology is refreshingly modern and he makes a good case for his conclusions about dialect groupings in a hitherto unexplored area. Petraček (1954) contributes a philological study of the old dialect of Medina.

2.4.2 Based on textual analysis and statements by the early Arab grammarians, conflicting conclusions as to the origin and nature of early literary Arabic and its relationship to the language of the Koran have arisen. Rabin (1951) presents his view that Classical Arabic is basically an amalgam of Eastern and Western Arabian dialects, the Eastern group contributing the grammatical structure, the Western group, the sound system. In 1955 Rabin published an excellent survey of the arguments in this controversy including those of Fück (1950) and Kahle (1948, 1949). Additional analyses of this early period of development in historical dialectology appear in works which seek to explain the origin of the diversity manifest in the modern dialect situation in the Arab world (2.5).

2.4.3 As mentioned above in footnote 1, the continuous 1500 year-long history of Classical Arabic development has only recently been divided into definable segments on the basis of modern linguistic criteria. Fück (1950) discusses the rise of Middle

Arabic in a study whose outlook is basically non-linguistic. For the opinions of an excellent linguist, the recent works by Blau (1963a and b, 1965) contribute to the specification of Middle Arabic. For a discussion of works relating to the modern period of Classical Arabic, see (1.6) above.

2.5 *Comparative Studies*

Comparative studies of Arabic in relation to the other members of the Semitic family of languages and even the larger grouping of the Afro-Asiatic languages generally lie beyond the scope of this survey. The comparative grammar recently produced by Grande (1963) in Russian does come highly recommended for those who can make use of it.

The historical relationship of Classical Arabic to the various modern Arabic dialects has been examined principally by Arabic dialectologists studying the modern period. Birkeland's outlines (1940, 1952, 1954) of the development of these modern spoken languages from the pausal forms of Classical Arabic have met with only limited approval. Ferguson (1956) in an important review of Birkeland's most recent attempt in this direction (1954) questions the validity of the thesis that the modern dialects developed from the Classical language at all. In 1959a, Ferguson supports his belief in an urban *koiné* as the common ancestor of all the modern dialects by marshalling an impressive array of internal linguistic evidence. This evidence has come under further critical evaluation by Cohen (1962) who, in agreement with Blau (1963b), contends that the early dialect situation of Arabic was far more complicated in nature than Ferguson's thesis would allow. He urges the compilation of linguistic atlases to chart isoglosses which would support his contention that the modern dialects evolved from several contemporary urban *koinés*.

2.6 *The Grammatical Tradition of the Arabs*

> ... the rather obvious fault of the linguistic observations of most Muslim scholars was that they as a rule did not admit the right of a language to change and even less the right of creative speakers to coin new forms. (Rosenthal 1953:310, in a review of Fück 1950)
>
> Pour le grammarien arabe musulman, sa langue est un absolu, elle est l'organe d'expression de l'Absolu. (Fleisch 1958a:105)

Much of the recent philological and lexicographical work produced in the field of Classical Arabic has centered around elucidation of the linguistic viewpoint of the earliest Arab grammarians in their codification of the system of Classical Arabic and later commentaries on these works. In the field of native Arabic lexicography, the works by Haywood (1956, 1960) and Kopf (1953) will be of particular interest to the student of the historical development of this field. An excellent summary of the rise and development of the native grammatical tradition appears in Fleisch (1961). Fleisch's particular interest in the work of the early Arab grammarians (1958a and b) has been furthered by Semaan (1959) and also by Blanc (1966).

Gérard Troupeau has contributed numerous articles in this field. In particular, his discussion of Sibawaih's terminology in relation to the temporal nature of the verb stems of Classical Arabic (1962b) is well worth reading. Sidney Glazer has edited an important work of the Arab grammarian, Abu Hayyān, and in doing so wrote a short article on the linguistic philosophy of this great man (1942). Additional works on the general development of this field include Reuschel (1959), Blachère (1950), and the important philological studies of Loucel (1963, 1964).

3. ARABIC LINGUISTICS IN THE MODERN ARAB WORLD

Arabic has been for long regarded as a God-given language, unique in beauty and majesty, the best equipped and most eloquent of all languages for expressing thought and emotions. (Chejne 1965:449)

If there has been little work appearing in the Western world in the field of Classical Arabic over the past twenty years that can be termed linguistic, there is even less in the Arab world. Modern works in Classical Arabic about Classical Arabic written by Arabs continue the traditional normative or prescriptive outlook of the earlier Arab grammarians. In addition, the specific goals of modern articles and works with 'linguistic' titles often include the improvement of pedagogy through language reform or the suppression of foreign borrowing and the control of certain other derivational processes in the development of the scientific lexicon of Modern Literary Arabic.

Language academies have been established in the major urban centers of the Arab world whose proceedings tell a familiar tale of the frustrations of trying to legislate language usage and change. For example, efforts to improve the complicated syntax of Arabic numerals include the proposals by Ḥusain (1962) and an-Najjār (1962) for simplification. These proposals like many others were discussed but not adopted. Meanwhile the increasing usage of colloquial number forms in oral rendition of Modern Literary Arabic (see Harrell 1961) is a descriptive fact these scholars choose to ignore. Other examples of attempts to regulate or prevent language change are seen in the articles of an-Nakadī (1963), and al-Kawākibī (1960–62, 1964). On the interesting phenomenon of word compounding in Arabic, see ash-Shihābī (1959) and al-Kawākibī (1964). An excellent summary and bibliography of these attempts at language reform appears in Merad (1965).

The motivation for some of the proposed reforms in Arabic grammatical terminology comes from the difficulty of improving the literacy rates in the Arab world when the learning of Classical Arabic is burdened with such a weight of grammatical terminology. Al-Ḥusainī (1962),[5] ʿAqil (1953), and at-Tanūkhī (1960b) propose several reforms. The pioneering efforts of men like Anīs Frayḥa (1955) and Ibrāhīm Anīs (1964, 1965) to make the ideas of modern linguistic analysis appeal to their countrymen are commendable.

Unfortunately, articles on linguistic analyses of Classical Arabic are frequently nothing more than collations of earlier views of Arab authors with very little, if any original thinking. The studies are characterized by a general disregard of Western works on similar subjects and a lack of bibliographical references. Ṭarazī's article on the definite article in Arabic (1962) is typical of this type of study.

Studies of the older Arabic grammatical traditions are fairly common. Again, Western works on the same subject (2.6) are completely ignored. Examples of this type of work are found in al-Faḥḥām (1960), Ibn ʿAshūr (1963), at-Tanūkhī on al-Ḥalabī (1960), ʿAḍīmah (1959), al-Mubārak (1963), and Alsamirrai (1954).

In one interesting case, a western linguist, William Cowan (1964), has written an article in Arabic concerning the development of Classical Arabic into the modern dialects (2.5).

Arabs frequently write about Arabic in languages other than Arabic. Works on the modern dialects are being produced by young Arab linguists in this country and others but there is relatively little being done on Classical Arabic. An interesting, if non-scientific sidelight, are the sociological analyses by Arabs of the role of Arabic as a language in their society. For typical expressions of this viewpoint, see Chejne (1965), Shouby (1951), Issawi (1951), and Hadeed (1951).

The question of the use of Classical Arabic in relation to the Colloquial languages (1.6) is discussed in Arabic works also. An example of this discussion is seen in Ash-Sharūni (1962). The prospects for improvement in Classical Arabic linguistics depends on the ability of the Arabs to stop regarding their language as beyond the scope of ordinary linguistic statement. There seems to be a general feeling that Classical Arabic has already been fully analyzed, by the Arab grammarians; who are they to say something new! The fact that, in 1966, Idris can produce an article on the non-arbitrary relationship of sound, meaning and graphic symbol in Classical Arabic is a discouraging portent for the future of this field for Arab scholars.

REFERENCES

Articles and books written in Arabic appear in a separate listing at the end of this bibliography. Titles in languages other than English, French, or German frequently are accompanied by a short résumé in French or English taken directly from the *BL*.

In addition, reviews of books are included directly following their entries when they either (a) present an excellent summary of the work in a language different from the original or (b) include some contributions or criticisms deemed significant for the evaluation of the work.

---

[5] The same article appears in 1965 with no reference to this earlier publication date — another discouragingly common practice among Arab authors, publishing the same article twice.

AARTUN, KJELL. 1963. Zur Frage altarabischer Tempora. Scand. University Books; Oslo and Bergen. Universitetsforlag; Stockholm. Svenska bokförlaget, Bonnier.

ABDESSELEM, M. 1960. Situation et perspectives de l'arabe moderne [en Tunisie]. Ibla XXIII.1–6.

ACHLEDIANI, V. G. 1962. K voprosu ob istorii uvuljarnych v arabskom jazyke. VON 3/9.198–202. Sur l'évolution des uvulaires en ar.

ALANI, SALMAN HASSAN. 1963. Phonology of contemporary standard Arabic. Indiana University diss.

ARO, JUSSI. 1964. Der *maṣdar al-mīnī* und seine Funktion im Arabischen. SO XXVIII.11. Helsinki.

BARANOV, CH. K. 1957. Arabsko-russkij slovar'. 2-e izd. Moskva. Izd. inostrannych i nacional'nych slovarej. BSL LV/2.225 (1960) D. Cohen.

BATESON, MARY CATHERINE. 1967. Arabic language handbook. Language Handbook Series. Washington, D.C. Center for Applied Linguistics.

BECK, EDMUND. 1956. Die Ausnahmepartikel *'illa* bei al-Farrā' und Sībawaih. Or XXV.42–73.

BECKER, VALERIE. 1964. A transfer grammar of the verb structures of modern literary Arabic and Lebanese Colloquial Arabic. Yale University diss.

BELARDI, W. 1959. Arabo *qal'a*. AION-L I.147–50.

BELKIN, V. M. 1957. Arabskoe jazykoznanie poslednich let. VJa 6.97–100. Ar. linguistics in recent years.

——. 1959. Obsuždenie problem nacional'nogo jazyka v arabskoj pečati. VJa 2.122–7. La discussion des problèmes de la langue nationale dans la presse ar.

——. 1960. Problema literaturnogo jazyka i dialekta v arabskich stranach. TIJa X.158–74. Langue littéraire et dialectes dans les pays ar.

——. 1963. Zamečanija o charaktere semantičeskich izmenenij v sisteme arabskogo glagola. Semit. jaz. 19–24. Remarks on the 'forms' of the Ar. verb.

BIELAWSKI, JÓZEF. 1956. Deux périodes dans la formation de la terminologie scientifique arabe (La période classique et la période moderne). RO XX.263–320.

BIRKELAND, H. 1940. Altarabische Pausalformen. Skrifter utg. av Det Norske Videnskaps-Akad. i Oslo, II. Hist.-filos. Klasse 4. Oslo, Dybwad. BSL XLV (131).228–30 (1949) J. Cantineau.

——. 1952. Growth and structure of the Egyptian Arabic dialect. Avhandlinger utg. av Det Norske Videnskaps-Akad. i Oslo, II. Hist.-filos. Klasse 1. Oslo. Lg XXX.558–64 (1954) C. A. Ferguson. BSL XLIX (139).151–4 (1953) J. Cantineau.

——. 1954. Stress patterns in Arabic. Avhandlinger utg. av Det Norske Videnskaps-Akad. i Oslo, Hist.-filos. Klasse 3. Oslo. Lg. XXXII.384–7 (1956) C. A. Ferguson.

BISHAI, WILSON B. 1965. Form and function in Arabic syntax. Word XXI.265–9.

——. 1966. Modern Inter-Arabic. JAOS LXXXVI.319–23.

BLACHÈRE, RÉGIS. 1950. Les savants iraqiens et leurs informateurs bédouins aux IIe-IVe siècles de l'hégire. Mélanges William Marcais, 37–48.

——. 1952. Sur la consonne hamza en arabe classique. GLECS VI.8–9.

——. 1957. Le développement et l'adaptation de la langue arabe à l'époque contemporaine (Une conférence de M. –). [Rés. par Michel Lelong]. Ibla XX.44–6.

BLANC, HAIM. 1961. Stylistic variations in spoken Arabic. A sample of interdialectal educated conversation. Contributions to Arabic linguistics, 81–156.

——. 1966. Les deux prononciations du 'qāf' d'après Avicenne. Arabica XIII.129–36.

BLAU, JOSHUA. 1963a. The role of the Bedouins as arbiters in linguistic questions and the *mas'ala az-zunbūriyya*. JSS VIII.42–51.

——. 1963b. Hyper-correction and hypo-correction (half-correction) in pseudo-correct features. Muséon LXXVI.363–7.

——. 1965. The emergence and linguistic background of Judaeo-Arabic: a study of the origins of Middle Arabic. Scripta Judaica 5. London, Oxford University Press.

BLOCH, A. 1946. Vers und Sprache im Altarabischen. Metrische und syntaktische Untersuchungen: Acta Tropica, Suppl. V. Basel, Verlag für Recht und Gesellschaft, XII. ZDMG XCIX/2.284–8 (1950) K. Munzel. BSL XLV (131).230–2 (1949) J. Cantineau.

BORRMANS, M. 1961. A propos de l'arabe moderne: notes syntaxiques. Ibla XXIV. 363–72.

BRAVMANN, M. M. 1953. Studies in Arabic and general syntax: Textes arabes et études islamiques 11. Le Caire. JAOS LXXVII.248 (1957) C. A. Ferguson. Arabica II.117 (1955) R. Blachère.

BRILL, M., D. NEUSTADT, and P. SCHUSSES. 1940. The basic word-list of the Arabic daily newspaper. Jerusalem.

BROCKELMANN, CARL. 1953–54. Das Arabische und seine Mundarten. Handbuch der Orientalistik III.207–45.

BULOS, AFIF A. 1960. *'ismu'l-mawṣūl* in Classical Arabic and the relative pronoun in English. A contrastive study. LL X.47–53.

——. 1965. The Arabic triliteral verb; A comparative study of grammatical concepts and processes. Foreword by John B. Carroll. Beirut, Khayats. JAOS LXXXVII. 315 (1967) G. Krotkoff.

CACHIA, P. J. E. 1967. The use of the colloquial in modern Arabic literature. JAOS LXXXVII.12–22.

CANTINEAU, JEAN. 1939. Le pronom suffixe de 3e. personne singulier masculin en arabe classique et dans les parlers arabes modernes. BSL 89–97.

——. 1941. Cours de phonétique arabe. (See 1960).

——. 1946. Esquisse d'une phonologie de l'arabe classique. BSL XLIII.93–140.

——. 1951. La disparition du féminin pluriel dans le verbe et le pronom personnel de certains parlers arabes [Résumé]. BSL XLVII (134).

——. 1956. The phonemic system of Damascus Arabic. Word 12.116–24.

——. 1960. Études de linguistique arabe. Mémorial Jean Cantineau. Paris, Klincksieck.

CHEJNE, ANWAR G. 1965. Arabic: Its significance and place in Arab-Muslim society. MEJ XIX.447–70.

CHOUEMI, MOUSTAFA. 1961. Sur des aspects de la 'permutation' (ʾibdāl) en arabe. GLECS IX.60–2.

——. 1965. La consonne nasale *N* en arabe. GLECS X.72–6.

CHRAKOVSKIJ, V. S. 1965a. O charaktere oppozicii form *kataba/jaktubu* v arabskom jazyke. KSINA 86.155–63. On the nature of the opposition *kataba/yaktubu* in Ar.

——. 1965b. Opyt formal'nogo analiza glagolov, upravljajuščich pridatočnym s sojuzom *'anna* v sovremennom literaturnom arabskom jazyke. Semit. jaz. 412–22. An attempt at a formal analysis of verbs governing subordinate clauses with *anna* in mod. lit. Ar.

——. 1965c. Opyt formal'noj charakteristiki glagolov v sovremennom literaturnom arabskom jazyke po sintagmatičeskim kriterijam. NAA 1.143–54. On formally characterizing verbs in mod. lit. Ar. according to syntagmatic criteria (E. summ.).

COHEN, DAVID. 1961. Essai d'une analyse grammaticale de l'arabe. TA II.48–70.

——. 1962. Koinè, langues communes et dialectes arabes. Arabica IX.119–44.

——. 1965. La linguistique sémitique et arabe: A propos de quelques travaux récents. REIsl XXXIII.175–84.

COLIN, GEORGES S. 1939. Incompatibilités consonantiques dans les racines de l'Arabe classique. GLECS 24.61–2.

——. 1945–48. Les racines trilitères à première et troisième radicales identiques en arabe classique. GLECS IV.82–3.

——. 1952. Étude des diminutifs et des augmentatifs en arabe dans leurs affinités morphologiques et sémantiques [Résumé]. BSL XLVIII (136).xi.

——. 1953. Les différentes étapes de la limitation d'emploi du duel en arabe [Résumé]. BSL XLIX (138).xiv-xv.

——. 1961. Singuliers secondaires analogiques tirés de faux pluriels en arabe. GLECS IX.11–15.

Contributions to Arabic linguistics. 1961. Ed. by Charles A. Ferguson. Harvard Middle Eastern Monographs 3. Cambridge, Mass.

DENZ, ADOLF. 1964. Die phonetische Beschaffenheit der Laryngale im Arabischen und ihre phonologische Systematisierung. ZDMG CXIV.232–8.

DROZDÍK, LADISLAV. 1964. The loss of relevancy of some grammatical meanings in modern written Arabic. JČ XV.109–15. Slov. summ.

ERICKSON, JON LAROY. 1965. English and Arabic: A discussion of contrastive verbal morphology. University of Texas diss.

FERGUSON, CHARLES A. 1956. The Emphatic /l/ in Arabic. Lg. XXXII.446–52.

——. 1957. Two problems in Arabic phonology. Word XIII.460–78.

——. 1959a. The Arabic Koine. Lg. XXXV.616–30.

——. 1959b. Diglossia. Word 15.325–40.

FLEISCH, HENRI. 1949–50. Études de phonétique arabe. MUSJ XXVIII.255–85. BSL XLVII (135).244–8 (1951) J. Cantineau.

——. 1956. L'arabe classique. Esquisse d'une structure linguistique. MUSJ XXXIII.1. Beyrouth. Lg. XXXIV.314–21 (1958) C. A. Ferguson. Hespéris XLV. 173–5 (1958) L. Brunot. BSOAS XXI.637–8 (1958) T. F. Mitchell.

——. 1957a. Esquisse d'un historique de la grammaire arabe. Arabica IV.1–22.

——. 1957b. Études sur le verbe arabe. Mélanges Massignon II.153–81.

——. 1958a. La conception phonétique des Arabes d'après le Sirr ṣināʿat al-iʿrāb d'Ibn Ǧinnī. ZDMG CVIII.74–105. Arabica VI.318–19 (1959) G. Troupeau.

——. 1958b. *Mağhūra, mahmūsa.* Examen critique. MUSJ XXXV/2.193–210.

——. 1961. Traité de philologie arabe. Vol. I. Beyrouth. Imprimerie Cath. JNES XXIII.289–90 (1964) M. Mahdi. Arabica X.96–8 (1963) G. Troupeau.

——. 1963. Observations sur les études philologiques en arabe classique. Oriens XVI.134–44.

FROLOVA, O. B., and S. JA. FITIALOV. 1963. O dvuch vozmožnych sposobach pererabotki informacii pri mašinnom perevode s arabskogo jazyka (Programma morfologičeskogo analiza). MMLMP 2.161–70. Deux possibilités de remanier l'information dans la trad. mécanique de l'arabe.

FÜCK, JOHANN. 1950. Arabiya, Untersuchungen zur arabischen Sprach- und Stilgeschichte. Abhandlungen der Sächsischen Akad. der Wissenschaften zu Leipzig. Phil.-hist. Klasse XLV, 1. Berlin. JNES XII.71–2 (1953) G. E. von Grunebaum. Or XXII.307–11 (1953) F. Rosenthal. IQ II.146–7 (1955) C. Rabin. JSS I.411–13 (1956) A. J. Arberry.

——. 1953–54. Geschichte der Arabistik. Handbuch der Orientalistik, 341–9.

——. 1955. ʿArabīya. Recherches sur l'histoire de la langue et du style arabe. Trad. par Claude Denizeau. Publ. de l'Inst. des Hautes Études Marocaines, Notes et documents 16. Paris. BSL LIII/2.205–8 (1957–58) É. Benveniste.

——. 1957. Zur arabischen Wörterbuchfrage. ZDMG CVII.340–7.

——. 1962. Bemerkungen zur altarabischen Metrik. ZDMG CXI/2.464–9.

GABUČAN, G. M. 1963a. K voprosu ob arabskich grammatičeskich učenijach. Semit. jaz. 37–55. Les théories grammaticales ar. dans le passé.

——. 1963b. Nekotorye teoretičeskie voprosy izučenija artiklja v arabskom literaturnom jazyke. Semit. jaz. 773–85. Some theoretical problems of the study of the art. in lit. Ar.

GARBELL, IRENE. 1958. Remarks on the historical phonology of an East Mediterranean Arabic dialect. Word XIV.303–37.

GÄTJE, HELMUT. 1965. Strukturen der Genitivverbindung. Untersuchungen am arabischen Genitiv. Sprache XI.61–73.

GLAZER, S. 1942. A noteworthy passage from an Arab grammatical text. JAOS LXII.106–8.

GRANDE, B. M. 1963. Kurs arabskoj grammatiki v sravnitel'no-istoričeskom osveščenii. Moskva, Izd. vostočnoj literatury (Inst. narodov Azii).

GREENBERG, J. H. 1950. The patterning of root morphemes in Semitic. Word VI. 162–81.

HADEED, M. F. ABOU. 1952. Psychology and the Arabic language. MEJ VI.112–14.

HAMP, ERIC P. 1959. The personal morphemes of classical Arabic. SIL XIV.21–2.

HARRELL, RICHARD S. 1961. A linguistic analysis of Egyptian radio Arabic. Contributions to Arabic linguistics, 1–77.

HAYWOOD, JOHN A. 1956. An Indian contribution to the study of Arabic lexicography — the 'Bulgha" of Muḥammad Ṣiddīq Hasan Khān Bahādur (1832–1890). JRAS 165–80.

——. 1960. Arabic lexicography, its history, and its place in the general history of lexicography. Leiden, Brill.

HYMES, D. H. 1959. On the rate of morpheme decay in Arabic. IJAL XXV.267–9.

IDRIS, HADY-ROGER. 1966. De l'expressivité de deux phonèmes arabes: ḥā', mīm. SIsl XXV.5–11.

ISSAWI, C. 1951. The Arabic language and Arab psychology. MEJ V.525–6.

JAKOBSON, ROMAN. 1957. Mufaxxama — The 'emphatic' phonemes in Arabic. Studies presented to Joshua Whatmough on his sixtieth birthday, ed. by Ernest Pulgram, 105–15. 's-Gravenhage, Mouton.

JANSSENS, G. 1959. Over de betrouwbaarheid en de waarde van de overgeleverde kennis der Arabische grammatika. HandVIFC XXIII.109–13 (Rés.). Sur la solidité et la valeur de la connaissance traditionelle de la grammaire ar.

KAHLE, P. E. 1948. The Qur'ān and the 'Arabīya: Ignace Goldziher memorial Volume, 163–82. Budapest.

——. 1949 The Arabic readers of the Koran. JNES VIII.65–71.

KARIEV, U. Z. 1965a. Slovoobrazovatl'naja funkcija suffiksa *-ijj(un)*. Semit. jaz. 382–94. The word-building function of the suffix *iyy(un)*.

——. 1965b. Sposob usečenija (naxt) v sisteme arabskogo slovoobrazovanija. Semit. jaz. 833–45. Truncation (*naḥt*) in Ar. word-formation.

KILLEAN, CAROLYN G. 1966. The deep structure of the noun phrase in modern written Arabic. Ph.D. thesis, University of Michigan.

KHALAFALLĀH, MUḤAMMAD. 1955. Early stages in the development and standardisation of the Arabic literary language. MKAI IX.3–21 [E. section].

KÖBERT, R. 1965. Einige weniger beachtete *maṣdar*-Bildungen des Arabischen. Or XXXIV.173–4.

KOPF, LOTHAR. 1953. The word-definitions in the indigenous Arabic lexicons [in Hebrew with English summary]. Jerusalem. Arabica I.367 (1954) G. Vajda.

——. 1956. Religious influences on medieval Arabic philology. SIsl V.33–59.

——. 1961. The treatment of foreign words in medieval Arabic lexicology. ScrH IX (Studies in Islamic Hist. and Civilization). 191–205.

KOVALEV, A. A. 1952. K voprosu o vremennych formach arabskogo glagola. TVIIJa I.72–85. A propos des formes temporelles du verbe arabe.

——. 1963. K voprosu ob analitičeskich formach arabskogo glagola. KSINA 72. 26–31. On the analytical forms of the Ar. verb.

——. 1965. Osnovnye voprosy lingvističeskoj podgotovki arabistov v vuzach. Semit. jaz. 66–74. The main problem of linguistic training of Arabic philologists in higher schools.

——, and G. Š. Šarbatov. 1960. Učebnik arabskogo jazyka. Moskva. Manuel de langue ar. BSL LVIII/2.234 (1963) D. Cohen.

Kramers, J. H. 1954–56. La pause en arabe et en hébreu considérée au point de vue phonologique. Analecta Orientalia, by J. H. Kramers, II.3–13.

Krotkoff, Georg. 1963–64. Nochmals: *mağhūra, mahmūsa.* WZKM LIX-LX. 147–53.

Kuryłowicz, J. 1950. La mimation et l'article en arabe. AO XVIII.1/2 (Mélanges Hrozný, III). 323–8.

——. 1951. Le diptotisme et la construction des noms de nombre en arabe. Word VII.222–6.

Landau, Jacob M. 1959. A word count of modern Arabic prose. New York, Am. Council of Learned Soc. WI VII.211–12 (1961) H. Wehr. Arabica IX.87–8 (1962) R. Blachère. Word XVI.285–7 (1960) M. F. Saʿid.

Lecerf, J. 1954. Esquisse d'une problématique de l'arabe actuel. L'Afrique et l'Asie 26.1–16.

——. 1963. Remarques sur le lexique arabe. GLECS IX.81–6.

——. 1966. Note sur l'auxiliaire *ʿāda, yaʿūdu.* GLECS X.185–8.

Lecomte, Gérard. 1961. Réflexions sur un vocabulaire technique en formation: Contribution à la connaissance de 'l'arabe moderne'. Orient (Paris). XVII/1. 13–24.

——. 1964. Arabe et modernisme. RENLO 1.57–77.

Lekiašvili, A. 1959. K istorii form distributiva v arabskom. Trudy Tbilisskogo gosud. universiteta 73 (Serija vostokovedenija I.17–27.) Sur l'hist. des formes du distributif en ar.

——. 1960. K obrazovanii form množestvennogo čisla v arabskom. XXV Meždunarodynj kongress vostokovedov, Doklady delegacii SSR. Moskva, Izd. vostočnoj literatury. On the formation of the plural in Ar.

——. 1963a. Ob odnom tipe narečija v arabskom jazyke. Semit. jaz. 59–61. Sur les adv. du type: *bukrata, saḥara, suḥrata.*

——. 1963b. Zur Bildung des gebrochenen Plurals im Arabischen. Trudy XXV Kongr. vostokovedov II.136–41.

Lewkowicz, Nancy Margaret K. 1967. A transformational approach to the syntax of Arabic participles. University of Michigan.

Loucel, H. 1963. L'origine du langage d'après les grammairiens ar. Arabica X.188–208, 253–81.

——. 1964. L'origine du langage d'après les grammairiens ar. Arabica XI.57–72, 151–87.

LOUIS, A. 1955. La langue arabe et les examens en Tunisie. Ibla XVIII.187–221.

MACDONALD, JOHN. 1963. The Arabic derived verb themes: A study in form and meaning. IQ VIII/3–4.96–116.

MAGEE, W. L. 1950. The pronunciation of the prelingual mutes in classical Arabic. Word VI.74–7.

MAINZ, E. 1931. Zur Grammatik des modernen Schriftarabisch. Dissertation: Hamburg.

MAMEDOV, A. DŽ. 1963. Predloženie s vydelennym imenem, ili 'dvustoronnee predloženie' (ğumbla dāt uağhain) v arabskom literaturnom jazyke. Semit. jaz. 62–71. Sur les propositions du type: az-zahra rā'iḥātuhā tayyiba.

MARTINET, ANDRÉ. 1959. La palatalisation "spontanée" de *g* en arabe. BSL LIV/1. 90–102.

MASSIGNON, LOUIS. 1954. Réflexions sur la structure primitive de l'analyse grammaticale en arabe. Arabica I.3–16.

MERAD, ALI. 1965. A propos d'une nouvelle méthode grammaticale arabe: *Al-Aḥrufiyya*. Arabica XII.67–77.

MIDDLE EAST CENTRE FOR ARAB STUDIES, SHEMLAN, LEBANON. A selected word list of Modern Literary Arabic. Beirut, Dar al-Kutub Press. JSS V.426–7 (1960) J. D. Latham.

MITCHELL, T. F. 1960. Prominence and syllabication in Arabic. BSOAS XXIII. 369–89.

MONTEIL, VINCENT. 1960. L'arabe moderne. Coll. 'Études ar. et islamiques' 3. Paris, Klincksieck.

——. 1964. Al-lughah al-ʿarabiyyah. LA 1.76–84. L'arabe moderne de Vincent Monteil resumé en ar. par Jamāl ad-Dīn Al-Baghdādī. Lg XXXIX.329–32 (1963) W. Cowan.

MORABIA, ALFRED. 1964. Recherches sur quelques noms de couleur en arabe classique. SIsl XXI.61–99.

MUNZEL, KURT. 1950. Zur Wortstellung der Ergänzungsfragen im Arabischen. ZDMG C.566–76.

MURTONEN, A. 1964. Broken plurals: origin and development of the system. Leiden, E. J. Brill.

NADER, L. 1962. A note on attitudes and the use of language. AnL IV/6.24–9.

NASR, RAJA T. 1962. Phonemic velarization in literary Arabic. PICL IX.453–5.

NEDOSPASOVA, M. E. 1963. O zaimstvovannych značenijach v sovremennoj arabskoj terminologii. KSINA 72.59–64. On borrowed meanings in present-day Ar. terminology.

OLIVERIUS, JAROSLAV. 1963. Contribution to the Arabic historical dialectology. AO XXXI.625–9. Dialect features mentioned in a work by Antonius Ullerstorff, 1690.

OMAN, GIOVANNI. 1960. I prestiti semantici nell'arabo moderno. AION-L II.235–55 (à suivre).

PANACHI, M. P. 1965. O kriterii složnogo slova v arabskom jazyke. Semit. jaz. 145–51. The criteria for the compound word in Ar.

PAULINY, JÁN. 1963. K otázkam semantickej diferenciácie medzi spisovným jazykom a dialektom v arabčine. Orientalistický sborník, 145–8. Specific features appearing in the development of the Ar. language in relationship with the semantic differentiation between literary language and dialect (E. summ.).

PELLAT, CH. 1951. La détermination et l'indétermination du nom en arabe. GLECS V.88–90.

——. 1952. L'arabe vivant. Mots arabes groupés d'après le sens et vocabulaire fondamental de l'arabe moderne. Paris, Adrien Maisonneuve. BSOAS XVII. 397–8 (1955) D. Cowan. Word IX.90–3 (1953) B. H. Smeaton.

——. 1957. Un fait d'expressivité en arabe: *l'itbāʿ*. Arabica IV.131–49.

——. 1960. Sur quelques noms d'animaux en arabe classique. GLECS VIII.95–9.

——. 1961. A propos de l'anticipation en arabe. GLECS IX.18–20.

PETRÁČEK, KAREL. 1952. Zur Artikulation des sogenannten emphatischen /l/ im Arabischen. AO 20.509–23.

——. 1953. Der doppelte phonologische Charakter des Ghain im klassischen Arabisch. AO XXI.240–62. Quantitative analysis.

——. 1954. Material zum altarabischen Dialekt von al-Madīna. AO XXII.460–6.

——. 1955. L'activité des arabisants en Tchécoslovaquie. Arabica II.242–4.

——. 1956. Bemerkungen zur Artikulation der Liquiden im Arabischen. Charisteria Orientalia, Festschrift Rypka, 227–32.

——. 1960. A study in the structure of Arabic. AUC-Ph 1 (Orientalia Pragensia I). 23–39.

——. 1964. Die Inkompatibilität in der semitischen Wurzel in Sieht der Informationstheorie. RO XXVII.133–8.

——. 1965. Die Isomorphie im System der arabischen Pluralbildung. Symbolae Kuryłowicz, 227–9.

RABIN, CHAIM. 1946. The ancient Arabic dialects and their relationship to Hebrew [in Hebrew]. Melilah II.243–55.

——. 1951. Ancient West-Arabian. London. Taylor's Foreign Press. IQ I.60–2 (1954) J. W. Fück. JNES XII.298 (1953) G. E. von Grunebaum. JAOS LXXII. 173–4 (1952) F. Rosenthal. Lg XXVIII.159–62 (1952) A. Jeffery.

——. 1955. The beginnings of classical Arabic. SIsl IV.19–37.

——. 1965. The diptote declension. Ar. and Islamic studies in honor of H. A. R. Gibb, 547–62. Leiden.

——, M. KHALAFALLAH, J. W. FÜCK, H. WEHR, H. FLEISCH, and PH. MARCAIS. 1957. ʿArabiyya. A. The Arabic language. The Encyclopaedia of Islam. New ed. Vol. 1, fasc. 9 and 10, 561–83. Leiden, Brill, and London, Luzac.

REUSCHEL, WOLFGANG. 1959. Al-Ḫalīl ibn-Aḥmad, der Lehrer Sibawaihs, als Grammatiker. VIO 49. Berlin. MUSJ XXXVI.244–5 (1959 [1961]) H. Fleisch. BSOAS XXV.343–7 (1962) A. F. L. Beeston.

ROMAČEV, B. N. 1965. Nekotorye charakteristiki minimal'noj prosodičeskoj edinicy v sovremennom arabskom jazyke. Semit. jaz. 459–65. Some features of the minimal prosodic unit in Modern Literary Arabic.

RUŽIČKA, R. 1950. Quelques cas du ǵ secondaire en arabe. JA CCXXXVIII.269–318.

ŠAGAL', V. E. 1963a. Ob arabskoj 'smyslovoj idafe'. KSINA 72.48–53. 'Semantic *iḍāfa*' in Ar.

——. 1963b. O strukturnych osobennostjach složnych substantivnych slovosočetanij tipa idafy v arabskom jazyke. Semit. jaz. 90–8. Les particularités structurales de l'*iḍāfa* en ar.

SA'ID, MAJED F. 1964. Lexical innovation through borrowing in modern standard Arabic. Princeton University.

SAMARRAI, ALAUDDIN ISMAIL. 1959. Rate of morphemic decay in Arabic. IJAL XXV.68–70.

ALSAMIRRAI. 1954. Statistiques des pluriels internes dans le Coran [Résumé]. BSL L/1.xxviii.

ŠARAFUTDINOVA, R. Š. 1965. Semantičeskaja charakteristika vzaimodejstvija glagolov s predlogami v sovremennom arabskom jazyke (Rol' predloga v izmenenii značenija glagola). Semit. jaz. 422–43. Semantic features of the interaction of verbs with prepositions in mod. Ar. (The role of the preposition in shifting the meaning of the verb).

ŠARBATOV, G. Š. 1954. Ob otnositel'noj podvižnosti udarenija v sovremennom arabskom literaturnom jazyke. TVIIJa V.89–95. Sur la mobilité relative de l'accent en arabe littéraire moderne.

——. 1961. Sovremennyj arabskij jazyk. Jazyki zarubežnogo Vostoka i Afriki. Moskva, Izd. vostočnoj literatury. L'ar. contemporain.

——. 1965. Problema sootnošenija arabskogo literaturnogo jazyka i sovremennych arabskich dialektov. Semit. jaz. 55–66. On the relation between lit. Ar. and the mod. Ar. dialects.

SATTERTHWAIT, ARNOLD C. 1960. Rate of morphemic decay in Meccan Arabic. IJAL XXVI.256–61.

——. 1963. Computational research in Arabic. MT 2.62–70.

——. 1965. Sentence-for-sentence translation: an example. MT 2.14–38.

SCHRAMM, GENE M. 1962. An outline of classical Arabic verb structure. Lg. XXXVIII.360–75.

SEGAL', V. S. 1965. K fonologičeskoj interpretacii dolgich glasnych v arabskom literaturnom jazyke. Semit. jaz. 451–8. On the phonological interpretation of long vowels in literary Arabic.

SELIM, GEORGE DIMITRI. 1967. Some contrasts between Classical Arabic and Egyptian Arabic. Linguistic studies in memory of Richard Slade Harrell, 133–52.

SEMAAN, KHALIL IBRAHIM HANNA. 1959. Phonetics in early Islam: The speech-sounds. Columbia University diss.

——. 1962. Tajwīd as a source in phonetic research. WZKM LVIII.111–19.

Semitskie jazyki. 1963. Sbornik statej. Ed. by G.Š. Šarbatov. Moskva, Izd. 'Nauka' (Inst. Narodov Azii),

——. 1965. Byp. 2, č. 1 + 2. Materialy Pervoj Konferencii po Semitskim Jazykam, 26–28 okt. 1964. Semitic languages. Issue 2, pt. 1 + 2. Papers presented for the First Conference on Semitic Languages, 26–28 Oct. 1964. Ed. by G.S. Šarbatov. Moskva, Izd. 'Nauka' (Inst. Narodov Azii).

Shamosh, I. 1951–52. The problem of the language of modern Arabic fiction [in Hebrew]. Tarbiz XXIII.231–5.

Shouby, E. 1951. The influence of the Arabic language on the psychology of the Arabs. MEJ V.284–302.

Sikirič, Šacir. 1952–53. Sintaksičke funkcije arapskih prijedloga. Prilozi za orijentalnu filologiju i istoriju jugoslovenskih naroda pod turskom vladavinom III-IV. 553–75. Les fonctions syntaxiques des prépositions en arabe (Avec résumé en français).

Skalmowski, Wojciech. 1964. A note on the distribution of Arabic verbal roots. FO VI.97–100.

Smeaton, B. Hunter. 1956. Some problems in the description of Arabic. Word XII.357–68.

——. 1959. Lexical expansion due to technical change: as illustrated by the Arabic of Al Hasa, Saudi Arabia, during the decade 1938–48. Columbia University diss.

Snow, James Adin. 1965. A grammar of modern written Arabic clauses. University of Michigan diss.

Soden, W. von. 1960. Status rectus-Formen ... und die sogenannte uneigentliche Annexion im Arabischen. JNES XIV.163–71.

Spitaler, Anton. 1961. Arabisch. Linguistica semitica, 115–38.

——. 1962. Al-ḥamdu lillāhi llaḏī und Verwandtes. Ein Beitrag zur mittel- und neuarabischen Syntax. Oriens XV.97–114.

Starinin, V.P. 1961. Oboznačenie čeredovanija osnovy arabskich neproizvodnych glagolov. KSINA XL.78–9. Alternation of radicals in non-derived Ar. verbs.

——. 1963. Linvističeskie zametki arabista. Semit. jaz. 72–81. Remarques linguistiques d'un arabisant.

Tanaka, Shirō. 1963. Arabiago bunten (1). Osaka, Osaka Gaikokugo daigaku Arabiago kenkyūshitsu. A grammar of Ar. (1).

Tibāwī, A.L. 1955. The meaning of *ṯaqāfa* in contemporary Arabic. IQ II.222–8.

Al-Toma, Salih. 1957. The teaching of classical Arabic to speakers of the colloquial in Iraq: A study of the problem of linguistic duality and its impact on language education. Ed.D. Thesis, Harvard University.

——. 1961. The Arabic writing system and proposals for its reform. MEJ XV. 403–14.

Trager, George L., and Frank A. Rice, 1954. The personal-pronoun system of Classical Arabic. Lg XXX.224–9.

TROUPEAU, GÉRARD. 1958. Le commentaire d'al-Sīrāfī sur le chapitre 565 du *Kitāb* de Sibawayhi. Arabica V.168–82.

——. 1961. A propos des grammairiens cités par Sībawayhi dans le *Kitāb*. Arabica VIII.309–12.

——. 1962a. La grammaire à Bagdād du IXe au XIIIe siècle. Arabica IX.397–405.

——. 1962b. La notion de temps chez Sibawaihi. GLECS IX.44–6.

ULLENDORFF, EDWARD. 1965. The form of the definite article in Arabic and other Semitic languages. Ar. and Islamic studies in honor of H.A.R.Gibb, 631–7. Leiden.

UŠAKOV, V.D. 1963. Ustojčivye slovosočetanija v sovremennom literaturnom arabskom jazyke. KSINA 72.37–47. Fixed word-groups in present-day lit. Ar.

——. 1965. Terminy 'motivirovannost'' i 'nemotivirovannost'' v svjazi s klassifikaciej idiomatičeskich slovosočetanij (na materiale arabskogo literaturnogo jazyka). Semit. jaz. 444–50. The terms 'motivation' and 'non-motivation' with regard to the classification of idiomatic word groups in lit. Ar.

VAJDA, GEORGES. 1961. Les lettres et les sons de la langue arabe d'après Abū Hātim al-Rāzī. Arabica VIII.113–30.

VYCICHL, WERNER. 1953. Die Deklination im Arabischen. RSO XXVIII.71–8.

——. 1958. Numerus und Kasus im klassischen Arabisch. Ein Problem und zwei Interpretationen. RSO XXXIII.175–9.

WEHR, H. 1934. Die Besonderheiten des heutigen hoch arabischen mit Berücksichtigung der Einwirkung der europäischen Sprachen. Berlin.

——. 1952. Der arabische elativ. AAWL 7. MUSJ XXXI.429–32 (1954) H. Fleisch. JNES XIII.208 (1954) G.E. von Grunebaum.

——. 1953. Zur Funktion arabischer Negationen. ZDMG CIII.27–39.

——. 1958. Arabisches worterbuch für die Schriftsprache der Gegenwart. 3. Aufl. Wiesbaden. Lg XXX.174–7 (1954) C.A. Ferguson.

——. 1959. Supplement zum Arabisches Wörterbuch für die Schriftsprache der Gegenwart. Wiesbaden, Harrassowitz.

——. 1961. A dictionary of modern written Arabic. Ed. by J Milton Cowan. Wiesbaden. BSOAS XXV.341–2 (1962) R.B. Serjeant.

WILD, STEFAN. 1962. Neues zur ältesten arabischen Lexikographie. ZDMG CXII. 291–8.

YUSHMANOV [= JUŠMANOV], N.W. 1961. The structure of the Arabic language. Transl. from the Russ. by Moshe Perlmann. Washington, D.C., Center for Applied Linguistics. Transl. of Stroj arabskogo jazyka. Leningrad 1938. JAOS LXXXIV.263 1964 (George Krotkoff).

Arabic Titles

ʿAḌĪMAH, MUḤAMMAD ʿABD AL-KHĀLIQ. 1959. Asrār al-ʿarabiyyah li-Kamāl ad-Dīn

Al-Anbārī. MMAD XXXIV.376–82. The secrets of Arabic by Kamāl ad-Din al-Anbāri.

Anīs, Ibrāhīm. 1963a. Dalālat al-alfāẓ. 2nd ed. Cairo, Maktabat al-Anglo-Miṣriyyah. The semantics of Ar.

——. 1963b. Ḥurūf tushbihu al-ḥarakāt. MMLA XVI.13–17. Consonants and vowels in Ar.

——. 1964. Dirāsah fi ṣīghat *fi''īl* ka-shirrīb wa-sikkīr. MMAD XXXIX.365–73. Study on the pattern *fi''īl* in *shirrīb* and *sikkīr*.

——. 1965. Fi al-qiyās al-lughawī: ṣīghat *fa'īl*. MMLA XVIII.81–8. Linguistic analogy: the pattern *fa'īl*.

'Aqil, F. 1953. The basic vocabulary of the Arabic primary reading [in Arabic]. Damascus.

Al-'Atharī, Muḥammad Bahjah. 1958. Muḥammad Shukrī al-'Alūsī wa-'ārā'uhu al-lughawiyyah. Cairo, Institute for Higher Arab Studies, The Arab League. Muḥammad Shukrī al-'Alūsī and his linguistic views.

Bin-'Abd Allāh, 'Abd al-'Azīz. 1964. Al-uṣūl al-fuṣḥā fi al-lahjah al-mahgribiyyan. LA 1.134–41. The classical basis of the Moroccan colloquial.

Cowan, William. 1964. Āthār al-ḥarakāt al-akhīrah al-faṣīḥah fī al-lahjāt al-'arabiyyah ad-dārijah. Al-Abhāth XVII.83–8. Survival of the final classical vocalizations in modern spoken Ar.

Darwīsh, 'Abdallāh. 1956. Al-ma'ajim al-'arabīya. Cairo. Bio-bibliographical survey of Arabic lexicography from the earliest times to the present day, with special reference to the dictionary *Al-'Ain* by Khalīl b. Aḥmad. JRAS 230–1 (1956) G. M. Wickens.

Al-Faḥḥām, Muḥammad. 1960. Sībawaih Al-muḥāḍarāt al-'āmmah lil-mausim ath-thaqāfī ath-thānī (ād-daurah al-ūlā) 1960 alqāhā ba'd rijāl al-fikr wal-qānūn wal-adab bi-qā'at al-Azhar al-kubrā, 173–96. Cairo, Maṭba'at al-Azhar, s.d. Public lectures delivered at al-Azhar University in 1960 during the second cultural season (first session).

Frayḥa, Anīs. 1955. On the necessity of rewriting Arabic grammar on a descriptive basis [in Ar.]. Al-Abhāth VIII.26–69.

Al-Ḥalabī, Abū Tayyib 'Abd al-Wāḥid ibn 'Alī al-Lughawī. 1960. Kitāb al-muthannā. (I, II). Ed. and with introd. by 'Izz ad-Dīn At-Tanūkhī. MMAD XXXV.421–65, 609–46. The book of the dual.

Ḥusain, Kāmil. 1962. Ra'y fī jins al-'adad. MMLA XV.68–9. A view on the gender of the numerals.

Al-Ḥusainī, Isḥāq Mūsā. 1962. Al-maqta'iyyah fī al-lughah al-'arabiyyah. MMLA XV.51–6. The Ar. syllable.

——. 1965. Syllabism in the Arabic language. Arabic and Islamic studies presented to H. A. R. Gibb, 319–25. Leiden.

Ibn 'Ashūr, Muḥammad aṭ-Ṭāhir. 1961. Ṣaugh *maf'alah* min asmā' al-a'yān aththulāthiyyat al-aḥruf mimmā wasaṭuhu ḥarf 'illah. MMAD XXXVI.36–42.

The pattern *maf'alah* in the formation of nouns having a weak second radical.

——. 1963. Naẓrah fī al-kitāb al-mu'anwan bi'unwān *Muqaddimah fī an-naḥw* al-mansūb ilā al-Imām Khalaf al-Aḥmar. MMAD XXXVIII.576–90. View on the book *Introduction to grammar* attributed to Imām Khalaf al-Aḥmar.

Al-Kawākibī, Ṣalaḥ ad-Din. 1960–62. Al-auzān al-'arabiyyah fī al-muṣṭalaḥāt al-'ilmiyyah. MMAD XXXV.341–51 [fa'ala]; XXXVI.50–7 [maf'alah], 187–99 [fu'ālah and fa'alān], 610–16 [fu'āl]; XXXVII.401–6 [fa'ūl, fā'ūliyyah, fa'lam, fi'lim, fu'lum and fa'lana]. The patterning of Ar. scientific terminology.

——. 1964. An-naḥt wal-muṣṭalaḥāt al-'ilmiyyah (I, II). MMAD XXXIX.507–9, 675–86. Word formation (compounding) and scientific terminology.

Al-Magribī, 'Abd al-Qādir. 1953. Ba'ḍ asrār al-luġa al-'arabiyya. MMAD XXVIII.181–6. Sur la tendance, commune à l'arabe ancien et aux dialectes modernes visant à transformer des racines trilitères normales en racines 'sourdes'.

——. 1955. Fī l-luġati abnā'u 'allat, kamā fī l-bašar. MMAD XXX.253–67. Sur les dérivés des racines arabes. Arabica II.368 (1955) Ch. Pellat.

Mandūr, Muḥammad. 1964. *Al-'Arab* wa-nash'at al-lughah. Al-Majallah 65.57–61. The Arabs' view on the origin of language.

Marmardji, A. S. 1947. Hal al-'arabiyyat mantiqiyyat? Djounieh (Liban) Imprimerie des Missionnaires Libanais. La langue arabe est-elle logique? Orientalia XIX.207–8 (1950) J. Adem.

Al-Mubārak, Māzin. 1963. Ar-Rummānī an-Naḥawī fī ḍau' Sharḥihi. Damascus, Damascus University Press. Ar-Rummānī in the light of his *Commentary*.

Mustafa, Ibrāhīm. 1962. Al-'adad. MMLA XV.74–6. The numerals.

An-Najjār, Muḥammad 'Alī. 1962. Al-'adad fī al-'arabiyyah. MMLA XV.70–1. The numerals in Ar.

An-Nakadī, 'Ārif. 1963. Ghair — al-ghair; al-ma'ājim am al-mu'jamāt au kilāhumā. MMAD XXXVIII.340–3. Problems in using *ghair*, *al-ghair*, *al-ma'ājim* and *al-mu'jamāt*.

——. 1965. Maf'ūl — mafā'īl. MMAD XL.109–16. The patterns *maf'ūl* — *mafā'īl*.

Nakhla, Ralph. 1958. Le style privé de la conjonction 'wāw' est-il arabe? [en ar.]. Al-Machriq LII.641–77.

As-Ṣaghānī, Raḍī ad-Din Abū al-Faḍā'il al-Ḥasan ibn Muḥammad ibn al-Ḥasan. 1964. Mā banathu al-'Arab 'alā fa'āli (I, II, III). Ed. and with introd. by 'Izzah Ḥasan. MMAD XXXIX.295–312, 469–86, 629–45. What the Arabs have patterned on *fa'āli*.

Saleh, Mansūr Abi-. 1949. A propos d'un livre du P. Marmardji [en arabe]. Al-Machriq XLIII.27–42. Oriens IV.182 (1951) H. Ritter.

As-Sāmarrā'ī, Ibrāhīm. 1961. Dirāsāt fī l-luġa. Baghdad, al-'Ānī. Arabica IX.198 (1962) R. Blachère.

Ash-Shārūnī, Yūsuf. 1962. Lughat al-ḥiwār baina al-'āmmiyyah wal-fuṣḥā. Al-Majallah 67.41–54. The views of Maḥmūd Taimūr, Ṭāha Ḥusain, 'Abbās

Maḥmūd al-ʿAqqād, Taufīq al-Ḥakīm, Najīb Maḥfūẓ and Yūsuf as-Sibāʿī on the use of Colloquial and Classical in written dialogue.

ASH-SHIHĀBĪ, MUṢṬAFĀ. 1959. Madā an-naḥt fī al-lughah al-ʿarabiyyah. MMAD XXXIV.545–54. Word formation (compounding) in Ar.

AT-TANŪKHĪ, ʿIZZ AD-DIN. 1960a. A-maṭār am maṭīr wa-masār am masīr? MMAD XXXV.164–6. Problems in using *maṭār*, *maṭīr*, *masār* and *masīr*.

——. 1960b. Al-ibdāl al-lughawī au al-ishtiqāq al-akbar. MMAD XXV.3–11. The alternation of consonants and the derivation of triconsonantal roots.

TARAZĪ, FUʾĀD. 1962. Adāt at-taʿrīf fī al-ʿarabiyyah. Al-Abhāth XV.478–84. The article in Ar.

AZ-ZAJJĀJĪ, ABŪ AL-QĀSIM. 1959. Al-īḍaḥ fī ʿilal an-naḥw. Ed. by Māzin al-Mubārak with an introd. by Shauqī Ḍaif. Cairo, Maktabat al-ʿUrubah. A grammatical treatise.

——. 1962. Kitāb al-ibdāl wal-muʿāqabah wan-naẓāʾir (I, II, III). Ed. and with introd. by ʿIzz ad-Dīn at-Tanūkhī. MMAD XXXVII.240–75, 428–75, 602–38. On the alternation of consonants in the Ar. root.

SPOKEN ARABIC

PETER F. ABBOUD

1. OVER-ALL VIEW

1.1

Arabic is spoken by some 100,000,000 people in an area that includes: (1) in Africa, the countries of North Africa, Egypt, much of the Sudan, some of the sub-Saharan regions around Lake Chad, and Mauritania; (2) in Asia, the countries of the Fertile Crescent, Arabia, and the Central Asian SSR of Uzbekistan; and (3) in Europe, Malta, and previously in Spain and Sicily, where Arabic was spoken until the 16th and 18th centuries respectively. Further, small Arabic-speaking communities live in Cyprus and on the east coast of Africa. As might be expected in a language used for a long period of time in these immense regions, spoken Arabic has a wide range of dialects and sub-dialects, which show differences in their sounds, grammar, and vocabulary. The major regional cleavage is between Western and Eastern dialects separated by a line that runs roughly from the western borders of Egypt to Lake Chad. In spite of these variations, which can be quite marked at the extremities of the Arab world, the dialects on the whole show remarkable similarities and possess a common core which identifies them unmistakably as Arabic. It is the purpose of this article to give a critical account of the significant linguistic studies which have been made on Arabic dialects in the period following World War II. This will be presented in the next sections. The rest of this section will be devoted to a sketch of the history of dialect studies in Europe, a brief evaluation of the major scholarly works done in the period prior to World War II, and a statement on bibliographical sources and materials used in this article.

1.2

The study of modern dialects was begun in Europe in the second half of the eighteenth and the beginning of the nineteenth centuries, in countries like Italy, France, Austria, England, and Russia which had cultural and commercial interests in the Arabic-speaking world, with the establishment of schools where the colloquials were taught with the help of native speakers from Egypt and Syria.[1] The need for teaching materials prompted men like Mīkhā'īl al-Ṣabbāgh, who taught at *L'École des Langues Orientales Vivantes*, and Muḥammad 'Ayyād al-Ṭanṭāwi, who taught at the University of St. Petersburg, and others, to write grammars for the dialects: al-Ṣabbāgh 1886 and al-Ṭanṭāwī 1848 are the first such attempts known.[2] Progress in dialect studies was slow, mainly because Orientalist scholars were more interested in ancient texts than in the current scene with the result that they confined their attention to the study of Islam and Classical Arabic. There were a few, like A. Fischer and Kampffmeyer, who did some dialect work, but Orientalists as a whole shunned working with the modern dialects. Towards the end of the nineteenth century, however, there appeared several works and collections of texts with commentaries by European scholars who worked and traveled in the Arabic-speaking countries and studied the dialects firsthand. Among these were Spitta and Willmore, who wrote grammars of Egyptian Arabic; Socin, whose activities included the collection of a large number of texts from Central Arabia and studies on Iraqi and Moroccan Arabic; Stumme, who worked on Tunisian and Maltese Arabic; and the indefatigable Landberg, whose works include texts and voluminous glossaries from the north and the south of the Arabian peninsula. It is also in this period, 1898–99, that the expedition of the Vienna Academy to the south of Arabia was undertaken, with the purpose of studying the South Arabian dialects and resulted in a number of texts on which are based the few studies we have of these dialects.[3] The period between the two world wars saw the rise of Orientalists who made substantial contributions to Arabic dialect studies. These include a German, Bergsträsser, who gave us the first linguistic atlas based on his work on the Greater Syrian area and wrote an excellent study of Damascus Arabic; three Frenchmen, W. Marçais, Brunot, and Colin, who worked on North African dialects; a fourth Frenchman, Cantineau, whose extensive publications covered Eastern and Western dialects; and finally an Italian, Rossi, and a Britisher, Gardiner, who worked on Yemeni and Egyptian Arabic respectively. The works of two native speakers of Arabic in this period are worthy of note: al-Raṣāfī's observations of his native dialect of Iraq, and Feghali's study of his dialect of Kfar 'Abīda and his syntax of Lebanese Arabic.[4] With Cantineau begins the period of the application of structural methodology to the study of Arabic dialects.

1.3

Much of the work on the dialects in the century or so prior to World War II that is of

[1] For an account of Arabic dialect studies in Europe see al-Ma'lūf 1935 and 1937. For a history of Arabic studies as a whole see Fück 1955; a shorter account is given in Fück 1954.

[2] al-Ṣabbāgh 1886 was written in 1812 but was not published until 1886; it deals with the Egyptian and Syrian dialects. al-Ṭanṭāwī 1848 describes the Egyptian colloquial. For other works by native speakers of the last century, see al-Ma'lūf 1935 and 1937.

[3] Little work has been done on the modern South Arabian dialects; these dialects have not been taken into consideration in this article. On South Arabian, old and modern, see Höfner 1954.

[4] The works of these and other pre-World War II scholars can be found in the various articles in Sobelmann 1962. In the U.S., work on Arabic dialects started during the war years.

linguistic interest consists of collections of texts and glossaries, but there were a few grammatical studies. The collections, which contain stories, songs, and poems, typically give descriptive and comparative notes and comments, with Classical Arabic as their point of reference. Some are written in Arabic script, adapted with various degrees of success to represent the sounds of the dialects, while others are transcribed. They are usually accompanied by a translation. The glossaries based on these texts are important in that among other things they give comments on the main morphological features of the entries and their stem alternations. The descriptive studies range from full-scale grammars to brief sketches. Almost all presuppose a knowledge of European grammars of Classical Arabic. The sounds of the dialects being studied are discussed, especially in earlier works, with reference to the letters of Classical Arabic, which results sometimes in confusion between writing system and spoken language. The traditional morphological and syntactic categories and terms, some of which have become irrelevant to the dialects, are used. In spite of this, a few studies are outstanding and present the material with clarity and keen insight. Their flaws are those of the framework within which they of necessity had to be written. The rest, their shortcomings notwithstanding, are useful in that they often contain the only information we have about the dialects, and quite a few could well serve as the basis for modern work.

1.4

We have a number of useful bibliographical collections for Arabic dialects. I relied upon the following, which the reader is asked to consult for further details. (1) al-Maʿlūf 1935–37 are rarely, if ever, mentioned in European and American works, probably because they are in Arabic and hence are less accessible to the average student. They deal mainly with Syrian and Egyptian dialect studies and are especially useful for early works. (2) Brockelmann 1954 gives bibliographical information and references throughout the article. Most of them are from pre-World War II works. (3) Cantineau 1955 is a state-of-the-art report that surveys the important work done on the various dialect areas. (4) The pertinent sections under *ʿArabiyya* in EI[5] give references in the text and selected bibliographies at the end of each section. (5) Fischer 1959 gives 451 titles of works used in the study. They include texts, glossaries, textbooks, and various other materials from which linguistic information was gleaned. A very useful aspect is the plotting of these works on maps of the Arabic-speaking regions. (6) Pérès 1959 is an exhaustive analytical bibliography for the Algerian and Saharan regions. (7) Sobelmann 1962 is a collection of six articles by as many scholars, four of which are updated versions of articles that appeared between 1955 and 1959. The articles are organized into sections, each with analytical comments on general and comparative studies, dictionaries, descriptive studies, teaching materials and textbooks, and collections of texts, followed by an extensive bibliography. They

[5] EI in this article refers to the second edition of the *Encyclopedia of Islam*.

cover Syria, Egypt, the Arabian Peninsula, Iraq, North Africa, and Malta. (8) Prochazka 1967 is a selected bibliography of articles and books that appeared between 1960 and 1967, for both literary Arabic and the colloquials, arranged by topic. The 615 entries are taken from sources in Arabic, which are generally left out in the aforementioned bibliographies, as well as sources in the major European languages.

Special sections on Arabic (both colloquial and literary) can be found in the *Linguistic Bibliography*, and in the *MLA Bibliography*. The *Abstracta Islamica*, which accompanies the *Revue des études islamiques* but is published separately, has a section on Arabic dialect studies, with summaries sometimes given after the entries. The *Middle East Journal* has useful bibliographies of books and articles in periodicals.

In the following survey, I have confined myself to linguistic works and have excluded philological works and, with very few exceptions, teaching materials, textbooks, and collections of texts. The works reviewed consist of published materials such as books, monographs, and articles, and of unpublished dissertations and, in a very few cases, M.A. theses of importance. The latter have been included because (1) a number of them make significant original contributions to the field, (2) most, especially those presented at American universities, are readily available to scholars in xeroxed form, and (3) a number are in the process of being published or are being considered for publication and will be available to the reader by the time this article appears. Articles and papers are scattered in a number of periodicals that range from linguistic publications to journals that deal with general Orientalist, Islamic, or Arabic studies: we do not have a journal devoted exclusively to dialect studies.

I have personally examined all publications in the more familiar languages unless otherwise indicated. Since I do not control the language, I am not competent to judge works that appeared in the USSR and most East European countries; my sources of information on these were Šarbatov 1961b, Blanc 1963, and Prochazka 1967 for more recent works. As for the unpublished materials, I examined actual or xeroxed copies of the majority of American dissertations[6] and theses; for those I was not able to obtain, I consulted *Dissertation Abstracts*.[7] I know only by title the dissertations referred to in the article which were presented at universities in Great Britain (mainly the University of London)[8] and at the University of Cairo.[9] Most other European dissertations of interest are generally published soon after they are accepted.

Having given this background information, I will now proceed to the subject of this article, which is organized into four sections dealing with descriptive, comparative, historical, and contrastive studies. Section 6 gives concluding remarks.

[6] For these see *Doctoral Dissertations Accepted by American Universities* (*1933–1955*); *Index to American Doctoral Dissertations* (*1955–1965*); and *Dissertation Abstracts* (*1952–1967*).

[7] I was not able to find abstracts for one or two dissertations because the particular institution does not contribute to DA.

[8] For these see *Index to Theses Accepted for Higher Degrees in the Universities of Great Britain and Ireland: 1950–1964*. To my knowledge they remain unpublished with the exception of Johnstone 1967, which has recently appeared.

[9] For these see 'Ibrāhīm, 'Abd al-Laṭīf. 1967. *al-Rasā'il al-'Ilmīya li Darajatayy al-Mājistīr wa al-Duktūrāh* 1932–1966. Cairo, U. of Cairo P.

2. DESCRIPTIVE STUDIES

The period following World War II has witnessed the appearance, at an ever-increasing pace, of a number of descriptive studies dealing with the various dialects. These are given and critically examined in the following subsections. First, however, a few general remarks on the character and quality of these studies for this period are in order. (1) General descriptive studies that treat dialect areas as a whole are rare. Two subsections in EI (Fleisch 1958 and Ph. Marçais 1958) give the main phonological and grammatical characteristics of the Eastern and Western dialects respectively. Brockelmann 1954 contains a few of the distinguishing features of each area but is based mostly on older materials. Colin 1945, W. Marçais 1950, and Ph. Marçais 1957 give surveys of Moroccan, Tunisian, and Algerian Arabic respectively. I know Šarbatov 1960 on the analytical character of Arabic dialects by title only. It should be noted in this connection, that some titles tend to be misleading: terms such as Egyptian, Syrian, etc., are merely labels for the most prestigious or influential dialect in the particular area (the former mostly referring to Cairo, and the latter to one of the urban centers in Greater Syria), and works having such titles do not necessarily present a general study of the dialect area in question. (2) The treatment of the different components of the grammars are not equally developed. In general, the progress made in phonology in the forties and fifties is reflected in Arabic phonological studies, with the result that the phonology is usually more satisfactorily handled than other parts of the grammar. Gone are the days when the analyst was contented with a discussion of how the letters of the Classical Arabic alphabet are represented in the dialects; most analyses now present a more or less clear picture of the sound system. The morphology usually forms the bulk of the work. It typically lists the various *ʾawzān* 'patterns' using traditional conventions, which presupposes some knowledge of Classical Arabic grammar. Syntax was for long a neglected area. This is seen even in the works of the leading and most productive dialectologists such as Cantineau and others. During the last decade or so, however, interest in syntax has increased as witnessed by an increasing number of studies and monographs and by the larger and larger sections devoted to it in general works. (3) There are, generally speaking, distinctions in presentation, outlook, approach, and methodology, between modern descriptive works by American-trained and those by European-trained scholars. For convenience, these will be referred to as American and European respectively, it being understood, of course, that differences and schools do exist within each group and that some (e.g. British) works would defy such dichotomy. In terms of approach, the former are rigidly descriptive, while the latter, even those that are descriptive in goal, generally include historical, dialectological, and comparative materials. In presentation, European works are often encumbered by exhaustive details, with the result that important generalizations and clear patterns are missed. On the other hand, American works, in general, in seeking these generalizations and cherishing neatness of pattern, tend to be impatient with details. In methodology both schools are in the long and venerable tradition of orientalist scholarship going back as far as De Sacy (1758–1838). The field of Arabic linguistics is on the whole conservative, but the two schools can be distinguished in the degree of departure from this tradition. In the previous section progress was noted in phonological studies, which are now mostly structuralist in outlook. The particular brand of structuralism used by European scholars, mainly French but more recently German also, is that of the Prague school. In Great Britain, Firthian influence is felt in the few works that are readily available. American works have so far been in the vein of what has been called American structuralism. In morphology and syntax American (and some British) works have shown greater readiness to depart from the tradition. Thus attempts have been made with varying degrees of success to restructure and reclassify patterns and structures on a more formal basis, using immediate constituent, slot-filler, and, more recently, generative approaches (and in the case of the British, the so-called syntagmatic analysis, Mitchell 1958), and to change and adapt traditional terminology, inordinate reliance upon which has hampered progress and has tended to obscure the significant facts and structures of the language. (4) Few discussions on theoretical implications of descriptive and field work and the adequacy of the methodology used to describe Arabic dialects exist. Arabic linguists have been too busy discovering the linguistic facts to bother with theory. The closest we come to such a discussion is the exchange between Ferguson, Cantineau, and Smeaton: Ferguson 1954, Cantineau 1956c, Smeaton 1956 and Ferguson 1957. Here arguments such as what constitutes a phoneme, whether morphological criteria are relevant to phonemic analysis, how foreign elements and borrowings are to be handled, etc. are discussed. Another article with theoretical interest is Cantineau 1950, with comments on American structural phonemics as applied in Harris 1942.

In what follows the works to be evaluated are considered in this order: grammars and grammatical sketches, phonological, morphological, syntactic studies, and dictionaries.

2.1 *Grammars*

For Egypt we have two important works from the pre-war era: Spitta 1880 and Willmore 1905, to which reference has already been made. Among the more recent works, Mitchell 1962:10–120 (an improved version of Mitchell 1956) gives a succinct and clear description of Cairo Arabic. The phonology is briefly but adequately covered, including the ingenious solution of setting up a low back vowel to take care of emphasis not attributable to the presence of the familiar four emphatic consonants and emphatic /r/, a solution not without its problems, of course. The sections on the elision of high short vowels and glottal stop, on verb phrases, participles, noun modifiers with or without the relative, etc., are among the best in the literature. An unpublished dissertation (Khalafallah 1961) is the first general descriptive study of an Upper Egyptian dialect. It has an interesting discussion on emphasis and on its spread and domain. The syntax is a bare outline, which, it is hoped, will be filled with more comprehensive statements when the work is published. Tomiche 1964 is a descriptive study of Cairo Arabic that also contains dialectological and historical materials. The phonology presents original statistical analysis of the sounds and syllables. The morphology is traditional, and the syntax rather confused and disorganized. A brief sketch of the features of the speech of the nomads in the area west of Alexandria, Egypt, is given in Maṭar 1966. I know Abu Farag 1960, on the Lower Egyptian dialect of Minufiya, by title only. Another unpublished dissertation not available to me (Ṭalab 1958) deals with the dialect of the Sudan.

The Syrian area has received more attention than any other dialect. From the pre-war period we have a number of useful studies such as Bauer 1913 for Jerusalem and surrounding areas, Feghali 1919 for Kfar ʿAbīda, Lebanon, Driver 1925 for Jerusalem, and Cantineau 1934 for Palmyra. Of these only Driver 1925 deals with syntax. In the post-war period, Cantineau 1946 is an outstanding and meticulous study of the Horan in Syria. Unfortunately, it lacks any treatment of syntax. El-Hajje 1954 describes the speech of the author, who hails from Tripoli, Lebanon. The transcription, especially for the vowels, is somewhat confusing and the presentation inconsistent in parts; but it is a useful treatment of an area with interesting features. Shawkat 1962 is an unpublished dissertation on Damascus Arabic. Its useful features include a discussion of consonant clusters with extensive tables and of the more important syntactic structures, the first for this dialect. Emphasis is very lightly touched upon, and the morphophonemics is inadequate. Cowell 1964 is a study of the dialect of Damascus based on both published works and actual field work with informants. The material is well organized and very well illustrated. It is one of the few works of its kind where syntax is discussed in more than a casual manner. Grotzfeld 1964 and 1965 on Damascus Arabic are similar. The latter has a shorter section of phonology but has a section on syntax, transcribed texts, and a glossary, which the former does not. The phonology, which includes a chapter on historical developments, is Praguian. The transcription shows only the four familiar emphatics. Syntactic remarks are brief and present the most salient features only. Jiha 1964 is in the same vein but attempts no discussion of syntax. Shorter works include Fleisch 1947–48, 1962, 1963–64, and Cantineau 1956a, b, which describe the peculiar features of some dialects in the Lebanon not hitherto worked on. I know Bishr 1955 on Lebanese Arabic by title only.

For Iraq we have an unpublished dissertation (Van Wagoner 1944), which I have not seen. Erwin 1963 and Malaika 1963 are both based on the speech of Baghdadi Muslims and are interesting to compare in method and approach. The bulk of the latter (henceforth M) deals with morphology, but it also contains a short section on syntax and an even shorter treatment of phonology. The former (henceforth E) is richer in detail and more comprehensive in scope. In M we are given a list of sounds including /m̃/ and /ñ/, which are described as strongly nasalized consonants, and, in addition to the usual emphatics, emphatic /r g l ṯ/, but are not told whether they present phonemic distinction. E gives emphatic /p f m l/, all of which, in addition to emphatic /z/, are termed secondary emphatic following Harrell 1957. The morphology in M and E is comparable in scope and treatment. The syntax in M lists the functions of the various parts of speech. In E, syntax is presented in a more satisfactory manner by means of types of structures such as sentence, phrase, and clause types. Blanc 1964 describes the linguistic features that delineate the dialects of Jews, Christians, and Muslims in Baghdad and in the process gives an overall picture of the phonological, morphological, and, to a more limited scale, syntactic features, of Baghdad Arabic. I have not seen Schramm 1954, nor Šarbatov 1961a which purports to give some peculiarities of Iraqi Arabic.

For Arabia, descriptive studies for any region are rare. From the pre-war period, Cantineau 1936–37 are important contributions to our knowledge of the speech of the nomadic tribes of the Syro-Arabian desert, and Rossi 1939, for Yemen. More recently, Goitein 1960 gives the main characteristics of a Yemeni dialect. Johnstone 1961 (revised in Johnstone 1964) gives the characteristics of the speech of a Kuwaiti tribe. Johnstone 1967 is an important work, the first such study for Arabian dialects, which specifically deals with the dialect of the eastern Arabian coast. Important general statements on the various features that characterize the group as a whole are followed by statements on the distinguishing features of the individual dialects: Kuwaiti, Baḥraini, Qaṭari, and the dialect of the Trucial Coast. The basic approach used is a study of dialectal departures from Classical Arabic. A short discussion of syntax is preceded by the questionable statement that the syntax of these dialects does not differ greatly from that of literary Arabic, a statement not borne out by the subsequent discussion.

The Arabic dialects of Central Asia are known to us through dictionaries and texts published by Russian scholars.[10] Fischer 1961 analyzes these materials and gives a preliminary description of the dialect which will have to be revised in the light of more recent publications. Another 'island' dialect surrounded by speakers of other languages is the Arabic spoken by Cypriots of Arab descent. It is described in Tsiapera 1963, a study which has some interesting observations but lacks depth.

For North Africa we have a number of studies dating back to pre-war days. The more important ones are W. Marçais 1901–02 for Tlemcen in Algeria, the series of articles W. Marçais 1906–09 on the Bedouin dialect in Oran, and M. Cohen 1912 on the Jewish dialect of Algiers. More recent works include Ph. Marçais 1956, a detailed account of the dialect of Djidjelli in Algeria, whose method and approach is typical of works by French scholars. Harrell 1962 draws on the work of French dialectologists, but this in no way diminishes its originality. The phonology is brief but clearly presented, though the treatment of vowels and the lack of marking of length for them raise many questions. The syntax is somewhat unorthodox in that it starts with a discussion of negation and interrogatives, but is one of the very few substantial treatments of the subject for a North African dialect. I have not seen ʿAbd al-ʿĀl 1966 on the dialect of

[10] For a bibliography see footnotes 42 and 43 in Blanc 1963:381–2 and Fischer 1961:232, to which must now be added Vinnikov 1962 and 1965.

Taṭwān in Northern Morocco, nor Brown 1955 on Algerian Arabic. D. Cohen 1963, which describes the Ḥassānīye Arabic of Mauritania, was unfortunately not available to me at the time of writing this article. For Maltese we have Aquilina 1959 and 1961 which describe Maltese as a mixed language, consisting of two layers, a Semitic and non-Semitic, and analyze the phonology and grammar of each separately, a questionable analysis which is abandoned in a more cogent and a little less difficult to follow work, Aquilina 1965.

2.2 *Phonology*

A number of excellent studies and monographs on the phonology of various dialects exist. Cantineau 1951 is a detailed and thoroughgoing, strictly synchronic analysis of a dialect in North Africa, applying with all rigor the phonological principles of the Prague school. Two studies illustrate the rigorous application of the American brand of structural phonemics. The first (Harrell 1957), in addition to a fullscale study of the segmental and suprasegmental features of Cairo Arabic, including juncture and intonation, includes an interesting study of emphasis in terms of its linguistic and extra-linguistic functions. The discussion on intonation and juncture is somewhat questionable, smacking as it does of the then influential Trager-Smith analysis of English. The second (Blanc 1953), a study of the speech of the Druze of North Palestine, unlike the two afore-mentioned studies, gives comparisons with other related dialects and has copious footnotes containing comments on linguistic, historical, dialectological, and other matters. Some of its interesting features include the treatment of the vowels, which are divided into short and compound, the latter transcribed as /a: i: u: iy uw/, chiefly for morphophonemic reasons, and of emphasis. Cantineau 1956c is a brief analysis of Damascus segmentals prompted by criticism in Ferguson 1954 of Cantineau and Helbaoui 1953. I have not been able to examine Dawood 1949 on the Upper Egyptian dialect of al-Karnak, nor Dawood 1951 on Aden Arabic, which to my knowledge have never been published. Having been written in Great Britain, they would illustrate Firth's approach to phonology; it would be interesting to compare them with the other works given in this section. D. Cohen 1966 discusses the phonology of Maltese from a synchronic and diachronic view.

The problem of emphasis has received quite a bit of attention. Ph. Marçais 1948 is a radioscopic analysis of the articulatory correlates of emphasis. Firth 1948:141 hints at an analysis of emphasis in Cairo Arabic as a prosody of the syllable. Ferguson 1956 shows that a consistent implementation of structural phonemic theory necessitates the setting up of an emphatic /l/ in Classical Arabic and the dialects. Jakobson 1957 applies the distinctive feature analysis to emphasis and gives its acoustic and physical correlates. In view of the fact that post-velar fricatives behave like other consonants in Arabic, Arabists would find his treating them as [-consonantal] objectionable. Nasr 1959 discusses three analyses of emphasis and comes to the dubious and highly questionable conclusion that they are equally acceptable, the choice depending mainly on typographical considerations. Obrecht 1961 is an instrumental analysis of emphasis in Lebanese Arabic which studies its acoustic correlates and probes the role the second formant plays in the perception of emphatic consonants. Lehn 1963 compares different analyses of emphasis as applied to Cairo Arabic and demonstrates that the domain of emphasis is the syllable, and that the most economic way to indicate it is by marking the onset of each emphatic syllable.

An unpublished dissertation (Abdalla 1960) is a spectographic analysis of Cairo Arabic with a view of describing its intonation system by means of instrumental procedures. The conclusions throw some doubt on the analysis of intonation as found in Harrell 1957 and other works that follow it and suggest a system of three stresses and four pitch levels, but no distinctive function for the so-called terminal junctures. Another unpublished dissertation (Badawi 1964) is an intonational study of the Arabic of Riyadh in Saudi Arabia.

Fleisch 1964 discusses an interesting vowel alternation, /ī ~ ē/, in word final and non-final position in the dialect of a Shiite community in Lebanon.

2.3 *Morphology*

Aboul-Fetouh 1961 is an unpublished dissertation dealing with the morphology of Cairo Arabic. Its originality lies in its departure from traditional treatises by seeking to establish form classes on the basis of their inflectional categories and in some cases their syntactic behavior. Members within each class are then classified according to their stem alternations. The approach contrasts with the more traditional one in Singer 1958b for the North African dialect of Taṭwān. Within morphology, the verb and the noun in Cairo Arabic and their classification on the basis of their canonical shapes as well as their inflectional and derivational categories are the subjects of two unpublished dissertations: Helmy-Hassan 1960 and Ghaly 1961, respectively. On the basis of the vowel alternation in the perfect and the imperfect of form I verbs in a Lebanese dialect, Fleisch 1954 suggests seven subclasses. An unpublished thesis (Gamal-Eldin 1959) gives a detailed description of morphophonemics in Cairo Arabic, the only such study for any dialect. Brunot 1950a and Quémeneur 1963 deal with some verb patterns with long vowels peculiar to North African Arabic, and Saydon 1958 shows that the quality of the vowels of Maltese form I verbs in the perfect is affected by the consonants in the root. I know Ayoub 1949 and Vinnikov 1965 by title only.

2.4 *Syntax*

Four general syntactic works and four dealing with specific syntactic problems are known to me. Blau 1960 is based on texts collected for the village of Bīr-Zēt in Central Palestine. The features of the dialect are treated in great detail, but the work is couched in the terminology and approach of traditional grammars. Gamal-Eldin 1961 analyzes the syntax of Cairo Arabic using mainly the immediate constituent approach, but, where this is not adequate, other techniques are also used. Hanna 1962 discusses the phrase structure of Cairo Arabic as well as singular and double based or generalized transformations. Abboud 1964 is a study of the syntax of an important dialect of Northern Najd. These last two works, though in no sense transformational grammars, use generative grammar formulations and abbreviatory devices, which result in added clarity of presentation. Studies of specific areas in syntax include El Sayid 1962, Piamenta 1964 and 1966, and Bloch 1965. The first deals with the parts of speech in Cairo Arabic. Piamenta 1964, based on a dissertation in Hebrew dealing with the tenses, aspects, and moods in Jerusalem Arabic, is detailed but highly traditional in approach. Piamenta 1966 is also based on the same dissertation but with an attempt at a structural reformulation, though the tone and spirit remain traditional. It deals specifically with the tense, aspect, and mood concord (or lack of it) of the verb in the main, with the verb in the subordinate, clause. The importance of Piamenta's works lies in their being the first attempt to study in detail a difficult and little explored area of Arabic syntax. One cannot, however, concur with the conclusion (Piamenta 1964) that the topic is too complex and unsystematic to be amenable to analysis; but Piamenta is probably right when he says: 'Some syntactic features may never be analyzable in purely structural terms ...' (Piamenta 1966:xiv), if by that he means that the framework he uses, whether traditional or structural, is inadequate to deal with the problem and that what is needed is a more explicit and more powerful linguistic theory. Bloch 1965 is a study of another little known area of Arabic syntax, i.e. subordination. It is traditional in outlook and terminology but is well organized. Shorter treatments include Mitchell 1952, which studies the morphological and syntactic behavior of the active participle in the dialect of Cyrenaica, and Wild 1964 which makes a similar study of the active participle in the Syrian dialect. I am not able to judge Badawi 1959, which I know only by title.

2.5 *Dictionaries*

The number of dictionaries for the dialects is small. Vocabularies and glossaries are more numerous but the following remarks will be concerned with available dictionaries only. This gap in our knowledge is being gradually filled by the dictionaries published in the Georgetown Arabic Series. So far four have appeared: Sobelmann and Harrell 1963 is English-Moroccan; Abu-Talib and Fox 1966, Moroccan-English; Stowasser and Ani 1964, English-Syrian; Clarity, Stowasser and Wolfe 1964, English-Iraqi. Two are scheduled to appear soon: a Syrian-English and an Iraqi-English. These dictionaries, all of which follow the same principles and are based on a bilingual German-English dictionary,[11] are a great improvement on previous works. Some of

[11] This is the German-English, English-German Dictionary of Everyday Usage, ed. by J. Alan Pfeffer (New York, Holt), which was prepared during World War II.

their useful features are: (1) The entries are followed by equivalents which are then presented in sentences that illustrate their usage in both languages and define their semantic range. (2) Particular attention is paid to idiomatic expressions and their renderings. (3) The Arabic is given in an easy-to-follow phonemic transcription. (4) The typography is clear and neat.

Besides these, we have the following for Syrian Arabic. Barthélemy 1935–54 is a comprehensive and valuable work based mainly on Aleppo Arabic; it is Arabic-French. A recent work supplements it: Denizeau 1960. Bauer 1933, in German-Arabic, a new edition of which was published in 1957, is based on Jerusalem Arabic and has extensive entries. Frayha 1947 is a well-researched dictionary of Lebanese Arabic with definitions given in Arabic. For Egypt we do not have a good modern dictionary. Spiro 1923 in Arabic-English, and Spiro 1929 in English-Arabic, which first appeared in the 1890's, are valuable but have long been out of print. Elias 1949 in English-Arabic and Elias and Elias 1954 in Arabic-English have gone through many editions. They are useful but lack sophistication. For North African Arabic and Maltese the important dictionaries, most of which are prewar works, are listed in Sobelmann 1962:60–2, 93–5. For the Central Asian dialects we have Vinnikov 1962 for the dialect of Bukhara. Other dialects lack good dictionaries.

3. DIALECTOLOGICAL STUDIES

3.1 *Dialect Geography*

No region of the Arabic-speaking world is well known from a dialect geography point of view. One of the better known regions is the Greater Syrian area, for which we have three excellent studies: (1) Bergsträsser 1915, with 40 maps showing major isoglosses based on phonological, grammatical and lexical features. Fleisch 1959 gives a preliminary report on recent extensive work, which will correct and supplement Bergsträsser's, conducted in some 50 places in Lebanon using a questionnaire with 110 sentences, later revised down to 35; (2) Cantineau 1936–37, where the major subgroupings and geographical distribution of a number of nomadic tribal dialects are indicated; and (3) Cantineau 1946, with 60 very carefully drawn maps on the Horan region. Cleveland 1963 is a very tentative and not too well-defined classification of the dialects of Jordan into four subgroups. For Iraq, Blanc 1964 suggests two major dialect groupings, clearly defined by well correlated linguistic criteria, which are called the *qeltu* and *gelet* dialects, the word being the 1 sg. form of the verb 'say'. For Arabia, Johnstone 1963 discusses the distribution in the peninsula of the affricated reflexes of /k/ and /q/, and Johnstone 1965, that of the reflexes of /j/. Johnstone 1967:1–18 gives the main linguistic characteristics and distribution of the North Arabian dialects, including the East Arabian group. For Egypt, Tomiche 1962 is a tentative attempt to delineate the features of the dialects of Upper and Lower Egypt. The title of an unpublished dissertation (Abul-Fadl 1961), not available to me, suggests a dialect geography study of the province of Šarqīya in Lower Egypt. For North Africa, we have Cantineau 1936, 1937, 1939b, and 1940. I do not know of more recent works for this area. For Malta, Aquilina, Isserlin and Annan 1966 announces a new dialect survey.

3.2 *Comparative Studies*

Many of the descriptive studies given in section 2 above contain comparisons of the particular dialect under discussion with other dialects. Systematic comparative studies in depth are few. Brockelmann's *Grundriss* remains an important instrument of work, though quite obviously outdated. Mitchell 1960 studies stress as a function of syllabic structure and syllable sequences in two dialects, and in Classical Arabic as pronounced in Egypt, based on principles that are clearly applicable to other dialects. Fischer 1967 discusses syllable structure, elision, and epenthesis of vowels in Classical Arabic, the modern dialects, and other Semitic languages. An important comparative study, the first of its kind, Fischer 1959 has very good coverage of the morphology and syntax of the demonstratives, using all available materials in the various dialects. The work is detailed and well documented, with an extensive bibliography, but one looks in vain for generalizations, valid conclusions, and a study of trends, based on the findings. A similar work on the interrogative in the dialects (Singer 1958a) was not available to me. An unpublished dissertation (Cadora 1966) attempts to show the degrees of lexical affinities among Syro-Lebanese urban dialects by means of quantitative procedures and to demonstrate the basic lexical homogeneity of the group when compared to four other major dialects.

3.3 *Social Dialectology*

The study of languages and dialects from a sociological point of view are rare. Some work in this field has been done on Arabic and will be of interest to sociolinguists in general.

3.3.1 *Diglossia, Bilingualism*

The problem of the existence in the Arab world of a literary language side by side with an everyday spoken language has recently attracted attention in the USSR and the West. Al-Toma 1957 presents the many educational and pedagogical aspects and implications of the problem. Ferguson 1959b attempts to identify the sociolinguistic characteristics of the phenomenon of Diglossia by studying the features common to Arabic and three other languages which have a standard-colloquial language dichotomy. Belkin 1960 reviews the various representative points of view on the subject in the Arab world, following a discussion of the historical, economic, and social factors, which are at the root of the problem.[12] Blanc 1960 studies the nature of the stylistic variations introduced in the dialects of educated speakers of Arabic with different dialect backgrounds when they converse on subjects requiring the use of 'higher' or more learned forms of Arabic. The modifications in the phonology, grammar, and lexicon of the language so used are catalogued and described. Saʿīd 1964 is a detailed and useful but not altogether objective account of the origin, development, and impact of the classical-colloquial controversy in Egypt. The language situation in the Arab world is discussed in Chejne 1958 and 1965. Abou 1962 discusses the history, development, impact, and future of French-Arabic bilingualism in Lebanon; its approach is basically literary and sociological, not linguistic.

3.3.2 *Socio-Economic and Communal Dialects*

The Arabic dialect cleavage into sedentary and nomadic has long been recognized. The most important differentiating features for the modern dialects are discussed and evaluated by D. Cohen (1962:125–32). Cantineau 1939a attempts to delineate the speech of sedentaries in Greater Syria by means of linguistic criteria. A dialect cleavage of a different kind, based on differences attributable to religious affiliation has also been investigated. Blanc 1964 finds in Baghdad as many dialects as religious communities, i.e. Muslim, Christian, and Jewish. The dialects show distinctions in their phonology, grammar, and lexicon, that are well correlated with these religious groupings. Fleisch 1959 offers preliminary data that points to communal differentiation in Lebanon. Brunot 1950b:16–19 and Ph. Marçais 1956:218f. discuss both the socio-economic and religious dialect situation that obtains in North Africa.[13]

4. HISTORICAL STUDIES

4.1 *The Ancient Dialects*[14]

These dialects were the object of study by the leading Orientalists of the nineteenth and the beginning of the twentieth centuries.[15] In more recent times, Kofler 1940–42 collects the known sources for the ancient dialects and arranges the linguistic material by grammatical features. ʾAnīs 1965, which has gone through three editions, deals primarily with the phonetic features of the dialects, and is based mostly on late sources. Littmann 1948 deals with some of the features of the ancient dialects which are attested in pre-Islamic literature. Ḥammūdah 1948 makes important contributions

[12] I examined this article in a preliminary English translation which, with other translated articles on socio-linguistics, was scheduled for publication by the Center for Applied Linguistics. The project apparently has been shelved for the time being.

[13] For a fuller account of the relevant literature, see footnotes 15–21 in Blanc 1964:184–5.

[14] I have not taken into consideration the languages of the North Arabian inscriptions and other graffiti. For a description of these see EI 561–4.

[15] For an annotated bibliography see Rabin 1951:xi-xii.

by studying the features of the dialects as reflected in the variant readings *qirā'āt* of the Quran. Rabin 1951 is an excellent study, based on the best sources, which presents a well documented account of the phonological and grammatical features of the ancient dialects spoken in the West of the Arabian peninsula. A recent dissertation (al-Jundi 1965), which I have not been able to examine, purports to examine the materials about the old dialects as reported in the works of the Arab grammarians. Many features of the dialect of Tamīm are collected in al-Ṣālih 1960:66–106.

4.2 *Modern Dialects*

4.2.1 *Origin of the Dialects; Middle Arabic*

A widely accepted hypothesis about the origin of the modern dialects is that they are the decendents, directly or indirectly, of Classical Arabic, which was itself a koine based on the ancient dialects. Several refinements of this hypothesis have been suggested. Fück 1950, an important work tracing the developments from Classical Arabic to Medieval Arabic by careful evaluation of deviations in the latter from the former as reflected in the writings of the Medieval litterateurs and philologists, suggests that a spoken koine developed in the military camps following the Arab Conquests. As a result of the intermarriage and intercommunication of the Arabs with the conquered peoples of the area, there arose in the first century of the conquests various vernaculars, which, through the process of leveling and simplification, developed features differing considerably from the language of the conquerors. It is these vernaculars which are the ancestors of the modern urban dialects outside Arabia. Ferguson 1959a, basing its arguments exclusively on linguistic criteria, makes the hypothesis that the urban dialects are descended from a common homogeneous spoken language, a koine not identical with any of the earlier dialects and different from Classical Arabic, which spread over the conquered area, with differences in the modern dialects developing at a later stage. D. Cohen 1962 in answer argues that there were not one but several such koines, because many of the features given by Ferguson are to be found in the speech of the nomads, hence pointing to a common development, and because the features are not as widespread among the urban dialects as Ferguson implies. Blau 1965 and 1966–67 attempt to delineate the structural characteristics of Middle Arabic, which term he uses to mean the urban dialects which arose in the early years of the Arab conquests, by the careful study of the consistent and clear deviations from Classical Arabic found in the extensive Medieval Jewish and Christian Arabic literature, which though ostensibly written in literary Arabic, betrays dialectal usage. It will be noticed that the dialects were very rarely, if ever, written, and hence our knowledge of them is not based on direct sources. The one important exception to this is Spanish Arabic, spoken in Spain from the eighth to the sixteenth centuries, for which we do possess such documents. Some of its main features are given in Colin 1959, which also gives a good biliography, and in Pérès 1950.

4.2.2 *Diachronic Studies*

Birkeland 1952 represents the first attempt to apply the principles and methodology of modern linguistics to the historical study of modern Arabic dialects. The scope of the work, contrary to what is implied in the title, is limited to phonological developments in Egyptian Arabic. It presents a succession of five stages each dealing with changes in the structure of final syllables, and discusses the emergence of a system with fixed word stress. A more inclusive treatment of historical phonology (Garbell 1958) attempts to trace and date the sound changes in the urban dialects of Greater Syria, through five structurally well-defined stages, with corroborative external evidence from Aramaic and other dialect sources. Birkeland 1954 discusses the development in the major dialects of a new pattern which, unlike the pre-dialectal stage, has fixed word stress, and which originated in the eastern dialects and spread to the others. Cowan 1960 is the first application of the comparative method to Arabic. Representatives of the major dialect areas are selected and first a proto-western, then, by comparing this with other dialects, a proto-colloquial, are established by recurring phonological correspondences. This attempt is somewhat premature in that the gaps in our knowledge of important dialect areas place severe limitations on the extent and validity of the findings. Two articles discuss sound changes in Maltese: D. Cohen 1966 and Cowan 1966. Erickson 1965 is an interesting study of the developments in verbal morphology from Classical to Cairo Arabic (see also 5.2 below). ʿAbdīn 1966 is an attempt to trace some phonological and morphological features in the dialects of the Sudan to ancient dialects. I know Axveldiani 1953 and the articles based on it (Šarbatov 1961b:135) on the reflexes of the pharyngeals in the dialects by title only.

4.2.3 *Substratum*

Various works discussing peculiar features in particular dialects tend, sometimes hastily, to ascribe them to substratum influences. An unpublished dissertation (Bishai 1959), four articles based on it (Bishai 1960, 1961, 1962, and 1964), and Petraček 1956 discuss Coptic influences in Egyptian Arabic; Simon 1953, Berber influences in North African Arabic; Aquilina 1961 and Saydon 1956, Punic and Latin influences in Maltese. Problems with substratum theory are well known. In Arabic, while substratum influences in the lexicon have been readily demonstrated, evidence for influences in the phonology and grammar remains meager. Further research on the modern and ancient dialects could well explain many peculiar dialectal features.

4.2.4 *Glottochronology*

Two attempts at applying the principles of glottochronology to Arabic are known Samarrai 1959 compares Egyptian, Jordanian, and Iraqi Arabic with Classical Arabic, and concludes that the rate-constant is higher for Arabic than for other languages. The conclusion is rejected in Hymes 1959, and in Satterthwait 1960, which contrasts modern Meccan with Quranic Arabic.

4.2.5 *Borrowings*

Most of the work on borrowings in the modern dialects is of an etymological nature and will not concern us here. Two unpublished works of interest are known: Smeaton 1959 and Butros 1963. The first studies from a sociolinguistic point of view the manner, process, impact of, and motivation for, the incorporation in the dialect of al-Hasa in Saudi Arabia of a large number of technical terms. The second deals with the impact of English loanwords on the phonological, grammatical, and semantic patterns of the dialect of Jerusalem. Other treatments include Colin 1947, which deals with borrowed morphemes in North African Arabic, Hadj-Sadok 1955, which discusses classes of borrowings and their provenience from certain social institutions, and Barbot 1961, which deals with the effects that borrowings from various languages have had on the phonology of the Syrian urban dialects throughout their history.

5. CONTRASTIVE STUDIES

Almost all of these studies consist of unpublished dissertations or theses presented at American universities during the last decade or so. The majority contrast dialects with English, but two contrast dialects with Modern Standard Arabic (MSA). Most are pedagogically oriented, and are thus of interest to linguists and language teachers alike. In what follows these studies are considered under two headings: those that are pedagogically oriented and those that are not.

5.1 *Pedagogically oriented studies*

The works are similarly organized and planned. The features in question, whether phonological or grammatical, in the native language, whether English or Arabic as the case may be, are described and compared with those of the target language. Problems for the native speaker in mastering the target language lie in the differences in the two systems. These differences are pointed out and discussed. The following account lists the native and target languages, in this order, next to the work. For convenience, English is abbreviated to E. On phonological contrastive analysis: (Nasr 1955), Lebanese-E; (Lehn and Slager 1959), Cairo-E; (Kennedy 1960), E-Cairo; (Khalafallah 1959), Ṣaʿiidi-E. All of these deal mainly with segmentals and stress. (Malik 1956–57), Iraqi-E, discusses consonant clusters. (Rammuny 1966), Jordanian-E, is an instrumental contrastive analysis of suprasegmentals, especially intonation patterns. On general (phonological and grammatical) contrastive studies: (Al-Toma 1957), Iraqi-MSA, and (Greis 1963), E-Cairo.

5.2 *Other Contrastive Studies*

Becker 1964 contrasts MSA and Lebanese verb structures and formulates transfer rules from one to the other. Erickson 1965 studies the development of verb morphology in two historical stages of English (Old and Modern English) and of Arabic (Classical and Cairo Arabic) and contrasts the rules that generate the various forms of the verb for one language at each stage with those of the other language. The conclusion reached is that Arabic is much more conservative than English. I know Satterthwait 1962 by title only.

6. CONCLUSIONS

This survey will have shown that significant progress has been made in Arabic dialect studies since World War II. In order to assess this, it will be useful to compare the present state of affairs with the one that obtained when Cantineau wrote his report on Arabic dialectology (Cantineau 1955) some 15 years ago. Even a casual examination will show progress on several fronts. (1) Dialect areas that were totally unknown or not too well known have now been worked on. To the first category belong the Arabian Peninsula, specifically the Najd and the eastern seaboard, and the Central Asian SSR of Uzbekistan, two areas of the greatest importance in dialect work; to the latter belong the main urban centers of Syria, Egypt, and others, whose main outlines are now clearly discerned thanks to a few excellent studies. (2) The researchers who now apply their sophisticated linguistic know-how to dialect study number far more than the four Cantineau mentions.[16] One of the most promising developments in the field is the emergence of a number of trained linguists who are native speakers of Arabic. They are bound to have an impact on the field not only in Europe and the United States, but also, and perhaps more importantly, in the Arab world itself, where for too long dialect studies have been neglected and looked down upon. Encouraging signs can already be seen in the increased activities both within and without the Arab academies, especially the Egyptian *Majmaʿ al-Lughah al-ʿArabīyah.* The number of non-native linguists and arabists with interest in dialect studies has also increased appreciably, whether in the U.S.A., Western Europe, or the U.S.S.R. (3) Cantineau complained, and rightly so, that in spite of the fact that Arabic dialectology could boast of many works, too few among them were grammars and dictionaries. Since then, a relatively large number of linguistic studies have appeared in the form of full scale grammars, monographs, and articles. A quick glance at the references at the end of this article, however, will indicate that many works are still unpublished. It is gratifying to note that some publishers have taken an interest in publishing some of these important studies, thus making them available to scholars so that they could examine and evaluate them. They will have a strong impact on the field. These

[16] Of these four, only Blanc is presently engaged in dialect research. Cantineau himself passed away in 1956; Harris's publications on Arabic dialects never went beyond his one article (Harris 1942), and Ferguson, who has made important contributions to the field, has for some time now not been active in research on Arabic dialects.

remarks should not be interpreted to mean that the work is done. Far from it. Important areas still remain virtually unknown. Except for the work of P. Fleisch in Lebanon, there is paucity in dialect geography work; thoroughgoing descriptive analyses of even the better known dialects are lacking, let alone the many regions that are still unknown; comparative studies in depth are still rare; and the whole field of social dialectology has hardly been touched. (4) Some progress has taken place in an area not considered by Cantineau: historical studies. The investigations, which in many cases are in their pioneer stage, have included attempts at reconstructing earlier stages of modern dialects, collecting and collating the main features of the ancient dialects from the writings of the Arab grammarians, and examining the emergence and characteristics of the medieval (Middle Arabic) dialects through the study of the works of medieval philologists and litterateurs and of the Christian and Jewish literature. But progress lies mostly in more research on modern dialects — hence the paramount importance of descriptive studies — using the tools of traditional historical linguistics and those emerging from more recent developments, which are having important implications for historical studies. (5) Finally, as far as methodology and techniques are concerned, the field of Arabic dialect studies is somewhat more progressive than in the early fifties: new ideas have permeated some areas. It is hoped, however, that researchers will continue to be receptive to new ideas from modern linguistic theories and so sharpen their current techniques and framework whose inadequacies scholars of various convictions are starting to notice.

REFERENCES

ABBOUD, PETER F. 1964. The syntax of Najdi Arabic. University of Texas Ph.D. diss.

ʿABD AL-ʿĀL, ʿABD AL-MUNʿIM SAYYID. 1966. Lahjat Shamāl al-Maghrib; Taṭwān wa mā Ḥawlahā. University of Cairo Ph.D. diss.

ABDALLA, ALBERT GEORGE. 1960. An instrumental study of the intonation of Egyptian Colloquial Arabic. University of Michigan Ph.D. diss.

ʿABDĪN, ʿABD AL-MAJĪD. 1966. Min ʾUṣūl al-Lahajāt al-ʿArabīyah fī al-Sūdān. Cairo.

ABOU, SELIM. 1962. Le bilinguisme arabe-français au Liban. Paris, Presses Universitaires de France.

ABOUL-FETOUH, HILMI MOHAMMED. 1961. A morphological study of Egyptian Colloquial Arabic. University of Texas Ph.D. diss.

ABU FARAG, M. A. 1960. A grammatical study of the Arabic dialect of Tahway (Minufiya Province). University of London Ph.D. diss.

ABU-TALIB, MOHAMMED, and THOMAS R. FOX, 1966. A dictionary of Moroccan Arabic. Arabic-English. Georgetown Arabic Series 10. Washington, D.C., Georgetown U.P.

ABUL-FADL, FAHMI. 1961. Volkstumliche Texte in arabischen Bauerndialekten der ägyptischen Provinz Šarqiyya mit dialektgeographischen Untersuchungen zur Lautlehre. University of Münster diss.

'ANĪS, 'IBRĀHĪM. 1965. Fī al-Lahajāt al-ʿArabīyah. 3rd ed. Cairo, Anglo-Egyptian Bookstore.

AQUILINA, JOSEPH. 1959. The structure of Maltese. A study in mixed grammar and vocabulary. Floriana, The Royal University of Malta.

——. 1961. Papers in Maltese linguistics. Valetta, Royal University of Malta.

——. 1965. Maltese. The teach yourself language books. London, The English Universities Press, Ltd.

——, B.S.J. ISSERLIN, and W.R.B. ANNAN. 1966. A new survey of present day Spoken Maltese: Preliminary notice. JMS 3.42–6.

AXVELDIANI, V.G. 1953. Refleksy faringal'nyx soglasnyx v sovremennyx arabskix dialektax. J.V. Stalin State University at Tbilisi diss.

AYOUB, ABDEL RAHMAN E.R. 1949. The verbal piece in the Egyptian language (a morphological study). University of London M.A. thesis.

BADAWI, E.S.M.M. 1964. An intonational study of Colloquial Riyadhi Arabic. University of London Ph.D. diss.

BARBOT, MICHEL. 1961. Emprunts et phonologie dans les dialectes citadins syro-libanais. Arabica 8.174–88.

BARTHÉLEMY, A. 1935–55. Dictionnaire Arabe-Français. Dialectes de Syrie: Alep, Damas, Liban, Jerusalem. Paris.

BAUER, L. 1913. Das palästinische Arabisch. Die Dialekte des Stadters und des Fellachen. 3rd ed. Leipzig.

——. 1933. Wörterbuch des palästinensischen Arabisch. Deutsch-Arabisch. Leipzig.

——. 1957. Deutsch-arabisches Wörterbuch der Umgangssprache in Palästina und im Libanon. Unter Mitwirkung von A. Spitaler. 2nd ed. Wiesbaden, Harrassowitz.

BECKER, VALERIE. 1964. A transfer grammar of the verb structures of Modern Literary Arabic and Lebanese Colloquial Arabic. Yale University Ph.D. diss.

BELKIN, V.M. 1960. Problema literaturnogo jazyka i dialekta v arabskix stranax. Trudy Instituto Jazykoznanja Akademia Nauk SSSR, Moscow. 10.158–74.

BERGSTRÄSSER, G. 1915. Sprachatlas von Syrien und Palästina. ZDPV 38.169–222.

BIRKELAND, HARRIS. 1952. Growth and structure of the Egyptian Arabic Dialect. Oslo.

——. 1954. Stress patterns in Arabic. Oslo.

BISHAI, WILSON B. 1959. The Coptic influence on Egyptian Arabic. The Johns Hopkins University Ph.D. diss.

——. 1960. Notes on the Coptic substratum in Egyptian Arabic. JAOS 80.225–9.

——. 1961. Nature and extent of Coptic phonological influence on Egyptian Arabic. JSS 6.175–82.

——. 1962. Coptic grammatical influence on Egyptian Arabic. JAOS 82.285–9.

——. 1964. Coptic lexical influence on Egyptian Arabic. JNES 23.39–47.

BISHR, K. M. A. 1955. A grammatical study of Lebanese Arabic. University of London Ph.D. diss.

BLANC, HAIM. 1953. Studies in North Palestinian Arabic: Linguistic inquiries among the Druzes of Western Galilee and Mt. Carmel. Oriental notes and studies 4. Jerusalem, The Israel Oriental Society.

——. 1960. Style variations in Spoken Arabic: A sample of interdialectal educated conversation. Contributions to Arabic linguistics. Harvard Middle Eastern Monograph Series 3, ed. by Charles A. Ferguson, 79–161. Cambridge, Mass., Harvard U.P.

——. 1963. Semitic. Current Trends in Linguistics, vol. I, ed. by Thomas A. Sebeok, 374–91. The Hague, Mouton.

——. 1964. Communal dialects in Baghdad. Harvard Middle Eastern Monograph Series. Cambridge, Mass., Harvard U.P.

BLAU, JOSHUA. 1960. Syntax des palästinensischen Bauerndialekts von Bīr-Zēt. Beiträge zur Sprach- und Kulturgeschichte des Orients 13. Walldorf-Hessen, H. Vorndran.

——. 1965. The emergence and linguistic background of Judaeo-Arabic. A Study of the Origins of Middle Arabic. Scripta Judaica 5. London, Oxford U.P.

——. 1966–67. A Grammar of Christian Arabic. Corpus Scriptorum Christianorum Orientalium, 267, 276. Louvain.

BLOCH, ARIEL. 1965. Die Hypotaxe im Damaszenisch-Arabischen mit Vergleichen zur Hypotaxe im Klassisch-Arabischen. Abhandlungen für die Kunde des Morgenlandes 35,4. Wiesbaden, Steiner.

BROCKELMANN, CARL. 1908, 1913. Grundriss der vergleichenden Grammatik der semitischen Sprachen. 2 vols. Berlin.

——. 1954. Das Arabische und seine Mundarten. Handbuch der Orientalistik, Bd. 3, Semistik, ed. by B. Spuler, 207–45. Leiden, Brill.

BROWN, A. F. 1955. A phonological and grammatical analysis of an Algerian dialect of Arabic. University of London Ph.D. diss.

BRUNOT, LOUIS. 1950a. Sur le thème *f'āl* en dialectal marocain. Mélanges William Marçais, 55–62. Paris, Maisonneuve.

——. 1950b. Introduction à l'arabe marocain. Paris, Maisonneuve.

BUTROS, ALBERT JAMIL. 1963. English loanwords in the Colloquial Arabic of Palestine (1917–1948) and Jordan (1948–1962). Columbia University Ph.D. diss.

CADORA, FREDRIC JOSEPH. 1966. An analytical study of interdialectal lexical compatibility in Arabic. University of Michigan Ph.D. diss.

CANTINEAU, JEAN. 1934. Le dialecte arabe de Palmyre. Mémoires de l'Institut Français de Damas. 2 vols. Beirut.

——. 1936. Geographie linguistique des parlers arabes algériens. Rev. afr. 79.91–3.

——. 1936–37. Études sur quelques parlers de nomades arabes d'Orient. AnnIEO 2.1–118; 3.119–237.

——. 1937. Les parlers arabes du département d'Alger. Rev. afr. 81.703–11.

——. 1939a. Remarques sur les parlers de sédentaires syro-libano-palestiniens. BSL 40.80–8.

——. 1939b. Les parlers arabes du département de Constantine. Actes, Fourth Congress of the Federation of Learned Societies of North Africa, Algiers. 2.849–63.

——. 1940. Les parlers arabes du département d'Oran. Rev. afr. 84.220–31.

——. 1946. Les parlers arabes du Ḥōrân. Société de Linguistique de Paris. Collection Linguistique 52. Paris.

——. 1950. Reflections sur la phonologie de l'arabe marocain. Hespéris 37.193–207.

——. 1951. Analyse phonologique du parler arabe d'El-Ḥāmma de Gabès. BSL 47.64–105.

——, and Y. Helbaoui. 1953. Manuel élémentaire d'arabe oriental (parler de Damas). Paris.

——. 1955. La dialectologie arabe. Orbis 4.149–69.

——. 1956a. Notes sur les parlers arabes des oasis syriennes: Qarītēn, Palmyre, Soukhné. Studi orientalistici in onore de Giorgio Levi della Vida, 120–31. Rome.

——. 1956b. Notes sur le parler arabe de Mecherfé. Mélanges Louis Massignon 1.305–14. Damascus.

——. 1956c. The phonemic system of Damascus Arabic. Word 12.117–24.

Chejne, Anwar G. 1958. The role of Arabic in present day Arab society. The Islamic Literature 10/4.15–54.

——. 1965. Arabic: Its significance and place in Arab-Muslim society. MEJ 19. 447–70.

Clarity, B. E., Karl Stowasser, and Ronald G. Wolfe. 1964. A dictionary of Iraqi Arabic: English-Arabic. Georgetown Arabic Series 6. Washington, D.C., Georgetown U.P.

Cleveland, Ray L. 1963. A classification for the Arabic dialects of Jordan. BASOR 171.56–63.

Cohen, David. 1962. Koine, langages communes, et dialectes arabes. Arabica 9.119–44.

——. 1963. Le dialecte arabe ḥassānīye de Mauritanie, parler de la Gebla. Études arabes et islamiques. Séries 3. Études et documents 5. Paris, Klincksieck.

——. 1966. Le système phonologique du maltais: aspects synchroniques et diachroniques. JMS 3.1–26.

Cohen, Marcel. 1912. Le parler arabe des juifs d'Alger. Paris.

——. 1945. Initiation au Maroc. Paris.

Colin, G. S. 1947. Quelques 'emprunts' de morphèmes étrangers dans les parlers occidentaux. GLECS 4.42–7.

——. 1959. al-'Andalus: Spanish Arabic. EI 501–3.

COWAN, WILLIAM GEORGE. 1960. A reconstruction of Proto-Colloquial Arabic. Cornell University Ph.D. diss.

——. 1966. Loss of emphasis in Maltese. JMS 3.27–32.

COWELL, MARK W. 1964. A reference grammar of Syrian Arabic. Georgetown Arabic Series 7. Washington, D.C., Georgetown U.P.

DAWOOD, T. H. M. 1949. The phonetics of the Il-Karnak Dialect (Upper Egypt). University of London M.A. thesis.

——. 1951. The phonetics and phonology of an Aden dialect of Arabic. University of London Ph.D. diss.

DENIZEAU, CLAUDE. 1960. Dictionnaire des parlers arabes de Syrie, Liban, et Palestine. Paris.

DRIVER, G. R. A. 1925. A grammar of the Colloquial Arabic of Syria and Palestine. London.

EL-HAJJE, HASSAN. 1954. Le parler arabe de Tripoli (Liban). Paris.

ELIAS, A., and EDWARD E. ELIAS, 1954. Modern dictionary, Arabic-English, 7th ed. Cairo, Elias' Modern Press.

ELIAS, EDWARD E. 1949. Practical dictionary of the Colloquial Arabic of the Middle East, English-Arabic. 2d ed. Cairo, Elias' Modern Press.

EL SAYED, DAWOOD H. A. 1962. A descriptive analysis of the part of speech system and the grammatical categories of Egyptian Colloquial Arabic. Cornell University Ph.D. diss.

ERICKSON JON LAROY. 1965. English and Arabic: A discussion of contrastive verbal morphology. University of Texas Ph.D. diss.

ERWIN, WALLACE M. 1963. A short reference grammar of Iraqi Arabic. Georgetown Arabic Series 4. Washington, D.C., Georgetown U.P.

FEGHALI, MICHEL. 1919. Le parler arabe de Kfar ʿAbîda; essai linguistique sur la phonétique et la morphologie d'un parler arabe moderne. Paris.

FERGUSON, CHARLES A. 1954. Review of Manuel élémentaire d'arabe oriental (parler de Damas), by J. Cantineau and Y. Helbaoui. Lg 30.564–70.

——. 1956. The emphatic *l* in Arabic. Lg 32.466–72.

——. 1957. Two problems in Arabic phonology. Word 13.460–78.

——. 1959a. The Arabic Koine. Lg 35.616–30.

——. 1959b. Diglossia. Word 15.325–40.

FIRTH, J. R. 1948. Sounds and prosodies. TPhS 127–52.

FISCHER, WOLFDIETRICH. 1959. Die demonstrativen Bildungen der neuarabischen Dialekte. 's-Gravenhage, Mouton.

——. 1961. Die Sprache der arabische Sprachinsel in Uzbekistan. Islam 36.232–63.

——. 1967. Silbenstruktur and Vokalismus im Arabischen. ZDMG 117.30–77.

FLEISCH, HENRI. 1947–48. Notes sur le dialecte arabe de Zahlé. MUSJ 27.73–116.

——. 1954. La première forme du verbe arabe dans un parler libanais (Maāsser Beit ed-Dīne). MUSJ 31.289–313.

——. 1958. The Eastern dialects. EI 574–8.

——. 1959. Premiers resultats d'une enquête dialectale au Liban. Orbis 8.385–99.

——. 1962. Le parler arabe de Šḥīm (Liban). MUSJ 38.369–88.

——. 1963–64. Le parler de Kfar-Ṣghab (Liban). BEO 18.95–125.

——. 1964. Observations sur le vocalisme d'un parler arabe chiite du Liban-sud. BSL 59.viii-xi.

FRAYHA, ANIS. 1947. Muʿǧam al-alfāẓ al-ʿāmmīya fī al-lahǧa al-lubnānīya. A Dictionary of non-classical vocables in the Spoken Arabic of Lebanon. American University of Beirut, Faculty of Arts and Sciences Oriental Series 19. Beirut.

FÜCK, JOHANN. 1950. Arabiya. Abhandlungen der Sächsischen Akademie der Wissenschaft zu Leipzig, Phil.-hist. Klasse 45.1. Berlin. Arabic tr. by A.-H. al-Najjār. 1951. Cairo, Dār al-Kitāb al-ʿArabī.

——. 1954. Geschichte der Arabistik. Handbuch der Orientalistik, Bd, 3, Semistik, ed. by B. Spuler, 341–9. Leiden, Brill.

——. 1955. Die arabischen Studien in Europa bis in den Anfang des 20 Jahrhunderts. Leipzig.

GAMAL-ELDIN, SAAD M. 1959. Morphophonemics of Colloquial Egyptian Arabic. University of Texas M.A. thesis.

——. 1961. A syntactic study of Colloquial Egyptian Arabic. University of Texas Ph.D. diss.

GARBELL, IRENE. 1958. Remarks on the historical phonology of an East Mediterranean Arabic Dialect. Word 14.303–37.

GASIM, AWN AL-SHARIF. 1965. Some aspects of Sudanese Colloquial Arabic. Sudan Notes and Records (Khartoum). 46.40–9.

GHALY, MUHAMMAD MAHMOUD ALSAYED. 1961. Substantive morphology of Colloquial Egyptian Arabic. University of Michigan Ph.D. diss.

GOITEIN, S. D. 1960. The language of Al-Gades: The main characteristics of an Arabic Dialect spoken in Lower Yemen. Muséon 73.351–94.

GREIS, NAGUIB AMIN FAHMY. 1963. The pedagogical implications of contrastive analysis of cultivated Cairene Arabic and the English language. University of Minnesota Ph.D. diss.

GROTZFELD, HEINZ. 1964. Laut- und Formenlehre des damaszenisch-Arabischen. Abhandlungen für die Kunde des Morgenlandes 35,3. Wiesbaden, Steiner.

——. 1965. Syrisch-Arabische Grammatik (Dialekt von Damaskus). Porta Linguarum Orientalium, N.S. 8. Wiesbaden, Harrassowitz.

HADJ-SADOK, M'HAMMAD. 1955. Dialectes arabes et francisation linguistique de l'Algérie. AnnIEO 13.61–97.

ḤAMMŪDAH, ʿABD AL-WAHHĀB. 1948. Al-Qirā'āt wa al-Lahajāt. Cairo.

HANNA, HANNA MORCOS. 1962. The phrase structure of Egyptian Colloquial Arabic. Cornell University Ph.D. diss.

HARRELL, RICHARD S. 1957. The phonology of Colloquial Egyptian Arabic. ACLS Program in Oriental Languages Publications Series B-Aids-Number 9. New York, American Council of Learned Societies.

——. 1962. A short reference grammar of Moroccan Arabic. Georgetown Arabic Series 1. Washington, D.C., Georgetown U.P.

HARRIS, ZELLIG. 1942. The phonemes of Moroccan Arabic. JAOS 62.309–18.

HELMY-HASSAN, SALAH ELDIN. 1960. Verb morphology of Egyptian Colloquial Arabic Cairene Dialect. University of Michigan Ph.D. diss.

HÖFNER, MARIA. 1954. Das Südarabische der Inschriften und der lebenden Mundarten. Handbuch der Orientalistik, Bd. 3, Semistik, ed. by B. Spuler, 314–41. Leiden, Brill.

HYMES, D. H. 1959. On the rate of morpheme decay in Arabic. IJAL 25.267–8.

JAKOBSON, ROMAN. 1957. Mufaxxama. The 'emphatic' phoneme in Arabic. Studies presented to Joshua Whatmough, ed. by Ernst Pulgram, 105–15. 's-Gravenhage, Mouton.

JIHA, MICHEL. 1964. Der arabische Dialekt von Bišmizzīn. Volkstümliche Texte aus einem libanesischen Dorf. Mit Grundzügen der Laut- und Formenlehre, Beiruter Texte und Studien 1. Wiesbaden, Steiner.

JOHNSTONE, T. M. 1961. Some characteristics of the Dōsirī dialect as spoken in Kuwait. BSOAS 24.249–97.

——. 1963. The affrication of 'kāf' and 'gāf' in the Arabic dialects of the Arabian Peninsula. JSS 8.210–66.

——. 1964. Further studies on the Dōsirī dialect of Arabic as spoken in Kuwait. BSOAS 27.77–113.

——. 1965. The sound change j > y in the Arabic dialects of Peninsular Arabia. BSOAS 28.233–41.

——. 1967. Eastern Arabian dialect studies. London Oriental Series Vol. 17. London, Oxford U.P.

AL-JUNDĪ, 'AḤMAD. 1965. al-Lahajāt al-ʿArabīyah kamā Tuṣawwiruhā Kutub al-Naḥw wa al-Lughah. University of Cairo Ph.D. diss.

KENNEDY, NANCY M. 1960. Problems of Americans in mastering the pronunciation of Egyptian Arabic. Washington, D.C., Center for Applied Linguistics.

KHALAFALLAH, ABDELGHANY ABDALLAH. 1959. Some phonological problems involved in the learning of English by native speakers of Ṣaʿiidi Egyptian Arabic. University of Texas M.A. thesis.

——. 1961. A descriptive grammar of Ṣaʿi:di Colloquial Egyptian Arabic. University of Texas diss.

KOFLER, H. 1940–42. Reste altarabischer Dialekte. WZKM 47.60–130, 233–62; 48.52–88; 49.15–30, 234–56.

LEHN, WALTER, and WILLIAM R. SLAGER. 1959. A contrastive study of Egyptian Arabic and American English. LL 9.25–33.

——. 1963. Emphasis in Cairo Arabic. Lg 39.29–39.

LITTMANN, ENNO. 1948. Baqāyā al-Lahajāt al-ʿArabīyah fī al-'Adab al-ʿArabī. Majallat Kullīyat al-'Ādāb, Jāmiʿat Fu'ād al-'Awwal. 10 (May). 1–44.

MALAIKA, NISAR. 1963. Grundzüge der Grammatik des arabischen Dialektes von Bagdad. Wiesbaden, Harrassowitz.

MALIK, A. P. 1956–57. A comparative study of American English and Iraqi Arabic consonant cluster. LL 7.65–87.

AL-MAʿLŪF, ʿĪSĀ ʾISKANDAR. 1935, 1937. al-Lahjah al-ʿArabīyah al-ʿĀmmīyah. MMLA 1.350-68, 3.349–71.

——. 1939. al-Lahjah al-ʿĀmmīyah fī Lubnān wa Sūrīyah. MMLA 4.294–315.

MARÇAIS, PHILIPPE. 1948. L'articulation de l'emphase dans un parler arabe maghrébin. AnnIEO 7.5–28.

——. 1956. Le parler arabe de Djidjelli (Nord Constantinois, Algérie). Paris.

——. 1957. Initiation à l'Algérie. Paris.

——. 1958. The Western dialects. EI 578–83.

MARÇAIS, WILLIAM. 1901–02. Le dialecte arabe parlé à Tlemcen; grammaire, textes et glossaire. Paris.

——. 1906–09. Le dialecte arabe des Ūlād Brāhīm de Saïda (Département d'Oran). Mémoires de la Société de Linguistique de Paris 14.97–164, 416–72, 481–500; 15.40–72, 104–29.

——. 1950. Initiation à la Tunisie. Paris.

MAṬAR, ʿABD AL-AZĪZ. 1966. Khaṣāʾiṣ al-Lahjah al-Badawīyah fī ʾIqlīm Sāḥil Maryūṭ. MMLA 20.99–105.

MITCHELL, T. F. 1952. The active participle in an Arabic Dialect of Cyrenaica. BSOAS 14.11–33.

——. 1956. An introduction to Egyptian Colloquial Arabic. London, Oxford U.P.

——. 1958. Syntagmatic relations in linguistic analysis. TPhS 101–18.

——. 1960. Prominence and syllabication in Arabic. BSOAS 23.369–89.

——. 1962. Colloquial Arabic. The teach yourself language books. London, The English Universities Press.

NASR, RAJA T. 1955. The phonological problems involved in the teaching of American English to native speakers of Lebanese Arabic. University of Michigan Ph.D. diss.

——. 1959. Velarization in Lebanese Arabic. Phonetica 3.203–9.

OBRECHT, DEAN HUBERT. 1961. Effects of the second formant in the perception of velarization in Lebanese Arabic. University of Pennsylvania Ph.D. diss.

PÉRÈS, HENRI. 1950. L'arabe dialectale en Espagne musulmane aux Xe et XIe siècles de notre ère. Mélanges William Marçais. L'Institut d'Études Islamiques de l'Université de Paris, 289–99. Paris, Maisonneuve.

——. 1959. L'arabe dialectal algérien et saharien: bibliographie analytique avec un index méthodique, références arrêtées au 31 décembre 1957. Algiers.

PETRAČEK, KAREL. 1956. Zum arabischen Dialekte von Ägypten: Zum koptischen Einfluss im Arabischen. AO 24.591–5.

PIAMENTA, MOSHE. 1964. The use of tenses, aspects and moods in the Arabic

Dialect of Jerusalem [in Hebrew with table of contents and summary of findings in English]. Jerusalem, Mif'al Hashichpul.

——. 1966. Studies in the syntax of Palestinian Arabic. Oriental Notes and Studies 10. Jerusalem, The Israel Oriental Society.

PROCHAZKA, THEODORE. 1967. 1960–1967 Selected bibliography of Arabic. Washington, D.C., Center for Applied Linguistics.

QUÉMENEUR, J. 1963. Les verbes à allongement vocalique interne en arabe parlé tunisien. Ibla 26.119–36.

RABIN, CHAIM. 1957. Ancient West Arabian. London, Taylor's Foreign Press.

RAMMUNY, RAJI. 1966. An analysis of the differences in the prosodies of general American English and Colloquial Jordanian Arabic and their effect on second-language acquisition. University of Michigan Ph.D. diss.

ROSSI, ETTORE. 1939. L'arabo parlato a Ṣan'ā'. Grammatica, testi, lessico. Publicazioni del Istituto per l'Oriente. Rome.

AL-ṢABBĀGH, MĪKHĀ'ĪL. 1886. al-Risālah al-Tāmmah fī Kalām al-'Āmmah wa al-Manāhij fī 'Aḥwāl al-Kalām al-Dārij. Strasbourg.

SA'ĪD, NAFFŪSA ZAKARĪYA. 1964. Tārīkh al-Da'wah ilā al-'Āmmīyah wa 'Āthāruha fī Miṣr. Cairo, Dār Nashr al-Thaqāfah.

AL-ṢĀLIḤ, ṢUBḤĪ. 1960. Dirāsāt fī Fiqh al-Lughah. Damascus.

SAMARRAI, ALAUDDIN ISMAIL. 1959. Rate of morphemic decay in Arabic. IJAL 25.68–70.

ŠARBATOV, G. Š. 1960. Ob analitičnosti stroja sovremennyx arabskix dialektov. Trudy XXV Kongressa vostokovedov, vol. 2.141–6. Moscow.

——. 1961a. Nekotorye osobennosti irakskogo dialekta, arabskogo jazyka. KSINA 40.80–6.

——. 1961b. Arabistika v SSSR (Filologija) 1917–1959. Arabic tr. al-'Isti'rāb fī al-'Ittiḥād al-Sūfyītī (al-Lughah wa al-'Adab) 1917–1961. Moscow.

SATTERTHWAIT, ARNOLD C. 1960. Rate of morphemic decay in Meccan Arabic. IJAL 26.256–61.

——. 1962. Parallel sentence-construction grammars of Arabic and English. Harvard University Ph.D. diss.

SAYDON, P. P. 1956. The Pre-Arabic Latin element of Maltese. Orbis 5/1.191–7.

——. 1958. The vocalization of the verb in Maltese. Orbis 7/1.168–82.

SCHRAMM, GENE M. 1954. Judeo-Baghdadi: A descriptive analysis of the Colloquial Arabic of the Jews of Baghdad. Dropsie College Ph.D. diss.

SHAWKAT, MAHMOUD HAMED. 1962. A descriptive grammar of educated Damascene Arabic. Cornell University Ph.D. diss.

SIMON, M. 1953. Punique ou berbère. Notes sur la situation linguistique dans l'Afrique romaine. Bulletin de l'Institut de Philologie et d'Histoire Orientales et Slaves. 14.613–29.

SINGER, HANS-RUDOLPH. 1958a. Neuarabische Fragewörte. Erlangen diss.

——. 1958b. Grundzüge der Morphologie des arabischen Dialektes von Tetuan.

ZDMG 108.229–65.

SMEATON, B. H. 1956. Some problems in the description of Arabic. Word 12.357–68.

——. 1959. Lexical expansion due to technical change: As illustrated by the Arabic of al-Hasa, Saudi Arabia, during the decade 1938–48. Columbia University Ph.D. diss.

SOBELMANN, HARVEY, ed. 1962. Arabic dialect studies. Washington D.C., Center for Applied Linguistics.

——, and RICHARD S. HARRELL. 1963. A dictionary of Moroccan Arabic: English-Moroccan. Georgetown Arabic Series 4. Washington, D.C., Georgetown U.P.

SPIRO, SOCRATES. 1923. Arabic-English dictionary of the Modern Arabic of Egypt. 2d ed. Cairo, Elias' Modern Press.

——. 1929. An English-Arabic vocabulary of the Modern and Colloquial Arabic of Egypt. 3d ed. Cairo, Elias' Modern Press.

SPITTA, WILHELM. 1880. Grammatik des arabischen Vulgärdialektes von Ägypten. Leipzig.

STOWASSER, KARL, and MOUKHTAR ANI. 1964. A dictionary of Syrian Arabic: Dialect of Damascus: English-Arabic. Georgetown Arabic Series 5. Washington, D.C., Georgetown U.P.

ṬALAB, ʿABD AL-ḤAMĪD AL-SAYYID. 1958. Min Lahajāt al-Jazīrah wa ʾĀdābihā fī al-Sūdān. University of Cairo Ph.D. diss.

AL-ṬANṬĀWĪ, MUḤAMMAD ʿAYYĀD. 1848. ʾAḥsan al-Nukhab fī Maʿrifat Lisān al-ʿArab. Leipzig.

AL-TOMA, SALIH JAWAD. 1957. The teaching of Classical Arabic to speakers of the colloquial in Iraq: A study of the problem of linguistic duality and its impact on language education. Harvard University Ed.D. thesis.

TOMICHE, NADA. 1962. Les parlers d'Égypte. Materiaux pour une étude de géographie dialectale. Études d'orientalisme dediées à la mémoire de Levi-Provençal. vol. 2.767–79. Paris.

——. 1964. Le parler arabe du Caire. Maison des Sciences de l'Homme, Recherches mediterranéennes. Textes et études linguistiques 3. Paris & La Haye, Mouton.

TSIAPERA, MARIA. 1963. A descriptive analysis of Cypriot Maronite Arabic. University of Texas Ph.D. diss.

VINNIKOV, I. N. 1962. Slovar' dialekta buxarskix arabov. Palestinskij Sbornik 10(73). Moskva-Leningrad. Izd. ANSSSR.

——. 1965. Materialen zur Grammatik des Dialektes der Kaška-Darjiner Araber. Paradigmen der Verbalformen. Studia Semitica philologica necnon philosophica Ioanni Bakoš dicata, ed. by Stanislaus Seger, 261–76. Bratislava, Vyd. Slovenskej Akad. Vied.

VAN WAGONER, M. Y. 1944. A grammar of Iraqi Arabic. Yale University diss.

WILD, STEFAN. 1964. Die resultative Funktion des aktiven Partizips in den syrisch-palästinischen Dialekten des Arabischen. ZDMG 114.239–54.

WILLMORE, J. S. 1905. The spoken Arabic of Egypt. 2d ed. London.

ETHIOPIC AND SOUTH ARABIAN

WOLF LESLAU

ETHIOPIC

The first grammar of Geez (Ancient Ethiopic) was published in 1661 by Hiob Ludolf. The same author published the first grammar of Amharic in 1698. What has been accomplished since then in the field of the Ethiopian languages is the subject of the present study.

There are three language families spoken in Ethiopia: Semitic, Cushitic, and Nilotic. Only the Semitic group will be investigated here.

From the descriptive point of view the Semitic languages are divided into two groups: a) North Ethiopic: Geez (Gəʿəz), Tigre, and Tigrinya; b) South Ethiopic: Amharic, Argobba, Gafat, Gurage, and Harari.[1]

Geez

Geez (Geʿez) or Ancient Ethiopic is no longer spoken but has remained the language of the liturgy. Though it ceased to be spoken sometime in the twelfth or thirteenth century, it continued to be the literary language of Ethiopia. The oldest inscriptions, in an unvocalized script, date from the fourth century A.D. The following inscriptions, in vocalized script, cover the period from the fourth to the ninth century. Literary written documents began to appear in the fifth century, and, with an interruption stretching from the ninth to the thirteenth century, continued up to the seventeenth century.

The first book in Geez published in Europe was the edition of the Psalter by Potken in 1513.[2] A sketch of the grammar was published in 1522 by Marianus Victorius,[3] but it remained for Hiob Ludolf, who acquired his knowledge of Geez and Amharic from the Ethiopian scholar Abba Gregorius, to publish in 1661 the first grammar

[1] W. Leslau, 'Sketches in Ethiopic classification', *ACISE* 89–93.
[2] *Psalterium Hebraicae, Graecae, Aethiopicae et Latinae* (Rome, 1513).
[3] *Chaldeae seu Aethiopicae linguae institutiones* (Rome, 1552).

of a scientific character.[4] Ludolf made use of his knowledge of Hebrew and Arabic in the presentation of some grammatical features of Geez.[5]

It was August Dillmann who published the most complete grammar of Geez.[6] Dillmann drew his material from Ludolf's study, but made particular use of the published texts in Geez and of the numerous manuscripts. Although the etymologies and the grammatical explanations given by him are often too mechanistic and can be disregarded in many cases, his grammar remains the most exhaustive treatise of Geez, especially of its syntax. In his etymologies Dillmann compares Hebrew, Arabic, and occasionally Syriac, but had no knowledge of the spoken languages of Ethiopia. A serious drawback that, unfortunately, applies to nearly all the existing grammars of Geez derives from the fact that Dillmann had no knowledge of the 'traditional' pronunciation of Geez (see below).[7] Since he relied only on written material without having contact with Ethiopian scholars, he was unaware of the problem of gemination, and of the pronunciation of the consonants in the so-called '6th order' (that is, their pronunciation with or without the vowel *ə*), features that are not expressed by the Ethiopian alphabet.

Grammars that are clearer in presentation and much more convenient for the beginner, but much less detailed, are those of F. Praetorius[8] and M. Chaîne.[9] These authors likewise had no knowledge of the 'traditional' pronunciation and their grammars are marred, therefore, by the same drawback as Dillmann's grammar.

C. Conti Rossini in his grammar[10] transcribes the Geez forms phonetically, but it is strange that the imperfect of the triradicals is transcribed *yĕqatĕl*, with a non-geminated 2nd radical *t*, whereas all the studies on the 'traditional' pronunciation give the form *yĕqattĕl*, with a geminated 2nd radical. Besides, he does not give the transcription of all the cited forms.

Useful sketches of Geez, in phonetic transcription only, were published by G. Bergsträsser,[11] C. Conti Rossini,[12] and E. Littmann.[13] A more detailed sketch was published by B. Starinin.[14]

[4] *Grammatica aethiopica* (London, 1661).

[5] The way in which Ludolf understood the structure of the language and his misunderstanding of some problems were pointed out by J. Flemming, 'Hiob Ludolf: Ein Beitrag zur Geschichte der orientalischen Philologie', *BA* 1.537–82 (1890), 2.63–110 (1894).

[6] *Grammatik der äthiopischen Sprache* (Leipzig, 1857); 2nd ed. by Carl Bezold (Leipzig, 1899); English translation by James A. Crichton (London, 1907).

[7] To give an example: the author does not point out that the imperfect of the verb is *yəqättəl*, with gemination of the 2nd radical.

[8] *Äthiopische Grammatik* (Karlsruhe and Leipzig, 1886).

[9] *Grammaire éthiopienne* (Beyrouth, 1907).

[10] *Grammatica elementare della lingua etiopica* (Rome, 1941).

[11] *Einführung in die semitischen Sprachen*, 96–104 (München, 1928).

[12] *Etiopia e genti d'Etiopia*, 217–30 (Firenze, 1937).

[13] 'Die äthiopische Sprache', *Handbuch der Orientalistik*, herausgegeben von Berthold Spuler dritter Band, zweiter und dritter Abschnitt. Semitistik, 350–75 (Leiden, 1954).

[14] *Efiopskii Iazyk* (Moscow, 1967).

The Ethiopian scholars, too, contributed much to our knowledge of Geez. In order to make the liturgical language understandable to their fellow-countrymen, the Ethiopian scholars compiled Geez-Amharic vocabularies (called *säwasəw* 'ladders') accompanied by grammatical explanations. These *säwasəw* have considerable interest for our knowledge of Geez since they contain many words and grammatical forms not found in the grammars and dictionaries published by Western scholars. They also reveal the grammatical method used by the Ethiopians. Besides, they contain ancient words and forms of Amharic and contribute thus to our knowledge of Ancient Amharic. Most of the *säwasəw* are, however, unpublished and are found as manuscripts in Ethiopia and in the libraries of Europe. Only a few have been published, and I cite especially those by H. Hirschfeld,[15] Hermine Brauner-Plazikowski,[16] and E. Littmann.[17] A. Dillmann in his Lexicon[18] likewise made use of the various *säwasəw*. An analysis of the native grammars and their terminology was given by I. Guidi,[19] and M. Chaîne.[20] The most complete glossary of the Geez grammatical terminology was published by M.M. Moreno.[21]

Various Geez grammars written in Geez and Amharic were also published by Ethiopian scholars. The most important are those by Abba Täklä Maryam Wäldä Sämharay,[22] Abba Ya'qob Gäbrä Iyäsu,[23] Kəflä Giyorgis and Kidanä Wäld Kəfle,[24] and the *Mäṣḥafä säwasəw*.[25]

It would be important to have a complete glossary of the traditional grammatical terminology. The Ethiopian linguists would then have at their disposal native grammatical terms when compiling Amharic grammars in Amharic for the use of their schools.

It was said above that the drawback of most of the Geez grammars is due to the fact that the authors did not have a chance to investigate the present-day pronunciation of Geez, and, therefore, had to rely on documents written in Ethiopic script. The Ethiopic script, though on the whole phonetic, has, however, several disadvantages: it does not have a special sign for the gemination of the consonants, and it does not

15 'An Ethiopic-Falasi glossary', *JRAS* 209–30 (1919), 573–82 (1920), 211–37 (1921). It is a Geez-Amharic glossary, and not a Falasha glossary, as the title would suggest.

16 'Ein äthiopisch-amharisches Glossar (Sawasew)', *MSOS* 17/2.1–96 (1914).

17 'Abessinische Glossen', *ZA* 21.101–9 (1908).

18 See fn. 44.

19 'Il Sawasew', *Orientalische Studien Theodor Nöldeke zum siebzigsten Geburtstag gewidmet* 2.912–23 (Giessen, 1906).

20 'L'enseignement du guèze chez les Abyssins', *Mélanges Maspéro* 2.363–73 (1935–37) (= Mémoires de l'Institut Français d'archéologie orientale 67).

21 'Struttura e terminologia del Sawasew', *RSEt* 8.12–62 (1949).

22 *Yägə'əz qʷanqʷa säwasəw* (Cheren, 1899 [= 1907]), written in Amharic; *Mäṣḥafä säwasəw zäləsanä mäṣḥaf bäləsanä rə'əsu* (Rome, 1938), written in Geez.

23 *Mäṣḥafä säwasəw zägə'əz* (Asmara, 1928), written in Amharic.

24 *Mäṣḥafä säwasəw wägəs wämäzgäbä qalat ḥaddis*, ed. by Dästa Täklä Wäld, 9–180 (Addis Ababa 1948 [= 1956]).

25 *Mäṣḥafä säwasəw* (Monkullo 1889 [= 1897]), written in Amharic; 2nd ed. Addis Ababa 1918 (= 1926).

indicate whether the vowel of the so-called 'sixth order' is to be pronounced with the vowel ə or without the vowel *zero*. This explains the inadequacy in the description of the various forms given in the existing grammars. Some Ethiopian and Western scholars tried to overcome this difficulty by having recourse to the way Geez is pronounced at present by priests and teachers in the church schools. The present-day pronunciation, though not the same throughout the country and partially influenced by the pronunciation of Amharic, renders adequately the Geez pronunciation at a time when Geez was a spoken language. It is, therefore, designated as the 'traditional' pronunciation of Geez.

Hiob Ludolf was the first to give in his grammar some details about the 'traditional' pronunciation of Geez. The accent is the object of a study by Ernst Trumpp.[26] The most important studies in the field of the 'traditional' pronunciation are those by E. Mittwoch,[27] E. Littmann,[28] Marcel Cohen,[29] and the Ethiopian grammarian Abba Täklä Maryam.[30] These studies contain the essential morphological features, in phonetic transcription, accompanied by a selection of texts, likewise in phonetic transcription. The investigation was made with the help of Ethiopian scholars having a good knowledge of Geez. The Ethiopian scholar Abba Täklä Maryam uses the Ethiopic script with the addition of special symbols for the gemination, for the vowel of the 'sixth order', and so on.

Numerous monographs and articles were published dealing with specific problems in phonology, morphology and lexicography. Some of them have only historic value while others are still valid today. I would like to cite only those by Bernard Stade for the pluriradical verbs;[31] the various articles by F. Praetorius[32] dealing with the problems of the imperfect and jussive of type B, the dual, the plural forms, and so on; the monograph of E. Koenig[33] on different problems of orthography, phonology and morphology; the articles by P. Leander[34] on the perfect of verbs 2nd radical *w*, *y*, the imperfect and its suffixes, the value of the sound *ḍ*, and so on; the numerous notes on

[26] 'Über den Accent im Äthiopischen', *ZDMG* 28.515–61 (1874).
[27] 'Die traditionelle Aussprache des Äthiopischen', *MSOS* 28/2.126–248 (1925); reprint (Berlin and Leipzig, 1926).
[28] 'Geʿez-Studen', *Nachrichten der Königlichen Gesellschaft der Wissenschaften zu Göttingen* (Phil.-Hist. Klasse), 627–702 (1917), 318–39 (1918).
[29] 'La prononciation traditionnelle du guèze (éthiopien classique)', *JA* 17/11.217–69 (1921).
[30] *Mämhərä ləsanä gəʿəz* (Rome, 1911); *Fəṭun mälmäde wänəbab zäləsanä gəʿəz* (Rome, 1911), and others.
[31] *Über den Ursprung der mehrlautigen Thatwörter der Geʿez-Sprache* (Leipzig, 1871).
[32] 'Beiträge zur äthiopischen Grammatik und Etymologie', *BA* 1.21–47, 369–78 (1890); 'Noch ein Dualrest im Aethiopischen', *ZDMG* 47.395 (1893); 'Zur äthiopisch-arabischen Grammatik', *ZDMG* 27.639–44 (1873).
[33] *Neue Studien über Schrift, Aussprache und allgemeine Formenlehre des Äthiopischen*, aus den Quellen geschöpft, comparativ und physiologisch erläutert (Leipzig, 1877).
[34] 'Kurze Bemerkungen zur aethiopischen Formenlehre', *Studier tilegnede Es. Tegnér*, 1–7 (1918); 'Några anteckningar till Geʿez-språkets historia', *Studier tilegnede Professor Dr. Phil. & Theol. Frants Buhl*, 91–7 (1925).

Geez morphology by S. Grébaut, in *GLECS*, *Aethiops* and *Aethiopica*;[35] the studies of Marcel Cohen[36] on the laryngeals and the consonant clusters which have a bearing not only on Geez but also on the spoken languages of Ethiopia; an analysis of the forms *qatälä*, *qotälä*, *qetälä* by H. Fleisch;[37] syntactical problems in the Book of Enoch (such as the place of the qualifier, the expression of the complement of the noun, and the expression of the direct object) statistically analyzed by A. Caquot;[38] a study by Marcel Cohen and his students[39] who attempted to establish, through selections from the dictionary, the related proportions of certain verbal formations in Geez; a monograph by R. Schneider[40] who gives a statistical study of the expression of the direct complement either by the accusative (*qätälä bəʾəs-e*) or by the analytical structure (*qätälo lä-bəʾəsi*), examines the expression of the 'complément de nom' either by *bet-ä nəgus*, or *bet-u lä-nəgus*, or *bet zä-nəgus*, and investigates the place of the 'epithète déterminative' such as *zəntu* 'this', *kʷəllu* 'all' and so on; and a brief article by K. Petraček[41] who argues that Geez has never known the phoneme *ghain*, and that in the vocalic system one could guess the gradual changing from quality into 'tone color as a phonemic element'.

The history of Geez and the relation between Geez, Tigre, Tigrinya and Amharic is treated by Abba Gäbrä Iyäsu Haylu in a booklet written in Amharic.[42]

In the field of detailed problems of Geez it would be desirable that the editors of new texts bring out the features in morphology and syntax of the edited texts in the light of what the existing grammars inform us about Geez.

An important field of study of Geez is the lexicography. The dictionary of H. Ludolf[43] has only historic value. A remarkable achievement for that period are the comparisons between Geez, Hebrew and Arabic roots appended to Ludolf's dictionary.

The Geez-Latin dictionary published by A. Dillmann[44] is a monumental achievement. Dillmann used Ludolf's Dictionary, made use of the published and unpublished texts in Geez writings, and incorporated many words from the *säwasəw*. References to the cited words are given throughout. Columns 1435–1522 have a Latin-Geez index in which the author gives only the number of the page on which the Geez word is to be found. The author also gives etymologies and comparisons with Hebrew, Arabic,

[35] From 1921 to 1949.

[36] 'Consonnes laryngales et voyelles en éthiopien', *JA* 210.19–57 (1927); 'Groupes de consonnes au début du mot en éthiopien', *Cinquantenaire de l'Ecole Pratique des Hautes Etudes*, 141–59 (Paris, 1921); 'Des groupes de consonnes et de quelques géminations en éthiopien', *MSL* 23.72–100 (1927).

[37] *Les verbes à allongement interne sémitique*, 205–58 (Paris, 1944).

[38] 'Recherches de syntaxe sur le texte éthiopien d'Enoch', *JA* 240.487–96 (1952).

[39] 'Esquisse d'une étude chiffrée du verbe guèze (éthiopien classique)', *RSEt* 9.41–64 (1950).

[40] *L'expression des compléments de verbe et du nom et la place de l'adjective épithète en guèze* (Paris, 1959).

[41] 'Zur Entwicklung des phonologischen Systems des altäthiopischen', *RSEt* 20.129–32 (1964).

[42] *Səlä gəʿəz qʷanqʷa tarik* (Addis Ababa, 1939 [= 1947]).

[43] *Lexicon Aethiopico-Latinum* (London, 1661), 2nd ed. Frankfurt, 1699.

[44] *Lexicon linguae Aethiopicae* (Leipzig, 1865).

and Aramaic, but many of them are doubtful and should be used with caution. Neither Akkadian, South Arabic, nor the modern languages of Ethiopia were known at Dillmann's time.

Dillmann's dictionary is supplemented by S. Grébaut.[45] His Geez-French dictionary also contains an edition of the Geez lexicon of Juste d'Urbin. The additions concern mainly the morphology; there are relatively few additions to the lexicography. Only occasionally are references given.

P. Gabriele da Maggiore published a Geez-Italian-Latin dictionary,[46] in alphabetical order of the consonant with the vowel and not in the order of the roots. The dictionary contains a number of words not found in Dillmann, but the author did not make sufficient use of the native Ethiopic dictionaries. No reference is given for the meanings.

Ethiopian scholars who published Geez-Amharic dictionaries are: Abba Täsfa Səllase,[47] and particularly Kəflä Giyorgis and Kidanä Wäld Kəfle.[48] The dictionary contains Geez words that are not found elsewhere. The words are occasionally illustrated. The dictionary is, unfortunately, arranged in the order of *abugida*, that is, the order of the Hebrew alphabet. This arrangement presents a serious disadvantage even for Ethiopians who, at present, are not familiar with the order of the Hebrew alphabet.

Useful additions to the existing dictionaries are found in editions published by C. Bezold,[49] C. Conti Rossini,[50] D. Lifchitz,[51] S. Strelcyn,[52] and others. It would be desirable to have additions of that kind in any new text published in the future.

The Ethiopian scholar Amsalu Aklilu[53] published his dissertation on etymologies and comparisons of Geez with Tigre, Tigrinya, Amharic and Arabic. He based his work on Dillmann's entries.

In the field of loanwords mention should be made of T. Nöldeke[54] who investigates Hebrew and Aramaic loanwords in Geez, and Ethiopic loanwords in Geez.

W. Leslau[55] analyzes the phonetic and morphological treatment of the Arabic loanwords in Geez, the loanwords being arranged according to subjects.

H.J. Polotsky[56] suggests that the Aramaic loanwords in Geez were not introduced by Syriac-speaking missionaries or Bible translators.

[45] *Supplément au Lexicon linguae aethiopicae de August Dillmann et édition du Lexique de Juste d'Urbin* (Paris, 1952).

[46] *Vocabolario etiopico-italiano-latino*, ad uso dei principanti (Asmara, 1953).

[47] *Aččər yägəʿəz gəs mämmariya lägämmariwočč* (Addis Ababa, 1938 [= 1946]).

[48] *Mäṣḥafä säwasəw wägəs wämäzgäbä qalat ḥaddis* (Addis Ababa, 1948 [= 1956]). A brief analysis of this dictionary was made by M. Cohen, *JSS* 9.20–6 (1964).

[49] *Kebra Negest*, pp. xxi-xxiv (München, 1905).

[50] 'Note di agiografia etiopica', *RSO* 17.433–4,439 (1938).

[51] *Textes éthiopiens magico-religieux*, 252 (Paris, 1940).

[52] *Prières magiques éthiopiennes pour délier les charmes*, 481–2 (Warszawa, 1955).

[53] *Etymologischer Beitrag zu A. Dillmanns Lexicon linguae aethiopicae* (Tübingen, 1962).

[54] *Neue Beiträge zur semitischen Sprachwissenschaft* (Strassburg, 1910).

[55] 'Arabic loanwords in Geez', *JSS* 3.146–68 (1958).

[56] 'Aramaic, Syriac and Geʿez', *JSS* 9.1–10 (1964).

S. Strelcyn[57] makes an attempt to establish etymologies for some names of plants.

To sum up the situation for Geez it can be stated that adequate grammars and a good dictionary are at our disposal. It would be desirable, however, to have a Geez reference grammar that would give the transcription of all the grammatical forms based on the present-day pronunciation of Geez.

Another important tool that is still missing is a Geez Textbook with graded exercises. While it is true that the study of Geez is facilitated by the chrestomathy of A. Dillmann[58] containing a Geez-Latin glossary, and the chrestomathies in the grammars of F. Praetorius[59] and M. Chaîne,[60] there are no graded exercises in any of the existing grammars.

In the field of lexicography, an etymological dictionary of Geez is a desideratum. Dillmann's dictionary contains comparisons with Hebrew, Arabic and Aramaic, but no mention is made of Akkadian, Ancient and Modern South Arabian, and the spoken languages of Ethiopia for the obvious reason that most of these languages were unknown in Dillmann's time. In addition, the etymologies and comparisons from the languages cited by Dillmann have to be revised.

It would also be useful to have a handy dictionary that would incorporate all the words dispersed in the general and specialized dictionaries of Geez.

Modern Languages

The spoken Semitic languages of Ethiopia are: Tigre, Tigrinya, Amharic, Argobba, Gafat, Gurage, and Harari.

The oldest document on the modern languages is that of Amharic dating from 1698.[61] Gafat is documented since 1790;[62] Tigrinya since 1812;[63] Tigre since 1814;[64] Harari since 1814;[65] Gurage since 1878;[66] and Argobba since 1931.[67]

With the exception of Amharic, the first-hand documentation of the other modern

[57] 'Quelques remarques sur les noms des plantes en guèze', *Studia semitica Ioanni Bakoš dicata*, 245–9 (Bratislava, 1965).

[58] *Chrestomathia aethiopica* (Leipzig, 1866).

[59] See fn. 8.

[60] See fn. 9.

[61] This refers to H. Ludolf's grammar, see fn. 158.

[62] See fn. 264.

[63] J. C. Adelung, *Mithridates: oder, Allgemeine Sprachenkunde mit dem Vater Unser als Sprachprobe in bey nahe fünf hundred Sprachen und Mundarten*, 119–22 (Berlin, 1812).

[64] H. Salt, *A voyage to Abyssinia and travels to the interior of that country*, pp. xiii-xiv (London, 1814).

[65] See fn. 325.

[66] See fn. 275.

[67] See fn. 253.

languages is due to the efforts of missionaries and travelers, for the most part not trained in linguistics. It is only toward the end of the nineteenth century that the modern languages attracted the attention of the scholars in Ethiopic. As for the Semitist, he was mostly interested in Geez, representing the classical language type. With the exception of the comparative grammar of C. Brockelmann,[68] all the other comparative grammars of Semitic took only Geez into consideration. It is not, however, only the Semitist who is to be blamed for the shortcoming. Indeed, no adequate descriptive or comparative material of the modern Ethiopian languages was at his disposal. On the other hand the thinking of the Semitist is still rooted in the concept of the importance and validity of the classical languages, and the general Semitist thus disregards the contributions that the spoken Semitic languages can make toward our understanding of Proto-Semitic problems. And yet, the modern Semitic languages of Ethiopia offer an explanation, or at least a parallel, for many features of Proto-Semitic or of individual Semitic languages. In other cases innovations occur in the modern languages of Ethiopia which are of linguistic interest in themselves even if they do not shed special light on Semitic problems.

A few examples will be given to illustrate the point.

The complete or partial disappearance of the laryngeals or the merger of one laryngeal into another — a phenomenon found in Akkadian, Canaanite and some Aramaic dialects — finds its parallel in the North Ethiopian languages of Tigre and Tigrinya, and especially in the South Ethiopian languages.

The spirantization of *b* and *k* in intervocalic position, found in Aramaic and Hebrew, occurs in Tigrinya and in South Ethiopic. It may have occurred in Geez, but since the Ethiopic script has no way of expressing the spirants it is difficult to know whether this was also the case in Geez.

In the field of morphology one observes in the South Ethiopian languages the disappearance of the internal plural as is the case in the North Semitic languages.

The 'conative' force of the so-called 'third form' of Arabic is still retained in Tigre. The other Ethiopian languages have a 'conative' type (namely, type C) that corresponds to the third form of Arabic, but no longer the meaning.[69]

The morpheme of the direct complement expressed in Semitic and in Geez by *a* (*ä*) is lost in all the other languages of Ethiopia except in Selti and Zway.[70]

The forms of the Arabic jussive *yaqtula*, *yaqtala*, *yaqtila* (with the vowels *u*, *a*, *i*, after the 2nd radical) occurring in Geez as *yəngər* (representing *yaqtula*, *yaqtila*) and *yəlbäs* (representing *yaqtala*) appear only in some West Gurage dialects.[71]

The vowel *a* (*ä*) of the prefix of the Semitic jussive as represented in the Arabic *yaqtula* is preserved only in the Gurage dialects.[72]

[68] *Grundriss der vergleichenden Grammatik der semitischen Sprachen* (Berlin, 1908–13).
[69] *JAOS* 65.4–5 (1945).
[70] *JAOS* 71.217–18 (1951).
[71] See fn. 305.
[72] *Or* 37.90–3 (1968).

The marker *-u* of the main imperfect as represented in Arabic *yaqtul-u* is represented in the Gurage dialect of Soddo and others.[73]

The problem of the linguistic substratum which has to be considered in the investigation of Akkadian and in some Arabic dialects has clear parallels in the modern languages of Ethiopia, expecially of South Ethiopia, where the Cushitic substratum explains many phonetic and morphological features.[74]

These few examples, and many more not mentioned here, show the contribution that the modern languages of Ethiopia can make toward our understanding of Proto-Semitic. Future studies of comparative Semitic should, therefore, take into consideration not only Geez, the classical language, but all the modern languages of Ethiopia. It is, however, the task of the small group of *éthiopisants* to put all available material at the disposal of the Semitist.

Tigre

Tigre (known as *al-ḫaṣiya* in the Kassal province of the Sudan) is spoken in the eastern, western and northern lowlands of Eritrea including the Massawa region and the Dahlaq islands in the east, and the Keren and Agordat divisions in the west up to the Kassala province in the border region of the Sudan. The only writings are some religious texts published by Protestant missionaries. Folk literature and popular traditions have been collected by Western scholars.

The first documents on the language were published by persons who visited the country for reasons other than linguistic (archeological, ethnographic, missionary activity, and so on) and who included collections of words or general grammatical notes on Tigre in their works. Thus the documents published by R. Perini,[75] and M. Beurmann-A. Merx[76] have no value for the general Semitist. All these documents, as well as those of L. Reinisch,[77] W. Munzinger,[78] A. d'Abbadie,[79] and the Bible translations were utilized in a scientific manner by E. Littmann who published a study on the pronoun[80] and the verb.[81] As might be expected — Littmann himself confesses it — these studies cannot be considered complete and, owing to unreliable sources, cannot give a clear picture of the language. It was in order to collect first-hand material that Littmann undertook an expedition to the Tigre speaking regions in 1905–6 and published a highly valuable collection of texts in prose and poetry translated into English and German.[82] The prose texts are written in the dialect of Mensa. All the

[73] *JNES* 26.121–5 (1967).
[74] See fns. 428–31.
[75] *Manuale teorico-pratico della lingua tigrè* (Rome, 1893).
[76] *Glossar der Tigré-Sprache* (Leipzig, 1868).
[77] *Die Bilin-Sprache*. Bd. 2. Wörterbuch (Wien, 1887).
[78] *Vocabulaire de la langue tigré* (1863). Appendix to A. Dillmann, *Lexicon linguae aethiopicae*.
[79] *Extrait du vocabulaire de la langue parlée à Muçaww'a*. In W. Munzinger, *Vocabulaire de la langue tigré*, col. 53–64 (1863).
[80] 'Die Pronomina in Tigré', *ZA* 12.188–230, 291–316 (1897).
[81] 'Das Verbum der Tigré-Sprache', *ZA* 13.133–78 (1898); 14.1–102 (1899).
[82] *Publications of the Princeton Expedition to Abyssinia*. 4 volumes (Leyden, 1913).

prose and poetry texts are printed in Ethiopic characters provided with a special sign for the gemination of the consonants, this feature being important in the analysis of any Ethiopian language. This is why the interesting texts published by C. Conti Rossini,[83] K. G. Roden,[84] and partially by G. R. Sundström,[85] printed in the Ethiopic alphabet only, without a special sign for the gemination, can hardly be utilized in a study of Tigre.

Littmann's texts are discussed from the cultural, historical and linguistic points of view by T. Nöldeke.[86]

W. Leslau elaborated, on the basis of Littmann's texts, the first systematic grammar in the dialect of Mensa.[87] The grammatical forms are given in phonetic transcription. The grammar is also comparative. First-hand material correcting and supplementing grammatical problems of Tigre was collected by the same author during his stay in Keren in 1947.[88]

A grammar and a dictionary of Tigre published, in Ethiopic characters only, by the Catholic Mission of Eritrea[89] is not systematically arranged and, in general, has no scientific value.

Some volumes published during the Italo-Abyssinian war by non-linguists cannot be utilized scientifically.

The valuable sketch, in phonetic transcription, by G. Bergsträsser[90] is too short to give a clear picture of the language.

The outline by A. C. Beaton and A. Paul,[91] in phonetic transcription, does not always interpret the facts correctly.

In the domain of specialized problems, H. Fleisch analyzed the verb forms *qatälä*, *qotälä*, and *qetälä* in Tigre.[92] Maria Höfner discussed the occurrence of the verb forms *qalqala*, *qatlala*, *qataltala* and their meanings.[93] E. Littmann investigated the diminutive forms of the proper and common nouns,[94] and gave an analysis of the Tigre biradical verbs going back to a triradical root.[95]

[83] 'Tradizioni storiche dei Mensa', *GSAI* 14.41–99 (1901); *Ricordo di un soggiorno in Eritrea* (1903).
[84] *Le tribù dei Mensa* (Asmara, 1913).
[85] 'Kännedom om läkemedel ock deras andvändning bland infödingarne i Mänsa", *MO* 3.152–73 (1909), and others.
[86] 'Tigré-Texte', *ZA* 24.286–300 (1910); 'Tigré-Lieder', *ZA* 31.1–25 (1918).
[87] *Short grammar of Tigre* (New Haven, 1945). A reprint of the author's articles: 'The verb in Tigre', *JAOS* 65.1–26 (1945); and 'Grammatical sketches in Tigre', *JAOS* 65.164–203 (1945).
[88] 'Supplementary observations on Tigre grammar', *JAOS* 68.127–39 (1948).
[89] *Grammatica analitica della lingua tigré* (Asmara, 1919).
[90] *Einführung in die semitischen Sprachen*, 119–23 (München, 1928).
[91] *A grammar and a vocabulary of the Tigre language, as spoken by the Beni Amer* (Khartoum, 1954).
[92] *Les verbes à allongement interne en sémitique*, 302–23 (Paris, 1944).
[93] 'Probleme der Verbalstammbildung im Tigre', *ZDMG* 101.89–106 (1951).
[94] 'Die Diminutivbildung im Tigre', *AIUO* 2.89–103 (1943).
[95] 'Bilitterale Verba im Tigrē', *Donum natalicium H.S.Nyberg oblatum*, 94–101 (Uppsala, 1954).

F. R. Palmer published articles on Tigre prosody,[96] and on the relative clause in Tigre.[97] The same author also published a monograph on the morphology of the noun.[98] This study is based on original research and deals with the morphology of the noun and with the morphologically and syntactically related class of adjectives, these being preceded by a chapter on the phonology.

The older vocabularies to be mentioned, despite their defects, are those of W. Munzinger,[99] A. d'Abbadie,[100] L. Reinisch,[101] and the glossary of the *Grammatica della lingua tigre*.[102]

We have at present an excellent Tigre-German-English dictionary published by E. Littmann and M. Höfner.[103] While it is basically a dictionary of the Mänsaʿ (Mensa) material collected by Littmann it also incorporates the words of the previously mentioned vocabularies. The dictionary is in Ethiopic script only, with a special symbol for the gemination. Unfortunately, no indication is given for the pronunciation of the 'sixth order'. The authors bring in comparisons with Geez, Tigrinya, and Amharic. Arabic is compared wherever there is no Ethiopic equivalent.

W. Leslau investigated the Arabic loanwords in Tigre[104] discussing at the same time the phonetic and morphological treatment of the loanwords.

While on the whole there is adequate material available for the study of Tigre, there are no texts in phonetic transcription that would enable us to clear up the obscure points of the Tigre structure. Besides, a description of the language based on field work would be desirable.

Tigrinya

Tigrinya (Təgrəñña) is spoken in the province of Tigre and in Eritrea in the divisions of Hamasen, Akkele Guzay, Serae, Temben and Wolqayt. There are regional variants in Tigrinya.

Owing to the fact that Tigrinya is spoken in Eritrea, the former Italian colony, the Italians attached some importance to its study. Another factor which contributed to our knowledge of Tigrinya is the activity of the missionaries who, for religious purposes, edited different texts and vocabularies in Tigrinya. Several scholars have also had the opportunity of investigating the language with the help of Tigrinya

[96] 'Openness in Tigre', *BSOAS* 18.561–77 (1954).
[97] 'Relative clauses in Tigre', *Word* 17.24–33 (1961).
[98] *The morphology of the Tigre noun* (London, 1962).
[99] See fn. 78.
[100] See fn. 79.
[101] See fn. 77.
[102] See fn. 89.
[103] *Wörterbuch der Tigrē-Sprache*. Tigrē-Deutsch-Englisch (Wiesbaden, 1962).
[104] 'Arabic loanwords in Tigre', *Word* 12.125–41 (1956).

speakers outside of the country. As a result of all this, Tigrinya is relatively well known.

The first collections of words and general observations made by missionaries and travelers, as well as the translation into Tigrinya of some books of the Old and New Testament, were elaborated by F. Praetorius in his grammar of Tigrinya.[105] Praetorius was the first scholar who analyzed the language on a sound basis. The grammar deals with the phonology, morphology and syntax, and is comparative at the same time. Since, however, the grammar is based mainly on translations, it does not represent the spoken language. Besides, the inadequacy of the sources used by the author makes the grammatical forms often doubtful. On the other hand, the grammar is a very valuable instrument for the comparatist.

With the exception of Praetorius's grammar all the grammars given below are first-hand descriptions.

J. Schreiber's grammar adequately describes the language.[106] The Tigrinya forms are given in Ethiopic script only, with special symbols for the vowel of the 'sixth order'. The gemination, however, is not indicated. On the other hand it is superfluous to mark the accent in Tigrinya. The author does not indicate the region of the language he describes.

L. de Vito published an adequate grammar of Tigrinya,[107] in Ethiopic characters, with partial transcription. It is a description of the Tigrinya speech of Adoua.

The grammar of Padre Mauro da Leonessa[108] gives a good description of the language. Unfortunately, the author does not indicate the region in which the language described by him is spoken. The Tigrinya forms are in Ethiopic script and in phonetic transcription. Considerable space is given to syntax.

The grammar of Francesco da Offeio[109] has no scientific value.

The present writer published a grammar in the speech of Akkele Guzay.[110] The grammar is descriptive and deals with the phonology, morphology and the syntax of the language. The forms are given in transcription only.

A textbook of Tigrinya, that is, a grammar with graded exercises and vocabularies, was published by C. Conti Rossini.[111] The exercises are in Tigrinya and in Italian. The Tigrinya is used in transcription only. Occasionally the transcription is not satisfactory.

A useful sketch of Tigrinya, in transcription, was published by C. Conti Rossini.[112] Unfortunately, the author does not indicate the region of the speech he describes.

[105] *Grammatik der Tigriña-Sprache in Abessinien, hauptsächlich in der Gegend von Aksum and Adoa* (Halle, 1871).
[106] *Manuel de la langue tigraï, parlée au centre et dans le nord de l'Abyssinie* (Vienne, 1887–93).
[107] *Grammatica elementare della lingua tigrigna* (Roma, 1895).
[108] *Grammatica analitica della lingua tigray* (Roma, 1928).
[109] *Grammatica della lingua tigrai* (Cheren, 1907).
[110] *Documents tigrigna (éthiopien septentrional)* (Paris, 1941).
[111] *Lingua tigrina.* Elementi grammaticali ed esercizi (Milano, 1940).
[112] *Ethiopia e genti d'Etiopia*, 231–51 (Firenze, 1937).

Tables of the conjugation and of the derived stems of the Tigrinya verb, in Ethiopic script only, were published by Padre Mauro da Leonessa.[113]

A grammar of Tigrinya in Tigrinya was published by Abba Yaʿqob Gäbrä Iyäsus.[114] The Tigrinya grammatical terms are translated into Italian. There are also exercises at the end of the book.

Another grammar of Tigrinya in Tigrinya was published by an author who abbreviated his name into A. Ma. Ha.[115] The grammar also has exercises for various topics. Some Tigrinya grammatical terms are translated into Italian.

It was mentioned several times above that the authors of the various grammars did not indicate the region of the speech they describe. This brings up the question of the existence of dialects in Tigrinya. On the basis of the general observations and the texts whose speech was localized, such as Praetorius's for Hamasen and Temben,[116] Littmann's for Temben,[117] de Vito's for Adoua,[118] Kolmodin's for Hamasen,[119] and Leslau's for Akkele Guzay,[120] the present writer expressed the opinion that there are dialects in Tigrinya.[121] E. Ullendorff is opposed to the idea of the existence of dialects and thinks that '(dialectal distinctions) have often been over-estimated because research was based on the evidence supplied by single informants'.[122] While, in my opinion, the existing material warrants the conclusion that there are dialects in Tigrinya, it is also true that more documentation on Tigrinya of the various regions is necessary to arrive at a definite conclusion. Besides, there is the moot question of the definition of a dialect.

Several studies on detailed grammatical and etymological questions were published.

Marcel Cohen[123] examines the gemination of some Tigrinya verbal forms.

I. Wajnberg investigates the Tigrinya nominal forms[124] and the quadriradicals[125] examining them from the phonetic and etymological point of view.

113 *Verbi tigray e loro flessione* (Rome, 1935).

114 *Ḥaddis mäğämmäriya ziwäṣṣə' zällo mäṣḥaf säwasəw* (Asmara, 1926 [= 1934]).

115 *Säwasəw təgrəñña* (Asmara, 1951 [= 1959]).

116 'Über zwei Tigriña-Dialekte. 1. Der Dialekt von Hamâsen. 2. Der Dialekt von Tanbên', *ZDMG* 28.437–47 (1874).

117 'Tigriña-Texte von Tanbên', *WZKM* 16.211–25 (1902).

118 See fn. 107.

119 See fn. 153.

120 See fn. 157.

121 'Observations sur quelques dialectes du tigrigna. Dialectes d'Akkele Gouzay, d'Adoua et du Hamasen', *JA* 231.61–115 (1939).

122 *The Semitic languages of Ethiopia. A comparative phonology*, 22.

123 'La gémination dans les formes verbales en tigrigna', *MSL* 23.91–7 (1927).

124 'Die Typen der Nominalbildung im Tigriña', *ZS* 8.73–96 (1932), 10.256–310 (1935); *ZDMG* 90.637–79 (1936).

125 'Etudes sur les quadrilitères tigriña', *RO* 11.52–78 (1935); *Researches in Tigriña quadriliterals of phonetic origin* (Kraków, 1937).

N. V. Yushmanov[126] makes an attempt to explain the *š* of the Tigrinya ordinals from 5 to 9 as against *s* of the other Ethiopian languages.

H. Fleisch[127] analyzes the verbal forms *qatälä*, *qotälä*, *qetälä* in Tigrinya.

F. R. Palmer[128] published a phonological analysis to handle the morphological relation between the 'broken' plurals and the singular form with which they are grammatically paired. He also discusses the relative clause in Tigrinya.[129]

The present writer makes an attempt at reconstructing the verbal endings in Tigrinya;[130] discusses the form of the imperfect of type C in Tigrinya bringing it into the general context of the Proto-Ethiopic forms, and investigates the quantity of the vowels *ä* and *a* in Proto-Ethiopic on the basis of the syllable structure in Tigrinya;[131] and analyzes the phonetic and morphological treatment of the Arabic loanwords in Tigrinya, the loanwords being arranged according to subject matter.[132]

There are several vocabularies and dictionaries in Tigrinya. The first collections of words by H. Salt,[133] U. J. Seetzen,[134] C. T. Beke,[135] and C. T. Lefebvre[136] are described by F. Praetorius.[137] The vocabularies by A. Allori and Serrano,[138] F. Caressa,[139] P. G. Jansen,[140] T. Piccirilli,[141] and others, published during the Italo-Abyssinian war have no scientific value.

The Tigrinya-Italian vocabulary (with an Italian-Tigrinya index), in Ethiopic script and transcription, published by L. de Vito,[142] and the Italian-Tigrinya vocabulary, in Ethiopic script and transcription, published by A. Cimino,[143] can be utilized, with some reservations.

The Tigrinya-French dictionary by P. S. Coulbeaux and J. Schreiber[144] is unfortunately incomplete. It contains only the letters H to N (in the alphabetic order of Ethiopic). It is printed in the Ethiopic script, with special signs for the accent, the vowel

[126] 'A sibilant anomaly in the Tigrinya numerals', *Africana* 1.77–87 (1937).
[127] *Les verbes à allongement interne en sémitique*, 259–301 (Paris, 1944).
[128] 'The "broken plurals" of Tigrinya', *BSOAS* 17.548–66 (1955).
[129] 'Relative clauses in Tigrinya', *JSS* 7.36–43 (1962).
[130] 'Essai de reconstitution des désinences verbales du tigrigna', *RESm* 70–99 (1938).
[131] 'Réflexions à propos du type C en tigrigna', *BSL* 56.202–11 (1961).
[132] 'Arabic loanwords in Tigrinya', *JAOS* 76.204–13 (1956).
[133] *A voyage to Abyssinia and travels into the interior of that country*, pp. xviii-xxiii (London, 1814).
[134] 'Seetzen's linguistischer Nachlass', in J. S. Vater, *Proben deutscher Volksmundarten* (Leipzig, 1816).
[135] 'On the languages and dialects of Abyssinia and the countries to the south', *PPS* 2.97–107 (1846).
[136] *Voyage en Abyssinie exécuté pendant les années 1839–1843*, 3.328–9, 397–400 (Paris [1845]).
[137] See fn. 105.
[138] *Piccolo dizionario eritreo* (Milano, 1936).
[139] *Dizionario africano* (Milano, 1938).
[140] *Guida alla conoscenza dei dialetti de l'Africa Orientale* (Milano, 1936).
[141] *Dizionario di alcune parlate nell'A.O.I.* (Empoli, 1938).
[142] *Vocabolario della lingua tigrigna* (Rome, 1896).
[143] *Vocabolario italiano-tigrai e tigrai-italiano* (Asmara, 1904).
[144] *Dictionnaire de la langue tigraï* (Wien, 1915).

of the 'sixth order' and the gemination. It is an abundant dictionary and one gains the impression that its sources came from various Tigrinya-speaking regions.

The most complete and the best available dictionary is the one published by Francesco da Bassano.[145] It is a Tigrinya-Italian dictionary with an Italian-Tigrinya index. The dictionary is in Ethiopic script with phonetic transcription. Besides, the geminated consonants are also indicated by a horizontal line on the top of the Tigrinya letter. Occasionally the words are illustrated with a sentence. While the dictionary is the most complete one we have, it is far from being exhaustive.

The Ethiopian scholar Abba Yohannəs Gäbrä Egzi'abəher published a Tigrinya-Amharic dictionary,[146] in Ethiopic script, without any special sign for the gemination or the value of the vowel of the "sixth order". Occasionally the author illustrated the word with a Tigrinya sentence which he translates into Amharic.

The edition of a Tigrinya-Turkish and Tigrinya-Arabic (in the dialect of Hijaz) vocabulary by E. Littmann[147] deserves attention. The vocabularies are in the Ethiopic script.

There are a few glossaries dealing with specific subjects, such as E. Chiovenda's for plants,[148] C. Conti Rossini's for terms refering to social life and law,[149] M. Griaule's for games,[150] G. A. Schweinfurth's for plants,[151] and others.

The first writings in Tigrinya are due to the efforts of the missionaries. At present, the student interested in Tigrinya has at his disposal a relatively abundant literature in secular writings, including newspapers. For study purposes he will find a useful collection of dialogues and phrases in Tigrinya, Italian and French, published by Angelo da Ronciglione.[152]

An abundant collection of Tigrinya texts (in the speech of Hamasen) of historical character (in Ethiopic script, with a special sign for the gemination), translated into French, was published by J. A. Kolmodin.[153]

C. Conti Rossini published a collection of 489 annotated proverbs, in phonetic script;[154] texts of historical character in Ethiopic script, translated into Italian;[155] and Tigrinya poetry.[156]

The present writer published texts describing the various aspects of the life of

[145] *Vocabolario tigray-italiano e repertorio italiano-tigray* (Rome, 1918).

[146] *Mäzgäbä qalat təgrəñña amharəñña.* Ethiopian dictionary. Tigrigna-Amharic (Asmara, 1949 [= 1957]).

[147] 'Abessinische Glossen', *ZA* 21.56–90 (1908).

[148] *La collezione dei cereali della colonia Eritrea* (Rome, 1912).

[149] *Principi di diritto consuetudinario della colonia Eritrea* (Rome, 1916).

[150] *Jeux et divertissements abyssins*, 250–3 (Paris, 1935).

[151] *Abyssinische Pflanzennamen* (Berlin, 1893).

[152] *Manuale tigray-italiano-francese* (Rome, 1912).

[153] *Traditions de Tsazzegga et Hazzegga*, 2 vols. (Rome, Upsal, 1912–15).

[154] *Proverbi, tradizioni e canzone tigrine* (Verbania, 1942).

[155] 'Note etiopice. 2. Leggende tigray', *GSAI* 10.143–53 (1897); 'Studi su popolazioni dell'Etiopia', *RSO* 4.599–625 (1911–12).

[156] 'Canti popolari tigrai', *ZA* 17.23–52 (1903); 18.320–86 (1904); 19.288–341 (1906).

Akkele Guzay, as well as folktales and proverbs.[157] All the texts are in transcription, with an interlinear and free translation into French.

From all the information given above it can be seen that the *éthiopisant* and the Semitist have at their disposal adequate grammars and dictionaries. However, a more complete dictionary would be highly desirable, as well as linguistic descriptions of the various Tigrinya-speaking regions.

Amharic

Amharic (Amarəñña) is the national language of Ethiopia. The name is derived from the region of Amhara (Amara). It is spoken in the central and southern highlands of Ethiopia. As the literary and national language it is used throughout the country. Within the Amharic-speaking region there are enclaves where other Semitic Ethiopic and some Cushitic languages are spoken. There are minor variations in the pronunciation, in the morphology and in the vocabulary of the various regions.

Due to its national character, Amharic is the best known language of Ethiopia. In fact, the student has at his disposal adequate grammars, dictionaries and editions of texts which enable him to gain a thorough knowledge of the language.

The first Amharic grammar was published in 1698 by H. Ludolf[158] who acquired the language with the help of the Ethiopian scholar Abba Gregorius. While not all the grammatical forms were understood and correctly interpreted by Ludolf,[159] his grammar has a scientific basis and is an important document for the study of seventeenth-century Amharic.

The missionary C. W. Isenberg[160] broadened the knowledge of Amharic, but he misunderstood the structure of the verb.

The grammar of G. Massaia[161] is of no scientific value.

F. Praetorius,[162] the well-known Semitist, rendered great services to Ethiopic studies. With his keen mind he interpreted correctly the grammatical forms of Amharic and explained them by comparison with other Ethiopic and Semitic languages known in his time. The phonetic problems, however, were not adequately treated since Praetorius did not speak the language and had to rely on previous grammars and documents published mostly in Ethiopic script or transcribed by non-linguists. In his etymologies he often tried to explain roots through Semitic, whereas many of them are of Cushitic origin. His grammar cannot be used by the beginner, but the *éthiopisant* will profit by it greatly. Praetorius also had the great merit to have brought to

[157] *Documents tigrigna*, 157–378 (Paris, 1941).
[158] *Grammatica linguae amharicae* (Frankfurt, 1698).
[159] See I. Guidi, 'Lo studio dell'Amarico in Europa', *Actes du onzième congrès des orientalistes*, 4th section, 68–72 (Paris, 1898).
[160] *Grammar of the Amharic language* (London, 1842).
[161] *Lectiones grammaticales pro missionariis qui addiscere solunt linguam Amaricam ...* (Paris, 1867).
[162] *Die amharische Sprache* (Halle, 1879).

the attention of the Semitist the existence of the other Semitic Ethiopic languages of Ethiopia known in his time.

I. Guidi[163] published a short but precise grammar of Amharic in 1889. Being aware of the problem of the gemination the author transcribed most of the forms correctly. Unfortunately he occasionally takes Latin grammar as basis for the interpretation of Amharic morphology and speaks about noun declension with as many as eight cases.

F. Mondon-Vidailhet[164] published a grammar in Ethiopic script only. It cannot, therefore, be used with great profit. He, too, distinguishes seven cases in the noun declension, and the interpretation of other morphological features is inadequate.

In the same class, more or less, is the grammar published by J. Baeteman.[165]

The Ethiopian scholar Afevork Ghevre Jesus[166] published an Amharic grammar in Italian, in Ethiopic script, with a special symbol for the gemination, and partially in transcription. There is useful information in the grammar, but the presentation of the grammatical features is not systematic. The book can be used only by someone who knows the language. There are sentences in Amharic and Italian, but the exercises are not graded.

The grammar of C. H. Armbruster[167] is a useful introduction to the Amharic language, the grammatical features being clearly and correctly presented. However, it is not complete, particularly in the verb treatment. The forms given by the author are correctly transcribed.

The Italo-Abyssinian war, as might have been expected, led to the publication of many Amharic grammars, but none of them, with the exception of the one by Bruno Ducati,[168] is of scientific value.

R. C. Abraham[169] published an Amharic grammar by the offset process. A special symbol was added for the indication of stress throughout the book which makes for complicated reading. Phonetic transcription is used throughout, without the Ethiopic script. While the information on the whole is correct, the arrangement is not clear.

The grammar by C. H. Dawkins[170] uses some of the grammatical terminology of Armbruster. It is in Ethiopic script, with a special symbol for the gemination. The chief value of the grammar lies in the fact that it includes grammatical points and colloquial usages not mentioned in other grammars, but it is lacking in clarity.

The most complete descriptive grammar of Amharic is the monumental *Traité* of Marcel Cohen.[171] The Amharic is given in Ethiopic script and in transcription. The

[163] *Grammatica elementare della lingua amarica* (Roma, 1889); 3rd ed. Rome, 1924.
[164] *Grammaire de la langue abyssine* (Paris, 1898).
[165] *Grammaire amarigna*, par un missionnaire Lazariste (Addis Ababa, 1923).
[166] *Grammatica della lingua amarica* (Rome, 1905).
[167] *Initia Amharica. An introduction to spoken Amharic.* Part I. Grammar (Cambridge, 1908).
[168] *Corso di amharico per autodidatti* (Rome, 1936); *Corso di lingua amharica per autodidatti* (Rome, 1938).
[169] *A modern grammar of spoken Amharic* (Addis Ababa, 1941).
[170] *The fundamentals of Amharic* (Addis Ababa, 1960).
[171] *Traité de langue amharique* (Paris, 1936).

examples are taken from written documents as well as from colloquial usage. It can be used with profit not only by the *éthiopisant* and the Semitist, but also by the general linguist. It is not, however, an easy book to be consulted by the beginner in Amharic.

The *Traité* is supplemented by the *Nouvelles études*.[172] It contains grammatical forms that the author collected orally, as well as from the Amharic writings, and from the Amharic studies written by other scholars. An extensive index of the words and forms treated in the body of the book is extremely useful.

Useful sketches of Amharic were published by J.P. Alone,[173] C. Conti Rossini,[174] N.V. Yushmanov,[175] A. Klingenheben,[176] and E. Gankin,[177] all of them in transcription.

Several Ethiopian scholars compiled grammars of Amharic in Amharic. Käntiba Gäbru,[178] and Abba Yaʿqob Gäbrä Iyäsus[179] are to be mentioned in particular.

With the recent development of the educational system in Ethiopia and the teaching of Amharic in the Ethiopian schools the need was felt for Amharic grammars adapted for the teaching of the language. Several Amharic grammars were written in Amharic, but the language is not treated scientifically. Special mention should be made of Märsəʿe Hazän Wäldä Qirqos whose grammar has exercises as well.[180] Unfortunately, the author applied to Amharic the grammatical concepts of English grammar, without considering the structure of Amharic itself. Täklä Maryam Fäntaye[181] also compiled a grammar (with exercises) for use in the classroom.

Beginning with 1950 and particularly with 1960 a change in the emphasis of the study of Amharic took place. Several factors contributed to this change. The increased interest that the Western world took in Ethiopia; the activities of the Peace Corps in Ethiopia, particularly in the field of education; the search for new linguistic methods in the teaching of languages; and, among the missionaries, the more acute conviction of the necessity to acquire the language of the country in which they were active. All this resulted in the compilation of textbooks and readers of all kinds. I should add that the term 'textbook' refers to a book that gives grammatical features of the language with graded exercises and vocabularies. It is not a reference grammar. The grammatical features are not treated in a systematic way, but are chosen so as to allow the student to construct connected sentences. Needless to say, not all the textbooks mentioned below are of the same quality. They are given in chronological order.

172 *Nouvelles études d'éthiopien méridional* (Paris, 1939).

173 *Short manual (with vocabulary) of the Amharic language* (London, 1909).

174 *Etiopia e genti d'Etiopia*, 253–79 (Firenze, 1937).

175 *Stroi amharskogo iazika* (Leningrad, 1936). The 2nd edition has the title *Amharskii iazik* (Moscow, 1959).

176 *Deutsch-Amharischer Sprachführer*, 11–49 (Wiesbaden, 1966).

177 E. Gankin and Käbbädä Dästa, *Russko-Amkharskii Slovar'*, 945–1009 (Moscow, 1965).

178 *Yamarəñña säwasəw märi. A short guide of the practical Amharic* (Addis Ababa, 1915 [= 1923]).

179 *Yamarəñña qʷanqʷa aččər säwasəw* (Asmara, 1921 [= 1929]).

180 (*Baddis sərat yätäsänadda*) *yamarəñña säwasəw* (Addis Ababa, 1935 [= 1943]). He also published abridged grammars.

181 *Ḫohətä ṭəbäb zäsənä ṣəḥuf* (Addis Ababa, 1946 [= 1954]).

D. M. Davies and E. F. Liester[182] compiled a short textbook divided into 29 lessons, in Amharic script, with a special symbol for the gemination. The presentation is inadequate.

Gene M. Schramm's textbook[183] is based largely on M. Cohen's *Traité*. The text is in Amharic script, with a special symbol for the gemination, but it is not consistently applied to all the forms. It is insufficient for the acquisition of the language.

The textbook published by Padre Agostino da Hebo[184] first presents the grammar which is followed by exercises. The book is in Amharic script only, without any special symbol for the gemination. While the forms given by the author are on the whole correct, the presentation is not systematic nor is the analysis of the forms always correct.

The Foreign Service Institute (FSI) in Washington compiled a textbook for its own use.[185] The grammar and exercises are in phonetic transcription only. The exercises of the first volume are repeated in the Ethiopic script in the second volume. The interpretation of the grammatical features is on the whole correct. In each lesson the basic sentences and structure sentences are followed by grammatical notes and drills. While the material covered in each unit is undoubtedly appropriate for the FSI teaching method, it is not appropriate for ordinary classroom conditions.

The active interest that the missionaries took in Amharic resulted in the publication of two textbooks outside of Dawkins' grammar mentioned above.

A textbook for use in the Cooperative Language Institute of Ethiopia was prepared by Milton C. Fisher.[186] The following passage from the introduction will give the tenor of the book. 'It is to be understood that the lessons which follow will achieve the desired goal only when coupled with 5 to 6 hours each day of study with an informant, classroom drill and instruction, private review, use of language lab tapes and from conversation with Ethiopian friends.' Consequently, only with a special kind of student can the book be used. Besides, the subject matter is often religious. While the book gives the essential features of the language, it is done mainly through drills. The book is in Amharic script with a symbol for the gemination employed only wherever the word or the form is used for the first time. The book cannot be used without the help of a teacher.

Marie Frydenlund and Kristine Svensen of the Norwegian Lutheran Mission Language School prepared another textbook.[187] The book is based on Dawkins' grammar. The Amharic is given in Ethiopic script, without a special symbol for the gemination. The student can, therefore, read the forms correctly only with the help of an informant. There is a key to the exercises.

182 *A beginner's Amharic grammar* (Washington, 1952).
183 *A practical course in the Amharic language* (Washington, 1954).
184 *Grammatica amarica* (Asmara, 1955).
185 *Amharic. Basic course.* By Serge Obolensky, Debebow Zelelié, and Mulugeta Andualem. 2 vols. (Washington, 1964).
186 *A guide to learning Amharic* (Addis Ababa, 1963; revised in 1965).
187 *Amharic for beginners* (Addis Ababa, 1967).

W. Leslau published a textbook[188] that was originally designed for the teaching of the Peace Corps volunteers to Ethiopia, but was then enlarged for the purpose of teaching Amharic to college students. The textbook has 50 lessons. Each lesson describes one or several grammatical features of the language and includes a vocabulary and exercises. The Amharic is given in the Ethiopic script, with a special symbol for the gemination. Besides, the grammatical forms as well as the vocabularies of the individual lessons are transcribed phonetically. There are connected stories and dramatized dialogues. An Amharic-English and an English-Amharic vocabulary include all the words of the textbook. An index of the grammatical features helps the student to find the systematic treatment of the grammatical forms.

There are many specialized studies in the phonology and morphology of Amharic, but only a few will be mentioned here; they are given in chronological order.

I. Guidi[189] was the first to recognize the importance of the gemination in the Amharic morphology.

F. Beguinot[190] discussed the cases of assimilation in Geez and in Amharic.

G. J. Afevork[191] devoted a monograph to the study of the Amharic verb. While it contains useful information about the morphology of the verb, the presentation is not systematic.

M. Cohen[192] published numerous notes of phonetic and morphological problems of Amharic.

I. Wajnberg[193] discussed grammatical and etymological problems of the Amharic quadriradicals.

H. Fleisch[194] analyzed the verbal forms *qatälä*, *qotälä*, *qetälä* in Amharic.

Fedele da Valdieri[195] gives a classification and conjugation of the Amharic verb with numerous tables, in Ethiopic script and transcription.

A. Klingenheben treated the laryngeals, and especially the glottal stop;[196] the expression of the 'general impersonal' of the type *yənägroʷal* 'one says'; [197]and the prefix *aš-* with the meaning of a causative.[198]

188 *Amharic textbook* (Wiesbaden and Berkeley, 1967).

189 'La forma intensiva del verbo amarico', *GSAI* 3.179–81 (1889); 'Sulla reduplicazione delli consonanti amariche', *SPAGI* 2.1–13 (1895); 'Sulle coniugazioni del verbo amarico', *ZA* 8.245–62 (1893).

190 'Di alcune fenomeni di variazione fonetica combinatoria e dissimilatoria in amarico', *RSO* 2.509–34 (1909).

191 *Il verbo amarico* (Rome, 1901).

192 See W. Leslau, *An annotated bibliography of the Semitic languages of Ethiopia*, nos. 1212–22.

193 'Beiträge zu den mehrlautigen Wurzeln im Amharischen', *Or* 6.184–213 (1939).

194 *Les verbes à allongement vocalique interne en sémitique*, 324–56 (Paris, 1944).

195 *Il verbo amarico in tavole sinottiche*: classificazione-coniugazione-sintassi, con trascrizione italiana di ogni parola amarica (Rome, 1945).

196 'Die Laryngalen im Amharischen', *ZDMG* 100.374–84 (1950).

197 'Das 'schiefe Verbum' des Amharischen', *ZPhon* 9.150–5 (1956).

198 'Zum Problem der Verbalstämme des Amharischen', *JSS* 9.42–6 (1964).

C. Sumner[199] published an experimental phonetic study of various Amharic sounds.

W. Leslau[200] suggested a hypothesis on the origin of the type B of Amharic as being **qettälä*.

H. J. Polotsky[201] treated typological problems in the syntax of Amharic and Turkish.

S. Strelcyn[202] examines the sources for the study of Ancient Amharic from phonetic, morphological and lexicographical points of view. These sources are the Geez writings with Amharic elements from the fifteenth century onward, the Geez vocabularies of the seventeenth and eighteenth centuries, and the medical treatises.

Joanna Mantel-Niećko[203] undertook a statistical analysis of the phonetic structure of the roots, a statistical discussion of the frequency and correlation of the derived stems, and frequency of the derived stems in literary, journalistic and other texts.

E. G. Titov discusses the nominal, verbal and adverbial nature of the Amharic gerundive;[204] and examines the features in the phonology, morphology and syntax that are different from those of the other Semitic languages and explains them through Cushitic.[205]

R. Hetzron examines the meaning of the factitive in relation to other stems of the same root;[206] suggests that the vowel *ə* is not phonemic;[207] and investigates the pronominalization in Amharic.[208]

Taddese Beyene[209] published a contrastive study between the Amharic and English segmental phonemes, and discussed the errors that Amharic speaking students make in English.

Recently, a few studies were published making use of the transformational theory without using this name.

Hailu Fullas[210] examines the various functions of the particle *yä-* and the many relations expressed by the *yä*-complex which differ not only semantically but also formally. Transposition is used as one of the formal criteria.

F. P. Cotterell[211] discusses several problems in Amharic syntax such as word clauses, primary neutral sentences, and others.

[199] *Etude expérimentale de l'amharique moderne* (Montréal, 1951); 2nd ed. Addis Ababa, 1957.
[200] 'Une hypothèse sur la forme primitive du type B en amharique', *Word* 13.479–88 (1957).
[201] 'Syntaxe amharique et syntaxe turque', *ACISE* 117–22.
[202] 'Ethiopian medical treatises as a source of early Amharic', *Proceedings of the First International Congress of Africanists 1962*, 105–12 (London, 1964); 'Matériaux pour l'étude de l'ancien amharique', *JSS* 9.257–64 (1964).
[203] 'Quantitative research on the phonetic structure and derivative stems of Amharic', *JSS* 9.27–41 (1964).
[204] 'Deeprichastie v amharskom iazyke', *AESY* 3.184–202 (1959).
[205] 'Ob osobennostiakh amharskogo iazyka v sravnenii nekotorymi drugimi semitiskimi iazykami', *AESY* 3.169–83 (1959).
[206] 'La réaction du thème factitif en amharique', *Muséon* 76.425–39 (1963).
[207] 'La voyelle du sixième ordre en amharique', *JAfrL* 3.179–90 (1964).
[208] 'Pronominalization in Amharic', *JSS* 11.83–97 (1966).
[209] 'Amharic and English segmental phonemes: a contrastive analysis', *LL* 16.93–120 (1966).
[210] 'The particle *yä-* in Amharic', *RSEt* 20.103–119 (1964).
[211] 'Expansion process in Amharic syntax', *AfrLS* 5.1–16 (1964); 'Amharic word clauses', *JEthS* 2.33–48 (1964); 'The Amharic primary neutral sentence', *JEthS* 4.11–33 (1966).

E. Ullendorff[212] in an inaugural lecture discusses the intricacies of Amharic in the various fields of the language.

Various doctoral theses have recently been published on Amharic subjects.

Abraham Demoz[213] submitted a thesis to the University of California, Los Angeles (UCLA), on the meaning of the derived stems with the prefix *tä-*, *a-*, *as-*, *tä-C*, and *a(t)-*.

Hailu Fullas[214] submitted a thesis to UCLA on the derivation of nominal patterns of Amharic.

Gideon Goldenberg[215] submitted a thesis to the Hebrew University, Jerusalem, on the tense-system. 'Tense-system is meant here as a purely formal signification for that system of verbal forms and syntactical construction which cuts across all verbal stems, thus comprising all the "tiroirs verbaux" including the modal forms as well'.

There is a number of vocabularies and dictionaries of Amharic, but it should be stressed that none of them is complete nor up-to-date. The dictionaries that have no scientific value will not be mentioned here.

The Amharic-Latin dictionary (with a Latin-Amharic index) of H. Ludolf[216] is important as reflecting the state of Amharic in the seventeenth century. The author occasionally indicates comparisons with Arabic and Hebrew.

The Amharic-English dictionary by C. W. Isenberg[217] is taken mainly from the Bible in Arabic translated into Amharic by an Ethiopian monk, but it also contains words collected by the author himself as well as words of the previous vocabularies. As a result of the Biblical source, the dictionary contains a number of words transliterated from Arabic and it is difficult to know whether some of these words were ever used in the spoken language. The dictionary is in the Amharic script only, without any special mark for the pronunciation. The translations of the English-Amharic index are stilted.

A. d'Abbadie[218] compiled an Amharic-French dictionary of about 15,000 words, written in Ethiopic script with partial transcription. The transcription is on the whole correct. The dictionary was compiled with the help of a single native speaker with whom the author checked the previously published dictionaries. The importance of the dictionary lies, among others, in the fact that it is mainly the vocabulary of one region, namely of Gondar, even though the vocabulary of other regions is also in-

212 *The challenge of Amharic*. An inaugural lecture delivered on 28 October 1964 (London, 1965).
213 *The meaning of some derived stems in Amharic* (Los Angeles, 1964).
214 *Derived nominal patterns in Amharic* (Los Angeles, 1966).
215 *The Amharic tense-system*. In Hebrew, with an English abstract (Jerusalem, 1966). The author gave a summary of the subject in 'On the Amharic tense-system', *JSS* 9.47–9 (1964).
216 *Lexicon Amharico-Latinum*, cum indice Latino (Frankfurt, 1698).
217 *Dictionary of the Amharic language*. Amharic and English, and English and Amharic (London, 1841).
218 *Dictionnaire de la langue amariñña* (Paris, 1881).

cluded. Besides, it contains words that have disappeared from the language and it is important to have them registered. The French index gives the number of the page on which the Amharic word is to be found.

I. Guidi[219] compiled an Amharic-Italian dictionary of about 25,000 words. The dictionary is in Ethiopic script, with phonetic transcription, mainly whenever a consonant is geminated in the Amharic words. With the help of the Ethiopian scholar Kəflä Giyorgis from Shoa, Guidi checked d'Abbadie's dictionary and added new words. It is the first scientific dictionary of Amharic. A supplement to Guidi was published by F. Gallina and E. Cerulli.[220] It is based on literary and oral sources.

J. Baeteman[221] published an Amharic-French dictionary based on the existing dictionaries and his collections of words made during his stay in Ethiopia. It contains about 20,000 words. The dictionary is in Ethiopic script, with partial transcription. It also contains a French-Amharic index.

The Amharic-English dictionary by C. H. Armbruster[222] contains only the letters H to S (in Ethiopic order). It is in Ethiopic script, with phonetic transcription. Many vocabulary items are illustrated with examples in Ethiopic script and phonetic transcription. It is the first etymological dictionary of Amharic.

An Amharic-German glossary of the songs in honor of the kings dating back to the fourteenth century was published by E. Littmann.[223]

There are some dictionaries in Amharic-Amharic. Mäsfən Ləsanu[224] published an Amharic-Amharic dictionary of uniradical and biradical roots. The Geez roots are indicated.

Täfärra Wärq[225] published an Amharic-Amharic dictionary of about 5000 words for high school students.

Täsämma Habtä Mika'el Gəṣəw[226] is the author of an extensive Amharic-Amharic dictionary. It has many new words not found in the other dictionaries. There is a considerable number of illustrations in the dictionary. Unfortunately, the meanings that the author indicated for a given root are all grouped together without showing the various shades of meaning.

Dictionaries in foreign languages translated into Amharic are:

C. H. Armbruster's dictionary[227] in English-Amharic is in Ethiopic script with

219 *Vocabolario amarico-italiano* (Rome, 1901).
220 *Supplemento al Vocabolario amarico-italiano* (Rome, 1940).
221 *Dictionnaire amarigna-français*, suivi d'un vocabulaire français-amarigna (Dire-Daoua, 1929).
222 *Initia Amharica. An introduction to spoken Amharic.* Part III. Amharic-English vocabulary (Cambridge, 1920).
223 'Altamharisches Glossar. Der Wortschatz in den "Canzoni geez-amariñña"', *RSO* 20.473–505 (1944).
224 *Yamarəñña mäṣḥetä qalat* (Addis Ababa, 1946 [= 1954]).
225 *Yamarəñña sənä qalat* (Addis Ababa, 1947 [= 1955]).
226 *Käsate Bərhan täsämma*: *Yamarəñña mäzgäbä qalat* (Addis Ababa, 1951 [= 1959]).
227 *Initia Amharica.* Part II. *English-Amharic vocabulary with phrases* (Cambridge, 1910).

phonetic transcription. Occasionally the author gives sentences to illustrate the word, but the usage of the Amharic words is often outdated.

C.H. Walker[228] published an English-Amharic dictionary in the dialect of Shoa, in phonetic transcription. The lexical items are occasionally illustrated with brief sentences that are very often a free translation of the English text. In this dictionary, too, the usage of the Amharic words is often outdated.

A. Klingenheben[229] is the author of a German-Amharic dictionary, in phonetic transcription. Special symbols indicate the verbal type.

The most abundant dictionary in any foreign language is the Russian-Amharic dictionary by E. Gankin and Käbbädä Dästa.[230] It contains about 23,000 words. The dictionary is in Ethiopic script, with phonetic transcription.

There are also smaller dictionaries that were compiled mainly for practical purposes.

J.P. Alone's dictionary[231] is in Amharic-English and English-Amharic, in transcription only.

A vocabulary[232] printed in Dire-Daoua is in Amharic-English-French, English-Amharic-French, and French-Amharic-English, in Ethiopic script only.

J. Bodiger[233] published a Hebrew-Amharic and an Amharic-Hebrew vocabulary. The Hebrew is transliterated into the Ethiopic script, and the Amharic is transliterated into the Hebrew script.

Italian-Amharic dictionaries were published by L. Fusella and A. Girace,[234] in a good transcription; and by A. Bevilaqua,[235] in Ethiopic script and transcription.

English-Amharic dictionaries were published by Asäffa Mälke[236] and by Asfaw Šibäši,[237] both in Ethiopic script, the English words being transcribed into Ethiopic script.

There are also vocabularies arranged according to subjects. The authors of these vocabularies are: Afevork Ghevre Jesus;[238] A. M. Raad and B. Ghaleb;[239] Angelo da Ronciglione;[240] and Emmanuel Abraham.[241]

Several authors deal with the foreign loanwords and calques in Amharic.

[228] *English-Amharic dictionary* (London, 1928).
[229] *Deutsch-Amharischer Sprachführer* (Wiesbaden, 1966).
[230] *Russko-Amkharskii Slovar* (Moscow, 1965).
[231] *Short manual of the Amharic language*, 75–145 (London, 1909).
[232] *Yamarəňňa yäənglizəňňa yäfäränsayəňňa mäzgäbä qalat.* Vocabulary. Vocabulaire (Dire-Daoua, 1956).
[233] *Millon ibri-amhari, amhari-ʿibri.* Dictionary, Hebrew-Amharic, Amharic-Hebrew (Jerusalem, 1964).
[234] *Dizionario pratico e frasario per conversazione italiano-amarico* (Napoli, 1937).
[235] *Vocabolario italiano-amarico* (Rome, 1912); *Nuovo vocabolario italiano-amarico* (Rome, 1937).
[236] *Ləsanä bəḫer* (Addis Ababa, 1950 [= 1958]).
[237] *Yäənglәzəňňanna yamarəňňa kisäňňa mäftəḥe qalat* (Addis Ababa, n.d.).
[238] *Guide du voyageur en Abyssinie*, 6–81 (Rome, 1908); *Manuale di conversazione italiano-amarico* (Rome, 1934).
[239] *La clé de la conversation abyssine* (Beyrouth, 1910).
[240] *Manuale amarico-italiano-francese* (Rome, 1912).
[241] *An introduction to spoken English* (Addis Ababa, 1939 [= 1947]).

Abraham Demoz[242] published an account of European loanwords used in the first seven issues of every month of the newspaper Addis Zämän.

L. Fusella made a collection of Amharic neologisms;[243] and discussed loanwords, calques and translation problems in modern Amharic.[244]

Arabic loanwords in Amharic were studied by W. Leslau[245] and S. Strelcyn.[246]

M. M. Moreno[247] gives a useful list (in Italian-Amharic) of legal terms adapted into Amharic.

J. Tubiana[248] discusses the nouns of relationship in Amharic.

It would be desirable to have a study on the history and development of the Amharic vocabulary, but the time had not yet come for a study of that kind. All the texts of 'ancient' Amharic would have to be examined as well as the usage of the language beginning with the rise of modern Amharic literature. The present writer compared modern Amharic equivalents of some 250 English words with the translations given by Armbruster in 1910 to show the changes that the vocabulary has undergone.[249]

It would be beyond the scope of this article to mention all the literary writings in Amharic. The student has at his disposal a voluminous literature in Amharic published in Ethiopia and editions of texts made by Western scholars. I will mention only several books published recently with the purpose of facilitating the study of the language.

T. L. Tiutrumova published a Chrestomathy,[250] without dictionary.

E. Ullendorff[251] is the author of a useful chrestomathy, with an Amharic-English vocabulary.

W. Leslau[252] published an Amharic conversation book. The subjects deal with various aspects of Ethiopian life. The Amharic text is translated into English.

J. Tubiana[252a] published a collection of texts used in the examinations.

From the preceding survey on Amharic it can easily been seen that Amharic has attracted the greatest attention of the *éthiopisant* and the Semitist. As a result, the student can gain quite a thorough insight into the various aspects of the language. There are still, however, a few desiderata.

An up-to-date reference grammar for the beginner is still missing.

242 'European loanwords in an Amharic daily newspaper', *Languages in Africa*, ed. by John Spencer (Cambridge, 1963).

243 'Breve raccolti di neologismi amarici', *AIUO* 3.405–16 (1949).

244 'Osservazioni linguistiche sull'amarico moderno', *ACISE* 81–8.

245 'Arabic loanwords in Amharic', *BSOAS* 19.221–44 (1957).

246 'Sur les emprunts arabes en amharique', *Symbolae linguisticae in honorem Georgii Kuryłowicz*, 309–16 (Wrocław-Warszawa-Kraków, 1965).

247 'La terminologia dei nuovi codici etiopici', *RSEt* 20.22–34 (1964).

248 'Les noms de parenté en amharique', *GLECS* 6.48–53 (1951–54).

249 'Toward a history of the Amharic language', *JEthS* 2.12–20 (1964).

250 *Amkharskii iazyk. Khrestomathia* (Leningrad, 1960).

251 *An Amharic chrestomathy* (London, 1965).

252 *An Amharic conversation book* (Wiesbaden, 1965).

252a *Recueil de versions amhariques* (Paris, 1966).

A description of the language as it is actually spoken in everyday life taking into consideration all the phonetic phenomena such as elision, assimilation, intonation, and so on, would greatly enhance our knowledge of the language.

Finally an Amharic-English and an English-Amharic dictionary that would fulfill the needs not only of the scholar or foreigner wanting to study Amharic, but also of the Ethiopian student whose language of instruction is English is a great necessity. This dictionary should record the literary as well as the present-day spoken language.

Argobba

Argobba is spoken in the region of Ankober to the north of Addis Ababa in the Moslem villages of Aliyu Amba, Çanno, and a few others. The language is disappearing in favor of Amharic.

Argobba was also spoken to the south of Harar, but the language disappeared in favor of Galla.

A small collection of words of so-called Argobba was given by U.J. Seetzen[253] and C.T. Lefebvre.[254] Their collections were utilized by F. Praetorius[255] and Marcel Cohen.[256] The present writer proved that the vocabularies are not Argobba, but Gurage of the Selti-Wolane type.[257] Seetzen and Lefebvre most probably collected these words from Gurage speakers living in the region of Argobba.

A vocabulary of South Argobba (that is, the Argobba of the region of Harar) was collected by Mme de Monfreid who lived in the region of Harar. The material was elaborated by Marcel Cohen[258] who gave a brief outline of Argobba on the basis of the various forms given in the vocabulary and published the vocabulary classifying it according to subjects.

A text in poetry in Ethiopic script only, without translation, collected by C. Mondon-Vidailhet, was published by E. Weinzinger.[259]

The present writer collected material for the description of the language and a vocabulary. On the basis of his still unpublished material he gave a preliminary description of the language;[260] suggested that Argobba is, of all the Ethiopian languages, the closest to Amharic;[261] investigated the Arabic loanwords in Argobba;[262]

[253] 'Seetzen's linguistischer Nachlass', in J.S. Vater, *Proben deutscher Volksmundarten*, 301–3 (Leipzig, 1816).
[254] *Voyage en Abyssinie exécuté pendant les années 1839–1843*, 3.405–9 (Paris [1845]).
[255] *Die amharische Sprache*, p. 14 and passim (Halle, 1879).
[256] *Etudes d'éthiopien méridional*, 364–6 (Paris, 1931).
[257] 'Examen du supposé argobba de Seetzen et de Lefebvre', *Word* 5.46–54 (1949).
[258] *Nouvelles études d'éthiopien méridional*, 419–26 (Paris, 1939).
[259] *Etudes sur le guragiē*, 95–119 (Wien, 1913). For these texts, see also E. Cerulli, *RRAL*, ser. 5, vol. 25.633–6 (1916), and M. Cohen, *Etudes d'éthiopien méridional*, 362–3 (Paris, 1931).
[260] 'A preliminary description of Argobba', *AE* 3.251–73 (1959).
[261] 'Sketches in Ethiopic classification', *ACISE* 93–8.
[262] 'Arabic loanwords in Argobba', *JAOS* 77.36–9 (1957).

and gave an analysis of the Argobba vocabulary with an index of the words mentioned in the article.[263]

As it can easily be seen, there is not yet adequate material to be used by the *éthiopisant* or by the Semitist.

Gafat

Gafat was a language spoken in the southern part of Godjam, in the region of the Blue Nile. At present the language is no longer spoken and the Gafat speak Amharic.

The only documents of this language consist of 1) a collection of words and the text of the 'Song of Songs' translated from Amharic into Gafat, partially published by James Bruce in 1790;[264] and 2) a collection of words published by C. T. Beke in 1845.[265]

These documents were elaborated by the present author in his book which contains a descriptive and comparative grammar of Gafat,[266] and the edition of the 'Song of Songs' in a photostatic copy.[267] The text is also transliterated and is given a literal and free translation into English. A comparative vocabulary of Gafat and an English-Gafat index conclude the book. Needless to say, the description of Gafat on the basis of a text written in Ethiopic script only could not be satisfactory. Indeed, neither the gemination nor the syllabic structure could be adequately described.

In an investigation made in Ethiopia in 1946–47 the present author found only four speakers of the language in the region of Womberma to the south of Godjam. On the basis of their speech he published a descriptive and comparative grammar of Gafat.[268] The book also contains an etymological vocabulary of Gafat, and a French-Gafat index.

The same author also examined the position of Gafat in Ethiopic and placed it with the Gurage dialect of Soddo.[269] In another study he suggested a parallel between Hebrew and Gafat in the non-gemination of *r*.[270]

Gurage

Gurage is a language cluster spoken in the region of Gurage, to the southwest of Addis Ababa, bordered on the north by the river Awash, on the east by Lake Zway and on the southwest by the river Omo. There are three subgroups in Gurage: 1) an Eastern group including Selti, Wolane (with variants of Ulbarag or Urbarag, and

[263] 'Analysis of the Argobba vocabulary', *JAfrL* 5.102–12 (1966).

[264] *Travels to discover the sources of the Nile*, 2.491–9 (2nd ed. Edinburgh, 1804).

[265] 'On the languages and dialectes of Abyssinia and the countries to the south', *PPS* 2.97–107 (1846).

[266] *Gafat documents. Records of a South Ethiopic language.* (New Haven, 1945).

[267] The manuscript is preserved in the Bodleian Library in Oxford.

[268] *Etude descriptive et comparative du gafat* (Paris, 1956).

[269] 'La position du gafat parmi les langues de l'Ethiopie', *GLECS* 5.47–8 (1948–51). Another opinion was expressed in *Lg* 20.56–65 (1944).

[270] 'A parallel to the non-gemination of the Hebrew *r*', *JBL* 68.55–6 (1949).

Inneqor), and the dialects spoken on the five islands of Lake Zway; 2) a Western group including Čaha, Eža, Ennemor, Endegeň, Gyeta, and possibly Muher, Masqan and Gogot; 3) and a Northern group represented by Soddo (previously called Aymellel).

The Gurage cluster is the most intriguing of all the Semitic languages of Ethiopia. Indeed, the great variety of dialects in a relatively small region is surprising. Besides, the high degree of unintelligibility is quite remarkable. A speaker of Selti will not understand a speaker of Čaha, and a speaker of Soddo will not be able to communicate with a speaker of Eža. And yet, there definitely is a Gurage cluster, as has been suggested by the present writer.[271]

Another intriguing problem is the classification of the Gurage dialects. The above mentioned classification was first suggested by Marcel Cohen[272] and accepted tentatively by myself. The suggestion made by R. Hetzron[273] of a Northern Gurage group including Soddo, Gogot, and Muher on the basis of a simple feature, namely the main verb markers, is too hasty to be accepted in the present state of our knowledge.

A valuable critical bibliography on the Gurage dialects and a discussion on the geographic and linguistic distribution of the Gurage dialects is given by Marcel Cohen.[274]

The earliest documents are those published by Johannes Mayer.[275] They contain some grammatical notes of a Gurage dialect that was recognized by C. Mondon-Vidailhet as belonging to Soddo (or Aymellel).[276] They also contain a small English-German-Amharic-Galla-Gurage vocabulary and the translation into Gurage of the second chapter of Matthew, in Ethiopic script only.

These documents as well as the translation of the 2nd chapter of the Gospel of John, in Ethiopic script only, were elaborated by F. Praetorius, who gave a brief grammatical description of the dialect.[277]

Another collection of words and some grammatical features in the dialect of Čaha were made by G. Chiarini and edited by A. Cecchi.[278]

A brief first-hand description of the dialect of Čaha was given by C. Mondon-Vidailhet[279] who on occasion compared Ulbarag, Gogot, Masqan, Wolane and Aymellel (= Soddo). However, the description and the transcription are inadequate.

On the basis of personal observations Marcel Cohen describes general features of

[271] 'Is there a Proto-Gurage?', *Proceedings of the International Conference of Semitic Studies*, 20 pages (Jerusalem, 1968).
[272] *Etudes d'éthiopien méridional*, 100–3 (Paris, 1931).
[273] 'Main verb-markers in Northern Gurage', *Africa* 38.156–72 (1968).
[274] *Etudes d'éthiopien méridional*, 57–62 (Paris, 1931).
[275] *Kurze Wörtersammlung in Englisch, Deutsch, Amharisch, Gallanisch, Guragesch* (Basel, 1878).
[276] *La langue harari et les dialectes éthiopiens du gouraghê*, 81 (Paris, 1902).
[277] *Die amharische Sprache*, 507–23 (Halle, 1879).
[278] *Da Zeila alla frontiere del Caffa*, 3.473–6 (Rome, 1887).
[279] *La langue harari et les dialectes éthiopiens du gouraghê*, 77–115 (Paris, 1902).

the phonology and morphology of Čaha, Muher, Aymellel and Wolane.[280] All these dialects are treated together.

H. J. Polotsky[281] investigated phonetic and morphological problems of Čaha on the basis of texts published by W. Leslau.

An outline of the essential features of Čaha is given by Leslau.[282] The same author published an outline of Soddo.[283]

A number of specific problems were discussed by various authors.

H. Fleisch[284] analyzes the verb forms *qatälä, qotälä, qetälä* of various Gurage dialects of previously published material. Since, however, his sources are defective, the author's observations have to be rectified.

H. J. Polotsky[285] investigates various problems such as gemination, alternance of liquids and the negative perfect, labialization and palatalization, and others; discusses the rounding of the impersonal in Muher because of an *l* in the root.[286]

F. Rundgren[287] discusses the infinitive in Ennemor, the imperfect in Gogot, Muher and Soddo, the negative jussive in Harari and Zway, the future with *šä, -se*, and others, using Leslau's source material. In another study he suggests an etymology for *ban(n)* 'he was'.[288]

A. J. Drewes[289] analyzes the type C in the East Gurage dialect of Azarnat-Mugo.

R. Hetzron[290] proposes a grouping of Soddo, Gogot and Muher into a Northern Gurage subgroup, but see above.

R. Hetzron and Habte Mariam Marcos[291] examine the nasalization in Ennemor over a chain of several phonemes and the labialization and prepalatalization.

W. Leslau attempts to prove that there is a Gurage cluster;[292] investigates the impersonal in Čaha from the phonetic, morphological and syntactic points of view;[293] analyzes the homonyms in Gurage;[294] the Arabic loanwords in Gurage;[295] the gemina-

[280] *Etudes d'éthiopien méridional*, 55–241 (Paris, 1931).
[281] *Notes on Gurage grammar* (Jerusalem, 1951).
[282] *Ethiopic documents: Gurage*, 12–32 (New York, 1950).
[283] *Ethiopians speak: Studies in cultural background. III. Soddo*, 6–34 (Berkeley and Los Angeles, 1968).
[284] *Les verbes à allongement vocalique interne en sémitique*, 383–414 (Paris, 1944).
[285] 'Etudes de grammaire gouragué', *BSL* 38.137–75 (1938).
[286] '*L* labialisé en gouragué muher', *GLECS* 3.66–8 (1937–40).
[287] *Intensiv und Aspektkorrelation*, 237–59 (Wiesbaden, 1959).
[288] 'Das Verbum *ban(n)*- in Gurage', *OS* 3.27–30 (1954).
[289] 'A propos de: Wolf Leslau, Le type verbal *qatälä* en éthiopien méridional', *BiOr* 17.5–10 (1960).
[290] 'Main verb-markers in Northern Gurage', *Africa* 38.156–72 (1968).
[291] 'Des traits pertinents superposés en ennemor', *JEthS* 4.17–30 (1965).
[292] See fn. 271.
[293] 'The impersonal in Chaha', *To honor Roman Jakobson*, Essays on the occasion of his seventieth birthday, 1150–62 (The Hague, 1967).
[294] 'Homonyms in Gurage', *JAOS* 80.200–17 (1960).
[295] 'Arabic loanwords in Gurage', *Arabica* 3.266–84 (1956).

tion of the Čaha verb[296] and of the dialect of Azarnat-Mugo;[297] the influence of Sidamo on Gurage;[298] the classification of Zway;[299] supplementary observations on Čaha;[300] and type C in Gurage.[301]

An exchange of articles between E. Ullendorff[302] and W. Leslau[303] deals mainly with the method of making a linguistic enquête, the case in question being that of Gurage.

The present writer is particularly interested in investigating Proto-Ethiopic or Proto-Semitic features in Gurage. He proves it through finding traces of laryngeals in Ennemor;[304] through various forms of the jussive (that is, **yəngər*, **yənəgr*, **yəngär*) in Western Gurage and particularly in Čaha and Eža, forms found only in Geez;[305] through the vowel *ä* of the prefix of the jussive in some Gurage dialects;[306] and through the marker *-u* of the main imperfect.[307]

There is not yet an exhaustive dictionary of any of the Gurage dialects.

J. Mayer[308] published a brief vocabulary in English-German-Amharic-Galla-Gurage, partially in Ethiopic script and transcription and partially in Ethiopic script only.

G. Chiarini[309] gave a short Italian-Čaha vocabulary, in a defective transcription.

A French-Gurage(Čaha, Ulbarag, Gogot)-Amharic vocabulary, partially in Ethiopic script and partially in a defective transcription, was collected by F. Mondon-Vidailhet and edited by E. Weinzinger.[310]

Marcel Cohen[311] published a brief French-Gurage (Muher, Čaha, Aymellel, Wolane) vocabulary, arranged according to subjects.

W. Leslau[312] compiled a Čaha-English glossary of all the words referring to the Čaha texts.

Very few texts were published until recently. J. Mayer has a one-page text of the 2nd chapter of the Gospel of Matthew, in Ethiopic script only.[313] The second chapter

[296] 'Le problème de la gémination du verbe chaha', *Word* 4.42–7 (1948).
[297] 'Remarks on the gemination of the Gurage dialect of Azarnat-Mugo', *BiOr* 18.19–20 (1961).
[298] 'The influence of Sidamo on the Ethiopian languages of Gurage', *Lg* 28.63–81 (1952).
[299] 'Sketches in Ethiopic classification', *ACISE* 98–102.
[300] 'Observations on Gurage documents', *Word* 6.234–8 (1950).
[301] 'Le type verbal *qatälä* en éthiopien méridional', *MUSJ* 31.15–98 (1954).
[302] 'Gurage notes', *Africa* 20.335–44 (1950); 'A further Gurage note', *Africa* 21.248–9 (1951).
[303] 'Observations on "Gurage notes"', *Africa* 21.139–45 (1951).
[304] 'Traces of the laryngeals in the Ethiopic dialect of Ennemor', *Or* 28.257–70 (1959).
[305] 'Le type läbsä en Gurage', *RSEt* 10.85–98 (1951); 'The jussive in Chaha', *Lg* 40.53–7 (1964); 'The jussive in Eža', *JSS* 12.66–82 (1967).
[306] 'An archaic vowel of the jussive in Gurage, Gafat, and Harari', *Or* 37.90–3 (1968).
[307] 'Hypothesis on a Proto-Semitic marker of the imperfect in Gurage', *JNES* 26.121–5 (1967).
[308] See no. 275.
[309] 'Note grammaticale e vocaboli della lingua ciaha', in Antonio Cecchi, *Da Zaila alla frontiere del Caffa*, 3.477–84 (Rome, 1887).
[310] *Etudes sur le guragiē*, 10–92 (Wien, 1913).
[311] *Etudes d'éthiopien méridional*, 216–30 (Paris, 1931).
[312] *Ethiopic documents: Gurage*, 145–68 (New York, 1950).
[313] *Kurze Wörtersammlung in Englisch, Deutsch, Amharisch, Gallanisch, Guraguesch*, 27–8 (Basel, 1878).

of the Gospel of John in the Gurage dialect of Soddo was published by F. Praetorius.[314] F. Mondon-Vidailhet published three pages in Čaha,[315] in phonetic transcription and French translation. Azaïs and R. Chambard[316] collected a few songs in Čaha. Marcel Cohen[317] published phrases and some texts (in prose and poetry) in the dialects of Muher, Soddo, and Wolane, in transcription and translation.

A Catechism of the Roman Catholic church was published in the Čaha dialect[318] in Ethiopic script, without translation.

W. Leslau[319] published texts in Čaha in transcription, with an interlinear and free translation into English. The texts are of ethnographic character. The same collection also includes folktales, poems and proverbs.

The same author inaugurated a series "Ethiopians speak: Studies in cultural background" in which the life of the various ethnic groups is described by the speakers of these languages. At his request students wrote down texts dealing with the various aspects of their life. The texts were in Ethiopic script and W. Leslau transcribed them phonetically and gave an interlinear and a free translation. The second volume of the series is an autobiography of Sahle Sellasie, a native of Čaha.[320] The text is in Ethiopic script, transcribed phonetically and translated into English. In the third volume, Hailu Fullas described the life of the Soddo, in the dialect of Soddo.[321] These texts are in phonetic transcription, with an interlinear and free translation.

W. Leslau also published songs[322] and riddles in Čaha[323] and riddles in Eža.[324]

The problems and challenges in Gurage are many. There are not yet any full descriptions of any of the dialects nor are there dictionaries of the various dialects. The present writer is working at present on a comparative dictionary of twelve Gurage dialects.

Harari

Harari, called Adäre or Gē sinān by the inhabitants, is spoken only in the city of Harar in eastern Ethiopia.

The Harari are Moslems and their literature, in prose and poetry, deals mainly with Moslem religious subjects. The writings are in Arabic script, but very few

[314] *Die amharische Sprache*, 507–8 (Halle, 1879).
[315] 'Les dialectes éthiopiens du gouraghê', *RS* 9.67–70 (1901); *Etudes sur le guragiē*, 1–7 (Wien, 1913).
[316] 'Notes sur quelques coutumes observées en gouragué', *RETP* 8.39–44 (1927).
[317] *Etudes d'éthiopien méridional*, 231–41 (Paris, 1931).
[318] *Aç̣ç̣ər təmhərtä krəstiyan bäčäha qʷanqʷa* ... (Dire-Dauoa, 1926 [= 1934]).
[319] *Ethiopic documents: Gurage*, 33–144 (New York, 1950).
[320] *Ethiopians speak: Studies in cultural background. II. Chaha* (Berkeley and Los Angeles, 1966).
[321] *Ethiopians speak: Studies in cultural background. III. Soddo* (Berkeley and Los Angeles, 1968).
[322] 'The farmer in Chaha song', *Africa* 34.230–42 (1964).
[323] 'Chaha riddles', *RSEt* 31.27–93 (1965).
[324] 'Eža riddles', *RSEt* 33.

specimens of them are published. Only recently did Western scholars collect and publish texts in Harari.

The first collection of Harari words was published by H. Salt.[325] Other documents consisting of vocabularies, collections of sentences, and general grammatical observations, were published by C. Beke,[326] R. F. Burton,[327] P. Paulitschke,[328] and L. Bricchetti-Robecchi.[329] These first-hand documents, collected by more or less trained linguists, were elaborated by F. Müller,[330] who was the first to assign Harari to the Semitic languages of Ethiopia and not to Cushitic, as was done before him. A grammatical analysis on the basis of the previously mentioned documents was also published by F. Praetorius[331] and E. Littmann.[332] The texts edited by C. Conti Rossini[333] were also analyzed by E. Littmann[334] from the grammatical point of view. Some grammatical features were also mentioned by Ricardo de Santis[335] on the basis of a few texts collected by him.

The first systematic grammar was published by C. Mondon-Vidailhet.[336] It is based on material collected from a Harari informant. The grammatical forms are given in the Ethiopic script which cannot render the actual pronunciation, and especially not the vowel quantity, an important feature in the Harari phonology. Indeed, Harari is one of the few Ethiopian languages that has long and short vowels with phonemic value. The Ethiopic script cannot render this feature.

The grammar of M. Cohen,[337] while not giving a complete description of the language, describes in exact terms the general character of Harari. The forms are given in phonetic transcription.

A more complete grammar is that of E. Cerulli.[338] The grammar is based on material collected by the author. The phonetic phenomena are explained through comparison with the other Ethiopian languages. The morphology is descriptive. The morphology as well as the syntax are based on the phrases and texts collected by the author; as a result, some grammatical forms not mentioned in the texts are not given by the author. While the grammar contains the main features of the language it is not exhaustive.

[325] *A voyage to Abyssinia and travels into the interior of that country*. Appendix I., pp. vi-x (London, 1814).
[326] 'On the languages and dialects of Abyssinia and the countries to the south', *PPS* 2.97–107 (1846).
[327] *First footsteps in Africa*, 536–82 (London, 1856).
[328] *Beiträge zur Ethnographie und Anthropologie der Somâl, Galla und Hararî*, 81–90 (Leipzig, 1888).
[329] 'Lingue parlate somali, galla e harari', *BSGI* ser. 3, vol. 3, pp. 257–71, 380–91, 689–708 (1890).
[330] 'Über die Harari-Sprache im östlichen Africa', *SWAW* 44.601–13 (1863).
[331] 'Über die Sprache von Harar', *ZDMG* 23.453–72 (1869).
[332] 'Harari-Studien', *ZS* 1.38–84 (1922).
[333] 'Testi in lingua harari', *RSO* 8.401–25 (1919–20).
[334] 'Bemerkungen zu den neuen Harari-Texten', *ZDMG* 75.21–36 (1921).
[335] 'Piccoli testi harari', *RSO* 18.386–98 (1940).
[336] *La langue harari et les dialectes éthiopiens du gouraghê*, 1–75 (1902).
[337] *Etudes d'éthiopien méridional*, 243–354 (Paris, 1931).
[338] *Studi etiopici. I. La lingua e la storia di Harar*, 56–203 (Rome, 1936).

The Harari verb is the subject of a monograph published by W. Leslau.[339] It is a descriptive and comparative study of the Harari verb based on documents the author collected in Ethiopia. An index gives all the verbs mentioned in the body of the book.

In the field of specific grammatical problems mention should be made of E. Littmann who investigated the meaning of the particle *-ma*[340] on the basis of the texts collected by R. Burton,[341] L. Bricchetti-Robecchi,[342] and P. Paulitschke.[343]

The verb forms *qatälä, qotälä, qetälä* are analyzed by H. Fleisch.[344]

W. Leslau published supplements to the Harari grammar as described by E. Cerulli[345] and discussed the dialectal position of Harari. The same author connects Harari with East Gurage.[346] Elsewhere he analyses the expression of 'while', the pseudo-object suffix pronouns, the possessive suffix pronouns (among them a suffix pronoun of the generalized impersonal 'one's', not found in the other Ethiopian languages), the positional relation in a combination of nouns, and the nominalization of the relative verb forms.[347]

The vocabularies of H. Salt,[348] C. Beke,[349] R. Burton,[350] L. Bricchetti-Robecchi,[351] and P. Paulitschke[352] were edited by W. Leslau with an etymological analysis.[353] A French-Harari index was added to it.

A Harari-Italian vocabulary of about 750 roots with an Italian-Harari index was published by E. Cerulli.[354] The vocabulary is comparative and etymological.

W. Leslau published a Harari-English vocabulary[355] of about 2500 roots collected through texts and through questioning. The dictionary is comparative and etymological. It also contains an index of the Semitic roots cognate with Harari roots, an index of the Arabic loanwords, and an English-Harari index.

The present writer also analyzed the Harari vocabulary in its relation to the other Ethiopian languages;[356] investigated the Arabic loanwords in Harari, discussing at

339 *The verb in Harari* (University of California Publications in Semitic Philology, 21, 1958).
340 'Die Partikel *ma* im Harari', *ZA* 33.103–22 (1931).
341 See fn. 327.
342 See fn. 329.
343 See fn. 328.
344 *Les verbes à allongement vocalique interne en sémitique*, 357–82 (Paris, 1944).
345 'Contributions à l'étude du harari', *JA* 229.433–57 (1937).
346 'Sketches in Ethiopic classification', *ACISE* 102–7.
347 'Gleanings from the Harari vocabulary', *RSEt* 16.23–37 (1960).
348 See fn. 325.
349 See fn. 326.
350 See fn. 327.
351 See fn. 329.
352 See fn. 328.
353 'Contributions à l'étude du harari', *JA* 229.460–79, 529–91 (1937).
354 *Studi etiopici. I. La lingua e la storia di Harar*, 229–81, 443–62 (Rome, 1936).
355 *Etymological dictionary of Harari* (Berkeley and Los Angeles, 1963).
356 'An analysis of the Harari vocabulary', *AE* 3.275–98 (1959).

the same time the phonetic and morphological treatment of the loanwords;[357] and published gleanings from the Harari vocabulary such as the use of *aša*, metathesis, words and things, kinds of drums, and so on.[358]

It was said above that there are writings in Harari written in Arabic script. These writings deal with religious subjects, but, unfortunately, with the exception of the text discussed below, they are still unpublished.

While some phrases and small texts were published by various authors, it is with E. Cerulli that we begin to have more abundant texts in Harari. Indeed Cerulli published 24 pages of folktales and phrases which he translated into Italian.[359]

W. Leslau[360] collected Harari songs which he translated into French. In the series 'Ethiopians speak' he published a collection of texts[361] written down in Ethiopic characters, at his request, by students from Harar. The present writer transcribed them phonetically and gave an interlinear and free translation into English. These texts deal with various aspects of Harari life, such as household, food and drinks, associations, engagement and wedding, birth, holiday, and so on.

In summing up our documentation on Harari it is reasonable to state that while we have adequate dictionaries and a good number of texts we still lack a complete description of the language.

'Ancient Harari'

The ethnographer Paulitschke acquired in Ethiopia a Harari manuscript (at present in the Bibliothèque Nationale of Paris) dating approximately from the beginning of the eighteenth century, written in Arabic characters, in a language slightly different from modern Harari. Marcel Cohen[362] who interpreted a fragment of it and investigated some grammatical features of this text calls it 'Chansons de noce', or 'Wedding songs'. These songs come very close to those published by W. Leslau.[363]

Another manuscript written in Arabic script is the *Kitāb al-Farā'id* 'The book of the religious precepts'. E. Cerulli,[364] the editor of this text, designates the language as 'Ancient Harari'. He edited the text in its original, transliterated it and translated it into Italian. He also worked out a grammatical description of the language and compiled a vocabulary on the basis of the text.

[357] 'Arabic loanwords in Harari', *Studi orientalistici in onore di Giorgio Levi della Vida*, 2.14–35 (Rome, 1956).
[358] 'Gleanings from the Harari vocabulary', *RSEt* 16.23–37 (1960).
[359] *Studi etiopici. I. La lingua e la storia di Harar*, 204–28 (Rome, 1936).
[360] 'Chansons harari', *RSEt* 7.130–60 (1947).
[361] *Ethiopians speak: Studies in cultural background. I. Harar* (Berkeley and Los Angeles, 1965).
[362] *Etudes d'éthiopien méridional*, 328–54 (Paris, 1931).
[363] See fn. 360.
[364] *Studi etiopici. I. La lingua e la storia di Harar*, 282–442 (Rome, 1936).

The phonetic status of this 'Ancient Harari' was examined by W. Leslau.[365]

It would be desirable to edit more texts of this kind so as to gain a better insight into the language of the Harari literature written in Arabic script.

General Problems

This section will deal with subjects that are not limited to one specific Ethiopian language, but concern at least two languages. Studies on general Semitic in which Ethiopic is also treated will not be mentioned here. The comparative grammars of Semitic will, therefore, not be discussed.

BIBLIOGRAPHIES on Ethiopia in which the languages are mentioned are those of G. Fumagali,[366] G. F. Black,[367] and J. Simon.[368]

Bibliographies dealing specifically with the Ethiopian languages were published by W. Leslau.[369] His annotated bibliography[370] has an index of authors and a subject index apart from the division into individual languages.

Critical studies as well as studies describing the state of Ethiopic linguistics are those of I. Guidi,[371] C. Conti Rossini,[372] Mauro da Leonessa,[373] I. Kračkovskij,[374] M. Cohen,[375] and W. Leslau.[376]

A SURVEY of the Ethiopian languages is given by M. Cohen,[377] C. Conti Rossini,[378]

[365] 'Contributions à l'étude du harari', *JA* 229.448–52 (1937).

[366] *Bibliografia etiopica.* Catalogo descrittivo e ragionato degli scritti pubblicati dalla invenzione della stampa fino a tutto il 1891 intorno alla Etiopia e regioni limitrofi (Milano, 1893).

[367] *Ethiopica & Amharica.* A list of works in the New York Public Library (New York, 1928).

[368] 'Bibliographie éthiopienne', *Or* 21.47–66, 209–30 (1952).

[369] *Bibliography of the Semitic languages of Ethiopia* (New York, 1946).

[370] *An annotated bibliography of the Semitic languages of Ethiopia* (The Hague, 1965).

[371] 'Lo studio dell'amarico in Europa', *Actes du onzième congrès international des orientalists*, 4th section, 67–76 (Paris, 1898); 'Langues éthiopiennes', *L'année linguistique* 1.109–33 (1902), 4.13–58 (1910); 'Bolletino. Africa. Abissinia', *RSO* 1.157–63 (1907), 2.120–6 (1908–9), 3.154–65 (1910).

[372] 'Rapport sur le progrès des études éthiopiennes depuis le dernier congrès (1894–97)', *Actes du onzième congrès international des orientalists*, 4th section, 27–66 (Paris, 1898); 'Etiopia (1915–27)', *Aevum* 1.459–520 (1927); 'Bibliografia etiopica (1927–giugno 1936)', *Aevum* 10.467–587 (1936); 'Publicazioni etiopistiche dal 1936 al 1945', *RSEt* 4.1–133 (1945).

[373] 'Linguistica etiopica. Gli studi sulle lingue della colonia Eritrea', *Atti del primo congresso di studi coloniali*, 4.147–56 (Firenze, 1931).

[374] *Vvedenie v étiopskuju filologiju.* (*Introduction to Ethiopic philology*). (Leningrad, 1955).

[375] 'Linguistique éthiopienne: état des travaux et perspectives pour le proche avenir', *ACISE* 59–73.

[376] 'The present state of Ethiopic linguistics', *JNES* 5.215–29 (1946); 'Report on Ethiopic linguistics', *JNES* 17.49–55 (1958).

[377] 'Langues éthiopiennes', in A. Meillet and M. Cohen, *Les langues du monde*, 122–7 (Paris, 1924); 2nd ed. 142–8 (Paris, 1952).

[378] *Etiopia e genti d'Etiopia*, 123–69 (Firenze, 1937).

N. V. Yushmanov,[379] M. A. Bryan[380] (with slight modification in A. N. Tucker and M. A. Bryan),[381] W. Leslau,[382] and E. Ullendorff.[383]

COMPARATIVE GRAMMARS. There is no comparative grammar of Semitic Ethiopic dealing in a systematic way with the phonology, morphology, and syntax of the languages. There are, however, studies or grammars of individual languages in which comparisons are made with the other Ethiopian languages.

E. Ullendorff[384] published the most systematic comparative phonology dealing with the consonants, vowels, accent and selected problems of combinatory effect, such as consonant clusters, vowel harmony, and so on.

F. Praetorius in his grammars of Tigrinya[385] and Amharic[386] compared the other Ethiopian languages.

E. Cerulli's grammar of Harari,[387] and particularly the phonology, is of a comparative nature.

W. Leslau in his grammars of Gafat[388] and Tigre,[389] and in his study of the Harari verb,[390] made comparisons with the other Ethiopian languages. The same author also published a brief comparative study of the Semitic Ethiopian languages.[391]

COMPARATIVE DICTIONARIES. There is no general comparative dictionary of the Ethiopian languages. As is the case with the grammars, there are, however, dictionaries of individual languages in which etymologies are suggested and comparisons are made with the other Ethiopian languages.

The dictionaries of this kind are: H. Ludolf's Amharic dictionary;[392] A. Dillmann's Geez dictionary;[393] C. H. Armbruster's Amharic dictionary;[394] E. Cerulli's Harari dictionary;[395] E. Littmann's Tigre dictionary[396] (where only Geez, Amharic and Tigrin-

[379] 'Iazyki Abisinii', *Akademiya Nauk. Institut Antropologii i Etnografii. Abyssinia*, 259–91 (Moscow, 1936).
[380] *The distribution of the Semitic and Cushitic languages of Ethiopia*, 25–6 (London, 1947).
[381] *The Non-Bantu languages of Northeastern Africa*, 132–6 (London, 1956).
[382] 'The languages of Ethiopia and their geographical distribution', *EO* 116–21 (1958).
[383] *Exploration and study of Abyssinia*, 65–70 (Asmara, 1945); *The Ethiopians*, 116–35 (London, 1960).
[384] *The Semitic languages of Ethiopia. A comparative phonology* (London, 1955).
[385] See fn. 105.
[386] See fn. 162.
[387] See fn. 338.
[388] See fns. 266, 268.
[389] See fn. 87.
[390] See fn. 339.
[391] 'Characteristics of the Ethiopic language group of Semitic languages', in A. N. Tucker and M. A. Bryan, *The Non-Bantu languages of North-eastern Africa*, 593–613 (Oxford, 1966).
[392] See fn. 216.
[393] See fn. 44.
[394] See fn. 222.
[395] See fn. 354.
[396] See fn. 103.

ya are compared); W. Leslau's Gafat[397] and Harari[398] dictionaries. The same author also published a study dealing with Ethiopic and South Arabic etymologies and comparisons to the Biblical Hebrew lexicon.[399] It should be pointed out that L. Reinisch in his various dictionaries of the Cushitic languages[400] made comparisons with Semitic Ethiopic.

SPECIFIC PROBLEMS OF GRAMMAR. There are numerous articles dealing with specific subjects in phonology, morphology, and syntax. Only the basic articles will be given here. Needless to say, many of these problems were also discussed in the various grammars.

M. Cohen deals with the laryngeals;[401] with consonant clusters and gemination;[402] and with phonetic problems of South Ethiopic such as liquids, weakening of labials, prepalatalization, and others.[403]

I. Wajnberg[404] deals with the traces of the dual in modern Ethiopic.

F. R. Palmer[405] concerns himself with the possibility of making descriptive and comparative statements about the Ethiopian languages.

W. Leslau discusses the frequentative stem in Ethiopic;[406] the type C in South Ethiopic taking up a problem investigated by H. Fleisch;[407] the existence of archaic features in South Ethiopic;[408] and general problems of the Ethiopian languages.[409]

M. L. Bender[410] applies glottochronological analysis to some Semitic Ethiopic languages. However, more information is necessary.

The classification of the Ethiopian languages is investigated by M. Cohen[411] and W. Leslau.[412]

The relation between Ethiopic and South Arabic as well as between Ethiopic,

397 See fns. 266, 268.

398 See fn. 355.

399 *Ethiopic and South Arabic contributions to the Hebrew lexicon* (Berkeley and Los Angeles, 1958).

400 To cite only *Wörterbuch der Bilin-Sprache* (Wien, 1887); *Wörterbuch der Beḍauye-Sprache* (Wien, 1895).

401 'Consonnes laryngales et voyelles en éthiopien. Conjugaison des verbes à laryngale médiane et finale', *JA* 210.19–57 (1927).

402 'Groupes de consonnes au début du mot en éthiopien', *Cinquantenaire de l'Ecole Pratique des Hautes Etudes,* 141–59 (Paris, 1921); 'Des groupes de consonnes et de quelques géminations en éthiopien', *MSL* 23.72–100 (1927).

403 *Etudes d'éthiopien méridional,* 377–403 (Paris, 1931).

404 'Dualreste und Dualspuren im Neuabessinischen', *RO* 13.19–23 (1937).

405 'Comparative statement and Ethiopic Semitic', *TPhS* 119–43 (1958).

406 'Le thème verbal fréquentatif dans les langues éthiopiennes', *RESm* 15–31 (1938).

407 'Le type verbal *qatälä* en éthiopien méridional', *MUSJ* 21.15–95 (1954).

408 'Archaic features in South Ethiopic', *JAOS* 71.212–30 (1951).

409 *The scientific investigation of the Ethiopic languages.* An inaugural lecture delivered on 12 February 1954, at the University College of Addis Ababa (Leiden, 1956).

410 'Notes on lexical correlation in some Ethiopian languages', *JEthS* 4.5–15 (1966).

411 *Etudes d'éthiopien méridional,* 1–52 (Paris, 1931).

412 'Sketches in Ethiopic classification', *ACISE* 89–107.

South Arabic and Akkadian or Semitic in general was discussed by V. Christian,[413] J. Cantineau,[414] M. Moscati,[415] W. Leslau,[416] M. Höfner,[417] W. Müller,[418] E. Ullendorff,[419] and A. Murtonen.[420]

Problems of the verbal system and the derived stems were investigated by F. Rundgren.[421] In his thesis Getatchew Haile[422] analyzes certain verb forms.

The labials and the labiovelars were studied by H. Grimme,[423] J. Kuryłowicz,[424] A. Klingenheben,[425] E. Ullendorff,[426] and by various members of GLECS.[427]

The influence of Cushitic on Semitic in phonology, morphology, syntax and vocabulary was investigated by F. Praetorius,[428] M. M. Moreno,[429] and W. Leslau.[430] C. Brockelmann published a study on the Cushitic loanwords in the modern languages of Ethiopia.[431]

E. Wagner[432] brings to our attention an intriguing problem dealing with grammatical features common to the Northwest African dialects and to the Ethiopian languages.

413 'Akkader und Südaraber als ältere Semitenschichte', *Anthropos* 14/15.729–39 (1919–20).

414 'Accadien et sudarabique', *BSL* 33.175–204 (1932).

415 'Nordarabico, sudarabico, etiopico', *RSO* 34.33–9 (1959).

416 'Southeast Semitic (Ethiopic and South Arabic)', *JAOS* 63.4–14 (1943); 'The position of Ethiopic in Semitic: Akkadian and Ethiopic', *Akten des vierundzwanzigsten internationalen Orientalistenkongress*, 251–3 (München, 1959).

417 'Über sprachliche und kulturelle Beziehungen zwischen Südarabien und Äthiopien im Altertum', *ACISE* 435–45.

418 'Über Beziehungen zwischen den südarabischen Sprachen und den abessinischen Sprachen', *JSS* 9.50–5 (1964).

419 'The Semitic languages of Ethiopia and their contribution to general Semitic studies', *Africa* 25.154–60 (1955).

420 *Early Semitic*. A diachronical inquiry into the relationship of Ethiopic to the other so-called South-east Semitic languages (Leiden, 1967).

421 *Intensiv und Aspektkorrelation*. Studien zur äthiopischen und akkadischen Verbalstammbildung, 47–60, 129–236 (Wiesbaden, 1959).

422 *Das Verbalsystem im Athiopischen*. Ein morphologischer Vergleich mit den orientalischen semitischen Sprachen. Inaugural-Dissertation zur Erlangung des Doktorats (Tübingen, 1961).

423 'Theorie der ursemitischen labialisierten Gutturale: Ein Beitrag zur Verständigung über den Begriff Ursemitisch', *ZDMG* 55.447–86 (1901).

424 'Les labio-vélaires éthiopiens', *RO* 9.37–42 (1933).

425 'Die *w*- und *y*-haltigen Konsonanten abessinischer Semitensprachen mit besonderer Berücksichtigung des Amharischen', *RSEt* 14.25–47 (1959).

426 'The labiovelars in the Ethiopian languages', *RSEt* 10.71–84 (1951).

427 'Entretien sur la formation des labio-vélaires en chamito-sémitique', *GLECS* 3.7–8 (1937–40).

428 'Hamitische Bestandteile im Aethiopischen', *ZDMG* 43.317–26 (1889); 'Kuschitische Bestandteile im Aethiopischen', *ZDMG* 47.385–94 (1893).

429 'L'azione del cuscitico sul sistema morfologica delle lingue semitiche d'Etiopia', *RSEt* 7.121–30 (1948).

430 'The influence of Cushitic on the Semitic languages of Ethiopia', *Word* 1.59–82 (1945); 'Sidamo features in South Ethiopic phonology', *JAOS* 79.1–7 (1959); 'The influence of the Cushitic substratum on Semitic Ethiopic re-examined', *Trudy XXV mezhunarodnogo Kongressa vostokovedov*, Moskva, 9–16 avgusta, 1960, 1.387–90 (Moscow, 1962).

431 *Abessinische Studien*, 4–40 (Berlin, 1950).

432 'Der Yemen als Vermittler äthiopischen Sprachgutes nach Nordwestafrica', *Sprache* 12.252–79 (1966).

According to him Yemen would be the 'Ausstrahlungsgebiet' for these common features. The problem requires further investigation.

W. Leslau[433] analyzes the contributions made by the Ethiopian languages to Semitic linguistics, to Hamito-Semitic linguistics, and to linguistics in general.

SPECIFIC PROBLEMS OF LEXICOGRAPHY. There is a number of individual studies dealing with etymologies. Here again, only the essential studies will be mentioned.

F. Hommel [434] gives the names of animals in Ethiopic, with Semitic etymologies.

Hebrew and Ethiopic etymologies are treated by I. Eitan.[435]

E. Ullendorff discusses the contribution of Ethiopic and Epigraphic South Arabic to the Hebrew vocabulary.[436]

W. Müller compares Ethiopic roots with Egyptian roots.[437] The root *šft* of modern Ethiopic is compared by F. Rundgren with Egyptian *ḫfty*.[438] The same author suggests etymologies for some modern Ethiopic roots,[439] and discusses Ethiopic roots with *š*- and *n-t* formation.[440]

The present writer examines the echo-words in Ethiopic;[441] the names of the fingers;[442] the names of the weekdays;[443] Ethiopic denominatives with nominal morphemes;[444] mutilated roots in various Gurage dialects due to phonetic developments;[445] words common to Ethiopic and South Arabic;[446] words common to Akkadian, Ethiopic and South Arabic;[447] and suggests Ethiopic cognates to Akkadian.[448]

Hindu words in Ethiopic are examined by J. Halévy[449] and E. Littmann.[450]

Loanwords in the various Ethiopic languages were already mentioned in the sections dealing with the individual languages. W. Leslau[451] gave an analysis of phonetic

[433] *The land of Prester John*. Faculty Research Lecture (Los Angeles, 1968).
[434] *Die Namen der Säugethiere bei den südsemitischen Völkern*, 359–70 (Leipzig, 1879).
[435] 'Ethiopic and Hebrew etymologies', *AJSL* 40.269–76 (1924).
[436] 'The contributions of South Semitic to Hebrew lexicography', *VT* 6.190–8 (1956).
[437] 'Äthiopisches zur semitisch-ägyptischen Wortvergleichung', *Muséon* 54.199–205 (1961).
[438] 'The root *šft* in the Modern Ethiopic languages (Tigre, Tigriña, and Amharic) and old Egyptian *ḫfty*, Coptic *šft*', *OS* 2.19–25 (1953).
[439] 'Neoaethiopica', *SL* 8.92–102 (1954).
[440] *Über Bildungen mit* š- *und* n-t- *Demonstrativen im Semitischen*, 19–112, 186–290 (Uppsala, 1955).
[441] 'Echo-words in Ethiopic', *AE* 4.205–38 (1961).
[442] 'The names of the fingers in Ethiopic', *Orbis* 9.388–97 (1960).
[443] 'The names of the weekdays in Ethiopic', *JSS* 6.62–70 (1961).
[444] 'Ethiopic denominatives with nominal morphemes', *Muséon* 75.139–75 (1962).
[445] 'Some mutilated roots in Ethiopic', *Lingua* 6.268–86 (1957).
[446] 'South-east Semitic (Ethiopic and South Arabic)', *JAOS* 63.11–14 (1943).
[447] 'Vocabulary common to Akkadian and South-east Semitic (Ethiopic and South Arabic)', *JAOS* 64.53–8 (1944).
[448] 'South-east Semitic cognates to the Akkadian vocabulary', *JAOS* 82.1–4 (1962), 84.115–18 (1964).
[449] 'Indien und Abessinien', *Beiträge zur Literaturwissenschaft und Geistesgeschichte Indiens, Festgabe Herman Iacobi*, 406–17 (Bonn, 1926).
[450] 'Traces d'influence indo-parsie en Abyssinie', *RS* 4.258–65 (1896).
[451] 'The phonetic treatment of the Arabic loanwords in Ethiopic', *Word* 13.100–23 (1957).

and etymological correspondences between the Arabic and Ethiopian sounds in the Arabic loanwords.

The present writer also investigated the argot of people possessed by a spirit,[452] a merchants' argot,[453] a minstrels' argot,[454] an argot of a Gurage secret society,[455] and examined the linguistic principles underlying the various argots.[456]

PERIODICALS. There is no periodical devoted solely to linguistic studies. However, the periodicals listed below also deal with linguistic problems.

Aethiops, Bulletin Geʿez, was edited by Sylvain Grébaut, vol. 1–6, 1922–38. It contains mainly editions of texts in Geez, but deals occasionally with language problems of Geez. It is no longer published.

Aethiopica, Revue philologique, was edited by S. Grébaut, vol. 1–4, 1933–36. It contains the same subject matter as in *Aethiops* and is no longer published.

Rassegna di Studi Etiopici, published by the Istituto per l'Oriente, is devoted to general subjects on Ethiopia including linguistics. Since 1941, 22 volumes have appeared.

Annales d'Ethiopie, published by the Section d'archéologie du gouvernement Imperial d'Ethiopie, is devoted mainly to archeology. Since 1955, 7 volumes have appeared.

Journal of Ethiopian Studies, published by Haile Sellassie I University, Institute of Ethiopian Studies, is devoted to general subject on Ethiopia, including linguistics. Since 1963, 5 volumes have appeared.

TO SUM UP the achievements in the studies dealing with all the Semitic Ethiopic languages it can easily be seen that a comparative grammar of Semitic Ethiopic and an etymological dictionary are still lacking. The time has not yet come, however, to accomplish this task since there are still considerable gaps in our knowledge of the individual languages.

A brief REVIEW of the trends in the last thirty or forty years reveals that relatively little was added to our knowledge of Geez. In the last two decades, practical grammars and textbooks of Amharic were compiled for reasons mentioned above. Regardless, however, of the practical aspects, considerable attention was given to the investigation of the modern languages of Ethiopia apart from Amharic. Collections of texts in languages that had no writings were made, and descriptive and comparative studies were compiled. The syntax was given more attention than previously. Here and there a struc-

[452] 'An Ethiopian argot of people possessed by a spirit', *Africa* 19.204–12 (1949).
[453] 'An Ethiopian merchants' argot', *Lg* 25.22–8 (1949).
[454] 'An Ethiopian minstrels' argot', *JAOS* 72.102–9 (1952).
[455] 'An Ethiopian argot of a Gurage secret society', *JAfrL* 3.52–65 (1964).
[456] 'Linguistic principles of the Ethiopian argots', *JSS* 9.58–66 (1964). The various articles on the argots were republished in the volume *Ethiopian argots* (The Hague, 1964).

turalist tried his hand, and adherents of the transformational theory, of contrastive analysis, of statistical research, and of glottochronology made weak attempts at investigation. Any approach to linguistic study is welcome as long as the researcher has a thorough knowledge of the language that he investigates and as long as his investigation furthers our knowledge.

It is also gratifying to see that a group of young Ethiopian linguists is at work. It is to be hoped that they will endeavour to contribute their share to our knowledge of the Ethiopian languages.

In concluding one is entitled to state that much has been accomplished, but much still remains to be done.

SOUTH ARABIAN

This section deals with Epigraphic South Arabian and Modern South Arabian.

Epigraphic South Arabian

Epigraphic South Arabian is known to us from inscriptions extending over fifteen hundred years. The earliest inscriptions seem to go back to the ninth century B.C. The latest inscriptions belong to the sixth century A.D.[457]

The principal dialects of Epigraphic South Arabian are Sabaean, Minaean, Qatabanian, and Hadrami. The most numerous inscriptions are those of the Sabaean and Minaean dialects.

U.E. Seetzen was the traveler who copied the first five inscriptions, in the year 1810.[458] Other travelers and scholars penetrated into South Arabia copying other inscriptions, often at the risk of their life.[459] The most recent expedition was that of the American Foundation for the Study of Man.[460]

At present we have many thousands of inscriptions, and yet no complete gram-

[457] W.F. Albright, 'The chronology of Ancient South Arabia in the light of the first campaign of excavation in Qataban', *BASOR* 119.5–15 (1950); 'The chronology of the Minaean kings of Arabia', *BASOR* 129.20–4 (1953); J. Pirenne, *Paléographie des inscriptions sud-arabes. Contribution à la chronologie et à l'histoire de l'Arabie du sud antique*, tome I: Des origines à l'époque himyarite (Bruxelles, 1956), and *Le royaume sud-arabe de Qataban et sa datation d'après l'archéologie et les sources classiques jusqu'au Périple de la Mer Erytrée* (Louvain, 1961); A. Jamme, 'On a drastic current reduction of South-Arabian chronology', *BASOR* 145.25–30 (1957), and *La paléographie sud-arabe de J. Pirenne* (Washington, 1957).

[458] *Fundgruben des Orients* 2.275–84 (Wien, 1811).

[459] D. Nielsen, 'Geschichte der Wissenschaft und Übersicht des Materials', in *Handbuch der altarabischen Altertumskunde*, ed. by D. Nielsen, vol. 1, pp. 1–56 (Kopenhagen, 1927); J. Pirenne, *A la découverte de l'Arabie* (Paris, 1957).

[460] A. Jamme, 'Les expéditions archéologiques américaines en Arabie du Sud (1950–1953)', *OM* 33.133–57 (1953).

matical description of the various dialects, nor a dictionary, are at our disposal. There are various reasons for the lack of these tools. The script of the inscriptions has no notation for vowels, the only possible exception being *w*, *y*, and perhaps *h* serving as vowel markers.

The subject matter of the inscriptions is of a practical nature: legal contracts, building records, ex votos, funerary monuments, and a few others.[461] Their style and language are rigid and do not offer a great variety of form and expression. An example that drastically illustrates the rigidity of expression is the usage of the 3rd person only. As a result, we have no knowledge of the 1st and 2nd forms of the verb or pronoun. And finally, the interpretation of the inscriptions still creates considerable difficulties.

Notwithstanding these difficulties the South Arabists and Semitists have made considerable efforts for the last fifty years to advance our knowledge of the structure of the language.

The first description of the language was given by the well-known Semitist W. Gesenius in 1841.[462] This description has at present only historic value. The same can be said of the description given by E. Osiander.[463]

J. Halévy[464] advanced our knowledge of South Arabian through his interpretation of the inscriptions as well as by compiling a description of the language. W.F. Prideaux's brief description is based on Halévy.[465]

A more systematic description is given by F. Hommel[466] who, unfortunately, based his sketch on the Minaean inscriptions alone even though the subtitle reads 'Minäo-Sabäische Grammatik'. Besides, the phonetic transcription and/or the Arabic script in which the vowels are indicated is misleading. Mayer Lambert[467] compiled critical notes on various sections of Hommel's grammar on the basis of his interpretation of new inscriptions.

The most complete grammar was written by Maria Höfner.[468] The South Arabian forms and citations are in phonetic transliteration. Generally morphology and syntax are treated together, but there is also a special section devoted to syntax.

461 A. Jamme, *Classification descriptive générale des inscriptions sud-arabes* (Tunis, 1948). Supplément a la revue *Ibla* 11.401–76 (1948).

462 'Ueber die himjaritische Sprache und Schrift', *ALZ* 1841. 43 p.

463 'Zur himjarischen Alterthums- und Sprachkunde. A. Schrift und Sprache im Einzelnen', *ZDMG* 10.31–50 (1856); 'Zur himjarischen Alterthumskunde. Schrift und Sprache', *ZDMG* 20.211–62 (1866).

464 *Etudes sabéennes*. Examen critique et philologique des inscriptions sabéennes connues jusqu'à ce jour, 1–104 (Paris, 1875). Extrait du *JA* mai-juin 1873, et décembre 1874.

465 'A sketch of Sabaean grammar with examples of translation', *TSBA* 5.203–24 (1876).

466 *Südarabische Chrestomathie*, 1–58 (München, 1893).

467 'Notes de grammaire sabéenne', *JA* 10/11.319–25 (1908). Observations on sections 7, 25, 32, 35 of Hommel's grammar.

468 *Altsüdarabische Grammatik* (Leipzig, 1943). A review article on the grammar was published by G. Ryckmans, 'Une grammaire des anciens dialectes de l'Arabie méridionale', *Muséon* 56.137–45 (1943).

A distinction is made between the various dialects. The author occasionally brings in comparisons from Semitic. Her indulgence in psychological explanations, however, is superfluous, especially since the explanations do not apply to South Arabian only. Besides, the vocalization should have been avoided since at times it can be misleading. It should be stressed, however, that the grammar deals with all the phenomena which can be deduced from the inscriptions.

A sound descriptive analysis of South Arabian was given by A. F. L. Beeston.[469] The grammar is in transcription only, without indication of vowels, and distinguishes the various South Arabian dialects.

The most recent description of the South Arabian structure was published by G. M. Bauer.[470] The South Arabian is in phonetic script only, in the consonantal skeleton.

A brief sketch was compiled by I. Guidi[471] who uses the South Arabian script as well as a transcription with vowels based on Arabic. This kind of transcription is misleading.

Maria Höfner[472] also published a grammatical outline of South Arabian in transcription only. The forms are given in their consonantal skeleton, with occasional vocalization in parentheses.

Considering the great number of inscriptions and the many scholars who have attempted to interpret them, there are relatively few articles dealing with specific grammatical problems of South Arabian. The reason is obvious. The main aim of the scholars has been so far to interpret the inscriptions. It is, therefore, within the framework of their interpretation of the inscriptions that grammatical problems, as well as meanings of words and their etymologies, have been discussed and no studies on specific grammatical problems have been deemed necessary. There are, however, several problems that have been hotly debated. They include the sibilants, and the 'parasitic' *h* in Minaean.

There are three sibilants *s* in South Arabian, most conveniently designated as s_1, s_2, and s_3. The questions confronting the South Arabist and the Semitist in general are: what are the phonetic values of these sibilants, and what is the etymological correspondence between the South Arabian sibilants and the sibilants of the other Semitic languages? While Proto-Semitic undoubtedly had three sibilants, some attested Semitic languages have only two, others three (Hebrew *s*, *š*, and *ś* of unknown pronunciation; Modern South Arabian *s*, *š*, and a lateral *ś*). It can safely be stated that etymologically Epigraphic South Arabian s_1 corresponds to Modern South Arabian *š*,

469 *A descriptive grammar of Epigraphic South Arabian* (London, 1962).
470 *Iazyk iuzhnoaraviiskoi piśmennosti* (Moscow, 1966).
471 'Summarium grammaticae arabicae meridionalis', *Muséon* 39.1–32 [grammar, pp. 1–18] (1926).
472 'Das Südarabische der Inschriften und der lebenden Mundarten. I. Das Altsüdarabische', in *Handbuch der Orientalistik*, ed. by Berthold Spuler, dritter Band, zweiter und dritter Abschnitt, Semitistik, pp. 314–31 (Leiden, 1954).

s_2 corresponds to Modern South Arabian *ś*, and s_3 corresponds to Modern South Arabian *s*. There is less agreement concerning the etymological correspondences between the sibilants of Epigraphic South Arabian and those of the other Semitic languages. Besides, etymological correspondences are not necessarily analogous to phonetic correspondences. Indeed, Arabic *s* corresponds etymologically to Hebrew *ś*, but the sounds are different. The various aspects of the problem have been discussed by D. H. Müller,[473] F. Hommel,[474] W. Leslau,[475] J. Cantineau,[476] D. Stehle,[477] M. Höfner,[478] A. F. L. Beeston,[479] and W. LaSor.[480]

Another problem debated back and forth has been the nature of the so-called 'parasitic' (that is, non-etymological) *h* in the Minaean dialect. The theories evolved around the solution of this problem are a 'graphic' theory, and a 'phonetic' theory. According to the 'graphic' theory the *h* is a vowel-marker, sometimes for *i* but mostly for *a* (or *ā*), whereas according to the 'phonetic' theory the *h*, while not etymological, was pronounced as a consonant. The exponents of the 'graphic' theory are F. Hommel,[481] D. Nielsen,[482] A. Ungnad,[483] O. Weber,[484] and some others. J. H. Mordtmann[485] was the first one to suggest a phonetic value for the *h*. When the existence of a consonantal 'parasitic' *h* in Soqoṭri became known, F. Praetorius[486] was the first scholar to posit the phonetic value of the *h* in both languages. In an extensive study on the subject, N. Rhodokanakis[487] investigated thoroughly the occurrences of the 'parasitic' *h* in Soqoṭri and Minaean and concluded that *h* was a glide between two vowels, the two vowels resulting from a strongly accented vowel that tended first to diphthongize, then split into two vowels between which the glide *h* was introduced.

[473] 'Zur Geschichte der semitischen Zischlaute', *Verhandlungen des VII. internationalen Orientalisten-Congresses*, gehalten in Wien im Jahre 1886. Semitische Section, pp. 229–48 (Wien, 1888).

[474] 'Das Samech in den minäo-sabäischen Inschriften, nebst einer Erklärung betr. die Inschriften Eduard Glaser's', *ZDMG* 46.528–38 (1892).

[475] 'Der *ś*-Laut in den modernen südarabischen Sprachen', *WZKM* 44.211–18 (1937); *Lexique soqoṭri*, 31–6 (Paris, 1938).

[476] 'La "mutation des sifflantes" en sudarabique', in *Mélanges Gaudefroy-Demombynes*, pp. 313–323 (Le Caire, 1939).

[477] 'Sibilants and emphatics in South Arabic', *JAOS* 60.507–43 (1940).

[478] *Altsüdarabische Grammatik*, pp. 18–21 (Leipzig, 1943).

[479] 'Phonology of the epigraphic South-Arabian unvoiced sibilants', *TPhS*, 1951 pp. 1–26; 'Arabian sibilants', *JSS* 7.222–33 (1962).

[480] 'The sibilants in Old South Arabic', *JQR* 48.161–73 (1957).

[481] 'Das graphische *h* im Minäischen und das Alter der minäischen Inschriften', *MVAG* 3.258–72 (1897).

[482] 'Der Vokalbuchstabe *h* im Minäischen', in his *Neue Katabanische Inschriften und der Vokalbuchstabe h im Minäischen, MVAG* 4.49–70 (1906).

[483] 'Zur südarabischen Grammatik', *OLZ* 495–7 (1907).

[484] 'Der Vokalbuchstabe *h* im Minäischen', in his *Studien zur südarabischen Altertumskunde*. III, MVAG 2.47–54 (1907).

[485] 'Parasitisches *h* im Minäischen und Sabäischen', in his *Beiträge zur minäischen Epigraphik*, 78–95 (Weimar, 1897).

[486] 'Zur Frage über das parasitische *h* des Minäischen', *ZDMG* 62.708–13 (1908).

[487] 'Der zweigipflige Akzent im Minäo-Sabäischen', in his *Studien zur Lexikographie und Grammatik des Altsüdarabischen*, 1.13–56 (Wien, 1915). SWAW, Bd. 178, Abh. 4.

As for the studies dealing with specific problems in morphology only a small selection will be given.

The suffix pronoun having the meaning of the article or of the demonstrative has been discussed by H. Winckler,[488] D. H. Müller,[489] F. Praetorius,[490] and H. Reckendorf.[491]

D. H. Müller investigated the construct state in South Arabic;[492] the nunation and mimation;[493] and the usage of the external plural, masculine.[494]

The question of the final *-n* of the imperfect and infinitive having originally the value of reinforcement, then taking over other meanings, has been discussed by Maria Höfner.[495]

The infinitive of South Arabian is studied by F. Praetorius[496] who recognizes it in the so-called 'energetic' perfect; and by J. M. Sola-Solé.[497]

Y. B. Grunfest discussed the infinitive in South Arabian;[498] the consecutive construction;[499] and the verb in South Arabian.[500]

In recent years the question of the position of the adjective, its agreement with the noun, and its usage with mimation or nunation has been argued by A. Jamme,[501] and A. F. L. Beeston.[502]

The need for a South Arabian dictionary has been felt since the beginning of South Arabian studies. The method of compiling such a dictionary has been suggested by G. Ryckmans.[503]

488 'Bemerkungen zu dem Ersatz des Artikels durch das Pronomen', *ZDMG* 53.525–33 (1899).

489 'Der angebliche Ersatz des Artikels durch das Pronomen', *WZKM* 13.363–9 (1899).

490 'Zu Wincklers Aufsatz in dieser Zeitschrift, Bd. 53, S. 525ff.', *ZDMG* 54.1–7 (1900).

491 'Artikelhafter Gebrauch des Personalpronomen und Verwandtes im Semitischen', *ZDMG* 54.130–6 (1900).

492 'Der status constructus im Himjarischen', *ZDMG* 30.117–24 (1876).

493 'Die Nunation und die Mimation', *ZDMG* 32.542–51 (1878).

494 'Ueber den Gebrauch des äussern Plural masc. in den südsemitischen Sprachen', *Actes du sixième congrès international des Orientalistes*, tenu en 1883 à Leide. Part 2, section 1. Semitic, 445–64 (Leiden, 1885).

495 'Zur Grammatik des Altsüdarabischen', *ZDMG* 93.197–203 (1939).

496 'Das vermeintliche energetische Perfectum des Sabäischen', *ZDMG* 42.56–61 (1888).

497 'L'infinitif en sud-arabique. I. Le sud-arabique épigraphique', in his *L'infinitif sémitique*, 29–40 (Paris, 1961).

498 'Infinitiv v iuzhnoarabskom iazyke', *Semitic languages.* Papers presented for the first conference on Semitic languages, 26–28 October 1964; issue 2, pt. 2, 285–305 (Moscow, 1965).

499 'Konsekutivnye konstruktsii v iuzhnoarabskom iazyke', *Kratkie soobshcheniia Instituta Narodov Azii*, 86, 1965 (known to me only by title).

500 *Glagol v iuzhnoarabskom iazyke.* Candidate thesis. Leningrad, 1966 (known to me only by title).

501 'Syntax of the adjective in South Arabic', *JSS* 2.176–81 (1957); 'The syntax of South Arabic adjectives again', *JSS* 4.264–7 (1959).

502 'The syntax of the adjective in Old South Arabian: Remarks on Jamme's theory', *JSS* 3.142–5 (1958).

503 'Comment réaliser un dictionnarie des anciens dialectes sud-sémitiques?', *Atti del XIX congresso internazionale degli orientalisti*, Roma, 1935, 441–5 (Rome, 1938).

F. Hommel[504] was the first to compile a brief South Arabian-German glossary forming a part of his grammar and chrestomathy. The glossary contains only the words of the chrestomathy. The words are in South Arabian script and transcribed into Arabic with occasional vocalization.

An extensive South Arabian-Latin glossary, but far from complete, has been compiled by C. Conti Rossini.[505] The glossary is in South Arabian script and is comparative. The words are often illustrated by sentences taken from the inscriptions and translated into Latin. The roots and their derived forms are indicated in the glossary. It also contains proper names.

A useful index of the South Arabian vocabulary has been compiled by A. F. L. Beeston.[506] While it forms a part of his chrestomathy it also contains words and forms of other inscriptions. The index is in South Arabian script, without translation, but with references to the words' occurrence in the Corpus and the Répertoire (for which see below). No proper names are given.

It is fortunate that some interpreters of the inscriptions appended to their studies glossaries containing the words discussed in the inscriptions. It would be of great help if this procedure were followed by all future interpreters. Only a few studies of this kind will be mentioned.

J. H. Mordtmann[507] has appended a glossary to his text; the words are given in South Arabian script only, with references to the inscriptions in which they are found.

N. Rhodokanakis[508] uses the same procedure in his collections of inscriptions. The author uses the South Arabian script, and only occasionally the Hebrew script.

I. Guidi[509] has a brief glossary in South Arabian script with vocalized transcription. The words are translated.

J. H. Mordtmann and E. Mittwoch[510] appended a glossary to their study using the Hebrew script with a translation into German. The proper nouns are included in the glossary.

A. Jamme[511] likewise published a word list (in phonetic transcription) including proper names.

[504] *Süd-Arabische Chrestomathie*, glossary, 121–8; index of proper names, 129–36 (München, 1893).

[505] *Chrestomathia arabica meridionalis epigraphica*, 99–261 (Rome, 1931).

[506] *Sabaean inscriptions*, 91–152 (Oxford, 1937).

[507] *Beiträge zur minäischen Epigraphik*, 123–7 (Weimar, 1897).

[508] *Studien zur Lexikographie und Grammatik des Altsüdarabischen* 1.71–2 (Wien, 1915); 2.179–85 (Wien, 1917); 3.50 (1931); *Altsabäische Texte* 1.147–8 (Wien, 1927); *Ḳatabanische Texte zur Bodenwirtschaft* 1.148–50 (Wien, 1919); 2.107–8 (Wien, 1922).

[509] *Summarium grammaticae arabicae meridionalis*, 27–32 of the offprint (1928).

[510] *Sabäische Inschriften*, 252–65 (Hamburg, 1921). Hamburgische Universität. Abhandlungen aus dem Gebiete der Auslandskunde. Band 36.

[511] *The Al-ʿUqlah texts* (*Documentation sud-arabe, III*), 69–74 (Washington, 1963).

A detailed index of the South Semitic (including South Arabic) proper names has been published by G. Ryckmans.[512] This monumental study contains the names of persons, places, and tribes, with detailed indexes. It would have been preferable, however, if the author had abstained from giving the etymologies of the proper names, especially since he tried to establish the South Arabian etymologies on the basis of Arabic rather than on internal evidence.

There are also isolated studies dealing with the meaning of particular South Arabian words. At times these studies are etymological. Their number is relatively small for the reason mentioned above in connection with the studies dealing with specific problems in morphology. Indeed, problems in morphology and lexicography have been most often discussed in connection with the interpretation of the inscriptions, and there may have been no need to discuss these problems in specific studies.

Out of the various studies I cite only those of D. H. Müller,[513] F. Praetorius,[514] C. Conti Rossini,[515] A. F. L. Beeston,[516] J. Ryckmans,[517] A. Jamme,[518] A. G. Lundin,[519] E. Ullendorff,[520] and P. Boneschi.[521]

The doctoral thesis of Walter W. Müller [522] deserves special attention. It is a sound study dealing with the meaning and etymologies of the verbs 2nd and 3rd radicals *y/w*.

The relation between South Arabian, Ethiopic and Akkadian from the points of view of morphology and lexicography has been discussed by V. Christian,[523] J.

[512] *Les noms propres sud-sémitiques* (Louvain, 1934): vol. 1. Répertoire analytique; vol. 2. Répertoire alphabétique; vol. 3. Concordance générale des inscriptions sud-sémitiques.

[513] 'Kleine Mitteilungen: Die Etymologie der Wurzel ms_1r; Die Etymologie von $mḥs_2kt$', *WZKM* 13.393–5, 396–7 (1899).

[514] 'Sabäisch *gbr* "Person"', *ZDMG* 54.37–8 (1900); 'Sabäisches und Äthiopisches', *ZDMG* 57. 271–5 (1903); 'Sabäisches ʿs_1d "wer immer"', *ZDMG* 57.199–200 (1903); 'Sabäisches *mnḍḫm*', *ZDMG* 61.754–5 (1907); "Zu einigen altsüdarabischen Wörtern", *ZS* 2.142–3 (1924), *ZS* 4.123–4 (1925).

[515] 'Sudar. *asad* = et. *anbasa* "uomo d'arme"', *ZA* 24.337–44 (1910); 'Sabaica', *RSO* 9.27–31 (1921).

[516] 'Notes on Old South-Arabian lexicography', I. *Muséon* 63.53–8 (1950); II. *Muséon* 63.261–8 (1950); III. *Muséon* 64.127–32 (1951); IV. *Muséon* 65.139–47 (1952); V. *Muséon* 65.109–22 (1953); VI. *Muséon* 67. 311–22 (1954).

[517] 'Le sens de *ḏʿl* en sud-arabe', *Muséon* 67.339–48 (1954).

[518] 'Le pronom démonstratif sabéen *mhn* et les conjonctions composites *lqbl(y)/ḏ(t)*, *kmhnmw* et *kmʿnmw*', *Cahiers de Byrsa* 6.173–80 (1958).

[519] 'The meanings of the verb *ʿsy* in Ancient Yemenite texts', *Semitic languages*. Papers presented for the first conference on Semitic languages, 26–28 October 1964; issue 2, pt. 2, pp. 306–12 (Moscow, 1965).

[520] 'South Arabian etymological marginalia', *BSOAS* 15.157–9 (1953).

[521] 'Variazioni etimologiche sul tema *'lmqh*', *RRAL*, ser. 8, vol. 13, pp. 327–55 (1958).

[522] *Die Wurzeln mediae und tertiae y/w im Altsüdarabischen* (Tübingen, 1962).

[523] 'Akkader und Südaraber als ältere Semitenschichte', *Anthropos* 14/15.729–39 (1919–20).

Cantineau,[524] M. Moscati,[525] W. Leslau,[526] M. Höfner,[527] W. Müller,[528] and A. Murtonen.[529]

H. Grimme[530] investigates the South Arabian loanwords and the South Arabian grammatical forms in the Koran.

The existing COLLECTIONS of the inscriptions are those of the *Corpus* and the *Répertoire*, both published by the Académie des Inscriptions et Belles-Lettres. The *Corpus inscriptionum semiticarum, pars quarta, inscriptiones himyariticas et sabaeas continens* (Paris, 1889–1931, 3 vols.) contains inscriptions 1–985. The inscriptions are in South Arabian script, transcribed into Hebrew, translated into Latin, with an extensive commentary.

The *Répertoire d'épigraphie sémitique*, edited by G. Ryckmans (Paris 1929–1950) contains inscriptions 2624–5106 in volumes 5, 6, and 7. The first two volumes (Paris 1900–1914) occasionally contain South Arabian inscriptions with an index. The inscriptions are given in Hebrew transcription only, with a French translation and commentary.

Outside of the Corpus and the Répertoire the inscriptions in the various dialects and their interpretation are spread throughout the various periodicals. It is, therefore, gratifying for the student to have a few CHRESTOMATHIES at his disposal.

The chrestomathy of F. Hommel[531] is in South Arabian script, without translation.

C. Conti Rossini[532] published a chrestomathy in South Arabian script only, without translation, but with reference to the authors who translated the inscriptions.

The only chrestomathy that gives the translation of the inscriptions is that of A. F. L. Beeston.[533] The inscriptions are in South Arabian script, with an English translation and a commentary.

The existing BIBLIOGRAPHIES deal with general problems of South Arabia, such as geography, history, travels, and language studies. There is no bibliography that deals with language only. Besides, with the exception of a few articles, the bibliographies are not annotated.

[524] 'Accadien et sudarabique', *BSL* 33.175–204 (1932).
[525] 'Nordarabico, sudarabico, etiopico', *RSO* 34.33–9 (1959).
[526] 'South-east Semitic (Ethiopic and South Arabic)', *JAOS* 63.4–14 (1943).
[527] 'Über sprachliche und kulturelle Beziehungen zwischen Südarabien und Äthiopien im Altertum', *ACISE* 435–45.
[528] 'Über Beziehungen zwischen den südarabischen Sprachen und den abessinischen Sprachen', *JSS* 9.50–5 (1964).
[529] *Early Semitic*. A diachronical inquiry into the relationship of Ethiopic to the other so-called South-east Semitic languages (Leiden, 1967).
[530] 'Über einige Klassen südarabischen Lehnwörter im Koran', *ZA* 26.158–68 (1912).
[531] *Süd-Arabische Chrestomathie*, 90–120 (München, 1893).
[532] *Chrestomathia arabica meridionalis epigraphica*, 39–97 (Rome, 1931).
[533] *Sabaean inscriptions*, 1–87 (Oxford, 1937).

F. Hommel's bibliography enumerates the various items from the year 1774 to 1892.[534]

O. Weber's bibliography continues the period of 1892 to 1908.[535]

G. Ryckman's bibliography starts with the year 1717 and ends with 1928.[536] The same author published an annotated bibliography of pre-Islamic epigraphy including South Arabian of the years 1938 to 1948.[537]

A useful bibliography of South Semitic including South Arabian has been published by Y. Moubarac.[538]

The present state of the inscriptional material and of the problems connected with it was presented by M. Höfner.[539]

From this brief survey it can be seen that the interpretation of the South Arabian inscriptions and the investigation of the grammatical problems of the language have preoccupied several well-known Semitists such as F. Hommel, J. Halévy, E. Glaser, H. Winckler, D. H. Müller, J. H. Mordtmann, F. Praetorius, H. Derenbourg, O. Weber, Mayer Lambert, C. Conti Rossini, N. Rhodokanakis. The scholars actively engaged at present in the field of South Arabian studies are A. F. L. Beeston, M. Höfner, A. Jamme, and G. Ryckmans. Their task is enormous. Indeed, the need is keenly felt for a bibliography that supplements in a systematic way the one published by G. Ryckmans. Still better, an annotated bibliography of the grammatical and lexicographical studies as well as the studies dealing with the interpretation of the inscriptions would be of great help.

While the grammars of M. Höfner and of A. F. L. Beeston give the essentials of the language, a grammar that reflects our present knowledge of the field is much to be desired.

What is needed most is a complete dictionary of Epigraphic South Arabian. The Semitist would particularly value a dictionary that also included etymologies.

Modern South Arabian

In Central South Arabia and on the island of Soqoṭra, Kuria Muria, and ʿAbd-el-Kūri in the Gulf of Aden a group of languages is spoken that we call Modern South Arabian.

534 *Süd-Arabische Chrestomathie*, 63–88 (München, 1893).

535 'Bibliographie der südarabischen Altertumskunde seit 1893', in his *Studien zur südarabischen Altertumskunde, III*, 68-101 (Berlin, 1907). *MVAG* 1907, Abh. 2.

536 *Répertoire d'épigraphie sémitique*, 5.i–lxxxiii (Paris, 1929).

537 'L'épigraphie arabe préislamique au cours de ces dix dernières années', *Muséon* 61.197–213 (1948).

538 'Eléments de bibliographie sud-sémitique', *REIsl* 23.121–76 (1955): South Arabic, 126,139–58; 'Les études d'épigraphie sud-sémitique et la naissance de l'Islam', *REIsl* 25.13–68 (1957): South Arabia, 24–54.

539 'Der Stand und die Aufgaben der südarabischen Forschung', in *Beiträge zur Arabistik, Semitistik und Islamwissenschaft*, ed. by Richard Hartmann and Helmuth Scheel, 42–66 (Leipzig, 1944).

The languages and dialects belonging to this group are:

1. Mehri, and its dialects Harsusi and Botahari
2. Šḫauri (or Šaḥri) and its dialect of Kuria Muria
3. Soqoṭri and its dialect of ʿAbd-el-Kūri.

The Modern South Arabian dialects form a dialectal unit within Semitic and are different from the Arabic dialects in phonology, morphology, and vocabulary.

We owe our first knowledge of these languages to J.R. Wellsted who visited the island of Soqoṭra in 1835, and collected some 250 words of the language of the island.[540] An epoch-making event in the investigation of Modern South Arabian was the expedition sponsored by the Kaiserliche Akademie der Wissenschaften of Vienna and headed by Carl von Landberg and D.H. Müller at the end of 1898.[541] Subsequently scholars, among them W. Hein and A. Jahn, went to South Arabia (thanks to the support of the Academy mentioned above), collected texts on the spot and brought native informants to Vienna. Recently our knowledge of Modern South Arabian has been enriched by knowledge of the dialects of Mehri, namely Botahari and Harsusi, as a result of the exploration of Bertram Thomas in 1937.[542]

Mehri

Mehri is spoken on the coastal region of Ǧabal al-Sūd, eastward through the 'Land of Mahra' and on through Ḍofar.[543]

The first information on Mehri was given in 1940 by J.R. Wellsted, who collected 37 words of the language.[544] Other small collections of words and phrases came from L. Krapf (published by G.H.A. Ewald in 1846)[545] and from H.J. Carter in 1847.[546] H. von Maltzan, a trained Arabist, published in 1873 the collections of Mehri words of the travelers just mentioned as well as his own collection.[547]

A considerable collection of texts comes from the members of the expedition sponsored by the Kaiserliche Akademie der Wissenschaften of Vienna. These texts

[540] See fn. 617.

[541] D.H. Müller, *Die südarabische Expedition der Kaiserlichen Akademie der Wissenschaften in Wien, und die Demission des Grafen Carlo Landberg*. Actenmässig dargestellt. (Wien und Leipzig, 1899).

[542] *Four strange tongues from South Arabia. The Hadara group* (London, 1937). PBA 23.

[543] For the region, see J. Tkatsch, 'Mehri', *EI* 3.138–44 (1928).

[544] *Travels to the city of the Caliphs*, 2.26–7 (London, 1840).

[545] 'Sammlung von Wörtern in der Sprache von Murbat dafar und Mahara im südlichen Arabien' (herausgegeben von G.H.A. von Ewald), *ZWS* 1.311–15 (1846).

[546] 'Notes on the Mahra tribe of southern Arabia, with a vocabulary of their language to which are appended additional observations on the Gara tribe', *JRAS*, Bombay Branch, 2.339–70 (1847).

[547] 'Dialektische Studien über das Mehri in Vergleich mit verwandten Sprachen', *ZDMG* 27.225–31 (1873).

are in phonetic transcription, translated into German. The authors of these texts are A. Jahn,[548] D. H. Müller,[549] and W. Hein.[550]

The first grammar based on first-hand documents was published by Alfred Jahn.[551] Unfortunately, the verbal and nominal systems are presented in a disorderly way, but the phonology is treated in a much more detailed manner than in M. Bittner's grammar.[552] Occasionally the author makes comparisons with other Semitic languages.

A complete grammar of Mehri was published by M. Bittner.[553] This grammar is constructed on the basis of the texts of A. Jahn[554] and D. H. Müller.[555] The grammar is also comparative.

Grammatical outlines of Mehri were published by H. von Maltzan[556] on the basis of his own material; by G. Bergsträsser,[557] and by Maria Höfner[558] on the basis of grammars previously mentioned. The most detailed outline is that of C. Brockelmann.[559]

Recent material on Mehri morphology (together with Šaḥri, Botahari and Harsusi) treating briefly the pronoun, the article, the noun, the adjective and the verb has been published by B. Thomas.[560] The author himself confesses that 'the material presented here is that of a single-handed Englishman without philological training other than a facile knowledge of colloquial Arabic, a musical ear, and a long experience of the native mind'. B. Thomas's material was analyzed by W. Leslau,[561] who attempted to derive therefrom some phonetic and morphological principles of the language.

In the field of specific studies mention should be made of A. Jahn,[562] who gives the phonetic correspondence between Mehri, 'Küstenarabisch' and Arabic.

K. Vollers[563] discusses some questions of the phonetic system of Mehri, on the basis of Jahn's texts.

548 *Die Mehri-Sprache in Südarabien.* Texte und Wörterbuch (Wien, 1902). KAWSE 3.
549 *Die Mehri- und Soqoṭri-Sprache.* I. Texte (Wien, 1902). KAWSE 4; III (Wien, 1907). KAWSE 7.
550 *Mehri- und Ḥaḍrami-Texte* (Wien, 1909). KAWSE 9.
551 *Grammatik der Mehri-Sprache in Südarabien* (Wien, 1905). SWAW, Bd. 150, Abh. 6.
552 See fn. 553.
553 *Studien zur Laut- und Formenlehre der Mehri-Sprache in Südarabien*, 4 vol. (Wien, 1909–14). SWAW, Bd. 162, Abh. 5; Bd. 168, Abh. 2; Bd. 172, Abh. 5; Bd. 174, Abh. 4.
554 See fn. 548.
555 See fn. 549.
556 'Über den Dialekt von Mahra, genannt Mehri in Südarabien', *ZDMG* 25.196–214 (1871); 'Arabische Vulgärdialekte. 6. Dialekt von Mahra', *ZDMG* 27.252–94 (1873).
557 *Einführung in die semitischen Sprachen.* Mehri, 126–31 (München, 1928).
558 'Das Südarabische der Inschriften und der lebenden Mundarten. II. Die lebenden südarabischen Mundarten', *Handbuch der Orientalistik*, herausgegeben von Berthold Spuler, dritter Band, zweiter und dritter Abschnitt. Semitistik, pp. 331–41 (Leiden, 1954).
559 'Mehri', *EI* 3.449–54 (1931).
560 *Four strange tongues from South Arabia. The Hadara group*, 13–36 (London, 1937). PBA 23.
561 'Four modern South Arabic languages', *Word* 3.189–94 (1947).
562 *Die Mehri-Sprache in Südarabien.* Texte und Wörterbuch, p. viii (Wien, 1902). KAWSE 3.
563 'Die arabischen Teile der Wiener Südarabischen Expedition', *ZA* 23/24.97–106 (1909–10).

M. Bittner analyzes W. Hein's texts[564] from the phonological and grammatical points of view;[565] elsewhere he gives an outline of the Mehri verb based on his own study of the Mehri verb.[566]

N. Rhodokanakis[567] examines the nominal forms of Mehri as given by M. Bittner.[568]

O. Rössler[569] examines the prefix and suffix forms of the verb of Mehri and compares them with those of Akkadian, Berber and Bedja.

There is an initial *ḥ* in Mehri that occurs with some nouns designating parts of the body, with nouns of relationship, and so on. The origin of this *ḥ* has been argued by K. Vollers,[570] A. Ember,[571] C. Brockelmann,[572] V. Vycichl,[573] W. Leslau,[574] and C. D. Matthews.[575]

In the field of syntax, M. Bittner [576] makes various observations on C. Brockelmann's data on Mehri syntax.[577]

A thorough investigation of the Mehri syntax was published by E. Wagner[578] on the basis of the texts of the Viennese expedition mentioned above. Occasionally the syntax of Šaḥri and Soqoṭri is taken into consideration. The author follows C. Brockelmann[579] in the arrangement of the material. The study contains also an index of the grammatical terminology and an index of the particles of Mehri, Šaḥri, and Soqoṭri.

The collections of words made by J. R. Wellsted,[580] L. Krapf,[581] and H. J. Carter[582] can be used only with great caution since these explorers were not trained linguistically. H. von Maltzan[583] published the above mentioned vocabularies together with his own

[564] See fn. 550.
[565] 'Neues Mehri-Materiale aus dem Nachlasse des Dr. Wilhem Hein', *WZKM* 24.70–93 (1910).
[566] *AWAW* 47.57–68 (1910).
[567] *Zur Formenlehre des Mehri* (Wien, 1910). SWAW, Bd. 165, Abh. 1.
[568] See fn. 553.
[569] 'Verbalbau und Verbalflexion in den semitohamitischen Sprachen', *ZDMG* 100.496–501 (1951).
[570] See fn. 563.
[571] 'Mehri parallels to Egyptian stems with prefixed ḥ', *ZÄS* 51.116, 117, 138 (1914).
[572] 'Mehri', *EI* 3.451 (1931).
[573] 'Über ein ḥa-Präfix im Arabischen', *WZKM* 43.109–10 (1936); 'Wieder über das ḥa-Präfix im Arabischen', *WZKM* 46.141–42 (1939).
[574] 'Über das ḥa-Präfix im Arabischen', *WZKM* 44.219–20 (1937).
[575] 'Again on non-Arabic place names in Central Southern Arabia', *Trudy XXV mezhunarodnogo kongressa vostokovedow*, Moskva, 9–16 avgusta 1960, 1.550–2 (Moscow, 1962).
[576] 'Einige das Mehri betreffende Bemerkungen zu Brockelmanns Grundriss II (Syntax)', *WZKM* 28.48–52 (1914).
[577] *Grundriss der vergleichenden Grammatik der semitischen Sprachen*. I. Laut- und Formenlehre. II. Syntax (Berlin, 1908–13).
[578] *Syntax der Mehri-Sprache*, mit Berücksichtigung auch der anderen neusüdarabischen Sprachen (Berlin, 1953).
[579] See fn. 577.
[580] See fn. 544.
[581] See fn. 545.
[582] See fn. 546.
[583] See fn. 547.

collection, and added a Šaḥri vocabulary of L. Krapf and the Kuria Muria vocabulary of J. G. Hulton.

W. Gesenius[584] reviews the Mehri words of J. Wellsted and suggests some etymologies.

The most reliable Mehri vocabulary is that of A. Jahn.[585] While it is far from being complete, it is an abundant Mehri-German vocabulary (with a German-Mehri index), in a good transcription. Occasionally the author also gives comparisons with other Semitic languages, especially with Arabic.

The most recent Mehri vocabulary is that of Bertram Thomas who published an English-Šaḥri-Mehri-Harsusi-Botahari vocabulary.[586] The vocabulary contains nearly 600 words; some Mehri words are not found in the other vocabularies. The material should, however, be reevaluated for reasons mentioned above in connection with his grammar.

M. Bittner[587] published indexes of all the words treated in his Mehri grammar, referring to the page where the word is mentioned and compared with the root of other Semitic languages. There is also an index[588] of the roots of the various Semitic languages with which the Mehri word is compared. The same author also published an index of the Mehri words that are suggested in his comparisons with Šaḥri.[589] An index of the Mehri particles was published by E. Wagner in his Mehri syntax.[590] K. Voller's[591] article contains some etymologies of Mehri.

Botahari and Harsusi

The dialects closest to Mehri are Botahari and Harsusi.

The Botahri live along the littoral of Kuria Muria Bay. The Harsusi occupy the territory from Jaddat Harasi to the northern Oman borderlands. We owe the only document on their languages to the efforts of Bertram Thomas, who published a brief grammatical outline of the dialects, some phrases and sentences, names of persons, and a vocabulary of about 600 words in English-Šaḥri-Mehri-Harsusi-Botahari.[592]

W. Leslau[593] analyzed Thomas's material, particularly the morphology and the phrases. He attempted to derive from it some phonetic and morphological principles for each language and arrived at the conclusion that Botahari and Harsusi are dialects closely related to Mehri.

[584] 'Über die himjaritische Sprache und Schrift', *ALZ.* 42–43 of the offprint (1841).

[585] *Die Mehri-Sprache in Südarabien.* Texte und Wörterbuch, 161–242 (Wien, 1902). KAWSE 3.

[586] *Four strange tongues from South Arabia. The Hadara group*, 58–103 (London, 1937). PBA 23.

[587] *Studien zur Laut- und Formenlehre der Mehri-Sprache in Südarabien*, 1.90–111; 2.122–42; 4.42–8, 60–4 (Wien, 1909–15).

[588] *Studien zur Laut- und Formenlehre der Mehri-Sprache in Südarabien*, vol. 4.68–81; Šḫauri (= Šaḥri), p. 77 (Wien, 1915).

[589] *Studien zur Šḫauri-Sprache in den Bergen von Dofâr am Persischen Meerbusen*, 1.81–7; 2.79–85 (Wien, 1916).

[590] *Syntax der Mehri-Sprache*, 164–5 (Berlin, 1953).

[591] 'Die arabischen Teile der Wiener Südarabischen Expedition', *ZA* 23/24.97–106 (1909–10).

[592] *Four strange tongues from South Arabia. The Hadara group* (London, 1937).

[593] 'Four modern South Arabic languages', *Word* 3.194–202 (1947).

Š̱hauri (or Šaḥri)

The name of the language was recorded by the Viennese expedition as Š̱hauri.[594] However, C. D. Matthews[595] has argued convincingly that the name of the language is actually Šaḥri. Since I have no personal opinion on the subject I have adopted Matthews' suggestion and call this language 'Šaḥri'. Note that the language is also known as Eḥkili (Eḥkali, Aḥkali), but it is difficult to know whether this is actually another name of the same language or whether, in fact, it belongs to a dialect close to it.

The tribe of al-Šaḥra is concentrated in Ḍofar, in the mountains north of al-Salāla.

The first information on Šaḥri comes from the French consul Fulgence Fresnel[596] who, when he was in Djedda in 1838, acquired some knowledge of Šaḥri (that he calls 'Eḥkili') from an informant who chanced to be in Djedda. The author gives, in addition to a rather detailed study of the phonology, the conjugation of the verb *zeged* 'take', *ẖeṣof* 'pierce', the article, and other scattered information as well as a small text consisting of a translation of Genesis 37:2 from Arabic into Šaḥri and Latin.

F. Fresnel's information was analyzed by E. Rödiger[597] who suggests calling the language 'Vulgär-himjaritisch' or 'Neu-himjaritisch'; by W. Gesenius;[598] and by N. V. Yushmanov,[599] who analyzes Fresnel's text on the basis of M. Bittner's indications and deduces some phonetic and morphological principles of Šaḥri.

Other small collections of words and phrases are those of L. Krapf (edited by G. H. A. von Ewald in 1846)[600] and E. Glaser (edited by F. Hommel in 1896).[601]

As in the case of Mehri, a considerable collection of texts has come from the members of the Kaiserliche Akademie der Wissenschaften of Vienna. The texts were published by D. H. Müller in phonetic transcription and translated into German.[602] M. Bittner made some philological observations on these texts.[603] The same

[594] For the geography, see A. Grohmann, "Al-Shiḥr", *EI* 4.369–70 (1927).

[595] 'Again on non-Arabic place names in Central Southern Arabia', *Trudy XXV mezhunarodnogo kongressa vostokovedow*, Moskva, 9–16 avgusta 1960, 1.549 (Moscow, 1962).

[596] 'Quatrième lettre sur l'histoire des Arabes avant l'islamisme', *JA*, ser. 3, vol. 5.497–544 (1838); 'Note sur la langue hymiarite. Extrait d'une lettre à M. J. Mohl datée de Djedda, 12 décembre 1837', *JA*, ser. 3, vol. 6.77–84 (1838); 'Cinquième lettre sur l'histoire des Arabes avant l'islamisme', *JA*, ser. 3, vol. 6.529–70 (1838).

[597] 'Fresnel über die himjaritische Sprache', *ZKM* 3.288–93 (1840).

[598] 'Über die himjaritische Sprache und Schrift', *ALZ* 370–5 (18*ü*1).

[599] 'Les matériaux de Fresnel relatifs au dialecte sud-arabe eḥkili', *Akademija nauk. Aziatski muzei. Zapiski kollegiya vostokovedow*, Moskva, 5.379–91 (1930).

[600] See fn. 545.

[601] 'Vorläufige Mittheilungen über die inschriftlichen Ergebnisse der vierten Reise Eduard Glaser's', *Actes du dixième congrès international des Orientalistes*. Section de Genève, 1894. Troisième partie, section II., 115–17 (Leiden, 1896).

[602] *Die Mehri- und Soqoṭri-Sprache*. III. Š̱hauri-Texte (Wien, 1907). KAWSE 7.

[603] 'Nachträge zu den Texten von D. H. Müller', in his *Studien zur Š̱hauri-Sprache in den Bergen von Dofâr am Persischen Meerbusen* 4.70–104 (Wien, 1917).

author republished some of the texts, translated them into German and accompanied them with philological notes, without grammatical commentary.[604]

The latest information on Šaḥri comes from B. Thomas in 1937. For more information, see below.

The only grammar of Šaḥri was published by M. Bittner[605] who elaborated it on the basis of D. H. Müller's texts. In many questions Bittner compares the Šaḥri phonemes with those of Mehri.

An outline of Šaḥri was likewise published by M. Bittner.[606]

B. Thomas' study[607] contains some grammatical indications of Šaḥri together with those of Mehri, Botahari, and Harsusi.

W. Leslau[608] analyzed Thomas' material and attempted to derive from it some phonetic and morphological principles of the language.

The most extensive vocabulary of Šaḥri-German is that of M. Bittner.[609] It contains all the Šaḥri words of the author's studies. The Roman and Arabic numbers refer to the volume and the page where the word is examined from grammatical and etymological points of view. The same author gives indexes of the words of all the other Semitic languages which he takes into consideration in his comparisons with Šaḥri.[610]

B. Thomas likewise published an English-Šaḥri-Mehri-Harsusi-Botahari vocabulary of about 600 words.[611] As in the case of Mehri, Thomas' material has to be reevaluated.

An index of the Šaḥri particles was published by E. Wagner in his Mehri syntax.[612]

Kuria Muria

Kuria Muria, in Arabic Hūryān Mūryān, is a group of five islands off the coast of Arabia. Only the island Hallāniya is inhabited.

The only linguistic information on Kuria Muria is provided by J. G. Hulton, who

[604] *Studien zur Šḫauri-Sprache in den Bergen von Dofâr am Persischen Meerbusen.* III. Zu ausgewählten Texten (Wien, 1917). SWAW, Bd. 179, Abh. 5.

[605] *Studien zur Šḫauri-Sprache in den Bergen von Dofâr am Persischen Meerbusen*, vol. 1–2 (Wien, 1916). SWAW, Bd. 179, Abh. 2,4.

[606] 'Charakteristik der Šḫauri-Sprache in den Bergen von Dofâr am Persischen Meerbusen', *AWAW* 50.81–94 (1913).

[607] *Four strange tongues from South Arabia. The Hadara group*, 13–36 (London, 1937).

[608] 'Four modern South Arabic languages', *Word* 3.183–9 (1947).

[609] *Studien zur Šḫauri-Sprache in den Bergen von Dofâr am Persischen Meerbusen* 4.6–69 (Wien, 1917). SWAW, Bd. 183, Abh. 5.

[610] *Studien zur Šḫauri-Sprache in den Bergen von Dofâr am Persischen Meerbusen*, 1.68–91; 2.69–87 (Wien, 1916). SWAW, Bd. 179, Abh. 2; Bd. 179, Abh. 4.

[611] *Four strange tongues from South Arabia. The Hadara group*, 58–103 (London, 1937).

[612] *Syntax der Mehri-Sprache*, 165–6 (Berlin, 1953).

gives a list of 103 words in English, and Arabic.[613] A part of the collection is reproduced in H. von Maltzan.[614]

The present writer[615] has analyzed Hulton's vocabulary and the phonetic and morphological phenomena as far as they can be deduced from the vocabulary, and has arrived at the conclusion that Kuria Muria is a dialect of Šaḥri.

Soqoṭri

Soqoṭri is spoken on the island of Soqoṭra, in the Gulf of Aden.[616]

The first information was given in 1835 by J. R. Wellsted,[617] whose study contains a collection of about 250 words. Other small collections of words and phrases are those of C. Guillain (in 1855),[618] I. B. Balfour (names of flowers, in 1888),[619] E. Glaser (published by F. Hommel in 1894),[620] and T. Bent.[621]

A considerable collection of texts in Soqoṭri translated into German was compiled by D. H. Müller,[622] a member of the Viennese expedition.

M. Bittner[623] republished the text of 'Aschenputtel' in Mehri, Šaḥri and Soqoṭri, with philological notes as well as morphological and lexicographical observations. The same author[624] edited an unpublished text of the first six chapters of the Gospel of Mark in Soqoṭri-Arabic-German, with morphological and lexicographical observations.

There is no grammar of Soqoṭri. The only complete outline was published by M. Bittner.[625]

D. H. Müller[626] gives a table of phonetic correspondences between Mehri, Soqoṭri and the other Semitic languages; the pronoun in Mehri, Šaḥri and Soqoṭri; and the conjugation of the verbs *kwn*, *qfd* (in the perfect and imperfect) in Soqoṭri.

613 'Notice on the Curia Muria Island', *TBGS* 3.183–97 (1840).

614 'Dialektische Studien über das Mehri in Vergleich mit verwandten Mundarten', *ZDMG* 27. 227–30 (1873). Maltzan speaks incorrectly about 200 words and calls the language 'Qarâwi' (= Šaḥri).

615 'The position of the dialect of Curia Muria in Modern South Arabic', *BSOAS* 12.5–19 (1947).

616 For the description of the island, see J. Tkatsch, 'Soḳotra', *EI* 4.476–81 (1927).

617 'Memoir on the island of Socotra', *JRGS* 5.220–29 (1835).

618 'Quelques mots de l'idiome de Socotra', in his *Documents sur l'histoire, la géographie et le commerce de l'Afrique orientale* 2/2.478–9 (Paris, 1855).

619 *Botany of Socotra*, 439 (Edinburgh, 1888).

620 See fn. 601.

621 *Southern Arabia*, 440–8 (London, 1900).

622 *Die Mehri- und Soqoṭri-Sprache*. I. Texte (Wien, 1902). KAWSE 4; II. Soqoṭri-Texte (Wien, 1905). KAWSE 6; III. Šḫauri-Texte (Wien, 1907). KAWSE 7.

623 *Vorstudien zur Grammatik und zum Wörterbuche der Soqoṭri-Sprache*, vol. 2 (Wien, 1918). SWAW, Bd. 186, Abh. 4.

624 *Vorstudien zur Grammatik und zum Wörterbuche der Soqoṭri-Sprache*, vol. 3 (Wien, 1918). SWAW, Bd. 186, Abh. 5.

625 'Charakteristik der Sprache der Insel Soqoṭra', *AWAW* 55.48–83 (1918).

626 *Die Mehri- und Soqoṭri-Sprache*. II. Soqoṭri-Texte, 372–6 (Wien, 1905). KAWSE 6.

W. Leslau[627] has published a short outline of Soqoṭri; a table of correspondences between Soqoṭri, Mehri, Šaḥri, Arabic, Epigraphic South Arabian, Hebrew and Aramaic; and a detailed phonetic description of Soqoṭri, Mehri, Šaḥri, and comparisons between these and other Semitic languages.

In the field of specific problems, D. H. Müller[628] gives a list of Soqoṭri nouns of the form *qatlal, šaqtal* which designate colors and bodily defects. He compares the Soqoṭri form with Arabic *'aqtalu.*

M. Bittner[629] has analyzed the feminine marker *-t*, the expression of possession, particularly with the noun of relationship. In another article[630] the author discusses several morphological features, such as the loss of the prefix *t-* of the imperfect, the passive, the internal gender and the number marker in the verb.

W. Leslau describes a special case of the treatment of the reflexive marker *t*;[631] the prefix *n-* in Soqoṭri;[632] and the internal passive in Soqoṭri.[633]

The problem of the so-called 'parasitic' *h* in Soqoṭri and its identification with the *h* in Epigraphic South Arabian has been discussed by F. Praetorius,[634] D. Nielsen,[635] and N. Rhodokanakis.[636]

An etymological dictionary of Soqoṭri with a French-Soqoṭri index has been published by W. Leslau.[637] The dictionary is elaborated on the basis of Müller's texts.[638] The principal forms of the noun and the verb are indicated with reference to Müller's volume. Müller's misinterpretation of certain passages are rectified by the author.

M. Bittner[639] published a glossary of Soqoṭri with reference to the page where each word is analyzed. The same author[640] also gave a list of Persian loanwords in Soqoṭri.

627 *Lexique soqoṭri*, 9–43 (Paris, 1938).

628 'Die Form *qatlal* und *qatlil* in der Soqoṭri-Sprache', *Florilegium, ou, Recueil de travaux d'érudition dédiés à Monsieur le marquis Melchior de Vogüé*, 445–55 (Paris, 1909).

629 *Vorstudien zur Grammatik und zum Wörterbuche der Soqoṭri-Sprache*, 1.4–31 (Wien, 1913). SWAW, Bd. 173, Abh. 4.

630 'Einige Besonderheiten der Sprache der Insel Soqoṭra', *WZKM* 30.347–58 (1917–18).

631 'Observations sur quelques faits éthiopiens et sudarabiques. III. Un cas particulier du traitement du *t* du refléchi en soqoṭri', *GLECS* 3.19–20 (1937).

632 'Sur le préfixe *n-* en soqoṭri', *GLECS* 2.45–7 (1936).

633 'Le passif interne en soqoṭri', *GLECS* 2.91–2 (1937).

634 'Zur Frage über das parasitische *h* des Minäischen', *ZDMG* 62.708–13 (1908).

635 *Der sabäische Gott Ilmuḳah*, 15–19 (Berlin, 1910).

636 *Studien zur Lexikographie und Grammatik des Altsüdarabischen*, vol. 1.12–56 (Wien, 1915). SWAW, Bd. 178, Abh. 4.

637 *Lexique soqoṭri* (*sudarabique moderne*), avec comparaisons et explications étymologiques (Paris, 1938).

638 See fn. 622.

639 *Vorstudien zur Grammatik und zum Wörterbuche der Soqoṭri-Sprache* 2.72–80 (Wien, 1918). SWAW, Bd. 186, Abh. 4.

640 *Vorstudien zur Grammatik und zum Wörterbuche der Soqoṭri-Sprache* 1.31–6 (Wien, 1913). SWAW, Bd. 173, Abh. 4.

An index of the Soqoṭri particles has been published by E. Wagner in his Syntax.[641] Isolated etymologies were published by W. Leslau[642] and G. Colin.[643]

ʿAbd-el-Kūri

ʿAbd-el-Kūri is a small island to the west of Soqoṭra. The only document of the ʿAbd-el-Kūri dialect is a collection of texts published by D. H. Müller.[644]

E. Wagner[645] elaborated the phonology, morphology and syntax on the basis of Müller's texts. He also gave a list of words that either are not found in Soqoṭri or have another meaning or another form in Soqoṭri. On the basis of these considerations he arrives at the conclusion that ʿAbd-el-Kūri is a Soqoṭri dialect.

General Problems

This section will deal with phonological, morphological and lexicographical problems that arise in more than one language.

The problem of the three sibilants in Modern South Arabian and their etymological correspondence with the Epigraphic South Arabian sibilants has been discussed by D. H. Müller[646] and N. Rhodokanakis.[647] Another opinion is expressed by W. Leslau[648] and accepted by A. F. L. Beeston.[649]

D. H. Müller[650] and W. Leslau[651] give a table of correspondence between the various Modern South Arabian languages and other Semitic languages.

D. H. Müller[652] also examines the meaning of the verbal noun in the various Modern South Arabian languages.

Maria Höfner[653] makes occasional comparisons between the Mehri morphology and that of Šaḥri and Soqoṭri.

In the field of lexicography and etymology mention should be made of J. Halévy[654]

[641] *Syntax der Mehri-Sprache*, 166–7 (Berlin, 1953).
[642] 'Observations sur quelques faits éthiopiens et sudarabiques. IV. Etymologie du soqoṭri *di-ʿimede* "bédouin"', *GLECS* 3.19–20 (1938).
[643] 'Observations critiques sur quatre communications antérieures. IV. Sur W. Leslau, Soqoṭri *di-ʿimede*', *GLECS* 3.28 (1938).
[644] *Die Mehri- und Soqoṭri-Sprache*. I. Texte, 92–111 (Wien, 1902). KAWSE 4.
[645] 'Der Dialekt von ʿAbd-el-Kūri', *Anthropos* 54.475–86 (1959).
[646] *Die Mehri- und Soqoṭri-Sprache*. I. Texte, p. viii, fn. 1 (Wien, 1902).
[647] 'Altsabäische Texte', *WZKM* 39.225–6 (1932).
[648] *Lexique soqoṭri*, p. 32 (Paris, 1938); 'Der *ś*-Laut in den modernen südarabischen Sprachen', *WZKM* 44.211–8 (1937).
[649] *A descriptive grammar of Epigraphic South Arabian*, 13–14 (London, 1962).
[650] *Die Mehri- und Soqoṭri-Sprache*. II. Soqoṭri-Texte, 372–6 (Wien, 1905).
[651] *Lexique soqoṭri*, 9–43 (Paris, 1938).
[652] 'Das Substantivum verbale', in *Orientalische Studien, Theodor Nöldeke gewidmet*, 781–6 (Giessen, 1906).
[653] See fn. 558.
[654] 'Lettre à Monsieur d'Abbadie sur l'origine asiatique des langues du nord de l'Afrique', *ASP* 1.29–43 (1869).

who examines the Šaḥri words of F. Fresnel, and the Mehri words of H. J. Carter and L. Krapf, and compares them with Egyptian and Berber.

M. Bittner,[655] D. H. Müller,[656] and W. Leslau[657] suggest etymologies for some Mehri and Soqoṭri roots.

W. Leslau[658] analyzes the roots expressing the parts of the body in Modern South Arabian, and finds many words in Modern South Arabian that are not found in the other Semitic languages. The same author lists the roots common to Ethiopic, Epigraphic South Arabian and Modern South Arabian;[659] the roots common to Akkadian, Ethiopic, South Arabian;[660] and Ethiopic and South Arabian cognates to the Hebrew lexicon.[661]

The dialectal unity of the various Modern South Arabian languages presents no problem in the present state of our knowledge. It is quite generally accepted that Modern South Arabian forms a unit with Epigraphic South Arabian, even though the precise relationship is difficult to establish: because of the nature of the Epigraphic South Arabian script, we do not know the vocalic system of Epigraphic South Arabian. More intriguing is the relation between South Arabian and Ethiopic. Their unity is accepted by E. Glaser,[662] J. Cantineau,[663] W. Leslau,[664] and M. Höfner.[665] It is denied by M. Moscati[666] and A. Murtonen.[667] There are some (A. Ungnad,[668] V. Christian,[669] O. Rössler)[670] who find a dialectal unity between South Arabian and Akkadian, others (J. Cantineau,[671] W. Leslau[672]) who deny it. In a monograph devoted to the subject, V. Christian[673] connects Modern South Arabian with Aramaic. There is no doubt that more investigation is necessary on this very complicated problem.

[655] 'Kleine Mitteilungen', *WZKM* 30.423–5 (1917–18).

[656] 'Mehri- und Soqoṭri-Glossen', *ZDMG* 58.780–6 (1904); 'Soqoṭri-Glossen', *WZKM* 23.347–59 (1904).

[657] 'Remarques sur quelques mots du sudarabique moderne', *MSL* 23.407–10 (1935).

[658] 'The parts of the body in the modern South Arabic languages', *Lg* 21.230–49 (1945).

[659] 'South-east Semitic (Ethiopic and South Arabic) vocabulary', *JAOS* 63.11–14 (1943).

[660] 'Vocabulary common to Akkadian and South-east Semitic (Ethiopic and South Arabic)', *JAOS* 64.53–8 (1945).

[661] *Ethiopic and South Arabic contributions to the Hebrew lexicon* (Berkeley and Los Angeles, 1958).

[662] 'Das Weihrauchland und Soḳotra', *Beilage zur Allgemeinen Zeitung*. Nos 120 and 121. The author considers Mehri and Amharic as 'Tochtersprachen' of Habashitic (Geez).

[663] 'Accadien et sudarabique', *BSL* 33.175–204 (1932).

[664] 'South-east Semitic (Ethiopic and South Arabic)', *JAOS* 63.4-14 (1943).

[665] 'Über sprachliche und kulturelle Beziehungen zwischen Südarabien und Äthiopien im Altertum', *ACISE* 435–44.

[666] 'Nordarabico, sudarabico, etiopico', *RSO* 34.33–9 (1959).

[667] *Early Semitic*. A diachronical inquiry into the relationship of Ethiopic to the so-called South-east Semitic languages (Leiden, 1967).

[668] *Das Wesen des Ursemitischen: eine sprachgeschichtliche und psychologische Untersuchung* (Leipzig, 1925).

[669] 'Akkader und Südaraber als ältere Semitenschichte', *Anthropos* 14/15.729–39 (1919–20).

[670] 'Verbalbau und Verbalflexion in den semitohamitischen Sprachen', *ZDMG* 100.461–514 (1951), and elsewhere.

[671] See fn. 524.

[672] 'The imperfect in South-east Semitic', *JAOS* 73.164–6 (1953), and elsewhere.

[673] *Die Stellung des Mehri innerhalb der semitischen Sprachen* (Wien, 1944). SWAW, Bd. 222, Abh. 3.

South Arabian in Studies of General Semitic

Modern South Arabian is treated in studies dealing with general Semitic even though no mention is made of 'South Arabian' in the title of these studies. Needless to say, only a selection can be given here.

In the field of phonology, the relation between South Arabian *š* and Semitic *h* is analyzed by W. Leslau.[674]

R. Růžička[675] considers Modern South Arabian with the other Semitic languages in seeking a solution to the problem of dissimilation.

In his volumes on comparative Semitic morphology and syntax, C. Brockelmann discusses South Arabian.[676]

M. Cohen discusses South Arabian in connection with the Semitic verbal system,[677] and the affix *n*;[678] J. Barth, in connection with the Semitic pronoun;[679] T. Nöldeke, in connection with the perfect;[680] L. Reinisch, in connection with the pronoun and verbal forms;[681] C. Brockelmann, in connection with the diminutive and augmentative;[682] W. Leslau, in connection with the verbal diminutive;[683] H. Torczyner, in connection with the various nominal endings;[684] E. Wagner, in connection with the dual;[685] and J. M. Sola-Solé, in connection with the infinitive.[686]

In the field of lexicography, C. Brockelmann,[687] C. Landberg,[688] and M. Cohen[689] make use of South Arabian in the various comparative dictionaries.

V. Christian[690] mentions South Arabian in his study on the 'deictic' elements in Semitic.

T. Nöldeke[691] treats South Arabian among the Semitic biradicals.

[674] 'Le rapport entre *š* et *h* en sémitique', *AIPH* 7.265–72 (1939–44).

[675] *Konsonantische Dissimilation in den semitischen Sprachen* (Leipzig, 1909). BA, Band 6, Heft 4.

[676] *Grundriss der vergleichenden Grammatik der semitischen Sprachen*. 2 vols. (Berlin, 1908–13).

[677] *Le système verbal sémitique et l'expression du temps* (Paris, 1924).

[678] 'Sur l'affixe *n* dans les verbes expressifs de diverses langues chamito-sémitiques', *MIFAO* 67. 705–19 (1935).

[679] *Die Pronominalbildung in den semitischen Sprachen* (Leipzig, 1913).

[680] 'Die Endungen des Perfects', in his *Beiträge zur semitischen Sprachwissenschaft*, 15–29 (Strassburg, 1914).

[681] *Das persönliche Fürwort und die Verbalflexion in den chamito-semitischen Sprachen* (Wien, 1909).

[682] 'Diminutiv und Augmentativ im Semitischen', *ZS* 6.109–34 (1928).

[683] 'Sur le diminutif verbal en sémitique', *Word* 1.277–80 (1945).

[684] *Die Entstehung des semitischen Sprachtypus*. Ein Beitrag zum Problem der Entstehung der Sprache (Wien, 1916).

[685] 'Die erste Person Dualis im Semitischen', *ZDMG* 102.229–33 (1952).

[686] 'L'infinitif en sud-arabique. II. Le sud-arabique moderne', in his *L'infinitif sémitique*, 40–4 (Paris, 1961).

[687] *Lexicon syriacum*. 2nd ed. (Halle, 1928).

[688] *Glossaire Datinois*. 3 vols. (Leiden, 1920–42).

[689] *Essai comparatif sur le vocabulaire et la phonétique du chamito-sémitique* (Paris, 1947).

[690] 'Die deiktischen Elemente in den semitischen Sprachen', *WZKM* 31.137–92 (1924).

[691] 'Zweiradikalige Substantiva', in his *Neue Beiträge zur semitischen Sprachwissenschaft*, 109–78 (Strassburg, 1910).

A. Z. Aešcoly[692] compares Hebrew roots with those of Mehri and Šaḥri.

Walter W. Müller[693] makes extensive use of Modern South Arabian in his study of Epigraphic South Arabian roots with 2nd and 3rd radical *w/y*.

Bibliography

The reader will find more detailed information on the various problems mentioned here in the bibliography published by W. Leslau in 1946.[694] The few additional items from 1946 to 1953 were recorded by E. Wagner.[695] An annotated study on E. Wagner's Mehri syntax[696] and on W. Leslau's studies on Modern South Arabian was published by F. A. Pennacchietti.[697]

To SUMMARIZE, we may state that a basis for comparison of the grammar and vocabulary of Modern South Arabian languages with those of the other Semitic languages has been laid by the above mentioned studies. What is still needed is a more complete dictionary of Mehri and Šaḥri, and a grammar of Soqoṭri. For that matter, since the field of study is rather limited, a general comparative dictionary of all the Modern South Arabian languages would be of great help for the Semitist. These deficiencies can be removed by the collection of many more first-hand documents in South Arabia by trained linguists. Collection of additional texts as well as of material for more complete dictionaries and grammars is essential to fill the gap in our knowledge of South Arabian.

I can only repeat what I said some twenty years ago. It is now time for the Semitist to investigate these languages in South Arabia itself, since the Modern South Arabian languages are in danger of disappearing and of being replaced by the Arabic dialects of the neighboring tribes.

[692] 'Mĕqoroṯ lĕ'oṣar hammilim ha'iḇri', *Leshonenu* 7.83–6, 163–70, 283–90, 372–7 (1937); 8.49–63 (1938).

[693] *Die Wurzeln mediae und tertiae y/w im Altsüdarabischen* (Tübingen, 1962).

[694] 'Modern South Arabic languages. A bibliography', *Bulletin of the New York Public Library*, 1945. 29 p.

[695] *Syntax der Mehri-Sprache*, p. 156 (Berlin, 1953).

[696] See fn. 578.

[697] 'Recenti studi sudarabici', *AIUO* 17.337–42 (1967).

B

OTHER LANGUAGES

EGYPTIAN

J. VERGOTE

The study of the Egyptian language presents two principal aspects: the description of Egyptian in its different stages, and the examination of the relations between Egyptian and the Hamito-Semitic languages. The two problems have been treated on the basis of a full and up-to-date bibliography by A. Korostovtsev (1963).

I. THE CONNECTION OF EGYPTIAN TO RELATED LANGUAGES

The numerous theories concerning the comparison of Egyptian with neighboring languages are the subject of the first part of Cohen's book (1947:3–42). This author advocates the subdivision of Hamito-Semitic into four relatively independent groups:

1) the Semitic group (see SEMITIC)
2) Egyptian
3) the Libyco-Berber or (more briefly) the Berber group (see BERBER)
4) the Cushitic group (see CUSHITIC)

Cohen's bibliography can be completed by the items which are given in the review of this work by F. Hintze (1951).

Before Cohen the Egyptian vocabulary had been compared with that of Semitic by A. Ember (1930) and in the posthumous work of F. Calice (1936). The latter had also introduced comparisons with the Cushitic and Berber languages. His work lost none of its value with the publication of Cohen's book since his included an even higher number of Egyptian etymologies, which are moreover painstakingly arranged according to their degree of certitude or probability (complement to this work, with an identical title, by Vycichl 1958). Cohen had taken as a base a list of about five hundred French words, composed of the names of very basic objects and common activities. The corresponding terms were then sought in the Egyptian lexicon and in lexicons of the various supposedly related languages. His lexical list is arranged according to the phonemes, for which the author tried to establish the rules governing the phonological correspondences.

Notwithstanding the studies of W. Vycichl (1934) and J. Lukas (1937, 1939), Cohen does not consider Hausa to be a Hamito-Semitic language. However, he felt that he could not neglect this language, which is spoken primarily in northern Nigeria and in the southern part of Niger. Lukas had studied, along with Hausa, the related languages of the Chad area, which he called Chado-Hamitic. The study of these languages has recently made fresh progress due to the publications of P. Newman and Roxana Ma (1966) and V. M. Illič-Svityč (1966). On the other hand, A. B. Dolgopoljskij (1966) has treated a problem of comparative Cushitic phonology, and I. M. Diakonoff (1965) has made an over-all survey of Hamito-Semitic. C. T. Hodge, after having gathered material intended to establish the relationship of Hausa to Egyptian (1966), has taken up this problem again (1967), using the results of Newman-Ma, who had treated certain Chadic languages. On the basis of these studies, it is possible to add a fifth group, Nigero-Chadic, to the four above-mentioned groups composing the Hamito-Semitic family.

The origin of Hamitic and its relationship with Semitic have generally been explained by the hypothesis of a more or less complete fusion of primitive autochthonous African tongues with proto-Semitic dialects introduced into north and northeast Africa. As long as the division into 1) Semitic, 2) Egyptian, 3) Hamitic (comprising the Berber and Cushitic languages) prevailed, the question of the relationship of Egyptian to the first or third group remained particularly acute. Two theses confront each other here. The first, defended by A. Erman (1892) and K. Sethe (1899–1902), claimed that Egyptian was of Semitic origin. The clearest assertion came from W. F. Albright (1923:70): 'Egyptian is throughout a Semitic language. The number of certain etymologies is increasing with great rapidity, and though there are many problems as yet unsolved, the writer is convinced that Egyptian is in no sense a *Mischsprache*, like Babylonian, but is probably Semitic throughout.' Among the scholars who declared themselves in favor of connecting Egyptian with Hamitic, we must cite especially É. Naville (1920), F. Lexa (1921–22), G. Möller (1924), Frida Behnk (1928) and E. Zyhlarz (1933). The spread of this second thesis was largely due to the fact that it was adopted by G. Lefebvre (1936) and expounded as follows in his grammar (1940, 1955²: §1): 'L'égyptien comporterait donc essentiellement lui aussi un substrat africain (plutôt libyque), que pénétrèrent et modifièrent de fortes influences sémitiques: c'est bien plutôt, semble-t-il, une langue africaine sémitisée qu'une langue sémitique déformée.' Sir Alan Gardiner, after having cited (1927, 1957) certain correspondences between Egyptian and Semitic, continues further (1957: §3): 'In spite of these resemblances, Egyptian differs from all the Semitic tongues a good deal more than any one of them differs from any other, and at least until its relationship to the African languages is more closely defined, Egyptian must certainly be classified as standing outside the Semitic group. There are grounds for thinking that it is a language which, possibly owing to a fusion of races, had, like English as compared with the other Teutonic dialects, disintegrated and developed at an abnormally rapid pace.'

The division of Hamito-Semitic into four distinct groups, as proposed by Cohen, or into five groups, gives an entirely different aspect to this problem. F. Hintze (1951:67) said regarding this proposition: 'Vor allem wird so der müssige Streit darüber, ob das Ägyptische zu den semitischen oder hamitischen Sprachen gehöre, gegenstandslos: es ist eine Untergruppe der hamitosemitischen Sprachen, wie das Semitische, Berberische oder Kuschitische. Auch die verbreitete Ansicht, das Ägyptische sei das Resultat einer Überschichtung und stelle eine Art Semitisch auf hamitischem Substrat dar, kann in dieser Form nicht als durch sprachliche Tatsachen bewiesen gelten. Es finden sich bei einer eingehenden Untersuchung der lexikalischen, morphologischen und phonologischen Einzelheiten so viele sich überschneidende Isoglossen, dass je nach dem gewählten Kriterium jede der Untergruppen zu jeder beliebigen anderen als enger verwandt gestellt werden könnte. Dagegen weisen diese vier Untergruppen einerseits genügend charakteristische Merkmale auf, um sie je als besondere Gruppe auffassen zu können, und andererseits sind ihnen genügend Merkmale gemeinsam, um sie zu einer grösseren Einheit des Hamitosemitischen zusammenzufassen.' It is in the same sense that Cohen, in the above-mentioned work and in his other writings, notably in A. Meillet-M. Cohen (1924, 1952) eliminates the term 'Hamitic' as designating the Libyco-Berber and Cushitic groups. The term Hamito-Semitic refers to the whole family, with no subdivision inferred.

The reaction against G. Lefebvre's opinion, which one sees in the citation from Hintze, is also found in Vycichl (1959c:27): 'A certain affinity between Egyptian and the Semitic languages is admitted by all scholars. It is explained by a blend of an older autochthonous element of African origin, called Hamitic, and a younger Semitic wave. This opinion can hardly be maintained in view of the facts we possess now.' The same attitude was adopted by Fecht (1960:193, fn. 545). Moreover, these two authors accept the theories of O. Rössler (1952, 1958), according to which none of the 'Hamitic' languages, even the Libyco-Berber group, offers any traces of an African substratum and must consequently be considered Semitic. Vycichl concludes: 'Under these new points of view, Egyptian is not situated as hitherto, on the borderline of the domain of Semitic languages but at its centre.' Fecht writes to the same effect: 'Aus diesen und manchen anderen Gründen ... neige ich der Anschauung T. Nöldeke's zu, der in Nordafrika die Urheimat des Grosssprachstammes suchte (Nöldeke, *Die semitischen Sprachen*, S. 11).'

We may note here that A. N. Tucker recently (1967) proposed to substitute the name 'Erythraeic' for the term Hamito-Semitic. He compares the Red Sea to the body of a butterfly whose wings extend into Asia and into Africa. In this study he has shown that the personal pronouns of Egyptian are found in the Ik (Teuso) language spoken in eastern Uganda.

A very solid brief account of the correspondences of Egyptian with related languages is found in the grammar of Lefebvre (1955:§§3–6). He distinguishes A) Common points between Egyptian on the one hand and Semitic, Libyco-Berber and Cushitic on the other; B) Agreement of Egyptian with the other languages of the family, excluding Semitic; C) Special affinities between Egyptian and Semitic; D) Linguistic features restricted to Egyptian. This account has been reproduced by Korostovtsev (1963).

II. DESCRIPTION OF THE EGYPTIAN LANGUAGE

Notwithstanding the above discussion, the Egyptian grammars are synchronic in character. The most important are those of A. H. Gardiner (1927) and G. Lefebvre (1940), which follow in general the pattern worked out from 1894 on by A. Erman (1928[4]) for the language of the Middle Kingdom, classical Egyptian. The last editions of these date respectively from 1957 and 1955. A sketch made by C. T. Hodge (1954) is designed to give the general linguist a brief account of the linguistic structure of Middle Egyptian. A minute analysis of Old Egyptian has been made by E. Edel (1955–64), while W. Westendorf (1962) has published a detailed grammar of Middle Egyptian medical texts. For Late Egyptian there is still the second edition of A. Erman's grammar (1933) which remains a valuable manual. W. Spiegelberg (1925) and F. Lexa (1947–51) have furnished us with grammars of Demotic.

A. *Phonetics and Phonology*

It was at about the same time that W. Czermak (1931–34) and W. H. Worrell (1934) independently tried to determine the phonetic value of, respectively, the Egyptian and the Coptic consonants. The first based his theory on orthographic variants and errors in the Egyptian texts, on the transcription of Egyptian words into cuneiform, and on the transcription of Canaanite words into hieroglyphs. The second established the value of Coptic consonants by comparing them with the consonants of Middle and Late Egyptian, the evidence of the Canaanite words found in Egyptian helping him to identify them.

In order to resolve the impasse to which the divergent theories of these two authors led, I have redone their work (Vergote 1945) beginning, as did Worrell, from Coptic and basing myself on the same data as they, but I have tried to carry the matter back, thanks to the etymologies of Calice (1936), to proto-Semitic. My conclusions are as follows:

1) It is necessary to admit with Worrell that, contrary to Czermak, Egyptian did not have any emphatic stops. The distinction between voiced and voiceless stops, postulated for proto-Semitic, was replaced in Egyptian by the opposition between voiceless stops and voiceless aspirated stops. This sound shift could have occurred at the time the Egyptian language was formed; it was certainly accomplished before the end of the Old Kingdom, given the fact that even at this time the voiced consonant /z/ was replaced by a voiceless /s/.

The phonemes which Egyptologists transcribe by *d*, *ḏ*, *g*, *ḳ* were therefore actually voiceless /t/č/k/q/ and those transcribed by *p*, *t*, *ṯ*, *k* had the values of /ph/th/čh/kh/. If the latter were not aspirated at the end of a syllable and at the beginning of an unaccented syllable, these simple voiceless consonants are to be considered as allophones of the aspirated ones; also in a like manner in Coptic-Bohairic: *čhoys* 'lord', pl. *čisēwi*.

2) Worrell was correct in distinguishing two prepalatalizations instead of one (Czermak). The first, giving rise to the change pSem. *g* > Eg. *ḏ* and pSem. *k* > Eg. *ṯ*, took place in prehistoric times. At the beginning of the Old Kingdom, with the exception of sporadic writings with *k*, attesting perhaps to dialect variants, this change had reached the stage where *ḏ* represented /t'/ and *ṯ* was equivalent to /t'h/. After the palatalization had disappeared in the majority of words, confusing these phonemes with *d* = /t/ and *t* = /th/, the progress of prepalatalization in the remaining cases changed *ḏ* into /č/ and *ṯ* into /čh/, probably before the end of the Old Kingdom.

The second prepalatalization, which I had assigned to the New Kingdom, appears rather to have taken place after the fourth century B.C. (cf. Albright 1946:317).

The origin and the evolution of *ḫ* and *ẖ* is explained by the extension of the two prepalatalizations to the velo-palatal spirant.

Beja *g* corresponds to many cases where Eg. *ḏ* equates with Sem. *ṣ*: Eg. *ḏbʿ* 'finger' = *gība*; Eg. *ḏrw* 'frontier' = *gil*; perhaps also Eg. *ḏd* 'endure' = *gad* 'hold'. This made me suppose that Common Semitic has participated in the same prepalatalization as Egyptian: in place of /g/ > /t'/ > /č/ the result here was a /ts/ or /s/, in other cases a /d/ or /z/ which preserved a secondary velar articulation (Vergote 1945:53, 147–8). In this hypothesis the emphasis of Arabic (and Hebrew), which is essentially a velarization, represents the most ancient state. The glottalization which characterizes the emphatic consonants of Cushitic (and of Chadic) could then be an innovation resulting from the substitution of neighboring points of articulation in the off-glide.

3) Egyptian possessed the four laryngals which exist in Arabic and Hebrew. The examples where Eg. *ꜣ* corresponds to a proto-Semitic *ʾaleph*, the numerous cases where it is substituted for pSem. *r* or *l*, particularly in a syllabic final position, and especially the fact that it alternates with *ʿayin* (1945:133, no. 3c, d) show that Eg. *ꜣ* was, like the last, a laryngal consonant, in fact the glottal stop /ʔ/. The Semitic correspondences show that the other laryngals of Egyptian were /ʿayin/, /h/ and /ḥ/.

In the course of its history, Egyptian underwent a gradual reduction of laryngal consonants, comparable to that which occurred in the various Semitic languages. The weakening of *ꜣ* at the end of the syllable and the concomitant change of *ʿayin* to /ʔ/ have been dated by me as occurring under the Old Kingdom (1945:97). This early dating is, however, contradicted by the treatment of certain vowels in Coptic. Sahidic, where earlier /a/ generally became /o/, shows this same change before /ʔ/ representing an earlier *ꜣ*: *rꜣ*: **raꜣ* > S *ro* 'mouth'; before a /ʔ/ derived from /r/t/w/y/: *ḏr.t.f*: **dártaf* > S *to'təf* 'his hand'; *itrw*: **yátru* > **yá'ru* > S *yo'r* 'canal'; *mkḥ.w*: **maḳáḥwu* > **maḳáwḥu* > B *əmkawh* > S *əmko'h* 'sufferings'; *bin.t*: **báynat* > **báʾnat* > S *boʾne* 'evil'; also before /ʔ/ from /ʿ/ preceding /ḥ/: *iʿḥ*: **yáʿḥu* > *áʾḥu* > S *oʾh* 'moon'; *sʿḥʿ*: **sáʿḥaʿ* > **sáʾḥaʾ* > S *soʾhe* 'set upright'. To the contrary, earlier /a/ is preserved before /ʔ/ derived from /ʿ/: *ḏbʿ* > S *təbá* 'ten thousand'; *wʿb.w* > S *wáʾb* 'pure'. This proves that at the time of the change /a/ > /o/, /ʿ/ was still distinct from /ʔ/ except, by dissimilation, when it preceded /ḥ/. But E. Edel has shown (1954:35–6) that this change, before /ʔ/ at the end of a word, is attested by cuneiform transcriptions of the Amarna period, and, before the syllabic final /ʔ/ preceding a consonant, by a transcription dating at the latest in the twelfth century B.C. I have since shown that this latter phenomenon is already found in the cuneiform transcriptions of the 'prenomen' of Amenhotep IV and Tutankhamon (1961b). But in every other position the /a/ seems still to be retained at this period, so that the thirteenth century B.C. appears to be the *terminus post quem* of the change of the Egyptian *ʿayin* into a glottal stop.

Thus we obtain the following scheme for the consonants of Middle Egyptian:

LABIALS	LABIO-DENTALS	DENTALS	PREPALATALS	POSTPALATALS	VELARS	LARYNGALS
ph:		(t:th):	(č:čh):	(k_2:kh_2):	k_3:	ʔ
	f:	s:š:		x_2 :	x_3:	h:(ḥ:ʿ)
ẉ:ƀ:			j			
m:		n				
		l:r				

These phonetic definitions have in large part been adopted by S. Sauneron in the second edition of Lefebvre's grammar. E. Edel (1955–64) has done the same. However, when *ỉ* does not represent a /j/ he does not see in it, as we do, a simple vowel support (with gradual beginning or ending) but, under the influence of Albright (1946), a weaker glottal stop, corresponding to that of Ger. *Ver'ein*. In contrast, according to him, *ȝ* is equivalent to the stronger laryngal stop which is substituted for classical /q/ in the spoken Arabic of Egypt, e.g. in /'amar/ 'moon'. Thus he practically returns to the view defended by Czermak.

On the other hand, after having presented in §119 my description of *ḫ* (= /x_3/), he prefers, in the *Nachträge* (p. xxxvi), with reference to Hintze, to place *ḫ* parallel to *k* (and so = /x_2/). Besides, he places *ẖ* parallel with *ḏ*, *ṯ* (thus = /ç/ or voiceless *yod*). The stops and fricatives should then be distributed as follows:

LABIALS	LABIO-DENTALS	DENTALS	PREPALATALS	POSTPALATALS	VELARS	LARYNGALS
ph:		(t:th):	(t′:t′h):	(k_2:kh_2):	k_3:	ʔ
	f:	(z:s):š:	ç:	x_2:		h:(ḥ:ʿ)

I myself assigned this value of *ẖ* = /ç/ to the earliest stage of the Egyptian language, but I also supposed that, parallel to *ḏ*, *ṯ*, this phoneme had, before the end of the Old Kingdom, lost the prepalatal quality; otherwise *ḫ* would have been confused with *ẖ* at the time of the second prepalatization. While this phenomenon caused the shift of *ḏ*, *ṯ* to /t/, /th/, the fricative *ẖ*, on the other hand, retracted and became /x_2/. But since the distinction between *ẖ* and *ḫ* was maintained, this implied that from the very beginning *ḫ* was parallel to the velar /k_3/, hence being /x_3/. Therefore the empty slot which rose from the disappearing of /ç/ was occupied by *ḫ* at the time of the second prepalatization in dialects other than Akhmimic; it is this new /ç/ which is rendered in Old Coptic by ϭ, and by ϣ in the Ascension of Isaiah (cf. Kahle 1954:203–5), anticipating its merger with original /š/. In Akhmimic and in Bohairic, ẖ = /x_2/ is preserved in this way. It probably attracted to itself the point of articulation of the original ḫ in Akhmimic and in the rare instances where, in Bohairic, this did not follow the new movement. In Sahidic, Fayumic and Subakhmimic, the laryngal articulation /h/ was substituted for the postpalatal articulation of ẖ. (Concerning the localization of the Coptic dialects see Vergote 1961d.)

The comparison of Egyptian with Hausa led C. T. Hodge (1966) to deny to Egyptian ꜣ the value of a laryngal. On the basis of certain correspondences between Eg. ꜣ and Ha. /r/ɼ/ he prefers to see there 'a trill, flap or lateral of some kind.' He also calls attention to the fact that in borrowings from Semitic the glottal stop (*ʾaleph*) is never transcribed by Eg. ꜣ but by *ỉ*. As Worrell, for example, had done earlier, Hodge also considers, by virtue of the Hausa etymologies, glottalization as the original characteristic of Hamito-Semitic emphatics, and velarization as a later development. Consequently, he rejects the evolution which I have proposed from pSem. /g/ into Sem. /ṣ/ and Eg. /č/.

In the prosodic domain, W. F. Edgerton (1947) has compared with the non-vocalized forms of Egyptian the data, established more than a half century ago by G. Steindorff and K. Sethe, concerning the structure of syllables, vowel quantity, and the place of the accent in Coptic words. He concludes from these that there were three patterns of words, governed by fixed rules lasting over a period of time which could not have begun any later than 2000 B.C. and which ended before 1350 B.C. The Egyptian of this period, which he designates by the new name of 'Paleo-Coptic', was certainly dead by this latter date. The only law which remains in force, from Paleo-Coptic to Coptic inclusively, is that which forbids the accent of the word to come farther forward than the penultimate syllable. As to the rest, the phonetic patterns of Paleo-Coptic are not represented in Late-Egyptian and in the later developments of the language except by fossilized vowel quantities.

B. *The Structure of Semantemes* (*or Lexemes*)

Of all the grammars of Egyptian, only that of E. Edel is concerned with this important problem. Given the extremely low number of prefixes and suffixes which enter into the formation of Egyptian substantives, it was to be supposed that their structure is based essentially, as in Semitic, on internal vocalic changes. On undertaking the reconstruction of these vowels, Edel has largely depended on the comparison with Coptic. He distinguishes: 1) substantives without ending, which are concrete nouns, with the exception of two types of feminines, which are verbal substantives; 2) substantives ending in *-w*, feminine *-wt*, where he identifies nouns of agent, nouns of action, and abstract nouns, as well as a variety of concrete nouns; 3) substantives ending in *-j* and *-tj*, serving to create nouns of occupations and trades; 4) feminine collectives ending in *-wt* and *-t*; 5) substantives with the prefix *m-*, which are divided into nouns of place, nouns of instrument and participles; 6) a few rare substantives with the prefix *ḥ-*. In the same manner the author makes a distinction between adjectives and verbs without any ending and, on the other hand, adjectives and verbs with the ending *-j* or *-w*. He recognizes also the use of other prefixes and suffixes in the formation of verbs.

At the time when he published his grammar E. Edel was apparently unaware of the existence of two articles, published only a short time before, in which Vycichl (1952, 1953; cf. 1956) connected two new types of Egyptian nouns of agent with well-known Semitic formations. In fact, this author identified the form *qattāl* in B *akhō* 'magician' by interpreting Eg. *ḥkꜣw* as *ḥakkāꜣo* (or *ḥakkāꜣaw*); the feminine of this form would be represented by C *satō* 'fan', derived from **saddāꜣatu* 'that which shakes'. The second form is *qittīl* which, starting as **gerrīgaw*, would produce C *cerēc* 'hunter'; the accented /a/ of the plural *cerácе* confirms the presence of an original /i/ in the second syllable.

In later studies, (1957b, 1959a and b), Vycichl discovered the existence in Egyptian of the Semitic pattern *qitl* comparing Ar. *zift* 'pitch' with C *sīfe* 'id.' and of the type *qatīl* by deriving C *ušap* 'loan' from Eg. **wašīb*, which he translated as 'that which was exchanged'. However, contrary to the preceding examples, these two words present in Egyptian a vowel quantity different from that of the Semitic types. One may also ascertain this in the efforts attempted by K. Sethe (1923) to relate the Egyptian structures to the Semitic. According to Sethe, the Semitic prototype of the infinitive C *sōtəm* 'hear' < Eg. **sādəm* was in fact the 'infinitive' *qatlun*; that of the so-called second infinitive C *ənšot* 'to be hard, strong' < Eg. **naḫát* was that which he called the infinitive of the Arabic verbs of quality *qatāl*, an example of which he sought to find in Ar. *salām* 'to be safe and sound'.

A general examination of all the structures was then made in order to determine under what conditions the vowel quantity of the proto-Semitic pattern was preserved in Egyptian or underwent a change. The benefit of a similar investigation became still more evident after I had established the existence, in Egyptian, of the type of abstract noun *qatūlat* and of the type of substantivized adjective *qútlu* and *qútlat* (1962). Parallel to H *melūḵāh* 'royalty', Egyptian presents in fact *mꜣʿ.t*: **maꜣūʿat* 'cosmic order' > C *(a)mēe*, *(a)mēi* 'truth, justice'; besides H *ḥokmāh* 'wisdom' and *qošṭ* 'truth' ('the true'), Egyptian possesses *múꜣʿat* > C *me*: *mei* 'truth' ('the true') and **wuʿbu* > C *wēʾb* 'priest' ('the pure').

This research, undertaken to restore as much as possible the original state of the Egyptian patterns, was rendered possible thanks to the work of G. Fecht (1960), which threw an entirely new light on the evolution of the accent of the Egyptian word and on its syllabic structure. This author's original intention was to explain the origin of compound words in Coptic and Egyptian which are accented on the first element of the compound and which have their second element strongly reduced; for example the name of a class of Egyptian priests made up of **ḥom* 'servant' and *nūte* 'god' became in C *hont*. These are called 'old compounds' because, as a general rule, the reverse of this is what occurs: C *how* 'day' and *mīse* 'beget' are combined as *humīse* 'birthday'. According to Fecht, these words belong to the language of civilization of the Old Kingdom, which was based upon a dialect of the Delta and which was characterized by that which he designated as the 'three syllable law'; that is to say that, in this language, the accent of the word could go back, under certain conditions, to the antepenult. In the speech of Upper Egypt, on the contrary, a 'two syllable law' has predominated since prehistoric times, which did not permit the accent to go beyond the penult. If, nevertheless, almost all the 'old compounds', insofar as they are attested in cuneiform and Greek transcription, or in Coptic, do not have the accent prior to the penult, it is because between the proto-historic period and the end of the Old Kingdom, the 'two syllable law' also affected the dialect of Lower Egypt. Because of the syncope of the unstressed vowel in an open syllable after the accent, the words conformed to this law.

In comparing the Egyptian and proto-Semitic structures of semantemes (1965a), I have taken account of the three following factors:

1) The transition from the law of the antepenult to the law of the penult due to the syncope of the vowel which was originally in the penultimate syllable;

2) The law discovered long ago by G. Steindorff, according to which the vowel of the accented syllable is long when it is open, short when it is closed;

3) The *w* and *j*, which Edel has always tended to treat as a prefix or a suffix, form a part of the root in certain words. The *ỉ* prefix and suffix and the *w* suffix, to which Edel assigned a purely consonantal value, could also represent, according to us, for *ỉ* the vowel /a/ or /i/, and *w* the vowel /u/. A similar opinion had already been propounded in 1900 by A. Erman (1900:321–2) and more recently by Thacker (1954).

These three factors perfectly accounted for the similarities and differences existing between the proto-Semitic and Egyptian structures. For example, Edel (1955–64: §§227 and 230) derived C *čoy* 'boat' from a noun of agent **ḏáꜣj͜w* meaning 'one who takes across the water' but Fecht (1960:§364), basing himself on the plural C *ečēw*, shows that this word comes from **ḏáꜣijaw*. I concluded from this that the latter had its origin in the proto-Semitic participle of the type *qātilu*; **ḏāꜣiyu*, having the above-cited sense, lost the /i/ (cf. 1) and the /ā/ shortened itself in the syllable which had become closed (cf. 2): **ḏáꜣyu* > **ḏáyyu* > C *čoy*. Many substantives which Edel believes cannot be assimilated with the nouns of agent (1955–64:§244) are explained in the same manner: *ḥfꜣw*: **ḥāfiꜣu* > **ḥáfꜣu* > C *hof* 'serpent' was 'one who crawls or wriggles'; **yāriḥu* > **yárhu* > * *yáʿḥu* > B *yoh*: S *o'h* 'moon', 'one who travels'; *hrw*: **hāriwu* > **hárwu* > **háwwu* > C *how* 'day', 'one who lights up'.

One source of irregularities in the Egyptian and Semitic correspondences is brought up by the fact that the ending *-u*, which is found in proto-Semitic in all substantives, adjectives and verbal nouns, is preserved in the masculine in certain Egyptian patterns, whereas it has disappeared in numerous other cases. According to the hypothesis which I have formulated to account for this, *-u* serves to characterize in a particular manner some deverbal forms as substantives, often in the sense of 'names of creatures or things' (cf. below: 'one who...', 'that which...') or, it may indicate that the substantive refers to some creatures or objects which normally occur in groups. Rather than the term 'collective' the term 'noun of great number' or 'noun of abundance', borrowed from Arabic grammar, is suitable to these latter formations. The shift of accent, conforming to the law of the antepenult, in feminine nouns, shows that they had everywhere preserved the ending *-u* in the earliest stage of the Egyptian language. However, this had disappeared before the law of the penult came to predominate; this explains why, for example, *qitālatu* became *qitālat* instead of becoming **qitált(u)*.

The following table enumerates the masculine substantives in Egyptian which have kept the ending *-u*, along with the corresponding feminines, and then the feminine substantives which do not correspond to masculines in *-u* and which have changed their accent. Contrary to what I did in *Verhouding* (1965a) I here set side by side the proto-Semitic forms using as a paradigm *q t l* 'kill' and the Egyptian, using *s d m* 'hear'. The class-meaning of the proto-Semitic pattern is given first.

1. active participle *qātilu*: *sádmu*; *ḥfꜣw* C *hof* 'serpent' ('one who crawls or wriggles')
   qātilatu: *sádmatu*; *bỉn.t* C *bo'ne* 'evil' ('that which is evil')
2. noun of agent *qattālu*: *saddāmu*; *ḥkꜣw* B *akhō* 'magician' ('one who performs magic')
   qattālatu: *saddāmatu*; *ṯꜣ.t*, *ṯꜣy*[*.t*] C *ečō/ačō* 'tongs' ('that which seizes')
3. concrete noun *qālu*: *sāmu*; *ḥr* C *hōr* '(the god) Horus' ('the one who is far away')
   qālatu: *sāmatu*; *ḥr.t* C **hōre* (Gr. *On-ouris*) ('the one (f.) who is far off')
4. noun of action *qítlu*: *sídmu*; *ʿḳy* C *ayk* 'consecration (of a church, etc.)' ('entrance [of the king]')
   qítlatu: *sídmatu*; *ḳrs.t* C *kayse* 'embalming' or 'preparation for burial'
5. concrete noun *qítalu*: *sídmu*; *ỉnḥ* C (*é*)*nəh* 'eyebrow' ('that which encircles, surrounds')
   qítalatu: *sidāmatu*; *šꜣ*(*y*)*.t* C *ešō* 'sow'
6. active participle *qittīlu*: *siddīmu*; *grg* C *cerēc* 'hunter' ('one who sets traps')
7. substantivized adjective *qútlu*: *súdmu*; *mrš* C *merəš*, *mērəš* 'red, ruddy person'
   qútlatu: *súdmatu*; *mꜣʿ.t* C *me*(*e*), *mei* 'truth' ('the true')
8. adjective, passive participle *qatūlu*: *sadūmu*; *bỉn* C *ebyēn* 'pauper, miserable person'
   (*prḫ*) C *prēš* 'thing spread out (mat, cloak)'
   noun of quality, noun of action *qatūlatu*: *sadūmatu*; *kmm.t* C *kmēme* 'obscurity'
   ḫpr.t C *špēre* 'miracle' ('event')
9. noun of abundance (?) *qatīlu*: *sadīmu*; *spr* C *spīr* 'rib'
10. noun of abundance (?) *qīlu*: *sīmu*; *sm*(*w*) C *sīm* 'herb'
    qīlatu: *sīmatu*; *sw.t* **sīwat* (cun. *in-si-ib-ya*) 'reed'
11. concrete noun *qátalatu*: *sadāmatu*; *ntr.t* C *əntōre* 'goddess'
    adjective *mdw.t* C *əmtō* 'depth' (Latin 'profundum')
12. concrete noun *qálqalatu*: *samsāmatu*; C *kelkōle* 'pustule'
13. concrete noun *qílqilatu*: *simsīmatu*; C *təltīle* 'drop, a tiny bit'
14. concrete noun *qátulatu*: *sadūmatu*; *mꜣy.t* C *myē* 'lioness'

If one compares the feminines of Nos. 1, 5 and 11–14, one sees that the pattern *qātilatu*, the only one which possesses a long vowel in proto-Semitic, does not agree with the law of the antepenult; *sādimatu* did not change, like the other feminines, into **sadīmatu* but, after having lost the *-u*, it preserved itself just as it was till the law of the penult came into force: *sádmat*. Another exception is found in the word *ỉmnt.t*, C *amənte* 'the realm of the dead' ('the region of the west'). *ỉmnty* C *emənt* 'west' is generally considered as an adjectival (nisbe) derivative from *yamīn* 'right hand': **yamīnatiy* > **e*(*y*)*mínt*(*e*). It follows that the corresponding feminine (having become masculine in Coptic) must be **yamīnatiyatu* or **yamīnatitu*. C *amənte* proves that the long proto-Semitic vowel kept the accent. Fecht's law relative to the antepenult must consequently be completed as follows: In the oldest stage of Egyptian, the accent moves back toward the beginning of the word until it encounters a syllable with a long vowel; if the word possesses only short vowels, the accent cannot go beyond the third syllable from the end of the word.

In a review of my study, G. Janssens (1967:103) has proposed different rules for the accent of the word in the oldest stage of Egyptian. These rules appear to have no foundation when one wishes to apply them to the formation of masculine plurals (Vergote 1969).

My inquiry has thus revealed the existence, in Egyptian, of at least sixty different structural patterns, created by internal change and of which the class-meaning is, in the majority of cases, identical with or related to that of a proto-Semitic type. It is necessary to remark however that certain ones of these are counted twice, for example, because they form at the same time both verbs and substantives or both substantives and adjectives. These are as follows:

	SUBSTANTIVES		ADJECTIVES		VERBS
	Masc.	Fem.	Masc.	Fem.	
Accented /a/	14	7	1	1	5
Accented /i/	10	8	1	1	6
Accented /u/	3	2			1

The semantemes derived by means of the suffixes *-y*, *-ty*, and *-wt* present only a distant and purely external analogy with various Semitic derivatives. Edel is the first grammarian to recognize that the derivation in *-y*, *-ty* could create substantives, notably nouns denoting professions (1955–64: §§246, 247). This term is preferably applied to derivations in *-ītiy* (Vergote 1965b: 365), but it is necessary to remark that other types also exist. Nevertheless Edel still sacrifices too much to established tradition when he designates as nisbe adjectives the majority of words derived from substantives or prepositions by means of these same morphemes. Indeed, it appears from his translations that a great number of the examples cited in §§342–8 refer to creatures or things and that they are intended to perform the function of subject and of direct or indirect object. Edel considers them substantivized adjectives (§354).

One may reverse the question and ask if this derivation is not essentially substantival. In the cases where a nisbe word modifies a substantive, we should then have a case of apposition, for example in *Ḥr ꜣḫty* 'Horus, dweller in the horizon', or it would be equivalent to the French expressions *un acte créateur, un compliment flatteur* (cf. Vergote 1952). The various relationships between the nisbe 'adjectives' and their attributes (e.g. *he who is upon his mountain*) have been studied by Schenkel (1966).

The feminine nouns formed by the addition of *-wt* after the last radical constitute two different classes. The first, where the suffix is *-ūwat*, includes some true collective nouns, for example *ꜣpd.wt* 'poultry', cf. C *rəmyē* 'tears' (Edel 1955–64: §§248–51). The second, with a suffix *-āwat* (*-āyat*), is generally considered a category of abstract nouns (Edel 1955–64:§§234–42). There is, however, a way of expressing more precisely the meaning by saying that if offers analogies with Greek words having the suffix *-ma* (Vergote 1961a:361). Like the latter, the Egyptian nouns express: 1) that which undergoes the action of the verb from which the word is derived: *ꜣṯp.wt*: **ꜣaṯpāwat*, C *etpō* 'burden' ('that which is loaded'), Gr. *bástagma*; *sbꜣ.yt*: **sabꜣāyat*, C *sbō* 'instruction' ('that which is taught'), Gr. *máthēma*; 2) the means serving to accomplish the action or the place where it is accomplished: *rs.yt*: **rasāyat*, C *ərsō* 'park, enclosure, camp' ('means of looking after (*rs*) livestock'); *mr.yt*: **marāyat*, C *əmrō* ('place at a port where ships are moored (*mr*)'); 3) by extension, something which accomplishes the action: *ḥfꜣ.wt*: **ḥafꜣāwat*, C *əhfō* 'serpent' ('one who crawls or wriggles'), *wbꜣ.yt* 'maidservant' ('one who opens [jugs]').

It is difficult to determine to what stage of Egyptian the Coptic form known as *participium conjunctum* goes back. It is a form of the verb which is attached, in the construct state, to a substantive, the two together forming a compound word which most often has a present or extra-temporal sense; for example, B *mas-nūti* 'mother of God', Gr. *theotókos* 'one who gave birth to (*mīse*) God'; S *šamše-nūte* 'servant of God' ('one who serves (*šəmše*) God'); S *pas-socən* 'perfumer', Gr. *murepsós* ('one who boils (*pīse*) perfumes'). If one sees here, with Edel (1955–64:§233), agent nouns of the type **sáḏm˘w*: *noyk* 'adulterous man', *čoy* 'boat' (derived in fact from the proto-Semitic participle *qātilu* [cf. above]), this form can already be found in Old and Middle Egyptian. This author supposes, on the other hand, that the *participium conjunctum* can also be derived in part from the Egyptian perfective participle, to which he assigns a vocalization resembling that of the above-mentioned agent nouns (but **māsej* for the *3ae* Infirmae verbs, cf. §627). The same hypothesis was already formulated by A. Erman and G. Steindorff, rejected by K. Sethe and revived by T. W. Thacker (1954), who proposed a vocalization analogous to that of Edel. However, I feel that I have demonstrated (1956:43–5; 1960:28–32) that the *participium conjunctum* always represents the construct state of the perfective active participle, which was vocalized **saḏmíy* and which survived in Coptic in substantives accented on the last syllable and called by Steindorff 'apparent nisbe forms' (1951:§120), e.g. C *nešté* 'one who is hard, rough'; C *alké* 'last day of the month', ('one who ends [the month]');

C *mané* 'shepherd'. The result is that, by a development parallel to proto-Semitic *qātilu*/Eg. **ḏāꜣiyu* > C *čoy* 'boat', the Egyptian participles, which were also substantival ('one who...'), became true substantives in Coptic. This also implies that the Coptic *participium conjunctum*, because of its construct state which attests to a 'genitive' relation, had to have a late origin. So long as the Egyptian participle preserved its verbal nature, it was able to take a direct object. This is borne out by the form *mny.w* (plural) *ḥtr.w* (plural) 'those who raise horses', attested to by an ostracon of Deir el-Medineh and which is parallelled by C *mane-hto* 'horse-keeper, groom', in which J. Černý discovers the origin of the (graecized) name *Manethōs* (1950:39).

It naturally follows that this comparison between the structure of Egyptian semantemes and proto-Semitic semantemes assures for the first time a precise etymology for a great number of Egyptian and Coptic words.

C. *Morphology*

I. *The Substantive*

In the domain of the substantive, there were no great innovations to be expected. The formation of the 'direct genitive' poses a special problem due to the fact that Coptic attests to the existence of two different processes: the first, which constitutes the general rule, consists in the reduction of the determined element, which is put in the construct state, as in the Semitic languages, and, secondly, the existence of a certain number of words where it is the determiner which suffers the reduction, as a result of the loss of the accent. In the preceding section, which deals with the lexicon, it has been shown how this question was resolved by Fecht (1960). It is necessary to remark, however, that in Egyptian this phenomenon belongs more to the morphology than it does to the lexicon, given the fact that the combining of substantives is here a live process, as in German or Dutch. We do not have here a limited inventory or a closed series of 'noun compounds', as in French.

One may ask, on the other hand, just what the endings *-w* and *-wt*, which characterize the plural of nouns, represent. The consonantal value of the *w* in the ending of the feminine plural has never been in doubt (cf. for example, Edel 1955–64:§269; Fecht 1960:§§361–3). On the contrary, different theories have been proposed for the *-w* of the masculine. Sethe (1923:203) read it *-ᵉw*; Edel (1955–64) sometimes *-ắw* (§269), sometimes *-⏑w* (§128), this latter transcription being also adopted by Fecht (1960:§§364–5). On the contrary, W. Vycichl (1955) attributes to *-w* the value /ū/, and he has been followed in this by T. O. Lambdin (1958:182–3). I myself have also accepted the value /u/ (short) (Vergote 1959:15–16) until recently, when an exhaustive examination showed me that only a reading /-wu/ could explain the quite varied forms of the plural preserved in Coptic (Vergote 1969).

II. *The Verb*

1. *'Predicative' and relative* sdm.f

The principal paradigm of Egyptian, that which I shall call the predicative *sḏm.f* as well as the relative *sḏm.f*, distinguishes, according to the leading grammars, between imperfective *sḏm.f* and a perfective *sḏm.f*. In the first, the 2 Gem. verbs (Secundae Geminatae [with double second radical], for example, *wnn* 'to be') and 3 Inf. (Tertiae Infirmae [with weak third radical], for example, *pry* 'to go forth') present the gemination of the second radical: *wnn.f*, *prr.f*. In the second, this root remains simple: *wn.f*, *pr.f*. The two predicative *sḏm.f*'s express, in a main affirmative clause, present time, past time or future time; the imperfective *sḏm.f* adds to these notions of time a nuance of repetition or of continuity. They further express a wish or an order.

Only A. Gardiner (1957: §447 and Obs.) acknowledges that the perfective *sḏm.f* probably represents two different forms, of which one, employed in three well-determined cases, is called the prospective *sḏm.f*, because it has a 'relatively future meaning'.

Erman had, in the first edition of his *Ägyptische Grammatik* (1894: §§172–82), distinguished in the perfective *sḏm.f* three or four different functions, but in his fourth edition (1928) he attributed these functions to a single form, which he called indifferently the 'ordinary or prospective' *sḏm.f* and which he accented *s⏑ḏm⏑́f*.

Given the existence of these debatable points, it is not surprising that a number of Egyptologists have looked for alternative solutions. A fundamental revision of the verbal system was attempted by C. E. Sander-Hansen (1941). This abandoned the perfective-imperfective opposition and saw in the simple *sḏm.f* the use of three moods, which he called indicative, jussive and subjunctive. The indicative *sḏm.f* does not refer to any distinction of time or aspect. It has different values depending on whether it is found at the head of the phrase ('unbekleidet') or is preceded by some element ('bekleidet'). This latter use is compared to the 'consecutive tenses' of Hebrew. The geminating *sḏm.f* is opposed to the simple *sḏm.f* as a 'theme', this word being understood in the sense which it assumes in Semitic grammar. It expresses the iterative-habitual 'Aktionsart'. The geminating *sḏm.f* does not include the indicative mood, but only the subjunctive and the jussive. One should consult the review of this work by H. J. Polotsky (1947).

The theory put forward by Polotsky (1944) produces an equally profound change in the analysis of the Egyptian verbal system. This author also drops the distinction between perfective and imperfective. The geminating *sḏm.f* is not, according to him, a predicative form, because it never serves as a predicate in an independent clause. It conceals two different forms. The first is the 'concrete relative' form; it modifies, in a relative clause (in the current sense of the term), a substantive of the main clause, which however can never correspond to the subject of this relative clause. For example, *this charge in which his majesty had placed me.* The second is the 'abstract relative' form; it converts the clause which it constitutes into a noun clause, in the same manner as the English conjunction *that* or the French conjunction *que* (these being equally related to the relative pronouns *who* and *qui*). It is used in the completive clause which serves as the direct object of the verbs 'order, wish, promise, see, know, find, etc.', for example, *ỉw grt wḏ.n ḥm.f prr(.ỉ) r ḫ3s.t tn* 'His majesty ordered that I go into this desert' (Gardiner 1957:§442.1), and after prepositions, which are thus changed into conjunctions, e.g. *mỉ ḫdd mw* 'as the water flows' or 'in the manner that the water flows' (§444.3). Polotsky has, however, drawn special attention to the use of the 'abstract relative' in the main clause, whether declarative or interrogative. This serves to emphasize the adverbial part of the clause, e.g. 'thou art the rudder of the entire land' *sḳdd t3 ḫft wḏ.k* 'it is in accordance with thy command that the land sails'; *ḥnw.t.ỉ ỉrr.t p3 ỉb ḥr m* 'my mistress, wherefore art thou in this mood?' ('that thou art in this mood (is) because of what?') (Gardiner 1957:§440.1, 6). Polotsky sees the proof that these forms are relative in the fact that they are negated by *tm*. Parallel to these geminating forms, which are indefinite as to time, he finds two forms with the infix *-n-* expressing the past and two non-geminating forms, called 'prospective' which refer to the future. This is outlined in the following table (Polotsky 1944:93):

	PASSIVE PARTICIPLE	PREDICATIVE FORMS	NON-PREDICATIVE FORMS	
			concrt. rel.	abstr. rel.
PAST	*ḥzy*	*ḥz.n.f*	*ḥz.n.f*	*ḥz.n.f*
INDEFINITE	*ḥzzw*	*ḥz.f**	*ḥzz(w).f*	*ḥzz.f*
FUTURE (prospective)	*ḥzy*	*ḥz.f*	*ḥzy.f*	*ḥz.f*

(*According to the correction made by Polotsky 1947:104, fn. 6.)

These observations of Polotsky have not been utilized in the new editions of Gardiner's grammar (1950², 1957³), of Lefebvre (1955) or of de Buck (1952). Edel (1955–64) has not included them in his grammar either, where he distinguishes an ordinary *sḏm.f*, a geminating *sḏm.f* and, in addition, a new form, the *sḏm.w.f*. In discussing the geminating *sḏm.f* he said of this proposal: 'Nach einer neuen Theorie soll die *mrrf*-Form im Gegensatz zum gewöhnlichen und stets prädikativ gebrauchten *mrjf* eine substantivierte Verbalform sein mit der Bedeutung "der Umstand, dass er liebt". Es lassen sich damit eine Menge von Beispielen mit der *mrrf*-Form erklären (vgl. §494–5), die früher Schwierigkeiten bereitet hätten; doch scheinen aus dieser Theorie nicht gut alle Verwendungsmöglichkeiten des *mrrf* abgeleitet werden zu können' (§493).

The description which Thacker (1954) dedicated to the verbal system means a return to the conceptions of Gardiner, but at the same time taking account of the opinion of Polotsky. Thacker goes back to the terms perfective *sḏm.f* and imperfective *sḏm.f*; he assigns to the latter, in addition to the aspect of repetition and continuity, recognized by Gardiner, the sense of incompletion. He also relies on the examples cited by Gardiner, in his review of Polotsky (1947; cf. Gardiner 1957:§44, fn. 7), to defend the existence of the imperfective *sḏm.f* in a predicative function. Since these independent clauses do not include any adverbial complement, there is no reason to believe that the geminating *sḏm.f* plays a role of 'abstract relative' in them. On the other hand, Thacker accepts the idea of a relative form in the *sḏm.f* serving as direct object to certain verbs or dependent upon a preposition-conjunction as well as in the partial question. But, in his eyes, these relative forms have the same structure as those figuring in the relative clause in the ordinary sense of the term. In other words, the last two columns of Polotsky's table must coalesce: the same paradigms have two functions, that of 'concrete relative' and of 'abstract relative'.

Thacker further states that the gemination in the 2 Gem. verbs must be distinguished from that of 3 Inf. verbs. In the first case, the two geminate consonants are elements of the root, and the spelling *mꜣꜣ.f* 'he sees' is explained by the presence of an accented vowel between them. The substitution of /r/ in *prr.f* for the /y/ of *pry* 'to go forth' is equivalent, on the contrary, to a true reduplication. As in many languages, this reduplication has the function of adding to the form a notion of repetition, of duration, or a kind of emphasis. This emphasis applies to the clause as a whole but also, at least in our translations, occasionally to a particular member of the sentence (this latter restriction would then reject the use of the 'abstract relative' for placing the accent on the adverbial complement).

However the 3 Inf. (and the 4 Inf.) do not differ only in the imperfective *sḏm.f* from the other classes of verbs. In the perfective *sḏm.f* they are indifferent with respect to the notion of time. On the contrary, the perfective *sḏm.f* of the other classes of verbs expresses only the past; their imperfective *sḏm.f* expresses continual or repeated action in the past, as well as present and future. Since the rules established by the grammars are based almost exclusively on examples with 3 Inf. verbs, they should be revised, in the sense indicated above, for the other classes of verbs. Thacker gives (1954:196) some examples where the imperfective *sḏm.f* of the 2 Gem. verb *mꜣꜣ* 'see' expresses the present (for *mꜣ.k* which is supposed to express future time [Gardiner 1957:§450.3] see Vergote 1957). The future sense of the verb *wnn.f* (Gardiner 1957: §§107.1, 118.2) would not then be an isolated phenomenon.

The most important innovation of Thacker is related to the discovery of a prospective *sḏm.f*, which has a modal jussive-optative sense. He demonstrated that the forms *dỉ.f*, *ỉwt.f*, *ỉnt.f*, *mꜣn.f*, of the irregular verbs *rdỉ* 'to give', *ỉwy* 'to come', *ỉny* 'to bring', *mꜣꜣ* 'to see' as well as the form of the 3 Inf. characterized by *y* (*pry.f*, *gmy.f*) do not have a 'relatively future meaning' (Gardiner) but that they sometimes express an order, sometimes a wish like the Latin subjunctive. Like the latter, the prospective also has a subordinating function, namely after the verbs *n sp* 'it does not happen/will not happen that' and *nn* (derived from *n-wn*) 'it does not exist that'. It is necessary then to attribute the same functions to the non-geminating *sḏm.f* of the other verbal classes if it is found in uses parallel to those of the above cited verbs.

The vocalization proposed by Thacker for these three varieties of *sḏm.f* differs from that previously assigned to the forms which had been recognized. He rejects the hypothesis of Sethe, developed by Gardiner, who derived the predicative *sḏm.f* from the passive participle; it would thus have originally meant 'heard of him', the participle having at one time a past sense, at another a sense of incompletion. In place of the structure *s◡ḏm◡́f* or *s◡ḏmáf* of the perfective (Sethe, Erman; Edel, Fecht), Thacker proposes *sáḏm◡f* and considers it to be derived from the pseudoparticiple plus suffix 'heard of him'. The authors who concerned themselves with the problem have proposed for the imperfective a structure *s◡ḏ́m◡f* or *s◡ḏḏām◡f* (Erman, Edel, Fecht; Gardiner, Parker [1955], Vycichl [1952]). Contrariwise, Thacker reads it *s◡ḏ́mm◡f* or *s◡ḏámm◡f*; this stem was perhaps a nominal base having the value of a noun of agent: 'a hearer (is) he'. The prospective was vocalized *s◡ḏmáf* and it had as stem the singular masculine imperative.

A detailed examination of Thacker's work convinced me (1956) of the exactness of these three vocalizations and I have even proposed to complete, by means of the neutral vowel /a/, the unaccented syllables: *sáḏmaf, saḏámmaf, saḏmáf.* But besides these three predicative forms, there also exist a perfective, an imperfective and a prospective in a relative function ('concrete' and 'abstract') and in the passive in *-tw*. For these, as well as for the predicative and relative *sḏm.n.f*, and the passive *sḏm.w.f*, I have completed the vocalizations of Thacker or have proposed different structures, partly because I arrived at the conclusion that the active participles (perfective and imperfective) ended in an accented /i/ and the passive participles (perfective and imperfective) in an accented /u/. The hypothesis of the existence of a prospective participle, which Gardiner also opposed, did not seem to me worth being retained.

My analysis of verbal forms preserved in the Egyptian personal names in Greek transcription (1960) confirmed these vocalizations established in a theoretical manner. However, it appeared that the ending of active participles ought rather to be accented /iy/, and that of the passive participles accented /uw/.

In comparing the theories of Thacker with the grammars of Gardiner and Lefebvre with regard to the function of the different forms *sḏm.f* and *sḏm.n.f*, I have been led to endorse them almost entirely (1957). The only reservations are the following. 1. It is necessary to admit that the relative imperfective *sḏm.f* and the relative *sḏm.n.f* also serve to place the emphasis on the adverbial part of an independent clause; they are found moreover in circumstantial clauses not introduced by a preposition-conjunction. 2. The use of the prospective *sḏm.f* is hypotactic — and not paratactic — not only after *nn* and *n sp*, but also after *rdì* 'cause that', after certain verbs of will or intention and in final-consecutive clauses. The indicator of this dependence is the negation of the prospective by *tm* instead of *ìmì*; however it is not likely that the use of *tm* implies here the presence of a relative prospective (cf. Polotsky 1964:271–2; Vergote 1965b:359).

We may add to this discussion that Westendorf (1962, 1963) recognized the prospective *sḏm.f* in the form *sḏm.w.f* discovered by Edel (1955–64:§§511–31; cf. 1959). He detected in it an optative and future value. It seems to me, however, that besides the prospective value, the *sḏm.w.f* represents in many cases the relative perfective, employed as an 'abstract relative'. This spelling can indicate an original structure *s aḏamáwf* and would confirm that the prospective *sḏm.f* is derived from the plural of the imperative (Vergote 1965b:360), a hypothesis proposed but not retained by Thacker.

If these new conceptions of the functions of the *sḏm.f* are adopted, the following rules would result (1957–58). The added paragraph numbers of Gardiner's grammar

(1957) enable one to assess the difference between the two theories, while furnishing occasionally adequate examples.

NEGATION	A. IN THE MAIN CLAUSE	
	1. The perfective *sḏm.f*	
	of the 3 Inf. and 4 Inf. — being an indefinite tense — expresses:	of the other verbs expresses:
n sḏmf	1) past 450.1	1) past 450.1
(perf.) 455.1	However, in Middle Egyptian, it was more often replaced by *sḏm.n.f* 414.1	
	2) present 450.2	
	3) future 450.3	
	2. The imperfective *sḏm.f*	
	of the 3 Inf. (except *ỉwy*, etc.) and 4 Inf. expresses:	of the other verbs expresses:
	1) continued or repeated action in the past 440.2	1) continued or repeated action in the past
n sḏm.n.f 418.1	2) in the present, a habitual fact or something which is stated in an emphatic manner 440.1	2) present
nn sḏm.f (prosp.) 457 cf. B1, a, 1	3) in the future, a fact of customary character or something which is stated in an emphatic manner 440.3	3) future 107.1; 118.2 (*wnn*)
	4) with this sense of future, a wish, an advice, or a polite order 440.5,7	4) with this sense of future, a wish, an advice, a polite order
ỉm.f sḏm.w 343,345	3. The prospective *sḏm.f* expresses a wish, an advice, an order 450.4, perhaps also: an obligation, a possibility	
	4. The relative imperfective and *sḏm(w).n.f* forms are used:	
tm 346.2	1) to emphasize the adverbial part of the proposition	
tm 346.1	2) in the partial question, to emphasize the interrogative adverbial part (440.6)	

NEGATION	B. IN THE SUBORDINATE CLAUSE
	1. The prospective *sḏm.f* is used:
	a. in the completive clause
nn tm.f 346.3	1) as subject of the impersonal verbs *nn* (<*n wn* 'it does not exist that') and *n sp* ('it does not happen that/ will not happen that')* 452.3; 457

wḏ + *tm* 347.1 — 2) as direct object of *rdỉ* and of verbs meaning 'order, wish, promise'** 452.1

tm 347.4 — b. in the circumstantial clause of purpose and of consequence which is not introduced by a preposition-conjunction 454.3

2. The perfective and imperfective *sḏm.f* are used:
   a. in the completive clause as the direct object of the verbs 'see, know', etc., if this clause is introduced by *ntt*, *r-ntt*, *wnt* 187

n 201 — b. in the relative clause introduced by *nty*, *ỉwty*, sometimes also when *nty* is not present (cf. Lefebvre 1955:§750) 443; 453

   c. in the circumstantial clause introduced by *ntt* after a preposition-conjunction 223
   d. with the exception of the final and consecutive clause, probably also with certain circumstantial clauses not introduced by a preposition-conjunction 444.1–2; 454.1

3. The relative imperfective, perfective, prospective and *sḏm*(*w*).*n.f* forms are used:
   a. in the completive clause
      1) as subject of an adjectival predicate and of the infinitive + *pw* as well as an interrogative clause*** 442.2

tm 347.2 — 2) as predicate of *pw* 442.3; 452.4

tm 347.1 — 3) as direct object of the verbs 'see, know', etc., and (only the imperfective relative?) of the verbs 'order, wish, promise,' etc. 442.1; 452.1*b*; 185

      4) as determinative of a substantive, whether or not introduced by the *n* of the genitive 191

tm 397.3 — b. in the relative clause the subject of which does not refer to the antecedent 387; 389

tm 347.5, 6 — c. in all circumstantial clauses introduced by a preposition-conjunction, including also here the clause introduced by *ỉr* 444.3–4; 454.4–5

tm 347.3 — d. in circumstantial clauses not introduced by a preposition-conjunction, with the exception of the final and consecutive clause 444.1–2; 454.1; 414.2

* cf. Lat. *ei contigit ut te videret*

** cf. Lat. *senectutem ut adipiscantur omnes optant*

*** Westcar 8, 10/11 *pty s.t ... tm rdỉ.w mꜣn.ỉ ṯw* 'what is it ... that thou hast not let me see thee (before)'.

2. *The Passive Forms*

W. Westendorf has devoted a detailed study to the passives *sḏm.f*, *sḏm.tw.f*, *sḏm.n.tw.f* (1953). In examining their origin and development, he was also led to discuss many other verbal forms, such as the pseudoparticiple. According to the author, the passive *sḏm.f* always possesses a past or perfect sense in texts of the Middle

Kingdom, but this signification can be affected by static as well as by dynamic nuances. This form is often employed in an impersonal manner. No definite example of its use with a pronominal subject is known. It is very frequent in subordinate clauses (temporal, concomitant, relative).

3. *Compound Tenses*

In comparing the use of simple verbs with that of verbs accompanied by auxiliary verbs, Polotsky (1965) is especially concerned with the contrast between *sḏm.n.f* and *ỉw sḏm.n.f*. He concluded that the first, in initial position, is 'emphatic' in the sense that it is a 'that-form', serving as subject to an 'adverbial adjunct as predicate'. Thus he expresses in other terms the 'abstract relative' function which he previously attributed to this form (cf. also Polotsky 1957). The construction *ỉw sḏm.n.f* is reserved for transitive verbs and it has a plainly predicative value; the verbs of motion borrow in this case the constructions *ỉw.ỉ pr(ỉ).kwỉ* ('I-am, I-having-gone-forth'), *mk wỉ ỉỉ.kwỉ* ('behold me, I-having-come'). In the opposition between the forms accompanied by *ỉw* and the simple forms, it is necessary to make a distinction between 'discourse' and 'narration'. All the compound verbal forms composed with *ỉw* 'introduce a statement regarded from the standpoint of the present'. Moreover, Polotsky infers the existence of a circumstantial *sḏm.f*, this being an independent variety of *sḏm.f*.

Thacker, on the other hand, compared the verbal forms having the auxiliary *wnn* 'be' with the tenses of Semitic languages similarly containing a verb 'be' (1963).

4. *The Late Egyptian Conjunctive*

The stages of Egyptian following the language of the Middle Kingdom have not been the object of many new studies since the publication of Erman's grammar (1933) and the two grammars of Demotic (Spiegelberg 1925; Lexa 1947–51). The most important work which should be mentioned in this area is that of F. Hintze (1950–52), which analyzes the works of Late Egyptian literature from the stylistic point of view. Since he conceives stylistics in a modern linguistic sense, contrasting 'parole' to the abstract system of 'langue', he furnishes us with some very interesting data from the grammatical viewpoint.

The problem which has especially held the attention of scholars is that of the origin of the Late Egyptian conjunctive. A. Volten (1964) proposed a new hypothesis after a detailed discussion of the theories of his predecessors (Gardiner 1928; G. Mattha 1947; Černý 1949). Another similar contribution was furnished by Miriam Lichtheim (1964).

Černý (1964) dedicated a study to the construction *ỉw sḏm.f* in Late Egyptian, which opens interesting perspectives.

D. *Syntax*

A work which appeared to provide some modification in the domain of syntax seemed to me to be my article on the function of the pseudoparticiple (Vergote 1955). Here I have shown that the verbal form in question normally serves as a predicate of attribution to the subject (*I spent three days alone* [*I being alone* expressed by the pseudoparticiple]) and to the object (*he found him lying down* [*him lying down* expressed by the pseudoparticiple]). The subject and its predicate of attribution can be considered as a predicative relation of a particular type, different from that which makes up the independent clause in the language in question, and the term 'nexus', created by Otto Jespersen (1924) to designate the predicate relation in general, can be reserved for it. The same observation is valid for the direct object and its predicate of attribution. This new nomenclature permits us to refer to a nexus-subject (*I-alone spent three days*) and to a nexus-direct object (*he found him-lying down*). But this same nexus, represented by the pseudoparticiple, can also be dependent on a preposition (*a heaven is over thee-placed in the hearse*), and it serves as an adverbial complement, employed in an independent fashion like the genitive absolute of Greek or the ablative absolute of Latin (*then His Majesty fared downstream, his heart rejoicing*). Finally the pseudoparticiple can accompany a substantive in the same manner as the Egyptian participle. The two are normally translated by relative clauses, but there exists between them a distinction which corresponds to that which Jespersen established between a non-restrictive relative clause and a restrictive relative clause. I have called the first a descriptive relative, e.g. *nḥm(w) ꜥꜣ.w.f sꜥḥ(.w) r ḏꜣ.t.f* 'taking away his asses, which were driven into his estate'. The second can be called a determinative relative clause, e.g. *P. pw sꜣ Ḫprr msy m Ḥtp.t* 'P. is the son of Kheprer who was born in Ḥtp.t' (in opposition to a son who was born elsewhere).

As a result one sees that the use of the pseudoparticiple in an independent clause, except when it is dependent on *ỉw*, *wnn*, *mk*, *ꜥḥꜥ.n-*, is rare and is limited to certain stereotyped formulas. This observation had already been made by W. Golenischeff (1922) and by T. G. Allen (1929).

With the exception of the latter case, all of these functions are also performed by the Coptic *circumstantialis*. The two verbal forms thus appear especially designated to express the nexus, in the sense described above. It has been shown that Egyptian grammar and Coptic grammar must give the nexus a well-determined place in the syntax. The actual syntactic scheme is practically limited to determining how the primary or 'substantival' functions, the secondary or 'adjectival' functions and those of a 'normal' predicate, the tertiary or 'adverbial' functions are performed 1) by the semantemes (substantive, adjective, verb, adverb of manner) and 2) by subordinate clauses. But the grammar ought also to examine, after 1, how these same functions are fulfilled by the nexus. And since the nexus also exists in other languages, the elaboration of the same syntactic scheme would give a very clear insight into the differences which exist between them in the use of this construction.

The distinction between the determinative relative clause and the descriptive one does not occur only in our interpretations of the Egyptian participle and pseudoparticiple. I have shown that this language also possesses a morpheme, namely *nty* (*ənt(e)*, *ete* in Coptic) to characterize as such the determinative relative clause (1946: 69–70), and de Buck has included this observation in the French edition of his Egyptian grammar (1952). F. Daumas made the same distinction independently (1962) between what he called the essential relative clause and the accessory relative clause when he applied to Egyptian the data given in the posthumous work of L. Tesnière (1959).

A study by W. Schenkel (1963–65) rejects the usual division made by grammars into verbal sentence and non-verbal (or nominal) sentence and substitutes for it a more complex scheme. An important problem of Late Egyptian syntax, concerning the different types of non-verbal clauses, is treated in a very detailed manner in the work of Sarah Israelit Groll (1967).

REFERENCES

ALBRIGHT, WILLIAM FOXWELL. 1923. The principles of Egyptian phonological development. RT 40.64–70.

——. 1946. Review of Phonétique historique de l'égyptien, by J. Vergote. JAOS 66.316–20.

ALLEN, THOMAS GEORGE. 1929. 'Independent' uses of the Egyptian qualitative. JAOS 49.160–7.

BEHNK, FRIDA. 1928. Über die Beziehungen des Ägyptischen zu den hamitischen Sprachen. ZDMG 82.136–41.

DE BUCK, ADRIAAN. 1952. Grammaire élémentaire du moyen-égyptien. Traduite par B. van de Walle et J. Vergote. Leiden, Brill.

CALICE, FRANZ. 1936. Grundlagen der ägyptisch-semitischen Wortvergleichung, ed. by Heinrich Balcz. (Beihefte zur WZKM 1.) Wien, Orientalisches Institut der Universität.

ČERNÝ, JAROSLAV. 1949. On the origin of the Egyptian conjunctive. JEA 35.25–30.

——. 1950. Notes on Coptic etymologies. Coptic studies in honor of W. E. Crum, 35–47. Boston, The Byzantine Institute.

——. 1964. A special case of the verbal construction *ỉw sḏm.f* in Late Egyptian. Studies H. J. Polotsky, 81–5. Jerusalem, The Israel Exploration Society.

COHEN, MARCEL. 1947. Essai comparatif sur le vocabulaire et la phonétique du chamito-sémitique. Paris, Champion.

CZERMAK, WILHELM. 1931–34. Die Laute der ägyptischen Sprache. (Schriften der Arbeitsgemeinschaft der Ägyptologen und Afrikanisten in Wien, 2–3.) 2 vols. Wien, Höfels.

DAUMAS, FRANÇOIS. 1962. La proposition relative égyptienne étudiée à la lumière de la syntaxe structurale. Orbis 11.21–32.

DIAKONOFF, I. M. 1965. Semito-Hamitic Languages. Moscow.

DOLGOPOLJSKIJ, A. B. 1966. Materialy po sravniteljno-istoričeskoj fonetike Kušitskix jazykov: gubnye i dentaljnye smyčnye v načaljnom položenii. Jazyki Afriki, 35–88. Moscow.

EDEL, ELMAR. 1954. Zur Vokalisation des Neuägyptischen. MIO 2.30–43.

——. 1955–64. Altägyptische Grammatik. (Analecta Orientalia, 34/39.) 2 vols. Roma, Pontificium Institutum Biblicum.

——. 1959. Neue Belege für die aktive *sḏmwf*-Form. Zur Verbreitung und Geschichte der aktiven *sḏmwf*-Form. ZÄS 84.108–11.

——. 1967. Altägyptische Grammatik. Register der Zitate (von R. Grundlach-Barbara Schwartzkopf). Roma, Pontificium Institutum Biblicum.

EDGERTON, WILLIAM FRANKLIN. 1947. Stress, vowel quantity and syllable division in Egyptian. JNES 6.1–17.

EMBER, AARON. 1930. Egypto-Semitic studies, ed. by Frida Behnk. (Alexander Kohut Memorial Foundation.) Leipzig, Verlag Asia Major.

ERMAN, ADOLF. 1892. Das Verhältniss des Ägyptischen zu den semitischen Sprachen. ZDMG 46.93–129.

——. 1900. Die Flexion des ägyptischen Verbums. SbDAW 317–53.

——. 1928. Ägyptische Grammatik. 4. Aufl. (Porta linguarum orientalium, 15.) Berlin, Reuter-Reichard.

——, 1933. Neuägyptische Grammatik. 2. Aufl. Leipzig, Engelmann.

FECHT, GERHARD. 1960. Wortakzent und Silbenstruktur. (Ägyptologische Forschungen, 21.) Glückstadt etc., Augustin.

GARDINER, ALAN HENDERSON. 1927. Egyptian grammar. Oxford, Clarendon Press.

——. 1928. An Egyptian split infinitive and the origin of the Coptic conjunctive tense. JEA 16.86–96.

——. 1947. Review of Études de syntaxe copte, by H. J. Polotsky. JEA 33.95–101.

——, Sir ALAN. 1950², 1957³. Egyptian grammar. Oxford-London, Griffith Institute-Oxford University Press.

GOLENISCHEFF, WLADIMIR. 1922. Quelques remarques sur la syntaxe égyptienne. Recueil d'études égyptologiques J. F. Champollion, 685–711. Paris.

HINTZE, FRITZ. 1950–52. Untersuchungen zu Stil und Sprache neuägyptischer Erzählungen. (Deutsche Akademie der Wissenschaften zu Berlin. Institut für Orientforschung, 2; 6.) Berlin, Akademie-Verlag.

——. 1951. Zur hamitosemitischen Wortvergleichung. ZPhon 5.65–87. (Review of Essai comparatif sur le vocabulaire et la phonétique chamito-sémitique, by M. Cohen).

HODGE, CARLETON TAYLOR. 1954. An outline of Egyptian grammar. SIL 12.8–23.

——. 1966. Hausa-Egyptian establishment. AnL 8/1.40–57.

——. 1967. Some Afroasiatic etymologies. AnL 10/3.19–24.

ILLIČ-SVITYČ, V. M. 1966. Iz istorii Čadskogo konsonantizma: Labialjnye smyčnye. Jazyki Afriki, 9–34. Moscow.

ISRAELIT GROLL, SARAH. 1967. Non-verbal sentence patterns in Late Egyptian. London, Oxford University Press.

JANSSENS, GÉRARD. 1967. Contribution to the Hamito-Semitic and the Egyptian phonetic laws. CdÉ 42.86–122. (Review of Verhouding van het Egyptisch tot de Semietische talen, by J. Vergote.)

JESPERSEN, OTTO. 1924. The philosophy of grammar. London and New York, G. Allen and Unwin-H. Holt and Co.

KAHLE, PAUL ERIC. 1954. Bala'izah. 2 vols. London, Oxford University Press.

KOROSTOVTSEV, MICHAIL ALEXANDROVITCH. 1963. Vvedenie v Egipetskuju filologiju. Moscow, Istadeljstvo Vostočnoj Literaturi.

LAMBDIN, THOMAS O. 1958. The bivalence of Coptic *Eta* and related problems in the vocalization of Egyptian. JNES 17.177–93.

LEFEBVRE, GUSTAVE. 1936. Sur l'origine de la langue égyptienne. CdÉ 11.266–92.

——. 1940. Grammaire de l'égyptien classique. (Bibliothèque d'Étude, 12.) Le Caire, Institut Français d'Archéologie Orientale.

——. 1955. Grammaire de l'égyptien classique. 2e éd. (Bibliothèque d'Étude, 12.) Le Caire, Institut Français d'Archéologie Orientale.

LEXA, FRANÇOIS (FRANTIŠEK). 1921–22. Comment se révèlent les rapports entre les langues hamitiques, sémitiques et la langue égyptienne, dans la grammaire des pronoms personnels, des verbes et des numéraux cardinaux 1–9. Philologica 1.151–77.

——. 1947–51. Grammaire démotique. 7 fasc. Praha, Orbis.

LICHTHEIM, MIRIAM. 1964. Notes on the Late-Egyptian conjunctive. Studies H.J. Polotsky, 1–8. Jerusalem, The Israel Exploration Society.

LUKAS, JOHANNES. 1937. Der hamitische Gehalt der tschado-hamitischen Sprachen ZES 28.286–99.

——. 1939. Die Verbreitung der Hamiten in Afrika. Scientia.

MATTHA, GIRGIS. 1947. The Egyptian conjunctive. BIFAO 45.43–55.

MEILLET, ANTOINE, and MARCEL COHEN. 1924. Les langues du monde. (Collection linguistique. Société de Linguistique de Paris, 16.) Paris, Champion.

——. 1952. Les langues du monde. Nouv. éd. Paris, Champion.

MÖLLER, GEORG. 1924. Die Ägypter und ihre libyschen Nachbarn. ZDMG 78.36–60.

NAVILLE, ÉDOUARD. 1920. L'évolution de la langue égyptienne et les langues sémitiques. Paris, Geuthner.

NEWMAN, PAUL, and ROXANA MA. 1966. Comparative Chadic: phonology and lexicon. JAfrL 5.218–51.

PARKER, RICHARD ANTHONY. 1955. The function of the imperfective *sḏm.f* in Middle Egyptian. RE 10.49–59.

POLOTSKY, HANS JAKOB. 1944. Études de syntaxe copte. (Publications de la Société d'Archéologie Copte.) Le Caire.

——. 1947. Review of Über die Bildung der Modi im Altägyptischen, by C.E. Sander-Hansen. BiOr 4.102–6.

——. 1957. The 'emphatic' *sḏm.n.f* form. RE 11.109–17.

——. 1964. Ägyptische Verbalformen und ihre Vokalisation. Or 33.267–85. (Review of De oplossing van een gewichtig probleem, by J. Vergote.)

——. 1965. Egyptian tenses. (The Israel Academy of Sciences and Humanities, 2.5.) Jerusalem, The Israel Academy.

RÖSSLER, OTTO. 1952. Der semitische Charakter der libyschen Sprache. ZA 16.121–50.

——. 1958. Die Sprache Numidiens. Sybaris, Festschrift Hans Krahe, 94–120. Wiesbaden, Harrassowitz.

SANDER-HANSEN, CONSTANTIN EMIL. 1941. Über die Bildung der Modi im Altägyptischen. (Det kgl. Danske Videnskabernes Selskab. Historisk-filologiske skrifter, 1.3.) København, Munksgaard.

——. 1956. Studien zur Grammatik der Pyramidentexte. (Analecta Aegyptiaca, 6.) København, Munksgaard.

SCHENKEL, WOLFGANG. 1963–65. Beiträge zur mittelägyptischen Syntax. ZÄS 88. 113–30, 92.47–72.

——. 1966. Die mittelägyptischen Nisben als Nuklei präpositionaler, limitierender und Genitiv-Relation. CdÉ 41.50–9.

SETHE, KURT. 1899–1902. Das ägyptische Verbum. 3 vols. Leipzig, Hinrichs.

——. 1923. Die Vokalisation des Ägyptischen. ZDMG 77 (N.F.2.).145–208.

SOTTAS, HENRI. 1923. Notes de grammaire égyptienne. RT 40.73–8.

SPIEGELBERG, WILHELM. 1925. Demotische Grammatik. Heidelberg, Winter.

STEINDORFF, GEORG. 1951. Lehrbuch der koptischen Grammatik. Chicago, The University of Chicago Press.

TESNIÈRE, LUCIEN. 1959. Éléments de syntaxe structurale. Paris, Klincksieck.

THACKER, THOMAS WILLIAM. 1954. The relationship of the Semitic and Egyptian verbal systems. Oxford, Clarendon Press.

——. 1963. Compound tenses containing the verb 'be' in Semitic and Egyptian. Studies G.R.Driver, 156–71. London, Oxford University Press.

TUCKER, ARCHIBALD N. 1967. Erythraeic elements and patternings: Some East African findings. Paper given at the 27th International Congress of Orientalists, August 12–19. AfrLR 6.17–25.

VERGOTE, JOZEF. 1945. Phonétique historique de l'égyptien. Les consonnes. (Bibliothèque du 'Muséon', 19.) Louvain, Bureaux du 'Muséon'.

——. 1946. Review of Egyptische grammatica, by A.de Buck. CdÉ 21.66–71.

——. 1947. Le système phonologique du moyen-égyptien. GLECS 4.57–61. (Obs. by M.Cohen: 61-2.)

——. 1952. A propos des adjectifs nisbés de l'égyptien. Diatribae F.Lexa. AO 20.417–23.

——. 1955. La fonction du pseudoparticipe. O.Firchow. Ägyptologische Studien H.Grapow, 338–61. (Deutsche Akademie der Wissenschaften zu Berlin. Institut für Orientforschung, 29.) Berlin, Akademie-Verlag.

——. 1956. Vocalisation et origine du système verbal égyptien. CdÉ 31.16–53.

——. 1957. Une nouvelle interprétation de deux passages du Naufragé (132b–136 et 167b–169). Festschrift H.Junker, I. MDAIK 15.275–87.

——. 1957–58. Naar een hernieuwing van de Egyptische grammatica. JEOL 15.34–46.

——. 1959. Où en est la vocalisation de l'égyptien? BIFAO 58.1–19.

——. 1960. De oplossing van een gewichtig probleem: de vocalisatie van de Egyptische werkwoordvormen (with French summary: La solution d'un problème important: la vocalisation des formes verbales égyptiennes). (MKVA 22.7.) Brussel.

——. 1961a. Le nom du roi 'Serpent'. Or 30.355–65.

——. 1961b. Toutankhamon dans les archives hittites. (Uitgaven van het Nederlands Historisch-Archaeologisch Instituut te Istanbul, 12.) Istanbul, Nederlands Historisch-Archaeologisch Instituut.

——. 1961c. Sur les mots composés en égyptien et en copte. BiOr 18.208–14. Review of Wortakzent und Silbenstruktur, by G. Fecht.

——. 1961d. Les dialectes dans le domaine égyptien. CdÉ 36.237–49.

——. 1962. Les prototypes égyptiens des mots *me-mēi* 'vérité, justice'. BIFAO 61.69–78.

——. 1965a. De verhouding van het Egyptisch tot de Semietische talen (with French translation: Le rapport de l'égyptien avec les langues sémitiques). (MKVA 27.4.) Brussel.

——. 1965b. Les formes verbales égyptiennes et leur vocalisation. Or 34.345–71.

——. 1969. The plural of nouns in Egyptian and in Coptic. Or 38.77–96.

Volten, Aksel. 1965. The Late Egyptian conjunctive. Studies H. J. Polotsky, 54–80. Jerusalem, The Israel Exploration Society.

Vycichl, Werner. 1934. Haussa und Ägyptisch. MSOS 37/3.36–116.

——. 1952. Ein Nomen Actoris im Ägyptischen. Der Ursprung der sogenannten emphatischen Konjugation. Muséon 65.1–4.

——. 1953. Neues Material zur Form des ägyptischen Nomen Agentis *qattāl*. OLZ 48.293–4.

——. 1955. Gab es eine Pluralendung *-w* im Ägyptischen? ZDMG 105 (N.F.30.). 261–70.

——. 1956. Was bedeutet 'Sanuth' im koptischen Kambyses-Roman? Ein weiteres Beispiel des Nomen Agentis *qattāl* im Ägyptischen. Aegyptus 36.25–6.

——. 1957a. Ein passives Partizip im Ägyptischen und im Haussa (British Nigeria). Die passive Konjugation *sǧmm.f*. Muséon 70.353–6.

——. 1957b. Die Selbstlaute. Zur Lautlehre der ägyptischen Sprache. Festschrift H. Junker. WZKM 54.214–21.

——. 1958. Grundlagen der ägyptisch-semitischen Wortvergleichung. Festschrift H. Junker, II. MDAIK 16.367–405.

——. 1959a. Nouveaux aspects de la langue égyptienne. BIFAO 58.49–72.

——. 1959b. Ein passives Partizip *qatīl* im Ägyptischen und Semitischen. Der Ursprung der periphrastischen Konjugation *sǧm.n.f* als Parallele zu aramäisch *šemī leh* 'er hat gehört'. ZDMG 109.253–8.

——. 1959c. Is Egyptian a Semitic language? Kush 7.27–44.

Westendorf, Wolfhart. 1953. Der Gebrauch des Passivs in der klassischen Literatur der Ägypter. (Deutsche Akademie der Wissenschaften zu Berlin. Institut für Orientforschung, 18.) Berlin, Akademie-Verlag.

——. 1962. Grammatik der medizinischen Texte. (Grundriss der Medizin der alten Ägypter, 8.) Berlin, Akademie-Verlag.

——. 1963. *sḏmwf* = *saḏmóf*. ZÄS 60.127–31.

Worrell, William Hoyt. 1934. Coptic Sounds. With an Appendix by Hide Shohara. (University of Michigan Studies. Humanistic Series, 26.) Ann Arbor, University of Michigan Press.

Zyhlarz, Ernst. 1933. Ursprung und Sprachcharakter des Altägyptischen. Berlin-Hamburg (Offprint from ZES 23 (1932–33).25–45, 81–110, 161–94, 241–54.)

COPTIC

H. J. POLOTSKY

Coptic linguistics is, in practice, not an independent field of study. It is a part of Egyptian linguistics, and a very important part at that, because Coptic is the only phase of Egyptian of which it is possible to obtain as precise and comprehensive a knowledge as can reasonably be expected where a dead language is concerned. Coptic literature, or the literature preserved in Coptic, on the other hand, lies outside the domain of Egyptology proper: it belongs to theology (including the textual study of the Greek Bible), to the history of religions, and generally to the history of late Hellenistic and Byzantine civilization. The student of the Egyptian language who wishes to use Coptic texts as material for linguistic research needs at least a modicum of acquaintance with those fields. Moreover, many problems concerning the Coptic language cannot be adequately dealt with on the basis of printed texts, but require recourse to MS material, i.e. a kind of work which is usually looked upon as 'philological' rather than linguistic. The actual editing of Coptic MSS is, in fact, as a rule left to scholars who are specialists in the subject matter. Yet they are constantly confronted with problems of a linguistic nature. This is especially the case with texts in less familiar or altogether new dialects. Such topics as 'dialectology' are therefore often treated by scholars who would not describe themselves as linguists. On the whole, the separation between linguistics and 'philology' is, in the Coptic field, less marked than elsewhere; least of all, perhaps, in the field of lexicography.

The one field which all students of Coptic are content to leave to the linguist is grammar. Since the Egyptologist, by definition, must view Coptic as a stage of Egyptian, his ultimate aim will inevitably be diachronic. Yet it will nowadays be generally realized that there is no better first step towards that ultimate aim than a strictly synchronic description of Coptic. A synchronic description is, of course, also what 'mere philologists' desire.

At the same time one notices a revival of avowedly and openly diachronic interest in Coptic grammar. It arose in connection with the increased attention paid during the last 40 years to the later stages of pre-Coptic Egyptian, Late Egyptian, and Demotic, and received fresh impetus from the unexpected light which new insights into Coptic were found to shed even on Classical and Old Egyptian.

As regards linguistic methodology, it is no secret that Egyptologists are not conspicuous in the forefront of modern movements.

BIBLIOGRAPHY

The *Bibliography* compiled by W.H. Worrell's students[1] will be found especially helpful for tracking down earlier items from periodical literature; a new edition of this work is in preparation. Similar services are rendered by the very full bibliography in the fourth edition of Mallon's Bohairic grammar.[2]

For the current literature since 1948 and 1947 respectively we have two invaluable bibliographies, viz., J. Simon's annual *Bibliographie copte*[3] and the late J.M.A. Janssen's[4] *Annual Egyptological Bibliography / Bibliographie égyptologique annuelle*,[5] now under the care of M.S.H.G. Heerma van Voss. The former is classified ("X. Linguistique. Philologie"), the latter is purely alphabetical, but sometimes gives fuller summaries.

A survey of 'the present status' of Coptic studies was published in 1954.[6]

DIALECTS

Three Coptic dialects have been known since the end of the eighteenth century. Between the 1880's and the 1920's the number rose to five. Today we must reckon with seven at least. The existence of comparatively many literary dialects seems to have been a feature of the earlier period, and their gradual recovery is due to the discovery of MSS of greater antiquity. If dialects thus require and receive a good deal of attention, it must be emphasized that the study of Coptic 'dialectology' in any serious sense of this term is a job which resembles nothing so much as the making of bricks without straw, because in practically all cases we lack the basic data on place and time. This ignorance is reflected in the hypothetic character and in the startling divergence of beliefs concerning the home of most Coptic dialects. An important auxiliary of Coptic dialectology is palæography, which might be expected to supply some information about chronology, if it were not itself so badly in need of secure foundations. Much of what passes for Coptic dialectology is in reality palæographical statistics.[7] This

1 *A Coptic bibliography*, compiled by Winifred Kammerer, with the collaboration of Elinor M Husselman and Louise A. Shier (Ann Arbor 1950).

2 A. Mallon, *Grammaire copte*. Quatrième édition par Michel Malinine (Beyrouth, Impr. Catholique, 1956): 'Bibliographie de la littérature copte', 254–401.

3 In *Orientalia*. The last instalment to date is the 18th, in vol. 35.139*–171* (1966). – Since this was written the 19th instalment, vol. 36.157*–211* (1967), has come to hand, being the joint work of J. Simon and H. Quecke. It contains the announcement that this bibliography is likely to be discontinued.

4 Obituary by S. Morenz, *ZÄS* 91.IX–X (1964).

5 Leiden (Brill).

6 W. Till, 'Das Koptische. Heutiger Stand der Forschung', *Orbis* 3.486–97 (1954).

7 In the sense in which the term was used by K. Krumbacher, 'Studien zu den Legenden des hl. Theodosios', *SbBAW* 1892 II.275.

applies also to the outstanding work in this field, the late P.E. Kahle's *Bala'izah*,[8] ostensibly the publication of the Coptic MS fragments discovered by Flinders Petrie in 1907 (*Gizeh and Rifeh*) and subsequently assigned to the Bodleian. The importance of the work is due less to the text themselves, though some of them are interesting enough, than to two long chapters which form part of the Introduction: VIII (pp. 48–192), 'Dialectical variation in Sahadic non-literary texts', and IX (pp. 193–290), 'The Coptic literary dialects: their origin, development and interrelationship'. These subjects had last been treated by W. H. Worrell in the second part of his *Coptic sounds* (Ann Arbor 1934). A comparison between the two works reveals at once the merits and the defects of each. Worrell had the better linguistic training, while Kahle commanded a far richer material, largely obtained by his own researches at the Griffith Institute and at the British Museum.

It had for some time been realized that Sahidic occupies a position apart from all other dialects: while the latter — including Bohairic down to a rather late date (11th cent.) — were regional dialects (but not necessarily 'sub-dialects', as Kahle likes to call them), Sahidic was the standard literary language over the whole of Egypt. Nevertheless, Sahidic must naturally have been based on a regional dialect ('Proto-Sahidic'), though in the process of becoming the standard language it may well have shed some of its primitive regional characteristics. The traditional belief that Sahidic was the dialect of Thebes, or of the Thebaid, had been practically abandoned, especially because Sahidic so strikingly agrees with Bohairic in having the vowels *o* and *a* where all other dialects have *a* and *e* respectively.

On the assumption that this agreement presupposes geographical contiguity, Sahidic had been moving downstream in recent attempts to reconstruct the dialect map of Christian Egypt. In Worrell's scheme it had got as far as 'the lower valley' from Oxyrhynchus northward. Vergote thought, not implausibly (if the premise is admitted), of Memphis.[9] Kahle is content with nothing short of Alexandria, although 'this conclusion is offered with some reserve and hesitation' (p. 257 fn. 1). I must confess that I find it extremely hard to think of Alexandria as the original home, not only of (Proto-)Sahidic, but of any Coptic dialect.

Since Kahle wrote, the whole question has been placed on a different basis by what is perhaps the most interesting recent addition to Coptic dialectology, the Bodmer MS of Proverbs, published by R. Kasser.[10]

8 *Bala'izah.* Coptic texts from Deir al-Bala'izah in Upper Egypt, edited by Paul E. Kahle, published on behalf of the Griffith Institute, Ashmolean Museum, Oxford [...] (London, Oxford University Press, 1954). — Reviews by W. F. Edgerton, *JNES* 15.58–64 (1956); W. Till, *Orientalia* 25.384–403 (1956); J. Vergote, *CdÉ* 30.173–6 (1955); A. Böhlig, *BiOr* 14.72–5 (1957).

9 In his review (note 8), p. 175. Kahle claims (256) to have advanced arguments against the localization of (Proto-)Sahidic at Memphis. All I can discover is the surmise (248) 'that a type of Bohairic, presumably not unlike that of the Bala'izah semi-Bohairic fragment [no. 19, 377–80], was the spoken language of Memphis and its neighbourhood in early times, perhaps extending as far south as Herakleopolis.'

10 *Papyrus Bodmer VI* [:] *Livre des Proverbes*, éd. par R. Kasser (*CSCO* t. 194) (Louvain 1960).

Its alphabet uses other Demotic signs than the familiar ones and certain orthographic devices unknown elsewhere. The dialect has many features familiar from Akhmimic and Subakhmimic, alongside of the 'Sahidic' vowels *o* and *a*.[11] After Kasser had studied certain points of similarity between the new text and the London 'Old Coptic' Horoscope,[12] P. Nagel[13] showed in a well-constructed analysis that many of the peculiarities of P had striking parallels in the much later documents from Thebes. Nagel's demonstration would have been even more convincing if he had avoided one misstatement[14] and if he had removed all doubt that the examples under 2.132 ('Tonsilbe *o:a*' p. 34) are really all from texts exhibiting the Theban dialect and not just standard Sahidic.

If Nagel is right, as I think he is, then Kahle's contention that Akhmimic was the dialect of Thebes[15] is definitely disproved. This contention, however, can hardly have found many adherents anyway. A more important consequence is that the vowels *o* - *a* are no argument against localization at Thebes and that the only reason for seeking the home of (Proto-)Sahidic in the neighborhood of Bohairic is thereby invalidated. It would seem, then, that Sahidic may safely return to the Thebaid; its vocalic agreement with Bohairic will have to wait for a less naive explanation.

GRAMMAR IN GENERAL

At a time when students are increasingly becoming aware that 'even standard literary Sahidic is not fully understood by any living person'[16] it is perhaps natural for them to concentrate on monographs rather than to attempt comprehensive grammars.

Neither of the two most recent grammars can be said to be representative of 'current trends', though the authors of both were in principle sympathetic to, and tried to keep abreast of, recent efforts. Steindorff's[17] can be consulted with profit by a critical reader, but for practical purposes of instruction and reference Till's[18] is on the whole to be preferred.

[11] A characteristic instance of 'AA_2' morphology together with 'S' vocalism is the distinction of the Infinitive *hmast* (= AA_2 *hmest*) from the Stative *hmost* (= AA_2 *hmast*) 'to sit'.

[12] 'Papyrus Londinensis 98 (the Old Coptic Horoscope) and Papyrus Bodmer VI', *JEA* 49.157–60 (1963).

[13] 'Der frühkoptische Dialekt von Theben', in *Koptologische Studien in der DDR* (= *Wissenschaftliche Zeitschrift der Martin-Luther-Universität Halle-Wittenberg*, 1965, Sonderheft), 30–49.

[14] Item 4.1 (44), 'Die *nci*-Konstruktion wird in P und Th nicht verwendet' is wrong, so far as P is concerned: Kasser in his Index (140) cites no less than 11 instances.

[15] The external evidence for the localization of Akhmimic at Akhmim is admittedly slender. Yet F. Ll. Griffith had pointed out, *JEA* 14.332 (1928), that the very name Akhmim, with its *kh* as against the *sh* of the Sahidic and Bohairic form *Shmin*, displayed the most characteristic feature of Akhmimic phonology. The weight of this argument is acknowledged by Worrell, 74–5.

[16] W. F. Edgerton, *JNES* 16.136 (1957).

[17] G. Steindorff, *Lehrbuch der koptischen Grammatik* (Chicago 1951). Reviews by W. Till, *Orientalia* 23.152–69 (1954); J. Vergote, *BiOr* 11.103–7 (1954).

[18] W. C. Till, *Koptische Grammatik* (Leipzig 1955, 2nd ed. 1961). Reviews by J. Vergote, *CdÉ* 31. 403–9 (1956) and *BiOr* 13.224–7 (1956); W. F. Edgerton, *JNES* 16.136–7 (1957); HJP, *OLZ* (1957) 219–34; (1962) 478–81.

The second edition of Till's little dialect grammar[19] avoids the factual errors of the first but cannot satisfy more than the most elementary needs.

PHONOLOGY

Works in which the Coptic material is used as a starting point for the reconstruction of the earlier stages of the Egyptian phonological system, especially of the vocalization, are more appropriately discussed elsewhere in this volume. Such works are J. Vergote's *Phonétique historique de l'égyptien*,[20] and G. Fecht's *Wortakzent und Silbenstruktur*.[21] There is, however, much incidental matter of Coptic interest to be found in them, especially in the latter's numerous footnotes.

The axioms and assumptions of the Steindorff-Sethe interpretation of the Coptic vowel system were subjected to a critical examination by W.F. Edgerton.[22] He clarifies and re-defines some of the current notions and comes to the conclusion that the prosodic system which underlies the Coptic ('Proto-Coptic') goes back to the New Kingdom.

Two phonological analyses of the Coptic, especially the Sahidic, vowel system, were published almost simultaneously, the one by E. E. Knudsen,[23] the other by J.H. Greenberg.[24] The two analyses arrived at rather divergent conclusions as regards the phonemes represented by the letters *ēta* and *ōmega*. While Knudsen accepts the current view that these letters express the long vowels corresponding to *epsilon* and *omikron* respectively, Greenberg assumes that the difference between the two pairs is one of quality rather than of quantity. In the discussion of double vowels one feels that more attention ought to have been paid to the actual facts of Sahidic orthography.

The unstressed vocalic ending appears in Sahidic as *-e* and usually corresponds to Bohairic *-i*. Certain dialects present a more differentiated picture. Fayyumic, for instance, which on the whole goes with Bohairic, has *-e*, like Sahidic, when the word originally ended in 'Ayin;[25] in this case the dialect of the Bodmer Proverbs has *-a*, while Bohairic, in its turn, normally has no vowel at all. A somewhat similar case

19 W. C. Till, *Koptische Dialektgrammatik*, 2nd ed. (München 1961). Review by D. W. Young, *JNES* 23.69–70 (1964).

20 J. Vergote, *Phonétique historique de l'égyptien. Les consonnes* (= *Bibliothèque du* Muséon, vol. 19) (Louvain 1945).

21 G. Fecht, *Wortakzent und Silbenstruktur. Untersuchungen zur Geschichte der ägyptischen Sprache* (= *Ägyptologische Forschungen*, Heft 21) (Glückstadt-Hamburg-New York 1960). Reviews by J. Vergote, *BiOr* 18.208–14 (1961); E. E. Knudsen, *AcOr* 26.193–203 (1961–62).

22 W. F. Edgerton, 'Stress, vowel quantity, and syllable division in Egyptian', *JNES* 6.1–17 (1947).

23 E. E. Knudsen, 'Saidic Coptic vowel phonemes', *AcOr* 26.29–42 (1961–62).

24 J. H. Greenberg, 'The interpretation of the Coptic vowel system', *JAfrL* 1.22–9 (1962).

25 HJP, 'Zur koptischen Lautlehre I', *ZÄS* 67.74–7 (1931).

was observed by P. Lacau[26] in certain varieties of Akhmimic and Subakhmimic. These dialects usually agree with Sahidic in having *-e*, but some MSS have regularly *-i* when the underlying form had consonantal *y* before an ending which later became silent (*časi* < **časy◡w*). Lacau's observation was further developed by E. Edel,[27] who had already been led by cuneiform evidence to assume a twofold origin for the unstressed vocalic ending in Coptic.

The much-discussed question of the supralinear stroke and its significance received a contribution from P. Nagel.[28]

In the field of MORPHOLOGY we have to record J. Vergote's classification of the nominal vocalization patterns.[29] He seeks, on the one hand, to establish their 'class-meanings' and, on the other hand, to correlate them, formally and semantically, to the Semitic vocalization patterns. This is an ambitious undertaking, but some of Vergote's comparisons are striking enough and the first impression is favourable.

SYNTAX has received a good deal of attention, and it is perhaps in this field that 'current trends' have produced the most significant advances. It must, however, be added that it is also precisely in this field that older (roughly pre-1880) scholars sometimes have achieved surprisingly good insights, which were forgotten by their immediate successors.

Coptic sentence-structure looks deceptively simple in the sense that the order of the elements agrees more or less with what is customary in Western European languages; that it seems to be free from such features as might shock speakers of those languages as eccentric;[30] and that on the whole it is not too difficult to construe a Coptic sentence. Irrelevant and subjective points of view like these are gradually giving way to the recognition that the language is rich in syntactic categories which are not all familiar or naturally to be expected.

As early as 1916 the NOMINAL SENTENCE was made the subject of a diachronic monograph by K. Sethe.[31] This monograph was in many ways a model of its kind, but was never imitated for any other topic in Egyptian grammar.

[26] P. Lacau, 'Fragments de l'Ascension d'Isaïe en copte', *Le Muséon* 69.453–67, esp. 464–5 (1946).

[27] E. Edel, 'Zur Vokalisation des Neuägyptischen', *MIO* 2.30–43, esp. 40ff. (1954); 'Neues Material zur Herkunft der auslautenden Vokale *-e* und *-i* im Koptischen', *ZÄS* 86.103–6 (1961).

[28] P. Nagel, 'Zum Problem der konsonantischen Silbenträger im Koptischen', *ZÄS* 92.76–8 (1965).

[29] *De verhouding van het Egyptisch tot de Semietische talen / Le rapport de l'égyptien avec les langues sémitiques* = *MKVA* XXVII/4.

[30] Ad. Erman, *Neuägyptische Grammatik*, 2nd ed. (Leipzig 1933:§6): 'Wer an das Neuägyptische geht, erwarte nicht, in ihm ungewöhnliche sprachliche Erscheinungen zu finden. Sieht man von dem Konjunktiv des §575ff. und Wenigem anderen ab, so ist fast nichts in ihm zu finden, was nicht ebenso, mutatis mutandis, in anderen Sprachen vorkäme, die auf der gleichen Stufe der Entwicklung stehen.' A. H. Gardiner, *Some aspects of the Egyptian language* (*PBA* XXIII:18): '... every expert in the Egyptian language must acknowledge the logicality of its syntax, and the rarity in it of abnormal or excentric constructions.'

[31] K. Sethe, *Der Nominalsatz im Ägyptischen und Koptischen* = *Abh. Sächs. Ges. Wiss.*, philol.-hist. Kl., XXXIII/3 (Leipzig 1916).

Following Arabic usage Egyptologists had long been in the habit of defining the Nominal Sentence as a sentence which (*a*) contains no verb, and (*b*) begins with a noun. As a result of this squinting definition the term was made to cover two different sentence types, viz. (1) the sentence with nominal predicate, and (2) the sentence with adverbial predicate. Sethe set forth the profound structural differences between the two, but continued nevertheless, on the strength of definition (*b*), to use *Nominalsatz* as a cover term, representing them as two species of one genus: the first was called Nominal Nominal Sentence ('Nominaler Nominalsatz'), and the second Adverbial Nominal Sentence ('Adverbialer Nominalsatz'). A more satisfactory principle of classification was introduced for Classical Egyptian by Gardiner,[32] and in his wake for Coptic by Till,[33] by using the predicate as single criterion: thus the 'Nominale Nominalsatz' becomes the Sentence with Nominal or Pronominal Predicate, and the 'Adverbiale Nominalsatz' is replaced by the Sentence with Adverbial Predicate (Till: 'Nominalsatz' pure and simple and 'Adverbialsatz', of which the latter, however, is ambiguous).

The usefulness of the new classification depends on the question whether the nominal or pronominal predicate can be identified as such by purely linguistic criteria. So far as Coptic is concerned, and at least to a certain extent, this is indeed possible, but the relevant criteria have not yet been set forth in public. A difficulty of another kind concerns the adverbial predicate: its privilege of position can be shared by certain verbal expressions by virtue of the adverbial character which they had in Classical Egyptian, but which is entirely obscured in Coptic. This construction, which differs from the Verbal Sentence by expressing durativity (for action and for state), used to be called 'Uneigentlicher Nominalsatz' (Erman, Steindorff), upon which Gardiner's 'Pseudo-verbal Construction' is no great improvement. No adequately descriptive term has yet been found.

While Sethe's monograph was avowedly diachronic, a purely synchronic study of the Coptic Nominal Sentence was attempted by J. Vergote.[34] He rejects Gardiner's re-definition and returns to Sethe: (1) 'la phrase nominale à prédicat adverbial', (2) 'la phrase nominale à prédicat substantival'. After a theoretical and critical introduction, much of which is valuable, he presents (237 ff.) what he believes to be 'un tableau plus clair, plus systématique des règles relatives à la phrase nominale'. Further contributions by Vergote to the study of the Nominal Sentence are to be found in some of his reviews.[35] In *BiOr* 13.226b (1965), for instance, he makes the interesting observation that Coptic uses its equivalent of *c'est moi* also in cases where French would use *je le suis*; it is gratuitous to assume that the two employments were distinguished prosodically.

Vergote's 'Phrase nominale' stimulated Till to write his 'Satzarten',[36] the plan

[32] *Egyptian grammar* (Oxford 1927), §28, 1.2
[33] 'Die Satzarten im Koptischen', *MIO* 2.378–402 (1954).
[34] 'La phrase nominale en copte. Étude critique', in *Crum Studies*, 229–42.
[35] Especially those quoted in notes 17 and 18.
[36] See note 33. Review by J. Vergote, *CdÉ* 31.218–19 (1956).

and idea of which were more felicitous than the execution. The sections on the Nominal Sentence, however, are the best and make a valuable contribution to the subject.

A peculiar case of the Binary Nominal Sentence was discussed by P. Jernstedt:[37] the pronominal subject ('topic') is in the 3rd f. sg. (*te*), while the predicate ('com ment') is a masc. noun, preceded by the 'indefinite article' (*ou-*) and accompanied by a Circumstantial Clause the pronominal actor of which agrees in gender with the 'topic'. It is sometimes difficult to decide whether a Circumstantial Clause is to be understood adverbially or adnominally (as 'Uneigentlicher Relativsatz' describing an indefinite antecedent). A passage from Shenoute quoted by Jernstedt consists of a long series of such sentences: in one of them the position of the Circumstantial Clause (due to its brevity) shows that it can only be understood adnominally, in spite of the apparent incongruity in gender: *ou-hethnos e-s-ouaab te* 'she is a holy (lit. 'being pure, holy') nation'.[38] Jernstedt concludes that the pronominal suffix 3rd f. sg. in *es-* refers, not to *ou-hethnos* as a whole (which would normally be treated as masculine), but only to the *ou-* (the proclitic form of both the masc. *oua* and the fem. *ouei* 'one') and that the noun must be subordinated to it, or, as he says, *ou-hethnos* must be an 'izafet':[39] 'a feminine specimen of the category nation'. The Shenoute passage gives the impression of a nonce-construction, but there are certain normal constructions in Coptic, which seem to call for the same explanation. Jernstedt quotes especially Nominal Sentences where the 'comment' is the indefinite article preceding a word either for materials (*hen-hat ne* 'they are (of) silver') or for abstract notions (*hen-me ne* 'they are true' [not 'truths']).[40] Jernstedt's article is reported here in some detail because it is little known and because it makes no easy reading.

Closely related to the Nominal Sentence is the CLEFT SENTENCE,[41] corresponding in function (and in essential structure[42]) to the European sentence type 'it was N. who wrote this chapter.' Such sentences are a characteristic feature of Egyptian syntax in all stages of the language. The difference between the Nominal Sentence and the Cleft Sentence can best be seen in real Nominal Sentences which resemble Cleft Sentences in having a substantivized relative clause as second member ('topic').[43] The Coptic Cleft Sentence stands in a relationship of complementary distribution, and partly in that of a variant, to the Second Tenses (see below).

[37] 'K determinacii v koptskom jazyke', *Sovetskoe Vostokovedenie* 6.52–62 (1949). Two unsuccessful attempts have, to my knowledge, been made to have this article translated into a Western language.

[38] *Sinuthii opera*, ed. J. Leipoldt, III (= *CSCO* t. 42) 61, 14; *(h)ethnos*, neuter in Greek, is masculine in Coptic.

[39] This Arabic-Persian term is much used by Russian linguists, apparently in order to avoid 'genitive' and its Indo-European associations.

[40] Cf. *Orientalia* 31.418–19 (1962). Cases where the 'comment' consists of the indefinite article plus two nouns connected by *hi-* likewise belong here, cf. *OLZ* (1957) 233–4.

[41] This term, which was coined by O. Jespersen, is a translation of the Danish *kløvet sætning*.

[42] The essential characteristic of the Cleft Sentence is that the 'topic' has the form of a relative clause, not that it is 'represented' at the beginning of the sentence by *it* (French *ce*, Danish *det*).

[43] HJP, 'Nominalsatz und Cleft Sentence im Koptischen', *Orientalia* 31.413–30 (1962). A case of this kind is the second of P. du Bourguet's 'Quelques [three] dérogations aux "règles" de la grammaire copte', *BSAC* 17.13–21, esp. 15–19 (1964, for 1963–64).

VERB

We have W. F. Albright's testimony for the bewildering impression which the Coptic 'tense' system makes on first acquaintance: 'the remarkable composite structures which are the despair of the Semitist who glances into a Coptic grammar.'[44] It is a commonplace to say that Coptic has twenty-two 'tenses'.

With the help of formal criteria, such as specific modes of negation, it is, however, possible to break up these 'tenses' into several groups and to single out certain forms which are not 'tenses' at all, but correspond in function to subordinate clauses (temporal, conditional, etc.). Moreover, some of the remaining real tenses are merely modifications, characterized by identical, or at least similar, morphemes common to all or most basic tenses.[45]

A useful list of the Conjugation Bases from recently discovered dialectal sources was compiled by R. Kasser.[46]

Within the Verbal System a special status is reserved to the DURATIVE TENSES, i.e. the 'Uneigentliche Nominalsatz' or 'the pseudo-verbal construction' (see above); this was already recognized by Ludw. Stern in his unsurpassed *Koptische Grammatik* (Leipzig 1880). Among their peculiarities he noticed (§ 494) their inability to have the object follow the verb-stem immediately; this is a prerogative of the non-durative ('point') tenses. In the Durative Tenses the object can only be expressed through the intermediary of a preposition (*n-* before nouns, *mmo-* before suffixes).

In Steindorff's *Koptische Grammatik* (Berlin 1894, 2nd ed. 1904), which was the standard textbook during two generations, this fact was not mentioned, and thus Stern's observation was forgotten.[47] It was not until 1927 that Stern's rule was re-formulated more fully by P. Jernstedt.[48] This (re-)discovery of a rule which is so strictly observed and which has so wide an application showed perhaps more clearly than any other that our knowledge of Coptic had more serious gaps than was generally believed. It took some time for these six pages of Jernstedt's to become as widely known as they deserve, yet they can be said to have opened the era of 'current trends', so far as syntax is concerned.

Jernstedt's article also prompted an inquiry into the pre-Coptic antecedents of this rule. It was found to have been in force already in Persian Demotic.[49]

The so-called SECOND TENSES had long been a puzzling feature of the Coptic verbal

[44] *RT* 40.70 (1923).
[45] HJP, 'The Coptic conjugation system', *Orientalia* 29.392–422 (1960).
[46] R. Kasser, 'Compléments morphologiques au Dictionnaire de Crum', *BIFAO* 64.19–66 (1966); 63 ff.: Préfixes verbaux.
[47] F. Ll. Griffith, *Stories of the High Priests of Memphis* (Oxford 1900), 102, note on *IKh.* 3, 36, pointed out the corresponding contrast, with the verb 'to say', between the 'First Present' and the ('Third') Future in Demotic, but apparently without discerning the principle.
[48] P. Jernstedt, 'Das koptische Praesens und die Anknüpfungsarten des näheren Objekts', *Doklady Akademii Nauk SSSR* (1927) 69–74.
[49] R. A. Parker, 'The durative tenses in P. Rylands IX', *JNES* 20.180–7 (1961).

system. A study by HJP[50] showed that they correspond in function, and in essential structure, to that type of the European Cleft Sentence in which the predicative (the 'comment') is an adverbial expression, while the 'topic' has the form of a (conjunctional) *that*-clause (French *que*, Danish *at*). Just as the two types of the European Cleft Sentence do to each other, so the Second Tenses stand in a relationship of complementary distribution, and in part in that of a variant, to the Coptic Cleft Sentence (Cleft Sentence, 'it is I to whom you have done it' ~ Second Tense, 'it is to me that you have done it'). The discovery of the true nature of the Second Tenses threw light on certain puzzling verb forms in all stages of pre-Coptic Egyptian. It helped in disentangling two Demotic auxiliaries,[51] a task of which one of the highest authorities had written that 'the prospects cannot be called encouraging'.[52]

The paradigm of the CAUSATIVE IMPERATIVE, *mare*, provides an interesting illustration of loose method. While earlier grammarians had been careful to state that they had been unable to find instances of the 2nd persons[53] or, like A. Peyron, *Grammatica linguae copticae* (Turin 1841:106) and M.G. Schwartze in his posthumous shorter *Kopt. Gramm.* (Berlin 1850:453), refrained at any rate from setting up a 'full' paradigm, later authors exerted no such commendable caution. A paradigm with all three persons, including even the 2nd f. sg., appears in H. Brugsch's *Grammaire démotique* (Berlin 1855:§291) (Demotic and Coptic) and in Stern's *Kopt. Gramm.* §383. Thereafter it became firmly established, until L.Th. Lefort showed conclusively that the 2nd persons were not used in classical Sahidic.[54] A posteriori it was, of course, realized that the absence of these persons is perfectly natural, because it is against Egyptian usage for a form of the verb 'to give', of which *ma-* is the imperative, to govern its own person in a dependent verb form. The fact is also relevant to the question whether *mare* might not, after all, be allowed to keep its traditional name 'Optative'. If E. Revillout long ago[55] could argue from the supposed presence of all three persons that *mare* must be an Optative, not an Imperative, it can be argued now that the absence of the 2nd persons alone is sufficient proof that *mare* is not an Optative: it is in complementary distribution with the ordinary Imperative, providing the 1st and 3rd persons of what might be called 'Jussive'.[56]

The Coptic CONJUNCTIVE still awaits a detailed study, but some articles on its

[50] *Études de syntaxe copte*, 21–96 (Cairo 1944).
[51] R. J. Williams, 'On certain verbal forms in Demotic', *JNES* 7.223–35 (1948).
[52] W. F. Edgerton, *JAOS* 55.264 (1935).
[53] M. G. Schwartze, *Das alte Aegypten* (II) pp. 1959, 1961, 1963 (Leipzig 1843) states that the 2nd pl. was avoided, that the 2nd m. sg. seems to have been very little used [a doubtful example had been quoted by Chr. Scholtz, *Grammatica Aegyptiaca*, 97 (Oxford 1778), who also states, p. 98, that the 2nd pl. is only set up 'juxta Analogiam'], and that he does not recall a single instance, either of the sg. or the pl., in the Bohairic Psalter.
[54] *Muséon* 60.23 (1947).
[55] *JA* 1872 I.277.
[56] Schwartze, *op. cit.* (note 53), (II) 1959–60; HJP, in *Crum Studies* 81–4.

Late Egyptian antecedents, by M. Lichtheim,[57] A. Volten,[58] and E. F. Wente,[59] have an indirect bearing on the subject.

The negative form of the so-called 'THIRD FUTURE'[60] or 'Futur énergique' (thus A. Mallon[61] and now R. Kasser[62]) usually renders the Greek *ou mē* with the Subjunctive. Both its affirmative and its negative forms were shown by L. Th. Lefort,[63] and more fully by HJP,[64] to be also the normal rendering of the Greek Optative. All aspects of this important tense were discussed in a very thorough and remarkably well documented monograph by M. R. Wilson.[65]

The so-called 'FINALIS', *tare*, is used in late texts in a manner which might justify that name. In the classical language, however, its function is quite different.[66] It is used exclusively in direct speech (one would expect a 'Finalis' not to be excluded from narration) and most often after an Imperative, to express the result which the speaker promises will ensue from the fulfilment of his command or advice: 'Seek, and ye shall find; knock, and it shall be opened unto you.' Besides being used exclusively in direct speech the form has the further peculiarity that the 1st person singular, *tari-*, is practically avoided in the classical language. These two facts in conjunction suggest that the first element of *tare*, *ta-*, is the 1st person singular of the verb 'to give (cause)' in the so-called prospective *sḏm.f*: 'Do this or that, and I shall cause this or that to happen'.[67] Lefort pointed out that the absence of the 1st person singular in the paradigm *tare* is the exact counterpart of the absence of the 2nd persons in the paradigm *mare*,[68] while A. Volten[69] showed that the postulated use of the 1st person singular of 'to give' actually occurs in Demotic wisdom literature.[70]

[57] 'Notes on the Late-Egyptian conjunctive', in *Studies in egyptology and linguistics*, 1–8 (Jerusalem 1964.
[58] 'The Late Egyptian conjunctive', in the same volume, 54–80.
[59] 'The Late Egyptian conjunctive as a Past Continuative', *JNES* 21.304–11 (1962).
[60] This name is misleading, because it seems to imply that the 'Third Future' is of the same kind as the 'First' and the 'Second' Futures.
[61] *Grammaire copte* §241 (see note 2).
[62] 'Compléments morphologiques' (see note 46) 65. What Kasser calls 'Futur énergique II négatif' is the form used in the Bodmer Proverbs (see note 10) after *čekas* 'in order that' (*ene-* 4, 21; *enf-* 3, 30). This form corresponds to the Sahidic *enne-* (in old MSS often *ene-*), first pointed out in *OLZ* (1957) 233. It is impossible to decide whether this is really 'II' or 'circumstantial'; to Akhmimic this special form is unknown.
[63] *Muséon* 60.28 fn. 34 (1947).
[64] *Crum Studies* 84–7.
[65] M. R. Wilson, Syntactical studies of future tenses in Sahidic. Ph.D. dissertation, Brandeis University, 1963. University Microfilms, Inc., Ann Arbor, Michigan, 1967.
[66] Already E. Revillout, in *Mélanges d'archéologie égyptienne et assyrienne* 2.231–2 (1875; N° 6, 1874), had tried to define 'la nuance délicate de cette tournure élégante, que le copte possède seul. et qui répond à une nuance de pensée également fort nette.'
[67] HJP, *Études de syntaxe copte* 1–19 (see note 50).
[68] L. Th. Lefort, 'A propos de syntaxe copte [:] *tare mare mprtre*', *Muséon* 60.7–28 (1947).
[69] A. Volten, 'Die moralischen Lehren des demotischen Pap. Louvre 2414', in *Studi in memoria di I. Rosellini*, II.271–80, esp. 277 (Pisa 1955). — Two more examples came to light in another Demotic wisdom book, '*Onkhsheshonqy* 17, 26 (note 220a); 25, 16.
[70] Space forbids reporting in detail two articles by D. W. Young, 'On Shenoute's use of Present

LEXICOGRAPHY

No sooner had the first part of W.E. Crum's *Coptic Dictionary* come out in 1929 than there began an era of discoveries which has been bringing us new texts of novel contents and of unprecedented antiquity and dialectal variety. Crum gathered in as much as was humanly possible, but it was clear that before long the question of a Supplement, or of Supplements, would become serious. Only a comparatively small part of the new material has so far been published, but the needs of those engaged in the editing and in the study of the new texts, especially of the Gnostic texts from Nagʿ Ḥammadi, required an interim solution. R. Kasser's *Compléments*[71] were therefore greeted with universal gratitude.

At the same time two new full-scale dictionaries have begun to appear, the one by W. Westendorf,[72] the other by R. Kasser and W. Vycichl.[73] While disclaiming any pretence to replace or supersede Crum, both go in certain respects beyond Crum. Both include as much as possible of the new material, and both give etymologies, not only Egyptian, but 'Hamito-Semitic' in general; owing to Vycichl's collaboration the African material of the Geneva dictionary is richer. Westendorf gives ample references to the scholarly literature, while Kasser gives a wealth of dialectal forms and spellings. The most prominent feature of Kasser is the inclusion of Greek words[74] and of late loans from Arabic.

On the other hand, both seem to expect the user to turn to Crum, not only for references,[75] but also for details of construction and phraseology, traditionally the backbone of a dictionary. Spiegelberg did pay due attention to these things, and at least to one grateful user it was they more than anything else which made the old *Hand-*

I', *JNES* 20.115–19 (1961), and especially '*ešōpe* and the Conditional Conjugation', *JNES* 21. 175–85 (1962); and numerous articles on syntax, esp. on the Relative Clause, by A. I. Jelanskaja (apparently a pupil of P. Jernstedt), e.g. 'Sintaksičeskaja rol' opredelitel'nyx predloženij v koptskom jazyke', *Palestinskij Sbornik*, vyp. 5(68).32–44 (1960); 'Slučai nesoglasovanija "podxvatyvajuščego mestoimenijas" antecedentom opredelitel'nogo predloženija v koptskom jazyke', in *Drevnij Egipet i drevnaja Afrika* 27–9 (Moscow 1967).

[71] R. Kasser, *Compléments au Dictionnaire copte de Crum* = *Institut français d'archéologie orientale. Bibliothèque d'études coptes*, tome 7 (Le Caire 1964). Cf. also his 'Compléments morphologiques' (note 46).

[72] W. Westendorf, *Koptisches Handwörterbuch.* Bearbeitet auf Grund des Koptischen Handwörterbuchs Wilhelm Spiegelbergs, Heidelberg, 2 Lieferungen (out of 5), 1965, 1967. Reviews by H. Quecke, *Orientalia* 35.459–63 (1966) [the faulty *ahe*, instead of *ahē*, mentioned on p. 461, was taken from W. F. Engelbreth, *Fragmenta basmurico-coptica* 10 (Havniae 1811)]; R. Kasser, *BiOr* 24.131–5 (1967).

[73] R. Kasser, avec la collaboration de W. Vycichl, *Dictionnaire auxiliaire, étymologique et complet de la langue copte*, fasc. I (Genève 1967).

[74] The meanings of the Greek words are treated somewhat summarily. Nobody will consult Kasser-Vycichl in order to learn that *apokrisis* means 'réponse'. What the reader of Coptic texts, hagiographical as well as documentary, may need to learn is that it can mean 'business (besogne)'.

[75] Under the necessity of making a selection Crum tended to curtail Biblical references in favour of other texts. One could imagine a Concise Dictionary based mainly on the Bible versions (taking due account of Kasser's publications) and giving occasionally other, and in certain cases even fuller, references than Crum.

wörterbuch so attractive. Its very imperfections[76] had the wholesome effect of stimulating the reader, especially the young student, to observe and to note for himself. I wonder whether either of the two new dictionaries is likely to have a similar effect. The shift of interest and emphasis to which they bear witness, both positively and negatively, must probably also be reckoned among *Current Trends.*

[76] Cf. Crum's review, *JEA* 8.116–19, 187–90 (1922).

CUSHITIC

F. R. PALMER

1. IDENTIFICATION AND CLASSIFICATION

There is, as yet, very little agreement concerning the identification and classification of the languages to which the name 'Cushitic' is to be applied. At most, it is clear that the name is used for a number of languages spoken in and around modern Ethiopia and Somalia, an area in which almost all the other languages are Ethiopian Semitic. The minimum list of Cushitic languages or language groups — those that appear to be accepted by all reputable scholars — includes only:

Saho-Afar:	coastal plains of Ethiopia (Eritrea) and Jibouti;
Agau:	northern Ethiopia, in several linguistic islands in the region around Lake Tana and also (Bilin) around Keren in Eritrea;
Burji-Sidamo:	southwestern Ethiopia;
Galla:	southern Ethiopia and northern Kenya;
Somali:	Somalia, eastern Ethiopia, and northwestern Kenya.

In addition to these, the following languages or language groups have also been included, with varying degrees of agreement:

Beja:	northern Ethiopia and western Sudan;
Sidama:	southwestern Ethiopia (the term Sidama was used to cover a whole group of languages and is to be distinguished from Sidamo which is now the name given to one language—see below p. 572);
Sanye and Boni:	northeastern Kenya;
Iraqw:	northern Tanzania.

At the present time there are two main views on the identification and classification of the Cushitic languages, those of Greenberg and Tucker. Since both are derived to some degree from earlier views, a brief historical statement may be useful.

The first serious identification of the languages stems from the extensive work at the end of the nineteenth century by Leo Reinisch (see below p. 578). Reinisch made a single distinction, between 'Low' and 'High' Cushitic. This was essentially a geographical division between the languages spoken on the coastal plains, Beja, Afar-Saho, and Somali, and those spoken in the Ethiopian highlands.

The first detailed classification of the languages was made by M. M. Moreno (for details consult table below, pp. 574–5). An account of his researches was published in an article (Moreno 1938a) and a classified list of the languages is also to be found in his grammar of Galla (Moreno 1939). A much more detailed classification appeared in his manual of Sidamo (Moreno 1940). Moreno made three points in his discussion, which, in effect, abandoned or, at least, modified Reinisch's division into High and Low Cushitic. First, he divided Low Cushitic into two, by separating off Beja, which now became the sole member of Northern Cushitic, leaving the remainder as Eastern Cushitic. Secondly, he argued at some length for separating the Burji-Sidamo group from the remainder of 'Sidama'. Cerulli (1925) had already pointed out that 'Sidama' was the term used by the Galla for all non-Galla speakers, including those who spoke Amharic, and Moreno suggested that the term should now be abandoned as it was quite misleading. But he further argued that the languages of the Burji-Sidamo group were close to 'Low' Cushitic and therefore placed them in the Eastern group; he also transferred, though without similar justificatory arguments, some other languages, including Konso and Geleba. Thirdly, he saw a major division between the languages that had forms of the type *ani* and *ati* for the first and second person singular pronouns and those that had forms of the type *tā* and *ne*. This division into *ani, ati/tā, ne* languages he rather inappropriately likened to the *centum/satem* division in Indo-European. Its effect was to distinguish between the old 'Sidama' group (less Burji-Sidamo) and the rest, and, in particular, to distinguish between this group and the Agau group within what had been High Cushitic. This led to a classification in terms of four groups of which the first three were *ani, ati* and the last one *tā, ne*: Northern (Beja), Eastern (Somali, Saho-Afar, Galla, and Burji-Sidamo), Central (Agau), and Western ('Sidama'). Moreno provided almost no evidence for his classification apart from his *ani, ati/tā, ne* distinction and a detailed argument to show the closeness of the languages of the Burji-Sidamo group to one another and to Eastern Cushitic. But he provided no grounds for isolating Beja and Agau as Northern and Central Cushitic respectively, nor for the inclusion of the Konso-Geleba group along with Burji-Sidamo as members of Eastern Cushitic. Of Konso he simply says 'è certamente una lingua basso-cuscitico' (1938a:51).

Another classification appears in Bryan (1947) — into Northern, Central, and Eastern, Central being essentially Moreno's Central and Western. In Tucker and Bryan (1956) the various languages are assembled into language groups, but there is no further overall classification of the 'Larger Unit Cushitic'.

Yet another grouping was suggested by Plazikowksy-Brauner who regularly referred in the titles of her articles to the 'so-called Cushitic languages' (1958a, 1958b, 1959, 1963, 1965). Cushitic is to be divided into four groups — Agau, Boro (Shinasha and Kafa — Western Cushitic), Hadya (languages of Burji-Sidamo group), and Ollabi (including Somali and Galla). The Ometi group (referred to by other scholars as 'Ometo') is considered to be marginally Cushitic but to have a non-Cushitic substratum, while Beja is said to be non-Cushitic but to belong to the 'Noba' group. Apart from the material in the articles themselves (see below), no evidence for the classification is given. As far as I am aware, no other scholar has excluded Beja from Cushitic.

The classification of Greenberg (1963a:49, cf. also 1955) agrees, according to its proposer, with that of Moreno 'with the omission of Southern Cushitic' (1963a:65, fn. 11). Southern Cushitic, a fifth group, includes Sanye from Kenya and some languages from northern Tanzania of which the best known is Iraqw. In fact, Greenberg also adds Bako and some languages related to it (southwestern Ethiopia) to the western Cushitic group. It is somewhat disconcerting, however, to be told with reference to Moreno (1940) that 'the careful review of the evidence there makes a formal justification of the present classification unnecessary' (1963a:65, fn. 11). The evidence for the addition of Southern Cushitic is promised in a subsequent publication, while on Bako and the related languages we are told that 'material now available shows that these languages are without doubt Western Cushitic'. A further sub-division of Eastern Cushitic (again without any evidence being provided) is suggested in a subsequent article (Greenberg 1963b:42); the article itself deals with Mogogodo, a language of northern Kenya and known only from a chapter in a book written in 1910 (see below p. 579).

A different approach is implied in Tucker and Bryan (1966), where the previous (Tucker and Bryan 1956) 'Larger Group Cushitic' (No. 32) is divided into three sub-groups 32a, 32b, and 32c of which it is said that the languages in 32b are 'partially' Cushitic and those in 32c are not Cushitic. 32a, the genuinely Cushitic sub-group, includes precisely those admitted by earlier scholars (cf. Cohen 1947) — Beja, Saho-Afar, Agau, Galla, Somali, and Sidamo. 32b includes Janjero, Ometo, Gimira, and Kafa, while the Konso-Geleba group is placed in 32c.

The evidence for this classification, though with some modification to the classifications and some additions, especially that of Greenberg's 'Southern Cushitic', is to be found in Tucker (1967). He there points out that within the Cushitic field there is a great lack of material, that there has, as yet, been little attempt to work out correspondences between the languages, and that, moreover, where comparative studies of vocabulary have been made the results have been most disappointing. Andrzejewski (1964b), for instance, undertook a comparison of Galla with certain other languages. With Somali he found 20% shared vocabulary, with Afar, Sidamo, and Saho 3%, and with Agau, Beja, Kafa, and Ometo less than 1%. Tucker's approach is traditional in the sense that as it takes account of morphological patterns of the verb — a feature that Cohen (1947:43) had regarded as important for the identification of the larger Hamito-Semitic, and which, in part at least, is to be found in some of Moreno's arguments (Moreno 1940, cf. Klingenheben 1956).

Looking at other 'Erythraic' languages (Tucker's term for Greenberg's 'Afro-Asiatic' or 'Hamito-Semitic') and specifically Geez, Arabic, Berber, and Hausa, he sees three patterns:

(a) the distribution of morphemic elements — most importantly *n* for first person, *n* for plural, *t* for second person, and *t* for feminine in second and third person;

(b) the 'block' pattern — the fact that the plural forms repeat (for each person) features of the singular;

(c) the 'interlocking' pattern — the fact that certain elements are merged, in particular the *t* of both second person and of the feminine.

Tucker begins with the very plausible assumption that all the languages of the previous sub-group 32a are 'orthodox' Cushitic. The remainder, whose status is to be investigated, are 'fringe' Cushitic, though he now adds to the list all Greenberg's Southern Cushitic, plus Teuso (Eastern Sudanic), whose real name is Ik according to Tucker, Hatsa (Khoisan), Mogogodo, and Boni (from the northern coast of Kenya). The chief conclusions are not summarised by Tucker himself, but may, perhaps, be fairly stated as:

(1) Sanye (divided into Waata and Dahalo) and Boni (divided into Boni and Aweera) are clearly 'orthodox'.

(2) Ometo, Janjero, and Kafa have some Erythraic features, and the name 'Western Cushitic' has the merit of at least classing some similar languages together, but further research is needed.

(3) Iraqw and, more obviously, Burunge have some Erythraic features. These, but not Mbugu and Sanye, may fairly be described as 'Southern Cushitic'.

(4) Mbugu has a Bantu verbal system, but pronouns like those of Iraqw, and is therefore perhaps to be regarded as mixed (cf. also on this Winston 1966:165).

(5) Teuso and Hatsa are possibly Cushitic.

(6) There is little evidence that the Konso-Geleba group is Cushitic, and Greenberg's placement of this group in Eastern Cushitic together with the orthodox Saho-Afar, Somali, and Galla is unconvincing. The same is true for Mogogodo.

A summary in table form of the relationship between the classifications of Moreno (1940), Tucker and Bryan (1956), Greenberg (1963a), and Tucker (1967) follows. Since Tucker reaches no firm conclusion, except about the 'orthodox' languages, I have interpreted his remarks in terms of 'doubtful', 'possible', 'probable', and 'mixed'.

MORENO	TUCKER-BRYAN	GREENBERG	TUCKER
Northern I Beja	32a Bedauye	1 Northern	Orthodox
Central II Agau	32a Agau	2 Central	Orthodox
Eastern III 'Low'	32a Saho-Afar, Somali, Galla	3 Eastern	Orthodox
Eastern IV Various languages	32c Konso-Geleba, Arbore	3 Eastern	Doubtful
Eastern V Burji-Sidamo	32a Sidamo	3 Eastern	Orthodox
Western VI Yamna	32b Janjero	4 Western	Probable
Western VI Ometo	32b Ometo	4 Western	Probable
Western VIII Gimira	32b Gimira	4 Western	—
Western IX Gonga	32b Kafa	4 Western	Probable
	28 Bako	4 Western	—

—	27	Didinga-Mirle	4 Western	—
—	34	Iraqw	5 Southern	Probable
—	35	Mbugu	5 Southern	Mixed
—	36	Sanye	5 Southern	Orthodox
—	29	Teuso	Eastern Sudanic	Possible
—	38	Hatsa	Khoisan	Possible

The table does not bring out all the points of disagreement. It does not mention Boni and Mogogodo, and there are two points relating to Greenberg's listing of individual languages that are worth noting. First, under 'Northern' Greenberg enters only Beja though Moreno differentiated Bishari-Hadendoa, Beni-amer, and Halenga as forms of Beja and, according to Paul (1954), some of the dialects of Beja are mutually unintelligible, yet, on the other hand, Gimira, Benesho, Nao, Kaba, Shako, She, and Maji appear as separate items (together with many more) under Greenberg's 'Western', while Moreno (followed by Tucker and Bryan) treats Gimira as the name of the whole group and the rest as subdivisions. There is clearly grave dissension about the status of these linguistic units. Secondly, in Greenberg (1963b: 42) there is a sub-division of Eastern Cushitic into four sections with Galla placed in the fourth together with Konso-Geleba languages, the other three being Afar-Saho, Somali, and Sidamo respectively. The fact that Tucker treats Galla as orthodox and Konso-Geleba as very doubtful, while Greenberg places them together in a small sub-group within Eastern Cushitic, emphasises the extent of the disagreement between them.

Tucker's strongest point, which he does not emphasise sufficiently, is the regular occurrence in the orthodox languages of the affix pattern:

1 s.	zero
2 s.	*t*
3 m.s.	*y* or zero
3 f.s.	*t*
1 pl.	*n*
2 pl.	*t*
3 pl.	*y* or zero

A further very striking point is that Saho, Beja, Somali, and Awiya (at least) have two 'conjugations', one using prefixes and the other suffixes (cf. Cerulli 1948 and, for the feature in 'Hamito-Semitic', Klingenheben 1956), but with the elements listed above in both. This affix pattern is clearly illustrated by verbal forms of Saho (Welmers 1952:236):

1 s.	*ḥabe*	*uble*
2 s.	*ḥabte*	*tuble*
3 m.s.	*ḥabe*	*yuble*

3 f.s.	*ḥabte*	*tuble*
1 pl.	*ḥabne*	*nuble*
2 pl.	*ḥabten*	*tublin*
3 pl.	*ḥaben*	*yublin*

Almost identical paradigms are to be found in Awiya (Palmer 1959:279, 285), and paradigms of the first type in Bilin (Palmer 1957:144) and Galla (Moreno 1939:66; Andrzejewski 1964b:135, where he comments that Galla is morphologically similar to other Cushitic languages). Those of Somali (Andrzejewski 1956:126–7), Beja (Hudson 1964), and Sidamo (Moreno 1940, Plazikowsky-Brauner 1960:64) follow exactly the same basic pattern, but differ only in having additional suffixes which distinguish forms that are otherwise identical. This affix pattern is so striking that it alone might be regarded as a test of orthodoxy, and it is of particular importance to note that the two conjugations (with both prefixes and affixes) are found in languages that are placed in different groups by Greenberg and Moreno — Northern (Beja), Eastern (Saho and Somali), and Central (Awiya). Whether Greenberg's lexical material is sufficient to challenge this is not yet in evidence. Plazikowsky-Brauner's exclusion of Beja seems in the light of this feature wholly unacceptable.

2. COMPARATIVE AND DIALECT STUDIES

The major views on the classification and identification of the Cushitic languages have already been discussed. There has been fairly general agreement that Cushitic, however it is to be defined precisely, is part of a larger group, be it Hamito-Semitic (Cohen 1947), Afro-Asiatic (Greenberg 1955, 1963a) or Erythraic (Tucker 1967), which includes ancient Egyptian, Semitic, Berber, and Hausa, at least. The view that Beja is particularly closely related to Egyptian (an extreme version is that the Beja are the direct descendants of the ancient Egyptians) was considered by Vycichl (1953, 1960) who concluded that in spite of geographical, anthropological, and cultural arguments for the relationship, Beja was no more closely related to ancient Egyptian than any other language within Hamito-Semitic.

The only really discordant view is that of Homburger, who argued originally simply for the unity of the 'Negro-African' languages and their descent from Egyptian (Homburger 1949). More recently she has suggested that these languages are related to the Dravidian languages of India (Homburger 1955, 1957a, chapter 12, *Le Sindo-Africain*) and in particular has found Dravidian features in Cushitic (1962a, 1962b), and especially in Somali (1954) and ancient Egyptian (1957b). The evidence she provides is only partially linguistic, and the linguistic evidence is flimsy — a small number of words to indicate correspondences, some tribal names, and a few morphological features.

The question whether the language of Meroitic inscriptions is Cushitic has again been raised. Zylharz (1930) following Meinhof maintained that Meroitic was an ancient Cushitic language. Hintze (1955), however, argued that the features which Zylharz considered to be Cushitic are either not present or very questionably so, while many of the clearly established features are certainly not Cushitic. Vycichl (1958) agreed with him, saying simply that Meroitic was a 'Negro' language. The present conclusion of Zylharz (1960) (cf. 1956) is that it is an extinct 'semitoid' language. An excellent resumé of the arguments is to be found in Trigger (1964) who accepts the view that Meroitic is not Cushitic, but now suggests that a link may be found with the Eastern Sudanic group.

A particularly interesting point that has been raised is whether Cushitic is related to Bushman and Hottentot. This has arisen from the recognition of the Southern Cushitic group. Greenberg (1963a:44) notices the occurrence of a masculine element *b* in both Hottentot and Beja though he says 'such a point of contact is arresting but not decisive'. We have already seen that one of his Khoisan languages, Hatsa, is regarded as possibly Cushitic by Tucker (1967). This is, however, not evidence for the relationship since Tucker denies any resemblance between Hatsa and the neighbouring language Sandawe, and the latter he is prepared to accept as Khoisan. There is however one further point, that one of the Cushitic languages found in Kenya, Sanye (Dahalo), which Tucker regards as 'orthodox', has click consonants (Dammann 1950, Tucker 1967), a feature otherwise associated with Bushman and Hottentot.

Within Cushitic very little work has been done to establish relationships or dialect divisions. Moreno (1951, 1953, 1955) investigated Somali dialects. Andrzejewski (1957) has firmly established that Borana (Galla) is quite different from the Galla studied by previous scholars. Fleming (1964) has investigated the Somali 'outliers' Baiso and Rendille, which Greenberg now (1963b) groups together with Somali. The precise status of Sanye and Boni is still perhaps in doubt; Dammann (1950) had merely noted that there were many Galla and Somali elements in Sanye, while Grottanelli (1957) came to very much the same conclusion with regard to Boni, though he concluded that Boni was neither Galla nor Somali. Fleming (1964) suggests that Boni is close to Somali, though now virtually extinct, and that Sanye is close to Galla.

The relationships within Agau are still not clear and even the precise geographical location of the various Agau languages is not certain (Tubiana 1954, 1955). The status of Bilin is still in doubt. Conti Rossini (1910:599) recorded the tradition that the Bilin came north in the eleventh century and imposed the language upon a Semitic-speaking people (see also Tubiana 1955:3) and argued (Conti Rossini 1912) that Bilin was an archaic form of Agau. That Bilin shares many features with the neighbouring Semitic languages is clear enough (Palmer 1960), but what it shares with Agau is to some degree of a typological nature (Palmer 1967) and there is no evidence of its archaic state — indeed its treatment of tone vis-à-vis Awiya (see below, p. 579) would suggest the reverse. Within the Sidamo group Plazikowksy-Brauner (1960) has suggested that Hadya is closer to Alaba and Kambata than it is to Sidamo, and that the phonetic situation in Sidamo represents a more recent state of the language.

Considerable discussion of features common to the Cushitic languages is to be found in the works of Plazikowsky-Brauner. She dealt with the auxiliary elements (1957), the determinative elements (1958b), the causative (1959), the numerals (1963), and the verb formation (1965). Some of this appears to be wholly speculative, for instance the suggestion (1965) that the verbs are all formed with the help of auxiliaries from what are essentially nominal roots. She may have been on safer ground in trying to reconstruct the auxiliaries (1957), but less certainly in trying to reconstruct auxiliary verbs that are purported to underlie the causative forms (1959). A comparative phonological study (of initial labials and dentals) is that of Dolgopoljskij (1966). Tucker's article (1967), with its emphasis on morphological features, is, of course, very important in this field.

There have been numerous articles on the influence of Cushitic on the Semitic languages, especially by Leslau. These are listed in the index of Leslau (1965:318). The influence of the Semitic languages on Cushitic, with regard to the numerals, is suggested in Plazikowsky-Brauner (1963:482–3).

3. DESCRIPTIVE WORK

Very few complete dictionaries or grammars of Cushitic languages have appeared in recent years. In fact, to a very large degree we must still rely for our information on the languages on the publications of Leo Reinisch at the end of the last century. In just over twenty years he produced authoritative works, often in two or even three volumes, with both grammars and dictionaries, on Saho, Bilin, Kamir (Agau), Afar, Quara (Agau), Kafa ('Sidama'), Beja, and Somali (Reinisch 1878 and 1889, 1882, 1884, 1887a, 1887b, 1888, 1893, and 1900 respectively). The only other scholars who produced substantial publications in the field are the Italians, Carlo Conti Rossini, Enrico Cerulli, and Martino Mario Moreno. Conti Rossini's linguistic contributions include descriptions of Kemant (Agau) and Saho (Conti Rossini 1912, 1913). Cerulli undertook studies of Sidamo and Janjero (Cerulli 1938a, 1938b), while Moreno published grammars of Ometo, Galla, and Sidamo (Moreno 1938b, 1939, 1940). Apart from these scholars' publications, the only major works that appeared before the 1939–1945 war were Roper (1928) on Beja (a handbook for officials in the Sudan), Kirk (1905) on Somali, and Nordfeldt (1939) on Galla. More recently (see below) Cerulli and Moreno have produced further publications. A complete bibliography up to that date is to be found in Bryan (1947:26–35), and linguistic details of the languages in Tucker and Bryan (1966).

In recent years, Somali has been the language to which the greatest attention has been paid. Grammars by Warsama and Abraham (1951), Bell (1953), and Moreno (1955) have appeared and dictionaries by Minozzi and Poletti-Turrini (1961, 1962), and a handbook by Pia (1966). An article on lexicography is that of Zholkovsky (1967). Andrzejewski has published a number of articles on Somali; the most important are his discussions of the interrelation between tone and grammar with reference to the verbal forms (1956) and the noun classes (1964a). He has, however, also discussed the problems of vowel representation (especially with regard to the problem of vowel harmony) (1955), the pronominal and prepositional particles (1960a), and the substantive ('emphatic') pronouns (1961). A study of a difficult grammatical point — the particle *baa* — was undertaken by Hetzron (1965). A collection of more general studies of Somali is that of Cerulli (1957).

Galla has also been studied by Andrzejewski (the Borana dialect). An interesting grammatical study is that of the forms for number (plural, singulative, and general only, with plural and singulative now obsolescent) (1960c), but more general studies are those of 1957, 1960b, and 1964b. Further discussions of problems in Galla are by Klingenheben (1949b) and Webster (1960).

The present writer has dealt with the verb and the noun in Bilin and the verb in Awiya (Palmer 1957, 1958, 1959, 1965a). Of particular interest, perhaps, is the fact that in both languages tone and vowel quality (which implies some degree of vowel harmony) distinguish not only lexical verb classes but also two 'aspects' of the verb into which all the tense forms fall. A much more detailed study of the same Agau dialect (Awiya) is that of Hetzron (1969); Hetzron prefers the name 'Southern Agau', since the term Awiya has simply the meaning 'person'.

The only study of Beja undertaken recently is that of Hudson, a detailed grammatical study written in terms of 'scale and category' grammar, as yet unpublished.

There is a brief study of Saho by Plazikowsky-Brauner and Wagner (1953), and a much more detailed study of the morphology of Saho written in a strictly phonemic-morphemic framework by Welmers (1952).

Within the Sidamo group Hadya has been described in some detail by Plazikowsky-Brauner (1960, 1961, and 1964), with a much briefer analysis of the closely-related Alaba (Plazikowsky-Brauner 1962). Leslau (1952, 1956) has produced notes on Kambata.

Of the 'fringe' languages the morphology of Shinasha (Kafa) has been treated by Plazikowsky-Brauner (1950), and Kafa in an extensive publication by Cerulli (1951). Leslau (1959) has produced a dictionary of Mocha, which he notes is very closely similar to the dialect of Kafa studied by Cerulli; this dictionary is important for comparative work in that it systematically quotes related forms of the other Cushitic languages. An illustration of the flimsiness of the material available to scholars working in this field is shown by Greenberg's article on Mogogodo (1963b). There is here a very small amount of grammatical material plus only 292 vocabulary stems. Of these, a relationship with Cushitic is suggested for 90, and a relationship with Masai, or, in a few cases, another Eastern Sudanic language, for 40. Greenberg argues with some plausibility that the Masai words are borrowings, but the affiliation of Mogogodo with Eastern Cushitic is dubious (see above p. 573).

Most important for the establishment of the Southern Cushitic group is the work on Iraqw which has been undertaken by Whiteley (1953, 1958, 1960).

Perhaps the most interesting point that has been fully established by recent research is that most, if not all, of the languages are tone languages. This feature was not always noted by earlier scholars and often caused them great difficulty. Moreno, for instance described the 'accent in Galla' as 'very unstable' (1939:30, cf. Moreno 1936 where, quoting Jespersen, he says that there are three kinds of accent in Galla — traditional, psychological, and physiological). Plazikowsky-Brauner (1950) merely states with regard to Shinasha that it is difficult to give rules for the accent, as in other Cushitic languages. In her analysis of Hadya (1960), however, she discusses the position of the 'accent', which would appear to be fixed in two-syllable words and to occur on the first syllable only, but in the case of three-syllable words to occur on either the first or second syllable. Leslau (1956:985) notes that, although Mocha is quite clearly a tone language and one must suspect that the other Kafa languages are similar since they are so close, no previous authors have mentioned tone in their descriptions of these languages. Perhaps even more striking or, perhaps, disturbing is the fact that although there was a very clear and positive statement concerning tone in Somali by Armstrong (1934), Klingenheben (1949a) was prepared to suggest that Somali was not in fact a tone language. On this he was, however, firmly answered by Vycichl (1956). Andrzejewski (1954) suggested that Somali was partly a tone, partly a stress, language, though his more recent publications would suggest very strongly that it can only be treated as a tone language.

The use made of tone in the different languages varies greatly. So far only Awiya (Palmer 1959, Hetzron 1969), and Mocha (Leslau 1958, 1959) have been clearly shown to be tone languages in the familiar sense that there are several tones independently possible for grammatical and lexical features within any one word. In some of the languages, Bilin (Palmer 1957) and Saho (Welmers 1952), the use of tone is minimal; one syllable at the most in any word may have a high tone and in some words there is no high tone at all. (It is, I think, misleading to use the term 'stress', as Welmers does for this feature, if Saho is at all like Bilin, since it is phonetically always a high pitch and it may be absent altogether from some words, even 'full words'). Tone in Bilin and Saho has both lexical and grammatical function. In Borana-Galla (Andrzejewski 1957) tone seems to be wholly grammatical (but too complex to be treated as intonation?). For Somali Andrzejewski has investigated, as we have already seen (1956, 1964a), the very complex morphophonological patterns relating to the lexical and grammatical characteristics of nouns and verbs with regard to tone, though phonemically (tonemically) there seems to be a very limited system; with the noun, for instance, there can only be two tones on the penultimate syllable, and three on final syllables, with only four possible combinations of these (cf. Palmer 1965b). The position in Beja is not clear; it would appear that there is a phonemic distinction between a high and a high-falling tone, though, as in Galla and Somali, tone is closely linked with grammar (Hudson 1964:24).

Earlier discussion has shown that work in the Cushitic field has been largely on morphology. There has been some work, but not enough, on phonetics and phonology, while syntax has been almost completely neglected. Unfortunately, it would appear that in recent years the work on Cushitic is actually decreasing in volume. The entries in the *Bibliographie Linguistique* for 1965 are fewer than they have been for many years.

For more general and very largely non-linguistic studies of the areas in which the Cushitic languages are spoken, the reader is referred to the *Ethnographic Survey of Africa: North-Eastern Africa* (Lewis 1955, Huntingford 1955, Cerulli 1956) and to the volumes in the series *Völker Süd-Äthiopiens* (Jensen 1959, Haberland 1963, Staube 1963).

BIBLIOGRAPHY

Andrzejewski, B.W. 1954. Is Somali a tone language? Proc. 23rd Int. Congr. Orientalists, 367–8.

——. 1955. The problem of vowel representation in the Isaaq dialect of Somali. BSOAS 17.567–80.

——. 1956. Accentual patterns in verbal forms in the Isaaq dialect of Somali. BSOAS 18.103–29.

——. 1957. Some preliminary observations on the Borana dialect of Galla. BSOAS 19.354–74.

——. 1960a. Pronominal and prepositional particles in Northern Somali. AfrLS 1.96–108.

——. 1960b. My recent researches into the Galla dialects. Atti del convegno intern. di studi Etiopici, 75–80. Rome, Accademia nazionale dei Lincei.

——. 1960c. The categories of number in noun forms in the Borana dialect of Galla. Africa 30.62–75.

——. 1961. Notes on the substantive pronouns in Somali. AfrLS 2.80–99.

——. 1964a. The declension of Somali nouns. London, School of Oriental and African Studies.

——. 1964b. The position of Galla in the Cushitic language group. JSS 9.135–8.

Armstrong, L.E. 1934. The phonetic structure of Somali. MSOS 37.116–61.

Bell, C.R.V. 1953. The Somali language. London, Longmans.

Bryan, M. 1947. The distribution of the Semitic and Cushitic languages of Africa. London, Oxford University Press.

Cerulli, E. 1925. Note su alcune popolazioni Sidama dell'Abissinia meridionali. I Sidama Orientali. RSO 10.597–692.

——. 1938a. Studi Etiopici II. La lingua e le storie dei Sidamo. Rome, Instituto per l'oriente.

——. 1938b. Studi Etiopici III. Il linguaggio dei Giangero ed alcune lingue sidama dell'Omo (basketo ciara saisse). Rome, Instituto per l'oriente.

——. 1948. Sur la conjugaison en couchitique. GLECS 5.1–2.

CERULLI, E. 1951. Studi Etiopici IV. La lingua Caffina. Rome, Instituto per l'oriente.

——. 1956. Peoples of south-west Ethiopia and its borderland (Ethnographic Survey of Africa: North Eastern Africa 3). London, Int. Afr. Inst.

——. 1957. Somalia. Scritti vari editi ed mediti. 3 vols. 1957, 1959, 1964. Amministrazione Fiducaria Italiana della Somalia (1–2); Ministero degli affari esteri (3).

COHEN, M. 1947. Essai comparatif sur le vocabulaire et la phonetique du Chamito-sémitique. Paris, Honoré Champion.

CONTI ROSSINI, C. 1910. Studi su popolazioni dell'Etiopia. RSO 3.849–900, 4.599–651, 6.365–425.

——. 1912. La langue des Kemant en Abissinie. Vienna, Alfred Holder.

——. 1913. Schizzo del dialetto Saho dell'alta Assaorta in Eritrea. Rendiconti dei Lincei 22.151–246.

DAMMANN, E. 1950. Einige Notizen über die Sprache der Sanye (Kenya). ZES 35.227–34.

DOLGOPOLJSKIJ, A. B. 1966. Materialy po sravniteljno-istoričeskoj fonetike kušitskix jazykov: gubnye i dentaljnye smyčnye v nacaljnom položenii. Jazyki Afriki, ed. by B. A. Uspenskij. Moscow.

FLEMING, H. C. 1964. Baiso and Rendille: Somali outliers. RSEt 20.35–96.

GREENBERG, J. H. 1955. Studies in African linguistic classification. New Haven, Compass Press.

——. 1963a. The languages of Africa. IJAL Publication 25.

——. 1963b. The Mogogodo: a forgotten Cushitic people. JAfrL 2.29–43.

GROTTANELLI, V. L. 1957. Noti sui Bon, cacciatori di bassa costa dell Oltregiuba. Ann. Lat. 21.191–212.

HABERLAND, E. 1953. Über einen unbekannten Gunza-Stamm im Wallegga. RSEt 12.139–48.

——. 1963. Galla Süd-Äthiopiens (Völker Süd-Äthiopiens 2). Stuttgart, Kohlhammar.

HETZRON, R. 1965. The particle *baa* in Northern Somali. JAfrL 4.118–30.

——. 1969. The verbal system of southern Agau. California and Los Angeles, Univ. of California Press.

HINTZE, F. 1955. Die sprachliche Stellung des Meroitischen. VIO 26.355–72.

HOMBURGER, L. 1949. The Negro-African languages. London, Routledge and Kegan Paul.

——. 1954. Elements dravidiens en Somali. BSL 50.xxv.

——. 1955. L'Inde e l'Afrique. JSAfr 25.13–18.

——. 1957a. Les langues négro-africaines. Paris, Payot.

——. 1957b. De quelques elements communs à l'égyptien et aux langues dravidiennes. Kêmi 14.26–33.

——. 1962a. L'origine de Couchites. BSL 57.xii-xiii.

——. 1962b. Sur l'origine de quelques langues couchitiques. GLECS 9.54–7.

HUDSON, R. A. 1964. A grammatical study of Beja. Ph.D. thesis. University of London.

HUNTINGFORD, G. W. B. 1955. The Galla of Ethiopia. The kingdom of Kafa and Janjero. (Ethnographic Survey of Africa: North Eastern Africa 2). London, Int. Afr. Inst.

JENSEN, E. 1959. Altvölker Süd-Äthiopiens (Völker Süd-Äthiopiens 1). Stuttgart, Kohlhammer.

KIRK, J. W. C. 1965. A grammar of the Somali language. Cambridge, The University Press.

KLINGENHEBEN, A. 1949a. Ist das Somali eine Tonsprache? ZPhon 3.289–303.

——. 1949b. Zur Nominalbildung im Galla. ZES 35.21–47, 107–27, 235–66.

——. 1956. Die Präfix- und die Suffix-Konjugationen des Hamitosemitischen. MIO 4.211–77.

LESLAU, W. 1952. Notes on Kambatta of Southern Ethiopia. Africa 22.348–59.

——. 1956. Additional notes on Kambatta of Southern Ethiopia. Anthropos 51. 985–93.

——. 1958. Moča, a tone language of the Kafa group in southwestern Ethiopia. Africa 28.135–47.

——. 1959. A dictionary of Moča (Southwestern Ethiopia). Berkeley and Los Angeles, Univ. of California Press.

——. 1965. The Semitic languages of Ethiopia. The Hague, Mouton.

LEWIS, I. M. 1955. People of the Horn of Africa: Somali, Afar, and Saho. (Ethnographic Survey of Africa: North Eastern Africa. 1). London, Int.Afr.Inst.

——. 1964. Recent progress in Somali studies. JSS 9.122–34.

MINOZZI, M. T., and C. POLETTI-TURRINI. 1961. Dizionario italiano-somalo. Milan.

——. 1962. Dizionario somalo-italiano migiurtino-italiano. Milan.

MORENO, M. M. 1936. L'accento in galla. RSO 16.184–211.

——. 1938a. Le mie indagini linguistiche nel Galla-Sidamo. Oriente moderno 16. 50–4.

——. 1938b. Introduzione alla lingua ometo. Milan, Montadori.

——. 1939. Grammatica teorico-practica della lingua galla, con esercizi. Milan, Montadori.

——. 1940. Manuale di sidamo. Milan, Montadori.

——. 1951. Brevi notazioni di Ǧiddu. RSEt 10.99–107.

——. 1953. Il dialetto degli Asraf di Mogadiscio. RSEt 12.107–38, 13.5–19.

——. 1955. Il somalo della Somalia, grammatica e testi del Benadir, Darôd e Dighil. Rome, Istituto poligrafico dello stato.

NORFELDT, M. 1939. A Galla grammar. MO 33–5.1–232.

PALMER, F. R. 1957. The verb in Bilin. BSOAS 19.131–59.

——. 1958. The noun in Bilin. BSOAS 21.376–91.

——. 1959. The verb classes of Agau (Awiya). MIO 7.270–97.

——. 1960. An outline of Bilin phonology. Atti del convegno intern. di studi Etiopia, 109–16. Rome, Accademia nazionale dei Lincei.

——. 1965a. Bilin 'to be' and 'to have'. AfrLS 6.101–11.

——. 1965b. Review of Andrzejewski 1964a. Lg 41.676–80.

——. 1967. Affinity and genetic relationship in two Cushitic languages. To Honor Roman Jakobson II. The Hague, Mouton.

Paul, A. 1954. A history of the Beja tribes of the Sudan. Cambridge, The University Press.

Pia, J. J. 1966. Beginning in Somali. (Rev. ed.) Syracuse.

Plazikowsky-Brauner, H. 1950. Schizzo morfologico dello šinaša. RSEt 9.65–83.

——. 1957. Die Hilfselemente der Konjugation im den Kuschitischen Sprachen. ZDMG 107.7–30.

——. 1958a. Zu den Wanderungen der sog. Kuschiten. Kush 6.99–105.

——. 1958b. Die determinativen Elemente der sog. Kuschitischen Sprachen. MIO 6.121–41.

——. 1959. Der Kausativ in den sog. Kuschitischen Sprachen. Anthropos 54. 129–40.

——. 1960. Die Hadiya Sprache. RSEt 16.38–76.

——. 1961. Texte der Hadiya Sprache. RSEt 17.83–115.

——. 1962. Grammatik der Alābā-Sprache. RSEt 18.83–96.

——. 1963. Zahlen und Zahlensysteme in den sog. Kuschitischen Sprachen. MIO 8.466–83.

——. 1964. Wörterbuch der Hadiya-Sprache. RSEt 20.133–82.

——. 1965. Die verbalen Bildungen in den sog. Kuschitischen Sprachen. RSEt 21.94–110.

Plazikowsky-Brauner, H., and E. Wagner. 1953 Studien zur Sprache der Irob. ZDMG 103.378–93.

Reinisch, L. 1878. Die Sprache der Irob-Saho in Abessinien. Vienna, Carl Gerold's Sohn.

——. 1882. Die Bilin-Sprache in Nordost Afrika. Vienna, Carl Gerold's Sohn (vol. II 1887 Vienna, Alfred Hölder).

——. 1884. Die Chamir-Sprache in Abessinien (2 vols). Vienna, Carl Gerold's Sohn.

——. 1887a. Die Afar-Sprache. Vienna, Alfred Hölder.

——. 1887b. Die Quara-Sprache in Abessinien. Vienna, Alfred Hölder.

——. 1888. Die Kafa-Sprache in Nordost Afrika. Vienna, Alfred Hölder.

——. 1889. Die Saho-Sprache (2 vols. second 1890). Vienna, Alfred Hölder.

——. 1893. Die Bedauye-Sprache in Nordost Afrika (2 vols. second 1895). Vienna, Alfred Hölder.

——. 1900. Die Somali-Sprache (3 vols. second 1902, third 1903). Vienna, Alfred Hölder.

Roper, E. M. 1928. Tu Bedauriɛ. Hertford, Stephen Austin.

Staube, H. 1963. Westkuschitische Völker Süd-Äthiopiens. (Völker Süd-Äthiopiens 3). Stuttgart, Kohlhammer.

Trigger, B. G. 1964. Meroitic and Eastern Sudanic: a linguistic relationship? Kush 12.188–94.

Tubiana, J. 1954. La repartition geographique des dialectes Agaw. BSL 50.vi–vii.

——. 1955. Note sur la distribution geographique des dialectes Agaw. Cahiers de l'Afrique et l'Asie (Paris) 5.297–306.

Tucker, A. N. 1967. 'Fringe' Cushitic: an experiment in typological comparison. BSOAS 30.655–80.

Tucker, A. N., and M. Bryan. 1956. The non-Bantu languages of north-eastern Africa. London, Oxford University Press.

——. 1966. Linguistic analyses: the non-Bantu languages of north-eastern Africa. London, Oxford University Press.

Vycichl, W. 1953. Der bestimmte Artikel in der Bedja-sprache, seine Beziehungen zum Ägyptischen und Berberschen. Muséon 66.373–9.

——. 1956. Zur Tonologie des Somali. Zum Verhältnis zwischen musikalischem Ton und dynamischem Akzent in afrikanischen Sprachen und zur Bildung des Femininums im Somali. RSO 31.221–7.

——. 1958. The present state of Meroitic studies. Kush 6.74–81.

——. 1960. The Beja language Tu Bedawiye. Its relationship with Old Egyptian. Kush 8.252–64.

Warsama, S., and R. C. Abraham. 1951. The principles of Somali. London (mimeographed).

Webster, E. J. 1960. The particle in Boran. AfrLS 19.33–43.

Welmers, W. E. 1952. Notes on the structure of Saho. Word 8.145–62, 236–51.

Whiteley, W. H. 1953. Studies in Iraqw. Kampala, East African Institute of Social Research (mimeographed).

——. 1958. A short description of item categories in Iraqw. Kampala, East African Institute of Social Research.

——. 1960. The verbal radical in Iraqw. AfrLS 1.79–95.

Winston, F. D. D. 1966. Greenberg's classification of African languages. AfrLS 7.160–9.

Zholkovsky, A. K. 1967. On the lexicographic description of Somali nouns. NAA 93–102.

Zyhlarz, E. 1930. Das meröitische Sprachproblem. Anthropos 25.409–63.

——. 1956. Die Fiktion der 'Kuschitischen' Völker. Kush 4.19–31.

——. 1960. Zum Typus der Kaschitischen Sprache. Anthropos 55.739–52.

THE BERBER LANGUAGES

JOSEPH R. APPLEGATE

The Berber languages are spoken in an area of northwest Africa that begins at the Oasis of Siwa in the western desert of Egypt and extends westward through Libya, Tunisia, Algeria, and Morocco to the Atlantic Ocean. From the Mediterranean coast the area extends southward through the Sahara Desert into Niger and Mali. A small area in Mauritania and northern Senegal is occupied by speakers of a Berber language that is isolated and rather different from that spoken in the larger area of Niger and Mali. The Berber language area is not a continuous one; it is characterized by small enclaves of Berber speakers often living in relatively isolated communities. At one time the Berbers may have occupied an area in which the various languages of the group were spoken in contiguous zones, but today this is not the case. Migration and, more recently, increased urbanization have led to changes in patterns of linguistic distribution as in other parts of Africa, but it is still possible to define distinct areas of Berber speech communities autside of the urban centers.[1]

In Morocco the distribution of Berber languages seems to be more uniform and more continuous than in any of the other regions of North Africa. In the southwestern part of Morocco from the coastal areas that extend as far south as Ifni and north to the area near Agadir the speakers of Shilha occupy a zone that goes as far east as the Draa. This area includes the valley of the Sous. North of this zone the speakers of Tamazight (or Beraber as it is sometimes called) occupy an area that includes the mountainous area of the Atlas and adjacent valleys as far as Taza and the vicinity of Rabat. North and to the west of this area is a small region near Xauen where the Ghomara are found. The largest group of Berbers in the north is the Riff, divided into two distinct dialect areas, the western Senhaja de Srair and that of other tribes like the Urriaghel and Beni Iznassen in the east near Alhucemas.[2] Migrations from this area have led to the establishment of small zones of Riff along the coast of Algeria as far east as Arzeu. Further south in Algeria near the Moroccan border more speakers of Tamazight and Shilha can be found, for the current boundary between Morocco and Algeria does not coincide with older tribal boundaries. The most important of the language areas in northern Algeria is that of the Grand Kabylie, east of Algiers and extending as far as Bougie. It is in this region that the speakers of Kabyle are found.

[1] For a small map of the area see A. Basset 1952.

[2] The chief criteria for the division are phonological.

Slightly south and east of this area is the Aurès, the region in which Chaouia is spoken. In Tunisia, there are communities in the southern part of the country in which the speakers of Berber live. These communities include Tmagourt, Sened, and Jerba. Similarities among the dialects of this area seem to justify their inclusion in one language. In Libya, Zuara on the coast near Tripoli, the area around Jebel Nefusa, Sokna, and Augila are relatively isolated, the first in Tripolitania, the second in Cyrenaica. The easternmost community of Berber speakers is found in the vicinity of Siwa. In the southern part of Algeria there are also isolated communities of Berber speakers. It is difficult to classify these languages in terms of the over-all structure so that Mzabi, Ouargla, Tougourt, and Gourara have been treated as isolated dialects with a clear relationship to each other but with their status as languages or dialects not clearly defined.[3] Further south, the areas in the vicinity of Touat and Tit are usually classified as distinct from both this group and from that of the Tuaregs.

The largest group of Berber speakers in the south consists of the various groups of Tuaregs. The area occupied by this group extends approximately from Ghadames on the Algerian-Libyan border to Ghat (and slightly eastward into Fezzan) into Niger with Zinder as the southeastern limit. From Zinder the boundary of the zone can be drawn westward through Maradi, Bonkoukou, and Tilabery to the area in the vicinity of Goundam and Timbuktu. Within this area, Tamašek is spoken.[4]

In Mauritania and northern Senegal between Mederdra and the Atlantic coast the Zenaga are found. This area is separated from the other Berber communities just as is Siwa in the east. Studies of the language of this area have been fewer than those made in some of the other areas. There is no doubt, however, that the language spoken by the Zenaga is a language related to the other Berber languages in basic structure although specific features of the language may, at first, seem very different from the features that can be readily observed in Tamašek or the languages of the north.

Traces of a local language that is no longer extant in the Canary Islands have led to questions about the status of this language, Guanche, as a member of the Berber group. The data on which the investigations depend are in the form of isolated lexical items, names, and similar data that have been preserved. Some of the data have been taken from reports made by early explorers about the local languages of the Canary Islands; but because the data collected were recorded at that time with a lack of precision, it has not been possible to reconstruct enough of the languages to provide final answers to the question of the linguistic group to which they belonged. It is possible that at one time a Berber language was spoken by some of the inhabitants of these islands. If so, this would mark the westernmost limit of the Berber languages. As

[3] A. Basset 1952 divides these languages into three groups, but the criteria for the division are no clear.

[4] Tamašek is another form of the name Tamazight. *amaziγ*, a masculine singular noun 'Berber', occurs in both languages. (In Tamašek /z/ → /š/, /ž/, or /h/). The feminine form, *tamaziγt*, is used to refer to a Berber woman or to the language, and in Tamašek /γt/ → /ķ/.

additional studies of the languages on the mainland are completed, it may become possible to reach a conclusion about the status of Guanche. Traces of Berber have been found in the dialects of Sicily and Malta, and further linguistic and historical studies of the Mediterranean area are needed.[5]

Although the large area in which Berber languages are now spoken can be defined, zones within the area are not clearly marked except for isolated communities such as Siwa, Sokna, Augila, and that of the Zenaga. Much of the work in linguistic geography was done by André Basset, and his maps of the area are important contributions to this part of Berber linguistics.[6] Early investigators usually treated the Berber languages as dialects of a single language, and this tended to obscure features needed for adequate recognition of dialect groupings. Later comparative studies based on similar assumptions continued to emphasize differences between dialects by focusing attention on the amount of each dialect's deviation from a basic set of structures. The true status of some of these linguistic groups as 'dialects' or as 'languages' still remains undetermined, and a complete linguistic atlas of the area is not yet available. Population trends caused by changes in the social structures of newly independent nations are now leading to new patterns of linguistic distribution; and as these patterns develop, new linguistic problems will arise.[7]

BERBER LINGUISTICS

The first descriptions of Berber languages were prepared by early travellers and explorers in North Africa; and since there is no extensive body of literature in the Berber languages, information about them must be taken from such sources. The works of some Arab geographers and historians have been the source of data recorded during and after the Arab conquest of North Africa.[8] Later this type of work was repeated by the Europeans during their colonization of the area. During the nineteenth century reports on the languages of North Africa began to appear more frequently in Europe. The first reports were usually in the form of word lists and short glossaries of "non-Arabic" languages of the area (Hornemann 1802; Jackson 1809; Minutöli 1824; Shaw 1738). The transcriptions used in glossaries of this kind were not phonetic, of course, and each reporter used the orthography of his own language. In some cases, the Arabic alphabet was used, and data recorded in this way often seemed more reliable to later investigators. By the middle of the nineteenth century, considerable inter-

[5] See G. Barbera 1935. G. S. Colin (1957) has treated the problem of Maltese Arabic.

[6] Several articles on linguistic geography are published in the posthumous collection of his articles (1959).

[7] There is already evidence that the southern boundary of Tamašek extends into northern Nigeria. None of the countries of N. Africa has adopted a Berber language as its official language, and Arabic is the language of instruction in the schools.

[8] See Ibn Battuta 1929; and Ibn Khaldun, *Histoire des Berbères* (tr. by W. M. de Slane), Paris, 1925–34.

est in the Berber languages and their origins had developed, and in 1858 Hanoteau in the introduction to his grammar of Kabyle cited the controversy that had developed concerning the classification of these languages as Indo-European, Semitic, or Hamitic (Hanoteau 1906:xvi). The last category had been proposed to include the non-Semitic languages such as Coptic and Ethiopic. Hanoteau's work had led him to the conclusion that the Berber languages were not related to the European languages, but he abstained from lengthy considerations of their origins.[9] His major objective in studying the languages was not only description and classification; for he pointed out the necessity for materials that could be used by colonial administrators in establishing and maintaining control of the area.

The statement by Hanoteau illustrates the background of two major trends in Berber linguistics. Studies produced by other colonial administrators followed the pattern that has been used by Hanoteau in his work: a brief phonological statement, detailed morphology and word syntax, sample texts with translations, and short comparative statements.[10] There was a great deal of concern for accuracy in describing the languages as they were spoken at that time, and historical statements were included only when it was thought that they contributed to clarity or increased accuracy. Usually such works were descriptions of a single linguistic or cultural area, and attempts to provide generalizations about underlying structures were not made. The objective of those who, like Hanoteau, were concerned with colonial administration was to provide reliable reference grammars, dictionaries, and lesson materials that were useful to others who had to learn the languages. Ethnographers were also interested in the description of the languages as elements of the cultures, and their studies tended to follow the same pattern. Concern for accuracy led to careful analysis of materials and the utilization of information supplied by other scholars who were concerned with linguistic analysis. Not all of the works of this type were produced by French colonials; other Europeans became involved in this type of study.[11] Later, Americans also became interested in the study and description of these languages.

The second trend in Berber linguistics led to historical and comparative studies attempting to show an underlying general structure for the Berber languages. One work of this type was published by Francis Newman (1882), and in it he attempted to reconstruct a proto-language by comparing lexical items from Kabyle, Shilha, Ghadamsi, and Tamašek. A few years later René Basset published a similar work adding a note in which he rejected a theory that had been proposed on the relationship of

[9] He did point out the similarity between Kabyle and Arabic sentences; the use of verbs and pronouns that was similar in Kabyle, Tamašek, and Arabic but not in European languages. See Hanoteau 1906: xvii.

[10] Biarnay 1908; Calassanti-Motylinski 1904; and Destaing 1907–11, are examples of this type of study.

[11] H. Stumme published several works including *Handbuch des Schilhischen von Tazerwalt* (1899). E. Ibañez prepared several dictionaries including *Diccionario rifeño-español* (1949), which contained grammatical notes and extensive bibliography.

Berber and Basque (R. Basset 1895). During the latter part of the nineteenth and the first part of the twentieth century, many studies of this type appeared. Many of them were short articles based on the comparison of a limited number of lexical items or a specific grammatical pattern. Usually the grammatical patterns dealt with in works of this kind were morphological structures; for the descriptions that were most carefully prepared were found to describe structures of this type. Phonology and syntactic analysis developed more slowly.[12]

In 1929 André Basset's monograph on the Berber verb appeared. This work illustrates the methodology that had been developed by scholars concerned with problems of describing a general structure for all of the Berber languages. Within a few years, several other works of the same type appeared including a general theory of Berber morphology by Marcy (1931). More data were available because of the work done by other scholars, and analyses and descriptions improved because of developments in linguistic theory. Marcel Cohen published his study of the Hamito-Semitic languages in 1947 (1947b), and four years later André Basset's monograph on the general features of Berber was written (1952).

Basset's work was a significant one in the development of Berber linguistics, for he summarized the results of work that had been completed up to that time. Furthermore, his attempt to present a brief general description of Berber structure was successful although certain features of the description may be questioned. There are indications of problems that remain, especially in the area of historical linguistics. The work that Basset himself had completed before the preparation of this monograph had enabled him to become familiar with the many developments in Berber linguistics as well as with general linguistic developments.

During the last two decades the growth of structural linguistics has produced some changes in Berber linguistic studies. Greenberg's study of African language classification (1955) was influenced by the developments in structural linguistics, and it has in turn influenced other historical and comparative studies. Mukarovsky (1963), although not concerned primarily with Berber, shows that he too has been influenced by structural linguistics in his historical and comparative studies. Descriptive studies have used the concepts of complementary distribution, phonemes, and morphemes to insure greater clarity. More recently, attempts to develop suitable models for description have resulted in production of works with grammatical rules more carefully formulated than those found in many of the early works. Improved techniques for analysis of data have also led to improved descriptions, especially in the area of phonology, but there are still a number of problems to be solved.

In the following sections a brief survey of some of the major problems in phonology, morphology and syntax with solutions that have been proposed will be presented. A short summary of Berber structure is provided as a conclusion.

[12] *Cf.* Laoust, *Étude sur le dialecte berbère du Chenoua comparé avec ceux des Beni-Menacer et des Beni-Salah*, Paris, 1912; and Schuchardt 1908. R. Basset (1919) presented periodic surveys of research in Berber linguistics at the various International Conferences of Orientalists.

PHONOLOGY

Vowel length has been one of the major problems of Berber phonology, and the complex vowel systems included in some of the descriptions of Berber languages are illustrations of the degree of importance attached to this feature. A set of vowels, ĕ ə̆ ĭ ŏ, all of which are said to be 'short' or 'very short' is usually included in such descriptions.[13] In some cases, the variation of vowel quality is noted. Careful examination of the data shows that the two problems are related. Although the exact rules that describe the occurrences of these vowels vary from language to language, a basic feature of sequences in which they occur is the consonantal feature. If the vowel is in medial position, the preceding and following segments are consonantal; if the vowel occurs in initial position, the following segment will be consonantal usually from the series that includes /l r m n h ʕ/. The quality of the vowel varies with the consonant that precedes it in medial position or which it precedes in initial position. This dependence on the occurrence of a consonant to determine not only the occurrence of one of these vowels but also the quality of the vowel indicates that these sounds should be considered part of the consonantal system, not the vowel system.

Another problem in phonology is that of [u] [w] [i] [y]. All of these occur as phonetic segments of the languages, but not all of them are phonemic as some descriptions indicate.[14] Careful examination of the data shows that [i] and [u] are restricted to environments in which the following segment is non-vocalic. [y] and [w], on the other hand, are restricted to environments in which the following segment is a vocalic segment so that these are clearly in complementary distribution with [i] and [u]. Two phonemes rather than four are adequate to deal with the four phones. Whether the phonemes are transcribed as /y/ and /w/ or /i/ and /u/ is not important. The significant fact is that each of the two phonemes contains both a vocalic and a semi-consonantal feature. Further analysis of the distribution of other vocalic segments shows that [e] and [ɨ] are complementary to [i]; [o] and [ʊ] are complementary to [u]. These additional vowels can then be included in the two phonemes that have been defined. Thus the vocalic system is simplified by reduction of the number of phonemic segments. Furthermore, accurate description of distribution patterns is possible so that classification of non-vocalic phonemes is facilitated. Parallel allophones usually have analogous functions, and the 'low' allophones [e] and [o] occur only with a 'flat' consonant in the adjacent segment. These allophones may then be described as recognition cues for pharyngealized or 'emphatic' consonants.

Unlike /i/ and /u/, the phoneme /a/ does not seem to have a semi-vocalic allophone. In all of its occurrences, this phoneme shows only vocalic qualities. While it varies from [ɛ] to [a] and [æ], it does not have an off-glide like [y] or [w]. It must, therefore, be a special type of vowel phoneme without the semi-vocalic features of /i/ and /u/. In Kabyle, for example, as well as in some other languages of the same area the dis-

[13] 'Les voyelles peuvent être longues, brèves, et ultra-brèves' (Laoust 1931:2).
[14] Cf. A. Basset's statement of this problem, 1952:7–8.

tinction can be stated clearly in terms of rules for syllable formation. /i/ and /u/ are said to consist of a nucleus with margins. Phonetic realization of the margins is determined by the environment in which the phoneme occurs. Before a vowel or in final position, the margin following the nucleus assumes a semi-consonantal characteristic while the nucleus itself is vocalic. Initially before a vowel, the nucleus of the phonemes is semi-consonantal, but the initial margin is vocalic. Between consonants, the nucleus is vocalic, and the margins are absorbed by the consonants. This is a simplified statement, but it provides a basis for certain rules of syllable formation. /a/ does not seem to have the margins of /i/ and /u/, and this accounts for its separation from /i/ and /u/ in the classification of phonemes.

Similar procedures can be used to reduce the number of consonantal phonemes and the complexity of the consonantal system. Confusion of phonemes and allophones in some descriptions is the result of failure to recognize the status of positional variants. Usually two sets of consonants are described where only one is necessary. In the northern languages, for example, where occlusive consonants are articulated in some utterances as stops and in others as fricatives or semi-occlusives some scholars have insisted that there are two distinct sets of phonemes. When a semi-occlusive allophone occurs in two adjacent segments, however, the result is a stop: /tt/ → [t]; /dd/ → [d]. This rule accounts for confusion that may arise when /ii/ → [gi] and /uu/ → [bu]. The semi-occlusive allophone of /g/ is palatalized and is often articulated as [y], which coincides with an allophone of /i/. [yi] can, therefore, be interpreted as occurrences of an identical phoneme in adjacent segments. This leads to articulation of the sequence as a stop, but the vocalic nucleus of the second /i/ remains. The same process may occur when /uu/ → [wu] → [bu].

Another problem of the consonantal system has been the result of failure to recognize or to acknowledge the occurrence of a vocalic component with each consonant. This component should be considered analogous to the marginal features described for /i/ and /u/. In those environments in which the following segment is a vowel, the vocalic component of the consonant is not articulated. In environments where the following phoneme is a consonant, the vocalic component may be articulated as a short vowel thus providing the source of the 'ultra-short' vowels that have usually been included in the set of vowel phonemes. The rules defining this process vary from language to language, but in each case the short vowels are readily identifiable as a part of the consonant (Applegate 1958). Furthermore, their occurrences may provide a basis for further classification of the consonantal segments. In the case of stops and fricatives, the vocalic segments are always found after the consonants of which they are a part. There are other phonemes (the liquids and nasals) in which the vocalic segment may either precede or follow the consonantal segment. The change from preceding to following position may be conditioned by the total environment, but in certain positions there is free variation, e.g. initially before a consonant /l/ occurs either as [əl] or [lə].

Identification of the emphatic consonants has also caused some difficulty in Berber phonology. These consonants have usually been described as a special set of consonantal phonemes, but there may be some question about the validity of such a description. In those languages where such consonants now occur, it seems justifiable to identify them as sequences of consonants with an additional feature of pharyngealization. This additional feature is phonemic, but its domain is usually found to extend over more than one segment of the utterance. In some cases, it is syllabic as in Shilha and Beni Snous; in others, it extends over the consonant and adjacent vowel, as in Kabyle (Applegate 1963). In the case of consonant clusters, both consonants in the cluster will be emphatic if one is emphatic. This feature has been found to affect nearly all of the consonants and not merely those for which special symbols exist in the Arabic alphabet as indicated in some of the early grammars of Berber languages.

Parallel to the problem of the pharyngealized consonants is that of the 'long' consonants. There is, indeed, a contrast between consonants that occur as single phonemic segments and those that occur as the result of juxtaposition of identical consonants. This is most clearly illustrated in languages having stops articulated as semi-occlusives in certain environments and as stops in others. One of the environments in which such phonemes are articulated as stops is that where the same consonant is the adjacent segment. This has led to the concept of 'gemination' or 'lengthening' as an explanation for all such consonants. While it is true that gemination of the type that results from addition of certain affixes or infixes to the utterance, does produce articulations of the type described, not all such occurrences can be accounted for in this way on the basis of data currently available. Furthermore, acoustic analysis of the data shows that there is no significant difference in the length of the consonantal segments occurring in single positions and those occurring in so-called 'geminated' positions. Because of the characteristics of the articulation it is possible to consider these consonants 'fortis' consonants marked by increased aspiration, additional noise, etc. The occurrence of such a consonant may be considered due to a special feature which affects not only the consonant itself but also the adjacent vowel. In some of the languages, the effect is syllabic, and any consonant in the same syllable is affected in the same way. In other languages, the effect of the feature is interrupted by the occurrence of a vocalic segment. One can see, therefore, that this feature is parallel to that of pharyngealization as far as the domains of the two are concerned. Their effects on vocalic segments may be considered opposite: fortis consonants occur with the high allophones of the vowel phonemes [i] [u] [ε]; pharyngealized consonants occur with the low allophones [e] [o] [a]. Introduction of these features leads to reduction of the number of phonemes required for the basic system of the languages.

All of these findings result in clearer descriptions of the phonemic structures of the various Berber languages. The simplification of the set of vowel phonemes as well as the elimination of the superfluous sets of consonants at the phonemic level leads to greater clarity and accuracy of description as well as a firmer basis for formulation of rules describing syllabic structure.

MORPHOLOGY

In Berber linguistic studies, morphology has received more attention than any other area. Traditional grammars were concerned with the construction of paradigmatic patterns, but the failure to recognize phonemic and allophonic differences often resulted in inaccurate paradigms. In other cases, morpheme boundaries were established to coincide with word boundaries so that phonological features of the morphemes were obscured. Lack of proper consideration of syntactic patterns has also resulted in inaccurate descriptions at the morphological level. Recognition of the relationship between the Berber languages and Arabic was another factor in distortion of morphological descriptions; for there was a tendency to employ rules derived from Arabic morphology to the Berber languages, especially in the verb systems. While there is an underlying similarity in the verb structures of Berber and Arabic, the two are not identical; and attempts to describe patterns of the former in terms of the latter have led to false conclusions.

The concern of many scholars in dealing with the morphology of Berber verbs is the definition of patterns that are like those of the Arabic verb, i.e. a consonantal root with vocalic patterns infixed to indicate the grammatical function of the completed form. Thus the consonantal root was considered the semantic base of the verb while the vocalic patterns were considered the morphological factors. Basset, in his monographs on verb morphology, states: 'La voyelle est un élément morphologique et uniquement morphologique' (1929: xxii). This serves as a basis for his classification of verb stems in terms of the vocalic patterns used with each. Dallet made a similar attempt in his study of verb morphology in Kabyle. Although there is some validity in the classification of verbs in this way, the weaknesses of the system are seen in Dallet's study; for stems with no semantic connection appear as identical forms differentiated only by the vocalic patterns used with each (Dallet 1953). This may be useful in computer analysis of verb forms, but it is clear that identification of a vocalic pattern at some point is essential for identification of the verb stem itself.

Another problem that arises in studies of Berber verb morphology is caused by attempts to define a system of tenses similar to those found in Indo-European languages. While it is true that there is some temporal element in many of the sentences in which verbs are used, the basic features of the system are aspectual rather than temporal. Analyses of co-occurring structures in the sentence may be used to determine the proper position of some morphological patterns that operate within the boundaries of the verb sequence. It is at this point that the importance of syntactic considerations for the proper definition of morphological entities becomes apparent. Although the two have been separated in some descriptions, there is obviously a need for information obtained from syntactic patterns in the description of morphological patterns.

One example of the confusion that may result from failure to consider the factors cited above is the description of the iterative stem in the Berber verb system. A great deal of attention has been given to this stem in studies of Berber languages, and detailed analyses of the forms have yielded lengthy descriptions of the patterns. Usually these patterns are assigned the same status as those which lead to the formation of negative stems or differentiation of imperfect and perfect stems. The iterative often occurs in contexts for which the imperfect is indicated, but further analysis shows that the chief function of the iterative is its effect on the complement structure of the sentence, especially those constituents that may be considered adverbial in function. Since the class of morphemes that includes the causative, reciprocal, and passive markers also has a similar function, i.e. modification of complement structure, the iterative should be included in this class rather than in the class of morphemes that signal a speaker's opinion of an action as completed or not completed.

Conclusions drawn from the various studies of Berber morphology lead to the description of three basic morpheme classes: stems, affixes, and particles. Stems are bound forms that may occur with another morpheme having the phonemic shape /Ø/. Affixes are also bound forms, but within word boundaries they must occur with at least one other morpheme the phonemic shape of which is not /Ø/. The morpheme to which an affix is attached may also be a bound form, and in some cases the word consists of a sequence of two bound forms. In Kabyle, for example, /γur-s/ 'to him', is a sequence of the prepositional prefix /γur-/ and a pronominal affix. Particles are free forms unattached to any other morpheme within the phonological word.

Further divisions are possible within each class of morphemes when rules for cooccurrence are considered. If the affixes are divided into three classes on the basis of distribution, some stems are found to occur only with affixes of Class I and Class III; others occur only with affixes of Class II and Class III. Further classifications of this type are possible, and stems can be divided into two sub-classes, nouns and verbs, for each of which there is a corresponding sub-class of affixes. A third sub-class of affixes is not restricted to a single group of stems but occurs with members of both.

Noun stems can be further sub-divided on the basis of certain features found in some but not in others. The phonemic shape of a member of this group may be determined by its position within the phrase or in the sentence. In phrase initial position, some stems have a form that may be described as independent, i.e. corresponding to the citation form of the morpheme. In non-initial position, the phonemic shape is reduced or changed, the exact nature of the reduction or degree of change depending on the rules of the specific language. In Shilha, /a/ which occurs at the beginning of many masculine nouns is changed to /u/ when the noun occurs in non-initial position in a phrase. In feminine nouns, this vowel which occurs after the initial feminine marker /t/ is reduced to (Ø) when the noun occurs in non-initial position. In Tamazight both the feminine marker and the vowel may be lost when this type of noun occurs in non-initial position:

n + *amaziγ* → *numaziγ* 'Amazigh's'
n + *tamaziγt* → *nmaziγt* 'Tamazight's'.

With the sub-class of personal pronoun stems, the reduction is more complete, and members of this group lose the feature that permits optional occurrence with a morpheme having the phonemic shape /Ø/. Thus personal pronouns in non-initial position in a sentence lose their status as free forms and must occur as affixes. Noun stems usually described as numerals are distinguished from other nouns by absence of a feature that permits optional occurrence with a plural marker.

Affixes, in addition to features determining their occurrences with members of the stem class, have features that determine with which members of the affix class they may occur. Furthermore, their features determine position within a sequence as well as selection of rules that govern their phonemic shape. Perhaps most important is the set of features that determine the morpho-syntactic class of the sequence of which the affix is a part. Certain affixes have the effect of shifting the stem from one morphological class to another, thus excluding the addition of other affixes of the same class. The morpheme *a* added to a verb stem, for example, functions as a nominalizer and precludes the addition of any other affixes of the type that occur with verb stems. Other affixes do not have this effect, but they may indicate a shift of the stem to another syntactic class. *s*, for example, when added to a verb stem shifts the stem to a class that requires an additional direct object. Intransitive verbs become transitive, and transitive verbs require two direct objects when this affix is added to them. Morphologically, however, the stem remains a member of the class to which other affixes of the same sub-class may be added. A reciprocal or passive marker may be added after *s* has been made a part of the verb stem. A third type of verb affix -*γ*, the first person singular subject marker, may occur in sequences with other verb affixes, but not with other subject-markers.

Special morphophonemic rules must be included in the description of affixes. The transitive marker cited above usually occurs as the voiceless fricative /s/; but if the stem to which it is added includes /z/, the marker is voiced:

rs > *srs* 'put down'
nz > *znz* 'sell, put on sale'

In the grammar for a language such as Shilha or Kabyle it is necessary to state the rules for morphophonemic changes in such a way that /s/ occurring as an indirect object affix will not be affected by the same features that affect /s/, the causative marker. A similar problem can be found when /t/, the iterative marker, /t/, the direct object affix, and /t/, the third person feminine subject marker are considered. At the phonemic level, these affixes seem identical; but morphologically they are distinct, so something must be added to their transcriptions to preserve the distinction until the rules for morphophonemic changes have been applied. In an article on Zuara (1953:378), T.F. Mitchell stated that 'phonological features have significance at other levels...'. It is possible to approach the problem in another way stating that syntactic or morphological features have significance at the phonological level (Applegate 1959). Both approaches have been used in the description of Berber languages, and both have proved useful. It is significant, however, that attempts at descriptions in which the three levels are kept rigidly separated have not been successful.

SYNTAX

Early studies of Berber languages were concerned chiefly with morphology as indicated above, and syntactic statements were usually given as part of the morphological descriptions. In other studies, syntactic statements were made as rules for translation of sentences or phrases from a European language into the Berber language being described. Only in the last decade or two have there been attempts to separate syntax from morphology and translation in grammatical descriptions of the Berber languages.

One work in which there is an attempt to treat syntax separately is that of A. Basset and Picard (1948). Later, Picard produced another description of a dialect of Kabyle in which he applied the theories developed by Bally and others (Picard 1960). The result is a description of Berber sentence structure in terms of minimal units which are modified or expanded in various ways, each modification or expansion requiring a special signal. This was perhaps the most comprehensive work of its kind that had been produced up to that time (1960). Although it was intended as a guide to expressive language in Kabyle, many of the statements made were based on categories borrowed from Indo-European, and some of the conclusions may be questioned.

In a brief grammar of Shilha published in 1958, an attempt was made to treat syntax as a separate level of grammatical description but with consideration for the influence of morphological structures (Applegate 1958). Only basic syntactic formulas were included, however. In a doctoral dissertation prepared in Paris under the direction of André Martinet, Thomas Penchoen presented a syntactic analysis of Chaouia using Martinet's concepts of 'functional syntax'. In that study, the sentence structure of the language was described in terms of syntactic units or syntagmemes required for a minimal sentence and the subsequent variations and combinations of the basic units in expanded constructions (Penchoen 1966).

The transformational model was used by Jeanette Johnson in the description of Tamazight prepared as a doctoral dissertation (Johnson 1966). The result is a statement of the rules needed for the production of verbal sentences in one of the dialects of that language. In addition to the value of the work as an example of how the transformational model functions with non-Indo-European languages, the data are important because they are taken from women's speech, an area that has been neglected.

Both the early works with incomplete syntactic statements and later works that may be considered more complete have produced useful information about the sentence structure of the Berber languages. In addition to those sentence types which may be considered invariable (formulas, greetings, etc.), the Berber sentence may be described as a sequence of two constituents: an initial phrase (or topic) and a complement. The initial phrase may have as a nucleus a verb stem with a tense-aspect marker and a subject-marker as affixes, or it may be a noun stem. The complement may consist of a single noun, a sequence of nouns, or a noun phrase. The exact structure of the complement is determined by the initial phrase. In some sentences in which the initial phrase is a verb phrase, the complement may be reduced to zero. This is not true when the initial phrase is a noun phrase. Expansions of the phrases are possible, but a fixed order of elements is essential in the basic sentence. When the normal order of the sentence is disturbed for purposes of emphasis or focus, special rules become operative to compensate for this interruption. Usually the compensation is in the form of the introduction of a special element to occupy the position vacated by the constituent to be emphasized; for the position of emphasis is at the beginning of the sentence:

i-uγa urgaz aγiul. The man bought the donkey.
aγiul i-uγa+*t* urgaz. The man bought *the donkey*.
aγiul ai-i-uγa urgaz. It was the donkey the man bought.

Recent works have been concerned with the statement of these rules in precise terms for specific languages. Although there are relatively few syntactic studies of this type, those that have been produced have done much to clarify the structure of the Berber sentence.

SUMMARY

From the various works on Berber languages it is possible to construct a genera picture of the basic structure. Although there are variations in phonology and lexical items, the features of syntax and morphology are relatively constant. The patterns of morphology and syntax, therefore, provide a general framework for comparison of Berber with other branches of the Afro-Asiatic family while the phonological patterns and distribution of lexical items are useful in defining the boundaries of languages and dialects within the group.

At the syntactic level, two types of sentences (in addition to the formulas used in greetings and expressions of courtesy) may be defined: nominal sentences and verbal sentences. In the first type, the initial constituent is a phrase with noun stem as head; the complement is a second noun phrase, with or without a verb accompanying it. When a verb is used in the second constituent of such sentences, it is characterized by a special marker, varying from language to language, which indicates a relative or participial function:

ism-ns muha. 'His name is Muha.' (Tamazight)
muha *ai*-i-ga. 'Muha (is) who he is.' (Tamazight)
tulauin *ad*-d-*i*-t:aui-*n* aman. '(It's) the women who bring the water' (Kabyle)

In the second sentence, it is the marker *ai-* that indicates the special function of the verb. In the third sentence, the combination of a similar prefix with the special subject marker *i-...-n* performs a similar function. In both of these sentences, the initial noun phrase may be described as a constituent of an underlying verbal sentence:

nt:a i-ga muha. 'He (is) Muha.'
t:aui-nt-id tulauin aman. 'The women bring the water.'

The shift of emphasis or focus causes a shift of the constituent to initial position with subsequent introduction of the special markers to signal this shift. Such a description provides a single base for both nominal and verbal sentences, but the particle *d* which occurs in some of the languages does not fit into such a scheme. In Kabyle, for example, this particle is used to signal the beginning of the complement phrase when that phrase is a single noun:

nt:a *d* aḳbaili. 'He (is) a Kabyle.'
argaz-ag:i *d* amdakl-iu. 'This man (is) my friend.'

In such sentences there is no apparent shift of emphasis to account for the introduction of the particle. Restrictions on the occurrence of the sentence make the concept of a deleted verb replaced by *d* a doubtful explanation for the pattern. Although not all of the languages use this particle in the nominal sentence, there is some trace of it in compound particles that function as conjunctions: *zun-d* (Tamazight) *hun-d* (Tamašek) 'as'; *nγ-d* (Shilha) 'or'; *is-d* (Shilha). The last example is used as the marker of a yes-no question before any constituent that is not a verb:

is-t-gi-t ašlḥi? 'Are you a Shleuh?'
izd kii ašlḥi? 'Are you a Shleuh?'

In such questions, the particle *izd* < is-d may be considered almost equivalent to the phrase 'is it true that' with the sentence that follows used as a noun. This pattern is paralleled in certain dialects by similar structures in negative sentences:

ur-d kii ašlḥi. 'You're not a Shleuh.'

There is another type of nominal sentence which seems to occur in all of the languages. In this second type, there may be a stronger basis for postulating deletion of a verb:

gigi laẓ. 'I'm hungry.' (Shilha)
γur-i lbhaim. 'I have some cattle.' (Kabyle)
ar:au g:-uxam. 'The children are in the house.' (Kabyle)

The verb *ili* (locative) 'be' may be supplied for all of these sentences with the assumption that the noun stem preceded by a prepositional prefix functions as a complement in the verbal sentence. In the first two sentences the complement has been moved to initial position for emphasis, and deletion of the verb may be described as an accompanying feature of such structures. In the third sentence, however, this is not the case, and the noun stem may still be moved to initial position:

axam uar:au g:i-s. 'The house is where the children are.'

The change of form in the other noun indicates some confusion about the status of the constituents; for *uar:au* is the form used in non-initial position in a phrase. Thus, the structure is parallel to that of a verbal sentence with the verb in initial position. In some of the languages additional evidence can be found to indicate that the prepositional phrase in such nominal sentences is treated as a verb substitute, and occurrence of such phrases with negative, interrogative, and tense-aspect markers usually found with verb stems has been noted in Shilha and some dialects of Kabyle. In other languages (or other dialects of Kabyle) there is rigid separation of this structure from the verbal structures. The fact that this pattern occurs in all of the languages although developed in different ways indicates that it is a basic part of Berber structure whatever its source.

The verbal sentence is equally important. In sentences of this type, the initial phrase includes a verb stem with appropriate markers to indicate subject and tense-aspect. The phrase may also include a noun stem which can be described as an extension of the subject marker. It is clearly not the dominant element of the phrase, for its form is the dependent or subordinate form when it occurs in non-initial position:

ad-i-d:u urgaz γr-suḳ. 'The man will go to market.' (Kabyle)
argaz ad-i-d:u γr-suḳ. 'The man will go to market.'

Furthermore, although the noun stem may be an optional constituent of the phrase, neither the subject nor the tense-aspect marker may be deleted from a phrase of this type:

nk:i fki-γ lflus i-urgaz. 'I gave the money to the man.' (Tamazight)
fki-γ lflus i-urgaz. 'I gave the money to the man.'

The second phrase in verbal sentences is a noun phrase that functions as a complement. It may occur with or without a prepositional prefix depending on the verb in the initial phrase. Its separation from the verb phrase is justified on the basis of form because the noun occurring as a direct object immediately after the verb retains its independent form:

i-ufa aḳžun g:-ubrid. 'He found the dog on the road.'
t-uui aman sg:-lbir. 'She brought the water from the well.' (Kabyle)

In both of these sentences the initial vowel of the complement remains unchanged, but this is not the case when they function as extensions of subject markers in a verb phrase:

i-la uḳžun g:-ubrid. 'The dog is on the road.'
la-n uaman g:-lbir. 'The water is in the well.'

Complements other than direct objects are preceded by prepositional markers, and are, therefore, always in non-initial position within the phrase:

fki-γ lflus i-urgaz. 'I gave the man the money.'
i-saual s-tšlḥit. 'He spoke Shilha.'

The complement may be moved to the initial position of the sentence in an emphatic structure, but the positions left vacant by such a move are filled by substitutes, usually pronouns:

argaz fki-γ-*as* lflus. 'I gave *the man* the money.'
aḳžun i-ufa-*t* g:-ubrid. 'He found *the dog* on the road.'
tašlḥit i-saual sii-*s*. 'He spoke *Shilha.*'
abrid i-ufa aḳžun g:i-*s*. 'He found the dog on *the road.*'

Although the sequences of preposition and noun may function as adverbial particles, the structure of sentences (2) and (4) above indicate the contrast between that function and that of the complement. The adverbial particle may be moved to the initial position of the sentence without the introduction of a replacement after the verb phrase:

g:-ubrid i-ufa aḳžun. 'He found the dog on the road.'

Both the initial phrase and the complement phrase of a sentence may be expanded by the addition of particles or modifiying phrases. The rules for such expansions vary from language to language, but the basic syntactic framework remains the same.

Stems and affixes form the bulk of forms in the morphology of the Berber languages. A third group of forms, particles, do not occur as frequently as members of the first two groups. The stems may be divided into two groups on the basis of syntactic functions: nouns and verbs. Noun stems are marked for gender and number, but not for person. Usually the distinction between masculine and feminine is indicated by the occurrence of *t*, which may be considered the feminine marker, and *n* is used to indicate plural forms. Special groups of forms, however, employ special forms of these markers thereby providing criteria for establishing sub-classes of morphemes. Kinship terms, for example, may occur with *ait*, *i*, or *id* apparently marking the plural:

g:ma	'my brother'	*ait*ma	'my brothers'
babat-nsn	'their father'	*id*babat-nsn	'their fathers'
ultma	'my sister'	*i*stma	'my sisters'

In some of the languages, the form *babat* is treated as a plural form without an additional prefix. The contrast between *ib:a* 'my father' and *im:a* 'my mother' in Tamazight illustrates the fact that gender may be determined without the special marker /t/. Other classes of noun stems may require not only the addition of /n/ as a suffix to indicate the plural form but also addition of a vowel or modification of a consonant of the stem:

asif > *isaf:n* 'rivers'
amksa > *imksaun* 'shepherds'.

The addition of a feminine marker may indicate the shift from generic to individual reference: *afirs* 'pear/pears' *tafirst* 'a pear', or it may be the marker of a diminutive form: *azru* 'rock' *tazrut* 'stone, pebble'.

The pronouns are a special class of noun stems which may not occur in non-initial position as free forms. In addition, there are special forms of the feminine and plural affixes that occur with these stems:

kii	'you' (m.s)	*kim*	'you' (f.s.)
kunui	'you' (m.p.)	*kunmti*	'you' (f.p.)

When the pronominal stems occur in non-initial position as complements, they have special forms which may reveal an underlying phonemic structure:

Direct Object	Indirect Object	Prepositional	
ii	ii	-i	1st s.
k	ak	-k	2nd s.m.
(k)m	am	-m	f.
t	as	-s	3rd s.m.
t:	as	-s	f.
aγ	aγ	-nγ	1st p.
un	aun	-un	2nd p.m.
unt	aunt	-unt	f.
tn	sn	-sn	3rd p.m.
tnt	snt	-snt	f.

The direct and indirect object forms may occur either as prefixes or suffixes. The prepositional forms are always suffixed forms. After the possessive or relational marker, these stems have forms that match the prepositional forms with the exception of the first person singular. In some languages this form is *-inu*; in others, it is *-iu*. In all of the languages it is Ø when it occurs after one of the basic kinship terms.

With numerals, the plural marker is Ø although it may be considered an essential component of the numeral. The numerals vary from language to language; for Arabic lexical items are used. All of the languages retain the Berber form for 'one' *iun*; *ij*; *idž;* and many have preserved the Berber form for 'two' *sin*. Only Tamašek has preserved the Berber numerals to 'one thousand' with the patterns necessary for counting to 999,999. There are special feminine forms for the numerals, but the marker /t/ occurs in them: *iut*; *išt*; *iat*; *snat*.

The verb stems form a significant morphological class not only in terms of number but also because they are the one class of morphemes that may serve as the source of another class: noun stems may be formed from verb stems, but verbs cannot be formed from nouns. There are three forms of each verb stem depending on the tense-aspect marker with which the stem occurs: imperfect, perfect, and negative. The negative stem is usually characterized by the occurrence of the vowel /i/. In many of the perfect stems there is alternation between the vowel /i/ in the first and second person singular forms and /a/ in the third person singular and the plural forms:

ufi-γ	'I found'	bni-γ	'I built'
t-ufi-t	'you found'	t-bni-t	'you built'
i-ufa	'he found'	i-bna	'he built'
ufa-n	'they found'	n-bna	'we built'

The vowel of the perfect stem may be associated with a vowel of the imperfect stem as in the case of *bni/bna* < *bnu*, or the imperfect stem may have Ø as in *ufi/ufa* < *af.* In either case, the negative stem usually contains the vowel /i/. The occurrence of these special stems may be ascribed to the occurrence of tense-aspect markers: *ad-i-af* 'that he find' or 'he will find'; *ur-i-ufi* 'he did not find', but it is not possible to find a marker that occurs with the perfect stem. The only solution seems to be to postulate a marker with the phonemic shape /Ø/ that has some effect on the vocalic pattern of the stem.

In addition to the tense-aspect marker, a subject marker must occur with the verb stem. If the stem is perfect, two groups of verbs can be defined in terms of the subject markers with which they occur. One class has been defined as 'stative'. These are stems that occur with subject markers that are always suffixes, and it is possible that these subject markers are the residue of an older system of suffixes which together with the special stem used in the perfect served to distinguish all perfect forms from negative and imperfect. The system is characterized by the occurrence of Ø as the mark of the third person, singular, masculine form. *-t* or *-it* is found as the mark of the plural third person form, and in some languages this affix is found in all forms regardless of person. In other languages, it is used as the mark of the third person, singular, feminine form. The following forms are found in Kabyle, for example:

mlul	'he is (has become) white'
mlul-t	'she is white'
mlul-it	'we, you, they are white'

With other verbs, a set of subject markers that is now considered basic occurs:

1st	s.	-γ	1st	p.	n-
2nd	s.m.	t- -t	2nd	p.m.	t- -m
	f.	t- -t		f.	t- -mt
3rd	s.m.	i-	3rd	p.m.	-n
	f.	t-		f.	-nt

Gender is distinguished only in the third person forms and in the second person plural form.

Another form occurs with a special marker that may be considered participial or relative. The marker is not distinguished for person or number in many of the languages, and in some it is not marked for gender. It may consist of a prefix and a suffix, *i-...-n*, but in those languages that distinguish gender and number in this form these are characteristic of the masculine singular form. The feminine is *t-...-t*, and the plural is ...*-n-in*. In languages such as Tamašek, when the form occurs with certain affixes such as the negative, the special subject marker is separated into two parts, one of which remains in the position characteristic of subject markers while the second is moved to a position directly after the affix that is characteristic of pronouns used as object affixes. This has led to the theory that the form was originally a compound form with a special pronominal component.

In the class of affixes, two types may be considered basic: derivative and inflectional. The first type may be added to a stem to produce another stem that functions in much the same way that the stem without affixes functions. The feminine marker for nouns, the causative, passive, and reciprocal markers for verbs are examples of this type of affix. Subject markers, tense-aspect markers, the pluralizer may all be considered examples of the second type. It is significant that affixes of either type may be associated with changes in the vocalic patterns of the stems to which they are attached.

In terms of co-occurrence, three classes of affixes may be defined: nominal, verbal, common. These affixes are characterized by the various types of stems with which they occur. Nominalizers, subject markers, and tense-aspect markers occur with verb stems; feminine markers, prepositional prefixes, and certain demonstrative suffixes occur only with noun stems. The third type, such as directional markers, may occur with either nouns or verbs.

The phonemic shape of an affix may be determined by the type of stem with which it occurs. The causative marker *s* becomes /z/ before a stem in which /z/ occurs. The prepositional prefixes have long forms when they occur before pronoun stems:

g:-uxam	'in the house' (Kabyle)
g:i-s	'in him (it)'
γr-urgaz	'at the man('s house)' (Tamazight)
γir-s	'at his house'

Usually the long form is characterized by the addition of a vowel, but in some cases there is complete reduplication:

didi 'with me' (Shilha)
g:ig:i 'in me' (Kabyle)

The phonology of the Berber languages is based on the following set of phonemes:

	t	(c)	k		i	u
b	d	(j)	g			
f	s	š	(x)		a	
	z	ž	γ			
m	n					
	r	l		(h)	(ʕ)	

Those that are not widely distributed are enclosed in parentheses. In addition, there are two special phonemes, /Ç/ (pharyngealization) and /:/ (increased tension) that may be considered supra-segmental. All of the segmental phonemes (except /a/) contain two components, a vocalic which is dominant in /i/ and /u/ and a consonantal which is dominant in all of the others. The non-dominant component may be realized as a glide [w] or [y] for /u/ and /i/ or as a short central vowel [ə] for the phonemes classified as consonants. With liquids and nasals, the vowel may occur either before or after the consonantal segment; with other consonants it occurs only after the consonantal segment. Phonetic realization of the non-dominant component depends on environment, but a few general rules can be stated. The short central vowel occurs (1) between a voiced and a voiceless consonant; (2) between a fortis and a lenis consonant; (3) between a pharyngealized and a non-pharyngealized consonant. The glide occurs before a vowel.

Only the Tuaregs have preserved an old Berber alphabet. The alphabet is similar to the Arabic, but it has only one vowel symbol which is usually found in the final syllable of words. It is boustrophic, either horizontally or vertically. Other Berber groups now use the Arabic alphabet or roman characters with the orthography of a contemporary European languge.

There are still questions to be answered about the structure of the Berber languages. Questions of boundaries, origins, and development of certain forms require additional data. With increased urbanization new problems are developing. However, it does not seem, on the basis of data now available, that the Berber languages are disappearing.

SELECTED BIBLIOGRAPHY

ABERCROMBY, JOHN A. 1917. The language of the Canary Islanders. Harvard African Studies 1.95–129.

ALVAREZ DELGADO, JUAN. 1941. Puesto de Canarias en la investigación lingüística. Monografías, Instituto de Estudios Canarios, Universidad de la Laguna, vol. 3, sec. 2, no. 1.

APPLEGATE, JOSEPH R. 1958. Outline of the structure of Shilha. American Council of Learned Societies.
——. 1959. Some phonological rules in Shilha. Report of the Tenth Annual Round Table Meeting on Linguistics and Language Studies. Georgetown University Monograph Series 12.37–42.
——. 1963. The structure of Kabyle. U.S. Office of Education.
BARBERA, GIUSEPPE. 1935. Arabo e berbero nel linguaggio italo-siculo. Beirut.
BASSET, ANDRÉ. 1929. La langue berbère. Morphologie. Le verbe. Étude de thèmes. Paris, Leroux.
——. 1935–45. Siwa et Aoudjila, problème verbal berbère. Mélanges Gaudefroy-Demombynes, 279–300. Cairo, Imprimerie de l'Institut français d'archéologie orientale.
——. 1936–39. Atlas linguistiques des parlers berbères. Algérie. Territoires du nord. Fasc. 1, Equides, Algiers, 1936. Fasc. 2, Bovins, Algiers, 1939.
——. 1938. Le nom de l'étable en Kabylie et la flexion du participe. BSL 39.177–8.
——. 1952. La langue berbère. London, Oxford University Press.
——. 1959. Articles de dialectologie berbère. Paris, Klincksieck.
——, and ANDRÉ PICARD. 1948. Éléments de grammaire berbère. Algiers, La.Typo-Litho.
BASSET, RENÉ. 1894. Études sur les dialectes berbères. Paris, Leroux. (Bull. corr. afr. 14).
——. 1895. Les noms de métaux et des couleurs en berbère. Mémoires de la Société de Linguistique de Paris 9.58–92.
——. 1902. Rapport sur les études berbères et haoussa 1897–1902. Ja (sér. 9) 20.307–25.
——. 1919. Rapport sur les études relatives à la linguistique berbère 1913–1918. Rev. afr. 60.161–9.
—— (ed.). 1918–20. Dictionnaire abrégé touareg-français, by CHARLES DE FOUCAULD. Algiers, Carbonel.
——. (ed.). 1920. Notes pour servir à un essai de grammaire touarègue, by CHARLES DE FOUCAULD. Algiers, Carbonel.
—— (ed.). 1922. Textes touareg en prose, by CHARLES DE FOUCAULD and A. DE CALASSANTI-MOTYLINSKI. Algiers, Carbonel.
BIARNAY, S. 1908. Étude sur le dialecte berbère de Ouargla. Paris, Leroux. (Bull. corr. afr. 37).
CALASSANTI-MOTYLINSKI, GUSTAVE A. DE. 1904. Le dialecte berbère de R'edames. Paris, Leroux. (Bull. corr. afr. 28).
CENIVAL, PIERRE DE, CHRISTIAN FUNCK-BRENTANO, and MARCEL BOUSSER. 1937. Bibliographie marocaine 1923–1933. Paris, Larose.
COHEN, MARCEL. 1947a. A propos du classement de la forme d'habitude dans la grammaire berbère. GLECS 4.37–40.

——. 1947b. Essai comparatif sur le vocabulaire et la phonétique du chamito-sémitique. Paris.

COLIN, GEORGES. 1957. Mots berbères dans le dialecte arabe de Malte. Mémorial André Basset, 7–16. Paris, A. Maisonneuve.

DALLET, JEAN M. 1953. Le verbe kabyle. Fichier de documentation berbère. Fort-National.

DESTAING, EDMOND. 1907–11. Étude sur le dialecte berbère des Beni-Snous. Paris, Lerouz. (Bull. corr. afr. 34 and 35).

——. 1928–31. Notes sur l'expression verbale de la durée du temps en berbère et en arabe marocain. BSL 29.45–73; 31.1–33.

——. 1930. L'expression verbale de l'état et de la durée dans les parlers berbères marocains. BSL 30.9–10.

FÉVRIER, J. G. 1956. Que savons-nous du libyque? Rev. afr. 100.263–73.

GALAND, LIONEL. 1953. La phonétique en dialectologie berbère, Orbis 2.225–33.

——. 1955. État et procès. Hespéris 42.245–51.

——. 1957. Un cas particulier de phrase non verbale 'L'anticipation renforcée' et l'interrogation en berbère. Mémorial André Basset, 27–37. Paris, A. Maisonneuve.

——. 1964. L'énoncé verbal en berbère. Étude de fonctions. CFS 21.33–53.

GLASS, GEORGE. 1764. History of the discovery and conquest of the Canary Islands. London.

GREENBERG, JOSEPH. 1955. Studies in African linguistic classification. New Haven, Compass.

HANOTEAU, ADOLPHE. 1896. Essai de grammaire de la langue tamachek'. Algiers, Jourdan, 2nd ed.

——. 1906. Essai de grammaire kabyle. Algiers, Jourdan, 2nd ed.

HORNEMANN, FRIEDRICH. 1802. Tagebuch seiner Reise von Cairo nach Murzuk in den Jahren 1797–98. Weimar.

HOSOTTE-REYNAUD, M. 1956. Publications de l'Institut des Hautes Études marocaines. Limoges.

IBÁÑEZ, ESTEBAN. 1949. Diccionario rifeño-español. Madrid, Instituto de estudios africanos.

IBN BATTUTA. 1929. Travels in Asia and Africa 1325–1354. (tr. by H. A. R. Gibb). London, Routledge.

IBN KHALDUN, 'ABD-AR-RAḤMAN IBN-MUḤAMMAD. 1956. Tarix Ibn-Khaldun Kitab al-'ibar wa-diwan al-mubtada' wal-xabar fi ajjam al-'Arab wal-'Aġam wal-Barbar. Beirut, Dar al-kitab al-lubnani.

JACKSON, JAMES G. 1809. An account of the Empire of Morocco and the District of Suse. London.

JOHNSON, M. JEANETTE. 1966. Syntactic structures of Tamazight. Los Angeles, University of California (doctoral dissertation).

LAOUST, ÉMILE. 1924. Rapport sur les études de dialectologie berbère de 1920 à 1924. Hespéris 5.445–9.

——. 1931. Siwa: son parler. Paris, Leroux. (Publications de l'Institut des Hautes Études marocaines, XXII).

MARCY, GEORGES. 1931. Essai d'une theorie générale de la morphologie berbère. Hespéris 12.50–89, 177–203.

——. 1939. Fonctions originales dans les parlers berbères des pronombres démonstratifs-relatifs. BSL 40.151–73.

MINUTÖLI, HEINRICH C. 1824. Reise zum Tempel des Jupiter Ammon in der libyschen Wüste ... in 1820–21. Berlin.

MITCHELL, T. F. 1953. Particle-noun complexes in a Berber dialect (Zuara). BSOAS 15/2.375–90.

——. 1957a. Long consonants in phonology and phonetics. Studies in linguistic analysis, 182–205. Oxford.

——. 1957b. Some properties of Zuara nouns. Mémorial André Basset, 83–96. Paris, Maisonneuve.

MUKAROVSKY, HANS G. 1963. Die Grundlagen des Ful und das Mauretanische. Vienna, Herder.

NEWMAN, FRANCIS. 1882. Lybian vocabulary. London.

NICOLAS, FRANCIS. 1953. La langue berbère de Mauritanie. Dakar, Institut français d'Afrique noire.

PENCHOEN, THOMAS. 1966. Étude syntaxique du parler berbère des Ait-Frah (Aurès). École Pratique des Hautes Études, Université de Paris.

PICARD, ANDRÉ. 1960. De quelques faits de stylistique dans le parler berbère des Irjen. Algiers, Carbonel. (Publications de l'Institut d'Études orientales d'Alger, no. 19.)

PRASSE, KARL-G. 1957. Les relations de sexe, d'age et de sang. AcOr 22.118–41.

——. 1960. Notes sur la langue touaregue. AcOr 25.45–109.

SARNELLI, TOMMASSO. 1957. Sull'origine del nome Imaziġen. Mémorial André Basset, 131–8. Paris, Maisonneuve.

SCHUCHARDT, HUGO E. M. 1908. Berberische Studien. WZKM 22.245–64, 351–84.

SHAW, THOMAS. 1738. Travels and observations relating to several parts of Barbary and the Levant. Oxford.

STUMME, HANS. 1899. Handbuch des Schilhischen von Tazerwalt. Leipzig, Hinrichs.

WALKER, W. SEYMOUR. 1921. The Siwi language. London.

WILLMS, ALFRED. 1962. Zur Phonologie der langen Konsonanten im Kabylischen. ZPhon 15.103–9.

——. 1966. Auswahlbibliographie des berberologischen Schrifttums. Afrika und Übersee 50.64–128.

WÖLFEL, DOMINIK J. 1957. Dilettantismus und Scharlatanarie und die Erforschung der Eingeborenensprache der Kanarische Inseln. Mémorial André Basset, 147–58. Paris, Maisonneuve.

ZYHLARZ, ERNST. 1950. Das kanarische Berberisch in seinem sprachgeschichtlichen Milieu. ZDMG 100.403–60.

GENERAL ANNOTATED BIBLIOGRAPHY

Berbers: History

1. BASSET, HENRI. Les influences Puniques chez les Berbères. Rev. afr. 62.340–74, 1921. (This article contains important historical data.)
2. BASSET, RENÉ. Nédromah et les Traras. 1901. (This report of an archaeological expedition is chiefly historical in nature, but it contains a glossary of words used by the Berbers in northwestern Algeria, in Roman and Arabic transcription, with French equivalents. The work is no. 24 of the Bull. corr. afr.)
3. BEGUINOT, FRANCESCO. I berberi e le recenti scoperte nel Fezzan. Afr. Ital. 197–208, 1932–33.
4. BERTHELOT, SABIN. Antiquitiés Canariennes. Paris, 1897.
5. BERTHELOT, SABIN and WEBB. Histoire Naturelle des Iles Canaries. Paris, 1842. (This work and the preceding one have served as sources of data for establishing the relationship between the Berber languages and those of the Canary Islands. The two works served as sources of information for René Basset, and the more recent controversies about the history of the Berber languages usually contain references to these two works.)
6. BOUSQUET, GEORGES H. Les Berbères. Paris, 1957. (A general study of the history and social organization of the Berbers with bibliography.)
7. CASTRIES, HENRI. Les Sources inédites de l'histoire du Maroc de 1530 à 1845. Paris, 1905. (An important bibliographical item.)
8. FOUCAULD, CHARLES DE. Reconnaissance au Maroc. Paris, 1888. (A second edition was published in 1902.)

9. FRIBOURG, ANDRÉ. L'Afrique latine. Paris, 1922.
10. GHIRELLI, ANGELO. El País berbere. Madrid, 1942.
11. GLASS, GEORGE. History of the Discovery and Conquest of the Canary Islands. London, 1764. (A glossary of Guanche is given, and a comparison is made between Guanche and Shilha and Libyan. This may be the earliest attempt to establish the relationship between Guanche and Berber.)
12. GSELL, STÉPHANE. Histoire ancienne de l'Afrique du Nord. Paris, 1913. (Although this work is not devoted to language but deals with history of the area, there is information that is useful in work with the Berber languages.)
13. HANOTEAU, ADOLPHE. Les Iles Fortunées ou Archipel des Canaries. Brussels, 1896. (Some comments on the language of the Canary Islands.)
14. ——. La Kabylie et les coutumes kabyles. Paris, 1872–73. (There is a short essay on language in the first volume of this three-volume work.)
15. HÖLSCHER, WILHELM. Libyer und Ägypter. Ägyptologische Forschungen, vol. 4. (Discussion of the link between Libyan and ancient Egyptian cultures.)
16. JUSTINARD, LÉOPOLD V. Notes d'histoire et de litterature berbères. Hespéris 5.227–38; 7.333–56, 1928.
17. ——. Notes sur l'histoire du Sous au XIXe siècle. Hespéris 5.265–76, 1925; and 6.351–64, 1926.
18. ——. Notes sur l'histoire de l'Atlas. Paris, 1940. (La rihla du Marabout de Tasaft translated and annotated. Contains historical information.)
19. LAOUST, ÉMILE. Le folklore marocain. Encyclopédie coloniale et maritime, Le Maroc, ser. 4, 23.429–56. Paris, 1940.
20. ——. Le taleb et la mosquée en pays berbère. Bulletin de l'Enseignement public de Maroc, 3–18, 1924.
21. LEGEY, FRANÇOISE. Essai de folklore marocain. Paris, 1926. (An English translation, The Folklore of Morocco, by L. Hotz, was published in London, 1935.)
22. LEGLAY, MAURICE. L'école française et la question berbère. Bulletin de l'Enseignement public de Maroc, 1921,
23. LÉVI-PROVENÇAL, E. Les historiens des Chorfa. Paris, 1922.
24. LEWICKI, T. Mélanges berbères-ibadites. REIsl 3.267–86, 1936.
25. MACGUCKIN DE SLANE, WILLIAM (tr.). Histoire des Berbères. Algiers, 1852–56. (This translation of the well-known work by Ibn Khaldoun was used by a number of scholars in their studies of Berber. At the end of volume 4, there is an appendix on the language, literature, and the origins of the Berbers.)
26. MASQUERAY, ÉMILE. Coup d'œil d'histoire de l'Afrique septentrionale. Algiers, 1881.
27. MERCIER, E. La langue libyenne et la topographie antique de l'Afrique du Nord. JA 189–320, 1924.
28. MEYER, ALPHONSE. Origine des habitants de la Kabylie. Rev. afr., 357, 1858. (Consideration of historical information contained in narratives of native speakers of Kabyle.)

29. OLIVIER, M. G. Recherches sur l'origine des Berbères. Bulletin Académie d'Hippone, 1867–68. (Some linguistic data.)
30. RINN, LOUIS. Essai d'études linguistiques et ethnologiques sur les origines berbères. Rev. afr., 1881–89. (This series of essays was published in the journal in sections. The material is basically the same as that of no. 31, below. At least one article of the series can be located in each volume of the journal between the years 1881 and 1889.)
31. ——. Les origines berbères. Algiers, 1889. (The material of this book is basically the same as that of the essays referred to above. There is an attempt to reconstruct the ancient culture of the Berbers and to trace the development of that culture on the basis of linguistic and sociological data.)
32. ROGET, RAYMOND. Le Maroc chez les auteurs anciens. Paris, 1924. (French translation of references to North Africa in the works of Greek and Roman writers. Index of place names.)
33. TAUXIER, H. Examen des traditions grecques, latines et musulmanes relatives à l'origine du peuple berbère. Algiers, 1861. (This paper was originally published in volume 6 of Rev. afr. An abstract also appeared in JA.)
34. WAGNER, M. L. Restos de latinidad en el Norte de Africa. Coimbra, 1936.
See also works by:
AMAT, CHARLES (See no. 724).
AUCAPITAINE, HENRI (See no. 726).
BASSET, HENRI (See no. 730).
BASSET, RENÉ (See nos. 216, 218, 219, 625, 732).
BEGUINOT, FRANCESCO (See nos. 140, 220).
CALASSANTI-MOTYLINSKI, G. A. DE (See nos. 69, 594, 667).
SHAW, THOMAS (See no. 211).
VYCICHL, WERNER (See no. 126).

Berber Language: General

35. AUCAPITAINE, HENRI. Études récentes sur les dialectes berbères de l'Algérie. Paris, 1859. (An important bibliographical note.)
36. AVEZAC-MACAYA, MARIE ARMAND PASCAL DE. Notes pour l'étude de la langue berbère. Paris, 1840.
37. BASSET, ANDRÉ. A propos du parler berbère de Ghadames. Travaux de l'Institut des Recherches sahariennes 3.137–40, 1945.
38. ——. Apparence et réalité en berbère. JA, 417, 1943–45.
39. ——. Articles de dialectologie berbère. Paris, 1959. (A collection of articles and papers published posthumously. This does not contain all of Basset's work, but there is a complete list of his publications arranged in chronological order.)
40. ——. Entretiens sur la mise à part: faits berbères. GLECS, 65–6, 1947.,

41. ——. La langue berbère. London, 1952. (Part I of the Handbook of African Languages of the International African Institute. This is probably the best general survey of the Berber languages: phonology, morphology, syntax, and lexicon with notes on the writing system and a brief chapter on relationships between the Berber languages, Libyan, and Guanche. There is also a bibliography which is adequate but not complete.)
42. ——. Note sur les parlers rifains du Zerhoun. IVe Congr. Fed. Soc. Sav. Afr. Nd. 2.877–81, 1938.
43. ——. Note sur les parlers zenaga. Bull. Com. et. hist. sc. A.O.F., 319–32, 1933.
44. ——. Notules berbères Ait Sadden. GLECS 1–3, 1955. (This is Basset's last work published before his death.)
45. ——. Les parlers berbères. Initiation à Tunisie, 220–6. Paris, 1950.
46. ——. Principes d'enquête linguistique appliques au berbère. Rev. afr. 76. 369–71, 1935.
47. ——. Quelques considerations sur la langue berbère. Le Monde non Chretien, no. 11.
48. Basset, René. Le dialecte berbère de Taroudant. Giornale della Societa Asiatica Italiana 8.1–63, 1887. (A description of Shilha.)
49. ——. Le Dialecte de Syouah. Paris, 1890. (A grammatical description of the dialect of Siwa, the oasis in Egypt. This is no. 5 of the Bull. corr. afr.)
50. ——. Mélanges africains et orientaux. Paris, 1915. (A collection of articles and essays on a variety of topics. Those that are concerned specifically with Berber languages are listed separately in this bibliography.)
51. ——. Mission au Senegal. Paris, 1909. (Part I of this work is a study of Zenaga, a Twareg dialect spoken in southern Mauritania and Senegal. This is no. 39 of the Bull. corr. afr.)
52. ——. Notes sur le chaouia de la province de Constantine. JA 9/8.361–94, 1896.
53. ——. Notice sur le dialecte berbère des Beni-Iznacen. Giornale della Societa Asiatica Italiana 11.1–14, 1898. (A preliminary study of one of the Riff dialects.)
54. ——. Notice sur les dialectes berbères des Haratka et du Djerid Tunisien. Publ. IX Congr. Intern. Orient., vol. 2, 1892.
55. ——. Rapport sur les études berbères, arabes et éthiopiennes 1887–1891. Publ. IX Congr. Intern. Orient. Paris, 1893. (A survey of research undertaken and completed.)
56. ——. Rapport sur les études berbères et haoussa 1897–1902. JA 9/20.307–25, 1902. (This report was presented at the 12th International Congress of Orientalists.)
57. ——. Rapport sur les études berbères et haoussa 1902–1908. Rev. afr. 52.243–64, 1908. (This survey was presented at the 15th International Congress of Orientalists.)
58. ——. Rapport sur les langues africaines 1891–1897. Act. XI Congr. Intern. Orient. 5.53–70, 1899.

59. ——. Rapport sur les langues berbères et haoussa 1891–1897. Act. XI Congr. Intern. Orient. 5.39–51, 1899.

60. BEGUINOT, FRANCESCO. Il gergo dei Berberi della Tripolitania. Annuar. Ist. Orient. Nap., 1917–18.

61. ——. Gli studi berberi dal 1919 al maggio 1922. RSO 9.382. (A general survey of research in Berber languages similar to the reports prepared by René Basset.)

62. BENOIT, FERNAND. Recherches sur les berbèrophones. Act. XV Congr. Intern. Anthro. Archeol. preh. Coimbra, 1930. (This article is concerned chiefly with the areas of Djerba and Ahaggar. There are also some references to Morocco.)

63. BERNARD, J. M. La langue Maure. Paris, 1893. (A two-volume work on the language of Mauritania and Senegal.)

64. BIARNAY, S. Étude sur le dialecte berbère de Ouargla. Paris, 1908. (This is no. 37 of the Bull. corr. afr. In addition to the description of phonology, morphology, and syntax, there are two glossaries. The first, in roman characters, gives French equivalents for Berber stems arranged alphabetically according to roots. The second, in Arabic, gives French equivalents of lexical items assumed to be derived from Arabic. There are also sample texts, and in an appendix there is a detailed presentation of marriage customs in which the complete vocabulary for ritual is given.)

65. ——. Étude sur le dialecte des Bet't'ioua du Vieil-Arzeu. Algiers, 1911. (This work was originally published as a series of articles in Rev. afr. 54.97–181, 301–54, 405–39; 55.100–36, 170–215, 327–42, 1910–11. It is the description of the language of a colony of emigres from the Rif living near Oran. In addition to the description, there are texts, in roman transcription, and glossaries of forms used in the description and in the texts. Three texts in dialects of Riff are included, and these are of interest as reports of causes of the emigration according to the oral tradition of the tribes of the Riff. A brief description of the dialects of Ait-Saaden and Beni-Mgild, two tribes of central Morocco is included in this book. The form of the description is the same as that of other works of this period, and there are glossaries and texts for the second description also. The glossaries are alphabetized according to the roots.)

66. ——. Étude sur les dialectes berbères du Rif. Paris, 1917. (This is no. 54 of the Bull. corr. afr. The work is a detailed description of the several dialects of Riff at the phonological level. There are texts in roman transcription, glossaries, and a table of comparative phonology. Morphological and syntactic features are presented only in footnotes or in the glossaries, so the chief value of the work is in the phonological information and in the fact that the texts themselves may be used as sources of data.)

67. ——. Notice sur les dialectes berbères parles par les Aith-Sadden et les Beni-Mgild. Rev. afr., vol. 55, 1911. (See no. 65 above.)

68. BROSSELARD, CHARLES. Lettre à M. E. Renan. JA 7/19.518–21, 1882. (Information about work on Berber languages.)

69. CALASSANTI-MOTYLINSKI, G. A. DE. Le dialecte berbère de R'edames. Paris, 1904. (No. 28 of the Bull. corr. afr. This is a detailed study of one of the Libyan dialects complete with grammar, texts in Arabic and roman transcription, and a glossary. In addition, the vocabularies of Graberg de Hemso and Richardson are included. Historical notes, in Arabic, about Ghadames are presented and translated. An Arabic manuscript on Ghadames, Ghat, and the Tuaregs is also included with translation. At the end of the volume, there is a short Tuareg text published as an example of one type of folktale. The grammatical statement at the beginning of the book is not complete, but the additional material in the work makes it an important item for Berber linguistics.)
70. ——. Le Djebel Nefousa. Paris, 1898. (A three volume work on the dialect of the area. The work includes the text cited above with translation and additional material on the grammar. This is no. 22 of the Bull. corr. afr.)
71. CESARO, ANTONIO. Ancora per gli studi berberistici in Italia. L'Oltremare, 172, 1932.
72. CHAMBERLAYNE, JOHN. Oratio dominica in diversas linguas versa. Amsterdam, 1715. (Contains an early description of Shilha.)
73. CHARNOCK, R. S. Notes on the Kabyle Language. Imperial and Asiatic Quarterly Review. vol. 3, no. 6, 1892.
74. COLIN, GEORGES S. Le parler berbère des Gmara. Hespéris 9.43–58, 1929.
75. COYNE, A. Le Mzab. Rev. afr. 23.172, 1879.
76. CUST, ROBERT N. A sketch of the modern languages of Africa. London, 1883. (This book has been used as a reference work in Berber language studies. It includes a bibliography.)
77. DELAPORTE, J. HONORAT. Specimen de la langue berbère. Paris, 1844.
78. DE SAMUDA, ——. Essai sur la langue des Beni-Mzabs. Mon. Alg., 1840. (One of the earliest descriptions.)
79. DESTAING, EDMOND. Étude sur le dialecte berbère des Ait Seghrouchen. Paris, 1920. (Description of a dialect of central Morocco. This work is no. 56 of Bull. corr. afr.)
80. ——. Étude sur le dialecte berbère des Beni-Snous. Paris, 1907–11. (Nos. 34–5 of the Bull. corr. afr. In the first volume a grammatical description is presented, followed by texts, roman transcription, with translations. In the second volume, additional texts, with translations, are given.)
81. ——. L'expression verbale de l'état et de la durée dans les parlers berbères marocains. BSL 30.9–10. (See nos. 225, 351, below.)
82. DEVAUX, CHARLES. Les Kebailes du Djerjera. Marseille, 1859. (A general study with section on language.)
83. DRUMMOND-HAY, JOHN. Western Barbary. London, 1844. (Includes comments on the Berber languages.)
84. DUBIE, P. L'ilot berbèrophone de Mauritanie. BIFAN, 1942.
85. DUCATI, BRUNO. Le lingue parlate nelle nostre colonie. L'Oltremare, 220–1.

86. DU PONCEAU, PETER S. Grammatical sketch and specimens of the Berber language. Philadelphia, 1830. (Publication of notes and four letters to William Hodgson.)

87. FAIDHERBE, LOUIS L. Le Zenaga des tribus Senegalaises. Paris, 1877. (Minor study of the languages.)

88. FLORES MORALES, A. El dialecto bereber en Marruecos. Africa, 30–3, February, 1943. (General survey.)

89. FREEMAN, HENRY S. Dialecte de Ghat. Rev. afr. 8.396, 1864. (This is a translation of the preface to Freeman's work prepared by H. Aucapitaine.)

90. GALAND, LIONEL. Berbères: La Langue. EI, Leiden. (This is a general survey of the Berber languages with very good bibliographies at the end of each section of the article.)

91. GAUDEFROY-DEMOMBYNES, M. Langues du Maroc. Revue générale des sciences pures et appliqués, 301-5, 1914.

92. GIESE, WILHELM. Los estudios de las lenguas canarias de E. Zyhlarz. Revue historique 18.413–27, 1952.

93. GRABERG, JACOB OF HEMSÖ. Remarks on the language of the Amazirghs. JRAS 106–30, 1836. (Also published separately. This work contains general introductory remarks on the Berbers, a text in Shilha and in the dialect of Ghadames, and a glossary. There are also a few sample sentences in the dialect of Ghadames.)

94. GRIMME, HUBERT. Nachtrag zur A. Klingenhebens Studie über die berberischen Zahlmethoden. ZES 17.230–4, 1927.

95. HAMMER-PURGSTALL, JOSEPH VON. Neustes zur Forderung der Länder-Sprachen und Völkerkunde Nord-Afrikas. Vienna, 1852.

96. IBÁÑEZ, ESTEBAN. El dialecto bereber del Rif. Mémorial André Basset, 51–6. Paris, 1957. (A general description of distribution, principal characteristics, and relationship to other Berber dialects.)

97. JONES, ZACHARIAS. Dissertatio de lingua shilhense. Amsterdam, 1715. (Published in Chamberlayne's Oratio dominica in diversas linguas versa, no. 72 above.)

98. KLINGENHEBEN, AUGUST. Zu den Zahlmethoden in den Berbersprachen. ZDMG 81.90–1, 1926.

99. LANGLÈS, LOUIS M. Mémoire sur les Oasis. Paris, 1803. (This is a description of Siwa published as part of the French translation of Hornemann's journal, no. 197 below. It includes a glossary taken from Venture de Paradis' work.)

100. LAOUST, EMILE. Coup d'œil des études berbères. (Bull) IHEM, 107–29, 1920.

101. ——. Le dialecte berbère du Rif. Hespéris 7.173–208, 1927.

102. ——. Étude sur le dialecte berbère du Chenoua comparé avec ceux des Beni-Menacer et des Beni-Salah. Paris, 1912. (Includes grammar, texts and glossary. Vol. 50 of Bull. corr. afr.)

103. ——. Étude sur le dialecte berbère des Ntifa. Paris, 1918. (Grammatical description and texts. There is an essay on divisions of time and seasons, and there are also a number of texts with translations, but no glossary.)
104. ——. Siwa. EI, 482–5. Leiden, 1934.
105. ——. Siwa: son parler. Paris, 1932. (Grammar, texts with translations, glossaries. Bibliographical notes.)
106. LAURO, A. Gli studi berberistici in Italia. L'Oltremare, 380–4, 1931.
107. LE GLAY, MAURICE. Le Berbère marocain. Rev. Viv., 367–77, 1930.
108. LOUBIGNAC, V. Étude sur le dialecte des Zaian et des Ait Sgougou. Paris, 1924. (Grammatical description.)
109. ——. Étude sur le dialecte des Zaian et des Ait Sgougou. Paris, 1926. (A continuation of the preceding item with texts.)
110. MARSDEN, WILLIAM. Observations sur la langue siwahane. Paris, 1802. (This was published as an appendix to the French translation of Hornemann's journal. See no. 197 below.)
111. MEILLET, A., and M. COHEN. Les langues du monde, 156–64. Paris, 1952. (A survey of the Berber languages is given.)
112. MONTEIL, VINCENT. Notes sur Ifni et les Ait-Ba-Amran. (Notes Doc.) IHEM, no. 2. Paris, 1948.
113. NEHLIL, ——. Étude sur le dialecte de Ghat. Paris, 1909. (No. 38 of Bull. corr. afr. Description of a Tuareg dialect.)
114. NEWMAN, FRANCIS W. Of the structure of the Berber language. London, 1844. (Published as an appendix to Pritchard's Researches of the physical history of mankind.)
115. NICOLAS, FRANCIS. La langue berbère de Mauritanie. Dakar, 1953. (Mémoires, IFAN, no. 33. Complete description of the language with historical notes, texts and micro-glossaries, and a lexical index with items classified by root.)
116. PLAULT, M. Études berbères: La langue berbère dans la commune mixte de Barika; La langue berbère dans la commune mixte du Guergour. Rev. afr. 90.194–207, 1946.
117. PRASSE, KARL G. Notes sur la langue touaregue. AcOr XXV/1–2.42–111, 1960. (A restatement of the phonological descriptions of Foucauld based on original data. An appendix contains a criticism of the transcription in Foucauld's collection of texts, and a second appendix contains a set of texts collected by Hanoteau and annotated by Prasse.)
118. ROBECCHI-BRICCHETTI, LUIGI. Sul dialetto di Siwah. Rc. Accademia dei Lincei, vol. 5, 1889.
119. SARRIONANDIA, PEDRO. Noticia sobre la lengua que se hablo en el Rif. Tangiers, 1909.
120. SCHMIDT, VIDAL F. Ensayo sobre linguistica en el Rif Occidental. Africa, 32–7, October, 1945.
121. SCHUCHARDT, HUGO E. M. Berberische Studien. WZKM 22.245–64, 351–84,

1908. (The first part deals with noun morphology. The second part is a reply to Basset's article on Arabic loanwords, no.420.)

122. SIERAKOWSKI, A. Das Schaui: Ein Beitrag zur berberischen Sprachen- und Völkerkunde. Dresden, 1871.

123. STANLEY, C. W. D. The Siwan language and vocabulary. Jl. R. Afr. Soc., 438–57, 1912.

124. ——. A report on the oasis of Siwa. Cairo, 1912. (Includes some comments about the language.)

125. VENTURE DE PARADIS, JEAN MICHEL DE. Principes de la langue berbère. Paris, 1832. (The description which serves as the basis for one of the earliest grammars and glossaries.)

126. VYCICHL, WERNER. Introduccion al estudio de la lengua y de la historia de Canarias. La Laguna de Tenerife, 1952.

127. WALKER, W. SEYMOUR. The Siwi language. London, 1921. (A short description of the dialect spoken near the Oasis of Siwa. Texts and glossaries are included as well as a short general description of the area, with map.)

128. ZANON, F. A proposito di studi berberistici. L'Oltremare, 333–4, 1932.

See also works by:

BASSET, HENRI (See no. 728).
BERTHOLON, LUCIAN J. (See no. 141).
MOULIERAS, AUGUSTE J. (See no. 791).
SHALER, WILLIAM (See no. 798).

Berber Languages: Historical Studies

129. ALVAREZ DELGADO, JUAN. Puesto de Canarias en la investigacion linguistica. Monog., vol. 3, sec. 2, no. 1. Instituto de Estudios Canarios, Universidad de la Laguna, 1941. (Contains useful bibliographical data.)

130. BASSET, ANDRÉ. Etymologies berbères. GLECS 4.79–80, 1948.

131. ——. Formations accidentelles en berbère. GLECS, 45–7, 1939.

132. ——. La parenté linguistique et le berbère. Rev. afr. 76.357–9, 1935.

133. BASSET, RENÉ. Rapport sur les études relatives à la linguistique berbère 1913–1918. Rev. afr. 60.161–9, 1919.

134. BEGUINOT, FRANCESCO. Alcune etimologie e questioni fonetische magrebine. AION-L, vol. 2, 1943. (Historical and comparative study.)

135. ——. Di alcune parole dellinguaggi nord-africani derivate del latino. Rome, 1938.

136. ——. Gli studi di linguistica berbera. Att. 1° Congr. stud. col. Florence, 1931.

137. ——. Gli studi di linguistica berbera. La Rivista Orienta 4.137–47, 1931.

138. ——. Gli studi di linguistica berbera. La Rivista Orienta, 145–8, 1934.

139. ——. Studi linguistici nel Fezzan. Bollettino, Società geografica italiana 6/12.660–5, 1935.
140. ——. Sugli 'Atapartesi di Erodoto e sul nome berbero del grande Atlante. Mémorial Henri Basset 1.29–42. Paris, 1928. (This article contains a discussion of one of the place names cited by Herodotus, and Beguinot examines carefully previous hypotheses about the derivation of the name concluding that it is, in fact, a Berber stem. The article contains bibliographical footnotes, and it is useful in the documentation of Berber history as well as in historical linguistics.)
141. Bertholon, Lucien J. Origine et formation de la langue berbère. Revue tunisienne, 1903–06.
142. Boulifa, Si Ammar ben Said. Étude linguistique et sociologique sur la Kabylie de Djurdjura. Algiers, 1913. (See no. 529, below.)
143. Brockelmann, Carl. Semitische Sprachwissenschaft. Leipzig. 1906. (Translated into French as Précis de linguistique sémitique by W. Marcais and M. Cohen and published in Paris in 1910. It is this translation that has been cited by a number of French scholars in their works on Berber languages.)
144. ——. Gibt es einen hamitischen Sprachstamm? Anthropos 27.797–818, 1932.
145. Broussais, Emile. Recherches sur les transformations du berbère. Bull. corr. afr., no. 1, 1883.
146. Cohen, Marcel. Genou, famille, force dans le domaine chamito-sémitique. Mémorial Henri Basset 1.203–19. Paris, 1928. (Historical essay with some examples from Berber languages.)
147. ——. Le Système verbal sémitique et l'expression du temps. Publications de l'École des langues orientales vivantes, ser. 5, vol. 11. Paris, 1924. (Examples from Berber are included.)
148. Colin, Georges S. Une date dans l'histoire de la langue berbère. Hespéris 18.201–2, 1934.
149. ——. Etymologies magribines. Hespéris 6.52–82, 1926; 7.85–102, 1927; and 10.125–7, 1930. (The second article of the series has the title: 'Notes de dialectologie arabe — etymologies magribines'. In the articles, Colin discusses not only Arabic but also the Berber languages.)
150. ——. Mots berbères dans le dialecte arabe de Malte. Mémorial André Basset, 7–16. Paris, 1957. (This essay is an attempt to establish Berber roots for a number of words found in Maltese Arabic. The problem presented came from Colin's previous interest in derivations of words in the Berber languages and his realization that little had been done on the problem of Berber loan words in the non-Berber languages.)
151. ——. Observations étymologiques sur le vocabulaire Kabyle. Mélanges Gaudefroy-Demombynes, 301–12. Cairo, 1939. (Arabic loan words in Kabyle.)
152. Fevrier, J. G. Que savons-nous du libyque? Rev. afr. 100.263–73, 1956. (The two articles by Fevrier are contributions to the study of the development of the Berber languages.)

153. GABELENTZ, GEORG VON DER. Baskisch und Berberisch. Berlin, 1893. (This book is more useful to those interested in the development of historical and comparative linguistics than those interested in Berber languages.)
154. GALAND, LIONEL. Deux exemples de linguistique psychologique. Hespéris 37. 438–42, 1950.
155. ——. Onomastique de l'Afrique ancienne. RIOno, 67–79, 1950. (A contribution to the study of Libyan languages and the development of Berber.)
156. ——. La phonétique en dialectologie berbère. Orbis 2.225–33, 1953. (Consideration of the problems encountered in historical and comparative Berber studies.)
157. GUAY, J. La forme feminine berbère a Sale. Archs. Berb., 31–52, 1918. (An example of possible Berber influence on the morphology of Moroccan Arabic is presented.)
158. HALEVY, JOSEPH. Études sur les langues de l'Afrique. Revue de linguistique et de philologie comparée, October, 1869. (Includes notes on Berber.)
159. IBÁÑEZ, ESTEBAN. El Padre Sarrionandia y el problema de la linguistica rifeñobereber. Verdad y Vida, 226–9, 1943.
160. ——. Voces hispano-latinas en el dialecto rifeño. Verdad y Vida, 365-81, 1947.
161. LAOUST, EMILE. Le nom berbère du qsar: ighrem. Hespéris 19.188–90, 1934.
162. ——. Le nom de la charrue et de ses accessoires chez les berbères. Archs. Berb. 3.1–29, 1918. (An attempt to trace the influence of the Romans by analysis of agricultural terminology.)
163. MARCY, GEORGES. Au sujet du nom berbère du fer. GLECS, vol. 2, 1937.
164. ——. Le mot 'halluf' est-il d'origine berbère. Bulletin des études arabes, 106–7, 1941.
165. ——. Notes linguistiques autour du periple d'Hannon. Hespéris 20.21, 1935.
166. ——. Les phrases berbères des documents inédits d'histoire almohade. Hespéris 14.61–77, 1932.
167. MERCIER, GUSTAVE. Notes sur l'etymologie du nom 'rusccuru'. Rec. Not. Mém. Soc. arch. hist. geog. dept. Const. 48.94–5, 1915. (An examination of the historical implications of the occurrence of similar noun stems in place names of different regions.)
168. NEWMAN, FRANCIS W. Notes on the Libyan languages. JRAS 12.417–34, 1880.
169. PEYRIGUERES, P. Psychologie linguistique berbère. Compte rendu des Conferences de l'année 1930, 27–32, 1930.
170. PICARD, ANDRÉ and A. BASSET. Sur berbère yir 'mauvais' chez les Irjen. Rev. afr. 93.293–313.
171. PIETSCHMANN, RICHARD. Über die kanarischen Zahlworte. ZEthn, 1879.
172. RAYNAUD, HENRI. Notes de philologie berbère. L'Ethnographie 41.84–92, 1943.
173. RENAN, ERNEST. Histoire générale et système comparé des langues sémitique. Paris, 1863.

174. RÖSSLER, OTTO. Der Semitische Charakter der libyschen Sprache. Z. Ass. vord. arch. 16.121–50, 1952.
175. SARNELLI, TOMMASO. A propos du nom berbère tizri dans le 'Guide d'oculiste de l'arabo-espagnol Muhammad al-Gafiqi'. Act. XXIe Congr. Intern. Orient., 315–16, 1948.
176. ——. Sull'origine del nome Imazigen. Mémorial André Basset, 131–8. Paris, 1957. (An attempt to define the native word, 'Berber', by consideration of both linguistic and extra-linguistic data.)
177. VYCICHL, WERNER. L'histoire de la langue berbère. Act. XXIe Congr. Intern. Orient., 319–20, 1948.
178. ——. Punischer Spracheinfluss im Berberischen. JNES 11.198–204.
179. ——. Eine vorhamitischen Sprachschicht im Altägyptischen. ZDMG 101.67–77, 1951.
180. WERNER, ALICE. The Language Families of Africa. London, 1925.
181. WÖLFEL, DOMINIK J. Dilettantismus und Scharlatanarie und die Erforschung der Eingeborenensprache der Kanarischen Inseln. Mémorial André Basset, 147–58. Paris, 1957.
182. ZYHLARZ, ERNST. Das geschichtliche Fundament der Hamitensprachen. Afrika 9.440, 1936.
183. ——. Die Sprache Numidiens. ZES, vol. 19, 1932.

See also works by:

BASSET, RENÉ (See no. 369).
BEGUINOT, FRANCESCO (See no. 246).
CAILLIÉ, RENÉ (See no. 186).
COHEN, MARCEL (See nos. 224, 307).
HODGSON, WILLIAM B. (See no. 315).
HUYGHE, G. (See no. 493).
REINAUD, JOSEPH (See no. 508).
RINN, LOUIS (See nos. 30, 31).
SCHUCHARDT, HUGO E. M. (See no. 121).

Berber: Travel Journals

184. BASSET, ANDRÉ. Sur une notation berbère de G. F. Lyons. AION-L, 379–81 1949. (Comment on the interpretation of a transcription from the travel journal of an early 19th century British explorer.)
185. CAILLIAUD, FRÉDÉRIC. Voyage à Meroc, au Fleuve Blanc, au dela de Fazoql dans le midi du Royaume de Sennaar, à Syouah et dans cinq autres Oasis, fait dans les années 1819-20-21 et 22. Paris, 1826–27. (The most important item in this four volume work is the description of the dialect of Siwa, with glossary, that has been included at the end of the first volume.)

186. CAILLIÉ, RENÉ. Journal d'un voyage à Tembouctou et à Jenne dans l'Afrique centrale pendant les années 1824–25–26–27–28. Paris, 1830. (This work, like the preceding one, is typical of the journals of voyages and explorations which appeared at this time. There are some notes on dialects spoken by Berbers, but the notes are not so precise as those in the preceding work. The work may be useful in historical and comparative studies, however.)
187. CARTERET, GEORGE. The Barbary voyage of 1638. Philadelphia, 1929. (There are some comments on the language of the area.)
188. DE LA PEÑA, NUÑEZ. Conquista y antiguedades de las Islas de Gran Canaria. Madrid, 1676. (One of the early travel journals that has served as the source of data for studies of the relationship between Berber languages and Guanche.)
189. AL-EDEISI, (ABU ABDALLAH MUHAMMAD IBN MUHAMMAD AL-SHARIF AL-IDRISI). Description de l'Afrique et de l'Espagne. Leiden, 1866. (Translation prepared by R. Dozy and J. de Goeje.)
190. FARINE, CHARLES. A travers la Kabylie. Paris, 1865.
191. FELZE, JACQUES. L'Atlas berbère. Vis Maroc. Ill., 1930.
192. FISCHER, FRIEDRICH T. Wissenschaftliche Ergebnisse einer Reise in Atlas. Gotha, 1900.
193. FOUREAU, FERNAND. Rapport sur ma mission au Sahara. Paris. 1894. (There are some useful data in volume 1 of this report.)
194. GENTIL, LOUIS. Une mission dans l'Atlas marocain. L'Afrique française 33. 447–64, 1923.
195. HODGSON, WILLIAM B. Notes on Northern Africa, the Sahara and Soudan. New York, 1844. (Includes comments on language.)
196. HOOKER, JOSEPH D. Journal of a tour in Morocco and the Great Atlas. London, 1878. (This journal contains a chapter, 'On the Shelluhe language,' in which the general characteristics of the language(s) of the area are described and a short vocabulary is given.)
197. HORNEMANN, FRIEDRICH. Tagebuch seiner Reise von Cairo nach Murzuk in den Jahren 1797–98. Weimar, 1802. (This journal contains data about the languages of the area, especially Siwa, cited in later studies. An English translation was published in London in 1802.)
198. HÖST, GEORG H. Efterretingen om Marokos och Fes. Copenhagen, 1779.
199. ——. Nachrichten von Marokos. Copenhagen, 1781. (This is a German translation of the preceding work. In it are samples of the languages spoken in Morocco, and the list of Berber forms has been cited by later authors as proof of the stability of the Berber languages.)
200. IBN BATUTA (MUHAMMAD IBN 'ABD ALLAH). Travels of Ibn Batuta. London, 1829. (Translated by Samuel Lee. Used as a source of data by a few scholars in the nineteenth century.)
201. JACKSON, JAMES G. An account of the Empire of Morocco and the District of Suse. London, 1809. (This journal contains a chapter on the language(s) of

Morocco in which a short glossary is presented to show that Shilha and Tamazight are different languages and distinct from Siwa.)
202. LEMPRIÈRE, WILLIAM. Voyage dans l'Empire du Maroc et le royaume de Fez. Paris, 1801. (Journal of travels, 1790–91; translated from English.)
203. LENS, OSCAR. De Timbouctou au Maroc. Paris, 1884.
204. LYONS, GEORGE F. A narrative of travels in Northern Africa. London, 1821.
205. MASQUERAY, EMILE. Voyage dans l'Aouras. Bulletin, Société de géographie, 39–59, 449–73, 1876.
206. MINUTÖLI, HEINRICH C. Reise zum Tempel des Jupiter Ammon in der libyschen Wüste ... in 1820–21. Berlin, 1824. (This travel journal contains one of the early wordlists in Siwa.)
207. PEYSONNEL, JEAN A. Voyages dans les Regences de Tunis et d'Alger. Paris, 1838. (This travel journal includes a short list of Zouave words.)
208. RICHARDSON, JAMES. Travels in Morocco. London, 1860. (Included are observations about the languages.)
209. ROHLFS, GERHARD. Reise durch Marokko. Bremen, 1867. (Travel journal of an expedition from Morocco to Tripoli.)
210. SCHOLZ, JOHANN M.A, Reise in der Gegend zwischen Alexandrien und Paratonium. Leipzig, 1824. (Travel journal with a glossary of the dialect of Siwa.)
211. SHAW, THOMAS. Travels and observations relating to several parts of Barbary and the Levant. Oxford. 1738. (A detailed description of North Africa including a glossary of Zouave. In an appendix summaries and quotations from the works of ancient medieval geographers and historians are given.)
See also works by:
NEWMAN, FRANCIS W. (See no. 503).
PACHO, RAYMOND (See no. 507).
STUMME, HANS (See no. 510).

Berber Comparison

212. BARBERA, GUISEPPE. Arabo e berbero nel linguaggio italosiculo. Beirut, 1935.
213. BASSET, ANDRÉ. De nouveau à propos du nom de l'île de Fer. Onomastica, 121–16, 1948. (Criticism of a hypothesis, formulated by Marcy, about the relationship between Guanche and the Berber languages.)
214. ——. Siwa, Aoudjila et Imeghran à propos d'un rapprochement. AnnIEo 2.119–27, 1936.
215. ——. Siwa et Aoudjila, problème verbal berbère. Mélanges Gaudefroy-Demombynes, 279–300. Cairo, 1933–45.
216. BASSET, RENÉ. Études sur les dialectes berbères, Paris, 1894. (This is a comparative study based on limited data available at the end of the nineteenth century. It is one of the first attempts to define the relationships among the

various Berber languages, and it deals chiefly with phonology and morphology. There is also a brief historical commentary and a short bibliography. Transcriptions are in Arabic, Roman, and in tifinagh, for Tuareg. This is no. 14 of the Bull. corr. afr.)

217. ——. Étude sur les dialectes berbères du Rif marocain. Act. XI Congr. Intern. Orient., sec. 5, 71–171, 1897. (A general description of several dialects of Riff, including those of Temsaman, Beni Ouriaghel, Ibeqqoyen, etc.)

218. ——. Étude sur la Zenatia de l'Ouarsenis et du Maghreb Central. Paris, 1895. (This work includes historical notes, grammatical descriptions, texts in both Arabic and Roman transcriptions, and bilingual glossaries alphabetized according to roots. The dialects described are those of northwestern Algeria and central Morocco. This is no. 15 of the Bull. corr. afr.)

219. ——. Étude sur la Zenatia du Mzab, d'Ouargla et de l'Oued-Rir'. Paris, 1893. (The plan of this work is the same as that of 132; historical notes, grammatical description, texts, and glossaries. The dialects described are those spoken in the southern part of Algeria. This is no. 12 of the Bull. corr. afr.)

220. Beguinot, Francesco. A proposito di una voce libica citata da Erodoto. Afr. Ital., vol. 3, 1924. (In this article an attempt is made to establish the relationship between a form found in Herodotus and contemporary Berber lexical items. The article is significant as an addition to the documentation of Berber history.)

221. ——. L'unita linguistica semito-camitica. Annuario, R. Accademia d'Italia 1.139–44, 1939.

222. Bute, John (Marquess of). On the ancient language of the natives of Tenerife. London, 1891. (This is one of the earlier works in the series of publications containing speculations about the relationships between the languages of the Canary Islands and those of the Berber group.)

223. Cohen, Marcel. Essai comparatif sur le vocabulaire et la phonétique du chamito-sémitique. Paris, 1947. (Careful consideration of the languages of the Hamito-Semitic group with a proposal for redefining the family.)

224. ——. Sur l'affixe dans les verbes expressifs de diverses langues chamito-sémitiques. Mélanges Maspero, 705–19. Cairo, 1935. (Historical-comparative study.)

225. Destaing, Edmond. Notes sur l'expression verbale de la durée du temps en berbère et en arabe marocain. BSL 29.45–73, 1928; 31.1–33, 1931. (These articles and no. 81, above, are a single series. The data is taken from Shilha, and the comments on Moroccan Arabic are based on the analysis of the dialect spoken in the same area.)

226. Géze, Louis. De quelques rapports entre les langues berbères et basque. Mém. Soc. arch. Midi Fr. 2/3.30–6, 1885.

227. Greenberg, Joseph H. The labial consonants of Proto-Afro-Asiatic. Word 14/2–3.295–302, August-December, 1958.

228. HALÉVY, JOSEPH. Lettre a M. d'Abbadie sur quelques langues du Nord de L'Afrique. Paris, 1870. (Published as a separate monograph.)
229. HECTOR, P. A propos de psychologie linguistique berbère. Maroc Cath., 527–8, 575–81, 642–6, 1929; 33–7, 94–8, 222–7, 329–32, 385–90, 639–45, 1930; and 19–20, 346–7, 1931.
230. IBÁÑEZ, ESTEBAN. Divergencias filologicas entre el arabe y el bereber. Verdad y Vida, 610–17, 1943.
231. ——. La lengua bereber y el dialecto rifeño. Mauritania, 1942.
232. JUDAS, AUGUSTE C. Étude comparative de la langue berbère. Revue de l'orient et de l'Algérie [et des colonies] 3.57.
233. ——. Étude démonstrative de la langue phénicienne et de la langue libyque. Paris, 1847.
234. MASQUERAY, EMILE. Comparaison d'un vocabulaire des Zenaga avec les vocabulaires correspondants des dialectes Chawia et des Beni Mzab. Archives des missions scientifiques et littéraires 3/5.473–533, 1879.
235. MICHELL, G. B. Notes on a comparative table of Berber dialects. London, 1902.
236. ROCHEMONTEIX, M. de. Les rapports grammaticaux qui existent entre l'Egyptien et le Berbère. Mém. Congr. Intern. Orient. 2.67–106, 1876.
237. ROSE, J. Herodotus and Westermarck. CR, 165, 1923. (A short comment on the similarity of a Berber exclamation reported by Westermarck to a Libyan exclamation recorded by Herodotus.)
238. RÖSSLER, OTTO. Die Sprache Numidiens. Sybaris, 94–120, 1958.
239. ROUX, ARSÈNE. Le verbe dans les parlers berbères des Ighezran, Beni Alaham et Marmoucha. BSL 35.43–78, 1935.
240. SCHUCHARDT, HUGO E. M. Baskisch und Hamitisch. Paris, 1913. (An examination of possible relationships between Basque and African languages. Word lists of Basque, Berber and Hamitic languages are compared.)
241. WÖLFEL, DOMINIK J. Le problème des rapports du Berbère. Hespéris 40.523, 1953.
242. ——. Le problème des rapports du Guanche et du Berbère. Hespéris 40.523–7, 1953. (An attempt to define relationships between extant Berber languages and a language of the Canary Islands.)
243. ZYHLARZ, ERNST. Baskisch-afrikanische Sprachverwandtschaft. Anthropos, September, 1933.
244. ——. Das kanarische Berberisch in seinem sprachgeschichtlichen Milieu. ZDMG 100.403–60, 1950. (This article, which was the subject of Wölfel's attack, is one of the important works in the controversy about relationships between the languages of the Canary Islands and the Berber languages.)
245. ——. Konkordanz ägyptischer und libyscher Verbalstammtypen. ZÄS 70.107–22, 1934.

See also works by:

ABEL, HANS (See no. 642).
BASSET, ANDRÉ (See no. 41).
BASSET, RENÉ (See no. 423).
BEGUINOT, FRANCESCO (See no. 472).
BERTHELOT, SABIN, and WEBB (See no. 5).
DA COSTA DE RACEDO, J. J. (See no. 754).
GLASS, GEORGE (See no. 11).
HANOTEAU, ADOLPHE (See no. 312).
IBÁÑEZ, ESTEBAN (See nos. 96, 496).
JACKSON, JAMES G. (See no. 201).
LAOUST, EMILE (See no. 102).
NEWMAN, FRANCIS W. (See no. 504).
PARADISI, UMBERTO (See no. 458).
STUMME, HANS (See no. 510).
ZYHLARZ, ERNEST (See no. 183).

Libyan Inscriptions

246. BEGUINOT, FRANCESCO. Appunti di epigrafia libica. Afr. Ital. 6.127–35, 1927. (An article on the decipherment of a Libyan inscription in terms of contemporary knowledge of Berber languages. This problem is important in tracing the development of Berber languages and the writing system of the Tuaregs.)
247. ——. Di alcune inscrizioni in caratteri latini e in lingua sconoscuta trovate in Tripolitania. RSO 24.14–19, 1949. (A contribution to the decipherment of Libyan inscriptions. The article is based on a paper presented to the International Congress of Orientalists.)
248. ——. Note di epigrafia libica. AION-L, 1929.
249. ——. Gli studi sull'epigrafia libica e sulle iscrizione Tuareg in Italianell' ultimo quarentennio. Libia 1.82–90, 1953. (The articles in this group, 136–9, are valuable because of their bibliographical content.)
250. BOTTIGLIERI, R. Studi italiani sull'epigrafia libica e sulle iscrizioni tifinagh. Afr. Ital. 54.367–77, 1936.
251. CHABOT, J. B. Punica. Paris, 1918. (Originally published in JA, ser. 11.)
252. ——. Recueil des inscriptions libyques. Paris, 1940. (This is an exhaustive study of the inscriptions found in N. Africa. The work includes comparisons of various interpretations, reproductions of the inscriptions, plates, and a bibliography.)
253. FAIDHERBE, LOUIS L. Collection complète des inscriptions numidiques. Paris, 1870. (A collection of all the inscriptions available at that date with notes on ancient Libyan culture. Plates.)

254. HALÉVY, JOSEPH. Études berbères: Part I — Essai d'epigraphie Libyque. JA 7/3.73–203, 4.369–416, 1874. (This article on the Libyan inscriptions was also published separately.)

255. JOMARD, E. F. Seconde note sur une pierre gravée trouvée dans un ancien tumulus et à cette occasion sur l'idiome libyan. Paris, 1845.

256. JUDAS, AUGUSTE C. Examen des mémoires de M. le Dr. Reboud et de M. le General Faidherbe sur les inscriptions libyques. Paris, 1871. (Comparison and interpretation.)

257. ——. Mémoire sur 19 inscriptions numidico-puniques. Annuaire, 1860–61.

258. LETOURNEUX, A. Du déchiffrement des inscriptions libyco-berbères. Proc. IVe Congr. Intern. Orient, 1.57–75, 1878.

259. LIDZBARSKI, MARK. Eine Punisch-Altberberische Bilinguis aus einem Tempel des Massinissa. Sitzungsberichte der K. Akademie der Wissenschaften in Wien, no. 15, 1913.

260. MARCY, GEORGES. A propos du déchiffrement des inscriptions libyques. Algiers, 1938

261. ——. Quelques inscriptions libyques de Tunisie. Hespéris 25.289–365, 1938.

262. MEINHOF, CARL. Die libyschen Inschriften. Abhandlungen für die Kunde des Morgenlandes, vol. 19, no. 1, 1931.

263. REBOUD, V. Recueil d'inscriptions libyco-berbères. Rec. Not. Mém. Soc. arch. hist. géog. dept. Const., 43 et. seq., 1875.

264. TOVAR, A. Papeletas de epigrafia libica. B. Sem. Est. Arte Arqueol. Valladolid, 33–52, 1943.

Dialect Geography

265. ASPINION, ROBERT. Maroc au 1/500,000. Carte linguistique. Bureau des cartes de la Résidence Générale. Rabat.

266. BASSET, ANDRÉ. Aires phonétiques homogènes et non homogènes. Proc. 3rd Int. Congr. Phonét. Sci., 258–61. (A short paper on dialect geography, with maps.)

267. ——. Arabophones et berberophones dans le Nord-Marocain. Rif et Jbala, 77–8, 1926.

268. ——. Atlas linguistique des parlers berbères. Algiers, 1936. (This is one part of studies in dialect geography. The area considered is northern Algeria, and the data consist of the names for equines.)

269. ——. Cartes usuelles et cartes scientifiques. IIIe Congr. Intern. Topon. Anthropon., 457–9, 1949.

270. ——. Études de géographie linguistique dans le Sud-marocain. Hespéris 29. 3–22, 1942. (Dialect geography: Shilha and Tamazight.)

271. ——. Études de géographie linguistique en Kabylie. Paris, 1929. (Dialect geography of northern Algeria; text with maps.)

272. ——. La langue berbère au Sahara. Cah. Ch. Foucauld, 115–27, 1948. (Dialect geography with maps.)

273. ——. La langue berbère dans les territoires du Sud. Rev. afr. 85.62–71, 1941.

274. ——. Le nom de coq en berbère. Mélanges Linguistiques Vendryes, 41–54. Paris, 1925. (Dialect geography.)

275. ——. Le nom de l'étable en Kabylie et la flexion du participe. BSL 39.177–8, 1938.

276. ——. Le nom de la 'porte' en berbère. Mélanges René Basset 2.1–16, 1923. (Dialect geography.)

277. ——. Notes de linguistique berbère. Hespéris 3.69–81, 1923. (Dialect geography based on words for 'needle'.)

278, ——. Parlers touaregs du Soudan et du Niger. Bull. Com. et. hist. sc. A.O.F., 496–509, 1934, and 338–54, 1935. (An article on linguistic geography, with maps.)

279. ——. Presentation de cartes linguistiques berbères. GLECS, 42–3, 1934.

280. ——. Presentation des premières cartes d'un atlas linguistique en cours de realisation des parlers du Sahara et du Soudan. Proc. 4th Int. Congr. Ling., 177–82, 1936.

281. ——. Quatre études de linguistique berbère. JA, 161–291, 1940. (Linguistic geography with maps.)

282. ——. Situation actuelle des parlers berbères dans le departement d'Oran. Rev. afr. 76.999–1006, 1936. (With one map.)

283. ——. Sur le verbe berbère signifiant 'vivre'. Afrikanistische Studien Diedrich Westermann zum 80. Geburtstag gewidmet, 15-50. Berlin, 1955.

284. ——. Sur quelques termes berbères concernant la basse-cour. Mémorial Henri Basset 1.5–28. Paris, 1928. (An important article for lexicography and dialect geography.)

285. ——. Sur une singularité des parler berbères du sud marocain. GLECS, 29–31, 1949.

286. BEGUINOT, FRANCESCO. L'area linguistica berbera. Rome, 1914. (A linguistic map published by the Ministero delle Colonie; Scale 1:15,000,000.)

287. BERNARD, AUGUSTIN, and PAUL MOUSSARD. Arabophones et Berbèrophones au Maroc. Annls. Géogr. 33.267–82, 1924. (An important contribution to the definition of linguistic boundaries in Morocco.)

288. BRUNOT, LOUIS. L'élaboration du questionnaire destine à l'establissement de l'atlas linguistique du Maroc. Hespéris, vol. 19.

289. ——. Topographie dialectale de Rabat. Hespéris 10.7–13, 1930.

290. CLINE, WALTER. Berber dialects and Berber script. SJA 9/3.268–76, 1953.

291. DOUTTE, EDMOND, and E. F. GAUTIER. Enquête sur la dispersion de la langue berbère en Algérie. Algiers, 1913.

292. GALAND, LIONEL. Un type de frontière linguistique arabe et berbère dans le haouz de Marrakech. Orbis 3.22–3, 1954.

293. GAUTIER, E. F. Répartition de la langue berbère en Algérie. Annls. Geogr. 22.255–66, 1913.
294. GESLIN, M. Rapport sur le tableau des dialectes de l'Algérie et des contrées voisines. Paris, 1856.
295. GREENBERG, JOSEPH H. The classification of African languages. AmA 50. 24–30, 1948.
296. ——. Essays in linguistics. Chicago, 1957.
297. ——. Studies in African linguistic classification. New Haven, 1955. (Some attention is given to the Berber languages and their place in the Hamito-Semitic group. Greenberg's hypothesis is considered an important one, not only for Berber but for African linguistics generally.)
298. IBÁÑEZ, ESTEBAN. Mosaico linguistico de Marruecos español. Africa, 52–3, 1947.
299. LAOUST, EMILE. Rapport sur les études de dialectologie berbère de 1920 à 1924. Hespéris 4.455–9, 1924.
300. REINAUD, JOSEPH T. Rapport sur le tableau des dialectes de l'Algérie. Paris, 1856.
See also works by:
BASSET, ANDRÉ (See no. 512).
BEGUINOT, FRANCESCO (See no. 472).
GALAND, LIONEL (See no. 156).
IBÁÑEZ, ESTEBAN (See no. 494).

Berber Grammar

301. AHMAD IBN KHAUWAS. Notions succinctes de grammaire kabyle. Algiers, 1881. (A short description of the principal features of Kabyle.)
302. BASSET, ANDRÉ. Le système grammatical de berbère. Conf. Inst. Ling. Univ. Paris 2.15–24, 1934.
303. ——, and ANDRÉ PICARD. Éléments de grammaire berbère. Algiers, 1948. (This is intended to be a brief reference grammar of Kabyle, but is limited in scope, without texts.)
304. BASSET, RENÉ (ed.). Notes pour servir à un essai de grammaire touaregue, by Charles de Foucauld. Algiers, 1920.
305. ——. Observations grammaticales sur la grammaire touaregue et textes de la Tamahaq des Taitoq, by E. Masqueray. Paris, 1896–97. (No. 18 of the Bull. corr. afr.)
306. BEGUINOT, FRANCESCO. Il berbere Nefusi di Fassato. Rome, 1931. (This is a detailed reference grammar of the language spoken in western Libya. The data on which the analysis and description are based were collected from native informants of the region. In addition to the systematic descriptions of phono-

logy, morphology, and syntax, there are texts and glossaries, with footnotes. All texts are in roman characters, transcribed according to the system established in the phonological description at the beginning of the book.)

307. COHEN, MARCEL. A propos du classement de la forme d'habitude dans la grammaire berbère. GLECS 4.37–40, 1947. (Historical-comparative study.)

308. DELAPORTE, J. HONORAT. Grammaire de la langue berbère. Paris, c. 1840.

309. FOUCAULD, CHARLES DE. Notes pour servir à un essai de grammaire touaregue. Algiers, 1920. (Edited by R. Basset.)

310. FREEMAN, HENRY S. A grammatical sketch of the Temahug or Tuareg language. London, 1862. (This early description is brief, but it has furnished data for several later works by other scholars.)

311. GOURLIAU, ERNEST. Grammaire complète de la langue mzabite. Milan, 1898.

312. HANOTEAU, ADOLPHE. Essai de grammaire kabyle. Algiers, 1858. (A description of Zouave with texts, including poems. The book also contains a comparison of the vocabularies of Kabyle and Tuareg with the glossary given by Cailliaud for Siwa. At the end of the book there is a discussion of the Tuareg inscriptions with transcriptions and translations. 2nd edition was published in Paris, 1906.)

313. ——. Essai de grammaire de la langue Tamachek. Paris, 1860. (Grammatical description with texts and sample sentences. There is also a map showing the distribution of Berbers in Algeria. Samples of Tifinagh script are given with transcriptions and translations.)

314. ——. Rapport sur un essai de grammaire de la langue des Kabyles et sur un mémoire relatif à quelques inscriptions en caractères touaregs. Versailles, 1857.

315. HODGSON, WILLIAM B. Grammatical sketch and specimens of the Berber language. TAPS, vol. 1, 1829. (Includes four letters on Berber etymology.)

316. JOLY, ALEXANDRE. Le Chaouiya des Ouled-Sellem. Paris, 1913. (This short grammar with glossary was originally published in Rev. afr., vols. 55 and 56, 1911–12.)

317. LANFRY, J. Deux Notes Grammaticales sur le Berbère de Ghadames. Mémorial André Basset, 57–60. Paris, 1957. (A brief discussion of locatives and demonstratives.)

318. MASQUERAY, EMILE. Observations grammaticales sur la grammaire touaregue et textes de la tamahaq des taitog. Paris, 1896. (This work was edited by R. Basset and Gaudefroy-Demombynes and published posthumously. The grammatical description is short, but there are many texts. Each text is in Tuwareg script with roman transcription and translation into French. No. 18 of Bull. corr. afr.)

319. MERCIER, GUSTAVE. Le chaouia de l'Aures. Paris, 1896. (Grammatical description with texts.)

320. NEWMAN, FRANCIS W. A grammar of the Berber language. WZKM 6.245–336, 1845.

321. ——. Outline of the Kabail grammar. W. Engl. Jl. Sci. Lit., 1836.

322. NOUR BEN SI LOUNIS and MOKA MESSAOUD BEN YAHIA. Grammaire mozabite. Algiers, 1897.
323. OSTOYA-DELMAS, S. Notes préliminaires l'étude des parlers de l'arrondissement de Phillipeville. Rev. afr. 82.60–83, 1938. (Grammatical sketch with maps.)
324. PICARD, ANDRÉ. De quelques faits de stylistique dans le parler berbère des Irjen. Algiers, 1960. (No. 19 of AnnIEO. A study of expressive language in Kabyle.)
325. ——, and A. BASSET. Éléments de grammaire berbère. Algiers, 1948. (A detailed description of the Kabyle dialect of Irjen.)
326. PROVOTELLE, ——. Étude sur la Tamazir't ou Zenatia de Qalaat es - Sened. Paris, 1911. (Grammar of the Tunisian dialect with texts in Arabic and roman transcriptions, translations, and glossary. No. 46 of Bull. corr. afr.)
327. REINAUD, JOSEPH T. Rapport sur en essai de grammaire de la langue des Kabyles et sur un mémoire relatif à quelques inscriptions en caractères Touaregs. Revue de l'orient et de l'Algérie [et des colonies] 6.162, 1858. (A review of Hanoteau's grammar, no. 312, with some new data.)
328. RENISIO, AMIDEE. Étude sur les dialectes berbères des Beni Iznassen, du Rif et des Senhaja de Srair. Paris, 1932. (No. 22 of (Publ) IHEM. This is a reference grammar of three dialects of northern Morocco and Algeria accompanied by transcriptions of ethnographic texts, fables, and poems with translations. There are also glossaries, Berber to French and French to Berber.)
329. ROUX, ARSENE. L'épreuve de grammaire au Brevet de berbère. Rabat, 1949.
330. SARRIONANDIA, PEDRO. Contestacion de P. Pedro H. Sarrionandia al Sr. René Basset. Tangiers, 1907. (A reply to Basset's review of Sarrionandia's grammar of Riff.)
331. ——. Gramatica de la lengua rifena. Tangiers, 1906. (A reference grammar intended for use as a textbook. Complete descriptions of phonology, morphology, and syntax are given, and there are translation exercises that indicate clearly the purpose of the book. Second edition, 1925.)
332. STUMME, HANS. Handbuch des Schilhischen von Tazerwalt. Leipzig, 1899. (A reference grammar of Shilha with descriptions of phonology, morphology, and syntax. Illustrative texts and dialogs are included, with glossary.)
333. VENTURE DE PARADIS, JEAN MICHEL DE. Grammaire et dictionnaire abréges de la langue berbère. Paris, 1844. (This is one of the earliest grammars of the Berber dialects. Although the author does not define the dialect exactly, it seems that much of his material has been taken from Kabyle and Tamazight. In the glossary, he does indicate that some words are restricted geographically. The work is of great historical value, not only because of the data from the languages but also because the introduction is a clear statement of European attitudes toward the Berber languages.)
334. WARDEN, ——. Esquisse sur le système grammatical de la langue berbère. Paris, 1836. (This description is very much like that of Venture de Paradis. The material is more restricted to dialects spoken in Algeria, however.)

See also works by:

ABES, M. (See no. 521).
BARTHÉ, ALBERT (See no. 524).
BASSET, RENÉ (See nos. 218, 219, 424, 526).
CALASSANTI-MOTYLINSKI, G. A. DE (See nos. 69, 70, 475).
CREUSAT, JEAN BAPTISTE (See no. 481).
DEPONT, OCTAVE (See no. 531).
DESTAING, EDMOND (See no. 80).
DU PONCEAU, PETER S. (See no. 86).
JUSTINARD, LÉOPOLD (See no. 533).
LAOUST, EMILE (See nos. 102, 103, 105, 690).
LOUBIGNAC, V (See no. 108).
ROCHEMONTEIX, M. DE (See no. 236).

Berber Phonology

335. APPLEGATE, JOSEPH R. Some phonological rules in Shilha. Rpt. 10th Ann. Rnd. Tble. Mtg. Ling. Lang. Stud., Georgetown University Monograph Series on Languages and Linguistics 12.37–42, 1959. (An attempt is made to correlate certain phonological phenomena with specific types of morpheme boundaries.)
336. BASSET, ANDRÉ. A propos d'un dérivé à nasale berbère. AnnIEO, 110–16, 1937.
337. ——. A propos de l'article de Schuchardt sur la rupture d'hiatus en berbère. Act. XIX congr. intern. orient., 111–13, 1938. (An addition to description of intervocalic 'y'.)
338. ——. Autour de E en Kabylie. GLECS 2.50, 1936.
339. ——. Réduction de diphtongue et constance de la voyelle initiale en berbère. GLECS 5.51–2, 1950.
340. ——. Sur la voyelle initiale en berbère. Rev. afr. 86.82–8, 1945.
341. ——. Le système phonologique du berbère. GLECS 4. 33–6, 1946.)
342. ——. Voyelle initiale du nom berbère. JA, 456, 1943–45.
343. BEGUINOT, FRANCESCO. Saggio di fonetica del Berbero Nefusi di Fassato. Rc. Accademia dei Lincei, ser. 6, vol. 1, no. 6, 1925. (This work was also published separately, and it is the preliminary work for some of the conclusions found in the reference grammar, no. 306.)
344. ——. Sul trattamento delle consonanti *b*, *v*, *f* in berbero. Riv. Accademia dei Lincei 33.186–99, 1924.
345. BRONZI, PIETRO. Frammento di fonologia berbera. Bologne, 1919.
346. FÉVRIER, J. G. La prononciation punique des noms propres latins en *-us* et en *-ius*. JA, 465–71, 1953.
347. MARCY, GEORGES. Note sur l'instabilité dialectale du timbre vocalique berbère et la conjugaison des verbes du type 'neg'. Hespéris 16.139–50, 1933.

348. MITCHELL, T. F. Long consonants in phonology and phonetics. Studies in linguistic analysis, 182–205. Oxford, 1957. (Consideration of special phonological problems in Berber.)

349. SCHUCHARDT, HUGO E. M. Berberische Hiatustilgung. Sitzungsberichte der K. Akademie der Wissenschaften in Wien, vol. 182, 1916.

350. VYCICHL, WERNER. L'article défini du berbère. Mémorial André Basset, 139–46. Paris, 1957. (Phonological patterns of noun stems are correlated with a few syntactic patterns, and on this basis the development of noun forms from sequences of article and stem is postulated.)

351. ——. Der Umlaut im Berberischen des Djebel Nefusa in Tripolitanien. AION-L 6.145–52, 1954.

See also works by:

BASSET, ANDRÉ (See nos. 41, 266, 361, 599).
BASSET, RENÉ (See no. 216).
BEGUINOT, FRANCESCO (See nos. 134, 305).
BIARNAY, S. (See nos. 64, 66).
GALAND, LIONEL (See no. 156).
GREENBERG, JOSEPH H. (See no. 227).
MITCHELL, T. F. (See no. 386).
PRASSE, KARL (See nos. 117, 389).
SARRIONANDIA, PEDRO (See no. 331).
STUMME, HANS (See no. 332).
WESTERMARCK, E. (See no. 397).

Berber Morphology

352. BASSET, ANDRÉ. Autour d'une racine berbère. AnnIEO 1.73–6, 1934–35.

353. ——. Détermination et indétermination du nom en berbère. GLECS 5.95–6, 1951. (Description of noun allomorphs.)

354. ——. La langue berbère. Morphologie. Le verbe. Paris, 1929. (An attempt to classify the verbs of Berber languages by description of stem patterns.)

355. ——. 'n' devant complément de nom en berbère. GLECS 7.1–5, 1954.

356. ——. Note sur l'élément démonstratif en berbère. BSL 34.213–15, 1933.

357. ——. Note sur l'état d'annexion en berbère. BSL 33.173–4, 1932. (This should be considered with no. 61.)

358. ——. Notes sur le genre dans le verbe et dans le nom en berbère. Cinquantenaire de la Faculté des Lettres d'Alger, 62–71, 1932.

359. ——. Un pluriel devenu singuliér en berbère. GLECS, 19, 1938.

360. ——. Problème verbal dans le parler berbère de Siwa. Mélanges Maspero 3. 155–9. Cairo, 1935.

361. ——. Six notes de linguistique berbère. AnnIEO 5.16–40, 1939–41. (Short articles on morphology and phonology.)
362. ——. Sur berbère Ait Sadden *it(t)h* 'parce que' et la formation du système conjonctif. GLECS 6.64, 1954.
363. ——. Sur l'évolution actuelle du prétérit négatif en berbère. GLECS 6.25–6, 1952.
364. ——. Sur la structure et la terminologie du verbe berbère. JA, 442, 1943–45.
365. ——. Sur le participe berbère. GLECS 5.34–6, 1949.
366. ——. Sur le participe dans le parler berbère d'Ait Sadden. JA, 393–6, 1954.
367. ——. Sur le pluriel nominal berbère. Rev. afr. 86.255–60, 1942.
368. ——. Sur un thème berbère d'aoriste intensif insolite. GLECS 6.2, 1951.
369. BASSET, RENÉ. Index des principales racines des mots berbères. Muséon 12.5–16, 1893. (This article provides a basis for later historical and comparative studies.)
370. DALLET, JEAN-MARIE. Le Verbe Kabyle. Algiers, 1953. (Careful listing and classification of verbs, roman transcription, with French equivalents given. The classification is based on morphological criteria, and illustrative sentences are supplied. This is volume 1 of a series of works, and the only volume that has appeared.)
371. DESTAING, EDMOND. Note sur la conjugaison des verbes de forme C^1 and C^2. Mémoires, Société de Linguistique de Paris, 21.139–48, 1919.
372. ——. Note sur le pronom démonstratif en berbère. BSL 22.186–200, 1921.
373. ——. Notes sur le verbe passif. GLECS, vol. 2, 1935.
374. ——. Les particules *d* et *n* en berbère. GLECS, vol. 2, 1934. (Morphological analysis.)
375. ——. Remarques sur le genre grammatical de quelques noms dans le parler arabe des Chleuhs du Sous. Mélanges Gaudefroy-Demombynes, 173–88. Cairo, 1937. (An attempt to correlate Arabic and Berber gender markers.)
376. ——. Sur l'expression dans le verbe berbère de l'irréel par l'emploi de la forme dite d'habitude. BSL, vol. 35, 1935.
377. ——. Sur les pronoms *walli, wanna*. GLECS, vol. 2, 1937.
378. GALAND, LIONEL. État et procès. Hespéris 42.245–51, 1955. (This article deals with a sub-class of verbs in Berber, the 'verbs of quality', which have special morphological and syntactic characteristics.)
379. MARCY, GEORGES. Essai d'une théorie générale de la morphologie berbère. Hespéris 12.50–89, 177–203, 1931.
380. ——. Fonctions originales dans les parlers berbères des pronoms démonstratifs-relatifs. BSL 40.151–73, 1939.
381. ——. Note sur le pronom relatif-démonstratif en berbère. GLECS, vol. 1, 1934.
382. ——. Note sur le pronom relatif sujet et pseudo-participe dans les parlers berbères. BSL 37.45–57, 1936.

383. ——. Sur l'alternance 'a/ad' dans le pronom relatif commun en berbère du Sous. BSL 34.203–12, 1933.
384. MITCHELL, T. F. Particle-noun complexes in a Berber dialect. BSOAS, vol. 15, pt. 2, 1953. (Morphology and syntax of nouns in Zuara, dialect of Tripolitania.)
385. ——. Particle-noun complexes in a Berber dialect (Zuara). BSOAS 15/2.375–90, 1953. (A detailed study of noun morphology.)
386. ——. Some properties of Zuara nouns. Mémorial André Basset, 83–96. Paris, 1957. (Morphophonological description.)
387. PICARD, ANDRÉ. Du prétérit intensif en berbère. Mémorial André Basset, 107–20. Paris, 1957. (Comparison of Tuareg and Kabyle verb systems.)
388. PRASSE, KARL G. Analyse semantique des verbes dérivés par préfixe en touareg. AcOr XXIV/3–4.147–60, 1959.
389. ——. Le problème berbère des radicales faibles. Mémorial André Basset, 121–30. Paris, 1957. (Morphophonology of Tuareg. The data are taken from Foucauld's dictionary.)
390. ——. Les affixes personnels du verbe berbère (Touareg). AcOr XXVII/1–2, 1963.
391. SCHUCHARDT, HUGO E. M. Ein auffallender Gebrauch des Genetivs im Berberischen. Z. Sem. verw. Geb. 1.227–9, 1922.
392. ——. Zu berberischen Substantiven auf *-im*. WZKM 26.163–70, 1912.
393. STUMME, HANS. Eine sonderbare Anwendung von Akkusativkonfixen im Berberischen. Festschrift Meinhof, 81–87. Hamburg, 1927. (Morphology and syntax of pronouns in Shilha and Kabyle.)
394. VYCICHL, WERNER. Das berberische Perfekt. RSO 27.74–83, 1952.
395. ——. Diminutiv and Augmentativ im Berberischen. ZDMG 111.243–53, 1961.
396. ——. Die Nisbe-Formationem im Berberischen. AION-L 4.111–17, 1952.
397. WESTERMARCK, E. Nomina im status absolutus und status annexus in der südmarokkanischen Berbersprache. Öfers. Fins. Vet. Soc. Förh., vol. 56, no. 3, 1913. (Morphophonemic changes in Shilha.)
398. ZYHLARZ, ERNST. Ältere und jüngere Pluralbildung im Berberischen. ZES 22.1–15, 1935.

See also works by:

BASSET, ANDRÉ (See nos. 41, 131, 215, 275, 340, 342, 401, 417).
BASSET, RENÉ (See no. 423).
BEGUINOT, FRANCESCO (See no. 306).
BIARNAY, S. (See no. 64).
COHEN, MARCEL (See nos. 147, 307).
DESTAING, EDMOND (See no. 225).
GUAY, J. (See no. 157).
SARRIONANDIA, PEDRO (See no. 331).
SCHUCHARDT, H. E. M (See no. 121).
STUMME, HANS (See no. 332).
VYCICHL, WERNER (See no. 350).

Berber Syntax

399. BASSET, ANDRÉ. Entretiens sur la détermination et indétermination: berbère. GLECS 2.52, 1936.
400. ——. La proposition sans verbe en berbère. GLECS 4.90–2, 1948.
401. ——. Sur l'anticipation en berbère. Mélanges William Marcais, 17–27. Paris, 1950. (A description is given of rules for determining the positions of verbal affixes.)
402. ——. Sur la proposition indépendante et la proposition relative en berbère. GLECS 4.30–2, 1946.
403. DALLET, JEAN-MARIE. Notes détachées pour servir à l'étude de la syntaxe d'un parler. Mémorial André Basset, 17–26. Paris, 1957. (Preliminary study of expressive language in the dialect of Tizi-Ouzou.)
404. DESTAING, EDMOND. Remarques sur la qualification en Tachelhit du Sous. GLECS, vol. 3, 1938.
405. GALAND, LIONEL. Un cas particulier de phrase non verbale. Mémorial André Basset, 27–37. Paris, 1957. (This article deals with the syntax of certain sentence types in the Berber languages. The role of the initial constituent is considered in declarative and interrogative sentences. The description is based on data from the Moroccan languages, for the most part.)
406. JOHNSON, M. JEANETTE. Syntactic structures of Tamazight, 1966. (Doctoral dissertation using transformation model. In manuscript.)
407. LAOUST-CHANTREAUX, G. Sur l'emploi du démonstratif *i*. Mémorial André Basset, 61–8. Paris, 1957. (Syntax of a Kabyle dialect.)
408. MARCY, GEORGES. Observations sur le relatif futur en Touareg Ahaggar. BSL 41.129–33, 1941.
409. PELLAT, CHARLES. *am* et *zun*(*d*) 'comme' en berbère. Mémorial André Basset, 97–105. Paris, 1957. (Syntactic classification of morphemes of comparison in the Berber languages. The study is based on data obtained from published descriptions of several Berber languages.)
410. ROUX, ARSÈNE. Initiation au thème berbère. Rabat, 1950.

See also works by:

BASSET, ANDRÉ (See no. 41).
BEGUINOT, FRANCESCO (See no. 306).
BIARNAY, S. (See no. 64).
GALAND, LIONEL (See no. 378).
MITCHELL, T. F. (See no. 384).
PICARD AND BASSET (See no. 170).
SARRIONANDIA, PEDRO (See no. 331).
STUMME, HANS (See nos. 332,393).
VYCICHL, WERNER (See no. 350).
WESTERMARCK, E. (See no. 397).

Berber Lexicography

411. ASPINION, ROBERT. Contribution à l'étude du droit coutumier berbère marocain. Casablanca, 1937. (This contains valuable lexical information.)
412. BASSET, ANDRÉ. 'Après midi' en berbère. BSL 50.181–7, 1955.
413. ——. Au sujet de berbère (*t*) *ahyam* (*t*)... GLECS 3.91–2, 1940.
414. ——. Berbère *inigi* 'témoin'. GLECS 2.20, 1935.
415. ——. Berbère *isnin* 'tous les deux'. GLECS 4.19–20, 1946.
416. ——. 'maintenant' en berbère. BSL 50.221–30, 1954.
417. ——. Noms de parenté en berbère. GLECS 6.27–30, 1953.
418. ——. Sur berbère YIR 'mauvais' chez les Irjen. Rev. afr. 93.291–313, 1949. (Extensive study of a lexical item in Kabyle, with A. Picard.)
419. ——. *Tidma*, terme kabyle pour désigner les femmes. JA, 176, 1946–47.
420. BASSET, RENÉ. Les mots arabes passés en berbère. Orientalische Studien Theodor Nöldeke Gewidmet 1.439–43, 1906. (Lexicography and morphology.)
421. ——. Les noms berbères des plantes dans le Traité des simples d'Ibn el Beïter. Giornale della Societa Asiatica Italiana 12.53–66, 1899.
422. ——. Le nom de chameau chez les Berbères. Act. Congr. Intern. Orient., 69–82, 1905.
423. ——. Les noms des métaux et des couleurs en berbère. Mémoires, Société de Linguistique de Paris 9.58–92, 1895. (This is a comparative study of various lexical items in the Berber languages preceded by a short description of the morphology of the sub-class of verbs to which adjective-like forms belong. There is also a comment on an article by von Gabelentz in which an attempt had been made to show a relationship between the Berber languages and Basque. On the basis of the data presented in his own study, Basset rejects the hypothesis of von Gabelentz.)
424. ——. Notes de lexicographie berbère. JA 8/1.281–342, 1883. (This is the first of a series of articles on various Berber dialects. The dialects considered are those of the Rif, Djerba, Ghat, and Kel Qui. Texts and grammatical notes are given.
425. ——. Notes de lexicographie berbère. JA 8/4.518–56, 1884. (The second of this series of articles deals with a dialect of northern Algeria.)
426. ——. Notes de lexicographie berbère. JA 8/5.148–219, 1885. (A continuation of the preceding article on the dialect of Beni Menacer.)
427. ——. Notes de lexicographie berbère. JA 8/6.302–71, 1885. (This article is a study of the dialect spoken in the vicinity of Oran.)
428. ——. Notes de lexicographie berbère. JA, ser. 8, vol. 7, 1886. (A study of the dialect of Figuig.)
429. ——. Notes de lexicographie berbère. JA 8/10.365–464, 1887. (In addition to the dialects of Gourara and Mzab, consideration is given to some of the Tuareg dialects.)

430. BERTHOLON, LUCIEN J. Note sur les noms des Ibères, Berbères, et Africains. Bulletin, Société d'anthropologie de Paris, 6.145–9, 1905.
431. BEURMANN, CARL MORITZ VON. Brief des Herrn von Beurmann an Prof. Fleischer. ZDMG 16.563–5, 1862. (This letter contains a short list of lexical items from the dialect of Augila.)
432. BOSSOUTROT, A. Vocabulaire berbère ancien. Revue tunisienne 7.489–507, 1900. (A list of items, Jebel Nefusi dialect, obtained from an Arabic text, Al-Mudawwanah of Ibn Ghanim.)
433. BOUTEMENE, Y. A propos des noms du fouet en touareg. Bulletin des études arabes 8.73–4, 1942.
434. BRUNOT, LOUIS. Noms de vêtements masculins à Rabat. Mélanges René Basset. Paris, 1923.
435. ——. Notes lexicologiques sur le vocabulaire maritime de Rabat et Salé. Paris, 1920. (Contains some Berber lexical items. This is no. 6 of the series (Publ.) IHEM.)
436. CALASSANTI-MOTYLINSKI, G. A. DE. Le nom berbère de Dieu chez les Abadhites. Rev. afr. 49.141–8, 1905.
437. CAPOT-REY, R. and MARCAIS, P. La charrue au Sahara. Travaux de l'Institut des Recherches sahariennes, vol. 9. (This article includes a map of the area, illustrations and some useful lexical data.)
438. CLAUZEL, J. Des noms Songay dans l'Ahaggar. JAfrL 7/1.43–4, 1962.
439. COLIN, GEORGES S. Noms d'artisans et de commerçants à Marrakech. Hespéris 12.229–40, 1931.
440. ——. Notes de dialectologie arabe: observations sur un vocabulaire maritime berbère. Hespéris 4.175–9, 1924.
441. CORSO, RAFFAELE. Varianti arabo-berbere delle docidi parole della verità. AION-L 2.3–15, 1930.
442. DESTAING, EDMOND. Étude sur la tachelhit du Sous. Paris, 1920. (Vol. 7 of Bibliothèque de l'École des langues orientales vivantes. Chiefly lexical.)
443. ——. Interdictions de vocabulaire en berbère. Mélanges René Basset, 2.177–277. Paris, 1925. (This is a general essay on taboos in languages of the Berbers. There is a text in Shilha which begins with general statements about language and includes statements about specific taboo words and substitutions. The text was translated by Destaing, and it is very useful because it presents the native speaker's conception of his language. The article includes bibliographical information and ends with statements about other languages based on data obtained from the sources cited in the bibliography.)
444. FOUREAU, FERNAND. Essai de catalogue des noms arabes et berbères de quelques plantes, arbustes et arbres algériens et sahariens. Paris, 1896.
445. HANOTEAU, ADOLPHE. Lettre à M. Reinaud sur les noms de nombre en berbère. JA, vol. 2, 1860.

446. JUNGFER, J., and PAJARES, A. MARTÍNEZ. Estudio sobre appellidos y nombres de lugar Hispano-Marroquies. Madrid, 1918.

447. LAOUST, EMILE. Des noms berbères de l'ogre et l'ogresse. Hespéris 34.253–65, 1947.

448. LAPERRINE, ——. Les noms des années chez les Touareg du Ahaggar de 1875 à 1907. Rev. afr. 53.153–8, 1909.

449. ——. Noms donnés par les Touareg Ahaggar aux diverses années de 1860 à 1874. Rev. afr. 54.191–4, 1910.

450. LÉVI-PROVENÇAL, E. Une liste de surnoms populaires des tribus djebalah. Archs. Berb., vol. 2, 1915.

451. MAIRE, ——. Flore de l'Afrique du Nord. Paris, 1952. (Includes some Berber plant names.)

452. MARCY, GEORGES. À propos de berbère tafaska. Proc. XIXe Congr. Intern. Orient., 145–8, 1935.

453. ——. Notes linguistiques relatives à la terminologie marocaine indigène des vents. Mémoires, Société des sciences naturelles du Maroc 41.90–7, 1935.

454. MERCIER, GUSTAVE: Le noms des plantes en dialecte chaouia. Act. XIVe Congr. Intern. Orient. 2.79–82, 1906.

455. MONTEIL, VINCENT. Contribution à l'étude de la faune du Sahara occidental. Paris, 1951. (Index of animals found in southern Morocco, Rio de Oro, Mauritania, Senegal with names in Berber as well as other languages of the area. Zoological classification, bibliography, illustrations.)

456. ——. Contribution à l'étude de la flore du Sahara occidental. Paris, 1950. (Prepared in collaboration with Charles Sauvage. The plan of this book is the same as that of the preceding.)

457. ——. Contribution à l'étude de la flore du Sahara occidental, vol. 2. Paris, 1953. (Continuation of no. 456. The three items above are nos. 9, 5, and 6 of the series: (Notes Doc.) IHEM.)

458. PARADISI, UMBERTO. El Fógăha oasi berberofona del Fezzân. RSO XXXVI/3–4. 293–302. Rome, 1961.

459. PRASSE, KARL G. Les relations de sexe d'âge et de sang. Enquête sur la terminologie dans le dialecte berbère des Ayt-Sadden. AcOr XXII/3–4.119–41, 1957.

460. ——. L'origine du mot *amāziy*. AcOr XXXIII/3–4.197–200, 1959.

461. ROHLFS, GERHARD. Die Zahlzeichen der Rhadamser. Ausland 29.695–6, 1872.

462. ROUX, ARSÈNE. Quelques argots arabes et berbères du Maroc. IIe Congr. Féd. Soc. sav. Afr. Nd. 2/2.1067–88. Algiers, 1936.

463. SÁNCHEZ, PÉREZ A. El nombre bereber de Zamora. Africa, 11–13, September, 1943.

464. SCHIRMER, H. De nomine et genere populorum qui berberi vulgo dicuntur. Paris, 1892.

465. SCHUCHARDT, HUGO E. M. Die romanischen Lehnwörter im Berberischen. Sitzungsberichte der K. Akademie Wissenschaften in Wien, vol. 188, 1918.

466. TROTTER, A. Flore economica della Libia: Rome, 1915. (Includes plant names in Berber.)
467. WÖLFEL, DOMINIK J. Les noms de nombre dans le parler Guanche des Iles Canaries. Hespéris 41.47–79, 1954.
See also works by:
BASSET, ANDRÉ (See nos. 41, 274, 276, 277, 283, 284).
BEGUINOT, FRANCESCO (See nos. 135, 220).
BERNARD, A (See no. 741).
BIARNAY, S. (See no. 64).
CHANTRÉAUX, GERMAINE (See no. 750).
COHEN, MARCEL (See no. 146).
COLIN, GEORGES S. (See no. 151).
DELAYE, THÉOPHILE JEAN (See no. 756).
GRIMME, HUBERT (See no. 94).
KLINGENHEBEN, AUGUST (See no. 98).
LAOUST, EMILE (See nos. 161, 162, 776).
MARCY, G. (See nos. 163, 164).
MERCIER, GUSTAVE (See no. 167).
MINUTÖLI, HEINRICH (See no. 206).
MONTAGNE, ROBERT (See no. 789).
NICHOLAS, FRANCIS (See nos. 115, 793).
PEYSONNEL, JEAN A. (See no. 207).
PICARD and BASSET (See no. 170).
SARNELLI, T. (See nos. 175, 176).
SCHUCHARDT, H. E. M. (See no. 240).

Berber Glossaries

468. APPOGGI, ——. Glossario dei nomi e delle terminologi più in uso nei paesi abitati dai touareg degli Azgher. Tripoli, 1933.
469. BASSET, ANDRÉ. La place du dictionnaire touareg-français du P. de Foucauld dans les études berbères. JA, 548, 1952.
470. ——. Sur une confusion de verbes dans le dictionnaire du P. de Foucauld. Travaux de l'Institut des Recherches sahariennes 6.3–7, 1950.
471. BASSET, RENÉ (ed.). Dictionnarie abrégé touareg-français, by Charles de Foucauld. Algiers, 1918–20.
472. BEGUINOT, FRANCESCO. Proposition en vue d'éditer un dictionnaire comparé des dialectes de la langue berbère. Paris, 1931. (Publication of the International Institute of African Languages and Cultures. This is a systematic presentation of the problems involved in defining linguistic boundaries in North Africa.)

473. BERQUE, J. Un glossaire notarial arabo-chleuh du Deren. Rev. afr. 94.357–98, 1950. (An examination of an 18th century manuscript.)
474. BROSSELARD, CHARLES, et al. Dictionnarie français-berbère. Paris, 1844. (This dictionary of Kabyle was prepared for the Ministry of War. It is historically important because of the data contained and because it was used as a model for later bilingual dictionaries.)
475. CALASSANTI-MOTYLINSKI, G. A. DE. Grammaire dialogues et dictionnaire touaregs. Algiers, 1908. (This work was edited by René Basset and published posthumously.)
476. CAPOT-REY, R., et al. Un glossaire des termes géographiques arabo-berbères. Bull. Liais. sahar., vols. 5–9, 1954–58. (An attempt to catalogue local geographical terminology. The results were presented in a series of articles, and A. Picard and P. Marcais were among the contributors.)
477. CID KAOUI, S. Dictionnaire français-tachelh'it et tamazight. Paris, 1907.
478. ——. Dictionnaire français-tamaheq. Algiers, 1894.
479. ——. Dictionnaire pratique tamaheq-français. Algiers, 1900.
480. COLIN, GEORGES S., and H. RENAUD. Ibn-al-h'acha. Rabat, 1941. (A glossary of Berber plant names obtained from a mediaeval Arabic manuscript.)
481. CREUSAT, JEAN BAPTISTE. Essai de dictionnaire français-kabyle. Algiers, 1873. (The dictionary is preceded by a brief outline of the grammar and five folktales in roman transcription with translations. There is also a reference to two translations from French to Kabyle: Catéchisme du diocèse d'Alger and Épitres et Évangiles des dimanches et fêtes de l'année. The dialect is Zuave from Djurdjura.)
482. CROS, LOUIS. Le Maroc pour tous. Paris, 1918. (The book includes "Dictionnaire colonial pratique", a short glossary.)
483. DELAPORTE, J. HONORAT. Vocabulaire berbère. JA 3/1.97–122, 1836.
484. ——. Vocabulaire berbère-français. Paris, 1836. (The four works of Delaporte are of historical value.)
485. DESTAING, EDMOND. Dictionnaire français-berbère. Algiers, 1914. (No. 49 of Bull. corr. afr. This dictionary may be considered a supplement to no. 80, above.)
486. FOUCAULD, CHARLES DE. Dictionnaire abrégé touareg-français. Algiers, 1918–20. (Dialect of Ahaggar. The work was edited by R. Basset and published posthumously. 2 vols.)
487. ——. Dictionnaire touareg-français. Paris, 1951–52. (Complete dictionary, dialect of Ahaggar, prepared from notes. This work in four volumes is an important item in Berber linguistics.)
488. ——. Dictionnaire abrégé touareg-français des noms propres. Paris, 1940.
489. GRIMAL DE GUIRAUDON, THOMAS. Dyebayli Vocabulary, from an Unpublished MS. A.D. 1831. JRAS, 669–98, 1893. (A short glossary from Jebel Nefusi.)
490. HUYGHE, G. Dictionnaire chaouia-arabe-kabyle-français. Algiers, 1907.

491. ——. Dictionnaire français-chaouia. Algiers, 1906.
492. ——. Dictionnaire français-kabyle. Paris.
493. ——. Dictionnaire kabyle-français. Paris, 1901. (The first item in this series of dictionaries, no. 490, is an attempt to clarify dialectal distinctions and show the influence of Arabic. Zouave and Kabyle forms are given with the Arabic form between the two. Berber forms are in roman characters.)
494. IBÁÑEZ, ESTEBAN. Diccionario español-baamarani. Madrid, 1954. (Includes introduction on structural characteristics of the language, distribution, with map.)
495. ——. Diccionario español-rifeño. Madrid, 1944.
496. ——. Diccionario español-senhayi. Madrid, 1959. (Introduction with map and general comments on contrasts between Senhaji and Riff.)
497. ——. Diccionario rifeño-español. Madrid, 1949. (In the introduction there is a summary of Berber language studies and an extensive bibliography in addition to the notes on distribution and characteristics of the language.)
498. JORDAN, ANTOINE. Dictionnaire berbère-français. Rabat, 1934. (Shilha.)
499. KOENIG, E. Vocabulaires appartenant à diverses contrées de l'Afrique. Paris, 1839. (Berber items are included.)
500. MASQUERAY, EMILE. Dictionnaire français-touareg. Algiers, 1893–95. (No. 11 of Bull. corr. afr.)
501. MEYERHOF, MAX. Un glossaire de matière médicale de Maîmonide. Mélanges Maspero, Cairo, 1940. (Contains an index of Berber botanical terms.)
502. MÜLLER, ——. Vocabulaire de la langue des habitants d'Audjela. Paris, 1827–29. (Glossary in the dialect of Cyrenaica included as an appendix to Pacho's travel journal; see 507 below.)
503. NEWMAN, FRANCIS W. Kabail vocabulary supplemented by the aid of a new source. London, 1887. (Kabyle glossary with items from travel journals and texts.)
504. ——. Lybian vocabulary. London, 1882. (An attempt to reconstruct a proto-language by comparison of the vocabularies of Kabyle, Shilha, Ghadames, and Tuareg.)
505. ——. Wörterbuch des Dialektes der Auelimmiden. Gotha, 1857. (This glossary was published as a supplement to volume 5 of Barth's Reisen und Entdeckungen in Nord- und Central Afrika.)
506. OLIVIER, M. G. Dictionnaire françaíse-kabyle. Le Puy, 1878. (All entries in roman transcription.)
507. PACHO, RAYMOND. Relation d'un voyage dans la Marmarique, la Cyreniaique et les Oasis d'Audjelah et de Maradeh. Paris, 1827–29. (Journal of an expedition during 1824–25. The journal includes Müller's glossary, no. 502 above.)
508. REINAUD, JOSEPH T. Notices sur les dictionnaires géographiques arabes et sur le système primitif de la numération chez les peuples de race berbère. Paris, 1861.
509. RENAUD, H., and G. S. COLIN. Tuhfat al-ahbab. Paris, 1934. (A glossary of

Moroccan medical terminology in which is included a list of Berber botanical terms.)

510. STUMME, HANS. Eine Sammlung über den berberischen Dialekt der Oase Siwe. Verhandlung der Kaiserliche Sächsische Akademie der Wissenschaften zu Leipzig 66.91–109, 1914. (A comparison of glossaries obtained from travel journals. The lists made by Hornemann and Scholz, which were not used by Basset in no. 216, are included.)

511. TRABUT, LOUIS. Répertoire des noms indigènes des plantes spontanées cultivées et utilisées dans le Nord de l'Afrique. Algiers, 1935. (A glossary of botanical terms, some of which are in Berber dialects.)

See also works by:

ABÈS, M. (See no. 521).
BASSET, RENÉ (See nos. 2, 218, 219, 526, 653, 658).
BEGUINOT, FRANCESCO (See no. 306).
BIARNAY, S. (See nos. 64, 65, 66, 745).
BOULIFA, SI AMMAR BEN SAID (See nos. 529, 530).
BOURILLY, J. (See no. 747).
CAILLIAUD, FRÉDÉRIC (See no. 185).
CALASSANTI-MOTYLINSKI, G. A. DE (See no. 69).
DALLET, JEAN-MARIE (See no. 370).
DEPONT, OCTAVE (See no. 531).
DESTAING, EDMOND (See no. 675).
GRABERG, JACOB OF HEMSÖ (See no. 93).
HANOTEAU, ADOLPHE (See no. 312).
HOOKER, JOSEPH D. (See no. 196).
JACKSON, JAMES (See no. 201).
JOLY, ALEXANDER (See no. 316).
JUSTINARD, LÉOPOLD (See no. 533).
LANGLÈS, LOUIS (See no. 99).
LAOUST, EMILE (See nos. 102, 105, 535, 536),
MERCIER, H. (See no. 697).
PELLAT, CHARLES (See no. 706).
PHARAON, F., and J. PHARAON (See no. 795).
PROVOTELLE, —— (See no. 326).
RENISIO, A. (See no. 328).
RICHARDSON, JAMES (See nos. 553, 709).
SCHOLZ, JOHANN M. A. (See no. 210).
SHAW, THOMAS (See no. 211).
STUMME, HANS (See no. 332).
VENTURE DE PARADIS (See no. 333).
WALKER, W. S. (See no. 127).

Berber Toponymy

512. BASSET, ANDRÉ. Sur la toponymie berbère et spécialement sur la toponymie Chaouia Ait Frah. Onomastica, 123–6, 1948. (Linguistic geography of northern Algeria.)
513. BEGUINOT, FRANCESCO. Per gli studi di toponomastica libico berbera. Att. XI Congr. Geogr. Ital. 3.243–7. Naples, 1930.
514. LAOUST, EMILE. Contribution à une étude de la toponymie du Haut Atlas. REIsl 2.201–312; 4.27–73, 1939–40. (Based on the maps of Jean Dresch.)
515. MERCIER, GUSTAVE. Étude sur la toponymie berbère de la region de l'Aures. Act. XIe Congr. Intern. Orient., 173–207, 1897.
516. MONTEIL, VINCENT. La part du berbère dans la toponymie du Sahara maure. Act. IIIe Congr. Topon. Anthropon., 478–9. 1951.
517. ——. Le part du berbère dans la toponymie du Sahara maure. Notes africaines 45.21, 1950.
518. PICARD, ANDRÉ. Compléments à la toponymie berbère. Onomastica 2.127–32, 1948. (With maps.)

See also works by:

BEGUINOT, FRANCESCO (See no. 140).
CALASSANTI-MOTYLINSKI, G. A. DE (See no. 594).
JOLEAUD, L. (See no. 771).
JUNGFER, J., and A. P. MARTÍNEZ, (See no. 446).
MERCIER, GUSTAVE (See no. 167).
ROGET, RAYMOND (See no. 32).

Berber Tribal Names

519. HART, DAVID M. Tribal and place names among the Arabo-Berbers of northwestern Morocco. Hespéris-Tamuda 1/3.457–511, 1960. (A correlation of tribal, clan, and place names in terms of linguistic origin.)
520. ROUX, ARSÈNE. Quelques remarques sur la formation des noms de tribus chez les Berbérophones du Maroc. Act. Mém. IIIe Congr. Topon. Anthropon., 485–90, 1951.

See also:

BASSET, RENÉ (See no. 53).

Berber Textbooks

521. ABÈS, M. Première année de berbère. Rabat, 1916. (Subtitle: 'dialecte du Maroc central.' An introductory textbook with grammatical explanation, model dialogues, sample texts, and glossary.)

522. ALBINO, J. Manual del lenguaje vulgar de los moros de la Riff. Cadiz, 1859. (Textbook.)
523. ASPINION, ROBERT. Apprenons le Berbère. Rabat, 1953. (Elementary textbook for Shilha with notes and exercises.)
524. BARTHÉ, ALBERT. Manual elementaire de conversation touarègue. Paris, 1952. (This elementary textbook was published as part of the 'Collection de Langues et Dialectes d'Outre Mer' by the Centre des Hautes Études d'Administration Musulmane in mimeographed form. It contains model sentences with French equivalents, notes on pronunciation and grammar, and a short list of frequent verbs. There are also notes on geography and a short bibliography.)
525. BASSET, ANDRÉ, and J. CROUZET. Cours de berbère. Algiers, 1937. (An elementary textbook for Kabyle.)
526. BASSET, RENÉ. Manuel de langue kabyle. Paris, 1887. (This work is divided into three parts: grammatical description, texts, and glossary. The format indicates that it is intended for use as a textbook.)
527. BELKASSEM BEN SEDIRA (also: ABU AL-KASIM IBN SADIRA). Cours de langue Kabyle. Algiers, 1887. (A basic textbook with grammatical description and exercises.)
528. BISSON, PAUL. Leçons de berbère tamazight. Rabat, 1940. (A conventional textbook for study of the language of central Morocco.)
529. BOULIFA, SI AMMAR BEN SAID. Méthode de langue Kabyle. Algiers, 1913. (This book was intended to be used as a textbook for an advanced course in Kabyle. It includes the linguistic study listed as no. 142 above, as well as texts and glossary.)
530. ——. Une première année de langue Kabyle. Algiers, 1897. (This textbook presents the language of the Grand Kabylie with exercises, sample texts, and glossary of verbs used in the textbook. The book is remarkable as an attempt to systematize the aural-oral approach to language instruction which Boulifa used. No. 529, above, may be considered a continuation of this textbook.)
531. DEPONT, OCTAVE. Vocabulaire français-kabyle. Bordeaux, 1933. (This manual was prepared for medical students. It contains a brief grammatical description, texts, sample dialogues, and glossary. The glossary is especially useful because it includes anatomical terms and names of diseases.)
532. GOURLIAU, ERNEST. La conversation française-kabyle. Milan, 1893. (Textbook.)
533. JUSTINARD, LÉOPOLD. Manuel de berbère marocain. Paris, 1914. (A textbook for Shilha. The grammatical description is very short, and there are many texts, roman transcription, with model conversations and a glossary.)
534. JUSTINARD, LÉOPOLD V. Manuel de berbère marocain. Paris, 1926. (Riff.)
535. LAOUST, EMILE. Cours de berbère marocain. Paris, 1920. (A textbook for Shilha. A second edition was published in 1936 with revised orthography and glossary.)
536. ——. Cours de berbère marocain. Paris, 1924. (A textbook for Tamazight. A

second edition was published in 1928 with revised orthography and glossary.)
537. MUÑOZ, BOSQUE A. Manual de conversación bereber-rifeña. Madrid, c. 1920.
538. PEREGRIN, G. Rudimentos de bereber rifeño. Tetuan, 1944. (An elementary textbook.)
539. ROUX, ARSÈNE. Petit guide de conversation berbère. Rabat, 1950.
See also:
SARRIONANDIA, PEDRO (See no. 331).

Berber Writing Systems

540. BASSET, ANDRÉ. Écritures libyques et touarègues. Notices sur les caractères étrangers anciens et modernes, edited by Charles Fossey (new edition), 135–43. Paris, 1948. (Comments on the tifinay.)
541. BENHAZERA, MAURICE and PÉLÉKUS. Les Touaregs, les Tifinars berbères et l'origine de l'écriture. Atlantis 6.129–44, 1933.
542. BOISSONET, E. Le k'lem tifinag. Paris, Challamel, c. 1880. (A study of the alphabet of the Tuaregs.)
543. BRINTON, DANIEL G. The alphabets of the Berbers. Proc. Orient. Clb. Phila. Philadelphia, 1894. (Published as a separate monograph, 11 pp.)
544. BURTON, D. G. The alphabets of the Berbers. Science 21.104, 1893.
545. CHABOT, J. B. Notes sur l'alphabet libyque. Compte Rendus, Académie des inscriptions et belles-lettres, 558–64, 1917.
546. COHEN, MARCEL. L'écriture dans la main chez les Touaregs et en Chine. GLECS 5.56, 1949.
547. FOSSEY, CHARLES. Notices sur les caractères étrangers anciens et modernes (new ed.). Paris, 1948. (Includes an article by A. Basset. See no. 540, above.)
548. HALÉVY, JOSEPH. L'origine des alphabets berbères. JA 10/7.119, 1905. (Based on data obtained from inscriptions.)
549. JUDAS, AUGUSTE C. Note sur l'alphabet berbère usité chez les Touaregs. JA, 1847.
550. ——. Sur l'écriture et la langue berbère dans l'antiquité et de nos jours. Paris, 1863.
551. LITTMAN, ENNO. L'origine de l'alphabet libyque. JA 10/4.423–40, 1904.
552. PELEKUS, ——. Les tifinars berbères et l'origine de l'écriture. Atlantis 47.141–4, 1933. (See 541 above.)
553. RICHARDSON, JAMES. Touarick alphabet with the corresponding Arabic and English letters. London, 1847. (A guide for transliteration. There are glossaries of Tuareg and Ghadames dialects. In addition there are translations of parts of the Gospel according to St. Matthew prepared by F. W. Newman for Kabyle and the dialect of Ghadames.)
554. RINN, LOUIS. Lettres de Touareg. Rev. afr. 31.321–40, 1887.

555. SAULCY, LOUIS F. DE. Observations sur l'alphabet Tifinag. JA 4/13.247–64,1849.
556. ZOHRER, L. Über den Anwendungsbereich des Tifinag in der Sahara. Archiv für Anthropologie 25.134–6, 1939.
See also works by:
BEGUINOT, FRANCESCO (See nos. 246, 558).
BOULIFA, SI AMMAR BEN SAID (See no. 560).
CLINE, WALTER (See no. 290).
MONOD, THÉODORE (See no. 568),

Berber Inscriptions

557. BEGUINOT, FRANCESCO. Le iscrizioni berbere del Sahara. La Rivista d'Orienta, 59–62, 1935.
558. ——. Le iscrizioni rupestri in caratteri tifinagh. Att. 2° Congr. stud. col., 104–12. Naples, 1932. (A contribution to the decipherment of inscriptions and a statement about the development of the Tuareg alphabet.)
559. BOULIFA, SI AMMAR BEN SAID. L'inscription d'Ifir'a. RA 53.411, 1909. (There is a copy of an inscription found in northern Algeria with commentary by Boulifa.)
560. ——. Nouveaux documents archéologiques découverts dans le Haut Sebaou. Rev. afr. 55.16–41, 1911. (Report and commentary on inscriptions found in 1910 by Boulifa in Kabylie. The inscriptions seem to be related to the writing system of the Tuaregs.)
561. FERAUD, ——. Bracelet de Touareg avec une inscription en Tifinar. Rev. afr. 3.396, 1858. (Description of a bracelet from Ahaggar. The inscription has been used as a source of data by Hanoteau and others.)
562. FLAMAND, GEORGES B. M. Hadjrat Mektoubat ou les pierres écrites. Bulletin, Société d'anthropologie et de biologie de Lyon. June, 1901.
563. ——. Les Pierres écrites. Paris, 1921. (Study of N. African inscriptions.)
564. HALÉVY, JOSEPH. L'Inscription punique-berbère du temple de Masinissa. Rev. sém., 136–8, 1913. (Commentary on a bilingual inscription.)
565. MARCY, GEORGES. Les inscriptions libyques bilingues de l'Afrique du Nord. Paris, 1936.
566. ——. Introduction à un déchiffrement méthodique des inscriptions 'tifinagh' du Sahara central. Hespéris 24.89–118, 1937.
567. MERCIER, E. La numération libyenne. JA 222.263–322, 1933.
568. MONOD, THÉDORE. L'Adrar Ahnet. Paris, 1932. (North African inscriptions and the development of the Berber writing system.)
569. ——. Gravures peintures et inscriptions rupestres. Paris, 1938. (A study of Saharan inscriptions.)

570. MORDINI, A. Les inscriptions rupestres tifinagh du Sahara et leur signification ethnologique. Ethnos 2/5.333–7, 1937.
571. NICOLAS, FRANCIS. Inscriptions et gravures rupestres. (Mémoires) IFAN 10. 541–51, 1950. (Study of Saharan inscriptions.)
572. REYGASSE, MAURICE. Contribution à l'étude des gravures rupestres et inscriptions Tifinar' du Sahara central. Cinquantenaire de l'Université d'Alger, Faculté des Lettres, 437–534. Algiers, 1932.
See also works by:
HANOTEAU, ADOLPHE (See nos. 312, 314).
REBOUD, V. (See no. 263).
REINAUD, JOSEPH T. (See no. 327).

Berber Literature

573. BASSET, ANDRÉ. Littérature berbère. Histoire des Littératures (edited by Raymond Queneau), 886–90. Paris, 1955.
574. BASSET, HENRI. Essai sur la littérature des Berbères. Algiers, 1920. (This is probably the best work on Berber literature and folklore. The book includes a brief history of the languages, a survey of their distribution, and detailed descriptions of written literature, legal literature, and oral forms, including poetry. In the description of the oral forms, the themes as well as the forms themselves are carefully analyzed.)
575. BASSET, RENÉ. La littérature populaire berbère et arabe. Mélanges africains et orientaux, 27–63. Paris, 1915. (The first part of this essay, 27–50, deals with the forms and themes of Berber literature, chiefly poetry. A few comments are added about the various types of folk stories.)
576. CERBELLA, GINO. I berberi e la novellistica berbera. Afr. Ital., 266–77, 1927.
577. CERTEUX, ALPHONSE, and EMILE H. CARNOY. L'Algérie traditionnelle. Paris, 1884. (Essays on folklore, stories, songs, etc., chiefly Arabic but with some Berber data.)
578. DUQUAIRE, HENRI. Anthologie de la littérature marocaine arabe et berbère. Paris, 1943.
579. FERRANAT, V. DE. Proverbes morocains. Rev. Gen., 611–20, 1926.
580. HANOTEAU, ADOLPHE. Littérature orale des Touaregs. Rev. afr. 1.510. (Tuareg fables.)
581. JUSTINARD, LÉOPOLD V. Note sur la littérature et la poésie chez les rifains. Rif et Ibala, 82–3, 1926.
582. LAFUENTE, DOMENECH. La literatura oral del pueblo berberí. Archos, Instituto de estudios africanos, no. 13, 1950.
583. LAOUST, EMILE. La littérature des Berbères d'après l'ouvrage de M. Henri Basset. Hespéris 1.192–208, 1921.

584. LEBEL, ROLAND. Notre littérature marocaine. Bulletin de l'Enseignement public de Maroc, 1928.

585. MERCIER, GUSTAVE. Moorish literature. London, c. 1901. (Collection of ballads, narratives, and folklore with an introduction by René Basset, translated into English.)

586. RICARD, ROBERT. La littérature des Berbères marocains. Revue de l'Aucam, 121–9, 1933.

587. STUMME, HANS. Sidi Hammu als Geograph. Orientalische Studien Theodor Nöldeke Gewidmet 2.445–52, 1906.

588. WILSON, EPIPHANIUS (ed. and tr.). Moorish literature. New York, 1901. (A collection of folk tales, poems, songs, etc., with an introduction by René Basset.)

See also works by:

BASSET, RENÉ (See no. 654).
BEGUINOT, FRANCESCO (See no. 738).
FERAOUN, MOULOUD (See no. 604).
JUSTINARD, LÉOPOLD V. (See no. 16).
KÖLLER, ANGE (See no. 775).

Berber Manuscripts

589. AVEZAC-MACAYA, MARIE ARMAND PASCAL DE. Les documents recueillis jusqu'à ce jour pour l'étude de la langue berbère et sur divers manuscrits anciens en cette langue qu'il importe de rechercher. Bulletin Société de géographie 2/14.223–39, 1840. (An important bibliographical article.)

590. BASSET, ANDRÉ. Deuxième note additionnelle à T. Lewicki. REIsl, 287–96, 1936.

591. ——. Note additionelle à T. Lewicki. REIsl, 275–305, 1934. (Comment about an article on Berber based on data taken from an old manuscript.)

592. BASSET, HENRI. Un nouveau manuscrit berbère: le Kitab elmawaiza. JA 202. 299–303, 1923.

593. BOULIFA, SI AMMAR BEN SAID. Manuscrits berbères du Maroc. JA 10/6.333–62, 1905.

594. CALASSANTI-MOTYLINSKI, G. A. DE. Les livres de la secte abadhite. Algiers, 1885. (Although this work is about the Arabic manuscripts in the possession of certain tribes in the area of Mzab and Nefusi, it may be considered important because of the notes on history and bibliography as well as the list of place names used in all local chronicles.)

595. ——. Le manuscrit arabo-berbère de Zouagha. Act. XIV Congr. Intern. Orient., 69–78. Algiers, 1905.

596. COLIN, GEORGES S. A propos d'un manuscrit berbère. Hespéris 14.90, 1932.

597. DRESCH, JEAN. Documents berbères: Atlas central. Paris. (No. 35 of (Publ) IHEM.)

598. IBRAHIM IBN MUHAMMAD AL-MASSI. Translation of a Berber manuscript. JRAS, vol. 4, 1837. (This translation of the Shilha text was prepared by W. B. Hodgson.)
See also works by:
BERQUE, J. (See no. 473).
COLIN, GEORGES S., and H. RENAUD (See no. 480).
DUVEYRIER, HENRI (See no. 759).
JUSTINARD, LÉOPOLD V. (See no. 610).

Berber Poetry

599. BASSET, ANDRÉ. Sur la métrique berbère. C. r. somm. Institut français d'anthropologie, 4–5. Paris, 1952. (A short discussion of prosodic features, chiefly in Tuareg.)

600. BASSET, RENÉ. Poème de Cabi en dialecte Chelha. JA 7/13.476–508, 1879. (A text in Shilha transcribed and translated into French.)

601. BEGOUEN, HENRI. De quelques poètes du Hoggar et de la poésie des Touaregs d'après le Père de Foucauld. Mém. Acad. sci. inscr. bell. let. Toul., 203–34, 1932.

602. BOULIFA, SI AMMAR BEN SAID. Recueil de poésies kabyles. Algiers, 1904. (This is an important collection of texts from the Grand Kabylie, with notes on metrics and musical forms. The texts are in roman and Arabic transcriptions, and there is an introductory essay on the role of women in Kabylie.)

603. CHERBONNEAU, A. Aicha poète de Bougie. Rev. afr. 4.34, 1859.

604. FERAOUN, MOULOUD. Les Poèmes de Si Mohand. Paris, 1960. (A collection of poems by a Kabyle poet who lived during the 19th century, c. 1840–1906. The poems are transcribed in roman characters and translated into French. There are notes on metrics. Important as a study of Berber literature.)

605. FOUCAULD, CHARLES DE. Poésies touarègues. Paris, 1925–30. (Texts from Ahaggar, edited by R. Basset. 2 volumes.)

606. GALAND-PERNET, PAULETTE. Une tradition orale encore vivante. Mémorial André Basset, 39–49. Paris, 1957. (This article is a re-examination of one of the Berber poems available in written form. There is an attempt to reconcile the several versions of the poem that have been reported, and the conclusion that one of the versions has not been accurately transcribed is reached after consideration of internal evidence and Berber metrics.)

607. HANOTEAU, ADOLPHE. Poésies populaires de la Kabylie. Paris, 1867. (Military poems, songs in Arabic and roman transcriptions. There are some ethnographic notes. No glossary.)

608. JOLY, ALEXANDRE. Poésies du Sud. Rev. afr. 53.285–307, 1909. (Texts and translations. A correction was published in Rev. afr. 54.96, 1910.)

609. JUSTINARD, LÉOPOLD V. Poèmes chleuhs recueillis au Sous. Revue du monde musulman 60.63–107, 1925.

610. ——. Poésies en dialecte du Sous marocain. JA, vol. 213, 1928. (Texts taken from an Arabic-Berber manuscript.)
611. LUCIANI, JEAN D. El H'aoudh, (tr.). Algiers, 1897. (This is the translation of a Shilha poem by Muhammad ibn Ali ibn Brahim. The original text is given.)
612. MAMMERI, MOULOUD. Evolution de la poésie kabyle. Rev. afr. 94.125–48, 1950.
613. MOJAND, SID. El jardín de los deseos. Madrid, 1914. (Berber poems translated by Isaac Muñoz.)
614. MUHAMMAD AL-AWZALI. L'Océan des Pleurs. Leiden, 1960. (A Berber poem edited and translated into French by B.H. Stricker.)
615. NICOLAS, FRANCIS. Folklore twareg. (Bull) IFAN, vol. 6, 1944. (Poems and songs of the Tuaregs in the area of the Azawak River.)
616. ——. Poèmes touaregs. (Bull.) IFAN, vol. 6, 1941–42.
617. RODD, PETER R. Translation of Tuareg poems. BSOAS 5.109–12, 1928. (Five Tuareg poems transcribed and translated with a brief introduction.)
618. ROUX, ARSÈNE. Un chant d'amdyaz, l'aède berbère du groupe linguistique beraber. Mémorial Henri Basset 2.237–42. Paris, 1932. (A poem from central Morocco transcribed and translated with notes.)
619. ——. Les imdyazen ou aèdes berbères du groupe linguistique beraber. Hespéris 8.231, 1928. (Poetry of the central Moroccan area.)
620. ——. Poésie populaire arabo-berbère du Maroc central. IVe Congr. Féd. Soc. Sav. Afr. Nd., 865–72. Rabat, 1938.
621. STUMME, HANS. Dichtkunst und Gedichte der Schluh. Leipzig, 1895. (Detailed study of Shilha poetry.)
See also works by:
BASSET, RENÉ (See no. 575).
HANOTEAU, ADOLPHE (See no. 312).
JUSTINARD, LÉOPOLD V. (See no. 581).
RENISIO, AMIDÉ (See no. 328).

Berber Songs

622. ABÈS, M. Chansons d'amour chez les Berbères. France-Maroc, 1919.
623. AMROUCHE, JEAN. Chants berbères de Kabylie. Paris, 1947. (Description with texts.)
624. ANDREWS, CLARENCE E. Berber songs. Asia, vol. 21, 1921. (A translation of typical songs.)
625. BASSET, RENÉ. L'Insurrection algérienne de 1871 dans les chansons populaires Kabyles. Muséon 11.254–70, 330–51, 428–34, 1892. (This collection of texts with translations was published separately by J.B. Istas, Louvain, 1892. The collection is useful in historical studies.)

626. BIARNAY, S. Notes sur les chants populaires du Rif. Archs. Berb. 1.22–39, 1915. (Some useful texts.)
627. BOUVERET, ——. Chansons marocaines du Sud. Maroc Médical, 142–4, 202–4, 452, 1926.
628. CALASSANTI-MOTYLINSKI, G. A. DE. Chanson berbère de Djerba. Bull. corr. afr. 5–6.461–4, 1885. (A text from Tunisia.)
629. CHOTTIN, A. Airs populaires recueillis à Fès. Hespéris 33.275–85, 1923.
630. ——. Chants et danses berbères au Maroc. Le Ménestrel, September, 1933.
631. HANOTEAU, ADOLPHE. Une chante kabile. Rev. afr. 3.75, 1858.
632. JOLY, ALEXANDRE. Chansons du répertoire algerois. Rev. afr. 53.46–66, 1909. (Texts and translations.)
633. LAOUST, EMILE. Chants berbères contre l'occupation française. Mémorial Henri Basset 2.9–20, 1928. (Texts of songs in a dialect of central Morocco transcribed and translated. There is a short description of song types.)
634. LUCIANI, JEAN D. Chansons kabyles de Smail Azikkiou. Rev. afr. 44.44–59, 1900. (Text and translation.)
635. MARAVAL-BERTHOIN, A. Chants du Hoggar. Paris, 1934.
636. MORESTEL, ——. Chant kabile sur l'expedition de 1857. Rev. afr. 2.221, 1857.
637. ——. Un chant kabile. Rev. Afr. 2.500. 1857.
638. PAUL, MARGUERITE, L. Chants berbères du Maroc. Paris, 1905.
639. RINN, LOUIS. Duex chansons kabyles sur l'insurrection de 1871. Rev. afr. 31. 55–71, 1887. (Texts with notes.)
640. ——. Note indiquant le nom de l'auteur des deux chansons kabyles sur l'unsurrection de 1871. Rev. afr. 31.240, 1887. (A short comment on the material of no. 639, above.)
641. SERVIER, JEAN. Chants des femmes de l'Aurès. Paris, 1955.
See also works by:
HANOTEAU, ADOLPHE (See no. 607).
NICOLAS, FRANCIS (See no. 615).

Berber Texts

642. ABEL, HANS. Eine Erzählung im Dialekt von Ermenne. Abh. Kais. Sach. Akad. Wissensch., vol. 29. Leipzig, 1913. (This detailed analysis of a text in one of the Nubian dialects may be useful in historical and comparative studies of the Berber languages and their relation to other languages of the area.)
643. AHMAD IBN KHAUWAS. Dialogues français-kabyles. Algiers, 1881. (Sample texts intended to be used as models in learning the language.)
644. ASPINION, ROBERT. Textes relatifs aux maladies dans le parler des Ait Arfa du Gurgon. Hespéris, vol. 18, 1941.
645. BARTH, HEINRICH. Kelgeres-Lieder. ZDMG, vol. 7, 1853.

646. BASSET, ANDRÉ. Textes berbères de l'Aurès. Paris, 1961. (Collection of texts with notes and translations. The material is ethnographic.)
647. BASSET, HENRI. Les proverbes de l'Ahaggar. Rev. afr. 43.389–502, 1922. (A collection of Tuareg texts.)
648. ——. Quelques nouveaux contes berbères. Rev. ethnog. 2.26–38, 1921.
649. BASSET, RENÉ. Contes populaires Berbères. Paris, 1887. (A collection of folk-tales, transcribed, annotated and translated into French. This is vol. 12 of the series: Collection de contes et de chansons populaires.)
650. ——. Contes poulaires d'Afrique. Paris, 1903. (This is a large collection of African literature and folklore which includes some Berber stories. It is vol. 27 of: Les littératures populaires de toutes les nations.)
651. ——. Les dictons satiriques sur les villes et les tribus d'Algérie attribuées à Sidi Ah'med ben Yousof. JA 8/16.203–97, 1890. (Although these texts are in Arabic, the translation and the index of place names are useful.)
652. ——. Injil ne Sidna Aisa l'Masih' akken itsouaktheb sarresoul Mattieu. Algiers, 1883. (Translation of the Gospel according to St. Matthew into Kabyle.)
653. ——. Loqman berbère. Paris, 1890. (A collection of fables in twenty-three dialects of the various Berber languages. A transcription of each text is given in Arabic and in roman characters. There is an introductory essay on the fables, a bibliography, a comparative table, and four glossaries. The first glossary gives a list of forms occurring in the texts; the second is a list of roots with French translations; the third contains the Arabic forms as they occur in the various texts; the fourth is a French word list with references to Glossaries 2 and 3.)
654. ——. Nouveaux contes berbères. Collection de contes et chansons populaires, vol. 23. Paris, 1897. (Contains a diverse collection of folktales with notes and translations.)
655. ——. Recueil de textes et documents relatifs à la philologie berbère. Algiers, 1887. (This work was published in the Bulletin de correspondance africaine and separately. The texts and notes cover the dialects of Beni-Menacer, Oran, Figuig, Oued Draa, and some dialects of Shilha.)
656. ——. Relation de Sidi Brahim de Massat. Paris, 1883. (A text in Shilha with translation and notes.)
657. ——. Salomon et le dragon. Bull. corr. afr. 2.3–4, 1885. (A Kabyle folktale with translation and notes.)
658. ——. Textes berbères dans le dialecte des Beni Menacer. Giornale della Societa Asiatica Italiana 6.37–84, 1892. (A collection of texts from northern Algeria in transcription with glossary, translations, and notes.)
659. ——. Textes touaregs en prose. Algiers, 1922.
660. BIARNAY, S. Six textes en dialecte berbère des Beraber de Dades. JA 10/19. 346–71, 1912. (Texts from central Morocco transcribed and edited.)
661. BOULIFA, SI AMMAR BEN SAID. Le Kanoun d'Ad'ni. Mémoires et textes, XIV Congr. Intern. Orient. Algiers, 1905.

662. ——. Textes berbères en dialecte de l'Atlas Marocain. Paris, 1908. (This is no. 36 of the Bull. corr. afr. The texts are transcribed and translated.)

663. BUSELLI, G. Berber Texts from Jebel Nefusi. Jl. R. Afr. Soc. 23.285–93, 1924. (Some religious texts transcribed and translated.)

664. ——. Testi berberi del Gebel Nefusa. Afr. ital. 50. 26–34, 1921. (A collection of folktales told by a native of Gemmari transcribed and translated.)

665. CALASSANTI-MOTYLINSKI, G. A. DE. Dialogue et textes en berbère de Djerba. JA 9/10.377–401, 1897. (A collection of texts transcribed and translated, with some notes.)

666. ——. Le Djebel Nefousa. Algiers, 1885. (Subtitle: Ir'asra d ibridn di drar n Infousen. A text in the dialect of Djebel Nefusi, edited and translated. The text is also included in no. 70.)

667. ——. Guerara depuis sa Fondation. Algiers, 1885. (Translation of a narrative by a native of the area about the history of the Mzab.)

668. ——, and C. FOUCAULD. Textes Touaregs en prose. Algiers, 1922. (This collection of texts was edited by René Basset and published posthumously. The texts are from Ahaggar.)

669. CARREY, EMILE. Recits de Kabylie. Paris, 1858. (Collected during the war of 1857.)

670. CESARO, ANTONIO. Due racconti in linguaggio nefusi. AION-L 3.395–404, 1949.

671. CHABROLLES, M. Proverbes imouchar. Bull. Liais. Sahar. 12.34–7, 1953. (With comments by A. Picard.)

672. DALLET, JEAN-MARIE. Trois contes berbères. Ibla 26.206–9, 1944. (Kabyle texts.)

673. DERMENGHEM, EMILE. Contes kabyles. Algiers, 1945. (A collection of folktales with comments.)

674. DESTAING, EDMOND. L'ennayer chez les Beni Snous. Rev. afr., 51–70, 1905. (A text from northwestern Algeria with translation.)

675. ——. Textes arabes en parler des chleuhs du Sous. Paris, 1937. (Transcriptions, translations, and glossary.)

676. ——. Textes berbères en parler des chleuhs du Sous. Paris, 1940.

677. FOUCAULD, CHARLES DE, and G. A. DE CALASSANTI-MOTYLINSKI. Textes touaregs en prose. Algiers, 1922. (Texts from Ahaggar edited by R. Basset.)

678. FROBENIUS, LEO. Volksmärchen der Kabylen. Atlantis, 1921–28.

679. GARCIA GOMEZ, EMILIO. Al Hakam II y los bereberos segun texto inedito de Ibn Hayyan. Al-An, vol. 13, 1948.

680. HANOTEAU, ADOLPHE. Akatcim ne diousis Ledzer s taqebailit. Algiers, 1868. (Translation into Zouave.)

681. ——. Aktabe en tibratin d endjilen s taqebailit. Algiers, 1869. (Translation of part of the New Testament into Zouave.)

682. HODGSON, WILLIAM B. The Narrative of Sidi Brahim ben Mohammed el-Susi. JRAS, no. 18, 1848. (Shilha text.)

683. HUMBERT, JEAN. Collectio epistolarum carminum bellicorum et eroticum. Leiden, 1822. (A collection of Zouave texts.)
684. IBRAHIM IBN MUHAMMAD AL-MASSI. Relation de Sidi Brahim de Massat. Paris, 1882. (This translation of the Shilha text was prepared and annotated by René Basset.)
685. JORDAN, ANTOINE. Textes berbères. Rabat, 1935. (A collection of Shilha texts.)
686. JUSTINARD, LÉOPOLD V. Textes chleuhs de l'Oued Nfis. Mémorial Henri Basset 1.331–7. Paris, 1928. (Texts transcribed and translated with ethnographic notes.)
687. KRAUSE, G. ADOLF. Proben der Sprache von Ghat. Leipzig, 1884. (Text with translation.)
688. LAOUST, EMILE. Contes berbères du Maroc. Paris, 1949. (A collection of one hundred and fifty texts representing the four basic types of oral narrative. The texts are in the language of central Morocco. Roman transcription.)
689. ——. Contes berbères du Maroc. Paris, 1950. (Translations and notes for texts of no. 688. The two items are vol. 50 of (Pub.) IHEM.)
690. ——. Un texte dans le dialecte berbère des Ait Messad. Mélanges René Basset 2.305–34, 1925. (A text on marriage is presented with translation, and the article includes a grammatical description based on the text. Illustrations of marriage scenes.)
691. LEBLANC DE PREBOIS, P. Essai de contes kabyles. Batna, 1897. (Texts with translations.)
692. LEGEY, FRANÇOISE. Contes et legendes poulaires du Maroc. Paris, 1926. (No. 16 of (Pub.) IHEM.)
693. LE GLAY, MAURICE. Badda, fille berbère et autres récits marocains. Paris, 1921.
694. LEWICKI, T. Quelques textes inedits en vieux berbère provenant d'une chronique ibadite anonyme. REIsl 3.275–305, 1934.
695. MASQUERAY, EMILE. Traditions de l'Aouras oriental. Bull. corr. afr. 3.72, 1885. (Texts and comments.)
696. MERCIER, GUSTAVE. Cinq textes berbères en dialecte chaouia de l'Aurès. JA 9/16.189–249, 1900.
697. MERCIER, H. Vocabulaires et textes berbères dans le dialecte des Ait Izdeg. Rabar, 1937. (Bilingual glossaries with ethnographic texts. There are illustrations, both photographs and line drawings, of tools, costumes and utensils. The texts are untranslated.)
698. MOULIERAS, AUGUSTE J. Les fourberies de si Djeh'a. Paris, 1890. (A collection of folktales in Kabyle with translations.)
699. ——. Legendes et contes merveilleux de la Grande Kabylie. Paris, 1893-98. (The first part of this work contains Kabyle texts; the second part, translations and notes. No. 13 of Bull. corr. afr.)
700. MUHAMMAD IBN ALI IBN IBRAHIM. El H'aoudh. Algiers, 1897. (Shilha text, edited and translated by J. D. Luciani.)
701. MUHAMMAD IBN IBRAHIM IBN MUHAMMAD IBN 'ABD AL-RAHMAN AL-ZARHUNI.

La rihla du Marabout de Tasaft. Paris, 1940. (An Arabic text, 18th century, on the history of the Atlas translated with notes by L. Justinard.)

702. NEWMAN, FRANCIS W. The narrative of Sidi Ibrahim ibn Muhammad el Messi el Susi. JRAS 19.215–66, 1848. (Shilha text transcribed and annotated with interlineary translation.)

703. NICOLAS, FRANCIS. Dictons proverbes et fables de la Tamacheq des Iullemeden. Anthropos 4.41–4, 6.807–16, 1946–49. (Folklore of the Tuaregs in Niger.)

704. ——. Textes ethnographiques de la Tamajeq des Iullemeden de l'Est. Anthropos 46.754–800, 1951. (Tuareg texts with comments.)

705. PELLAT, CHARLES. Deux textes dans le parler berbère des Ait Zeggu le Mestigmeur. Rev. afr. 19.254–9, 1947. (Texts from central Morocco.)

706. ——. Textes berbères dans le parler des Ait Seghrouchen de la Moulouya. Paris, 1955. (Texts from central Morocco in roman transcription with translations and glossary.)

707. PICARD, ANDRÉ. Textes berbères dans le parler des Irjen. Algiers, 1959. (Collection of Kabyle texts.)

708. REYNIERS, F. Tauograt oulles Berbères racontes par eux-mêmes. Paris, 1930. (Collection of texts in Shilha about Berber life.)

709. RICHARDSON, JAMES. First chapter of the Gospel according to St. Matthew. London, 1846. (Translation with Kabyle vocabulary.)

710. RIVIERE, JOSEPH. Recueil de contes populaires de la Kabylie du Djurdjura. Paris, 1882. (Translations.)

711. ROCHEMONTRIX, M. DE. Documents pour l'étude du Berbère. JA 8/13.198–228, 402–27, 1889. (Subtitle: 'Contes du Sous et de l'Oasis de Tafilelt'. A collection of texts, from manuscripts, edited, translated and annotated.)

712. ROUX, ARSÈNE. Choix de versions berbères. Bayonne, 1951. (Texts in Shilha.)

713. ——. Recits contes et legendes berbères en Tachelhait. Rabat, 1942.

714. ——. Recits contes et legendes dans le parler des Beni Mtir. Rabat, 1942. (This collection of texts, like nos. 721, 722, 724, 725, and 729, was intended to be used as part of a training program in Berber languages. The texts are given in romanized transcription without translations.)

715. ——. La vie berbère par les textes. Paris, 1955. (Vol. 1 of Collection de textes berbères marocains of the IHEM. The texts are in Shilha.)

716. SARNELLI, TOMMASO. Linguaggi coloniali ignorati. Naples, 1924–25. (Published as a supplement to Afr. Ital., this work is a collection of texts, transcribed and translated with comments and notes on the dialect of Sokna.)

717. STUMME, HANS. Elf Stücke im Šilḥa-Dialekt von Tazerwalt. ZDMG 48.22–8, 1894.

718. ——. Märchen der Berbern von Tamazratt in Sudtunisien. Leipzig, 1900. (Texts, translated with notes.)

719. ——. Märchen der Schluh von Tazerwalt. Leipzig, 1895. (Texts, translated and annotated.)

720. ——. Mitteilungen eines Schilh über seine marokkanische Heimat. ZDMG 61.503–41, 1907. (Text with translation and notes.)
721. VALLICROSA, JOSE M. Textes magics del Nord d'Africa. Bull. Ass. cat. antrop. etno. preh. 1.147–60, 2.85–100, 1923–24.
722. ANONYMOUS. New Testament. London. (Portions of the New Testament have been published by the Bible Society, London, in various Berber languages from the early part of the 19th Century. In some cases, the name of the translator is not known.)

See also works by:

ABÈS, M (See no. 521).
BASSET, RENÉ (See no. 218, 219, 305, 424, 526).
BEGUINOT, FRANCESCO (See no. 306).
BIARNAY, S. (See nos. 64, 65, 66, 626, 745).
BOSSOUTROT, A. (See no. 432).
BOULIFA, SI AMMAR BEN SAID (See nos. 529, 530, 602).
CALASSANTI-MOTYLINSKI, G. A. DE (See nos. 69, 70).
CREUSAT, JEAN BAPTISTE (See no. 481).
DEPONT, OCTAVE (See no. 531).
DESTAING, EDMOND (See nos. 80, 443, 757).
GRABERG, JACOB OF HEMSÖ (See no. 93).
HANOTEAU, ADOLPHE (See nos. 312, 313).
IBRAHIM IBN MUHAMMAD AL-MASSI (See no. 598).
JUSTINARD, LÉOPOLD V. (See no. 533).
LAOUST, EMILE (See nos. 102, 103, 105, 779, 780).
LOUBIGNAC, V. (See no. 108).
MASQUERAY, EMILE (See no. 318).
MERCIER, GUSTAVE (See no. 319).
NEWMAN, FRANCIS W. (See no. 513).
NICOLAS, FRANCIS (See no. 115).
PRASSE, KARL G. (See no. 117).
PROVOTELLE, —— (See no. 326).
RENISIO, AMIDÉE (See no. 328).
RICHARDSON, JAMES (See no. 553).
STUMME, HANS (See no. 332).
WALKER, W. SEYMOUR (See no. 127).

Berber Ethnography

723. ABÈS, M. Les Ait Ndhir. Archs. Berb., vol. 2 (1917), vol. 3 (1919). (The first part is entitled 'Monographie d'une tribu berbère', and the work contains some

linguistic data from the area of central Morocco in which Tamazight is spoken.)

724. AMAT, CHARLES. Le M'zab et les M'zabites. Paris, 1888. (This is primarily a historical-sociological study, but it includes some material on the language.)

725. ARRIPE, H. J. Dans l'Aures: les Chaouia tels qu'ils sont. Recueil des Notices et Mémoires, Rec. Not. Mém. Soc. Arch. Hist. Geogr. Dept. Const., 56.113–98, 57.211–46, 1925–27.

726. AUCAPITAINE, HENRI. Étude sur l'origine et l'histoire des tribus de la haute Kabylie. JA 5/14.273–86, 1859.

727. BASSET, ANDRÉ, Les ksours berbèrophones du Gourara. Rev. afr. 80.353–5, 1937.

728. BASSET, HENRI. Les éléments du peuple marocain. France-Maroc 2.261–7, 1918. (There are some general comments about the languages of Morocco.)

729. ——. État actuel des études d'ethnographie du Maroc. (Bul.) IHEM, 130–6, 1920.

730. ——. La population berbère: Origines, Langue, Mœurs, Religion. Armée d'Afrique, 13–21. Paris, 1925.

731. ——. Rapport sur une mission chez les Ntifa. Archs. Berb. 2.97–122, 1917. (Contains some linguistic data.)

732. BASSET, RENÉ. Genealogistes berbères. Arch. Berb., vol. 1, 1915. (This is a study of the genealogists used as sources of information by Ibn Khaldoun.)

733. ——. Recherches sur la religion des Berbères. Rev. Hist. relig. 61.291–342, 1910. (This is a translation of an article that first appeared in the Encyclopaedia of Religion and Ethics, vol. 2, 1909. Although the article is not a linguistic study, it contains some useful data.)

734. ——, and G. YVER. Berbères. EI, 1908. (General description including linguistic data.)

735. BAUER LANDAUER, IGNACIO. El Rif y la Kabila de Beni Urriaguel. Memorias, Sociedad española de antropología, etnografía y prehistoria 1.3–13, 1921. (Although not primarily linguistic, the article contains useful data about one of the eastern tribes of the Riff.)

736. BEGUINOT, FRANCESCO. Chi sono i Berberi. Oriente Moderno 1.240–7, 303–11, 1921.

737. ——. Frammenti di psicologia arabo-berbera. Terra Vita 1.180–6, 1922.

738. ——. Le gente libiche. L'Impero Coloniale Fascista, 375–400. Novara, 375–400. (In this essay a survey of the population of Libya is presented with sections devoted to language and literature as well as to other features of the culture.)

739. BELKASSEM BEN SEDIRA. Une mission en Kabylie sur les dialectes berbères et l'assimilation des indigenes. Algiers, 1887. (This is a report of investigations made in preparation for establishment of an educational system.)

740. BENHAZERA, MAURICE. Six mois chez les Touareg du Ahaggar. Algiers, 1908.

741. BERNARD, AUGUSTIN. Enquête sur l'habitation rurale des indigenes de l'Algérie. Algiers, 1921. (Although this monograph is a sociological study, it is a source of

useful information about the vocabulary of Kabyle. A second edition was published in Paris by Larose in 1921.)

742. BERQUE, J. Verite et poésie sur les Seksawa. Rev. afr. 97.159–60, 1953.
743. BERTHOLON, LUCIEN J., and E. CHANTRE. Recherches anthropologiques dans la Berbère orientale, 2 vols. Lyon, 1913.
744. BIARNAY, S. Cas de regression vers la coutume berbère chez une tribu arabisée. Archs. Berb., vol. 1, 1915–16.
745. ——. Notes d'ethnographie et de linguistique nord-africaines. Paris, 1924. (This collection of papers was published posthumously, edited by Louis Brunot and Emile Laoust, as vol. 12 of the series: (Pub.) IHEM. The most important item, for Berber linguistics, is a text in one of the Mzabi dialects on the cultivation of dates. The text is in roman characters with a glossary of roots and stems and their French equivalents. The footnotes which accompany the translation are, for the most part, ethnographic.)
746. BOURILLY, J. Cours d'ethnographie marocaine. Bull. Soc. Preh. Maroc., no. 3, 1929.
747. ——. Éléments d'ethnographie marocaine. Paris, 1932. (This collection of lectures was edited by Emile Laoust and published posthumously. There are chapters on language, music, and folklore with bibliographies, and there is also a glossary of Arabic and Berber words.)
748. BRIGGS, LLOYD CABOT. The living races of the Sahara Desert. Cambridge, Mass. (Published in Papers of the Peabody Museum of Archaeology and Ethnology, Harvard University.)
749. BRUNOT, LOUIS. Les caracteres essentiels de la mentalite marocaine. Bulletin de l'Enseignement public de Maroc., 1923.
750. CHANTRÉAUX, GERMAINE. Le tissage sur métier de haute lisse à Ait-Hichem et dans le Haut Sebaou. Rev. afr. 85.78–116, 212–29, 86.261–313, 1941–42. (Lexical data for Kabyle.)
751. ——. Les tissages decorés chez les Beni-Mguild. Hespéris 31.1933, 1945.
752. CHOISNET, E. Coutumes Kabyles. Rec. Not. Mém. Soc. Arch. Hist. Geog. Dept. Const., 1911.
753. CORJON, F. Maladies, rites magiques pour enfants berbères du Moyen Atlas. Bulletin de l'Enseignement public de Maroc., May, 1932.
754. DA COSTA DE MACEDO, J. J. Ethnographical remarks on the original languages of the inhabitants of the Canary Islands. Jl. R. Geog. Soc. 11.171–83, 1841. (A discussion of the views of the time about the Berbers. Vocabularies are compared and the hypothesis is that there are several Berber languages, not one.)
755. DAOUD, BEN. Notes sur le pays Zaian. Archs. Berb. 2.276–306, 1917.
756. DELAYE, THEOPHILE JEAN. Aux casbahs berbères du grand Atlas marocain. Annls. Col., August, 1930. (Some lexical data.)
757. DESTAING, EDMOND. Fêtes et coutumes saisonnieres chez les Beni-Snous. Rev. afr. 50.244–60, 362–85, 1906. (Ethnological study with Berber texts.)

758. DOUTTE, EDMOND. Missions au Maroc. Paris, 1914. (Vol. 1 'En tribu', contains some linguistic data.)
759. DUVEYRIER, HENRI. Exploration du Sahara. Paris, 1864. (About the Tuaregs. Contains a Tuareg document.)
760. ——. Notizen über vier berberische Völkerschaften. ZDMG 12.176–86, 1858. (Report of observations made among the Mzabi and Beni Menacer during a trip in southern Algeria.)
761. FAIDHERBE, LOUIS L. Les berbères et les arabes des bords du Senegal. Bulletin, Société de géographie, 1854.
762. FOUREAU, FERNAND. Mission chez les Touareg. Paris, 1895.
763. ——. Les Touareg de l'Est. La Reforme sociale 3/8.435–46, 1894.
764. GALINIER, ——. Les Touareg. Rev. afr. 1.74, 1856.
765. HAMY, JULES T. E. Laboureurs et pasteurs berbères. Association française pour l'avancement des sciences, 54–70. Paris, 1900. (Contains some lexical data.)
766. HARRIS, WALTER B. The Berbers of Morocco. Jl. R. Anthrop. Inst. 27.61–73, 1898.
767. ——. The local distribution of tribes inhabiting the mountains of West Morocco. London, 1889.
768. HECTOR, P. Essai de monographie psychologique berbère. Casablanca, 1933. (An analysis of family speech and social relationships.)
769. HOOTON, EARNEST A. Ancient inhabitants of the Canary Islands. Cambridge, 1925. (Harvard African Studies, no. 7.)
770. JOLEAUD, L. Gravures rupestres et rites de l'eau en Afrique du Nord. JSAfr 3.197–282, 1933.
771. ——. Rites de l'eau et toponymie chez les Ait Hadidou. JSAfr. 3.346–7, 1933.
772. JOLY, ALEXANDRE. Un calendrier agricole marocain. Archives marocaines 3.301–19, 1905.
773. JUSTINARD, LÉOPOLD V. Les Ait Baamran. Paris, 1930. (No. 8 of Villes et Tribus au Maroc. Includes some texts.)
774. KÖLLER, ANGE. Los berberes marroquies. Tetuan, 1952. (Ethnographic description.)
775. ——. Essai sur l'esprit du Berbère marocain. Fribourg, 1949. (Ethnographic study with sections on language and literature and bibliography.)
776. LAOUST, EMILE. Au sujet de la charrue berbère. Hespéris 10.37–47, 1930. (With illustrations.)
778. ——. Le mariage chez les Berbères du Maroc. Archs. Berb., vol. 1, 1915.
779. ——. Mots et choses berbères. Paris, 1920. (A description of the culture of the Berbers with illustrative texts in the language of Morocco translated and transcribed.)
780. ——. Noms et cérémonies des feux de joie chez les Berbères du Haut et de l'Anti-Atlas. Hespéris, vol. 1, 1921. (Also published as a separate monograph. Includes texts.)

781. ——. Pêcheurs berbères du Sous. Hespéris 3.237–60, 297–361, 1923. (Some lexical data.)
782. ——. Éléments d'ethnographie marocaine. (See no. 243 above.)
783. LAREDO, ABRAHAM. Bereberes y Hebreos en Marruecos. Madrid, 1954.
784. LEGLAY, MAURICE. Les populations berbères du Maroc. Paris, 1916.
785. LÉVI-PROVENÇAL, E. Pratiques agricoles et fêtes saisonnaires des tribus djebalah de la vallee moyenne de l'Ouargla. Archs. Berb., vol. 3, 1917.
786. MARCY, GEORGES. Une tribu berbère de la confédération des Ait Warain. Hespéris 9.79, 1929.
787. MARZO, COSTANZO DI. I Twareg attraverso i loro proverbo. Afr. Ital., 82–94, 1927.
788. MONTAGNE, ROBERT. Coutumes et legendes de la cote berbère du Maroc. Hespéris 4.101–16, 1924.
789. ——. Une tribu berbère du Sud marocain. Hespéris, vol. 4. (Ethnographic description with illustrations and useful lexical data.)
790. MONTEIL, VINCENT. Notes sur les Tekna. Paris, 1948. (No. 3 of (Notes Doc.) IHEM.)
791. MOULIERAS, AUGUSTE J. Les Beni-Izguen. Oran, 1895. (A description of the language and folklore of one of the Mzabi tribes.)
792. NEHLIL, ——. L'azref des tribus et qsour berbères du Haut Guir. Archs. Berb., vol. 1, 1915–16.
793. NICOLAS, FRANCIS. Les industries de protection chez les Tuareg de l'Azawagh. Hespéris 25.43–85, 1938. (Contains lexical data.)
794. ——. Pieces du folklore des Twaregs Ioullemeden. Anima, 3–12, January, 1942.
795. PHARAON, FLORIAN, and J. PHARAON. Les Cabiles de Bougie. Algiers, 1839. (At the beginning is a short French-Kabyle glossary.)
796. RAHMANI, S. Notes ethnographiques et sociologiques sur les Beni M'hamed du Cap-Aokas et les Beni Amrous. Rec. not. mem. Soc., Arch. hist., geog. dept. const., vol. 62, 1934.
797. SHALER, WILLIAM. On the language, manners and customs of the Berbers. Philadelphia, 1823. (A series of letters to Peter Du Ponceau. See no. 86.)
798. ——. Sketches of Algiers. Boston, 1826. (A description of the Berbers in Algeria including comments about the language. The description was based on observations made while Shaler served as U.S. Consul in Algiers. A French translation, Esquisse de l'état d'Alger, prepared by Bianchi and published in Paris in 1830 was used as a handbook for French troops when they invaded Algeria.)
799. WYSNER, GLORIA M. The Kabyle people. New York, 1945.
800. ZANON, F. Contributo alla conoscenza linguistico-etnografica dell'oasi di Augila. Afr. Ital., 259–70, 1933.
See also works by:
BASSET, ANDRÉ (See no. 646).
BIARNAY, S. (See no. 64).

Boulifa, Si Ammar ben Said (See nos. 142, 602).
Bousquet, Georges H. (See no. 6).
Hanoteau, Adolphe (See no. 607).
Justinard, Léopold V. (See no. 686).
Mercier, H. (See no. 697).
Monteil, Vincent (See no. 112).
Mordini, A (See no. 570).
Nicolas, Francis (See no. 704).
Paradisi, Umberto (See no. 458).
Renisio, Amidée (See no. 328).
Rinn, Louis (See nos. 30, 31).

Berber Bibliography

801. Applegate, Joseph R. Berber Studies I: Shilha. MEJ II.324–7, 1957. (Short bibliographical article.)
802. Blaudin de The, Bernard. Essai de Bibliographie du Sahara Français et des régions avoisinantes. Service des Affaires sahariennes, 1959. (The linguistics listings are unsatisfactory because of the many omissions and inaccuracies.)
803. Ceccherini, Ugo. Bibliografia della Libia. Rome 1915. (This is a continuation of the bibliography published by Minutelli. Items published between 1903 and 1914 are included, with notes. Accurate and complete.)
804. Cenival, Pierre, and Christian Funck-Brentano. Bibliographie Marocaine. Paris, 1937. (This is a supplemented version of the annual bibliographies that had appeared in Hespéris. The entries are complete and accurate with notes of important revues.)
805. Hosotte-Reynaud, M. Publication de l'Institut des Hautes Études Marocaines. Limoges, 1956. (A complete list of all publications of the Institute from 1936 to 1954, including tables of contents for Hespéris.)
806. Minutelli, Frederico. Bibliografia della Libia. Turin, 1903. (Predecessor of Ceccherini's bibliography, no. 803.)
807. Playfair, Robert L. A bibliography of Algeria. London, 1888. (From 1541 to 1887.)
808. ——. Supplement to the Bibliography of Algeria. London, 1898. (This supplement to the preceding entry contains listings from 470 B.C. to 1895 A.D.)
809. ——, and Robert Brown. A bibliography of Morocco. London, 1892.
810. Stumme, Hans. Arabische und berberische Dialekte. Berlin, 1928. (Bibliographical notes.)
811. Tovar, A. Los estudios bereberes en relacion con España. Cuadernos de estudios africanos, 113–24.

See also works by:

Alvarez Delgado, Juan (See no. 129).
Aucapitaine, Henri (See no. 35).
Avezac-Macaya (See no. 589).
Barthé, Albert (See no. 524).
Basset, André (See no. 41).
Basset, René (See nos. 133, 216, 653, 732).
Beguinot, Francesco (See nos. 136, 140, 249).
Bourilly, J. (See no. 747).
Bousquet, Georges H. (See no. 6).
Calassanti-Motylinski, G. A. de (See no. 594).
Castries, Henri (See no. 7).
Chabot, J. B. (See no. 252).
Cust, Robert N. (See no. 76).
Destaing, Edmond (See no. 443).
Galand, Lionel (See no. 90).
Ibáñez, Esteban (See no. 497).
Köller, Ange (See no. 775).
Laoust, Emile (See no. 105).
Lauro, A. (See no. 106).
Monteil, Vincent (See no. 455).
Wölfel, Dominik J. (See no. 181).

PART FOUR

REGIONAL LANGUAGE ISSUES AND STUDIES

REGIONAL LANGUAGE ISSUES AND STUDIES: AN OVERVIEW

The nations of Southwest Asia and North Africa share many features in their respective language situations and also show interesting parallels in their responses to language problems, but contrasts are also apparent among them. The four chapters which follow are written from different points of view and with quite disparate coverage of particular questions, but each illustrates to some extent the fundamental similarities and differences.

Unlike many nations in Asia and Africa, every one of the countries in this area clearly has a dominant national language, although complications exist in a number of them. In Afghanistan the dominance of Pashto is shared with Persian; in Arabic-speaking Iraq, Sudan, Algeria, and Morocco minority languages are spoken by substantial proportions of the populations; in Iran the native speakers of languages other than Persian constitute a large segment of the population; and in Israel, Arabic is a recognized minority language beside the dominant Hebrew. Finally, in all these, and other countries in the area, a European 'language of wider communication', either English or French, plays a special role; in several, for example, it is a medium of secondary and higher education. All this means that the choice of a national language is not, as such, at issue in these countries, although for several the extension of the national language to domains of use formerly or still filled by English or French is a question of considerable importance. This latter has often involved political speechmaking, editorializing, and other public expression of national sentiments but little study of the actual allocation or shifting of domains; two exceptions are the volume on Arabic-French bilingualism in Lebanon by Selim Abou and the studies on Arabization in Tunisia reported at conferences and in the *Revue Tunisienne de Sciences Sociales* of the University (Abou 1962, *Actes du Seminaire de Linguistique* 1966).

Language development may be considered under the three headings of graphization, standardization, and modernization (Ferguson 1968). On the first point, all national languages of the area have a fairly well-established standard orthography. Apart from Turkish, however, which drastically changed its system of writing in the twenties, all the languages (Arabic, Persian, Pashto, and Hebrew) have orthographic reform movements, and discussions of orthographic change have taken place in official institutions or agencies of language planning. Interestingly enough, the issues raised are strikingly similar: possible romanization, more efficient representation of vowels in ordinary writing, and the spelling of foreign words; in addition, for languages using Arabic script, the issue has been raised of simplifying the varied shapes of consonantal letters or totally eliminating ligature forms. For Arabic and Persian the chapters by Al-Toma and Yar-Shater in this volume give convenient summaries and bibliographical references; for Hebrew, cf. Rabin (forthcoming) and for Pashto, Penzl (1954). Despite decisions by language academies, at least on minor points, and by governmental policy on several occasions, almost no significant changes in orthography have occurred; one is reminded of the similarly insignificant orthographic changes in most of the world's languages even after lengthy and heated presentation of the issues (Berry 1957, Dickens 1953, Smalley 1964).

On the question of standardization, the five major national languages of the area differ on both the nature of the norm and the degree of diglossia (Ferguson 1959). Arabic is a clear case of full diglossia with all its accompanying educational problems and conflicting goals of language change, as Al-Toma discusses in some detail. This situation has been repeatedly recognized and discussed for Arabic, but the nature and function of intermediate varieties and also such basic issues as degree of mutual intelligibility of Classical and colloquial, shifts in domain of use, and historical development still cry out for systematic, dispassionate study. Persian and Pashto, like many languages, show considerable regional and social variation, but they are not cases of diglossia in the Arabic sense. Their status is of special interest in that both have competing centers of standardization: Persian has the standards of Teheran and Kabul as well as the norm of Soviet Tajikistan; Pashto, those of Kandahar in Afghanistan and Peshawar in Pakistan. Descriptive and dialectological studies of some of the variation in Persian and Pashto are reported elsewhere in this volume, but socio-linguistic studies of the differing patterns of standardization as such, and attempts to determine the current trends within them, would be of value for both linguistic scholarship and national policy-making in education and communication.

Since all major national languages of the area are increasingly used for scientific and technological purposes and are functioning more and more as part of the intertranslatable worldwide communication network, modernization of vocabulary and forms of discourse presents serious and special problems: Hebrew as a revived language requires unusually rapid lexical expansion; Arabic has such wide geographical extension that new terms are coined in different centers. Each language has at least one national organization devoted to its cultivation. Most of these take the form of a language academy comprising a small number of highly respected scholars selected for life and intended to function as authoritative sources of decisions on points of grammar, new vocabulary, and literary standards. One, however, the Türk Dil Kurumu, is a large association with nationwide membership which, at least in its early years, included not only leading scholars but also enthusiastic amateur word collectors. The Syrian academy is the oldest of these organizations (founded in 1918–19), the Academy of the Hebrew Language the most recent (1953); most of them were established during the two decades 1927–47.

The processes of modernization take place outside the academies as well as within; a few studies of these processes, especially on the sources of new vocabulary, are referred to in the following chapters. Almost no sociolinguistic studies of the process itself have been made, and only a handful of studies on the operations and accomplishments of the academies (e.g. Hamzaoui 1965, Morag 1959) or other planning agencies. This aspect of national development, however, is only now beginning to receive recognition as a legitimate and important field of inquiry (Tauli 1968, Jernudd and Das Gupta forthcoming).

Linguistics as a scholarly discipline has been slow to appear in the universities and intellectual circles of the countries of Southwest Asia and North Africa. Competent scholars in all major universities work on historical and philological questions in the national language, carry out limited research on local dialects, and make comparative linguistic studies, but they do little teaching or research in general linguistics, at least in part because systematic scientific study of human language behavior and its underlying principles has low priority in terms of national needs, and possibly also because language issues themselves are tied to nationalistic sentiments and emotional attitudes. Even departments of linguistics as in Teheran and at the Hebrew University are affected by strong normative views held by particular scholars and national leaders.

On the other hand, substantial efforts have been made to cope with the problem of language in education, many of them based on careful investigation and sophisticated educational philosophies. A number of countries have introduced materials and techniques for literacy instruction and for teaching the national language and foreign languages; a few have made serious attempts to broaden the range of foreign languages taught. Although coverage of these movements is uneven in the chapters of this section, they indicate the nature and extent of innovation and demonstrate that great changes are taking place.

REFERENCES

ABOU, SELIM. 1962. Bilinguisme arabe-français au Liban. Paris, Presses Universitaires de France.

Actes du séminaire de linguistique. 1966. Revue Tunisienne de Sciences Sociales, 3e année, no. 8. Tunis, Centre d'Études et de Recherches Économiques et Sociales.

BERRY, JACK. 1957. The making of alphabets. Proceedings of the 8th International Congress of Linguists, 752–64. Oslo.

DICKENS, K. J. 1953. Unification in the Akan dialects of the Gold Coast. The use of vernacular languages in education, 115–23. Paris, Unesco.

FERGUSON, CHARLES A. 1959. Diglossia. Word 15.325–40.

——. 1968. Language development. Language problems of developing nations, ed. by J. A. Fishman, C. A. Ferguson, and J. Das Gupta. New York, Wiley.

HAMZAOUI, RICHARD. 1965. L'académie arabe de Damas et le problème de la modernisation de la langue arabe.

JERNUDD, BJÖRN and JYOTIRINDRA DAS GUPTA. Forthcoming. Towards a theory of language planning. To appear in proceedings of the meeting on language planning processes, Hawaii, 1969.

MORAG, SHLOMO. 1959. Planned and unplanned development in Modern Hebrew. Lingua 8.247–63.

PENZL, HERBERT. 1954. Orthography and phonemes in Pashto. JAOS 74.74–81.

RABIN, CHAIM. Forthcoming. Spelling reform — Israel 1968. To appear in proceedings of the meeting on language planning processes, Hawaii, 1969.

SMALLEY, WILLIAM A., et al. 1964. Orthography studies. London.

TAULI, VALTER. 1968. Introduction to a theory of language planning. Uppsala, Acta Universitatis Upsaliensis.

CHARLES A. FERGUSON

IRAN AND AFGHANISTAN*

EHSAN YAR-SHATER

1. Twentieth century language studies in Iran and Afghanistan have been largely dominated by a method based on traditional Islamic literary and linguistic science modified by European concepts and methods. Modern linguistics was introduced on a modest level in the early 1930's but its application to language studies has only recently made headway. The chief linguistics centers are Tehran, Tabriz, and Mashhad in Iran, and Kabol in Afghanistan.

The subject at hand may conveniently be studied under the following headings: Grammar, Dialectology, Lexicography, Modern Linguistics, and Language Teaching.

GRAMMAR

2.1. In Iran, Persian grammar has been the main concern of grammarians, while in Afghanistan, following the general policy of the State, the study of Pashtu has been the focus of official and academic attention.

Persian grammar generally treats of the polite or written language. Qarib's definition of grammar as that which 'treats of the rules of speaking and writing correctly' (1911:5) is followed by almost all Persian grammarians (Homā'i 1959:117, Qarib et al. 1950:4, Homāyunfarrokh 1959:33, Khayyāmpur 1965:11).[1] The criterion of

* I am indebted to Mr. I. Afshar, Miss Eden Naby, Mrs. M. Schinasi, Dr. Ahmad Tafazzoli, Dr. H. Milanian, Professors S. Reshtin and A. H. Navā'i and Mr. Q. Ghazanfar for kindly assisting me in obtaining some of the relevant material.

The following transcription has been used in this contribution.

vowels		some consonants			
a	Wa	s̱	Wa	z̤	Wa
e	Wa	ḥ	Wa	ţ	Wa
o	Wa	ẕ	Wa	ẓ	Wa
ā	Wa	zh	Wa	‘	Wa
i	Wa	sh	Wa	gh	Wa
u	Wa	ṣ	Wa	q	Wa
		ṣ̌	Wa	’	Wa
		ḍ	Wa		
		dz	Wa		

[1] Baṣṣāri's definition of grammar as 'the sum of the rules and principles on which the language has been based' (1967:3) is broader, but gives the impression that the language was consciously formed with the help of some rules.

correctness is neither logic nor current use, but 'the usage of the classic writers'. Accordingly, double plurals (e.g. *manzel-hā* 'stages', *'ajāyeb-hā* 'wonders') and double comparatives (e.g. *owlā-tar* 'prior, better') and nouns made of a Persian base and an Arabic suffix (e.g. *irāniyyat* 'Persian-ness', *maniyyat* 'I-ness, ego', *bahāriyye* 'ode to spring'), all of which challenge some current rule of Persian grammar, are, however reluctantly, considered acceptable, because they are used by some classic writers[2] (Homā'i 1959:118, Qarib et al. 1950:30, Mo'in 1961:81, Minavi 1950:6–8). On the other hand, omitting the verbal part of a compound verb (e.g. omitting *kard* 'he did' from *ṣāder kard* 'he issued') when its nominal complement by itself indicates the sense of the omitted verb — a practice often found in administrative correspondence and journalistic prose[3] — is not admissible, because the *qodamā*, 'the ancients', did not do so.[4]

The conservative character of grammatical writings hardly condones[5] and often ignores innovation. Thus a continuous past and present of recent formation which employs the auxiliary *dāshtan* 'to have, to hold' (*dāram miravam* 'I am going', *dāshtam miraftam* 'I was going') is hardly ever treated in formal Persian grammars,[6] whereas the imperfective suffix *-i*, nonexistent in current use, is often given a full treatment. In grammatical comments and in admonitions about correct writing, the 'proper', that is, the original pronunciation or orthography of words, is often stressed in preference to their current forms (e.g. *vejdān* and *nekāt*, versus *vojdān* and *nokāt*). An article in which this writer (1957:99–104) defended the validity of any usage that gained currency and served communication was viewed with some dismay among the conservatives whose outlook dominates the instruction of Persian in the country.[7] Illustrative of this outlook is the fact that supporting examples in Persian grammars are generally quoted from the classics, preponderantly in verse. In his article on spoken and written language, Khānlari (1961:139–50) draws attention to different levels of usage, but even though he concedes that the gradual change of the language is inevitable, he draws and defends a firm line between spoken and written Persian.

The increasingly emancipated language of some modern writers, with its frequent colloquialisms and grammatical transgressions, has not as yet been found worthy of serious consideration in Persian grammars, and despite rapid social change, the proponents of a more flexible language have thus far found no firm footing in the nation's schools and universities.

[2] Cf. Khānlari (1961:140). Homāyunfarrokh (1959:273), however, disapproves of the use of double plurals.

[3] E.g. *avāmer-e lāzem ṣāder va be-ṭaraf-e ṭehrān rahsepār gardid* 'he issued the necessary orders and set out for Tehran'.

[4] See Minavi 1951, Homā'i 1959:119, Khānlari 1961:132–3.

[5] Minavi's following comment (1950b:6) is illustrative of the point: 'The use of the two words *vaẓ 'iyyat* and *mowqe'iyyat*, as is now practiced after the Turks, has no warrant.'

[6] Keshāvarz (1962) briefly discusses the two tense-aspects. His term *malmus* 'concrete', adopted also by Baṣṣāri (1967:129) is, however, unsuitable. A more pertinent term would be *modāvem* 'continuous' or *jāri* 'current'. Cf. Parvizi (1967:499–504). Behrangi's term *dar jarayān* 'in progress' for the Azari Turkish equivalent (1964) is clumsy if relevant.

[7] Cf. Khānlari (1957).

Sporadically, however, concession is made to current taste and usage. Homā'i (1959:121), for example, recommends relinquishing the concord of gender between Arabic nouns and adjectives used in Persian, and Mo'in quotes from the unconventional contemporary writer Ṣādeq Hedāyat and occasionally also records colloquial usage.[8]

2.2 A more significant exception to the conservative character of grammatical studies is found in Farhādi's grammar of Kaboli Persian: *Le Persan Parlé en Afghanistan.* The objectives of the author may be gathered from his assertion that 'il importe d'étudier la langue *vivante* et effectivement parlée par la plus grande partie de la population — celle des couches sociales "moyennes" en distinguant ce qu'il ya d'argotique, de dialectal, d'archaique, ou emprunts recents au persan semilitéraire' (1955:3). Farhādi's grammar shows marked methodological advances. Working with the speech of the ordinary Kabolis, he organizes his material systematically and with a broader conceptual outlook than is found in ordinary Persian grammars. In his treatment of phonology, however, the author is more concerned with the differentiation between Kaboli and literary Persian than in the description of Kaboli sounds. But unlike many others who confuse their treatment by focussing on the 'letters' rather than the sounds, Farhādi does not allow the written form of the sounds to obscure his analysis. This is more than can be said for even so observant a grammarian as Homā'i, who for instance, rather than proceeding from sounds to their written symbols, at times takes the latter as the point of departure (e.g. 1959:133). Farhādi also discusses accent and intonation in Kaboli and has a useful section on syntax. On the whole, his is a competent and reliable grammar, organized after traditional French models. The fact that it is written in French, however, has limited its effect on native grammars.

3. Phonology is the weakest area in Persian grammars. Consideration of it is almost absent in school grammars, and even in so detailed and bulky a grammar as Homāyunfarrokh's, it does not receive more than a fleeting mention in a section wherein discussion of sounds, the alphabet, and orthography are mingled (1959:35–41). This is partly due to the fact that traditionally phonetics (on which informed treatises exist[9]) was not considered part of grammar, but of metrics. Articulation of speech sounds was treated in works on *tajvid* 'the science of correct pronunciation' with a view towards the proper recitation of the Koran. With the decline of traditional sciences, phonetics all but disappeared.

An intelligent discussion of some aspects of Persian phonology is found, however, in Khānlari's book on Persian meters (1958:85–119). He correctly notes, for instance, that unlike Arabic, what differentiates Persian long and short vowels is not only length, which may be blurred in rapid speech, but timbre (1958:97; cf. Ekhtiār 1967:227). In reviewing the various possibilities for accounting for the so-called

[8] E.g. *āqāyun-hā* 'gentlemen' (Mo'in 1958:87).
[9] Among others, Avicenna's *Asbāb ḥudūth al-ḥurūf* or *Makhārij al-ḥurūf*. Naṣir Ṭusi's *Mi'yār al-ash'ār* contains a very useful section on the subject.

diphthong [ow], Khānlari rightly disagrees with considering the second member as the semi-vowel *w*, since it doesn't otherwise occur in Persian (1958:102). But his own choice, namely, taking the second member for the vowel *u* is no more satisfactory, since as he himself remarks, the diphthong has only the duration of two short vowels, whereas /u/ is a long vowel roughly equalling by itself two short vowels. Actually the most economical account of [w] is to consider it an allophone of /v/ occurring only after /o/ within the same syllable and if not followed by /v/.[10]

On the basis of some laboratory experiments, Khānlari claims that the accent in Persian is one of pitch rather than intensity, a view which runs counter to generally accepted opinion. In the absence of published laboratory tests or a more detailed study that Khānlari has promised but not yet presented, it is difficult to either support or reject this view. Fo'ādi, whose early death in the late 1930's deprived Persian linguistics of its best informed scholar, considers word accent in Persian one of intensity (1933–34:967).[11] This notion is implied also by Ekhtiār who treats of some aspects of Persian phonetics in an appendix to his treatment of English phonetics (1967:229, 233).[12]

4.1 Of the major points of divergence among Persian grammarians, I may mention two. One concerns the number of word classes. Traditional practice, following Arabic grammars, distinguished only three parts of speech: nouns, verbs, and indeclinables (*ḥoruf*). Ḥabib Eṣfahāni, influenced by European models, delineated ten (Homā'i, 1959:127, 129); and Qarib (whose views gained wide acceptance through the almost exclusive use of his graded grammars in schools) divided words, following French models, into nine classes: namely, nouns, adjectives, pronouns, numbers, verbs, adverbs, prepositions, conjunctions, and interjections (1911:26). In his acceptance address to the Iranian Academy (the *Farhangestān*), Homā'i (1959:134–5) challenged the appropriateness of this division and proposed a division based on six classes: nouns, adjectives, particles, interjections, verbs, and quasi-verbs (*shebh-e feʿl*). He admits, however, that the latter (such as *āfarin!*, *darigh!*) may be included either under verbs or nouns, reducing the parts of speech to five. Later classifications have varied somewhat in this respect. Homāyunfarrokh makes pronouns, adjectives, and adverbs into separate classes,[13] whereas Khayyāmpur (1965:28–9) subsumes pronouns under nouns, but differentiates the phrase-words (what Homāyunfarrokh

[10] Otherwise [w] reverts to [v], e.g. [now] 'new', [noˈvi] 'new-ness', [qovˈvæt] 'strength'. There are three words in Persian where /ov/ is followed by /v/: /qovævt/, /dovvom/, and /zovvar/.

[11] Fo'ādi distinguishes three accents in Persian: 'lafzi' (accent of a syllable within a word), 'manteqi' (accent of a word within a sentence), and 'musiqi' (clause accent). He considers the first two intensity accents, and the third, one of pitch (musical) (1933:964–8).

[12] Cf. Ferguson's remark (1957:124) on this point: 'Identification of the exact nature of the prominence attributed to stress must await experienced investigation, but the auditory impression is that of relative loudness, so called "expiratory" stress.' Ferguson (1957:123–35) makes reference to other works and opinions on stress in Persian. Jazāyery and Paper (1961:51) are noncommittal. They recognize that 'a great deal of work needs to be done on Persian superfixes'.

[13] According to the section headings.

calls 'quasi-verbs') from other classes. Since the approach in these grammars is not structural, the problem as posed is perhaps not significant, although it does somewhat affect the definition of grammatical classes and organization of materials. In a notional grammar the older categorization of words into nouns, verbs, and indeclinables remains the most economical. But in a descriptive grammar clarity of definition may require more detailed divisions. Formal description of Persian word classes calls for fresh studies. This is particularly true in the case of adverbs and indefinite pronouns, considering their fluid contours and frequent over-lapping with some other word classes.

4.2 A second point of divergence among grammarians concerns the derivation of verbs. Led by the example of Arabic, in which all verbal forms are traced back to their single root, traditional grammarians tried to derive various Persian verb forms from a single base, the infinitive. This course, followed by Qarib, results in a complicated series of totally unnecessary rules of sound changes. In a strictly structural account of Persian verb derivation, such a system of morphophonemic alterations may have a place, but in a grammar meant for instruction much can be said for a system of verb derivation based on two stems, past and present. In such a system one finds that practically all Persian verbs are regular; all reference to 'irregular' verbs is thus not only futile, but also unnecessarily difficult for students. What the grammarians have called 'regular' verbs are in fact verbs with a secondary past stem (e.g. *xābid* 'he slept' < the present stem *xāb*, versus the older past form *xoft*). Although adherence to the two-base system has now relieved most Persian grammars of cumbersome morphophonemic rules of verb derivation, vestiges of the old approach are still found in some, notably Homāyunfarrokh (1959:422ff.) and Qarib et al. (1950:119).

4.3 In 1942 in his acceptance address to the Iranian Academy, Homā'i partially reviewed early Persian grammars and pointed out areas which needed further research or fresh treatment (see 1959). Since then a fairly large number of Persian grammars have been published, but the paucity of original approaches hardly justifies their number. In a new secondary school grammar, Khānlari attempts a fresh arrangement of grammatical material, mainly to facilitate instruction. On the assumption that the basic unit of a language is a clause rather than a word, he begins his grammar with the definition of the sentence, and then through its analysis leads into morphology. Despite this promising approach, however, the book soon falls into the conceptual patterns of older Persian grammars and follows their familiar paths. The author makes no attempt at formal definition, and his grammar remains solidly notional. Some of his terminology and definitions even represent a setback. For instance, his definition of sentence as 'a collection of words that together contain a complete and perfect thought' is somewhat blurred by his use of the term *jomle* for both sentence and clause (Khānlari 1967:8, 40–5).

Fo'ādi, on the other hand, clearly distinguishing the two, employs *jomle* for the clause and *kalām* for the sentence. In his perceptive article on the subject (1935–36c), in which he aims at formal definitions, he characterizes a sentence by two features:

containing a verb, and having a falling intonation accent at the end followed by a juncture. A subordinate clause is distinguished from an independent clause by having a different intonation accent at the end.[14]

However, a number of useful and detailed studies in a traditional manner on various aspects of Persian grammar have added much to our knowledge of literary Persian: Minavi's essay on the infinitive-forming suffix *-iyyat* (1950b); Moʿin's monographs on definition (1958), the ezafe (1962b), number (1961), and verbal nouns (1962a); Mortaẕavi's article on suffixes (1956); and Khaṭib Rahbar's article on prepositions (1964, 1967) deserve particular mention.

5. Among the Iranian and Afghan linguists who have contributed new directions to the study of Persian, are Moḥammad Jazāyery and Eḥsan Enteẓār. Jazāyery, in collaboration with Herbert H. Paper and under a contract with the United States Office of Education, prepared *A reference grammar of Modern Persian* (University of Michigan, 1961), a grammar conceived on a structural basis. It is to be regretted that only a limited number of mimeographed copies of this work were distributed. Despite some inadequacies to which the authors freely admit, its wider circulation would have stimulated a fresh treatment of Persian grammar.

Enteẓār's contribution is seen in *Farsi reference manual*, a basic course in Kaboli Persian prepared in collaboration with David J. Burns, coordinator of the Language Program of the Peace Corps, Experiment in International Living (mimeographed edition, Putney, Vermont, 1964). The first part briefly describes segmental and supra-segmental phonemes; other parts illustrate and concisely comment on the structural patterns of the language. Unpretentious as the work is from a grammatical point of view, the fact that its approach is more structurally than traditionally oriented makes it a significant contribution.

6. The study of Pashtu has received a good deal of attention in Afghanistan since 1936 when a royal decree inaugurated a movement to promote the cause of Pashtu as a national language. Pashtu Tolana, the Pashtu Society, has made remarkable efforts to bring the language into focus and facilitate its instruction. Most such efforts concentrated on the literary and historical heritage of the Pashtu people. But a number of grammars revealing an earnest interest in the study of Pashtu have been published in Afghanistan by such authors as Qandahāri (1937–38), Mohmand (1938), Ayāzi (1939, 1948), Olfat (1941), Khādem (1948), Wakil (1951), and Reshtin (1958).

DIALECTOLOGY

7.1 In recent years interest in the study of local dialects has spread in both Iran and Afghanistan. The interest has centered on the collection of vocabulary and texts, and

[14] Fo'ādi's worthy approach, however, went mostly unnoticed.

a number of useful lexical works, text editions, and also grammatical studies have resulted.[15] A large number of folk poems in local dialects have been recorded and published in Persian and Afghan periodicals. Field recordings of daily speech, however, have been relatively few,[16] and disciplined phonetic descriptions of local dialects are only beginning to increase.[17]

Until recently, in treating the grammar of these dialects, researchers have mostly been guided by traditional Persian grammars, generally describing their dialects through comparison with Persian. Such grammatical studies are particularly weak in phonology. Conjugation of verbs receives the greatest attention; pronouns, numerals, comparison of adjectives, and suffixes are generally covered.

In the 1960's, however, a number of researchers with training in linguistics have applied themselves to the study of local dialects. Baqā'i's study of Kermāni Persian (1963–67) and Zomorrodiān's study of Qāyeni Persian (1965–66), both of which employ modern linguistic methods, are indicative of a new direction.

Of the several articles which have sought to guide dialect researchers, that of Khānlari (1959) treats of general guidelines and is followed by a short vocabulary questionnaire. Ekhtiār's (1964–66) is a far more detailed piece of work and practically includes a course on general phonetics.

The most active center of dialect studies is to be found in Tabriz where a number of keen and active scholars (including Navvābi, Mortaẓavi, Adib Ṭusi, Kārang, Baqā'i, Ayyubiān, Salim, Fattāḥi Qāẓi, Māchiāni, and Arzhangi) have published a series of studies on Kurdish, Tāti, Azari Turkish, and some other dialects. Most Turkish studies are concerned with comparison of Turkish and Persian vocabulary, idioms, and idiomatic expressions.[18] Ayyubiān's (1961–62) and Fattāḥi's (1964–66) editions of Kurdish texts are useful additions to the available texts on that language.

[15] Among such works are Sābeti's guide to Iranian forest trees (1947) which contains a wealth of dialectal tree names; Mokri's glossary of Kurdish bird names (1947) and his edition of a number of Kurdish songs (1950); Moqaddam's work on the dialects of Vafs, etc; Ẕokā's sketches of Karingāni (1953) and Harzandi (1957); Sotude's dictionaries of Gilaki (1953), Kermāni (1957), and Semnāni etc. (1964); Kārang's study of Tāti and Harzani (1954); Eqtedāri's dictionary of Lāri (1955); Sorushiān's dictionary of the language of the 'Behdinān'; Kiā's dictionary of Āshtiāni (1956); Yār-Shāṭer's essay on the Iranian languages and dialects (1957a); Badakhshi's dictionary of Pashtu, etc. which provides a useful comparative list of Pashtu, Persian, and five Pāmir dialects (1960); Sirat's article on the Arabic dialect around Balkh (1962); Tafaẓẓoli's glossary of the dialectal words of the *Toḥfat al-Mo'menin* (1962); Farahvashi's article on the Sedehi verb (1962); Mortaẓavi's article on Harzani verbs (1962–63); Ayyubiān's article on gender in Kurdish (1963); Rajā'i's study of Bokhārā'i (1964); Izadpanāh's dictionary of Lori (1965); Baqā'i's study of Kermāni Persian (1963–67); Zomorrodiān's study of Qāyeni Persian (1965–66); and Adib Ṭusi's edition and glossary of Shāh Dā'i's poems (1965–66). For details see References.

[16] Rajā'i's useful grammar and glossary of the dialect of Bokhārā, however, contains extensive examples of daily speech (1964:161–303).

[17] This writer has published several papers in English on Southern and Northern Tāti dialects, sketching their phonology and the main features of morphology (1959, 1960, 1964). Description of sounds is made in terms of modern linguistics, those of morphology in terms of traditional grammar.

[18] For studies of Azerbaijani Turkish by 'Abd al-'Ali Kārang, Ṣamad Behrangi and others, see Doerfer in this volume.

The Bulletin of the Tabriz Faculty of Literature has been notable in the past nineteen years for generously publishing such dialect studies.

In Mashhad, traditionally a center of language and literary scholarship, an active group of language researchers (including Rajā'i, Yusofi, Matini, 'Afifi, and Zomorrodiān) are making increasing use of the Bulletin of the Faculty of Literature for publishing their research.

In Tehran the newly formed group of linguists, centered in the University's Department of Linguistics has been more occupied with linguistic theories and methods than with their application to dialect studies. With the ground work already achieved, there is promise of more extensive work in the field.

7.2 Through the efforts of the Société internationale de la dialectologie iranienne (established in 1957), a summer course was given by Professors G. Morgenstierne and G. Redard to train young investigators (mostly university students and elementary school teachers) to collect dialect data for the projected Linguistic Atlas of Iran. For two years the trainees collected materials, mostly from Tāti dialects; but since 1962 the project has been inactive in Persia because of a shortage of funds. In Afghanistan, on the other hand, the Linguistic Institute of the Faculty of Literature of the University of Kabol has encouraged the project. Thus far materials from some 200 linguistic groups have been collected by the investigators trained by the Société and the Institute in Afghanistan.[19] None of these, however, has yet been published.

8. Several studies aim at establishing a historical perspective of local dialects. Aḥmad Kasravi's pioneering book on the ancient language of Azerbaijan (1925) established that before Turkish became the vernacular of the region an Iranian language (Āẕariyya, or Āẕari), still spoken in some Azerbaijan villages, had been in use in the area. Kasravi, however, was a better historian than linguist. He assumed for instance, that Median, Old Persian, and Parthian were all one and the same language with only slight differences, and that these differences reflected temporal rather than geographical factors (1938:7–8; see 1930–31). Yet he was able to stimulate interest in linguistic work. A number of Afghan scholars such as Badakhshi and Ḥabibi have also shown an interest in tracing the Pashtu language and Pamir dialects to Old Indo-Iranian.[20]

This is an area where regional feelings and sentiments toward the past have shown more than desirable bearing on linguistic research, and the interest in historical study of the dialects has not always been matched by comparable philological skill.

LEXICOGRAPHY

9.1 A preliminary task before lexical researchers has been to sift the chaff from the wheat in existing Persian dictionaries. Good progress has been made. Many

[19] According to a report read by G. Redard and M. R. Elhām to the International Congress of Iranology, Tehran, September, 1966.

[20] Ḥabibi's attempt in *Zabān-e do hazār sāl qabl-e afghānestān* (1963) to derive Persian directly from the Bactrian language of the Sor Khkotal inscriptions, however, is unique.

Persian dictionaries of the past few centuries are notorious for their uncritical approach, careless copying, excessive reliance on earlier works, and even inclusion of forgeries: forgeries derived from the *Dasātir*, a seventeenth century work composed in fabricated language and then passed off as a holy book. Oddly enough, it was accepted as a genuine work by a number of the Parsis as well as some Persian writers and lexicographers, notably the author of the *Borhān-e qāteʿ* (seventeenth century), the most current of all traditional Persian dictionaries.

Ibrāhim Pur-Dāvud has been the most prolific of the denouncers of the *Dasātir*,[21] and Moʿin, editor of the standard edition of the *Borhān-e qāteʿ* (Tehran, 1957), makes a point of drawing attention to such forgeries. ʿAli Asghar Hekmat (1945) has followed the lead of pioneer scholars, such as Dāʿi al-Eslām, Moḥammad Qazvini, ʿAli Akbar Dehkhodā, ʿAbbās Eqbāl Ashtiāni, and Moḥammad-Taqi Bahār, to provide a fairly clear picture of the sources and relationships of Persian dictionaries and offers as well an analytical description of the content of the *Borhān-e qāteʿ*. In a long introduction to his edition of this work, Moʿin adds more details on the subject, and rectifies a number of corrupt forms in Persian dictionaries.

9.2 Many editors of Persian texts have also done much lexical ground work: in their indices and annotated glossaries of rare, obsolete, and otherwise interesting words they have provided future lexicographers with a rich fund of Persian words with textual illustrations.[22]

The *Bonyād-e farhang-e irān*, a cultural foundation established by royal decree in 1964, is now compiling individual glossaries for significant Persian texts, from which a historical dictionary of Persian is projected. The foundation also has plans for publishing Persian scientific texts (with special attention to terminology), unpublished Arabic-Persian dictionaries, glossaries of a number of Middle Persian texts, and technical and scientific dictionaries.

The conspicuous absence of colloquialisms and slang in Persian dictionaries has now been remedied by several dictionaries, notably those of Raḥmati (1951), Amini (n.d.), Afghāni-nevis (1961), and Jamālzāde (see Djamālzādeh 1962), the latter, one of the earliest writers of short stories in colorful, colloquial language.

Afghan lexicographical efforts have concentrated on the compilation of Pashtu, or, more frequently, Pashtu-Persian dictionaries. The Pashtu Tolana has been the main source of encouragement for such works and has served as their publisher.[23]

The Persian translation and adaptation of the Columbia Viking Desk Encyclopaedia (1965), which has in many cases required creation of new terms or redefinition of older

[21] See especially *Farhang-e Irān-e Bāstān*, vol. I, 1947:17–51 and *Hormazd-nāme*, 1953:310–19.

[22] Moʿin (1954) provides a useful glossary of Persian scientific and philosophical terms of the Persian works of Avicenna, Biruni, Naṣir Ṭusi and others. Publication of Gowharin's glossary and concordance of Jalāl al-Din's *Maṣnavi* (4 vols. 1958–69) and a glossary of Ḥāfez by Amir Moqaddam, begun in 1966, is still in progress. An excellent treatment of Western loanwords in Persian is to be found in Jazāyery's study of the subject (1966–67).

[23] Among such works is *Pashtu Qāmus* (2 vols. 1951–54) and the dictionaries compiled by Mohmand (1937), Kākar (1940), Ayāzi (1940), and Afghāni-nevis (3 vols. 1956–57).

ones, must also be considered a valuable lexical event, particularly since its meticulous editor, Gholām-Hosein Moṣāḥeb, has not shrunk before the demands and difficulties of his job.

9.3 The most ambitious lexical project yet undertaken is Dehkhodā's dictionary, *Lughat-nāme*. Dehkhodā aimed at an exhaustive dictionary of the Persian language, including geographical and biographical names. He died in 1959 leaving his incomplete notes and index cards in the care of Moḥammad Moʿin, who, with the help of researchers, has continued Dehkhodā's work. Thus far, 153 fascicles in more than 16,000 pages in folio format have been published.

The *Lughat-nāme* is of uneven quality and value. Its chief merit lies in its coverage of obsolete and literary terms. Here the author's erudition is manifestly evident in the numerous quotations from Persian classics which support or illustrate the meaning of such words. Grammatical comments are also generously provided. The *Lughat-nāme*, however, suffers from the following: meanings are not ordered in terms of frequency or historical occurrence; reference to page numbers of quoted sources is mostly lacking, even for published works;[24] synonyms are often offered for definition and in excessive numbers (the authors' aim obviously has been a thorough compilation of equivalents, however redundant); except in cases when Dehkhodā undertook to write on certain significant figures (such as Biruni and Ibn Sinā), biographical and geographical data are compiled from published works with uneven critical evaluation. In short, the *Lughat-nāme* is more of a pool for lexicographic materials of differing character than a disciplined and evenly reliable dictionary. Its greatest value is perhaps as a source for later dictionaries.

Moʿin's own dictionary, *Farhang-e Moʿin*, of which volumes I, II, III, and V (the latter a dictionary of proper names) have been published to date, is a far less ambitious, but much better organized enterprise and must be considered the best dictionary of Persian, as far as it goes. The author has taken the *Dictionnaire Larousse* as his chief model,[25] and has accordingly planned separate sections for Persian words, foreign expressions, and proper names. For added clarity, the meanings of each word are numbered, but the ordering of the meanings is neither historical nor strictly distributional. The author's attempts to actually define words rather than merely provide synonyms have been only partially successful. This, in fact, is an area in Persian lexicography which requires further elaboration and a great deal more sophistication.[26]

10.1 Faced with growing Western influence, Persia and Afghanistan, along with a number of other countries, have had to cope with an acute need for lexical innovation. In both countries, as in Turkey and India, this need coincided with the rise of nationalism. The process has therefore been influenced by para-linguistic considerations and

[24] In later fascicles better source references are given.

[25] Cf. vol. I, Introduction, 48.

[26] It is to be deeply regretted that Moʿin's illness since 1966 has placed the publication of a promised larger version of his dictionary in serious doubt.

linked with various movements for the purification of the language from its foreign elements, particularly Arabic.

The earliest organized effort in Persia to coin new words appeared in 1934 among some military nationalists and like-minded civilians. A strong distaste for words of Arabic origin led the group to make or adopt what were thought to be purely Persian words. With inadequate linguistic information, occasionally they created such anomalies as *artesh* 'army' and *timsār* (honorific title for generals).[27]

Alarmed at their excesses, which at times violated the long-established norms of Persian, a number of responsible scholars sought to harness these lexical outbursts. This led, in 1935, to the formation of the Farhangestān, the Iranian Academy, somewhat on the model of the French Academy. The Farhangestān adopted in its constitution and by-laws a comprehensive program of lexical, grammatical, and literary research procedures, but in practice, and because of national pressure, it focussed mainly on adopting or coining new terms.

In the same year Taqizāde's famous article '*Jonbesh-e melli-ye adabi*' (National Literary Movement) was published.[28] Veteran of the 1906 Constitutional Revolution, respected statesman and scholar, who at one time had championed a complete overhaul of national habits and customs, Taqizāde now sharply attacked the extremists' position as eccentric, shallow, and thoughtless (1941:4). He defended the norms of proper Persian, stressed the acquired right of 'citizenship' for current Arabic elements, and cautioned against rash decisions with a proposal for a scholarly society responsible for linguistic revision or innovation — a proposal which well fitted the constitution of the envisaged Farhangestān.

The article created an acute sensation and was even banned for a while. But Taqizāde's suggestion, which coincided with that of the eminent scholar and statesman Mohammad 'Ali Foroughi (then Prime Minister), and was supported by a solid if mute body of Persian men of learning, helped to organize the moderate wing and shape its views. The tension established between traditionalist and nationalist viewpoints has pervaded the Persian linguistic atmosphere ever since. The moderates' case is set forth in Foroughi's *Payām-e man be farhangestān* (My message to the Farhangestān, 1937), a work of considerable common sense, insight, and cogency. As the first President of the Farhangestān, he naturally tried to translate his thoughts into action, at times in the face of strong opposing pressures.

Foroughi recognizes the mood of the time and makes concessions to the current preference for words of Persian origin. He suggests ways and methods for gradually accommodating this preference and replacing Arabic words with Persian ones — but with certain restrictions: he warns against rash assumptions which may ruin the language, deplores importing unfamiliar Middle and Old Iranian words into Persian, and above all defends long-current Arabic words as part and parcel of the language

[27] The first is based on a misanalysis of Middle Persian *arteštār* (< Av. *raθaē štar-* 'warrior') and the second is a *Dasātir* word. See Pur-Dāvud, 1953:275–86, 320–58.

[28] Also published separately later in 1941. See References.

and its literary heritage (1937:6–31). Essentially a conservative, however, he strongly pleads resistance to the absorption into the language of European words (with the exception of international terms referring to concrete objects, e.g. *atom* and *telephone*) and semantic loans, a practice he believes to be the greatest danger to the constitution of Persian.

The alarm raised against the intrusion of Western languages on Persian, born partly of patriotism and partly of distaste for change in linguistic habits, has been the rallying cry of most literary scholars (Qazvini 1924; Taqizāde 1947; Forughi 1941, 1951; Eqbāl 1933, 1948; Minavi 1950a; Maḥjub 1957). Purists of a different kind, they have stood for the elegant language of the great Persian classics. They have abhorred any trend which threatens to interfere with its modes of expression, often forgetting that language is not an isolated phenomenon in human behavior, and that the nature and pace of current social change in Iranian society are bound to affect language in ways unlikely to be agreeable to the purists.

The new words adopted or issued by the Farhangestān in the eight years (1935–43) before its sessions were disrupted by the political turmoil which followed the Second World War, attest, by and large, to its sound methods and good taste, and to the prevalence of moderate opinion. The norms of word-formation and derivation in Persian were generally preserved, and excessess frequently resisted.

10.2 Others have chosen different methods of word coinage, with a view toward 'rectifying' or enriching the language. For example, Aḥmad Kasravi's efforts to gradually purge his prose of Arabic words finally led him to resuscitate obsolete and dead vocabulary, to treat non-productive affixes as productive, and to extend full or 'logical' conjugations where the language recognized only partial or arbitrary ones. He ended by making his prose intelligible only to the initiated.[29] Another group, best represented by Moḥammad Moqaddam, has tended to divide a Western term into its constituent parts, literally translate each part into a Persian equivalent, preferably a cognate, and then put them together as a new word (e.g. *tarā-nevisi* for 'tran(s)-scription', *miyān-vāke'i* 'inter-vocalic'). Already criticized and rejected by Forughi as inadequate and contrary to the spirit of the language (1937:48–9), this method has remained unpopular.

10.3 Worthy of mention in this respect is a small glossary of proposed geographical terms by a group of forward-looking scholars.[30] Conscious of the acute need for new scientific terminology and impatient with the slow progress in the field, they have not confined themselves to reviving old and unfamiliar words, redefining current terms, or making new ones by the accepted derivation and combination methods, but have also adopted some foreign bases as if they were Persian, and then derived new terms from them according to Persian rules. Hence such words as *oksidan*

[29] Kasravi's numerous articles on language and on Persian appeared chiefly in his own journal *Peymān*, 1933–41, Tehran.

[30] A. Ārām, Ṣ. Aṣfiyā, H. Golgolāb, Gh. Moṣāḥeb, M. Moqarrabi. Golgolāb (1961) has also contributed to Persian nomenclature by his devising of many plant names.

'oxidize', *oksande* 'oxidizer', *oksāyesh* 'oxidation' (Ārām et al. 1960:5), *yonize* 'ionized', and *yongar* 'ionizer' (1960:59). This is bound to prove shocking to the purist but does open a way for accurate and flexible terminology. Its proponents may point out that the principle involved is not, after all, new to Persian, but is seen in such hybrids as *fahm-idan* 'to understand' and *ṭalab-idan* 'to seek'.

11. In connection with linguistic reforms may be mentioned attempts at alphabet reform. The rapid modernization in Iran under Rezā Shāh (1925–41) stirred among some patriots a desire for changing the Persian script, a step which had even earlier found some protagonists (notably Mirzā Fatḥ-ʿAli Akhūndzāde, d. 1878).[31] By some superficial reasoning a number of well-meaning reformists came to regard the Persian system of writing — which generally omits short vowels — as the major obstacle to instant literacy. Proposed changes varied from adopting Latin script (advanced by, among others, Nafisy [1950], and the Anjoman-e Īrān-e Javān 'Young Iran Society') to reviving the Avestan alphabet (Pur-Dāvud), to vocalizing Persian script in various ways,[32] to accepting a new alphabet supposedly based on the description of the relevant organs of speech (Behruz 1946). Iran actually twice came close to seriously considering alphabet change, but conservative opinion prevailed against the idea.

12. Within the existing system of writing, orthography has received a good deal of attention. With the practical demise of the Farhangestān, however, no official standardization has been possible. The best study of the subject is contained in the late Aḥmad Bahmanyār's detailed article (1952) which is an elaboration of his acceptance address to the Farhangestān. He carefully examines all orthographic problems of Persian and proposes rules, among others, for the writing of *hamze*, the *yāʾ-e vaḥdat* and *kasre-ye eẕāfe* in various environments. He argues that in the *eẕāfe* construction when the first member ends in [e] (indicated in writing by a silent *h*), the [e] of the *eẕāfe* (pronounced *-ye* in this case) should not be indicated by a *hamze* above the *h*, as in common use, but by a full *y*. He also claims that when *ā* or *u* is followed by *i* (*yāʾ-e vaḥdāt*, *yāʾ-e nesbat*, etc.) what separates the two vowels is not a glottal stop, but the glide *y*, which should be written accordingly as such, and not as a *hamze*. This proposal, which was later supported by others, has gained a measure of acceptance, even though its phonetic basis is far from certain and does not reflect the standard dialect of Tehran.

MODERN LINGUISTICS

13. Even though Foʾādi's pioneering articles on language and language teaching (1933–34; 1934–35; 1935–36a, b, and c), guided by the Russian school of linguistics,

[31] See I. Afshār, *Nur-e Jahān* II/6-7.16–19; 8-9.25–6, 29–30 (1951).
[32] Among others M. Naṣri (1925) and A. Farhang (1928).

appeared in the early 1930's, the more effective introduction of this discipline dates only from the early 1950's. In the absence of serious academic sponsorship, however, the spread of linguistics progressed very slowly until 1963 when a department of linguistics was established in the University of Tehran.

Ekhtiār discussed modern phonemic theory in an article published in 1954 (1954: 73–88) and in 1955 provided a more detailed treatment of general phonetics in an introduction to his book on English phonetics (see 1967:24–54). Khānlari in his book on Persian metrics (1958:85–126) touched upon some general aspects of Persian phonetics and discussed stress in some detail.

In 1965, this writer chaired the Iran-American Society's conference on Iranian linguistics at which Ekhtiār discussed the transformational theory of language and its application to Persian. In his *From linguistics to literature* (1962), Ekhtiār refers to a number of theories affecting the development of modern linguistics and discusses recent definitions of poetry and literature. A recent article by Fereydun Badre'i (1967) largely confines discussion on general semantics to various basic definitions.

The most significant development in the spread of linguistic science in Iran is the establishment of the Department of General Linguistics and Ancient Languages in the University of Tehran which offers an M.A. and Ph.D. in linguistics. A group of young and active scholars are now busy teaching, writing, and translating works of foreign linguists.[33] Instruction does not follow any single linguistic school, but exposes students to French, English, and American directions according to the background of staff members who keep well abreast of Western developments in the field. The Ancient Languages section of this department, however, is for the moment given to excessive nationalistic enthusiasm and employs linguistic theories prompted by such enthusiasm.

Application of modern linguistic methods to the study of Iranian languages has not gone very far yet. At this stage most Persian and Afghan linguists are busy with the introduction of new methods and principles and the standardization of essential terminology. But applications of these methods may be expected soon; in fact a number of linguistic research projects and doctoral dissertations involving such applications are now in progress.

LANGUAGE TEACHING

14.1 In the area of applied linguistics, advances in both Iran and Afghanistan are

[33] Including Manṣur Ekhtiār, Hormoz Milāniān, Moḥammad Reẕā Bāṭeni, 'Ali Ashraf Ṣādegi, and Fereydun Badre'i in Tehran; Reẕā Zomorrodiān in Mashẕhad; Nāṣer Baqā'i in Tabriz; andMoḥammad Raḥim Elhām, Nur Aḥmad Shāker, and Ḥabibollāh Tigi in Kabol.

noticeable in the teaching of Persian to beginners (both to children and adults) and in the teaching of English.

Traditionally the alphabet was taught in an almost abstract manner. Early contributions towards the simplification of teaching methods were made by Hushyār,[34] Bāghchebān, and Bizhan who insisted on teaching sounds as the constituents of words, and the alphabet as symbols of sounds. Considerable improvement in reading and writing instruction was affected in 1963 when the Iranian Ministry of Education assisted by the Royal Organization for Social Services, published its four graded readers for elementary schools. The most noticeable advance took place in the, first book, in which Persian sounds, and the symbols which represent them, are taught through the analysis of words into their phonetic constituents. The relevance of words and sentences to the beginners' environment is equally taken into consideration. These methods are now used also in Afghan elementary Pashtu and Persian texts provided through an arrangement with the Franklin Book Program which manages the Education Press in Kabol under a contract with the Government of Afghanistan, and which also operates in Iran.

With the formation of the Literacy Corps in Iran in 1960 as part of the 'White Revolution Program', and with the inauguration of the Literacy Campaign in 1963, the need for a simple and effective method of teaching adults to read and write assumed particular urgency and led to considerable improvement in teaching technique and material. In the first book for adults, which has a companion guide-book for teachers, effective use is made of picture reading to stimulate thinking and expression of ideas, of spoken word analysis for sound identification, and of written word analysis to identify letters. The writing system is first reduced to simple geometric line-drawings and then transformed into letters. Text material is suitable and pertinent.

14.2 In teaching foreign languages, particularly English, traditional reliance on grammar and reading has been superceded by emphasis on language patterns learned through imitation and repetition drills.

In Afghanistan, the change has been affected by the establishment in 1955 of an English Teacher Training Program within the Institute of Education of the University of Kabol, and affiliated with Columbia University's Teachers College. The objectives of the Institute of Education are varied and complex. The Columbia Team provides professional aid and helps to maintain the Institute's self-sufficiency through in-service projects designed to upgrade existing teacher training institutions. The English Language Program has now developed into an Institute located in the Faculty of Education, and the Institute 'is now ready to make headway towards a phase-out program of the American personnel'.[35]

Among the achievements of the Program is the publication of the twelve volume secondary school series, *Afghans learn English.* The books follow the normal pattern

[34] See in particular Hushyār 1946.

[35] From a paper prepared in 1966 by Qāsem Ghaẕanfar, a graduate of Kabol University associated with the Program.

of teaching English to foreigners as developed in the United States. Each of the several units in each book contains speaking, reading, comprehension, and vocabulary exercises. Relevant grammatical points are discussed after the introduction of various patterns. A teacher's guide in English accompanies each volume.

Under the Fulbright Teacher Exchange Program and the British Council Scholarship Program, a number of Iranian teachers of English have had a chance to get acquainted with more advanced teaching methods, and this is reflected in the more recent English books in use in secondary schools. Here again, the importance of the basic patterns of the language, the relevance of the material to the student's environment, and the gradual introduction of new materials are taken into consideration. The adoption of appropriate teaching methods of such materials, however, is not always as easy as might be hoped.

REFERENCES

ADIB ṬUSI. 1964. Farhang-e loghāt-e bāzyāfte (A dictionary of rediscovered words). Tabriz.

——. 1965–66. Kān-e malāḥat: se goftār az shāh dā'i shirāzi ... be lahje-ye qadim-e shirāzi (Three discourses by Shah Dā'i ... in the old dialect of Shiraz). RFLIsf 17.149–82, 376, 466–89; 18.33–48, 197–212, 287–310, 459–75. Republished 1967. Tabriz.

AFGHĀNI-NEVIS, A. 1956. Afghān qāmus: fārsi pe pashtu (Persian-Pashtu dictionary). Kabol. Pashtu Tolana.

——. 1961. Loghat-e 'āmiyāne-ye fārsi-ye afghānestān (Colloquial Persian vocabulary of Afghanistan). Kabol.

AMINI, AMIR QOLI. no date. Farhang-e 'avām (A dictionary of colloquialisms). 2nd. ed. Tehran.

ĀRĀM, A., S. AṢIFIYĀ, H. GOLGOLĀB, GH. MOṢĀḤEB, and M. MOQARRABI. 1960. Farhang-e eṣṭelāhāt-e joghrāfiā'i (A dictionary of geographical terms). Tehran.

AYĀZI, MOḤAMMAD A'ẒAM. 1939. Qavā'ed-e paṣ̌tō (Rules of Pashtu). Kabol.

——. 1940. Les zra paṣ̌tō loghatuna (Ten-thousand Pashtu words). Kabol.

——. 1948. Də paṣ̌tō naḥw (Pashtu syntax). Kabol. Pashtu Tolana.

AYYUBIĀN, 'O. 1961–62. Charike-ye kordi (A Kurdish epic). RFLIsf 13.164–240, 351–406, 527–44; 14.249–84, 343–436, 489-534.

——. 1963. 'Alāmāt-e moẕakkar va mo'annaṯ dar kordi (Signs of the masculine and feminine in Kurdish). RFLIsf 15.418–38.

BADAKHSHI, SHĀH 'ABDOLLĀH. 1942–43. Tadvin-e loghāt-e navāḥi-ye pāmir (Recording the vocabulary of the Pamir region). Āriānā I/12.7–10; II/2.20–3.

——. 1960. Də afghānestān də dzinō zhebō aw lahjō qāmus (A dictionary of Afghan languages and dialects). Kabol. Pashtu Tolana.

BADRE'I, FEREYDUN. 1967. Moqaddame'i bar ma'ni-shenāsi (An introduction to semantics.) RFLTan XV/1.47–69.

BAHMANYĀR, AḤMAD. 1952. Emlā-ye fārsi (Persian orthography). Nāme-ye Farhangestān I/4.42–66; II/1.5–36. Reissued 1959: Loghat-nāme-ye Dehkhodā: Moqaddame, 148–77.

BAQA'I, NĀṢAR. 1963–67. Fārsi-ye kermān (Kermani Persian). RFLIsf 15.15–40, 214-43; 16.46–64, 225–46, 507–16; 17.398–402; 18.175–80, 441–58; 19.345–60 (to be continued).

BAṢṢĀRI, ṬAL'AT. 1967. Dastur-e zabān-e fārsi (A grammar of Persian). Tehran.

BEHRANGI, ṢAMAD. 1964. Māẕi va moẕāre'-e dar jarayān dar zabān-e konuni-ye āzarbāijān (Continuous past and present in the current language of Azerbaijan). FIZ 13.72–6.

BEHRUZ, ẔABIḤ. 1946. Khaṭṭ o farhang (The alphabet and culture). Irān-kude 8.1–234.

BITĀB, MALEK AL-SHO'ARĀ. 1961. Dastur-e zabān-e fārsi (Persian grammar). Kabol. Faculty of Literature.

DJAMĀLZĀDEH, M. A. 1962. Farhang-e loghāt-e 'āmiyāne (A dictionary of colloquial and slang usage). Tehran.

EKHTIĀR, MANṢUR. 1954. Naẓariyye-ye vāḥed-e aṣvāt-e goftāri (The phonetic theory). RFLTan II/1.73–88.

——. 1962. From linguistics to literature. Tehran. University Publications No. 758.

——. 1964–66. Shive-ye barrasi-ye guyeshhā (The method of dialect investigation). RFLTan 12.170–215; 13.1–73.

——. 1967. Ṣowt shenāsi: raf'e moshkelāt-e talaffoẓ-e engelisi (Phonetics: English pronunciation made easy). 2nd. ed. Tehran. First edition 1955.

ENTEẒĀR, E., and D. J. BURNS. 1964. Farsi reference manual: Basic course. Putney, Vt. The Experiment in International Living.

EQBĀL ĀSHTIĀNI, 'A. 1933. Fārsi-ye sākhtegi (Fabricated Persian). Mehr 1.435–47.

——. 1948. Defā' az zabān-e fārsi-ye faṣiḥ (A defense of proper Persian). Yādegar V/1–2.7–17.

EQTEDĀRI, AḤMAD. 1955. Farhang-e lārestāni (Larestani dictionary). Tehran.

FARAHVASHI, BAHRĀM. 1962. Taḥlil-e fe'l dar lahje-ye sedehi (An analysis of the verb in the dialect of Sedeh). RFLTan 10.311–23.

FARHĀDI, 'A. GH. 1955. Le persan parlé en Afghanistan: Grammaire du Kâboli. (mimeographed ed.) Paris. Librarie C. Klincksieck.

FARHANG, A. 1928. Khaṭṭ-e pahalavi-ye now (New Pahlavi script). Nāṣeri (Ahvāz).

FATTĀḤI QĀẔI, QĀDER. 1964–66. Chand beyt-e kordi (Some Kurdish poems). RFLIsf 16.307–20, 400–22; 17.91–8, 119–220, 331–52, 521–9; 18.85–96, 181–96, 273–86, 421–29.

——. 1966. Manẓume-ye kordi-ye mehr o vafā (The Kurdish poem Mehr o Vafā). Tabriz. Faculty of Literature.

FERGUSON, CHARLES A. 1957. Word stress in Persian. Lg 33.123–35.
FO'ĀDI, ḤOSEIN. 1933–34. Āhang dar zabān-e fārsi (Accent in Persian). Mehr 1.924–68.
——. 1934–35. Seyr-e takāmoli-ye zabān (Evolution of language). Mehr 2.73–8, 171–4, 249–53, 365–70, 777–81, 869–73, 969–73.
——. 1935–36a. Zabān va lahje (Language and dialect). Mehr 3.54–7.
——. 1935–36b. Kalame (The word). Mehr 3.252–6.
——. 1935–36c. Ḥokm va jomle (Predication and the clause). Mehr 3.602–5.
——. 1935–36d. Taqsim-e kalamāt az leḥāẓ-e maʿni (Division of words according to meaning). Mehr 3.478–80.
——. 1935–36e. Taqsim-e kalame be rishe va jozʾ (Division of words into stem and affix). Mehr 3.361–4.
FORUGHI, MOḤAMMAD ʿALI. 1937. Payām-e man be farhangestān (My message to the Farhangestān). Tehran.
——. 1941. Taqlid o ebtekār (Imitation and innovation). Amuzesh o Parvaresh X/10-11.1–8.
——. 1951. Nofuẕ-e zabānhā-ye bigāne dar zabān-e fārsi (The intrusion of foreign languages into Persian). Amuzesh o Parvaresh XXV/5.33–9, 6–7.16–18.
GOLGOLĀB, ḤOSEIN. 1961. Giā: rāhnemā-ye giāhi (Plants: Guide to plants). Tehran. University Publications No. 707.
GOWHARIN, ṢĀDEQ. 1958–60. Farhang-e lughāt o taʿbirāt-e masnavi (Glossary of the words and the expressions of Masnavi). 3 vols. Tehran. University Publications Nos. 497, 545, 608.
ḤABIBI, ʿABD AL-ḤAYY. 1956. Qorb-e zabān-e pashtu be pārsi-ye bāstān (Affinity of Pashtu with Old Persian). Yaghmā 9.20–4.
——. 1963. Zabān-e do hazār sāl qabl-e Afghānestān (The language of Afghanistan two thousand years ago). Kabol. Historical Society.
ḤEKMAT, ʿALI AṢGHAR. 1945. Sisadomin sāl-e ta'lif-e ketāb-e borhān-e qāteʿ (The 300th year of the composition of the B.Q.). Nāme-ye farhangestān III/1.1–24.
HOMĀ'I, JALĀL. 1959. Dastur-e zabān-e fārsi (Persian grammar). Lughat-nāme-ye Dehkodā: Moqaddame, 110–47. Originally published 1943: Goftār dar ṣarf o naḥv-e fārsi (Discourse on the morphology and syntax of Persian). Nāme-ye farhangestān 1.40–58; 2.26–68; 3.34–61; 4.6–20.
HOMĀYUNFARROKH, ʿABD AL-RAḤIM. 1959. Dastur-e jāmeʿ-e zabān-e fārsi (A comprehensive grammar of Persian). 7 books in one vol. 2nd. ed. Tehran.
HUSHYĀR, M.B. 1946. Sāde-tarin ravesh-e taʿlim-e rasm-ol-khaṭṭ-e fārsi (The simplest method of teaching the Persian alphabet). Sālnāme-ye Pārs 22.43–6.
IZADPANĀH, ḤAMID. 1965. Farhang-e lori (A dictionary of Lori). Tehran.
JAHĀNSHĀHI, I., and ʿA. SAYYĀḤI. 1967a. Bekhānim o benevisim: Barā-ye āmuzesh-e bozorg sālān (Let us read and write: for instruction of adults). Tehran. Ministry of Education.
——. 1967b. Rāhnemāy-e tadris-e bekhānim o benevisim (Instructional guide for Let us read and write). Tehran. Ministry of Education.

JAZĀYERY, M. A. 1966–67. Western loan words in Persian: with reference to westernization. Islamic Culture 40.207–20; 41.1–19.

——, and H. H. PAPER. 1961. A reference grammar of Modern Persian. University of Michigan (Mimeographed ed).

KĀKAR, LAʿL MOḤAMMAD. 1940. Spetsalē paṣ̌tō (Pashtu [-Persian] vocabulary). Kandahar.

KĀRANG, ʿA.ʿA. 1954. Tāti va harzani (Tati and Harzani dialects). Tabriz.

KASRAVI, AḤMAD. 1925. Āẕari yā zabān-e bāstān-e āẕarbāygān (Āẕari or the ancient language of Azerbaijan). Ṭehran.

——. 1930–31. Nāmhā-ye shahrhā va dehhā-ye irān (The names of Iranian towns and villages). 2 sections. Tehran. 2nd. ed. 1938.

KESHĀVARZ, KARIM. 1962. Moẓāreʿ va māẓi-ye malmus (The continuous present and past). Rāhnemā-ye Ketāb 5.687–94.

KHĀDEM, QIYĀM AL-DIN. 1948. Də paṣ̌tō keli (Key to Pashtu). Kabol.

KHĀNLARI, P. NĀTEL. 1957. Taḥavvol-e zabān (The evolution of language). Sokhan 8.315–19.

——. 1958. Vazne sheʿr-e fārsi (Metre in Persian poetry). Tehran. University Publication No. 514.

——. 1959. Tarḥ-e ejmāli barāye taḥqiq dar lahjehā-ye irāni (A short guide for Iranian dialect investigation). Sokhan 10.565–75.

——. 1961. Darbāre-ye zabān-e fārsi (On the Persian language). Tehran. [A collection of articles originally published in Sokhan 1943–61].

——. 1967. Dastur-e zabān-e fārsi: ravesh-e now (Grammar of Persian: A new method). Tehran. Ministry of Education.

KHAṬIB RAHBAR, KHALIL. 1964, 1967. Sākhtemān va taqsim-e ḥarfhā-ye eẓāfe va jāy-e ānhā (The formation and divisions of the prepositions and their place). RFLTan XII/2.150–61; XV/1.70–96.

KHAYYĀMPUR, A. 1965. Dastur-e zabān-e fārsi (A grammar of Persian). 5th. ed. Tabriz.

KIĀ, ṢĀDEQ. 1956. Guyesh-e āshtiān. daftar-e nokhost: vāzhe-nāme (The dialect of Ashtian. Part I: Wordlist). Tehran. University Publication No. 384.

MĀCHIĀNI, FARẒPUR M. 1964–65. Zabān o fanhang-e māchiāni (The Māchiāni language and vocabulary). RFLIsf 16.277–96, 451–70; 17.109–28, 261–84.

MAḤJUB, MOḤAMMAD JAʿFAR. 1957. Zabān-e fārsi rā daryābim (Let us save the Persian language). Ṣadaf 1.1–13.

MINAVI, MOJTABĀ. 1950a. Shive-ye fārsi nevisi (How to write Persian). Yaghmā 3.353–9, 401–7, 449–58.

——. 1950b. -iyyat-e maṣdari (The infinitive-forming *-iyyat*). Tehran.

——. 1951. Al-jonun fonun (The folies are many kinds). Yaghmā 4.289-94.

MOGHDAM, MAHMAD. 1949. Guyeshhā-ye vafs va āshtiān va tafresh (The dialects of Vafs, Āshtiān and Tafresh). Tehran.

MOHMAND, GOL MOḤAMMAD. 1937. Paṣ̌tō sind (Pashtu[-Persian] dictionary). Kabol.
——. 1938. Də paṣ̌tō zhebē lyār (The path of Pashtu). Lahor.

MOʿIN, MOḤAMMAD. 1954. Lughāt-e fārsi-e ibn sinā va ta'ṯir-e ānhā dar adabiyyāt (Persian vocabulary of Avicenna and its influence on Persian literature). RFLTan II/2.1–38. Reissued and elaborated 1959: Loghat-nāme-ye Dehkhodā: Moqaddame, 63–86.
——. 1958. Ma ʿrefe va nakare (Definite and indefinite [nouns]). Tehran.
——. 1961. Mofrad va jamʿ (The singular and the plural). 2nd. ed. Tehran.
——. 1962a. Esm-e maṣdar va ḥāṣel-e maṣdar (Verbal nouns). 2nd. ed. Tehran.
——. 1962b. Eẕāfe (The ezafe). 2 parts. 2nd. ed. Tehran.

MOKRI, MOḤAMMAD. 1947. Nāmhā-ye parandegān dar lahjehā-ye kordi (Bird names in Kurdish dialects). Tehran.
——. 1950. Gurgāni yā tarānehā-ye kordi (Gurgani Kurdish songs). Tehran.

MOQADDAM, AMIR. 1966. Farhang-e eṣṭelāḥāt-e ḥāfeẓ (A dictionary of Hafiz). RFLIsf 530–7. (to be continued).

MORTAẔAVI, MANUCHEHR. 1955–56. Chand pasvand (Some suffixes). RFLIsf 45–60, 159–74, 274–87; 110–20. Republished 1956. Tabriz.
——. 1962–63 feʿl dar zabān-e harzani (The verb in Harzani). RFLIsf 14.453–88; 15.61–97.

MOṢĀḤEB, GḤ. H. (ed.). 1966. Dāyerat al-maʿāref-e fārsi (Persian encyclopaedia). vol. 1. Tehran.

NAFISY, SAʿID. 1950–51. Khaṭṭ-e lātin barāy-e zabān-e fārsi (Latin alphabet for Persian). Nur-e Jahān II/11.16–18, 21; 12.4, 27–30; III/2.17–18.

NAṮRI, MUSĀ. 1935. Khaṭṭ-e fārsi (Persian script). Mehr, 3.200–5, 281–4, 379–88.

OLFAT, GOLPĀCHĀ. 1941. Nokte'i chand dar gerāmer va loghat-e pashtu (A few remarks on Pashtu grammar and vocabulary). Kabol Kālani, 182–7.

PARVIN GONĀBĀDI, M. 1957. Review of Dastur-e jameʿ-e zabān-e fārsi by A. Homāyunfarrokh. Rāhnemā-ye Ketāb 1.241–51. Rejoinder by A. Homāyunfarrokh in Rāhnemā-ye Ketāb 2.161–5 (1958).

PARVIZI, FARANGIS. 1967. Review of Dastur-e zabān-e fārsi by Ṭ. Baṣṣari. Rāhnemā-ye Ketāb 10.499–504.

PASHTU TOLANA (Pashtu Society). 1954. Paṣ̌tō qāmus (Pashtu dictionary). Kabol.

PUR-DĀVUD, IBRĀHIM. 1947. Farhang-e irān-e bāstān (The culture of ancient Iran). vol. I. Tehran.
——. 1953. Hormazd-nāme. Tehran.

QANDAHĀRI, Ṣ. M. 1937–38. Paṣ̌tō zhebē (Pashtu language). 2 vols. Kabol. Pashtu Tolana.

QARIB, A., B. BAHĀR, B. FORUZĀNFAR, J. HOMĀ'I, and R. YĀSEMI. 1950? (available editions give no date). Dastur-e zabān-e fārsi (A grammar of Persian). 2 vols. Tehran.

QARIB-E GARAKĀNI, ʿABD AL-ʿAẒIM. 1911. Dastur-e zabān be oṣlul-e alsene-ye maghreb-zamin (Grammar [of Persian] after the method of western languages). 3rd. level. Tehran.

QAZVINI, MOḤAMMAD. 1924. Ṭarz-e negāresh-e fārsi (The Persian style of writing). Farhangestān 1.405–38.

RAḤMATI, YUSOF. 1951. Farhang-e ʿāmiyāne (A dictionary of colloquialisms). Tehran.

RAJĀʾI, AḤMAD ʿALI. 1964. Lahje-ye bokhārāʾi (The dialect of Bokhārā). Mashhad. University Publication No. 8.

RESHTIN, ṢADIQOLLĀH. 1947. Də paṣ̌tō eshteqāqunē aw terkibunē (Derivation and combination in Pashtu). Kabol.

——. 1948. Paṣ̌tō gerāmar (A Pashtu grammar). vol. 1. Kabol.

S̱ĀBETI, ḤABIBOLLĀH. 1947. Derakhtān-e jangali-ye irān (Iranian forest trees). Tehran. University Publications No. 20.

SIRAT, ʿABD AL-SATTĀR. 1962. ʿArabi-ye ʿāmiyāne dar ḥavāli-ye balkh (Colloquial Arabic in the Balkh region). Adab X/1.1–11.

SORUSHIĀN, JAMSHID. 1956. Farhang-e behdinān (A dictionary of the dialect of the Zoroastreians of Kerman and Yazd). Tehran.

SOTUDE, MANUCHEHR. 1953. Farhang-e gilaki (Gilaki dictionary). Tehran.

——. 1956. Farhang-e kermāni (Kermani dictionary). Tehran.

——. 1964. Farhang-e semnāni, sorkheʾi, lāsgerdi, sangesari, and shahmirzādi (Semnani, etc. dictionary). Tehran. University Publication No. 883.

TAFAẔZOLI, AḤMAD. 1962. Vāzhehā-ye guyeshi dar toḥfat al-moʾmenin (Dialectal words in Toḥfat al-Moʾmenin). Enteshātār-e farhang-e ʿāmmea 2.95–149.

TAQIZĀDE, S. H. 1941. Jonbesh-e melli-ye adabi (The national literary movement). Tehran. Originally published, 1935, in Majelle-ye taʿlim va tarbiat 5.

——. 1947. Lozum-e ḥefẓ-e fārsi-ye faṣih (The necessity of preserving proper Persian). Yādgar IV/6.1–40.

WAKIL, FAẔL MOḤAMMAD. 1951. Də paṣ̌tō zhebē lanḍ geramer (A concise grammar of Pashtu). Kandahar.

YAʿQUB ḤASAN KHĀN. 1938. Pashtu az naẓar-e feqh al-loghe (Pashtu from the philological point of view). Sālnāme-ye Kābol 7.251–310.

YĀR-ṢHĀṬER, EḤSAN. 1957. Zabānhā va lahjehā-ye irāni (Iranian languages and dialects). RFLTan V/1–2.11–48.

——. 1957b. Gham-e zabān (The care of the language). Sokhan VIII/2.99–104.

——. 1959. The dialect of Shāhrud (Khalkhāl). BSOAS XXII.52–68.

——. 1960. The dialect of Kajal. BSOAS XXIII/2.275–86.

——. 1964. The dialects of Alvir and Vidar. Mélange presenté à Georg Morgenstierne, ed. by G. Redard, 177–87. Wiesbaden.

——, and W. B. HENNING, eds. 1962. Tāti dialects of Rāmand. A locust's leg, 240–5. London.

Ẕ̌OKĀʾ, YAḤYĀ. 1953. Guyesh-e karingān (The dialect of Karingān). Tehran.

——. 1957. Guyesh-e galinqaye: harzinda (The dialect of Galinqaye: Harzandi). Tehran.

ZOMORRODIĀN, REẔA. 1965–66. Fonolozhi-ye lahje-ye qāyen (The phonology of Qāyeni). *Maj. Dan. Ada. Mash.* 1.378–95; 2.68–77.

LANGUAGE EDUCATION IN ARAB COUNTRIES AND THE ROLE OF THE ACADEMIES

SALIH J. ALTOMA

The aim of this paper is to delineate issues and trends which have dominated the teaching of Arabic in more than a dozen Arab states during the postwar period (1945–65) (see Table I) and to outline the role of the language academies regarding language problems in general and language education in particular.* Although specific examples are taken from the U.A.R. (Egypt) and Iraq, much of the discussion holds true for other countries not only because they share basically the same problems, but also because they follow similar or nearly identical curriculums and textbooks. However, special reference will be made to other countries whenever the need arises. The paper is divided into three sections: the first deals with three general problems directly affecting the language program; the second covers language education: content, textbooks and methodology; and the third discusses the role of the academies.

1. DIGLOSSIA, THE WRITING SYSTEM AND ARABIZATION

1.1 *Diglossia*

Language education in Arab countries is complicated by the fact that Classical Arabic (hereafter = CA), around which the program revolves, differs considerably from the colloquial Arabic spoken daily by school children. An attempt to describe salient differences between CA and one spoken variety was made by the writer in his work: *The Problem of Diglossia in Arabic: A Comparative Study of Classical and Iraqi Arabic.*[1] The study, which took the high school curriculum of Arabic grammar as a base of comparison, shows the wide variation not only in aspects related to the complex system of case endings but also in many other features of phonology, morphology, syntax and lexicon. This implies that the pupils have to unlearn or suppress most of their linguistic habits while trying to acquire new ones based on CA

* The author would like to thank Indiana University for a research grant that allowed him to prepare this article.

[1] The work appeared in 1969 as a monograph in the Harvard Middle Eastern Studies series.

TABLE I

Educational Systems and the Language of Instruction in thirteen independent Arab states 1965–1966

Country	Primary – No. of years	Language of Instruction	Secondary (intermediate or preparatory and senior levels) – No. of years	Language of Instruction
Algeria	6	Arabic/French	7	French/Arabic
Iraq	6	Arabic/Kurdish*	5	Arabic
Jordan	6	Arabic	6	Arabic
Kuwait	4	Arabic	8	Arabic
Lebanon	5	Arabic	7	Arabic
Libya	6	Arabic	6	Arabic
Morocco	5	Arabic/French	7	French/Arabic
Saudi Arabia	6	Arabic	5	Arabic
Sudan	4	Arabic	8 Int.	Arabic
			Senior	English/Arabic
Syria	6	Arabic	6	Arabic
Tunisia	6	French/Arabic	6	French/Arabic
U.A.R. (Egypt)	6	Arabic	6	Arabic
Yemen	6	Arabic	7	Arabic

* Kurdish is used only in Kurdish regions.

as the language program requires.[2] The burden of internalizing or reinforcing these acquired habits is compounded by conflicting practices: on the one hand the program deliberately neglects the actual speech of the pupils, and, on the other, CA in practice does not encompass all classes, since teachers themselves (especially of other subjects) tend to use the colloquial for one reason or another.[3] In the absence of pertinent studies, it is not possible to determine accurately the 'kind' of CA employed in the class situation or the extent of its use, but there are indications which suggest that even teachers of Arabic at high school level tend to use other than CA in their instruction or in conversation with their students outside the class.[4] As a result of this conflicting

[2] The curriculum of different educational levels cites, as a major objective, the correct use of CA in reading, writing and conversation.

[3] Ṭāhā Ḥusayn attributes this practice to the fact that teachers are not competent in using CA. He remarks: 'Like almost everyone else, I should like teachers to use Classical Arabic in every class regardless of the course, but I am reluctant to insist because they do not know the language well enough and, if required to speak it, would fail to communicate the subject matter to their pupils.' (Ḥusayn 1954:89).

policy, the student's exposure to, and practice in, CA within the school are, by mere quantitative measures, inadequate for attaining the desired objectives. Official instructions issued by educational authorities do urge teachers to avoid the colloquial, but are often disregarded by either the teachers' inability to speak CA correctly and with ease for a prolonged time or their desire to eliminate misunderstanding or achieve maximum communication in teaching their subjects.

In view of the fact that the dichotomy is not confined to school situations, numerous solutions have been proposed for eliminating or reducing its effects. The proposed solutions can be roughly divided into two categories, the first, representing a small group, calls for promoting a variety of spoken Arabic as the standard language in place of CA, or advocates modifications in CA; the other insists on the preservation of CA and raising it to the status of a naturally spoken language.

Those who favor the former think often of a cultivated middle language based on the form spoken by educated speakers of a particular region (such as Egypt) or of different Arab countries. Anis (1960: 64–71), a leading Egyptian linguist, presents the language of educated Egyptians as the possible future language for all Arab countries and cites a number of factors favoring such development including the following: (1) Egypt is numerically the largest single Arab country, (2) it enjoys political and cultural prestige not equalled by that of other Arab countries, and (3) Egyptian Arabic represents the spoken variety most widely used in literature, movies, radio programs and other modes of expression. Frayḥa (1955:183–96), of the American University of Beirut, focuses his attention on a common variety spoken by educated speakers from different Arab countries. Although he is aware of the variations in pronunciation or lexicon existing within this variety, he maintains that its structure is essentially the same whether the speakers come from Egypt, Iraq, Syria or other areas, and suggests four steps for developing it into an official language[5] (see 2.2 below). Each of the above suggestions has the potentiality of greatly reducing the difficulties, but these as well as other similar reforms have been constantly rejected primarily for extra-linguistic factors: political, religious, and cultural.[6]

The classicists, whose views are reflected in the work of the various language academies and have thus far determined language programs, maintain that CA can and should replace the colloquials as the common spoken language. Their views as to what kind of CA and how it should be elevated to a spoken language vary from one to another depending on whether they envisage a modified CA or they object to

[4] A questionnaire addressed to high school teachers of Arabic in Iraq reveals the following findings: 30.5% of the teachers considered CA with its case endings to be the easiest medium for the students to comprehend their subjects, whereas 69.5% chose other varieties of Arabic. On the question of the use of CA outside the class, only 6% claimed that they used it always, while 47.6% often, 26.2% rarely and 20.2% did not use it at all. As to the use of the colloquial in instruction, 90% indicated that they used it either often or rarely, see Al-Toma 1957:122–7.

[5] On the development of a related variety labelled CA without case endings or Modern Inter-Arabic, see Bishai, 1966.

[6] A summary of these factors as reflected in Arabic writings is presented by Chejne 1965.

any change.[7] But all share a strong faith in the role of universal literacy and of mass communications media in gradually bridging the gaps between the two forms of Arabic. They point to the fact that the spread of education has already classicized the colloquial and therefore propose linguistic planning which would accelerate the spread of CA and extend its use to all activities which require or adopt the colloquial as an idiom.[8]

The classicists' approach is greatly undermined by theoretical and practical weaknesses. First, their assessment of classicization has been based on impressions rather than detailed objective studies which would measure the type and extent of classical penetration. All present traces of CA in the colloquials indicate that the morphological and syntactical systems of the latter remain basically intact. The process of classicization has been primarily confined to the use of classical phonemes in place of their reflexes, set of CA phrases, and lexical borrowings. Second, the classicists, in their understandable search for the ideal, unduly ignore linguistic principles when they persist in their notion of the colloquial as a corruption of CA lacking the qualities which 'make it worthy of the name of a language' (Ḥusayn 1954:86) or when they blame other factors such as the curriculum, textbooks, students or the lack of qualified teachers[9] (Farrūkh 1961:115–16). Third, their opposition to the use of the colloquial runs counter to several trends, educational, literary and political, which extend, rather than restrict, its role. In view of the high percentage of illiteracy,[10] and the drive for universal education, the colloquial will continue to serve as an effective means of instruction, formal or informal, being readily accessible to its speakers. Stylistically, it has acquired prominence in fiction and drama as an important structural element of realistic or effective presentation.[11] Politically, the spread of revolutionary or socialist oriented movements in the postwar years has developed a sympathetic attitude toward the language or literature used or understood by the masses and elevated the spoken language to a higher status as is evident in President Nasser's highly colloquial speeches.

To all these must be added the fact that, in spite of numerous efforts made recently, there exists no central authority or unified policy which would contribute effectively toward minimizing the effects of the dichotomy whether within each state or on a pan-Arab level.

[7] Classicists do not represent a unified rigid stand regarding CA or the colloquials; among them there are few who tolerate the use or study of the colloquial and admit the need for modifications in CA (note, for example, Al-Ḥuṣrī 1958:44–9, and Al-Khūlī, see 2.2. below. Others question the value of the colloquials and reject changes in CA: Al-Afghānī 1962:216–18, Farrūkh 1961).

[8] Al-Bazzāz (1961b), a leading Arab statesman and former prime minister of Iraq, outlines his linguistic planning by which CA would ultimately replace the colloquials, and suggests the imposition of measures restricting the use or the study of the colloquial.

[9] Philistin's article (1958) reflects the view that the problem is essentially pedagogical, and that the solution should be sought in the training of competent teachers. According to Philistin the teacher's inability to teach or use adequately Classical Arabic fosters a belief among the students, that Arabic cannot be learned, see pp. 50–1.

[10] According to Unesco's *Statistical yearbook* 1965 (Paris, 1966), the percentage of illiteracy of most Arab states is still very high, often exceeding 60%.

[11] For arguments for or against the literary use of the colloquial, see Al-Toma 1961a, Cachia 1967

1.2 *The Writing System*

Two defects in the writing system have given rise to a large number of proposed reforms: the plurality of letter variations and the usual absence of vowel signs. Most letters in the present system have initial, medial and terminal variations. It is assumed that two major difficulties result from this plurality: economic and cultural or educational. The former pertains to the expense, effort and time involved in using hundreds of variations for printing purposes. The latter implies an unnecessary burden on the learners, be they children or illiterate adults, to understand and use the various letters according to their position or relation to each other. The absence of vowel signs, the second defect, creates a more serious problem due to the fact that it makes it difficult to read correctly without a large measure of alertness and discrimination even for well-educated readers.

The proposals which have been suggested for rectifying these and other defects[12] range from those calling for romanization or the creation of a new script,[13] to others based on the preservation of the Arabic script and the use of one character or a restricted number of variations for each letter.

Although most reform-minded scholars in the Arab world favor the preservation of the Arabic script, a few proposals have been made in favor of romanization since the latter part of the nineteenth century.[14] Among the leading proponents of romanization was Fahmī, a former Egyptian minister and a member of the Egyptian Academy. In his proposal submitted to, and examined by, the Egyptian Academy, 1943–44, Fahmī stressed the efficiency of the Roman alphabet as used by many languages, and maintained that its adaptation to Arabic would solve the problems of learning and understanding Arabic, and would greatly bridge the distance between the Arabs and other peoples.[15] Taking cognizance of the fact that the Roman alphabet lacks symbols for certain Arabic consonants, he suggested the use of ten Arabic characters in this proposed alphabet. The proposal ultimately failed to receive the support of the Academy not only because of its rather complicated mixture of Arabic and Roman scripts, but rather because of the opinion, shared by most scholars, that the defects of the present system can be rectified without recourse to romanization. Nevertheless, other writers, after Fahmī, continued to lend their support to the principle of romanization as the best solution for the defects of the writing system.[16]

[12] Other defects noted by reformers include the absence of long vowels in certain words, or the complex set of rules regarding the shape the glottal stop should take in different positions or vowel environments.

[13] The earliest proposal for a new script was voiced by Az-Zahāwī (1863–1936) in his perceptive study of the defects of the Arabic alphabet (Az-Zahāwī 1896). For other details on proposed reforms note Al-Toma 1961b:403–15.

[14] On proposals made before the second World War, see Qudsi 1923 and Madkūr 1962:12.

[15] Among the merits Fahmī listed for his proposal are the use of vowels and one form for each symbol and the simplified transition from Arabic to learning other languages which use the Roman alphabet; The Egyptian Academy 1946:28–34.

[16] See Mūsā 1945:137–9, 1955:44; Frayḥa 1955:189–93; Ṣabrī 1964:289–303; ʿAql 1961, the Lebanese poet, used a romanized alphabet in printing an entire collection of his colloquial poetry.

However, recent developments seem to point to the emergence of a modified system based on the Arabic script, and the principle of reducing letter variations to a minimum number. Four proposals aiming at such systems deserve special attention, those of Taymour, Khattar and Lakhdar and the proposal approved by the Egyptian Academy. Taymour, an influential novelist, playwright and academician, submitted his proposal to the congress of the Egyptian Academy held in Cairo, 1951. It called for the use of thirty characters consisting primarily of the variants presently used in initial position (Taymour 1951a:36, 1951b:18). In describing the merits of his proposal, Taymour stressed the fact that it does not involve a break with tradition, and that it facilitates considerably the task of printing, reading, and promoting literacy. Khattar's unified Arabic is similar in principle, but differs in its attempt to creat thirty symbols having the essential identifying trait of the existing letters (Khattar 1955). Lakhdar devised, while working as a director of the Moroccan Institute of Fundamental Education, a printing system which reduced the characters to 67. It was actually tested in printing a newspaper designed for newly literate readers and was adopted by the Moroccan government with an ultimate objective in mind of using the system for printing textbooks and extending its use to other Arab countries (Monteil 1960:51–2). However, the Egyptian Academy, which has been concerned with the problems since 1938, did not endorse any of these or other proposals, but preferred to entrust a committee set up for this purpose with the task of reforming the writing system. In 1956, a joint committee representing both the Academy and the Cultural Department of the Arab League called for two important changes: the reduction of letter variants and the use of vocalization in printed literature especially in school textbooks. By 1960, the Academy gave its full support to a new system for printing consisting of 135 symbols or characters (The Egyptian Academy 1961:20–5). The proposed system still retains two or more variants for most letters, nevertheless it has reduced the number of characters required for printing vocalized texts to about one third of the number used at present. The efficiency of the system was tested in printing a pamphlet dealing with the problems, and it is the Academy's hope that Ministries of Education in different Arab countries will put it into wider use.[17]

1.3 *Arabization*

Arabization can be viewed as a process aiming at achieving maximum use of Arabic in different Arab countries in oral and written communication. It covers issues ranging from the general question of making Arabic the official language of the state, the language of instruction, to matters related to the preparation of technical and scientific terminology in Arabic. In this broad sense, all Arab countries are faced with one phase or another of Arabization. But it is in North African countries and, to a certain extent,

[17] The writer received a letter from the Academy's Secretary, Dr. Madkūr, dated April 22, 1967, in which he pointed out that the Academy's recommendations were being implemented in the preparation of textbooks.

in the Sudan, that Arabization presents a special challenge to the teaching of Arabic and its role as a language of instruction.[18] Therefore, our discussion will be confined to Arabization as it proceeded in these countries.

Prior to the independence of Morocco and Tunisia (1956) and Algeria (1962), French dominated the educational system, while Arabic was relegated to a marginal position and treated more or less as a foreign language. Upon attaining their independence, these countries had to face the unavoidable question of the place of the national language, i.e. Arabic, in the educational program. As a matter of ultimate objective, all declared that the educational system should be Arabized. However, there emerged differences regarding the courses to be followed in achieving this objective.

1.3.1 In Morocco two opposing trends became apparent.[19] The first, strongly associated with nationalism and Islam, favored an immediate and maximum Arabization; the other, while acknowledging the importance of Arabization, felt that it was more important to provide the pupils with basic education in French, and to maintain an effective educational system than to proceed with Arabization at any cost.[20] However, the former prevailed at the Ministry of National Education during the early years of independence. In accordance with the Ministry's plan for 1956–57, the first grade was to be completely Arabized, and instruction in the remaining four grades was to be equally divided between Arabic and French. But by the end of 1958, it was realized that Arabization in the primary schools had resulted in lowering the quality of education due to a number of factors including the shortage of qualified teachers and inadequate planning.[21] A commission for the reform of education endorsed in 1958

[18] The role of Arabic as a language of instruction in another Arab country, Iraq, has not been satisfactorily defined in areas where non-Arab minorities, particularly Kurds, are concentrated. In such areas, Kurdish has been used as a language of instruction in the primary schools, but, in recent years, demands were made to extend the use of Kurdish as the language of instruction at various levels in the 'Kurdish region'. At certain points in the negotiations of 1964 between the central authority and Kurdish leaders, the government seemed willing to extend Kurdish as the language of instruction to the end of the intermediate level (three years beyond the elementary school. See Ad-Durrah 1966:381–2). Another Arab country, Mauritania, has not yet embarked on Arabization, and has retained French as its official language in spite of the fact that Arabic is the national language (Sasnett and Sepmeyer 1966:690–7).

[19] For a detailed examination of these and other trends see Zartman 1964:155–61. On the view of the traditionalists, see Al-Fāsī 1963a and b, Aṣ-Ṣaḥrāwī 1959, and Al-Baghdādī 1960.

[20] An editorial published in *Al-Istiqlal*, October 16, 1956, reflected the dimensions of the problem by declaring: 'If we are happy to see our language finally given the importance it deserves, we are no less eager that our children go to school. If the number of teachers capable of teaching in Arabic is insufficient, we would prefer to see our children learn French rather than leaving them in the streets' (Zartman 1964:158–9).

[21] The shortage of teachers is viewed as the primary reason for the setback in Arabization. Writing for Unesco's *The World Survey of Education*, III (New York, 1961), the Ministry of National Education stated: 'Arabization is essential in a country whose religion, everyday language and traditions are based on the Arabic language. Nevertheless, while it is natural that Arabic should be the cultural vehicle for Morocco, Arabization must not lose sight of facts. Arabization, of course, is bound up with the staffing question. The problem is to recruit and train Moroccan teachers' (p. 842).

the principle of Arabization but proposed that French be used in teaching science and arithmetic, and suggested the formation of a subcommission to formulate plans for Arabizing education. The problems were reviewed by the Superior Council of National Education and a new plan was agreed upon for progressive Arabization beginning with 1960–61 (Arab Information Center 1966:149, Zartman 1964:187–8). In January 1960, an Institute of Studies and Arabization was set up to prepare necessary materials in Arabic, such as textbooks and dictionaries, and to develop the linguistic base for Arabization of the three educational levels over fifteen to twenty years. It was natural for Morocco to turn to other Arab countries for guidance and assistance and consequently an Arab conference on Arabization was held in Rabat in 1961 leading to the creation of a permanent bureau for coordinating Arabization under the aegis of the Arab League. Since its inception in 1962, the Bureau has sponsored several conferences reviewing pertinent problems, issued a periodical *Al-Lisān Al-ʿArabī*[22] devoted to various aspects of Arabization, and prepared pedagogical materials and several technical dictionaries. Of the latter, the following dictionaries have been prepared: a dictionary based on textbooks (primary school) used in all Arab countries, France, Britain, and Italy,[23] and three other dictionaries for high school subjects: chemistry, mathematics and physics. As a result of these efforts and other measures which aimed at training Moroccan teachers, considerable progress was made toward Arabizing the primary schools. Although the Unesco yearbook of 1965 states that by October 1964 primary education was entirely Arabized, other sources cite 1967 as the terminal year for Arabizing the primary school.[24]

As for the language of instruction in the secondary schools, French remains predominant (20 out of 33 weekly hours given in French).[25] This seems to have been the policy since 1957 when a commission on secondary education decided that, pending the training of competent teachers, all specialized subjects be taught in French or Spanish.[26] In the meantime, efforts have been made to Arabize secondary education within seven years, effective 1967, as indicated in the plan submitted by the Permanent Bureau for Arabization.[27]

1.3.2 In Tunisia, the drive for immediate Arabization was not destined to prevail, in spite of demands made for such a course of action (Lelong 1956:415–22, Gordon 1964:74). The Tunisian government felt that: 'After the almost complete neglect of

[22] By 1967, five volumes of the periodical had appeared.

[23] Bin ʿAbdullah, the secretary general of the Bureau, considers this dictionary a tool serving to spread technical terms used in Western countries and to unify the terminology current in the Arab world. See Bin ʿAbdullah 1966:62–3.

[24] Unesco 1962:104, 1965:248; Bin ʿAbdullah 1966:66; *Al-Lisān Al-ʿArabī* 1966:4, 59.

[25] In areas formerly under Spanish rule, Spanish continues to dominate.

[26] See the Ministry's report to Unesco 1964:113, which points out that, as a rule, all subjects are taught in French with the exception of the Arabic language and Islamic subjects. The report adds: 'It has sometimes been possible for history and geography as well as philosophy to be taught in the original literary sections by Arabic speaking teachers.'

[27] *Al-Lisān Al-ʿArabī* 1966:69–70.

Arabic during the Protectorate, it was almost impossible to raise Arabic to being the sole vehicle of instruction immediately. A shortage of qualified teachers and the absence of adequate textbooks forbade such action as much as it might have been desired. Gradual well-timed progress was in order to avoid confusion and harm to the students in their various stages of education.'[28]

During the first two years of independence (1956–58) the first and second grades were Arabized, but bilingual instruction was pursued in the remaining grades.[29] In the secondary school, the language of instruction remained divided almost exactly as it was before independence, between one third in Arabic and two thirds in French. Although officials have continued to declare that the ultimate objective is to completely Arabize the instruction, questions have been raised as to whether Tunisia is not practically or deliberately prolonging bilingual instruction (Brown 1965:160, 165). According to latest available data, Arabic has already become the vehicular language for all subjects in the so-called Normal Section of the secondary schools, and the bilingual classes in which French serves as the language of instruction are to be Arabized as qualified Tunisian teachers become available.[30] Therefore, it is safe to assume that Tunisia is moving, though slowly and with caution, toward complete Arabization.

1.3.3 Of all North African countries, Algeria suffered most in its quest for Arabization, because it was under French rule for a longer period (1830–1962), during which time systematic attempts were made to transform Algeria into a integral part of France. The hours assigned to Arabic in public schools were minimal, often two hours per week, and the private traditional Arabic institutions were not allowed to develop (Gordon 1964:39, Ghannām 1963–64). By 1962, the year of independence, it was not surprising to see most members of the Algerian Constituent Assembly incapable of expressing themselves in their national language, Arabic.[31] Nor was it unexpected for Algeria to face unprecedented obstacles in its drive for Arabizing its schools. The first year 1962–63 witnessed an increase in the hours devoted to Arabic in both primary and secondary schools (Unesco 1964:3, 1965:4) and the plan called for a gradual increase in these hours in the ensuing years. To cope with some of the problems arising from this policy, Algeria had to call upon all available sources for help

[28] Arab Information Center 1966:247–8. See also the remarks made by the Dean of the Tunisian Normal School, Abdesselem (1960) on the shortcomings of Arabic and the urgent need for its reform.
[29] However, an official document maintains that the majority of subjects are taught in Arabic during the last four years of the primary school (Arab Information Center 1966:248).
[30] Arab Information Center 1966:248. See also similar remarks made by Messadi, the Secretary of State for Education, 1965:51, though he is quoted as having said earlier: 'We have committed our country to a de facto bilingualism' (Brown 1965:160).
[31] Ben Bella, the former Algerian president underscored the seriousness of the problem in the following terms: 'There has been a contradiction [in Algeria] and there will be one for a long time to come: one feels in Arabic, one thinks in Arabic but often one expresses oneself and cultivates oneself in French. The danger is that the personality suffers from a disequilibrium which to one extent or another [might become irrevocable]. ... We [Algerians] need to enter into possession of our language in order to develop ourselves, to raise ourselves' (Gordon 1966:112–13).

including teachers from other Arab countries, and to resort to massive recruitment of local teachers some of whom had only primary school diplomas. In order to limit as much as possible the unavoidable lowering of educational standards, the non-qualified teachers were to receive special training over a period of six years. Other measures were taken for the training of new teachers, and the preparation of required materials.[32] As a result of such efforts, those in control of education found it possible to Arabize, by 1965, the first grade, and to continue a policy of rapid Arabization in other grades (Unesco 1965:11), in spite of scepticism or opposition expressed by some Algerian and foreign experts.[33]

1.3.4 The problem in the Sudan is slightly different from, and perhaps less complicated than, that of North Africa. It stems from the government's plan to Arabize secondary education for which English was used as a language of instruction, and to introduce Arabic schools to the southern regions which were dominated by missionary schools. Many felt that with the bilingual approach practiced before Sudan's independence (1956) — Arabic in elementary and intermediate schools, English in secondary schools — neither Arabic nor English was adequately learned (Ali 1960:73, Henderson 1965:125). This was shared by an international commission which recommended in 1956 a gradual change from English to Arabic as the language of instruction (Akrawi 1960:274). But the government had to overcome numerous obstacles pertinent to the opposition of the South (mostly of non-Arabic speaking Sudanese), textbooks, training of teachers and requirements of higher learning.[34] It was only in 1965 that the use of Arabic as the language of instruction was applied to the pupils enrolled in the two lower classes of the secondary school. The educational authorities seem to feel that, on the basis of the outcome of the first year, Arabization would be completed within four years without impairing seriously the quality of education (Unesco 1966:329).[35]

The use of Arabic in southern provinces raises a serious educational issue due to the fact that Arabic is not the native language nor was it used as the language of

[32] Sections for Classical Arabic were added to six existing teacher training colleges during the year 1963–64 (Arab Information Center 1966:9), and this number was raised to sixteen according to Unesco 1966a:13. A new department of Arabization was created to draw up syllabuses, produce textbooks, and work out timetables.

[33] Algeria's first Minister of Education suggested that it would be better to wait twenty years for a solid solution than to opt immediately for Arabization which might collapse in a couple of years (Gordon 1966:200). Gallagher (1964:692–4), in reviewing the situation, maintains that the near-million Algerian children in school cannot possibly be receiving ten hours instruction in Arabic each week. Nevertheless, as Gordon points out (1966:148–9, 198–201) the dominant opinion seems to be in favor of speeding up Arabization.

[34] Ali 1960:73. According to an official statement made on June 23, 1964, the program toward Arabization was hampered by the lack of suitable textbooks. See Henderson 1965:125.

[35] Among other measures undertaken for the transition from English to Arabic were two training courses: one for all practicing teachers in secondary schools, the other for recent university graduates planning to teach at the secondary level.

instruction prior to the 1950's.[36] The problem is compounded by the presence of a large number of non-Arabic languages or vernaculars of which only a few are spoken by more than 100,000 people within the Sudan.[37] The need for a unifying language has long been recognized, but it was only recently (around 1950) that steps toward using Arabic were taken. By 1962, all elementary schools in southern provinces, with the exception of a small number, were Arabized. The number of schools which used local languages was presumably to decrease as teachers qualified in Arabic became available.[38] This policy, however, has not proceeded without some opposition on the part of some southerners,[39] and eventually it may have to consider the use of the more widespread southern languages in early educational stages as Akrawi suggested (Akrawi 1960:273). But until the problems associated with the multiplicity of languages, and the question of preparing adequate materials in languages selected for instructional uses are resolved, Arabization seems the only practical policy the Sudanese government can pursue.

2. LANGUAGE EDUCATION IN THE ARAB WORLD

The teaching of Arabic receives a considerable share of the time devoted to the general curriculum in both primary and secondary schools except in countries which are still in the process of Arabizing its schools (1.3). An examination of the program in several Arab states reveals that the time alloted to Arabic ranges from one third in the primary level to one fifth in the secondary level.[40] The division of the language program into different branches with special hours alloted to each, begins rather early in the primary school, though attempts are being made to avoid sharp division at least during the first three years.[41] The branches taught at this level are: composition (writing), conversation, dictation (spelling), grammar, memorization (recitation), and

[36] Royal Institute of International Affairs cites 1948 as the year when Arabic was taught throughout the south, *The Middle East*, 1954:446. For a brief discussion of the British policy aiming at excluding Arabic from the south, see Said 1965–66:32–77 and Sanderson 1962:110–17. Note especially the following remark: 'At that time [1900–48] the government did not necessarily consider the future progress of the south to be through Arabization. Today it is easy to see the advantages had Arabic been introduced uniformly at an earlier date but this was far from obvious at that time' (Sanderson 1962:117).

[37] The number of these languages is estimated at more than one hundred. Akrawi 1960:273, McLoughlin 1964:33, Said 1965–66:16. For information on some of these languages and the number of their speakers, see Tucker and Bryan 1966.

[38] The number of schools using local languages in 1962 was given at 338 out of 1,407; see Gannon 1965:324.

[39] The opposition is based on political, religious and pedagogical considerations; Oduho and Deng 1963:45–8, Le Page 1964:33.

[40] See Khater 1963:2, 7, 10; Matthews and Akrawi 1947:58, 149, 167, 367; Unesco 1956:48–52.

[41] Matthews and Akrawi (1947:44) observe for instance that study of formal grammar begins in the third year in Egyptian primary schools. But this has been postponed until the fifth year in recent years; Khater 1963:3.

reading. In the secondary schools two other branches are added: a formal study of literature and rhetoric. A typical distribution of all these branches is given in Table II.[42]

TABLE II

The Distribution of the Arabic Language Arts

Grades (primary)	Literature	Composition & Dictation	Conversation*	Grammar	Memorization	Reading	Rhetoric
1					3[a]	8[b]	
2			2		2	8[b]	
3		2	2		2	4	
4		4[a]		1	1	4	
5		2		2	1	1	
6		2		2	1	1	
Grades (Secondary)							
1		2		2	1	1	
2		2		2	1	1	
3	2	1		2	1	1	
4	2[c]	1		1	1	1	1
5	2[c]	1		1	1	2[d]	1[c]

* Conversation is mostly included in the hours assigned to composition.
[a] A portion of these hours is assigned to conversation.
[b] A portion of these hours is assigned to writing and/or dictation.
[c] Not given in science section.
[d] Only one hour for literary section.

According to prevalent practices, the content, textbooks, and distribution of hours devoted to different branches of Arabic, are determined centrally by the Ministry of Education and applied with optimum uniformity within each country (Unesco 1959). Thus the teachers are, on the whole, deprived of active participation in defining

[42] The table is based on courses of study in use in Iraqi schools; Al-Toma 1957:6.

the curriculum or selecting appropriate texts,[43] though they are encouraged to comment on the program, and to use, whenever possible, supplementary materials. As a consequence of such policy, the possibilities of testing new ideas or approaches in developing an effective language program have been greatly limited, while the traditional approach dominates with its emphasis on classicism, grammar, and passive knowledge about the language and its literature.

2.1 *Classicism*

Classicism, a hallmark of the entire language program, raises a special difficulty in the earliest stages of learning. The child comes to school with a different set of linguistic habits, i.e. his colloquial, and is faced rather abruptly with the task of learning classical Arabic. With no gradual transition from the colloquial to the classical, he is introduced by means of alphabet and phonic methods to the sounds and the structure of the language.[44] As Akil's study of fifteen readers used in five Arab countries indicates,[45] not only is the child burdened with items too numerous to assimilate or too difficult to make use of, but learning them is made cumbersome by the uncontrolled fashion in which they are presented. In an effort to rectify some of these defects, the Egyptian Ministry of Education selected in 1954 a new series of readers based on the global or sentence method to be used in schools (Khater 1958:43–56). The salient features of these readers are reflected in their use of Egyptian colloquial words and phrases especially at the beginning to serve as a transition to purely classical Arabic, their limited vocabulary and the graded method of presentation. But before too long, the readers were criticized for failing to help children read as fast or as accurately as those trained by the traditional alphabet or phonic methods, and for lowering the rate for their vocabulary growth (Khater 1958:55–6, A. Ibrāhīm 1966:114–16). Most suggestions made to overcome the limitations of this as well as traditional methods seem to favor an eclectic approach as present practices in Egypt indicate (Khater 1963:3). Another prevalent facet of classicism is related to the tendency to teach texts from earlier periods whether in reading or the formal study of literature

[43] Teachers in Lebanon enjoy relative freedom in selecting textbooks written in accordance with the prescribed curriculum, and, as a result, free competition among authors is encouraged. Note Hindāwī's remark (1958) regarding the merits of free competition vis-a-vis centralized policy in preparing textbooks. In Egypt, a new policy of open participation has been tried out lately to encourage authors to submit textbooks based on the prescribed curriculum, instead of limiting this role to appointed authors. Early indications suggest that this policy has succeeded in improving the quality of books selected for school use, Franklin Institute, Egypt, 1963:44–52.

[44] Matthews and Akrawi 1947:44, Khater 1958:62–3. For a detailed description of the readers used in Egyptian schools, see the latter: 8–70.

[45] A study covering the first three readers which were used in five Arab countries around 1950 shows that there were more than 9,000 items of which about one third occurred only once or twice. See Akil 1953:1-6.

(see 2.3 below). Of the textbooks used (1954) for the seventh grade in Iraq, for example, nearly 60% of the total was not of recent origin, but was rather extracted from works written prior to the tenth century (Al-Yāsīn 1953–54, Al-Toma 1957:165). One can readily detect religious, nationalistic or literary factors conducive to the excessive use of the literary heritage. But by so doing, the modern usage which is more important and relevant to the learner's needs is unduly neglected. However, a new trend has emerged placing more emphasis on the study of modern literature, as more works in the forms of novels, dramas, essays, or poems become available (Khater 1963:13).

2.2 *Grammar and Rhetoric*

2.2.1 No other branch of Arabic has been so much criticized or blamed for the failure of language education in Arab countries as grammar. Much of the criticism stems from a widely held belief that the teaching of grammar proceeds along lines laid down more than 1,000 years ago whether in terminology, organization or methods of teaching. One of the institutions charged with the responsibility for perpetuating the traditional approach is Al-Azhar University of Cairo which was, until the late thirties, in charge of training teachers of Arabic in Egypt,[46] but in 1938 the Egyptian Ministry of Education assumed the role of modernizing language instruction by setting up a committee[47] aiming at the simplification of grammar and rhetoric. The committee's efforts culminated in a report approved by the Egyptian Academy in 1945,[48] which was not implemented until the late fifties when textbooks based on the proposed reforms began to appear in Egypt, Iraq and Syria. Among the significant changes introduced by the report were: the use of a different terminology; a different meaningful order for most grammatical categories with a view to achieving maximum clarity in presenting them; and the deliberate attempt to deemphasize the practice of parsing or grammatical analysis.[49] These and other changes were adopted as guidelines for the teaching of grammar, especially in Egypt, but were temporarily halted in 1961

[46] The opposition of Al-Azhar to efforts restricting its role in training Arabic teachers is outlined by Ḥusayn 1938:84–93. The latter was a vocal voice for 'secularizing' Arabic, and has repeatedly called for simplifying the language lest 'we face the dreadful prospect of Classical Arabic becoming, whether we want it or not, a religious language and the sole possession of the men of religion' (Ḥusayn 1938: 86).

[47] *MMLA*, 1951:6, 180–5. Among the members of the committee were three leading neo-classicists, Ḥusayn, Muṣṭafā, and Amīn, who are noted for their active role in modernizing Arabic. Muṣṭafa (d. 1962) deserves special credit for what the committee has ultimately proposed, since the final report incorporated much of what he advocated in his pioneer work (1937).

[48] The report was published in 1958 under the title: *Taḥrīr an-naḥw al-ʿarabī* [Freeing the Arabic Grammar]. See Muṣṭafā *et al.*, 1958, but an early version of it appeared in *MMLA*, 1951:6, 180–97.

[49] Among the basic terms suggested are /musnad ilayh/ 'subject' and /musnad/ 'predicate'. The former replaces three traditional terms /fāʿil/ 'subject', /nāʾib fāʿil/ 'subject of a passive verb', and /mubtadaʾ/ 'subject of a nominal sentence'.

due to the opposition of the traditionalists.[50] Nevertheless, textbooks used in Egypt and Iraq seem to proceed along lines suggested by the report.[51]

2.2.2 The preceding reform represents only one of the current trends concerned with the teaching of grammar. Two other proposals reflecting different trends should be mentioned here: (a) a proposal for modifications in the grammatical rules of Classical Arabic; (b) another suggesting drastic departure from CA.

a) Al-Khūlī, an outstanding Azharite (d. 1966), felt that the academy's reform was not adequate because it was confined to matters of nomenclature, organization and methodology, and suggested that structural changes were needed if Arabic was to become an effective tool. According to him, the difficulties encountered in learning Arabic can be traced primarily to the classical-colloquial dichotomy, and the complexity of grammatical rules with their numerous exceptions. Therefore, his proposed reforms aimed at reducing exceptional cases, simplifying the declensional system and selecting usages which have counterparts in the colloquial (Al-Khūlī 1961:42–5). By so doing, he hoped that Classical Arabic would be governed by rules showing maximum consistency in application instead of the many exceptions encountered now, and that it would be free, like the colloquials, from a multiplicity of grammatical forms. Among the changes he proposed are: the use of one dual and one sound plural ending instead of two, and one declension instead of three for each of the so-called five nouns; the treatment of diptotes as fully declinable nouns, and of the sound feminine plural as an ordinary noun having three case endings; and the retention of the final long vowels in weak verbs instead of omitting them in the jussive mood (Al-Khūlī 1961:48–56).

The need for certain modifications in the rules of Classical Arabic was also underscored by Aḥmad Amīn (d. 1954) in a report he submitted to the Egyptian Academy in 1944 (Amīn 1951). Amīn addressed himself especially to the possibility of applying a rule by which the formation of the imperfect can be made predictable for the majority of the triliteral sound verbs.

Such modifications,[52] if implemented, would greatly simplify the learning of Arabic but, needless to say, they are neither acceptable to the traditionalists, nor are they based on actual usage in Classical Arabic, by which they could eventually attain acceptance.

b) Frayḥa, of the American University at Beirut, is one of the few Arab linguists who has been attempting to apply linguistic principles to the study of Arabic. Since his early article (Frayḥa 1938), Frayḥa has been crusading for promoting a descriptive method in dealing with language issues, especially grammar and the problem of diglossia. Two major works published in the fifties (1955, 1959) sum up his view of

[50] Traditionalists in Syria, which was at that time part of the U.A.R., opposed the new approach, and were instrumental in slowing down its application. See Al-Afghānī 1962:202–11, Ash-Shihābī 1964:531.

[51] See *MMLA* 1966:21, 365, regarding Egypt.

[52] Similar changes have been advocated by others: Ḥarakāt 1959:47–8, Khalīfa 1961, Al-ʿUzayzī 1967:124–5, Bin Jallūn 1965.

these issues including a scheme for achieving simplified Arabic and a model for writing grammar on a new basis. In his scheme (1955:169–96) Frayḥa favors the adoption of the vaguely defined colloquial spoken by educated Arabs on the premise that CA with its complicated inflectional system cannot replace the various colloquials as a naturally spoken language and that it is not practical to adopt local dialects or impose one variety such as Egyptian on all Arabic speaking regions. The cultivated spoken Arabic, on the other hand, represents the best alternative, being free from archaic features of CA, and closely related to various colloquials. Realizing that certain conditions are required for standardizing or accepting the proposed language, he suggests the following steps: 1) its use as the literary medium, 2) the adoption of the Roman script, 3) a description of its phonological, morphological and syntactical features and 4) its acceptance by the Arabs.

However, this ambitious scheme has not received, nor is it likely to receive, wide support both for linguistic and extra-linguistic considerations. The author himself acknowledged the impractical nature of his proposals, and therefore, in his later work (1959), Frayḥa attempted to simplify Arabic grammar without suggesting structural modifications. Many of the changes he proposed resemble those of the Egyptian Academy's report, especially in matters related to nomenclature and organization, though Frayḥa adopted more of the linguistic systems of classification.

The aforementioned and other similar[53] attempts reflect three trends concerned with the teaching of grammar. The strongest is that of the traditional school which feels that Arabic grammar is still adequate, and therefore tolerates no significant changes. The second, represented by the Egyptian Academy, has been preoccupied with the issue of simplifying grammar without deviating from the prescribed rules, and seems to have gained wide support. The third, the weakest at this point, stresses the need for modifications of certain grammatical rules. It is too early to assess the impact of these trends on the teaching of Arabic, but they can be taken at least as an indication of determined efforts to reexamine different aspects of the traditional grammar. However, it must be pointed out that nearly all reformists still seek the basis for such reexamination in the literature or grammatical works of earlier periods, rather than in the modern usage of Classical Arabic.

2.2.3 *Rhetoric and literary criticism*

Rhetoric as an independent branch of Arabic is taught in the upper classes of the secondary level (4–6). Its primary objective is to acquaint the students with the rhetorical devices or skills essential for effective use of the language, to enable them to analyze and evaluate texts accordingly, and to express their thoughts and feelings in a persuasive and effective manner.[54] As a subject, rhetoric encompasses three

[53] See for example: ʿArafa, Egypt, 1945; Aṣ-Ṣaʿīdī, Egypt, 1947; Sa'āda, Lebanon, 1947; Al-Ḥusaynī, Lebanon, 1954; K. Ibrāhīm, Iraq, 1955–56; Dīb, Lebanon, 1959; and Al-Afghānī, Syria, 1951, 1962; Al-Makhzūmī, Iraq, 1964.

[54] ʿAbdul Majīd 1961:349–51, A. Ibrāhīm 1966:299–304. The classic textbook used for many

traditional branches dealing with the arrangement of meanings and thoughts, the clarity of speech or expression and the beautification or embellishment of speech or writing. Much of the criticism levelled against the traditional grammar applies to the teaching of rhetoric.[55] The Egyptian committee entrusted with the task of simplifying grammar and rhetoric came out in favor of teaching rhetoric as an integral part of literature. It proposed a new syllabus in which few of the traditional topics were included and others dealing with new literary genres were added (The Egyptian Academy 1951:186, 192–3). The first Arab cultural conference (Arab League 1948: 101–2), after reviewing the program, echoed the findings of the Egyptian committee and proposed a new course of study in which rhetoric and literary criticism would be combined and closely linked with literature. This approach was first implemented in Egypt in 1955, and other Arab countries such as Syria and Iraq responded favorably.[56] The trend toward teaching rhetoric as an integral part of literature succeeded in 1960 in the elimination of both textbooks and special hours assigned for rhetoric and literary criticism from the Egyptian curriculum (A. Ibrāhīm 1966:301–2). Although not all Arab countries follow the Egyptian example,[57] there seems to be a strong trend moving toward combining rhetoric and literary criticism with the formal study of literature.

2.3 *Literature*

The formal study of literature occupies a prominent place in Arab high schools, as it attempts to acquaint the students with the literary heritage of about fourteen centuries. Thus far two chronological schemes have guided the program, in selecting, organizing and teaching literature. The first, followed in the U.A.R., proceeds from the pre-Islamic period (sixth century) to the present (grades 10–12), the other, practiced in Iraq, begins with modern literature and later introduces the students to earlier periods (grades 9–11). The second scheme, which was also prevalent in Egypt for some time,[58]

---

years in different Arab countries (Al-Jārim and Amīn 1953) sums up the purpose of teaching rhetoric in the following terms: 'to discover the merits of Arabic, to appreciate the greatness and beauty of its styles, and to study different types of discourse and expression which would endow them with the blessing of good taste, and develop in them the gift of sound criticism.'

[55] Mūsā (1945:61) viewed it as a subject concerned with elegant but empty verbosity whereas Aḥmad (1948) deplored the tendency to overburden high school students with rules or terms in place of helping them appreciate stylistic features in context.

[56] See Al-Ālūsī and Ṣādiq 1960:3–7 and Aṭ-Ṭāhir 1960:3–7. The subject taught in Iraq in 1959 combined rhetoric (4th year) and literary criticism (5th year).

[57] See for example Al-Lādiqī, Lebanon, 1962.

[58] Writing in 1938, Ḥusayn deplored the practice of beginning with the pre-Islamic writings as required by the old curriculum, and referred to changes which introduced the youth to the modern period, and spared them the strain of having to study earlier literature. See Ḥusayn 1954:92. The practice of beginning with modern literature and moving gradually to other periods until pre-Islamic is introduced in the last stage started in Egypt in 1935 and continued up to 1947. See Abdul Majid 1961:294–5.

is pursued on the premise that the literary works of the earlier periods are thematically remote from everyday life and stylistically more difficult to understand and appreciate.

For many years, the historical approach has been under attack for stressing information about literary figures or works at the expense of developing insight into literature itself. 'That we teach in our school everything but literature', a leading critic was led to remark, 'is a matter no one who knows our curriculum or is acquainted with our books and with what our teachers do, can deny' (Al-Ḥānī 1953:59). An Egyptian commission reporting on the subject in 1946 ('Abdul Majīd 1961:295) noted that the study of literary history had occupied a large portion of the program and prevailed over the study of literature which should be the main concern. To remedy this situation, the commission proposed a program based on textual study. Similar observations were voiced in the first Arab cultural conference held in Egypt (1947), when participants from different Arab countries reviewed the teaching of literature (Arab League 1948: 132–42).[59] The decisions of the conference, however, envisaged two stages in the teaching of literature: in the first, attention is focused on literary appreciation, and texts chosen primarily from contemporary literature, whereas in the second, the study of literature is to be pursued in accordance with a historical scheme extending from the pre-Islamic period to the present (Arab League 1948:101). Although the historical approach, on the basis of these decisions, has remained dominant in different Arab countries, the present program in Lebanon follows a new trend which takes literary genres, rather than strict historical periods, as the guiding principle. Thus the student in the last two years of secondary school (Grades 11–12) proceeds from a brief introduction to the concept of literature and the history of Arabic literature to the study of selected works covering different genres and periods within the same year (Mas'ūd 1965a I:5–6; II:5–6). In view of its emphasis on literature itself, this approach has been regarded as more effective in developing the student's literary sensitivity and appreciation, and seems to be gaining adherents among prominent authors.[60]

2.4 *Trends in Research and Teacher Training*

Aside from work done in the U.A.R., educational research or experiments dealing with the teaching of Arabic are still scanty in most Arab countries, though special research sections have been recently set up for this purpose in various ministries of education (Unesco 1960:76–82, 1966b:xiv–xviii). The language program is evaluated or revised by means of questionaires, teachers' reports, or conferences and recommendations made by inspectors and other administrators. Only in the

[59] Two related trends emerged in the meeting; one suggested literary texts rather than literary history as the basis for the programs (Ḥasan 1948:137), the other proposed a combination of chronological and thematic approaches with less emphasis on historical or factual information, provided the course begins with the modern period (Al-Maqdisī 1948:142).

[60] Note for example Khūrī's text (1957) on modern Arabic literature. Sulaymān 1962, Ad-Dahhān 1962–63:241–2.

U.A.R. has there been noticeable progress in developing research techniques regarding methods, texts or syllabuses used for different subjects, including Arabic (Unesco 1958:xlviii). Further experiments have been conducted lately to test the various methods or organization of teaching Arabic, or of teaching some or its branches such as literature.[61] Few studies or surveys of textbooks have been made available. Khater's work (1958) provides a detailed description and evaluation of nineteen primers or readers used in elementary schools or for adult education in Egypt. A statistical analysis of words found in more than fifteen readers which were in use in Egypt, Iraq, Lebanon, Palestine, Syria and Saudi Arabia was undertaken by Akil (1953). Kanʿān (1966) was primarily concerned with methods and texts used in three Arab countries (Lebanon, Iraq, U.A.R.) to teach Arabic to illiterate adults. The Center for Educational and Psychological Research at the University of Baghdad undertook recently an evaluation of the books used in teaching Arabic at the elementary level in Iraq (Khalil and Akrawi 1968). These and other types of research undertaken recently (Khater 1963:13) reflect a new emphasis on scientific investigation and wider use of systematic research in the area of language education.

As for the training of Arabic teachers, pertinent programs vary from one country to another. But in all Arab countries teachers for elementary schools are not provided with a college education;[62] they usually receive their training in special teachers institutes for two years after completing secondary education, as in Iraq, or for five or three years after the intermediate level (9th grade), as in the U.A.R. and Lebanon respectively. Elementary teachers are not always specialized in the teaching of Arabic, particularly at lower grades, though efforts have been made toward this end by requiring advanced study in Arabic as a part of teacher training.[63] The case of high school teachers of Arabic is different, since they are normally required to attend at least a four-year college program. Two types of professional training are still noted. The first consists of a four year program beyond the high school level during which students receive intensive training in Arabic and pedagogical disciplines as Table III indicates. The second type comprises two stages: four years of specialization in Arabic and one more year of professional training whether in the university faculty of education, as in the U.A.R., or in special institutes such as Secondary Teacher Training Institutes in Syria.[64]

[61] For a brief description of several experiments conducted since 1956–57, see A. Ibrāhīm 1966:364–83. Several M.A. and Ph.D. dissertations on various aspects of the Arabic language program were submitted to ʿAyn Shams University at Cairo, between 1950 and 1960, cf. ʿAyn Shams University 1961:715–18, dealing with reading interests of high school students, and 719–22, on the ability of high school students to use Arabic particles of conjunction. Note also Lotfi's dissertation (1948) on Egyptian readers.

[62] The latest conference of Arab ministers of Education meeting in Libya, April 9–14, 1966, suggested that Arab countries which are not faced with shortage of teachers should require college education as the minimum degree for teaching at any level. See Abd Ad-Dā'im 1966:709.

[63] Elementary teachers specializing in Arabic in the U.A.R. are required to attend a two-year advanced course in Arabic (Khater 1963:11).

[64] Khater 1963:11 and Arab Information Center 1966:223. For information on the training of teachers in Lebanon, see Kurani 1963.

In view of the shortage of teachers at both levels, graduates of other educational institutions are still recruited in spite of their inadequate training, whether in Arabic or other subjects. This practice, which applies to all Arab countries with the possible exception of the U.A.R., affects adversely the quality of Arabic instruction. Despite demands made for specialized training of elementary teachers, particularly in Arabic (Al-Jūmard 1967:117), the enormous task of preparing teachers for combating illiteracy, and for general education, is likely to prolong some of the present inadequate measures.

TABLE III

Program for teachers of Arabic at secondary school level followed at the University of Baghdad 1959–1960

Subject	Hours per Week	
	1st sem.	2nd sem.
First Year		
Grammar	3	3
Literature	3	3
Syntax	3	3
Eloquence and Prosody	4	4
Islamic History	2	2
English or French	3	3
Essay and Reading	4	4
Second Year		
Grammar	3	3
Literature	3	3
Rhetoric	2	2
Exegesis	3	3
Essay and Reading	4	4
General Psychology	3	3
Secondary Education	2	2
Islamic History	2	2
English or French	3	3

Subject	Hours per Week	
	1st sem.	2nd sem.
Third Year		
Grammar	3	3
Literary Criticism	3	3
Exegesis	2	2
Literature	3	3
Reading	2	2
Teaching Methods	3	3
General Psychology	2	2
English or French	3	3
Fourth Year		
Modern Literature	3	3
Abbassid Literature	2	–
Andalusian Literature	–	2
Grammar	3	3
Literary Criticism	3	3
Teaching Methods	3	–
An Elective Course	–	2
Philosophy of Education	2	3
English or French	3	3

3. THE ROLE OF THE ACADEMIES

Three Arab academies have been directly concerned with various aspects of Classical Arabic. The Syrian (est. 1918–19), the Egyptian (1932), and the Iraqi (1947).[65] All regard, among their primary objectives, the preservation and renovation of Classical Arabic as an effective and unified language for all Arabic speaking people. In their attempts to achieve this aim, they have continued to resist the penetration of colloquialism from within, and loan words from without. The major problem which none of the academies has been able to resolve is how to make Classical Arabic effective

[65] Each of these academies has an official journal: *MMLA*, *MMAD*, and *MMII*, and other series of publications covering modern language problems and philological or historical studies relevant to earlier periods or works. The Egyptian academy, however, places more emphasis on modern issues. For additional details, see Al-Futayyiḥ 1956, Dahân and Laoust 1949–50, Al-Jūbūrī 1965, and Hamzaoui 1965.

in meeting the needs of modern life without changes in areas of orthography, grammar, and vocabulary. Of all Arab academies, the Egyptian has been most involved in attempts to modernize the language, and has exerted greater influence in the Arab world through the membership of distinguished scholars from other Arab countries. Therefore the following discussion will be focused on its role in coping with three central issues: orthography, grammar and terminology or lexicon.

a) In addition to what has been stated earlier regarding the academy's efforts at simplifying the Arab writing system and grammar and rhetoric (see 1.2 and 2.2), reference should be made to its stand on questions of modern usage. As a rule, the academy opposes usages which do not conform to basic rules of Arabic; nevertheless, it has examined and approved a large number of grammatical features or lexical items of modern usage which do not violate the structure of Classical Arabic. In modifying or adding to established rules, the academy does not initiate new usages, but rather it lends its support to what has already been widely used in modern written Arabic. The changes or modifications are approved after lengthy discussion in special and general meetings, and presented in the form of decisions which are published regularly in the official Journal *MMLA*.[66] Such decisions ultimately find their way into textbooks and dictionaries.[67] In pedagogical terms, the academy's decisions facilitate, in a modest way, the task of authors working on textbooks not only by providing them with guidelines for what features of modern usage they select, but also by protecting them against the criticism of extreme purists who deplore any deviations from established rules.[68] The two major contributions made toward simplifying the teaching of Arabic are represented by the Academy's proposed reforms of grammar and the writing system (see 1.3 and 2.2). But the academy has been always faced with the question of how to implement its decisions on a large scale locally or in different Arab countries. Its proposed grammar reform was submitted to the Egyptian Ministry of Education in 1945, but was not implemented before the late fifties, and even then, the opposition of Syrian educational authorities (when Syria was part of the U.A.R.) obstructed its implementation.[69] There does not seem to be complete agreement among the various academies on language issues, particularly grammar reform.[70] Nevertheless, several steps have been taken to foster a closer cooperation between the academies themselves, and between them and the Ministries of Education, by means

[66] A collection of these decisions were published under the title: *Majmūʿa Al-qarārāt Al-ʿilmiyya*. See *MMLA*, 1966:20, 364.

[67] Note, for example, Muṣṭafā *et. al.*, 1958, and the Egyptian Academy's Dictionary, 1960–62, which incorporate such modifications.

[68] Even the academy was the target of such criticism for sponsoring reforms which were regarded by purists as detrimental to the preservation of Classical Arabic (Al-Afghānī 1962:198–211).

[69] Note remarks made relevant to the problem of implementation by the academy's secretary general (Madkur 1966) in his annual report: *Al-Buḥūθ wa Al-Muḥāḍarāt*, an annual publication of the academy, vol. 9:270, and also his earlier observations (1955:14) and those made by Ṭāhā Ḥusayn 1959:102.

[70] The Syrian Academy, for example, did not endorse the proposed reform of grammar approved by the Egyptian Academy, see Al-Afghānī 1962:199–200.

of joint committees, or by convening conferences for all academies, or by holding some of the regular meetings in a host country.[71]

b) Since its inception, the Egyptian academy has addressed itself to the task of creating scientific and technical terminology needed for various disciplines as well as different branches of government. The predominant principle which guided but slowed down its work calls for using Arabic equivalents except in cases for which no Arabic word can be found (Ash-Shihābī 1965:71). Depending on the work of committees of experts and specialists, such as committees for physical and chemical terms, for biological terms, legal terms, etc., the academy reviews the proposed terms in its annual meetings and publishes lists of those approved items in its official journal, *MMLA*. Between 1957 and 1964 about 20,000 such terms were published. These figures clearly reflect the slow procedures by which the terms are approved,[72] and suggests that the academy, despite its valuable contribution, is far from meeting the demands created by rapidly developing sciences and growing terminologies. Leading academicians realize that other measures or methods should be pursued, such as direct translation of specialized dictionaries, or encouraging competent specialists to work on basic terminology in their respected fields, if Arabic is to serve as an efficient medium of technical and scientific literature (Ash-Shihābī 1965:81). However, an overemphasis on Arabic equivalents, lack of staff and inadequate funds have hampered the academy's efforts to keep pace with the needs of progress (Zaki 1953:93). Consequently individual attempts to introduce needed terms in their fields were unavoidable, and these in turn created a multiplicity of terms for the same object or concept which may vary not only from one country to another, but from one book to another within the same country. This chaotic situation is due also to the lack of coordination among different academies, and between the academies and other governmental departments or professional associations. The need for unifying terminology was stressed as early as 1936 when the Egyptian Academy began working on a dictionary to include terms used in other Arab countries such as Iraq, North Africa and Syria (*MMLA*, 1936:33). Recent attempts have been made along these lines, but in the absence of a central coordinating agency, no substantial results were achieved. Apart from the role of the academies (especially the Egyptian) in developing unified terminology, a new institution — the Cultural Division of the Arab League — has become increasingly involved in this area of endeavor. It has sponsored numerous Arab scientific and professional conferences which discussed, among other things, measures for setting up unified terminology.[73] A special Arab conference for unifying scientific

[71] Examples of such measures are the conference of the three academies held in Damascus, September 29-October 4, 1956, and the regular meeting of the Egyptian Academy convened in Baghdad in 1965. The Egyptian Ministry of Education also began to issue special bulletins to teachers on the academy's decisions regarding different subjects. The first bulletin was issued to teachers of Arabic in January, 1966; see *MMLA* 21:357–9.

[72] According to Madkur, an average of 2,000 terms are approved annually, see *MMLA* 18(1965):10.

[73] Among such conferences is the Arab Scientific Congress held in Alexandria, 1953, and developed into a permanent Arab Scientific Union. Between 1955 and 1961, the union attempted to provide

terms was held in Algiers (1964) under the aegis of the League (Cultural Division), and recommendations were made for using a unified terminology especially in school textbooks. To such efforts must be added the fact that the Bureau for Arabization (see 1.3.1) has also been concerned with the creation of unified terminology. These trends seem to favor the Arab League (Cultural Division) as the practical channel through which unified terminology can be promoted, but the scholarly contributions of the academies are still recognized as an important basis for achieving this objective.

A final reference should be made to the academy's new dictionary *Al-Muʿjam Al-Wasīṭ* which was prepared in response to the request made in 1936 by the Egyptian Ministry of Education.[74] The dictionary includes many items of modern usage, whether they were approved by the academy or not, and represents the only modern authoritative dictionary prescribed for use in schools. As with other traditional dictionaries, the words are listed according to their root rather than their alphabetical order. The latter system, which would have facilitated the search for items, was rejected on the basis that Arabic is a derivative language and that alphabetical arrangement would deprive the students or others of having a comprehensive view of related items under one entry. The argument against alphabetical arrangement was advanced again in 1966 when the Egyptian Minister of Culture cited the need for a new dictionary based on a simplified scheme of listing.[75] However, the academy's insistence on a root system did not deter an outstanding Lebanese lexicographer from compiling an alphabetical dictionary. Al-ʿAlāyilī (1963), motivated by the need for a modern and comprehensive, yet simplified, dictionary, tried to combine both the western method, in listing the lexical items according to their pronunciation, and the traditional method, in listing roots along with their widely used derivatives. Aside from his ambitious attempt to indicate, whenever possible the historical origin of the usage, he incorporated a large number of technical terminologies cited in French or English and their counterparts in Arabic. A similar, but far less ambitious, dictionary, was prepared by a Lebanese teacher (Masʿūd 1965a) to serve primarily as an educational tool. Both of these works reflect a growing awareness that one important source of student apathy regarding the use of Arabic dictionaries, even at higher educational levels, lies in their cumbersome arrangement, and the concomitant realization that alphabetically arranged dictionaries would be more effective, and less time consuming in serving the needs of the students and others.[76]

---

a list of terms used or to be used in different Arab countries, and its efforts culminated in the compilation of scientific terms collected from high school textbooks used in five Arab states: U.A.R., Iraq, Jordan, Lebanon and Syria. See Ash-Shihābī 1965:189–92.

[74] The dictionary was compiled by a committee under the supervision of the Egyptian Academy and was published in two volumes in 1960–62. The original request envisaged a dictionary for school use, *MMLA*, 3(1936):33–4, but it is questionable whether the final form is suitable for the level of high school students.

[75] *Al-Buḥūθ wa Al-Muḥāḍarāt*, vol. 9:5,7–8 (Cairo, 1966).

[76] Note, for example, Al-ʿUzayzī's remarks (1967:125–6, 129) regarding the urgent need for such dictionaries, and Ad-Dabbāgh's (1962) reference to his work on a pedagogical dictionary following alphabetical order.

CONCLUSION

The present survey, brief as it may be, points to the complex language issues with which different Arab countries have had to cope during the postwar years. Serious efforts, and steady, though slow, progress were made toward minimizing the adverse effects of these issues on education in general, and the teaching of Arabic in particular. But most proposed solutions or measures have been greatly impaired partly because of the lack of a coordinated policy, but also because they were opposed, or restricted, by traditionalists who tend to resist changes aiming at modernizing Arabic, whether in its writing system, grammar or in matters related to lexicon and terminology. Nonetheless, one cannot escape the conviction that the pertinent discussions and solutions succeeded in preparing the groundwork for more effective measures, by contributing toward an adequate grasp of the problems faced, and by developing a general awareness of the urgent need for immediate reforms. As a result, new trends have emerged strongly favoring the simplification of the writing system and grammar as it is taught in school. A new emphasis has been placed on the importance of unifying the terminology and the language of textbooks used in different Arab countries, and on the scientific investigation of different aspects of the language programs: textbooks, curriculum, and methods of teaching. It is hoped that steps proposed for a coordinated policy will yield more constructive results in dealing with the numerous language problems shared, in one form or another, by all Arab countries.

REFERENCES

ʿAbd ad-Dāʾim, ʿAbdullah, 1966. At-taxṭīṭ at-tarbawī. Beirut.

Abdesselem, M. 1960. Situation et perspectives de l'arabe moderne. Ibla 23.1–6.

ʿAbdul Majīd, ʿAbdul ʿAzīz. 1961. Al-Luġa Al-ʿArabiyya: uṣūluhā an-nafsiyya wa ṭuruq tadrīsihā. Vol. I. Cairo.

Al-Afghānī, Saʿīd. 1951. Fī ʾuṣūl an-naḥw. Damascus.

——. 1962. Ḥāḍir al-luġa al-ʿArabiyya fi aš-šām. Cairo.

Aḥmad, Muḥammad Khalafalla. 1948. Taysīr an-naqd wa al-balāġa fī marḥala at-taʿlīm aθ-θānawī. Al-Mutamar aθ-θaqāfī Al-ʿArabī Al-Awwal, ed. by Arab League, 143–7. Cairo.

Akil, Fakhir. 1953. The basic vocabulary of the arabic primary reading. Damascus.

Akrawi, Matta. 1945. Iṣlāḥ al-xaṭṭ Al-ʿArabī. Al-Muqtaṭaf 106.245–52, 352–61, 435–42.

——. 1960. Educational planning in a developing country: the Sudan. International Review of Education 6.257–82.

Al-ʿAlāyilī, ʿAbdullah. 1963. Al-Marjiʿ. Vol. I, Beirut.

Ali, Nasr El Hag. 1960. Educational problems in the Sudan. Sudan Notes and Records. 41.66–77.

AL-ĀLŪSĪ, JAMĀL AD-DĪN and ABDUL RIḌĀ ṢĀDIQ. 1960. Al-Balāġa. Baghdad.

AMĪN, AḤMAD. 1951. ʾIqtirāḥ bi baʿḍ al-iṣlāḥ. MMLA 6.86–93.

ANĪS, IBRAHIM. 1960. Mustaqbal al-luġa al-ʿArabiyya al-muštaraka. Cairo.

ʿAQL, SAʾĪD. 1961. Yara. Beirut.

ARAB INFORMATION CENTER. 1966. Education in the Arab States. Information Paper. No. 25(I-XIII). New York.

ARAB LEAGUE. 1948. Al-Muʾtamar aθ-θaqāfī al-ʿArabī al-awwal. Cairo.

ʿARAFA, MUḤAMMAD. 1937. An-Naḥw wa an-nuḥāh bayn al-azhar wa al-jāmiʿa. Cairo.

——. 1945. Muškila al-luġa al-ʿArabiyya. Cairo.

ʿAYN SHAMS UNIVERSITY. 1961. At-Taqrir Al-ʿIlmī 1950–60. Cairo.

AL BAGHDĀDĪ, JAMĀL AD-DIN. 1960. Al-Luġa Al-ʿArabiyya bi xayr ya duktūr. Daʿwa Al-Ḥaqq 3/9.53–8.

AL-BAZZĀZ, ʿABDUL RAḤMĀN. 1961a. Al-Fuṣḥā ʿunwān waḥdatinā. Al-ʿArabī 46. 16–24.

——. 1961b. Al-Luġa Al-Fuṣḥā al-muštaraka. Al-ʿArabī 49.16–24.

BELQZIZ, MOHAMMED. 1960. Problemes de l'evolution de la langue Arabe. Confluent (juin-juillet).416–22.

BIN ʿABDULLAH, ʿABDUL ʿAZĪZ. 1966. Riḥla al-amīn al-ʿām ilā al-ʿawāṣim al-ʿArabiyya. Al-Lisān al-ʿArab. 4.61–8.

BIN JALLŪN, ʿABDUL MAJĪD. 1965. Tawḥīd al luġa al-ʿArabiyya. Daʿwa al-Ḥaqq 8/9–10.40–1.

BISHAI, WILSON B. 1966. Modern Inter-Arabic. JAOS 86.319–23.

BRAVMANN, M. M. 1956. Language. The Republic of Syria, ed. by Raphael Patais, vol. I,139–49. New Haven, Human Relations Area Files.

BROWN, LEON CARL. 1965. Tunisia. Education and political development, ed. by James S. Coleman, 144–68. Princeton.

CACHIA, P. J. E. 1967. The use of the colloquial in modern Arabic literature. JAOS 87.12–22.

CHEJNE, ANWAR G. 1965. Arabic: Its significance and place in Arab Muslim society. MEJ 19.447–70.

AD-DABBĀGH, MUḤAMMAD ABDUL ʿAZĪZ. 1962. Xiṭṭa jadīda fī al-muʿjam al-ʿArabī. Daʿwa al-Ḥaqq 5 (No. 5, February).58–60.

DAHÂN, SAMI, and HENRI LAOUST. 1949–50. L'œuvre de l'academie arabe de Damas. BEO 13.160–219.

AD-DAHHĀN, SĀMĪ. 1962–63. Al-Marjiʿ fi tadrīs al-luġa al-ʿArabiyya li al-madāris al-iʿdādiyya wa aθ-θānawiyya. Damascus.

——. 1964. Āθār al-majāmiʿ al-ʿilmiyya al-ʿArabiyya. Āfāq 2/4.64–8. Morocco.

DĪB, WADĪʿ AMĪN. 1959. Naḥw jadīd: ittijāh jadīd fī tadrīs qawāʾid al-luġa Al-ʿArabiyya. Beirut.

AD-DURRAH, MAḤMŪD. 1966. Al-Qaḍiyya Al-Kurdiyya. Beirut.

THE EGYPTIAN ACADEMY. 1946. Taysīr al-kitāba al-ʿArabiyya. Cairo.
——. 1951. Qarārāt mu'tamar al-majaʿ fī taysīr qawāʿid al-luġa al-ʿArabiyya. MMLA 6.180–97.
——. 1960–62. Al-Muʿjam al-wasīṭ. 2 vols. Cairo.
——. 1961. Taysīr al-kitāba al-ʿarabiyya. Cairo.
ERIC. CENTER FOR APPLIED LINGUISTICS. 1967. 1960–67 Selected Bibliography of Arabic. Washington, D.C.
FARRŪKH, ʿUMAR. 1961. Al-Qawmiyya al-fuṣḥā. Beirut.
AL-FĀSĪ, ʿALLĀL. 1963a. Mustaqbal al-luġa al-ʿarabiyya. Al-Bayyina 1/9.109–21.
——. 1963b. Mustaqbal al-luġa al-ʿarabiyya. Al-Bayyina 1/10.74–97.
FRANKLIN INSTITUTE, EGYPT. 1963. Al-Kitāb ad-dirāsī. Cairo.
FRAYḤA, ANĪS. 1938. Al-ʿĀmmiyya wa al-fuṣḥā. Al-Muqtaṭaf 93.292–8.
——. 1955. Naḥw ʿarabiyya muyassara. Beirut. Dar ath-thaqafa.
——. 1959. Tabsīṭ qawāʿid al-luġa al-ʿarabiyya ʿalā 'usus jadīda. Beirut.
AL-FUTAYYIḤ, AḤMAD. 1956. Tārīx al-majmaʿ al-ʿilmi al-ʿarabī. Damascus.
GALLAGHER, CHARLES F. 1963. The United States and North Africa. Cambridge, Harvard University Press.
——. 1964. North African problems and prospects: language and identity. American Universities Field Staff (North African Series) 10.683–704.
GANNON, EDMUND J. 1965. Education in the Sudan. Comparative Education Review 9.323–30.
GHANNĀM, MUḤAMMAD AḤMAD. 1963–64. Taʿrīb at-taʿlīm fī al-waṭan Al-ʿArabī. Ṣaḥīfa at-Tarbiya 16/1.35–50 (1963), 16/2.49–60 (1964).
GORDON, DAVID C. 1964. The search for identity: Arabization and modernization in North Africa. North Africa's French legacy, 1954–62, 65–79. 2nd printing. Cambridge, Harvard University Press.
——. 1966. The passing of French Algeria. London, Oxford University Press. (Esp. 109–14, 197–201).
HAMZAOUI, RACHAD. 1965. L'Académie arabe de Damas et le problème de la modernisation de la langue arabe. Leiden, E. J. Brill
AL-ḤĀNĪ, NĀṢIR. 1953. Naqd wa adab. Baghdad,
ḤARAKĀT, IBRĀHĪM. 1959. Mašākil al-luġa al-ʿarabiyya. Daʿwa al-Ḥaqq 2/5.47–9.
ḤASAN, ʿABDUL ḤAMĪD. 1948. Tadrīs al-adab al-ʿarabī. Al-Mu'tamar aθ-θaqāfī al-ʿarabī al-awwal. Arab League. Cairo.
HENDERSON, K. D. D. 1965. Sudan Republic. London, Ernest Benn.
HINDĀWĪ, KHALĪL. 1958. Kitāb al-muṭālaʿa at-tawjīhiyya. Al-Ādāb 6.51.
HOLT, P. M. 1961. A modern history of the Sudan. New York, Grove Press, Inc.
ḤUSAYN, ṬĀHĀ. 1938. Mustaqbal aθ-θaqāfa fī miṣr.
——. 1954. The future of culture in Egypt, trans. by Sidney Glazer. Washington, D.C. 6.
——. 1956. Yassirū an-naḥw wa al-kitāba. Al-Ādāb 4.890–4, 911.
——. 1957. Al-luġa al-fuṣḥā wa taʿlīm aš-šaʿb. MMAD 32.44–56.

——. 1959. Muškila al-iʿrāb. MMLA 11.89–100 (and the comments on it, 101–2).

AL-ḤUSAYNĪ, ISḤĀQ MŪSA. 1954. Asālīb tadrīs al-luġa al-ʿarabiyya fī aṣ-ṣufūf al-ibtidā'iyya. Beirut.

AL-ḤUṢRI, SĀṬIʿ. 1958. Arā' wa aḥādīθ fī al-luġa wa al-adab. Beirut.

IBRĀHĪM, ʿABDUL AL-ʿALĪM. 1966. Al-Muwajjih al-fannī li mudarrisī al-luġa al-arabiyya. Cairo.

IBRĀHĪM, KAMĀL. 1955–56. Inḥiṭāṭ al-ʿarabiyya fī al-ʿIrāq wa asbābuh. al-Ustāð 4.27–30 (1955), 5.151–5 (1956).

ISSAWI, CHARLES. 1967. European loan-words in contemporary Arabic writing: a case study in modernization. Middle Eastern Studies 3.110–33.

AL-JĀRIM, ʿALI, and MUSṬAFĀ AMĪN. 1953. Al-balāġa al-wāḍiḥa. Cairo.

——. 1954. Dalīl al-balāġa al-wāḍiḥa. Cairo.

AL-JŪBŪRĪ, ʿABDULLAH. 1965. Al-majmaʿ al-ʿilmī al-ʿirāqī. Baghdad.

AL-JŪMARD, MAḤMŪD. 1967. Al-ʿināya bi al-muʿallim wa al-kitāb al-ʿarabī. Al-Lisān al-ʿarabī 5.117–19.

KAHALÉ, OMAR RIDA. 1963. Termes techniques: parus dans la revue de l'academie arabe tomes XXI-XXX. Damascus.

KANʿĀN, ḤALĪM. 1966. Dirāsa fi mukāfaḥa al-'ummiyya. Al-Abhath 19.208–95.

KHALĪFA, AL-JUNAYDĪ. 1961. Naḥw ʿarabiyya afḍal. Beirut.

KHALIL, S., and S. AKRAWI. 1968. Taqyīm al-Kutub al-madrasiyya Fī al-marḥala al-ibtidā'iyya Fī al-ʿirāq: Kutub al-luġa al-ʿarabiyya. Baghdad, Center for Educational and Psychological Research, University of Baghdad.

KHATER, MAḤMOUD ROUSHDI. 1958. Kutub taʿlīm al-qirā'a wa al-kitāba. Cairo.

——. 1963. The teaching of Arabic in the Arab world. Washington, D.C., Center for Applied Linguistics.

KHATTAR, NASRI. 1955. Unified Arabic: weapon against illiteracy. al-Kulliyah 30 (May).8–12.

AL-KHŪLĪ, AMIN. 1944. Hāðā an-naḥw. Bulletin of the Faculty of Arts Fouad I (Cairo) University 7.29–68.

——. 1961. Manāhij tajdīd fī an-naḥw wa al-balāġa wa at-tafsīr wa al-adab. Cairo, dar al-Maʿrifa.

KHŪRĪ, RA'ĪF. 1957. ʿAṣr al-iḥyā' wa an-nahḍa. Beirut.

KURANI, HABIB R. 1963. The training of teachers in Lebanon. The education and training of teachers: the yearbook of education, ed. by George Z. F. Bereday and Joseph A. Lauwerys, 298–312. New York.

AL-LĀDIQĪ, MUHAMMAD TAHIR. 1962. A.-Mubassaṭ fi ʿulum al-balāġa. Beirut.

LELONG, MICHEL. 1956. Faut-il Arabiser l'Enseignement des Sciences: Une enquete de la Revue Ach-Chabab. Ibla 19.415–22.

LEPAGE, R. B. 1964. The national language question. London, Oxford University Press.

LOTFI, M. K. 1948. Changes needed in Egyptian readers to increase their value. Ph.D. Dissertation. University of Chicago.

McLoughlin, Peter F. M. 1964. Language-switching as an index of socialization in the Republic of the Sudan. Berkeley and Los Angeles, University of California Press.

Madkūr, Ibrāhīm. 1955. Majmaʿ al-luġa al-ʿarabiyya fī xamsata ʿašara ʿāman. MMLA. 8.11–16.

——. 1962. Al-Adab Al-ʿArabi tijāh muškilatay al-luġa wa al-ḥarf. MMLA 15.5–13.

——. 1966. Talxīṣ aʿmāl al-mu'tamar. Al-Buḥūθ wa Al-Muḥādarāt, 271–3.

Al-Makhzūmi, Mahdi. 1964. Fī an-naḥw al-ʿarabī. Beirut.

Al-Maqdisi, Anis. 1948. Tadrīs al-adab fī al-madāris al-ibtidā'iyya wa aθ-θānawiyya. Al-Mu'tamar aθ-θaqāfī al-ʿarabī al-awwal, 139–42. Cairo, Arab League.

Masʿūd, Jubrān. 1965a. Al-Muḥīṭ fī adab al-bakālūrya. 2 vols. Beirut, Al-Makshuf.

——. 1965b. Ar-Rā'id. Beirut.

Matthews, Roderic D., and Matta Akrawi. 1947. Education in Arab countries of the Near East. Washington, D.C.

Messadi, Mahmoud. 1965. Un Tour D'horizon Complet des problemes d'enseignement. (An interview). Afrique. Supplement No. 2 (October, 1965).50–7.

Monteil, Vincent. 1960. L'Arabe moderne. Paris, Libraire C. Klinksilek.

Mūsā (Mousa), Salāma. 1945. Al-Balāġa al-ʿaṣriyya wa al-luġa al-ʿarabiyya. Cairo.

——. 1955. Arabic language problems. MEA 6.41–4.

Muṣṭafā, Ibrāhīm. 1937. Iḥyā' an-naḥw. Cairo.

——, et al. 1958. Taḥrīr an-naḥw al-ʿarabī. Cairo.

Oduho, Joseph, and William Deng. 1963. The Problem of the Southern Sudan. London, Oxford University Press.

Philistin, Wadei. 1958. Wa al-lisān al-ʿarabī. Journal of Modern Education (of the American University of Cairo) 32.48–51.

Qudsi, Ilyās. 1923. Tabdīl al-ḥurūf al-ʿArabiyya. MMAD 3.177–84.

Saʿāda, Yusuf. 1947. Taʿdīl al-qawāʿid al-ʿArabiyya wa tashīluhā. Beirut.

Ṣabrī, ʿUthmān. 1964. Naḥw abjadiyya jadīda. Cairo.

Aṣ-Ṣaḥrāwī, Abdulqādir. 1959. Ma'sāh al-luġa al-ʿarabiyya fī al-maġrib. Daʿwa al-Ḥaqq 3/1.51–6.

Said, Beshir Mohammed. 1965–66. The Sudan. Great Britain U.A.A. Dufour Editions.

Aṣ-Ṣaʿīdī, ʿAbdul Mutaʿāl. 1947. An-naḥw al-jadīd. Cairo.

As-Salāwī, Muḥammad Adīb. 1965. Qaḍiyya at-taʿrīb fī al-maġrib. Al-Maʿrifa 4/40.40–50.

Sanderson, Lilian. 1962. Educational development in the Southern Sudan 1900–1948. Sudan Notes and Records 43.105–17.

Sasnett, Martena, and Inez Sepmeyer. 1966. Educational systems of Africa. Berkeley and Los Angeles, University of California Press.

Ash-Shabībī, Muḥammad Riḍā. 1950. Tawḥīd al-muṣṭalaḥāt. MMLA 8.131–5.

ASH-SHIHĀBĪ, MUṢṬAFĀ. 1964. Muškilāt al-ʿarabiyya wa iqtirāḥ al-marḥūm Aḥmad Amīn. MMAD39.529–34.

——. 1965. Al-muṣṭalaḥāt al-ʿilmiyya fī al-luġa al-ʿarabiyya. Damascus.

AS-SŪDĀ, YUSUF. 1959. Al-aḥrufiyya aw al-qawāʿid al-jadīda fī al-ʿarabiyya. Beirut.

SULAYMĀN, MUSA. 1962. Al-adab fī al-manhaj al-lubnānī. At-tarbiya 4/2.38–41.

AṬ-ṬĀHIR, ʿALĪ JAWĀD. 1960. An-naqd al-adabī. Baghdad.

TAYMOUR [TAYMŪR], MAḤMŪD. 1951a. Ḍabt al-kitāba al-ʿarabiyya. Cairo.

——. 1951b. A new script to facilitate the use of the diacritical points essential for correct speech and writing. The Islamic Review 39 (October).16–18.

AL-TOMA, SALIH J. 1957. The teaching of Classical Arabic to speakers of the colloquial in Iraq: a study of the problem of linguistic duality and its impact on language education. Ed. dissertation, Harvard University. 1957.

——. 1961a. Al-luġa al-ʿāmmiyya wa istiʿmāluhā fi al-ʿamal al-adabī. Maqālāt muxtāra, 65–82. Baghdad, Publications of the Union of Iraqi Writers.

——. 1961b. The Arabic writing system and proposals for its reform. MEJ 15. 403–15.

——. 1969. The problem of diglossia in Arabic: A comparative study of Classical and Iraqi Arabic. Cambridge, Harvard University Press.

TRIAL, GEORGE T., and R. BAYLEY WINDER. 1950. Modern education in Saudi Arabia. History of Educational Journal 1/3.121–33.

TUCKER, A.N., and M.A.BRYAN. 1966. Linguistic analysis: the non-Bantu languages of North-Eastern Africa. London, Oxford.

UNESCO. 1956. Compulsory education in the Arab states. Amsterdam.

——. 1957. Training of primary teacher training staff. Paris and Geneva.

——. 1958. Preparation and issuing of the primary school curriculum. Paris and Geneva.

——. 1959. Primary school textbooks. Paris and Geneva.

——. 1960. Preparation of general secondary school curricula. Paris and Geneva.

——. 1961. The world survey of education III. New York.

——. 1962. In-service training for primary teachers. Paris and Geneva.

——. 1964. International Bureau of Education. Modern languages at general secondary schools. Geneva and Paris.

——. 1965. International Bureau of Education. International yearbook of education. Geneva and Paris.

——. 1966a. International Bureau of Education. International yearbook of education. Geneva and Paris.

——. 1966b. International Bureau of Education. The organization of educational research. Geneva and Paris.

AL-ʿAZAYZĪ, R.Z. 1952. Kayf nuʿallim al-luġa al-Arabiyya al-ʿIrfān 40.162–7, 273–8.

——. 1967. Al-luġa al-ʿArabiyya asmā al-luġāt wa akmaluhā. Al-Lisān Al-ʿArabī 5.123–30.

AL-YĀSĪN, ʿIZZUDDĪN, et al. 1953–54. Al-muṭālaʿa al-ʿarabiyya. Vol. I. Baghdad.
AZ-ZAHĀWĪ, J. S. 1896. Al-xaṭṭ al-jadīd. Al-Muqtaṭaf 20.738–52.
ZAKI, AHMED. 1953. The renovation of Arabic. The use of vernacular languages in education, 87–95. Paris, Unesco.
ZARTMAN, I. WILLIAM. 1962. Les problems posés par l'arabisation des enseignements primaire et secondaire au maroc. Confluent 7/26.766–78.
——. 1963. Muškilāt at-taʿrīb fī madāris al-maġrib. Hiwār 1/6.14–22.
——. 1964. Arabization of primary and secondary education. Morocco: problems of new power, 155–95. New York, Prentice-Hall, Inc.

LANGUAGE STUDY IN ISRAEL

JACOB M. LANDAU

INTRODUCTION

During British rule in Palestine (1917–48), there was widespread appreciation of the importance of language teaching (and, to a lesser degree, of language research). The country was officially trilingual: the language of Government was English, while those of the two peoples were Arabic and Hebrew, respectively. The growing strength of nationalist movements among both peoples, during this period, added a quasi-fanatic undertone to the evaluation of the national language. Determined efforts were made towards language revival, concomitant with re-discovery of a national cultural heritage: all intellectual creation, in Arabic or Hebrew, was comprehensively considered as national literature, by each of the two peoples. During late Ottoman rule, Arabic fought for an official standing equal to that of Turkish — with varying success.[1] At the very same time, Hebrew was considered, by a small Jewish minority, as an important element in the national awakening. Although the first Congresses of the Zionist movement, from 1897 onwards, used mainly German for speeches and debates, some delegates spoke Hebrew; the latter soon became the recognized language of Zionism.

The spread of Hebrew in Palestine itself is to be credited in no small degree to the enthusiasm and perseverance of Elieser Ben-Iehuda[2] in Jerusalem. From the end of the nineteenth century, he persisted in talking Hebrew, coining new words, and compiling a large historical dictionary of the language;[3] the dictionary's introductory volume fittingly carried as its main topic 'Up to what date was Hebrew spoken?' The personal example of Ben-Iehuda and his family, as well as the activity of his admirers brought about the revival of Hebrew — which for centuries had existed almost solely in written form[4] — as a spoken language, employed in all fields of life.

[1] See, e.g., G. Antonius, *The Arab awakening*, 3rd ed. (New York, 1965), pp. 87–8 and passim.

[2] Authors' names are transliterated here according to accepted usage, except when they have been employing a special romanized form of their own.

[3] *Thesaurus totius Hebraitatis et veteris et recentioris auctore Elieser Ben Iehuda Hierosolymitano.* The dictionary started publication in 1908, and was completed, after its compiler's death, by Professor N. H. Tur-Sinai and his assistants. It has 16 vols., totalling almost 8,000 pages.

[4] It was rarely spoken by few; consult Ch. Rabin 1960:79–80.

This is, apparently, the only known example in history of a language revival on such a scale (see Tur-Sinai 1960).

Not surprisingly, there were many difficulties in adapting Hebrew to modern needs.[5] Not all experiments were successful, including those advocating the introduction of a Romanized alphabet. By and large, however, experts and institutions worked at coining words and phrases, drawn from the Bible, the Talmud, and later sources, as well as from cognate languages (Aramaic, Arabic). Part of their work was to sort out expressions in current local usage in Palestine (and, later, in Israel) largely resulting from the contact of Hebrew speakers with the neighboring language (Arabic), or with the languages of their countries of origin — Russian, Yiddish, German, and others (Morag 1959 includes a detailed bibliography; Garbell 1930). These contacts influenced both the vocabulary and the syntax of modern Hebrew;[6] they are reflected, for instance, in the Hebrew spoken by children in Palestine and Israel (Bar-Adon 1963). By consensus, the chief authority for linguistic innovation in Hebrew was vested in the Committee for the Hebrew Language. Founded in 1890, the Committee was formally recognized by the Jewish community in Palestine in 1904 (Rabin 1958 and 1962). One of its scholarly activities was the publication of *Lĕšōnenū* (Hebrew for: 'Our Language'), which was then — and still is — the only serious periodical published in Israel wholly concerned with linguistics. Independently of the Committee for the Hebrew Language, many linguists, writers, and others coined words, a number of which were commonly accepted (Avinery 1946)[7] — in itself an indication of the widespread interest in the revival and growth of Hebrew.

During the years of the First World War and those immediately following, Hebrew became the main language of instruction at all levels in most Jewish schools in Palestine, following a prolonged struggle with German and other languages.[8] A contributory factor in this success was Germany's defeat in the war and the resulting decline of its influence in the Middle East. In the interwar period, Hebrew became the sole language of instruction for all subjects, from Jewish kindergarten to University (Rieger 1940, Scharfstein 1928, Nardi 1945: chapter II seq.). The number of those speaking it as their main, or only, language, rose rapidly: according to the calculation of R. Bachi (1955) it grew from 34,000 in the year 1914 to 511,000 in 1948.[9] While Hebrew is the mother-tongue of practically all Jews born in Palestine and Israel, who consider it simply as their native language, many of their parents regard it differently. As immigrants, they have acquired Hebrew as a foreign language and many of them have fought for its sake; they tend to be proud of their achievement and alert to defend it, sometimes fanatically. In this, perhaps, lies the reason for the

[5] Some of the difficulties and methods used to overcome them have been described by H. Blanc (1954 and 1957).

[6] Rosen 1957, and Sappan 1963; Peretz 1962 treats both aspects.

[7] Avinery collected his own innovations in a thick volume, *Yad ha-lašōn*, in 1964.

[8] For examples, see Actions Committee of the Zionist Organization 1914.

[9] According to this computation, their number reached 679,000 in the year 1950, and 861,000 in June 1954. Fuller details were published after the 1961 census.

relatively great importance attached to the study of Hebrew as a mother-tongue,[10] at the expense of learning foreign languages (as will be shown later).

The State of Israel serves, in many respects, as a large laboratory for language study. Its two official languages are Hebrew and Arabic. Laws and regulations appear in both languages, and they may both be used in debates in the "Knesset" (Parliament), where interpreters translate busily (Piamenta 1955); the State-owned radio broadcasts full, varied programs in both Hebrew and Arabic (while other languages rate hardly more than newscasts); and a sizable number of newspapers and periodicals is published in each of the languages. Hebrew is the main language of the Jewish majority (about two and a half million in 1967), while Arabic is spoken by the Arab minority (over three hundred thousand in 1967). One result of the June 1967 war was to add about one million Arabic speakers to Israeli rule in the occupied territories, thus raising the proportion of Arabs from one ninth to over one third of the total population.

Israel is a country of immigration par excellence, whose Jewish population has quadrupled (from 650,000 to about 2,500,000) in the first nineteen years of the State's existence. Few of the immigrants knew any Hebrew; practically all brought with them a bewildering number of various mother-tongues and dialects, from Morocco to India, and from Northern Europe to South Africa. Israel is also tourist-minded, hence its authorities and people strive to supply the requirements of tourists in their own languages. Lastly, Israel is a developing country, whose growing industry and commerce need languages to expand its exports to distant lands, with the aim of bypassing the Arab economic blockade. The situation has thus encouraged a certain alertness about the importance of language study. Many Jewish immigrants to Israel have remained, however, plurilingual, using different languages at home, at work, etc. (For data and estimates see Bachi 1955:198–9.) Some still read, in addition to a Hebrew newspaper, or in its stead, a newspaper or journal in the language of their country of origin (many such publications appear in Israel). This applies to the Jews in the new State rather than to the Arabs. The latter have made full use of the State's education services; their growth in numbers has been due to natural increase and the 'unification of families' (return of Palestinian Arab refugees to Israel). The problem of acquiring a wholly new and unfamiliar language has been absent.

The Arabic language in Israel has been able to draw on the studies of linguists in the Arab countries. A rather different situation has prevailed in regard to Hebrew, which had to rely for creative impetus mainly upon Israel. By an act of the Knesset, passed in 1953, the Committee for the Hebrew Language was replaced by an Academy for the Hebrew Language. The main task of this new body was 'to direct the development of the Hebrew language by means of investigation of the language, in all its

[10] Goitein (1958:7–8) maintains rightly that in this manner the whole education of Jewish pupils is Hebrew. As to fanaticism for Hebrew, the following recent event is a case in point: In 1968, a student of history and political science at the Hebrew University wrote to the Rector and demanded a ruling that the students read, and their instructors publish, in Hebrew — though he himself read five languages. Cf. *Nīṣōṣ* (students' weekly) 3, fasc. 10 (28 January 1968) Jerusalem, p. 1. The Rector, Professor N. Rotenstreich, replied that he disagreed with him.

forms, through all periods of history'. The Academy's members and associate-members are appointed from the best linguists in Israel, including scholars teaching linguistics at University level. It is situated on the campus of the Hebrew University. Besides continuing to publish *Lĕšōnenū*, it issues another periodical, popular in nature, *Lĕšōnenū la-ʿam* (that is: 'Our Language for the People'), presenting information in simple language about new words as well as common mistakes (and how to avoid them). In addition, the Academy for the Hebrew Language issues books and pamphlets listing new terms in all branches of science, administration, education, arts and crafts, etc. The lists of new words and terms, following approval in plenary session, are sent to the Minister of Education, who countersigns them and has them published in the Official Gazette; their use is then compulsory on all Government offices. Close to 40,000 terms have been determined in this manner. A selection is printed in large characters and posted in schools and public institutions. The Academy has also embarked upon compiling a scholarly and comprehensive historical dictionary of the Hebrew language. As the dictionary is to include every word used in Hebrew before the year 1908, its preparation will undoubtedly take some decades (Rabin 1962).

Yet another body dedicated to innovating in Hebrew is the word-coining department in the Israeli Defence Forces. Its work proceeds much more rapidly than that of the Academy for the Hebrew Language. Many of the terms it coins filter into civilian use in Israel. All these sources of innovation, including the impact of daily use, contribute to the formation of a new type of Hebrew, which some linguists tend to call 'Israeli Hebrew'.[11] Lexical and other changes in modern Hebrew are a function of speedily-developing life in modern Israel and the inadequacy of the language to cope with it.

That the problems of Israeli Hebrew are not solely academic was shown during the mass-immigration of Jews to Israel in the late 1940's and the early 1950's. Most new immigrants wanted to learn Hebrew in a hurry. While former students of Hebrew in Palestine had frequently been inspired by ideological considerations, these immigrants were motivated by material needs and their desire to integrate in Israel. Similar considerations affected many of the Arabs in Israel, who have increasingly been learning Hebrew.

Those members of both communities who already knew Hebrew could not but acknowledge the benefits to them and their children from a study of foreign languages. These attitudes have resulted in the investment of considerable effort, both linguistic and didactic, by public bodies and private individuals in language teaching. Many textbooks have been published, as well as a number of high-quality pedagogical journals, such as *Mĕgammōt*, *ha-Ḥīnnūx*, *Ūrīm*,[12] and others. Much of this literature, although mainly educational in character, includes material of interest to the linguist.

[11] For an analysis of its characteristics, see Rosen 1956 and cf. Weiman 1950.

[12] *Ūrīm* devoted a complete issue — 20, fasc. 9–10 (1963) — to the problems of teaching Hebrew in Israel.

For the purposes of this article, it has seemed most useful to approach language teaching in Israel by discussing the main languages imparted in Israeli schools, with some concluding observations on language teaching in Israeli Universities.

HEBREW

Several educational agencies of the State have contributed to the teaching of Hebrew (Goitein 1958; Mor 1945; Adar 1965; and others) — both as a mother-tongue and a foreign language — in kindergartens, elementary and high schools, and the Universities (Roth 1941); the achievements of the Defence Forces (Haramati 1958) in this sphere will be discussed later. Applied research in linguistics has been conducted, at least partly intended to assist the preparation of textbooks,[13] which have appeared in growing number. The formidable task in the early 1950's, at the peak of Jewish immigration to Israel, has been reduced to manageable proportions in the 1960's. Normalcy seems to have been achieved, quantitatively, in regard to the teaching of Hebrew, now not too different from the equivalent problem in many other countries. Not a few adults, however, both Jews and Arabs, do not yet know enough Hebrew for free communication, and still prefer their mother-tongue.

Hebrew Kindergarten and Elementary Schools

As early as kindergarten (one year of which is free and compulsory), an effort is made to have Jewish children acquire good Hebrew and to enrich their vocabulary. In elementary school, consisting in Israel of eight grades (again, free and compulsory),[14] the aims in the study of Hebrew are officially defined as follows, 'a. To encourage the child to acquire concepts and terms and to enrich his thought. b. To develop his written and oral expression, the talent to think and to express his thoughts in precise and colorful style and in a clear and pleasant manner ... c. To promote his knowledge and enjoyment of the national and general culture of all times. d. To foster his aesthetic feeling, to increase his sensitivity to works of art, to create the inner need and practical habit of reading Jewish sources and general literature, science and the press. e. To convince him that using language in all its nuances in a clear, pleasant and natural way raises one's self confidence and value in society. f. To encourage loyalty towards Hebrew and the desire to assist its development, its improvement and its

[13] E.g., for spelling, see Rieger 1935. Rieger repeated his findings, in an enlarged version, in his *Modern Hebrew* (1953).

[14] During 1967–68, Israel's Ministry of Education and Culture has been seriously considering the advisability of dividing the 12 grades, following kindergarten, into a pattern of 6+3+3 (i.e., resembling that in the United States); this new pattern is already being experimented with in Israel. The innovation would mean, inter alia, having the first nine grades (instead of the present eight) free and compulsory.

spread among the whole people.' (Ministry of Education and Culture 1954b:xvii — Translation mine). A few years later, when the curriculum was changed, an important educational item was added to these aims, viz., 'to implant the awareness that employment of clear and precise language, with many nuances, is conducive to better understanding between fellow-men and raises the cultural level of society.'[15]

This ambitious formulation has found practical expression in the allocation of relatively numerous class-periods to the study of Hebrew language, often combined with literature. The curriculum lays stress on acquiring proper habits in reading, writing and speaking Hebrew as well as information in literature and general knowledge — obtainable through the media of language. Hence, language at this stage is considered more as a vehicle of instruction than as a target for formal learning. Hebrew language and literature receive a large proportion of time in the first four elementary grades, and 4–5 hours a week in grades 5 to 8;[16] but teachers of other subjects also are expected to assist the development of the pupils' language. Reading is chiefly directed towards understanding, aiming at perception of the important points and explanation of content. The expectation is that each pupil should be capable, at the end of the eighth grade, of understanding various types of material, from literature to current affairs, of expressing himself clearly, and of listening politely to others.

Hebrew High Schools

The Israeli education system allows for four years of high school (grades 9 to 12) on a selective basis.[17] In these schools, the Ministry of Education and Culture has set ambitious targets for the study of Hebrew as the pupil's first language, viz., '... e. to develop the pupil's skill in correct, clear, precise and logical expression — oral and written. f. To help him acquire an organic knowledge of the rules and forms in Hebrew, in its development, as well as the ability to distinguish between its historical strata. g. To equip him with idioms ...' (Ministry of Education and Culture 1955:25). The above seems directed towards practical aims as well as scholarly (or quasi-scholarly) ones, as may be seen from a detailed description of the aims in the study of Hebrew in the high school: a thorough knowledge of all the language forms in use (including morphology and syntax), fostering of proper habits in writing and speech, essay writing of high quality, and 'perception of the language layers and the style of various periods and authors' (Ministry of Education and Culture 1955: 29–30).

[15] Ministry of Education and Culture, *Tōxnīt ha-līmmūdīm lĕ-veyt ha-sefer ha-yĕsōdī ha-mamlaxtī vĕ-ha-mamlaxtī — ha-datī: lašōn vĕ-sifrūt*, p. 3.

[16] *Ibid.*, pp. 19, 72, 119, 169. Cf. also, Ministry of Education and Culture 1954a.

[17] That is, instruction is neither free nor compulsory, although the needy gifted receive a remission of tuition fees. High schools accept their pupils on the basis of the grades at the end of the elementary schools as well as competitive examinations.

Only the best students, apparently, attain the above requirements, for several reasons. Three main causes seem to account for this comparative lack of success.

(a) On the one hand, the targets set for the high school Hebrew teacher appear to be too ambitious and manifold, so that he cannot achieve them all, particularly as most classes are heterogeneous and overpopulated (40 pupils or more). On the other hand, the requirements in the official syllabus for teaching Hebrew are set out in far less detail than any other subject, so that an added burden of decision and selection falls on the language teacher.[18]

(b) While the vocabulary of most pupils has been enriched and become idiomatic, partly due to reading, the teaching of Hebrew grammar in the Israeli high school has been considerably less successful. Several factors, some already pointed out by linguists and educators, appear to be responsible: (1) In many schools, grammar is taught in a formal way, based on a multitude of rules, which are not always apparent in the context of practical usage; few teachers are trained linguists, hence they rarely use a descriptive approach, which might be more attractive to their pupils, in addition to training them to observe linguistic features (Nir 1963). (2) The teaching of grammar is still largely based on a normative approach to Biblical grammar, studiously avoiding the grammar of Israeli Hebrew, with all its innovations and 'mistakes'. Hence, the study of grammar has gradually become a linguistic discipline (offered by teachers, many of whom lack training in linguistics, as already noted) — instead of being an applied study, closely interrelated with daily matters.[19] (3) The presentation of grammar overemphasizes the study of vocalization ('niqqūd'), in very considerable detail, completely overlooking the obvious fact, that hardly any pupil will ever need to vocalize a text and show active knowledge of the study. One feels that vocalization — and, indeed, Hebrew grammar, in general — is frequently taught in Isreal in the same way in which this was done in the Diaspora, that is, as a foreign language. This approach overlooks a basic fact that practically all pupils in Israel speak Hebrew, and that this ought to have been taken into account in teaching grammar in Hebrew as a mother-tongue.[20]

(c) Although some recent studies point out that reading ability in Hebrew could be improved (Feitelson 1964:54 seq.), research has shown that more meaningful criticism is to be leveled at attainments in speech and writing in the high school (Regev 1967). Some critics remark the lack of polish, even negligence, in the oral and written expression of a number of graduates from Hebrew high schools. C iticism is directed, also, at the relatively large number of failures in composition at the high school final examinations, and the modest knowledge of those passing them. The reason lies not only in the high standards set by the Israeli Ministry of Education and Culture, but much deeper. These results may well be the outcome of an age-old

[18] R. Nir (1966) has already made the point, that the requirements of the final high school examinations alone (at the end of the 12th grade) determine the duty of teachers and pupils in this respect.

[19] Rieger 1951. A critical view of this approach was voiced by M. Gottstein 1952–53.

[20] Cf. Ornan 1951 and the introduction to his book, *Diqdūq ha-ōzen vĕ-ha-pe*.

attitude of Jews in the Diaspora, of giving marked preference to content-matter over form (including the studied avoidance of most visual arts, on religious grounds). In addition, some of the blame may attach to the long tradition in the Diaspora of overstressing reading-and-interpretation, at the expense of instruction in writing and speaking, in any language (at least until the 19th century, when imitation of the environment changed this somewhat).

Hebrew as a Foreign Language

The study of Hebrew as a foreign language in Israel is loaded with a variety of problems, linguistic and didactic, as well as socio-economic. One may subdivide the discussion into the following headings: the instruction of Hebrew to (a) Jewish immigrant children, (b) Jewish immigrant adults and Arab adults, and (c) Arab schoolchildren.

Instruction of Hebrew to Jewish Immigrant Children

Mass immigration to Israel created not only serious economic difficulties, but also educational problems. Many immigrant families, particularly those from Afro-Asian countries, were blessed with many children. The new situation demanded not only the opening of new classes, but posed serious questions about the teaching of Hebrew. Those immigrant children who settled in established communities were registered in the same school as the sons and daughters of the old settlers and, after receiving some assistance, integrated well enough. However, many families remained in the transit camps which had changed meanwhile into 'immigrant villages'. In this case, all schoolchildren were immigrants; hence, special curricula and teaching methods had to be devised for their needs, including instruction in Hebrew. The limited intellectual background of many of these children, the economic difficulties of their parents and the different customs brought from many lands, all made the problem of their education a baffling one.[21] Only their eagerness to study and their teachers' devotion brought these children nearer to life in Israel and to a fair knowledge of Hebrew. The Ministry of Education and Culture and the teachers succeeded in overcoming psychological and didactic obstacles by preparing new textbooks,[22] suited to the background of the immigrant children, forming homogeneous classes when possible, and frequently employing the project-system. The urgent task lay in teaching the immigrant children to speak Hebrew, while other schoolchildren could already speak the language fluently (Rōn 1954–55, Abbīr 1950).

[21] For the problems and some solutions, consult Avišay 1951–52.
[22] Details in *Ūrīm* 13 (1955–56), which contains numerous articles on reading instruction for immigrant children in Israel.

Instruction of Hebrew to Adults and the Ūlpanīm

Teaching Hebrew to adults in Israel is not seen as just another facet of the struggle against illiteracy which is being carried out in Hebrew courses for Jews and Arabic courses for Arabs. It was considered rather as an over-all campaign for mass-instruction. It was organized and financed in a joint effort by Israel's Ministry of Education and Culture, the Jewish Agency's Absorption Department, the General Federation of Labor, and the municipalities. No less than 82,000 adult immigrants studied in these courses, from their inception in 1949 up to 1965.[23] However, the campaign proved more than just a success in numbers. Few dropped out, unlike the case in foreign-language courses for adults elsewhere. There were two apparent main reasons. The first may be found in other immigration countries, too (as in English courses for immigrants to the United States): the desire to integrate in the adopted country serves as a strong incentive for learning the new language. The second reason seems to be more specific to Israel. The teaching of Hebrew to adult immigrants proceeds from two points of departure: association with Jewish civilization, and actualization through extensive use of the newspaper; or, in other words, creation of ties with the past and familiarization with the present.

The courses founded on this approach were called 'Ūlpan' (workshop; plural 'Ūlpanīm'). Their practical, intensive character was necessitated by two factors: the students urgently wanted to use their Hebrew to find employment, and the State had limited financial resources and in any case could provide only a limited number of teachers. In general, the Jewish cultural heritage tended to be imparted more thoroughly in those classes whose pupils had had some intellectual background. However, in most classes, emphasis was regularly laid on practical study, with the main purpose as the acquisition of the following skills: To understand spoken Hebrew, including lectures and theater shows; to talk fluently; to read letters, newspapers and books; to write letters, receipts, bills, etc. These objectives determined the length of the course and the method of instruction, and these, in turn, brought about the preparation of specially suited textbooks. In addition, texts were rewritten in 'easy Hebrew', a simplified, basic language — in which dailies and weeklies appear regularly; news bulletins in 'easy Hebrew' are also broadcast daily.[24]

The length of the Ūlpan is a function of its intensity. If a minimum achievement is insisted upon, the less hours per week one studies, the longer the course will take. There are three main types of intensive Ūlpanīm. The most commonly found give 30 hours per week instruction. Others offer only 24 hours per week, and are called 'working Ūlpanīm'; they are usually held in a 'kibbūtz' (or collective settlement) and the students work part-time, in their free hours. A third type is the 'evening Ūlpanīm', offering 16 hours per week, usually 4 hours a day, 4 days a week;[25] these

[23] *EḤ* 3.585.

[24] 'Easy Hebrew' is based on a careful selection of vocabulary, by word-frequency, as well as of syntactic phenomena. Cf. Qōdeš and Ḥōmsqī 1967.

[25] Generally, four evening sessions of four hours each, see Shaked 1955.

are generally attended by townspeople, already working for their livelihood. The following should give an idea of the length of study in all three types (Weinberg 1958:104).

Types of Ūlpanīm

Type	Hours per week	Duration of course	Days of tuition	Hours of tuition
Ūlpan[26]	30	5 months	107	536
Working Ūlpan	24	6 „	137	548
Evening Ūlpan	16	10 „	143	572

The subjects studied in all Ūlpanīm are: Hebrew, Bible, Talmudic legends, geography of Israel, civics, Jewish history, Zionism, and music. It will be noted that the more intensive an Ūlpan is, the smaller is its total of classroom periods. The assumption is, of course, that if the effort is more concentrated, it will presumably be more fruitful. The organized framework and the rapid progress encourage uninterrupted perseverance. In addition to the 30 or 24 hours of study per week of the first two types held in the mornings, homework is done in the afternoons, often guided by teachers. The latter encourage the students in their social and cultural activities, such as parties, choir singing, joint visits to the theater, trips, etc. These teachers in time gain considerable experience and constantly strive for the improvement of methods and textbooks. The direct method is generally employed in all Ūlpanīm and frequent use is made of audio-visual aids. The same usually applies to less intensive evening-courses of Hebrew, called 'Ūlpanīt' (i.e., little Ūlpan), offering 4 to 15 classroom periods per week. Both Ūlpan and Ūlpanīt attempt to help their students benefit from the Hebrew character of their environment.

Hebrew for Arab Adults

Although conceived mainly for Jewish immigrant adults, the Ūlpanīm have consistently been attended by adult Arabs, who felt they needed Hebrew for their daily work. Their overall number seems to have been small, until the June 1967 war. After that and the annexation of Eastern Jerusalem (the 'Old City') to Israel, many more Arabs started attending the Ūlpanīm. Since their main aim was pragmatic — they wanted jobs in the Jerusalem municipality, commercial ties with Jews, etc. — Hebrew intensive courses were arranged specifically for them. Practically everything connected

[26] During 1964–65, there were in Israel ten intensive Ūlpanīm, of which eight had arrangements for living in.

with the Jewish heritage was dropped from the curriculum, which became strictly a language-course.

Hebrew in the Armed Forces

An important share in the teaching of Hebrew to adults falls to the Israel Defence Forces. Since all Jews of both sexes and all male Druzes have to serve in Israel's army, all recruits ignorant of Hebrew are given an elementary Hebrew course. This program embraces, then, a majority of young Jewish immigrants and all those Druze youths who had not acquired enough Hebrew in the State schools. The need for elementary Hebrew courses was more acute during the first years of the State, partly owing to the large Jewish immigration and, partly, to the fact that many Druze recruits had not yet learnt Hebrew (since their primary schooling had been under the British Mandate). The elementary Hebrew course in the Israel Defence Forces extends over 180 class-periods, divided into three stages; soldiers who are wholly illiterate, in any language, receive an additional introductory course. Since the study of Hebrew is executed by command, side by side with fatiguing military training, strong motivation is necessary to encourage the soldiers to learn; therefore, instructors stress motivation both in introducing the course and also later on. Because the total number of hours devoted to this course is markedly smaller than in the Ūlpanīm, and some of the soldiers are tired by their military exercises, results are consistently lower than those in the Ūlpanīm. Nonetheless, most soldiers graduating from the elementary Hebrew courses attain fairly fluent conversational ability on everyday matters, can read a vocalized newspaper and even parts of the regular press, and are able to write letters. The common denominator in all these skills, in terms of materials, is the current-affairs content of the course, whose topicality captures the soldier-students' interest and is, indeed, meant to assist them, both in their military, and then in their future civilian career. The direct method is generally employed; grammar is taught functionally and selectively only.[27]

Instruction of Hebrew to Arab Schoolchildren

Yet another section of Israel's population studying Hebrew as a foreign language is that of the Arab pupils in all State schools and, with minor differences, in the schools maintained by various religious communities and missionaries. Upon the foundation of a State-wide system of education, all Arabic elementary schools were required to teach Hebrew, as a foreign language, in grades 4 to 8, at the rate of three hours per week. With the 1968–69 school-year, Arabic schools offer Hebrew from grade 3, four hours per week. The study of Hebrew is continued in the Arabic high schools, in

[27] Details in Haramati 1958. For the theoretical conception involved in these courses see Haramati 1964:63–349.

grades 9 to 12, at the rate of six hours per week. Some Hebrew is taught in the Arab teachers' college as well. From January 1968, these norms are gradually being applied to the Arabic schools in Eastern Jerusalem.[28] The general conception seems to have been that Hebrew should become not just another foreign language, but rather a second language for all Arab schoolchildren in Israel. In the early days of the new State, scattered voices of extremist Arabs spoke up, expressing worry, lest the study of Hebrew influence adversely the study of Arabic — an important cement for Arab nationalism. These views are no longer heard as it became evident that the study of Hebrew, limited in scope to a few hours per week, did not bring about the neglect of Arabic, but only assisted the Arabs in integrating in the economic life of Israel and in studying in its institutions of higher education, where practically all teaching is carried out in Hebrew.

The main aims in the study of Hebrew in Arabic schools seem clear enough: didactically, to reach high quality performance in all active language skills; educationally, to assist a *rapprochement* between the two peoples and to foster a sense of civics, by imparting objective information about the Jews and the State of Israel. The Ministry of Education has published a fairly detailed curriculum.[29] With the co-operation of both Arab and Jewish supervisors of education and of younger teachers, educated in Israel's Universities, considerable progress has been achieved in the study of Hebrew in the Arabic schools. Teachers are encouraged to avoid the age-hallowed traditional way of learning through excessive oral recital. More dynamic methods are preferred, viz., the direct method, and constant etymological comparison to Arabic. The textbooks are suited to the age of the pupils and contain materials of interest to them. Newspapers are read, but attempts are made to read and appreciate literature as well. These features are even more evident in the study of Hebrew in the Arabic high school than in the elementary. At this level, the study of Hebrew is correlated with geography, history and civics. Some experts claim that the formal study of Hebrew grammar is still excessive in Arabic schools.[30] In practical evaluation, it would appear that the study of Hebrew in Arabic schools is quite successful, as many Arab students participate in University courses in Hebrew, without difficulty, while others use their knowledge of Hebrew in clerical jobs or in commerce.

ARABIC

In discussing the study of Arabic in Israel, as with Hebrew, one should distinguish between Arabic as a mother-tongue in Arabic schools and as a foreign language in Hebrew schools. In both cases, one should take into account the fact that Arabic

[28] A. Dōrōn in *Maʿariv* (daily), 22 January 1968, p. 11. For further changes, see *Ha-Areṣ* (daily), 29 August 1968, p. 2.

[29] Ministry of Education and Culture, *Manhaj al-dirāsa al-madrasiyya al-ʿarabiyya al-ibtidāʾiyya al-rasmiyya li-ʾl-ṣaffayn al-xāmis waʾl-sādis*. A similarly-titled curriculum exists for the 7th and 8th grades. As for Arabic high schools, see the Ministry's *Manāhij al-dirāsa fiʾl-madāris al-ṯānawiyya*.

[30] E.g., consult Abner Cohen, *EḤ* 2.675–6.

is a dynamic language, in the throes of innovation resembling those of Israeli Hebrew, digesting new words and terms.[31] In addition, however, in modern Arabic a contest seems in progress between the literary and the colloquial,[32] somewhat different from one another in phonology, syntax and even vocabulary. The implication for Israel is that the Arab pupil learns literary Arabic and interprets it in the colloquial. The distinction between these two layers of Arabic continues throughout school, just as in the Arab countries, without any attempt at integration or at reaching literary Arabic via the colloquial, as is successfully done in the study of German in the German cantons of Switzerland. This refers to Arab pupils; the non-Arab, who desires to study Arabic as a foreign language, has to choose whether to learn the literary, or the colloquial, or both.

Arabic as a Mother-Tongue

Arabic is the language of instruction in all Arabic schools in Israel. It is, also, the subject of special class-periods in grades 1-8, where it rates seven to eight hours per week, and another two for Koran (for the Muslims) or the Old and New Testaments (for the Christians). However, the language gets adequate treatment in many other disciplines as well, where it serves as the language of instruction. The curriculum[33] shows no essential difference, in all stages from kindergarten to the end of high school, from those currently in use throughout the Arab countries (which, indeed, differ considerably from one another in detail). Perhaps the main innovation in the curriculum of the Arab school is that, in addition to Arabic as the main language, *two* foreign languages — Hebrew and English — are taught in the elementary and high school; other innovations lie in methodological improvements.

In recent years, newly prepared textbooks for the study of Arabic in the first grades of the Arabic school have consistently chosen their materials from the environment best known to the pupil. With the cooperation of the younger teachers (the older, too, have received refresher courses), the Ministry of Education and Culture has pressed for didactic reforms: in the elementary schools, reading and writing have become less mechanical and more meaningful than during British rule in Palestine; recital has partly given way to free oral expression, intended to develop independent thinking; written exercises emphasize brevity and clarity, at the expense of synonym-stringing, so common previously. In the Arabic high school, it is intended to broaden and deepen language proficiency in all skills, but through a serious study of Arabic

[31] Consult Ch. Issawi, 'European loan-words in contemporary Arabic writing: a case study in modernization', *Middle Eastern Studies* 3.110–33 (January 1967).

[32] See Moussa 1955, and, more recently, P. J. E. Cachia, 'The use of the Colloquial in Modern Arabic literature', *JAOS* 87.12–22 (January-March 1967).

[33] Ministry of Education and Culture, *Manhaj al-dirāsa al-madrasiyya* for grades 5–8. For lower grades, consult the Ministry's *Manhaj al-dirāsa li'l-madrasa al-asāsiyya al-ʿarabiyya al-rasmiyya li'l-ṣufūf al-awwal — al-rābiʿ*.

literature, classical and modern, its analysis and appreciation — on the same lines as the study of Hebrew in the Hebrew schools.[34] It was necessary to compile a new set of textbooks on these lines. The inspectors of the Ministry of Education and Culture prepared several and commissioned others; this work is still proceeding.

Arabic as a Foreign Language

While the teaching of Arabic as a mother-tongue already had a long tradition, over a wide area, the same did not apply to its instruction as a foreign language. At pre-university level, at least, hardly any meaningful experience could be gleaned outside Palestine and Israel.[35] It is true that in France, Iran, Pakistan and Indonesia some Arabic was being studied (in the last three — for reading the Koran and other sources); however, this was not widespread and was of little use as an example. Hence some of the difficulties besetting the teaching of Arabic as a foreign language in Israel. On the other hand, Arabic had inherited the place of Turkish immediately after the First World War, though it had been taught sporadically in Jewish schools previously.[36] However, as many of the pupils in the Hebrew schools knew some Arabic, since it was spoken in their homes and neighborhood, they approached its study as that of a mother-tongue. Nevertheless, the sum-total of the experience gained was quite meaningful. Hebrew schools in Palestine, under British rule, usually taught Arabic as a second foreign language (the first being, with very few exceptions, English), in grades 7 and 8 of the elementary, and the four grades of high school (though not in the science 'trend').

In Israel, the practice continues, but with a difference. Fewer pupils in the Hebrew schools are taking Arabic as their second foreign language. Some sixty elementary Hebrew schools only offer Arabic in grades 7 and 8. In most Hebrew high schools, pupils are choosing French rather than Arabic as their second foreign language, probably because of a pragmatic approach to their future prospects of employment or planned voyages abroad. Insofar as Arabic is studied, it rates three class-hours per week in grades 7 and 8 of the elementary Hebrew school and three to four hours a week in the four grades of the Hebrew high school.[37] Instruction in grades 7 and 8 of the elementary school is given in both colloquial and literary Arabic; the former is taught in Hebrew transliteration, the latter in the Arabic script. Due to this over-ambitious approach, only the rudiments of each type of Arabic are acquired. The graduates of elementary schools who do not pursue their studies in the high school

[34] For additional details, see Salmōn 1959.

[35] Most of the materials relating to the teaching of Arabic as a foreign language in Israel, expressed in research and various views, by scholars and teachers, have been collected in Landau 1961; see pp. 121–3 for a bibliographical list.

[36] For an interesting account see J. J. Rivlin, 'Hōra'at ha-safa ha-ʿaravīt bĕ-vatey ha-sefer ha-yĕhūdiyyīm bĕ-Ereṣ Yisra'el', *Sĕde Ilan* 2.117–32 (1968).

[37] Details in the official curricula of the Ministry of Education and Culture.

forget what little they have learnt; the feeling of time waste does not increase their desire to study Arabic. In the four-year Hebrew high school, practically the whole effort in learning Arabic goes into the literary language. The graduates can usually understand the daily newspaper and radio broadcasts; a few can also read and understand a simply story.

An interesting program in teaching Arabic exists in half a dozen Hebrew high schools in Israel. Pupils grouped in an 'Orientalist trend' devote a larger number of class-periods to Arabic, including the study of Islam and some classical and modern Arabic literature. The standards expected from these pupils, in their high-school final examinations, include the ability to read not only the Arabic newspaper, but classical and modern literature (if difficult excerpts, with the aid of a dictionary). In these efforts, they find lexical aids in the word-frequency studies compiled in Israel (Brill 1940; Landau 1959b). However, at all pre-university levels of the study of Arabic as a foreign language, all pupils (a few gifted ones excepted) achieve but modest results in written and oral expression. In other words, the main instruction offered is passive; reading-and-translation, along with good grounding in grammar, is the mainstay of the study of Arabic by non-Arabs. In order to improve this situation, all pupils in the Orientalist trend, of both sexes, live among the Arabs for a month during their last summer vacation, i.e. before entering their last grade of high-school. Together with their teachers, they reside and work in an Arab village or town. In this way, they learn colloquial Arabic and practise it, gain more correct notions of Arabic life in Israel, and form ties of friendship with the local Arab youth.

The outcome of the June 1967 war aroused increased interest in the study of Arabic. Even before, certain institutions (such as the police) held intensive courses of Arabic for their own purposes. Now, however, a number of additional courses were inaugurated by popular demand. Among these may be mentioned extracurricular activities in Hebrew high schools, evening courses of Arabic opened by the Y.M.C.A., various clubs, and private language schools, such as Berlitz. There are some indications that Arabic instruction in Hebrew schools, too, may get a boost. A continuous stream of textbooks (for literary or colloquial Arabic) as well as long-playing records and dictionaries have been printed during the years 1967–68.

The main language of Jewish pupils learning Arabic in Israel is Hebrew — whether this is their mother-tongue or an acquired language. This influences the study of Arabic in two ways: On one hand, it makes it easier, for a part of the vocabulary and some morphological phenomena (such as the stems of the verb, the regular plural of the noun, etc.) are kindred enough to be well understood and speedily acquired. On the other hand, there are some difficulties: the common pronunciation in Israeli Hebrew does not distinguish precisely between several consonants and treats all long vowels as short ones; these habits are carried over by the pupils into the study of Arabic. The lack of syntactic preparation on the part of many Hebrew-speaking pupils makes it difficult for them to grasp the intricacies of the relatively-developed Arabic syntax. The existence of a proportionately large Arab minority in Israel ought to have afforded Jewish pupils an opportunity to practise their Arabic. Actually most of the pupils study literary Arabic, with little occasion to practise the colloquial (with the exception of those in the 'Orientalist trend'). The various primers and readers, many of them adequate,[38] have taken these factors into account and have tried to facilitate the study of Arabic as a foreign language — although some of them have missed the point by compiling texts which are too simple and do not afford any intellectual or emotional challenge to the pupils.

OTHER LANGUAGES

While Hebrew and Arabic are employed as first or foreign languages by various sections of Israel's population, several other foreign languages are studied in various schools at pre-university level. The main ones, English, French, Latin, and Yiddish, (Roth 1939; Landau 1959a) will be discussed presently. Italian was at one time studied in a few Hebrew high schools, chiefly in Tel-Aviv, as an optional second foreign language, like French. However, this practice seems to have been confined to the period between the two World Wars, as an expression of Italy's desire to export its civilization throughout the Mediterranean Basin; today Italian has disappeared from the high schools, though it is still studied in the evenings by adults in the 'Dante Alighieri' circles. Russian was taught as an optional foreign language in one of the Tel-Aviv high schools, but this ceased several years ago. New immigrants studying at high school, as well as those sitting for the high school final examinations externally (that is, without registering first as regular pupils), may take the following languages, either as a first or a second foreign language (in addition to Arabic, English, and French): Italian, Russian, Spanish, Roumanian and Polish. It should be emphasized that this choice is specially intended for newcomers, and that these languages are not a part of the school-curriculum.

English

In British-ruled Palestine, English had a most-favored language standing in practically all elementary and high schools, both Hebrew and Arabic. This preferential status has continued in Israel, although the State's early years were marked by a somewhat hostile attitude towards English in anti-British circles, which preferred to strengthen French cultural influence at the expense of British (as will be explained below). A possible result was the official decision to postpone starting the study of English from the fifth to the sixth elementary grade. It was not long, however, before the public and educators realized the importance of the language as a vehicle of com-

[38] Some of these are up to University standards, such as M. M. Plessner's *Diqdūq ha-lašōn ha-ʿaravit lĕ-vatey sefer ʿivriyyīm.*

munication and science, as the language of most of the Jews living outside Israel. While peaceful relations between Israel and the Arab States are lacking, English also remains the major vehicle of communication with the outside world for Israeli Arabs. Hence, efforts at reappraisal have been made. These have included attempts to change the curriculum (in 1967–68, the study of English was again started in the fifth grade, and experiments were made for advancing it to the fourth), improved methods of instruction (audio-visual) and a careful analysis of the aims in the study of English and of the available materials.[39]

English is one of the main subjects of study at school-level, in terms of time allotted: 4 years, 4 hours per week, in grades 5–8 of the elementary school; 5 hours per week in Hebrew schools, and 6 hours per week in Arab schools, in the four grades of the high school. Nevertheless, neither the elementary, nor the high schools really achieve their goals (Cohen and Aronson 1964:9). Most graduates of the eighth grade in elementary school do not attain the prescribed standards of 'conversation on everyday matters and on matters related to other school subjects ... Ability to read and understand the material studied; private reading of additional material with the aid of a dictionary ... The writing of summaries, letters and guided compositions on subjects taken from the material studied ....'

As a direct consequence of the limited achievements in English of elementary school graduates, many high school pupils, also, do not reach the standards required by the Ministry of Education and Culture. Since some of them still lack basic language structures, they can hardly be expected to master literature in English. A relatively large number fail in their final high school examinations in English (examinations in a first foreign language are compulsory); even those who pass are hardly fluent. They still experience difficulties with Shakespeare's language[40] (until recently, one Shakespeare play was compulsory; it may now be replaced by G. B. Shaw). This is not unexpected; nor is their failure to digest 350 years of English and American literature. What is more unsatisfactory is the inability of many high school graduates to read a newspaper, talk English fluently,[41] and write on practical subjects. Instructors in Israel's institutions of higher learning have been complaining that many of their students cannot understand English textbooks, or articles in the specialized journals (Kurzweil 1963:40–1), although these are easier to read than literature. As a result, experiments are now being made in a number of Hebrew high schools to introduce, optionally, modern text reading, instead of Shakespeare and poetry.

'The struggle with the English language' (G. Cohen 1966:21) is a serious problem for the young Israeli in his formative years. This is not solely due to the unfamiliarity

[39] Two of the best reports on these investigations are those of Vera Adamson, *A survey of the teaching of English in Israel* and G. Cohen and R. Aronson, 1964. Miss Adamson's report was incorporated later, with some modifications, by Cohen and Aronson, in their report, pp. 265–304.

[40] Cf. the ironical comments of Wardī (1957), who claims that Israeli teachers of English murder Shakespeare.

[41] A suggestion by A. Rōn (1963–64) that English be spoken in summer-camps on the sea-shore was not acted upon.

of Jewish and Arab children with an Indo-European language, possessing a new alphabet, a vocabulary different from their own, and a strange grammar. One may lay part of the blame on over-populated classes, lack of audio-visual equipment, shortage of experienced teachers, and the inadequacy of some of the textbooks employed. Aspirations may also be too high, and the curriculum too formal and literature-oriented — despite recent promises of reforms in this direction.

French

French has a special status in Israel, in some respects equal to that of English. Soon after the State's foundation, in May 1948, there was a certain revulsion against English, as a symbol of the British Mandate. At the time, many seriously inclined to making French Israel's main foreign language. In post offices and other Government departments, signs and posters in French, in addition to those in Hebrew and Arabic, were hung. France's sympathy for Israel, together with the political, scientific and military assistance it offered the new State during its first nineteen years, brought the two States closer in the cultural field as well. In 1959 a cultural agreement was signed between the two Governments: more Hebrew would be taught in French high schools, and an examination in this language was included, on an optional basis, in the official *baccalauréat*; Israel undertook to encourage the study of French both as a first and second foreign language.

This entrenchment of the French language in Israel may be seen as a culmination of French cultural penetration into the Middle East since the eighteenth (and, increasingly, the nineteenth) century. As early as 1882, French schools for Jewish children were opened in Palestine by the *Alliance Israélite Universelle*. This French Jewish association, essentially philanthropic, had been founded in 1860 to assist needy Jews in the Balkans, the Middle East, and North Africa, in the sphere of education, and in doing so to promote the spread of French civilization in that area. The schools of the *Alliance* in Palestine and Israel offered instruction in French in several subjects of the curriculum, so that French became, indeed, a second language for the pupils in such schools. English was learnt as a second foreign language only (M. Cohen 1959). Following the Israeli-French cultural agreement, schools offering French as a first foreign language were opened in the larger towns; during 1967–68, three of these were in existence. Obviously, in these institutions very few chose Arabic as a second foreign language, generally preferring English. In Arabic schools the situation is slightly different: since these offer compulsory instruction in Hebrew and English as foreign languages, French is generally left out. However, an Arabic high school in Nazareth, the St. Joseph, offers French as a third foreign language in all its four grades. In the newly-founded (1968) Arabic comprehensive high school in Jaffa, also, French is to be taught as a third foreign language.[42]

[42] According to a news item in *Maʿarīv*, 22 January 1968, p. 11.

In general, the study of French as a first foreign language in Israel's schools has remained fairly limited, since the public reawakened to the importance of English. Nevertheless, its status as a second foreign language in Israel's Hebrew schools has grown considerably, at the expense of Arabic — probably because many parents and pupils estimate the study of French (side by side with English) as a more profitable investment, both pragmatically and culturally (Kurzweil 1954).

The requirements of the final examinations in French as a first foreign language, in materials and skills, parallel those in English, and are similarly quite ambitious. Nor are the standards for French as a second foreign language elementary (Ministry of Education and Culture 1955:53–7): to achieve, during four years, at three hours per week (or three years, at four hours per week), satisfactory performance in 'reading the literary material required by the examinations program, dictations, summaries, free composition (narrative or descriptive), translations ... questions and answers, stories, singing' (Ministry of Education and Culture 1955:54 and 56). Obviously, not all high school graduates reach these standards. They might have done so, had they all excelled in English, since in that case, the study of French would have been based on the knowledge of English, as is often the practice in the United States, Great Britain, and elsewhere. However, because of their difficulties in learning English, many pupils consider the study of French as yet another burden. In consequence, the final attainments in French are regularly even lower than those in English, as less time and effort have been invested. An interesting experiment has been conducted, since the early 1960's, in ten Hebrew high schools, to devote an equal amount of time to both French and English, that is to add class-hours to the study of the former, at some expense to the latter. While this seems to raise final achievements in French, it may lower them in English. To avoid this, the arrangement is mainly intended for the more gifted pupils. In conclusion, one may speculate, whether the high schools in Israel ought not to add years of study and class-hours towards learning foreign languages; or, if this is not feasible, whether it would not be preferable for the less gifted to learn one foreign language thoroughly, instead of two, superficially.

Latin

Considering the modest achievements in the study of a second foreign language in the Hebrew high schools in Israel, whether Arabic or French, one may wonder at the introduction of Latin as an alternative to Arabic and French in two of the schools. However, its cultural and philological value is so remarkable, that the study of Latin has been considered worthwhile; it was also thought advisable to vary the background of high school graduates. Even those educators who appreciated classical Greek civilization and admired it, conceded that Latin — rather than Greek — ought to be taught in Israeli high schools (Goitein 1939–40). Greek, indeed, appears even more difficult than Latin for Israelis. The Ministry of Education and Culture saw advantages in learning Latin to those high school graduates who continued their studies in law, medicine, pharmacy, some of the sciences, ancient and medieval history. Those who wanted the younger generation to be better acquainted with Western civilization envisaged this benefit from the study of Latin in the Israeli high school; and those who believed in the importance of formal analysis of a foreign language for the education of the young hoped to attain this, again, by the study of Latin (Ziv 1959:578–80).

The proponents of Latin as a second foreign language in Israeli high schools are apt to point out that, on account of its being a dead language, one need not invest time and effort on spontaneous oral expression. Instead, one may concentrate on reading, translation, and grammar — all the while becoming acquainted with the classical world (Wirzubski 1961). Actually, since Latin, as an optional second foreign language in several Israeli high schools, is chosen by small groups interested in it, the pupils reach satisfactory standards: in the final examinations most can translate from Latin an unseen prose passage of medium difficulty, with or without the aid of a dictionary.

Yiddish

Yiddish has had a special standing in the Jewish communities of Eastern Europe and the Americas,[43] roughly similar to that of Ladino (Judeo-Spanish) among Jews in Southern Europe and the Middle East. Because of its standing, many Zionists who had settled in Palestine favored the use of Hebrew as a working-language against Yiddish — which they considered, often derogatorily, as the language of the Jewish Diaspora. Numerous speakers of Yiddish came out at the time to defend it,[44] maintaining that it was the oral and written language of the Jewish masses, therefore more idiomatic than Hebrew (Kosover 1966: especially Part III). Two separate groups argued the right of Yiddish to be the national language of all Jews in Palestine and abroad: on the one hand, orthodox circles, who considered Hebrew solely as a holy language, not to be desecrated by daily use; on the other, Communists and other leftist elements, for whom Yiddish was the language of the Jewish workers.

Despite opposition, Hebrew succeeded to the place of Yiddish (and other languages) and became a first language of the Jews in Palestine, and then an official language in the State of Israel. It is now the mother-tongue of most Jews born in Palestine and Israel, as well as the language of instruction in their schools. At the same time, the status of Yiddish declined with the reduction in the number of its speakers, both in Israel and in the Diaspora — where many Yiddish-speaking Jews were brutally murdered during the Second World War in Poland and Eastern Europe; contacts with those in the Soviet Union are severed; while in the Americas Yiddish has been relegated to an inferior status, due to the fact that the younger Jews, in contradistinction to

[43] Y. Mark, 'Changes in the Yiddish School', *Jewish Education* 19.31–8 (1947–48).

[44] One publication out of many: League for Rights of Yiddish in Palestine, *Yidiš in Ereṣ Yisro'el.*

the immigrant generation, generally employ the local language, practically always English or Spanish, respectively.

As a result, an overwhelming majority both in Israel and in the Zionist movement abroad has ceased looking upon Yiddish as a rival to Hebrew. There is currently no opposition to Yiddish in Israel: newspapers, journals and books appear in Yiddish; a Yiddish theater flourishes; the Hebrew University of Jerusalem has instituted a chair in Yiddish language and literature; and, most significantly, in Haifa's suburb of Qiryat Ḥayyim, a Hebrew high school has officially introduced the study of Yiddish as a foreign language.

LANGUAGES IN HIGHER EDUCATION

The study of languages has an important place in the institutes of higher education in Israel. A large number is taught at the Hebrew University of Jerusalem, founded soon after the First World War, as well as at Tel-Aviv University and at Bar-Ilan University (in Ramat-Gan, near Tel-Aviv), both founded in 1955. This applies, but to a lesser extent, to the Haifa Institute of Technology, the University College in Haifa, the Hebrew University's extension courses in Be'er Sheba and Bar-Ilan University's extension courses in Ashqelon.

The study of languages learned in high school — Hebrew, Arabic, English, French, more rarely Latin or Yiddish — starts at a high level, above beginners' standards. For those unacquainted with these languages, intensive preparatory classes bring them up to requirements. For instance, during 1967–68, the Hebrew University offered preparatory classes in the following languages: Hebrew, Arabic, English, French, Latin, Yiddish, Greek, Russian, Italian, Spanish, and German.

These preparatory courses serve as a first stage towards regular studies in all these languages for the B.A. and some for the M.A. degree as well. In addition, other languages recently offered for those degrees at the Hebrew University are: Turkish and Altaic languages, Iranian languages, Chinese, Japanese, Armenian, Sanskrit, Hindi, Urdu, Geez, Amharic, Aramaic, Syriac, Ugaritic, Akkadian, Sumerian, ancient Egyptian and Coptic, Portuguese, Ladino, Old French, and Church Slavonic.[45]

Tel-Aviv University offers courses in the following languages: Hebrew, Arabic, Aramaic, Turkish, Persian, Greek, Latin, French, Old French, Akkadian, ancient Egyptian, Ethiopic languages, English.[46]

Bar-Ilan University offers courses in the following languages: Hebrew, Arabic, Aramaic, Akkadian, Sumerian, Geez, Syriac, Greek, Latin, English, French, Italian, German, and Russian.[47]

The general trend in Israeli Universities is to learn languages less from a functional

[45] Mainly based on the Hebrew University's catalog for 1967–68.
[46] Based on Tel-Aviv University's catalog for 1967–68.
[47] Based on Bar-Ilan University's catalog for 1967–68.

point of view than as an instrument for linguistic and philological research; or, at least as a vehicle for literary appreciation or historical analysis. The research-oriented approach characterizes not only the M.A. and Ph.D. studies, but most B.A. courses as well. This is particularly evident in the departments of linguistics in each of the Universities, but exists in other departments, too, as shown by the serious progress in research at these institutions.[48]

The high standards of language instruction and linguistic research at the Israeli Universities is reflected in the final achievements of their graduates. These results merit special mention, on account of two main difficulties: a. With the exception of Bar-Ilan University, where the B.A. is stretched over a four-year course, all Israeli Universities compress the B.A. studies into three years, which implies pressure-cooking the language studies, sometimes without due opportunity for digestion. b. The Hebrew University of Jerusalem, Tel-Aviv University and the University College in Haifa require two majors for the B.A. degree;[49] only Bar-Ilan University requires one major and one minor. For this reason, students cannot devote their complete attention, during their B.A. studies,[50] to a single language or to one aspect of linguistics.

CONCLUSION

While it has obviously been impossible to include a very detailed outline and analysis of language study in Israel in this brief survey, an attempt has been made to bring together the significant factors.

The most salient feature seems to be the manifest emphasis laid on the study of the mother-tongue, be it Hebrew or Arabic, at both the elementary and the high school levels — detrimental to some extent to the progress of foreign language study at these levels. Israel differs in this from other small countries, such as The Netherlands, where the instruction of major foreign languages has apparently had more effective results. Israel has been hampered by a rapid rise in its pupil-population, chiefly through immigration; this state of affairs has been aggravated by the State's insistence on free, compulsory schooling. Although the overall language situation seems better than in many other developing countries, due to high literacy and educational organization, there still remains a gap between the modest achievements of the high school in imparting knowledge of foreign languages and the higher standards required at Israeli Universities. Awareness of this gap and serious attempts to close it, at present in progress, appear promising.

[48] Linguistic research is outside the scope of this article and deserves a special study. Some idea may be gained from the Hebrew University's *Research Report* 1964–1965, vol. 3. For Arabic studies, see G. Baer (1967).

[49] An alternative course of studies for the B.A., based on one major only, is being discussed (1968) at the Hebrew University of Jerusalem and Tel-Aviv University.

[50] For the M.A. and Ph.D. degrees, one major suffices.

BIBLIOGRAPHY

ABBĪR, S. 1950. Hōra'at 'ivrīt li-yĕladīm bĕ-maḥanōt 'ōlīm. Ḥī 33.74–89.

ACTIONS COMMITTEE OF THE ZIONIST ORGANIZATION. The struggle for the Hebrew Language in Palestine. New York.

ADAMSON, VERA. A survey of the teaching of English in Israel: a survey of the teaching of English in the primary and secondary schools of Israel conducted between December, 1960 and July, 1961. (mimeographed, Jerusalem, n.d. — 1962?).

ADAR, ZVI. 1965. Ha-Miqṣō'ōt ha-humānisṭiyyīm ba-ḥīnnūx ha-tīxōn. Tel Aviv.

AVINERY, ISAAC. 1946. Kibbūšey ha-'ivrīt bĕ-dōrenū. Tel Aviv.

——. 1964. Yad ha-lašōn. Tel Aviv.

AVIŠAY, Y. 1951–52. Lĕ-Ve'ayat ha-qĕlīṭa ha-lĕšōnīt šel yĕladīm 'ōlīm. Tel-Aviv.

BACHI, R. 1955. A statistical analysis of the revival of Hebrew in Israel. Scripta Hierosolymitana 3.179–247.

BAER, GABRIEL. 1967. Etudes arabes en Israël. Les Temps Modernes (Paris) 253bis 732–41.

BAR-ADON, A. 1963. Lĕšōnō ha-mĕdūbberet šel ha-dōr ha-ṣa'īr bĕ-Yisra'el kĕ-nōse lĕ-meḥqar bĕ-misgeret ḥeqer ha-'ivrīt ha-dĕvūra bĕ-Yisra'el. Ḥī 35.21–35.

BLANC, HAIM. 1954. The growth of Israeli Hebrew. MEA 5.385–92 (December).

——. 1957. Hebrew in Israel: trends and problems. MEJ 11.397–409 (Autumn).

BRILL, MOSHE, in collaboration with D. NEUSTADT and P. SCHUSSER. 1940. The Basic Word List of the Arabic Daily Newspaper. Jerusalem.

CENTRAL BUREAU OF STATISTICS. 1963–66. Languages, literacy and educational attainment. Parts I-II-III. Jerusalem.

COHEN, GIDEON. 1966. English as a second language. Ariel 14.21–5 (Spring). Jerusalem.

——, and R. ARONSON, under direction of G. ORTAR. 1964. The teaching of English in Israel. Mimeographed. Jerusalem.

COHEN, M. 1959. Lašōn ṣarfatīt hōra'ata: I. Be'ayōt yĕsōd bĕ-hōra'at ṣarfatīt. EḤ 2.736–7.

FEITELSON, DINA. 1964. Dĕraxīm lĕ-šīppūr hōra'at ha-lašōn ha-'ivrīt bĕ-veyt ha-sefer ha-yĕsōdī: 'al yĕsōd meḥqar histakkĕlūt bĕ-kīttōt 4. Jerusalem.

GARBELL, J. 1930. Fremdsprachliche Einflüsse im modernen Hebräisch. Berlin.

GOITEIN, S.D. 1939–40. Lĕ-hōra'at tarbūt Yawan bĕ-veyt ha-sefer ha-tīxōn. Ḥī 13.65–71.

——. 1958. Hōra'at ha-'ivrīt: ḍarxey ha-līmmūd ba-miqṣō'ōt ha-'ivriyyīm: dībbūr — qĕrī'a — ḥībbūr. 3rd ed. Tel-Aviv.

GOTTSTEIN, M. 1952–53. Šīnnūy 'araxīm bĕ-hōra'at ha-diqdūq ha-'ivrī — keyṣad? Ḥī 25.102–6.

HARAMATI, SHLOMO. 1958. The teaching of Hebrew in the Israeli army. MLJ 42.123–31 (March).

——. 1964. Hōra'at 'ivrīt lĕ-an'alfabeytīm. Tel-Aviv.

The Hebrew University of Jerusalem. 1967. Research report 1964–65, vol. III: Humanities, social sciences, law, education, social work, library. Jerusalem.

Kosover, Mordecai. 1966. Arabic elements in Palestinian Yiddish: the Old Ashkenazic Community in Palestine: its history and its language. Jerusalem.

Kurzweil, Z. A. 1954. 'Aravīt ō ṣarfatīt. Ha-Areṣ (Tel-Aviv, daily) 21 October.

——. 1963. Hōra'at ha-anglīt bĕ-vatey sifrenū. Ḥī 35.40–8.

Landau, J. M. 1959a. Bĕḥīrat lašōn zara bi-mĕdīnat Yisra'el. EḤ 2.573–4.

——. 1959b. A word count of Modern Arabic prose. New York.

——, ed. 1961. Hōra'at ha-'aravīt kĕ-lašōn zara: leqeṭ ma'amarīm. Jerusalem.

League for Rights of Yiddish in Palestine. Yīdīš īn Ereṣ Yisro'el. New York. n.d.

Ministry of Education and Culture. 1954a. Toxnīt ha-līmmūdīm lĕ-veyt ha-sefer ha-yĕsōdī ha-mamlaxtī ha-datī: kīttōt 1–4. Jerusalem.

——. 1954b. Toxnīt ha-līmmūdīm lĕ-veyt ha-sefer ha-yĕsōdī ha-mamlaxtī vĕ-ha-mamlaxtī ha-datī: kīttōt 5–8. Jerusalem.

——. 1955. Haṣa'ōt lĕ-tōxniyyōt līmmūd bĕ-veyt ha-sefer ha-tīxōn (arba' šĕnōt līmmūd: 9–12). Tel-Aviv.

——. 1957. Manhaj al-dirāsa al-asāsiyya al-'arabiyya al-rasmiyya li'l-ṣufūf al-awwal — al-rābi'. Jerusalem. n.d.

——. Manāhij al-dirāsa fī'l-madāris al-ṯānawiyya. Jerusalem. n.d.

——. Manhaj al-dirāsa li'l-madrasa al-'arabiyya al-ibtidā'iyya al-rasmiyya li'l-ṣaffayn al-sābi' wa'l-ṯāmin. Jerusalem n.d.

——. Manhaj al-dirāsa li'l-madrasa al-'arabiyya al-ibtidā'iyya al-rasmiyya li'l-ṣaffayn al-xāmis wa'l-sādis. Jerusalem. n.d.

Mor, A. 1945. Ha-Lašōn ha-'ivrīt bĕ-ḥinnūx ha-dōr: yĕsōdōt hinnūxiyyīm w-pĕsīxōlōgiyyīm. Tel-Aviv.

Morag, Shlomo. 1959. Ha-'Ivrīt bi-tĕḥiyyata. EḤ 2.594–8.

Moussa, Salama. 1955. Arabic language problems. MEA 6.41–4 (February).

Nardi, Noah. 1945. Education in Palestine: 1920–1945. Washington, D.C.

Nir, Raphael. 1963. Ha-tittaxen gīša tey'ūrīt bĕ-hōra'at ha-lašōn ha-'ivrīt bĕ-veyt ha-sefer ha-tīxōn? Ḥī. 35.41–4.

——. 1966. 'Al tōqef bĕḥīnōt ha-bagrūt bĕ-miqṣō'a lašōn 'ivrīt. Mĕgammōt 14.372–6 (August).

Ornan, 'Uzzi. 1951. Diqdūq lĕ-yōd'ey 'ivrīt. Ḥī 23.48–58.

Peretz, Y. 1962. 'Ivrīt kĕ-hilxata: madrīx bĕ-'inyĕney lašōn. rev. ed. Tel-Aviv.

Piamenta, M. 1955. Arabic in the Knesset. MEA 6.45–7 (February).

Polturak, H. and H. Levinton. 1958. Hōra'at ha-anglīt bĕ-veyt ha-sefer ha-yĕsōdī. rev. ed. Tel-Aviv.

Qōdeš, S and M. Ḥōmsqī, eds. 1967. Lĕ-Darka šel ha-'ivrīt ha-qalla: qōveṣ ma'amarīm. (Ōrḥōt 5). Jerusalem. (December).

Rabin, Chaim. 1958. The revival of Hebrew. (Israel Today 5). Jerusalem.

——. 1960. Tōlĕdōt ha-lašōn. Mimeographed. Jerusalem.

——. 1962. New life for an old language. Ariel 3.13–22.

REGEV, ZINA. 1967. The improvement of written expression and composition in the mother tongue. Jerusalem.

RIEGER, ELIEZER. 1935. Ōṣar millōt ha-yĕsōd šel ha-lašōn ha-‘ivrīt ha-šimmūšīt: meḥqar be-‘arīxat toxnīt limmūdīm. Jerusalem.

——. 1940. Ha-Hinnūx ha-‘ivrī bĕ-Ereṣ Yisra’el. 2 vols. Tel-Aviv.

——. 1949. The revival of Hebrew, in N. Hans and J. A. Lauwerys, eds., Yearbook of Education, 471–9. London.

——. 1951. Lĕ-Šinnūy ‘araxīm bĕ-hōra’at ha-diqdūq ha-‘ivrī. Ḥī 24.181–95.

——. 1953. Modern Hebrew. New York.

RŌN, A. 1963–64. Lĕ-Qīddūm hōra’at ha-anglīt. Hed ha-Ḥinnūx 38 (fasc. 14–15).

RŌN, Y. 1954–55. ‘Al hōra’at ha-lašōn lĕ-yaldey ‘ōlīm. Hed ha-Ḥinnūx 29 (fascs. 6, 9–10, 18, 25, 43–5).

ROSEN, H. B. 1956. Ha-‘Ivrīt šelanū: dĕmūta bĕ-ōr šīṭōṭ ha-balšanūt. Tel-Aviv.

——. 1957. ‘Ivrīt ṭōva: ‘iyyūnīm bĕ-taḥbīr ha-lašōn ha-‘nĕxōna’. Jerusalem.

ROTH, LEON. 1939. ‘Al limmūd ha-lĕšōnōt. Leon Roth, ed. ‘Al ha-ḥinnūx ha-tīxōnī ha-‘ivrī bĕ-Ereṣ-Yisra’el, 172–89. Jerusalem.

——. 1941. Me ‘asta ha-ūnīversīṭa lĕ-ma‘an ha-lašōn ha-‘ivrīt. Jerusalem.

SALMON, S. 1959. Lašōn ‘aravīt, hōra’ata: I. hōra’ata ki-lĕšōn em. EḤ 2.702–25.

SAPPAN, R. 1963. Darxey ha-sleng: tōfa‘ōt, mašma‘ūt vĕ-ṣūra ba-‘ivrīt ha-tat-tiqnīt. Jerusalem.

SCHARFSTEIN, ZEVI. 1928. Ha-Ḥinnūx bĕ-Ereṣ-Yisra’el. New York.

SHAKED, JOSEPH. 1955. The education of new immigrant workers in Israel. Unesco's Educational Studies and Documents 16.30–42.

TUR-SINAI, N. H. 1960. The revival of the Hebrew language. Jerusalem.

ŪRĪM 20. 1963. (fasc. 9–10).385–512. [Special issue on the teaching of Hebrew.]

WARDĪ, D. 1957. Ha-Mōrīm wĕ-Shakespeare. Ofaqīm 11.288–93 (August).

WEIMAN, R. W. 1950. Native and foreign elements in a language: a study in general linguistics applied to modern Hebrew. Philadelphia.

WEINBERG, Z. 1958. Ha-Ūlpan lĕ-‘ivrīt wĕ-darxey ha-‘avōda bō. Ḥī 30.100–7.

WIRSZUBSKI, CHAIM. 1961. Lāṭīnīt bĕ-veyt ha-sefer ha-‘ivrī. Meir Shapira, ed. Halaxa w-ma‘ase ba-ḥīnnūx ha-tīxōn: qōveṣ ma’amarīm muqdašīm lĕ-ve‘ayōt beyt ha-sefer ha-tīxōn ha-‘iyyūnī (A. M. Dushkin jubilee volume), 46–51. Jerusalem.

ZIV, MICHAEL. 1959. Lašōn laṭīnīt, hōra’ata. EḤ 2.578–86.

LINGUISTICS AND LANGUAGE ISSUES IN TURKEY*

G. HAZAI

The origin of Turkish linguistics is closely tied to the founding of the modern Turkish republic of Kemal Atatürk. This republic, which had pledged itself to the cause of economic, political, and cultural reform, offered vast possibilities for the growth of scientific research. Within a relatively short time the new state created the material condition for the development of the most important areas of scientific investigation and encouraged the establishment of the necessary institutions. In these a new generation of scholars, whose numbers increased daily and whose horizons broadened steadily, found new opportunities for investigation.

The government, in planning its program for a cultural revival, gave top priority to the problems of reforming the Turkish language itself by abolishing the use of the Arabic script and creating a new literary language based on common spoken usage. This predestined the then still nascent Turkish linguistics to a special central position relative to other fields of scientific endeavor, and it was this preferential attitude of the government that contributed in large degree to the rapid development of the institutions and the personnel of this branch of scholarship as well as to its material requirements. It is undoubtedly true that these circumstances also determined the program of linguistics in Turkey for a long time, and were of immense importance to the evolution of its structure, scope, and further development. The close bond between Turkish linguistics and the problems of language reform were, for a long time, the most important factor in its development. This bond still exists today since the problem of language reform continues to remain one of active concern, even if in somewhat different dimensions. Its character, however, has changed considerably, for in the light of general linguistic activity a completely different proportion of the researcher's time and energy is applied.

The case for the Turkish language reforms, which decades earlier had come to the attention of the intelligentsia, occupied a special place within the republic's planned reforms. Quite obviously the solution of these problems would be a key to the solution of other problems.

The goal of the reform in written Turkish was to replace the Arabic script (which presented a real obstacle to literacy) by the Latin alphabet. Arabic writing had for

* The English text is the work of Karin L. Ford, as revised by the Assistant Editor.

centuries been the basis of Ottoman-Turkish literature, deeply rooted in Islamic culture. This script from the beginning had been totally unsuited to the Turkish language since it had been created for a completely different phonology. To complicate matters, because of cultural-historical circumstances, a great many Arabic and Persian words had been taken over into Turkish for centuries and had preserved a completely sovereign status as regarded their orthography. This development did not tend toward assimilation but rather toward maintaining and preserving the traditional orthography, which was rather complicated for the ordinary Turk. Writing continued to remain the property of the privileged few, as did the classical literary language, which again was suited to meet the requirements of only a few. The Arabic script was closely tied to the old literary language, and they shared the same fate.

The language reform resulted in the elimination of the old literary language and in the creation of a new one; in other words, it bridged the gap between the common and the literary languages.

The problem, then, was to create the kind of literary language that would bring the language of the state, of public life, of the press, and of literature closer to that of the people; in short, to modernize it.

It is easy to understand that these two tasks of the cultural program were of vital importance for Turkish society and for modern Turkey. The actual attack on these two problems was launched under the state's guidance and with its direct material and moral support. The initiator and guiding spirit of both endeavors was the great reformer of modern Turkey, Kemal Atatürk.

The new script was introduced in November 1928, and after a short transitional period the printing of Arabic script was legally prohibited as of January 1, 1929. This was the year that marked the complete and successful implementation of the reform in written Turkish. The 1935 census registered 2,517,387 persons who were able to write the new Latin script.

The course of the language reform did not always run smoothly or efficiently. Controversy between the radical and conservative elements often led to extremes that obscured the sensible middle road and proved wasteful of time. The development of uniform standards in the literary language is going on even today. Only after a long development at moderate pace can this change become crystallized and accepted. However, the basis for change has been established; during recent decades a noticeable change in the character of the language has already occurred and this has contributed to a definite lessening of tension.

The founding of the Turkish Linguistic Society (Türk Dil Kurumu), strongly encouraged by the state, represented the opening act of the language reform movement (July 12, 1932). The Society, which owed its existence largely to the initiative of Kemal Atatürk, was charged with the task of converting the idea of language reform into actual fact and of 'Turkifying' the language once again. The considerable financial support of the government enabled the Society to initiate such concrete measures as were required first of all to do the research necessary to make the language reform a success. Through systematic study of linguistic monuments and of the colloquial language, through comparative study of the Turkic dialects, the researchers sought to discover the genuine Turkish vocabulary in order to put it into the service of the language reform. To disseminate neologisms, the moral support provided by the state — through active involvement of the press and the educational system — was of utmost importance.

A few difficulties ensued as a result, however. A sharp conflict arose between the moderates or conservatives and the radicals, who often appealed to national feeling. The fact that the latter gained the upper hand soon led to a rather critical situation. As announcements and press releases of that time clearly show, the idiom that emerged as predominant was completely unintelligible to many people. There was a real danger that the state would sanction it for use in official circles, in the schools, and by the press.

However, things developed differently. The government recognized the linguistic chaos and its possible political consequences in time and put a halt to the activities of the extreme purists.

The fact that the official guidance, instigated in large part by Kemal Atatürk, kept a healthy distance from radical purism, did not mean, however, an interruption of the language reform. The purification of the language, the development of new norms in literature and language that would more closely approach the language of the people remained a primary concern and continued to be supported by the state.

However, the calm did not last long. At the instigation of İ. İnönü, who had become President of the Republic after Atatürk's death, the problems of language reform came into the foreground once more in the early 1940's. The radical purists again saw a field of activity wide open before them. The intelligentsia once again met these new efforts with negative attitudes. Particularly sharp controversy arose over the innovations in the area of technical and scientific language, over the new dictionary of the Türk Dil Kurumu, and over the new text of the constitution. Discussion was perhaps most heated on these issues.

The conflict and the generally negative feeling on the part of the intelligentsia towards the radical measures of the extremists forced the latter to retreat. For certain political reasons the government itself considered this retreat wise. In 1949 a moderate trend was adopted which gave preference to intelligibility rather than linguistic purity. This led to a quieting of the situation and a return to calmer days.

When the Democratic party came to power in 1950, a change in the relationship between state and the reform movement took place. The Democratic party, which had assumed power from the Republican people's party, had different ideas than its predecessor about national cultural programs in general, and consequently about language reform in particular, with a resultant cessation of financial and moral support of the language reform. The lack of the former did not noticeably affect the language reform. The Türk Dil Kurumu, which essentially incorporated all the followers of the reform movement, had secured a firm material base of operations through the considerable legacy left by Atatürk. The lack of moral support, however, which brought opposition to the neologisms on the part of governmental circles, the educational system, and the press, did have negative effects. There can be no doubt that this turn of events dealt a weakening blow to the position of such words and phrases that had already taken some hold in daily usage. Nevertheless, the course of the reform could not be interrupted, much less reversed — it had, by fulfilling a real social need, become quite well established. The young writers' interest in innovation, motivated in large part by national feeling, remained unshaken, and they continued to be consciously dedicated to language reform. This was and remained the most important factor in the development of the language reform, regardless of political and societal trends, and can be said to have served as the driving force behind the reform.

Changes of the 1960's caused new turmoil in the language reform, particularly in its institution, the Türk Dil Kurumu. Differences of opinion and discussion still continue today, but the answer to contemporary problems can only be sought in the future.

In evaluating the results of the language reform it is imperative to play down the importance of institutions, individuals or their radical initiative, and individual successes or failures, and rather to turn to the appropriate standard for judgment, the language itself. Was the goal of the reform — bringing the literary language closer to the language of the people and eliminating the existing gap between the two — met adequately?

We believe that the answer to this question has already been given most convincingly. The official, literary, and press language of today can scarcely be compared with that of the 1920's or 1930's, and even less with that of earlier decades. The language of today mirrors essentially the common language spoken in wide sectors of the population and is much closer to most strata of the population than the earlier idiom, which was quite foreign to the speech of the people.

Critics of the language reform often argue that the banishing of Arabic-Perisan elements in the language caused a linguistic vacuum which resulted in an avalanche of loan words from European languages. To ascribe the European influence on Turkish to the language reform is only accurate in the very limited sphere of technical language. The influx of European loan words was as much a result of objective historical and cultural-historical circumstances as was the Arabic-Persian influence some centuries earlier. The rapid and close alliance of Turkey with Europe and the assimilation of the technological and scientific achievements inevitably led to new language contacts. But this development can be explained by objective circumstances and not by the course of development in Turkish language reform. At the same time, however, we should not equate the European and Islamic influences, especially when keeping in mind the development and function of the literary language. Usage of the now-condemned Arabic-Persian language stratum was confined to a literary language whose function was limited to satisfying the needs of a relatively small segment of the population. The elements borrowed from European origins, however, entered the language under completely different historical and social circumstances and were therefore assimilated into the common language much more rapidly. Obviously, these words, so far as they have not been completely replaced by Turkish equivalents, occupy an entirely different place in the language than the earlier loan words held in the literary language.

This European influence on the language did not automatically reflect the extent of the actual cultural and scientific relations of the country. In keeping with cultural tradition, the earlier orientation of the language was towards the French vocabulary. This tradition continues in many respects today. In more recent decades, however, an English influence has made itself quite strongly felt.

A normal consequence in the development of a vocabulary is that several kinds of language appear concurrently. The use of these kinds of language depends on many factors, primarily, however, on the user's generation. Thus the older generation, which was educated prior to the language reform, generally continues to use the old vocabulary. Certain levels in the population continue deliberately in this usage, especially in the written language. The same is true also for many sectors of the government. A more balanced usage is found in literature and journalism. Further innovations, the conscious use of the new vocabulary, and the taking of initiative, are in the hands of the new generation of writers as clearly evidenced in their essays, sketches, and critiques. It is probably in this area that the tendencies of the reform are most strongly in evidence and where there is the most experimentation and effort towards the new. From here the neologisms are either integrated into the language or relegated to obscurity. Regional authors whose work describes the Anatolian village life make use of dialects, and in this way a regional vocabulary often found its way into the literary language, and still does.

The development of technical language took place rather independently and resulted in a rather mixed picture. Despite the retention of the traditional vocabulary which was fairly precise, the trend towards innovation could be felt here as well. At the same time the influence of international technical language could be noted. These various trends led to a variety of results in different technical areas. Slowly, however, a trend towards unification seems to be emerging which will eventually lead towards a consolidation of the vocabulary.

What is true for one aspect of cultural advance, where the language reform has made important progress, cannot be said for the fight against illiteracy, which in recent times has diminished only slightly in terms of percentage of population. The over-all number of illiterates has increased because of substantial growth in population. This situation seems to be a result of the form of the educational system, especially the unsatisfactory conditions of the public school system, which in earlier times was far from adequate but is becoming even less so with the increase in population. The growing contradiction between the population increase and the condition of the educational system will probably continue to contribute to the rise in the illiteracy rate.

The tables that follow will provide a more detailed look at illiteracy in Turkey. They are taken from official surveys of the United Nations and are based on data from the censuses of 1955 and 1960.[1]

	1955 CENSUS	1960 CENSUS
Total population	24,064,763	27,754,820
Turks	21,622,292	25,172,535
Arab	300,583	347,690
Armenian	56,242	52,756
Circassian	79,837	63,137
Georgian	51,982	32,944
Greek	79,691	65,139
Kurd	1,679,265	1,847,674
Ladino (Judeo-Spanish)	32,975	19,399
Laze	30,566	21,703
Pomak	16,163	24,098

The table above shows the population increase by ethnic group. Only those groups were considered whose total population exceeded 30,000. The breakdown by nationality serves to indicate what groups and what languages must be taken into account when considering the question of illiteracy in Turkey. No statistics for illiteracy by ethnic group are available. (See *Demographic Yearbook* 1963, United Nations, New York, 1964, p. 327.)

The actual literacy rate by age and sex for each census is shown in the following table (see *op. cit.*, p. 362):

Literacy Rate

Census of October 23, 1955

	ALL AGES	10 AND OVER	UNDER TEN	UNKNOWN
Both sexes	24,064,763	16,934,266	7,092,595	37,092
Literate	7,915,238	6,973,690	930,134	11,414
Illiterate	16,090,725	6,909,971	6,158,398	22,356
Unknown	58,800	50,605	4,063	4,132
Male	12,233,421	8,557,443	3,656,689	19,289
Literate	5,478,766	4,926,230	544,336	8,200
Illiterate	6,728,282	3,609,222	3,110,300	8,760
Unknown	26,373	21,991	2,053	2,329

[1] For the 1965 census only a few basic numbers are known. According to this census the population of Turkey was 31,291,207.

Female	11,831,342	8,376,823	3,435,906	18,613
Literate	2,436,472	2,047,460	385,798	3,214
Illiterate	9,362,443	6,300,749	3,048,098	13,596
Unknown	32,427	28,614	2,010	1,803

Census of October 23, 1960

Both sexes	27,754,820	19,451,950	8,253,099	49,771
Literate	8,901,006	7,956,356	936,114	8,536
Illiterate	18,837,890	11,487,442	7,314,317	36,131
Unknown	15,924	8,152	2,668	5,104
Male	14,163,888	9,882,377	4,252,693	28,818
Literate	6,157,842	5,595,225	556,395	6,222
Illiterate	7,997,072	4,282,717	3,695,144	19,211
Unknown	8,974	4,435	1,154	3,385
Female	13,590,932	9,569,573	4,000,406	20,953
Literate	2,743,164	2,361,131	379,719	2,314
Illiterate	10,840,818	7,204,725	3,619,173	16,920
Unknown	6,950	3,717	1,514	1,719

The table below shows the 1955 and 1960 illiteracy rates for the population 15 years old or over, grouped by sex (see *op. cit.* p. 375):

Illiteracy rate among population 15 years of age and over, by sex

		ILLITERATE	
BOTH SEXES	TOTAL	NUMBER	PER CENT
1955	14,589,543	8,931,447	61.4
1960	16,327,814	10,100,972	61.9

		ILLITERATE	
MALE	TOTAL	NUMBER	PER CENT
1955	7,282,983	3,190,902	43.9
1960	8,223,517	3,714,290	45.2

		ILLITERATE	
FEMALE	TOTAL	NUMBER	PER CENT
1955	7,306,560	5,740,545	77.5
1960	8,104,297	6,386,682	78.8

The Turkish sociologist M. Hiç established in his statistical analysis of relevant data

(*Cumhuriyet*, April 2, 1965) that the most successful period in the struggle against illiteracy was that immediately following the writing reform. Even though the introduction of the Latin script had caused a new kind of illiteracy in certain segments of the population, the net effect was a positive one. This too confirmed the correctness of the language reform.

The key to the solution of the problem of illiteracy would seem to lie in the improvement of the educational system, especially in the elementary level. Present-day conditions of the school system are as follows (see *The Europe Yearbook*, Vol. I, Europa Publications Limited, London, p. 1005):

	SCHOOLS	TEACHERS	STUDENTS
Primary	29,070	79,153	3,814,133
Secondary	1,084	19,599	452,192
Technical	677	6,469	113,356
Teacher Training	73	1,492	42,295
Universities	7	3,652	52,768

The problems are particularly clear when seen in the light of acceptance of the compulsory education laws on the elementary level. The statistics for school attendance by school-aged children during recent years is as follows (see Şahin Tekin, *Dünya*, Nov. 3, 1964):

YEAR	NO. OF CHILDREN AGE 6–10 (SCHOOL AGE)	NO. OF CHILDREN ATTENDING SCHOOL	PERCENTAGE ATTENDING
1950	2,591,149	1,576,127	60.0
1955	3,081,926	1,847,156	59.9
1960	3,932,247	2,500,258	63.6
1964	4,473,035	3,622,349	81.0

It is perhaps characteristic that in Ankara, the capital, only 74.6% of the children of compulsory attendance age were actually going to school, and in the largest metropolitan center of Turkey, Istanbul, only 91.2% were attending school. The most extreme example is the Hakkâri district, where the percentage was only 12.4% (all data are for 1960). At present, 66% of Turkish villages have schools, whereas the remainder do not. (Broken down numerically, there are 35,537 villages, of which 23,668 have schools and 11,869 do not.) Conditions in North and East Anatolia as in areas with ethnic minorities are particularly bad.

Provisions in the government's five-year plan for the educational system include an assurance of primary school attendance for every child by 1972. Some politicians and sociologists doubt the feasibility of the plan and draw a rather grim picture of the near future.

Foreign language instruction in Turkey has a long history and a great tradition to look back to. In this area the main role has been played by the French, German, English, and American foreign schools. In the Turkish schools, foreign language instruction has long been the weakest area of the entire Turkish education system. Only a few well-known schools could be credited with any success. More recently there has been an endeavor to improve and stabilize the general status of language instruction. The recruitment of foreign teachers to the teaching of languages has been one expression of this tendency, and has been especially true for English. The recruitment of foreign teachers, though initially done mostly by the major institutions, is gradually spreading out to other spheres of the national education system.

In 1931 the activities of foreign schools in Turkey were regulated by law. Accordingly, these schools are autonomous, but the Turkish Ministry of Education does have the right to exercise some control. Certain subjects, such as history, geography, and civics, must be taught in Turkish by Turkish teachers.

Among the foreign schools in Istanbul which have particularly strong traditions of foreign language instruction Robert College, Amerikan Kız Koleji, The British High School, Notre Dame de Sion, etc., are outstanding. Similar schools can be found in other major cities of the country.

Among Turkish high schools, Darüşşafaka and Ankara Koleji where instruction is carried on in English occupy special positions. For French instruction, the Galatasaray Lisesi is best known. Here too, with the aid of foreign teachers, the classes are taught in French.

The highest rung in foreign language instruction is occupied by the philological institutes of the universities, which at the same time foster the scientific study of the respective language. At the present time the Universities of Ankara, Istanbul, and Erzurum offer interested students a possiblility to pursue the study of foreign languages at this advanced level.

Among the universities, two occupy special positions: the Orta Doğu Teknik Üniversitesi for technological studies and the Hacettepe Üniversitesi for medicine. Because these universities train specialists for foreign countries the language of instruction is English.

The last few decades were marked by an increased interest in Anglo-American culture, and English has assumed a predominant position. This becomes obvious when one looks at the translations of foreign literature, where English is clearly in the lead. The figures for 1963–64 are as follows (*Statistical Yearbook 1966*, United Nations, New York, 1967, p. 751):

	TOTAL BOOKS	ENGLISH	FRENCH	RUSSIAN	GERMAN	OTHER
1963	599	197	133	25	45	199
1964	723	257	136	23	68	239

As was mentioned earlier, the birth and existence of Turkish linguistics was for a long time closely tied to the language reform. Its institutions, its researchers, and its endeavors came out of the interest in language reform. The substantial support of the state had a beneficial effect on the development of linguistics and made possible the realization of many useful projects.

The language reform, in need of a broad outlook for its most effective functioning, encouraged the scientific study of language, its past and present.

There is still a tendency in other countries to judge present-day Turkish linguistics in terms of the 'sun-language theory' of the 1930's, and in fact to identify one with the other. This evaluation is incorrect and not based on fact. The 'sun-language theory' was of importance to the Turkish language reform movement for only a short time and was of very little consequence to the further development of Turkish linguistics.

This 'sun-language' theory (or in its official formulation 'Güneş-dil teorisi' or 'la théorie de soleil-langue') which clearly owed its existence to the influence of a few discarded linguistic theories, supported the view that the origins of human language could be traced back to man's worship of the sun. Accordingly, all language is derived from the word *ağ*, the original designation for 'sun'. Words were developed from this root by application of simple phonetic rules, which increased the number of possible kinds of syllables. Words were thus quite easy to etymologize: all words, according to this phonetic scheme, had to be traced back to the original word.

The supporters of this theory maintained at the same time that Turkish, as an old culture language of Eurasia, was the source of many, if not all, languages, and that other languages of this area could indeed be traced back to Turkish.

This last contention explains the practical intention of the whole theory and of its historical function. The theory, which arose in 1935 at the height of the radical purist activity, reversed the facts about the Turkish language and its relation to loan words. It now was possible that the loanwords in Turkish might have been of Turkish origin to begin with. Thus words which had been condemned to death by the purists now came under protection. To the moderates this theory became a weapon with which to slow down the radicals. There can be no doubt that the theory, which had support in official circles, played a positive role in the language reform. This historical relationship should be stressed regardless of any superfluous criticism.

The sole result of the 'sun-language' theory was an insignificant and uninfluential array of pamphlets. It wanted no autonomy and it had no negative effect on the tenor of other linguistic endeavors. Nothing can demonstrate better the transitory nature of the theory than the fact that once-obligatory lectures expounding the theory were, after a few years, dropped from the curriculum of the universities. Turkish linguistics today looks back on this theory so critically that a discussion of it is deemed completely unnecessary. It is generally held that the theory gains meaning only within the framework of the language reform, where it played a positive role. Its influence on the scientific study of language was insignificant. The theory should only be considered in connection with the language reform and judged accordingly.

The influence of the Turkish language reform on linguistic research was quite positive, especially in terms of historical, comparative, and dialectal studies. It could be said that these areas supplied the fuel for the motor of the language reform. The studies were actually undertaken in the interest of the language reform and this meant that primary scholarly interests were pushed into the background. The lack of qualified experts had the same result. Decades would pass before the scholarly interests could come into their own.

Until now the most important projects of Turkish linguistics have been closely affiliated with the Türk Dil Kurumu. Under its guidance were begun the systematic publication of Turkish literary monuments and the work on the historical and dialectal Turkish dictionary. The work of linguists at both the Universities of Istanbul and Ankara followed very much along the same lines.

Most of the methodology for scholarly investigation was provided by the impetus of the German and Hungarian schools of Turcology. The research was actually undertaken because of a neogrammarian program. Little interest was shown in problems of general linguistics or in the newer developments in grammatical research, and the research remained almost totally untouched by the new methods of descriptive linguistics which made their appearance with the Prague phonological school. The methodology can be described as prephonemic even today.

Present-day linguistic research is carried out in four institutions. The Türk Dil Kurumu continues to be the guardian of the above-mentioned important endeavors. In the last few years scholarly research has beyond doubt lagged behind in the activity of this Society. The Türk Dil Kurumu seems rather to concentrate on the tasks of language reform, cultivation of language, and such tasks as might lie at the border between linguistics and literature but tend to point more in the direction of literary scholarship. A journal of the Society, *Türk Dili,* is exclusively literary. Scholarly articles appear in the Türk Dil Kurumu's other journal, the *Türk Dili Araştırmaları Yıllığı Belleten.* The most important publications of the Society, both as regards past and present, are discussed in the regularly published catalogue of the Türk Dil Kurumu.

Two vehicles are available for the scholarly writings of the linguists at Ankara University: the *Ankara Üniversitesi Dil Tarih-Coğrafya Fakültesi Dergisi*, which is the general periodical of the university and not aimed particularly at linguists; and the *Türkoloji Dergisi*, the journal for language and literary scholarship. Monographs appear in the publications series of the university, the *Ankara Üniversitesi Dil Tarih-Coğrafya Fakültesi Yayınları.* A catalogue of University publications reports on the monographs as well as on the contents of the periodicals.

The University of Istanbul likewise is represented by two linguistics journals. The *İstanbul Üniversitesi Edebiyat Fakültesi Türk Dili ve Edebiyatı Dergisi* is a journal published jointly by linguists and literary scholars. The *Türkiyat Mecmuası* encompasses Turcology as a whole and consequently linguistics is represented on a somewhat modest scale. The philological faculty of the University of Istanbul publishes a regular series entitled *İstanbul Üniversitesi Edebiyat Fakültesi Yayınları.*

The Institute for Turkish cultural history, the Türk Kültürünü Araştırma Enstitüsü, founded several years ago, also has an active interest in linguistic research. Its publications, *Türk Kültürü* and *Cultura Turcica*, carry linguistics papers as well. In the publication series of the Institute, the *Türk Kültürünü Araştırma Enstitüsü Yayınları*, a number of volumes have already appeared that are of great interest to linguistics.

The following bibliography is limited to the international literature for language reform. In another essay in this volume (see pp. 183–216) I endeavored to compile a fairly complete bibliography of recent Turkish linguistics, basically covering the postwar period. For the literature to the problems dealt with above I refer the reader to this bibliography. It seemed more suitable to present a uniform bibliography which would present a unified picture of the literature for the related problems of both studies.

BIBLIOGRAPHY

BABA, N. 1944. Linguistic reform and historical research in the new Turkey. Asiatic Review 40.173–6.

BALASSA, J. 1934. Két mai nyelvujitás. Nyr 63.41–4.

BAZIN, L. 1952. Les travaux linguistiques en Turquie depuis la République. Anadolu 3–26.

CATTAN, S. 1933. Il movimento per la riforma della lingua turca. La Vita Italiana 41.39–43.

DENY, J. 1935. Le réforme actuelle de la langue turque. En Terre d'Islam 10.223–47.

DUDA, H.W. 1929–30. Die neue Lateinschrift in der Türkei. OLZ 32.441–53, 33. 401–13.

——. 1942. Die Gesundung der türkischen Sprachreform. Islam 26.77–100.

GAL'PERINA, E. 1952. K voprosu ob istorii razvitija tureckogo literaturnogo jazïka. Period ot 1928 do 1951 g. Moskva, Izd. Vïsšej Diplomatičeskoj Školï MID SSSR.

GIESE, FR. 1934. Die Reinigung und Erneuerung der türkischen Sprache. Forschungen und Fortschritte 10.407.

HERSHLAG, Z.Y. 1968. Turkey: The challenge of growth. Leiden, E.J. Brill.

HEYD, U. 1953. Language reform in modern Turkey. Middle East Affairs 402–9.

——. 1954. Language reform in modern Turkey. Jerusalem, Israel Oriental Society. (Reviews: G. Fraenkel, UAJb 27 (1955).129–30; V.L. Ménage, BSOAS 17 (1955). 402; H.W. Duda, WZKM 52 (1955).421–2).

HONY, H.C. 1947. The new Turkish. JRAS 216–21.

——. 1949. 'Zavallı Türkçe'. İş Mecmuası 15/89.2–6.

KISSLING, H. J. 1937. Die türkische Sprachreform. Leipziger Vierteljahrsschrift für Südosteuropa 1/3.69–81.

KÚNOS, I. 1930. Török nyelvújitás. Nyr 59.152–5.

——. 1934. A török nyelv megujhodása. Emlékkönyv Balassa Józsefnek, Budapest, 87–90.

MANSUROĞLU, M. 1954. Réformes et débats linguistiques en Turquie. Orbis 3.395–9.

NIELSEN, K. 1937. Die türkische Sprachreform. NTS 8.443–59.

ÖZDEM, R. H. 1944. Tanzimattan beri yazı dilimiz. İstanbul.

ROSSI, E. 1935. La riforma linguistica in Turchia. OM 15.45–7.

——. 1942. Un decennio di riforma linguistica in Turchia. OM 22.466–77.

——. 1953. Venticinque anni di rivoluzione dell'alfabeto e venti di riforma linguistica in Turchia. OM 33.378–84.

SAMAN, G. 1951. Les études de la langue turque. AO 19.108–13.

SHIBATA, T. 1960. Toruko no moji kaikaku. Gaikoku ni okeru kakugo mondai, 36–67. Doitsu, Toruko, Chūgoku; Tokyo, Mombushō.

STEUERWALD, K. 1963–66. Untersuchungen zur türkischen Sprache der Gegenwart 1–3. Berlin, Langenscheidt. (Review: G. Hazai, OLZ 60(1965).176–9; 62(1967). 61–2; 64(1969).375–7.

SZABE, L. 1952. Regression or new development? Twenty years of linguistic reform in Turkey. Civilisations 2/1.46–54.

WEBSTER, D. E. 1939. Returkification: History and language reform. The Turkey of Atatürk: Social progress in the Turkish reformation. Philadelphia, The American Academy of Political and Social Science.

BIOGRAPHICAL NOTES

PETER F. ABBOUD (1931–) was born and brought up in Palestine and lived in Egypt for thirteen years prior to coming to the United States in 1961. He earned his master's degree in Arabic and Comparative Semitics at the American University in Cairo and received his doctorate in Linguistics at the University of Texas. He is co-author of textbooks for Cairo Arabic and for Modern Standard Arabic. His principal scholarly interests include Classical Arabic and the modern Arabic dialects.

SALIH J. ALTOMA (1929–) received his B.A. with honors in Arabic at the University of Baghdad in 1952, his M.A. at Harvard in 1955, and his Ed.D. in Language Education also at Harvard in 1957. From 1956–57 he was a Research Associate at Harvard's Center for Middle Eastern Studies. During 1957–60 he was an instructor, Registrar, and an Assistant Dean in the College of Education, University of Baghdad; in 1960–63 a Cultural Attaché in the Embassy of Iraq, Washington, D.C.; a research fellow at Harvard's Center for Middle Eastern Studies in 1963–64; and, since 1964, an Associate Professor of Arabic at Indiana University. During the Summers of 1965–66 he was Visiting Associate Professor at Harvard Summer School, and during 1967 Visiting Associate Professor at Princeton. His publications include numerous books and articles on Arabic.

JOSEPH R. APPLEGATE (1925–) studied at Temple University (B.S., 1945) and then completed his graduate work in linguistics under the direction of Zellig S. Harris at the University of Pennsylvania (Ph.D., 1955). He taught German and did research in mechanical translation at MIT (1955–60); then taught Berber, Arabic, and linguistics at UCLA (1960–66); and is now Professor of African Studies at Howard University in Washington, D.C. Special research interests include Berber languages, phonology, children's speech, and language pedagogy. Papers and publications include structural descriptions of Berber languages, works on phonology, and problems of language learning.

ÉMILE BENVENISTE (1902–) Ph.D., is Professor of Linguistics and Comparative Philology at the Collège de France since 1937, and at the École des Hautes Études since 1927. His current interests include: general linguistics, semiotics, and Indo-

European studies. He has also done fieldwork in Persia, Afghanistan, and among North-Western American Indian tribes (in British Columbia and Alaska). His recent major publications include: *Problèmes de linguistique générale* (1966) and *Titres et noms propres en iranien ancien* (1966).

M. J. CONNOLLY (ó Coinġeallaiġ) (1943–) graduated in 1965 from the Honors Program of the College of Arts and Sciences at Boston College with training in general linguistics and Germanic and Slavic languages and literature; Ph.D. in Linguistics from Harvard University in 1969. Research and publication fields include Indo-European, Armenian, problems of general linguistics, and child speech. He is presently Assistant Professor of Linguistics and Eastern Languages at Boston College.

GERHARD DOERFER (1920–) was born in Königsberg (now Kaliningrad), Eastern Prussia. He studied Altaic, Semitic, and Iranian languages at Freie Universität, Berlin. In 1955–57 he was editor of *Philologiae Turcicae Fundamenta*. Since 1960 he has been lecturer and (since 1966) Professor of Turcology and Altaistics at University of Göttingen. His research centers around the correlations between Iranian and Altaic languages, and between the Altaic languages themselves.

MARK J. DRESDEN (1911–) received M.A. degrees from the Universities of Amsterdam and Utrecht, and the Ph.D. from the University of Utrecht. He has also studied at the École Pratique des Hautes Études and the Collège de France under a fellowship from the French government, and at Cambridge University under a Dutch government grant. He has taught at Michigan, Georgetown, and Columbia Universities. His current position is Professor of Iranian Studies at the University of Pennsylvania. He has published a number of books and articles on Iranian languages and culture.

CHARLES A. FERGUSON (1921–) studied linguistics at the University of Pennsylvania where he received his Ph.D. in Oriental Studies. His linguistic research has been largely in Arabic and Bengali, and he has published about thirty articles ranging from detailed phonological studies to such fields as child language and sociolinguistics. He is a life member of the Linguistic Society of India and an honorary member of the Linguistic Research Group of Pakistan; he has been a member of the Committee on South Asia Languages of the Association of Asian Studies and served as its chairman 1956–57. For nine years he worked for the Foreign Service Institute of the Department of State. He has taught at Harvard University, the University of Washington, Seattle, and other Universities including Georgetown and Deccan College in India. From 1959–66 he was Director of the Center for Applied Linguistics in Washington, D.C. He is currently Professor of Linguistics and Chairman of the Committee on Linguistics at Stanford University.

ROBERT GODEL (1902–) received his early schooling in Geneva, studied Armenian in Turkey, and taught classics on his return to Geneva. Since 1951 he has been associated with the University of Geneva, and is now Professor of Latin language and literature. During the 1964–65 Spring Semester he was Visiting Professor of Classical Armenian at Harvard University. He serves also on the editorial board of *Cahiers F. de Saussure*.

GEORGE HAZAI (1932–) studied Turcology, linguistics and history at the L. Eötvös University (Budapest) in 1950–54, and was later sent by the Hungarian Academy of Sciences to Bulgaria. There he studied Turkic dialects and also lectured on Turcology at the University of Sofia (1956–57). In 1959 he received his doctor's degree from the University of Budapest. Since 1963 he has been Visiting Associate Professor at the Humboldt-University (Berlin, German Democratic Republic) and now heads the Turcological section of the Vorderasiatisches Institut, as well as leading the Turfan study group of the German Academy of Sciences. His Doctor of Philology thesis was defended in 1966 before the Hungarian Academy of Sciences. He is co-editor of the *Orientalistische Literaturzeitung* and the *Mitteilungen des Instituts für Orientforschung*. His main areas of work are Turkic linguistic history, dialectology, grammar, Slavo-Turcica, Turfan philology and bibliography.

CARLETON T. HODGE (1917–) was born in Springfield, Illinois. He received his A.B. degree in Greek and Latin from DePauw University, and his Ph.D. in Linguistics, with concentration in ancient Near Eastern languages, from the University of Pennsylvania. He has also studied at the University of Michigan and at Dropsie College. He has held teaching and administrative posts with the United States Department of State, Foreign Service Institute. In 1963–64 he was Jacob Ziskind Visiting Professor at Brandeis University. In the summer of 1965 he was Visiting Professor at the Linguistic Institute, University of Michigan. From 1964 to 1968 he was Professor of Linguistics and Director of the Intensive Language Training Center at Indiana University, and has been, since 1966, Co-Director of the NDEA African Language and Area Center. He is currently Professor of Linguistics and Anthropology and Associate Chairman of the Research Center for Language Sciences. He has published a number of books and articles, chiefly on Hausa, Persian, Serbo-Croatian, Bulgarian, and Afroasiatic.

CAROLYN G. KILLEAN (1936–) received undergraduate and graduate training in Near Eastern Studies and Linguistics from the University of Michigan. Her graduate study was supported by a succession of foreign language fellowships in Arabic from 1961 to 1966 under Title VI of the National Defense Education Act. Since receiving her Ph.D. in 1966, she has spent a year doing research in Egypt under the auspices of the American Research Center there and is currently teaching modern Arabic language and linguistics at the University of Chicago.

JOHN R. KRUEGER (1927–) holds degrees from The George Washington University and the University of Washington. As Fulbright scholar to the Central Asian Institute, he studied Turko-Mongolian languages and history at the University of Copenhagen. He has written widely on Altaic linguistic and literary topics, with additional interests in American Indian languages and onomastics. After teaching at the University of Washington, Reed College, and the University of California (Berkeley), he came to Indiana University where he concentrates on Turkic languages, Mongolian, and general linguistics.

EDUARD Y. KUTSCHER (1909–) a native of Slovakia, is Professor of Hebrew Philology at the Hebrew University; he also teaches at Bar-Ilan University. He has taught as Visiting Professor at the Jewish Theological Seminary, New York, at the Dropsie College, Philadelphia, at Yale University, at New York University, and the University of Pennsylvania. A recipient of the Israel Award for the Humanities, 1961, he has been the Editor of *Lěšonénu*, Quarterly of the Academy of the Hebrew Language, since 1964. His major research interests are Hebrew and Aramaic. His publications include a volume on the language of the Dead Sea Isaiah Scroll and several publications on Aramaic dialects. He is Co-Editor of Köhler-Baumgartner, *Hebräisches und aramäisches Lexicon zum A.T.*

JACOB M. LANDAU (1924–) was born in Rumania and brought up in Palestine. He holds an M.A. degree from the Hebrew University of Jerusalem and a Ph.D. from the School of Oriental and African Studies, University of London. In the field of linguistics, he has conducted research into word frequency in modern literary Arabic as well as into the study of Arabic as a foreign language. Since 1959, he has been connected with the Hebrew University of Jerusalem, where he is Associate Professor in the Faculty of Social Sciences; he is also part-time Associate Professor in Arabic at Bar-Ilan University. He has held visiting appointments at Brandeis University, at the University of California, Los Angeles (on a Fulbright Travel Grant), and at Wayne State University.

GILBERT LAZARD (1920–) studied classics in Paris, then Persian and Iranian linguistics in Paris and Tehran, and earned his doctorate at the University of Paris (Sorbonne). He has been associated with the Centre National de la Recherche Scientifique and with the École Nationale des Langues Orientales Vivantes, and is now professor of Iranian languages and civilization at the Sorbonne. His publications include books and articles on Persian linguistics and philology.

WOLF LESLAU (1906–) a native of Poland, came to the United States in 1942. He studied at the University of Vienna and the Sorbonne in Paris where he earned his degree of Docteur-ès-Lettres. He has taught at the École des Hautes Études, Paris, École Nationale des Langues Orientales, Asia Institute, Brandeis University, and since 1955, at the University of California at Los Angeles where he is Professor of Hebrew and Semitic Linguistics. He was the first chairman of the UCLA Department of Near Eastern languages and literatures. He has held fellowships from the John Simon Guggenheim Memorial Foundation, the National Foundation of the Arts and Humanities and Fulbright-Hays. He is a fellow of the Academy of Arts and Sciences and the American Academy for Jewish Research. He made eight linguistic expeditions to Ethiopia where he collected material for the description of various Ethiopian languages. He has published numerous books on Semitic linguistics, South Arabian, and particularly on Ethiopian linguistics. He is the recipient of the Haile Selassie Award for Ethiopian Studies.

FRANK R. PALMER (1922–) is a graduate of the University of Oxford (New College and Merton College). He was Lecturer in Linguistics at the School of Oriental and African Studies, London, where his research was directed towards the languages of Ethiopia 1950–60, and subsequently Professor of Linguistics at the University College of North Wales, Bangor 1960–65. He is now Professor and Head of the Department of Linguistic Science at the University of Reading.

HERBERT H. PAPER (1925–) a native of Baltimore, Maryland, received his B.A. in Classics (University of Colorado, 1943), his M.A. in Linguistics and his Ph.D. in Oriental Languages (University of Chicago, 1948 and 1951). In 1951–52, he was a Fulbright Fellow to Iran; and in 1952–53, a research assistant in linguistics at Cornell University. In 1953, he joined the Department of Near Eastern Studies at The University of Michigan. From 1963 to 1968, he served as the first chairman of the Department of Linguistics at Michigan; and during the summers of 1965 and 1967 was Director of the Linguistic Institute in Ann Arbor. During 1959–60 he held a postdoctoral ACLS fellowship at Cambridge University. His publications have been in the fields of Elamite, Old Persian, Modern Persian, and Judeo-Persian.

HANS JAKOB POLOTSKY (1905–) studied at the Universities of Berlin and Göttingen and received his Ph.D. from the latter in 1929. He has been on the staff of the Hebrew University, Jerusalem, since 1934, since 1951 as Professor of Egyptian and Semitic Linguistics, and from 1952 to 1967, and again from 1969, as Head of the Department of Linguistics. During 1967–68 he was seconded to the University of Copenhagen as Professor of Egyptology and Director of the Institute of Egyptology. He has written on Egyptian and Coptic, modern Ethiopian languages, and Modern East Aramaic.

CHAIM RABIN (1915–) was born in Germany. He studied at the Universities of Jerusalem, London, and Oxford. In 1941–56 he taught post-Biblical Hebrew, Arabic, and Ethiopic at Oxford, and since 1956 has been Professor of Hebrew Language at the Hebrew University of Jerusalem and member of the Hebrew Language Academy. His main interests are language history (with stress on sociolinguistic aspects), syntax, semantics, lexical borrowing, and the linguistic theory of translation.

GEORGES REDARD (1922–) pursued his studies at the Universities of Neuchâtel (Greek, Latin, Russian, Lithuanian, Sanskrit, Persian, linguistics) and Berne (Greek and Russian) in Switzerland. In Paris (Faculté des lettres, École Pratique des Hautes Études, Collège de France, École Nationale des Langues Orientales Vivantes) he was, for several years, a student of Professors J. Vendryes, J. Bloch, P. Chantraine, J. Marouzeau, G. Dumézil, H. Massé, and E. Benveniste. He holds the degrees of *docteur-ès-lettres* from the University of Neuchâtel (1949) and of *diplômé* from the École des Hautes Études de Paris (1950). He was formerly an editor of the *Glossaire des patois de la Suisse romande* (1948–54 under the direction of K. Jaberg), and has taught comparative grammar of Indo-European languages and general linguistics at the University of Neuchâtel (since 1948) and the University of Berne (since 1954). He has also conducted courses at the Universities of Tehran, Kabul, and Los Angeles. His publications are concerned chiefly with classical languages, French, and Iranian. He is director of the *Atlas des parlers iraniens*, the plan for which he proposed in 1957, and he has carried out 12 dialect surveys in Iran and Afghanistan. He has been editor of the review *Kratylos* (publisher: Harrassowitz), since its establishment in 1956, and edits two series: *Iranische Texte* and *Beiträge zur Iranistik*.

ERICA REINER is a native of Budapest and studied at the University of Budapest and at the École Pratique des Hautes Études of the Sorbonne in Paris. In 1952, Miss Reiner joined the Oriental Institute of the University of Chicago as research assistant with the Assyrian Dictionary Project. She is now Professor in the Department of Near Eastern Languages and Civilizations and in the Department of Linguistics at the University of Chicago, and member of the Editorial Board of the Chicago Assyrian Dictionary. She is the author of numerous articles in the field of Assyriology and Elamitology, *A linguistic analysis of Akkadian*, and a grammar of Elamite for the *Handbuch der Orientalistik*.

GENE M. SCHRAMM (1929–) is Associate Professor of Semitic Languages and Linguistics at the University of Michigan. He received his doctorate at the Dropsie College, Philadelphia, in 1956, and taught at the University of Kentucky and the University of California, Berkeley, prior to moving to Ann Arbor in 1965. He has published synchronic and diachronic studies in the fields of Semitic and Afro-Asiatic linguistics.

THOMAS A. SEBEOK (1920–) is a native of Budapest who has lived in the United States since 1937. After studying literary criticism, anthropology, and linguistics at the University of Chicago, he earned his doctorate at Princeton University in Oriental languages and civilizations. He has been a member of the Indiana University faculty since 1943, since 1967 with the rank of Distinguished Professor of Linguistics and Professor of Anthropology. He also serves as Chairman of the University's Research Center for the Language Sciences. He has held fellowships from the John Simon

Guggenheim Memorial Foundation (1958–59) and the Center for Advanced Study in the Behavioral Sciences (1960–61), and was Senior Post-doctoral Fellow of the National Science Foundation (1966–67). In 1964, he was Director of the Linguistic Institute of the Linguistic Society of America, which he currently serves as Secretary-Treasurer. He organized and, until 1963, was Chairman of the Committee on Linguistic Information. Beginning 1968, he became Editor-in-Chief of *Semiotica* (formerly *Studies in Semiotics*).

EDWARD ULLENDORFF (1920–) studied Semitic languages in the Hebrew University of Jerusalem (M.A.) and in the University of Oxford (D.Phil.). During World War II he served in Eritrea and Ethiopia and has since revisited these countries a number of times. He has been on the faculty of the Universities of Oxford and St. Andrews (Scotland) and was Professor of Semitic Languages in the University of Manchester. Since 1964 he has been the first incumbent of the newly established chair of Ethiopian Studies at the School of Oriental and African Studies, London University. He is a Fellow of the British Academy. His publications include books and many articles in the field of Semitic languages in general and Ethiopian studies in particular.

JOZEF VERGOTE (1910–) is a Doctor of Philosophy and Letters (Classic Philology) and is licensed in Oriental History and Philology at the University of Louvain. He completed his formal studies from 1934–36 at the University of Berlin, where he studied Egyptian under K. Sethe and H. Grapow, Coptic with Carl Schmidt, and Greek Papyrology with W. Schubart. Since 1943, he has been a professor at the University of Louvain, where he teaches, aside from the above mentioned subjects, Classical Greek. After having published, in collaboration with W. Peremans, a manual on 'papyrology' (in Dutch), he is working in linguistics, particularly on the vocalization of Ancient Egyptian. He was appointed corresponding member in 1955 and active member in 1957 of the 'Koninklijke Vlaamse Academie voor Wetenschappen, Letteren en Schone Kunsten van België'. Bibliography to 1958 published by S. Pop in *Orbis* (Louvain) 7.637–9 (1958).

EHSAN YAR-SHATER (1920–) is Chairman of the Department of Middle East Languages and Cultures and Professor of Iranian Studies at Colombia University. He studied in the University of Tehran where he received a Dr. Litt. in Persian language and literature, and in the University of London, where he received an M.A. and a Ph.D. in Old and Middle Iranian. His publications include works on Persian literature, a number of articles on Iranian dialects, a *Grammar of Southern Tati dialects* (Mouton, The Hague, 1969) and critical editions of several Persian texts. He is the editor of the Persian Texts Series published by the Pahlavi Foundation, Iran, and the editor of the Persian Heritage Series published in several European languages under the auspices of Unesco and the Pahlavi Foundation. He also is the general editor of *Rahnemay-e Ketab*, a bi-monthly journal of Persian language and literature and book reviews.

Lucia Hadd Zoercher (1942–) was graduated with high distinction from Indiana University with honors in English in 1965 (Phi Beta Kappa). She has held editorial and research assistantships in that institution's Research Center for the Language Sciences and was Assistant to the Director of the 1964 Linguistic Institute. In 1966 she was Assistant to the Director of Mouton & Co. N.V., The Hague, and, during 1967, Assistant Editor in the English Language Teaching Department of Oxford University Press, London. She has done free-lance editing in London, the United States, and Canada, and has been employed by the Center for Applied Linguistics (Washington, D.C.) since 1968.

INDEX OF LANGUAGE NAMES

INDEX OF NAMES